The Hornbook Series
of
Treatises on all the Principal Subjects of the Law

Admiralty — Gustavus H. Robinson.
Agency — Tiffany, 2nd Ed. by Richard R. Powell.
Bailments and Carriers — Armistead M. Dobie.
Bankruptcy — 2nd Ed., Henry C. Black.
Banks and Banking — Francis B. Tiffany.
Bills and Notes — William E. Britton.
Code Pleading — Charles E. Clark.
Common Law Pleading — Shipman, 3rd Ed. by Henry W. Ballantine.
Conflict of Laws — 2nd Ed., Herbert F. Goodrich.
Constitutional Law — Henry Rottschaefer.
Construction and Interpretation of Laws — 2nd Ed., Henry C. Black.
Contracts — Clark, 4th Ed. by A. H. Throckmorton.
Corporations — Robert S. Stevens.
Criminal Law — Justin Miller.
Criminal Procedure — Clark, 2nd Ed. by William E. Mikell.
Damages — Charles T. McCormick.
Domestic Relations — Joseph W. Madden.
Elementary Law — Smith, 2nd Ed. by Archie H. McGray.
Equity — Henry L. McClintock.
Equity Pleading and Practice — Walter C. Clephane.
Evidence — 4th Ed., John J. McKelvey.
Executors and Administrators — Simon G. Croswell.
Federal Jurisdiction and Procedure — Armistead M. Dobie.
Insurance — 2nd Ed., William R. Vance.
International Law — 3rd Ed., George G. Wilson.
Judicial Precedents — Henry C. Black.
Legal History — Max Radin.
Municipal Corporations — Roger W. Cooley.
Partnership — Judson A. Crane.
Real Property — William L. Burdick.
Roman Law — Max Radin.
Sales — Lawrence Vold.
Suretyship and Guaranty — Herschel W. Arant.
Torts — William L. Prosser.
Trusts — 2nd Ed., George G. Bogert.
Wills — Thomas E. Atkinson.

Published and for sale by

WEST PUBLISHING CO.   ST. PAUL, MINN.

HANDBOOK

OF THE

LAW OF TRUSTS

BY

GEORGE GLEASON BOGERT

JAMES PARKER HALL PROFESSOR OF LAW, UNIVERSITY OF
CHICAGO LAW SCHOOL

MEMBER OF THE NEW YORK AND ILLINOIS BARS

SECOND EDITION

HORNBOOK SERIES

DR. NORMAN A. WIGGINS

ST. PAUL, MINN.
WEST PUBLISHING CO.
1942

COPYRIGHT, 1921
BY
WEST PUBLISHING CO.

COPYRIGHT, 1942
BY
WEST PUBLISHING CO.

BOGERT TRUSTS 2D

To
L. E. B.
with grateful appreciation

✣

PREFACE TO SECOND EDITION

TWENTY-ONE years have elapsed since the publication of the first edition of this book. During that time there have been many important developments in the law of Trusts.

Hundreds of cases concerning trusteeship have been decided annually. Many of these have explored fields where the American cases were scanty or conflicting. The depression of the thirties has produced a multitude of claims for preferences against failed banks on trust theories, numerous efforts to surcharge trustees because of shrunken investment values, and many other problems.

The development of statutory trust law in these two decades has been remarkable. Not only have several trust codes been drafted by banking and trust company interests and passed by the legislatures, but the National Conference of Commissioners on Uniform State Laws has promulgated five important trust statutes, each covering a segment of the topic, and they have met with some favor.

Furthermore, the American Law Institute completed its Restatement of Trusts in 1935 and of Restitution in 1937. References to the various sections of these important works have been inserted in this revision at appropriate places.

The material has been reclassified in an attempt to produce a more logical development and eliminate slight repetitions. Several new sections have been added, and some of the old sections subdivided, so that the revised book contains 169 sections, as against 128 in the 1921 edition; but due to some omissions of procedural and other less important material the increase is only 63 pages. The statutory citations have been brought down to date. The text has been checked for clarity and accuracy. Many recent case and law review references have been added, and a new index has been prepared.

GEORGE G. BOGERT

UNIVERSITY OF CHICAGO LAW SCHOOL
   March, 1942.

PREFACE TO FIRST EDITION

THE object of this book is to give to practitioners and students a compact summary of the fundamental principles of the American law relating to trusteeships. It is hoped that lawyers will be able by the use of the book to obtain ready information on the large, outstanding problems in the field, and to gain starting points for research into the more recondite and complicated questions. The law student will, it is believed, find in the book sufficient material to furnish him that groundwork which is the maximum possible of attainment in his preliminary studies.

Space limitations have prevented detailed treatment of the English law and extended discussion of matters of principle. These must be reserved for a text-book which purports to be all-inclusive.

In the arrangement of topics the author has varied somewhat from the standard analysis. This change has been made partly with the purpose of facilitating the work of the reader in finding the law and partly because it has appealed to the author as logical. An effort has been made to classify the material under headings which represent the principal practical problems arising in the administration of trusts, as well as to develop the trust relation in sequence from beginning to end. The chapters on the trust purpose are illustrative of these departures from the customary outline. What may be the trust purpose is a frequently occurring question in practical affairs, and the trust purpose is one element of the trust relationship which logically deserves treatment.

Some statutory matters have been dealt with in considerable detail, as, for example, the Statute of Frauds. Effort has been made to set forth as far as possible the peculiarities existing in the states which have statutory trust systems, as, for instance, New York, Michigan, and California. The important distinction between the states which have modified and partially codified the law of trusts, and those jurisdictions which retain the English system almost wholly untouched by legislation, is not always ap-

PREFACE TO FIRST EDITION

preciated. Certain rules of property which sometimes intimately affect trusts have been discussed, although perhaps not usually treated in works on trusts. These are the rules regarding remoteness of vesting, suspension of the power of alienation, and accumulations.

References to articles in leading law periodicals have been inserted with an attempt at completeness. The value of these carefully prepared monographs on narrow points of law is increasingly apparent to bench, bar, and the law school world.

George G. Bogert

Cornell University College of Law,
    Ithaca, N. Y., March, 1921.

SUMMARY OF CONTENTS

Chapter		Page
1.	Introduction and History	1
2.	Distinctions between Trusts and other Relations	18
3.	Creation of Express Trusts—Trust Intent—Formalities—Conveyancing	52
4.	Creation of Express Trusts—The Trust Elements	104
5.	Creation of Resulting Trusts	170
6.	Creation of Constructive Trusts	194
7.	The Trust Purpose—Private Trusts	228
8.	Charitable Trusts	260
9.	The Powers of the Trustee—In General	314
10.	The Duties of the Trustee—In General	326
11.	Trust Administration—Protection and Investment	335
12.	Trust Administration—Liabilities from Contracts, Torts and Property Ownership	374
13.	Trust Administration—Sales, Mortgages and Leases	392
14.	Trust Administration—Payments—Changes in Trustee Personnel	411
15.	Trust Administration—Principal and Income Accounts	430
16.	Trust Administration—Accounting and Compensation	458
17.	Remedies under Trusts	486
18.	The Barring of Remedies	594
19.	Alteration or Termination of the Trust	619
Table of Cases		647
Index		719

TABLE OF CONTENTS

		Page
Chapter 1.	Introduction and History	1
Sec.		
1.	Definition of Fundamental Terms	1
2.	Origin of Uses and Trusts	6
3.	Uses and Trusts before the Statute of Uses	9
4.	The Statute of Uses	11
5.	The Effect of the Statute of Uses	13
6.	Trusts in America	15
Chapter 2.	Distinctions between Trusts and other Relations	18
Sec.		
7.	Debt	18
8.	Debt or Trust—The Specific Property Criterion	21
9.	The Debtor Making Himself Trustee—The Specific Property Criterion	31
10.	Bailment	32
11.	Equitable Charge	34
12.	Assignment of a Chose in Action	36
13.	Executorship	39
14.	Agency	41
15.	Guardianship	44
16.	Promoters and Officers of Corporations	45
17.	Receivership	48
18.	Life Tenant and Remainderman	49
19.	Deeds of Trust in the Nature of Mortgages	50
Chapter 3.	Creation of Express Trusts—Trust Intent—Formalities—Conveyancing	52
Sec.		
20.	Express and Implied Trusts	52
21.	Methods of Trust Creation	54
22.	Expression of Trust Intent	55
23.	Precatory Expressions	59
24.	Reality of Trust Intent—Savings Bank Trusts	65
25.	Formality—Statute of Frauds	79
26.	Formality—Wills Acts	89
27.	Consideration	92

TABLE OF CONTENTS

Sec.		Page
28.	Delivery of the Trust Instrument	95
29.	Notice of the Trust	99
30.	Transfer of Title to the Trustee	101

Chapter 4. Creation of Express Trusts—The Trust Elements 104

Sec.

31.	The Qualifications of the Settlor	104
32.	The Subject-Matter of the Trust	107
33.	Who may be a Trustee	111
34.	Original Appointment of Trustee	119
35.	Trust will Not Fail for Want of Trustee	121
36.	Estate of Trustee	122
37.	Acceptance by Trustee	124
38.	Qualification by the Trustee	128
39.	Necessity of Beneficiary	131
40.	Who may be a Beneficiary	134
41.	Acceptance by the Beneficiary	137
42.	Nature of Beneficiary's Interest	139
43.	Incidents of the Beneficiary's Interest	143
44.	Availability to Creditors	149
45.	Spendthrift Trusts	156
46.	Discretionary Trusts	166
47.	Trusts for Support	168
48.	Blended Trusts	168

Page

Chapter 5. Creation of Resulting Trusts 170

Sec.

49.	Introduction	170
50.	Statute of Frauds	172
51.	Voluntary Conveyances	173
52.	Payment of Consideration for Conveyance to Another	175
53.	Failure of Express Trust	190
54.	Where Express Trust Res Proves Excessive	192

Chapter 6. Creation of Constructive Trusts 194

Sec.

55.	Definition	194
56.	Statute of Frauds	195
57.	Fraudulent Misrepresentation	196
58.	Mistake, Undue Influence or Duress	198
59.	Proceeds of Larceny of Conversion	199
60.	Property Obtained by Homicide	200
61.	Breach of Contract to Convey	201

TABLE OF CONTENTS

Sec.		Page
62.	Disloyalty of Fiduciary	203
63.	Direct Dealing with Beneficiary	207
64.	Purchase at Judicial Sale under Oral Promise	212
65.	Conveyance of Land on Oral Trust	214
66.	Gift by Will or Intestacy on Oral Trust	219

Chapter 7. The Trust Purpose—Private Trusts - - - - 228
Sec.

67.	Trusts Classified as to Purpose	228
68.	Passive Trusts	230
69.	Active Trusts—Validity of Purpose	233
70.	Active Trusts—Statutory Restrictions	240
71.	Rule against Remoteness of Vesting	242
72.	Rule against Suspension of Power of Alienation	247
73.	Rule against Accumulations	253
74.	Duration of Trusts	257

Chapter 8. Charitable Trusts - - - - - - - - - - - 260
Sec.

75.	Definition of Charitable Trust	260
76.	History—Statute of Charitable Uses	268
77.	Indefiniteness—Purpose and Beneficiaries	273
78.	Religious Purposes	276
79.	Gifts for Masses	279
80.	Cemeteries and Monuments	282
81.	Educational Purposes	285
82.	Eleemosynary Purposes	288
83.	Governmental Trusts	291
84.	Purposes Not Charitable	293
85.	The Administration of Charities	294
86.	The Cy Pres Doctrine	296
87.	The Rule against Remoteness of Vesting	303
88.	The Rule against Restraints on Alienation	307
89.	The Rule against Accumulations	308
90.	Duration of Charitable Trusts	311
91.	Other Statutory Restrictions on Charitable Trusts	311

Chapter 9. The Powers of the Trustee—In General - - - - 314
Sec.

92.	Express and Implied Powers	314
93.	Discretionary and Imperative Powers	315
94.	Personal Powers and Powers Attached to the Office of Trustee	317
95.	Exercise of Powers by Cotrustees	320

TABLE OF CONTENTS

Sec.		Page
96.	Delegation of Trust Powers	323
97.	Notice of Trustee's Powers	325

Chapter 10. The Duties of the Trustee—In General - - - - 326

Sec.		
98.	Duty to Use Ordinary Skill and Prudence	326
99.	Duty of Loyalty	328
100.	Duty to Carry out the Trust	333

Chapter 11. Trust Administration—Protection and Investment - - - - - - - - - - - - - - - - 335

Sec.		
101.	Duty to Defend the Trust	335
102.	Duty to Take Possession and Collect	336
103.	Duty to Keep Trust Property Safely	339
104.	Duty to Make Trust Property Productive	342
105.	Duty to Use Reasonable Care in Investing	345
106.	Statute and Court Rules—Effect	348
107.	Investments Generally Approved	350
108.	Investments Generally Disapproved	354
109.	Common Trust Funds	362
110.	Control by the Settlor, the Court, or the Beneficiary	364
111.	Duty to Review Trust Investments	371
112.	Duty to Change Trust Investments	372

Chapter 12. Trust Administration—Liabilities from Contracts, Torts and Property Ownership - - - 374

Sec.		
113.	Personal Liability of Trustees on Contracts	374
114.	Exclusion of Personal Liability	376
115.	Trustee's Right of Indemnity as to Contracts	379
116.	Contract Creditor's Rights against the Trustee as Such	381
117.	Personal Liability of Trustee for Torts	385
118.	Trustee's Right of Indemnity as to Torts	387
119.	Tort Creditor's Rights against the Trustee as Such	389
120.	Liability of the Trustee as Property Owner	390

Chapter 13. Trust Administration—Sales, Mortgages and Leases - - - - - - - - - - - - - - - - 392

Sec.		
121.	Trustee's Power to Sell	392
122.	Court Control of Trustee's Sale	395
123.	Conduct of Sales by Trustees	397

TABLE OF CONTENTS

Sec.		Page
124.	Express or Implied Power to Borrow and Give Security	399
125.	Court Control over Borrowing and Giving Security	401
126.	Effect of Loans and Giving Security	403
127.	Express or Implied Power to Lease	405
128.	Length of Leases Permitted	407
129.	Trustee's Duties as Lessor	408

Chapter 14. Trust Administration—Payments—Changes in Trustee Personnel - - - - - - - - - - 411

Sec.		
130.	Trustee's Duties in Making Payments	411
131.	Advances of Trust Capital or Income	414
132.	Resignation by Trustee	416
133.	Death of Trustee	419
134.	Vacancies in Trusteeship—Appointment of Successors	422

Chapter 15. Trust Administration—Principal and Income Accounts - - - - - - - - - - - 430

Sec.		
135.	Ordinary Returns	430
136.	Apportionment of Receipts	431
137.	Extraordinary Receipts	434
138.	Unproductive Property	437
139.	Wasting Property	440
140.	Cash Dividends	445
141.	Stock Dividends	448
142.	Stock Subscription Rights	453
143.	Source from Which Expenses should be Paid	455

Chapter 16. Trust Administration—Accounting and Compensation - - - - - - - - - - - - 458

Sec.		
144.	Duty to Keep Records and Give Information	458
145.	Duty to Render Court Accounting	460
146.	Compensation of the Trustee	472

Chapter 17. Remedies under Trusts - - - - - - - - 486

Sec.		
147.	Advice and Instruction by the Court	486
148.	Enjoining or Setting Aside Wrongful Acts	488
149.	Decree for Carrying Out of Trust	490

TABLE OF CONTENTS

Sec.		Page
150.	Money Judgment against Trustee for Breach of Trust	501
151.	Personal Liability of Trustee with Lien	528
152.	Recovery of the Trust Res or Its Substitute	530
153.	Meaning of Bona Fide Purchaser	533
154.	Tracing Trust Funds—Identification	547
155.	Necessity of Election between Tracing and Damages	563
156.	Subrogation and Marshaling	566
157.	Control of Trust Administration	568
158.	Recovery from Bondsman or Guaranty Fund	575
159.	Actions against Third Persons for Participating in a Breach of Trust	578
160.	Actions against Third Parties for Injuring the Trust Property	590

Chapter 18. The Barring of Remedies - - - - - - - - 594

Sec.		
161.	Act or Omission of the Beneficiary	594
162.	The Statute of Limitations	605

Chapter 19. Alteration or Termination of the Trust - - - - 619

Sec.		
163.	Alteration of Trust by Trust Parties	619
164.	Alteration of Private Trusts by the Court	620
165.	Revocation of the Trust	622
166.	Natural Termination	627
167.	Purpose Accomplished or Becomes Impossible of Accomplishment	632
168.	Merger of Interests	636
169.	Termination at Request of Beneficiary	638

Table of Cases - - - - - - - - - - - - - - - - 647

Index - 719

†

HANDBOOK

OF THE

LAW OF TRUSTS

CHAPTER 1

INTRODUCTION AND HISTORY

Sec.
1. Definition of Fundamental Terms.
2. Origin of Uses and Trusts.
3. Uses and Trusts before the Statute of Uses.
4. The Statute of Uses.
5. The effect of the Statute of Uses.
6. Trusts in America.

DEFINITION OF FUNDAMENTAL TERMS

1. **A trust is a fiduciary relationship in which one person is the holder of the title to property, subject to an equitable obligation to keep or use the property for the benefit of another.**[1]

    The settlor of a trust is the person who intentionally causes the trust to come into existence.

    The trustee is the person who holds the title for the benefit of another.

    The trust property is the property interest, real or personal, which the trustee holds, subject to the rights of another.

    The beneficiary is the person for whose benefit the trust property is held or used by the trustee.

The trusts treated herein should not be confused with the monopolies or combinations called "trusts," or with the positions

---

[1] "A trust is an obligation imposed, either expressly or by implication of law, whereby the obligor is bound to deal with property over which he has control for the benefit of certain persons, of whom he may himself be one, and any one of whom may enforce the obligation." Hart, What is a Trust? 15 Law Quart.Rev. 301.

"A trust may be defined as a property right held by one party for the use of another." Keplinger v. Keplinger, 185 Ind. 81, 113 N.E. 292, 293.

which are loosely called "places of trust." The monopolistic trusts were originally so called because the stock of the combining corporations was transferred to technical trustees to accomplish a centralization of control.[2] In common parlance, to be in a position of "trust" or to be a "trustee" often means merely to occupy a station where elements of confidence and responsibility exist.[3] The one trusted in this sense may be an agent, a servant, a partner, a guardian, or a trustee. He is not necessarily in the technical trust relation.

It is not intended that the definitions of the essential terms here given shall be final or exhaustive. The nature and incidents of the trust will be developed throughout the book, and the meaning of the elementary terms more fully explained. Detailed qualifications and exceptions are not attempted in this section. But a certain rough, general description of the trust and its parts is necessary before one can proceed to trace the history of trusts and distinguish them from other similar relationships.[4]

A Fiduciary Relation

The relation between trustee and beneficiary is particularly intimate. The beneficiary is obliged to place great confidence in the trustee. The trustee has a high degree of control over the affairs of the cestui que trust. The relation is not an ordinary business one. The court of equity calls it "fiduciary", and places on the trustee the duties to act with great honesty and candor

"A trust, in its simplest sense, is a confidence reposed in one person, called a trustee, for the benefit of another, called the cestui que trust, with respect to property held by the former for the benefit of the latter." Dowland v. Staley, 201 Ill.App. 6, 7.

For other definitions, see Teal v. Pleasant Grove Local Union, No. 204, 200 Ala. 23, 75 So. 335; Keeney v. Bank of Italy, 33 Cal.App. 515, 165 P. 735; Drudge v. Citizens' Bank of Akron, 64 Ind.App. 217, 113 N.E. 440; Frost v. Frost, 165 Mich. 591, 131 N.W. 60; Ward v. Buchanan, 22 N.M. 267, 160 P. 356; Templeton v. Bockler, 73 Or. 494, 144 P. 405.

See Restatement, Trusts, § 2.

Some definitions of the trust seem concerned rather with the duty or obligation of the trustee, or the right of the cestui, than with the trust. The trust in its modern sense is conceived to be the relationship or status in which are concerned certain property and persons, and incidental to which are certain rights and duties. The whole bundle of property, persons, rights, and duties makes up the trust. It is often said that a trustee holds the trust property "subject to a trust," but it would seem to be more accurate to state that he holds it subject to the duties of a trustee.

[2] Jenks, The Trust Problem, 111.

[3] See Thompson v. Thompson, 178 Iowa 1289, 160 N.W. 922.

[4] For similar definitions, see Restatement, Trusts, § 3.

BOGERT TRUSTS 2D

and solely in the interest of the beneficiary. There are many other fiduciary relations, as, for example, guardianship and executorship.

The Trust Property

It should first be noticed that a specific thing or things and specific property interests therein are always involved in the trust. In some relations men only, or men and any property, may be involved, as, for example, in agency, where A. may be the agent of B. for the performance of personal services, which have no connection with any property, or no connection with any particular property. But the trust presupposes identified things, tangible or intangible, and ascertained interests therein, to be handled or held by the trustee. What may be the trust property and how it may become such are matters to be dealt with later. The trust property is sometimes called the trust res, the corpus, the subject or subject-matter, of the trust.

It is sometimes said that the legal title to the trust property is always in the trustee. His title may be a legal or an equitable one, dependent on the nature of the title which the settlor has seen fit to give him. Thus, if the settlor has a fee-simple estate in certain lands, and conveys his interest to A. to hold in trust for B., A., the trustee, will be seised of the legal estate; but, if the settlor has contracted in writing to buy land for which he has paid the purchase price, but a deed of which he has not yet received, and the settlor transfers his interest in the land to A. in trust for B., A., the trustee, will hold merely the equitable title of the contract vendee of the land. It is because of this possibility of legal or equitable ownership that the definition given above merely states that the trustee is a title holder, without regard to the court in which his title will be recognized. In a great majority of trusts the trustee has the legal title to the trust property.

The Trust Parties

It is customary to think of three persons as connected with every trust, namely, the settlor, the trustee, and the beneficiary. But since, where the settlor declares himself a trustee, settlor and trustee are one and the same person, a trust may exist with only two persons. Since a man cannot be under an obligation to himself, the same individual cannot be settlor, trustee, and beneficiary, and the persons involved can never be less than two. But a sole trustee may be one of a number of cestuis que trust, and one of several joint trustees may be the sole cestui.[5] There are no limitations upon the maximum number of persons who may be connected with a trust, except the limitations of convenience.

In some trusts there is no settlor. These are the implied trusts created by the law for the purpose of accomplishing justice.[6] In these implied trusts no individual intentionally brings a trust into being. The court gives life to the trust. But the acts of one or more persons have caused the court to decree the trust's existence. Such persons are not settlors. Their acts merely afford the reasons which the courts give for declaring the existence of the trust. Hence, in the definition of the word "settlor" given above the word "intentionally" is used, so that the doers of acts which unintentionally result in the declaration of a trust by a court may not be included within the class of settlors.

The settlor is also sometimes called the creator of the trust, the donor, or the trustor. The phrase cestui que trust [7] is synonymous with beneficiary of the trust.

The Trust Rights and Duties

The trustee holds the property "for the benefit of" the cestui que trust. It is unnecessary now to consider how the cestui may obtain that benefit. The methods vary greatly, according to the terms of the particular trust. In one case the trustee may have no duty, except to hold the property, and the cestui que trust may take the profits directly. In another instance the trustee may be charged with the obligation of detailed management, and the cestui que trust may receive the benefits indirectly. The means of obtaining the benefits for the cestui are not at this point important. The fundamental principle is that somehow the benefit is his.

The duty of the trustee is enforceable by the cestui que trust. This quality distinguishes the trust in some jurisdictions from

[5] Post, § 40.

[6] Post, § 55.

[7] Pronounced as if spelled "cestwe kuh trust." Anderson, Dict. of Law, 162. The words are Norman French. The plural is properly "cestuis que trust," although frequently spelled "cestui que trustent," "cestui que trusts," or "cestuis que trustent"! by the courts. See City of Marquette v. Wilkinson, 119 Mich. 413, 78 N.W. 474, 43 L.R.A. 480. For a discussion of the origin, meaning, and proper form of "cestui que use" and "cestui que trust" see a note by Charles Sweet, Esq., in 26 Law Quart.Rev. 196, in which the views of Prof. Maitland are set forth. The author says: "'Cestui que use,' therefore, means 'he for whose benefit,' and 'cestui que trust' means 'he upon trust for whom,' certain property is held."

certain possible contracts. Thus, if A. promises B., for a consideration running from B. to A., that he (A.) will deliver over certain property to C., C. will in some jurisdictions have no right to enforce the performance of A.'s promise, because C. is a stranger to the contract.[8] But, if A. declares himself a trustee of property for C., C. may everywhere enforce the trust against A., regardless of privity. This quality of enforceability by the cestui que trust, notwithstanding a lack of privity, is a characteristic of the trust.

The trustee's obligation is said to be "equitable." Originally it was recognized only by the English Court of Chancery, which alone administered the rules and applied the principles of equity. Many definers of the trust make enforceability in a court of chancery or equity a part of their definition. But in the present state of the law it is deemed preferable to define the trustee's obligation as equitable, and to omit any reference to the court in which this obligation may be enforced. In England and in many American states the separate Court of Chancery has been abolished, and both legal and equitable obligations are enforced by the same court. On the other hand, in a few states the separate court of equity is maintained.[9] The trustee's obligation is based on equitable principles, whether enforced by a court having both legal and equitable jurisdiction, or by a court having solely equitable functions. In rare cases a court of law enforces the obligation of the trustee to the beneficiary. It seems wiser to omit all reference to the forum of enforcement.

Whether the right which the cestui has is a property right in the subject-matter of the trust (a right in rem), or merely a personal right against the trustee (a right in personam), is a question much debated. The arguments pro and con are stated in a later section, dealing with the nature of the interest of the cestui que trust.[10]

[8] Wald's Pollock on Contracts, 3d Ed., 243 et seq.

[9] For a discussion of the effect of constitutional changes on the separate existence of the court of equity, see 1 Pomeroy's Eq.Juris. §§ 40–42. In McClintock on Equity (p. 8) it is stated that separate courts of equity are still maintained in Alabama, Arkansas, Delaware, Mississippi, New Jersey, Tennessee, and Vermont.

[10] Post, § 42.

ORIGIN OF USES AND TRUSTS

2. Trusts, in their early development in England, were divided into two classes, namely, special or active trusts, and general, simple, or passive trusts. The latter were generally called uses. Prior to 1535, uses constituted the more important class of trusts.

Uses were introduced into England shortly after the Norman Conquest (1066 A. D.), although not enforced by the courts until the fifteenth century.

They were patterned after the German treuhand or salman.

The principal objects of their introduction were—

(a) To avoid the burdens of holding the legal title to land, such as the rights of the lord under feudal tenure, the rights of creditors, and the rights of dower and curtesy;

(b) To enable religious houses to obtain the profits of land, notwithstanding the mortmain acts which prohibited their owning land;

(c) To secure greater freedom in conveying land inter vivos;

(d) To obtain power to dispose of real property by will.

The use was a general or passive trust in which the trustee had no active duties, but was merely a receptacle of the legal title for the cestui que trust.

The words "use" and "trust" are employed as synonyms frequently by writers and judges. However, there is a distinction in their meanings. Prior to the Statute of Uses (1535) there existed in England a relationship known as a trust. Trusts were of two classes, namely, active or special, and passive, simple, or general. In cases where a trustee held property for some temporary purpose and with active duties to perform, the trust was called active or special. Thus, if A. conveyed land to B. for ten years, to take the profits of the land and apply them to the use of C., B. was an active or special trustee. These trusts were comparatively rare prior to the Statute of Uses. But if the legal title was transferred to one as a holder for the benefit of another, but with no positive duties of care or management, the trust was called general, simple, or passive, or a use. Thus, an enfeoffment of A. and his heirs to the use of B. and his heirs would create a use or general trust.[11] Uses were far more common than special trusts prior to the Statute of Uses. Indeed, by the time of Henry V (1413–1422) they were the rule rather than the exception in landholding.[12]

[11] Bacon, Uses, 8, 9; Sanders, Uses and Trusts, 3–7.

[12] Digby, History of Law of Real Property, 320.

Uses and trusts were introduced into England shortly after the Norman Conquest.[13] Recent scholars agree that they were modeled after the German treuhand or salman, rather than after the Roman fidei-commissum.[14] Under the Roman law it was not possible to give property by will to certain persons, as, for instance, persons not Roman citizens.[15] It became customary among the Romans to devise property to one capable of taking it, with a request that he deliver it to a desired devisee who was incompetent to take directly. This was the creation of a fidei-commissum. The obligation of the devisee to the desired beneficiary in this relationship was not at first legally enforceable, but later became so. This confidence was analogous in many ways to the English trust or use, but differed in that it arose by will only.

Trusts were not known to the civil law,[16] although substitutes for them have been evolved.[17]

"The feoffee to uses of the early English law corresponds point by point to the salman of the early German law, as described by Beseler fifty years ago. The salman, like the feoffee, was a person to whom land was transferred in order that he might make a conveyance according to his grantor's directions."[18]

It was said by an English lawyer many years ago that the parents of the trust were Fraud and Fear and the Court of Conscience was its nurse.[19] Certain it is that the reasons for the

[13] Ames, Origin of Uses and Trusts, 2 Select Essays in Anglo-American Legal History, 737, 741; Maitland, The Origin of Uses, 8 Harv.Law Rev. 127, 129; Development of Trusts, G. H.J.Hurst, 136 L.T. 76.

[14] Ames, Origin of Uses and Trusts, 2 Select Essays in Anglo-American Legal History, 739, 740; Maitland, The Origin of Uses, 8 Harv.Law Rev. 127, 136. The earlier view was that the use was an evolution of the fidei-commissum. Story, Eq.Juris. §§ 966, 967; Pomeroy, Eq.Juris. §§ 976–978.

[15] Digby, History of Law of Real Property, 317.

[16] Thus in Louisiana, whose system is founded on the civil law, trusts were not recognized (Marks v. Loewenberg, 143 La. 196, 78 So. 444) until Act 107 of 1920 legalized them. Under this statute the trust term could not exceed ten years after the death of the donor or the majority of a minor beneficiary. This statute was repealed by Act 7 of the Extraordinary Session of 1935. But trusts were restored to Louisiana by Act 81 of the Laws of 1938. See 13 Tul.L.R. 70, 178; 52 Harv.L.R. 145; 1 La.L.R. 774.

[17] Lepaulle, Civil Law Substitutes for Trusts, 36 Yale L.J. 1126.

[18] Holmes, Early English Equity, 2 Select Essays in Anglo-American Legal History, 705, 707.

[19] Attorney General v. Sands, Hard. 488, 491.

introduction of uses and trusts were not in all cases honorable. The common law of England attached to the holding of the legal title to land many burdens. As the feudal system prevailed when uses arose, the lord of the land was entitled to a "relief," or money payment, when the land descended to an heir of full age; to the rights of "wardship" and "marriage" when the heir was a minor; and to "aids" upon the marriage of a daughter of the lord, the knighting of his eldest son, or when the lord was held to ransom. These burdens, and others of a similar nature, fell upon the holder of the legal title. By enfeoffing another of the legal title and reserving only the use, the tenant escaped such exactions. "The legal ownership, however, represented by the feoffee to uses, was subject to the incidents of tenure, which could be enforced against the land, but by vesting the seisin in two or more feoffees jointly, whose number was renewed from time to time, and the survivor of whom took the whole legal estate, the burdens incident to the descent of land were generally avoided."[20]

So, too, upon the commission of certain crimes the holders of the legal title suffered a forfeiture, which could be avoided by vesting the legal estate in another and retaining only the use. And the common law gave no remedy to a creditor against the interest of a cestui que use. Some dishonest persons escaped payment of their debts by a transfer of land to a feoffee to uses. The incidents of dower and curtesy attached only to the legal estate. A man, desiring to prevent the attaching of a dower interest in a prospective wife, could accomplish the result by a conveyance to a feoffee to uses. And a corresponding fraud could be worked by a woman with respect to her husband's estate by the curtesy of the law of England.

Not only was the equitable estate of cestui que use free from dangers and duties, but it could be held by a large and influential class which could not hold the legal estate in lands, namely, religious corporations. The mortmain acts forbade the alienation of land to religious corporations, and thus prevented the religious orders from acquiring directly the real property they needed, and which charitably minded persons often desired to give them. Furthermore, certain of the orders had taken the vows of poverty, and could not consistently hold property in their own names. By a conveyance of land to an individual, to be held for the use of the religious order, however, the monks and friars could have the benefit of the land, though not the sei-

[20] 1 Tiffany, Real Property, 200.

sin. In the opinion of some scholars, the religious bodies were the first to employ the use extensively.[21]

The equitable estate or use was also more easily dealt with and transferred than the legal estate. The latter could be conveyed only by feoffment with livery of seisin, fine, or recovery. Publicity was essential. The use, on the other hand, could be created and transferred secretly, and with little or no ceremony. This capacity for secret transfer favored fraud on later purchasers of the land and encouraged the employment of the use by the unscrupulous. Likewise the use was capable of being disposed of by will. The legal estate was not so disposable at that period. To be able to control land after death was no doubt a great incentive to the creation of uses.

USES AND TRUSTS BEFORE THE STATUTE OF USES

3. **Originally uses and trusts were not enforceable in any court, but were purely honorary.**

   The courts of law did not recognize the claims of the cestui que trust, because no writ existed for that purpose.

   Chancery began to enforce uses and trusts in the early part of the fifteenth century.

Early English law was extremely rigid. Forms and technicalities were strictly observed. The courts of common law gave no remedy, unless a writ fitted exactly to the case could be found. The introduction of new remedies through the law courts was a matter of great difficulty.[22] The interests of the beneficiary of a use were not protected by the common-law courts, because no writ existed to fit the case. Uses were a novelty. The ecclesiastical courts had no jurisdiction to enforce them. Therefore, for many years uses and trusts existed as honorary obligations, but had no legal standing. If the trustee saw fit to deny that he held the property as trustee, and to appropriate it to his own use, he might do so with impunity.[23] Fiduciary relations with respect to money and chattels were early enforced by the common-law courts, but these were the so-called "common-law trusts," and not uses. If money were delivered to A.,

---

[21] Maitland, The Origin of Uses, 8 Harv. Law Rev. 127, 130; Jenks, Short History of English Law, 96.

[22] Spence, History of the Court of Chancery, 2 Select Essays in Anglo-American Legal History, 219.

[23] Ames, Lectures on Legal History, 236, 237.

to be paid to B., the common-law action of account lay.[24] If a chattel were delivered to another for the use of a third, detinue could be brought by the beneficiary.[25]

But the development of the Court of Chancery wrought a change. About the time that uses and trusts were arising, it became the custom to petition the king or his council for relief in cases where the law courts gave no remedy. If no writ was available, or if the opponent was powerful enough to prevent justice, the aggrieved suitor besought the king or his council for a special and extra-legal dispensation. Of this council the Chancellor was a member, and about the time of the reign of Edward I (1272–1307) it became usual to refer these petitions to the Chancellor for consideration. The Chancellor became the custodian of the king's conscience, and his court the court of conscience. Equity and fairness were supposed to rule there, rather than technicality.

It was natural that cestuis que trust who had been injured, due to a failure of their trustees to hold the property for their use, should apply to the Chancellor for relief. At some time early in the fifteenth century the justice of these petitions began to be recognized by chancery, and uses and trusts were enforced.[26] The Chancellors of those days were churchmen, and their consciences were naturally shocked by the unfairness of allowing a trustee to make away with his beneficiary's property. Probably, too, the common-law trust appealed to the Chancellor as a quasi-precedent. The process by which the Chancellor acted was known as a subpœna. It commanded the defendant to do or refrain from doing a certain act. The relief was personal and specific, not merely money damages. Hence it is often said that cestui que trust has a remedy only by subpœna.

[24] Anonymous, Year Book, 6 Henry IV, folio 7, plac. 33; Ames' Cases on Trusts, 2d Ed., p. 1.

[25] Ames, Origin of Uses and Trusts, 2 Select Essays in Anglo-American Legal History, 743.

[26] Ames, Origin of Uses and Trusts, 2 Select Essays in Anglo-American Legal History, 741, 742.

THE STATUTE OF USES

4. The Statute of Uses provided that, wherever any person should thereafter be seised of land to the use of another, the latter should be deemed the legal owner of such lands, and the taker subject to a use should have no interest in the lands.

The object of this statute was to convert the equitable interest of the cestui que use into a legal interest, and thus—

(a) Prevent the loss of feudal rights by landlords;

(b) Obviate fraud on creditors, alienees, dowresses, and tenants by the curtesy;

(c) Probably to injure the religious orders which were the beneficiaries of uses.

By the beginning of the sixteenth century uses and trusts had come to involve serious inconveniences and frauds. It has been said that the principal objects of their introduction were to relieve landowners of the burdens of feudal landholding, to enable religious orders to have the benefit of land, and to effect greater freedom in the conveyance of real property. These advantages obtained from uses were abused. From time to time prior to the Statute of Uses acts in aid of creditors, purchasers, and landowners defrauded by uses, and against the holding of lands to the use of religious houses, were enacted by Parliament,[27] but they were ineffective. The preamble to the statute catalogues the evils thought to be caused by the use in 1535.[28]

---

[27] Digby, History of the Law of Real Property, 318, 319; Cruise, Uses, 34-37.

[28] "Where by the common laws of this realm, lands, tenements, and hereditaments be not devisable by testament, nor ought to be transferred from one to another, but by solemn livery and seisin, matter of record, writing sufficient made bona fide, without covin or fraud, yet nevertheless divers and sundry imaginations, subtle inventions, and practices have been used, whereby the hereditaments of this realm have been conveyed from one to another by fraudulent feoffments, fines, recoveries, and other assurances craftily made to secret uses, intents, and trusts, and also by wills and testaments sometimes made by nude parolx and words, sometimes by signs and tokens, and sometimes by writing, and for the most part made by such persons as be visited with sickness, in their extreme agonies and pains, or at such time as they have had scantly any good memory or remembrance; at which times they, being provoked by greedy and covetous persons lying in wait about them, do many times dispose indiscreetly and unadvisedly their lands and inheritances; by reason whereof, and by occasion of which fraudulent feoffments, fines, recoveries, and other like assurances to uses, confidences, and trusts, divers and many heirs have been unjustly at sundry times disinherited, and lords have lost their

Aside from the reasons named in the statute itself, there was, according to some authorities,[29] the desire on the part of Henry VIII to destroy the monasteries and confiscate their property, which he thought could best be accomplished by abolishing the method by which they held land, namely, the use.

The famous Statute of Uses (27 Henry VIII, c. 10) was enacted in 1535.[30] Its object was to abolish uses, and this it proposed to do by wiping out the estate of the feoffee to uses, and giving to the former holder of the use the entire legal estate. The statute "executed the use," in the phrase of the day. Instead of leaving it to the feoffee to uses to transfer the legal title to the cestui que use when the latter required it, the law transferred such interest immediately on the creation of the use.[31] By this "transmutation of the use into possession" it was thought that this troublesome class of equitable interests would cease to exist, and that all estates in lands would be subject to the same burdens, the same rules of tenure and conveyance. There would be no uses in land, because the law would change them to legal interests at the instant of their birth.

---

wards, marriages, reliefs, harriots, escheats, aids, *pur fair fitz chivalier* and *pur file marier*, and scantly any person can be certainly assured of any lands by them purchased, nor know surely against whom they shall use their actions or execution for their rights, titles and duties; also men married have lost their tenancies by the curtesy, women their dowers; manifest perjuries by trial of such secret wills and uses have been committed; the king's highness hath lost the profits and advantages of the lands of persons attainted, and of the lands craftily put in feoffment to the use of aliens born, and also the profits of waste for a year and a day of felons attainted, and the lords their escheats thereof. * * *" Preamble to St. 27 Henry VIII, c. 10, as quoted in Digby, History of the Law of Real Property, 347, 348.

[29] Jenks, Short Hist. of English Law, 99. Holdsworth is opposed to this view. Causes Which Shaped the Statute of Uses, 26 Harv.Law Rev. 108, 121.

[30] For a discussion of the events leading up to its passage, see Holdsworth, Causes Which Shaped the Statute of Uses, 26 Harv.Law Rev. 108.

[31] The active portion of the statute was as follows: "That where any person or persons stand or be seized, or at any time hereafter shall happen to be seized, of and in any honours, castles, manors, lands, tenements, rents, services, reversions, remainders or other hereditaments to the use, confidence or trust of any other person or persons, or of any body politick, by reason of any bargain, sale, feoffment, fine, recovery, covenant, contract, agreement, will or otherwise, by any manner means whatsoever it be; that in every such case all and every such person or persons, and bodies politick, that have or hereafter shall have any such use, confidence or trust, in fee simple, fee tail, for term of life or for years, or otherwise, or any use, confidence or trust, in remainder or reverter, shall from henceforth stand and be seized, deemed and

THE EFFECT OF THE STATUTE OF USES

5. The Statute of Uses did not have its intended effect because—
   (a) By virtue of its express provisions, and because of the construction given it by the courts of law, certain equitable interests were not converted into legal interests, namely, equitable interests in personal property, active trusts, and uses upon uses;
   (b) These equitable interests not so converted into legal interests were recognized and enforced by the Court of Chancery as trusts after the Statute of Uses, and form the basis of the modern law of trusts.

To the common-law judges, who alone had to do with legal estates, fell the task of construing the Statute of Uses, and determining when the statute executed the use and gave to the cestui que use the legal estate. It was evident from the express words of the statute that uses in personalty were not included. The statute spoke only of real property. And since it referred only to instances in which the feoffee to uses was "seized," it was readily held that the statute had no application to interests in real property other than freeholds. Therefore, a gift to A. of a term for five years, to the use of B., was not affected by that statute. The statute was held, also, not to apply to active trusts but only to passive or general trusts. Duties of administration required the legal title in the trustee. Thus, if land were conveyed to A. for life, to collect the profits thereof and pay them to B. and his heirs, the trust would be active, and the statute would not execute the use, but leave the legal estate in A. and the equitable interest in B. separately.

Lastly, the courts of law held that the statute did not affect a use upon a use. It could operate only once. After such operation, its force was spent. Thus, if lands were conveyed to A.

adjudged in lawful seisin, estate and possession of and in the same honours, castles, manors, lands, tenements, rents, services, reversions, remainders and hereditaments, with their appurtenances, to all intents, constructions and purposes in the law, of and in such like estates as they had or shall have in use, trust or confidence of or in the same; and that the estate, title, right and possession that was in such person or persons that were, or hereafter shall be seized of any lands, tenements or hereditaments, to the use, confidence or trust of any such person or persons, or of any body politick, be from henceforth clearly deemed and adjudged to be in him or them that have, or hereafter shall have, such use, confidence or trust, after such quality, manner, form and condition as they had before, in or to the use, confidence or trust that was in them."

and his heirs, to the use of B. and his heirs, to the use of C. and his heirs, the statute was held to transfer the use of B. into possession and give him the legal estate, but not to convert the use of C. into possession and destroy B.'s legal estate.[32] This construction has generally been thought to be a mere quibble, which improperly caused a partial destruction of the statute.[33] But one scholar of high repute has pointed out that the use upon a use was held void by the Court of Chancery before the passage of the Statute of Uses, and that, therefore, the decision of the common-law courts in Tyrrel's Case was entirely correct.[34] Where a use upon a use was attempted the second party named would not be seised of land to the use of the third party, but rather of a use for his benefit, so that logically a case would not be presented for the operation of the statute as to the second use.[35]

A large number of uses and trusts were, as shown above, left unaffected by the Statute of Uses and were recognized and enforced by chancery. The name "trust" was, after the Statute of Uses, applied to all the equitable interests so sustained, whether they had before been denominated uses or trusts. Perhaps the Court of Chancery had no desire to stimulate the enactment of a second Statute of Uses by continuing the name "use." Perhaps it felt that the Statute of Uses had transferred to the law courts jurisdiction over uses.[36] It will be seen that the interests thus supported by chancery after the Statute of Uses, and called "trusts," were composed of the old active or special trusts and that part of the old general trusts or uses which the statute did not destroy. These interests are the modern trusts, which form the basis of the present English and American systems.

[32] Tyrrel's Case, Dyer 155, 1557.

[33] Jenks, Short History of English Law, 100. "By this means, a statute made upon great consideration, introduced in a solemn and pompous manner, by this strict construction, has had no other effect than to add, at most, three words ["to the use"] to a conveyance." Lord Hardwicke, Hopkins v. Hopkins, 1 Atk. 581, 591.

[34] Ames, The Origin of Uses and Trusts; 2 Select Essays in Anglo-American Legal History, 747 et seq.

[35] See Perry, Trusts, 7th Ed., § 301.

[36] See 17 Mich.Law Rev. 87, for a discussion of the reasons for the survival of the trust. It is there suggested that the statute did not contemplate the active trust which was then rare and little developed.

TRUSTS IN AMERICA

6. The English system of equity jurisprudence, of which the trust was a part, was adopted almost bodily by the American states.

Just as the colonists of the thirteen original states adopted substantially entire the common law of England, so they took over with little change the English scheme of equity jurisprudence, a part of which was the system of trusts. The development of chancery in colonial America, however, was slow and difficult. In Massachusetts no equity court existed for any substantial time until 1877.[37] Redress in extraordinary cases was had only through petition to the Legislature. In minor cases the Legislature doled out to the common-law courts from time to time meager equity powers, but no inclusive jurisdiction. In Pennsylvania no court of chancery was founded until 1836.[38] The law courts often worked out equitable relief through their own forms. In New York, in 1701, by an ordinance of Governor and council, the Governor was appointed chancellor.[39] The Legislature and people objected to this method of forming the new court and sought its abolition. This movement failed, but the court was thereafter unpopular and little patronized. In Virginia chancery was at first administered by the Governor and council and later by the general court and county courts. In the other colonies the governor, aided by his council, usually exercised the powers of a chancellor.[40]

Towards the close of the eighteenth century, when trusts came into more common use in America, the English system had been well developed, and was naturally adopted in substantial entirety by the American colonial and early state chancellors. The first state reports show that, considering the poverty and newness of America, trusts were involved in litigation with a fair measure of frequency.[41]

---

[37] Chancery in Massachusetts, E. H. Woodruff, 5 Law Quart.Rev. 370.

[38] The Administration of Equity through Common-Law Forms in Pennsylvania, S. G. Fisher, 2 Select Essays in Anglo-American Legal History, 810.

[39] History of New York, Wm. Smith, Yates' Ed., 385–389; preface to vol. 1, Johns.Ch.Rep.

[40] Courts of Chancery in the American Colonies, S. D. Wilson, 2 Select Essays in Anglo-American Legal History, 779.

[41] In the following cases, decided before 1800, a trust was discussed or construed:

Connecticut, Bacon v. Taylor, Kirby, 368, 1788.

In England a small part of the law of trusts has been codified in the Trustee Act[42] and the Charitable Trusts Act,[43] but most of the principles are stated in judicial decision alone. In the United States trust codes of fair size have been enacted in New York[44] (followed by Michigan,[45] Wisconsin,[46] and Minnesota[47]) and in California[48] (followed by Montana,[49] North Dakota,[50] Oklahoma,[51] and South Dakota[52]), but even in those states the amount of statutory trust law is small.

An attempt has been made in recent years to codify small parts of trust law in the Uniform Fiduciaries Act,[53] Uniform Principal and Income Act,[54] Uniform Trusts Act,[55] Uniform Trustees' Accounting Act,[56] and Uniform Common Trust Fund

Maryland, State ex rel Hindman v. Reed, 4 Har. & McH. 6, 1797; Reeder v. Cartwright, 2 Har. & McH. 469, 1790; Swearingham v. Stull's Ex'rs 4 Har. McH. 38, 1797; Ridgely v. Carey, 4 Har. & McH. 167, 1798; Dorsey's Ex'rs v. Dorsey's Adm'r, 4 Har. & McH. 231, 1798; Hatcheson v. Tilden, 4 Har. & McH. 279, 1799; Bank of Columbia v. Ross, 4 Har. & McH. 456, 1799.

New Jersey, Arrowsmith v. Van Harlingen's Ex'rs, 1 N.J.L. 26, 1790. Green v. Beatty, 1 N.J.L. 142, 1792.

New York, Jackson v. Sternbergh, 1 Johns.Cas. 153, 1799; Neilson v. Blight, 1 Johns.Cas 205, 1799.

North Carolina, Hogg's Ex'rs v. Ashe, 2 N.C. 471, 1797.

Pennsylvania, Kennedy v. Fury, 1 Dall. 72, 1 L.Ed. 42, 1783; Field v. Biddle, 2 Dall. 171, 1 L.Ed. 335, 1792; Knight v. Reese, 2 Dall. 182, 1 L.Ed. 340, 1792; Cox's Lessee v. Grant, 1 Yeates 164, 1792; Fogler's Lessee v. Evig, 2 Yeates 119, 1796; Lee's Lessee v. Tiernan, Add. 348, 1798.

South Carolina, Lindsay v. Lindsay's Adm'rs, 1 Desaus. 150, 1787; Bethune v. Beresford, 1 Desaus. 174, 1790; Stock's Ex'x v. Stock's Ex'r, 1 Desaus. 191, 1791; Gadsden's Ex'rs v. Lord's Ex'rs, 1 Desaus. 208, 1791; Wilson v. Wilson, 1 Desaus. 219, 1791.

Virginia, McCarty v. McCarty's Ex'rs, 2 Va.Col.Dec. 34, 1733; Hill v. Hill's Ex'rs, 2 Va.Col.Dec. 60, 1736; Coleman v. Dickenson, 2 Va.Col.Dec. 119, 1740; Pendleton v. Whiting, Wythe 38, 1791.

[42] 15 Geo. V, c. 19, 1925.

[43] 15 & 16 Geo. V, c. 27, 1925.

[44] New York Real Property Law, §§ 90–117; Personal Property Law, §§ 10–24.

[45] Mich.Ann.St. §§ 26.51 to 26.81.

[46] Wis.St.1941, §§ 231.01–231.33.

[47] Minn.St.1927, §§ 8081–8106.

[48] Cal.Civ.Code, secs. 852–871.

[49] Mont.Rev.Codes 1935, §§ 7878–7927.

[50] N.D.Comp.L.1913, §§ 6271–6318.

[51] Okl.St.1931, §§ 11803–11836, as amended L.1941, H.B. 174, p. 505, 60 Okl.St.Ann. §§ 131–175.53, 46 Okl.St. Ann. §§ 31–39.

[52] S.D.Code 1939, §§ 59.0101–59.0317.

[53] Post, § 159.

[54] Post, § 135.

[55] Post, § 99.

[56] Post, § 145.

Act.[57] These acts were prepared by the National Conference of Commissioners on Uniform State Laws. Their effects and the extent of their adoption are stated in later sections. But even if all these statutes were adopted, the great bulk of trust law would be case law.

The trust is a common law institution, although substitutes for it have been invented in civil law countries.[58] It was unknown in Louisiana until 1920, when it was validated to a limited extent, but this act was repealed in 1935. A comprehensive trust code was adopted in 1938.[59]

In 1935 The American Law Institute completed a restatement of the American law of trusts. This treatise sets forth the rules of law affecting trust creation and administration as the institute believes them to exist. It gives illustrations and comments.[60] References to the various sections of the Restatement of Trusts are appended in the footnotes to this text.

---

[57] Post, § 109.

[58] Lepaulle, Civil Law Substitutes for Trusts, 36 Yale L.J. 1126; Nussbaum, Sociological and Comparative Aspects of the Trust, 38 Col.L.R. 408.

[59] La.Acts 1920, No. 107; La.Acts Sp.Sess.1935, No. 7; La.Acts 1938, No. 81. See Stubbs, 1 La.L.R. 774; Wisdom, 13 Tul.L.R. 70; Nabors, 13 Tul. L.R. 178.

[60] For comments on the Trusts Restatement, see Arnold, 31 Col.L.R. 800; Scott, 31 Col.L.R. 1266; Isaacs, 8 Am.L.S.R. 424; Butler, 6 Ford.L.R. 228; Vanneman, 34 Mich.L.R. 1109.

BOGERT TRUSTS 2D—2

CHAPTER 2

DISTINCTIONS BETWEEN TRUSTS AND OTHER RELATIONS

Sec.
7. Debt.
8. Debt or Trust—the Specific Property Criterion.
9. The Debtor Making Himself Trustee—The Specific Property Criterion.
10. Bailment.
11. Equitable Charge.
12. Assignment of a Chose in Action.
13. Executorship.
14. Agency.
15. Guardianship.
16. Promoters and Officers of Corporations.
17. Receivership.
18. Life Tenant and Remainderman.
19. Deeds of Trust in the Nature of Mortgages.

DEBT[1]

7. The trust is distinguished from a debt in that—
   (a) Debt arises out of a contract, whereas the trust arises from a conveyance;
   (b) A contract generally requires consideration to make it enforceable; a trust does not;
   (c) Sometimes contracts are not enforceable by third party beneficiaries, whereas trusts do not require privity between the trustee and beneficiary;
   (d) The trustee's obligations are equitable, while the debtor's are legal;
   (e) The trustee's obligation relates to specific property, whereas the debtor's does not necessarily do so;
   (f) The trustee occupies a fiduciary relation, but the debtor does not.

Debt Arises Out of Contract

Debts are obligations arising from the making of contracts. Hence their enforceability and the methods of their enforcement depend upon the rules of contract law which, for the most part, have been developed by the common law courts.

Trust creation is, on the other hand, essentially a conveyance. The declarant of the trust conveys an equitable interest to the

[1] Restatement, Trusts, §§ 12-14.

beneficiary.[2] The transferor to a trustee conveys the legal interest to the trustee and the equitable interest to the beneficiary.[3] It is true that one may create a trust by promising to pay money to another as trustee for a third party and here rules of contract law will determine whether the trust has a subject matter of value;[4] but still the promisor is also conveying legal and equitable interests in the chose in action against himself.

Consideration

The contracts out of which the debt arises are, with some exceptions, dependent on consideration or the seal for their enforceability.[5] Completely created trusts are enforceable, without regard to the receipt of consideration by settlor or trustee.[6] Thus, if A. agrees voluntarily to pay $100 to B., the promise may be repudiated by A. with impunity in most cases; while if A. conveys land without consideration to B., in trust for C., C. can enforce the trust against B. regardless of lack of benefit received by A. in return for the conveyance.

Privity

In a few jurisdictions it is still necessary, at least in some cases, to show that the plaintiff was a party to the contract which he seeks to enforce.[7] This idea of privity is foreign to the law of trusts. Chancery enforces trust obligations in favor of beneficiaries who were not parties to the trust instrument and knew nothing of its creation until after the event.[8] Here again the conveyance theory of trust creation is apparent.

Debt a Legal, Trust an Equitable, Obligation

As previously stated, the trust is an obligation resting solely on equitable principles, and originally enforceable only in chancery. In a great variety of ways equity will act upon the trustee, and compel him to do or refrain from doing certain acts.[9] The debtor's duties, however, are legal, and are enforced by an action to recover the amount of the debt ordinarily. Equity may, of course, aid the creditor; but the primary method of enforcement is by legal remedies. The courts of law have been

[2] See § 41, post.
[3] See § 21, post.
[4] See § 21, post.
[5] Restatement, Contracts, §§ 75-110.
[6] See, § 27, post.
[7] Restatement, Contracts, §§ 133-147.
[8] See § 40, post.
[9] Post, § 148.

largely responsible for defining and enforcing contract rights; whereas chancery first recognized, and has fostered and developed the trust.[9]

The Trust Requires a Definite Subject

The property which the trustee controls for the benefit of his cestui que trust is always definite property. A debtor does not owe his creditor definite money. He owes him any money. If A. is a trustee for B., A. always owns specific property, as, for example, the Jones farm, or certain five thousand one-dollar bills. A. may have the power under the trust to change the form of the investment, and to buy a bond with the bills originally received; but the bond then becomes the specific subject-matter. On the other hand, if A. borrows $5,000 from B., it is obvious that A. may satisfy his obligation to B. by paying any bills or coin. He need not return the identical bills or coin received from B., or their substitutes, in case he invests the money so received from B.

The results of this contrast between trust and debt are striking. If the debtor loses any particular article through negligence or accident, he will not be absolved from payment of his debt; but, if the trust property is lost or destroyed without the fault of the trustee, his obligation is wiped out.[10]

Again, each creditor is obliged to share pro rata with his fellow creditors all the property of his bankrupt debtor,[11] even though the debtor have in his hands and capable of identification certain specific money lent him or goods sold him. On the other hand, the cestui que trust may take from the assets of the bankrupt trustee the specific trust property, if he can identify it.[12]

A debtor may, with certain exceptions unnecessary to mention here, do as he likes with the money he receives from his creditor, or with his property generally. A trustee will be guilty of the crime of embezzlement, if he converts to his own use the trust funds.[13] The specific nature of the trust property requires him to keep it separate from private use.

[10] Shoemaker v. Hinze, 53 Wis. 116, 10 N.W. 86.

[11] City of Sturgis v. Meade County Bank, 38 S.D. 317, 161 N.W. 327.

[12] Post, § 152.

[13] People v. Meadows, 199 N.Y. 1, 92 N.E. 128.

No Element of the Fiduciary in Debt

The debtor's obligations are all self-imposed. He agrees to pay the creditor $100 on January 1st. That is his only duty to the creditor. There is no relationship of trust and confidence between debtor and creditor. The law imposes no obligation on the debtor to deal with the creditor with any more than ordinary fairness. The debtor may look out for himself. He has no duty to protect the creditor. They deal with each other at arm's length. In opposition to this the trustee is a fiduciary, whose obligations are not only those which he has voluntarily assumed by express agreement, but also those which the law imposes on him, whether he will or no. Those law-imposed duties are that the trustee treat the beneficiary with the utmost fairness and frankness, conceal nothing from him, and take no advantage of him. To illustrate: A debtor may buy from his creditor any property which the latter will sell him, and which he (the debtor) can pay for. But a cestui que trust may avoid a sale from himself to his trustee, unless the latter can prove the transaction was absolutely fair and open.[14]

Because of this intimacy and control over the beneficiary's affairs, a trustee is subject to arrest under some statutes for breach of his duties, where a mere debtor would not be.[15]

DEBT OR TRUST—THE SPECIFIC PROPERTY CRITERION

8. Frequently where insolvency of an obligor has intervened, it is important to determine whether he was a debtor out of whose estate a mere dividend can be recovered, or a trustee from whose estate specific property can be taken. The more important situations involving this controversy are the cases of

    (a) Commercial paper delivered to a bank for collection;
    (b) Money paid to agents;
    (c) Money deposited or paid to enable the deliveree to meet an obligation of the deliveror;
    (d) Security deposits of tenants and servants;
    (e) Funds delivered to be lent or invested;
    (f) Funds delivered to be transmitted or to furnish credit for the deliveror at a distance;
    (g) Bank deposits.

---

[14] Post, § 63. § 826; Wallace & Sons v. Castle, 14 Hun, N.Y., 106.

[15] New York Civil Practice Act,

Collection of Commercial Paper

Drafts, checks, and notes are frequently deposited by a customer with his bank for the purpose of having the bank collect the paper from the drawee or maker. Many of these instruments are payable by parties at a distance and hence the instruments have to be sent by the original bank through banking channels for collection. For instance, if A. has received from B. a check drawn by B. in favor of A. on the First National Bank of Jonesville and A. lives in Brownstown, A. will deposit the check to the credit of his account in a Brownstown bank and it will be forwarded by the Brownstown bank through other banks (generally through the Federal Reserve system) to the Bank of Jonesville for collection.

The cases of negotiable paper deposited for collection may be divided into three classes, namely: (1) Cases where the paper is uncollected at the time the dispute arises, and the contending parties are the depositor of the paper and the collecting bank; (2) cases where the paper has been collected when the rights of the parties are fixed, and the litigants are depositor and collector; (3) cases where the rights of a subagent of the original collector are involved.

The majority of the courts which have considered the first class of cases, namely, those of uncollected paper in the hands of the original collector, have declared the relationship that of principal and agent, and have said that no title passed to the collector by virtue of the deposit of such paper for collection.[16] Little or no attention seems to have been paid to the form of the indorsement to the collector, whether general and unqualified, or restrictive. This would seem to be an influential factor. An unrestrictive indorsement would pass title to the instrument to the collector, and, since ordinarily he would not also be the beneficial owner, he would seem to be properly a trustee. But if the

---

[16] Giles v. Perkins, 9 East 12;. Commercial Nat. Bank v. Armstrong, 148 U.S. 50, 13 S.Ct. 533, 37 L.Ed. 363; St. Louis & S. F. R. Co. v. Johnston, 133 U.S. 566, 10 S.Ct. 390, 33 L.Ed. 683; Richardson v. New Orleans Coffee Co., C.C.A.La. 102 F. 785, 43 C.C.A. 583; Balbach v. Frelinghuysen, C.C.N.J., 15 F. 675; Manufacturers' Nat. Bank v. Continental Bank, 148 Mass. 553, 20 N.E. 193, 2 L.R.A. 699, 12 Am.St.Rep. 598; Bank of America v. Waydell, 187 N.Y. 115, 79 N.E. 857; National Butchers' & Drovers' Bank v. Hubbell, 117 N.Y. 384, 22 N.E. 1031, 7 L.R.A. 852, 15 Am.St.Rep. 515; Scott v. Ocean Bank in City of New York, 23 N.Y. 289; Hazlett v. Commercial Nat. Bank, 132 Pa. 118, 19 A. 55; Second Nat. Bank of Columbia v. Cummings, 89 Tenn. 609, 18 S.W. 115, 24 Am.St.Rep. 618.

§ 8 DEBT OR TRUST—THE SPECIFIC PROPERTY CRITERION

indorsement were restrictive, in that it was "for collection," title would not pass to the collector, although he would have power to sue on the instrument, and he would be a mere agent.[17] Occasionally the collecting bank, prior to collection, is called a trustee,[18] or a bailee of the paper.[19]

Whether called agent, trustee, or bailee, the result reached by these courts is the same. The depositor may take back the uncollected paper,[20] unless the collector has transferred it to an innocent purchaser for value. Since the property concerned is negotiable paper, it matters not whether the right of the depositor is an equitable or a legal one. Either would be cut off by a negotiation to a bona fide purchaser for value.[21]

In a few cases it has been held that the collector, prior to collection, was a debtor of the depositor of the negotiable paper. In these instances immediate, unconditional credit was given to the depositor for the amount of the paper. In some cases the indorsement was restrictive, "for collection" only,[22] while in others the indorsement was general.[23]

As to the second class mentioned above, namely those cases where the collector has received the money and the contest is between depositor and collector, there is a conflict of authority. It would seem logical that the collecting bank should be regarded as a debtor after collection in most cases, since it does not, in the ordinary instance, keep separate the bills, coins or credit received

---

[17] Negotiable Instruments Law, § 37; 1 Daniel, Neg.Inst., 6th Ed., § 698d.

[18] Jones v. Kilbreth, 49 Ohio St. 401, 31 N.E. 346.

[19] Beal v. City of Somerville, C.C.A.Mass., 50 F. 647, 1 C.C.A. 598, 17 L.R.A. 291.

[20] Kirstein Leather Co. v. Deitrick, C.C.A.Mass., 86 F.2d 793; American Barrel Co. v. Commissioner of Banks, 290 Mass. 174, 195 N.E. 335. If the representative of the failed bank collects the item after the bank's insolvency has been adjudged, the forwarder of the item is entitled to a preference to the extent of the amount collected. Hardesty v. Smith, 118 Fla. 464, 159 So. 522. Fine v. Receiver of Dickenson County Bank, 163 Va. 157, 175 S.E. 863, 94 A.L.R. 1393.

[21] There is some ambiguity in the discussion of the relationship here existing. Thus, one writer speaks of the collector as an "agent, i. e., trustee" (Ames, Cases on Trusts, 2d Ed., 18, 19), and another calls the collector an "agent or trustee" (Tiffany, Banks and Banking, 28).

[22] First Nat. Bank of Elkhart v. Armstrong, C.C.Ohio, 39 F. 231; Ayres v. Farmers' & Merchants' Bank, 79 Mo. 421, 49 Am.Rep. 235.

[23] Carstairs v. Bates, 3 Camp. 301; Hoffman v. First Nat. Bank of Jersey City, 46 N.J.L. 604; Metropolitan Nat. Bank of New York v. Loyd, 90 N.Y. 530.

for the collected paper. As a rule the collecting bank expects to pay the depositor any funds which it has conveniently at hand. It expects to have the right to use the particular cash or credit received as the proceeds of the collection for its own purposes, and to substitute others when payment is made to the depositor. Such incidents are inconsistent with a trust, which is always founded on definite subject-matter. Many courts have held the collector to be a mere debtor after collection.[24]

On the other hand, however, upon varying degrees of evidence of an intent to keep the collected funds separate, it has been held in many cases that the collector was a trustee of the amount collected.[25]

[24] Mackersy v. Ramsays, 9 Clark & F. 818; Bank of Commerce v. Russell, Fed.Cas.No.884; Nixon State Bank v. First State Bank of Bridgeport, 180 Ala. 291, 60 So. 868; Plumas County Bank v. Bank of Rideout, Smith & Co., 165 Cal. 126, 131 P. 360, 47 L.R.A.,N.S., 552; Gonyer v. Williams, 168 Cal. 452, 143 P. 736; Cronheim v. Postal Telegraph-Cable Co., 10 Ga.App. 716, 74 S.E. 78; Citizens' Nat. Bank of Danville, Ky., v. Haynes, 144 Ga. 490, 87 S.E. 399; Tinkham v. Heyworth, 31 Ill. 519; Union Nat. Bank v. Citizens' Bank, 153 Ind. 44, 54 N.E. 97; American Nat. Bank v. Owensboro Savings Bank & Trust Co.'s Receiver, 146 Ky. 194, 142 S.W. 239, 38 L.R.A.,N.S., 146; Alexander County Nat. Bank v. Conner, 110 Miss. 653, 70 So. 827; Gordon v. Rasines, 5 Misc. 192, 25 N.Y.S. 767; North Carolina Corporation Commission v. Merchants' & Farmers' Bank, 137 N.C. 697, 50 S. E. 308; Commercial & Farmers' Nat. Bank of Baltimore v. Davis, 115 N. C. 226, 20 S.E. 370; Schafer v. Olson, 24 N.D. 542, 139 N.W. 983, 43 L.R.A., N.S., 762, Ann.Cas.1915C, 653; In re Bank of Oregon, 32 Or. 84, 51 P. 87; Akin v. Jones, 93 Tenn. 353, 27 S.W. 669, 25 L.R.A. 523, 42 Am.St.Rep. 921; Bowman v. First Nat. Bank, 9 Wash. 614, 38 P. 211, 43 Am.St.Rep. 870; Hallam v. Tillinghast, 19 Wash. 20, 52 P. 329.

In the following cases an agreement for weekly or other periodic remittances of the collected funds showed clearly that the collector was at liberty to satisfy his obligation with any money, and hence the collector was held to be a debtor after collection; People v. City Bank of Rochester, 93 N.Y. 582; National Butchers' & Drovers' Bank v. Hubbell, 117 N.Y. 384, 22 N.E. 1031, 7 L. R.A. 852, 15 Am.St.Rep. 515; McCormick Harvesting Mach. Co. v. Yankton Sav. Bank, 15 S.D. 196, 87 N.W. 974.

[25] American Can Co. v. Williams, 178 F. 420, 101 C.C.A. 634; Western German Bank v. Norvell, C.C.A.Fla., 134 F. 724, 69 C.C.A. 330; State Nat. Bank of Little Rock v. First Nat. Bank of Atchison, Kan., 124 Ark. 531, 187 S.W. 673; Henderson v. O'Conor, 106 Cal. 385, 39 P. 786; Kansas State Bank v. First State Bank, 62 Kan. 788, 64 P. 634; German Fire Ins. Co. v. Kimble, 66 Mo. App. 370; Griffin v. Chase, 36 Neb. 328, 54 N.W. 572; Anheuser-Busch Brewing Ass'n v. Morris. 36 Neb. 31, 53 N.W. 1037; Thompson v. Gloucester City Sav. Inst., N.J.Ch., 8 A. 97; Arnot v. Bingham, 55 Hun 553, 9 N.Y.S. 68, 29 N.Y.St.Rep. 878; People v. Bank of Dansville, 39 Hun, N.Y., 187; Warren-Scharf Asphalt Paving Co. v. Dunn, 8 App.Div. 205,

§ 8 DEBT OR TRUST—THE SPECIFIC PROPERTY CRITERION 25

Occasionally a memorandum for separation [26] or a provision for immediate remittance of the collected fund [27] has given more secure basis for the declaration of a trust.

The third situation, under the analysis given above, is that where the collector or agent with whom the paper is originally deposited forwards it to a subagent for collection. Two questions may arise while the subagent bank has the paper or its proceeds, namely: Is the agent bank a debtor or trustee? and is the subagent bank debtor or trustee?

With reference to the first question, it would seem that the agent bank, the original collector, should have no responsibility, either as debtor or trustee, if it has used due care in selecting the subagent, and the latter has in his possession the paper or its proceeds. The agent in such a situation ought not to be held to be a debtor, because he has received no money belonging to the depositor as a result of the collection; nor should he be considered a trustee, because there is no trust res in his hands. Some courts have adopted this view.[28] But others have held the agent bank

---

40 N.Y.S. 209; In re Commercial Bank, 4 Ohio Dec. 108; Mad River Nat.Bank of Springfield v. Melhorn, 8 Ohio Cir.Ct.R. 191; White v. Commercial & Farmers' Bank, 60 S.C. 122, 38 S.E. 453; Plano Mfg. Co. v. Auld, 14 S.D. 512, 86 N.W. 21, 86 Am.St.Rep. 769; Continental Nat. Bank v. Weems, 69 Tex. 489, 6 S.W. 802, 5 Am.St.Rep. 85; First Nat. Bank v. Union Trust Co., Tex.Civ. App., 155 S.W. 989.

In the following cases the collected funds were held to have been trust funds in the hands of the collector, but the trust could not be enforced because of the inability to trace the funds into the assets of the collector: Illinois Trust & Savings Bank v. First Nat. Bank, C.C.N.Y., 15 F. 858; G. Ober & Sons Co. v. Cochran, 118 Ga. 396, 45 S.E. 382, 98 Am.St.Rep. 118; Kansas State Bank v. First State Bank, 62 Kan. 788, 64 P. 634; In re Seven Corners Bank, 58 Minn. 5, 59 N.W. 633; Frank v. Bingham, 58 Hun 580, 12 N.Y.S. 767, 35 N.Y. St.Rep. 714; In re Commercial Bank, 4 Ohio Dec. 108; Nonotuck Silk Co.

v. Flanders, 87 Wis. 237, 58 N.W. 383.

If the collection is made after the insolvency of the collecting bank, it is held that the agency to collect is revoked and the funds are held in trust. Lippitt v. Thames Loan & Trust Co., 88 Conn. 185, 90 A. 369; First Nat. Bank of Raton v. Dennis, 20 N.M. 96, 146 P. 948.

[26] First Nat. Bank v. Armstrong, C. C.Ohio, 36 F. 59.

[27] Philadelphia Nat. Bank v. Dowd, C.C.N.C., 38 F. 172, 2 L.R.A. 480; National Butchers' & Drovers' Bank v. Wilkinson, 10 N.Y.St.Rep. 290; Hunt v. Townsend, Tex.Civ.App., 26 S.W. 310.

[28] First Nat. Bank of Pawnee City v. Sprague, 34 Neb. 318, 51 N.W. 846, 15 L.R.A. 498, 33 Am.St.Rep. 644; Falls City Woolen Mills v. Louisville Nat. Banking Co., 145 Ky. 64, 140 S.W. 66; Daly v. Butchers' & Drovers' Bank, 56 Mo. 94, 17 Am. Rep. 663; Indig v. National City Bank of Brooklyn, 80 N.Y. 100.

liable to the depositor as a debtor, upon the failure of the subagent bank.[29]

After the subagent bank has remitted to the agent bank by sending cash or its equivalent, or by crediting the agent bank on an account, the agent bank would seem properly to be held to be a debtor of the depositor, and so many cases have held.[30]

The second question presented under the third class of cases here to be discussed is regarding the relation of the subagent to the depositor. If the subagent has the paper or its proceeds in his hands—that is, has not remitted to the agent or credited the agent—some courts have held the subagent a trustee for the depositor,[31] while others have called the subagent an "agent" of the depositor, and have stated that the title to the paper remained constantly in the depositor.[32] Occasionally the view has been taken that the subagent assumed the position of debtor upon the collection of the paper.[33]

Whatever the name they have applied to the subagent, in a great majority of the cases the courts have allowed the depositor to follow the proceeds of the paper into the hands of the subagent, if capable of identification, and the paper into the hands

---

[29] Simpson v. Waldby, 63 Mich. 439, 30 N.W. 199; Power v. First Nat. Bank, 6 Mont. 251, 12 P. 597; St. Nicholas Bank of New York v. State Nat. Bank, 128 N.Y. 26, 27 N.E. 849, 13 L.R.A. 241; Bradstreet v. Everson, 72 Pa. 124, 13 Am.Rep. 665.

[30] Mackersy v. Ramsays, 9 Clark & F. 818; Commercial Nat. Bank v. Armstrong, 148 U.S. 50, 13 S.Ct. 533, 37 L.Ed. 363; Fifth Nat. Bank v. Armstrong, C.C.Mo., 40 F. 46; First Nat. Bank v. Armstrong, C.C.Ohio, 42 F. 193; Briggs v. Central Nat. Bank of New York, 89 N.Y. 182, 42 Am.Rep. 285. The decision in Blair v. Hill, 50 App.Div. 33, 63 N.Y.S. 670, that the agent bank became a trustee of the moneys delivered to it by the subagent bank, seems erroneous.

[31] Holder v. Western German Bank, 136 F. 90, 68 C.C.A. 554; National Exch. Bank v. Beal, C.C.Mass., 50 F. 355; State v. Bank of Commerce of Grand Island, 61 Neb. 181, 85 N.W. 43, 52 L.R.A. 858.

[32] Manufacturers' Nat. Bank v. Continental Bank, 148 Mass. 553, 20 N.E. 193, 2 L.R.A. 699, 12 Am.St.Rep. 598; Bank of Sherman v. Weiss, 67 Tex. 331, 3 S.W. 299. In Gilpin v. Columbia Nat. Bank, 220 N.Y. 406, 115 N.E. 982, L.R.A.1917F, 864, the depositor sued the subagent bank for its negligence in failing properly to present the note for payment. It was held that the defendant bank was the agent of the first bank and not of the plaintiff depositor, and hence no recovery for defendant's negligence was allowed.

[33] Old Nat. Bank v. German-American Bank, 155 U.S. 556, 15 S.Ct. 221, 39 L.Ed. 259; San Francisco Nat. Bank v. American Nat. Bank of Los Angeles, 5 Cal.App. 408, 90 P. 558.

§ 8   DEBT OR TRUST—THE SPECIFIC PROPERTY CRITERION   27

of all except bona fide purchasers for value. As in the case of the agent bank, so with the subagent, it would seem logically that the subagent should be held to be a trustee of the paper when the form of the indorsement was such as to give it title, as in the case of a general indorsement, but should be held a technical agent when the indorsement was restrictive and did not give the subagent title to the paper.

Once the subagent remits properly to the agent or properly credits himself on a joint account, of course, the subagent relieves himself from all obligation to the depositor.

The American Bankers' Association Collection Code which has been adopted in several states [34] attempts to settle the rights of parties to these collection transactions. It makes a bank in possession of uncollected paper an agent, and permits the forwarder of paper after its collection to obtain payment in full out of the assets of the bank which has collected, even though the proceeds of the collection cannot be traced into the property of the failed collecting bank.[35] This statute in terms applies to all banks, national and state, but has been held by the United States Supreme Court [36] to be unconstitutional in so far as it attempts to regulate the disposition of the assets of failed national banks, since Congress alone has power over that matter and has acted in regard to it by providing for equal distribution among unsecured creditors.

Money Paid to Agents or Factors

Where money is paid to one for the use of another, or as the proceeds of another's property sold, it is sometimes difficult to distinguish trust from debt. The general rule, however, is that such persons as commission agents receiving the proceeds of

[34] Alabama, Hawaii, Illinois, Indiana, Kentucky, Maryland, Michigan, Missouri, Nebraska, New Jersey, New Mexico, New York, North Dakota, Oklahoma, Oregon, Pennsylvania, South Carolina, West Virginia, Washington, Wisconsin, Wyoming.

[35] For the terms of the act, see N.Y.L.1929, c. 589; N. Y. Negotiable Instruments Law, §§ 350-350L; and see 43 Harv.L.R. 307, 8 Tul.L.R. 21.

[36] Old Company's Lehigh, Inc., v. Meeker, 294 U.S. 227, 55 S.Ct. 392, 79 L.Ed. 876, 1935. In Illinois the entire act has been held invalid because of the unconstitutionality of that part affecting national banks. People ex rel. Barrett v. Union Bank & Trust Co., 362 Ill. 164, 199 N.E. 272, 104 A.L.R. 1090, 1935. In other states having the act, however, apparently the portion of it relating to state banks is valid.

goods sold,[37] insurance agents collecting premiums,[38] an agent to sell bonds,[39] and a collector of rents [40] are trustees of the money so coming into their hands. The expectation of the parties is usually that the agent will keep separate the cash or credit he receives, earmark it as that of his principal, and remit it to his principal. He is not at liberty to use the proceeds as his own in return for a contract obligation to pay some money to the principal.

Money Delivered to Pay Deliveror's Debt

Frequently a debtor, instead of paying a debt directly, will employ a bank or other intermediary to pay it for him and will deliver to the intermediary cash or credit for the purpose of procuring the payment of the debt. Thus, a person who has drawn a check, or accepted a draft, or signed a note, payable at a given bank,[41] or who owes taxes [42] or the purchase price of property bought,[43] may make an arrangement with the bank whereby it agrees to meet his obligation in return for a deposit of cash or commercial paper which he makes. Another example of this situation is that where an obligor on bonds arranges with a local bank to have it provide credit at a distant bank to meet the principal or interest on the bonds.[44]

In all these cases it is unnatural to expect the bank or other intermediary to use the exact cash or credit delivered to it, in accomplishing the desired purpose. It is much more natural to construe the transaction as permitting the intermediary to use any of its cash or credit for that purpose and to be able to appropriate the cash or credit delivered to it for any of its purposes. Banks and similar intermediaries expect freedom to meet their obligations from any assets which are at the time conven-

[37] Union Stockyards Nat. Bank v. Gillespie, 137 U.S. 411, 11 S.Ct. 118, 34 L.Ed. 724; Wallace & Sons v. Castle, 14 Hun, N.Y., 106; Baker v. New York Nat. Exch. Bank, 100 N.Y. 31, 2 N.E. 452, 53 Am.Rep. 150; Boyle v. Northwestern Nat. Bank, 125 Wis. 498, 103 N.W. 1123, 104 N.W. 917, 1 L.R.A.,N.S., 1110, 110 Am.St.Rep. 844.

[38] Dillon v. Connecticut Mut. Life Ins. Co., 44 Md. 386; Central Nat. Bank v. Connecticut Mut. Life Ins. Co., 104 U.S. 54, 26 L.Ed. 693.

[39] Van Alen v. American Nat. Bank, 52 N.Y. 1.

[40] Farmers' & Mechanics' Nat. Bank v. King, 57 Pa. 202, 98 Am.Dec. 215.

[41] Furber v. Barnes, 19 N.W. 728, 32 Minn. 105; Bank of Blackwell v. Dean, 60 P. 226, 9 Okl. 626.

[42] Gutknecht v. Sorge, 218 N.W. 726, 195 Wis. 477.

[43] Lamb v. Ladd, 209 P. 825, 112 Kan. 26.

[44] Hershey v. Northern Trust Co., 112 S.W.2d 545, 342 Mo. 90.

ient. Hence, it should seem reasonable that transactions of this type should be held to create contract relations only, and that the intermediary would not be held a trustee of the cash or credit delivered to it in return for its promise.[45] However, in some cases on more or less satisfactory evidence of an intent to have the very property delivered used to satisfy the obligation of the deliveror, the courts have held that the deliveree was a trustee.[46]

Security Deposits

If an employee or tenant is required by his employer or landlord to make a cash deposit as security for performance of his duties, it is not normally expected that the deposited money will be segregated or deposited in a special bank deposit. It is rather usually intended that the cash or credit deposited can be used as the absolute property of the party with whom it is deposited and that he can satisfy his duty to the depositor by paying any cash or credit of the same amount. The normal construction is, therefore, contract and not trust.[47]

Funds Delivered for Investment

If cash or credit is left with an attorney or investment counsellor for investment, or to be lent out on bond and mortgage, the relation should be that of debtor and creditor if the investor is to be at liberty to use the funds he receives as his own, and to make the investment from any of his own funds later; [48] but should be a trust relation if the funds delivered to the attorney or other party are to be translated directly into a special bank account and then into the investment in the name of the client.[49]

---

[45] Stonebraker v. First National Bank, C.C.A.Fla., 76 F.2d 389; In re Kountze Bros., C.C.A.N.Y., 104 F.2d 157; Baiar v. O'Connell, 365 Ill. 208, 6 N.E.2d 140.

[46] Town of La Fayette v. Williams, 232 Ala. 502, 168 So. 668; Dolph v. Cross, 153 Iowa 289, 133 N.W. 669; Stein v. Kemp, 132 Minn. 44, 155 N. W. 1052.

[47] Povey v. Colonial Beacon Oil Co., 294 Mass. 86, 200 N.E. 891; De Vol v. Citizens' Bank, 92 Or. 606, 179 P. 282, rehearing denied 92 Or. 606, 181 P. 985. By statute these deposits are sometimes declared to be held in trust. N.J.S.A. 34:18–1 to 34:18–5; Wis.L.1937, c. 117.

[48] Wetherell v. O'Brien, 140 Ill. 146, 29 N.E. 904, 33 Am.St.Rep. 221; Budd v. Walker, 113 N.Y. 637, 21 N. E. 72.

[49] Hitchcock v. Cosper, 164 Ind. 633, 73 N.E. 264; Harrison v. Smith, 83 Mo. 210, 53 Am.Rep. 571; Rusling v. Rusling's Ex'rs, 42 N.J.Eq. 594, 8 A. 534; Cavin v. Gleason, 105 N.Y. 256, 11 N.E. 504; Merino v. Munoz, 5 App. Div. 71, 38 N.Y.S. 678; Keller v. Washington, 83 W.Va. 659, 98 S.E. 880.

The payment of interest by the attorney or bank tends strongly to prove a debt, since interest is a payment for the use of the cash or credit as that of the attorney or bank.[50] A trustee does not normally agree to pay a fixed return on the funds in his hands, but only to deliver over whatever income they actually produce.

Transmission of Funds—Purchase of Foreign Credit

When a customer delivers to a bank or foreign exchange house cash or a check for the purpose of procuring the transmission of funds to a foreign country and the establishment of credit in the customer's favor or for the benefit of another there, the implied understanding is not that the bank will use the cash or credit received by it as the source of the foreign credit to be established, but rather that the bank will treat what it receives as its own property and consider itself under a contract duty to establish the credit for its customer from any source it finds convenient. This is characteristic of contract and not of trust.[51]

Bank Deposits

The relation between customer and bank in the case of a general bank deposit, which results in the creation of, or addition to, a checking account, is that of debtor and creditor. The bank becomes the absolute owner of the cash and commercial paper handed to its teller at the time of the deposit, and the customer becomes a general creditor of the bank, with no property interest in the cash or paper, or the proceeds of the cash or paper, which he brought to the bank.

This is true whether the funds deposited are public monies, like those of a county treasurer,[52] or are funds held in a fiduciary capacity by the depositor, as in the case of a deposit by an executor or trustee of the funds of the estate or trust.[53]

If the deposit is wrongfully made, however, in that the depositor has no authority to make it, or the bank no authority to re-

[50] Pittsburgh Nat. Bank of Commerce v. McMurray, 98 Pa. 538.

[51] Beecher v. Cosmopolitan Trust Co., 239 Mass. 48, 131 N.E. 338; Legniti v. Mechanics' & Metals Nat. Bank of New York, 230 N.Y. 415, 130 N.E. 597, 16 A.L.R. 185, noted in 19 Col.L. R. 322; Stone, Legal Problems in the Transmission of Funds, 21 Col.L.R. 507.

[52] City of Fulton v. Home Trust Co., 336 Mo. 239, 78 S.W.2d 445; State ex rel. Village of Warrensville Heights v. Fulton, 128 Ohio.St. 192, 190 N.E. 383.

[53] Corbett v. Hospelhorn, 172 Md. 257, 191 A. 691; Parker v. Hood ex rel. Central Bank & Trust Co., 209 N. C. 494, 183 S.E. 737.

ceive it, the bank becomes the owner of that which is deposited, subject to a constructive trust in favor of the depositor or those whom he represents.[54]

THE DEBTOR MAKING HIMSELF TRUSTEE—THE SPECIFIC PROPERTY CRITERION

9. A debtor may, in addition to making himself liable at law on his contract, set up a trust of some of his property to secure the performance of this promise. Some important cases where there is controversy over the question whether the debtor has set up a trust are the cases of

(a) Agreements to support;
(b) Coupon accounts;
(c) Dividend accounts;
(d) Payroll accounts.

Sometimes it is alleged that one who is admittedly a debtor has set aside part of his property as the subject matter of a trust for the benefit of the creditor, thus giving the creditor an additional remedy beside the contract claim in a court of law, namely, an equitable claim against the trust property.

For example, if land is conveyed by an elderly person to another under an agreement that the grantee will support the grantor for his life, the grantee may also agree to hold the land in trust for the grantor for the purpose of furnishing the support.[55]

Or a corporation which has issued bonds with interest coupons may deposit a sum of money in a bank and head the account "coupon" account, thus dedicating it to use in paying the coupons.[56]

Or a corporation which has declared a dividend may likewise make a deposit headed "dividend account" and direct the bank to pay from it checks drawn in payment of the dividend.[57]

Or an employer who owes his employees salaries may create a payroll account in a bank for the purpose of having the different salary checks paid from this account.[58]

---

[54] Screws v. Williams, 230 Ala. 392, 161 So. 453; Dewey v. Commercial State Bank, 141 Kan. 356, 41 P.2d 1006.

[55] Buffinton v. Maxam, 140 Mass. 557, 5 N.E. 519; Kendall v. Chase, 203 Mich. 660, 169 N.W. 861.

[56] Guidise v. Island Refining Corp., D.C.N.Y., 291 F. 922.

[57] In re Interborough Consol. Corp., D.C.N.Y., 267 F. 914.

[58] Northern Sugar Corp. v. Thompson, C.C.A.Minn., 13 F.2d 829.

In each of these cases it is a question of fact whether the debtor really intended to declare himself trustee of the property from which it is alleged he agreed that the debt should be paid,—in the case of support the land conveyed, and in the other cases the bank account or claim against the bank. If the debtor merely contracted to pay out of particular property, or merely stated his intention to pay out of such property, he did not become a trustee. The tendency has been to treat the dividend account as held in trust for the stockholders, but the coupon account as not held in trust for the bondholders. There seems to be no reason for this distinction. A reasonable construction is that the debtor intends to hold all such accounts in trust for the creditors.[59] The bank in which such an account exists should not be held to be a trustee for the depositor or his creditors.[60]

BAILMENT[61]

10. Bailment differs from trust in that
    (a) It was developed in the common law actions, whereas trust was developed in chancery, so that the rights of bailor are now legal, while those of the beneficiary are equitable;
    (b) Bailment is not a fiduciary relation;
    (c) Bailment deals only with personal property, while trust deals with all kinds of property;
    (d) The bailee has a special, limited property interest, and the bailor has general property, whereas in trusts the trustee usually has full ownership subject to the equitable interest of the beneficiary.

Similarities in Two Relations

Bailment and trust are in some respects similar. In each the owner of property places it in the control of another, usually for a temporary purpose. Some definitions of bailment would seem to make it a form of trust.[62]

[59] Matter of Le Blanc, 14 Hun 8, affirmed 75 N.Y. 598 (dividend account); but see Schloss v. Powell, C.C.A.Va., 93 F.2d 518 (coupon account; no trust). See section 2, Uniform Trusts Act.

[60] Carnegie-Illinois Steel Corp. v. Berger, C.C.A.Pa., 105 F.2d 485, certiorari denied 308 U.S. 603, 60 S.Ct. 140, 84 L.Ed. 504; Millerstown Borough v. Receivers of Millerstown Deposit Bank, 128 Pa.Super. 258, 193 A. 332; but see, *contra*, Woolley v. City of Natchez, C.C.A.Miss., 89 F. 2d 937; In re Sturdivant Bank, 89 S.W.2d 89, 232 Mo.App. 55.

[61] Restatement, Trusts, § 5.

[62] "Bailment from the French 'bailler,' to deliver, is a delivery of goods in trust, upon a contract, ex-

Distinctions—Court of Origin and Development

Bailment is a common law institution. It was developed through the common law actions like detinue, replevin, and trover. Relief for violation of the terms of a bailment is now given almost always in a court of law.[63] As previously stated, the trust was first recognized by the court of chancery and is now enforced by it almost exclusively.

Distinctions—Fiduciary Relation

Bailment is a business relation in which the parties deal with each other at arm's length, with no duties of disclosure or candor or extreme good faith.[64] Bailor and bailee may contract and convey freely. They are not in special relations of intimacy or confidence. That the trust is a fiduciary relation is fundamental.

Distinction—Type of Property Involved

It happens that bailment has been confined to cases of the delivery of personal property by one to another for a temporary purpose, as, for example, where the general owner of a typewriter lends it to a friend for a month. There is no such thing as bailment of realty. The trust subject matter may be any kind of property, real or personal.[65]

Distinctions—Nature of Property Rights Involved

It is sometimes said that trust and bailment differ in that a bailee has no "title," whereas the trustee has "legal title." It is more accurate to state that the bailee has a special, legal property interest which entitles him to possession and use for a period which is generally relatively short. The larger, general property interest remains in the bailor. In trust the property interest of the trustee is usually legal in nature and much larger than that of the bailee. The beneficiary's interest is always equitable. Thus, in the normal bailment the total property in-

---

pressed or implied, that the trust shall be faithfully executed on the part of the bailee." Blackstone's Com. 451. The following definition of bailment would seem preferable: "A bailment is the transfer of the possession of personal property, without a transfer of ownership, for the accomplishment of a certain purpose, whereupon the property is to be redelivered or delivered over to a third person." Hale, Bailments and Carriers, 5, 6.

[63] Ashley's Admrs. v. Denton, 1 Litt. 86; Piester v. Ideal Creamery Co., 289 Mich. 489, 286 N.W. 801.

[64] Young v. Mercantile Trust Co., C.C.A.N.Y., 145 F. 39; Taylor v. Turner, 87 Ill. 296.

[65] See § 32, post.

terest is divided into two types of legal interest, special and general. While in the normal trust full legal ownership is in the trustee subject to some equitable interests in the beneficiaries.

EQUITABLE CHARGE[66]

11. An equitable charge is distinguished from a trust by—
   (a) Its lack of fiduciary relationship;
   (b) The presence in it of beneficial ownership.

Similarities

An equitable charge bears many striking resemblances to a trust. In both relations the holder of the property is seized of a title, generally legal. In both the claimant or beneficiary has rights enforceable in equity.[67] In both a purchaser of the property with notice of the burden attached will hold it subject to the claim of the beneficiary. Thus, if A. devise land to B., "subject to the payment of an annuity of $500 to C.," B. will hold subject to equitable rights to the enjoyment of $500 income resting in C., just as if A. had devised the land to B., "in trust to pay C. $500 a year." In the first instance, as well as in the second, X., a purchaser with knowledge of the terms of the devise to B., will take it subject to the burden in favor of C.[68]

---

[66] Restatement, Trusts, § 10.

[67] In the case of an equitable charge, the beneficiary of the charge, if the instrument show such intent, may have a remedy against the holder of the property by way of an action at law, as well as the equitable claim against the property. The acceptance of the gift with a charge attached raises an implied promise, under some circumstances to pay the amount of the charge. Commissioner of Internal Revenue v. Smiley, C.C.A., 86 F.2d 658; Williams v. Nichol, 47 Ark. 254, 1 S.W. 243; Lord v. Lord, 22 Conn. 595; Adams v. Adams, 14 Allen, Mass., 65; Birdsall v. Hewlett, 1 Paige, N.Y., 32, 19 Am.Dec. 392; Harris v. Fly, 7 Paige, N.Y., 421; Kelsey v. Western, 2 N.Y. 500; Gridley v. Gridley, 24 N.Y. 130; Loder v. Hatfield, 71 N.Y. 92; Brown v. Knapp, 79 N.Y. 136; Redfield v. Redfield, 126 N.Y. 466, 27 N.E. 1032; Logan v. Glass, 338 Pa. 489.

Personal liability on the part of a trustee is legally possible but is practically unheard of. The trustee agrees to pay over the income of the trust property and does not ordinarily assume responsibility if the income is inadequate. See, 104, post.

[68] Wolfe v. Croft, 11 East.L.R., Can., 532; Harris v. Fly, 7 Paige, N.Y., 421. But a purchaser of the land from the holder subject to a charge personally binding on such holder is entitled to have the remedies against such holder exhausted before relief is sought in equity against the property. Kelsey v. Western, 2 N.Y. 500.

BOGERT TRUSTS 2D

Dissimilarities

But the relations are not equivalent.[69] A trustee is a fiduciary. He alone can perform the duties of the trust. To transfer the trust property to another, except in exercise of a power of sale, would be a breach of the trust. In the ordinary case the trustee is expected to retain the trust property and perform the trust duties personally. By contrast, the holder of property subject to a charge has no personal relation to the beneficiary of the charge. He may sell the property to a stranger, and pass on the burden of paying the charge, in so far as the liability of the land to pay is concerned. Such an act will be no breach of any duty to the beneficiary of the charge. And so, too, the holder subject to a charge may deal with the charged property and with the beneficiary of the charge as with a stranger's property and a stranger, buying in the charge and taking any advantage of the beneficiary which is lawful. A sale of the trust property to the trustee, on the other hand, is voidable by the cestui que trust, and the trustee must show the utmost good faith in order to sustain the sale.

In the second place, the holder subject to an equitable charge is a beneficial holder; whereas the trustee is not. If B. receive property subject to a charge of $500 a year in favor of C., and the property produces $1,000 a year, B. may retain the surplus $500 for his own use. Contrariwise, if B. were a trustee of the same property for the purpose of paying C. $500 a year, B. could not keep the extra $500, but would be obliged to hold it for the benefit of the creator of the trust, or for his heirs or next of kin, if the settlor were dead. The holder subject to a charge is entitled to all benefits from the property beyond the amount necessary to satisfy the charge. The trustee is never entitled to any beneficial use of the trust property.[70]

It is often important to decide whether a relation is a trust or an equitable charge, because of the statute of limitations.[71] The statute does not begin to run against the cestui's rights until there has been a repudiation of the trust; but the statute commences to operate against an equitable charge from the time when it becomes due.

---

[69] For a discussion of the distinctions between equitable charges and trusts, see 3 Pomeroy, Eq.Jurisprudence, 3d Ed., § 1033, note; 19 Am. & Eng.Encyc.Law, 2d Ed., 1343.

[70] King v. Denison, 1 Ves. & B. 260; In re West, [1900] 1 Ch. 84; Woodbury v. Hayden, 211 Mass. 202, 97 N. E. 776.

[71] Hodge v. Churchward, 16 Sim. 71; McKeage v. Coleman, 294 Ill. App. 232, 13 N.E.2d 662; Loder v. Hatfield, 71 N.Y. 92; Merton v. O'Brien, 117 Wis. 437, 94 N.W. 340.

No set formula will always create a charge and refute the notion of a trust. The courts seek the creator's intent, whether it be to make a beneficial gift of the property, subject to an incumbrance, or to place upon the shoulders of the recipient of the property a fiduciary relation.[72]

The grantor of land subject to a charge cannot release or destroy the charge, unless he reserved power to do so,[73] a result similar to that found in trust creation.[74]

ASSIGNMENT OF A CHOSE IN ACTION[75]

12. **An assignment of a chose in action at common law differs from a trust in which the subject-matter is a chose in action, in that—**

(a) **The assignee's remedy is normally at law, while the cestui que trust's is equitable;**

(b) **The assignor's duty is purely negative, whereas a trustee always has some positive duty;**

(c) **In the case of partial assignment of a chose the assignor alone can sue at law and has a duty to turn over part**

---

[72] In the following cases the wording was construed to create an equitable charge: King v. Denison, 1 Ves. & B. 260 (subject to payment of annuities); Wood v. Cox, 2 Myl. & C. 684 ("trusting and wholly confiding that he will act in strict conformity with my wishes"); Hodge v. Churchward, 16 Sim. 71 (paying £10 a year); Wolfe v. Croft, 11 East.L.R., Can., 532; Merchants' Nat. Bank v. Crist, 140 Iowa 308, 118 N.W. 394, 23 L.R.A., N.S., 526, 132 Am.St.Rep. 267 (support made a lien); Lang v. Everling, 3 Misc. 530, 23 N.Y.S. 329 ("upon the express condition that"); Loder v. Hatfield, 71 N.Y. 92 ("on the following conditions and proviso"); Chew v. Sheldon, 214 N.Y. 344, 108 N.E. 552, Ann.Cas.1916D, 1268 (subject to a duty to support daughter); Dixon v. Helena Soc. of Free Methodist Church of North America, 65 Okl. 203, 166 P. 114 (direction to a devisee to pay a legacy).

In the following instances the courts found a trust: Buffinton v. Maxam, 140 Mass. 557, 5 N.E. 519 (for the support of); Baker v. Brown, 146 Mass. 369, 15 N.E. 783 (subject to the condition that); Woodbury v. Hayden, 211 Mass. 202, 97 N.E. 776 (to be used as far as necessary for the support and maintenance of); Pierce v. McKeehan, 3 Watts & S., Pa., 280 (subject to the maintenance of); Hoyt v. Hoyt, 77 Vt. 244, 59 A. 845 (on condition that); Barnes v. Dow, 59 Vt. 530, 10 A. 258.

In the following cases neither an equitable charge nor a trust was held to exist, the recipient of the property taking it absolutely: Zimmer v. Sennott, 134 Ill. 505, 25 N.E. 774 (upon condition that); Dee v. Dee, 212 Ill. 338, 72 N.E. 429 (for the benefit of); Crandall v. Hoysradt, 1 Sandf.Ch., N.Y., 40 (for the maintenance of).

[73] Logan v. Glass, 338 Pa. 489, 14 A.2d 306.

[74] See, § 165, post.

[75] Restatement, Trusts, §§ 15, 16.

of the proceeds to the assignee, and the assignee can sue only in equity normally. But this situation is evolved on contract principles and the assignor is not trustee for the partial assignee;

(d) Assignor and assignee are not in a fiduciary relation, but trustee and beneficiary are in such relation.

Similarities

At common law a chose in action was not assignable, in the sense that the assignee could sue upon it in his own name. He could enforce it only by an action in the name of the assignor. The legal title to the chose in action remained in the assignor, while the assignee received merely a power of attorney to enforce the claim in the name of the assignor. In nearly all American jurisdictions statutes requiring actions to be brought in the name of the real party in interest, or making choses in action assignable, now enable the assignee to sue in his own name.[76]

Yet decisions in a few states indicate that in some cases it is still necessary for the assignee to sue in his assignor's name.[77] Wherever such is the case, the assignor resembles a trustee of a chose in action, in that he holds an interest in property the beneficial interest in which belongs to another. Both assignor and trustee own something, which they are not entitled to use for their benefit, but solely for the benefit of another, namely, the assignee or the cestui que trust.

Distinctions

But, while both assignee and cestui que trust are entitled to the benefit of property, their methods of obtaining that benefit differ. The cestui que trust's right is equitable. The assignee's

[76] Reios v. Mardis, 18 Cal.App. 276, 122 P. 1091; Rambo v. Armstrong, 45 Colo. 124, 100 P. 586; Birdsall v. Coon, 157 Mo.App. 439, 139 S.W. 243; Sternberg & Co. v. Lehigh Val. R. Co., 80 N.J.L. 468, 78 A. 1135; Continental Oil & Cotton Co. v. E. Van Winkle Gin & Machine Works, 62 Tex.Civ. App. 422, 131 S.W. 415; Carozza v. Boxley, C.C.A.Va., 203 F. 673, 122 C.C.A. 69 (construing a Virginia statute); Hankwitz v. Barrett, 143 Wis. 639, 128 N.W. 430. In two important states the change was made but recently. See Gilman v. American Producers' Controlling Co., 180 Mass. 319, 62 N.E. 267 (construing St.1897, c. 402), and Neyens v. Hossack, 142 Ill. App. 327 (construing section 18 of Practice Act of 1907 [Laws 1907-08, p. 448]).

[77] Snead v. Bell, 142 Ala. 449, 38 So. 259, 1904; Boqua v. Marshall, 88 Ark. 373, 114 S.W. 714, 1908; Durant Lumber Co. v. Sinclair & Simms Lumber Co., 2 Ga.App. 209, 58 S.E. 485, 1907; Croyle v. Guelich, 35 Pa.Super. Ct. 356, 1908; Martin & Garrett v. Mask, 158 N.C. 436, 74 S.E. 343, 41 L.R.A.,N.S., 641, 1912.

interest is normally legal, namely, a power of attorney to sue on the chose in action in a court of law, and it is only in cases where the assignor threatens to collect the claim for his own benefit, or where some other extraordinary circumstance endangers the collection by the assignee suing at law in the name of the assignor, that the assignee may resort to equity.[78]

Secondly, the assignor has the sole duty of refraining from action which will prevent the collection of the chose in action by the assignee. The assignor has no positive duty. On the other hand, in active trusts the trustee has the duty of collection of the chose in action for the cestui que trust, and, if the trustee refuses to collect, the cestui may go into equity and join the debtor and trustee as defendants.[79]

Partial Assignments

Where the owner of a chose assigns part of it, the assignee at common law obtained merely a power to sue in equity, joining the assignor and obligor as defendants.[80] The power to sue at law was in the assignor only.[81] If he collected, he had a duty to deliver to the partial assignee his share of the proceeds. Under some modern statutes action by the partial assignor and partial assignee at law against the obligor is permitted.[82]

While it might seem at first impression that the partial assignor was trustee of the part assigned for the partial assignee, this is not the case. The cause of action at law is in the assignor, not because he was intended to be a trustee of it, but because the principles of common law pleading and practice will not allow the splitting of the cause of action and the vexation of the obligor by two suits. The remedy of the partial assignee is in equity, not because the parties intended a trust, but because equity gives the partial assignee a remedy on account of the inadequacy of his remedy at law and because equity practice permits the joinder of all concerned in one suit.

[78] Hammond v. Messenger, 9 Sim. 327; Hayward v. Andrews, 106 U.S. 672, 1 S.Ct. 544, 27 L.Ed. 271; Walker v. Brooks, 125 Mass. 241; Carter v. United Ins. Co., 1 Johns.Ch., N.Y., 463.

[79] Thomassen v. Van Wyngaarden, 65 Iowa 687, 22 N.W. 927; Fogg v. Middleton, 2 Hill Eq., S.C., 591.

[80] Phillips v. Edsall, 127 Ill. 535, 20 N.E. 801; James v. City of Newton, 142 Mass. 366, 8 N.E. 122, 56 Am.Rep. 692.

[81] Cable v. St. Louis Marine Ry. & Dock Co., 21 Mo. 133.

[82] Fireman's Ins. Co. v. Oregon R. Co., 45 Or. 53, 76 P. 1075, 67 L.R.A. 161.

Fiduciary Relation

Assignor and assignee stand in a purely business relation and not in a fiduciary relation. They are not subject to the disabilities and duties which equity has placed upon those persons in positions of intimacy and trust who are called "fiduciaries".

EXECUTORSHIP

13. **Executorship is similar to trust in that the executor is a fiduciary who holds the title to property for the benefit of others.**

    It is unlike trust with regard to
    - **(a) The forum of enforcement;**
    - **(b) The kind of property held;**
    - **(c) The functions to be performed;**
    - **(d) The nature of the powers granted.**

Similarities

Both executors and trustees are fiduciaries.[83] Both occupy positions of high trust and confidence, in which they have great control over the affairs of others. The courts require of them the highest good faith.

The executor also is like a trustee in that he has title to property for others. When the will is admitted to probate and the executor receives his letters testamentary, he is deemed to have title to the personal property of the testator, dating back to the latter's death.[84] The executor holds this property interest not for himself, but for the creditors and legatees of the testator.

Differences

The executor is an officer of the probate court from which he receives his evidence of authority, his letters of administration.[85] He is named by the testator, just as a trustee is named by the settlor, but his position is dependent on the action of the probate court in admitting the will to probate and issuing letters to him. He is subject to the direction of that court. Relief against him by legatees or creditors is generally obtained by petition to the probate court. Actions at law or suits in equity are sometimes

---

[83] Colburn v. Hodgdon, 241 Mass. 183, 135 N.E. 107.

[84] Oulvey v. Converse, 326 Ill. 226,

157 N.E. 245; Rolfe v. Atkinson, 259 Mass. 76, 156 N.E. 51.

[85] In re Durel, C.C.A.Cal., 10 F.2d 448.

available to the legatee or creditor, but they are secondary and auxiliary.[86] The trustee is accountable in equity.

Courts frequently make the statement that executors are trustees,[87] but this is not accurate. They are probate fiduciaries.

The statute of limitations does not run against the claim of a beneficiary of a trust, until the trustee repudiates the trust.[88] Other statutes of limitation control the claims of creditors and legatees against the executor.[89] In the case of creditors there is often a short statutory period, as, for example, six months, which applies if the executor advertises for claims.

The executor holds title to personalty only, although he sometimes has a power of sale over realty. Title to the realty passes direct to the devisees. A trustee may hold either realty or personalty.

The executor has a simple temporary function, always the same, namely, to collect the personal property of the testator, reduce it to money so far as necessary, and pay expenses, taxes, and the creditors of the testator and his legatees. This function can usually be performed in a year or a year and a half. Trustees' functions are highly varied. There are many different purposes of trusts and they customarily last for many years or for several lives.

The powers of the executor, where there are two or more executors, are several;[90] while the powers of trustees are joint and must be exercised by all as a body.[91] Thus, in the case of two executors, one may sell estate property and collect the price, without joinder of his associate. In a trust both trustees would be obliged to sign the bill of sale.

Often a will names the same person as executor and trustee and it becomes a delicate question to tell when he acts in one capacity and when in the other.[92] Both functions may be administered concurrently or consecutively. Even though a man is

---

[86] Colt v. Colt, 32 Conn. 422; Andrews v. Hunneman, 6 Pick., Mass., 126.

[87] Hardwick v. Cotterill, 221 Ky. 783, 299 S.W. 958; Central Nat. Bank, Savings & Trust Co. v. Gilchrist, 23 Ohio App. 87, 154 N.E. 811.

[88] Post, § 162.

[89] Wilmerding v. Russ, 33 Conn. 67;

In re Moore's Appeal, 84 Mich. 474, 48 N.W. 39.

[90] Pearse v. National Lead Co., 162 App.Div. 766, 147 N.Y.S. 989.

[91] Post, § 95.

[92] Coudon v. Updegraff, 117 Md. 71, 83 A. 145; In re Bird's Will, 241 N.Y. 184, 149 N.E. 827.

named as executor only, if trust functions are given to him as executor he will be deemed to be a trustee with regard to those functions.[93] When property is given to an executor to pay debts, he will be deemed to take it as executor and not as trustee, unless the method of distribution is different from that which the law would apply if the will had been silent as to method of paying debts.[94]

An administrator is like an executor, except that he is named by the probate court and acts in the case of intestacy. He has the same title and functions. In some cases statutes vest causes of action in administrators for the benefit of the next of kin, in the case of the causing of the death of the intestate by wrongful act. Here the administrator is a statutory trustee.[95] The cause of action is not something owned by the intestate during his life and passed on by intestacy. But normally an administrator is a probate fiduciary and not an equity trustee.

AGENCY[96]

14. Agency and trust resemble each other, in that both are relations of trust and confidence. Their points of difference are:

(a) That an agent is ordinarily not the owner of property for the benefit of his principal, while a trustee always holds the title to property for his cestui que trust;

(b) That agency is generally a personal relation, dependent on the will and continued existence of both parties, whereas a trust is ordinarily an impersonal relation;

(c) That the agent is a mere instrument in the hands of the principal, and incurs no personal responsibility when the agency is disclosed, but the trustee binds himself personally by his official contracts.

Points of Similarity

It is probable that both agency and trust arose from the same ill-defined intermediary relation.[97] Agency was molded by the

---

[93] Jones v. Broadbent, 21 Idaho 555, 123 P. 476; Dingman v. Beall, 213 Ill. 238, 72 N.E. 729; Fenton v. Hall, 235 Ill. 552, 85 N.E. 936; Drake v. Price, 5 N.Y. 430; In re Leonard, 168 App.Div. 12, 153 N.Y.S. 852; Teel v. Hilton, 21 R.I. 227, 42 A. 1111.

[94] Cohn v. McClintock, 107 Miss. 831, 66 So. 217.

[95] Kansas Pacific Ry. Co. v. Cutter, 16 Kan. 568.

[96] Restatement, Trusts, § 8; Restatement, Agency, §§ 1, 13.

[97] "The germ of agency is hardly to be distinguished from the germ of another institution, which in our English law has an eventful future be-

courts of law and received one set of characteristics. The trust was fostered by chancery and developed along different lines. But, though wide apart now, each possesses the element of trust and confidence. Each is a fiduciary relation. Both agents and trustees are placed in positions of intimacy, where it is easy for them to take advantage of those who have trusted them. Because of this fiduciary element, agents and trustees are under a common prohibition against acting for their private interests when managing the affairs of those for whom they act. For example, neither can purchase the property which is the subject of his dealings, if the principal or cestui que trust objects.[98] And they are classed together as "fiduciaries" under statutes making such persons liable to arrest in given cases.[99] This common feature has led some authors to confuse the two relationships,[1] and others to call the agent a "quasi trustee";[2] but the distinctions stated below show good reasons for keeping them separate.[3]

Points of Difference

It has been seen that an essential feature of the trust is the ownership by the trustee of property for the benefit of the cestui que trust. The agent, on the other hand, need own no property. He acts for his principal, and often cares for, or transports, or sells property; but it is ordinarily property to which the legal and equitable titles are in the principal.

A trust is ordinarily indestructible and irrevocable by its settlor, in the absence of a power of revocation expressly reserved.[4] The death of the settlor or of the trustee will not affect the life of the trust.[5] If the latter die, a new trustee will succeed him. On the contrary, an agency is revocable at the option of the principal, unless it be coupled with an interest, and is revoked by the

---

fore it, the 'use, trust, or confidence.'"
2 Pollock & Maitland, History of English Law, 226.

[98] Bain v. Brown, 56 N.Y. 285; Copeland v. Mercantile Ins. Co., 6 Pick., Mass., 198; Story, Agency, 9th Ed., § 211.

[99] New York Civil Practice Act, § 826.

[1] "The terms 'trustee' and 'agent' are frequently used in a loose way, as though those terms marked off absolutely distinct and separate duties and liabilities. All trustees, however, are agents; but all agents are not trustees. A trustee is an agent and something more." Ewell's Evans on Agency, 349.

[2] Marvin v. Brooks, 94 N.Y. 71.

[3] First Wisconsin Trust Co. v. Wisconsin Dept. of Taxation, 237 Wis. 135, 294 N.W. 868.

[4] § 165, post.

[5] § 166, post.

death of either party.[6] The personality of the particular parties with whom the relation begins is of the essence, and no others can be substituted therefor. The principal supervises and guides the agent. The trust beneficiary usually has little or no control over the trustee.

Furthermore, the agent, contracting in the name of his principal, incurs no personal responsibility for the performance of his contracts.[7] The trustee is personally liable upon contracts made in the performance of the trust unless he expressly excludes liability, though he has the right of indemnity, and the cestui que trust is not responsible on such contracts.[8] The agent is a mere tool or instrument in the principal's hands, but the trustee is a separate, responsible party.

It should be noticed that the principal's rights against the agent are legal rights, and that ordinarily his remedy is in a court of law.[9] The cestui's rights are equitable.

Frequent occasions arise for making this distinction between trust and agency.[10]

---

[6] Viser v. Bertrand, 16 Ark. 296; Rowe v. Rand, 111 Ind. 206, 12 N.E. 377; Flaherty v. O'Connor, 24 R.I. 587, 54 A. 376.

[7] Everett v. Drew, 129 Mass. 150.

[8] Taylor v. Davis, 110 U.S. 330, 335, 4 S.Ct. 147, 28 L.Ed. 163; Shepard v. Abbott, 179 Mass. 300, 60 N.E. 782; Hartley v. Phillips, 198 Pa. 9, 47 A. 929.

[9] A principal may, however, obtain an accounting from his agent in equity. Warren v. Holbrook, 95 Mich. 185, 54 N.W. 712, 35 Am.St.Rep. 554; Marvin v. Brooks, 94 N.Y. 71.

[10] In the following cases the question was one of revocation: Viser v. Bertrand, 16 Ark. 296; Rowe v. Rand, 111 Ind. 206, 12 N.E. 377; Lyle v. Burke, 40 Mich. 499. In others the problem was one of personal liability by agent or trustee. Shepard v. Abbott, 179 Mass. 300, 60 N.E. 782; Hartley v. Phillips, 198 Pa. 9, 47 A. 929; Taylor v. Davis, 110 U.S. 330, 4 S.Ct. 147, 28 L.Ed. 163. In Coggeshall v. Coggeshall, 2 Strob., S.C., 51, the occasion for distinction was a question of evidence, while in Weer v. Gand, 88 Ill. 490, the preference of a claim against an estate depended upon the distinction between agency and trust.

That the officer is called a "trustee" has not prevented the courts from finding that he was in fact an agent. Viser v. Bertrand, 16 Ark. 296; Rowe v. Rand, 111 Ind. 206, 12 N.E. 377.

Where A. sent a check to B., payable to the order of B., to be used in paying an assessment against realty, and B. deposited it to his own credit and gave a clerk his own check to pay the assessment, and the clerk embezzled the proceeds of this second check; and thereafter A. and B. died; it was held that B. was not a trustee, but a mere agent, and the agency was revoked by death. Title Guarantee & Trust Co. v. Haven, 214 N.Y. 468, 108 N.E. 819.

Corporate fiduciaries are agents when they operate "custodian accounts" for their customers.[11] Here they take possession of securities belonging to a customer, store them safely, and sell and buy investments, either on their own initiative or at the direction of the customer.

GUARDIANSHIP[12]

15. Guardianship resembles trusteeship, in that it is a fiduciary relation, but it is distinguished by the guardian's lack of title to the property concerned.

Guardians (sometimes called committees, conservators, or curators) of infants, spendthrifts, and incompetents resemble trustees by virtue of the relation of trust and confidence which they sustain to their wards. Both guardians and trustees control property of others, toward whom the most scrupulous honesty and good faith must be observed. The guardian, like the trustee, when acting officially, must act solely for his beneficiary and never in his own interest. If a guardian purchases outstanding claims against his ward's property, for example, he can derive no benefit therefrom. The purchase will inure to the benefit of the ward.[13]

A guardian is sometimes said to be a strict trustee.[14] But the better view in America is that the interest of the guardian in his ward's property is less than that of the trustee in the trust property. The guardian has possession, and the right to continue in possession, and a power of disposition, but not what is generally called "title", since this rests in the ward.[15] The trustee usually

---

[11] McKay v. Atwood, D.C.Pa., 10 F.Supp. 475, affirmed 76 F.2d 1014; Smith v. Simmons, 99 Colo. 227, 61 P.2d 589.

[12] Restatement, Trusts, § 7.

[13] Lee v. Fox, 6 Dana, Ky., 171, 176.

[14] Eversley, Domestic Relations, 2d Ed., 659; Tiffany, Persons and Domestic Relations, 319; Schouler, Domestic Relations, 5th Ed., § 322. "The view I take of this case is that the relation of guardian and ward is strictly that of trustee and cestui que trust. I look on it as a peculiar relation of trusteeship, and this appears from the case of Duke of Beaufort v. Berty. A guardian is not only a trustee of the property, as in an ordinary case of trustee, but he is also the guardian of the person of the infant, with many duties to perform, such as to see to his education, and maintenance." Mathew v. Brise, 14 Beav. 341, 345.

[15] Longmire v. Pilkington, 37 Ala. 296, 297; Welles v. Cowles, 4 Conn. 189, 10 Am.Dec. 115; Muller v. Benner, 69 Ill. 108; Hutchins v. Dresser, 26 Me. 76, 78; Moore v. Hazelton, 9 Allen, Mass., 102, 104; Manson v.

has greater property interests and these are generally called "title". The guardian is more like an agent; the trustee is an owner and manager for others.

Guardians are officers of the court which appoints them, or to which they are accountable, which is generally the probate or equity court.[16] Trustees are usually not court officers.

The powers of joint guardians are held jointly, as are those of co-trustees.[17] The guardian should act in the name of the ward, followed by the words "by ———, guardian". The trustee contracts or conveys in his own name, followed by the words "as trustee under the will of John Brown", or similar language.

PROMOTERS AND OFFICERS OF CORPORATIONS

16. Promoters and officers of corporations are in relations of trust and confidence toward the stockholders and the corporation, but are not technical trustees for either the stockholders or corporation, because they do not hold title to any specific property to the benefit of which the latter are equitably entitled.

Promoters

Promoters of corporations have sometimes been loosely called "trustees" for the corporation to be organized or its stockholders.[18] The promoter, like the trustee, is no doubt a fiduciary.

Felton, 13 Pick., Mass., 206, 211; Rollins v. Marsh, 128 Mass. 116, 118; Grist v. Forehand, 36 Miss. 69; Judson v. Walker, 155 Mo. 166, 55 S.W. 1083; Seilert v. McAnally, 223 Mo. 505, 515, 122 S.W. 1064, 135 Am.St. Rep. 522; Newton v. Nutt, 58 N.H. 599, 601; McDuffie v. McIntyre, 11 S.C. 551, 560, 32 Am.Rep. 500; Neblett v. Valentino, 127 Tex. 279, 92 S.W.2d 432; In re Paulsen's Guardianship, 229 Wis. 262, 282 N.W. 36. Woerner, The American Law of Guardianship, 172. But see McColl v. Weatherly, 5 Strob., S.C., 72; Hunter v. Lawrence's Adm'r, 11 Grat., Va., 111, 62 Am.Dec. 640. In the following cases the right of the guardian is said to be a power coupled with an interest: Lincoln v. Alexander, 52 Cal. 482, 28 Am.Rep. 639; Van Doren v. Everitt, 5 N.J.L. 528, 8 Am.Dec. 615; People v. Byron, 3 Johns.Cas., N.Y., 53; Pepper v. Stone, 10 Vt. 427.

[16] Cobleigh v. Matheny, 181 Ill.App. 170.

[17] Pepper v. Stone, 10 Vt. 427.

[18] Central Trust Co. v. East Tennessee Land Co., C.C.Tenn., 116 F. 743; Yeiser v. United States Board & Paper Co., C.C.A.Ohio, 107 F. 340, 46 C.C.A. 567, 52 L.R.A. 724; Wills v. Nehalem Coal Co., 52 Or. 70, 96 P. 528; Jordan & Davis v. Annex Corporation, 109 Va. 625, 64 S.E. 1050, 17 Ann.Cas. 267; Mangold v. Adrian Irr. Co., 60 Wash. 286, 111 P. 173. See Wilgus, Corporations and Express Trusts as Business Organizations, 13 Mich.Law Rev. 205; Maitland, Collected Papers, vol. 3, p. 321.

He occupies a position of trust and confidence, where he has unusual opportunities to take advantage of others, and where he is prohibited from acting for his individual interest in any way.[19] But he is not a technical trustee. He holds title to no definite property for the benefit of others. The corporation is not yet in existence. He cannot be a trustee for it. He does not hold any definite property for the prospective stockholders' benefit. Such property as the promoters become the owners of, in preparation for the organization of the corporation, they own absolutely.[20] Their position seems to be that of "anticipatory" agents.[21]

The promoter may become a trustee for stockholders or a corporation. Thus, if he makes a secret profit for himself out of transactions with the corporation, equity will fasten a constructive trust upon such profits in favor of the stockholders.[22] But such a trust arises out of wrongdoing by the promoters. In their normal relation, promoters are not in any true sense trustees.

Officers

Directors, trustees, and other officers of corporations are often spoken of by judges and legal writers as "trustees," or as in a "trust relation," or as "charged with a trust."[23] But they are not technical trustees. They lack wholly the element of property ownership. The corporation itself is holder of the title to the property with which the officers have to do. The officers have no equitable or legal ownership.[24]

[19] Goodwin v. Wilbur, 104 Ill.App. 45; Old Dominion Copper Mining & Smelting Co. v. Bigelow, 203 Mass. 159, 89 N.E. 193, 40 L.R.A.,N.S., 314; Torrey v. Toledo Portland Cement Co., 158 Mich. 348, 122 N.W. 614; Colton Imp. Co. v. Richter, 26 Misc. 26, 55 N.Y.S. 486; Goodman v. White, 174 N.C. 399, 93 S.E. 906.

[20] Reynolds v. Title Guaranty Trust Co., 196 Mo.App. 21, 189 S.W. 33; Arnold v. Searing, 78 N.J.Eq. 146, 78 A. 762; Alger, Law of Promoters, § 21.

[21] Arnold v. Searing, 78 N.J.Eq. 146, 78 A. 762; 1 Thompson on Corporations, 2d Ed., § 103; 2 Cook on Corporations, 6th Ed. § 651; 1 Clark & Marshall on Priv. Corp. § 110b.

[22] Exter v. Sawyer, 146 Mo. 302, 47 S.W. 951; Groel v. United Electric Co. of New Jersey, 70 N.J.Eq. 616, 61 A. 1061; Colton Imp. Co. v. Richter, 26 Misc. 26, 55 N.Y.S. 486; Shawnee Commercial & Savings Bank v. Miller, 24 Ohio Cir.Ct.R. 198; Pietsch v. Milbrath, 123 Wis. 647, 101 N.W. 388, 102 N.W. 342, 68 L.R.A. 945, 107 Am.St.Rep. 1017.

[23] Jackson v. Ludeling, 88 U.S. 616, 21 Wall. 616, 22 L.Ed. 492; Gillett v. Bowen, C.C.Colo., 23 F. 625; Beers v. Bridgeport Bridge Co., 42 Conn. 17; Colquitt v. Howard, 11 Ga. 556; Cumberland Coal & Iron Co. v. Parish, 42 Md. 598; Hun v. Cary, 82 N.Y. 65, 37 Am.Rep. 546; 2 Thompson on Corporations, 2d Ed., § 1269.

[24] Appeal of Spering, 71 Pa. 11, 20, 10 Am.Rep. 684; Wallace v. Lincoln

§ 16   PROMOTERS AND OFFICERS OF CORPORATIONS   47

Directors, trustees, and other corporate officers are fiduciaries, as are agents, executors, guardians, and strict, technical trustees. As corporate officers they owe a duty of extraordinary good faith to the stockholders, because of the peculiar intimacy of the relations and the ease with which the officers could take advantage of the stockholders. The officers must act solely for the interest of the stockholders, as the trustee must work solely for the benefit of his cestui.[25] But, aside from this fiduciary element, the two relations are not similar.

Officers of corporations, like promoters, may become trustees in a technical sense for the stockholders, if they are guilty of wrongdoing which results in a secret profit to themselves. Equity will declare the officers constructive trustees of such unlawful profits.[26] But the corporate officer who performs his duty is not a technical trustee.

A corporation is not a trustee of its property for its stockholders or creditors, although it owes important duties to such persons.[27] These obligations are founded on contract, and not on an equitable property interest held by stockholders or creditors in the corporate assets.

Majority stockholders owe duties toward minority stockholders, but they are not in any sense trustees of the stock they own, for the benefit of the minority.[28]

Sav. Bank, 89 Tenn. 630, 649, 15 S. W. 448, 24 Am.St.Rep. 625; Boyd v. Mutual Fire Ass'n of Eau Claire, 116 Wis. 155, 90 N.W. 1086, 94 N.W. 171, 61 L.R.A. 918, 96 Am.St.Rep. 948; 3 Clark & Marshall on Priv. Corp. § 748; 2 Cook on Corporations, 6th Ed., p. 1856, note.

[25] Coons v. Tome, C.C.Pa., 9 F. 532; Bainbridge v. Stoner, 16 Cal.2d 423, 106 P.2d 423; Hawley v. Wells, 151 Kan. 539, 99 P.2d 784; Slee v. Bloom, 20 Johns., N.Y., 669; Hedges v. Paquett, 3 Or. 77; Philadelphia, W. & B. R. Co. v. Cowell, 28 Pa. 329, 70 Am.Dec. 128; Hope v. Valley City Salt Co., 25 W.Va. 789.

[26] See § 62, post.

[27] People v. Dennett, 276 Ill. 43, 114 N.E. 493; Hyams v. Old Dominion Co., 113 Me. 294, 93 A. 747, L.R.A. 1915D, 1128; Hospes v. Northwestern Mfg. & Car Co., 48 Minn. 174, 50 N.W. 1117, 15 L.R.A. 470, 31 Am.St.Rep. 637; Berle, Corporate Powers as Powers in Trust, 44 Harv.L.R. 1049.

[28] Heffern Co-Op. Consol. Gold Min. & Mill Co. v. Gauthier, 22 Ariz. 67, 193 P. 1021; Wood, Status of Management Stockholders, 38 Yale L. J. 57.

RECEIVERSHIP

17. **A receiver is not usually a trustee. He is a court officer appointed by equity to manage property which is being administered by the court. Neither the court nor the receiver has title to the property, although the court has possession and powers of management and disposition. If the court vests title in the receiver, as is sometimes done, the receiver becomes a court-controlled trustee.**

Receivers are like trustees, in that they are fiduciaries, and are subject to control by the court of chancery.

When the estate of an insolvent is brought before it, and in other cases, equity sometimes appoints a receiver of the property, in order to conserve it for appropriate distribution. Receivers have sometimes been referred to as "trustees".[29] They are undoubtedly fiduciaries, governed by the same rules as to fidelity and loyalty as trustees.[30] They also resemble trustees in that they are subject to the jurisdiction of a court of equity.

But it is not believed that the ordinary receiver is strictly speaking a trustee.[31] He is a court officer and must secure authority from the court for every act he does.[32] The "title" to the property being administered is regarded as being in the insolvent corporation, or other individual who had it prior to the receivership.[33] The creation of the receivership merely indicates that the court has taken the property into its possession and has assumed powers of management and disposition which it is going to exercise through an officer or agent, the receiver. A trustee is not usually an officer of the court, and his interests in the property he manages are greater than those of the usual receiver. Those interests are usually dignified by the name "title".

A receiver is more like an agent than a trustee. He does not contract or convey as a separate legal entity and is not ordinarily liable on contracts or conveyances.[34]

---

[29] Byrnes v. Missouri Nat. Bank, C.C.A.Mo., 7 F.2d 978; Broussard v. Mason, 187 Mo.App. 281, 173 S.W. 698.

[30] Patterson v. Woodward, 175 Ark. 300, 299 S.W. 619; Roller v. Paul, 106 Va. 214, 55 S.E. 558.

[31] Harmon v. Best, 174 Ind. 323, 91 N.E. 19.

[32] Nevitt v. Woodburn, 190 Ill. 283, 60 N.E. 500.

[33] Pennsylvania Steel Co. v. New York City Ry. Co., C.C.A.N.Y., 198 F. 721; Dietrich v. O'Brien, 122 Md. 482, 89 A. 717; Hannon v. Mechanics Bldg. & Loan Ass'n of Spartanburg, 177 S.C. 153, 180 S.E. 873, 100 A.L.R. 928.

[34] Rosso v. Freeman, D.C.Mass.,

Sometimes equity appoints a receiver and vests him with title. Either by court decree or by conveyance the receiver gets all the interests of the party whose estate is being managed, subject to a duty to manage those interests for the benefit of creditors, stockholders, or others. Here the receiver probably becomes a court-appointed trustee.[35]

LIFE TENANT AND REMAINDERMAN

18. **A life tenant is not a trustee of property in his possession for the remainderman who is to follow in occupation and enjoyment.**

It is sometimes said in a loose and non-technical sense that a life tenant is a trustee for the remainderman who is to follow him.[36] Undoubtedly the life tenant owes certain duties to the remainderman which are somewhat similar to those of trustees. The life tenant should preserve the property by the payment of taxes and mortgage interest,[37] he should refrain from waste or destruction of the property, and he should not buy in outstanding claims against the property for his sole benefit but should give the remainderman the benefit of such claims.[38]

But the similarity to the trust is superficial.[39] The life tenant owns a separate interest. It is a case of successive interests in the same thing, usually both legal in nature. There is no simultaneous ownership of the same property interest, divided into legal and equitable parts.

Life tenants are sometimes required to give bond to preserve the property for the remainderman.[40] This shows that they have power to injure the remainderman by abuse of the land or chattels involved, but it does not show that the life tenant is a trustee.

30 F.2d 826; Avey v. Burnley, 167 Ky. 26, 179 S.W. 1050; International Shoe Co. v. U. S. Fidelity & Guaranty Co., 186 S.C. 271, 195 S.E. 546.

[35] Squire v. Princeton Lighting Co., 72 N.J.Eq. 883, 68 A. 176, 15 L.R.A., N.S., 657; Decker v. Gardner, 124 N.Y. 334, 26 N.E. 814, 11 L.R.A. 480.

[36] Buder v. Franz, C.C.A.Mo., 27 F.2d 101; In re Hamlin, 141 App. Div. 318, 126 N.Y.S. 396,

[37] Grodsky v. Sipe, D.C.Ill., 30 F. Supp. 656.

[38] Morrison v. Roehl, 215 Mo. 545, 114 S.W. 981.

[39] Spring v. Hollander, 261 Mass. 373, 158 N.E. 791; Welsh's Estate, 239 Pa. 616, 86 A. 1091.

[40] Scott v. Scott, 137 Iowa 239, 114 N.W. 881, 23 L.R.A.,N.S., 716, 126 Am.St.Rep. 277. In re Knowles' Estate, 148 N.C. 461, 62 S.E. 549.

DEEDS OF TRUST IN THE NATURE OF MORTGAGES[41]

19. **A deed of trust in the nature of a mortgage is similar to a trust to secure or pay creditors but differs from it slightly.**

A deed of trust in the nature of a mortgage is a common security device in many states. The borrower conveys property to a trustee in the deed of trust, in order to secure payment of the debt owed to the holders of notes or bonds. This instrument is a substitute for the common law mortgage and is especially convenient where the debt is owned by several or many creditors. Because it is a security transaction and a variation of the common law mortgage, it is governed by that body of principles built up by law and equity relating to mortgages and other security instruments. Among these rules is that giving the borrower in these security transactions an "equity of redemption", that is, a right to any surplus realized from the mortgaged property after the creditors have been paid. This interest is similar to that of the beneficiary of a trust but not identical with it.[42]

If property is conveyed to a trustee to pay off creditors at once, or in the future provided they are not paid by the debtor himself, the legal title is ordinarily vested in the trustee, and the equitable interest in the creditors to be paid. There remains in the settlor-debtor a contingent equitable interest called his interest as the beneficiary of a resulting trust. If there is a surplus after paying the cestuis of the trust, the balance results to the settlor.[43] He takes it on the basis of a presumed intent that it should come back to him. This is very similar to the equity of redemption in the case of the deed of trust in the nature of a mortgage in that both are equitable. It differs in that it is at least theoretically based on the settlor's intent, whereas the equity of redemption is granted by chancery in order to prevent injustice.

In the deed of trust in the nature of a mortgage there is always the so-called "defeasance clause", providing that the title of the trustee shall cease if the debt is paid. This is a feature not used in a strict trust to pay debts.[44]

---

[41] Restatement, Trusts, § 9.

[42] First Nat. Bank of Atlanta v. Southern Cotton Oil Co., C.C.A.Ga., 78 F.2d 339; Touli v. Santa Cruz County Title Co., 20 Cal.App.2d 495, 67 P.2d 404; Kidd, Trust Deed and Mortgages in California, 3 Cal.L.R. 381.

[43] Post, § 54.

[44] Neikirk v. Boulder Nat. Bank, 53 Colo. 350, 127 P. 137; Hoffman v.

The duties of the trustee in the deed of trust in the nature of a mortgage are similar to those of the trustee in a trust to pay creditors, as far as the creditors are concerned. Both hold property interests which they have a duty to apply for the creditors and this duty is enforceable in equity.

There is no fiduciary relation between mortgagor and mortgagee or giver of a deed of trust and the trustee under it,[45] although there is between the trustee of a trust to pay creditors and the settlor as the holder of a contingent resulting trust interest. But both the deed of trust and the trust to pay creditors involve a fiduciary relation between the trustee and the creditors for whom he acts.[46]

Mackall, 5 Ohio St. 124, 64 Am.Dec. 637.

but see Earll v. Picken, 72 App.D.C. 91, 113 F.2d 150.

[45] Chicago Title & Trust Co. v. Suter, 287 Ill.App. 162, 4 N.E.2d 650;

[46] Brewer v. Slater, 18 App.D.C. 48; Morriss v. Virginia State Ins. Co., 90 Va. 370, 18 S.E. 843.

CHAPTER 3

CREATION OF EXPRESS TRUSTS—TRUST INTENT—FORMALITIES—CONVEYANCING

Sec.
20. Express and Implied Trusts.
21. Methods of Creation of Express Trusts.
22. Expression of Trust Intent.
23. Precatory Expressions.
24. Reality of Trust Intent—Savings Bank Trusts.
25. Formality—The Statute of Frauds.
26. Formality—The Wills Acts.
27. Consideration.
28. Delivery of the Trust Instrument.
29. Notice of the Trust.
30. Transfer of Title to the Trustee.

EXPRESS AND IMPLIED TRUSTS[1]

20. Trusts are classified, with respect to their method of creation, as express and implied. Express trusts are created by the stated intent of the settlor that they shall exist, accompanied by the necessary disposition of the trust property. Implied trusts are those adjudged to exist by courts of equity, either because of a presumed intent that they shall exist or for the purpose of preventing the unjust enrichment of the holder of a title.

In considering the origin of trusts two classes are usually fixed. Those trusts which come into being because the parties concerned have formed the actual intent that they shall arise, have expressed that intent in written or spoken words or otherwise, and have made the requisite property transfers, are called express trusts. Thus, if A. executes a writing whereby he declares himself trustee of certain of A.'s lands for B., using the words "trustee" and "cestui que trust," and describing the particular land as the subject of the trust, there is an express trust.

But there are certain trusts which do not have back of them any written instrument or oral expression or other acts explicitly showing a trust intent. These latter trusts are called implied, and are divided into two classes, namely, resulting and constructive.[2] The former occur where the courts presume or infer from

---

[1] Restatement, Trusts, § 1.

[2] Messrs. Lewin and Perry, respectively the authors of important texts on the subject of trusts, have introduced some confusion into the classification of trusts by giving to the phrase

certain acts that the parties intended a trust to exist, although the parties expressed no such trust intent directly and may not actually have had it. The latter, namely, constructive trusts, are imposed by chancery on the holders of legal or equitable titles as a means of accomplishing justice and preventing unjust enrichment. Constructive trusts are not based on the intent of the parties, either actual or presumed. They are often called involuntary trusts, or trusts ex maleficio. Thus, if A pays the purchase price of land to C and C conveys the land by absolute deed to B in consideration of such purchase price, equity will presume that A intended B to act as trustee for A and a trust will result. While if A when occupying a fiduciary relation to B, fraudulently obtains B's property, B may have A declared a constructive trustee of the property. The further definition of implied trusts is

"implied trusts" a peculiar meaning. They define as implied those trusts which exist because of certain language used by the parties which does not clearly create a trust, but is construed by the courts to have that intent. Under this definition implied trusts arise from ambiguous or doubtful language used by the parties, which is held by the courts to disclose an actual trust intent. Lewin, Trusts, 14th Ed., 16, 82; 1 Perry on Trusts, 7th Ed., § 112. These authorities have led several American courts into the classification of trusts into four groups, namely, express, implied, resulting, and constructive. Kayser v. Maugham, 8 Colo. 232, 6 P. 803; Plum Trees Lime Co. v. Keeler, 92 Conn. 1, 101 A. 509, Ann.Cas.1918E, 831; Weer v. Gand, 88 Ill. 490; Holsapple v. Schrontz, 65 Ind.App. 390, 117 N.E. 547; Stevens v. Fitzpatrick, 218 Mo. 708, 723, 118 S.W. 51; Burks v. Burks, 7 Baxt., Tenn., 353, 355; Olcott v. Gabert, 86 Tex. 121, 127, 23 S.W. 985; Gottstein v. Wist, 22 Wash. 581, 590, 61 P. 715.

But the prevailing view in America is that implied trusts should be defined as including resulting and constructive trusts only. Eaton v. Barnes, 121 Ga. 548, 49 S.E. 593; Rice v. Dougherty, 148 Ill.App. 368;

Heil v. Heil, 184 Mo. 665, 675, 84 S.W. 45; Lovett v. Taylor, 54 N.J.Eq. 311, 34 A. 896; Gorrell v. Alspaugh, 120 N.C. 362, 366, 27 S.E. 85; McCoy v. McCoy, 30 Okl. 379, 121 P. 176, Ann. Cas.1913C, 146; 15 Am. & Eng.Enc. Law, 2d Ed., 1123; 39 Cyc. 24. Even though it might be desirable, if one were treating the matter de novo, to use "implied" in its natural sense, as, for example, as it is used in the law of contract, the terminology herein used is so deeply imbedded in the law that it would seem unwise to attempt a change.

The late Professor Costigan recommended classifying trusts as "Intent Enforcing" and "Fraud Rectifying". Under the first class would fall trusts based on an actual intent of the parties, whether the intent was expressed clearly or vaguely, or was inferred or implied. Under the latter group would fall all court created trusts, where the intent of the parties is immaterial, and the trust is merely a remedial device. This classification seems more logical than that of express and implied trusts, but it is perhaps too late to persuade the courts to make a change. The Classification of Trusts as Express, Resulting and Constructive, 27 Harv.L.R. 437.

left to later sections, where their origin is considered.[3] The steps leading to the creation of express trusts will first be described.

METHODS OF TRUST CREATION[4]

21. The principal methods of trust creation are—
    (a) A declaration by a property owner that he holds the property in trust for another;
    (b) A transfer by a property owner of that property to another to hold in trust for a third person;
    (c) A contract by one to pay money to another which the payee is to hold in trust for a third person.

Trust Declarations

If A is the full owner of a share of stock in the United States Steel Corporation, he may declare in writing or orally that henceforth he holds that stock in trust for his nephew, B., with a duty to pay the nephew the dividends during his life. This is the creation of a trust by "declaration". The settlor is also the trustee.

Trust Transfers

If A is the owner of the stock mentioned above, he may deliver it to the X. Trust Company, to be held by it in trust for the nephew, B., with the duty to pay over the income to B. during his life. Upon the manifestation of this intent by A., the handing over of the stock certificate, with appropriate endorsement, and the acceptance of the trust by the Trust Company, the creation of a trust by "transfer" is completed.

The most common way of creating a trust by transfer is to leave property by will to another in trust for a third. Thus, a property owner may make a will by which he leaves all his property to B, to hold it in trust for the testator's family. On the death of the testator, with the will unrevoked, title passes to the trustee and the trust begins. Testamentary trusts are much more frequently created than any other type of trust.

---

[3] See §§ 49–54, post, on Resulting Trusts, and §§ 55–66, post, on Constructive Trusts.

[4] Restatement, Trusts, § 17.

Contracts in Favor of a Trustee

A may make out a promissory note whereby he agrees to pay $1,000 to B., as trustee for C. On the delivery of this note to B., a trust will arise.

A may take out a policy of insurance with the X. Insurance Company on his, A.'s, life, and the company may promise to pay the amount of the insurance to B. as trustee for C., with a duty to support C. from these proceeds for the life of C. This is the creation of a trust through the making of a contract in favor of a trustee. The trust will arise when the insurance company makes its contract.

EXPRESSION OF TRUST INTENT[5]

22. The speaking, writing, or other act of the settlor relied on to prove an express trust must—
   (a) Manifest an intent that an express trust arise; and
   (b) Describe with certainty the trust property and the beneficiaries.

   No particular words or phrases need be used to express this intent and embody this description.

Language [6] Used Must Express Intent That Trust shall Arise

Obviously, unless the language used by the settlor indicates an intent that a trust come into existence, no express trust will be created, whatever the words employed.[7] The very definition of express trusts indicates that they spring from the will of the parties. Thus, words expressing an intent to make an absolute gift will not, when the gift is imperfect, create a trust;[8] and

---

[5] Restatement, Trusts, §§ 23–27.

[6] While the acts showing the trust intent may be acts other than talking or speaking, such cases are so rare that they may be ignored. The trust intent will almost always be expressed in a deed, will, other writing, or in an oral statement made by the settlor to the trustee, beneficiary, or to both. Where there is an expression of the trust intent in a document, it is usually called the "trust instrument". The details about the settlor's intent as to the trust are sometimes called the "trust terms".

[7] Seabrook v. Grimes, 107 Md. 410, 68 A. 883, 16 L.R.A.,N.S., 483, 126 Am.St.Rep. 400; Colmary v. Fanning, 124 Md. 548, 92 A. 1045; Winters v. Winters, 166 Or. 659, 109 P.2d 857; Richardson v. Inglesby, 13 Rich.Eq., S.C., 59. In expressing this intent the settlor's mind must act freely. Thus, if undue influence affects it, the creation of the trust will be set aside. Beard v. Beard, 173 Ky. 131, 190 S.W. 703, Ann.Cas.1918C, 832. See Settlor, § 31, post.

[8] Pratt v. Griffin, 184 Ill. 514, 56 N.E. 819; In re Ashman's Estate, 223

words showing an intent to convey in trust at some time in the future do not establish a present trust.[9] A purpose to give property to a corporation absolutely for its corporate purposes will not found an express trust with the corporation as trustee.[10]

No Particular Words Required

If the words used convey the intent to establish a trust, they will have that effect. No formal or technical expressions are required.[11] For example, it is not necessary that the settlor use the words "trust" or "trustee,"[12] and the designation of one as a "trustee" does not conclusively show the creation of a trust.[13]

The language used may be sufficient, although the person actually intended to be a trustee is called an "executor," [14] an "attorney,"[15] an "agent,"[16] or a "guardian."[17] If the duties required of the officer appointed are those of a trustee, the party nominated will be held to be a trustee, regardless of teminology used.[18]

Pa. 543, 72 A. 899; Johnson v. Williams, 63 How.Prac., N.Y., 233. This is true even though the donor expresses a hope that the donee will at some time return the property or its avails. Murray v. Ray, C.C.A. Idaho, 251 F. 866, 164 C.C.A. 82.

[9] Reynolds v. Thompson, 161 Ky. 772, 171 S.W. 379.

[10] Clarke v. Sisters of Society of the Holy Child Jesus, 82 Neb. 85, 117 N.W. 107; In re Durand, 194 N.Y. 477, 87 N.E. 677.

[11] Teal v. Pleas. Grove Local Union No. 204, 202 Ala. 23, 75 So. 335; In re Heywood's Estate, 148 Cal. 184, 82 P. 755; Anderson v. Crist, 113 Ind. 65, 15 N.E. 9; Citizens' Loan & Trust Co. v. Herron, 186 Ind. 421, 115 N.E. 941; Reeder v. Reeder, 184 Iowa 1, 168 N.W. 122; Blake v. Dexter, 66 Mass. 559, 12 Cush. 559; O'Neil v. Greenwood, 106 Mich. 572, 64 N.W. 511; Moulden v. Train, 199 Mo.App. 509, 204 S.W. 65; Putnam v. Lincoln Safe Deposit Co., 191 N.Y. 166, 83 N.E. 789; Martin v. Moore, 49 Wash. 288, 94 P. 1087.

[12] Carr v. Carr, 15 Cal.App. 480, 115 P. 261; Hughes v. Fitzgerald, 78 Conn. 4, 60 A. 694; In re Soulard's Estate, 141 Mo. 642, 43 S.W. 617; Morse v. Morse, 85 N.Y. 53.

[13] Bank of Visalia v. Dillonwood Lumber Co., 148 Cal. 18, 82 P. 374; In re Hawley, 104 N.Y. 250, 10 N.E. 352; Sansom v. Ayer & Lord Tie Co., 144 Ky. 555, 139 S.W. 778. A gift to two brothers, "to be placed in savings bank in trust," with no mention of a trustee or beneficiary is an absolute gift. Birge v. Nucomb, 93 Conn. 69, 105 A. 335.

[14] Angus v. Noble, 73 Conn. 56, 46 A. 278.

[15] Mersereau v. Bennet, 124 App. Div. 413, 108 N.Y.S. 868.

[16] Anderson v. Fry, 116 App.Div. 740, 102 N.Y.S. 112.

[17] Fleck v. Ellis, 144 Ga. 732, 87 S.E. 1055.

[18] Ryder v. Lyon, 85 Conn. 245, 82 A. 573; Rantz v. Dale, 158 Ill.App. 244; Mee v. Gordon, 187 N.Y. 400, 80

So free from technicality are the rules regarding the creation of trusts that the trustee of a real property trust will take whatever estate is necessary for the performance of his duties, regardless of the presence or absence of the word "heirs" or other technical words limiting the estate granted.[19]

Language Must Describe Trust Elements Completely and with Certainty

Uncertainty and ambiguity in the description of the trust elements tends to show that no trust was designed;[20] but, if the intent to create a trust be assumed, it cannot be effective unless the trust elements are properly described. Those elements are the subject-matter, the trust purpose, the cestuis que trust, and the trustee.[21]

Thus, if the property to be administered by the trustee be indefinite and incapable of identification, no trust can arise.[22] The residue of the testator's property is a sufficiently definite subject-matter for a trust.[23] So, too, if the trust purpose be omitted,[24] or the description of the beneficiaries be vague,[25] the trust will be defectively declared.

That a trustee is not named is not important, since the court will supply that element.[26] It is also not needful that the settlor

---

N.E. 353, 116 Am.St.Rep. 613, 10 Ann. Cas. 172.

[19] Tyler v. Triesback, 69 Fla. 595, 69 So. 49; West v. Fitz, 109 Ill. 425; Packard v. Old Colony R. Co., 168 Mass. 92, 46 N.E. 433; Chamberlain v. Thompson, 10 Conn. 243, 26 Am.Dec. 390; Ewing v. Shannahan, 113 Mo. 188, 20 S.W. 1065; Fisher v. Fisher, 41 N.J.Eq. 16, 2 A. 608; Welch v. Allen, 21 Wend., N.Y., 147; Williams v. First Presbyterian Soc. in Cincinnati, 1 Ohio St. 478; contra, Evans v. King, 56 N.C. 387; Allen v. Baskerville, 123 N.C. 126, 31 S.E. 383. But see Fulbright v. Yoder, 113 N.C. 456, 18 S.E. 713.

[20] Pratt v. Trustees of Sheppard & Enoch Pratt Hospital, 88 Md. 610, 42 A. 51.

[21] Inglis v. Sailor's Snug Harbor, 28 U.S. 99, 3 Pet. 99, 7 L.Ed. 617;

Drinkhouse v. German Savings & Loan Soc., 17 Cal.App. 162, 118 P. 953; Crowley v. Crowley, 131 Mo.App. 178, 110 S.W. 1100.

[22] Mills v. Newberry, 112 Ill. 123, 1 N.E. 156, 54 Am.Rep. 213; Barkley v. Lane's Ex'r, 69 Ky. 587, 6 Bush 587; Roddy v. Roddy, 3 Neb. 96.

[23] Glover v. Baker, 76 N.H. 393, 83 A. 916.

[24] Bank v. Rice, 143 Cal. 265, 76 P. 1020, 101 Am.St.Rep. 118; Ingram v. Fraley, 29 Ga. 553.

[25] Condit v. Reynolds, 66 N.J.L. 242, 49 A. 540; Fowler v. Coates, 201 N.Y. 257, 94 N.E. 997.

[26] Trustees of McIntire Poor School v. Zanesville Canal & Mfg. Co., 9 Ohio, 203, 34 Am.Dec. 436; Appeal of Varner, 80 Pa. 140.

should expressly give the trust property to the trustee. If the trust is fully described, the gift of the property to the trustee will be implied.[27]

Where the settlor uses repugnant words, at one point showing an intent to create a trust and at another an opposing intent, whether any trust was created is a difficult question of construction. In many instances of repugnant wordings a trust has been found,[28] while in other cases of the same sort the construction was against a trust.[29]

In a few states the statutes contain statements as to the content of the settlor's expression which is necessary to trust creation.[30] In other states legislation has been enacted as to the effect of a conveyance to one as trustee, without description of the beneficiaries or other terms of the trust.[31]

Where an absolute conveyance is made, it may be argued that the parol evidence rule will prevent proof by oral evidence of a claim that the grantor intended the grantee to be a trustee for the grantor[32] or for a third party.[33] If the conveyance is clearly to the grantee in trust, this same rule will prevent a contradiction by oral evidence of the intent expressed in the deed as to the trust terms.[34]

---

[27] Haywood v. Wachovia Loan & Trust Co., 149 N.C. 208, 62 S.E. 915; In re Eppig, 63 Misc. 613, 118 N.Y.S. 683.

[28] Harris v. Ferguy, 207 Ill. 534, 69 N.E. 844; Brown's Lessee v. Brown, 12 Md. 87; Robinson v. Cogswell, 192 Mass. 79, 78 N.E. 389; Fairchild v. Edson, 77 Hun 298, 28 N.Y.S. 401; In re Lejee's Estate, 181 Pa. 416, 37 A. 554; In re Luscombe's Will, 109 Wis. 186, 85 N.W. 341.

[29] Thompson v. Adams, 205 Ill. 552, 69 N.E. 1; Blakeshere v. Trustees, 94 Md. 773, 51 A. 1056; Spooner v. Lovejoy, 108 Mass. 529; Dunshee v. Goldbacher, 56 Barb., N.Y., 579.

[30] The settlor is required to indicate by acts or words "an intention on the part of the trustor to create a trust" and "the subject, purpose, and beneficiary of the trust". Cal.Civ.Code, § 2221; Mont.Rev.Codes 1935,

§ 7884; N.D.Comp.L.1913, § 6277; S.D.Code 1939, § 59.0105.

[31] The purport of these statutes is that third parties may rely on the grantee as being the absolute owner or as a trustee with power to sell, and they need make no inquiry as to the terms of the trust. Mich.Ann.St. § 26.70; New York Real Property Law, § 104; Pa. 21 P.S. § 262. See § 153, post.

[32] That oral proof is admissible, see Hughes v. Pritchard, 122 N.C. 59, 29 S.E. 93; Harvey v. Gardner, 41 Ohio St. 642.

[33] *Admissible:* Huff v. Fuller, 197 Ky. 119, 246 S.W. 149; Young v. Holland, 117 Va. 433, 84 S.E. 637. *Inadmissible:* Wright v. Young, 20 Ariz. 46, 176 P. 583; Pusey v. Gardner, 21 W.Va. 469.

[34] Price v. Kane, 112 Mo. 412, 20 S.W. 609; Gale v. Sulloway, 62 N.H. 57.

§ 23

Burden of Proof and Character of Evidence Necessary

The burden lies upon the party asserting the existence of a trust to show that the language used is sufficient for that purpose.[35]

It is frequently stated by courts that the evidence to establish the existence of a trust must be "clear," "convincing," "explicit," and "unequivocal." [36] In practically all instances in which such requirements regarding the evidence have been laid down, the proof offered has been oral; but occasionally similar remarks have been made regarding written evidence.[37] Occasionally it has been stated that the evidence must establish a trust beyond a reasonable doubt,[38] or be so positive as to leave no doubt.[39]

On principle it would seem that no stronger evidence should be required to prove the creation of a trust than to prove any other fact in a civil action. However, many times the effort to prove a trust involves an attack on a title which by the records or otherwise seems absolute. The public interest in the security of titles is doubtless behind the statements of the courts about the character of evidence required for the proof of trusts. The rule requiring an extraordinarily high degree of proof has been actually applied rarely, except in cases where an attempt was made by oral proof to fasten a trust upon property which appeared to be owned absolutely.

PRECATORY EXPRESSIONS[40]

23. Precatory expressions are words of request or recommendation. Whether they create a trust is a matter of construction. In determining the supposed settlor's intent the following facts, among others, should be considered:

(a) The definiteness of the subject-matter and the beneficiaries referred to;

---

[35] Prevost v. Gratz, 19 U.S. 481, 6 Wheat. 481, 5 L.Ed. 311; Miller v. Hill, 64 Misc. 199, 118 N.Y.S. 63; Russell v. Fish, 149 Wis. 122, 135 N.W. 531; Neyland v. Bendy, 69 Tex. 711, 7 S.W. 497.

[36] Sheehan v. Sullivan, 126 Cal. 189, 58 P. 543; Lurie v. Sabath, 208 Ill. 401, 70 N.E. 323; Crissman v. Crissman, 23 Mich. 217; Hoffman v. Union Dime Saving Inst'n, 109 App. Div. 24, 95 N.Y.S. 1045; Boughman v. Boughman, 69 Ohio St. 273, 69 N.E. 430; Gribbel v. Gribbel, 341 Pa. 11, 17 A.2d 892; Watts v. McCloud, Tex.Civ. App., 205 S.W. 381.

[37] Otjen v. Frohbach, 148 Wis. 301, 134 N.W. 832.

[38] Rogers v. Rogers, 87 Mo. 257.

[39] Harrison v. McMennomy, 2 Edw. Ch., N.Y., 251.

[40] Restatement, Trusts, § 25.

(b) The amount of discretion allowed the trustee;

(c) The relationship of the alleged cestui que trust to the supposed settlor and the ethical or legal obligations of the latter to the former;

(d) The wording of the gift, whether first made absolutely and then affected by precatory words in a later and separate part of the will, or whether the words of gift and precatory expressions are bound up together in a single clause, sentence or paragraph.

Precatory Expressions

The cases in which greatest difficulty arises in discovering whether a testator or grantor intended a trust to be created are those in which he uses "precatory expressions." Precatory expressions are "words of entreaty, request, wish, or recommendation." [41] If, for example, instead of giving property to A. "in trust for B.," the owner devises it to A. "with a request that A. care for B. from the income of such property," the latter expression of desire is called precatory.[42]

The basic principle in the construction of precatory expressions is well stated by a distinguished judge. "The primary question in every case is the intention of the testator, and whether in the use of precatory words he meant merely to advise or influence the discretion of the devisee, or himself to control or direct the disposition intended." [43]

The words "request," "desire," and the like, do not naturally import a legal obligation. But the early view in England was that such words, when used in a will, were to be given an un-

---

[41] Black's Law Dict., 2d Ed., 928.

[42] The trusts sometimes created by such words of entreaty or request are often called "precatory trusts." Keplinger v. Keplinger, 185 Ind. 81, 113 N.E. 292; Simpson v. Corder, 185 Mo.App. 398, 170 S.W. 357; Hunt v. Hunt, 18 Wash. 14, 19, 50 P. 578. But it is submitted that it is more satisfactory to reserve the word "precatory" for the description of the expression to be construed. If the construction is that a trust is created, there is no object in distinguishing it from any other trust by calling it a "precatory" trust. "A great deal has been said in argument and a great many cases have been cited as to what are awkwardly, and in my opinion incorrectly, called 'precatory trusts.' As I understand the law of the court, this phrase is nothing more than a misleading nickname. When a trust is once established, it is equally a trust, and has all the effect and incidents of a trust, whether declared in clearly imperative terms by a testator, or deduced upon a consideration of the whole will from language not amounting necessarily in its prima facie meaning to an imperative trust." Rigby, L.J., in In re Williams [1897] 2 Ch. 12, 27.

[43] Finch, J., in Phillips v. Phillips, 112 N.Y. 197, 205, 19 N.E. 411, 8 Am. St.Rep. 737.

natural meaning, and were to be held to be courteous and softened means of creating duties enforceable by the courts.⁴⁴ According to that opinion words of request prima facie created a trust. But since the beginning of the nineteenth century the English courts have changed their stand upon this question, and now hold that the natural significance of precatory words is not a trust, but that such an obligation may be shown by other portions of the instrument or by extrinsic circumstances.⁴⁵ The American courts have adopted this natural construction of precatory expressions.⁴⁶

Precatory Expressions—Guides to Intent

The particular words used will be of little assistance in guiding the searcher to a discovery of the intent. Thus the words "desire," ⁴⁷ "request," ⁴⁸ "wish," ⁴⁹ "hope," ⁵⁰ "recommend," ⁵¹ "in confidence that," ⁵² and "rely," ⁵³ have been held in some instances to create trusts, and in others to be of no legal effect. The use of any particular precatory word will not determine the question of intent. Aid in solving the problem must be sought in consideration of other portions of the instrument and the facts

---

⁴⁴ Malim v. Keighley, 2 Ves.Jr. 333; Knight v. Knight, 3 Beav. 148.

⁴⁵ "Words of request in their ordinary meaning convey a mere request, and do not convey a legal obligation of any kind, either at law or in equity. But in any particular case there may be circumstances which would oblige the court to say that such words have a meaning beyond their ordinary meaning and import a legal obligation." Lord Esher, in Hill v. Hill, [1897] 1 Q.B. 483, 486.

⁴⁶ Thomas v. Reynolds, 234 Ala. 212, 174 So. 753; In re Mallon's Estate, 34 Cal.App.2d 147, 93 P.2d 245; McClean v. McClean, 142 Kan. 716, 52 P.2d 625; Farmers Bank of Clinch Valley v. Kinser, 169 Ga. 69, 192 S.E. 745; Cowles v. Mathews, 197 Wash. 652, 86 P.2d 273. New Jersey tends to follow the original English rule. Deacon v. Cobson, 83 N.J.Eq. 122, 89 A. 1029.

⁴⁷ In re Browne's Estate, 175 Cal. 361, 165 P. 960; Lines v. Darden, 5 Fla. 51; Manley v. Fiske, 139 App. Div. 665, 124 N.Y.S. 149; Hardy v. Hardy, 174 N.C. 505, 93 S.E. 976; In re Dewey's Estate, 45 Utah 98, 143 P. 124, Ann.Cas.1918A, 475.

⁴⁸ McCurdy v. McCallum, 186 Mass. 464, 72 N.E. 75.

⁴⁹ Phillips v. Phillips, 112 N.Y. 197, 19 N.E. 411, 8 Am.St.Rep. 737; Sears v. Cunningham, 122 Mass. 538.

⁵⁰ Van Duyne v. Van Duyne, 15 N.J.Eq. 503; Eaton v. Watts, L.R. 4 Eq. 151.

⁵¹ Ford v. Fowler, 3 Beav. 146; Gilbert v. Chapin, 19 Conn. 342.

⁵² People v. Powers, 83 Hun 449, 29 N.Y.S. 950, 31 N.Y.S. 1131; Buffum v. Town, 16 R.I. 643, 19 A. 112, 7 L.R.A. 386.

⁵³ Blanchard v. Chapman, 22 Ill. App. 341; Willets v. Willets, 35 Hun, N.Y. 401.

surrounding the supposed settlor at the time of the execution of the instrument.

In the first place, a failure on the part of the settlor definitely to describe the subject-matter of the supposed trust or the beneficiaries or objects thereof is strong evidence that he intended no trust. Unless these elements, namely, subject and object, are definite, the trust will be unenforceable, even if it could come into being. A property owner will not be presumed to have disposed of his estate in an ineffectual and useless way. "Whenever the subject to be administered as trust property, and the objects for whose benefit it is to be administered, are to be found in a will, not expressly creating a trust, the indefinite nature and quantum of the subject, as well as the indefinite nature of the objects, are always used by the court as evidence that the mind of the testator was not to create a trust." [54] In many cases the uncertainty of the subject-matter has influenced the courts in holding that no trust was intended by the precatory words,[55] while the lack of clearness regarding the cestuis que trust has had a similar effect in other cases.[56]

Secondly, the nature of the donee's duties may be determinative. A trustee is under an imperative obligation to act for the cestuis. That he may elect to keep the property as his own or give all or part of it to the cestuis is inconsistent with the fundamental notion of a trust, namely, that it is an equitable obligation. Hence, if the discretion given to the supposed trustee in connection with the precatory words is so broad as to allow him to bestow no benefit on the supposed cestuis, if he likes, the courts will consider it unlikely that a trust was intended;[57]

[54] Lines v. Darden, 5 Fla. 51, 73. Accord: Floyd v. Smith, 59 Fla. 485, 51 So. 537, 37 L.R.A.,N.S., 651, 138 Am.St.Rep. 133, 21 Ann.Cas. 318; Handley v. Wrightson, 60 Md. 198; Lucas v. Lockhart, 18 Miss. 466, 10 Smedes & M. 466, 48 Am.Dec. 766; Noe v. Kern, 93 Mo. 367, 6 S.W. 239, 3 Am.St.Rep. 544; Harrisons v. Harrison's Adm'x, 2 Grat., Va., 1, 44 Am. Dec. 365.

[55] Bryan v. Milby, 6 Del.Ch. 208, 24 A. 333, 13 L.R.A. 563; Coulson v. Alpaugh, 163 Ill. 298, 45 N.E. 216; Hazlewood v. Webster, 7 Ky.Law Rep. 164; Williams v. Worthington, 49 Md. 572, 33 Am.Rep. 286; Whitesel v. Whitesel, 23 Grat., Va., 904; but see Cox v. Wills, 49 N.J.Eq. 130, 22 A. 794.

[56] Seymour v. Sanford, 86 Conn. 516, 86 A. 7; In re Gardner, 140 N.Y. 122, 35 N.E. 439; In re Roger's Estate, 245 Pa. 206, 91 A. 351, L.R.A. 1917A, 168; Baker v. Baker, 53 W.Va. 165, 44 S.E. 174.

[57] Toms v. Owen, C.C.Mich. 52 F. 417; In re Purcell's Estate, 167 Cal. 176, 138 P. 704; George v. George, 186 Mass. 75, 71 N.E. 85; Corby v. Corby, 85 Mo. 371; Eberhardt v. Perolin, 49 N.J.Eq. 570, 25 A. 510; Wilde v. Smith, 2 Dem.Sur., N.Y., 93.

whereas, if the discretion is merely as to manner, time, or choice of persons from a class, and the alleged trustee may under no circumstances keep the property for himself, the courts will be more apt to presume that the precatory words were intended as words of binding obligation.[58]

Thirdly, if the alleged beneficiary has any natural claim on the supposed author of the trust and the conditions are such that the latter would naturally provide for the former, the courts will be more ready to construe precatory words as creating a trust. Thus, in one case,[59] where the estate was large and given to the deceased's widow with a request that she care for the deceased's mother and sister, for whom no other provision was made, the court held that the precatory words could naturally be construed to create a trust.[60]

Fourthly, an absolute gift of property will not be construed to be a trust because there are later precatory expressions. Where the testator has once made an unrestricted transfer of the property, subsequent inconsistent precatory words will not be construed to show an intent to create a trust. Thus, if the gift is made to A. "absolutely," [61] or "in his own right," [62] the courts

---

[58] Bull v. Bull, 8 Conn. 47, 20 Am. Dec. 86; Dexter v. Evans, 63 Conn. 58, 27 A. 308, 38 Am.St.Rep. 336; Erickson v. Willard, 1 N.H. 217; Ide's Ex'rs v. Clark et al., 5 Ohio Cir. Ct. R. 239; In re Pennock's Estate, 20 Pa. 268, 59 Am.Dec. 718; Walker v. Quigg, 6 Watts, Pa., 87, 31 Am.Dec. 452; Seefried v. Clarke, 113 Va. 365, 74 S.E. 204.

[59] Colton v. Colton, 127 U.S. 300, 8 S.Ct. 1164, 32 L.Ed. 138.

[60] In the following cases trusts were declared where the supposed cestuis were parents: Whittingham v. Schofield's Trustee, 67 S.W. 846, 68 S.W. 116, 23 Ky.Law Rep. 2444; Foster v. Willson, 68 N.H. 241, 38 A. 1003, 73 Am.St.Rep. 581; Carroll v. Adams, Sup., 105 N.Y.S. 967. In other cases children were the cestuis. Warner v. Bates, 98 Mass. 274; Patterson v. Humphries, 101 Miss. 831, 58 So. 772; Kidder's Ex'rs v. Kidder, 56 A., N.J.Ch., 154; Appeal of Coate, 2 Pa. 129; Knox v. Knox, 59 Wis 172, 18 N.W. 155, 48 Am.Rep. 487. And a trust result has been reached where an adopted child (Murphy v. Carlin, 113 Mo. 112, 20 S.W. 786, 35 Am.St. Rep. 699) and a niece (Collister v. Fassitt, 163 N.Y. 281, 57 N.E. 490, 79 Am.St.Rep. 586) were to be benefited. But in the following cases of close relationship the precatory words were construed not to have created trusts: Bliss v. Bliss, 20 Idaho 467, 119 P. 451 (wife); Holmes v. Dalley, 192 Mass. 451, 78 N.E. 513 (child); In re Mitchell's Estate, 160 Cal. 618, 117 P. 774 (grandchild); Post v. Moore, 181 N.Y. 15, 73 N.E. 482, 106 Am.St.Rep. 495, 2 Ann.Cas. 591 (sister); Russell v. United States Trust Co. of New York, C.C.A.N.Y., 136 F. 758, 69 C.C.A. 410 (nephews and nieces).

[61] McDuffie v. Montgomery, C.C.Ill., 128 F. 105; In re Molk's Estate, Myr. Prob., Cal., 212; Haight v. Royce, 274

[62] Frierson v. General Assembly of Presbyterian Church of U. S., Tenn., 7 Heisk. 683.

will be inclined to construe the precatory words to have no legal effect. So, too, if to create a trust from the precatory words would be repugnant to other provisions of the instrument of undisputed validity,[63] or if the words "and it is only a request" follow the precatory expressions,[64] or, of course, if the implication of a trust is expressly excluded by words to the effect that no trust was intended,[65] the precatory words will be given no legal effect.

Fifthly, many other guiding facts of a miscellaneous character may exist. For example, if the precatory expression concerns property which the devisee already owns, as well as that given to the devisee by the testator, the courts will consider the words as of no legal effect.[66] The testator will not be deemed to have intended a trust as to property which he did not own. That the testator clearly created a trust in another part of the instrument, using appropriate words of trust, has been held to show that precatory words were not intended to create a trust.[67] And so, also, that the testator was a lawyer, and hence would presumably understand how to create a trust clearly, tends to prove that a use of precatory words was not intended to give rise to a trust.[68] That the legatee was personally interested in carrying out the objects mentioned in the precatory phrases has been held to point to an absolute gift, a trust being apparently unnecessary.[69] In a gift to a corporation, a request that the funds be applied to some particular corporate purpose is generally held not to indicate an attempted trust, but to be a mere suggestion, which the directors

---

Ill. 162, 113 N.E. 71; Riechauer v. Born, 151 Iowa 456, 131 N.W. 705; Pierce v. Pierce, 114 Me. 311, 96 Atl. 143; Williams v. Worthington, 49 Md. 572, 33 Am.Rep. 286; Bacon v. Ransom, 139 Mass. 117, 29 N.E. 473; Noe v. Kern, 93 Mo. 367, 6 S.W. 239, 3 Am.St.Rep. 544; Snyder v. Toler, 179 Mo.App. 376, 166 S.W. 1059; Carter v. Strickland, 165 N.C. 69, 80 S.E. 961, Ann.Cas.1915D, 416; Ringe v. Kellner, 99 Pa. 460; Wilmoth v. Wilmoth, 34 W.Va. 426, 12 S.E. 731.

[63] Clay v. Wood, 153 N.Y. 134, 47 N.E. 274.

[64] Sale v. Thornberry, 86 Ky. 266, 5 S.W. 468.

[65] Burnes v. Burnes, C.C.A.Mo., 137 F. 781, 70 C.C.A. 357; Enders' Ex'r v. Tasco, 89 Ky. 17, 11 S.W. 818; In re Havens, 6 Dem.Sur., N.Y., 456.

[66] Palmer v. Schribb, 2 Eq.Cas.Abr. 291, pl. 9; Parnall v. Parnall, 9 Ch. Div. 96; Hopkins v. Glunt et al., 111 Pa. 287, 2 A. 183.

[67] In re Whitcomb's Estate, 86 Cal. 265, 24 P. 1028; Williams v. Committee of Baptist Church, 92 Md. 497, 48 A. 930, 54 L.R.A. 427.

[68] Burnes v. Burnes, C.C.A.Mo., 137 F. 781, 795, 70 C.C.A. 357.

[69] Poor v. Bradbury, 196 Mass. 207, 81 N.E. 882.

may or may not carry out.[70] That a trust, if created by precatory words, would be void as violating the rule against accumulations, is an argument for showing that no trust was intended.[71]

REALITY OF TRUST INTENT—SAVINGS BANK TRUSTS[72]

24. That one has deposited his own money in a bank and directed that the account be entitled "in trust" for another does not of itself prove that the depositor intended to create an irrevocable trust of the bank account. The depositor may have intended to use the account as a dummy account for the purpose of getting greater interest or avoiding bank rules about limitation of the size of single accounts. He may have intended the trust to be revocable at will. The courts require proof of other acts by the depositor in order to prove an intent to have a genuine trust of an irrevocable character.

Acts tending to show an intent to have a real trust and an irrevocable trust are express statements by the depositor that he intended a trust; allowing the deposit to remain until the depositor's death; notice of the deposit to the beneficiary; notice to a third person; delivery of the bank book to the beneficiary or a third person; making a will consistent with a trust intent; and payment of part of the deposit to the supposed cestui. Near relationship between depositor and cestui tends to strengthen the notion of a trust.

Facts which rebut the inference that a trust was intended or show an intent to have the trust revocable are the depositor's express statement that he intended no trust; death of the beneficiary before notice to him of the trust account; leaving the account untouched after the beneficiary's death; reservation of the right to withdraw all or a part of the account; dealing with the interest or principal as the depositor's property; obliteration of the trust words on the bank book by the depositor; admissions by the supposed cestui inconsistent with a trust; the making of a will by the depositor which is inconsistent with a trust; that the depositor's financial condition is such that a trust would be unnatural; that the taxation laws or rules restricting the size of deposits favored small deposits as against large ones.

---

[70] Pratt v. Trustees of Sheppard & Enoch Pratt Hospital, 88 Md. 610, 42 A. 51; Williams v. Committee of Baptist Church, 92 Md. 497, 48 A. 930, 54 L.R.A. 427; In re Crane's Will, 159 N.Y. 557, 54 N.E. 1089.

[71] In re Lynch's Will, 102 Misc. 650, 169 N.Y.S. 321.

[72] Restatement, Trusts, § 58.
For recent discussions, see 87 U. Pa.L.R. 847; 22 Minn.L.R. 125; 28 Cal.L.R. 202; 53 Harv.L.R. 691.

BOGERT TRUSTS 2D—5

Reasons for Special Rule

If A deposits his own money in a bank, and by his direction the deposit is entitled "A., in trust for B.," is an irrevocable trust created? If any further acts on the part of A. are necessary to the creation of a trust what are such acts?

Under the elementary principles concerning the creation of trusts, previously stated, it might be assumed that the mere deposit of money in a bank under the circumstances mentioned in this question would lead to the establishment of a trust. The depositor calls himself a trustee of specific trust property, namely, the claim against the bank. His declaration is communicated to a third party, namely the officer of the bank. The beneficiary is definite and clearly identified.

But one peculiarity with respect to these so-called "savings bank trusts" is that the courts require that the declarant shall express his intent to create a trust more clearly and by a larger number of acts than in the case of an ordinary trust. The deposit of money in a bank under a trust title is considered equivocal. Men frequently deposit money under a trust title from other motives than that of creating a trust. The attitude of the courts towards a deposit entitled "in trust" is well stated by Andrews, J., in Beaver v. Beaver.[73] "The form of the account is the essential fact upon which the plaintiff relies. It may be justly said that a deposit in a savings bank by one person, of his own money to the credit of another, is consistent with an intent on the part of the depositor to give the money to the other. But it does not, we think, of itself, without more, authorize an affirmative finding that the deposit was made with the intent, when the deposit was to a new account, unaccompanied by any declaration of intention, and the depositor received at the time a passbook, the possession and presentation of which, by the rules of the bank, known to the depositor, is made evidence of the right to draw the deposit. We cannot close our eyes to the well-known practice of persons depositing in savings banks money to the credit of real or fictitious persons, with no intent of divesting themselves of ownership. It is attributable to various reasons—reasons connected with taxation; rules of the bank limiting the amount which any individual may keep on deposit; the desire to obtain high rates of interest where there is a discrimination based on the amount of deposits, and the desire, on the part of many persons, to veil or conceal from others

[73] 117 N.Y. 421, 430, 431, 22 N.E. 940, 6 L.R.A. 403, 15 Am.St.Rep. 531.

§ 24 REALITY OF TRUST INTENT—SAVINGS BANK TRUSTS

knowledge of their pecuniary condition. In most cases, where a deposit of this character is made as a gift, there are contemporaneous facts or subsequent declarations by which the intention can be established, independently of the form of the deposit. We are inclined to think that to infer a gift from the form of the deposit alone would, in the great majority of cases, and especially where the deposit was of any considerable amount, impute an intention which never existed, and defeat the real purpose of the depositor."

The possibility that the depositor may be influenced by other motives than the trust motive has caused the courts very generally to hold that the bare deposit under a trust title does not result in the creation of a trust. The depositor must show by other acts than the mere deposit that his object is the creation of a true trust.[74]

The ordinary trust is irrevocable by the settlor, unless he expressly stipulates for a power of revocation. In the case of savings bank trusts, however, the courts find an implied intent that the trust be revocable, unless the depositor does more than merely make the deposit. This implied power of revocation is permitted to be effective.[75] One problem with regard to these trusts, therefore, is whether the depositor has done something after the deposit which shows an intent to change the revocable trust to an irrevocable one, or has revoked the trust.

The evidence, aside from the mere deposit, must be examined for two purposes—(1) to see what light it sheds on the reality of the depositor's expressed trust intent; and (2) to see what it proves about revocability or revocation. This evidence will now be examined. Generally speaking that which tends to support a real trust intent may also often be used to show that the trust was irrevocable; and that which rebuts a real trust intent may also sometimes be applied to prove the existence of a power of revocation.

---

[74] Austin v. Central Sav. Bank of Baltimore, 126 Md. 139, 94 A. 520; Powers v. Provident Institution for Savings, 124 Mass. 377; Parkman v. Suffolk Savings Bank for Seamen, 151 Mass. 218, 24 N.E. 43; Cleveland v. Hampden Savings Bank, 182 Mass. 110, 65 N.E. 27; Matter of Totten, 179 N.Y. 112, 71 N.E. 748, 70 L.R.A. 711, 1 Ann.Cas. 900; Rambo v. Pile, 220 Pa. 235, 238, 69 A. 96; People's Savings Bank v. Webb, 21 R.I. 218, 42 A. 874.

[75] Evinger v. MacDougall, 28 Cal. App.2d 175, 82 P.2d 194; Hoppe v. Manhattan Co., 154 Misc. 745, 278 N.Y.S. 26; In re Pozzuto's Estate, 124 Pa.Super. 93, 188 A. 209; In re Bearinger's Estate, 336 Pa. 253, 9 A.2d 342.

The evidence bearing upon the intent of the depositor, aside from the deposit itself, may be divided into three classes, namely: (a) Express statements of intent; (b) acts of the depositor with respect to the deposit, or the supposed beneficiary, aside from express statements; (c) the circumstances of the depositor.

Express Statements of Intent

The most direct form of evidence as to the depositor's intent, aside from the deposit itself, is the express statement of the depositor concerning his intent. If the depositor stated, otherwise than by a direction as to the title of the deposit, at the time of the deposit, that he actually intended a trust, such evidence will be admissible, and ordinarily conclusive, as showing a trust.[76] So, too, evidence that the depositor stated at the time of the deposit that he intended no trust is receivable as a part of the res gestæ and is of great force.[77] Direct statements by the depositor that he intended a trust, made after the deposit, are given much weight;[78] but they are not necessarily conclusive in showing the existence of a trust.[79] On the other hand, statements by the depositor, after the deposit, to the effect that no trust was intended, if the depositor is dead, are inadmissible.[80] But, if the depositor is alive, he may testify to his in-

---

[76] Booth v. Oakland Bank of Savings, 122 Cal. 19, 54 P. 370; Bath Savings Inst. v. Hathorn, 88 Me. 122, 33 A. 836, 32 L.R.A. 377, 51 Am.St. Rep. 382; Littig v. Vestry of Mt. Calvary Protestant Episcopal Church, 101 Md. 494, 61 A. 635; Martin v. Martin, 46 App.Div. 445, 61 N.Y.S. 813, appeal dismissed 166 N.Y. 611, 59 N.E. 1126; Robinson v. Appleby, 69 App.Div. 509, 75 N.Y.S. 1, affirmed 173 N.Y. 626, 66 N.E. 1115. Contra: Clark v. Clark, 108 Mass. 522.

Parol evidence that the beneficiary named in the title of the trust account was to hold in trust for another must be clear and convincing. Dougherty v. Dougherty, 175 Md. 441, 2 A.2d 433.

[77] Merigan v. McGonigle, 205 Pa. 321, 54 A. 994; Connecticut River Savings Bank v. Albee's Estate, 64 Vt. 571, 25 A. 487, 33 Am.St.Rep. 944.

[78] Alger v. North End Savings Bank, 146 Mass. 418, 15 N.E. 916, 4 Am.St.Rep. 331; Peck v. Scofield, 186 Mass. 108, 71 N.E. 109; Mabie v. Bailey, 95 N.Y. 206. The failure to admit declarations of the depositor favorable to a trust was held ground for ordering a new trial in Walso v. Latterner, 140 Minn. 455, 168 N.W. 353.

[79] Macy v. Williams, 83 Hun 243, 31 N.Y.S. 620, affirmed 144 N.Y. 701, 39 N.E. 858.

[80] Tierney v. Fitzpatrick, 195 N.Y. 433, 88 N.E. 750; Matter of Bunt, 96 Misc. 114, 160 N.Y.S. 1118; Merigan v. McGonigle, 205 Pa. 321, 54 A. 994; Ray v. Simmons, 11 R.I. 266, 23 Am. Rep. 447; Connecticut River Sav. Bank v. Albee's Estate, 64 Vt. 571, 25 A. 487, 33 Am.St.Rep. 944.

§ 24   REALITY OF TRUST INTENT—SAVINGS BANK TRUSTS   69

tent in making the deposit, whether such testimony is favorable to a trust[81] or unfavorable.[82]

A statement by the supposed beneficiary that she had no property, made with knowledge of the deposit,[83] or a statement by the beneficiary that the deposit was made for the purpose of getting better interest rates and not as a trust,[84] is receivable as strong evidence that the depositor intended no trust.

Intent Implied from Acts of the Depositor Other Than Express Statements

(a) *Giving Notice of the Deposit.*—If the depositor notifies the beneficiary that the deposit has been made in trust form, a strong presumption of a trust arises;[85] but this presumption may be overcome by other facts in the case.[86]

Notice of the existence of the deposit given by the depositor to the beneficiary is not absolutely essential to the existence of a trust.[87] In several cases notice of the existence of a deposit in trust form given by the depositor to a third person has been

[81] Sayre v. Weil, 94 Ala. 466, 10 So. 546, 15 L.R.A. 544.

[82] Cunningham v. Davenport, 147 N.Y. 43, 41 N.E. 412, 32 L.R.A. 373, 49 Am.St.Rep. 641; Barefield v. Rosell, 177 N.Y. 387, 69 N.E. 732, 101 Am.St.Rep. 814; People's Sav. Bank v. Webb, 21 R.I. 218, 42 A. 874.

[83] Barefield v. Rosell, 177 N.Y. 387, 69 N.E. 732, 101 Am.St.Rep. 814.

[84] Matter of Mueller, 15 App.Div. 67, 44 N.Y.S. 280.

[85] Alger v. North End Saving Bank, 146 Mass. 418, 15 N.E. 916, 4 Am.St. Rep. 331; Peck v. Scofield, 186 Mass. 108, 71 N.E. 109; Grafing v. Heilmann, 1 App.Div. 260, 37 N.Y.S. 253, affirmed 153 N.Y. 673, 48 N.E. 1104; Farleigh v. Cadman, 159 N.Y. 169, 53 N.E. 808; Meislahn v. Meislahn, 56 App.Div. 566, 67 N.Y.S. 480; Matter of Pierce, 132 App.Div. 465, 116 N.Y.S. 816; Matter of Hewitt, 40 Misc. 322, 81 N.Y.S. 1030; Matter of Halligan's Estate, 82 Misc. 30, 143 N.Y.S. 676; Matter of Brennan, 92 Misc. 423, 157 N.Y.S. 141; Willard v. Willard, 103 Misc. 544, 170 N.Y.S. 886; Ray v. Simmons, 11 R.I. 266, 23 Am.Rep. 447; Petition of Atkinson, 16 R.I. 413, 16 A. 712, 3 L.R.A. 392, 27 Am.St.Rep. 745; Connecticut River Sav. Bank v. Albee's Estate, 64 Vt. 571, 25 A. 487, 33 Am. St.Rep. 944.

[86] Nutt v. Morse, 142 Mass. 1, 6 N.E. 763; Kelley v. Snow, 185 Mass. 288, 70 N.E. 89; Smith v. Speer, 34 N.J.Eq. 336; Matthews v. Brooklyn Sav. Bank, 208 N.Y. 508, 102 N.E. 520; Devlin v. Hinman, 34 App.Div. 107, 54 N.Y.S. 496; Hessen v. McKinley, 155 App.Div. 496, 140 N.Y.S. 724; Weber v. Weber, 58 How.Prac., N.Y., 255; Weber v. Weber, 9 Daly, N.Y., 211.

[87] In re Podhajsky's Estate, 137 Iowa 742, 115 N.W. 590; Milholland v. Whalen, 89 Md. 212, 43 A. 39, 44 L.R.A. 485; Brabrook v. Boston Five Cents Sav. Bank, 104 Mass. 228, 6 Am.Rep. 222; Gerrish v. New Bedford Inst. for Sav., 128 Mass. 159, 35 Am.Rep. 365.

accorded weight as tending to show an intent to create a trust.[88] But in other instances, notwithstanding such notice to a third person, no trust was found.[89] The Massachusetts courts have been inclined to give very little weight to the bare deposit in trust form, or to such deposit accompanied by notice to a third person unconnected with the beneficiary. The statement of Holmes, J., in Cleveland v. Hampden Savings Bank[90] is characteristic: "An owner of property does not lose it by using words of gift or trust concerning it in solitude or with the knowledge of another not assuming to represent an adverse interest. He may amuse himself as he likes."

Naturally notice of the existence of the deposit, obtained without the depositor's knowledge or consent, has no effect in showing the depositor's intent.[91]

(b) *Transactions Respecting the Bank Book.*—A trust may exist without delivery of the bank book by the depositor to another.[92] In fact, it is more natural that the trustee should retain possession of the evidence of the trust property than that he should deliver it to the beneficiary or to a third person.[93]

But the delivery of the bank book by the depositor to the beneficiary constitutes strong evidence of intent to make an irrevocable gift of the account by way of a trust.[94] A direction by the depositor to deliver the book to the bank for the beneficiary is also strong evidence of the trust intent.[95]

---

[88] Bath Sav. Inst. v. Hathorn, 88 Me. 122, 33 A. 836, 32 L.R.A. 377, 51 Am.St.Rep. 382; Merigan v. McGonigle, 205 Pa. 321, 54 A. 994; Mabie v. Bailey, 95 N.Y. 206; In re Biggars, 39 Misc. 426, 80 N.Y.S. 214; In re King's Will, 51 Misc. 375, 101 N.Y.S. 279.

[89] Minor v. Rogers, 40 Conn. 512, 16 Am.Rep. 69; Cleveland v. Hampden Sav. Bank, 182 Mass. 110, 65 N. E. 27; People's Sav. Bank v. Webb, 21 R.I. 218, 42 A. 874.

[90] 182 Mass. 110, 111, 65 N.E. 27.

[91] Matter of United States Trust Co., 117 App.Div. 178, 102 N.Y.S. 271.

[92] Willard v. Willard, 103 Misc. 544, 170 N.Y.S. 886; In re Gaffney's Estate, 146 Pa. 49, 23 A. 163.

[93] Milholland v. Whalen, 89 Md. 212, 43 A. 43, 44 L.R.A. 205; Weaver v. Emigrant, etc., Savings Bank, 17 Abb.N.C.,N.Y., 82; Merigan v. McGonigle, 205 Pa. 321, 54 A. 994.

[94] Decker v. Union Dime Sav. Inst., 15 App.Div. 553, 44 N.Y.S. 521; Proseus v. Porter, 20 App.Div. 44, 46 N.Y.S. 656; Jennings v. Hennessy, 40 App.Div. 633, 58 N.Y.S. 1142; Matter of Davis, 119 App.Div. 35, 103 N.Y.S. 946; Matter of Pierce, 132 App.Div. 465, 116 N.Y.S. 816; Matter of Rudolph, 92 Misc. 347, 156 N.Y.S. 825; In re Beaman's Estate, Sur., 163 N.Y.S. 800.

[95] Board of Domestic Missions of Reformed Church in America v. Mechanics' Sav. Bank, 40 App.Div. 120, 54 N.Y.S. 28, 57 N.Y.S. 582.

§ 24   REALITY OF TRUST INTENT—SAVINGS BANK TRUSTS   71

But the delivery of the book to the beneficiary is not conclusive proof of an irrevocable trust. The delivery may be so qualified as to show no intent to create a trust, but merely an intent to have the beneficiary hold the book as a bailee of the depositor.[96] The bare fact that the bank book is found in the possession of the beneficiary's sole heir and next of kin does not show that a trust exists.[97]

When the book has been delivered by the depositor to the beneficiary, the presumption of a trust is strong, notwithstanding a redelivery to the depositor or his nominee;[98] but in one case the New York Court of Appeals has held that under some circumstances such redelivery shows that no trust exists.[99]

In other cases the delivery of the book by the depositor to a third person [1] or to the depositor's executor,[2] or the leaving of the book with the bank,[3] has been considered as tending to prove that a trust was established. But other facts may overcome the presumption of a trust raised by the delivery of the book to a third person.[4]

The obliteration of the words of trust from the bank book by the depositor tends to show that he intended no trust or revoked it.[5]

(c) *Additions to and Withdrawals from the Account.*—No presumption for or against a trust arises from the mere addition to the original account during the life of the supposed beneficiary. The additions become trust property or not, according to the status of the original deposit.[6]

---

[96] Nutt v. Morse, 142 Mass. 1, 6 N.E. 763; Matter of Halligan's Estate, 82 Misc. 30, 143 N.Y.S. 676; Markey v. Markey, Com.Pl., 13 N.Y.S. 925.

[97] In re Duffy, 127 App.Div. 74, 111 N.Y.S. 77.

[98] Scrivens v. North Easton Sav. Bank, 166 Mass. 255, 44 N.E. 251; Macy v. Williams, 55 Hun 489, 8 N.Y.S. 658, affirmed 125 N.Y. 767, 27 N.E. 409; Stockert v. Dry Dock Sav. Inst., 155 App.Div. 123, 139 N.Y.S. 986; Ray v. Simmons, 11 R.I. 266, 23 Am.Rep. 447.

[99] Matthews v. Brooklyn Sav. Bank, 208 N.Y. 508, 102 N.E. 520.

[1] Peck v. Scofield, 186 Mass. 108, 71 N.E. 109.

[2] Martin v. Martin, 46 App.Div. 445, 61 N.Y.S. 813, appeal dismissed 166 N.Y. 611, 59 N.E. 1126; Scallan v. Brooks, 54 App.Div. 248, 66 N.Y.S. 591.

[3] Robinson v. Appleby, 69 App.Div. 509, 75 N.Y.S. 1, affirmed 173 N.Y. 626, 66 N.E. 1115.

[4] Lattan v. Van Ness, 107 App.Div. 393, 95 N.Y.S. 97, affirmed 184 N.Y. 601, 77 N.E. 1190.

[5] In re Bulwinkle, 107 App.Div. 331, 95 N.Y.S. 176.

[6] Farleigh v. Cadman, 159 N.Y. 169, 53 N.E. 808; Proseus v. Porter, 20

But a deposit made after the death of the supposed beneficiary tends to show that the trust is not real, but rather a mere form for the convenience of the depositor.[7]

The use by the depositor of the interest accruing upon the deposit for his personal benefit has some tendency to show that no trust was intended, and in some cases, in connection with other facts, it has defeated a trust; [8] but neither the reservation by the depositor of the right to use the interest on the account during his life,[9] nor the actual use of such interest by the depositor,[10] is necessarily inconsistent with a trust as to the principal. The crediting of the interest to the trust account is an act of no significance.[11]

The reservation by the depositor of the right to withdraw any or all of the principal fund for his own use has been viewed differently by the several courts which have considered the question. It has been regarded as militating against a trust,[12] while other courts have treated it as not inconsistent with a trust,[13] but as indicating merely a power to revoke a trust which was fully created.[14] So, too, actual withdrawal of part or all of the principal deposit for the use of the depositor has been held in

App.Div. 44, 46 N.Y.S. 656; Hyde v. Kitchen, 69 Hun 280, 23 N.Y.S. 573; Ray v. Simmons, 11 R.I. 266, 23 Am. Rep. 447; Connecticut River Sav. Bank v. Albee's Estate, 64 Vt. 571, 25 A. 487, 33 Am.St.Rep. 944.

[7] In re Bulwinkle, 107 App.Div. 331, 95 N.Y.S. 176.

[8] Macy v. Williams, 83 Hun 243, 31 N.Y.S. 620, affirmed 144 N.Y. 701, 39 N.E. 858; Garvey v. Clifford, 114 App.Div. 193, 99 N.Y.S. 555; Thomas v. Newburgh Sav. Bank, 73 Misc. 308, 130 N.Y.S. 810, affirmed 147 App. Div. 937, 132 N.Y.S. 1148.

[9] Gerrish v. New Bedford Inst. for Sav., 128 Mass. 159, 35 Am.Rep. 365.

[10] Gerrish v. New Bedford Inst. for Sav., 128 Mass. 159, 35 Am.Rep. 365; Martin v. Funk, 75 N.Y. 134, 31 Am.Rep. 446; Willis v. Smyth, 91 N.Y. 297; Grafing v. Heilmann, 1 App.Div. 260, 37 N.Y.S. 253, affirmed 153 N.Y. 673, 48 N.E. 1104; Meislahn v. Meislahn, 56 App.Div. 566, 67 N. Y.S. 480; Witzel v. Chapin, 3 Bradf. Sur., N.Y., 386; Ray v. Simmons, 11 R.I. 266, 23 Am.Rep. 447.

[11] Hyde v. Kitchen, 69 Hun 280, 23 N.Y.S. 573.

[12] Nutt v. Morse, 142 Mass. 1, 6 N.E. 763; Smith v. Speer, 34 N.J.Eq. 336.

[13] Carr v. Carr, 15 Cal.App. 480, 115 P. 261; Drinkhouse v. German Savings & Loan Soc., 17 Cal.App. 162, 118 P. 953; Culver v. Lompoc Valley Sav. Bank, 22 Cal.App. 379, 134 P. 355; Scrivens v. North Easton Sav. Bank, 166 Mass. 255, 44 N.E. 251; Witzel v. Chapin, 3 Bradf.Sur. N.Y., 386; In re Bunt, 96 Misc. 114, 160 N.Y.S. 1118; In re Beaman's Estate, Sur., 163 N.Y.S. 800.

[14] Littig v. Vestry of Mt. Calvary Protestant Episcopal Church, 101 Md. 494, 61 A. 635.

many instances to show the lack of trust intent,[15] and yet in other cases the withdrawals from the principal were regarded as consistent with the trust.[16]

Formal notice to the bank of intent to withdraw has been held to be equivalent to actual withdrawal.[17] That the account has remained untouched as to principal and interest since the principal deposit has been held to indicate a trust intent.[18] Withdrawal of part of the principal by the depositor and application of it to the use of the beneficiary tends to show a trust.[19] That the account is used by the depositor as his sole active account for the transaction of business is strong evidence against a trust.[20] An offer by the depositor to lend the principal to a third party has been held not antagonistic to a trust.[21] If the trust is complete and irrevocable, withdrawals from the fund for his own use will render the trustee liable to the cestui que trust therefor,[22] but if the trust is incomplete, or revocable, the withdrawals

[15] Jewett v. Shattuck, 124 Mass. 590; Macy v. Williams, 83 Hun 243, 31 N.Y.S. 620, affirmed 144 N.Y. 701, 39 N.E. 858; Matter of Totten, 179 N.Y. 112, 71 N.E. 748, 70 L.R.A. 711, 1 Ann.Cas. 900; Lattan v. Van Ness, 107 App.Div. 393, 95 N.Y.S. 97, affirmed 184 N.Y. 601, 77 N.E. 1190; Matthews v. Brooklyn Sav. Bank, 208 N.Y. 508, 102 N.E. 520; Devlin v. Hinman, 34 App.Div. 107, 54 N.Y.S. 496; Hessen v. McKinley, 155 App. Div. 496, 140 N.Y.S. 724; Lee v. Kennedy, 25 Misc. 140, 54 N.Y.S. 155; In re Barbey's Estate, Sur., 114 N.Y.S. 725; In re Biggars, 39 Misc. 426, 80 N.Y.S. 214; Weber v. Weber, 58 How. Prac., N.Y., 255.

[16] Milholland v. Whalen, 89 Md. 212, 43 A. 43, 44 L.R.A. 205; Scott v. Harbeck, 49 Hun 292, 1 N.Y.S. 788; Mabie v. Bailey, 95 N.Y. 206; Macy v. Williams, 55 Hun 489, 8 N.Y.S. 658, affirmed 125 N.Y. 767, 27 N.E. 409; Farleigh v. Cadman, 159 N.Y. 169, 53 N.E. 808; Robinson v. Appleby, 69 App.Div. 509, 75 N.Y.S. 1, affirmed 173 N.Y. 626, 66 N.E. 1115; Decker v. Union Dime Sav. Inst., 15 App.Div. 553, 44 N.Y.S. 521; Robertson v. McCarty, 54 App.Div. 103, 66 N.Y.S. 327;

Jenkins v. Baker, 77 App.Div. 509, 78 N.Y.S. 1074; Marsh v. Keogh, 82 App. Div. 503, 81 N.Y.S. 825; Connecticut River Sav. Bank v. Albee's Estate, 64 Vt. 571, 25 A. 487, 33 Am.St.Rep. 944.

[17] Rush v. South Brooklyn Sav. Inst., 65 Misc. 66, 119 N.Y.S. 726.

[18] Harrison v. Totten, 53 App.Div. 178, 65 N.Y.S. 725.

[19] Grafing v. Heilmann, 1 App.Div. 260, 37 N.Y.S. 253, affirmed 153 N.Y. 673, 48 N.E. 1104; Farleigh v. Cadman, 159 N.Y. 169, 53 N.E. 808.

[20] Rambo v. Pile, 220 Pa. 235, 69 A. 807.

[21] Willis v. Smyth, 91 N.Y. 297.

[22] Mabie v. Bailey, 95 N.Y. 206; Macy v. Williams, 55 Hun 489, 8 N.Y.S. 658, affirmed 125 N.Y. 767, 27 N.E. 409; Farleigh v. Cadman, 159 N.Y. 169, 53 N.E. 808; Robinson v. Appleby, 69 App.Div. 509, 75 N.Y.S. 1, affirmed 173 N.Y. 626, 66 N.E. 1115; Decker v. Union Dime Sav. Inst., 15 App.Div. 553, 44 N.Y.S. 521; Robertson v. McCarty, 54 App.Div. 103, 66 N.Y.S. 327; Marsh v. Keogh, 82 App. Div. 503, 81 N.Y.S. 825.

by the depositor for his own benefit entail no responsibility.[23]

(d) *Failure of Depositor to Withdraw Money Before his Death.*
—The depositor's failure to act, as well as his actions, are of significance in ascertaining whether he intended a trust. Many courts have held the failure of the depositor to withdraw the deposit before his death to be strong evidence of his desire to create a trust.[24] The mere disappearance of the depositor is not

---

[23] Macy v. Williams, 83 Hun 243, 31 N.Y.S. 620, affirmed 144 N.Y. 701, 39 N.E. 858; Cunningham v. Davenport, 147 N.Y. 43, 41 N.E. 412, 32 L.R.A. 373, 49 Am.St.Rep. 641; Matter of Totten, 179 N.Y. 112, 71 N.E. 748, 70 L.R.A. 711, 1 Ann.Cas. 900; Lattan v. Van Ness, 107 App.Div. 395, 95 N.Y.S. 97, affirmed 184 N.Y. 601, 77 N.E. 1190; Matthews v. Brooklyn Sav. Bank, 208 N.Y. 508, 102 N.E. 520; Hessen v. McKinley, 155 App.Div. 496, 140 N.Y.S. 724; In re Biggars, 39 Misc. 426, 80 N.Y.S. 214.

[24] Bank of America Nat. Trust & Savings Ass'n v. Hazelbud, 21 Cal. App.2d 109, 68 P.2d 385; Wilder v. Howard, 188 Ga. 426, 4 S.E.2d 199. Bath Sav. Inst. v. Hathorn, 88 Me. 122, 33 A. 836, 32 L.R.A. 377, 51 Am. St.Rep. 382; Littig v. Vestry of Mt. Calvary Protestant Episcopal Church, 101 Md. 494, 61 A. 635; Fiocchi v. Smith, N.J.Ch., 97 A. 283; Martin v. Funk, 75 N.Y. 134, 31 Am.Rep. 446; Willis v. Smyth, 91 N.Y. 297; Fowler v. Bowery Sav. Bank, 113 N.Y. 450, 21 N.E. 172, 4 L.R.A. 145, 10 Am.St.Rep. 479; Grafing v. Heilmann, 1 App.Div. 260, 37 N.Y.S. 253, affirmed 153 N.Y. 673, 48 N.E. 1104; Williams v. Brooklyn Sav. Bank, 51 App.Div. 332, 64 N.Y.S. 1021, appeal dismissed 165 N.Y. 676, 59 N.E. 1132; Martin v. Martin, 46 App.Div. 445, 61 N.Y.S. 813, appeal dismissed 166 N.Y. 611, 59 N.E. 1126; Board of Domestic Missions of Reformed Church in America v. Mechanics' Sav. Bank, 40 App.Div. 120, 54 N.Y.S. 28, 57 N.Y.S. 582; Harrison v. Totten, 53 App.Div. 178, 65 N.Y.S. 725; Scallan v. Brooks, 54 App.Div. 248, 66 N.Y.S. 591; Meislahn v. Meislahn, 56 App.Div. 566, 67 N.Y.S. 480; Marsh v. Keogh, 82 App. Div. 503, 81 N.Y.S. 825; O'Brien v. Williamsburgh Sav. Bank, 101 App. Div. 108, 91 N.Y.S. 908; Beakes Dairy Co. v. Berns, 128 App.Div. 137, 112 N. Y.S. 529; Warburton Ave. Baptist Church v. Clark, 158 App.Div. 230, 142 N.Y.S. 1089; In re Biggars, 39 Misc. 426, 80 N.Y.S. 214; Matter of Hewitt, 40 Misc. 322, 81 N.Y.S. 1030; In re King's Will, 51 Misc. 375, 101 N.Y.S. 279; Wait v. Society for Political Study of New York City, 68 Misc. 245, 123 N.Y.S. 637; Matter of Halligan's Estate, 82 Misc. 30, 143 N.Y.S. 676; In re Hammer, 102 Misc. 193, 169 N.Y.S. 684; Weaver v. Emigrant, etc., Savings Bank, 17 Abb.N.C., N.Y., 82; In re Barbey's Estate, Sur., 114 N.Y.S. 725; Witzel v. Chapin, 3 Bradf.Sur., N.Y., 386; In re Gaffney's Estate, 146 Pa. 49, 23 A. 163; Merigan v. McGonigle, 205 Pa. 321, 54 A. 994; Petition of Atkinson, 16 R.I. 413, 16 A. 712, 3 L.R.A. 392, 27 Am.St.Rep. 745; Connecticut River Sav. Bank v. Albee's Estate, 64 Vt. 571, 25 A. 487, 33 Am.St.Rep. 944. The American Bankers' Association has prepared a statute for the protection of its members with regard to the paying of savings bank trust deposits. It reads as follows: "When any deposit shall be made by any person in trust for another, and no other or further notice of the existence and terms of a legal and valid trust shall have been given in writing to the bank, in the event of the death of the trustee, the same, or any part thereof, together with the dividends or in-

§ 24   REALITY OF TRUST INTENT—SAVINGS BANK TRUSTS   75

equivalent to his death for this purpose.[25] But failure to remove the deposit before death is not conclusive evidence of the trust intent. Other facts may overpower it, and cause an adjudication that no trust exists.[26] In a few cases it has been held that, where the only facts proved were the deposit in trust form and the failure to remove before the death of the depositor, there was not sufficient evidence to show the creation of a trust.[27]

(e) *Attitude of Depositor to the Account before and after Death of Beneficiary.*—It is quite generally recognized that failure to indicate the trust intent by notice, delivery of the book, or in some other way, before the death of the supposed beneficiary, is very strong proof that no trust was intended.[28] Allowing the account to stand as a trust account after the death of the supposed cestui que trust,[29] or adding to the account after his death,[30] does not, if no act decisively indicative of trust intent has been done before the cestui que trust's death, show a complete trust. Nor does a withdrawal of the fund after the beneficiary's death render the depositor liable to the representative of the beneficiary, no acts showing an intent to have an irrevocable having occurred prior to the death of the beneficiary.[31]

terest thereon, may be paid to the person for whom the deposit was made." This act has been adopted in nearly all states. For citations see Bogert on Trusts and Trustees, pp. 213–214. For recent construction see Hickey v. Kahl, 129 N.J.Eq. 233, 19 A.2d 33.

[25] Hemmerich v. Union Dime Sav. Inst., 205 N.Y. 366, 98 N.E. 499, Ann. Cas.1913E, 514.

[26] Macy v. Williams, 83 Hun 243, 31 N.Y.S. 620, affirmed 144 N.Y. 701, 39 N.E. 858; Matter of Mueller, 15 App.Div. 67, 44 N.Y.S. 280; Rush v. South Brooklyn Sav. Inst., 65 Misc. 66, 119 N.Y.S. 726; Rambo v. Pile, 220 Pa. 235, 69 A. 807.

[27] Stone v. Bishop, 4 Cliff. 593, Fed. Cas.No. 13482; Brabrook v. Boston Five Cents Sav. Bank, 104 Mass. 228, 6 Am.Rep. 222; Clark v. Clark, 108 Mass. 522; Bartlett v. Remington, 59 N.H. 364.

[28] Cunningham v. Davenport, 147 N.Y. 43, 41 N.E. 412, 32 L.R.A. 373, 49 Am.St.Rep. 641; Haux v. Dry Dock Sav. Inst., 2 App.Div. 165, 37 N.Y.S. 917, affirmed 154 N.Y. 736, 49 N.E. 1097; In re Bulwinkle, 107 App.Div. 331, 95 N.Y.S. 176; Garvey v. Clifford, 114 App.Div. 193, 99 N.Y.S. 555; Matter of United States Trust Co. of New York, 117 App.Div. 178, 102 N.Y.S. 271; In re Duffy, 127 App.Div. 74, 111 N.Y.S. 77; In re Smith's Estate, 40 Misc. 331, 81 N.Y.S. 1035; In re Thompson's Estate, 85 Misc. 291, 147 N.Y.S. 402; Rambo v. Pile, 220 Pa. 235, 69 A. 807. The case of Bishop v. Seamen's Bank for Saving, 33 App. Div. 181, 53 N.Y.S. 488, is out of accord with the other cases.

[29] Garvey v. Clifford, 114 App.Div. 193, 99 N.Y.S. 555; Rambo v. Pile, 220 Pa. 235, 69 A. 807.

[30] In re Bulwinkle, 107 App.Div. 331, 95 N.Y.S. 176.

[31] Cunningham v. Davenport, 147 N.Y. 43, 41 N.E. 412, 32 L.R.A. 373,

But if the depositor has decisively shown his trust intent before the beneficiary's death, as by an express statement in a formal application to the bank,[32] or by the delivery of the book to the beneficiary,[33] then the death of the cestui que trust has no effect on the completed trust. The retention of the maiden name of a woman beneficiary in the trust account after her marriage is not inconsistent with the trust intent.[34]

(f) *The Making of a Will Inconsistent or Consistent with a Trust.*—That the depositor left a will inconsistent with a trust is strong evidence that he intended no trust in making the deposit or revoked the trust;[35] but if the trust was completed by acts of the depositor before his death, an inconsistent will cannot destroy the trust.[36] That a will is consistent with a trust is of some force in favor of the trust.[37]

That the depositor had expressed a desire to provide for the cestui que trust and made no provision for him in his will is evidence favorable to a trust as to the bank account,[38] but a gift in the will to the person named as a beneficiary in the bank account is not, under similar circumstances, fatal to the finding of a trust through the savings bank account.[39]

Intent Implied from Circumstances of the Depositor

(a) *His Relationship to the Beneficiary.*—That the beneficiary occupies a close relationship to the depositor has often been considered as having some evidentiary value in favor of the trust intent.[40] But other facts in the case may weigh so strongly

---

[49] Am.St.Rep. 641; In re Smith's Estate, 40 Misc. 331, 81 N.Y.S. 1035.

[32] Robinson v. Appleby, 69 App.Div. 509, 75 N.Y.S. 1, affirmed 173 N.Y. 626, 66 N.E. 1115.

[33] Matter of Davis, 119 App.Div. 35, 103 N.Y.S. 946.

[34] Willis v. Smyth, 91 N.Y. 297.

[35] Thomas v. Newburgh Sav. Bank, 73 Misc. 308, 130 N.Y.S. 810, affirmed 147 App.Div. 937, 132 N.Y.S. 1148.

[36] Stockert v. Dry Dock Sav. Inst., 155 App.Div. 123, 139 N.Y.S. 986; Weaver v. Emigrant, etc., Savings Bank, 17 Abb.N.C., N.Y., 82.

[37] In re King's Will, 51 Misc. 375, 101 N.Y.S. 279.

[38] In re Biggars, 39 Misc. 426, 80 N.Y.S. 214.

[39] Marsh v. Keogh, 82 App.Div. 503, 81 N.Y.S. 825.

[40] Garrigus v. Burnett, 9 Ind. 528 (granddaughter); Mabie v. Bailey, 95 N.Y. 206 (stepdaughter); Farleigh v. Cadman, 159 N.Y. 169, 53 N.E. 808 (adopted daughter); Williams v. Brooklyn Sav. Bank, 51 App.Div. 332, 64 N.Y.S. 1021, appeal dismissed, 165 N.Y. 676, 59 N.E. 1132 (brother); Bishop v. Seaman's Bank, 33 App.Div. 181, 53 N.Y.S. 488 (husband): Harrison v. Totten, 53 App.Div. 178, 65 N.Y.S. 725 (grandniece and nearest relative); Meislahn v. Meislahn, 56 App.Div. 566, 67 N.Y.S. 480 (child); Jenkins v. Baker, 77 App.Div. 509, 78

against a trust that the effect of the kinship will be overcome and a finding of no trust result.[41] That the party claiming to be a beneficiary was not related at all to the depositor, but merely occupied the business relationship of lessor to him, is some proof that no trust was intended by the depositor.[42]

(b) *Depositor's Financial Condition.*—The financial condition of the depositor may be such that he would be very unlikely to desire to make a gift of the moneys deposited. Thus, that the depositor is an aged man, having no money except that deposited in the account in question,[43] or that the depositor was not in business, but lived from the interest of his money and had a large part of his money entitled "in trust," [44] is strong evidence that no trust was intended.

(c) *The Depositor's Other Bank Accounts.*—That the depositor has twenty-seven accounts entitled "in trust," that he has $80,000 on deposit in banks, that all but $26,000 of it is in accounts entitled "in trust," and that the depositor made some deposits in trust and delivered the books to the beneficiaries, tends to show that no trust was intended by an account entitled "in trust for B," when the bank book was not delivered to B.[45] That the depositor had other bank accounts labeled "in trust" for certain letters of the alphabet, and others merely "in trust," without mention of the name of any beneficiary, tends to show that an account in trust for a stepdaughter was intended to create legal rights in the stepdaughter regarding the money so de-

N.Y.S. 1074 (husband); Marsh v. Keogh, 82 App.Div. 503, 81 N.Y.S. 825 (adopted child); Matter of Davis, 119 App.Div. 35, 103 N.Y.S. 946 (husband); Stockert v. Dry Dock Sav. Inst., 155 App.Div. 123, 139 N.Y.S. 986 (niece); Miller v. Seaman's Bank for Savings, 33 Misc. 708, 68 N.Y.S. 983 (brother); In re Biggars, 39 Misc. 426, 80 N.Y.S. 214 (child); Merigan v. McGonigle, 205 Pa. 321, 54 A. 994 (in loco daughter); Ray v. Simmons, 11 R.I. 266, 23 Am.Rep. 447 (in loco daughter); Petition of Atkinson, 16 R.I. 413, 16 A. 712, 3 L.R.A. 392, 27 Am.St.Rep. 745 (son).

[41] People's Sav. Bank v. Webb, 21 R.I. 218, 42 A. 874 (son); Cunningham v. Davenport, 147 N.Y. 43, 41 N.E. 412, 32 L.R.A. 373, 49 Am.St.Rep.

641 (brother); Haux v. Dry Dock Sav. Inst., 2 App.Div. 165, 37 N.Y.S. 917, affirmed 154 N.Y. 736, 49 N.E. 1097 (child); Devlin v. Hinman, 34 App.Div. 107, 54 N.Y.S. 496 (child); In re Smith's Estate, 40 Misc. 331, 81 N.Y.S. 1035; Weber v. Weber, 58 How.Prac., N.Y., 255 (daughter).

[42] Rambo v. Pile, 220 Pa. 235, 69 A. 807.

[43] Weber v. Weber, 58 How.Prac., N.Y. 255.

[44] Macy v. Williams, 83 Hun 243, 31 N.Y.S. 620, affirmed 144 N.Y. 701, 39 N.E. 858.

[45] Macy v. Williams, 83 Hun 243, 31 N.Y.S. 620, affirmed 144 N.Y. 701, 39 N.E. 858.

posited.[46] That the depositor had no other bank account than the one in question, and did an active business through it, militated against a trust in one case.[47]

(d) *Rules Limiting the Amount of Savings Bank Deposits.*— It is customary for legislatures to place a limit upon the amount which may be deposited under a single name in a savings bank. Thus, in New York, savings banks are forbidden to receive deposits of more than $7,500.[48]

That there is such a limit, and that the depositor in question had reached it in a deposit in his own name, shows a motive other than a trust motive for entitling another deposit "in trust." Such motive is the avoidance of the deposit limit rule. Such evidence is therefore relevant on the question of trust intent and may, with other facts, show the absence of a trust intent.[49] But in some cases this evidence has not been considered as conclusive against a trust, although it has been given weight.[50] "Inasmuch as the interest limit of this bank was $3,000, it is argued from these facts that these accounts were opened to gain interest. But the argument at best is speculation upon a possible motive. There were other savings banks open to him. We have seen that on the same day the depositor made a deposit in another savings bank, and this tends to refute the inference of his ignorance of the existence of other banks, or of his exclusion of them. Moreover, if he sought a scheme to gain interest, he could have deposited $3,000, instead of $2,700, in this particular account under discussion, out of the $7,482 received by him on that day. The argument based upon a scheme for interest does not carry special force in any case; for it is available in every case where the depositor's own funds in the same bank have reached the limit. It has not received much consideration where the depositor has named a beneficiary of the trust." [51]

---

[46] Mabie v. Bailey, 95 N.Y. 206.

[47] Rambo v. Pile, 220 Pa. 235, 69 A. 807.

[48] New York Banking Law, § 237.

[49] Brabrook v. Boston Five Cents Sav. Bank, 104 Mass. 228, 6 Am.Rep. 222 (no trust); Parkman v. Suffolk Sav. Bank for Seamen, 151 Mass. 218, 24 N.E. 43 (no trust); Thomas v. Newburgh Sav. Bank, 73 Misc. 308, 130 N.Y.S. 810, affirmed 147 App.Div. 937, 132 N.Y.S. 1148 (no trust).

[50] Merigan v. McGonigle, 205 Pa. 321, 54 A. 994; Williams v. Brooklyn Sav. Bank, 51 App.Div. 332, 64 N.Y.S. 1021, appeal dismissed 165 N.Y. 676, 59 N.E. 1132; Meislahn v. Meislahn, 56 App.Div. 566, 67 N.Y.S. 480.

[51] Williams v. Brooklyn Sav. Bank, 51 App.Div. 332, 336, 337, 64 N.Y.S. 1021, appeal dismissed 165 N.Y. 676 59 N.E. 1132.

(e) *Rules Giving Greater Interest Rates on Small Deposits.*—That the savings bank in question gave a higher rate of interest on deposits below a certain amount, and that the depositor had already reached this limit in an account under his own name, is of some evidentiary value, as tending to show a motive for the deposit in trust form other than the trust motive; [52] but, notwithstanding such evidence, the existence of a trust intent may otherwise be shown.[53]

(f) *Rules of Taxation Favoring Small Deposits.*—If the laws of the state in question tax savings bank deposits only when larger than a specific sum, and the depositor's individual account has already reached that amount, those facts may be shown as some proof that the depositor did not intend a trust by placing the account in a trust form, but merely intended to avoid taxation. But, notwithstanding such a motive, other circumstances may show a trust.[54]

FORMALITY—STATUTE OF FRAUDS[55]

25. In England, prior to 1677, trusts of real and personal property required no writing for their creation.

The seventh section of the English Statute of Frauds, enacted in 1677, required express trusts of real property to be "manifested and proved" by a writing signed by the party enabled to declare the trust.

A great majority of American states have passed similar statutes, though with many minor variations. In a few jurisdictions parol trusts in land are allowed.

Implied trusts and trusts of personal property have always, both in England and America, been provable by oral evidence.

If the beneficiary of an oral, voidable trust enters on the trust land and makes improvements, or otherwise acts to his damage on the strength of the enforceability of the trust, and this is done with the consent of the trustee, the trust will be enforceable, even though there is no written evidence.

The statute makes oral trusts in realty voidable only, not void.

Any writing, however informal, is sufficient to satisfy the statute, if it contain a complete statement of the trust, and is signed or subscribed by the proper party.

[52] Weber v. Weber, 58 How.Prac., N.Y., 255; Weber v. Weber, 9 Daly, N.Y., 211.

[53] Mabie v. Bailey, 95 N.Y. 206.

[54] Connecticut River Sav. Bank v. Albee's Estate, 64 Vt. 571, 25 A. 487, 33 Am.St.Rep. 944.

[55] Restatement, Trusts, §§ 39-52.

Situation at Common Law

Prior to 1677 there was no statute in England specifically concerned with a requirement that trusts be created with any formality. The rules of conveyancing as to real estate imposed indirectly certain requisites as to the method of creating trusts of land. In 1677 Parliament adopted the Statute of Frauds.[56]

The Statute of Frauds

The seventh section of the English Statute of Frauds provided that "all declarations or creations of trusts or confidences of any lands, tenements or hereditaments, shall be manifested and proved by some writing signed by the party who is by law enabled to declare such trust, or by his last will in writing, or else they shall be utterly void and of none effect." This section has been adopted, with many modifications, by a majority of the American states.[57] The general rule in America therefore is that trusts in land must be proved or created by a writing.

---

[56] St. 29, Chas. II, c. 3. For a discussion of the origin of the statute, see Hening, 61 Pa.Law Rev. 283.

[57] *Statute of Frauds Re-enacted.*—A section similar to the seventh section of the English Statute of Frauds is to be found in the following jurisdictions: Ala.Code 1940, title 47, § 149; Alaska Comp. L. 1933, § 4317; Ark. Pope's Dig.St. 1937, § 6064; Cal. Civ.Code, § 852; Colo.St.Ann.1935, c. 71, § 6; Fla.Comp.L.1927, § 5664-5; Ga.Code 1933, § 108-105; Idaho Code 1932, § 16-503; Ill. Smith-Hurd Stats. c. 59, § 9; Ind.Burns' Ann.St.1933, § 33-406; Iowa Code 1939, § 10049; Kan.Gen.St.1935, 67-210; Me.Rev.St. 1930, c. 87, § 17; Md.Code, 1939, art. 21, § 1; Mass.G.L. (Ter.Ed.) c. 203, § 1; Mich.St.Ann. § 26.906; Minn.St.1927, § 8459; Miss.Code 1930, § 3348; Mo. R.S.1939, § 3494; Mont. Rev.Codes 1935, § 6784; Neb.Comp.St.1929, § 36-103; Nev.Comp.L.1929, § 1527; N.H. Pub.L. 1926, c. 213, § 16; N.J.S.A., 25:1–3; N.Y. Real Property Law, § 242; N.D.Comp.L.1913, § 5364; 60 Okl.St.Ann. § 136; Ore.Code 1930, § 9–905; Pa. 33 P.S. § 2; R.I. Gen.L. 1938, c. 481, § 1; S.C.Code 1932, § 9041; S.D.Code 1939, § 59.0303; Utah Rev.St.1933, 33-5-1; Vt.Pub.L.1933, § 2598; Wis.St.1941 § 240.06. And see D.C.Code 1929, Title 11, § 3.

No Statute of Frauds.—In fifteen American jurisdictions the seventh section of the statute has not been expressly reenacted. This is true in Arizona, Connecticut, Delaware, Hawaii, Kentucky, Louisiana, New Mexico, North Carolina, Ohio, Tennessee, Texas, Virginia, Washington, West Virginia, and Wyoming.

In Connecticut the court seems to treat parol trusts as unenforceable. Wilson v. Warner, 84 Conn. 560, 80 A. 718. Delaware seems to have no substitute for the seventh section. Rentoul v. Sweeney, 15 Del.Ch. 302, 137 A. 74. In Kentucky apparently a parol declaration of trust is unenforceable, although on a transfer it may be proved by oral evidence that the grantee was to be a trustee. Huff v. Byers, 209 Ky. 375, 272 S.W. 897.

In New Mexico the seventh section seems to be enforced, although not expressly re-enacted. Eagle Mining

§ 25   FORMALITY—STATUTE OF FRAUDS

When Statute Does Not Apply—Implied Trusts

It is frequently stated by the courts that parol evidence is not admissible to establish a trust in real property in the absence of

& Imp. Co. v. Hamilton, 14 N.M. 271, 91 P. 718. As to the situation in North Carolina, see Lord & Van Hecke, Parol Trusts in North Carolina, 8 N.C.L.R. 152. In Ohio parol trusts in land seem to be permitted. Mannix v. Purcell, 46 Ohio St. 102, 19 N.E. 572, 2 L.R.A. 753, 15 Am.St. Rep. 562, but see Ohio Code, § 8620. Oral evidence is usable to establish an express trust of realty in Tennessee. Hunt v. Hunt, 169 Tenn. 1, 80 S.W.2d 666. In Texas no writing seems to be required. Bennett v. McKrell, Tex.Civ.App., 125 S.W.2d 701.

Virginia seems to be free from formality requirements. Fleenor v. Hensley, 121 Va. 367, 93 S.E. 582; 17 Va.L.R. 611. In Washington a section about conveyances has been held to cover trusts. In re Swartwood's Estate, 198 Wash. 557, 89 P.2d 203; Wash.Rem.Rev.St.1932, § 10550. As to West Virginia, see sec. 3524 of the 1937 Code, and Madden, Trusts and the Statute of Frauds, 31 W.Va. L.Q. 166.

As to Louisiana, see Act No. 81 of 1938, §§ 5-9. Oral trusts of realty seem to be denied enforcement in Arizona. Cashion v. Bank of Arizona, 30 Ariz. 172, 245 P. 360.

Nature of the Writing Required.—In the following states the English Statute of Frauds is substantially copied, and the trust need only be manifested and proved by a writing: Arkansas, District of Columbia, Florida, Illinois, Maryland, Missouri, New Jersey, New York, Pennsylvania, and South Carolina. In New York, between 1830 and 1860, the trust had to be "created" by a writing. Hutchins v. Van Vechten, 140 N.Y. 115, 35 N.E. 446. In other states the trust must be "created or declared in writing," but no special form of writing is mentioned: Alabama, California, Georgia, Indiana, Kansas, Maine, Massachusetts, Montana, New Hampshire, North Dakota, Oklahoma, South Dakota, and Vermont. On the subject of what facts the writing must state, and taking the position that any writing "identifying the land and clearly indicating that the person alleged to be a trustee has no beneficial interest therein, or only a specified interest," is sufficient, see 17 Mich.Law Rev. 266. Elsewhere the trust must be "created or declared by a conveyance of other instrument in writing." Alaska, Idaho, and Oregon.

In yet other states the wording is "created or declared by a deed or conveyance in writing." Colorado, Michigan, Minnesota, Nebraska, Nevada, Utah, and Wisconsin.

In Iowa, Mississippi, and Rhode Island the trust must be "created and declared" by an instrument executed, acknowledged, and recorded as a deed of real property. But in a number of states above mentioned, in which the statute requires creation or declaration by writing, the courts have allowed instruments which merely proved or manifested the trust to satisfy the statute. Gaylord v. City of Lafayette, 115 Ind. 423, 17 N.E. 899; McClellan v. McClellan, 65 Me. 500; Urann v. Coates, 109 Mass. 581; White v. Fitzgerald, 19 Wis. 504.

Party Who Must Sign or Subscribe.—In Alabama, Alaska, Colorado, Idaho, Indiana, Kansas, Maine, Michigan, Minnesota, Mississippi, Nebraska, Nevada, New Hampshire, New York, Oregon, Utah, Vermont, and Wisconsin the writing must be signed

BOGERT TRUSTS 2D—6

fraud, mistake or accident.[58] The implication is that express trusts in land based solely on oral evidence will be enforced if fraud, accident, or mistake exist. What is generally meant by these expressions is that if there is fraud, accident, or mistake of the proper kind, a trust of some sort, namely, an implied trust, will be enforced, even though the express trust fails for want of a writing. It is not meant that in the ordinary instance fraud, mistake, or accident cause equity to ignore the Statute of Frauds and allow parol evidence to create an express trust.

The eighth section of the English Statute of Frauds expressly exempts from the operation of the seventh section trusts which "arise or result by implication or construction of law."[59] This exception has been generally copied in America. These are the implied trusts, the creation of which is considered later.[60]

or subscribed "by the party creating or declaring the trust."

In Arkansas, Florida, Illinois, Maryland, Missouri, New Jersey, and South Carolina the words are "the party who is or shall be by law enabled to declare" the trust.

In California, Montana, North Dakota, Oklahoma, and South Dakota the requirement is that the signing or subscribing shall be "by the trustee" or by the party executing the instrument under which the trustee claims the estate.

In Maine the signature must be "by the party"; in Pennsylvania, "by the party holding the legal title"; in Rhode Island the instrument must be "duly signed"; while in Georgia and Iowa no express provision is made as to the identity of the signer or subscriber.

In Alabama, Alaska, California, Colorado, Idaho, Indiana, Kansas, Michigan, Minnesota, Montana, Nevada, New York, North Dakota, Oklahoma, Oregon, South Dakota, Utah, and Wisconsin the signature of an agent or attorney authorized in writing will also be sufficient. In Maine, Massachusetts, New Hampshire, and Vermont signature by an agent or attorney is expressly authorized, but no requirement of written authorization is fixed.

In Arkansas, Florida, Georgia, Illinois, Iowa, Maryland, Mississippi, Missouri, Nebraska, New Jersey, Pennsylvania, Rhode Island, and South Carolina, signature by an agent or attorney is not provided for in the statute.

Signature or Subscription.—In Alabama, Arkansas, Florida, Illinois, Kansas, Maine, Maryland, Massachusetts, Mississippi, Missouri, New Hampshire, New Jersey, Pennsylvania, Rhode Island, South Carolina, and Vermont the requirement is that the writing be "signed."

In Alaska, California, Colorado, Idaho, Michigan, Minnesota, Montana, Nebraska, Nevada, New York, North Dakota, Oklahoma, Oregon, South Dakota, Utah, and Wisconsin the writing must be "subscribed"; that is, signed at the end.

In Georgia and Iowa the statutes make no express provision either for signing or subscribing.

[58] Jones v. Van Doren, C.C.Minn., 18 F. 619; Amidon v. Snouffer, 139 Iowa 159, 117 N.W. 44; Baker v. Baker, 75 N.J.Eq. 305, 72 A. 1000.

[59] St. 29 Chas. II, c. 3.

[60] Post, §§ 50, 56.

BOGERT TRUSTS 2D

The requirement of writing, therefore, has no application to those trusts. Fraud, accident, and mistake constitute important grounds for the creation of one form of these implied trusts, namely, constructive trusts. Hence the exception frequently made, as above stated. The Statute of Frauds will not prevent the creation of an implied trust without a writing, even if the parties attempted to create an express trust orally and the statute forbade such a result.[61] If A. grants lands to B. under an oral express trust, the Statute of Frauds will prohibit the enforcement of the express trust. But equity may hold B. as trustee of the lands under an implied trust, if there are present elements on which such a trust can be raised, as, for example, fraud, accident, or mistake.[62]

When Statute Does Not Apply—Personal Property

The seventh section of the English Statute of Frauds applies only to trusts of "lands, tenements and hereditaments," and such is the scope of similar statutes in America. Trusts of personal property may everywhere be created and proved without writing.[63]

---

[61] Goldsmith v. Goldsmith, 145 N.Y. 313, 39 N.E. 1067; Rozell v. Vansyckle, 11 Wash. 79, 39 P. 270.

[62] Post, §§ 55–66, for a discussion of the circumstances under which equity will declare implied trusts.

[63] Souza v. First Nat. Bank of Hanford, 36 Cal.App. 384, 172 P. 175; Noble v. Learned, 153 Cal. 245, 94 P. 1047; Bay Biscayne Co. v. Baile, 73 Fla. 1120, 75 So. 860; People v. Schaefer, 266 Ill. 334, 107 N.E. 617; Taber v. Zehner, 47 Ind.App. 165, 93 N.E. 1035; Richards v. Wilson, 185 Ind. 335, 112 N.E. 780; Sturtevant v. Jaques, 96 Mass. 523, 14 Allen 523; Bradford v. Eastman, 229 Mass. 499, 118 N.E. 879; Harris Banking Co. v. Miller, 190 Mo. 640, 89 S.W. 629, 1 L.R.A.,N.S., 790; Moulden v. Train, 199 Mo.App. 509, 204 S.W. 65; Day v. Roth, 18 N.Y. 448; First Nat. Bank v. Hinkle, 65 Okl. 62, 162 P. 1092; In re Washington's Estate, 220 Pa. 204, 69 A. 747; McElveen v. Adams, 108 S.C. 437, 94 S.E. 733; Dupont v. Jonet, 165 Wis. 554, 162 N.W. 664.

The English statute was held to apply to trusts of leaseholds. Forster v. Hale, 3 Ves.Jr. 696; Skett v. Whitmore, 2 Freeman 280; and see Smith v. Hainline, Mo., 253 S.W. 1049; Christian Moerlein Brewing Co., v. Rusch, 272 Pa. 181, 116 A. 145. A trust of a bond and mortgage on real estate is not subject to the statute. Hartman v. Loverud, 227 Wis. 6, 277 N.W. 641.

The Georgia statute requires a writing for any trust, whether of realty or personalty. Alston v. McGonigal, 179 Ga. 617, 176 S.E. 632. And it requires a recording where the beneficiary resides within three months after its execution. Metropolitan Life Ins. Co. v. Hall, 191 Ga. 294, 12 S.E.2d 53, citing Ga.Code 1933, § 108-114.

The enforceability of a trust is determined by the nature of the subject-matter at the time the attempt to create was made. Thus, if the subject-matter of an oral trust is originally realty, the trust is unenforceable even though the land is sold and the trustee gets money for it.[64] And if the oral trust had for its subject-matter stocks and bonds, and these are sold and the proceeds invested in land, the trust will be enforceable against the land.[65] If one accepts an oral trust of land, and at the same time orally agrees that if he sells the land he will hold the proceeds in trust, there is an enforceable contract to hold personalty in trust which will apply to the sale proceeds.[66]

Part Performance

If under the terms of the trust the beneficiary is to have possession of the trust land, and after the creation of the trust the cestui does take possession with the consent of the trustee, and makes improvements or repairs, or pays taxes, some courts hold that the trustee may not thereafter set up the Statute of Frauds.[67] This is sometimes explained by the phrase "part performance", but may also be said to be based on an estoppel against the trustee to deny the enforceability of the trust.

The majority of the cases do not consider that an oral trust of land is made enforceable by part performance by the trustee.[68] The fact that for a time he turns over the income of the property to the beneficiary, for example, is not regarded as changing the trust to an enforceable one, although this evidence may be said to corroborate the oral evidence about the existence of a trust.

[64] Alexander v. Spaulding, 160 Ind. 176, 66 N.E. 694.

[65] Eadie v. Hamilton, 94 Kan. 214, 146 P. 323.

[66] Chace v. Gardner, 228 Mass. 533, 117 N.E. 841; Bork v. Martin, 132 N. Y. 280, 30 N.E. 584, 28 Am.St.Rep. 570, 43 N.Y.St.Rep. 938; but see, contra, McGinness v. Barton, 71 Iowa 644, 33 N.W. 152; Glieberman v. Fine, 248 Mich. 8, 226 N.W. 669; Marvel v. Marvel, 70 Neb. 498, 97 N.W. 640, 113 Am. St.Rep. 792.

[67] Spies v. Price, 91 Ala. 166, 8 So. 405; Haskell v. First Nat. Bank, 33 Cal.App.2d 399, 91 P.2d 934; Goff v. Goff, 98 Kan. 700, 158 P. 662.

[68] Feeney v. Howard, 79 Cal. 525, 21 P. 984, 4 L.R.A. 826, 12 Am.St. Rep. 162; Pearson v. Pearson, 125 Ind. 341, 25 N.E. 342; but see Andrew v. State Bank of Blairsburg, 209 Iowa 1149, 229 N.W. 819. Harrington, Part Performance of Oral Trusts, 30 Mich. L.R. 289.

Oral Trusts Voidable, Not Void

The express wording of the English statute and of many of its American copies would lead to the natural belief that oral trusts in land are wholly unenforceable under all conditions. The wording is that they are "utterly void and of none effect."[69] But, in line with the construction of other sections of the same statute, it has been generally held that "void" in this connection means "voidable" and that the oral trust may be enforced, if the parties are willing and raise no objection to the lack of written evidence.[70]

Thus, if the trustee desires, he may waive the Statute of Frauds, and the trust will be enforced against him, and, if the trust is completely executed, the validity of acts performed under it will not be open to question. If a father conveys realty to a son on an oral promise by the son that he will convey the land to his mother after the father's death, and the son makes such conveyance, the creditors of the son have no standing to attack the validity of the trust. The son having seen fit to carry it out, the effect is the same as if the trust had been declared with due formality.[71] Titles conveyed by the trustee and other rights accruing, due to such performance of the oral trust, will be recognized by the courts, just as if the trust had been reduced to writing. If the oral trust is not avoided, it is as valid as a trust complying with the statute.[72]

The trustee may avoid performance by refusing to carry out the trust and by pleading the statute as a defence if he is sued for performance of the trust. Only the trustee or those suc-

---

[69] St. 29 Chas. II, c. 3, § 7.

[70] Myers v. Myers, 167 Ill. 52, 47 N.E. 309; Forest v. Rogers, 128 Mo. App. 6, 106 S.W. 1105.

[71] Arntson v. First Nat. Bank of Sheldon, 39 N.D. 408, 167 N.W. 760, L.R.A.1918F. 1038. For a similar case, see Delvol v. Citizen's Bank, 92 Or. 606, 179 P. 282, 181 P. 985.

[72] Polk v. Boggs, 122 Cal. 114, 54 P. 536; Hayden v. Denslow, 27 Conn. 335; King v. Bushnell, 121 Ill. 656, 13 N.E. 245; Stringer v. Montgomery, 111 Ind. 489, 12 N.E. 474; Johnston v. Jickling, 141 Iowa 444, 119 N.W. 746; Ratigan v. Ratigan, 181 Iowa 860, 162 N.W. 580, 165 N.W. 85; Bailey v. Wood, 211 Mass. 37, 97 N.E. 902, Ann.Cas.1913A, 950; Lasley v. Delano, 139 Mich. 602, 102 N.W. 1063; Robbins v. Robbins, 89 N.Y. 251; Oklahoma Nat. Bank v. Cobb, 52 Okl. 654, 153 P. 134; Robertson v. Howerton, 56 Okl. 555, 156 P. 329; Shippey v. Bearman, 57 Okl. 603, 157 P. 302; Ryan v. Lofton, Tex.Civ.App., 190 S.W. 752; Blaha v. Borgman, 142 Wis. 43, 124 N.W. 1047.

ceeding to his interest in the trust property can set up the Statute of Frauds.[73]

What Writings Satisfy the Statute—General Requisites

The written evidence required under the statute has previously been considered from the point of view of the statutory statement,[74] but some discussion of the construction of such statutes will be useful.

First, the writing must contain a complete statement of the trust.[75] "To take the case out of the Statute of Frauds, the trust must appear in writing, under the hand of the party to be charged, with absolute certainty as to its nature and terms, before the court can undertake to execute it."[76] Where there is not sufficient identification of the trust res, for example, the memorandum is defective,[77] but that the length of the trust period is not stated in the memorandum is not important,[78] since the trust will last as long as necessary to accomplish its purpose.

Upon the question when the writing must be created, there can be no doubt, in states where the statute requires the trust to be "created or declared" in writing and the statute has been strictly construed, that the writing must be contemporaneous with the creation of the trust. In several of these states, however, the statute has been held to be satisfied by a writing made after the trust arose. In such case the writing merely proves the trust.[79] In states, on the other hand, where the requirement is only that the trust be manifested or proved by a writing, it is clear that the writing may be made at the time of the creation of the trust or at any time thereafter before the commencement of the action.[80]

---

[73] Lach v. Weber, 123 N.J.Eq. 303, 197 A. 417; Faunce v. McCorkle, 321 Pa. 116, 183 A. 926.

[74] Ante, p. 81.

[75] Marie M. E. Church v. Trinity M. E. Church, 253 Ill. 21, 97 N.E. 262; Holsapple v. Shrontz, 65 Ind. App. 390, 117 N.E. 547; H. B. Cartwright & Bro. v. United States Bank & Trust Co., 23 N.M. 82, 167 P. 436.

[76] Kent, Ch., in Steere v. Steere, 5 Johns, Ch., N.Y., 1, 9 Am.Dec. 256.

[77] Snyder v. Snyder, 280 Ill. 467, 117 N.E. 465.

[78] Willats v. Bosworth, 33 Cal.App. 710, 166 P. 357.

[79] Gaylord v. City of Layfayette, 115 Ind. 423, 428, 17 N.E. 899; McClellan v. McClellan, 65 Me. 500; Urann v. Coates, 109 Mass. 581, 585; White v. Fitzgerald, 19 Wis. 504, 511.

[80] Smith v. Howell, 11 N.J.Eq. 349; McArthur v. Gordon, 126 N.Y. 597, 27 N.E. 1033, 12 L.R.A. 667; Reid v. Reid, 12 Rich.Eq., S.C., 213.

A memorandum made after action brought is thought not usable. Lucas v. Dixon, 22 Q.B.D. 357; Huffine v.

The memorandum may be made by the settlor before or at the time of the trust creation,[81] and by the trustee before, at the time, or after he receives title.[82]

"It is not essential that the memorandum relied on should have been delivered to any one as a declaration of trust."[83] The intent with which the writing was made is immaterial.[84] Indeed, a paper which expressly repudiates the intention of fastening a trust upon the property by virtue of the writing, but which shows as a whole that the relation of trustee and cestui que trust exists, is sufficient.[85] But the admission that an oral trust exists made in a pleading which sets up the Statute of Frauds, will not be an effective writing.[86] It is not requisite that the writing be addressed to the cestui que trust, or any particular person.[87] A signature by initials is satisfactory.[88]

The following have been held sufficient to satisfy the statute: a deed of trust;[89] a memorandum below the signature on a deed;[90] an answer or other legal pleading;[91] a letter;[92] a receipt;[93] a contract regarding the improvement or control of the property;[94] a recital in a mortgage or lease;[95] a power of

---

McCampbell, 149 Tenn. 47, 257 S.W. 80.

[81] Ellison v. Ganiard, 167 Ind. 471, 79 N.E. 450; Johnson v. Candage, 31 Me. 28.

[82] Myers v. Myers, 167 Ill. 52, 47 N.E. 309; Williams v. Williams, 118 Mich. 477, 76 N.W. 1039; Baldwin v. Humphrey, 44 N.Y. 609.

[83] Urann v. Coates, 109 Mass. 581, 584. See, also, Viele v. Curtis, 116 Me. 328, 101 A. 966.

[84] Kingsbury v. Burnside, 58 Ill. 310, 11 Am.Rep. 67; McClellan v. McClellan, 65 Me. 500.

[85] Urann v. Coates, 109 Mass. 581.

[86] Whiting v. Gould, 2 Wis. 552.

If the trustee in the course of litigation confesses the trustee, it becomes enforceable, although oral. Williams v. Moodhard, 341 Pa. 273, 19 A.2d 101.

[87] Bates v. Hurd, 65 Me. 180.

[88] Smith v. Howell, 11 N.J.Eq. 349.

[89] Miles v. Miles, 78 Kan. 382, 96 P. 481.

[90] Ivory v. Burns, 56 Pa. 300.

[91] Garnsey v. Gothard, 90 Cal. 603, 27 P. 516; McLaurie v. Partlow, 53 Ill. 340; Patten v. Chamberlain, 44 Mich. 5, 5 N.W. 1037.

[92] Brackenbury v. Hodgkin, 116 Me. 399, 102 A. 106; Montague v. Hayes, 76 Mass. 609, 10 Gray 609; Moulden v. Train, 199 Mo.App. 509, 204 S.W. 65; Malin v. Malin, 1 Wend., N.Y., 625.

[93] Nesbitt v. Stevens, 161 Ind. 519, 69 N.E. 256; Appeal of Roberts, 92 Pa. 407.

[94] Nolan v. Garrison, 151 Mich. 138, 115 N.W. 58; Jones v. Davis, 48 N. J.Eq. 493, 21 A. 1035.

[95] Commercial & Farmers' Bank of Raleigh v. Vass, 130 N.C. 590, 41 S. E. 791; Aller v. Crouter, 64 N.J.Eq. 381, 54 A. 426.

attorney;[96] a deposition;[97] a book account;[98] an account rendered.[99] A defective will is not sufficient to create a trust, but it may operate as an admission that a trust already exists.[1]

The writing may be composed of more than one document.[2] If two or more papers are relied upon, they must be shown to be connected with each other. This connection may be shown by physical attachment or inclosure in the same receptacle,[3] or by reference to and adoption of one by another,[4] or by clear reference to the same transaction upon the face of each.[5]

What Writings Satisfy the Statute—Parol Evidence

Oral evidence cannot be used to bind several writings together. Their connection must appear from their physical attachment or from their contents.[6] The writing or writings relied on to satisfy the statute must contain a complete statement of the trust, without the necessity of relying on parol testimony to supply any missing element.[7] The parol evidence rule naturally forbids the admission of oral evidence to vary or contradict the terms of a trust which is evidenced by a writing.[8] But abbre-

---

[96] Hutchins v. Van Vechten, 140 N. Y. 115, 35 N.E. 446.

[97] Baker v. Baker, 3 Cal.Unrep. 597, 31 P. 355.

[98] Corse v. Leggett, 25 Barb., N.Y. 389; In re Smith's Estate, 8 Pa.Co. Ct.R. 539.

[99] Denton v. McKenzie, 1 Desaus., S.C., 289, 1 Am.Dec. 664.

[1] Bryan v. Bigelow, 77 Conn. 604, 60 A. 266, 107 Am.St.Rep. 64; Hiss v. Hiss, 228 Ill. 414, 81 N.E. 1056; Leslie v. Leslie, 53 N.J.Eq. 275, 31 A. 170.

[2] Tyler v. Granger, 48 Cal. 259; McCreary v. Gewinner, 103 Ga. 528, 29 S.E. 960; Nesbitt v. Stevens, 161 Ind. 519, 69 N.E. 256; Stratton v. Edwards, 174 Mass. 374, 54 N.E. 886; Randall v. Constans, 33 Minn. 329, 23 N.W. 530; Van Cott v. Prentice, 104 N.Y. 46, 10 N.E. 257; In re Greenfield's Estate, 14 Pa. 489.

[3] Wiggs v. Winn, 127 Ala. 621, 29 So. 96; Hall v. Farmers' & Merchants' Bank, 145 Mo. 418, 46 S.W. 1000.

[4] McClellan v. McClellan, 65 Me. 500; Packard v. Putnam, 57 N.H. 43; Kimball v. De Graw, 9 N.Y.St. Rep. 339.

[5] Ransdel v. Moore, 153 Ind. 393, 53 N.E. 767, 53 L.R.A. 753; Tenney v. Simpson, 37 Kan. 579, 15 P. 512; Gates v. Paul, 117 Wis. 170, 94 N. W. 55.

[6] Illinois Steel Co. v. Konkel, 146 Wis. 556, 131 N.W. 842.

[7] Cook v. Barr, 44 N.Y. 156; Kimball v. De Graw, 9 N.Y.St.Rep. 339; Appeal of Dyer, 107 Pa. 446; Martin v. Baird, 175 Pa. 540, 34 A. 809; Braun v. First German Evangelical Lutheran Church, 198 Pa. 152, 47 A. 963; Jourdan v. Andrews, 258 Pa. 347, 102 A. 33. But see Kendrick v. Ray, 173 Mass. 305, 53 N.E. 823, 73 Am.St.Rep. 289.

[8] Chadwick v. Perkins, 3 Me., Greenl., 399; Gale v. Sulloway, 62

viations, ambiguities or uncertainties in a written instrument creating, or proving a trust, and the relation and situation of the parties, may be explained by parol evidence.[9] "When the writing relied upon to satisfy the Statute of Frauds has been lost or destroyed, its contents may be shown by parol proof which is reasonably clear and certain in its character. * * * And the same rule should prevail where the party to the suit who is alleged to have signed the writing, and who has or should have possession thereof, fails to produce on notice and denies its existence."[10]

FORMALITY—WILLS ACTS[11]

26. If a will is relied upon to create a trust, rather than to evidence a pre-existing trust, the will must comply with the formalities prescribed by the Wills Acts. Otherwise, no valid trust will arise.

    An instrument which purports to create an inter vivos or living trust may be held to be an attempt at the creation of a testamentary trust, if the settlor reserves to himself too large powers. However, the courts have been very liberal in permitting great control by the settlor of living trusts.

    Property may be left by will to the trustee of a previously created living trust by a mere description of that trust, without giving the details of its dispositions.

Since the Statute of Wills [12] and the Statute of Frauds [13] in England some formality has been necessary to the execution of a valid will. Modern American legislation now very generally requires wills of real and personal property to be executed with certain formalities; the common provisions being that such instruments be in writing, signed or subscribed by the testator, and attested by one or more witnesses.[14] These statutes are often referred to as the Wills Acts.

It is self-evident that, if an instrument is relied upon as a will to pass the title to property to a trustee, it must be executed with

N.H. 57; Peer v. Peer, 11 N.J.Eq. 432; Wallace v. Berdell, 97 N.Y. 13; Richards v. Crocker, 66 Hun 629, 20 N.Y.S. 954, affirmed 143 N.Y. 631, 37 N.E. 827.

[9] Fox v. Fox, 250 Ill. 384, 95 N.E. 498; Nesbitt v. Stevens, 161 Ind. 519, 69 N.E. 256; Wolf v. Pearce, 45 S.W. 865, 20 Ky.Law Rep. 296; Adams v. Canutt, 66 Wash. 422, 119 P. 865.

[10] Hiss v. Hiss, 228 Ill. 414, 423, 81 N.E. 1056; J. A. B. Holding Co. v. Nathan, 120 N.J.Eq. 340, 184 A. 829.

[11] Restatement, Trusts, §§ 53–58.

[12] St. 32 Henry VIII, ch. 1.

[13] St. 29 Chas. II, ch. 3.

[14] See, for example, New York Decedent Estate Law, § 21.

the formality required by the laws of the state in question. But, if the instrument is relied on, not to pass the property to another and fasten a trust upon it, but to constitute an admission of a pre-existing trust of which the one executing the will is a trustee, then it is immaterial that the instrument is imperfectly executed as a will. It may be void as a will, and yet constitute sufficient evidence to make a valid memorandum of a pre-existing trust.[15] In other words, a defective will may prove an express trust, although it cannot create such a relation.

Not infrequently a living settlor delivers possession of property to a trustee and executes what purports to be instrument creating a present trust, but he reserves such large powers over the trust property that it is alleged the instrument was in fact a testamentary disposition. After the making of a will, but before the death of the testator, the testator has complete control over his property. He may revoke or change the will, sell or give away his property. He retains possession of all his assets. In some trusts created by a living settlor he reserves a power to revoke or alter the trust, to remove the trustee, to direct the trustee as to investments and management, to control directly some items of management, as, for example, the payment of taxes or the voting of stock; and to take all income of the trust during the life of the settlor and such of the capital of the trust as the settlor elects to demand from the trustee.[16] In these extreme cases the settlor approaches very close to the entire dominion of a testator, and the beneficiaries who are to take after the death of the settlor and life beneficiary have a very shadowy interest during the settlor's life. A strong argument can be made that what purports to be a trust inter vivos, or a so-called "living trust", is a disguised attempted will, and should be required to be executed with the formality of a will, if it is to be enforced. In a few cases this argument has been successful and the instrument has been held invalid as an attempted will which did not have the proper witnesses and testimonium clause.[17]

---

[15] Hiss v. Hiss, 228 Ill. 414, 81 N.E. 1056; Leslie v. Leslie, 53 N.J.Eq. 275, 31 A. 170.

[16] See Ballantine, 18 Mich.L.R. 470; Rowley, 3 Univ.Cin.L.R. 361; Scott, 43 Harv.L.R. 521; Howe, 25 Ill.L.R. 178; Leaphart, 78 Univ. of Pa.L.R. 626; Seftenberg, 5 Wis.L.R. 321.

[17] Dunham v. Armitage, 97 Colo. 216, 48 P.2d 797; Smith v. Simmons, 99 Colo. 227, 61 P.2d 589; McEvoy v. Boston Five Cent Sav. Bank, 201 Mass. 50, 87 N.E. 465; Warsco v. Oshkosh Savings & Trust Co., 183 Wis. 156, 196 N.W. 829. See Wis.L. 1931, c. 216.

§ 26   FORMALITY—WILLS ACTS   91

But in a much larger number of cases the courts have held that the instrument created a valid living trust; that the settlor was not the full owner after the execution of the instrument, and that the cestuis other than the settlor had present interests after such execution, although they were very frail and highly destructible.[18] The courts are doubtless influenced in these cases by the argument that the Wills Acts were intended to prevent forgery and imposition and that the trust instruments being construed were admittedly genuine.

Although the depositor in a savings bank trust which is completed and made irrevocable by the death of the depositor would seem to have had full ownership till his death, and the interest of the beneficiary would seem to mature on account of that death, these transactions are not usually treated as testamentary by the courts. They are regarded as valid inter vivos transfers.[19]

Not infrequently after a man has created a living trust, he makes a will leaving the residue of his estate to the trustee of the living trust for the purposes of that trust, merely naming the trustee and giving the date of the execution of the living trust instrument, without naming the beneficiaries of the living trust and their shares or other trust terms. If the will takes effect, it is held that the residue is added to the property of the living trust. The donees of the residue are held to be adequately described.[20] If, after the living trust and the will are executed, the living trust is amended, the instrument of amendment must be executed as a codicil to the will, if it is to affect the property covered by the will.[21]

[18] Bear v. Millikin Trust Co., 336 Ill. 366, 168 N.E. 349, 73 A.L.R. 173; Jones v. Old Colony Trust Co., 251 Mass. 309, 146 N.E. 716; Goodrich v. City Nat. Bank & Trust Co., 270 Mich. 222, 258 N.W. 253; Davis v. Rossi, 326 Mo. 911, 34 S.W.2d 172; Cleveland Trust Co. v. White, 134 Ohio St. 1, 15 N.E. 627, 118 A.L.R. 475.

[19] Wilder v. Howard, 188 Ga. 426, 4 S.E.2d 549; Coughlin v. Farmers & Mechanics Sav. Bank, 199 Minn. 102, 272 N.W. 166; Murray v. Brooklyn Sav. Bank, 258 App.Div. 132, 15 N.Y.S. 2d 915; contra. Travers v. Reid, 119 N.J.Eq. 416, 182 A. 908; Thatcher v. Trenton Trust Co., 119 N.J.Eq. 408, 182 A. 912.

Even though the transaction is not labeled testamentary, it is generally subject to estate and inheritance taxes. In re Henderson's Estate, Sur., 198 N.Y.S. 799.

[20] Swetland v. Swetland, 102 N.J. Eq. 294, 140 A. 279; Matter of Rausch's Will, 258 N.Y. 327, 179 N.E. 755, 80 A.L.R. 98.

[21] Old Colony Trust Co. v. Cleveland, 291 Mass. 380, 196 N.E. 920; Koeninger v. Toledo Trust Co., 49 Ohio App. 490, 197 N.E. 419.

CONSIDERATION[22]

27. If a trust is completely created, lack of consideration will not render it revocable or invalid.

In order that an unexecuted promise to create a trust may give rise to a trust, consideration is necessary; and voluntary agreements to settle property in trust, as well as voluntary incomplete trusts, are not bases for the declaration by equity of either express or implied trusts.

An incomplete gift will not be converted into a trust by equity.

When Trust is Completely Created

It is thoroughly established that no consideration is necessary to make a trust enforceable, if all acts essential to be done by the settlor in order to create the trust have been done.[23] "It is certainly true that a court of equity will lend no assistance towards perfecting a voluntary contract or agreement for the creation of a trust, nor regard it as binding so long as it remains executory. But it is equally true that if such agreement or contract be executed by a conveyance of property in trust, so that nothing remains to be done by the grantor or donor to complete the transfer of title, the relation of trustee and cestui que trust is deemed to be established, and the equitable rights and interests arising out of the conveyance, though made without consideration, will be enforced in chancery." [24] And another court has thus expressed itself: "If the deed under which they [the volunteer cestuis] claim be defective and inoperative at law, they cannot have the aid of a court of equity to complete and perfect it, any more than they can have the aid of the court to enforce a promise, or even a covenant, without consideration, to execute a deed." [25]

Once the owner of the property has placed the legal title in the trustee and created the equitable right in the cestui que trust, the trust becomes enforceable. If the trust has come into existence, the question whether the settlor received value for his act of settlement is immaterial. "The creation of a trust is but the gift of the equitable interest. An unequivocal declaration as ef-

---

[22] Restatement, Trusts, §§ 28–30.

[23] Ellison v. Ellison, 6 Vesey, 656; Padfield v. Padfield, 72 Ill. 322; Harris Banking Co. v. Miller, 190 Mo. 640, 89 S.W. 629, 1 L.R.A.,N.S., 790; Van Cott v. Prentice, 104 N.Y. 45, 10 N.E. 257; Dennison v. Goehring, 7 Pa. 175, 47 Am.Dec. 505.

[24] Bigelow, J., in Stone v. Hackett, 12 Gray, Mass., 227, 230.

[25] Ames, C.J., in Stone v. King, 7 R.I. 358, 365, 84 Am.Dec. 557.

fectually passes the equitable interest to the cestui que trust as delivery passes the legal title to the donee of a gift inter vivos." [26]

It is sometimes said that voluntary "executed" trusts are enforceable, but that voluntary "executory" trusts are of no effect legally.[27] "A trust may be said to be executed when it has been perfectly and explicitly declared in a writing duly signed, in which the terms and conditions upon which the legal title to the trust estate has been conveyed, or is held, and the final intention of the creator of the trust in respect thereto, appear with such certainty that nothing remains to be done, except that the trustee, without any further act or appointment from the settlor carry into effect the intention of the donor as declared." [28] But there is objection to the use of the words "executory" and "executed" in this connection, since the phrase "executory trust" is somewhat ambiguous. It is sometimes employed in another sense, namely, to indicate a trust, the details of the execution of which are not definitely and fully laid down in the original instrument, but which may, nevertheless, be completely created.[29]

Agreements to Create Trusts and Incomplete Trusts

On the other hand, if the property owner has merely agreed to create a trust, or has taken only part of the steps necessary to give the trust existence, or has taken all such steps, but some of them in a defective manner, and the cestui que trust is a volunteer, equity will not intervene in his behalf.[30] The trust not being in existence, the intended cestui can have nothing more on which to rely than a naked promise, which is of no more effect in equity than at law.

Equity's refusal to aid the volunteer prevents her from declaring implied trusts in the case of incomplete gifts of the full property interest.[31] If the owner of money intended to give A the full ownership therein, but failed to carry out his intent by de-

[26] Hallowell Sav. Inst. v. Titcomb, 96 Me. 62, 69, 51 A. 249.

[27] Massey v. Huntington, 118 Ill. 80, 7 N.E. 269.

[28] Gaylord v. City of Lafayette, 115 Ind. 423, 429, 17 N.E. 899.

[29] Post, § 70.

[30] Estate of Webb, 49 Cal. 541; Hamilton v. Hall's Estate, 111 Mich. 291, 69 N.W. 484; Brannock v. Magoon, 141 Mo.App. 316, 125 S.W. 535; Harding v. St. Louis Union Trust Co. 276 Mo. 136, 207 S.W. 68; Central Trust Co. v. Gaffney, 157 App.Div. 501, 142 N.Y.S. 902; Rousseau v. Call, 169 N.C. 173, 85 S.E. 414.

[31] Talcott v. American Board Com'rs for Foreign Missions, 205 Ill. App. 339; Young v. Young, 80 N.Y. 422, 36 Am.Rep. 634.

livering the money to A or delivering a deed of gift, there is no reason why equity should aid the intended donee and give him an equitable estate. His condition is no worse since the failure to execute the gift than it was before the intention to make a gift was formed; the injustice and unjust enrichment necessary to give rise to a constructive trust do not exist, nor does the intent necessary to an express trust. Nor will the court treat the incomplete gift of the full property interest as amounting to a declaration by the giver that he was a trustee for the intended donee.[32]

Doubtless if the intended voluntary cestui has sufficiently changed his position in justifiable reliance on the settlor's agreement to create a trust, the settlor may be estopped to deny that a trust was created.[33]

The consideration required to support an agreement to create a trust is a valuable consideration; that is, money or its equivalent. It is, indeed, stated in some cases that meritorious or good consideration—love and affection or a duty to support—are recognized by equity as sufficient consideration.[34] But the weight of modern authority in England and America denies the validity of meritorious consideration as a support for an agreement to create a trust.[35]

It is occasionally hinted by the courts that a seal will induce equity to carry out an agreement otherwise unenforceable.[36] But the better view is that chancery will go behind the seal to learn the true consideration, and that the presence of a seal will not of itself render a voluntary agreement enforceable.[37] "It [equity] will doubtless not enforce a contract to create a trust, though it were under hand and seal; and in this respect it carries the doc-

[32] In re Hayward's Estate, —— Ariz. ——, 110 P.2d 956; Krickerberg v. Hoff, 201 Ark. 63, 143 S.W.2d 560.

[33] Dillwyn v. Llewellyn, 4 De Gex, F. & J. 517.

[34] Ellis v. Nimmo, Lloyd & Goold, temp. Sugden, 333; Mahan v. Mahan, 7 B.Mon., Ky., 579; McIntire v. Hughes, 4 Bibb, Ky., 186; Landon v. Hutton, 50 N.J.Eq. 500, 25 A. 953; Bunn v. Winthrop, 1 Johns.Ch., N.Y., 329; Pomeroy, Eq.Jur., 3d Ed., § 588.

[35] Jefferys v. Jefferys, 1 Craig & P. 137; Phillips v. Frye, 14 Allen, Mass., 36; Whitaker v. Whitaker, 52 N.Y. 368, 11 Am.Rep. 711; Matter of James, 146 N.Y. 78, 94, 40 N.E. 876, 48 Am.St.Rep. 774.

[36] Caldwell v. Williams, Bailey, Eq., S.C., 175.

[37] Selby v. Case, 87 Md. 459, 39 A. 1041; Hayes v. Kershow, 1 Sandf. Ch., N.Y., 258; Minturn v. Seymour, 4 Johns. Ch., N.Y., 498; Pomeroy, Eq. Jur., 3d Ed., § 370, note, 383, 1293.

trine of nudum pactum further than even the law does. * * *" [38] Modern legislation, making the seal merely presumptive evidence of consideration or otherwise altering its common-law effect, will probably lead equity to decrease still further, if possible, its esteem for the seal.

If one contracting to create a trust has received consideration for his promise, and then fails to perform, equity will decree a trust. "If there be a valuable consideration between the alleged trustee and cestui que trust, then, under the equitable rule that what ought to be done will be considered as done, the court may decree a contract to declare a trust as equivalent to an actual declaration." [39]

DELIVERY OF THE TRUST INSTRUMENT[40]

28. If the trust is created by a written instrument and is an inter vivos trust, the instrument must be delivered in the sense that the settlor must by some act manifest an intent that it shall take effect. While handing the document to the trustee or cestui que trust is the most common way of showing this intent, it is not the sole manner of expressing this idea.

    If the trust instrument is a will, it is not necessary to the completion of the trust that the will be placed in the hands of the trustee or of a beneficiary. It must have been executed and published as a will.

    Recording of a deed declaring a trust or transferring property to a trustee is not necessary to trust creation, but is important to the protection of the interests of the beneficiaries.

"Delivery" is here used in its technical, conveyancing sense, as meaning an expression by the party executing an instrument that he desires it to have immediate effect. It is not used in the somewhat common, layman's sense as meaning the handing of possession of the instrument to another party. While the act of placing another in control of the document is the most usual and natural method of showing an intent that the instrument take effect, this state of mind may be shown also by other means, as, for example, by telling another that the instrument is in effect, or by acting toward another as if he were the beneficiary of the instrument.

[38] Gibson, C.J., in Dennison v. Goehring, 7 Pa. 175, 178, 47 Am.Dec. 505.

[39] Janes v. Falk, 50 N.J.Eq. 468, 472, 26 A. 138, 35 Am.St.Rep. 783.

[40] Restatement, Trusts, §§ 32, 35.

It is well established that it is not essential that the settlor actually hand the trust instrument to the cestui or to the trustee in order to complete the trust. In numerous cases, in which the property owner has declared himself a trustee by formal written document, it has been held unnecessary to give the cestui possession of that document.[41] If the declarant has shown an intent to effect a complete trust, his failure to place the instrument stating the trust in the possession or control of the cestui will not be of determining importance.

When the property owner transfers the res to a third person as trustee, an additional element is involved, namely, the passage of title from settlor to trustee. The necessity of transferring possession of the trust instrument will be determined here by the law of conveyancing. The declaration of a trust involves only a theoretical transfer of the property from the declarant as an individual to the declarant as a trustee. It is almost universally held, in cases of transfers to third persons in trust, that the trust deed need not be actually placed in the manual possession of the trustee, if the settlor has otherwise shown a desire that the deed go into effect.[42]

Thus, in Adams v. Adams [43] the settlor signed, sealed, acknowledged, and recorded the trust deed but did not actually put it into the hands of the trustee or notify him of its existence. Mr. Justice Hunt, speaking for the Supreme Court, made the following statement: "In the case before us the settlor contemplated no further act to give completion to the deed. It was not an intention simply to create a trust. He had done all that was needed.

---

[41] In re Way's Trusts, 2 De Gex, J. & S. 365; Linton v. Brown's Adm'rs, C.C.Pa., 20 F. 455; Janes v. Falk, 50 N.J.Eq. 468, 26 A. 138, 35 Am.St.Rep. 783; Moloney v. Tilton, 22 Misc. 682, 51 N.Y.S. 19; Smith's Estate, 144 Pa. 428, 22 A. 916, 27 Am.St.Rep. 641; In re Eshbach's Estate, 197 Pa. 153, 46 A. 905. *Contra:* Govin v. De Miranda, 76 Hun 414, 27 N.Y.S. 1049, in which the court states at page 419: "In no case has it ever been held as yet that a party may, by transferring his property from one pocket to another, make himself a trustee. In every case where a trust has been established the party creating it has placed the evidence thereof in the custody of another and has thereby shown that it was intended to be a completed act."

[42] Doe v. Knight, 5 B. & C. 671; Adams v. Adams, 21 Wall. 185, 22 L. Ed. 504; Huse v. Den, 85 Cal. 390, 24 P. 790, 20 Am.St.Rep. 232; Barr v. Schroeder, 32 Cal. 609; Tarbox v. Grant, 56 N.J.Eq. 199, 39 A. 378; Souverbye v. Arden, 1 Johns.Ch., N.Y., 240; Bunn v. Winthrop, 1 Johns.Ch., N.Y., 329; Steele v. Lowry, 4 Ohio, 72, 19 Am.Dec. 581. *Contra:* Loring v. Hildreth, 170 Mass. 328, 49 N.E. 652, 40 L.R.A. 127, 64 Am.St.Rep. 301.

[43] 21 Wall 185, 193, 22 L.Ed. 504.

With his wife he signed and sealed the deed. With her he acknowledged it before the proper officers, and himself caused it to be recorded in the appropriate office. He retained it in his own possession, but where it was equally under her dominion. He declared openly and repeatedly to her, and to her brothers and sisters, that it was a completed provision for her, and that she was perfectly protected by it. He intended what he had done to be final and binding upon him. Using the name of his friend as trustee, he made the placing of the deed upon record and keeping the same under the control of his wife, as well as himself, a delivery to the trustee for the account of all concerned, or he intended to make himself a trustee by actions final and binding upon himself." And in Huse v. Den [44] it is said that there need be no "formal and physical handing of it [the trust deed] over" to the trustee.

While the failure to part with possession of the trust instrument is not necessarily fatal to the existence of the trust, it will constitute important evidence that a completed trust was not intended. "It is not essential that the memorandum relied on should have been delivered to any one as a declaration of trust. It is a question of fact, in all cases, whether the trust had been perfectly created; and upon that question the delivery or non-delivery of the instrument is a significant fact, of greater or less weight according to the circumstances." [45]

It has been held that technical delivery of a trust deed was conclusively shown by an acceptance by the trustee written upon the trust instrument,[46] by signing and acknowledging a trust deed and leaving it to be recorded,[47] by signing, acknowledging, and recording the trust instrument,[48] and by a recital of delivery in

---

[44] 85 Cal. 390, 398, 24 Pac. 790, 20 Am.St.Rep. 232.

[45] Urann v. Coates, 109 Mass. 581, 584. See, also, Roosevelt v. Carow, 6 Barb., N.Y., 190, in which case the retention of the trust deed, together with other circumstances, was held to prove that no completed trust was intended. And see Welch v. Henshaw, 170 Mass. 409, 49 N.E. 659, 64 Am.St. Rep. 309, and Ambrosius v. Ambrosius, C.C.A.N.Y., 239 F. 473, 152 C.C.A. 351. In Geoghegan v. Smith, 133 Md. 535, 105 A. 864, the trust was held incomplete where the memorandum was not turned over and the supposed settlor exercised absolute control over the property after the making of the memorandum.

[46] New South Building & Loan Ass'n v. Gann, 101 Ga. 678, 29 S.E. 15.

[47] Lawrence v. Lawrence, 181 Ill. 248, 54 N.E. 918.

[48] Walker v. Crews, 73 Ala. 412; Chilvers v. Race, 196 Ill. 71, 63 N.E. 701.

BOGERT TRUSTS 2D—7

the deed coupled with signature, acknowledgment, and recording.[49]

A valid delivery of the trust instrument will not be affected by a later return of that writing to the settlor.[50] A delivery to a third person on behalf of the trustee is sufficient delivery to the trustee.[51] Mere custody of the deed by the trustee on behalf of the settlor is not sufficient to show delivery to the trustee.[52]

Recording

It is hardly necessary to state that recording of the trust paper, in the absence of statute, is not an essential to completion of the trust.[53] The effect of the recording statutes is the same upon trust deeds as upon other conveyances. A failure to record may make it possible for the title of the cestuis to be cut off by a transfer of the same property to a bona fide purchaser who records his deed.[54]

The recording of a trust instrument is strong evidence that a complete trust was intended,[55] but it has been held not to be conclusive.[56]

In some states the Statute of Frauds requires the recording of all instruments creating or proving trusts in real property.[57] In these states recording is a necessary step in the creation of trusts in land enforceable by action.

---

[49] Schreyer v. Schreyer, 43 Misc. 520, 89 N.Y.S. 508, affirmed, 182 N.Y. 555, 75 N.E. 1134.

[50] Stone v. King, 7 R.I. 358, 84 Am. Dec. 557; Talbot v. Talbot, 32 R.I. 72, 78 A. 535, Ann.Cas.1912C, 1221.

[51] Woodward v. Camp, 22 Conn. 457; Withers v. Jenkins, 6 S.C. 122.

[52] Abert v. Lape, Ky., 15 S.W. 134.

[53] Sprague v. Woods, 4 Watts & S., Pa., 192.

[54] See §§ 103, 153, post.

[55] Ante, p. 97.

[56] Loring v. Hildreth, 170 Mass. 328, 49 N.E. 652, 40 L.R.A. 127, 64 Am.St. Rep. 301. But see Bailey v. Wood, 211 Mass. 37, 97 N.E. 902, Ann.Cas. 1913A, 950.

[57] Ga.Code 1933, § 108-114; Code Iowa 1939, § 10049; Code Miss. 1930, § 3348; 60 Okl.St.Ann. § 172; Metropolitan Life Ins. Co. v. Hail, 191 Ga. 294, 12 S.E.2d 53 (if trust created by deed, voidable by one injured if not recorded in county where beneficiary resides in three months after execution); Cornelison v. Roberts, 107 Iowa, 220, 77 N.W. 1028; Board of Trustees of M. E. Church South v. Odom, 100 Miss. 64, 56 South. 314.

BOGERT TRUSTS 2D

NOTICE OF THE TRUST[58]

29. Neither notice to the trustee nor to the cestui que trust of the settlor's intent to have a trust is essential to the existence of a completed trust, but the lack of such notice may have evidentiary value in showing that the settlor did not intend a completed trust.

Notice to the Cestui Que Trust

Is notice to the beneficiary of the settlor's intent that a trust should be created a prerequisite to a complete trust? Obviously the cestui cannot bring suit to enforce the trust until he knows of it, but the trust may nevertheless exist without his knowledge. If the settlor's intent is clear that a trust shall arise, failure to notify the beneficiary of such intent will not be important.[59] "The question in such a case is not so much whether in the lifetime of the decedent the declaration was actually exhibited to the inspection of others, as whether, under all the circumstances of the case, it would appear to have been written and preserved for the inspection of others." [60]

If it be said that the cestui should be notified in order that he might exercise the option of accepting or rejecting the trust, the reply is that acceptance of a beneficial property interest is presumed. If for any reason the beneficiary does not desire to retain the bounty of the settlor, he may disclaim after he receives knowledge of the trust.

[58] Restatement, Trusts, §§ 35, 36.

[59] Fowler v. Gowing, C.C.N.Y., 152 F. 801; Johnson v. Amberson, 140 Ala. 342, 37 So. 273; O'Brien v. Bank of Douglas, 17 Ariz. 203, 149 P. 747; Cahlan v. Bank of Lassen County, 11 Cal.App. 533, 105 P. 765; Security Trust & Safe Deposit Co. v. Farrady, 9 Del.Ch. 306, 82 A. 24; Lewis v. Curnutt, 130 Iowa 423, 106 N.W. 914; Marshall's Adm'r v. Marshall, 156 Ky. 20, 160 S.W. 775, 51 L.R.A., N.S., 1208; City of Boston v. Turner, 201 Mass. 190, 87 N.E. 634; City of Marquette v. Wilkinson, 119 Mich. 413, 48 N.W. 474, 43 L.R.A. 840; Janes v. Falk, 50 N.J.Eq. 468, 26 A. 138, 35 Am.St.Rep. 783; Neilson v. Blight, 1 Johns. Cas., N.Y., 205; Smith's Estate, 144 Pa. 428, 22 A. 916, 27 Am.St.Rep. 641; Williams v. Haskin's Estate, 66 Vt. 378, 29 A. 371; Fleenor v. Hensley, 121 Va. 367, 93 S.E. 582. The courts of Massachusetts have shown a greater tendency than those of any other state to require notice to the beneficiary. In Boynton v. Gale, 194 Mass. 320, 323, 80 N.E. 448, the courts said: "Whatever may be the doctrine elsewhere, it is settled in this state that a mere declaration of trust by a voluntary settlor, not communicated to the donee and assented to by him, is not sufficient to perfect a trust, especially when the property is retained by him subject to his own control."

[60] Smith's Estate, 144 Pa. 428, 442, 22 A. 916, 27 Am.St.Rep. 641.

The failure of the settlor to notify the cestui of his intent to create a trust will be considered, with all other circumstances, in determining whether the settlor intended a complete trust, but such notice is not an absolute essential to the perfected trust. In an English case [61] that the alleged settlor had written words of trust in a book, but had not communicated them to the intended beneficiary, was held to show an intent that there should be no completed trust.

Notice to the Trustee

It is likewise well settled that notice to the trustee of the trust conveyance is unnecessary to the perfection of the trust.[62] "Although the trustee may never have heard of the deed, the title vests in him, subject to a disclaimer on his part." [63]

A trustee, as will appear later,[64] cannot be compelled to accept a trust, but it is unnecessary that he know of it or accept it. If he declines to act, another trustee will be appointed by equity. Since the principal object of requiring notice to the trustee would be to enable him to determine whether he wished to accept or reject the trust, and since the acceptance or rejection of any particular individual as trustee has no effect on the life of the trust, the rule which makes notice to the trustee unnecessary is easily understandable.

As a matter of course the giving or failure to give notice to the trustee will have some value as evidence of the settlor's state of mind with respect to the completeness of the trust, but it is not conclusive. At least in the case of living trusts it is natural to notify the trustee as soon as the trust is created, so that he may take possession and begin his work. If the trustee has not been notified by the settlor, it is often probable that the settlor regarded the transaction as inchoate or incomplete, and subject to further deliberation on his part.

---

[61] In re Cozzens, 109 Law Times, 306, commented on in 62 Pa.Law Rev. 482.

[62] In re Way's Trusts, 2 De Gex, J. & S. 365; Thatcher v. Wardens, etc., of St. Andrew's Church of Ann Arbor, 37 Mich. 264.

[63] Adams v. Adams, 21 Wall. 185, 192, 22 L.Ed. 504.

[64] Post, § 37.

TRANSFER OF TITLE TO THE TRUSTEE[65]

30. If the trust is to be created by transfer, obviously the settlor must go through the formalities required by the laws of conveyancing in order to bring about a transfer of the title to the particular trust property involved to the trustee. A failure to comply with these rules of law will make the trust incomplete and of no effect. The conveyancing rules vary for different types of property.

If the settlor wishes to establish his trust by transfer of title to the trust property to another, he must consult the laws of property transfer or conveyancing in order to know what acts are necessary. This usually resolves itself down to the question, How can a gift of this type of property be accomplished?[66] Most trusts are created voluntarily and not for a consideration.

For example, if the settlor wishes to transfer title by will, he must follow the local Wills Act as to a written instrument, witnesses, subscription, publication, etc.

If the settlor wishes to transfer a fee title by inter vivos transaction to the trustee, he will usually be required to make, sign, sometimes seal, and deliver a written deed.

If the res is a stock certificate, representing shares in a corporation, the normal method is to indorse the certificate to the trustee and hand it to him;[67] but the title transfer may be effected by mere delivery of the certificate with intent to give,[68] or by delivery of an instrument of assignment with a power to complete the transfer on the books of the corporation.[69]

In the case of an intended trust of a bond the most formal method is to deliver the bond and a written instrument of assignment to the trustee, but title may be passed by mere delivery of

---

[65] Restatement, Trusts, §§ 31-34.

[66] See Mechem, Delivery in Gifts of Chattels, 21 Ill. L.R. 341, 457, 568; Williston, Gifts of Rights under Contracts in Writing by Delivery of the Writing, 40 Yale L.J. 1.

See Madison Trust Co. v. Skogstrom, 222 Wis. 585, 269 N.W. 249 (gift of certificate of interest under a trust); Henderson v. Hughes, 320 Pa. 124, 182 A. 392 (mortgage): Poirot v. Gundlach, 284 Ill.App. 349, 1 N.E.2d 801 (non-negotiable chose);

Wilson v. Hughes Bros. Mfg. Co., Tex. Civ.App., 99 S.W.2d 411 (book account).

[67] Uniform Stock Transfer Act, §§ 1 and 22.

[68] Herbert v. Simson, 220 Mass. 480, 108 N.E. 65, L.R.A.1915D, 733; Miller v. Silverman, 247 N.Y. 447, 160 N.E. 910.

[69] Grymes v. Hone, 49 N.Y. 17, 10 Am.Rep. 313.

the bond with donative intent.[70] Either delivery of the bond or a deed of gift is necessary.

Where a settlor desires to transfer a savings bank account to a trustee, he may vest him with title by delivery of the book with an intent to pass title,[71] but this is not true with regard to an ordinary checking account.[72] In the case of either type of bank account, the execution and delivery of a deed of gift would be sufficient.[73]

Whether the trustee must become the holder of a legal or an equitable title to the property before the trust can be complete depends upon the nature of the title which the settlor intends the trustee shall have. Ordinarily the settlor transfers to the trustee the legal title, but occasionally he places in the trustee's hands the equitable title to the property to hold in trust for the beneficiaries.[74] Whatever title the trustee is to have during the administration of the trust must be given to him before the trust can be said to be completely created.

If the settlor declares himself the trustee, the transfer of title is formal or theoretical; but, if a third person is to become trustee, the transfer is actual, and the formalities necessary to convey the title to real or personal property from one to another must be complied with.

Transfer of Possession

In some instances no title to property can be passed without giving possession of the thing concerned. The transferee must have possession before he can have title. An oral gift of tangible personal property is an example. Where the creation of a trust is attempted by such a gift, the settlor must give the trustee possession of the trust property before the trust can be completed. The reason lies in the law of gifts, rather than in the rules governing the creation of trusts.[75] A retention by the cre-

---

[70] Pryor v. Morgan, 170 Pa. 568, 33 A. 98.

[71] Hellman v. McWilliams, 70 Cal. 449, 11 P. 659; Polley v. Hicks, 58 Oh. St. 218, 50 N.E. 809, 41 L.R.A. 858.

[72] Jones v. Weakley, 99 Ala. 441, 12 So. 420, 19 L.R.A. 700, 42 Am.St. Rep. 84; Wilson v. Featherston, 122 N.C. 747, 30 S.E. 325.

[73] Tarbox v. Grant, 56 N.J.Eq. 199, 39 A. 378.

See Havighurst, Gifts of Bank Deposits, 14 N.C.L.R. 129.

[74] Sloane v. Cadogan, 3 Sugden, Vendors & Purchasers, 10th Ed., Append. 66.

[75] Badgley v. Votrain, 68 Ill. 25, 18 Am.Rep. 541; Wellington v. Heermans, 110 Ill. 564; Brannock v. Magoon, 141 Mo.App. 316, 125 S.W. 535; Hoffman v. Union Dime Sav. Inst., 109 App.Div. 24, 95 N.Y.S. 1045; Brown

ator of the power to have access to the trust property in connection with the trustees, whereas the latter are allowed to handle the property without the joinder of the settlor, is sufficient delivery to the trustees and possession by them to make the trust effective.[76]

Where possession of the trust property is not necessary to the passage of title to the trustee, the trust may well be complete without a transfer of possession to the trustee.[77] "But the validity of the trust is not affected by the failure of the trustee to take possession of the property. * * *"[78] Indeed, delivery of the trust property to the trustee does not conclusively show that a trust has been created.[79]

Obviously it is only in cases of transfers to third persons that the change of possession can be important. If the property owner declares himself a trustee, any change of possession will be formal and theoretical only.

Ordinarily the cestui que trust is not expected to obtain possession of the trust res at any time during the life of the trust. It is well settled that possession of the corpus by him, either in cases of declarations of trust or transfers in trust, is not indispensable to the creation of the trust relationship.[80]

v. Spohr, 180 N.Y. 201, 73 N.E. 14; Dickerson's Appeal, 115 Pa. 198, 8 A. 64, 2 Am.St.Rep. 547.

[76] Meldahl v. Wallace, 270 Ill. 220, 110 N.E. 354.

[77] Cahlan v. Bank of Lassen County, 11 Cal.App. 533, 105 P. 765; Otis v. Beckwith, 49 Ill. 121; Roche v. George's Ex'r, 93 Ky. 609, 20 S.W. 1039; Schreyer v. Schreyer, 43 Misc. 520, 89 N.Y.S. 508, affirmed, 182 N.Y. 555, 75 N.E. 1134; Young v. Cardwell, 6 Lea, Tenn., 168.

[78] Young v. Cardwell, 6 Lea, Tenn., 168, 171.

[79] Lloyd v. Brooks, 34 Md. 27.

[80] Williamson v. Yager, 91 Ky. 282, 15 S.W. 660, 34 Am.St.Rep. 184; Mize v. Bates County Nat. Bank, 60 Mo.App. 358; Martin v. Funk, 75 N.Y. 134, 31 Am.Rep. 446; Robb v. Washington & Jefferson College, 185 N.Y. 485, 78 N.E. 359.

CHAPTER 4

CREATION OF EXPRESS TRUSTS—THE TRUST ELEMENTS

Sec.
31. The Qualifications of the Settlor.
32. The Subject-Matter of the Trust.
33. Who may be a Trustee.
34. Original Appointment of Trustee.
35. Trust will Not Fail for Want of Trustee.
36. Estate of Trustee.
37. Acceptance by Trustee.
38. Qualification by the Trustee.
39. Necessity of Beneficiary.
40. Who may be a Beneficiary.
41. Acceptance by the Beneficiary.
42. Nature of Beneficiary's Interest.
43. Incidents of Beneficiary's Interest.
44. Availability to Creditors.
45. Spendthrift Trusts.
46. Discretionary Trusts.
47. Trusts for Support.
48. Blended Trusts.

THE QUALIFICATIONS OF THE SETTLOR[1]

31. **Any person capable of conveying property absolutely may create a trust therein by a declaration of trust or transfer in trust. The power to be a settlor is restricted by the same rules which govern the disposition of property free from trust.**

    The crown, the United States, a state, and municipal and private corporations may settle property in trust. Infants, married women, lunatics, and aliens may create trusts in their property, subject to the same rules as to disaffirmance and avoidance which affect their ordinary transactions.

The settlor of a trust has previously been defined to be the person who intentionally causes the trust to come into existence.[2] The settlor is also sometimes called the creator or trustor. Having discussed elsewhere the definition of this party to the trust, it remains to consider the small number of problems which arise with respect to him. Ordinarily, upon the complete creation of the trust, the settlor drops out of the transaction and has few, if any, rights or duties. There are, however, a few

[1] Restatement, Trusts, §§ 18–22, 350.   [2] See ante, p. 3.

questions which concern the settlor more than any other element of the trust relation. These questions will be treated at this point.

The first query is: Who may be the settlor of a trust? What qualifications, if any, must the settlor possess, in order that equity will recognize and enforce the trust which he has attempted to create?

The answer is that the capacity to create a trust is restricted only by the ability of the party to convey or transfer property or to make a contract. "In general, every person competent to make a will, enter into a contract, or hold the legal title to and manage property, may dispose of it as he chooses, and, sui juris, has the power to create a trust, and dispose of his property in that way. * * *"[3] If one may legally convey his property absolutely, he may convey it upon trust, or declare himself to hold it upon trust.

A person capable of making a contract may create a trust by contracting to pay money to a trustee for a third person.[4]

The sovereign has the power to convey property upon trust. Thus, in England the crown may grant upon trust, as in the case of a conveyance of a prize in trust for the captors.[5] And so, in the United States, the legislature of the nation or a state has the authority to convey property upon trust.[6]

Corporations, both municipal[7] and private,[8] have the power to become settlors of property in trust for purposes which are within their corporate powers.

The conveyances of infants,[9] married women,[10] insane persons, and aliens upon trust are subject to the same restrictions

---

[3] Skeen v. Marriott, 22 Utah 73, 89, 61 P. 296. See, also, Reiff v. Horst, 52 Md. 255, 267. The beneficiary of a trust may contribute to the trust fund and thus make himself in part a settlor. Central Trust Co. of New York v. Falck, 177 App.Div. 501, 164 N.Y.S. 473.

[4] Fletcher v. Fletcher, 4 Hare 67; Fogg v. Middleton, 2 Hill Eq., S.C., 591, Riley Eq. 193.

[5] Stevens v. Bagwell, 15 Ves. 139; Lewin, Trusts, 13th Ed., 17.

[6] Commissioners of Sinking Fund v. Walker, 6 How., Miss., 143, 38 Am. Dec. 433.

[7] Mayor of Colchester v. Lowten, 1 Ves. & B. 226.

[8] State v. President, etc., of Bank of Maryland, 6 Gill & J., Md., 205, 26 Am.Dec. 561; Dana v. Bank of United States, 5 Watts & S., Pa., 223.

As to the ultra vires creation of trusts by banks, see Ulmer v. Fulton, 129 Ohio St. 323, 195 N.E. 557, 97 A.L.R. 1170.

[9] Ownes v. Ownes, 23 N.J.Eq. 60; Starr v. Wright, 20 Ohio St. 97.

[10] Durant v. Ritchie, 4 Mason 45, Fed.Cas.No. 4190. In Brandan v. McCurley, 124 Md. 243, 92 A. 540, L.R.A.

as absolute transfers by such persons would be. The trust instruments may be set aside on account of the disability of the settlor whenever a grant without trust could be overturned for the same reason.[11]

Naturally a bankrupt cannot create a trust in property already in the hands of the trustee in bankruptcy.[12]

The beneficiary of a trust may settle his equitable interest in trust in the same way that the owner of the legal title may create a trust.[13] There may be a trust within a trust.

A court of equity cannot properly be said to have the power of settling a trust. It finds trusts to exist, but does not create them itself. "Our courts have no common-law authority to create any kind of trusts, certainly not express trusts. In the exercise of equity jurisdiction, they find and adjudge trusts to exist by reason of contracts, devises, bequests, gifts, or wrongful or fraudulent acts, and may always appoint trustees when necessary to execute them, but never, by common-law authority, create them."[14]

Attention has elsewhere been called to some statutory limitations upon the rights of certain persons to settle property upon charitable trusts.[15] For the purpose of protecting the families of settlors and to prevent fraud and duress the creators of charitable trusts are in some states limited as to the amount of property which they may give to charity and the time before death within which it must be given.

If one is to create a trust by declaration or transfer, he must own a property interest in which he can create equitable, or equitable and legal property interests.

If the creation of the trust was induced by fraud, undue influence, or other invalidating cause the settlor or his successors may have it set aside.[16]

1915C, 767, it was held that, although a married woman could not convey property to her husband directly, she and he might join in a deed to him as trustee, since his capacity as grantee was different from his status as grantor.

[11] Commissioner of Internal Revenue v. Allen, C.C.A., 108 F.2d 961; Kimmell v. Tipton, Tex.Civ.App., 142 S.W.2d 421.

[12] Gardner v. Rowe, 5 Russ, 258.

[13] Tierney v. Wood, 19 Beav. 330; Kronheim v. Johnson, 7 Ch.D. 60.

[14] Vanclief, C., in Simpson v. Simpson, 80 Cal. 237, 242, 22 P. 167, 168.

[15] See, § 91.

[16] Groening v. McCambridge, 282 Mich. 135, 275 N.W. 795; Kinney v. St. Louis Union Trust Co., Mo., 143 S.W.2d 250.

THE SUBJECT-MATTER OF THE TRUST[17]

32. Every trust must have some property as its subject-matter. This property may be of any kind recognized as valuable by a court of equity. It may be legal or equitable, real or personal. The subject-matter of the trust must be certain, in order that the trust be enforceable.

A trust without subject-matter is inconceivable. It could not exist, any more than a trust without a beneficiary.[18] Some property must be fixed as the res, to be held by the trustee for the beneficiary. In a few cases efforts have been made to prove that a trust existed where no property could be found as the subject-matter. Thus, in several cases a testator has requested that a certain person be employed by the executors as solicitor or attorney or clerk. It has been held in these cases that the testator's direction did not create a trust, because of the lack of subject-matter.[19] No sum was left in trust to employ the person named. And so, also, the proceeds of property not in existence cannot be made the subject-matter of a trust;[20] nor does any trust arise from a request that the testator's wife and sister should live together.[21]

One criterion for distinguishing debt from trust is that the former relates to no particular subject-matter while the latter does.[22]

"In general, any right, interest, or thing which may be the subject of property may be granted in trust. Every kind of vested right which the law recognizes as valuable may be transferred in trust."[23] This property may be land, money, a patent right,[24] growing crops,[25] a promissory note,[26] a claim against a

---

[17] Restatement, Trusts, §§ 74–88.

[18] "In order that there may be a trust of any kind, there must be a trust fund." Koehler v. Koehler, 75 Ind.App. 510, 526, 121 N.E. 450, 455.

[19] Foster v. Elsley, 19 Ch.Div. 518; Jewell v. Barnes' Adm'r, 110 Ky. 329, 61 S.W. 360, 53 L.R.A. 377; In re Thistlethwaite, Sur., 104 N.Y.S. 264; Matter of Wallach, 164 App.Div. 600, 150 N.Y.S. 302.

[20] Mitchell v. Bilderback, 159 Mich. 483, 124 N.W. 557.

[21] Graves v. Graves, 13 Ir.Ch. 182.

[22] See § 8, ante.

[23] Dunn, J., in Burke v. Burke, 259 Ill. 262, 268, 102 N.E. 293, 295. See, also, Haulman v. Haulman, 164 Iowa 471, 145 N.W. 930, 933.

[24] In re Russell's Patent, 2 De G. & Jon. 130.

[25] Mauldin v. Armistead, 14 Ala. 702.

[26] Broughton v. West, 8 Ga. 248; Duly v. Duly, 2 Ohio Dec. 425.

bank,[27] an equitable interest,[28] a ship in construction,[29] or unaccrued rents and profits.[30] If a property interest is by its nature inalienable, obviously no trust can be created in it by declaration or transfer.[31]

It is obvious that the subject-matter of the trust must be certain, if a court of equity is to enforce it. An uncertain trust res is as fatal to the trust as no subject-matter whatever. Thus, where a testator provided that after a certain date the trustees might give such portions of the estate as they thought proper to any of the testator's brothers and sisters who might stand in need of the aid, and that the trustees should devote the remainder of the property to the advancement of the cause of temperance or in aid of a manual training school, it was held that the gift in trust for the cause of temperance or the school was void for uncertainty, since there was no assurance that there would be any of the property of the testator left after his brothers and sisters were provided for.[32] On the other hand, a legacy in trust of a sufficient sum of money to produce $50 per annum is not void for uncertainty of the subject-matter.[33]

When it is said that the trust subject-matter must be fixed and specific, it is not meant that the trust property may not change from time to time throughout the life of the trust. It must be specific and identifiable at any given time, but may be changed by the trustee through sale and reinvestment. The subject-matter may be a farm at the outset, which the trustee

[27] McCarthy v. Provident Institution for Savings, 159 Mass. 527, 34 N.E. 1073.

[28] Tarbox v. Grant, 56 N.J.Eq. 199, 39 A. 378. In Clark v. Frazier, 74 Okl. 141, 177 P. 589, it was held that a school land certificate entitling its holder to a preferential right to buy the land was an equitable interest, which could be the subject-matter of a trust.

[29] Starbuck v. Farmers' Loan & Trust Co., 28 App.Div. 272, 51 N.Y.S. 58.

[30] Gisborn v. Charter Oak Life Ins. Co., 142 U.S. 326, 12 S.Ct. 277, 35 L. Ed. 1029.

[31] Thayer v. Pressey, 175 Mass. 225, 56 N.E. 5 (claim against United States before allowance inalienable by statute); In re M. J. Hoey & Co., C.C.A. N.Y., 19 F.2d 764 (seat on stock exchange could not be made res of trust).

[32] Wilce v. Van Anden, 248 Ill. 358, 94 N.E. 42, 140 Am.St.Rep. 212, 21 Ann.Cas. 153.

[33] Crawford v. Mound Grove Cemetery Ass'n, 218 Ill. 399, 75 N.E. 998. For other cases, in which doubt has been raised as to the certainty of the subject-matter, but the trusts have been sustained, see Speer v. Colbert, 200 U.S. 130, 26 S.Ct. 201, 50 L.Ed. 403; French v. Calkins, 252 Ill. 243, 96 N.E. 877; Haynes v. Carr, 70 N.H. 463, 49 A. 638; Beurhaus v. Cole, 94 Wis. 617, 69 N.W. 986.

sells and for which he receives a check, which he deposits in a bank and for which he then receives a claim against the bank, which he draws out in order to buy certain bonds, which then become the trust res.

An undivided interest in certain property, or in all the property of the settlor, is a sufficiently definite subject-matter for a trust.[34]

If one attempts to create a trust of a property interest which he does not own, the transaction amounts to a contract to create a trust in the property in question, if and when such property is acquired, provided the element of consideration is present; but if the settlor receives no consideration for his act, the transaction amounts to an unenforceable promise to create a trust in the future.[35] Two examples will make this point clearer. If a man who expects to gamble on the stock market and to make profits in the year 1928, declares in 1927 that he then holds the expected 1928 profits in trust for his wife and children, the transaction is a voluntary agreement to hold the profits in trust if and when earned during 1928. It is not a present trust in 1927 nor a contract to hold the profits in trust in the future. When the man earns such profits in 1928, they are his until he sets them aside as trust property, as he may voluntarily do. Since they become his when earned, and do not automatically become trust property, he must pay an income tax on them.[36]

If a sister expects to receive property from her brother at his death, either by his will or by intestacy, she is said to have an "expectancy," and not a present property interest. If she purports to transfer her expectancy in her brother's property during his life to a trustee for a third person, voluntarily, and later her brother dies leaving her property, she may choose between turning this property over to the trustee and keeping it as her own. She has no obligation to deliver the after-acquired property to the trustee. Her action amounted merely to an unenforceable promise to turn over to the trustee property received from her brother. That the instrument of transfer was under seal does not make any difference.[37] The purported transfer did

---

[34] Commissioner of Internal Revenue v. McIlvaine, 296 U.S. 488, 56 S.Ct. 332, 80 L.Ed. 345; Rabalsky v. Kook, 87 N.H. 56, 173 A. 803.

[35] Bacon v. Bonham, 33 N.J.Eq. 614; Mastin v. Marlow, 65 N.C. 695.

[36] Brainard v. Commissioner of Internal Revenue, C.C.A., 91 F.2d 880.

[37] In re Ellenborough, 1903, 1 Ch. 697.

not amount to an actual transfer because there was nothing owned by the sister at that time.

An insurance policy is a valid trust subject-matter, even though the insured has reserved the power to change the beneficiary in the policy. The interest of the beneficiary is treated by the better authorities as a chose in action against the insurer which is vested, although subject to being divested and cut off by action of the insured in substituting another person as the beneficiary in the policy, or permitting the policy to lapse.[38]

A very large amount of life insurance is held in trust under the so-called "insurance trusts". If the insured makes a trustee the beneficiary, but transfers no fund to meet the premiums on the policy, the trust is called "unfunded"; whereas, if the settlor-insured not only makes the policy payable to a trustee, but also transfers to the trustee bonds or stocks from the income of which the trustee will be able to meet the premiums on the policy as they become due, the trust is referred to as "funded". Trusts of insurance for the benefit of relatives of the settlor are called "personal" insurance trusts, while those connected with the operation of partnerships and corporations are called "business" insurance trusts.[39] Due to the fact that insurance payable to another than the executor or administrator of the insured is not subject to the debts of the insured,[40] and is to some extent freed from inheritance and estate taxes on the estate of the insured,[41] there are practical advantages in the creation of insurance trusts, beyond the ordinary benefits which come from insurance.

In many insurance policies the company agrees to hold the proceeds of the policy "in trust" for named relatives on the death of the insured, and to pay the proceeds in installments with interest. These policies are said by the insurance companies to create trusts, but it is believed that in fact they are merely contracts. The company never contracts to hold particular proper-

[38] Cannon v. Nicholas, C.C.A.Colo., 80 F.2d 934; Goldman v. Moses, 287 Mass. 393, 191 N.E. 873; but see Dumesnil v. Reeves, 283 Ky. 563, 142 S.W.2d 132; Belknap v. Northwestern Mut. Life Ins. Co., 108 Vt. 421, 188 A. 897.

[39] For fuller discussions, see Horton, Some Legal Aspects of Insurance Trusts; Shattuck, Living Insurance Trusts; Hanna, Some Legal Aspects of Life Insurance Trusts, 78 Pa.L. R. 346; Fraser, Personal Life Insurance Trusts, 16 Cornell L. Q. 19; Bogert, Trusts and Trustees, §§ 235–245.

[40] See N.Y. Insurance Law, § 55a; Wash.L.1939, p. 546.

[41] 26 U.S.C.A. Int.Rev.Code, § 811(g); and see various state inheritance tax laws.

ty in trust, but expects merely to make bookkeeping entries, showing the rights of the beneficiaries.[42] While the insurance companies have procured legislation in many states making the interests of the beneficiaries inalienable and not subject to the debts of the beneficiaries, and so the appearance of a spendthrift trust is created,[43] the real effect is that choses in action are given protection similar to that of the interests of trust beneficiaries.

WHO MAY BE A TRUSTEE[44]

33. Any person capable of taking the title to property may be a trustee.

> The crown in England, the United States, or a state may be a trustee, although the trust may be unenforceable in the courts.
>
> Corporations, both private and municipal, may be trustees for purposes within their corporate powers.
>
> An unincorporated association has not the capacity to be a trustee, but a trust naming such an organization as trustee will not fail for that reason.
>
> Married women, infants, aliens, and lunatics may be trustees, subject to the disabilities which affect them in all their transactions.
>
> The settlor may declare himself a trustee, or may make the beneficiary trustee. Where the sole cestui que trust is the sole beneficiary, the trust will be destroyed by a merger of the legal and equitable interests of the trustee-beneficiary. But where the sole beneficiary is one of several trustees, or where the sole trustee is one of several beneficiaries, or where the same group of persons are trustees and beneficiaries, the trust is valid and no difficulty arises.

What are the qualifications of a trustee? What persons, natural and artificial, may hold the office of trustee?

Any person capable of taking the title to real or personal property may be a trustee. If one has the power to become the owner of property absolutely and for his own benefit, he may likewise become seized of property in trust for another.

---

[42] Pierowich v. Metropolitan Life Ins. Co., 282 Mich. 118, 275 N.W. 789; Van Hecke, Insurance Trusts—The Insurer as Trustee, 7 N.C.L.R. 21; but see Johnson v. New York Life Ins. Co., C.C.A.Fla., 75 F.2d 425; New York Life Ins. Co. v. Conrad, 269 Ky. 359, 107 S.W.2d 248.

[43] For a collection of statutory references, see Bogert, Trusts and Trustees, § 240.

[44] Restatement, Trusts, §§ 89–98.

The sovereign in England may be a trustee, although the beneficiary has no power to enforce the trust against the crown. Recent statutes[45] have provided against escheat to the crown upon the death of a trustee without heirs, and have also made it possible for the crown to transfer the duties of a trusteeship to another.

By way of dictum the New York Court of Appeals has said that the United States is incapable of holding property in trust for the establishment of a school.[46]

It would seem, however, that there are instances in the reports showing such holding in trust.[47] Both the national government and the states governments may not be sued without their consents, but this merely renders their trusteeships difficult of enforcement and does not prevent them. Boards or courts of claims have been set up by Congress and by many states for the hearing of claims against the government.

A state may be a trustee,[48] as for example, when the holder of property in trust to establish a home for insane persons,[49] or when taxes are illegally collected,[50] or when money is given for the benefit of the children living in the state,[51] or when the foreshore of the ocean is held for the public,[52] or where land is held for the benefit of soldiers.[53]

"It may be stated as a general proposition of law that, * * * unless specially restrained, municipal corporations may take and hold property in their own right by direct gift, conveyance, or devise, in trust, for purposes germane to the objects of the corporation, or which will promote aid, or assist in carrying out or perfecting those objects."[54]

Instances in which gifts to cities to hold in trust for governmental or other charitable purposes have been sustained are fre-

[45] 39 & 40 Geo. III, c. 88, 1800; 4 & 5 Wm. IV, c. 23, 1834; 13 & 14 Vict. c. 60, §§ 15, 46, 47, 1850.

[46] Wright, J., in Levy v. Levy, 33 N.Y. 97, 122.

[47] U. S. v. Jackson, 280 U.S. 183, 50 S.Ct. 143, 74 L.Ed. 361; U. S. v. Getzelman, C.C.A.Okl. 89 F.2d. 531.

[48] Preston v. Walsh, C.C.Tex., 10 F. 315.

[49] Yale College's Appeal, 67 Conn. 237, 34 A. 1036.

[50] Shoemaker v. Board of Com'rs of Grant County, 36 Ind. 175.

[51] Bedford v. Bedford's Adm'r, 99 Ky. 273, 35 S.W. 926.

[52] Allen v. Allen, 19 R.I. 114, 32 A. 166, 30 L.R.A. 497, 61 Am.St.Rep. 738.

[53] Pinson v. Ivey, 1 Yerg., Tenn., 296.

[54] Clayton v. Hallett, 30 Colo. 231, 249, 70 P. 429, 59 L.R.A. 407, 97 Am. St.Rep. 117.

quent.[55] These trusts are generally in aid of objects which the municipality is under a duty to forward or might well forward. Thus, one trust was for the establishment of a hospital for foundlings,[56] another for the purpose of making loans to needy young artificers,[57] and still a third for the planting and care of shade trees in the city.[58]

A town or village may become a trustee to carry out purposes for which it was incorporated.[59] "A trust for the support of schools, or of a particular school as a high school, or for any purpose of general public utility is a valid trust. So towns can hold property in trust for purposes within the general scope of their corporate existence."[60]

It is obvious that a private corporation may be a trustee whenever the purposes of the trust are consistent with the objects of the corporation. If carrying out the trust is within the powers granted to the corporation by its charter or certificate of incorporation, then the corporation may validly act as trustee.[61] If to carry out the trust would be beyond the corporate powers

---

[55] McDonogh v. Murdoch, 56 U S. 367, 15 How., 367, 14 L.Ed. 732; In re Coleman's Estate, 167 Cal. 212, 138 P. 992, Ann.Cas.1915C, 682; Dykeman v. Jenkines, 179 Ind. 549, 101 N.E. 1013, Ann.Cas.1915D, 1011; Richards v. Wilson, 185 Ind. 335, 112 N E. 780; Board of Trustees of Schools for Industrial Education in City of Hoboken v. City of Hoboken, 70 N.J.Eq. 630, 62 A. 1; State v. City of Toledo, 23 Ohio Cir.Ct.R. 327; McIntosh v. City of Charleston, 45 S.C. 584, 23 S.E. 943; Maxcy v. City of Oshkosh, 144 Wis. 238, 128 N.W. 899, 1136, 31 L.R.A.,N.S., 787. By Laws N.H. 1915, c. 162, cities and towns are authorized to act as trustees for certain purposes.

[56] Phillips v. Harrow, 93 Iowa 92, 62 N.W. 434.

[57] Higginson v. Turner, 171 Mass. 586, 51 N.E. 172.

[58] Cresson's Appeal, 30 Pa. 437.

[59] Roe v. Doe, 2 Boyce, Del., 348, 80 A. 250; Chapman v. Newell, 146 Iowa 415, 125 N.W. 324; Higginson v. Turner, 171 Mass. 586, 51 N.E. 172; Hatheway v. Sackett, 32 Mich. 97; Adams v. Highland Cemetery Co., Mo., 192 S.W. 944; Glover v. Baker, 76 N.H. 393, 83 A. 916; Stearns v. Newport Hospital, 27 R.I. 309, 62 A. 132, 8 Ann.Cas. 1176.

[60] Piper v. Moulton, 72 Me. 155, 159, in which case the trust was for educational purposes. In Sargent v. Cornish, 54 N.H. 18, the town held property for the purpose of buying and displaying flags for patriotic uses.

[61] Perin v. Carey, 65 U.S. 465, 24 How. 465, 16 L.Ed. 701; Hossack v. Ottawa Development Ass'n, 244 Ill. 274, 91 N.E. 439; State v. Higby Co., 130 Iowa, 69, 106 N.W. 382, 114 Am. St.Rep. 409; White v. Rice, 112 Mich. 403, 70 N.W. 1024; Chapin v. School Dist. No. 2 in Winchester, 35 N.H. 445; De Camp v. Dobbins, 29 N.J.Eq. 36; Ex parte Greenville Academies, 7 Rich.Eq., S.C., 471; Bell County v. Alexander, 22 Tex. 350, 73 Am.Dec. 268; Latshaw v. Western Townsite Co., 91 Wash. 575, 158 P. 248.

BOGERT TRUSTS 2D—8

of the trustee, then the trust will be established but the stockholders of the corporation may prevent the trust from being administered by their corporation. The ultra vires nature of the trust does not prevent the settlor's act from being effective in creating a trust.[62]

The private corporations which are most commonly made trustees are trust companies and banks. When authorized to act as trustee they constitute a class of professional trustees. National banks may be authorized by the Federal Reserve Board to act as trustees and many of them have such permits.[63] All trust companies are authorized to act in a fiduciary capacity, including trusteeship.[64] State banks are in many states also given permission to act as trustee, subject to certain qualifications.[65]

Unincorporated Associations

The question has frequently arisen whether an unincorporated association may be a trustee. Such a body is not recognized by the law as a legal entity. It has a shifting membership. Examples are labor unions, social clubs, fraternities, and lodges. While, under the older orthodox view, such an organization cannot receive the title to property and hence cannot be a trustee,[66] there are some modern decisions recognizing the association as a de facto trustee,[67] and all cases admit that the incapacity of the association to take title does not prevent the trust from beginning but rather merely calls for the appointment of another trustee.

The correct view would seem to be that a trust ought not to fail because an unincorporated association was named as its trustee. Such an association is not a legal entity. The title to the trust property could not rest in it, but would necessarily rest in the members of the association, if the association were allowed to be a trustee. But such members are constantly changing, and there is no provision for the transfer of the title to the property on the change of membership. But, even if it be conceded that an unincorporated association is not competent

---

[62] Daniel v. Wade, 203 Ala. 355, 83 So. 99; Hayden v. Hayden, 241 Ill. 183, 89 N.E. 347.

[63] 12 U.S.C.A. § 248k.

[64] See, for example, Fla.Comp.Gen. L.1927, §§ 6124–6145; N.Y. Banking Law, § 180 et seq.

[65] See, for example, Conn. Gen.St. 1930, § 3885; Pa. 7 P.S. §§ 251–254.

[66] Rixford v. Zeigler, 150 Cal. 435, 88 P. 1092, 119 Am.St.Rep. 229; Douthitt v. Stinson, 63 Mo. 268.

[67] Schneider v. Kloepple, 270 Mo. 389, 193 S.W. 834; Parker v. Cowell, 16 N.H. 149.

BOGERT TRUSTS 2D

to serve as a trustee, the trust may well be saved under the established principle that equity will not allow a trust to fail for want of a trustee.[68] The better method of dealing with such attempts to create a trust would seem to be to appoint new trustees.

Married women, even at common law, were capable of becoming trustees, although hampered in the administration of trusts by the rules restricting their dealing with property apart from their husbands.[69] Under modern legislation, giving married women power to take, convey, and manage their property as if single, married women may, of course, act without any disability as trustees, and they frequently are appointed.[70]

An infant may be a trustee, although subject to the usual disabilities of infancy, in that his contracts and conveyances will be voidable by him before he reaches his majority.[71] Equity will, on application, decree that the infant convey to a new trustee of full capacity.[72]

A lunatic may be a trustee, although subject to the same incapacities and disabilities as if acting with reference to his own property.[73] His business transactions will be voidable. Equity will remove the title from the lunatic trustee and vest it in a competent person.[74]

An insolvent[75] or bankrupt[76] person may be a trustee, although equity will ordinarily remove him on application.[77] Such a person has the capacity to hold and manage property, although his financial condition makes it highly dangerous to the cestui que trust that he continue in the trust office. On bank-

[68] See post, p. 121.

[69] Still v. Ruby, 35 Pa. 373.

[70] Rose v. Rose, 93 Ind. 179; In re Stewart, 56 Me. 300; Springer v. Berry, 47 Me. 330; Jones v. Roberts, 60 N.H. 216; Schluter v. Bowery Savings Bank, 117 N.Y. 125, 22 N.E. 572, 5 L.R.A. 541, 15 Am.St.Rep. 494; Clarke v. Saxon, 1 Hill Eq., S. C., 69.

[71] Jevon v. Bush, 1 Vernon, 342; Des Moines Ins. Co. v. McIntire, 99 Iowa 50, 68 N.W. 565; McClellan v. McClellan, 65 Me. 500; Levin v. Ritz, 17 Misc. 737, 41 N.Y.S. 405.

[72] Walsh v. Walsh, 116 Mass. 377, 17 Am.Rep. 162. Where infant trustees have conveyed to their cestui que trust, equity will confirm this voidable title. Clary v. Spain, 119 Va. 58, 89 S.E. 130.

[73] Pegge v. Skynner, 1 Cox, Eq.Cas. 23; Eyrick v. Hetrick, 13 Pa. 488.

[74] See discussion of removal of trustees, post, § 157.

[75] Shryock v. Waggoner, 28 Pa. 430.

[76] Rankin v. Barcroft, 114 Ill. 441, 3 N.E. 97.

[77] In re Barker's Trusts, 1 Ch.Div. 43.

ruptcy of the trustee the trust property does not pass to the trustee in bankruptcy.

At common law an alien did not take title to real property by descent, and a title obtained by conveyance was subject to being taken from him by the sovereign. Thus, he could not be a trustee, if descent were relied upon as a means of conveying title to him, but could be a trustee if title were tendered to him by conveyance.[78] Naturally his disability to hold against the crown made him a very undesirable trustee. In the United States the powers of an alien to take and hold real property have been much enlarged by statute but are not yet complete.[79] But, as later shown,[80] the selection of an alien as trustee will not defeat the origin of the trust, no matter what the disabilities of aliens in that state. These disabilities never extended to personal property.

"There is no rule of law that prohibits the donor from constituting himself a trustee for the donee, and in such case no further delivery is necessary, provided the trust is expressed."[81]

Merger

Frequently the trustee is also named as a beneficiary of the trust. Is a cestui que trust competent to act as a trustee? The question may arise in several ways. A. may have been appointed a trustee for himself alone. In such case the sole trustee is also sole beneficiary. There can be no doubt about the result in such an instance. The equitable estate merges in the legal, and A. becomes the owner of the property freed from any trust.[82] "The trustee and the beneficiary must be distinct personalities, or, otherwise, there could be no trust, and the merger of interests in the same person would effect a legal estate in him, of the same duration as the beneficial interest designed. * * * That the legal and beneficial estate can exist and be maintained separately in the same person is an inconceivable

---

[78] See, for example, Beidler v. Dehner, 178 Iowa 1338, 161 N.W. 32.

[79] See, for example, Ariz. Code 1939, § 71-201; Del.Rev.Code 1935, § 3655; Va.Code 1936, § 66; Kohler, Legal Disabilities of Aliens in the United States, 16 Amer. Bar. Ass. J. 113.

[80] See § 35, post.

[81] Yokem v. Hicks, 93 Ill.App. 667, 670.

[82] Nellis v. Rickard, 133 Cal. 617, 66 P. 32, 85 Am.St.Rep. 227; Matter of Hitchins, 39 Misc. 767, 80 N.Y.S. 1125; Butler v. Godley, 12 N.C. 94; Danforth v. Oshkosh, 119 Wis. 262, 97 N.W. 258. Upon the termination of trusts by merger see post, § 168.

proposition."[83] But if the same group of persons appointed trustees are also the sole beneficiaries, there is no merger or other difficulty about the origin or continuance of the trust. As trustees they are joint tenants, as cestuis they are tenants in common. There is sufficient diversity of personnel to satisfy the law of obligations.[84]

A different question is raised where A. is appointed trustee for A. and B. Here A.'s legal estate is not the same as his equitable interest. In the majority of the cases the validity of the trust has been sustained, and A. treated as a normal trustee.[85] In a few cases the courts have held that a partial merger arose in such a situation, and that A. became the absolute owner of part of the property, freed from the trust, but continued to be trustee as to the balance for the benefit of B.[86]

In Woodward v. James the testator's widow was made trustee for herself and certain other relatives. The widow was to have one-half the income from the trust property. The court said: "It is undoubtedly true that the same person cannot be at the same time trustee and beneficiary of the same identical interest. To say that he could would be a contradiction in terms, as complete and violent as to declare that two solid bodies can occupy the same space at the same instant. Where, however, the trustee is made beneficiary of the same estate, both in respect to its quality and quantity, the inevitable result is that the equitable is merged in the legal estate, and the latter alone remains. If, then, it be granted that, as to her half of the income, the widow was not trustee, and took what was given to her by a direct legal right, it does not follow that her trust estate in the corpus of the property is in any manner destroyed, or that there is any the less a necessity for its existence. She can be trustee for the heirs, and that trust ranges over the whole estate for the purpose of its management and disposition."[87]

Still a third view has been expressed in New York, namely, that A. may act for B., in the situation described, but is incom-

[83] Greene v. Greene, 125 N.Y. 506, 510, 26 N.E. 739, 21 Am.St.Rep. 743.

[84] Johnson v. Muller, 149 Kan. 128, 86 P.2d 569; Sturgis v. Citizens' Nat. Bank of Pocomoke, 152 Md. 654, 137 A. 378.

[85] Tyler v. Mayre, 95 Cal. 160, 27 P. 160, 30 P. 196; Nichols v. Nichols, 42 Misc. 381, 86 N.Y.S. 719; Doscher v. Wyckoff, 63 Misc. 414, 113 N.Y.S. 655; Allen v. Hendrick, 104 Or. 202, 206 P. 733; Lamb v. First Huntington Nat. Bk., W.Va. 7 S.E.2d 441; Fox's Estate, 264 Pa. 478, 107 A. 863.

[86] Woodward v. James, 115 N.Y. 346, 22 N.E. 150; Weeks v. Frankel, 197 N.Y. 304, 90 N.E. 969.

[87] 115 N.Y. 346, 357, 22 N.E. 150.

petent to act for himself, and that the court will act with respect to trust questions involving the interests of A. alone.[88] In a later New York case[89] the Court of Appeals indicates by way of dictum that its view is that A. would not be competent to act at all when he was appointed as trustee for himself and for B.

A third possible trust, namely, one where A. and B. are appointed trustees for A. alone, does not seem to have arisen often in litigation. A trust of this kind seems to have been sustained as a valid trust by way of dictum in one case.[90]

The fourth and last contingency is that in which A. and B. are appointed trustees for A. and C. A. here has conflicting interests. He has a private interest as a beneficiary and an official interest as the representative of C. A variety of views have been expressed by the courts relative to the effect of such a settlement. The majority of courts which have had occasion to consider the question have held that the trust was a valid trust and that no merger occurred as to A.'s interest.[91] "The title held by the trustees is joint, and there is no merger of separate interests in the different trustees arising out of the fact that they are also beneficiaries."[92]

Two objections to a merger of the trustee-beneficiary's interests are urged in a New York case, namely, that the doctrine of merger is aimed at passive trusts only, and that the title of the trustees is joint, whereas the interest of the cestuis que trust is separate and several.[93] In some cases, however, the courts have taken the position that, where A. and B. are trustees for A. and C., there is a partial merger, and A. becomes the absolute owner of part of the property dedicated to the trust.[94] The New Jersey court, in making its decision, says: "It may be he is trustee for his children, but he cannot be trustee for himself. He is one of the beneficiaries of the trust, and also trustee, and

---

[88] Rogers v. Rogers, 111 N.Y. 228, 18 N.E. 636.

[89] Robertson v. De Brulatour, 188 N.Y. 301, 317, 80 N.E. 938.

[90] Bull v. Odell, 19 App.Div. 605, 46 N.Y.S. 306.

[91] Burbach v. Burbach, 217 Ill. 547, 75 N.E. 519; Story v. Palmer, 46 N.J.Eq. 1, 18 A. 363; Amory v. Lord, 9 N.Y. 403; Tiffany v. Clark, 58 N.Y. 632; Weeks v. Frankel, 197 N.Y. 304,

90 N.E. 969; Cocks v. Barlow, 5 Redf.Sur., N.Y., 406; Moke v. Norrie, 14 Hun 128; Denniston v. Pierce, 260 Pa. 129, 103 A. 557.

[92] Burbach v. Burbach, 217 Ill. 547, 550, 75 N.E. 519.

[93] Amory v. Lord, 9 N.Y. 403, 412.

[94] Bolles v. State Trust Co., 27 N.J.Eq. 308; Craig v. Hone, 2 Edw.Ch., N.Y., 554; Mason v. Mason's Ex'rs, 2 Sandf.Ch., N.Y., 432.

therefore, to the extent of his personal interest in the trust property, both the equitable and legal estates are vested in the same person. This union works a merger of the equitable estate. Where the equitable and legal estates unite in the same person, the equitable sinks or merges into the legal, provided the legal estate is as extensive as the equitable."[95]

Lastly, with respect to class four of these trustee-beneficiary cases, there are some cases which maintain that the trust is valid, but that the trustee who is also a beneficiary is disabled from acting where his interests as a beneficiary are involved, but may act in all other cases. The noninterested trustees must act alone when the rights of the combination trustee and beneficiary are at stake.[96] "But, however this may be, it is clearly the law that where two or more trustees are appointed to execute a trust, and one or both is under the infirmity of being a beneficiary, neither the trust nor its execution fails, as each may act for the other where disqualification exists, and all can act with respect to that portion of the property in which they have no interest."[97]

A settlor may create different types of trustees, with different functions, as where he appoints a trust company as custodian trustee to have possession of the trust property, and an individual as managing trustee to make investments, collections and distributions.[98] But trustees may not distribute the trust duties among themselves.

ORIGINAL APPOINTMENT OF TRUSTEE[99]

34. The trustee is ordinarily originally appointed by the settlor. If the settlor fails to appoint a trustee, but creates a trust otherwise complete, equity will supply the deficiency and appoint the original trustee.

[95] Bolles v. State Trust Co., 27 N. J.Eq. 308, 310.

[96] Bundy v. Bundy, 38 N.Y. 410; Robertson v. De Brulatour, 188 N.Y. 301, 317, 80 N.E. 938; Rankine v. Metzger, 69 App.Div. 264, 74 N.Y.S. 649, affirmed 174 N.Y. 540, 66 N.E. 1115.

[97] Rankine v. Metzger, 69 App.Div. 264, 269, 74 N.Y.S. 649.

[98] City of Boston v. Dolan, 298 Mass. 346, 10 N.E.2d 275; Walker v. James, 337 Mo. 750, 85 S.W.2d 876; Thomas v. National Bank of Commerce of Seattle, 187 Wash. 521, 60 P.2d 264.

[99] Restatement, Trusts, § 108.

The original appointment of the trustee is, of course, ordinarily the function of the settlor.[1] By very definition the settlor is the person who selects the trustee, trust property, and beneficiary, and establishes the trust. In appointing the trustee, the settlor is not under any obligation to consider the wishes of the cestui que trust.[2]

In appointing the trustee the settlor need not use any particular language or describe the trustee as such.[3] It is sufficient if he clearly shows a purpose that a trust arise and that a given person shall administer it. Thus, that the word "committee," rather than "trustee," was used, is not important, if the intent to create a trust was evident.[4] And so, also, where a will makes a bequest in trust, but no trustee is named to carry out the trust, the executor is often deemed to have been appointed a trustee for that purpose.[5]

In some instances the original trustee may be appointed by the court of chancery rather than by the settlor. Thus, if the settlor establishes a trust, but fails to name any trustee, the court will supply the deficiency, and appoint a trustee to administer the trust.[6] Or if the trustee named by the settlor can never enter upon the performance of his duties, due to the fact that he has died prior to the taking effect of the trust instrument,[7] or because he declines the trust,[8] or because he is disqualified [9] or incompetent,[10] equity will supply the trustee. In some cases, also, the number of trustees appointed by the settlor is not sufficient

---

[1] Cruse v. Axtell, 50 Ind. 49; Leonard v. Haworth, 171 Mass. 496, 51 N.E. 7.

[2] In re Naglee's Estate, 52 Pa. 154.

[3] Grant Trust & Savings Co. v. Tucker, 49 Ind.App. 345, 96 N.E. 487.

[4] Boreing v. Faris, 127 Ky. 67, 104 S.W. 1022, 31 Ky.Law Rep. 1265.

[5] Groton v. Ruggles, 17 Me. 137; Dorr v. Wainwright, 13 Pick., Mass., 328; Holbrook v. Harrington, 16 Gray, Mass., 102; Wheeler v. Perry, 18 N.H. 307; Terry v. Smith, 42 N.J.Eq. 504, 8 A. 886; Montfort v. Montfort, 24 Hun, N.Y., 120.

[6] Bundy v. Bundy, 38 N.Y. 410; In re Weed, 181 App.Div. 921, 167 N.Y.S. 862. See post, p. 121.

[7] Ex parte Schouler, 134 Mass. 426; Woodruff v. Woodruff, 44 N.J.Eq. 349, 16 A. 4, 1 L.R.A. 380.

[8] Carruth v. Carruth, 148 Mass. 431, 19 N.E. 369; In re Snyder's Will, Sup., 136 N.Y.S. 670; King v. Merritt, 67 Mich. 194, 34 N.W. 689; Prince v. Barrow, 120 Ga. 810, 48 S.E. 412; Cffutt v. Jones, 110 Md. 233, 73 A. 629; Lee v. Randolph, 2 Hen. & M., Va., 12.

[9] Ogilby v. Hickok, 144 App.Div. 61, 128 N.Y.S. 860.

[10] Fitchie v. Brown, 211 U.S. 321, 29 S.Ct. 106, 53 L.Ed. 202; Eccles v. Rhode Island Hospital Trust Co., 90 Conn. 592, 98 A. 129; Childs v. Waite, 102 Me. 451, 67 A. 311; Force v. Force, N.J.Ch., 57 A. 973.

to manage the trust, and in such instances equity may appoint additional trustees to assist those whom the settlor has selected.[11]

The subject of the filling of vacancies in the trusteeship will later be considered.[12] At this point only the original appointment of the trustee is discussed.

TRUST WILL NOT FAIL FOR WANT OF TRUSTEE[13]

35. **Equity will not allow a trust to fail for want of a trustee. If at the beginning of the trust no trustee is named, or the trustee named is nonexistent or incompetent to accept, or refuses to accept the trust, chancery will supply a trustee, and the settlor's intent will be effectuated. The same result follows where there is a vacancy in the trusteeship during the life of the trust.**

No trust can be operated without a trustee, but the failure of the settlor to select a trustee or his selection of a trustee who cannot or will not act is not fatal to the origin of the trust. If the settlor has clearly indicated an intent that a trust shall exist, equity will, because of its desire to support the trust, supply the trustee in case of need. This principle is generally expressed in the maxim that "equity will not allow a trust to fail for want of a trustee." [14] Whether A. or B. is the trustee to administer the trust is not especially important. Any competent and honest man can carry out the intent of the settlor. The important purpose to be accomplished is the establishment and enforcement of an equitable interest in the beneficiaries, and not the identity of the mere representative or administrator, the trustee.

---

[11] In re Townsend's Estate, 73 Misc. 481, 133 N.Y.S. 492; Crickard's Ex'r v. Crickard's Legatees, 25 Grat, Va., 410.

[12] See post, § 134.

[13] Restatement, Trusts, §§ 33, 101.

[14] Handley v. Palmer, C.C.Pa., 91 F. 948; Kidd v. Borum, 181 Ala. 144, 61 So. 100; Appeal of Eliot, 74 Conn. 586, 51 A. 558; Hitchcock v. Board of Home Missions of Presbyterian Church, 259 Ill. 288, 102 N.E. 741, Ann.Cas.1915B, 1; In re Freeman's Estate, 146 Iowa 38, 124 N.W. 804; Harris v. Rucker, 52 Ky. 564, 13 B. Mon. 564; Attorney General v. Goodell, 180 Mass. 538, 62 N.E. 962; Penny v. Croul, 76 Mich. 471, 43 N.W. 649, 5 L.R.A. 858; Taylor v. Watkins, Miss., 13 So. 811; Rothenberger v. Garrett, 224 Mo. 191, 123 S.W. 574; Jones v. Watford, 62 N.J.Eq. 339, 50 A. 180; In re Powell's Will, 136 App.Div. 830, 121 N.Y.S. 779; Goodrum v. Goodrum, 43 N.C. 313; Hill v. Hill, 49 Okl. 424, 152 P. 1122; In re Stevens' Estate, 200 Pa. 318, 49 A. 985; Shields v. Jolly, 1 Rich.Eq., S.C., 99, 42 Am.Dec. 349; Gidley v. Lovenberg, 35 Tex.Civ.App. 203, 79 S.W. 831; Whelan v. Reilly, 3 W.Va. 597.

Thus, where the settlor describes the trust completely, except that he fails to name any trustee, equity will supply the want and appoint a trustee to administer the trust.[15] And by virtue of the same rule, if the trustee named by the settlor is a corporation which has passed out of existence, or a body which has no legal existence,[16] or if such trustee be dead,[17] or incompetent to act,[18] or refuse the trust,[19] equity will provide a trustee and the trust will be carried out.

ESTATE OF TRUSTEE[20]

36. The estate which the trustee has is governed by the needs of the trust. If a fee is required in order that the trust may be properly executed, the trustee will be deemed to have that estate, regardless of the wording of the trust instrument. The settlor will be deemed to have conveyed to the

[15] Carpenteria School Dist. v. Heath, 56 Cal. 478; Grand Prairie Seminary v. Morgan, 171 Ill. 444, 49 N.E. 516; Howard v. American Peace Society, 49 Me. 288; Brown v. Kelsey, 2 Cush., Mass., 243; Buckley v. Monck, Mo., 187 S.W. 31; Case v. Hasse, 83 N.J.Eq. 170, 93 A. 728; Shotwell v. Mott, 2 Sandf.Ch., N.Y. 46; Goffe v. Goffe, 37 R.I. 542, 94 A. 2, Ann.Cas.1916B, 240; Porter v. Bank of Rutland, 19 Vt. 410; In re Kavanaugh's Estate, 143 Wis. 90, 126 N.W. 672, 28 L.R.A.,N.S., 470. But in Tennessee, if the trust is charitable and no trustee is named, equity will not supply one. Ewell v. Sneed, 136 Tenn. 602, 191 S.W. 131, 5 A.L.R. 303. See, also, in accord with the Tennessee view, Robinson v. Crutcher, 277 Mo. 1, 209 S.W. 104.

[16] In re Crawford's Estate, 148 Iowa, 60, 126 N.W. 774, Ann.Cas. 1912B, 992; Darcy v. Kelley, 153 Mass. 433, 26 N.E. 1110; Bruere v. Cook, 63 N.J.Eq. 624, 52 A. 1001; McBride v. Elmer's Ex'rs, 2 Halst.Ch. 107, 6 N.J.Eq. 107.

[17] O'Brien v. Bank of Douglas, 17 Ariz. 203, 149 P. 747; Babcock v. African Methodist Episcopal Zion Society, 92 Conn. 466, 103 A. 665; Garrison v. Little, 75 Ill.App. 402; Herrick v. Low, 103 Me. 353, 69 A. 314; In re De Silver's Estate, 211 Pa. 459, 60 A. 1048.

[18] Culver v. Lompoc Valley Sav. Bank, 22 Cal.App. 379, 134 P. 355; Burke v. Burke, 259 Ill. 262, 102 N.E. 293; Guild v. Allen, 28 R.I. 430, 67 A. 855; Willis v. Alvey, 30 Tex.Civ.App. 96, 69 S.W. 1035; Lightfoot v. Poindexter, Tex.Civ.App., 199 S.W. 1152. In Gould v. Board of Home Missions of Presbyterian Church, 102 Neb. 526, 167 N.W. 776, the trustee named was incompetent because a foreign corporation. The court supplied a trustee, but said that it would not have done so, if the trust had been private.

[19] Dailey v. City of New Haven, 60 Conn. 314, 22 A. 945, 14 L.R.A. 69; Dykeman v. Jenkins, 179 Ind. 549, 101 N.E. 1013, Ann.Cas.1915D, 1011; Kelly v. Anderson, 173 Ky. 298, 190 S.W. 1101; Richards v. Church Home for Orphan & Destitute Children, 213 Mass. 502, 100 N.E. 631; McLean v. Nelson, 46 N.C. 396; Atwood v. Shenandoah Val. R. Co., 85 Va. 966, 9 S.E. 748.

[20] Restatement, Trusts, § 88.

trustee an interest in the property sufficient to enable him to perform the trust.

Since the trustee holds the trust property for the benefit of others and has no personal interest therein, the trust property is not liable for the payment of his debts.

The powers of the trustee are affected by the nature of the property rights which he holds in trust. Whether the estate granted to him in trust is a fee, a life estate, or other interest, is ordinarily determined by the trust instrument. But the important principle that a trustee takes such an estate or interest as is necessary to enable him to perform the trust should be observed.[21] If the trust can be administered only through the ownership of a fee simple, such an interest will be deemed granted,[22] although the limitations of the deed or will may not clearly show that a fee simple was transferred. If a life estate will suffice to enable the trustee to perform his duties, such an estate will be deemed vested in the trustee, regardless of the particular wording of the trust instrument.[23]

Ordinarily, of course, the legal estate is vested in the trustee,[24] although a trust may be created with an equitable interest as the subject-matter. The principle that, where the trust is passive, the legal estate vests in the cestui que trust by virtue of the Statute of Uses or its modern successors, has been explained at another point.[25] Attention has also been directed to the merger which sometimes takes place when the trustee is also the sole beneficiary.[26]

The estate of the trustee being a bare legal interest, and not a beneficial interest, his creditors cannot satisfy their claims from

[21] Christopher v. Mungen, 61 Fla. 513, 55 So. 273; Nixon v. Nixon, 268 Ill. 524, 109 N.E. 294; Defrees v. Brydon, 275 Ill. 530, 114 N.E. 336; Lyon v. Safe Deposit & Trust Co., 120 Md. 514, 87 A. 1089; Cleveland v. Hallett, 6 Cush., Mass., 403; Wright v. Keasbey, 87 N.J.Eq. 51, 100 A. 172; Brown v. Richter, 25 App.Div. 239, 49 N.Y.S. 368; Walker v. Scott, 7 Ohio App. 335; Holder v. Melvin, 106 S.C. 245, 91 S.E. 97; Joy v. Midland State Bank, 26 S.D. 244, 128 N.W. 147; Ellis v. Fisher, 3 Sneed, Tenn., 231, 65 Am.Dec. 52; Montgomery v. Trueheart, Tex.Civ.App., 146 S.W. 284.

[22] McFall v. Kirkpatrick, 236 Ill. 281, 86 N.E. 139.

[23] In re Spreckel's Estate, 162 Cal. 559, 123 P. 371.

[24] Ware v. Richardson, 3 Md. 505, 56 Am.Dec. 762; Welch v. City of Boston, 221 Mass. 155, 109 N.E. 174, Ann.Cas.1917D, 946.

[25] See § 5, ante; Palmer v. City of Chicago, 248 Ill. 201, 93 N.E. 765; Guild v. Allen, 28 R.I. 430, 67 A. 855; Schumacher v. Draeger, 137 Wis. 618, 119 N.W. 305.

[26] See § 33, ante.

the trust property. A judgment against the trustee personally is not a lien upon trust real estate and cannot be collected out of it.[27]

ACCEPTANCE BY TRUSTEE[28]

37. It is not necessary to the creation of a trust that the particular trustee named by the settlor accept the trust. Equity will not allow the trust to fail for want of a trustee.

But it is necessary that a trustee accept the trust before the title to the trust property permanently vests in him and before he is bound by the trust obligations. Acceptance of a trust by the trustee may be shown by any acts by the trustee expressly or impliedly recognizing the existence of his trusteeship.

The trustee may refuse to accept the trust. He cannot be compelled to undertake the duties of the trusteeship against his will.[29] If he clearly indicates that he declines the trust, he will not become a trustee. A trustee cannot accept part of the trust

---

[27] Lavender v. Lee, 14 Ala. 688; Aicardi v. Craig, 42 Ala. 311; H. B. Claflin Co. v. King, 56 Fla. 767, 48 So. 37; Taylor v. Brown, 112 Ga. 758, 38 S.E. 66; Cox v. Arnsmann, 76 Ind. 210; Brown v. Barngrover, 82 Iowa, 204, 47 N.W. 1082; Harrison v. Andrews, 18 Kan. 535; Emery v. Farmers' State Bank, 97 Kan. 231, 155 P. 34; Feagan v. Metcalfe, 150 Ky. 745, 150 S.W. 988; First Nat. Bank of Catonsville v. Carter, 132 Md. 218, 103 A. 463; Hussey v. Arnold, 185 Mass. 202, 70 N.E. 87; Lee v. Enos, 97 Mich. 276, 56 N.W. 550; Fleming v. Wilson, 92 Minn. 303, 100 N.W. 4; Moran v. Joyce, 125 N.J.L. 558, 18 A.2d 708; Dalrymple v. Security Loan & Trust Co., 11 N.D. 65, 88 N.W. 1033; Arntson v. First Nat. Bank, 39 N.D. 408, 167 N.W. 760, L.R.A. 1918F, 1038; Manley v. Hunt, 1 Ohio 257; J. I. Case Threshing Mach. Co. v. Walton Trust Co., 39 Okl. 748, 136 P. 769; Dimmick v. Rosenfield, 34 Or. 101, 55 P. 100; Barnes v. Spencer, 79 Or. 205, 153 P. 47; Eldredge v. Mill Ditch Co., 90 Or. 590, 177 P. 939; Nashville Trust Co. v. Weaver, 102 Tenn. 66, 50 S.W. 763; Williams v. Fullerton, 20 Vt. 346; Davenport v. Stephens, 95 Wis. 456, 70 N.W. 661. This rule applies, even though the trustee is also the settlor of the trust, in the absence of fraud. Wulff v. Roseville Trust Co. of Newark, N. J., 164 App.Div. 399, 149 N.Y.S. 683.

In the early days, when the separation of law and equity was complete, a creditor of the trustee could reach the trust property for the trustee's personal debt in the court of law, but equity would, at the suit of the beneficiary, enjoin the taking of the trust property for that purpose. Giles v. Palmer, 49 N.C. 386, 69 Am.Dec. 756. But now this same relief may be obtained in the law action.

[28] Restatement, Trusts, §§ 35, 354.

[29] Dailey v. City of New Haven, 60 Conn. 314, 22 A. 945, 14 L.R.A. 69; In re Yale College, 67 Conn. 257, 34 A. 1036; Silvers v. Canary, 114 Ind. 129, 16 N.E. 166; Carruth v. Carruth, 148 Mass. 431, 19 N.E. 369.

property and duties and reject the remainder. He must accept or reject the whole trust.[30]

If the trust is personal to the named trustee, that is, if the settlor indicated an intent that the trustee named should be the only qualified trustee, then refusal of the trust by that trustee causes the trust to fail.[31] Such an intent by a settlor is very rare.

Generally there is evidence of acceptance or refusal on the part of the trustee by some positive acts. Thus it has been held that an oral acknowledgment by the trustee that he had accepted the trust,[32] failure to object to the trust after knowledge of its existence for some time,[33] taking out letters testamentary when the trustee was also the executor under the will,[34] the writing of the trust deed under which the trustee was appointed,[35] taking control of that deed,[36] joining in the execution of the trust deed,[37] taking possession of the trust property [38] or exercising control over it,[39] or the performance of any acts which amount to a carrying out of the trust,[40] are all acts on the part of the trustee which show an acceptance of the trust by him. In many cases where the question of acceptance was in dispute, acts of a similar nature have been held to show an acceptance of the trust.[41]

[30] Chase Nat. Bank of City of New York v. Citizens Gas Co. of Indianapolis, C.C.A.Ind., 113 F.2d 217.

[31] Louisville & N. R. Co. v. Powers, 268 Ky. 491, 105 S.W.2d 591.

[32] Elizalde v. Elizalde, 137 Cal. 634, 66 P. 369, 70 P. 861.

[33] Salter v. Salter, 80 Ga. 178, 4 S.E. 391, 12 Am.St.Rep. 249; Roberts v. Moseley, 64 Mo. 507. Standing mute on the statement of the trust was held sufficient in Heitman v. Cutting, 37 Cal.App. 236, 174 P. 675.

[34] Coudon v. Updegraf, 117 Md. 71, 83 A. 145.

[35] Young v. Cardwell, 6 Lea, Tenn., 168.

[36] Hitz v. National Metropolitan Bank, 111 U.S. 722, 4 S.Ct. 613, 28 L.Ed. 577.

[37] Dayton v. Stewart, 99 Md. 643, 59 A. 281.

[38] McBride v. McIntyre, 91 Mich. 406, 51 N.W. 1113; Pullis v. Pullis Bros. Iron Co., 157 Mo. 565, 57 S.W. 1095; Chaplin v. Givens, Rice Eq., S.C., 132.

[39] Freeman v. Brown, 115 Ga. 23, 41 S.E. 385.

[40] Patterson v. Johnson, 113 Ill. 559.

[41] Kennedy v. Winn, 80 Ala. 165; St. Mary's Hospital v. Perry, 152 Cal. 338, 92 P. 864; Hearst v. Pujol, 44 Cal. 230; Baldwin v. Porter, 12 Conn. 473; Wilson v. Snow, 35 App.D.C. 562; Johnson v. Cook, 122 Ga. 524, 50 S.E. 367; Copeland v. Summers, 138 Ind. 219, 35 N.E. 514, 37 N.E. 971; Henderson v. McDonald, 84 Ind. 149; Ridenour v. Wherritt, 30 Ind. 485; Barclay v. Goodloe's Ex'r, 83 Ky. 493; Sangston v. Hack, 52 Md. 173; Lyle v. Burke, 40 Mich. 499; Jamison v. Zausch, 227 Mo. 406, 126 S.W. 1023, 21 Ann.Cas. 1132; Daly v. Bernstein, 6 N.M. 380, 28 P. 764;

In some cases doubt has arisen as to whether certain acts amounted to a refusal of the trust by the trustee. It has been held that the failure to qualify [42] or to give a bond [43] shows a rejection of the trust. But a refusal to act as executor, when the same person is appointed trustee and executor, does not prove a refusal of the trusteeship.[44] Where a trustee refused to take any steps under his appointment for more than two years, or to file a bond, or take possession of or manage the property, and suffered the buildings to become out of repair and untenantable and the land to be sold for the payment of taxes, his acts justify the inference that he has declined the trust.[45] In numerous other cases similar acts have been held to show a rejection of the trust duties by the trustee.[46]

The validity of a trust is not affected by the acceptance or rejection of the trust by any particular trustee, except in the rare cases where the trust is personal and can be carried out only by the trustee named.[47] Ordinarily, if John Doe declines to accept the trust, Richard Roe may be substituted for Doe, and the trust carried out without difficulty.[48] The refusal of the trustee to accept the office does not cause the title to the trust property to vest in the cestui que trust,[49] but it remains in the settlor (if the trust was created inter vivos) or passes to the heir or next of kin of the settlor subject to the trust (if the trust was created

Rowe v. Rowe, 103 App.Div. 100, 92 N.Y.S. 491; Christian v. Yancey, 2 Pat. & H., Va., 240.

[42] Sells v. Delgado, 186 Mass. 25, 70 N.E. 1036; In re Robinson, 37 N.Y. 261. Quite often, by statute, failure to qualify within a short time is treated as a declination of the trust. Pungs v. Hilgendorf, 289 Mich. 46, 286 N.W. 152.

[43] Attwill v. Dole, 74 N.H. 300, 67 A. 403. But see Coates v. Lunt, 213 Mass. 401, 100 N.E. 829.

[44] Pomroy v. Lewis, 14 R.I. 349; Garner v. Dowling, 11 Heisk., Tenn., 48.

[45] Adams v. Adams, 64 N.H. 224, 9 A. 100.

[46] White v. White, 107 Ala. 417, 18 So. 3; Dodge v. Dodge, 109 Md. 164, 71 A. 519, 130 Am.St.Rep. 503; Bowden v. Brown, 200 Mass. 269, 86 N.E. 351, 128 Am.St.Rep. 419; Brandon v. Carter, 119 Mo. 572, 24 S.W. 1035, 41 Am.St.Rep. 673; Mutual Life Ins. Co. v. Woods, 121 N.Y. 302, 24 N.E. 602; Anderson v. Earle, 9 S.C. 460.

[47] Richardson v. Mullery, 200 Mass. 247, 86 N.E. 319.

[48] Braswell v. Downs, 11 Fla. 62; Wells v. German Ins. Co. of Freeport, 128 Iowa, 649, 105 N.W. 123; Stebbins v. Lathrop, 4 Pick., Mass., 33; Minot v. Tilton, 64 N.H. 371, 10 A. 682; Rhode Island Hospital Trust Co. v. Town Council of Warwick, 29 R.I. 393, 71 A. 644; Cloud v. Calhoun, 10 Rich.Eq., S.C., 358. So held in the case of a charitable trust in Winslow v. Stark, 78 N.H. 135, 97 A. 979.

[49] Bennett v. Bennett, 217 Ill. 434, 75 N.E. 339, 4 L.R.A.,N.S., 470.

by will).⁵⁰ Equity will then, upon application, appoint a new trustee to execute the trust in the place of the trustee who has declined the trust.⁵¹ If two trustees are named in the original settlement, and one rejects the trust, the title to the trust property vests in the other trustee as if the trustee who declines had not been named.⁵²

While acceptance is unnecessary to the validity of the trust, this principle should be carefully distinguished from the doctrine that acceptance of the trust is necessary to the vesting of the title to the trust property in any particular trustee and to the fastening of the trust duties upon him. In order that John Jones may become the owner of the trust property,⁵³ and in order that he may assume the office of trustee,⁵⁴ he must accept the trust and consent to become a trustee. If he declines, the trust will proceed to its execution by another trustee; but it cannot be carried out by him without an express or implied acceptance of its duties on his part.

When the trustee does accept, his title relates back to the time of the creation of the trust, so that he is deemed to have been the owner of the property from the time when the will or deed creating the trust took effect.⁵⁵

It is axiomatic that when a trustee has once accepted the trust he cannot by a later act reject it. Having manifested his intent to assume the trust duties, he can only be relieved of his trust by a resignation or removal, and not by a mere casting off of the

---

⁵⁰ Owens v. Cowan's Heirs, 7 B. Mon., Ky., 152; Cushney v. Henry, 4 Paige, N.Y., 345; Goss v. Singleton, 2 Head, Tenn., 67. In an English case, where the trustee under a deed disclaimed, the court said: "Under these circumstances I think that the trust was really created, and that the fact that the trustee subsequently disclaimed did not destroy the trust, but that upon the revesting the settlor himself held in trust. * * * Mallott v. Wilson, [1903] 2 Ch. 494, 502.

⁵¹ Adams v. Adams, 88 U.S. 185, 21 Wall. 185, 22 L.Ed. 504; Storr's Agr. School v. Whitney, 54 Conn. 342, 8 A. 141; Richardson v. Essex Institute, 208 Mass. 311, 94 N.E. 262, 21 Ann.Cas. 1158; American Academy of Arts and Sciences v. President, etc., of Harvard College, 12 Gray, Mass., 582; Towle v. Nesmith, 69 N.H. 212, 42 A. 900; Stone v. Griffin, 3 Vt. 400.

⁵² In re Kellogg, 214 N.Y. 460, 108 N.E. 844, Ann.Cas.1916D, 1298.

⁵³ F. G. Oxley Stave Co. v. Butler County, 166 U.S. 648, 17 S.Ct. 709, 41 L.Ed. 1149; McFall v. Kirkpatrick, 236 Ill. 281, 86 N.E. 139; Brandon v. Carter, 119 Mo. 572, 24 S.W. 1035, 41 Am.St.Rep. 673.

⁵⁴ Maccubbin v. Cromwell's Ex'rs, 7 Gill & J., Md., 157.

⁵⁵ Stocks v. Inzer, 232 Ala. 482, 168 So. 877; Daley v. Daley, 300 Mass. 17, 14 N.E.2d 113; Christian v. Yancey, 2 Pat. & H., Va., 240.

trust upon his own motion.[56] And, having once disclaimed the trust, the trustee may not thereafter change his mind and accept it.[57] His action of acceptance or renunciation is final. Even though the trust property is realty the trustee may disclaim by parol.[58]

QUALIFICATION BY THE TRUSTEE

38. **In some cases a trustee is required to perform certain acts of qualification, as, for example, to give a bond, take an oath to administer the trust according to law, or receive letters of trusteeship from the court having jurisdiction of the trust.**

   A bond may be required by the court, or may be made compulsory by statute. The settlor may determine whether his trustee is to give a bond or not. Commonly corporate trustees are by statute excused from giving a bond, if they have qualified to do business as a trustee by depositing a security fund with a state officer.

   The courts are not agreed on the effect of failure by a trustee to qualify as required by statute or by court order or settlor's direction.

   In some states taking an oath of office and securing letters of trusteeship is required by statute.

Whether a trustee will be required to give a bond for the faithful performance of his duties is, in the absence of statute, in the discretion of the court of equity. If the character and situation of the trustee seem to render security necessary, the court may require it. If the trust property does not appear to be in any danger, equity may dispense with the bond.[59] Where the trustee is insolvent or of weak or doubtful financial condition, the

---

[56] Cauhape v. Barnes, 135 Cal. 107, 67 P. 55; Hanson v. Worthington, 12 Md. 418; Drury v. Inhabitants of Natick, 10 Allen, Mass., 169; In re Kellogg, 214 N.Y. 460, 108 N.E. 844, Ann.Cas.1916D, 1298; Appeal of Brooke, 109 Pa. 188.

[57] In re Van Schoonhoven, 5 Paige, N.Y., 559; In re Kellogg, 214 N.Y. 460, 108 N.E. 844, Ann.Cas.1916D, 1298.

[58] In re Robinson, 37 N.Y. 261; Read v. Robinson, 6 Watts & S., Pa., 329.

[59] Reeder v. Reeder, 184 Iowa 1, 168 N.W. 122; Dresser v. Dresser, 46 Me. 48; Munroe v. Whitaker, 121 Md. 396, 88 A. 237; Holcomb v. Coryell, 12 N.J.Eq. 289; In re Burke's Estate, 1 N.Y.St.Rep. 316; In re Whitehead, 3 Dem.Sur., N.Y., 227; Strayhorn v. Green, 92 N.C. 119; Ex parte Conrad, 2 Ashm., Pa., 527; Clarke v. Saxon, 1 Hill Eq., S.C., 69; Dunscomb v. Dunscomb, 2 Hen. & M., Va., 11.

court will generally require a bond.⁶⁰ If the trustee is a non-resident of the state having jurisdiction of the trust, the court will be inclined to require security.⁶¹ But if a trustee has been appointed by a Massachusetts court and given bond in that state, it is within the discretion of an Illinois court to relieve the trustee from giving a bond in Illinois.⁶² That the trustee has refused to obey an order of the court,⁶³ or that the cestuis que trust are infants,⁶⁴ may easily influence the court to require security of the trustee.

It is improper for the court to require the trustee to give a bond, when no reason for apprehension as to the safety of the fund exists, and the administration of the trust has been entirely satisfactory.⁶⁵

The settlor may provide in the trust instrument that the trustee shall not be obliged to give a bond, and this direction will be respected by the courts in the absence of extraordinary circumstances.⁶⁶ And in some instances the consent of the cestuis que trust has been held sufficient authority for excusing the trustee from giving security.⁶⁷ The settlor may also provide in the trust instrument that the trustee shall give a bond and state its terms.⁶⁷ᵃ

In many states trustees are required by statute to give bond for the faithful performance of their duties.⁶⁸ It is impossible

---

60 Bailey v. Bailey, 2 Del.Ch. 95; Trabue v. Reynolds, 9 Ky.Law Rep. 360; In re Sears, 5 Dem.Sur., N.Y., 497; In re Deaven's Estate, 32 Pa. Super.Ct. 205.

61 In re Satterthwaite's Estate, 60 N.J.Eq. 347, 47 A. 226; In re Strobel's Estate, 11 Phila., Pa., 122; Gaskill v. Gaskill, 7 R.I. 478; Ex parte Robert, 2 Strob.Eq., S.C., 86.

62 Regan v. West, 115 Ill. 603, 4 N.E. 365.

63 Holcomb v. Coryell, 12 N.J.Eq. 289.

64 In re Jones, 4 Sandf.Ch., N.Y., 615.

65 Crawford v. Creswell, 55 Ala. 497; Ladd v. Ladd, 125 Ala. 135, 27 So. 924; Berry v. Williamson, 11 B. Mon.,Ky., 245; Holcomb v. Coryell, 12 N.J.Eq. 289.

66 Parker v. Sears, 117 Mass. 513; Liesemer v. Burg, 102 Mich. 20, 60 N. W. 290; In re Kelley's Estate, 250 Pa. 177, 95 A. 401; Kerr v. White, 9 Baxt., Tenn., 161.

By Ga.Code 1933, § 108-304, the court may upon the application of the cestui que trust require the trustee to give a bond, even though the trust instrument directs that none shall be required.

67 Dexter v. Cotting, 149 Mass. 92, 21 N.E. 230.

67a Pool v. Potter, 63 Ill. 533.

68 Thiebaud v. Dufour, 54 Ind. 320; Sneer v. Stutz, 102 Iowa 462, 71 N. W. 415; Butler v. Taggart's Trustee, 86 S.W. 541, 27 Ky.Law Rep. 708;

BOGERT TRUSTS 2D—9

here to state the various statutory provisions.[69] It is generally provided that corporate trustees are not required to give a bond, if they have qualified for the administration of trusts by depositing with the state treasurer, or some similar official, a group of securities of a described type, which are to stand as security for the faithful administration of all their trusts.[70]

If the same person be named as executor and trustee, he must give separate bonds for the faithful performance of the duties of each office.[71]

Occasionally it is provided by statute that trustees must qualify by taking an oath to administer their office in a legal manner,[72] and by applying for and receiving from the court letters of

Stevens v. Burgess, 61 Me. 89; Bryan v. Hawthorne, 1 Md. 519; McClernan v. McClernan, 73 Md. 283, 20 A. 908; Coudon v. Updegraf, 117 Md. 71, 83 A. 145; Bullard v. Attorney General, 153 Mass. 249, 26 N.E. 691; Gibney v. Allen, 156 Mich. 301, 120 N.W. 811; Gartside v. Gartside, 113 Mo. 348, 20 S.W. 669; West v. Bailey, 196 Mo. 517, 94 S.W. 273; Fernald v. First Church of Christ, Scientist, in Boston, 77 N.H. 108, 88 A. 705; New York Surrogate's Court Act, § 169; In re Keene's Estate, 81 Pa. 133; Kerr v. White, 9 Baxt., Tenn., 161; Lackland v. Davenport, 84 Va. 638, 5 S.E. 540. In Wisconsin, in the case of testamentary trusts, the giving of a bond is a prerequisite to obtaining title to the trust property. In re Davies' Estate, 161 Wis. 598, 155 N.W. 152. By Wis.St.1941, § 323.01, a bond is required of testamentary trustees.

By Colo. St.Ann.1935, c. 176, § 229, a testamentary trustee is required to give bond, unless the will excuses him.

[69] An extract from a statute may serve as an illustration. The New York rule is now embodied in section 169 of the Surrogate's Court Act, which reads as follows: "Whenever by any last will and testament, or by an order of the Surrogate's Court, a trustee is appointed, or an executor is appointed who is required to hold, manage, or invest any money, securities or property real or personal for the benefit of another, such trustee, or executor, before receiving any such property into his possession or control shall, unless contrary to the express terms of the will, execute to the people of the state of New York, in the usual form, a bond with sufficient surety or sureties in an amount to be fixed by the surrogate. Upon any judicial settlement and partial distribution of such estate or fund the decree may provide for the discharge of the existing bond, and the filing of a new bond covering the amount still remaining in the hands of such executor or trustee. This section shall not affect any executor or trustee named in a will executed before Sept. 1, 1914."

Mass.G.L.(Ter.Ed.), c. 205, § 1, provides the form and contents of the bonds of testamentary trustees of private and public trusts.

[70] See, for example, Butler v. Builders Trust Co., 203 Minn. 555, 282 N.W. 462, 124 A.L.R. 1178; Neb.L.1939, c. 3; Ore.L.1939, pp. 552-553; R.I. L.1938, c. 2584.

[71] Groton v. Ruggles, 17 Me. 137; Williams v. Cushing, 34 Me. 370.

[72] See, for example, Kan.L.1939, c. 180, § 132.

BOGERT TRUSTS 2D

trusteeship which state the qualification of the trustee and his power to act in the particular trust.[73] These features of qualification are, however, not common.

If a trustee fails to qualify as required by any controlling authority, it is sometimes held that he is not a trustee and has no powers under the trust,[74] but other courts hold that if the trustee has accepted the trust his failure to qualify does not affect his powers as trustee, although it is a breach of his duty as trustee not to qualify.[75] Statutes sometimes provide that failure to qualify within a limited period shall be deemed a refusal of the trust.[76]

NECESSITY OF BENEFICIARY[77]

39. No private trust can exist without an identifiable beneficiary. In charitable trusts the public, or some class thereof, constitutes the beneficiary.

It is rudimentary that every private trust must have a cestui que trust.[78] One might as well speak of a contract with but one party as a trust lacking a beneficiary. In the words of Fowler, Surrogate, "to constitute a trust not charitable in nature there must always be a definite person, entitled to enforce the trust or power in trust in equity, and this beneficiary must be ascertained or ascertainable. * * *"[79] Trust creation constitutes a conveyance of an equitable interest in property. There can be no conveyance without a person to receive the interest

---

[73] Public Acts Mich.1939, No. 288, c. IV, §§ 28–32; N.Y.L.1937, c. 596.

[74] Philbin v. Thurn, 103 Md. 342, 63 A. 571; Chappus v. Lucke, 246 Mich. 272, 224 N.W. 432; In Wisconsin the trustee who accepts but fails to qualify seems to get title but no powers. Madler v. Kersten, 170 Wis. 424, 175 N.W. 779.

[75] Pool v. Potter, 63 Ill. 533; Reeder v. Reeder, 184 Iowa 1, 168 N.W. 122. In Ohio a non-qualifying trustee has power to preserve the trust property but not to do any other acts. Gen.Code § 10506-22.

[76] Williams v. Cushing, 34 Me. 370; Attwill v. Dole, 74 N.H. 300, 67 A. 403.

[77] Restatement, Trusts, §§ 2, 66, 364.

[78] Eldridge v. See Yup Co., 17 Cal. 44; Filkins v. Severn, 127 Iowa 738, 104 N.W. 346; Read v. Williams, 54 Hun 636, 8 N.Y.S. 24, judgment modified 125 N.Y. 560, 26 N.E. 730, 21 Am. St.Rep. 748; Wilcox v. Gilchrist, 85 Hun 1, 32 N.Y.S. 608; Boskowitz v. Continental Ins. Co., 175 App.Div. 18, 161 N.Y.S. 680. A declaration of trust by a realty owner, the beneficiaries to be such persons as later buy interests under the trust, is void. Kaufman v. Federal National Bank, 287 Mass. 97, 191 N.E. 422.

[79] Matter of Catlin, 97 Misc. 223, 227, 160 N.Y.S. 1034.

to be conveyed. There can be no equitable ownership without an owner.

The cestui que trust must be described by name, address, relationship, or in such other way that the court can be sure who is the person meant.[80] If the trust is to be enforceable, the court must be able to assure itself that the beneficiaries seeking enforcement are the persons intended by the settlor. If a trust instrument is vague or ambiguous in its naming or description of the cestui, equity cannot enforce the trust,[81] just as uncertainty in any essential part of any legal instrument renders the courts powerless to give it effect. Thus, a trust for certain persons or either of them is too indefinite.[82] But the cestuis que trust may be named as a class, as for example the children of A. at a given time,[83] and the members of the class will be presumed to have equal interests as cestuis.[84] The beneficiaries may also be such members of a class as are selected by the trustee, either in his absolute discretion, or in accordance with a standard fixed by the settlor.[85] Thus, a trust for my grandchildren, with power in the trustee to select any grandchildren he wishes as recipients of the bounty, is valid; as would be a trust for such of my grandchildren as my trustee considers most worthy and deserving.

But a trust to pay the income to any persons in the world, in the discretion of the trustee, is not a valid private trust, the element of vagueness and indefiniteness being considered too great.[86]

---

[80] U. S. v. Oregon & C. R. Co., C.C.Or., 186 F. 861; Barkley v. Lane's Ex'r, 6 Bush., Ky., 587; Isaac v. Emory, 64 Md. 333, 1 A. 713; German Land Ass'n v. Scholler, 10 Minn. 331, Gil. 260; First Presbyterian Soc. of Town of Chili v. Bowen, 21 Hun, N.Y., 389; Ludlam v. Holman, 6 Dem.Sur., N.Y., 194; Jarvis v. Babcock, 5 Barb., N.Y., 139; Appeal of Dyer, 107 Pa. 446.

[81] Oral evidence will not be admitted to prove the settlor's intent as to who were to be the beneficiaries, where the will was ambiguous or silent on that point. Gore v. Bingaman, 29 Cal.App.2d 460, 85 P.2d 172; Ray v. Fowler, Tex.Civ.App., 144 S.W.2d 665.

[82] Wright v. Pond, 10 Conn. 255. But a trust for three named children "or their heirs" is not in the alternative. O'Rourke v. Beard, 151 Mass. 9, 23 N.E. 576.

[83] Heermans v. Schmaltz, C.C.Wis., 7 F. 566.

[84] Loring v. Palmer, 118 U.S. 321, 6 S.Ct. 1073, 30 L.Ed. 211; Cowan v. Henika, 19 Ind.App. 40, 48 N.E. 809.

[85] In re Davis' Estate, 13 Cal.App.2d 64, 56 P.2d 584; Atwater v. Russell, 49 Minn. 57, 51 N.W. 629, 52 N.W. 26; Lundie v. Walker, 126 N.J.Eq. 497, 9 A.2d 783; Hughes v. Jackson, 125 Tex. 130, 81 S.W.2d 656.

[86] Morice v. Bishop of Durham, 9 Ves. 399; Davison v. Wyman, 214

§ 39   NECESSITY OF BENEFICIARY   133

The cestui que trust may be described otherwise than by naming him.[87] "The conveyance in question was to Marvin Hollister in trust for the use and benefit of ———, heirs at law of Seneca M. Conway, deceased, for whom the said Marvin Hollister is legal guardian, party of the second part. One of the principal points in controversy, on the trial below, was as to the sufficiency of this description of the persons beneficially interested, and whether the plaintiffs had shown themselves to be such persons. It is well settled that any description of parties in an instrument of this kind is sufficient, from which the court and jury, aided by a knowledge of surrounding facts and circumstances, are able to say with reasonable certainty that some and what particular persons were intended. It is not necessary that the parties should be described by their names. * * *"[88] It is sufficient that the cestuis become ascertained and definite at the beginning of the trust, and is not required that they be fixed from the date of the trust instrument.[89]

Sometimes there is a rather close question of fact as to whether the settlor's description of the beneficiary is clear and capable of being applied with certainty. Examples are found in the cases where the fund is left in trust for the settlor's best friend,[90] or for such person as has given most care to the settlor in his last years.[91]

Although it is sometimes said that in charitable trusts the beneficiaries must be indefinite persons to be selected later by the trustee, it is believed more accurate to say that such persons are merely the instrumentalities through which the public is to receive benefit, and that the public or some class of it constitutes the real beneficiary. This problem is discussed in a later section.[92]

Mass. 192, 100 N.E. 1105; Forster v. Winfield, 142 N.Y. 327, 37 N.E. 111.

[87] Turner v. Barber, 131 Ga. 444, 62 S.E. 587.

[88] Sydnor v. Palmer, 29 Wis. 226, 241.

[89] Salem Capital Flour Mills Co. v. Stayton Water-Ditch & Canal Co., C.C.Or., 33 F. 146; Heyward-Williams Co. v. McCall, 140 Ga. 502, 79 S.E. 133; Ludlow v. Rector, etc., of St. Johns Church, 144 App.Div. 207, 130

N.Y.S. 679; Ashurst v. Given, 5 Watts & S., Pa., 323.

[90] Early v. Arnold, 119 Va. 500, 89 S.E. 900 (void).

[91] Farley v. Fullerton, 145 Kan. 760, 67 P.2d 525 (valid); In re Utter's Will, 173 Misc. 1069, 20 N.Y.S.2d 457 (valid); In re Long's Estate, 190 Wash. 196, 67 P.2d 331 (person who rendered greatest service to testator during declining period; void).

[92] See § 77, post.

WHO MAY BE A BENEFICIARY[93]

40. Any person, natural or artificial, capable of taking and holding property may be a cestui que trust of a private trust.

Any one may be a cestui que trust who can take the title to property. Disabilities with respect to the management or control of the trust property do not affect the capacity to be a cestui que trust. "Equity subjects trusts to the same construction that a court of law does legal estates. And a donee must have capacity to take, whether it is attempted to convey title directly to the party himself, or to another in trust for him."[94] Under the common law the disability of an alien to hold real property after office found prevented his continuing to be the cestui que trust of a trust of realty.[95] But modern statutes have often decreased this disability to take and hold.[96]

Married women have always been valid cestuis que trust.[97] Minors[98] and lunatics may, of course, hold property, and so may be beneficiaries of a trust. A person yet unborn may be described in a trust instrument as the cestui que trust of a trust to come into effect upon his birth.[99] If the unborn person is the sole beneficiary, the trust does not have existence until the described person is born. Thus, a trust for the possible future wife and children of a bachelor does not begin until there is a marriage, but then automatically springs into existence.[1] It

---

[93] Restatement, Trusts, §§ 116–117.

[94] Trotter v. Blocker, 6 Port., Ala., 269, 305.

[95] Hammekin v. Clayton, Fed.Cas. No. 5,996; Philips v. Crammond, Fed. Cas.No.11,092; Leggett v. Dubois, 5 Paige, N.Y., 114, 28 Am.Dec. 413; Anstice v. Brown, 6 Paige, N.Y., 448; Hubbard v. Goodwin, 3 Leigh, Va., 492.

[96] As a sample statute, see New York Real Property Law, Consol. Laws, c. 50, § 10. Even before the modern change in New York it was held that, under the statute providing that a cestui que trust took no interest in the lands, but merely a right against the trustee, an alien might be a cestui que trust of land. Marx v. McGlynn, 88 N.Y. 357.

[97] Wells v. McCall, 64 Pa. 207; Springer v. Arundel, 64 Pa. 218; Appeal of Ogden, 70 Pa. 501; Pickering v. Coates, 10 Phila., Pa., 65; Appeal of Neale, 104 Pa. 214; Yard v. Pittsburgh & L. E. R. Co., 131 Pa. 205, 18 A. 874.

[98] Turner v. Barber, 131 Ga. 444, 62 S.E. 587.

[99] Easton v. Demuth, 179 Mo.App. 722, 162 S.W. 294; Folk v. Hughes, 100 S.C. 220, 84 S.E. 713.

[1] Morsman v. Commissioner of Internal Revenue, C.C.A., 90 F.2d 18, 113 A.L.R. 441; and see Folk v. Hughes, 100 S.C. 220, 84 S.E. 713; Carson v. Carson, 60 N.C. 575; Ashhurst v. Given, 5 Watts & S., Pa., 323.

was held by some courts that a slave, having no capacity to enforce a trust, could not be a cestui;[2] but other judges expressed the view that such trusts, while not enforceable by the cestuis que trust, might be considered honorary—that is, sanctioned by equity as valid if the trustee saw fit to carry them out.[3]

It is shown elsewhere that trusts for the good of animals generally, because probably of indirect benefit to mankind, are regarded as charitable.[4] But trusts having particular animals as cestuis que trust cannot be regarded as valid and enforceable since the animals are not legal persons who can sue in a court of equity. An English court has held valid a trust for specified horses and dogs on the theory of an honorary trust.[5] A trust to shut up a house,[6] or to keep a clock in repair,[7] being for the benefit of an inanimate object, lacks a proper cestui que trust, and fails. A trust to erect or care for a monument lacks a living beneficiary, and ought to fail as a private trust.[8] Its aspects as a charitable trust have been discussed elsewhere.[9] And trusts for masses as private trusts are for the benefit of deceased persons, and not sustainable on principle.[10] They are generally valid charities.[11]

The state may be a cestui que trust,[12] as may a corporation, if the purpose of the trust is within its corporate powers.[13] A joint-stock company,[14] a school district,[15] and a tribe of Indians [16]

---

[2] Bynum v. Bostick, 4 Desaus., S.C., 266; Blakely v. Tisdale, 14 Rich.Eq., S.C., 90.

[3] Cleland v. Waters, 19 Ga. 35; American Colonization Soc. v. Gartrell, 23 Ga. 448; Shaw v. Ward, 175 N.C. 192, 95 S.E. 164. In the case in 23 Ga. Lumpkin, J., said: "That many trusts are valid if executed by the trustee that cannot be carried into effect compulsorily I have no doubt." Page 456.

[4] Post, § 82.

[5] In re Dean, 41 Ch.Div. 552.
On this same theory a trust to promote fox hunting has been held valid, in the sense that the trustee may carry it out. In re Thompson, [1934] 1 Ch. 342.

[6] Brown v. Burdett, Wkly. Notes, 1882, 134.

[7] Kelly v. Nichols, 17 R.I. 306, 21 A. 906.

[8] Gilmer's Legatees v. Gilmer's Ex'rs, 42 Ala. 9.

[9] Post, § 80.

[10] In re Schouler, 134 Mass. 426.

[11] Post, § 79.

[12] Neilson v. Lagow, 12 How. 98, 13 L.Ed. 909.

[13] Sheldon v. Chappel, 47 Hun, N.Y., 59; Adams v. Perry, 43 N.Y. 487; Frazier v. St. Luke's Church, 147 Pa. 256, 23 A. 442.

[14] Hart v. Seymour, 147 Ill. 598, 35 N.E. 246.

[15] In re Sayre's Will, 179 App.Div. 269, 166 N.Y.S. 499.

[16] Ruddick v. Albertson, 154 Cal. 640, 98 P. 1045.

have been held to be qualified to act as beneficiaries. "At common law, it is true, a deed of conveyance to an unincorporated voluntary association was bad for lack of a capable grantee, and cases will be found which hold that, where the grantee could not take directly, he or it cannot take through the medium of a trustee. But from this grew an abuse which equity was prompt to remedy. So that it is now recognized that a valid grant may be made to trustees for such an unincorporated voluntary association, and that such title will descend in perpetuity." [17]

It is not necessary that the beneficiary be incompetent or subnormal,[18] in the absence of a statute restricting trusts to such persons.[19] The settlor may also be the sole cestui que trust or one among other cestuis que trust,[20] if he does not thereby commit a fraud upon his creditors.[21] The possibility that a trustee may also be a cestui que trust has been discussed elsewhere.[22] Subject to the chance of merger[23] if he be the sole trustee and sole cestui que trust, and to the further possibility

---

[17] Ruddick v. Albertson, 154 Cal. 640, 644, 98 P. 1045. In re Clarke, [1901] 2 Ch. 110; In re Drummond, [1914] 2 Ch. 90; Austin v. Shaw, 10 Allen, Mass., 552; Sangston v. Gordon, 22 Grat., Va., 755, accord. The older view is represented by Kain v. Gibboney, 101 U.S. 362, 25 L.Ed. 813; German Land Ass'n v. Scholler, 10 Minn. 331, Gil. 260; King v. Townshend, 141 N.Y. 358, 36 N.E. 513. A trust for an unincorporated village was sustained in Miller v. Rosenberger, 144 Mo. 292, 46 S.W. 167. And see Furniture Workers' Union Local 1007 v. United Brotherhood of Carpenters and Joiners of America, 6 Wash.2d 654, 108 P.2d 651 (labor union valid cestui).

[18] Appeal of Ogden, 70 Pa. 501; Appeal of Williams, 83 Pa. 377.

Indians may be the beneficiaries of a trust. Chippewa Indians of Minnesota v. United States, 301 U.S. 358, 57 S.Ct. 826, 81 L.Ed. 1156.

[19] In Georgia a statute permits trusts for incompetents only, with one exception. Lester v. Stephens, 113 Ga. 495, 39 S.E. 109; Armour Fertilizer Works v. Lacy, 146 Ga. 196, 91 S.E. 12; Clark v. Baker, 186 Ga. 65, 196 S.E. 750.

See § 70, post.

[20] Lawrence v. Lawrence, 181 Ill. 248, 54 N.E. 918; Foster v. Coe, 4 Lans., N.Y., 53; Colvin v. Martin, 68 App.Div. 633, 74 N.Y.S. 11; Appeal of Ashhurst, 77 Pa. 464.

[21] Hackley v. Littell, 150 Mich. 106, 113 N.W. 787; Sloan v. Birdsall, 58 Hun, 317, 11 N.Y.S. 814. And see post, § 45, regarding spendthrift trusts.

[22] See ante, § 33.

[23] Shope v. Unknown Claimants, 174 Iowa 662, 156 N.W. 850; Smith v. Smith, 194 Mo.App. 309, 188 S.W. 1111; McAfee v. Green, 143 N.C. 411, 55 S.E. 828; Lee v. Oates, 171 N.C. 717, 88 S.E. 889, Ann.Cas.1917A, 514. But an expressed intent contra may prevent merger. Highland Park Mfg. Co. v. Steele, S.C., 235 F. 465, 149 C.C.A. 11; Bowlin v. Citizens' Bank & Trust Co., 131 Ark. 97, 198 S.W. 288, 2 A.L.R. 575.

of being removed because of a disqualification to act as a trustee when his own interest as cestui que trust is concerned, the trustee may be named as cestui que trust.[24]

The beneficiary of a trust is the one intended by the settlor to receive the direct benefit of the trust property, and not one who incidentally in the course of the trust administration receives an advantage.[25] Thus, where a trust is created for the support of a person who is mentally incompetent and a pauper, the town where the pauper lives is not a beneficiary of the trust, although support of the pauper by trust money will to some extent relieve the town from a burden to support the pauper which it would otherwise have.[26]

ACCEPTANCE BY THE BENEFICIARY[27]

41. Acceptance of a trust by the beneficiary is necessary, but it is presumed until a disclaimer is shown. Upon learning of the creation of a trust in his favor the beneficiary may decline the trust. Acceptance or rejection may be manifested expressly or by conduct which impliedly shows the attitude of the beneficiary.

No man can be compelled to become the owner of property.[28] The transferee must assent.[29] The creation of a trust involves the transfer of property rights to the cestui. It follows that acceptance of the trust by the beneficiary must occur before the trust will be final,[30] just as the buyer of real property must acquiesce in the deed to him before the grantor's title will pass to him.

But the law presumes that the transferee of beneficial property rights accepts them. Commonly the rights of cestui que trust are purely beneficial and not burdensome. Hence, in the ordinary trust, there is a presumption that the cestui que trust assents to the trust. No express proof of acceptance of the

---

[24] Summers v. Higley, 191 Ill. 193, 60 N.E. 969.

[25] Brennan v. Vogler, 174 Mass. 272, 54 N.E. 556; Sapp v. Houston Nat. Exch. Bank, Tex.Com.App., 266 S.W. 141.

[26] Town of Sharon v. Simons, 30 Vt. 458.

[27] Restatement, Trusts, § 36.

[28] An exception must be made where title passes by operation of law.

[29] Tiffany on Real Property, § 463.

[30] Libby v. Frost, 98 Me. 288, 56 A. 906; Bailey v. Worster, 103 Me. 170, 68 A. 698; Cunniff v. McDonnell, 196 Mass. 7, 81 N.E. 879.

trust is necessary.[31] But, if the gift of the trust interest imposes onerous conditions, the consent of the beneficiary will not be presumed.[32]

This presumption of acceptance of the trust by the cestui may be overcome by evidence of rejection and refusal to take the property interest which is tendered.[33]

If the refusal to accept the trust occurs before the attempt of the settlor to create it, no trust will ever arise, and the settlor will remain the absolute owner of the property. If the disclaimer of the trust by the beneficiary takes place after the acts of the settlor necessary to the creation of the trust have been performed, the title to the trust property will be in the settlor. The disclaimer will relate back to the date of attempted trust creation, and the beneficiary be deemed never to have had any interest in the trust property.[34]

A beneficiary must accept or reject the entire trust. He cannot accept part of the trust and reject the remainder.[35]

An infant beneficiary is not required to accept or reject the trust until a reasonable time after he reaches his majority.[36]

Acceptance or disclaimer may be express, as where the beneficiary states orally or in writing that he accepts or declines the trust; or it may be by implication, as where the cestui makes no direct statement but takes the benefits of the trust when they are tendered to him after he knows of the existence of the trust.

---

[31] O'Brien v. Bank of Douglas, 17 Ariz. 203, 149 P. 747; Barr v. Schroeder, 32 Cal. 609; Brunson v. Henry, 140 Ind. 455, 39 N.E. 256; Devol v. Dye, 123 Ind. 321, 24 N.E. 246, 7 L.R.A. 439; Lewis v. Curnutt, 130 Iowa 423, 106 N.W. 914; Libby v. Frost, 98 Me. 288, 56 A. 906; Thorp v. Lund, 227 Mass. 474, 116 N.E. 946, Ann.Cas.1918B, 1204; Suydam v. Dequindre, Har., Mich., 347; H. B. Cartwright & Bro. v. United States Bank & Trust Co., 23 N.M. 82, 167 P. 436; Stone v. King, 7 R. I. 358, 84 Am.Dec. 557; Cloud v. Calhoun, 10 Rich.Eq., S.C., 358; Furman v. Fisher, 4 Cold., Tenn., 626, 94 Am.Dec. 210; Fleenor v. Hensley, 121 Va. 367, 93 S.E. 582; In re Duwe's Estate, 229 Wis. 115, 281 N.W. 669.

[32] Kemp v. Porter, 7 Ala. 138.

[33] Gwynn v. Gwynn, 11 App.D.C. 564; Lytle's Ex'r v. Pope's Adm'r, 11 B.Mon., Ky., 297; Breedlove v. Stump, 3 Yerg., Tenn., 257.

[34] Jervis v. Wolferstan, 18 Eq. 18.

[35] Bacon v. Barber, 110 Vt. 280, 6 A.2d 9, 123 A.L.R. 253.

[36] Bacon v. Barber, 110 Vt. 280, 6 A.2d 9, 123 A.L.R. 253.

NATURE OF BENEFICIARY'S INTEREST

42. While legal scholars have disagreed as to whether the right of cestui que trust is in personam, in rem, or partly both, the modern tendency is to give the right of cestui que trust incidents which make it, not only a right against the trustee to have the trust carried out, but also the equivalent of ownership of the trust res in equity.

Whether cestui que trust's rights are in rem or in personam has been the subject of much discussion among legal scholars. Rights in rem have been defined as: "Rights residing in persons, and availing against other persons generally. * * * The duties which correlate with rights *in rem* are always *negative;* that is to say, they are duties to forbear or abstain." And rights in personam have been thus described: "Rights residing in persons, and availing *exclusively* against persons specifically determinate. * * * Of the obligations which correlate with rights *in personam, some* are negative, but *some* (and *most*) are *positive;* that is to say, obligations to do or perform."[37]

Is the cestui que trust the owner merely of a claim against the trustee to have the trust carried out, or the equitable owner of the trust property, or do his rights combine both a right against the trustee and an ownership of the trust res, good against the world? The theory of a right in personam is supported by Holland,[38] Maitland,[39] Langdell,[40] Ames,[41] and some present-day writers,[42] the equitable title hypothesis is maintained by Salmond,[43] while several able recent authors in the field of trusts have argued that the cestui has both a right against the trustee and an ownership of the trust res.[44]

The terminology used by the courts will be of little guidance. Some have called the right of the cestui que trust an "equita-

[37] 1 Austin on Jurisprudence, 5th Ed., 370, 371.

[38] Jurisprudence, 13th Ed., 246 et seq.

[39] Equity, 111–155.

[40] Brief Survey of Equity Jurisdiction, 1 Harv.Law Rev. 59, 60.

[41] Cases on Trusts, 2d Ed., 244–281.

[42] See, for example, Harlan F. Stone, The Nature of the Rights of the Cestui que Trust, 17 Col.Law Rev. 467.

[43] Jurisprudence, 278–282.

[44] Roscoe Pound, 26 Harv.Law Rev. 462; Huston, The Enforcement Decrees in Equity, 138; Scott, The Nature of the Rights of Cestui que Trust, 17 Col. Law Rev. 269; Whitlock, Classification of the Law of Trusts, 1 Cal.Law Rev. 215.

ble estate,"[45] some an "equitable fee,"[46] others an "equitable title,"[47] and others "absolute ownership in equity,"[48] or even an "equitable lien";[49] while yet other judges have described the right as only a right to enforce the trust against the trustee.[50] In several states there are statutes purporting to adopt the in personam theory and to declare the cestui que trust the owner of no interest or estate in the trust property.[51] The incidents

[45] Dunkerson v. Goldberg, Mo., 162 F. 120, 89 C.C.A. 120; Honnett v. Williams, 66 Ark. 148, 49 S.W. 495; Leigh v. Laughlin, 211 Ill. 192, 71 N.E. 881; McFall v. Kirkpatrick, 236 Ill. 281, 86 N.E. 139; Handy v. McKim, 64 Md. 560, 4 A. 125; Mercer v. Safe-Deposit & Trust Co., 91 Md. 102, 45 A. 865; Wood v. Kice, 103 Mo. 329, 15 S.W. 623; Knowlton v. Atkins, 134 N.Y. 313, 31 N.E. 914; Appeal of Fowler, 125 Pa. 388, 17 A. 431, 11 Am.St.Rep. 902; Citizens' Nat. Bank v. Watkins, 126 Tenn. 453, 150 S.W. 96; Hutchinson v. Maxwell, 100 Va. 169, 40 S.E. 655, 57 L.R.A. 384, 93 Am.St.Rep. 944; Bank of Berkeley Springs v. Green, 45 W.Va. 168, 31 S.E. 260.

[46] Durant v. Muller, 88 Ga. 251, 14 S.E. 612; Laughlin v. Page, 108 Me. 307, 80 A. 753; Reardon v. Reardon, 192 Mass. 448, 78 N.E. 430; Cornwell v. Orton, 126 Mo. 355, 27 S.W. 536; Wright v. Miller, 4 Barb., N.Y., 600; Davis v. Heppert, 96 Va. 775, 32 S.E. 467.

[47] Hallowell Sav. Inst. v. Titcomb, 96 Me. 62, 51 A. 249; Mathias v. Fowler, 124 Md. 655, 93 A. 298; Blake v. O'Neal, 63 W.Va. 483, 61 S.E. 410, 16 L.R.A.,N.S., 1147.

[48] Ex parte Jonas, 186 Ala. 567, 64 So. 960; Badgett v. Keating, 31 Ark. 400; Ellsworth College of Iowa Falls v. Emmet County, 156 Iowa 52, 135 N.W. 594, 42 L.R.A.,N.S., 530.

[49] In re Hart's Estate, 203 Pa. 503, 53 A. 373.

[50] United States v. Devereux, N.C., 90 F. 182, 32 C.C.A. 564; Southern Pac. R. R. Co. v. Doyle, C.C.Cal., 11 F. 253; Fortner v. Phillips, 124 Ark. 395, 187 S.W. 318; Hunt v. Hunt, 124 Mich. 502, 83 N.W. 371; McCosker v. Brady, 1 Barb.Ch., N.Y., 329; Bennett v. Garlock, 79 N.Y. 302, 35 Am.Rep. 517; Cheyney v. Geary, 194 Pa. 427, 45 A. 369.

[51] Civ.Code Cal. § 863; New York Real Property Law, Consol.Laws, c. 51 § 100. For cases construing the latter statute, see Crooke v. County of Kings, 97 N.Y. 421; Schenck v. Barnes, 156 N.Y. 316, 50 N.E. 967, 41 L.R.A. 395; Newton v. Hunt, 134 App.Div. 325, 119 N.Y.S. 3, affirmed in 201 N.Y. 599, 95 N.E. 1134. In Marx v. McGlynn, 88 N.Y. 357, it was held an alien might be a cestui que trust of a real property trust, although an alien could not then hold title to land. The court said (page 376): "The fact that Bradley is an alien does not incapacitate him from receiving the income. He had no interest in the real estate. The income does not come to him as real estate or even as an incident of real estate. It comes to him as personal property. The title, both legal and equitable, is in the trustee, and it is expressly provided that a beneficiary or cestui que trust in such a case takes no interest in the lands, but has the simple right to enforce the performance of the trust in equity."

For a literal following of the wording of the New York statute, see Archer-Shee v. Garland, 144 L.T. 508.

which the decisions give to the cestui's right and their bearing on its actual nature will be treated in later sections.

The advocates of the in personam position claim:

(a) That the rights of the cestui que trust are not enforceable against the whole world, since a bona fide purchaser of the trust res from the trustee is excepted, and therefore, from the very definition of a right in rem, the cestui's right cannot be in rem; but in reply it is shown that many rights admittedly in rem are cut off by transfers to bona fide purchasers, as for example, in cases of sales in market overt, sales of realty where a second deed is recorded before the first, negotiations of negotiable paper, sales by a fraudulent vendee of personal property, sales by a seller left in possession of personal property, sales by agents having apparent authority to sell, and sales by conditional vendees of goods when the contract has not been filed or recorded; and it is also answered that where the trust res is an equitable interest in property and the trustee sells it to a bona fide purchaser, the right of the cestui que trust is not cut off, showing that at least in that instance the cestui has a right in rem; and it is further alleged that the bona fide purchaser rule regarding trusts is based on the respect of equity for the legal title and on the commercial expediency of having property easily transferable, that is, that such rule is a mere exception to the general rule that the cestui que trust has a right to the trust res enforceable against all the world.

(b) It is said that equity acts in personam, and the cestui's right, being admittedly equitable, must be in personam; to which the reply is that the nature of a right is not necessarily determined by the nature of the remedy given for its enforcement, and that modern statutes give equity almost generally power to act in rem, and to transfer title or possession directly in case the trustee refuses to obey a decree.[52]

(c) The impossibility of two persons owning the same thing is also urged as favorable to the in personam theory; but to this reply has been made that one may be the legal owner of a thing and a second the equitable owner, and that both law and

---

The Minnesota act (§ 8095) has been held not to prevent the beneficiary's interest from being devised. First & American Nat. Bank of Duluth v. Higgins, 208 Minn. 295, 293 N.W. 585.

[52] See Huston, The Enforcement of Decrees in Equity, appendix, for a list of statutes giving chancery power to act in rem and transfer title.

equity regard the trustee as the legal owner and the beneficiary as the equitable proprietor.

(d) Finally, it is urged that the duties which the trustee owes to the cestui que trust are positive and characteristic of rights in personam, while the obligations to the holder of a right in rem are always negative, merely to refrain from action. The answer is that the trustee has positive duties of management, and also negative duties to refrain from treating the trust res as his private property or acting in his own interest, and that these latter duties attach to the general public also in part.

In support of the contention that the cestui's rights are in rem, rights of ownership, it has been shown: (a) That, if the trust res be realty, curtesy and dower attach to the cestui's interest; (b) that his interest descends to heirs at law or personal representatives, dependent on whether the trust res is realty or personalty; (c) that, if the res is real, escheat operates on the cestui's rights; (d) that the cestui's powers of alienation show him to be an owner of the res; (e) that a disseisor of the trustee does not take the property free from the trust; (f) that creditors of the cestui que trust may take the trust res; (g) that a trust may be created without consideration, thus partaking more of the nature of a grant than of a contract; (h) that the modern tendency is to preserve the rights of cestui que trust even after the trustee is barred by the statute of limitations; (i) that the trustee's interest is purely formal and gives rise to no beneficial incidents to his wife as a dowress, to his creditors, or to the crown or state in case of forfeiture or escheat.

The situation would seem to be summarized by the statement that, while the right of cestui que trust was originally purely in personam against the trustee, it has become increasingly a right in rem and is now substantially equivalent to equitable ownership of the trust res. The cestui que trust, of course, also has rights in personam against the trustee. Speaking of a transfer by the beneficiary of his interest under the trust, the Supreme Court of the United States has recently stated: "The assignment of the beneficial interest is not the assignment of a chose in action but of the 'right, title, and estate in and to the property'."[53]

Where the subject-matter of the trust is realty the trust instrument sometimes provides that the interest of the beneficiary

---

[53] Blair v. Commissioner of Internal Revenue, 300 U.S. 5, 57 S.Ct. 330, 81 L.Ed. 465.

shall be considered personal property, and that he shall have no interest in the realty but merely in the proceeds of the realty and its income. Such clauses are respected and enforced by the courts.[54]

INCIDENTS OF THE BENEFICIARY'S INTEREST[55]

43. Upon the cestui que trust's death his interest passes to his heirs or devisees, if the trust property was realty, and to his administrator or executor, if the trust property was personalty.

The interest of the cestui que trust escheats to the state on his death intestate without heirs or next of kin.

Curtesy and dower are incidents of the beneficiary's interest, in states where those rights still exist.

The beneficiary's interest may be made the subject of a homestead claim, when the trust res is realty.

The rule in Shelley's Case operates on the equitable interest of cestui que trust, just as it would on a corresponding legal estate.

In the absence of lawful provision in the trust instrument restraining him from alienating his interest, or of statutory restraint on alienation, cestui que trust may transfer his rights inter vivos or by will, as freely as he could a legal estate.

The interest of cestui que trust passes to his heirs at law or personal representatives, dependent on the nature of the property held in trust, if the cestui dies intestate and his interest is to continue beyond his life.[56] From this rule it would appear that the cestui que trust has a property right in the trust property, since the nature of the latter determines the course of devolution of the cestui's interest. "In the case at bar, these legatees took no legal interest in the real property. Their interest in the body of the estate, so far as the matter is now before us for determination, is an equitable one, and equitable estates are governed by

---

[54] Wright v. Security-First Nat. Bank of Los Angeles, 35 Cal.App.2d 264, 95 P.2d 194; Duncanson v. Lill, 322 Ill. 528, 153 N.E. 618; Kountze v. Smith, 135 Tex. 543, 144 S.W.2d 261.

[55] Restatement, Trusts, §§ 132–163.

[56] Shackleford v. Elliott, 209 Ill. 333, 70 N.E. 745; Doran v. Kennedy, 122 Minn. 1, 141 N.W. 851; Boone v. Davis, 64 Miss. 133, 8 So. 202; Bredell v. Collier, 40 Mo. 287; Gill's Heirs v. Logan's Heirs, 11 B. Mon., Ky., 231; Glynn v. Maxfield, 75 N.H. 482, 76 A. 196; Cordon v. Gregg, 164 Or. 306, 97 P.2d 732, 101 P.2d 414; Lamb v. First Huntington Nat. Bank., W.Va., 7 S.E.2d 441.

the same rules of descent that govern the duration of legal estates." [57]

Escheat

The early rule in England was that the interest of cestui que trust did not escheat to the crown, but that the trustee held the property free from a trust.[58] A statute now provides for escheat of the beneficiary's interest.[59] In America the interest of the cestui, whether the trust res be real or personal, passes to the state on the death of the cestui without heirs or next of kin.[60] While technically escheat applies only to realty, an analogous principle has been introduced with respect to personal property. "From this review of the law it would seem that there is no substantial difference between real and personal property in respect to the rights acquired by the state, upon the death of its owner intestate, without heirs or next of kin. A clear deduction from the authorities seems to lead to the conclusion that the doctrine of escheat applies only to legal estates, and does not in a strict sense affect either equitable estates or personal property. It seems also to follow from the authorities cited, that upon the death of Ellen Spicer [the cestui que trust] the state took not the land, but succeeded to the equitable right which she had to a conveyance thereof." [61] While the result would be the same whether the interest of the beneficiary were regarded as a property right in the trust res or as a mere claim against the trustee, since both would pass to the state, regardless of the nature of the trust property, yet the courts have discussed the cases where the trust property was realty upon the theory that the equitable estate of the cestui que trust passed to the state by technical escheat; that is, as real property.

---

[57] Lich v. Lich, 158 Mo.App. 400, 138 S.W. 558, 562.

[58] Burgess v. Wheate, 1 Wm. Blackstone, 123.

[59] St. 47 & 48 Vict. c. 71, § 4.

[60] United States v. Klein, C.C.A.Pa., 106 F.2d 213; In re Williams' Estate, 37 Cal.App.2d 181, 99 P.2d 349; Matthews v. Ward, 10 Gill & J., Md., 443; Scott v. Gittings, 125 Md. 595,
94 A. 209 (dictum); Johnston v. Spicer, 107 N.Y. 185, 13 N.E. 753; Commonwealth v. Naile, 88 Pa. 429; In re Linton's Estate, 198 Pa. 438, 48 A. 298.

[61] Johnston v. Spicer, 107 N.Y. 185, 200, 13 N.E. 753. The right of cestui que trust is declared by statute in New York to be a mere right to the enforcement of the trust. Real Property Law, Consol.Laws, c. 51, § 100.

Curtesy and Dower

If a wife has been cestui que trust of a fee-simple interest in real property, her widower is now generally given curtesy in the trust res.[62] This can only be on the theory of an equitable property right by the wife in the trust res. If she owned a mere claim to have the trust enforced, her interest would be personal property, regardless of the subject-matter of the trust, and so not subject to curtesy. If the wife's interest as cestui was a separate estate in equity, the prevailing view is that curtesy arises in favor of the surviving husband,[63] unless a contrary intent appears in the trust instrument.[64] The exclusion of the husband from interest in or control of the property is deemed to be limited to the period of coverture.

The widow of cestui que trust was not entitled to dower in England[65] until the passage of a comparatively recent statute.[66] In America a few states follow the old English rule and refuse the widow dower,[67] but either by virtue of statute or by common law the incident of dower attaches to the estate of the cestui que trust in a great majority of American states.[68] In some states it is only

[62] Robison v. Codman, Fed.Cas.No. 11,970; Ogden v. Ogden, 60 Ark. 70, 28 S.W. 796, 46 Am.St.Rep. 151; Jackson v. Becktold Printing & Book Mfg. Co., 86 Ark. 591, 112 S.W. 161, 20 L.R.A.,N.S., 454; Payne v. Payne, 11 B.Mon., Ky., 138; Rawlings v. Adams, 7 Md. 26; Richardson v. Stodder, 100 Mass. 528; Alexander v. Warrance, 17 Mo. 228; Donovan v. Griffith, 215 Mo. 149, 114 S.W. 621, 20 L.R.A.,N.S., 825, 128 Am.St.Rep. 458, 15 Ann.Cas. 724; Cushing v. Blake, 30 N.J.Eq. 689; Sentill v. Robeson, 55 N.C. 510; Hunt v. Satterwhite, 85 N.C. 73; Lowry's Lessee v. Steele, 4 Ohio 170; Dubs v. Dubs, 31 Pa. 149; Carson v. Fuhs, 131 Pa. 256, 18 A. 1017; Tillinghast v. Coggeshall, 7 R.I. 383; Baker v. Heiskell, 1 Cold., Tenn., 641; Norman's Ex'x v. Cunningham, 5 Grat., Va., 63. But see (Hall v. Crabb, 56 Neb. 392, 76 N.W. 865; In re Grandjean's Estate, 78 Neb. 349, 110 N.W. 1108, 15 Ann.Cas. 577.

[63] Luntz v. Greve, 102 Ind. 173, 26 N.E. 128; Cushing v. Blake, 29 N.J. Eq. 399; Ege v. Medlar, 82 Pa. 86; In re Steinmetz's Estate, 3 Pa.Dist.R. 440. *Contra:* Cochran v. O'Hern, 4 Watts & S., Pa., 95, 39 Am.Dec. 60; Stokes v. McKibbin, 13 Pa. 267; Ash v. Ash, 1 Phila., Pa., 176; Jones v. Jones' Ex'r, 96 Va. 749, 32 S.E. 463.

[64] Frey v. Allen, 9 App.D.C. 400; Tremmel v. Kleiboldt, 6 Mo.App. 549; McTigue v. McTigue, 116 Mo. 138, 22 S.W. 501; Woodward v. Woodward, 148 Mo. 241, 49 S.W. 1001; McBreen v. McBreen, 154 Mo. 323, 55 S.W. 463, 77 Am.St.Rep. 758; Jamison v. Zausch, 227 Mo. 406, 126 S.W. 1023, 21 Ann.Cas. 1132; McCulloch v. Valentine, 24 Neb. 215, 38 N.W. 854; Ball v. Ball, 20 R.I. 520, 40 A. 234.

[65] D'Arcy v. Blake, 2 Sch. & Lef. 387.

[66] St. 3 & 4 Wm. IV, c. 105.

[67] Seaman v. Harmon, 192 Mass. 5, 78 N.E. 301; Hopkinson v. Dumas, 42 N.H. 296.

[68] Bush v. Bush, 5 Del.Ch. 144; Ill. Smith-Hurd Stats. c. 41, § 1; Mo. Rev.St.1939, § 318; N.J.S.A. 3:37–1.

BOGERT TRUSTS 2D—10

when the husband was a cestui que trust at his death that the widow is endowed.[69] That dower attaches as an incident to the cestui's right where the res is real property shows the tendency of modern law to treat the cestui's interest as a property right in the res.

An equitable owner of land may establish a homestead in his interest.[70] The cases arising have generally been those of contract vendees, but there seems to be no reason to differentiate the cestui que trust. If so, the rule is strong evidence that his interest is treated as a property right in land, when the trust res is land.

Where a trustee holds in trust for A. for life, with a remainder in trust for A.'s heirs, the rule in Shelley's Case applies and A. will become the owner of an equitable fee.[71] Some courts have held that the rule would not be applied in the case of active trusts, where to apply it would defeat the testator's intent.[72] The application of the rule is strongly confirmatory of the modern view that the cestui's interest is an estate in the res.

Power to Alienate

In the absence of provisions in the trust instrument or statutes to the contrary, the cestui que trust may alienate his interest as freely as he might a legal estate or interest.[73] "The law, how-

---

[69] Lugar v. Lugar, 160 App.Div. 807, 146 N.Y.S. 37; Tenn.Code 1938, § 8351.

[70] Rockafellow v. Peay, 40 Ark. 69; Allen v. Hawley, 66 Ill. 164; Hewitt v. Rankin, 41 Iowa 35; Moore v. Reaves, 15 Kan. 150; Tarrant v. Swain, 15 Kan. 146; Wilder v. Haughey, 21 Minn. 101; Jelinek v. Stepan, 41 Minn. 412, 43 N.W. 90; Smith v. Chenault, 48 Tex. 455; Doane's Ex'r v. Doane, 46 Vt. 485.

[71] Sutliff v. Aydelott, 373 Ill. 633, 27 N.E.2d 529; Cushing v. Blake, 30 N.J.Eq. 689; Boyd v. Small, 56 N.C. 39; Mack v. Champion, 26 Wkly. Law Bul., Ohio, 113; Crosby v. Davis, 4 Pa.Law J. 193; Carson v. Fuhs, 131 Pa. 256, 18 A. 1017; Danner v. Trescot, 5 Rich.Eq., S.C., 356.

[72] Berry v. Williamson, 11 B.Mon., Ky., 245; Porter v. Doby, 2 Rich.Eq., S.C., 49.

[73] Drennen v. Heard, D.C.Ga., 198 F. 414; Honnett v. Williams, 66 Ark. 148, 49 S.W. 495; Rea v. Steamboat Eclipse, 4 Dak. 218, 30 N.W. 159; Security Trust & Safe Deposit Co. v. Martin, 10 Del.Ch. 330, 92 A. 245; Hiss v. Hiss, 228 Ill. 414, 81 N.E. 1056; Nelson v. Davis, 35 Ind. 474; Martin v. Davis, 82 Ind. 38; Parkhill v. Doggett, 150 Iowa 442, 130 N.W. 411; Bayer v. Cockerill, 3 Kan. 282; Beuley v. Curtis, 92 Ky. 505, 18 S.W. 357; Brain v. Bailey, 82 S.W. 582, 26 Ky.Law Rep. 853; Palmer v. Stevens, 15 Gray, Mass., 343; Young v. Snow, 167 Mass. 287, 45 N.E. 686; Security Bank of New York v. Callahan, 220 Mass. 84, 107 N.E. 385; Boston Safe Deposit & Trust Co. v. Luke, 220 Mass. 484, 108 N.E. 64, L.R.A.1917A, 988; Dibrell v. Carlisle, 51 Miss. 785; Kingman v. Winchell, Mo., 20 S.W. 296; Ryland v. Banks, 151 Mo. 11, 51

ever, is perfectly settled that the estate of a cestui que trust may be conveyed as well as any other." [74] He may join with the trustee and transfer the whole title, legal and equitable.[75] The consent of the trustee is not necessary to the conveyance by the cestui of his interest, unless the trust instrument provides otherwise.[76] Cestui que trust may convey to a co-cestui,[77] or to the trustee,[78] although in the latter case the transaction will be voidable by the cestui unless it was entirely fair and above board. This power of alienation exists in the cestui que trust of an implied as well as an express trust.[79] Some courts have gone so far as to allow the beneficiary to vest absolute title to the trust res in another, free and clear of the trust.[80]

The interest of cestui que trust may also be devised,[81] mortgaged, or incumbered,[82] and made the subject of a gift.[83]

[74] Elliott v. Armstrong, 2 Blackf., Ind., 198, 208.

S.W. 720; Freeman v. Maxwell, 262 Mo. 13, 170 S.W. 1150; Converse v. Noyes, 66 N.H. 570, 22 A. 556; Rogers v. Colt, 21 N.J.L., 704; McCrea v. Yule, 68 N.J.L. 465, 53 A. 210; Camden Safe Deposit & Trust Co. v. Schellenger, 78 N.J.Eq. 138, 78 A. 672; Jenkinson v. New York Finance Co., 79 N.J.Eq. 247, 82 A. 36; Branch v. Griffin, 99 N.C. 173, 5 S.E. 393, 398; Cherry v. Cape Fear Power Co., 142 N.C. 404, 55 S.E. 287; Sayles v. Tibbitts, 5 R.I. 79; Ives v. Harris, 7 R.I. 413; Henson v. Wright, 88 Tenn. 501, 12 S.W. 1035; Mortimer v. Jackson, Tex.Civ.App., 155 S.W. 341; Burnett v. Hawpe's Ex'r, 25 Grat., Va., 481; Morgan v. Morgan, 60 W.Va. 327, 55 S.E. 389, 9 Ann.Cas. 943; Lamberton v. Pereles, 87 Wis. 449, 58 N.W. 776, 23 L.R.A. 824; Mangan v. Shea, 158 Wis. 619, 149 N.W. 378. The power of alienation is not handicapped by the contingent nature of the beneficiary's interest. Brown v. Fletcher, C.C.A.N.Y. 253 F. 15, 165 C.C.A. 35.

A beneficiary may sell or give away part of his interest. Blair v. Commissioner of Internal Revenue, 300 U.S. 5, 57 S.Ct. 330, 81 L.Ed. 465.

[75] Jones v. Jones, 111 Md. 700, 77 A. 270.

[76] Foster v. Friede, 37 Mo. 36.

[77] Murry v. King, 153 Mo.App. 710, 135 S.W. 107.

[78] Sprague v. Moore, 130 Mich. 92, 89 N.W. 712; People's Trust Co. v. Harman, 43 App.Div. 348, 60 N.Y.S. 178.

[79] Sinclair v. Gunzenhauser, 179 Ind. 78, 98 N.E. 37, 100 N.E. 376; Buck v. Swazey, 35 Me. 41, 56 Am. Dec. 681; Osgood v. Eaton, 62 N.H. 512.

[80] Hancock v. Ship, 1 J.J.Marsh., Ky., 437; Monroe's Trustee v. Monroe, 155 Ky. 112, 159 S.W. 651; Packer v. Johnson, 1 Nott & McC., S.C., 1. Thus, in Smith v. Witter, 174 N.C. 616, 94 S.E. 402, real property was held to be alienable by a widow, without the joinder of the trustee, where the trust had been a married woman's trust.

[81] Newhall v. Wheeler, 7 Mass. 189.

[82] Riordan v. Schlicher, 146 Ala. 615, 41 So. 842; Tift v. Mayo, 61 Ga.

[83] Henderson v. Sherman, 47 Mich. 267, 11 N.W. 153.

Naturally a right accruing to the cestui que trust under the trust, which is purely personal in character, and is intended for his sole benefit, cannot be assigned. Examples are a right to occupy the trust property and use it for grazing and pasturage,[84] and a right to a bona fide exercise of the trustee's discretion in applying the residue of the estate.[85] If the trustee has the discretion of giving the cestui que trust something or nothing, the cestui que trust has no assignable right.[86]

In a number of states the interest of the beneficiary of a trust or realty or personalty can be assigned only in writing,[87] and in other jurisdictions writing is required if the trust subject-matter is realty.[88]

The prevailing rule in the United States is that assignments by the beneficiary of his interest take effect in the order of their making,[89] but a minority view makes the controlling feature a notice to the trustee of the assignment, so that a second assignment of the same interest would be superior to a prior one if the second assignee notified the trustee of his assignment before the first assignee gave notice.[90]

If the assigning cestui que trust is also a trustee, the assignee takes subject to any equities in favor of the co-cestuis and against the assigning trustee-cestui.[91] Thus, if T. is trustee for T. and A., and T. assigns his interest to X., X. takes the interest of T. subject to any claims for past defaults on the part of T. as trustee,

---

246; Tillson v. Moulton, 23 Ill. 648; Jackson v. West, 22 Md. 71; Stump v. Warfield, 104 Md. 530, 65 A. 346, 118 Am.St.Rep. 434, 10 Ann.Cas. 249; Perrine v. Newell, 49 N.J.Eq. 57, 23 A. 492; Newton v. Jay, 107 App.Div. 457, 95 N.Y.S. 413; Edwards v. Barstow, 21 R.I. 562, 45 A. 579; Brown v. Ford, 120 Va. 233, 91 S.E. 145.

[84] Davis v. Harrison, Hawaii, 240 F. 97, 153 C.C.A. 133.

[85] True Real Estate Co. v. True, 115 Me. 533, 99 A. 627.

[86] In re Coleman, 39 Ch.Div. 443.

[87] New York Real Property Law § 242, Personal Property Law § 31; Wis.St.1941, § 243.01; and see authorities collected in Bogert on Trusts and Trustees, § 190. Section 9 of the English Statute of Frauds required a writing for the transfer of the interest of any cestui.

[88] Idaho Code 1932, § 16-503; Pa. 33 P.S. § 2.

[89] Lexington Brewing Co. v. Hamon, 155 Ky. 711, 160 S.W. 264; Putnam v. Story, 132 Mass. 205; Meier v. Hess, 23 Or. 599, 32 P. 755; Restatement, Trusts, sec. 163.

[90] Adamson v. Paonessa, 180 Cal. 157, 179 P. 880; Lambert v. Morgan, 110 Md. 1, 72 A. 407, 132 Am.St.Rep. 412, 17 Ann.Cas. 439; Canton Exchange Bank v. Zazoo County, 144 Miss. 579, 109 So. 1.

[91] Belknap v. Belknap, 5 Allen, Mass., 468.

and also for any future defaults. If when X. enforces his assignment, T. is liable for breaches of trust, the share received by X. will be reduced by the amount of such liabilities.

So, too, if a cestui has taken part with the trustee in a breach of trust or actively solicited such a breach, and such a beneficiary assigns his interest, the assignee takes subject to a duty to reimburse the other beneficiaries for the loss occasioned out of the property of the wrongdoing and assigning beneficiary.[92]

AVAILABILITY TO CREDITORS [93]

44. The interest of cestui que trust is, in the absence of statute or valid direction by the settlor to the contrary, liable to be taken for the payment of his debts in equity or at law.

In bare or passive trusts the creditor may resort to a legal execution. In active trusts a creditor's bill in chancery was originally the only remedy and is still the exclusive method available in some jurisdictions; but the modern tendency of court and legislature is to subject the beneficiary's interest to execution, attachment, and garnishment as if it were a legal estate.

Is liability for the payment of debts an incident of the interest of cestui que trust? Aside from statute and control by the settlor, his interest is voluntarily alienable. Is it likewise involuntarily alienable?

Passive Trusts

By the tenth section of the Statute of Frauds[94] it was provided that "it shall and may be lawful for every sheriff or other officer to whom any writ or precept is or shall be directed, at the suit of any person or persons, of, for, and upon any judgment, statute, or recognizance hereafter to be made or had, to do, make, and deliver execution unto the party in that behalf suing, of all such lands, tenements, rectories, tithes, rents, and hereditaments as any other persons or persons be in any manner of wise seised or possessed, or hereafter shall be seised or possessed, in trust for him against whom execution is so sued," in like manner as if the debtor had been seised or possessed of the legal estate. This statute gave a creditor of cestui que trust the right to collect his debt by an execution at law from the trust property, but it obviously applied only to trusts of land, and was

[92] Ehlen v. Mayor of Baltimore, 76 Md. 576, 25 A. 917.
[93] Restatement, Trusts, sec. 147.
[94] St. 29 Car. II, c. 3, 1677.

construed to be effective only against freehold interests and when the trust was a bare or passive trust. In many American jurisdictions similar statutes have been enacted, or the same result achieved by adoption of the tenth section as a part of the common law, or by judicial action.[95] Thus, if the trust is passive, so that the Statute of Uses executes the use and passes title to the cestui, his creditors may take the trust res by legal process.

But, although resulting trusts are passive, the interest of the beneficiary thereunder has not generally been held to be subject to legal execution.[96] The creditor has been remitted to equity for his remedy. In some states, where A. pays the consideration for land and has the title taken in the name of B., by statute no trust results for A., but there is a statutory trust for the creditors of A. Thus they obtain their remedy by a bill in chancery as statutory cestuis que trust.[97]

[95] A typical American statute with corresponding result is section 709 N.Y.Civil Practice Act: "Real property, held by one person, in trust or for the use of another, is liable to levy and sale by virtue of an execution, issued upon a judgment recovered against the person, to whose use it is so held, in a case where it is prescribed by law, that, by reason of the invalidity of the trust, an estate vests in the beneficiary; but special provision is not otherwise made by law, for the mode of subjecting it to his debts." See, also, Doe ex dem. McMullen v. Lank, 4 Houst., Del., 648; Pitts v. McWhorter, 3 Ga. 5, 46 Am.Dec. 405; Moll v. Gardner, 214 Ill. 248, 73 N.E. 442; Copeland v. Bruning, 44 Ind.App. 405, 87 N.E. 1000, 88 N.E. 877; Hunnicutt v. Alabama Great Southern R. Co., Miss., 50 So. 697 (citing section 2779, Code of 1906); First Nat. Bank v. Burns, Mo. App., 199 S.W. 282; Bogert v. Perry, 17 Johns., N.Y., 351, 8 Am.Dec. 411; Jackson ex dem. Livingston v. Bateman, 2 Wend., N.Y., 570; Jackson ex dem. Ten Eyck v. Walker, 4 Wend., N.Y., 462; Kellogg v. Wood, 4 Paige, N.Y. 518; Hawkins v. Sneed, 10 N.C. 149; Freeman v. Perry, 17 N.C. 243; Lummus v. Davidson, 160 N.C. 484, 76 S.E. 474; Loughney v. Page, 320 Pa. 508, 182 A. 700; Bristow v. McCall, 16 S.C. 545; Smitheal v. Gray, 1 Humph., Tenn., 491, 34 Am.Dec. 664.

[96] Smith's Ex'r v. Cockrell, 66 Ala. 64; Goodbar v. Daniel, 88 Ala. 583, 7 So. 254, 16 Am.St.Rep. 76; Robinson v. Springfield Co., 21 Fla. 203; Mayer v. Wilkins, 37 Fla. 244, 19 So. 632; Low v. Marco, 53 Me. 45; Gray v. Chase, 57 Me. 558; Anderson v. Biddle, 10 Mo. 23; White v. Kavanaugh, 8 Rich., S.C., 377; Richardson v. Mounce, 19 S.C. 477; Cunningham v. Wood, 4 Humph., Tenn., 417; Dewey v. Long, 25 Vt. 564. *Contra:* Tevis v. Doe, 3 Ind. 129; Peterson v. Farnum, 121 Mass. 476; Thomas v. Walker, 6 Humph., Tenn., 93.

[97] New York Real Property Law, § 94; Garfield v. Hatmaker, 15 N.Y. 475; McCartney v. Bostwick, 32 N.Y. 53. See § 52, post.

Active Trusts

If the trust is active, it is elementary that the creditor of the cestui que trust can subject his interest in the trust to the satisfaction of the debt, either in law or equity, unless a statute or valid spendthrift trust prevents this result. The question of the rights of creditors of a trust beneficiary is, therefore, largely one of methods and procedure. "There are several ideas that are inseparable from the institution of property, among the most prominent of which are, the right of alienation, and its being subject to the payment of debts. In all cases like the present, the inquiry must be, whether the debtor has a *vested, determinate interest* in the equitable estate sought to be subjected, with the present right of enjoyment in severalty. If he has, the right of the creditor follows as a corollary in mathematical science does the main proposition. Under the above qualifications and conditions, the creditor is entitled to relief, and in some form or other the debtor's *estate,* be that more or less, should be disposed of or sequestrated for the satisfaction of his debt."[98] Another court has forcibly said: "There cannot be a legal or equitable right in or to property, or to its rents, income, or profits, not so blended with the rights of others as to be incapable of separation and identification, that may not, by some appropriate remedy, in law or in equity, according to the nature of the case, be condemned to the satisfaction of debts. It is violative of public policy, and in fraud of the rights of creditors, to create a well-defined beneficial interest, legal or equitable, in property, real or personal, or in its rents, income, or profits, which can be enjoyed by an insolvent debtor, free from liability for the payment of debts."[99] The estate or interest of cestui que trust is now recognized as a property right and liable for the owner's debts equally with his legal interests, unless specially exempted by statute or act of the settlor.[1]

The creditor of the cestui que trust may always come into equity and ask to have the trust res or its income applied to the satisfaction of his debt.[2] And in some jurisdictions this

---

[98] Heath v. Bishop, 4 Rich.Eq., S.C., 46, 50, 55 Am.Dec. 654.

[99] Taylor v. Harwell, 65 Ala. 1, 13.

[1] Sefton v. San Diego Trust & Sav. Bk., Cal.App., 106 P.2d 974; Fox v. Greene, 289 Mich. 179, 286 N.W. 203.

[2] Raynolds v. Hanna, C.C.Ohio, 55 F. 783; Taylor v. Harwell, 65 Ala. 1; Burke v. Morris, 121 Ala. 126, 25 So. 759; Clarke v. Windham, 12 Ala. 798, contra (cestui in possession; Huntington v. Jones, 72 Conn. 45, 43 A. 564; Bronson v. Thompson, 77 Conn. 214, 58 A. 692; Coyne v. Plume, 90 Conn. 293, 97 A. 337 (by statute trust income is liable, if the trust is not for

equitable remedy is his only relief.³ "It is well settled that a judgment at common law is not a lien upon a mere equitable estate or interest, nor is such interest the subject of a levy and sale by virtue of an execution at law unaided by a decree of a court of equity."⁴

"It is a well-settled general rule that trust property, unless otherwise provided by statute, can only be subjected to the payment of debts in a court of equity. * * * It was early held in this state that the estate of cestui que trust is not subject to attachment or execution."⁵ In a recent case a federal court has said: "The incidents of a legal title attach to an absolute equitable interest to such an extent as to permit alienation, and such interest may be taken for the payment of the debts of the owner. * * * If an equitable estate be chargeable with the debts of the owner, it follows that such estate may be sold to discharge the debt. It is true that an execution issuing on a judgment is not leviable on an equitable estate; but it is also true that the corpus of an equitable estate may be subjected in equitable proceedings, and sold to pay the debt of the owner of the equitable estate."⁶

Some courts have subjected the trust res to an equitable execution,⁷ while others have decreed that the debt be satisfied

---

the support of the beneficiary or his family, and in the latter case only the surplus above the amount necessary for support can be reached); Conn.Gen.St.1930, § 5723; Macfarlane v. Dorsey, 49 Fla. 341, 38 So. 512; Johnston v. Redd, 59 Ga. 621; Jennings v. Coleman, 59 Ga. 718; De Rousse v. Williams, 181 Iowa 379, 164 N.W. 896; Knefler v. Shreve, 78 Ky. 297; Dickison v. Ogden's Ex'r, 89 Ky. 162, 12 S.W. 191; Southern Nat. Life Ins. Co. v. Ford's Adm'r, 151 Ky. 476, 152 S.W. 243; People's Bank of Madison, Ind., v. Deweese, 144 Ky. 172, 137 S.W. 850 (citing section 439, Civ.Code Prac.); Dockray v. Mason, 48 Me. 178; Haley v. Palmer, 107 Me. 311, 78 A. 368; Presley v. Rodgers, 24 Miss. 520; Hunnicutt v. Ala. Great Southern R. Co., Miss., 50 So. 697; McGregor-Noe Hardware Co. v. Horn, 146 Mo. 129, 47 S.W. 957; Heaton v. Dickson, 153 Mo.App. 312, 133 S.W. 159; Hogan v. Jaques, 19 N.J.Eq. 123, 97 Am.Dec. 644; Smith v. Collins, 81 N.J.Eq. 348, 86 A. 957; Spencer v. Richmond, 46 App. Div. 481, 61 N.Y.S. 397; Bergmann v. Lord, 194 N.Y. 70, 86 N.E. 828; Lummus v. Davidson, 160 N.C. 484, 76 S.E. 474; Decker v. Directors of Poor, 120 Pa. 272, 13 A. 925; Egbert v. De Solms, 218 Pa. 207, 67 A. 212; Wylie v. White, 10 Rich.Eq., S.C., 294; Bristow v. McCall, 16 S.C. 545; Leake v. Benson, 29 Grat.,Va., 153.

³ Noyes v. Noyes, 110 Vt. 511, 9 A. 2d 123.

⁴ Smith v. Collins, 81 N.J.Eq. 348, 350, 86 A. 957. Accord: Johnston v. Smith, 76 Fla. 474, 80 So. 184.

⁵ Feldman v. Preston, 194 Mich. 352, 160 N.W. 655, 658.

⁶ First Nat. Bank of Spartanburg, S. C. v. Dougan, D.C.Ga., 250 F. 510, 512.

⁷ In the following cases the res was applied to the discharge of the debt:

out of the income from the trust.[8] The procedure may be said to be discretionary with chancery. "And consequently the estate, whether it consist of land or personal property, may be subjected and sold, or if practicable and to the interest of the parties, the rents, interest, or profits may be subjected and applied by a court of equity to payment of debts of the cestui que trust."[9] Where the subject-matter of the trust is applied to the satisfaction of the beneficiary's debts, considerable support of the modern theory that the cestui's right is a property right in the trust res is found.

Statutory Control

In many states the right of a creditor to proceed in equity to obtain satisfaction of his claim from cestui que trust's interest is described and defined by statute. These judgment creditor's suits are ordinarily required to be based upon evidence of the return of an execution at law unsatisfied, or proof that the remedies at law for the satisfaction of the debt have been exhausted,[10] or at least evidence that the debtor is insolvent.[11] But in Massachusetts prior judgment at law and return of execution unsatisfied are not prerequisites to the maintaining of this bill.[12] A typical statute provides:[13] "When an execution against the property of a judgment debtor, issued out of a court of record, as prescribed in the next section, has been returned wholly or partly unsatisfied, the judgment creditor may maintain an action against the judgment debtor, and any other person, to compel the discovery of any thing in action, or other

---

Taylor v. Harwell, 65 Ala. 1; Southern Nat. Life Ins. Co. v. Ford's Adm'r, 151 Ky. 476, 152 S.W. 243; McGregor-Noe Hardware Co. v. Horn, 146 Mo. 129, 47 S.W. 957; McKimmon v. Rodgers, 56 N.C. 200. But in Huntington v. Jones, 72 Conn. 45, 43 A. 564, it was held that the corpus could not be taken by the creditor.

[8] See remaining cases cited in note 2, ante.

[9] Marshall's Trustee v. Rash, 87 Ky. 116, 118, 7 S.W. 879, 12 Am.St. Rep. 467.

[10] Burke v. Morris, 121 Ala. 126, 25 So. 759 (referring to section 814, Ala.Code 1896); Sefton v. San Diego Trust & Savings Bank, Cal.App., 106 P.2d 974; Ill. Smith-Hurd Stats. c. 22, § 49; Durand v. Gray, 129 Ill. 9, 21 N.E. 610; Ladd v. Judson, 174 Ill. 344, 51 N.E. 838, 66 Am. St.Rep. 267; Binns v. La Forge, 191 Ill. 598, 61 N.E. 382; Trotter v. Lisman, 199 N.Y. 497, 92 N.E. 1052; Tenn.Code 1938, § 10353; Hooberry v. Harding, 3 Tenn.Ch. 677.

[11] De Rousse v. Williams, 181 Iowa 379, 164 N.W. 896.

[12] Barry v. Abbot, 100 Mass. 396. See, also, Heaton v. Dickson, 153 Mo. App. 312, 133 S.W. 159.

[13] N.Y. Civil Practice Act; §§ 1189, 1196, in part.

property belonging to the judgment debtor, and of any money, thing in action, or other property due to him, or held in trust for him; to prevent the transfer thereof, or the payment or delivery thereof, to him, or to any other person; and to procure satisfaction of the plaintiff's demand. * * * The provisions of this article * * * do not * * * authorize the discovery or seizure of * * * any money, thing in action, or other property, held in trust for a judgment debtor, where the trust has been created by, or the fund so held in trust has proceeded from, a person other than the judgment debtor. * * * "

The interest of cestui que trust passes to his assignee in bankruptcy.[14] "And the beneficial interest of a bankrupt in property held in trust passes also, in all cases where that interest might have been transferred to another by the bankrupt, or might have been levied upon under judicial proceedings against him."[15]

The principle that relief must first be sought at law has been thus expressed by a New York court: "The rule was early established in this state, that creditors, seeking the aid of a court of equity to reach equitable assets of their debtor in satisfaction of their claims, must first have exhausted their legal remedies, according to the laws of this state, by the recovery of a judgment in one of its courts and the return of execution thereon unsatisfied."[16] While the opposing view is voiced by a Connecticut court in these words: "Such a bill [a creditor's bill] is one brought to enforce the payment of a debt out of the property of the debtor, under circumstances which impede or render impossible the collection of the debt by the ordinary process of execution. * * * As, for illustration, to reach equitable interests in property belonging to the debtor which could not be reached by an execution at law. * * * In this state it is not necessary that a judgment should be rendered before the creditor's bill is brought. The judgment may be rendered in the very action in which the equitable relief is asked."[17]

---

[14] In re Reynolds, D.C.N.Y., 243 F. 268; Horton v. Moore, C.C.A.Mich., 110 F.2d 189; Jenks v. Title Guaranty & Trust Co., 170 App.Div. 830, 156 N.Y.S. 478; In re Cunningham's Estate, 340 Pa. 265, 16 A.2d 712.

[15] In re Jersey Island Packing Co., Cal., 138 F. 625, 627, 71 C.C.A. 75, 2 L.R.A.,N.S., 560.

[16] Trotter v. Lisman, 199 N.Y. 497, 501, 92 N.E. 1052.

[17] Huntington v. Jones, 72 Conn. 45, 49–50, 43 A. 564.

Execution at Law

Courts and legislatures have increasingly taken the position that the interest of cestui que trust is subject to levy and sale under an execution at law, so that now in a number of states the creditor may seize the interest of the beneficiary without resort to chancery.[18] "It is the policy of our law that all the property of a debtor should be responsible for his debts, and in consonance with this policy we have held that our statutes regulating attachments and execution subject to these processes certain equitable interests in property. The interests which have been thus brought within the reach of execution have included the equitable title which a cestui que trust has in lands or property, the legal title of which is held by another under a trust for his benefit, the equity of redemption in property subject to a mortgage, the equity in shares of stock pledged as collateral for a loan, and the income of a trust fund which the cestui que trust is entitled to receive as a right."[19] A typical statute on the subject is that of Kentucky: "Estates of every kind held or possessed in trust, shall be subject to the debts and charges of the persons to whose use, or for whose benefit, they shall be respectively held or possessed, as they would be subject if those persons owned the like interest in the property held or possessed as they own or shall own in the use or trust thereof."[20]

The rights of attachment[21] in several jurisdictions and the

---

[18] By. St. 1 & 2 Vict. c. 110, execution at law against an equitable interest in land was allowed, and where the judgment debtor has the entire equitable interest in personal property it has been recently held that such interest may be reached on legal execution. Stevens v. Hince, 110 L. T.R. 935. See Reed v. Munn, Colo., 148 F. 737, 80 C.C.A. 215; Ives v. Beecher, 75 Conn. 564, 54 A. 207 (action to foreclose a judgment lien on land under sections 5120–5122, Conn. Gen.St.1930); Hempstead v. Dickson, 20 Ill. 193, 71 Am.Dec. 260; Iowa Code 1939, § 11660; Ind. Burns' Ann. St.1933, § 2-3608; State Bank v. Macy, 4 Ind. 362; Maxwell v. Vaught, 96 Ind. 136; Ky.St.1936, § 1681; Eastland v. Jordan, 3 Bibb, Ky., 186; Blanchard v. Taylor's Heirs, 7 B.Mon., Ky., 645; Hancock v. Twyman, Ky., 45 S.W. 68; Md. Code 1939, art. 83, § 1 (land only); Mo.Rev.St.1939, § 1336; (land only); Hutchins v. Heywood, 50 N.H. 491; Girard Life Ins. & Trust Co. v. Chambers, 46 Pa. 485, 86 Am. Dec. 513. See N.J.S.A. 2:26–151, regarding proceedings supplementary to execution against a beneficiary.

[19] Humphrey v. Gerard, 83 Conn. 346, 355, 77 A. 65.

[20] Ky.St.1936, § 2355.

[21] Price v. Taylor, 110 Ky. 589, 62 S.W. 270; Fidelity Trust & Safety Vault Co. v. Walker, 116 Ky. 381, 76 S.W. 131; Watson v. Kennard, 77 N.H. 23, 86 A. 257; Baumann v. Ballantine, 76 N.J.L. 91, 68 A. 1114; Girard Life Ins. & Trust Co. v. Chambers, 46 Pa. 485, 86 Am.Dec. 513. *Contra:* Fairfax v. Savings

rights of garnishment [22] in several jurisdictions have also been accorded to the creditor of a cestui que trust.

When Nature of Trust Prevents Subjection to Debts

The courts have been disinclined to seize the interest of a cestui que trust in payment of his debts when that right has been uncertain, contingent or on condition precedent,[23] but it will be no objection to the taking of cestui's interest that it is liable to be defeated or lessened by the happening of a condition subsequent, as, for example, where the birth of children may decrease the share of the debtor.[24]

SPENDTHRIFT TRUSTS [25]

45. A spendthrift trust is one in which, either by virtue of the direction of the settlor or because of statute, the beneficiary is unable to sell or give away his right to future income and his creditors are unable to collect from such right to future income. There is no restraint on the alienability of the income after it is received, but rather merely a restraint on the alienability of the right to future income.

Bank of Baltimore, 175 Md. 136, 199 A. 872; 116 A.L.R. 1334. Feldman v. Preston, 194 Mich. 352, 160 N.W. 655.

[22] Henderson v. Sunseri, 234 Ala. 289, 174 So. 767; Conn. Gen.St.1930, § 5723; Easterly v. Keney, 36 Conn. 18; Ladd v. Judson, 174 Ill. 344, 51 N.E. 838, 66 Am.St.Rep. 267 (but see May v. Baker, 15 Ill. 89); Bare v. Cole, 220 Iowa 338, 260 N.W. 338; Estabrook v. Earle, 97 Mass. 302 (if trust revocable and controllable by cestui at will); Warner v. Rice, 66 Md. 436, 8 A. 84; Meier v. Blair, 287 Mich. 13, 282 N.W. 884; Richards v. Merrimack & C. R. R. R., 44 N.H. 127; N.J.S.A. 2:26–182; Cowan v. Storms, 121 N.J.L. 336, 2 A.2d 183; N. Y. Civil Practice Act, § 684 (where the income is $12 a week or more); King v. Irving, 103 App.Div. 420, 92 N.Y.S. 1094; Heppenstall v. Baudouine, 73 Misc. 118, 132 N.Y.S. 511; John G. Myers Co. v. Reynolds, Sup., 166 N.Y.S. 654; Brearley School v. Ward, 201 N.Y. 358, 94 N.E. 1001, 40 L.R.A.,N.S., 1215, Ann.Cas.1912B. 251; In re Ungrich, 201 N.Y. 415, 94 N. E. 999; Grieves v. Keane, 23 R.I. 136, 49 A. 501. *Contra:* Plunkett v. Le Huray, 4 Har., Del., 436; Peninsular Sav. Bank v. Union Trust Co., 127 Mich. 355, 86 N.W. 798; Ross v. Ashton, 73 Mo.App. 254 (unless trust deed is fraudulent); Willis v. Curtze, 203 Pa. 111, 52 A. 5; Oglesby v. Durr, Tex.Civ.App., 173 S.W. 275; White's Ex'r v. White, 30 Vt. 338; Knettle v. Knettle, 190 Wash. 395, 68 P.2d 218.

Contra: McLeod v. Cooper, C.C.A. Fla., 88 F.2d 194 (Florida law).

[23] Russell v. Milton, 133 Mass. 180; Hill v. Fulmer, Miss., 39 So. 53; Myer v. Thomson, 35 Hun., N.Y., 561.

[24] First Nat. Bank of Spartanburg, S. C. v. Dougan, D.C.Ga., 250 F. 510.

[25] Restatement, Trusts, §§ 149–153, 156, 157.

An attempted sale of his right to future income by the beneficiary does not give the assignee a right to compel the trustee to pay income to him, but if the assignment has not been repudiated by the cestui, the trustee may treat it as an order to pay to the assignee and the trustee will be protected in making payments to the assignee until the order is revoked.

Spendthrift trusts are void, as creating an unlawful restraint on alienation and as against public policy, in England and a few American states. In the majority of American states such trusts are valid, either to an unlimited extent or subject to some statutory restrictions.

" 'Spendthrift trusts' is the term commonly applied to those trusts that are created with a view of providing a fund for the maintenance of another, and at the same time securing it against his own improvidence or incapacity for self-protection. The provisions against alienation of the trust fund by the voluntary act of the beneficiary, or in invitum by his creditors, are the usual incidents of such trusts." [26] Spendthrift trusts have as their object the giving of the income of real or personal property to a beneficiary, without liability to alienation of his right to future income, voluntary or involuntary, prior to its receipt by him. Thus, if A. transfer to B., as trustee, $100,000 in bonds to hold in trust for X., with a provision that B. shall pay to X. the net income of such bonds, but that X. shall not have the right to sell or mortgage his right to receive such income, and that the creditors of X. shall not have the power to attach the right to future income in the hands of the trustee, the trust is a spendthrift trust. Such trusts are frequently highly desirable, where provision is to be made for an inexperienced, incompetent, or wasteful person. If such person had the power to dispose of his right to receive the income from the trust, his incapacity or carelessness would lead him to anticipate his income and convey to money lenders and creditors the right to receive the income as it became due. If the hands of the incompetent or spendthrift can be tied, so that he can do nothing with the income until it is paid into his hands by the trustee, then the beneficiary may be assured against want to some extent at least.

The beneficiary of a spendthrift trust does not need to be a spendthrift, or incompetent or subnormal in any way.

[26] Wagner v. Wagner, 244 Ill. 101, 111, 91 N.E. 66, 18 Ann.Cas. 490, quoting 26 Am. & Eng. Encyc. of Law, 2d Ed., p. 138. The intent to restrict alienation may be implied. Hopkinson v. Swaim, 284 Ill. 11, 119 N.E. 985.

It is never the object of the spendthrift trust to restrain the beneficiary from spending the income after it has been paid to him by the trustee, or to restrain his creditors from taking such income from him after he has obtained it from the trustee. The sole object of these trusts is to prevent anticipation of the income by assignments of the right to receive future income or by attempts by creditors of the cestui to reach this income as it accumulates in the hands of the trustee.

The validity of spendthrift trusts has been much debated. It has been contended by some writers that an equitable life or full interest involves as an inherent characteristic alienability, that a clause against transferring equitable interests is repugnant to their very nature, that legal estates for life or in fee cannot be encumbered by restraints on alienation and there is no reason why equitable interests should be different; that spendthrift trusts tend to encourage weaklings and the improvident to continue to be weak and wasteful, and that such trusts mislead and defraud creditors of the beneficiaries.[27]

On the other hand it has been urged that the donor of property to a trust beneficiary should be able to attach to it such incidents as he pleases, that equitable interests are legally possible although they are inalienable as is shown by the clause against anticipation in relation to the married woman's separate estate, that there is no undesirable check on alienation of the trust property since the trustee can usually sell it free of the trust, that spendthrift trusts are necessary to the protection of inexperienced and incompetent persons, that creditors are not misled by the appearance of wealth which a beneficiary may show because the creditors can always inquire into the source of such income and find wills and deeds in the public records when spendthrift trusts have been created by them, that creditors can collect in time by taking the income as it is paid over to the beneficiary, and that if a gift of an equitable estate until attempted alienation or until bankruptcy is good, spendthrift trusts should be allowed.[28]

[27] See Gray, Restraints on Alienation, 2d Ed., §§ 134–277a; Scott, Control of Property by the Dead, 65 Univ. of Pa. L.R. 632, 642.

[28] For further discussions, see Costigan, 22 Cal.L.R. 471; Griswold, Spendthrift Trusts, §§ 1–36.

Minority View

The English courts have consistently opposed such trusts.[29] The English view is maintained by a small number of American courts.[30]

[29] Brandon v. Robinson, 18 Ves. 429; Graves v. Dolphin, 1 Sim. 66.

[30] In Alabama the English rule was observed with some qualifications. A beneficial interest could not be given to one, so that it was incapable of being reached by his creditors, unless such interest was conferred and was to be enjoyed jointly with others, and was also incapable of severance from the interest of such others. Rugely v. Robinson, 10 Ala. 702; Robertson v. Johnston, 36 Ala. 197; Jones v. Reest, 65 Ala. 134; Bell v. Watkins, 82 Ala. 512, 1 So. 92, 60 Am.Rep. 756. By Gen.Acts Ala.1935, No. 230, spendthrift trusts of capital and income for relatives were validated, provided the income should not exceed $1800 a year.

In Kentucky, after some vacillation, the courts seem to have adopted the English rule that spendthrift trusts are not allowed. Hubbard v. Hayes, 98 S.W. 1034; Ratliff's Ex'rs v. Commonwealth, 139 Ky. 533, 101 S.W. 978; Cecil's Trustee v. Robertson & Bro., 105 S.W. 926. "It is not the policy of the law that a person may hold free from the claims of his creditors and enjoy property which is not exempt from execution, and no device will be allowed to work an evasion so long as a beneficial interest is vested in the beneficiary." Cecil's Trustee v. Robertson & Bro., 105 S.W. 926, 928. But if the interest of the beneficiary is owned jointly with others and is inseparable from their interests, the trust may be in effect a spendthrift trust. Hackett's Trustee v. Hackett, 146 Ky. 408, 142 S.W. 673. And the last-named case also hints at a requirement that the creditor show that there is a surplus over and above what is necessary for the support of the beneficiary before he be allowed to take any part of the income. The courts have held valid clauses restraining the cestui que trust from aliening his interest, thereby approving one element of the spendthrift trust. Gillespie v. Winston's Trustee, 170 Ky. 667, 186 S.W. 517; Sparrow v. Sparrow, 171 Ky. 101, 186 S.W. 904; Muir's Ex'rs v. Howard, 178 Ky. 51, 198 S.W. 551.

In Ohio there is a decision and dictum to the effect that spendthrift trusts are not allowed. Wallace v. Smith, 2 Handy, 78; Hobbs v. Smith, 15 Ohio St. 419. But see dictum apparently favorable to spendthrift trusts in Stanley v. Thornton, 7 Ohio Cir.Ct.R. 455. See Babcock v. Monypeny, 34 Ohio Cir.Ct.R. 434.

See White, Spendthrift Trusts in Ohio, 2 Cinc. L.R. 333.

Spendthrift trusts were declared invalid in Tillinghast v. Bradford, 5 R.I. 205. See Newport Trust Co. v. Chappell, 40 R.I. 383, 101 A. 323.

The South Carolina courts are opposed to spendthrift trusts and will not uphold them. Heath v. Bishop, 4 Rich.Eq. 46, 55 Am.Dec. 654; Wylie v. White, 10 Rich.Eq. 294; Ford v. Caldwell, 3 Hill, 248.

The rule in Virginia remained in doubt for many years, but now has been clarified by statute. See Hutchinson v. Maxwell, 100 Va. 169, 40 S.E. 655, 57 L.R.A. 384, 93 Am.St.Rep. 944, and Honaker v. Duff, 101 Va. 675, 44 S.E. 900; Va.Code 1930, § 5157 (capital limited to $100,000).

In Brahmey v. Rollins, 87 N.H. 290, 179 A. 186, it was held that a trust to pay an annuity to a bene-

The attitude which the American courts which follow the English rule have taken is well expressed by Ames, C. J., speaking for a Rhode Island court: "It is quite clear that it was the intention of the testator to make an alimentary provision for his son during life, which should give him all the advantages of an estate in fee, without the legal incidents of such an estate—alienability, unless by will, and subjectiveness to the payment of the son's debts. Such restraints, however, are so opposed to the nature of property—and, so far as subjectiveness to debts is concerned, to the honest policy of the law—as to be totally void, unless, indeed, which is not the case here, in the event of its being attempted to be aliened, or seized for debts, it is given over by the testator to some one else. This has been the settled doctrine of a court of chancery, at least since Brandon v. Robinson, 18 Ves. 429; and in application to such a case as this is so honest and just that we would not change it if we could. Certainly no man should have an estate to live on, but not an estate to pay his debts with. Certainly property available for the purposes of pleasure or profit should be also amenable to the demands of justice."[31]

Majority View

In a great majority of the American states, however, spendthrift trusts are allowed either without qualification, or subject to statutory restrictions.[32] In California, Michigan, Minnesota, ficiary, where the trustee had no discretion as to the amount, could not be encumbered with a clause against creditors taking the right to future income, regardless of the validity of the clause as far as voluntary alienation was concerned.

[31] Tillinghast v. Bradford, 5 R.I. 205, 212.

[32] Nichols v. Eaton, 91 U.S. 716, 23 L.Ed. 254; Shelton v. King, 229 U.S. 90, 33 S.Ct. 686, 57 L.Ed. 1086.

Arizona.—Ariz.Code 1939 § 41-112 (can be created by parent for child who is actually a spendthrift).

Arkansas.—The dicta were unfavorable until the decision of Bowlin v. Citizens' Bank & Trust Co., 131 Ark. 97, 198 S.W. 288, 2 A.L.R. 575, announced that spendthrift trusts are valid. See Lindsay v. Harrison, 8 Ark. 302; Phillips v. Grayson, 23 Ark. 769; Honnett v. Williams, 66 Ark. 148, 49 S.W. 495.

California.—Civ.Code, § 859; Seymour v. McAvoy, 121 Cal. 438, 53 P. 946, 41 L.R.A. 544.

Connecticut.—Conn. Gen.St.1930, § 5723 (good only for cestui or his family and to extent necessary for support).

Delaware.—Gray v. Corbit, 4 Del. Ch. 135, dictum; Del.L.1933, c. 186.

District of Columbia.—Fearson v. Dunlop, 21 D.C. 236.

Georgia.—Ga.Code 1933, § 108-114; Sinnott v. Moore, 113 Ga. 908, 39 S.E. 415; Moore v. Sinnott, 117 Ga. 1010, 44 S.E. 810.

Montana, New York, North Dakota, South Dakota, and Wisconsin, "where a trust is created to receive the rents and profits of real property, and no valid direction for accumulation is given,

Illinois.—Wagner v. Wagner, 244 Ill. 101, 91 N.E. 66, 18 Ann.Cas. 490; Wallace v. Foxwell, 250 Ill. 616, 95 N.E. 985, 50 L.R.A.,N.S., 632; O'Hare v. Johnston, 273 Ill. 458, 113 N.E. 127; Hartley v. Unknown Heirs of Wyatt, 281 Ill. 321, 117 N.E. 995; Hopkinson v. Swaim, 284 Ill. 11, 119 N.E. 985.

Indiana.—McCoy v. Houck, 180 Ind. 634, 99 N.E. 97; Devin v. McCoy, 48 Ind.App. 379, 93 N.E. 1013; Gavit, Spendthrift Trusts in Indiana, 3 Ind.L.J. 525.

Iowa.—Merchants' Nat. Bank v. Crist, 140 Iowa 308, 118 N.W. 394, 23 L.R.A.,N.S., 526, 132 Am.St.Rep. 267; Keating v. Keating, 182 Iowa 1056, 165 N.W. 74; Kiffner v. Kiffner, 185 Iowa 1064, 171 N.W. 590; Horack, Spendthrift Trusts in Iowa, 4 Iowa Law Bul. 139.

Kansas.—Everitt v. Haskins, 102 Kan. 546, 171 P. 632; Sherman v. Havens, 94 Kan. 654, 146 P. 1030, Ann.Cas.1917B, 394.

Maine.—Roberts v. Stevens, 84 Me. 325, 24 A. 873, 17 L.R.A. 266; Tilton v. Davidson, 98 Me. 55, 56 A. 215.

Maryland.—Smith v. Towers, 69 Md. 77, 14 A. 497, 15 A. 92, 9 Am.St. Rep. 398; Maryland Grange Agency v. Lee, 72 Md. 161, 19 A. 534; Jackson Square Loan & Sav. Ass'n v. Bartlett, 95 Md. 661, 53 A. 426, 93 Am.St.Rep. 416; Houghton v. Tiffany, 116 Md. 655, 82 A. 831; Safe Deposit & Trust Co. of Baltimore v. Independent Brewing Ass'n, 127 Md. 463, 96 A. 617; Plitt v. Yakel, 129 Md. 464, 99 A. 669.

Massachusetts.—Hall v. Williams, 120 Mass. 344; Broadway Nat. Bank v. Adams, 133 Mass. 170, 43 Am.Rep. 504; Foster v. Foster, 133 Mass. 179; Wemyss v. White, 159 Mass. 484, 34 N.E. 718; Berry v. Dunham, 202 Mass. 133, 88 N.E. 904; Hale v. Bowler, 215 Mass. 354, 102 N.E. 415; Boston Safe Deposit Co. v. Collier, 222 Mass. 390, 111 N.E. 163, Ann. Cas.1918C, 962.

Michigan.—Ann.St. § 26.63.

Minnesota.—St.1927, § 8092.

Mississippi.—Leigh v. Harrison, 69 Miss. 923, 11 So. 604, 18 L.R.A. 49; Cady v. Lincoln, 100 Miss. 765, 57 So. 213.

Missouri.—Partridge v. Cavender, 96 Mo. 452, 9 S.W. 785; Jarboe v. Hey, 122 Mo. 341, 26 S.W. 968; Kessner v. Phillips, 189 Mo. 515, 88 S.W. 66, 107 Am.St.Rep. 368, 3 Ann.Cas. 1005; Dunephant v. Dickson, 153 Mo. App. 309, 133 S.W. 165; Higbee v. Brockenbrough, 191 S.W. 994. The presumption is against a spendthrift trust. First Nat. Bank v. Burns, App., 199 S.W. 282.

Montana.—Rev.Codes 1935, § 6788.

Nebraska.—Weller v. Noffsinger, 57 Neb. 455, 77 N.W. 1075.

Nevada.—By Nevada L.1939, c. 66, that state obtained a very liberal spendthrift trust statute.

New Jersey.—Expressions favorable to spendthrift trusts have appeared in Hardenburgh v. Blair, 30 N.J.Eq. 645, and Wright v. Leupp, 70 N.J.Eq. 130, 62 A. 464, but the question has recently been declared to be an open one in Camden Safe Deposit & Trust Co. v. Schellenger, 78 N.J. Eq. 138, 78 A. 672, and Brooks v. Davis, 82 N.J.Eq. 118, 88 A. 178. See N.J.S.A. 2:26–182 to 26–187.

New York.—Williams v. Thorn, 70 N.Y. 270; Tolles v. Wood, 99 N.Y. 616, 1 N.E. 251; Sherman v. Skuse, 166 N.Y. 345, 59 N.E. 990; Ullman v. Cameron, 186 N.Y. 339, 78 N.E. 1074,

BOGERT TRUSTS 2D—11

the surplus of such rents and profits, beyond the sum necessary for the education and support of the beneficiary, shall be liable to the claims of his creditors in the same manner as other personal property, which cannot be reached by execution." [33] In construction of these statutes it has been held that the education and support to which the cestui is entitled is that to which he has been

---

116 Am.St.Rep. 553; Stringer v. Young, 191 N.Y. 157, 83 N.E. 690; Bergmann v. Lord, 194 N.Y. 70, 86 N.E. 828; Brearley School v. Ward, 201 N.Y. 358, 94 N.E. 1001, 40 L.R.A., N.S., 1215, Ann.Cas.1912B, 251; New York Real Property Law, Consol. Laws, c. 50 §§ 98, 103; Civil Practice Act, §§ 684, 793. In New York the creditors of a cestui que trust have at least three possible remedies. If the trust was created by the cestui for himself, they may resort to a creditor's bill under sections 1189-1191 of the Civil Practice Act. Williams v. Thorn, 70 N.Y. 270. If the settlor was another than the beneficiary, the creditor may proceed under section 98 of the Real Property Law to take all the surplus beyond the amount necessary to the support and education of the cestui que trust, or he may proceed under the Garnishment Act, section 684 of the Civil Practice Act, and get 10 per cent. of the trust income, if it is $12 a week or more. Brearley School v. Ward, 201 N.Y. 358, 94 N.E. 1001, 40 L.R.A., N.S., 1215, Ann.Cas.1912B, 251; Hoye v. Hipkins, 182 App.Div. 901, 168 N.Y.S. 1112.

North Carolina.—Vaughan v. Wise, 152 N.C. 31, 67 S.E. 33; Fowler & Lee v. Webster, 173 N.C. 442, 92 S.E. 157; N.C.Code 1939, § 1742 (good for relative of settlor for life and income to be not more than $500 a year).

North Dakota.—Comp.L.1913, § 5369.

Oregon.—Mattison v. Mattison, 53 Or. 254, 100 P. 4, 133 Am.St.Rep. 829,

18 Ann.Cas. 218; Winslow v. Rutherford, 59 Or. 124, 114 P. 930.

Pennsylvania.—Norris v. Johnston, 5 Pa. 287; Appeal of Ashhurst, 77 Pa. 464; Thackara v. Mintzer, 100 Pa. 151; Appeal of Grothe, 135 Pa. 585, 19 A. 1058; Winthrop Co. v. Clinton, 196 Pa. 472, 46 A. 435, 79 Am.St.Rep. 729; Board of Charities & Corrections of City of Philadelphia v. Lockard, 198 Pa. 572, 48 A. 496, 82 Am.St. Rep. 817; In re Minnich's Estate, 206 Pa. 405, 55 A. 1067.

South Dakota.—Code 1939, § 59.-0306.

Tennessee.—Hooberry v. Harding, 3 Tenn.Ch. 677; Staub v. Williams, 5 Lea 458; Menken Co. v. Brinkley, 94 Tenn. 721, 31 S.W. 92; Jobe v. Dillard, 104 Tenn. 658, 58 S.W. 324; First Nat. Bank v. Nashville Trust Co., Ch.App., 62 S.W. 392.

Texas.—Patten v. Herring, 9 Tex. Civ.App. 640, 29 S.W. 388; Wood v. McClelland, Civ.App., 53 S.W. 381; McCreary v. Robinson, Civ.App., 57 S.W. 682; Lindsey v. Rose, Civ.App., 175 S.W. 829; Nunn v. Titche-Goettinger Co., Civ.App., 196 S.W. 890.

Vermont.—White's Ex'r v. White, 30 Vt. 338.

West Virginia.—Guernsey v. Lazear, 51 W.Va. 328, 41 S.E. 405; Hoffman v. Beltzhoover, 71 W.Va. 72, 76 S.E. 968; Kerns v. Carr, 82 W.Va. 78, 95 S.E. 606, L.R.A.1918E, 568.

Wisconsin.—St.1941, § 231.13.

[33] See statutes cited in note 32, ante.

BOGERT TRUSTS 2D

accustomed and to which persons of his class are used.[34] These statutes and their construction have been the subject of bitter criticism by a learned author.[35] In California and New York the statute has been applied to trusts of personal property as well,[36] but not so in Minnesota and Wisconsin.[37]

In this same group of states legislation either makes the right of a beneficiary to the income of a trust to collect income and profits inalienable by his voluntary action, or permits settlors to attach such an incident to the beneficiary's interest. Thus in these states, as shown elsewhere,[38] spendthrift trusts are encouraged and recognized.

A model statute on spendthrift trusts, limiting the income of them to $5,000 a year, permitting creditors to garnishee 10% of all income over $12 a week, preventing a right to principal from being subjected to a spendthrift provision, and excepting claims for support and other meritorious claims from the usual rule, has been adopted recently in two states.[39]

The position taken by a majority of the American courts is well stated by Morton, C. J., in a leading Massachusetts case:[40] "His clear intention, as shown in his will, was not to give his brother an absolute right to the income which might hereafter accrue upon the trust fund, with the power of alienating it in advance, but only the right to receive semiannually the income of the fund, which upon its payment to him, and not before, was to become his absolute property. His intentions ought to be carried out, unless they are against public policy. There is nothing in the nature or tenure of the estate given to the cestui que trust which would prevent this. The power of alienating in advance is not a necessary attribute or incident of such an estate or interest, so that the restraint of such alienation would introduce repugnant or inconsistent elements.

[34] Magner v. Crooks, 139 Cal. 640, 73 P. 585; Schuler v. Post, 18 App. Div. 374, 46 N.Y.S. 18; Williams v. Thorn, 70 N.Y. 270.

[35] Gray, Restraints, 2d Ed., preface, xi.

[36] Canfield v. Security-First Nat. Bk. of Los Angeles, 13 Cal.2d 1, 87 P.2d 830; Williams v. Thorn, 70 N.Y. 270; In re Williams, 187 N.Y. 286, 79 N.E. 1019.

[37] Erickson v. Erickson, 197 Minn. 71, 266 N.W. 161; Williams v. Smith, 117 Wis. 142, 93 N.W. 464.

[38] See § 72, post.

[39] La.Act. No. 81, 1938, § 28; 60 Okl.St.Ann. § 175.25.

[40] Broadway Nat. Bank v. Adams, 133 Mass. 170, 173-174, 43 Am.Rep. 504.

"We are not able to see that it would violate any principles of sound public policy to permit a testator to give to the object of his bounty such a qualified interest in the income of a trust fund, and thus provide against the improvidence or misfortune of the beneficiary. The only ground upon which it can be held to be against public policy is, that it defrauds the creditors of the beneficiary.

"It is argued that investing a man with apparent wealth tends to mislead creditors, and to induce them to give him credit. The answer is, that creditors have no right to rely upon property thus held, and to give him credit upon the basis of an estate which, by the instrument creating it, is declared to be inalienable by him, and not liable for his debts. By the exercise of proper diligence they can ascertain the nature and extent of his estate, especially in this commonwealth, where all wills and most deeds are spread upon the public records. There is the same danger of their being misled by false appearances, and induced to give credit to the equitable life tenant when the will or deed of trust provides for a cesser or limitation over, in case of an attempted alienation, or of bankruptcy or attachment, and the argument would lead to the conclusion that the English rule is equally in violation of public policy. We do not see why the founder of a trust may not directly provide that his property shall go to his beneficiary with the restriction that it shall not be alienable by anticipation, and that his creditors shall not have the right to attach it in advance, instead of indirectly reaching the same result by a provision for a cesser or a limitation over, or by giving his trustees a discretion as to paying it. He has the entire jus disponendi, which imports that he may give it absolutely, or may impose any restrictions or fetters not repugnant to the nature of the estate which he gives. Under our system, creditors may reach all the property of the debtor not exempted by law, but they cannot enlarge the gift of the founder of a trust, and take more than he has given."

It should be noted here that a property owner may not create a spendthrift trust in his own favor, such a trust being considered void as to the present and future creditors of the property owner.[41] To hold otherwise would be to give unexampled op-

---

[41] Hexter v. Clifford, 5 Colo. 168; De Rousse v. Williams, 181 Iowa 379, 164 N.W. 896; Wenzel v. Powder, 100 Md. 36, 59 A. 194, 108 Am.St.Rep. 380; Pacific Nat. Bank v. Windram, 133 Mass. 175; Cunningham v. Bright, 228 Mass. 385, 117 N.E. 909; Jamison v. Mississippi Valley Trust Co., Mo., 207 S.W. 788; Schenck v. Barnes, 156 N.Y. 316, 50 N.E. 967, 41

portunity to unscrupulous persons to lay aside their property before engaging in hazardous business enterprises, to mislead creditors into thinking that the settlor still owned the property since he appeared to be receiving its income, and thereby to work a gross fraud on creditors who might place reliance on the former prosperity and financial solidity of the debtor.

It should also be noticed that the courts have tended at times to make exceptions to the validity of spendthrift trusts in cases where the creditor of the beneficiary made an especially strong appeal to the sympathy of the court. Claims of this type are income tax claims,[42] claims for necessaries furnished the cestui,[43] or on account of debts due the settlor[44] or tort claims against the cestui.[45] There has been some tendency also to permit alimony and support money to be collected from a husband who is the beneficiary of a spendthrift trust by a court order directing the trustee to pay the wife or child instead of paying the husband the trust income.[46]

While some authorities contend that the spendthrift trust can protect only the beneficiary's right to future income, and not his right to capital in the future,[47] the trend of recent authorities supports these trusts as to both principal and income.[48]

The restraint imposed by a spendthrift trust may be limited to continue for the life of the beneficiary or any part of it.

The result of the rules of law just stated may be illustrated by a practical application. Suppose that A., the owner of a

L.R.A. 395; Rienzi v. Goodin, 249 Pa. 546, 95 A. 259. The settlor-cestui of a spendthrift trust can assign his interest. Byrnes v. Commissioner of Internal Revenue, C.C.A., 110 F.2d 294; City Bank Farmers' Trust Co. v. Kennard, Sup., 1 N.Y.S.2d 369.

[42] In re Rosenberg's Will, 269 N.Y. 247, 199 N.E. 206, 105 A.L.R. 1238.

[43] Sherman v. Skuse, 166 N.Y. 345, 59 N.E. 990.

[44] Matter of Foster's Estate, 38 Misc. 347, 77 N.Y.S. 922.

[45] Davies v. Harrison, 3 Pa.Dist. & Co. R. 481. On the general subject see Griswold, 43 Harv.L.R. 63.

[46] Mo.Rev.St.1939, § 570; Pa. 20 P.S. § 243; In re Stewart's Estate, 334 Pa. 356, 5 A.2d 910. But in other cases claims for alimony and support have not received any preferential treatment. Schwager v. Schwager, C.C.A.Wis., 109 F.2d 754; Bucknam v. Bucknam, 294 Mass. 214, 200 N.E. 918, 104 A.L.R. 774; Erickson v. Erickson, 197 Minn. 71, 266 N.W. 161.

[47] Restatement, Trusts, § 151, 153.

[48] Mellon v. Driscoll, C.C.A.Pa., 117 F.2d 477; Kelly v. Kelly, 11 Cal. 2d 356, 79 P.2d 1059, 119 A.L.R. 71; Snyder v. O'Conner, 102 Colo. 567, 81 P.2d 773; Medwedeff v. Fisher, 179 Md. 192, 17 A.2d 141; Erickson v. Erickson, 197 Minn. 71, 266 N.W. 161.

farm, conveys it to X., as trustee, to hold for the benefit of the son of A., who is a spendthrift and profligate. The trust instrument directs that the entire net income shall be paid over to the son in semiannual payments, on January 1st and July 1st. It also provides that the son shall have no power to sell his right to future income and that the right to such income shall not be liable for the debts of the son. In those states in which a spendthrift trust is condemned and held void, the provisions with respect to anticipation and the rights of creditors will be disregarded, and the son will be allowed to assign his rights, and his creditors to attach the right to future income. On the other hand, in the majority of American states, since spendthrift trusts are allowed, the settlor's directions will be respected, the son can create no present rights by means of an assignment of his right to receive payments, and the creditors of the son can have a remedy only against such funds as are paid into the son's hands on the 1st of each January and July and cannot compel the trustee to pay any of the income to them directly.

It should be noted, however, that an attempt by a spendthrift beneficiary to assign his right to future income may be treated by the trustee as an order to pay the income to the assignee, and that until such order is revoked by the beneficiary the trustee will be protected in paying income to the assignee, although he need not do so.[49] A purported present assignment by a spendthrift beneficiary also acts as a contract to assign the income when received, if the assignment is for a consideration, and damages can be recovered for the breach of this contract and collected out of property which has been delivered to the beneficiary by the trustee.[50]

DISCRETIONARY TRUSTS [51]

46. If a trustee has discretion to pay or apply income to or for a beneficiary, or to pay or apply nothing, the interest of the beneficiary before the trustee elects to pay or apply a given amount is not assignable or reachable by his creditors. If, however, the trust has no spendthrift clause in it, and a trustee of such a trust has received notice of an assignment by the beneficiary, or has been served with process by a creditor of the beneficiary attempting to reach the

---

[49] In re Easton's Estate, Sur., 13 N.Y.S.2d 295; In re Keeler's Estate, 334 Pa. 225, 3 A.2d 413, 121 A.L.R. 1301.

[50] Kelly v. Kelly, 11 Cal.2d 356, 79 P.2d 1059, 119 A.L.R. 71.

[51] Restatement, Trusts, § 155.

beneficiary's interest, and the trustee thereafter pays or applies trust property to or for the beneficiary, he will be liable to the assignee or creditor for the amount paid.

Sometimes the settlor provides that the trustee shall pay to or apply for the beneficiary only so much of the income or capital of the trust as the trustee sees fit to use for that purpose, and that the remainder of the trust property shall be used for another purpose. This is a discretionary trust, in the sense that there is a discretion to give the named beneficiary some benefits under the trust or to give him nothing. Here obviously the beneficiary cannot force the trustee to use any of the trust property for his benefit, nor should anyone taking under him, such as a transferee or creditor, be in any better position. To a suit to compel the trustee to pay or apply, the trustee could reply that he had elected not to pay or apply. Therefore, the nature of the trust gives the beneficiary no interest subject to assignment or to the claims of his creditors, before the time when the trustee has elected to use some of the trust property for the beneficiary.[52]

If, however, the trustee does at any time elect to pay trust income to the beneficiary, or to apply it for his benefit, then the beneficiary has a property interest which, if not protected by a spendthrift trust clause prohibiting alienation or taking by creditors, is assignable and reachable by creditors; and if the beneficiary assigns, or creditors seek to take, in advance of the election by the trustee to pay or apply, and later the trustee chooses to pay or apply, he will be liable to the assignee or creditor for the amount paid or applied, if the trustee had notice of the assignment or had been served with process by the creditor.[53] The assignment, or attachment, is deemed to affect future payments or applications, if and when the trustee in his discretion elects to make them.

[52] Foley v. Hastings, 107 Conn. 9, 139 A. 305; Funk v. Grulke, 204 Iowa 314, 213 N.W. 608; Foster v. Foster, 133 Mass. 179; Todd's Ex'rs v. Todd, 260 Ky. 611, 86 S.W.2d 168.

[53] In re Coleman, 39 Ch.D. 443; Hamilton v. Drogo, 241 N.Y. 401, 150 N.E. 496.

TRUSTS FOR SUPPORT [54]

47. **In a trust where the trustee is directed to spend only so much of the income as is necessary for the education and maintenance of the beneficiary, and to spend the income only for that purpose, the interest of the beneficiary is not assignable by him or reachable by his creditors.**

If a trustee is directed to spend trust income for the benefit of a certain beneficiary, but only to the extent necessary to educate and support him, the nature of the beneficiary's interest makes his interest not transferrable or takable by his creditors. The trustee is directed to pay out the trust income only if his payments will achieve a certain result, namely, education or support of the beneficiary. Paying money to an assignee of the beneficiary or to his creditors will not accomplish the education or support of the beneficiary. Therefore, the nature of the trust involves in effect a restraint on voluntary or involuntary alienation of the trustee's interest.[55]

Such a trust should be distinguished from one where the trustee is to pay a fixed amount for the education and support of the beneficiary, or is to pay all the income of the trust for such purposes. These latter trusts are not technically "support" trusts, since the beneficiary has a right to money which he will himself apply for his education or support. The words "education and support" in such a case are used merely to show the motive of the settlor and not to show the results which the trustee must accomplish by his payments or applications.[56] In these trusts the cestui's rights may be alienated or taken by creditors, unless protected by a spendthrift clause.

BLENDED TRUSTS [57]

48. **If a trust is for the benefit of a group of persons and no member of the group has a right to any individual benefits separate and apart from the others, then no member has an alienable interest or one which his creditors can reach.**

If a trust is established for a group of persons, as, for example, for the benefit of a man and his wife and children, with a direc-

---

[54] Restatement, Trusts, § 154.

[55] Keeler's Estate, 334 Pa. 225, 3 A.2d 413, 121 A.L.R. 1301; Keyser v. Mitchell, 67 Pa. 473. And see Jones v. Coon, 229 Iowa 756, 295 N.W. 162.

[56] Sparhawk v. Cloon, 125 Mass. 263; Young v. Easley, 94 Va. 193, 26 S.E.2d 401.

[57] Restatement, Trusts, § 161.

tion to the trustee to pay or apply the trust income for the benefit of this group, the interests of the members of the group are so inseparably blended that no one person can be said to have any individual interest. Each payment or application must work a group benefit. If there are six persons in the group, it cannot be said that each one has a one-sixth interest in the trust. The whole interest is vested in the group. Here, therefore, no transfer by one of the members will give the transferee a right to any trust income, and no creditor of any one member can collect trust income from the trustee.[58]

The so-called "protective trusts" to some extent take the place of spendthrift trusts in England. In them a gift is made to a trustee to pay or apply income for the benefit of a given person until that person seeks to transfer his interest under the trust, or his creditors seek to take it; and then the trustee is to hold for the benefit of the first beneficiary and his family, with discretion to pay or apply for their maintenance and support.[59] This is in substance an ordinary trust, determinable on attempted voluntary or involuntary alienation, with a gift over to the same trustee on a blended trust for the original beneficiary and his family. By recent legislation[60] such a protective trust can be accomplished without giving the details of it in the trust instrument, merely by a statement that the property is given to the trustee on a protective trust for A for life or for a lesser period.

---

[58] Bell v. Watkins, 82 Ala. 512, 1 So. 92, 60 Am.Rep. 756; Linn v. Downing, 216 Ill. 64, 74 N.E. 729; Russell v. Meyers, 202 Ky. 593, 260 S.W. 377; Talley v. Ferguson, 64 W. Va. 328, 62 S.E. 456, 17 L.R.A.,N.S., 1215.

[59] In re Bullock, 60 L.J.Ch. 341; Scott, Protective Trusts, Harv. Legal Essays, 1934, p. 419.

[60] English Trustee Act 1925, § 33.

CHAPTER 5

CREATION OF RESULTING TRUSTS

Sec.
49. Introduction to Implied Trusts.
50. Statute of Frauds.
51. Voluntary Conveyances.
52. Payment of Consideration for Conveyance to Another.
53. Failure of an Express Trust.
54. Where Express Trust Res Proves Excessive.

INTRODUCTION [1]

49. **Implied trusts are trusts declared to exist by courts of equity, either for the purpose of carrying out the presumed intent of the parties or to prevent unjust enrichment. They are of two classes, namely:**

   (a) Resulting trusts, which are declared by equity to exist because of a presumed intent of the parties that they shall exist; and

   (b) Constructive trusts, which are created by equity as a convenient means of relieving the victim of some kind of wrongful conduct and preventing unjust enrichment.

In previous sections [2] the creation of express trusts has been considered. The origin of implied trusts will now be studied.

Reference has previously been made to the unsatisfactory and conflicting classifications of trusts made by various judges and authors.[3] "Implied trusts" have been defined by some to mean trusts in which the settlor consciously intended a trust, but expressed his intent in doubtful or ambiguous language, as, for example, by the use of such precatory words as "I request." In such cases the court has sometimes been said to imply or construe the trust from the words of the parties.[4] But another definition of implied trusts is that they are trusts which owe their existence to the courts, and not to expressed intent of the parties (either clear or ambiguous); that they are law-created trusts, and not trusts created by act of the parties. This definition has also divided implied trusts into two classes, namely, resulting and constructive trusts; the former implied by the courts, because the

---

[1] Restatement, Trusts, Introduction to Chapter 12; Restatement, Restitution, § 160.

[2] Ante, §§ 20–48.

[3] See note, ante, ——.

[4] Lewin, Trusts, 13th Ed., p. 92; 1 Perry, Trusts, 7th Ed., § 112.

parties involved are inferred or presumed to have intended them, and the latter created by the courts for the purpose of preventing the unjust enrichment of the holder of a title, usually the legal title.[5]

The classification of trusts has been discussed by several able writers.[6] Undoubtedly a desirable division would be that of Professor Costigan, into "intent-enforcing" and "fraud-rectifying" trusts. Within the former class would fall: (1) Cases where the parties have clearly expressed an intent to have a trust exist; (2) cases in which the parties have expressed an ambiguous intent, which the court, construing their acts, holds to be a trust intent; and (3) cases in which the parties have expressed no intent by words, but have done acts from which the court infers that a trust was intended. In this latter case the court declares that as a result of these acts a trust exists. To the second class, that of "fraud-rectifying," would be assigned those cases now usually classed as constructive or involuntary trusts, in which the parties have expressed no intent to have a trust, nor does the court presume that any such intent existed, but the court uses the trust as the most convenient method of working out justice and preventing one party from unfairly enriching himself.

The statement that resulting trusts are created by operation of law may be criticized. It may be urged that they are created by the acts of the parties; that their basis is the intent of the parties; that the law does not bring them into being, but adjudges that they have existed ever since the parties did the acts in question; and that resulting trusts are like the contracts which are properly called "implied." Such contracts are inferred by the courts from the acts of the parties, as where one takes a newspaper from a

---

[5] See authorities cited, ante, p. 52, note.

"Some courts have been disposed to divide these trusts into categories, with distinctive names, as 'resulting trusts' and 'constructive trusts,' but have so confused the lines which divide them from each other as to have materially impaired their usefulness for the purpose of legal exposition. Generally speaking, however, a resulting trust is one which the law implies to meet the requirement of justice that a legal status be given to what is the clear intention of the parties; while constructive trusts rest upon the sound public policy which requires that the laws themselves should not become the instruments of designing persons to be used for the purpose of fraud and oppression." Ferguson v. Robinson, 258 Mo. 113, 129, 167 S.W. 447, 452.

[6] See Maitland, Equity, pp. 75–76; "The Classification of Trusts as Express, Resulting and Constructive," G. P. Costigan, Jr., 27 Harv.Law Rev. 437; "Resulting Trusts and the Statute of Frauds," H. F. Stone, 6 Col.Law Rev. 326.

news-stand without making any statement. Ordinarily the courts would infer that as a matter of fact there was a contract for the purchase of the newspaper.

On the other hand, it may be said that constructive trusts are analogous to quasi contracts, which are imposed by law upon parties for the purpose of preventing unjust enrichment. If A. has paid $500 to B. under a contract which is unenforceable because of the Statute of Frauds, and B. sets up the statute as a bar against performance, A. may recover of B. the $500 thus paid, not because of any true contract for its return, but because the law imposes on B. a quasi contractual obligation to return the $500. In the same way constructive trusts are imposed on parties who were never intended to be trustees, but who now hold property which does not fairly belong to them.

Although the common classification of trusts is illogical, it seems inadvisable to depart from it in an elementary text-book. Resulting and constructive trusts will be treated together, and under the common heading of implied trusts, although they do not logically belong together. To do otherwise would produce confusion rather than clarity.

STATUTE OF FRAUDS [7]

50. The Statute of Frauds has no application to resulting trusts. They may be proved by oral evidence, whether they relate to real or personal property.

The eighth section of the English Statute of Frauds [8] excepts from the operation of the seventh section trusts arising or resulting "by the implication or construction of law," and the American state statutes have universally followed the English model in this respect.[9] It is everywhere held that a resulting trust may be proved by parol evidence.[10] Resulting trusts need not be created or proved by a written instrument.

[7] Restatement, Trusts, § 406.

[8] St. 29 Charles II, c. 3, 1677.

[9] See § 25, ante. But the statutes of Pennsylvania require an acknowledged and recorded declaration of a resulting trust or an action of ejectment begun by the cestui que trust in order to make the resulting trust valid against creditors of or bona fide purchasers from the legal title holder, without notice. 21 P.S. § 601; Rochester Trust Co. v. White, 243 Pa. 469, 90 A. 127; Rosa v. Hummel, 252 Pa. 578, 97 A. 942.

[10] Caple v. McCollum, 27 Ala. 461; Bayles v. Baxter, 22 Cal. 575; Poulet v. Johnson, 25 Ga. 403; Brennaman v. Schell, 212 Ill. 356, 72 N.E. 412; McCollister v. Willey, 52 Ind. 382;

VOLUNTARY CONVEYANCES [11]

51. It was a doctrine of early English equity that a common-law conveyance, in which no consideration was named and no use expressed, was presumed to create a resulting trust in favor of the grantor. Trusts of this variety are now obsolete, because of a change in the presumption from that of trust to that of gift.

In the early history of the English common law practically all land was held to uses. It was almost universal to mention in conveyances the use to which the property conveyed was to be held. Wherever A. conveyed land to B. by a common-law conveyance (feoffment with livery of seizin, fine, or recovery), and no consideration was mentioned and no use named, chancery presumed that the universal custom of holding to uses would be followed, and that a use was intended for the benefit of A., the person naturally entitled to the profits of the property.[12] It was presumed that A. did not intend to give away his property, and, if any use were to exist, it would seem natural that it should exist in favor of A. This use was called a resulting use.

Later, when the Statute of Uses was enacted, and uses were recognized as trusts, chancery continued to enforce A.'s rights in the form of a resulting trust.

Changes in conveyancing have made conveyances without a consideration named and use described exceedingly rare. The

---

Culp v. Price, 107 Iowa 133, 77 N.W. 848; Lehrling v. Lehrling, 84 Kan. 766, 115 P. 556; Nickels v. Clay, 14 Ky.Law Rep. 925; Davis v. Downer, 210 Mass. 573, 97 N.E. 90; Butler v. Carpenter, 163 Mo. 597, 63 S.W. 823; Baker v. Baker, 75 N.J.Eq. 305, 72 A. 1000; Ross v. Hegeman, 2 Edw.Ch., N.Y., 373; Coffin v. McIntosh, 9 Utah 315, 34 P. 247.

The courts frequently state that the evidence to establish a resulting trust must be clear, strong, unequivocal and convincing. Hunter v. Feild, 114 Ark. 128, 169 S.W. 813; Steward v. Hackler, 117 Ark. 655, 173 S.W. 425; McGill v. Chappelle, 71 Fla. 479, 71 So. 836. "Since such a trust works in a sense uphill against the statute of frauds, the rule has ever been to require strong, unequivocal, and convincing proof before finding and decreeing the existence of such a trust." Hunnell v. Zinn, Mo., 184 S.W. 1154, 1156. The courts are anxious to preserve the security of record titles. Most efforts to have resulting trusts adjudged involve holding that the apparent full owner of property is not what he appears to be, and is merely a trustee. It is against social interest to do such a thing lightly. Wiley v. Dunn, 358 Ill. 97, 192 N.E. 661; Bisceglia v. Bisceglia, 340 Pa. 293, 17 A.2d 182.

[11] Restatement, Trusts, § 405.

[12] Digby, History of Real Property, 5th Ed., 329, 355; Bacon, Uses, 217.

old common-law forms of conveyancing are superseded by conveyances operating under the Statute of Uses, in which there is no room for a presumption of a trust in favor of the grantor. The conveyances by lease and release and bargain and sale practically always mention a consideration or name the person to whose use the land is to be held. The conveyance by bargain and sale relied for its operation on the raising of a use in the grantee. Hence such a conveyance without mention of a use was impossible. Modern conveyances in the form of grants always state that consideration passed, or name the use, or do both, and hence leave no room for presumptions as to the identity of the person who is entitled to the use of the property.

Furthermore, the presumption of a trust for the grantor on a voluntary conveyance has changed to a presumption of a gift to the grantee, where no consideration or use is mentioned.[13] According to present day ideas if a grantor expects a trust for himself or others, he will state it in the deed, and if he does not do so, the natural inference is that he desired to make a gift. The holding of property under trust is now the exception, and not the rule as it was in the middle ages in England.

The resulting trust of this nature is, therefore, very generally held to be nonexistent.[14] Naturally, if any consideration [15] or any use [16] is named, no trust can result to the grantor. A statute declaring that all conveyances shall pass a fee, unless a contrary in-

[13] Collins v. Collins, 46 Ariz. 485, 52 P.2d 1169; Fooshee v. Kasenberg, 152 Kan. 100, 102 P.2d 995; Hojnacki v. Hojnacki, 281 Mich. 636, 275 N.W. 659; Niemaseck v. Bernett Holding Co., 125 N.J.Eq. 284, 4 A.2d 794.

[14] Leman v. Whitley, 4 Russ.Ch. 423; Tainter v. Broderick Land & Investment Co., 177 Cal. 664, 171 P. 679; McClenahan v. Stevenson, 118 Iowa 106, 91 N.W. 925; Philbrook v. Delano, 29 Me. 410; Groff v. Rohrer, 35 Md. 327; Titcomb v. Morrill, 10 Allen, Mass., 15; Bartlett v. Bartlett, 14 Gray, Mass., 277; Taylor v. Thompson, 88 Mo. 86; Hogan v. Jaques, 19 N.J.Eq. 123, 97 Am.Dec. 644; Lovett v. Taylor, 54 N.J.Eq. 311, 34 A. 896; Coffey v. Sullivan, 63 N.J.Eq. 296, 49 A. 520. But see Bayles v. Crossman, 5 Ohio Dec. 354; Boyd v. Winte, 65 Okl. 141, 164 P. 781. But a voluntary conveyance, coupled with other facts, may raise a resulting trust. Gray v Beard, 66 Or. 59, 133 P. 791. It has been recently held that a voluntary conveyance by one trustee for a charity to another trustee, without mention of a trust purpose, created a resulting trust. Deutsche Presbyterische Kirche v. Trustees of Presbytery of Elizabeth, 89 N.J.Eq. 242, 104 A. 642.

[15] Verzier v. Convard, 75 Conn. 1, 52 A. 255; Gould v. Lynde, 114 Mass. 366; Jackson v. Cleveland, 15 Mich. 94, 90 Am.Dec. 266; Farrington v. Barr, 36 N.H. 86.

[16] Bragg v. Geddes, 93 Ill. 39; Donlin v. Bradley, 119 Ill. 412, 10 N.E. 11; Salisbury v. Clarke, 61 Vt. 453, 17 A. 135.

tent clearly appears in the conveyance, prevents the occurrence of resulting trusts of this class.[17]

"The old common-law conveyances operated to pass the title without the machinery of a declaration of uses, and where no use was declared, and in the absence of an actual consideration paid, the courts raised a resulting trust in favor of the grantor. But modern conveyances, of which the one in hand is a sample, operate under the Statute of Uses, and contain an express declaration of uses, and it is contrary to first principles to permit this declaration to be contradicted by parol, except in cases of fraud, accident, or mistake." [18]

Under the early common law, when resulting trusts of this class arose, the presumption of a trust in favor of the grantor could always be overcome by parol evidence that a gift was intended. The duty of a man to support his wife and children raised a presumption that a voluntary conveyance to wife or child was by way of gift, and not with the intent that wife or child should hold as a resulting trustee.[19]

PAYMENT OF CONSIDERATION FOR CONVEYANCE TO ANOTHER [20]

52. Where one pays the consideration for a transfer of real or personal property, but has the title taken in the name of another, it is presumed or inferred that the payor intended the grantee to be a trustee for the payor.

This presumption is rebuttable by proof that the payor of the consideration intended a gift to the grantee, either of part or all of the property. The presumption may also be confirmed by evidence that the parties expressly agreed that the payor should have an equitable interest, and such agreement does not make the trust an express one.

If the payor of the consideration is the husband or parent of the grantee, there is a presumption that the transfer of the property was by way of gift or advancement.

The consideration paid must be the money or other property of the alleged cestui at the time of the conveyance, if a trust is to exist. If money is lent to the payor by the grantee or another at the time of, or before, the deed, a resulting trust is presumed for the payor; but if the consideration

---

[17] Campbell v. Noble, 145 Ala. 233, 41 So. 745.

[18] Lovett v. Taylor, 54 N.J.Eq. 311, 318, 34 A. 896.

[19] Christ's Hospital v. Budgin, 2 Vern. 683; Jennings v. Sellick, 1 Vern. 467.

[20] Restatement, Trusts, §§ 440–460.

is lent to the grantee and paid on his behalf there is no basis for a resulting trust.

The consideration must be paid or agreed to be paid by or for the resulting trust claimant at or before the time when the property is conveyed.

If a part only of the price is paid by or for the resulting trust claimant, he is presumed to have intended a trust in a proportionate part of the property for himself, and not a gift or loan.

In seven states resulting trusts of this kind are abolished or modified by statute.

General Principle

The most important class of resulting trusts is that arising where A. pays the consideration for the conveyance of property, real or personal, and has the property conveyed to B. "On account of the improbability of a gift to a stranger, the law implies that the one who holds the title, without having paid any value for it, is a trustee for the one who in fact paid the purchase price." [21] This principle is one universally recognized,[22] except in certain states, where statutes have been passed controlling the situation. The statutes declaring or modifying the general rule above stated will be discussed later.[23]

If the object of the payor was to obtain a resulting trust for an unlawful purpose, as, for example, to avoid the public land

[21] Howe v. Howe, 199 Mass. 598, 602, 85 N.E. 945, 127 Am.St.Rep. 516.

[22] Dyer v. Dyer, 2 Cox, 93; In re Spencer, D.C.Vt., 128 F. 654; Spradling v. Spradling, 101 Ark. 451, 142 S.W. 848; Leroy v. Norton, 49 Colo. 490, 113 P. 529; Lander v. Persky, 85 Conn. 429, 83 A. 209; Pittock v. Pittock, 15 Idaho 426, 98 P. 719; Masters v. Mayes, 246 Ill. 506, 92 N.E. 945; Ratliff v. Elwell, 141 Iowa 312, 119 N.W. 740, 20 L.R.A.,N.S., 223; Buck v. Pike, 11 Me. 9; Euler v. Schroeder, 112 Md. 155, 76 A. 164; Mahorner v. Harrison, 21 Miss. 53, 13 Smedes & M. 53; Brown v. Alexander, 118 Miss. 848, 79 So. 842; Plumb v. Cooper, 121 Mo. 668, 26 S.W. 678; Cowles v. Cowles, 89 Neb. 327, 131 N.W. 738; Mershon v. Duer, 40 N.J.Eq. 333; Summers v. Moore, 113 N.C. 394, 18 S.E. 712; Creed v. President, etc., of Lancaster Bank, 1 Ohio St. 1; De Roboam v. Schmidtlin, 50 Or. 388, 92 P. 1082; Asam v. Asam, 239 Pa. 295, 86 A. 871; Butler v. Rutledge, 2 Cold, Tenn., 4; Burns v. Ross, 71 Tex. 516, 9 S.W. 468; Larisey v. Larisey, 93 S.C. 450, 77 S.E. 129; Fisk v. Patton, 7 Utah 399, 27 P. 1; Flanary v. Kane, 102 Va. 547, 46 S.E. 312. That the grantee was ignorant of the conveyance does not affect the resulting trust. Mereness v. Delemos, 91 Conn. 651, 101 A. 8; Froemke v. Marks, 259 Ill. 146, 102 N.E. 192. But if the placing of title in another than the payor of the consideration was with the object of preventing the collection of a judgment, and so the defrauding of creditors of the payor, the creditors can reach the property. Higginbotham v. Boggs, C.C.A.Va., 234 F. 253, 148 C.C.A. 155.

[23] See post, p. 187.

laws regarding the amount of land which he might enter in his name, no resulting trust will be enforced.[24] Another example of this type is an attempt to obtain a resulting trust in order to evade the creditors of the payor, by concealing his interest in the property. The creditors can take the property, if they can prove it was paid for by their debtor.[25]

This form of trust arises only when the purchase in the name of a stranger is made with the payor's consent. If such consent be lacking—that is, if the grantee uses the money of another to buy the property, without such other's knowledge or consent—a trust is declared by equity, which, although sometimes called a resulting trust, is more properly a constructive trust, one created to avoid the unjust enrichment of the legal title holder, and not one to carry out a presumed intent.[26] If the title is taken in the name of a stranger by mistake, equity will declare a trust in favor of the payor of the purchase price.[27] The general rule above stated applies to cases of personal property as well as real property.[28]

That the stranger who has acquired title as a result of consideration paid by another is a resulting trustee for that other is a presumption merely. The stranger may prove that a gift of the property to him was intended. He may rebut the presumption of a trust;[29] and the evidence which rebuts the presumption

[24] Miller v. Davis, 50 Mo. 572; Leggett v. Dubois, 5 Paige, N.Y., 114, 28 Am.Dec. 413 Smith v. Barnes, 129 Or. 138, 276 P. 1086.

[25] Lafkowitz v. Jackson, C.C.A.Mo., 13 F.2d 370; Hutchins v. Heywood, 50 N.H. 491.

[26] Keller v. Keller, 45 Md. 269; Shrader v. Shrader, 119 Miss. 526, 81 So. 227; Gogherty v. Bennett, 37 N.J. Eq. 87; Lloyd v. Woods, 176 Pa. 63, 34 A. 926.

[27] Fairhurst v. Lewis, 23 Ark. 435; Hayward v. Cain, 110 Mass. 273; Turner v. Home Ins. Co., 195 Mo.App. 138, 189 S.W. 626; Oberthier v. Stroud, 33 Tex. 522.

[28] Gowell v. Twitchell, 306 Mass. 482, 28 N.E.2d 531; Baker v. Terrell, 8 Minn. 195, 8 Gil. 165; Reynolds v. Kenney, 87 N.H. 313, 179 A. 16, 98 A.L.R. 751; McClung v. Colwell, 107 Tenn. 592, 64 S.W. 890, 89 Am.St.Rep. 961.

[29] Tryon v. Huntoon, 67 Cal. 325, 7 P. 741; Livermore v. Aldrich, 59 Mass. 431, 5 Cush. 431; Irvine v. Marshall, 7 Minn. 286, 7 Gil. 216; Baldwin v. Campfield, 8 N.J.Eq. 891; Warren v. Steer, 112 Pa. 634, 5 A. 4. The presumption has been overcome where the payor of the consideration was indebted at least morally to the grantee for maintenance in old age (Morford v. Stephens, Mo., 178 S.W. 441), and where there was long-continued acquiescence by the payor of the consideration in the use of the property by the grantee (Akin v. Akin, 276 Ill. 447, 114 N.E. 908), and where an employer paid the consideration for a house in which her secretary lived, the object being to reward services (Reizenberger v. Shel-

may be parol evidence.[30] While a resulting trust is not based on an express agreement, yet, if the payor of the consideration and the grantee make an agreement equivalent in effect to what the law would imply, under the facts of the case, a resulting trust will be decreed, and the express agreement will be ignored.[31] That there was an express agreement giving the payor as much as, or less than, the law would have given him by way of resulting trust, does not change the trust from resulting to an express trust. The agreement is treated merely as corroborative of the inferred intent of the payor, in whole or in part. Thus, if an uncle pays for land and has title run to his nephew, on the oral understanding that the uncle is to enjoy the land for his life and that thereafter the nephew is to have it, the resulting trust for the uncle which the law would imply is confirmed in part, namely, to the extent of a life estate, and rebutted in part, namely, as to the remainder interest following the uncle's life estate.[32] But if the oral agreement attempted to give the payor more than the law would imply for him, then as to the excess it amounts to an attempt to create an express trust.[33]

Effect of Relationship of Payor and Grantee

If the payor of the consideration is related to the person to whom title is conveyed in such a way that a gift is extremely natural, as a contribution toward the support of the grantee, or out of love and affection, or as an advancement in anticipation of death, the presumption of a resulting trust does not prevail, but the presumption of advancement or gift is established. Thus, if H., the husband of W., pay the consideration for a conveyance of property to W., there is a presumption that H. intended to give this property to W., because of the duty which H. has to support

ton, 86 N.J.Eq. 92, 97 A. 293). A common case is that where the grantee, with the knowledge and consent of the payor, for many years takes the benefits of the land and bears the burden of taxes and mortgage interest.

[30] Bayles v. Baxter, 22 Cal. 575; Blasdel v. Locke, 52 N.H. 238; Peer v. Peer, 11 N.J.Eq. 432; Strimpfler v. Roberts, 18 Pa. 283, 57 Am.Dec. 606; Smith v. Strahan, 16 Tex. 314, 67 Am. Dec. 622.

[31] Breitenbucher v. Oppenheim, 160 Cal. 98, 116 P. 55; Barrows v. Bohan, 41 Conn. 278; Cook v. Blazis, 365 Ill. 625, 7 N.E.2d 291; Mays v. Jackson, 346 Mo. 1224, 145 S.W.2d 392. A resulting trust is not changed to an express trust by a writing acknowledging its existence. Lasker-Morris Bank & Trust Co. v. Gans, 132 Ark. 402, 200 S.W. 1029.

[32] Larisey v. Larisey, 93 S.C. 450, 77 S.E. 129.

[33] See Wright v. Chilcott, 61 Or. 561, 121 P. 895, 122 P. 765.

BOGERT TRUSTS 2D

W., and because of the frequency and naturalness of gifts from husband to wife.[34] But this presumption of gift may be overcome by oral proof that no advancement was intended, and that a trust in favor of the husband was the object of the husband.[35]

So, too, if the payor of the consideration is the parent of the grantee of the property, or a person in loco parentis, equity presumes that the payor intended to make a gift or advancement, and not to raise a trust.[36] However, this presumption of gift is rebuttable by evidence that the parent intended a trust and did not have in mind a gift.[37]

[34] Ciffo v. Ciffo, 44 App.D.C. 217; Goelz v. Goelz, 157 Ill. 33, 41 N.E. 756; Sunderland v. Sunderland, 19 Iowa 325; Spring v. Hight, 22 Me. 408, 39 Am.Dec. 587; Hayes v. Horton, 46 Or. 597, 81 P. 386; Edgerly v. Edgerly, 112 Mass. 175; Ilgenfritz v. Ilgenfritz, 116 Mo. 429, 22 S.W. 786; Gray v. Gray, 13 Neb. 453, 14 N.W. 390; Dickinson v. Davis, 43 N.H. 647, 80 Am.Dec. 202; McGee v. McGee, 81 N.J.Eq. 190, 86 A. 406; Scott v. Calladine, 79 Hun 79, 29 N.Y.S. 630; Egerton v. Jones, 107 N.C. 284, 12 S.E. 434; Coe v. Coe, 75 Or. 145, 145 P. 674; Spradling v. Spradling, 101 Ark. 451, 142 S.W. 848; Kennedy v. Kennedy, Tex.Civ.App., 210 S.W. 581. Improvements put on the wife's land with the husband's money do not inure to his benefit by way of resulting trust. Nelson v. Nelson, 176 N.C. 191, 96 S.E. 986; Anderson v. Anderson, 177 N.C. 401, 99 S.E. 106.

[35] Poole v. Oliver, 89 Ark. 85, 115 S.W. 952; Hubbard v. McMahon, 117 Ark. 563, 176 S.W. 122; Jackson v. Jackson, 150 Ga. 544, 104 S.E. 236; Kern v. Beatty, 267 Ill. 127, 107 N.E. 794; Towles v. Towles, 176 Ky. 225, 195 S.W. 437; Price v. Kane, 112 Mo. 412, 20 S.W. 609; Woodward v. Woodward, 89 Neb. 142, 131 N.W. 188; Shotwell v. Stickle, 83 N.J.Eq. 188, 90 A. 246; Flanner v. Butler, 131 N.C. 155, 42 S.E. 557, 92 Am.St.Rep. 773; Toney v. Toney, 84 Or. 310, 165 P. 221; Wallace v. Bowen, 28 Vt. 638. If the wife expressly agrees to hold under conditions identical with those of a resulting trust, the presumption of a gift is rebutted. Wilson v. Warner, 89 Conn. 243, 93 A. 533.

[36] Foster v. Treadway, 98 Ark. 452, 136 S.W. 934; Doll v. Gifford, 13 Colo.App. 67, 56 P. 676; Euans v. Curtis, 190 Ill. 197, 60 N.E. 56; McGinnis v. McGinnis, 159 Iowa 394, 139 N.W. 466; Clark v. Creswell, 112 Md. 339, 76 A. 579, 21 Ann.Cas. 338; Page v. Page, 8 N.H. 187; Astreen v. Flanagan, 3 Edw.Ch., N.Y., 279; Wheeler v. Kidder, 105 Pa. 270; Miller v. Blose's Ex'r, 30 Grat., Va., 744. But see Madsen v. Madsen, 35 Cal. App. 487, 170 P. 435, *contra*, the decision being affected by statute.

The majority of the cases apply the presumption of a gift where a mother is the payor and a child the grantee, but some courts take the view that a trust for the mother is to be presumed. Harris v. Cassells, 202 Cal. 648, 262 P. 319; Eckert v. Eckert, 152 Iowa 745, 133 N.W. 112; Paulson v. Paulson, 50 R.I. 86, 145 A. 312.

[37] In re Peabody, C.C.A.Mass., 118 F. 266, 55 C.C.A. 360; Hartley v. Hartley, 279 Ill. 593, 117 N.E. 69; Rankin v. Harper, 23 Mo. 579; Long v. Long, Mo., 192 S.W. 948; Peer v. Peer, 11 N.J.Eq. 432; Jackson ex dem. Benson v. Matsdorf, 11 Johns., N.Y., 91, 6 Am.Dec. 355; Elrod v. Cochran, 59 S.C. 467, 38 S.E. 122; Shepherd v.

Since the wife was economically inferior in the days of the development of the common law, and normally did not make gifts to her husband, the law presumed that if she paid for property and had it conveyed to her husband, she expected him to be trustee for her and did not intend a gift. This presumption still prevails,[38] although the large increase in the amount of property held by women, and the changed relationship between man and wife, have led some courts to the view that the primary presumption should be that of gift from wife to husband.[39]

A child's payment of the consideration for a deed taken in the name of the parent is presumed to result in a trust in favor of the child.[40]

Where the payor of the consideration was the common-law wife,[41] fiancé,[42] or brother or sister,[43] of the grantee, a trust has been held to result, there being no presumption of a gift.

White, 10 Tex. 72; Law v. Law, 76 Va. 527; Clary v. Spain, 119 Va. 58, 89 S.E. 130.

[38] Shaw v. Bernal, 163 Cal. 262, 124 P. 1012; Loften v. Witboard, 92 Ill. 461; Resor v. Resor, 9 Ind. 347; Southern Bank of Fulton v. Nichols, 235 Mo. 401, 138 S.W. 881; Mayer v. Kane, 69 N.J.Eq. 733, 61 A. 374; Barnes v. Spencer, 79 Or. 205, 153 P. 47; McCormick v. Cooke, 199 Pa. 631, 49 A. 238; Chalk v. Daggett, Tex. Civ.App., 204 S.W. 1057. Prior to the Married Women's Acts the wife's money became her husband's property, and hence the purchase of property by him with the money formerly held by her as separate property created no resulting trust for her. Brooks v. Brooks, 275 Ill. 23, 113 N.E. 919. But a gift has been presumed where the wife paid the consideration and had the title taken in the names of both husband and wife. Doyle v. Doyle, 268 Ill. 96, 108 N.E. 796; Haguewood v. Britain, 273 Mo. 89, 199 S.W. 950. This seems correct, because the indication by the payor of the consideration that she was to have a certain interest in the property bought, namely, that of a tenant by the entirety, warrants the presumption that she did not expect to receive any greater interest. But in Deese v. Deese, 176 N.C. 527, 97 S.E. 475, the court held that payment of the consideration by the wife and a conveyance to the husband and wife created a resulting trust in her favor as to one-half.

[39] Bingham v. National Bank of Montana, 105 Mont. 159, 72 P.2d 90, 113 A.L.R. 315; Hummel v. Marshall, 95 W.Va. 42, 120 S.E. 164.

[40] Champlin v. Champlin, 136 Ill. 309, 26 N.E. 526, 29 Am.St.Rep. 323; Harlan v. Eilke, 100 Ky. 642, 38 S.W. 1094; Detwiler v. Detwiler, 30 Neb. 338, 46 N.W. 624; Crowley v. Crowley, 72 N.H. 241, 56 A. 190; O'Neill v. O'Neill, 227 Pa. 334, 76 A. 26.

[41] McDonald v. Carr, 150 Ill. 204, 37 N.E. 225.

[42] Lufkin v. Jakeman, 188 Mass. 528, 74 N.E. 933.

[43] Kuncl v. Kuncl, 99 Neb. 390, 156 N.W. 772; Harris v. McIntyre, 118 Ill. 275, 8 N.E. 182. But see Printup v. Patton, 91 Ga. 422, 18 S.E. 311, *contra*. It will not be presumed

Source of Consideration

It is essential that the money or other consideration furnished for the conveyance shall, at the time of the conveyance, have been the property of the person who claims to be a cestui que trust.[44] Hence, that A. has lent money to B., and that B. has purchased property with such money and taken title in his own name, is not ground for the declaration of a resulting trust in A.'s favor. The money furnished for the property had become B.'s by virtue of the loan, and it cannot be said that A. furnished the consideration for the conveyance to B.[45]

On the other hand, if the payor of the consideration has received it as a loan from the grantee of the property, a trust will arise in favor of the payor. If A. borrows $500 from B., and later A. pays this money to C., who, in return therefor and at A.'s request, conveys land to B., a presumption of a resulting trust arises. The money furnished was A.'s money. It had ceased to be the property of B., because of the loan from B to A.[46]

that a son is making a gift of property to his mother. Martin v. Thomas, 74 Or. 206, 144 P. 684; nor an uncle to his nephew, Doll v. Doll, 99 Neb. 82, 155 N.W. 226.

[44] Crawford v. Manson, 82 Ga. 118, 8 S.E. 54; Mercer v. Coomler, 32 Ind.App. 533, 69 N.E. 202, 102 Am.St. Rep. 252; Dehaven v. Sterrit, 3 J.J. Marsh., Ky., 27; Anderson v. Gile, 107 Me. 325, 78 A. 370; Shaw v. Shaw, 86 Mo. 594; Eisenberg v. Goldsmith, 42 Mont. 563, 113 P. 1127. The source of the money is not important so long as it belonged to the one claiming to be a cestui que trust. Harrison v. Harrison, 265 Ill. 432, 107 N.E. 128.

[45] Chapman v. Abrahams, 61 Ala. 108; Pain v. Farson, 179 Ill. 185, 53 N.E. 579; Reminger v. Joblonski, 271 Ill. 71, 110 N.E. 903; Meredith v. Citizens' Nat. Bank, 92 Ind. 343; Kennerson v. Nash, 208 Mass. 393, 94 N.E. 475; Phillips v. Phillips, 81 N.J.Eq. 459, 86 A. 949; In re Gorham, 173 N.C. 272, 91 S.E. 950; Jordan v. Jordan, Tex.Civ.App., 154 S.W. 359; Aaron Frank Clothing Co. v. Deegan, Tex.Civ.App., 204 S.W. 471. A trust will not be declared on a showing that A. owed B. and that A. thereafter bought realty for an amount equal to the debt. The funds of the alleged cestui que trust must be clearly traced to the property. Orear v. Farmers' State Bank & Trust Co., 286 Ill. 454, 122 N.E. 63. A fortiori if money is given to A. by B. and property is purchased by B. with the money, no resulting trust arises in A.'s favor. Metropolitan Trust & Savings Bank v. Perry, 259 Ill. 183, 102 N.E. 218; Stephens v. St. Louis Union Trust Co., 260 Ill. 364, 103 N.E. 190.

[46] Bates v. Kelly, 80 Ala. 142; Caruthers v. Williams, 21 Fla. 485; Reeve v. Strawn, 14 Ill. 94; Weekly v. Ellis, 30 Kan. 507, 2 P. 96; Burleigh v. White, 64 Me. 23; Dryden v. Hanway, 31 Md. 254, 100 Am.Dec. 61; Howe v. Howe, 199 Mass. 598, 85 N.E. 945, 127 Am.St.Rep. 516; Page v. Page, 8 N.H. 187; Rogan v. Walker, 1 Wis. 527.

It is obvious that the payor of the consideration, who claims the resulting trust in his favor, need not himself have delivered the consideration. It is sufficient if his money was paid by another for him, with his consent.[47]

Time of Payment

The trust results, if at all, at the time of the transfer of the title to the real or personal property involved. It is the taking of the legal title, considered with the payment of the consideration by another at that time or previously, or later pursuant to a duty assumed at the time of the deed, which gives rise to the presumption of a trust. Hence the time of the payment of consideration is important. Payment must be made or undertaken before or at the time of the conveyance.[48] Payments made to the seller of real or personal property after the time of purchase do not create any resulting trust in favor of the payor, unless made in pursuance of a duty assumed by the payor at the time the deed was delivered. The trust arises at the time of the conveyance, if ever.[49] Payments made to assist the owner of property in improving it do not give the payor any rights as a resulting cestui.[50]

---

[47] Breitenbucher v. Oppenheim, 160 Cal. 98, 116 P. 55; Barroilhet v. Anspacher, 68 Cal. 116, 8 P. 804. Thus, where a wife's interest in land is credited to her husband on payment of the price, the wife is a payor of part of the consideration and a resulting trust occurs. Hinshaw v. Russell, 280 Ill. 235, 117 N.E. 406.

[48] Long v. King, 117 Ala. 423, 23 So. 534; Pickler v. Pickler, 180 Ill. 168, 54 N.E. 311; Hays v. Hollis, 8 Gill, Md., 357; Brooks v. Shelton, 54 Miss. 353; Lynch v. Herrig, 32 Mont. 267, 80 P. 240; Lee v. R. H. Elliott & Co., 113 Va. 618, 75 S.E. 146; Whiting v. Gould, 2 Wis. 552. Payment before the conveyance is satisfactory. Guin v. Guin, 196 Ala. 221, 72 So. 74.

[49] Butterfield v. Butterfield, 79 Ark. 164, 95 S.W. 146, 9 Ann.Cas. 248; Motherwell v. Taylor, 2 Idaho, Hasb., 254, 10 P. 304; Alexander v. Tams, 13 Ill. 221; Westerfield v. Kimmer, 82 Ind. 365; Warner v. Morse, 149 Mass. 400, 21 N.E. 960; Ostheimer v. Single, 73 N.J.Eq. 539, 68 A. 231; Lescaleet v. Rickner, 16 Ohio Cir.Ct.R. 461; Sisemore v. Pelton, 17 Or. 546, 21 P. 667; Appeal of Cross, 97 Pa. 471; Musselman v. Myers, 240 Pa. 5, 87 A. 425; Guest v. Guest, Tex.Civ.App., 208 S.W. 547; Pinnock v. Clough, 16 Vt. 500, 42 Am. Dec. 521; Beecher v. Wilson, 84 Va. 813, 6 S.E. 209, 10 Am.St.Rep. 883; Bowen v. Hughes, 5 Wash. 442, 32 P. 98; Smith v. Turley, 32 W.Va. 14, 9 S.E. 46. In Shelton v. Harrison, 182 Mo.App. 404, 167 S.W. 634, payments made after the conveyance seem to have been given effect as creating a resulting trust as to a portion of the property.

[50] Bodwell v. Nutter, 63 N.H. 446, 3 A. 421; Krauth v. Thiele, 45 N.J. Eq. 407, 18 A. 351; Rogers v. Murray, 3 Paige, N.Y., 390. Nor does a payment to discharge a mortgage give rise to a resulting trust for the

§ 52   PAYMENT FOR CONVEYANCE TO ANOTHER   183

In a few cases it has been held that a payment of part of the consideration at the time of the conveyance and the giving of a note to the grantor for the balance, or the mere payment of the balance later, gave rise to a presumption of a resulting trust as to the whole property.[51] A resulting trust as to the amount actually paid or secured to be paid would seem correct on principle, but it is difficult to see why later voluntary payments should be given any retroactive effect. If A. pays for the property by giving his note, rather than by delivering cash, and A. later pays the note, it would seem that a trust in A.'s favor should arise. In an early New York case the court expressed itself on this point as follows: "In this case there can be no doubt that, whilst the grant was made to one person, the consideration therefore was paid by another. The defendant objects that but a part of the purchase money was paid when the deed was executed, and that, if there could have been a resulting trust in favor of the plaintiff, it would have been only pro tanto. But a note was given for the residue at the time, in her behalf, by her then friends, and it is apparent that it was the understanding at the time when the conveyance was made. It is not necessary that the consideration should be paid in specie, but anything representing it, coming from or in behalf of the cestui que trust, will be equally available to protect the beneficial interest. The cases which declare the unavailability of subsequent payments have reference to such as are made pursuant to arrangements concocted after the conveyance had been made and consummated."[52] It is sufficient if the obligation to pay is incurred by the alleged cestui at the time of the conveyance, whether the obligation is evidenced by a writing or not.[53] The

payor. Thomson v. Thomson, Mo., 211 S.W. 52.

[51] Skahen v. Irving, 206 Ill. 597, 69 N.E. 510; Lynch v. Herrig, 32 Mont. 267, 80 P. 240; Hickson v. Culbert, 19 S.D. 207, 102 N.W. 774; Pearce v. Dyess, 45 Tex.Civ.App. 406, 101 S.W. 549.

[52] Lounsbury v. Purdy, 16 Barb., N.Y., 376, 380. See, also, "Subsequent Payments under Resulting Trusts," C. E. Grinnell, 1 Harv.L.R. 185, and the following cases cited therein: Runnels v. Jackson, 1 How., Miss., 358; White v. Sheldon, 4 Nev. 280; Gibson v. Foote, 40 Miss. 788; Dudley v. Bachelder, 53 Me. 403; Cramer v. Hoose, 93 Ill. 503; Barrows v. Bohan, 41 Conn. 278; Morey v. Herrick, 18 Pa. 123; Willis v. Willis, 2 Atk. 71.

[53] Wrightsman v. Rogers, 239 Mo. 417, 144 S.W. 479, citing Weiss v. Heitkamp, 127 Mo. loc. cit. 31, 29 S.W. 709, and Clowser v. Noland, 133 Mo. 221, 34 S.W. 64. See, also, Yetman v. Hedgeman, 82 N.J.Eq. 221, 88 A. 206.

"consideration must be paid or assumed to be paid by the cestui que trust at the time of the conveyance."[54]

Amount of Payment

If the claimant has paid *all* the consideration for the conveyance at or before the time when such conveyance was made, there is no difficulty in declaring a presumption in favor of a resulting trust. But, if a *part* only of the money used to pay for the property was furnished by the alleged cestui, a question of some difficulty arises. A few American courts have laid down the rule that a part payment, in order to create a resulting trust, must have been an "aliquot part" of the purchase price and paid for a corresponding interest in the property. The word "aliquot," as used in this connection, means "a 'particular fraction of the whole,' as distinguished from a general contribution to the purchase money."[55] "There is no doubt of the correctness of the doctrine that where the purchase money is paid by one person, and the conveyance taken by another, there is a resulting trust created by implication of law in favor of the former. And where a part of the purchase money is paid by one, and the whole title is taken by the other, a resulting trust pro tanto may in like manner, under some circumstances, be created. But in the latter case we believe it to be well settled that the part of the purchase money paid by him in whose favor the resulting trust is sought to be enforced must be shown to have been paid for some specific part or distinct interest in the estate, for 'some aliquot part,' as it is sometimes expressed; that is, for a specific share, as a tenancy in common or joint tenancy of one-half, one-quarter, or other particular fraction of the whole, or for a particular interest, as a life estate, or tenancy for years, or remainder, in the whole, and that a general contribution of a sum of money toward the entire purchase is not sufficient."[56] In New York resulting trusts are abolished,

[54] Williams v. Wager, 64 Vt. 326, 333, 24 A. 765. See Hornbeck v. Barker, Tex.Civ.App., 192 S.W. 276, where the grantee gave his own notes for part of the price at the time of the conveyance, and payment of such notes later by another was allowed to create a resulting trust in favor of the payor of the notes. This seems an erroneous result.

[55] Skehill v. Abbott, 184 Mass. 145, 147, 68 N.E. 37. In Hinshaw v. Russell, 280 Ill. 235, 117 N.E. 406, "aliquot" is said to mean "a definite and distinct interest, as opposed to an indefinite and unascertainable one," and not a part contained in the whole a certain number of times without remainder.

[56] Hoar, J., in McGowan v. McGowan, 14 Gray, Mass., 119, 121, 74 Am.Dec. 668, citing Crop v. Norton, 2 Atk. 74; Sayre v. Townsend, 15 Wend., N.Y., 647; White v. Car-

except in cases where the title is taken in the name of another without the consent of the payor. Speaking of this statute, the Court of Appeals has said: "The exception in the fifty-third section applies in favor of a person who *pays the consideration*. That means the whole consideration, and not, as in this case, a part of it. * * * It may be that, in cases where an aliquot part or some other definite part of the consideration has been advanced, the parties intending that some specific interest shall vest in the person paying it, or in proportion to the sum paid, there might be a resulting trust to that extent."[57]

On the other hand, most courts have repudiated the notion that payment of an aliquot part or agreement for an aliquot share is necessary. "In order to establish a resulting trust arising from the payment of the purchase money by another, it is not necessary that the beneficiary should have furnished the whole of the purchase money, nor an exact aliquot part thereof. If the amount paid is certain, a trust will result with respect to an undivided share of the land proportioned to his share of the whole price."[58] "In this state a resulting trust does not depend upon the fact that the one who seeks to establish it had paid the entire consideration, nor that what he may have contributed was for an aliquot part of the estate."[59]

It is obvious that, if the amount of money contributed by the alleged cestui is uncertain, no trust can result in his favor. The portion of the property claimed as the subject-matter of the trust must be a fixed share.[60]

It has been held in a few cases that the mere payment of an even fraction of the purchase price, as one-half or one-third, with no understanding as to an interest in the property to be obtained by the payor, does not give the payor a right to have a resulting trust declared in his favor. The payment seems to

penter, 2 Paige, N.Y., 217; Perry v. McHenry, 13 Ill. 227; Baker v. Vining, 30 Me. 121, 50 Am.Dec. 617. See, also, Feingold v. Roeschlein, 276 Ill. 79, 114 N.E. 506; Pollock v. Pollock, 223 Mass. 382, 111 N.E. 963; Druker v. Druker, 308 Mass. 229, 31 N.E.2d 524.

57 O'Brien, J., in Schierloh v. Schierloh, 148 N.Y. 103, 107, 42 N.E. 409.

58 Neathery v. Neathery, 114 Va. 650, 656, 77 S.E. 465.

59 Gerety v. O'Sheehan, 9 Cal.App. 447, 449, 99 P. 545.

60 Harton v. Amason, 195 Ala. 594, 71 So. 180; Olcott v. Tope, 213 Ill. 124, 72 N.E. 751; Baker v. Vining, 30 Me. 121, 50 Am.Dec. 617; Cutler v. Tuttle, 19 N.J.Eq. 549.

be presumed to be a loan.[61] And so, also, it has been held that the payment of an uneven fraction of the purchase price, as, for example, $1,251.16 out of a total of $9,500, with no agreement regarding an interest in the property to be obtained by the payor, does not give rise to a resulting trust in favor of the payor.[62] But in other cases such payment of an uneven fraction of the purchase price, without express agreement, has been held to create a resulting trust.[63] Whether the payment was a loan or gift to the grantee or a part payment of the price should be, it would seem, a question of fact, to be determined by the peculiar facts of each case. The presumption may be stronger in favor of an intended trust where all the consideration is paid than where only a part is paid. But there seems to be no reason why part payment should not give rise to a presumption of some force that a trust was intended for the payor, leaving open the possibility of rebutting this presumption by evidence that a gift or loan was intended. That the payment was very small or of an odd amount may be of some slight effect as tending to rebut the presumption of a trust and to support the argument for a loan or gift.

It may be supposed that payor and grantee agreed that the title to the property to be purchased should be taken in the names of both payor and grantee; that is, that the deed should run to them as tenants in common or as joint tenants. In such case, if one party takes the title in his own name, without the knowledge or consent of the other, although half the price was paid by the other, a trust has been held in some cases to result in favor of the one paying part of the consideration, whose name was not mentioned in the deed.[64] In one case of this class it was said that, while no trust resulted in favor of the defrauded payor of part of the consideration, he had an equitable lien on the land for the amount of his payment.[65] It is submitted that in this class of

---

[61] German v. Heath, 139 Iowa 52, 116 N.W. 1051; Wheeler v. Kirtland, 23 N.J.Eq. 13.

[62] Olcott v. Bynum, 17 Wall. 44, 21 L.Ed. 570; McGowan v. McGowan, 14 Gray, Mass., 119, 74 Am. Dec. 668; Storm v. McGrover, 189 N. Y. 568, 82 N.E. 160; Sayre v. Townsend, 15 Wend., N.Y., 647; O'Donnell v. White, 18 R.I. 659, 29 A. 769.

[63] Lowell v. Lowell, 185 Iowa 508, 170 N.W. 811; Chadwick v. Felt, 35 Pa. 305; Neathery v. Neathery, 114 Va. 650, 77 S.E. 465. See, also, dictum of Chancellor Kent, Botsford v. Burr, 2 Johns.Ch., N.Y., 405.

[64] Ahrens v. Simon, 101 Neb. 739, 164 N.W. 1051; Skehill v. Abbott, 184 Mass. 145, 68 N.E. 37; Puckett v. Benjamin, 21 Or. 370, 28 P. 65; O'Donnell v. McCool, 89 Wash. 537, 154 P. 1090.

[65] Leary v. Corvin, 181 N.Y. 222, 73 N.E. 984, 106 Am.St.Rep. 542, 2 Ann.Cas. 664.

cases there is actual wrong-doing by the title taker, and that the misappropriation of funds should result in a constructive trust being declared.

In the situation where A. pays part of the consideration, and agrees with B. that B. shall pay the balance, and that title to the property shall be taken in the name of A., it has been held that no trust results in favor of A. when B. uses A.'s money and his own to buy the land and takes title in B.'s name, without A.'s consent.[66] Here B. should be held to be a constructive trustee for A. as to a half interest, since B. has in substance converted A.'s money by using it to buy land in the name of B.

On one theory and another most American courts have, in cases where part payment of the consideration has been made by one and title taken in the name of another, found resulting trusts in favor of such part payor to the extent of the payment, regardless of the size of the payment and regardless of agreement or lack of agreement that the payor should have a particular interest in the property.[67]

Statutes

In California, Georgia, Montana, North Dakota, Oklahoma, and South Dakota there are statutes declaring the rule of equity with respect to resulting trusts which is set forth above.[68]

In Kentucky, Michigan, Minnesota, New York, and Wisconsin the statutes do away with resulting trusts of this variety, unless

---

[66] Schierloh v. Schierloh, 148 N.Y. 103, 42 N.E. 409.

[67] Moultrie v. Wright, 154 Cal. 520, 98 P. 257; Price v. Hicks. 14 Fla. 565; Crawford v. Manson, 82 Ga. 118, 8 S.E. 54; Smith v. Smith, 85 Ill. 189; Frasier v. Findlay, 375 Ill. 78, 30 N.E.2d 613; Derry v. Derry, 98 Ind. 319; Sullivan v. McLenans, 2 Iowa 437, 65 Am.Dec. 780; Pierce v. Pierce, 46 Ky. 433, 7 B.Mon. 433; Buck v. Swazey, 35 Me. 41, 56 Am. Dec. 681; Johnson v. Johnson, 96 Md. 144, 53 A. 792; Barton v. Magruder, 69 Miss. 462, 13 So. 839; Baumgartner v. Guessfeld, 38 Mo. 36; Hall v. Young, 37 N.H. 134; Warren v. Tynan, 54 N.J.Eq. 402, 34 A. 1065; Bryant v. Allen, 54 App. Div. 500, 67 N.Y.S. 89; Morey v. Herrick, 18 Pa. 123; McGee v. Wells, 52 S.C. 472, 30 S.E. 602; Shoemaker v. Smith, 30 Tenn. 81, 11 Humph. 81; Neill v. Keese, 13 Tex. 187; Rogers v. Donnellan, 11 Utah, 108, 39 P. 494; Pinney v. Fellows, 15 Vt. 525; Pumphry v. Brown, 5 W.Va. 107.

[68] Cal.Civ.Code § 853; Ga.Code 1933, § 108-106; Mont.Rev.Codes 1935, § 6785; N.D.Comp.L.1913, § 5365; Clark v. Frazier, Okl., 177 P. 589; S.D. Code 1939, § 59.0102. The California statute reads as follows: "When a transfer of real property is made to one person, and the consideration therefor is paid by or for another, a trust is presumed to result in favor of the person by or for whom such payment is made."

the title was taken in the name of another than the payor without the payor's consent, or the title-taker in violation of a trust purchases the property with the money of another.[69] Indiana and Kansas abolish the purchase money trust also, unless one of the two exceptions named in the last sentence is found, or there was an oral agreement that the grantee should be a holder for the payor of the consideration.[70]

It should be observed that these statutes do not apply to personal property.[71] Partnership realty being deemed personalty, if a partner use partnership money to buy land and take the title in his own name, a trust will result to the other members of the firm, even in those states which have abolished resulting trusts of this type in real property.[72]

These statutes have been narrowly construed. Thus, in New York it has been held that if A. pay the purchase price of land, and have B., the seller, convey the land to C. upon an oral understanding that the conveyance is to be for the benefit of D., the statute does not apply, and a trust results in D.'s favor.[73] And so, too, if the payor of the consideration and the grantee sustain any confidential relations towards each other, the courts are quick to seize upon that fact as a basis for a constructive trust, even though the statute prohibits a resulting trust.[74] And in some cases the payment plus an oral agreement for a trust for

---

[69] Ky.St.1936, §§ 2353, 2354; Mich. Ann.St., §§ 26.57–26.60; Minn.St.1927, §§ 8086–8088; N.Y. Real Property Law § 94; Wis.St.1941, §§ 231.07 to 231.09. The New York statute is typical and reads as follows: "A grant of real property for a valuable consideration, to one person, the consideration being paid by another, is presumed fraudulent as against the creditors, at that time, of the person paying the consideration, and, unless a fraudulent intent is disproved, a trust results in favor of such creditors, to an extent necessary to satisfy their just demands; but the title vests in the grantee, and no use or trust results from the payment to the person paying the consideration, or in his favor, unless the grantee either, 1. Takes the same as an absolute conveyance, in his own name, without the consent or knowledge of the person paying the consideration; or 2. In violation of some trust, purchases the property so conveyed with money or property belonging to another."

[70] Ind. Burns' Ann.St.1933, §§ 56-606 to 56-608; Kan.G.S.1935, 67-406 to 67-408.

[71] Baker v. Terrell, 8 Minn. 195, 8 Gil. 165; Robbins v. Robbins, 89 N.Y. 251; Bork v. Martin, 132 N.Y. 280, 30 N.E. 584, 28 Am.St.Rep. 570; Tobin v. Tobin, 139 Wis. 494, 121 N.W. 144.

[72] Fairchild v. Fairchild, 64 N.Y. 471.

[73] Siemon v. Schurck, 29 N.Y. 598.

[74] Jeremiah v. Pitcher, 26 App.Div. 402, 49 N.Y.S. 788, affirmed 163 N.Y. 574, 57 N.E. 1113.

§ 52   PAYMENT FOR CONVEYANCE TO ANOTHER   189

the payor,[75] or plus part performance by the payor,[76] or coupled with a recognition of the trust by the grantee,[77] have been held to show a resulting trust.

The construction of these various statutes cannot be traced here, but some of the more important decisions are cited.[78]

[75] Wittner v. Burr Ave. Development Corporation, 222 App.Div. 285, 226 N.Y.S. 124.

[76] Waters v. Hall, 218 App.Div. 149, 218 N.Y.S. 31.

[77] Foote v. Bryant, 47 N.Y. 544.

[78] *California:* Broder v. Conklin, 77 Cal. 330, 19 P. 513; Hellman v. Messmer, 75 Cal. 166, 16 P. 766; Porter v. Douglass, 7 Cal.App. 429, 94 P. 591; Parks v. Parks, 179 Cal. 472, 177 P. 455.

Georgia: Brooks v. Fowler, 82 Ga. 329, 9 S.E. 1089; Manning v. Manning, 135 Ga. 597, 69 S.E. 1126; Hall v. Edwards, 140 Ga. 765, 79 S.E. 852.

Indiana: Wynn v. Sharer, 23 Ind. 573; Malady v. McEnary, 30 Ind. 273; Kimmick v. Linn, 217 Ind. 485, 29 N.E.2d 207; Mitchell v. Colglazier, 106 Ind. 464, 7 N.E. 199; Noe v. Roll, 134 Ind. 115, 33 N.E. 905; Koehler v. Koehler, Ind.App., 121 N.E. 450; Makeever v. Yeoman, Ind.App., 121 N.E. 672.

Kansas: Franklin v. Colley, 10 Kan. 260; Chantland v. Midland Nat. Bank, 66 Kan. 549, 72 P. 230; Hanrion v. Hanrion, 73 Kan. 25, 84 P. 381, 117 Am.St.Rep. 453; Garten v. Trobridge, 80 Kan. 720, 104 P. 1067; Anderson v. Hultberg, C.C.A. Kan., 247 F. 273, 159 C.C.A. 367.

Kentucky: Watt v. Watt, 39 S.W. 48, 19 Ky.Law Rep. 25; Clay v. Clay's Guardian, 72 S.W. 810, 24 Ky.Law Rep. 2016; Martin v. Martin, 68 Ky. 47, 5 Bush. 47; Wright v. Yates, 140 Ky. 283, 130 S.W. 1111; Neel's Ex'r v. Noland's Heirs, 166 Ky. 455, 179 S.W. 430; Dalzell v. Dalzell, 170 Ky. 297, 185 S.W. 1107; McFarland v. McFarland, 263 Ky. 434, 92 S.W.2d 785.

Michigan: Fisher v. Fobes, 22 Mich. 454; McCreary v. McCreary, 90 Mich. 478, 51 N.W. 545; Winans v. Winans' Estate, 99 Mich. 74, 57 N.W. 1088; Waldron v. Merrill, 154 Mich. 203, 117 N.W. 631; Signs v. Bush's Estate, 199 Mich. 192, 165 N.W. 820.

Minnesota: Durfee v. Pavitt, 14 Minn. 424, 14 Gil. 319; Johnson v. Johnson, 16 Minn. 512, 16 Gil. 462; Drees v. Gosling, 208 Minn. 399, 294 N.W. 374; Petzold v. Petzold, 53 Minn. 39, 54 N.W. 933; Haaven v. Hoaas, 60 Minn. 313, 62 N.W. 110.

Montana: Lynch v. Herrig, 32 Mont. 267, 80 P. 240.

New York: McCartney v. Bostwick, 32 N.Y. 53; Foote v. Bryant, 47 N.Y. 544; Everett v. Everett, 48 N.Y. 218; Reitz v. Reitz, 80 N.Y. 538; Haack v. Weicken, 118 N.Y. 67, 23 N.E. 133; Church of St. Stanislaus v. Algemeine Verein, 31 App.Div. 133, 52 N.Y.S. 922, affirmed 164 N.Y. 606, 58 N.E. 1086; O'Brien v. Gill, 166 App.Div. 92, 151 N.Y.S. 682; Hegstad v. Wysiecki, 178 App.Div. 733, 165 N.Y.S. 898.

North Dakota: Currie v. Look, 14 N.D. 482, 106 N.W. 131.

South Dakota: Hickson v. Culbert, 19 S.D. 207, 102 N.W. 774; Bucknell v. Johnson, 39 S.D. 212, 163 N.W. 683.

Wisconsin: Knight v. Leary, 54 Wis. 459, 11 N.W. 600; Campbell v. Campbell, 70 Wis. 311, 35 N.W. 743; Meier v. Bell, 119 Wis. 482, 97 N.W. 186; Perkinson v. Clarke, 135 Wis. 584, 116 N.W. 229; Friedrich v. Huth, 155 Wis. 196, 144 N.W. 202.

FAILURE OF EXPRESS TRUST [79]

53. Whenever an express private trust is voluntarily created, and it fails, there is a resulting trust for the settlor, or his successors if he is dead.

Where an express private trust is created gratuitously, and it fails for any reason, a problem arises as to the disposition of the trust property. Shall the trustee be allowed to retain it for his own benefit? This is a result for which no argument can be found, since the settlor evidently intended the trustee to get no advantage from the trust except his compensation. The property cannot be given to the beneficiaries, since by hypothesis to carry out the trust is illegal or impossible. The only defensible result is to return the property to the settlor, either on the theory that he would have intended that action if he had thought of the question, or on the basis of fair play and justice. Surely no one other than the settlor has any equitable or moral claim to the property.

The courts do make this return to the settlor, or if he is dead, to his successors in interest, and they often do it on the theory of a resulting trust for the settlor.[80] Since the trust cannot be carried out, the settlor is presumed to have desired a return to himself or his successors, or the court regards this as the only just thing to do.

Thus, if a settlor transfers property by will to named trustees, as a gift, but fails to describe the beneficiaries with certainty,[81] or he prescribes a term for the trust which is too long under the law of the state,[82] or gifts under the trust violate the rule against perpetuities,[83] the usual result is that the trust property results to the successors of the settlor who would take property of the type in question. The personalty goes to his next of kin, the realty to his heirs, or if he left a residuary clause the residuary devisees and legatees are the beneficiaries of the resulting trust.[84]

[79] Restatement, Trusts, §§ 411–429.

[80] Bainbridge v. Stoner, Cal., 106 P.2d 423; Blake v. Dexter, Mass., 12 Cush. 559; Broadrup v. Woodman, 27 Ohio St. 553.

[81] In re Ralston's Estate, 1 Cal.2d 724, 37 P.2d 76, 9 A.L.R. 953; Pedrick v. Guarantee Trust Co., 123 N.J.Eq. 395, 197 A. 909.

[82] Van Epps v. Arbuckle, 332 Ill. 551, 164 N.E. 1; Barnum v. Barnum, 26 Md. 119, 90 Am.Dec. 88.

[83] Wardens, etc., of St. Paul's Church v. Attorney General, 164 Mass. 188, 41 N.E. 231; Bailey v. Buffalo Loan, Trust & Safe Deposit Co., 213 N.Y. 525, 107 N.E. 1043.

[84] Clark v. McCue, 242 Mich. 551, 219 N.W. 653; McElroy v. McElroy,

It is often said that the result of the partial or imperfect or illegal declaration of trust, or of the failure or accomplishment of the trust is, in the case of wills, that the property concerned passes as if the deceased had died intestate so far as it is concerned; that is, that real property passes directly to the testator's heirs and personal property directly to an administrator for the next of kin.[85] It is submitted, however, that a more complete statement of the result is that the will is given effect to pass the legal title to the trustee named therein, but that the trustee holds such legal title in trust for the heirs or next of kin. To speak of intestacy in such a case is to declare the will void. The will takes effect, the trustee gets the legal title, but must hold it for the benefit of the heirs or next of kin, and the same decree which declares the resulting trust will doubtless decree a conveyance by the resulting trustee to the cestui que trust of such resulting trust, since the resulting trust is always passive.

This same result comes about if there is a failure of an express charitable trust, voluntarily created, if the cy pres rule is not in force in the state,[86] or even if cy pres is recognized in the state, if the settlor's charitable intent was construed to have been a narrow charitable intent.[87]

If consideration is paid by the trustee for the transfer in trust, and the trust fails, the trustee retains the property as his own,[88] and no trust results to the settlor, since he has received the value of the property and would be unjustly enriched as against the trustee if allowed to keep the consideration and get back the property. He cannot reasonably be said to have intended a return of the property, after having been paid its value.

The resulting trust here considered arises, even though the settlor expresses a desire that it shall not, unless the settlor makes a gift over to the trustee [89] or someone else in the event of the failure of the express trust. Thus, in a case where property was

113 Mass. 509; Trunkey v. Van Sant, 176 N.Y. 535, 68 N.E. 946.

[85] In re Fair's Estate, 136 Cal. 79, 68 P. 306; Bristol v. Bristol, 53 Conn. 242, 5 A. 687; Wilce v. Van Arden, 248 Ill. 358, 94 N.E. 42, 140 Am.St.Rep. 212, 21 Ann.Cas. 153; In re Eaton's Estate, 160 Mich. 230, 125 N.W. 85; Vail v. Vail, 4 Paige, N.Y., 317; Miller v. London, 60 N. C. 628.

[86] See § 86, post.

[87] See § 86, post.

[88] Trustees of Methodist Episcopal Church v. Trustees of Jackson Square Church, 84 Md. 173, 35 A. 8.

[89] In re Foord, [1922] 2 Ch. 519; Woodbury v. Hayden, 211 Mass. 202, 97 N.E. 776.

left in trust to keep it away from the testator's heirs and next of kin, and this trust failed for lack of beneficiaries, it was held that a trust resulted to the heirs and next of kin, which was exactly the result which the testator sought to avoid.[90]

It will be observed that the principle underlying this class of resulting trusts is the same as that which formed the basis of such trusts arising out of voluntary conveyances. Here, as there, a presumption against gift arises. The grantor or testator is presumed not to have intended that the voluntary trustee under the imperfect or illegal trust should hold for the trustee's benefit. The trustee has given no value for the property he holds under the defective trust. The presumption is that the settlor intended that, if the trust proved defective, the property subject to it should go back to the settlor, if living, or to his successors, if he be dead. Such presumption causes equity to fasten a trust on the property in the hands of the trustee named in the defective instrument. This action gives effect to the settlor's deed or will, and at the same time confers the beneficial ownership of the property on him who is equitably entitled to it.

WHERE EXPRESS TRUST RES PROVES EXCESSIVE [91]

54. Where an express private trust is created gratuitously, and the subject-matter of the trust proves to be larger in amount than is necessary to accomplish the purposes of the trust, there is a resulting trust of the excess for the settlor or his successors.

It not infrequently happens that the settlor conveys to the trustee a larger amount of property than is needed to carry out the objects which the settlor has stated. In such a case it would obviously be unfair and without justification, where the trust was created for no consideration, to permit the trustee to use the excess for his own benefit. The settlor expected the trustee to act in a representative capacity only and not to have any profit from the trust except his commissions. There are no beneficiaries named for this portion of the trust capital. The only choice which has merit behind it is to return the excess property to the settlor, or if dead, to his successors, on the argument that this

---

[90] Gross v. Moore, 68 Hun 412, 52 N.Y.St.Rep. 657, 22 N.Y.S. 1019, affirmed 141 N.Y. 559, 36 N.E. 343. And see McDermith v. Voorhees, 16 Colo. 402, 27 P. 250, 25 Am.St.Rep. 286; Woodruff v. Marsh, 63 Conn. 125, 26 A. 846, 38 Am.St.Rep. 346.

[91] Restatement, Trusts, §§ 430–439.

would have been desired by the settlor, if he had envisaged the situation, and furthermore that such return will satisfy the conscience of the chancellor.[92]

For example, if the settlor conveys by deed to trustees $50,000 in bonds to apply the income to the support of his Aunt Mary, until she is admitted to an old ladies' home which guarantees her support for the rest of her life, and while the trustees still hold these bonds and $1,000 of unexpended income, Aunt Mary is admitted to a home of the type described, the trustees will hold the trust property under resulting trust for the settlor, assuming he is living, and assuming that in the trust deed he made no provision for the disposition of the trust capital in the event which has occurred.

If the trustee gave consideration for the creation of the trust, there is no resulting trust as to excess property, and the trustee retains the excess as his own.

In the case of a charity, cy pres usually disposes of excess principal,[93] but if not, there will be a resulting trust.

[92] Jordan v. Jordan, 193 Minn. 428, 259 N.W. 386; In re Mooney's Estate, 131 Neb. 52, 267 N.W. 196; Lillard v. Lillard, 63 OhioApp. 403, 26 N.E.2d 896.

[93] See § 86, post.

BOGERT TRUSTS 2D—13

CHAPTER 6

CREATION OF CONSTRUCTIVE TRUSTS

Sec.
55. Definition.
56. Statute of Frauds.
57. Fraudulent Misrepresentation.
58. Mistake, Undue Influence or Duress.
59. Proceeds of Larceny or Conversion.
60. Property Obtained by Homicide.
61. Breach of Contract to Convey.
62. Disloyalty of Fiduciary.
63. Direct Dealing with Beneficiary.
64. Purchase at Judicial Sale under Oral Promise.
65. Conveyance of Land on Oral Trust.
66. Gift by Will or Intestacy on Oral Trust.

DEFINITION [1]

55. Constructive trusts are created by courts of equity whenever the title to property is found in one who is not in fairness entitled to retain it. They are often based on disloyalty or other breach of trust by an express trustee, but are also created where no express trust is involved but where property is obtained or retained by misrepresentation, undue influence, murder, or other unconscionable conduct. The court merely uses the constructive trust as a device for forcing the defendant to convey to the plaintiff.

Constructive trusts do not arise because of the intent of parties that they shall arise, but often directly contrary to such intent. They are not "intent-enforcing" trusts, but in a general way may be called "fraud-rectifying" trusts.[2]

These trusts are *created* by courts of equity, not merely declared to exist as a result of acts of the parties. Whenever equity finds that one has obtained or now retains title to property, real or personal, by any kind of wrongdoing, so that a retention of such title will result in his unjust enrichment, equity may declare such title holder to be the trustee of a trust constructed by it for the purpose of working out justice. The trust is merely a convenient means of remedying wrong.[3] It is not a per-

---

[1] Restatement, Restitution, § 160.

[2] These terms are used in an article by the late Professor G. P. Costigan, Jr., on "The Classification of Trusts as Express, Resulting and Constructive," in 27 Harv.Law Rev. 437.

[3] "A constructive trust is the formula through which the conscience of

manent trust, in which the trustee is to have any duties of administration, but a passive, temporary trust, in which the trustee's sole duty is to transfer the title to the cestui que trust.[4]

The situations in which equity works out a remedy by a constructive trust are without number. An attempt will be made in the subsequent sections of this chapter to consider some of the more important instances in which constructive trusts have been created or seriously considered.

Constructive trusts are sometimes called "trusts ex maleficio," or "involuntary trusts," or "trusts in invitum."

STATUTE OF FRAUDS [5]

56. The Statute of Frauds has no application to constructive trusts. They are created by equity, whether the evidence on which they are based is oral or written, and whether the property involved is real or personal.

By the express provisions of the eighth section of the English Statute of Frauds [6] trusts arising "by the implication or construction of law" are not subject to the Statute of Frauds. The equity finds expression. When property has been acquired in such circumstances that the holder of the legal title may not in good conscience retain the beneficial interest, equity converts him into a trustee. * * * A court of equity in decreeing a constructive trust is bound by no unyielding formula." Cardozo, C.J., in Beatty v. Guggenheim Exploration Co., 225 N.Y. 380, 386, 389, 122 N.E. 378. Dean Pound has referred to this type of trust as "specific restitution of a received benefit in order to prevent unjust enrichment." 33 Harv.L.R. 420, 421.

of New York, N. Y., v. Clemens, 230 Iowa 279, 297 N.W. 253; Clester v. Clester, 90 Kan. 638, 135 P. 996, L.R.A.1915E, 648; May v. May, 161 Ky. 114, 170 S.W. 537; Ferguson v. Robinson, 258 Mo. 113, 167 S.W. 447; Wilcox v. Wilcox, 138 Nev. 510, 293 N.W. 378; Allen v. Jones, Okl., 110 P.2d 911; Hall v. Miller, Tex.Civ. App., 147 S.W.2d 266.

In California constructive trusts are defined by statute: "One who gains a thing by fraud, accident, mistake, undue influence, the violation of a trust, or other wrongful act, is, unless he has some other and better right thereto, an involuntary trustee of the thing gained, for the benefit of the person who would otherwise have had it." Cal.Civ.Code, § 2224. See, also, Mont.Rev.Codes 1935, § 7887; N.D.Comp.L.1913, § 6280; S. D.Code 1939, § 59.0102.

[4] For cases discussing the definition and underlying theory of constructive trusts, see Bainbridge v. Stoner, Cal., 106 P.2d 423; Maltbie v. Olds, 88 Conn. 633, 92 A. 403; Miller v. Miller, 266 Ill. 522, 107 N.E. 821; Kern v. Beatty, 267 Ill. 127, 107 N.E. 794; Farrell v. Wallace, 161 Iowa 528, 143 N.W. 488; New York Life Ins. Co.

[5] Restatement, Trusts, § 40.

[6] St. 29 Chas. II, ch. 3, 1677.

American statutes have universally adopted this exception,[7] and the decisions that no written evidence is necessary as a basis for constructive trusts are numerous.[8]

Due to the interest of the courts in the security of titles, and their reluctance to disturb record or other apparent ownership, the courts of equity require the case for a constructive trust to be proved by "clear and convincing evidence".[9]

FRAUDULENT MISREPRESENTATION [10]

57. Where property is obtained by conscious misrepresentation of fact, its holder may be charged as a constructive trustee for the defrauded person.

Fraud is a well-known ground of equitable jurisdiction. "It is a well-settled rule of equity that a misrepresentation constitutes fraud relievable in equity only when (a) it is untrue; (b) the party making it knew, or should have known, it to be untrue, and it was made by him to induce the other party to act or omit to act; (c) it induced the other party to act or omit to act; and (d) it is a material fact."[11] "That courts of equity have concurrent jurisdiction with the law courts to grant relief from the consequences of fraud and misrepresentation is a proposition too firmly established in the jurisprudence of this state to be now questioned."[12]

---

[7] See § 25, ante.

[8] Whitney v. Hay, 181 U.S. 77, 21 S.Ct. 537, 45 L.Ed. 758; McNeil v. Gates, 41 Ark. 264; De Mallagh v. De Mallagh, 77 Cal. 126, 19 P. 256; Bohm v. Bohm, 9 Colo. 100, 10 P. 790; Larmon v. Knight, 140 Ill. 232, 29 N.E. 1116, 33 Am.St.Rep. 229; Buck v. Voreis, 89 Ind. 116; Becker v. Neurath, 149 Ky. 421, 149 S.W. 857; Gilpatrick v. Glidden, 81 Me. 137, 16 A. 464, 2 L.R.A. 662, 10 Am.St.Rep. 245; Cameron v. Lewis, 56 Miss. 76; Pratt v. Clark, 57 Mo. 189; Brannin v. Brannin, 18 N.J.Eq. 212; Wood v. Rabe, 96 N.Y. 414, 48 Am.Rep. 640; Avery v. Stewart, 136 N.C. 426, 48 S.E. 775, 68 L.R.A. 776; Hanson v. Svarverud, 18 N.D. 550, 120 N.W. 550; Ewing v. Ewing, 33 Okl. 414, 126 P. 811; Kroll v. Coach, 45 Or. 459, 78 P. 397, 80 P. 900; Schrager v. Cool, 221 Pa. 622, 70 A. 889; Morris v. Reigel, 19 S.D. 26, 101 N.W. 1086; Orr v. Perky Inv. Co., 65 Wash. 281, 118 P. 19; Floyd v. Duffy, 68 W.Va. 339, 69 S.E. 993, 33 L.R.A.,N.S. 883; Fairchild v. Rasdall, 9 Wis. 379.

[9] Leake v. Garrett, 167 Ark. 415, 268 S.W. 608; Gordon v. Kaplan, 99 N.J.Eq. 195, 138 A. 195.

[10] Restatement, Restitution, §§ 166–171.

[11] Taylor v. Mullins, 151 Ky. 597, 599, 152 S.W. 774.

[12] Culver v. Avery, 161 Mich. 322, 126 N.W. 439, 442.

§ 57

The cases in which equity has held a fraudulent grantee or transferee as a constructive trustee are very numerous.[13] Although some courts have required proof that the legal remedy is inadequate, before they will decree a constructive trust,[14] the better rule is that this is not necessary.[15] The enforcement of trusts of all kinds is a separate head of equity jurisdiction, not at all dependent on the attitude of courts of law.

Examples of the fraud which gives rise to a constructive trust are the cases where there is fraud by a buyer at a judicial sale in obtaining the property at an unusually low figure by means of false representations,[16] and where a person procures the property of a deceased party by making false statements to the probate court.[17]

Mere inadequacy of consideration for the transfer of property is not sufficient ground for declaring a trust; [18] but coupled with other facts, it may be sufficient to show fraud on which a trust may be based.[19]

[13] Cunningham v. Pettigrew, C.C.A. Utah, 169 F. 335, 94 C.C.A. 457; Smith v. Smith, 153 Ala. 504, 45 So. 168; Hays v. Gloster, 88 Cal. 560, 26 P. 367; Frick Co. v. Taylor, 94 Ga. 683, 21 S.E. 713; Smith v. Wright, 49 Ill. 403; Norris v. Kendall, 48 Ind.App. 304, 93 N.E. 1087; Hall v. Doran, 13 Iowa 368; Clester v. Clester, 90 Kan. 638, 135 P. 996, L.R.A. 1915E, 648; Vanderpool v. Vanderpool, 163 Ky. 742, 174 S.W. 727; Batty v. Greene, 206 Mass. 561, 92 N.E. 715, 138 Am.St.Rep. 407; Hanold v. Bacon, 36 Mich. 1; Nesbitt v. Onaway-Alpena Til. Co., 202 Mich. 567, 168 N.W. 519; Winona & St. P. R. Co. v. St. Paul & S. C. R. Co., 26 Minn. 179, 2 N.W. 489; Moore v. Crump, 84 Miss. 612, 37 So. 109; Aspinall v. Jones, 17 Mo. 209; South End Mining Co. v. Tinney, 22 Nev. 19, 35 P. 89; Valentine v. Richardt, 126 N.Y. 272, 27 N.E. 255; Edwards v. Culberson, 111 N.C. 342, 16 S.E. 233, 18 L.R.A. 204; Currie v. Look, 14 N.D. 482, 106 N.W. 131; Parrish v. Parrish, 33 Or. 486, 54 P. 352; Tetlow v. Rust, 227 Pa. 292, 76 A. 22; Davis v. Settle, 43 W.Va. 17, 26 S.E. 557; Blakeslee v. Starring, 34 Wis. 538.

[14] Lockward v. Evans, 88 N.J.Eq. 597, 103 A. 1053; Capuano v. Boghosian, 54 R.I. 489, 175 A. 830.

[15] City of Boston v. Santosuosso, 298 Mass. 175, 10 N.E.2d 271; Falk v. Hoffman, 233 N.Y. 199, 135 N.E. 243.

[16] McRarey v. Huff, 32 Ga. 681; Estill v. Estill, 3 Bibb, Ky., 177; Huxley v. Rice, 40 Mich. 73; Dickel v. Smith, 38 W.Va. 635, 18 S.E. 721.

[17] Purinton v. Dyson, 8 Cal.2d 322, 65 P.2d 777, 113 A.L.R. 1230; Zaremba v. Woods, 17 Cal.App.2d 309, 61 P.2d 976.

[18] Burch v. Nicholson, 157 Iowa 502, 137 N.W. 1066; Chandler v. Roe, 46 Okl. 349, 148 P. 1026 (semble).

[19] Parkhurst v. Hosford, C.C.Or., 21 F. 827; Bither v. Packard, 115 Me. 306, 98 A. 929.

Where property has been conveyed to an innocent grantee, due to the fraud of a third person, such innocent grantee may be decreed to hold the property under a constructive trust.[20]

MISTAKE, UNDUE INFLUENCE OR DURESS [21]

58. Where property is obtained by mistake, undue influence, or duress, the injured party may have the wrongdoer decreed to be a constructive trustee of the property so gained.

If by mistake the legal title is conveyed to another than the intended grantee, or the wrong property is conveyed to the intended grantee, the actual grantee may be declared by equity to hold the legal title under a constructive trust for the grantor.[22] "But there is another principle, recognized in equity, that when one person, through fraud or mistake, obtains the legal title and apparent ownership of property, which in justice and good conscience belongs to another, such property is impressed with a use in favor of the equitable owner."[23]

No trust was intended here, but the declaration of one by equity will prevent the person accidentally holding the legal title from unjustly enriching himself at the expense of him in equity entitled to the property.

If one acquire property through any kind of reprehensible conduct, equity may create a constructive trust as to the property for the purpose of working out the ends of justice.

Thus, property obtained through the exercise of undue influence or duress may be declared by equity to be subject to a constructive trust.[24]

---

[20] Saar v. Weeks, 105 Wash. 628, 178 P. 819; Ruhe v. Ruhe, 113 Md. 595, 77 A. 797.

[21] Restatement, Restitution, §§ 163–171.

[22] Wilson v. Castro, 31 Cal. 421; Andrews v. Andrews, 12 Ind. 348; Harris v. Stone, 8 Iowa 322; Smith v. Walser, 49 Mo. 250; Lamb v. Schiefner, 129 App.Div. 684, 114 N.Y.S. 34;
In re Bangor Trust Co., 317 Pa. 495, 178 A. 290.

[23] Cole v. Fickett, 95 Me. 265, 270, 49 A. 1066.

[24] Olson v. Washington, 18 Cal.App. 2d 85, 63 P.2d 304; Smith v. Stratton, 302 Mass. 17, 18 N.E.2d 328; Mullin v. Mullin, 119 App.Div. 521, 104 N.Y.S. 323.

PROCEEDS OF LARCENY OF CONVERSION [25]

59. Where one misappropriates the personal property of another, thereby becoming a thief or embezzler or converter, and he exchanges the property taken for other property, he may be charged as a constructive trustee of the proceeds of his wrongful conduct.

Property acquired through crime may be the basis of a constructive trust. Thus the proceeds of stolen property in the hands of a thief are often held to be bound by a constructive trust.[26] While the thief does not obtain ownership of the stolen things, he does get title to that which he receives in exchange for the stolen property. It is obviously unconscionable that he should retain this title, and to take it from him a trust is constructed by the courts.

Where personalty is wrongfully appropriated, and so the tort of conversion is committed, the wronged party may elect to treat the converter as a constructive trustee.[27] If one assumes to act as trustee of the property of another, without right, he may be treated as a constructive trustee,[28] or, as it is sometimes phrased, as a trustee *de son tort,* that is, a trustee by reason of his own wrong.

[25] Restatement, Restitution, §§ 128–138.

[26] Pioneer Mining Co. v. Tyberg, C.C.A. Alaska, 215 F. 501, 131 C.C.A. 549, L.R.A.1915B, 442; National Mahaiwe Bank v. Barry, 125 Mass. 20; Lamb v. Rooney, 72 Neb. 322, 100 N.W. 410, 117 Am.St.Rep. 795; Lightfoot v. Davis, 198 N.Y. 261, 91 N.E. 582, 29 L.R.A.,N.S., 119, 139 Am.St. Rep. 817, 19 Ann.Cas. 747.

[27] Burke Grain Co. v. St. Paul-Mercury Indemnity Co., C.C.A.S.D., 94 F.2d 458; Thompson v. Thompson, 107 Ala. 163, 18 So. 247; Ellett v. Tyler, 41 Ill. 449; Ramsden v. O'Keefe, 9 Minn., 9 Gil. 63, 74; Phillips v. Hines, 33 Miss. 163; Tecumseh Nat. Bank v. Russell, 50 Neb. 277, 69 N.W. 763; Newton v. Taylor, 32 Ohio St. 399; Lang v. Shell Petroleum Corporation, Tex.Civ.App., 141 S.W.2d 667.

[28] Penn v. Fogler, 182 Ill. 76, 55 N.E. 192; Tarbox v. Tarbox, 111 Me. 374, 89 A. 194; Nebraska Power Co. v. Koenig, 93 Neb. 68, 139 N.W. 839; Bailey v. Bailey, 67 Vt. 494, 32 A. 470, 48 Am.St.Rep. 826; Brown v. Lambert's Adm'r, 33 Gratt., Va., 256; Morris v. Joseph, 1 W.Va. 256, 91 Am.Dec. 386.

PROPERTY OBTAINED BY HOMICIDE [29]

60. Where one obtains property by intentionally killing another, a constructive trust may be decreed as to the property thus obtained.

It sometimes happens that a prospective heir, devisee, legatee, surviving joint tenant, dowress, or tenant in curtesy, intentionally kills the person through whom he expects to obtain a property right, and is convicted of the crime of murder or manslaughter. The question arises whether the murderer shall be allowed to retain the property which came to him by intestacy, through the operation of a will, or otherwise. Some early decisions held that the murderer might retain what he had gained through his crime, on the ground that the statutes of intestacy and of wills contained no express exception for this case, and the courts were not justified in creating an implied exception; [30] but a group of decisions which are much more defensible hold that the murderer obtains title to the property, but because of his reprehensible conduct in gaining it he must hold it as constructive trustee for those who would have taken the property if the murdered man had died when he actually did die, but the murderer had predeceased him.[31] Thus, if F. owns a farm in fee simple, and S. is his only son and prospective heir, and S. kills F. at a time when F. has made no will, the better view is that S. obtains title under the intestacy law, but that he must hold it under a constructive trust for the relatives of F. who would have taken his property if S. had died before F. and at the death of F. his heirs had been, let us say, his mother and father, M. and X.

In a few cases the courts have held that the murderer takes no interest from the one murdered, because the law does not permit instruments or statutes to operate in favor of one guilty of such a heinous crime.[32]

---

[29] Restatement, Restitution, §§ 187–189.

[30] Wall v. Pfanschmidt, 265 Ill. 180, 106 N.E. 785, L.R.A.1915C, 328, Ann. Cas.1916A, 674; Kuhn v. Kuhn, 125 Iowa 449, 101 N.W. 151, 2 Ann.Cas. 657; Shellenberger v. Ransom, 41 Neb. 631, 59 N.W. 935, 25 L.R.A. 564; Carpenter's Estate, 170 Pa. 203, 32 A. 637, 29 L.R.A. 145, 50 Am.St.Rep. 765.

[31] Ellerson v. Westcott, 148 N.Y. 149, 42 N.E. 540; Bryant v. Bryant, 193 N.C. 372, 137 S.E. 188, 51 A.L.R. 1100.

[32] Garwols v. Bankers' Trust Co., 251 Mich. 420, 232 N.W. 239; Perry v. Strawbridge, 209 Mo. 621, 108 S.W. 641, 16 L.R.A.,N.S., 244, 123 Am.St. Rep. 510, 14 Ann.Cas. 92; Riggs v. Palmer, 115 N.Y. 506, 22 N.E. 188, 5 L.R.A. 340, 12 Am.St.Rep. 819.

In many states there are statutes which prevent the murderer from taking or retaining the property of the murdered person.[33]

If the beneficiary of an insurance policy kills the insured intentionally, and thus causes the policy to mature by his wrongful act, he is not allowed to collect the policy. The proceeds go to the estate of the insured.[34]

BREACH OF CONTRACT TO CONVEY

61. Mere breach of a gratuitously made agreement to convey, or leave by will, or permit to pass by intestacy, does not make the violator of the promise a constructive trustee of the property; but if the promise was made in return for a promise to deliver property or perform services, and the property was delivered or the services performed and a money judgment will not give adequate relief to the promisee, equity often gives relief on specific performance or constructive trust theories.

It is elementary that the fourth section of the English Statute of Frauds, which is adopted generally in America, provides that oral contracts for the conveyance of an interest in land are voidable, unless in writing or manifested by a memorandum signed by the party sought to be charged. This section covers contracts to convey by deed, or to devise,[35] or to pass by intestacy.[36] A contract to bequeath goods for a consideration is a contract for the sale of goods under the seventeenth section of the Statute of Frauds, and unenforceable unless written or proved by a memorandum signed by the party to be charged, or partly performed by payment or acceptance and receipt.[37]

[33] Cal.Prob.Code, § 258; Colo.L. 1923, c. 195; D.C.Code 1929, T. 25, § 250; Ill.Smith-Hurd Stats. c. 3, § 167; Ind.Burns' Ann.St.1933, § 6-2352; Iowa Code 1939, §§ 12032–12034; Kan.Gen.St.1935, 22-133; La.Civ.Code 1932, § 966, 1560, 1710; Minn.St.1927, § 8734; Miss.Code 1930, § 3566; Neb.Comp.St.1929, §§ 30-119 and 30-120; N.C.Code 1939, §§ 10, 2522, 4099; N.D.Comp.L.1913, § 5683; 84 Okl.St.Ann. § 231; Ore.Code 1930, § 10-213; Pa. 20 P.S. §§ 136, 244; S.C.L.1924, p. 1188; Tenn.Code 1938, § 8388; Tex.Vernon's Ann.Civ.St. art. 5047; Utah Rev.St.1933, 101-3-22; Va.Code 1936, § 5274; Wyo.Rev.St.1931, § 88-4009.

[34] National Life Ins. Co. of Montpelier, Vt., v. Hood's Adm'r, 264 Ky. 516, 94 S.W.2d 1022; In re Greifer's Estate, 333 Pa. 278, 5 A.2d 118; but see Minasian v. Aetna Life Ins. Co., 295 Mass. 1, 3 N.E.2d 17 (beneficiary may collect where he unintentionally killed insured, although he was convicted of manslaughter therefor).

[35] Lozier v. Hill, 68 N.J.Eq. 300, 59 A. 234.

[36] Dicken v. McKinlay, 163 Ill. 318, 45 N.E. 134, 54 Am.St.Rep. 471.

[37] Wallace v. Long, 105 Ind. 522, 5 N.E. 666, 55 Am.Rep. 222.

It sometimes happens that where there has been a breach of a *voluntary* oral agreement to convey land, the promisee seeks to make the promisor a constructive trustee of the land. Thus, if A. is the owner of land in fee, and orally, but for no consideration, agrees to convey the land to B. by the will of A., and A. dies leaving a will which devises the land to C., B. may attempt to make C. a constructive trustee for B., on the basis of A.'s breach of contract and C.'s voluntary succession to the property. In these cases the result is almost invariably that C. is not made a constructive trustee.[38] The court does not regard A.'s breach of his voidable contract as an ethical or moral wrong. The legislature allowed him to violate it, and he did avoid it by devising to C. To make C. a constructive trustee would be to ignore the fourth section of the Statute of Frauds and to enforce an oral contract to convey an interest in land. B. is merely a disappointed expectant donee.

But in cases where the promisee under the oral agreement to convey gave consideration, and changed his position in such a way that hardship would result from ignoring the agreement, courts of equity often help the promisee. Thus, in many cases an elderly man contracts to leave his real estate to a female relative if the latter will take the old man into her home and care for him during the remainder of his life. The woman performs her part of the bargain, but on the death of the man it is found that he left no will and the woman is not his heir. In these cases equity often decrees that the taker of the realty by intestacy must convey to the woman promisee, the court using either language of specific performance of constructive trust.[39]

If, however, the promisee can be adequately protected by a money judgment against the promisor on some quasi-contrac-

[38] Scribner v. Meade, 10 Ariz. 143, 85 P. 477; Bland v. Talley. 50 Ark. 71, 6 S.W. 234; Hunter v. Feild, 114 Ark. 128, 169 S.W. 813; Taylor v. Kelley, 103 Cal. 178, 37 P. 216; Lyons v. Bass, 108 Ga. 573, 34 S.E. 721; Houston v. Farley, 146 Ga. 822, 92 S.E. 635; Miller v. Miller, 266 Ill. 522, 107 N.E. 821; Moore v. McClain, Ind.App., 119 N.E. 258; Revel v. Albert, Iowa, 162 N.W. 595; Goff v. Goff, 98 Kan. 201, 158 P. 26, rehearing denied, 98 Kan. 700, 158 P. 662; Fields v. Hoskins, 182 Ky. 446, 206 S.W. 763; McIntyre v. McIntyre, 205 Mich. 496, 171 N.W. 393; Ostheimer v. Single, 73 N.J.Eq. 539, 68 A. 231; Watson v. Erb, 33 Ohio St. 35; Chadwick v. Arnold, 34 Utah 48, 95 P. 527; In re Mason's Estate, 95 Wash. 564, 164 P. 205; Parkes v. Burkhart, 101 Wash. 659, 172 P. 908. On this and other topics considered in this section, see Costigan, "Trusts Based on Oral Promises to Hold in Trust, to Convey, or to Devise, Made by Voluntary Grantees," 12 Mich.Law Rev. 423, 515.

[39] Martin v. Martin, 250 Mo. 539, 157 S.W. 575; Worden v. Worden, 96 Wash. 592, 165 P. 501.

tual theory, the breach of the oral contract to convey will not be used as the basis for specific performance or constructive trust.[41]

DISLOYALTY OF FIDUCIARY [42]

62. If any fiduciary acquires property by means of disloyalty to his beneficiary, that is, by seeking the interest of himself rather than that of the beneficiary, he may be made a constructive trustee as to the property so gained.

Where one is acting in a representative and fiduciary capacity, equity demands that he seek only the profit and advantage of his beneficiary.[43] The fiduciary is not allowed to have conflicting interests. He must not be seeking his own financial advancement, as well as that of his beneficiary. The word "fiduciary" is here used in a broad, general sense, to include strict trustees, executors, administrators, guardians, committees of lunatics and feeble-minded persons, partners, co-tenants, agents, attorneys, directors, and promoters of corporations, and many others in similar relations. The word "beneficiary" is here used to designate the persons who are represented in the relationships above suggested, namely, the cestuis que trust, legatees, next of kin, wards, and others.

It is a broad principle of equity, having a highly varied application, that the fiduciary may be obliged to hold any private profit which he obtains, while acting in his representative capacity, under a constructive trust for the beneficiary, if the beneficiary so elect. The beneficiary may allow the fiduciary to retain the profit he has made—may ratify the transaction. But, if the beneficiary desires, he may by a bill in equity have the fiduciary declared a constructive trustee of the profit which the fiduciary has obtained.

This rule applies, regardless of the actual good faith of the fiduciary. He may have intended no fraud. He may have paid value for what he has received and done no actual harm to the beneficiary. Equity will nevertheless declare the fiduciary a constructive trustee of the property he has obtained. To discourage such dangerous dealings equity declares them all, regardless of the peculiar circumstances of individual cases, voidable at the election of the beneficiary.

[41] Andrews v. Aikens, 44 Idaho 797, 260 P. 423, 69 A.L.R. 8; Stellmacher v. Bruder, 89 Minn. 507, 95 N.W. 324, 99 Am.St.Rep. 609.

[42] Restatement, Trusts, § 206.

[43] See, post, § 99.

Thus, if the fiduciary buys the trust property at his own sale thereof, he may, at the option of the beneficiary, be held a constructive trustee of it for the beneficiary, regardless of the price paid or the loss or gain to the beneficiary.[44] It is immaterial whether the fiduciary buys the trust property directly or indirectly. The constructive trust will be created, at the option of the beneficiary.[45] Of course, if the beneficiary consents to the purchase of the property by the fiduciary, either in advance [46] or after the sale,[47] by way of ratification, the sale will be valid, and no trust will arise from it. And if the beneficiary sees fit to set aside the sale and have the fiduciary declared a constructive trustee of the property bought, he must, of course, reimburse the fiduciary for money advanced from his own pocket as payment for the property bought.[48]

"The rule which disables one occupying a confidential or fiduciary relation, in respect to property the subject of a sale, from purchasing for his own benefit, and regarding him as a trustee if he do purchase, is absolute, and looks to no other facts

---

[44] *Attorney and Client:* Stockton v. Ford, 52 U.S. 232, 11 How. 232, 13 L. Ed. 676; Holmes v. Holmes, 106 Ga. 858, 33 S.E. 216; Harper v. Perry, 28 Iowa 57; Rolikatis v. Lovett, 213 Mass. 545, 100 N.E. 748; Johnson v. Outlaw, 56 Miss. 541; Aultman, Miller & Co. v. Loring, 76 Mo.App. 66; Levara v. McNeny, 73 Neb. 414, 102 N.W. 1042; Case v. Carroll, 35 N.Y. 385; Miles v. Ervin, 1 McCord Eq., S.C., 524, 16 Am.Dec. 610; Wheeler v. Willard, 44 Vt. 640; Newcomb v. Brooks, 16 W.Va. 32; O'Dell v. Rogers, 44 Wis. 136.

Agent: Peabody v. Burri, 255 Ill. 592, 99 N.E. 690; Witte v. Storm, 236 Mo. 470, 139 S.W. 384; Luscombe v. Grigsby, 11 S.D. 408, 78 N.W. 357; Frost v. Perfield, 44 Wash. 185, 87 P. 117.

Administrator: Powell v. Powell, 80 Ala. 11; Williford v. Williford, 102 Ark. 65, 143 S.W. 132; Carrier v. Heather, 62 Mich. 441, 29 N.W. 38.

Trustee: Eisert v. Bowen, 191 N.Y. 544, 85 N.E. 1109, affirming 117 App. Div. 488, 102 N.Y.S. 707; Barrett v. Bamber, 81 Pa. 247.

Executor: Merrick v. Waters, 171 N.Y. 655, 63 N.E. 1119, affirming 51 App.Div. 83, 64 N.Y.S. 542.

Cotenants: Carpenter v. Carpenter, 58 Hun 608, 12 N.Y.S. 189.

Guardian: Sparhawk v. Allen, 21 N.H. 9.

Assignee for Creditors: Ex parte Lacey, 6 Ves. 625; Broder v. Conklin, 121 Cal. 282, 53 P. 699.

Members of Church Society: Fort v. First Baptist Church of Paris, Tex. Civ.App., 55 S.W. 402.

[45] Lovell v. Felkins, 181 Ala. 165, 61 So. 262; Turner v. Turner, 34 Okl. 284, 125 P. 730; Irwin v. Monongahela River Consol. Coal & Coke Co., 238 Pa. 558, 86 A. 491.

[46] Page v. Stubbs, 39 Iowa 537.

[47] Ward v. Brown, 87 Mo. 468; Olson v. Lamb, 56 Neb. 104, 76 N.W. 433, 71 Am.St.Rep. 670.

[48] Gaston v. King, 63 Miss. 326; Maynard's Case, 1 Walk., Pa., 472.

than the relation and the purchaser. 'No fraud in fact need be shown by the cestui que trust, and no excuse will be heard from the trustee. The fact established, and the result inevitably follows.' " [49]

If officers of a corporation buy property on which the corporation had an option, they may be held by the corporation as constructive trustees of the property.[50] So, too, the rule is well established that, if a fiduciary buys an outstanding claim against the trust property, the principal may hold him as a constructive trustee of such title or claim.[51] And if the fiduciary uses the trust property in his own business, and thereby makes a profit, he may be held as a constructive trustee of such profit by the principal.[52] If the fiduciary makes a profit on the sale of the trust property to a third person,[53] or purchases for himself property which he should have bought for the beneficiary,[54] equity will declare the fiduciary, at the option of the beneficiary, a constructive trustee of the property which he holds as a result of the reprehensible transaction.

A very common application of this principle with respect to constructive trusts is found in the cases where a promoter or agent has made a secret profit upon a sale of property to a corporation or other principal. In some instances the promoter or other agent himself sells to the principal, in other cases he obtains a consideration from a third party for arranging a sale to the principal. The promoter or other agent is universally held as a constructive trustee of the secret profit thus obtained; the

[49] King v. Remington, 36 Minn. 15, 25, 29 N.W. 352.

[50] Lagarde v. Anniston Lime & Stone Co., 126 Ala. 496, 28 So. 199; Trenton Banking Co. v. McKelway, 8 N.J.Eq. 84.

[51] Downard v. Hadley, 116 Ind. 131, 18 N.E. 457; Henry v. Raiman, 25 Pa. 354, 64 Am.Dec. 703.

[52] Kyle v. Barnett, 17 Ala. 306; Bond v. Lockwood, 33 Ill. 212; Chanslor v. Chanslor's Trustees, 11 Bush, Ky., 663; Clarkson v. De Peyster, Hopk.Ch., N.Y., 424.

[53] Griggs v. Griggs, 66 Barb., N.Y., 287.

[54] Turner v. Sawyer, 150 U.S. 578, 14 S.Ct. 192, 37 L.Ed. 1189; Koyer v. Willmon, 150 Cal. 785, 90 P. 135; McPherrin v. Fair, 57 Colo. 333, 141 P. 472; Ainsworth v. Harding, 22 Idaho 645, 128 P. 92; Vallette v. Tedens. 122 Ill. 607, 14 N.E. 52, 3 Am.St.Rep. 502; Byington v. Moore, 62 Iowa 470, 17 N.W. 644; Nester v. Gross, 66 Minn. 371, 69 N.W. 39; Winn v. Dillon, 27 Miss. 494; Seacoast R. Co. v. Wood, 65 N.J.Eq. 530, 56 A. 337; Maltz v. Westchester County Brewing Co., Sup., 140 N.Y.S. 521; Sawyer v. Issenhuth, 31 S.D. 502, 141 N.W. 378; Henyan v. Trevino, Tex.Civ.App., 137 S.W. 458.

principal, of course, being the beneficiary of such trust.[55] Thus the directors of a corporation, who act for their own benefit in the purchase of corporation property, may, at the election of the corporation or its stockholders, be held as constructive trustees of the profits which they have obtained;[56] and a partner or quasi partner, who conceals from his associates at the time of the purchase of a play by the partnership that he is entitled to one-fourth of the royalties from the play, is a constructive trustee of the royalties which he receives after the sale;[57] and a city officer, who, while advising a committee regarding building sites, buys land himself and sells it to the city through a third person, may be made a trustee for the city of the profits made—that is, the difference between the price paid by him for the land and the price paid by the city.[58]

If P. employs A. as agent to buy property with the money of P. and in the name of P. and instead A. purchases the property with the money of A. and in the name of A., there has been a violation of the fiduciary relationship of agency, a case of self-dealing where there should have been loyalty to the principal, and the principal should be allowed to charge the agent as constructive trustee of the property held by him, on reimbursing the agent for his expenses.[59] A few cases erroneously see in this transaction a breach of a voidable contract to convey an interest in land and give no relief for the breach.[60]

These cases are all variations of the same principle, namely, that one who is acting in a representative capacity must act for his beneficiary alone, and must not seek his own private gain. Whatever such a fiduciary obtains, while acting for his benefi-

[55] Davis v. Las Ovas Co., 227 U.S. 80, 33 S.Ct. 197, 57 L.Ed. 426; Johnston v. Little, 141 Ala. 382, 37 So. 592; Bone v. Hayes, 154 Cal. 759, 99 P. 172; Old Dominion Copper Mining & Smelting Co. v. Bigelow, 203 Mass. 159, 89 N.E. 193, 40 L.R.A.,N.S., 314; Exter v. Sawyer, 146 Mo. 302, 47 S.W. 951; Arnold v. Searing, 78 N.J.Eq. 146, 78 A. 762; Colton Imp. Co. v. Richter, 26 Misc. 26, 55 N.Y.S. 486; Shawnee Commercial & Savings Bank Co. v. Miller, 24 Ohio Cir. Ct. R. 198.

[56] Billings v. Shaw, 209 N.Y. 265, 103 N.E. 142

[57] Selwyn & Co. v. Waller, 212 N.Y. 507, 106 N.E. 321, L.R.A.1915B, 160.

[58] City of Minneapolis v. Canterbury, 122 Minn. 301, 142 N.W. 812, 48 L.R.A.,N.S., 842, Ann.Cas.1914D, 804.

[59] Vallette v. Tedens, 122 Ill. 607, 14 N.E. 52, 3 Am.St.Rep. 502; Rogers v. Genung, 76 N.J.Eq. 306, 74 A. 473; Jackson v. Pleasonton, 95 Va. 654, 29 S.E. 680.

[60] Burden v. Sheridan, 36 Iowa 125, 14 Am.Rep. 505; Watson v. Erb, 33 Ohio St. 35.

ciary, he must hold for the benefit of the beneficiary. In order to insure respect for the duty of loyalty equity gives the beneficiary the option of taking from the fiduciary the proceeds of any transaction in which the fiduciary has a selfish interest. Further details of the application of this principle are given in the sections dealing with the trustee's duty of loyalty to the beneficiary,[61] and in the sections on the remedies of the beneficiary.[62]

The general doctrine here stated applies to persons in a "confidential relation",[63] as well as to those in a "fiduciary relation". The latter term may be used to indicate many well-defined relationships which have separate categories in the law, like that of trustee and beneficiary, and executor and legatee. While the former may be applied to miscellaneous cases where one party has superiority of position and consequent control over another but the relationship does not belong to a special class. An illustration of a confidential relation may be found in the case of a husband and wife, where the husband is an able-bodied, experienced business man of great force and ability, and the wife is an inexperienced woman who leaves all her affairs to the management of her husband; or in the case of an able-bodied young man of good education and much business experience who is entrusted by his feeble and aged mother with the control of her property.

DIRECT DEALING WITH BENEFICIARY [64]

63. If any fiduciary acquires a property interest from his beneficiary directly, without making the fullest possible disclosure and treating the beneficiary with the utmost fairness, the fiduciary may be made a constructive trustee of the property acquired.

Dealings between persons on an unequal footing are viewed with suspicion by courts of equity. The opportunities for fraud are so great that equity places a burden on the stronger party to prove the fairness and good faith of the transaction. Where a person placed in a position of trust obtains a direct conveyance of property from the person trusting him, equity looks with suspicion on the transaction. The conveyance may be fair, made

---

[61] See § 99, post.

[62] See § 152, post.

[63] Commercial Merchants' Nat. Bank & Trust Co. v. Kloth, 360 Ill. 294, 196 N.E. 214; Van't Hof v. Jemison, 291 Mich. 385, 289 N.W. 186.

[64] Restatement, Trusts, § 170.

upon full information, and for a sufficient consideration. But, since the position of influence of the fiduciary makes fraud and undue influence easy, equity will presume fraud and place the burden on the grantee of showing the fairness of his conduct. If he can show that the grantor has acted upon full information as to the facts and his rights, has not been misled or deceived, and has received a consideration reasonably adequate, he (the grantee and fiduciary) will be allowed by equity to retain the property. But, if he cannot show these facts, he may be decreed by equity to hold the property under a constructive trust for the one trusting him.

Attorney and Client

A typical illustration of the cases here under discussion is that of a transfer from client to attorney during the existence of the relationship. It is said by the courts that this transaction will be closely scrutinized,[65] that the greatest good faith will be required on the part of the attorney,[66] and that the burden is on the attorney to prove the fairness of the transaction between himself and his client.[67] But an attorney is not incapacitated from becoming a grantee of his client. The grant from client to attorney is only presumptively fraudulent, and the presumption may be overcome by evidence of good faith. Proof by the attorney that he paid value, that the client acted with full knowledge of his rights and free from the influence of his attorney, will rebut the presumption of fraud and establish the sale as a valid transaction.[68] Of course, the presumption of fraud arises

[65] Dawson v. Copeland, 173 Ala. 267, 55 So. 600; Lewis v. Helm, 40 Colo. 17, 90 P. 97; Mills v. Mills, 26 Conn. 213; Gruby v. Smith, 13 Ill. App. 43; State v. Johnson, 149 Iowa 462, 128 N.W. 837; Yeamans v. James, 27 Kan. 195; Palms' Adm'rs v. Howard, 129 Ky. 668, 112 S.W. 1110; Gray v. Emmons, 7 Mich. 533; Eysaman v. Nelson, 79 Misc. 304, 140 N.Y.S. 183.

[66] In re Danford, 157 Cal. 425, 108 P. 322; McCormick v. Malin, 5 Blackf., Ind., 509; Ryan v. Ashton, 42 Iowa 365; Payne v. Avery, 21 Mich. 524; Hames v. Stroud, 51 Tex.Civ.App. 562, 112 S.W. 775;

Young v. Murphy, 120 Wis. 49, 97 N.W. 496.

[67] Day v. Wright, 233 Ill. 218, 84 N.E. 226; Donaldson v. Eaton & Estes, 136 Iowa 650, 114 N.W. 19, 14 L.R.A.,N.S., 1168, 125 Am.St.Rep. 275; Manheim v. Woods, 213 Mass. 537, 100 N.E. 747; Phipps v. Willis, 53 Or. 190, 96 P. 866, 18 Ann.Cas. 119.

[68] Myers v. Luzerne County, C.C. Pa., 124 F. 436; Cooley v. Miller, 156 Cal. 510, 105 P. 981; Appeal of St. Leger, 34 Conn. 434, 91 Am.Dec. 735; Stubinger v. Frey, 116 Ga. 396, 42 S.E. 713; Morrison v. Smith, 130 Ill. 304, 23 N.E. 241; Mitchell v.

only during the continuance of the relation of attorney and client.[69] Ratification by the client may prevent an attack on the sale on the ground of presumptive fraud.[70]

"Wherever a fiduciary relation exists, legal or actual, whereby trust and confidence are reposed on the one side, and influence and control are exercised on the other, courts of equity, independent of the ingredients of positive fraud, through public policy as a protection against overweening confidence, will interpose to prevent a man from stripping himself of his property. * * * The relation requires the parties to abstain from all selfish projects. The general principle is, if a confidence is reposed and that confidence is abused, courts of equity will grant relief. In such cases it is not necessary to prove the actual exercise of overweening influence, misrepresentation, importunity, or fraud aliunde the act complained of. * * * The general rule is that he who bargains in a matter of advantage with a person placing confidence in him is bound to show that a reasonable use has been made of that confidence, a rule applying equally to all persons standing in confidential relations to each other."[71]

Trustee and Cestui

The rule of presumptive fraud which applies to direct transfers from client to attorney also controls tranfers from cestui que trust to trustee. "Defined principles of public policy are clearly opposed to the unrestricted right of a trustee to acquire the property of a cestui que trust. A sale by a trustee to himself of the trust property is uniformly held to be voidable at the option of the cestui que trust, even though the trustee may have given an adequate price and gained no advantage. * * * But where trust property has been acquired by a trustee through the medium of direct dealing with the cestui que trust, it is

---

Colby, 95 Iowa 202, 63 N.W. 769; Yeamans v. James, 27 Kan. 195; Merryman v. Euler, 59 Md. 588, 43 Am.Rep. 564; Crocheron v. Savage, 75 N.J.Eq. 589, 73 A. 33, 23 L.R.A., N.S., 679; Nesbit v. Lockman, 34 N. Y. 167; Helms v. Goodwill, 64 N.Y. 642; Tippett v. Brooks, 95 Tex. 335, 67 S.W. 495, 512; Vanasse v. Reid, 111 Wis. 303, 87 N.W. 192. But see West v. Raymond, 21 Ind. 305; Yerkes v. Crum, 2 N.D. 72, 49 N.W. 422; Lane v. Black, 21 W.Va. 617;

Keenan v. Scott, 64 W.Va. 137, 61 S.E. 806.

[69] Zeigler v. Hughes, 55 Ill. 288.

[70] Wills v. Wood, 28 Kan. 400; Lewis v. Broun, 36 W.Va. 1, 14 S.E. 444.

[71] Thiede v. Startzman, 113 Md. 278, 77 A. 666, 670, quoting Highberger v. Stiffler, 21 Md. 352, 83 Am.Dec. 593.

manifest that the right of the cestui que trust to avoid the contract should not be without limitation. While some courts have held such dealing to be contrary to public policy, and voidable at the instance of the cestui que trust, the better and prevailing view appears to be that such dealings are presumed to be invalid, but will be supported if the trustee can establish that the cestui que trust acted voluntarily and with entire freedom from any influence arising by reason of the trust relationship, and with intelligence and full knowledge of all the circumstances."[72] The trustee who has received the property of cestui que trust by means of a direct grant from the cestui is held to be a constructive trustee of the property, unless he can establish the fairness of the transaction.[73]

And so, too, a direct transfer from distributee to administrator, or legatee to executor, raises a prima facie presumption of fraud, and the grantee will be held a constructive trustee for the grantor, unless the grantee can establish that the transfer was fair and above board.[74]

Guardian and Ward

A transfer from ward to guardian will be closely scrutinized by equity,[75] and will not be sustained if the guardian obtains any advantage from the transfer.[76] By the weight of authority it

---

[72] Swift v. Craighead, 75 N.J.Eq. 102, 103, 75 A. 974.

[73] Malone v. Kelley, 54 Ala. 532; Metropolis Trust & Savings Bank v. Monnier, 169 Cal. 592, 147 P. 265; Bryan v. Duncan, 11 Ga. 67; Brown v. Cowell, 116 Mass. 461; Field v. Middlesex Banking Co., 77 Miss. 180, 26 So. 365; Ludington v. Patton, 111 Wis. 208, 86 N.W. 571.

That the rule does not apply to a passive trustee, see Carpenter v. Kingham, Wyo., 110 P.2d 824.

Section 2235 of the Civil Code of California provides as follows: "All transactions between a trustee and his beneficiary during the existence of the trust, or while the influence acquired by the trustee remains, by which he obtains any advantage from his beneficiary, are presumed to be entered into by the latter without sufficient consideration, and under undue influence." See, also, Mont.Rev.Codes 1935, § 7895; N.D.Comp.L.1913, § 6288; S.D.Code 1939, § 59.0113.

[74] Williams v. Powell, 66 Ala. 20, 41 Am.Rep. 742; Golson v. Dunlap, 73 Cal. 157, 14 P. 576; Nelson v. Gossage, 152 Kan. 805, 107 P.2d 682; Richards v. Pitts, 124 Mo. 602, 28 S.W. 88; State ex rel. Jones v. Jones, 53 Mo.App. 207; Lovell v. Briggs, 2 N.H. 218; Leach v. Leach, 65 Wis. 284, 26 N.W. 754.

[75] Taylor v. Calvert, 138 Ind. 67, 37 N.E. 531; Hart v. Cannon, 133 N.C. 10, 45 S.E. 351.

[76] Fidelity Trust Co. v. Butler, 91 S.W. 676, 28 Ky.Law Rep. 1268; Williams v. Palmer, 2 Baxt. 488, 61 Tenn. 488.

BOGERT TRUSTS 2D

§ 63   DIRECT DEALING WITH BENEFICIARY   211

is held that the transfer from ward to guardian is not void nor voidable under all circumstances by the ward, but is voidable by the ward unless the guardian proves that the transaction was a bona fide conveyance for value, freely made by the ward. The transaction is presumed to be fraudulent, and the burden is on the guardian to show its fairness.[77] The ward may affirm the sale from himself to the guardian, although it was originally voidable.[78] But in some cases it has been held that a guardian cannot buy from his ward, and that a conveyance from ward to guardian is unenforceable.[79]

The rule of this section applies to persons in confidential relations with each other, as well as to the relations technically called "fiduciary" and referred to above. Where one person occupies a position of influence and control over another, by reason of kinship, age, experience, health, education, or otherwise, and he receives a transfer of property from the weaker party, the transaction is subject to scrutiny by the court, at the request of the transferror, and a constructive trust will be imposed, unless entire candor and fair dealing are shown.[80]

The question as to what constitutes a relation of trust and confidence sufficient to give rise to a presumption of fraud has arisen in a variety of ways. A transfer from cotenant to cotenant,[81] from son-in-law to father-in-law,[82] from stepdaughter to stepfather,[83] from minor niece to aunt,[84] from uncle to nephew,[85] and from parishioner to priest[86] has been held to give rise

---

[77] Willis v. Rice, 157 Ala. 252, 48 So. 397, 131 Am.St.Rep. 55; Waldstein v. Barnett, 112 Ark. 141, 165 S.W. 459; McParland v. Larkin, 155 Ill. 84, 39 N.E. 609; Meade v. Fullerton's Adm'x, 266 Ky. 34, 98 S.W.2d 1; Meek v. Perry, 36 Miss. 190; Brandau v. Greer, 95 Miss. 100, 48 So. 519, 21 Ann. Cas. 1118; Goodrick v. Harrison, 130 Mo. 263, 32 S.W. 661; Mann v. McDonald, 10 Humph. 275, 29 Tenn. 275; Baylor v. Fulkerson's Ex'rs, 96 Va. 265, 31 S.E. 63.

[78] Appeal of Schur, Pa., 2 A. 336.

[79] Hindman v. O'Connor, 54 Ark. 627, 16 S.W. 1052, 13 L.R.A. 490; Dohms v. Mann, 76 Iowa 723, 39 N.W. 823; Williams v. Davison's Estate, 133 Mich. 344, 94 N.W. 1048.

[80] Brown v. Brown, 329 Ill. 198, 160 N.E. 149; Wells v. Wells, 197 Ind. 236, 150 N.E. 361; McConville v. Ingham, 268 Pa. 507, 112 A. 85.

[81] Koefoed v. Thompson, 73 Neb. 128, 102 N.W. 268.

[82] Bowler v. Curler, 21 Nev. 158, 26 P. 226, 37 Am.St.Rep. 501.

[83] Newis v. Topfer, 121 Iowa 433, 96 N.W. 905.

[84] Butler v. Hyland, 89 Cal. 575, 26 P. 1108.

[85] Ward v. Conklin, 232 Ill. 553, 83 N.E. 1058.

[86] Henderson v. Murray, 108 Minn. 76, 121 N.W. 214, 133 Am.St.Rep. 412.

to a presumption of fraud upon which a constructive trust could be founded. On the other hand, in some cases transfers from uncle to nephew,[87] grandfather to grandson,[88] cousin to cousin,[89] and brother to sister[90] have been held not to give rise to any presumption of fraud on the ground of confidential relationship. A transfer from principal to agent has been held to be presumptively fraudulent.[91]

The doctrine applied in these cases is well stated in a New York case:[92] "Whenever, however, the relations between the contracting parties appear to be of such a character as to render it certain that they do not deal on terms of equality, but that either on the one side from superior knowledge of the matter derived from a fiduciary relation, or from overmastering influence, or on the other from weakness, dependence, or trust justifiably reposed, unfair advantage in a transaction is rendered probable, there the burden is shifted, the transaction is presumed void, and it is incumbent upon the stronger party to show affirmatively that no deception was practiced, no undue influence was used, and that all was fair, open, voluntary, and well understood."

Doubtless the exact relationship of the parties is not so important as their relative ages, their mental and physical condition, and their respective abilities and characters.

PURCHASE AT JUDICIAL SALE UNDER ORAL PROMISE [93]

64. If one purchases at a judicial sale the property of another, under oral agreement to hold it for that other, he may be made a constructive trustee of it, if he refuses to perform his promise, if the promisee and others relied on the promise, and breach of the promise works hardship on the promisee.

In numerous cases the owner of an interest in land, as, for example, an equity of redemption or a fee simple subject to the lien of a judgment, has made an agreement with a stranger to

---

[87] Doheny v. Lacy, 168 N.Y. 213, 61 N.E. 255.

[88] Cowee v. Cornell, 75 N.Y. 91, 31 Am.Rep. 428.

[89] Schneider v. Schneider, 125 Iowa 1, 98 N.W. 159.

[90] Reeves v. Howard, 118 Iowa 121, 91 N.W. 896.

[91] Kimball v. Tripp, 136 Cal. 631, 69 P. 428; Vorse v. Vorse, Iowa, 171 N. W. 186; Hunter v. Hunter, 50 Mo. 445.

[92] Cowee v. Cornell, 75 N.Y. 91, 99, 100, 31 Am.Rep. 428.

[93] Restatement, Restitution, § 181.

§ 64   PURCHASE AT JUDICIAL SALE UNDER ORAL PROMISE   213

the title that such stranger should bid in the land on the judicial sale of it, hold it for the promisee, and dispose of it for the promisee, or reconvey it to him upon certain conditions. If the promisor buys in the land but refuses to respect his promise to hold for or convey to the promisee, the cases usually decree a constructive trust for the promisee if the promisee, and sometimes the general public, relied on the promise and failed to take action to protect his interest.[94] In many cases also there is the factor that the property was sold for less than its value to the promisor under the oral promise.

The conduct of the buyer at the judicial sale is evidently considered by equity as particularly mean and blameworthy. The court decrees a constructive trust without apparent appreciation of the inconsistency between the result in these cases and that in the case of a deed from A. to B. on oral trust for A.[95] As argued later the inconsistency should be removed by a change of position in the latter case, rather than in the former.

A minority of the courts, however, have refused to charge the purchaser at the judicial sale as a constructive trustee for the promisee, either out of assumed necessity to preserve the Statute of Frauds or lack of evidence of reliance by the promisee to his damage.[96]

[94] Booth v. Mason, 234 Ala. 601, 176 So. 201; Brittin v. Handy, 20 Ark. 381, 73 Am.Dec. 497; Strasner v. Carroll, 125 Ark. 34, 187 S.W. 1057, Ann. Cas.1918E, 306; Price v. Reeves, 38 Cal. 457; Thomas v. Goodbread, Fla., 82 So. 835; Rives v. Lawrence, 41 Ga. 283; Arnold v. Cord, 16 Ind. 177; Eadie v. Hamilton, 94 Kan. 214, 146 P. 323; Griffin v. Schlenk, 139 Ky. 523, 102 S.W. 837; Miller's Heirs v. Antle, 2 Bush, Ky., 407, 92 Am.Dec. 495; Doom v. Brown, 171 Ky. 469, 188 S.W. 475 (trust called resulting); Deval v. Farris, 185 Miss. 757, 189 So. 516; Northcraft v. Martin, 28 Mo. 469; O'Day v. Annex Realty Co., Mo., 191 S.W. 41; Robinson v. Cruzen, Mo. App., 202 S.W. 449; Dickson v. Stewart, 71 Neb. 424, 98 N.W. 1085, 115 Am.St.Rep. 596; Day v. Devitt, 79 N.J.Eq. 342, 81 A. 368; Eckerson v. McCulloh, 39 N.J.Eq. 115; Van Horne v. Fonda, 5 Johns.Ch., N.Y., 388; Allen v. Arkenburgh, 2 App.Div. 452, 37 N.Y. S. 1032; Ryan v. Dox, 34 N.Y. 307, 90 Am.Dec. 696; Goldman v. Cohen, 167 App.Div. 666, 153 N.Y.S. 41; Rush v. McPherson, 176 N.C. 562, 97 S.E. 613; Beegle v. Wentz, 55 Pa. 369, 93 Am.Dec. 762; Wolford v. Herrington, 86 Pa. 39; Jenckes v. Cook, 9 R.I. 520; Denton v. McKenzie, 1 Desaus., S.C., 289, 1 Am.Dec. 664; Haywood v. Ensley, 8 Humph., Tenn., 460; Chandler v. Riley, Tex.Civ.App., 210 S.W. 716; Harras v. Harras, 60 Wash. 258, 110 P. 1085.

[95] See § 65, post.

[96] La Cotts v. La Cotts, 109 Ark. 335, 159 S.W. 1111; Emerson v. Ayres, 196 Ark. 791, 120 S.W.2d 16; Walter v. Klock, 55 Ill. 362; Kellum v. Smith, 33 Pa. 158; Lewis v. Williams, 186 Miss. 701, 191 So. 479; Woodard v. Cohron, 345 Mo. 967, 137 S.W.2d 497; Barnet v. Dougherty, 32 Pa. 371; Fox v. Peoples, 201 Pa. 9, 50 A. 226; Lancaster Trust Co. v.

The case of Ryan v. Dox[97] is illustrative of the prevailing view upon this subject. There a mortgagor agreed with the defendant that the defendant should buy the mortgaged real estate at the foreclosure sale; that title should be taken in the name of the defendant; that defendant should pay the amount of the bid with his own funds; that defendant should hold the real property as security for the repayment of his advances; and that defendant should convey the property to the mortgagor, the plaintiff, upon repayment of his advances. The defendant bid at the sale and obtained the property for a reduced price, because it was understood he was bidding for the mortgagor. The mortgagor remained away from the sale and took no steps to protect his interest, relying on the defendant. Upon the repudiation of his promise by the defendant, it was held that the defendant would be declared a constructive trustee for the mortgagor, the plaintiff.

On principle the purchasers at judicial sales, who violate their promises to hold for the promisees, are attempting unjustly to enrich themselves, and should be made constructive trustees for the promisees on repayment of their advances, even though the express trust involved cannot be enforced.

CONVEYANCE OF LAND ON ORAL TRUST [98]

65. Where land is conveyed by absolute deed to one under his oral promise that he will hold it for the grantor or another, a breach of the promise does not, according to prevailing American opinion, justify the court in charging the promisor as a constructive trustee. The rule is different if the grantee intended to break the promise when he obtained the deed, or was in a confidential or fiduciary relation with the grantor at that time.

Contract to Hold Real Property in Trust

It is held by the majority of American courts that the violation of an oral promise to hold real property in trust for the promisee or for another is not such wrong doing as will cause equity to create a constructive trust. If A. owns real property, and orally promises to hold it in trust for B., and later declines to carry out the trust, equity will not make A. a constructive trustee of the property; and the same result is reached, if A. conveys real

---

Long, 220 Pa. 499, 69 A. 993; Stafford v. Stafford, 29 Tex.Civ.App. 73, 71 S.W. 984.

[97] 34 N.Y. 307, 90 Am.Dec. 696.

[98] Restatement, Restitution, §§ 180, 182, 183.

property to B. upon B.'s oral promise to hold the land in trust for A. or for C., which promise is later violated. If the only wrong proved is the breach of the oral agreement, and if promisor and promisee do not occupy a confidential relationship, equity will not declare the promisor a trustee.[99]

In England and a few American states it is held that a constructive trust will be declared on account of a breach of an oral agreement by the grantee to hold land in trust for the grantor or another.[1]

The reason given for the prevailing view is that, to declare a constructive trust because of a breach of an agreement voidable

[99] Patton v. Beecher, 62 Ala. 579; Brindley v. Brindley, 197 Ala. 221, 72 So. 497; Wright v. Young, 20 Ariz. 46, 176 P. 583; Ussery v. Ussery, 113 Ark. 36, 166 S.W. 946; Burt v. Wilson, 28 Cal. 632, 87 Am.Dec. 142; Von Trotha v. Bamberger, 15 Colo. 1, 24 P. 883; Verzier v. Convard, 75 Conn. 1, 52 A. 255; Lawson v. Lawson, 117 Ill. 98, 7 N.E. 84; Davis v. Stambaugh, 163 Ill. 557, 45 N.E. 170; Ryder v. Ryder, 244 Ill. 297, 91 N.E. 451; Roche v. Roche, 286 Ill. 336, 121 N.E. 621; Westphal v. Heckman, 185 Ind. 88, 113 N.E. 299; Orear v. Farmers' State Bank & Trust Co., 286 Ill. 454, 122 N.E. 63; Dunn v. Zwilling, 94 Iowa 233, 62 N.W. 746; Andrew v. Andrew, 114 Iowa 524, 87 N.W. 494; Titcomb v. Morrill, 10 Allen, Mass., 15; Ryan v. Williams, 92 Minn. 506, 100 N.W. 380; Weiss v. Heitkamp, 127 Mo. 23, 29 S.W. 709; Ferguson v. Robinson, 258 Mo. 113, 167 S.W. 447; Dailey v. Kinsler, 31 Neb. 340, 47 N.W. 1045; Lovett v. Taylor, 54 N.J.Eq. 311, 34 A. 896; Sturtevant v. Sturtevant, 20 N.Y. 39, 75 Am.Dec. 371; Wheeler v. Reynolds, 66 N.Y. 227; Braun v. First German Evangelical Lutheran Church, 198 Pa. 152, 47 A. 963; McCloskey v. McCloskey, 205 Pa. 491, 55 A. 180; Farrell v. Mentzer, 102 Wash. 629, 174 P. 482; Krouskop v. Krouskop, 95 Wis. 296, 70 N.W. 475. See 39 L.R.A.,N.S., 906, for a good discussion of the subject. See, also, Harlan F. Stone, "Resulting Trusts and the Statute of Frauds," 6 Col.Law Rev. 326; J. B. Ames, "Constructive Trusts Based upon the Breach of an Express Oral Trust of Land," Lectures on Legal History, p. 425, 20 Harv.Law Rev. 549.

A fortiori no relief will be given if the oral promise was made after the deed. Crockett v. Crockett, 145 Fla. 311, 199 So. 337.

[1] Davies v. Otty, 35 Beav. 208; Rochefoucauld v. Bonstead [1897] 1 Ch. 196; Robertson v. Summeril, 39 Cal.App.2d 62, 102 P.2d 347; Chandler v. Georgia Chemical Works, 182 Ga. 419, 185 S.E. 787, 105 A.L.R. 837; Tinkler v. Swaynie, 71 Ind. 562; Myers v. Jackson, 135 Ind. 136, 34 N.E. 810 (but see General Convention of New Church in United States v. Smith, 52 Ind.App. 136, 100 N.E. 384); Becker v. Neurath, 149 Ky. 421, 149 S.W. 857; Huffine v. Lincoln, 52 Mont. 585, 160 P. 820; Feesner v. Cooper, 39 Okl. 133, 134 P. 379.

The English court bases its decision on the ground that it "is not honest" to keep the land.

In Massachusetts if the grantee on oral trust for the grantor will not carry out the trust, he may be sued by grantor for the value of the land. Cromwell v. Norton, 193 Mass. 291, 79 N.E. 433, 118 Am.St.Rep. 499. And see section 16, Uniform Trusts Act.

on account of the Statute of Frauds, would be practically to destroy the Statute of Frauds concerning trusts. It will be of slight importance to the beneficiary whether his trust is called implied or express, so long as it is enforced. This view has been forcibly stated by Brickell, C. J., in a leading case.[2] "The plain meaning of the statute is that a trust in land, not arising by implication or construction of law, cannot be created by parol— that a writing signed by the party creating or declaring the trust is indispensable to its existence. Fraud, imposition, mistake, in the original transaction, may constitute the purchaser, or donee, a trustee ex maleficio. It is *fraud then,* and not *subsequent fraud,* if any exist, which justifies a court of equity in intervening for the relief of the party injured by it—as it is the payment of the purchase money, at the time the title is acquired, which creates a resulting trust, and not a subsequent payment, whatever may be the circumstances attending it. * * * When the original transaction is free from the taint of fraud or imposition, when the written contract expresses all the parties intended it should, when the parol agreement which is sought to be enforced, is intentionally excluded from it, it is difficult to conceive of any ground upon which the imputation of fraud can rest, because of its subsequent violation or repudiation, that would not form a basis for a similar imputation, whenever any promise or contract is broken. It is annihilation of the statute to withdraw a case from its operation because of such violation or repudiation of an agreement or trust it declares shall not be made or proved by parol. There can be no fraud if the trust does not exist, and proof of its existence by parol is that which the statute forbids. In any and every case, in which the court is called to enforce a trust, there must be a repudiation of it, or an inability from accident to perform it. If the repudiation is a fraud, which justifies interference in opposition to the words and spirit of the statute, the sphere of operation of the statute is practically limited to breaches from accident, and no reason can be assigned for the limitation."

In answer to this argument, however, it may be said that parol agreements to hold in trust are of two classes, namely, those in which a refusal to enforce the promise will result in the unjust enrichment of the promisor, and those in which the failure to enforce the promise will not cause unjust enrichment of the promisor. If A. agrees, voluntarily, to hold in trust for B. real

---

[2] Patton v. Beecher, 62 Ala. 579, 592, 593.

property which at the time of the promise belongs to A., and A. later declines to carry out his agreement, the refusal of the courts to enforce A.'s promise will not result in A.'s being unjustly enriched at the expense of B. But if A. voluntarily transfers real property to B., in consideration of an oral promise by B. to hold such property in trust for A., and B. later repudiates his promise and seeks to hold the real property for his own benefit, the failure of the courts to compel B. to convey to A. will result in the unjust enrichment of B. at the expense of A.[3]

It is submitted that, in cases where unjust enrichment would result, equity might well create a constructive trust. This would not be enforcing the original oral express trust, but would be creating an implied trust for the sole purpose of preventing unjust enrichment. The original oral express trust might call for the collection of the rents and the delivery of them to the cestui que trust for a period of ten years. The constructive trust would be a mere passive trust, on the basis of which equity would decree a conveyance of the property to the beneficiary. It would require a grantee who saw fit to set up the voidability of his oral promise to hold in trust, to return the consideration which he received for making such promise. It would require him to restore the grantor to his former position, if the grantee decided not to go forward with performance of his voidable promise.

The holding suggested in cases of unjust enrichment would be in accord with the stand taken by the courts with respect to other agreements, voidable because not complying with the Statute of Frauds. Money paid and the reasonable value of services rendered, under a contract avoided because of the Statute of Frauds, may be recovered in quasi contract.[4]

Actual Fraud at the Time of the Promise

If the promisor, who has agreed to hold the real property in trust for the promisee or another, has a fraudulent intent at the time he makes the promise, then equity will declare the promisor a constructive trustee, notwithstanding that the promise was oral and the Statute of Frauds requires trusts in land to be manifested or proved by a writing.[5] He has misrepresented the

---

[3] For an interesting case in which a court felt bound to follow the old, majority rule, but clearly expressed its desire to give relief to the promisee, see Horsley v. Hrenchir, 146 Kan. 767, 73 P.2d 1010.

[4] Cook v. Doggett, 2 Allen, Mass.,

439; Herrick v. Newell, 49 Minn. 198, 51 N.W. 819; Erben v. Lorillard, 19 N.Y. 299; Ellis v. Cary, 74 Wis. 176, 42 N.W. 252, 4 L.R.A. 55, 17 Am.St. Rep. 125.

[5] Von Trotha v. Bamberger, 15 Colo. 1, 24 P. 883; Brown v. Doane,

state of his own mind. He impliedly stated that his mind was innocent and contained an intent to perform the oral trust. In fact his mind was guilty and contained an intent to violate the oral trust. A misrepresentation of any fact at the time of the transfer ought to entitle the grantor to a constructive trust.[6] The trust should be for the grantor even though the oral trust was in favor of another.

Active solicitation of the conveyance by the grantee under the oral trust may be considered evidence of an intent to defraud the grantor and break the oral promise.[7]

Confidential Relations Between Promisor and Promisee

A further exception to the strict rule regarding oral promises to hold in trust is found in the case of confidential relations existing between promisor and promisee. Many courts have been eager to avoid the hardship which the Statute of Frauds imposed upon promisees under oral agreements. Equity is well known to be the protector of confidential relations. It has been able to hold, therefore, that while the mere breach of the voidable promise might not be a wrong sufficient to warrant judicial relief, the violation of the confidential relation would be.[8] Whatever is obtained for himself by a confidant by the abuse of his confidential relation ought to be decreed by equity to be held for the one imposing confidence.

What is a confidential relationship is not well defined. The courts retain freedom to use the idea when they desire, and

---

86 Ga. 32, 12 S.E. 179, 11 L.R.A. 381; Lantry v. Lantry, 51 Ill. 458, 2 Am. Rep. 310; Gregory v. Bowlsby, 126 Iowa 588, 102 N.W. 517; Pollard v. McKenney, 69 Neb. 742, 96 N.W. 679, 101 N.W. 9; Wilcox v. Wilcox, 138 Neb. 510, 293 N.W. 378; Grote v. Grote, 121 App.Div. 841, 106 N.Y.S. 986; Parrish v. Parrish, 33 Or. 486, 54 P. 352; Meek v. Meek, 79 Or. 579, 156 P. 250.

[6] See § 57, ante.

[7] Fischbeck v. Gross, 112 Ill. 208; Lipp v. Lipp, 158 Md. 207, 148 A. 531.

[8] Bradley Co. v. Bradley, 165 Cal. 237, 131 P. 750; Hillyer v. Hynes, 33 Cal.App. 506, 165 P. 718; Milloglav v. Zacharias, 33 Cal.App. 561, 165 P. 977; Appeal of Fisk, 81 Conn. 433, 71 A. 559; Stahl v. Stahl, 214 Ill. 131, 73 N.E. 319, 68 L.R.A. 617, 105 Am.St.Rep. 101, 2 Ann.Cas. 774; Steinmetz v. Kern, 375 Ill. 616, 32 N.E.2d 151; Newis v. Topfer, 121 Iowa 433, 96 N.W. 905; Erdman v. Kenney, 159 Ky. 509, 167 S.W. 685; Apgar v. Connell, 79 Misc. 531, 140 N.Y.S. 705; Jeremiah v. Pitcher, 163 N.Y. 574, 57 N.E. 1113, affirming 26 App.Div. 402, 49 N.Y.S. 788; Goldsmith v. Goldsmith, 145 N.Y. 313, 39 N.E. 1067; Hanson v. Svarverud, 18 N.D. 550, 120 N.W. 550; Hatcher v. Hatcher, 264 Pa. 105, 107 A. 660; Metzger v. Metzger, 338 Pa. 564, 14 A.2d 285, 129 A.L.R. 683.

refuse to bind themselves by strict definitions. Thus, they have available a way out of the unpleasant application of the majority common law rule.

For example, where a son received real property from his mother under an oral promise to hold the same for the benefit of the mother and the promisor's brothers and sisters, a repudiation of the promise was held to give rise to a constructive trust.[9] The fact of near relationship and the natural trust placed by mother in son enabled the court to find a confidential relation. Although no actual fraud in the making of the promise was shown, and although the breach of the oral promise to hold in trust was not wrong, the court found a basis for a constructive trust in the violation of the confidential relationship.

This theory seems a beneficent subterfuge, since there must always be a relation of trust and confidence between promisor and promisee in these cases; otherwise, the land would scarcely be conveyed to the promisor upon his oral promise. The promisee must always trust the promisor. The fact that he conveys the land to the promisor, or has the land conveyed to the promisor, shows confidence reposed. Carried to its logical conclusion, the doctrine of confidential relationship would bring relief to the promisee in all cases.

GIFT BY WILL OR INTESTACY ON ORAL TRUST [10]

66. Where property is obtained by apparent absolute gift by will or intestacy by means of a promise to the testator or intestate that the transferee will use the property for the benefit of others, and the transferee refuses so to use it, he may be made a constructive trustee for the intended beneficiaries.

If the gift appears on the face of the will to be in trust, but no terms of the trust appear there, and the donee verbally agrees to hold for named donees, he will not be allowed to hold for them, but will be a resulting trustee for the testator's successors.

The Wills Acts, with some exceptions, prevent an oral testamentary disposition of property. An oral promise to hold or transfer property after the death of its owner and a written direction as to the disposition of property after the owner's death, not executed with testamentary formality, cannot, therefore, be enforced as testamentary provisions.

[9] Goldsmith v. Goldsmith, 145 N.Y. 313, 39 N.E. 1067.

[10] Restatement, Restitution, § 186.

If the promisor, who has secured property by the laws of intestacy or by will, had a fraudulent intent at the time he made the promise upon the basis of which he secured the property, and declines to hold for the agreed purpose, he will be charged with a constructive trust for the intended beneficiaries.

If the recipient of property by will or intestacy learns of the donor's desire that he use the property for another only after the donor's death, no constructive trust will attach as a result of a refusal to carry out the donor's wishes.

If the recipient by will or intestacy promises orally to hold the property for others, but the names of such others are not communicated until after the donor's death, the recipient will hold under an implied trust for the heirs, next of kin, or residuary devisees or legatees of the donor, and not for the intended beneficiaries.

A promise by one joint donee of property, by will or intestacy, will not ordinarily bind the other donees; but it may have that effect if made on behalf of all.

(a) The Wills Acts and the Statute of Frauds

It is well known that wills of real and personal property are, with some exceptions, required to be in writing. The Statute of Wills [11] first made possible wills of real property. Modern American statutes require testamentary dispositions of property, with some important exceptions, to be written.[12]

It is rudimentary law, also, that in a large majority of jurisdictions express trusts in land must be evidenced by or created in writing.[13]

On account of these statutory provisions affecting the disposition of property by will and the creation of trusts in land, it is obviously impossible that equity should declare that property left by a deceased person, either in a case of testacy or intestacy, should be burdened by any *express* oral obligation or affected by any *express* oral trust. Thus, if A. leaves a will by which real property is devised to B. absolutely, and A. tells B. orally that he desires him to hold the land in trust for C., and B. orally agrees so to hold it, the obligation of B. to hold the property for C. cannot be enforced directly without violating the Wills, Acts and the Statute of Frauds. To enforce such oral obligation would be to allow the making of an oral will or the creating of an oral trust in land.[14]

[11] St. 32 Henry VIII, c. 1.

[12] See, for example, N.Y., Decedent Estate Law, §§ 10–22.

[13] See ante, § 25.

[14] Reynolds v. Reynolds, 224 N.Y. 429, 121 N.E. 61.

It is an important question what attitude equity should assume toward B., in the illustration just given, if B. refuses to hold for C. after the will has taken effect and B. has become the legal owner of the property. Is B., in repudiating his promise, guilty of any wrong which will be recognized by equity, as the basis of a constructive trust? Or is the breach of an obligation attempted to be imposed in violation of the Statute of Frauds and the Wills Acts not legal wrong, though wrong morally?

The situation is the same on principle if the promise of the recipient of the property induces, not a gift by will, but intestacy, as a result of which the property comes to the promisor. Thus if A., the owner of real property, is induced by the promise of B., his sole heir, not to make a will, but to allow the real property to descend to B., upon B's oral promise to hold the land for X., the same question is presented. Is the refusal of B., the heir who has obtained the property, to perform the promise on the strength of which he obtained it, such unfair conduct as to give rise to a constructive trust? [15]

If a gift is made by will to B. in trust, without naming the beneficiaries in the will, but the testator had procured from B. an oral promise to hold for C. before the will was executed, B. will not be allowed to hold for C. against the objections of the heirs and next of kin of the testator. Since the property was not given absolutely to B., and since no trust for C. was provided in accordance with the formalities of the Wills Acts, the successors of the testator are entitled to claim that the property has not been legally willed away as far as the beneficial interest is concerned.[16]

(b) Actual Fraud at the Time of the Promise

It has already been shown that one who obtains property by actual fraud may be held as a constructive trustee of it.[17] It is therefore obvious that, if the person obtaining property by will or the laws of inheritance on account of an oral promise made to the testator or intestate to hold it for another had the actual

---

[15] For able discussions of the questions covered by this section, see Costigan, 28 Harv.Law Rev. 237, 366; Scott, 37 Harv.L.R. 653; McWilliams, 16 Cal.L.R. 19.

[16] Saylor v. Plaine, 31 Md. 158, 1 Am.Rep. 34; Olliffe v. Wells, 130 Mass. 221; Reynolds v. Reynolds, 224 N.Y. 429, 121 N.E. 61: *contra*, and to the effect that C. gets a constructive trust, are In re Fleetwood, 15 Ch. 594; Curdy v. Berton, 79 Cal. 420, 21 P. 858, 5 L.R.A. 189, 12 Am.St.Rep. 157; Cagney v. O'Brien, 83 Ill. 72.

[17] See ante, § 57.

intent at the time he made the promise not to perform it, he has been guilty of actual fraud, and equity will hold him as a constructive trustee of the property so obtained.[18] By impliedly representing that he intended to carry out the trust he has misrepresented the state of his own mind. "It is conceded that in cases of actual intentional fraud equity will raise a trust, notwithstanding the Statute of Frauds, or the Statute of Wills." [19]

In a few cases the courts seem to have held that actual fraud at the time of the promise was an essential to any relief.[20] A fraudulent intent later conceived seems not to have been considered sufficient. This theory is, however, the view of a small minority of the courts which have considered the question. The prevailing view is that a mere violation of the oral promise is ground for a constructive trust, and that therefore actual fraud at the time of the promise is *a fortiori* a reason for a constructive trust.

(c) Directions of Testator or Ancestor Not Communicated During His Life

Under this heading two situations may be imagined:

First, the testator or ancestor may not communicate to the devisee or heir that he intends the devisee or heir to hold otherwise than for his own benefit. For example, A., a testator, may die leaving a will by which real property is given to B. absolutely, but by a separate instrument, not executed as a will, and not discovered until after A.'s death, it may appear that A. intended B. to hold the property for C., or pay money to C. In this case B. has made no promise in return for the gift. The directions to hold for C. are of no force, since they attempt to make a testamentary disposition of property without the formalities required. In this case it is generally held that B. may hold for his own benefit, and that there is no constructive trust either for C. or for A.'s heirs or residuary devisees.[21] The Wills Act makes

---

[18] Hoge v. Hoge, 1 Watts, Pa., 163, 26 Am.Dec. 52.

[19] Winder v. Scholey, 83 Ohio St. 204, 216, 93 N.E. 1098, 33 L.R.A.,N.S., 995, 21 Ann.Cas. 1379.

[20] Moran v. Moran, 104 Iowa 216, 73 N.W. 617, 39 L.R.A. 204, 65 Am.St. Rep. 443; Evans v. Moore, 247 Ill. 60, 93 N.E. 118, 39 Am.St.Rep. 302 (discussed by Prof. Costigan in 6 Ill.Law Rev. 67; see, however, People v. Schaefer, 266 Ill. 334, 107 N.E. 617, discussed by Prof. Costigan in 10 Ill. Law Rev. 139); Sprinkle v. Hayworth, 26 Gratt., Va., 384; Tennant v. Tennant, 43 W.Va. 547, 27 S.E. 334.

[21] Juniper v. Batchelor, 1868, Wkly. Notes 197; Bryan v. Bigelow, 77 Conn. 604, 60 A. 266, 107 Am.St.Rep. 64; Nash v. Bremner, 84 N.J.Eq. 131,

the informal testamentary document inadmissible as evidence. Hence it cannot be proven, against the devisee's objection, that the testator intended the devisee to hold for another. That proof being lacking, there is no injustice on which to found a constructive trust.

Secondly, it may be supposed that the devisee or heir orally promises to hold for a purpose later to be communicated to him by the testator or ancestor, but that such purpose is not communicated during the life of the testator or ancestor. Thus, A. may devise real property to B., without naming the beneficiaries in the will, and B. may orally promise to hold the property in trust for persons later to be named. If no persons are named as beneficiaries during A.'s life, and the names of such beneficiaries appear only by a writing, not executed with testamentary formality, discovered after A.'s death, B. will be held as a trustee for A.'s heirs or residuary devisees.[22] It would obviously be an unjust enrichment to allow B. to hold for his own benefit. He cannot be compelled to hold for the purposes mentioned in the informal writing, for that would violate the Wills Act. Therefore the only just thing is to compel him to hold for the representatives of A., his heirs or residuary devisees.

(d) Directions of Testator or Ancestor Communicated During His Life

If the testator or ancestor tells the devisee or heir during the former's life that he desires the devisee or heir to hold for a third person, and the devisee or heir orally promises so to hold the property, and the gift is made to the heir or devisee in reliance on such promise, and the recipient of the property later repudiates the promise and attempts to hold for himself, equity will declare such recipient a constructive trustee of the property for the benefit of the beneficiary named in the promise.

"Trusts, in cases of this character, are impressed on the ground of fraud, actual or constructive, and the basis or ground upon which fraud is imputed is that of holding the estate of testator against conscience. It is not based necessarily on any imputation of fraud, or intention to defraud, at the time of making the promise, but of afterwards holding, or attempting to hold, the estate, as if the promise, on which the estate was received in its original condition, had not been made. The fraud consists in holding, or attempting to hold, the estate free from the effect or

92 A. 938; Schultz's Appeal, 80 Pa. 396.

[22] In re Boyes, L.R. 26 Ch.D. 531. See cases cited under ante, § 53.

obligation of a promise, subject to which it was intended to be devised and received, and which it is obligatory in conscience to carry out. Where the estate or interest therein is thus received by the person who made the promise, the attempt to hold the estate without performing the promise is an actual fraud, for the reason that the recipient, having actually made the promise, knows personally of the obligation, and is guilty of actual fraud in holding, or attempting to hold, the estate without performing the promise, so far as his interest in the estate extends. As to such promisor, it is clearly not a question of modifying or cutting down plain and ambiguous (sic) devises in a will by parol evidence or unattested papers, in violation of the statute of frauds or of wills, for the devise to the promisor is not modified, but he is dealt with as a holder by fraud of property under the will, and a trust ex maleficio is raised from these facts." [23] The court here uses "fraud" as meaning generally reprehensible conduct and not as indicating misrepresentation of fact.

The breach of the promise of the heir, next of kin, devisee, or legatee is regarded by equity as "fraud." In order to prevent the unjust enrichment of the promisor and to obviate "fraud," equity constructs a trust and compels the recipient of the property to hold it for the intended beneficiary.[24] The courts ignore the fact that relief is in effect giving validity to an informal

---

[23] Powell v. Yearance, 73 N.J.Eq. 117, 67 A. 892, 896.

[24] Shields v. McAuley, C.C.Pa., 37 F. 302; Curdy v. Berton, 79 Cal. 420, 21 P. 858, 5 L.R.A. 189, 12 Am.St.Rep. 157; De Laurencel v. De Boom, 48 Cal. 581; People v. Schaefer, 266 Ill. 334, 107 N.E. 617 (discussed by Prof. Costigan in 10 Ill.Law Rev. 139); Rice Stix Dry Goods Co. v. W. S. Albrecht & Co., 273 Ill. 447, 113 N.E. 66; Ransdel v. Moore, 153 Ind. 393, 53 N.E. 767, 53 L.R.A. 753; Orth v. Orth, 145 Ind. 184, 42 N.E. 277, 44 N.E. 17, 32 L.R.A. 298, 57 Am.St.Rep. 185; Meador v. Manlove, 97 Kan. 706, 156 P. 731; Taylor v. Fox's Ex'rs, 162 Ky. 804, 173 S.W. 154; Baylies v. Payson, 5 Allen, Mass., 473; Hooker v. Axford, 33 Mich. 453; Barrett v. Thielen, 140 Minn. 266, 167 N.W. 1030; Benbrook v. Yancy, 96 Miss. 536, 51 So. 461; Crinkley v. Rogers, 100 Neb. 647, 160 N.W. 974; Smullin v. Wharton, 73 Neb. 667, 103 N.W. 288, 106 N.W. 577, 112 N.W. 622, 113 N.W. 267; Williams v. Vreeland, 29 N.J.Eq. 417; Casey v. Casey, 161 App.Div. 427, 146 N.Y.S. 348; Jimmerson v. Ferguson, 57 Misc. 504, 109 N.Y.S. 845; Miller v. Hill, 64 Misc. 199, 118 N.Y.S. 63; Arntson v. First Nat. Bank, 39 N.D. 408, 167 N.W. 760, L.R.A.1918F, 1038; Winder v. Scholey, 83 Ohio St. 204, 93 N.E. 1098, 33 L.R.A.,N.S., 995, 21 Ann.Cas. 1379; Church v. Ruland, 64 Pa. 432; Jones v. McKee, 3 Pa. 496, 45 Am.Dec. 661; Appeal of Socher, 104 Pa. 609; Towles v. Burton, Rich.Eq.Cas., S.C., 146, 24 Am.Dec. 409; McLellan v. McLean, 39 Tenn. 684, 2 Head. 684; Bennett v. Harper, 36 W.Va. 546, 15 S.E. 143. *Contra:* Chapman v. Whitsett, C.C.A.Mo., 236 F. 873, 150 C.C.A. 135; Brown v. Kausche, 98 Wash. 470, 167 P. 1075.

will, and that if they merely wish to prevent unjust enrichment they should decree a constructive trust for the successors of the promisee. But for some reason the Wills Acts are not treated with as much respect by the courts as is the Statute of Frauds.

Of course it is essential that the testator or ancestor should have relied on the promise of the donee in transferring, or allowing the laws of intestacy to transfer, the property to the donee. If a testator, for example, would have transferred the property to the donee, regardless of the promise, and the making of the promise had no influence in causing him to make the gift, then the failure to perform the promise will not give rise to a constructive trust.[25]

The promise to hold for another need not be expressly made. It may appear by silent acquiescence.[26] "While a promise is essential, it need not be expressly made, for active co-operation or silent acquiescence may have the same effect as an express promise. If the legatee knows what the testator expects of him, and, having an opportunity to speak, says nothing, it may be equivalent to a promise, provided the testator acts upon it. Whenever it appears that the testator was prevented from action by the action or silence of the legatee, who knew the facts in time to act or speak, he will not be permitted to apply the legacy to his own use when that would defeat the expectations of the testator." [27]

Where the purpose communicated to the donee during the life-time of the donor is an illegal purpose, and therefore one which cannot be enforced by the courts, the donee will not be held under a constructive trust for the intended beneficiaries of the illegal trust, but will be held under a resulting trust for the next of kin or heirs of the donor. Thus, where the purpose of the donor was a charitable purpose, and the gift was made in a state where charitable gifts were invalid, the donee under an

---

[25] Whitehouse v. Bolster, 95 Me. 458, 50 A. 240; Mead v. Robertson, 131 Mo.App. 185, 110 S.W. 1095; Tyler v. Stitt, 132 Wis. 656, 112 N.W. 1091, 12 L.R.A.,N.S., 1087, 122 Am.St. Rep. 1012. And, of course, a mere statement by the legatee to the claimant that he would share the legacy, not referring to any promise to the testator, has no effect to create a constructive trust. Hollis v. Hollis, 254 Pa. 90, 98 A. 789.

[26] Russell v. Jackson, 10 Hare 198; Barron v. Stuart, 136 Ark. 481, 207 S.W. 22; Mead v. Robertson, 131 Mo. App. 185, 110 S.W. 1095; In re O'Hara's Will, 95 N.Y. 403, 47 Am. Rep. 53; Edson v. Bartow, 154 N.Y. 199, 48 N.E. 541; Stirk's Estate, 232 Pa. 98, 81 A. 187.

[27] Trustees of Amherst College v. Ritch, 151 N.Y. 282, 324, 45 N.E. 876, 37 L.R.A. 305.

oral promise to hold for charitable uses will be compelled by equity to hold for the benefit of the next of kin or heirs of the donor, depending upon whether the property was real or personal.[28]

Trusts under this heading may be divided into three classes: First, there are those cases in which a testator has been induced to make a devise or legacy upon a promise by devisee or legatee to hold the property for another.[29] Secondly, the testator may be induced by the promise to abstain from revoking a gift by will.[30] And in the third place the promise may have been made for the purpose of securing intestacy; the promisor agreeing that, if the owner will allow the property to pass to him by the laws of inheritance, he will apply the property to the benefit of another.[31] By the great weight of authority in each of these three instances the breach of the promise of the person receiving the property will cause equity to create a constructive trust in favor of the intended beneficiary of the property.

[28] In re O'Hara's Will, 95 N.Y. 403, 47 Am.Rep. 53. See, also, cases cited under ante, § 53.

[29] In re Fleetwood, L.R. 15 Ch.Div. 594; Buckingham v. Clark, 61 Conn. 204, 23 A. 1085; Chapman's Ex'r v. Chapman, 152 Ky. 344, 153 S.W. 434; Gilpatrick v. Glidden, 81 Me. 137, 16 A. 464, 2 L.R.A. 662, 10 Am.St.Rep. 245; Owings' Case, 1 Bland, Md., 370, 17 Am.Dec. 311; Ham v. Twombly, 181 Mass. 170, 63 N.E. 336; Hooker v. Axford, 33 Mich. 453; Benbrook v. Yancy, 96 Miss. 536, 51 So. 461; Smullin v. Wharton, 73 Neb. 667, 103 N.W. 288, 106 N.W. 577, 112 N.W. 622, 113 N.W. 267; Williams v. Vreeland, 29 N.J.Eq. 417; Edson v. Bartow, 154 N.Y. 199, 48 N.E. 541; Winder v. Scholey, 83 Ohio St. 204, 93 N.E. 1098, 33 L.R.A.,N.S., 995, 21 Ann.Cas. 1379; Jones v. McKee, 3 Pa. 496, 45 Am.Dec. 661; Rutledge's Adm'r v. Smith's Ex'rs, 1 McCord Eq., S.C., 119; McLellan v. McLean, 2 (Head, Tenn., 684; Bennett v. Harper, 36 W.Va. 546, 15 S.E. 143.

[30] Norris v. Frazer, L.R. 15 Eq. Cases 318; De Laurencel v. De Boom, 48 Cal. 581; Dowd v. Tucker, 41 Conn. 197; Gaither v. Gaither, 3 Md.Ch. 158; Ragsdale v. Ragsdale, 68 Miss. 92, 8 So. 315, 11 L.R.A. 316, 24 Am.St.Rep. 256; Belknap v. Tillotson, 82 N.J.Eq. 271, 88 A. 841; Heinisch v. Pennington, 73 N.J.Eq. 456, 68 A. 233; Rutherfurd v. Carpenter, 134 App.Div. 881, 119 N.Y.S. 790; Richardson v. Adams, 10 Yerg., Tenn., 273; Brook v. Chappell, 34 Wis. 405.

[31] McDowell v. McDowell, 141 Iowa 286, 119 N.W. 702, 31 L.R.A.,N.S., 176, 133 Am.St.Rep. 170; Gemmel v. Fletcher, 76 Kan. 577, 92 P. 713, 93 P. 339; Browne v. Browne, 1 Har. & J., Md., 430; Grant v. Bradstreet, 87 Me. 583, 33 A. 165; Tyler v. Stitt, 132 Wis. 656, 112 N.W. 1091, 12 L.R.A., N.S., 1087, 122 Am.St.Rep. 1012. In the case of Cassels v. Finn, 122 Ga. 33, 49 S.E. 749, 68 L.R.A. 80, 106 Am.St. Rep. 91, 2 Ann.Cas. 554, it was held that in this situation no constructive trust would be enforced against the promisor.

BOGERT TRUSTS 2D

(e) Direction of Testator or Ancestor Communicated to One or More of Several Donees, but Not to All

A difficult question arises where the property passes by will or inheritance to several persons, and one or more, but not all, of these donees have agreed to hold the property for others. Shall the promise of part of the donees bind all, or only the actual promisors?

The English courts have held that one tenant in common will not be bound by a promise made by a cotenant, while a joint tenant will be bound by a promise made by another for the purpose of inducing the gift, but not by a promise which merely prevented the revocation of the gift.[32]

In America, in some cases where the cotenant made a promise for himself, which did not purport to bind all the donees, it has been held that only the actual promisor was bound.[33] But in other cases, where the cotenant purported to make a promise for all, so that the entire title could be said to be tainted with fraud, it has been held that all the cotenants must hold under a constructive trust.[34]

---

[32] See In re Stead [1900] 1 Ch. 237, and authorities there collected.

[33] Powell v. Yearance, 73 N.J.Eq. 117, 67 A. 892; Heinisch v. Pennington, 73 N.J.Eq. 456, 68 A. 233; Fairchild v. Edson, 154 N.Y. 199, 48 N.E. 541, 61 Am.St.Rep. 609.

[34] Hooker v. Axford, 33 Mich. 453; Amherst College, Trustees of, v. Ritch, 151 N.Y. 282, 45 N.E. 876, 37 L.R.A. 305; Winder v. Scholey, 83 Ohio St. 204, 93 N.E. 1098, 33 L.R.A.,N.S., 995, 21 Ann.Cas. 1379.

CHAPTER 7

THE TRUST PURPOSE—PRIVATE TRUSTS

Sec.
67. Trusts Classified as to Purpose.
68. Passive Trusts.
69. Active Trusts—Validity of Purpose.
70. Active Trusts—Statutory Restrictions.
71. Rule against Remoteness of Vesting.
72. Rule against Suspension of Power of Alienation.
73. Rule against Accumulations.
74. Duration of Trusts.

TRUSTS CLASSIFIED AS TO PURPOSE [1]

67. Trusts are classified as to purpose as—
  (a) Private or charitable; and
  (b) Active or passive.

  A private trust is a trust for the financial benefit of described and identifiable persons.

  A charitable or public trust is a trust for the benefit of society or some part thereof, in which the funds are to be spent in ways and for persons selected by the trustee.

  An active trust is a trust in which the trustee has affirmative duties of management and administration to perform.

  A passive trust is one in which the trustee is a mere receptacle of the legal title and has no duties of administration.

With respect to the purposes for which trusts may be created there are two large classes. A trust may be private in its purpose; that is, have as its objects or beneficiaries certain identified or identifiable persons. A trust created by a father for the benefit of his son is of this variety. Or a trust may have as its purpose the assistance or benefit of the public or a large class thereof. This second sort of trust is called a public or charitable trust. If A. bequeathed money to X., as trustee, to invest and apply the income in aid of worthy retired clergymen, the trust is public or charitable. The public is to be benefited by the encouragement of religion and the relief of want through the distribution of aid to indefinite and unascertained persons, to be selected by the trustees from the entire class of clergymen.

[1] Restatement, Trusts, §§ 1-4, 67-73, 112, 348.

"The requisites of a valid private trust and one for a charitable use are materially different. In the former, there must not only be a certain trustee who holds the legal title, but a certain specified cestui que trust, clearly identified or made capable of identification by the terms of the instrument creating the trust, while it is an essential feature of the latter that the beneficiaries are uncertain—a class of persons described in some general language, often fluctuating, changing in their individual members, and partaking of a quasi public character. Indeed, it is said a public charity begins where uncertainty in the recipient begins."[2]

The purposes for which private trusts are and may be created will first be considered. In a separate chapter the purposes properly called charitable and the characteristics of such trusts will be set forth.

All trusts are also distinguished with respect to the active or passive nature of their purpose. "Where the trustee is not merely the recipient of the title for the use of the beneficiary, where he has a duty to perform in relation to the property which calls for the exercise of judgment or discretion, it is an active trust, and is not affected by the Statute of Uses."[3]

A passive trust is purely formal. "The prime requisite of a passive trust is that the trustee is made in form a mere holder of the legal title, the right to the possession and the profits being in another. If there are any active duties for the trustee to perform with respect to administering the property, and the primary use be expressly or impliedly, by reason of such active duty, vested in the trustee, the trust is necessarily active and not affected by the statute which would otherwise execute the use and thus vest the legal title in the equitable owner."[4]

Since passive trusts are comparatively unimportant and have no permanent existence, they will be considered first. Later active trusts, which constitute by far the larger and more important part of private trusts, will be discussed.

---

[2] Pennover v. Wadhams, 20 Or. 274, 278, 25 P. 720, 11 L.R.A. 210.

[3] Webb v. Hayden, 166 Mo. 39, 48, 65 S.W. 760.

[4] Holmes v. Walter, 118 Wis. 409, 416, 417, 95 N.W. 380, 62 L.R.A. 986. And see Randolph v. Read, 129 Ark. 485, 196 S.W. 133.

PASSIVE TRUSTS [5]

68. The English Statute of Uses attempted to abolish uses, which were practically equivalent to passive trusts, by providing that, wherever uses of freeholds were created, the statute would execute the use and transfer from the feoffee to uses to the cestui que use the legal estate.

In many American states the Statute of Uses is considered a part of the common law. In other states statutes abolishing passive trusts and transferring the legal title to the cestui que trust have been adopted. On one ground or another it is held that the creation of a passive trust of real or personal property results in the conveyance of the legal title directly to the beneficiary. The trustee takes nothing.

Passive trusts are also sometimes called simple,[6] dry,[7] naked,[8] formal,[9] or executed[10] trusts.

A passive trust has already been defined as one in which the trustee is the bare receptacle of the legal title and has no affirmative duties to perform. Thus, where a testatrix bequeathed $500 to A., to be kept in trust for A. by her daughter, the bequest amounts to a passive trust, and A. will be entitled to the payment of the legacy free from any trust.[11] And where land is patented to one in trust, without setting out the nature of the trust,[12] or where the purpose of the original trust is accomplished,[13] or where the trust is an implied trust, that is

---

[5] Restatement of Trusts, §§ 67–73.

[6] Atkins v. Atkins, 70 Vt. 565, 41 A. 503.

[7] Commonwealth v. Louisville Public Library, 151 Ky. 420, 152 S.W. 262.

[8] Wilkinson v. May, 69 Ala. 33.

[9] Dyett v. Central Trust Co., 64 Hun 635, 19 N.Y.S. 19.

[10] Woodward v. Stubbs, 102 Ga. 187, 29 S.E. 119; Park's Ann.Civ.Code Ga.1933, § 108-111; Kronson v. Lipschitz, 68 N.J.Eq. 367, 60 A. 819; Ranzau v. Davis, 85 Or. 26, 165 P. 1180; Kay v. Scates, 37 Pa. 31, 78 Am.Dec. 399; Porter v. Doby, 2 Rich. Eq., S.C., 49. Unfortunately "executed trust" is also used by some courts to mean a trust completely created. Lynn v. Lynn, 135 Ill. 18, 25 N.E. 634; Gaylord v. City of Lafayette, 115 Ind. 423, 17 N.E. 899; Miles v. Miles, 78 Kan. 382, 96 P. 481; Watson v. Payne, 143 Mo.App. 721, 128 S.W. 238; Morris v. Linton, 74 Neb. 411, 104 N. W. 927; Skeen v. Marriott, 22 Utah 73, 61 P. 296. The confusion of terminology is increased by an occasional use of the phrase as meaning a trust fully outlined and planned by the settlor as distinguished from one where the details of administration are left to the trustee. Saunders v. Edwards, 55 N.C. 134, 2 Jones, Eq., 134.

[11] Guild v. Allen, 28 R.I. 430, 67 A. 855.

[12] Brown v. Harris, 7 Tex.Civ.App. 664, 27 S.W. 45.

[13] Rector v. Dalby, 98 Mo.App. 189, 71 S.W. 1078.

§ 68 PASSIVE TRUSTS 231

either constructive or resulting,[14] the trust will be treated as a passive trust by equity.

The reasons for the enactment and the effect of the Statute of Uses have been previously explained.[15] It provided, in substance, that whenever any person should be seised of real property to the use of another by reason of any conveyance, the person to whom the use was given should thereafter have the legal title and the feoffee to uses should take no interest.[16] The use of that day was practically equivalent to the modern passive trust. The feoffee to uses was a mere holder of the legal title. The Statute of Uses abolished uses and rendered impossible thereafter passive trusts of freehold estates.

The Statute of Uses is regarded as a part of the common law of a majority of the American states. "The Statute of Uses being in force in England when our ancestors came here, they brought it with them as an existing modification of the common law, and it has always been considered a part of our law."[17]

In several states statutes directly abolishing passive trusts, and declaring that attempts to create them shall result in passing the legal title directly to the beneficiary, have been adopted.[18]

---

[14] Shelton v. Harrison, 182 Mo.App. 404, 167 S.W. 634.

[15] See §§ 4, 5, ante.

[16] St. 27 Henry VIII, c. 10, 1535. See Digby's History of the Law of Real Property, 5th Ed., p. 347.

[17] Marshall v. Fisk, 6 Mass. 24, 31, 4 Am.Dec. 76. And see Alford v. Bennett, 279 Ill. 375, 117 N.E. 89; Newcomb v. Masters, 287 Ill. 26, 122 N.E. 85. In some states, although the Statute of Uses has never been in force, the result accomplished by that statute is achieved by direct action of a court of equity, decreeing that the legal title is in the beneficiary of the passive trust. Farmers' & Merchants' Ins. Co. v. Jensen, 56 Neb. 284, 76 N.W. 577, 44 L.R.A. 861; Hill v. Hill, 90 Neb. 43, 132 N.W. 738, 38 L.R.A., N.S., 198; Helfenstine's Lessee v. Garrard, 7 Ohio 276, pt. 1; Gorham v. Daniels, 23 Vt. 600.

[18] Ala.Code 1940, Tit. 47, § 144; Mich.Ann.St. § 26.55; Minn.St.1927, § 8083; N.J.S.A. 46:3–9; New York Real Property Law, § 93. The New York statute is typical and reads as follows: "Every disposition of real property, whether by deed or devise, shall be made directly to the person in whom the right to the possession and profits is intended to be vested, and not to another to the use of, or in trust for, such person; and if made to any person to the use of, or in trust for another, no estate or interest, legal or equitable, vests in the trustee. But neither this section nor the preceding sections of this article shall extend to the trusts arising, or resulting by implication of law, nor prevent or affect the creation of such express trusts as are authorized and defined in this chapter." See Kidd v. Cruse, 200 Ala. 293, 76 So. 59; Berry v. Wooddy, 16 Ala.App. 348, 77 So. 942; Cutler v. Winberry, Sup., 160 N.Y.S. 712.

On one ground or another, either because of the operation of the Statute of Uses, or because of a local statute having an effect similar to that of the Statute of Uses, or because of a rule of equity, an attempt to create a passive trust is generally held to result in the passage of the legal estate to the cestui que trust.[19]

The Statute of Uses by its express wording is confined to real property, and it has been construed to have no application to personal property.[20] But the rule of the statute has often been applied to personal property, on the theory that the reason of the rule was equally applicable.[21]

The Statute of Uses has no application to resulting and constructive trusts.[22] In a few states it is held not to apply to uses

---

[19] Speed v. St. Louis M. B. T. R. Co., C.C.A.Mo., 86 F. 235, 30 C.C.A. 1; Huntington v. Spear, 131 Ala. 414, 30 So. 787; Ringrose v. Gleadall, 17 Cal.App. 664, 121 P. 407; Teller v. Hill, 18 Colo.App. 509, 72 P. 811; Slater v. Rudderforth, 25 App.D.C. 497; Smith v. McWhorter, 123 Ga. 287, 51 S.E. 474, 107 Am.St.Rep. 85; Smith v. Smith, 254 Ill. 488, 98 N.E. 950; Allen v. Craft, 109 Ind. 476, 9 N.E. 919, 58 Am.Rep. 425; Commonwealth v. Louisville Public Library, 151 Ky. 420, 152 S.W. 262; Hamlin v. Mansfield, 88 Me. 131, 33 A. 788; Brown v. Reeder, 108 Md. 653, 71 A. 417; Simonds v. Simonds, 199 Mass. 552, 85 N.E. 860, 19 L.R.A.,N.S., 686; Everts v. Everts, 80 Mich. 222, 45 N. W. 88; Thompson v Conant, 52 Minn. 208, 53 N.W. 1145; Van Vacter v. McWillie, 31 Miss. 563; Jones v. Jones, 223 Mo. 424, 123 S.W. 29, 25 L.R.A., N.S., 424; Fellows v. Ripley, 69 N.H. 410, 45 A. 138; Melick v. Pidcock, 44 N.J.Eq. 525, 15 A. 3, 6 Am.St.Rep. 901; Jacoby v. Jacoby, 188 N.Y. 124, 80 N. E. 676; Hallyburton v. Slagle, 130 N. C. 482, 41 S.E. 877; Troy & North Carolina Gold Min. Co. v. Snow Lumber Co., 170 N.C. 273, 87 S.E. 40; Springs v. Hopkins, 171 N.C. 486, 88 S. E. 774; Lee v. Oates, 171 N.C. 717, 88 S.E. 889, Ann.Cas.1917A, 514; Smith v. Security Loan & Trust Co., 8 N.D. 451, 79 N.W. 981; Fogarty v. Hunter, 83 Or. 183, 162 P. 964; In re West's Estate, 214 Pa. 35, 63 A. 407; Darling v. Witherbee, 36 R.I. 459, 90 A. 751; Breeden v. Moore, 82 S.C. 534, 64 S.E. 604; Brown v. Hall, 32 S.D. 225, 142 N.W. 854; Turley v. Massengill, 7 Lea, Tenn., 353; Henderson v. Adams, 15 Utah 30, 48 P. 398; Sims v. Sims, 94 Va. 580, 27 S.E. 436, 64 Am.St.Rep. 772; Blake v. O'Neal, 63 W.Va. 483, 61 S.E. 410, 16 L.R.A.,N.S., 1147; Holmes v. Walter, 118 Wis. 409, 95 N.W. 380, 62 L.R.A. 986.

[20] Smith v. Smith, 254 Ill. 488, 98 N.E. 950; In re Hagerstown Trust Co., 119 Md. 224, 86 A. 982; Slevin v. Brown, 32 Mo. 176; Harley v. Platts, 6 Rich., S.C., 310. In these states apparently a decree of the court is needed to pass the title to the personal property from the trustee to the beneficiary.

[21] Bowman v. Long, 26 Ga. 142; Prince de Bearn v. Winans, 111 Md. 434, 74 A. 626; In re De Rycke's Will, 99 App.Div. 596, 91 N.Y.S. 159. And see Bellows v. Page, 88 N.H. 283, 188 A. 12; Security National Bank v. Sternberger, 207 N.C. 811, 178 S.E. 595, 97 A.L.R. 720; McDowell v. Rees, 22 Tenn.App. 336, 122 S.W.2d 839.

[22] Trask v. Green, 9 Mich. 358; Strimpfler v. Roberts, 18 Pa. 283, 57 Am.Dec. 606.

created by devise.²³ It has no application to trusts to preserve contingent remainders.²⁴ The authorities are in conflict as to whether it operates in the case of a passive trust for the benefit of a married woman, created for the purpose of preserving her separate estate.²⁵ Charitable trusts, being active, are not subject to the Statute of Uses;²⁶ but a grant to trustees for a charitable corporation, if passive, will be executed by the statute.²⁷

A trust to permit the beneficiary to enjoy the trust property directly, with right to possession vested in him, and taxes and other burdens to be borne by him, is generally regarded as passive.²⁸ Where the trustee's only duty is to execute and deliver a deed to beneficiaries, the trust is generally regarded as active, whether regarded from the point of view of the date for conveyance or prior to that time.²⁹

ACTIVE TRUSTS—VALIDITY OF PURPOSE [30]

69. Except in states which have statutory systems, private trusts in real and personal property may be created for any purpose which does not violate law or public policy.

Conveyances in trust made with intent to defraud are subject to the same rules as other transfers tainted with fraud, and may be set aside at the instance of the person defrauded.

---

[23] Bass v. Scott, 2 Leigh, Va., 356; Blake v. O'Neal, 63 W.Va. 483, 61 S.E. 410, 16 L.R.A.,N.S., 1147.

[24] Vanderheyden v. Crandall, 2 Denio, N.Y., 9; Kay v. Scates, 37 Pa. 31, 78 Am.Dec. 399.

[25] That the statute applies to trusts for married women, see Marvel v. Wilmington Trust Co., 10 Del.Ch. 163, 87 A. 1014; Wilder v. Ireland, 53 N.C. 85, 8 Jones Law 85; Milton v. Pace, 85 S.C. 373, 67 S.E. 458. That the statute has no application to such trusts, see Glasgow v. Missouri Car & Foundry Co., 229 Mo. 585, 129 S.W. 900; Temple v. Ferguson, 110 Tenn. 84, 72 S.W. 455, 100 Am.St.Rep. 791.

[26] Huger v. Protestant Episcopal Church, 137 Ga. 205, 73 S.E. 385; In re Stewart's Estate, 26 Wash. 32, 66 P. 148, 67 P. 723.

[27] Schenectady Dutch Church v. Veeder, 4 Wend., N.Y., 494; Voorhees v. Presbyterian Church of Village of Amsterdam, 8 Barb., N.Y., 135; Van Deuzen v. Trustees of Presbyterian Congregation, 4 Abb.Dec., N.Y., 465.

[28] Alford v. Bennett, 279 Ill. 375, 117 N.E. 89; Everts v. Everts, 80 Mich. 222, 45 N.W. 88; Verdin v. Slocum, 71 N.Y. 345; Hannig v. Mueller, 82 Wis. 235, 52 N.W. 98.

[29] Appeal of Clark, 70 Conn. 195, 39 A. 155; McFall v. Kirkpatrick, 236 Ill. 281, 86 N.E. 139; Martling v. Martling, 55 N.J.Eq. 771, 39 A. 203; but see, contra, Watkins v. Reynolds, 123 N.Y. 211, 25 N.E. 322; Westcott v. Edmunds, 68 Pa. 34.

[30] Restatement, Trusts, §§ 59–65, 166.

A voluntary transfer of property to be held in trust for the transferor is fraudulent and void as against the existing and subsequent creditors of the transferor.

If the purpose of a trust is wholly illegal, the trust will not be enforced by equity. If the trust is partially for a valid purpose and partially for an illegal purpose, that portion of the trust having a valid purpose will be enforced, if it is independent of the invalid portion, so that the two can be separated without frustrating entirely the testator's intention.

If a trust was created for an illegal purpose, and that purpose was not accomplished, most courts will not decree a return of the property to the settlor, unless he was less guilty than the trustee with regard to the transaction.

The validity of the purpose of a trust of real property is usually determined by the situs of the real property which is the subject of the trust. Personal property trusts are generally controlled as to validity of purpose when created by will by the law of the domicile of the testator; when created by instrument inter vivos, by the law of the place where the instrument is executed.

Active trusts have previously been described as trusts in which the trustee has affirmative duties of administration to perform. Examples of such trusts are trusts to collect rents and pay them over to the beneficiary for life,[31] trusts to sell property and pay the debts of the settlor with the proceeds thereof,[32] and trusts for the conduct of business, in which the trustees occupy a position analogous to that of directors and the cestuis que trust correspond to stockholders.[33]

An active, private trust may be created, except in a few jurisdictions which have established statutory systems of trusts, for

[31] McFall v. Kirkpatrick, 236 Ill. 281, 86 N.E. 139.

[32] McHardy v. McHardy's Ex'r, 7 Fla. 301.

[33] For an illustration of this use of the trust as a substitute for a corporation, see Cunningham v. Bright, 228 Mass. 385, 117 N.E. 909. For a statutory authorization of such trust, see 60 Okl.St.Ann. § 171, which reads in part as follows: "Express trusts may be created in real or personal property or both with power in the trustee, or a majority of the trustees, if there be more than one, to receive title to, hold, buy, sell, exchange, transfer and convey real and personal property for the use of such trust; to take, receive, invest or disburse the receipts, earnings, rents, profits or returns from the trust estate; to carry on and conduct any lawful business designated in the instrument of trust, and generally to do any lawful act in relation to such trust property which any individual owning the same absolutely might do." For a comparison of express trusts and corporations as business organizations, see Wilgus, 13 Mich.Law Rev. 71, 205.

any purpose which does not contravene some statute of the nation or state[34] or public policy.[35] It is obvious that a trust designed to encourage treason, or to aid in the commission of murder, would not be enforced by the courts. Nor would a trust in restraint of marriage. In the Southern states, prior to emancipation, trusts for the freeing of slaves were sometimes held invalid.[36] But, aside from such restrictions regarding crime, contravention of civil law, and public policy which surround all transactions, the purposes for which trusts of real and personal property may be created in England and the majority of American states are limited only by the imagination of the creators of such trusts.

The most common purpose of an express private trust is that of distribution of an estate among the members of the owner's family and his friends, with provisions for collection and payment of income to certain temporary beneficiaries, conservation of the capital of the trust, and its ultimate distribution among relatives or friends. This is sometimes called a "family trust".[37] It is usually established by the will of the property owner, but is sometimes created by deed during the property owner's life, the former being called a testamentary trust and the latter a "living trust".[38]

In connection with this and other trusts the settlor may have the purpose of protecting persons who are weak mentally or physically, inexperienced, immature, or of profligate or other bad habits. This he can do to a large extent by creating a "spendthrift trust," so-called, the limitations upon, and operations of which are discussed in other sections.[39]

Other common objectives of the settlor are: (1) The conservation of insurance policies and their collection at the death of the insured, with subsequent investment of the proceeds, collection of income and distribution of income and capital. These are the so-called "insurance trusts" which are given further

---

[34] A trust designed to carry out a void act of a Legislature has an invalid purpose. Disston v. Board of Trustees of Internal Improvement Fund, 75 Fla. 653, 79 So. 295.

[35] A trust having the object of suppressing a criminal prosecution is void. Bettinger v. Bridenbecker, 63 Barb., N.Y., 395.

[36] Lemmond v. Peoples, 41 N.C. 137, 6 Ired.Eq. 137.

[37] See Breckinridge, The Family Trust, 28 Ill.L.R. 1062.

[38] See Goff, Living Trusts, 18 Oh.L. R. 353.

[39] See ante, § 45.

treatment elsewhere;[40] (2) relieving the settlor from the burdens of the management of his property; (3) providing security for creditors by having a trustee hold property from which they are to be paid if the debtor does not pay from other sources; these trusts being sometimes called "trust mortgages" or "trust deeds", and being equivalent in effect to the common law mortgage;[41] (4) trusts to pay creditors, used sometimes by an embarrassed debtor who wishes to have an impartial third party liquidate his assets and distribute the proceeds among his creditors;[42] (5) investment trusts, where a mass of securities is held by a trustee for investors who have advanced the money with which to buy the securities and have proportionate interests in the group of securities;[43] (6) real estate trusts, where landowners place title to realty in a trustee to hold for sale or development;[44] (7) voting trusts, where stockholders in a corporation transfer their stock to trustees in order to have it voted under a unified plan of operation;[45] (8) liquidating or reorganization trusts where the property of an insolvent corporation is vested in trustees for management and conservation pending its sale for the benefit of bondholders and stockholders;[46] and trusts to minimize income, estate or inheritance taxes.[47]

Wherever a property owner desires to vest ownership and management of his property in an intermediary for any lawful purpose, the trust is available for the accomplishment of his purposes.

Important also is the so-called "business" or "Massachusetts" trust, where a business is vested in trustees to manage for the benefit of beneficiaries whose interests are represented by certificates of beneficial interest. Here the trust is used as a sub-

---

[40] See § 32, ante. Phillips, Life Insurance Trusts, a Recapitulation for the Draftsman, 81 U.Pa.L.R. 284, 408.

[41] See Davis, Corporate Trusts; Bogert, Trusts and Trustees, §§ 246–247.

[42] See Bogert, Trusts and Trustees, § 248.

[43] See Robinson, Investment Trust Organization and Management; Steiner, Investment Trusts; Bogert, Trusts and Trustees, § 249.

[44] See MacChesney, Practical Real Estate Law; Bingham & Andrews, Financing Real Estate; Bogert, Trusts and Trustees, § 250.

[45] Cushing, Voting Trusts; Bogert, Trusts and Trustees, § 251.

[46] See Bogert, Trusts and Trustees, § 253.

[47] See Robinson, Saving Taxes in Drafting Wills and Trusts, 2d Ed.,; Bogert, Trusts and Trustees, §§ 261–284.

stitute for a private corporation, and the trustees correspond to directors while the cestuis are similar to stockholders.[48]

The immediately following sections of this chapter show some of the rules of law which limit or restrict the settlor in trying to accomplish the various social or economic ends of private trusts.

Naturally the purpose for which the trust is founded must be certain. An indefinite trust instrument can no more be enforced than an indefinite contract.[49] But the trust instrument need not provide for every possible contingency.[50]

The trust purpose must, of course, be free from fraud. If the trust was created with the actual intent to defraud another, it may be set aside by the person injured.[51] The subject of fraud on creditors by means of trusts will be found treated fully in books devoted to the subject of fraudulent conveyances.[52] It is impossible here to enter into a discussion of the effect of fraud on conveyances in trust. Fraud affects such conveyances as it affects all others.

An early English statute [53] provided that voluntary transfers of personal property to the use of the transferor should be void as against creditors. Many states have adopted similar statutes,[54] and the principle that such trusts are void against creditors is generally in force in the United States.[55] The rule applies

---

[48] See Sears Trust Estates as Business Companies, 2d Ed.; Dunn, Business Trusts; Bogert, Trusts and Trustees, §§ 291–310.

[49] Angus v. Noble, 73 Conn. 56, 46 A. 278; Sheedy v. Roach, 124 Mass. 472, 26 Am.Rep. 680; Smullin v. Wharton, 73 Neb. 667, 103 N.W. 288, 106 N.W. 577, 112 N.W. 622, 113 N.W. 267; Gueutal v. Gueutal, 113 App.Div. 310, 98 N.Y.S. 1002; Weaver v. Spurr, 56 W.Va. 95, 48 S.E. 852.

[50] In re Hoffman's Will, 201 N.Y. 247, 94 N.E. 990.

[51] Brundage v. Cheneworth, 101 Iowa 256, 70 N.W. 211, 63 Am.St.Rep. 382; Halliday v. Croom, 9 Lea, Tenn., 349. The trustee may not attack the trust as fraudulent regarding creditors. Henderson v. Segars, 28 Ala. 352.

[52] Bump, Fraudulent Conveyances; Glenn, Creditors' Rights and Remedies, and The Law of Fraudulent Conveyances.

[53] St. 3 Henry VII, c. 4.

[54] A typical statute is that of New York: "A transfer of personal property, made in trust for the use of the person making it, is void as against the existing or subsequent creditors of such person." Personal Property Law, § 34.

[55] McDermott v. Eborn, 90 Ala. 258, 7 So. 751; Innis v. Carpenter, 4 Colo.App. 30, 34 P. 1011; Johnson v. Sage, 4 Idaho 758, 44 P. 641; Camp v. Thompson, 25 Minn. 175; First Nat. Bank of Joplin v. Woelz, 197 Mo.App. 686, 193 S.W. 614; Racek v. First Nat. Bank of North Bend, 62 Neb. 669, 87 N.W. 542; Ward v. Marie, 73 N.J.Eq. 510, 68 A. 1084; Vilas Nat.

to real as well as personal property.[56]

If the trust instrument have but one purpose and that purpose be invalid, because, for example, of a violation of the rule against perpetuities, it is obvious that the entire trust must fall to the ground. But in many instances trusts have several purposes. The same trust instrument may provide for payments to A. during his life, payments to his children after his death, and finally a payment of the principal to X. at a given time. If one of these several purposes is valid and the remainder invalid, will the entire trust fail? The answer depends upon whether the purposes are separable or are inextricably connected. If the valid purpose is independent of the invalid, if the two can be separated, and the valid enforced without doing violence to the settlor's intent, then the valid purpose may be enforced, and the invalid stricken out.[57] But if, on the other hand, the valid purpose and the invalid purpose are so connected that to enforce one without enforcing the other would doubtless have been contrary to the settlor's intent, and would cause an injustice, then the entire trust must be declared void because of its partial invalidity.[58]

It not infrequently happens that a trust is created for a wrongful purpose but fails to accomplish the harm intended, and then the settlor seeks to get the help of equity to obtain a return of the trust property to him. For example, a settlor may convey property to a trustee for the purpose of hindering the settlor's creditors and preventing them from collecting just debts, but due to some unforeseen contingency the debts are paid and the trust actually did no harm to the creditors. Here equity usually applies its general rule that it will give no relief to a party tainted with evil conduct, but will rather leave the parties exactly as it

---

Bank of Plattsburgh v. Newton, 25 App.Div. 62, 48 N.Y.S. 1009; Nolan v. Nolan, 218 Pa. 135, 67 A. 52, 12 L.R.A.,N.S., 369; Hornsby v. City Nat. Bank, Tenn.Ch.App. 60 S.W. 160; Petty v. Moores Brook Sanitarium, 110 Va. 815, 67 S.E. 355, 27 L.R.A., N.S., 800, 19 Ann.Cas. 271; Stapleton v. Brannan, 102 Wis. 26, 78 N.W. 181.

[56] Sandlin v. Robbins, 62 Ala. 477, 485.

[57] Younger v. Moore, 155 Cal. 767, 103 P. 221; Andrews v. Rice, 53 Conn. 566, 5 A. 823; Sinnott v. Moore, 113 Ga. 908, 39 S.E. 415; Viney v. Abbott, 109 Mass. 300; Amory v. Trustees of Amherst College, 229 Mass. 374, 118 N.E. 933; Robb v. Washington and Jefferson College, 185 N.Y. 485, 78 N.E. 359; Culross v. Gibbons, 130 N.Y. 447, 29 N.E. 839; In re Denis' Estate, 201 Pa. 616, 51 A. 335; Appeal of Ingersoll, 86 Pa. 240.

[58] Carpenter v. Cook, 132 Cal. 621, 64 P. 997, 84 Am.St.Rep. 118; Hofsas v. Cummings, 141 Cal. 525, 75 P. 110; Rong v. Haller, 109 Minn. 191; 123 N.W. 471, 26 L.R.A.,N.S., 825; Kelly v. Nichols, 17 R.I. 306, 21 A. 906.

finds them. Thus, the trustee will be allowed to keep the property.[59] A few courts have decreed a return of the property to the settlor on the ground that the failure to accomplish the evil purpose frees the settlor from guilt,[60] but most courts deny relief, in order to discourage similar transactions in the future.[61] If the settlor was less guilty than the trustee, or as the courts say was not *in pari delictu,* as where the trustee suggested the illegal transaction and procured its making, the courts are apt to decree a return of the property to the settlor where the evil purpose was not achieved and perhaps never could be achieved.[62]

Conflict of Laws [63]

Real property is almost entirely controlled by the laws of the jurisdiction in which it lies. The validity of the purpose of trusts of real property is, in accordance with this principle, determined generally by the law of the situs.[64] If the trust be one of personal property, however, and be created by will, the law of the domicile of the testator controls ordinarily. Personal property is deemed to follow the person of the owner.[65] If the instrument is one taking effect inter vivos, ordinarily the law of the state of execution of the instrument will decide the question of validity of purpose.[66]

[59] Baird v. Howison, 154 Ala. 359, 45 So. 668; Brown v. Brown, 66 Conn. 493, 34 A. 490; Sewell v. Sewell, 109 Wash. 252, 186 P. 289.

[60] Hoff v. Hoff, 106 Kan. 542, 189 P. 613; Bird v. Bird, 232 Mich. 71, 205 N.W. 130.

[61] In re Great Berlin Steamboat Co., 26 Ch.D. 616; Tantum v. Miller, 11 N.J.Eq. 551; Pride v. Andrew, 51 Ohio St. 405, 38 N.E. 84.

[62] Coleman v. Coleman, 48 Ariz. 337, 61 P.2d 441; Carpenter v. Arnett, 265 Ky. 246, 96 S.W.2d 693.

[63] See Beale, 45 Harv.L.R. 969; Cavers, 44 Harv.L.R. 161; Swabenland, 45 Yale L.J. 438.

[64] Campbell-Kawannanakoa v. Campbell, 152 Cal. 201, 92 P. 184; Appeal of Fisk, 81 Conn. 433, 71 A. 559; Kerr v. White, 52 Ga. 362; Hobson v. Hale, 95 N.Y. 588; Penfield v. Tower, 1 N.D. 216, 46 N.W. 413.

[65] Farmers' & Mechanics' Sav. Bank v. Brewer, 27 Conn. 600; Cross v. United States Trust Co. of New York, 131 N.Y. 330, 30 N.E. 125, 15 L.R.A. 606, 27 Am.St.Rep. 597; Dammert v. Osborn, 140 N.Y. 30, 35 N.E. 407; Townsend v. Allen, 59 Hun 622, 13 N.Y.S. 73, affirmed 126 N.Y. 646, 27 N.E. 853; Merritt v. Corlies, 71 Hun 612, 24 N.Y.S. 561; Jones v. Jones, 8 Misc. 660, 30 N.Y.S. 177; Sullivan v. Babcock, 63 How.Prac., N.Y., 120; Wood v. Wood, 5 Paige, N.Y., 596, 28 Am.Dec. 451; English v. McIntyre, 29 App.Div. 439, 51 N.Y.S. 697; Lanius v. Fletcher, 100 Tex. 550, 101 S.W. 1076.

[66] Mercer v. Buchanan, C.C.Pa., 132 F. 501; Codman v. Krell, 152 Mass. 214, 25 N.E. 90; Wyse v. Dandridge, 35 Miss. 672, 72 Am.Dec. 149.

ACTIVE TRUSTS—STATUTORY RESTRICTIONS

70. **In Montana, New York, North Dakota, and South Dakota the purposes for which real property trusts may be created are limited by statute.**

    While an attempt to create a trust in these states for a purpose not named in the statute does not result in the creation of a trust, the instrument will be enforced as a power in trust, if otherwise lawful.

    In Georgia trust purposes are limited to the protection of minors, mentally incompetents, and persons of bad habits, and to the improvement of the trust property.

In four states, namely, Montana, New York, North Dakota, and South Dakota, the legislatures have established statutory systems of trusts in real property and have expressly limited the purposes for which such trusts may be created.[67] The theory of the founders of this system, for the statutory purposes named in the several states are very similar, was that all trusts, except those involving active administration and requiring the holding of the legal title, should be abolished, because they render un-

---

[67] N. Y. Real Property Law, § 96: "Purposes for Which Express Trusts may be Created.—An express trust may be created for one or more of the following purposes: 1. To sell real property for the benefit of creditors; 2. To sell, mortgage or lease real property for the benefit of annuitants or other legatees, or for the purpose of satisfying any charge thereon; 3. To receive the rents and profits of real property, and apply them to the use of any person, during the life of that person, or for any shorter term, subject to the provisions of law relating thereto; 4. To receive the rents and profits of real property, and to accumulate the same for the purposes, and within the limits, prescribed by law."

For constructions of this statute by the New York Court of Appeals, see Leggett v. Perkins, 2 N.Y. 297; Selden v. Vermilya, 3 N.Y. 525; Savage v. Burnham, 17 N.Y. 561; Beekman v. Bonsor, 23 N.Y. 298, 80 Am.Dec. 269; New York Dry Dock Co. v. Stillman, 30 N.Y. 174; Kiah v. Grenier, 56 N.Y. 220; Moore v. Hegeman, 72 N.Y. 376; Heermans v. Burt, 78 N.Y. 259; Cooke v. Platt, 98 N.Y. 35; Weeks v. Cornwell, 104 N.Y. 325, 10 N.E. 431; People v. Stockbrokers' Bldg. Co., 49 Hun 349, 2 N.Y.S. 113, affirmed 112 N.Y. 670, 20 N.E. 414; Cochrane v. Schell, 140 N.Y. 516, 35 N.E. 971; Cassagne v. Marvin, 143 N.Y. 292, 38 N.E. 285, 25 L.R.A. 670; Salisbury v. Slade, 160 N.Y. 278, 54 N.E. 741; Hubbard v. Housley, 43 App.Div. 129, 59 N.Y.S. 392, affirmed 160 N.Y. 688, 55 N.E. 1096; Thompson v. Hart, 58 App.Div. 439, 69 N.Y.S. 223, affirmed 169 N.Y. 571, 61 N.E. 1135; Russell v. Hilton, 80 App.Div. 178, 80 N.Y.S. 563, affirmed 175 N.Y. 525, 67 N.E. 1089; Murray v. Miller, 85 App.Div. 414, 83 N.Y.S. 591, affirmed 178 N.Y. 316, 70 N.E. 870; Robb v. Washington and Jefferson College, 185 N.Y. 485, 78 N.E. 359.

See, to the same effect, Mont.Rev. Codes 1935, § 6787; N.D.Comp.L.1913, § 5367; S.D.Code 1939, § 59.0301.

certain the record title to land and result in fraud and confusion. If the legal title is really necessary or highly convenient, said these reformers, we will allow a trust; but in cases where a trust is an unnecessary formality, and the work desired to be done could be done equally well by means of a power, we will abolish the trust.

The trusts allowed fall into four main classes, namely, those to sell property for the benefit of creditors; those to sell, mortgage, or lease for the benefit of annuitants or other legatees, or to pay off a charge; those to collect income and apply it to the use of beneficiaries; and those to collect income and accumulate it for persons entitled to receive accumulations. To accomplish these purposes the trust form is deemed necessary or very convenient. To accomplish other purposes sometimes reached by trusts, it is felt that powers in trust will be equally efficacious and convenient and more conducive to an orderly system of landholding.

The statutes of these same states ordinarily provide that, if an attempt is made to create a trust in land for an unauthorized purpose, the trustee shall take no estate as a trustee; but, if the trust directs the performance of an act which may lawfully be performed as a power in trust, the instrument shall be given effect as a power in trust.[68]

Thus, under this statutory system, if A. devised real property to B. for the purpose of having B. partition the property between C. and D., the will would fail to create a valid trust, because a trust to partition real estate is not provided for in this statutory scheme. But the direction of A. would be enforced as a power in trust. The real property would descend to A.'s heirs, as if he had died intestate, and B. would hold a power in trust over the property. The legal title would pass to A.'s heirs, but B. would have the power to partition the property between C. and D.

These statutes do not apply to personal property. Trusts of personal property may be created in these four states for any lawful purpose.[69]

---

[68] N. Y. Real Property Law, § 99; N.D.Comp.L. § 5370; S.D.Code 1939, § 59.0309.

For construction of these statutes, see Randall v. Constans, 33 Minn. 329, 23 N.W. 530; Hawley v. James, 5 Paige, N.Y., 318; Selden v. Vermilya, 3 N.Y. 525; Downing v. Marshall, 23 N.Y. 366, 80 Am.Dec. 290; New York Dry Dock Co. v. Stillman, 30 N.Y. 174; Townshend v. Frommer, 125 N.Y. 446, 26 N.E. 805; Cutler v. Winberry, Sup., 160 N.Y.S. 712; Murphey v. Cook, 11 S.D. 47, 75 N.W. 387.

[69] In re Schwartz, 145 App.Div. 285, 130 N.Y.S. 74; Hammerstein v. Equitable Trust Co. of New York, 156 App.Div. 644, 141 N.Y.S. 1065.

Bogert Trusts 2d—16

In California and Oklahoma these four types of real property trusts were the only ones originally permitted, but recent statutes remove such restrictions.[70] In Michigan, Minnesota and Wisconsin name the four purposes but also permit trusts of real or personal property for any other lawful purpose, thus negativing the notion of any restriction.[71]

In Georgia trusts of all kinds of property are limited to those for the benefit of minors, incompetents, and persons of bad habits, or for the purpose of improving the trust property. In the case of trusts for other purposes the legal title passes to the beneficiary and the trust is destroyed.[72]

RULE AGAINST REMOTENESS OF VESTING

71. The common-law rule against remoteness, which is the rule against perpetuities in a majority of American states, is that "no interest is good unless it must vest, if at all, not later than twenty-one years after some life in being at the creation of the interest."

This rule restricts the creator of a trust by requiring him to make all interests under or following his trust vest not later than twenty-one years after the end of some life in being at the time the trust instrument goes into effect.

Trusts, like all property interests, are subject in their creation to two restrictive rules, namely, the rule against remoteness, and the rule against suspension of the power of alienation. Each of these rules is sometimes referred to as "the rule against perpetuities," and sometimes this rule is construed to include both a prohibition of undue remoteness of vesting and a prohibition of undue suspension of the power of alienation. For the purpose of clearness these two entirely distinct rules will be treated in separate sections and the term "perpetuities" will be avoided as much as possible.

First, how does the rule against remoteness restrict the purposes for which trusts may be created. This rule has been stated in the following words by the most learned American commentator upon it: "No interest is good unless it must vest, if at all, not

---

[70] Cal.St.1929, p. 282; Erskine, 16 Cal.L.R. 1; 60 Okl.St.Ann. § 171; L. 1941, H.B. 174, 60 Okl.St.Ann. § 175.1 et seq.

[71] Mich.St.Ann. § 26.61; Minn.St. 1927, § 8090; Wis.St. 1941, §§ 231.01, 231.11, 231.12.

[72] Ga.Code 1933, § 108-114; McLain, 1 Georgia Lawyer 60; Sanders v. First Nat. Bank, 189 Ga. 450, 6 S.E. 2d 294.

BOGERT TRUSTS 2D

later than twenty-one years after some life in being at the creation of the interest." [73] A child en ventre sa mere is regarded as in being for the purposes of the rule.[74] This rule, it will be seen, has to do only with the date at which property interests must vest in interest. They must not remain contingent for too long a period, for longer than during the continuance of lives in being at the time the instrument takes effect and twenty-one years. "The rule governs both legal and equitable interests, and interests in both realty and personalty." [75] The rule does not apply to vesting in possession, that is, to the accrual of a right by a property owner to go into possession of the property.

This rule against remoteness is in force generally in the American states.[76]

[73] Gray, Perpetuities, 3d Ed., p. 175.

[74] Long v. Blackall, 7 Term R. 100.

[75] Gray, Perpetuities, 3d Ed., p. 175.

[76] Gen.Acts Ala.1931, No. 684; Clark v. Stanfield, 38 Ark. 347; Chilcott v. Hart, 23 Colo. 40, 45 P. 391, 35 L.R.A. 41.

Connecticut.—Since the enactment of chapter 249 of the Public Acts of 1895, which repealed a peculiar local rule, the common-law rule against remoteness has been in force. Bates v. Spooner, 75 Conn. 501, 54 A. 305; Loomer v. Loomer, 76 Conn. 522, 57 A. 167; Wolfe v. Hatheway, 81 Conn. 181, 70 A. 645; Bartlett v. Sears, 81 Conn. 34, 70 A. 33; Allen v. Almy, 87 Conn. 517, 89 A. 205, Ann.Cas.1917B, 112; Westport Paper-Board Co. v. Staples, 127 Conn. 115, 15 A.2d 1.

Delaware.—Wilmington Trust Co. v. Wilmington Trust Co., 15 A.2d 153.

District of Columbia.—In addition to the statutory statement of a rule against undue suspension of the power of alienation there seems to be recognition of the common-law rule against remoteness. Wills v. Maddox, 45 App.D.C. 128; Hopkins v. Grimshaw, 165 U.S. 342, 17 S.Ct. 401, 41 L. Ed. 739.

Florida.—The common-law rule seems to be in force. Cawthon v. Stearns Culver Lumber Co., 60 Fla. 313, 53 So. 738.

Georgia.—Code 1933, § 85-707, lays down the practical equivalent of the common-law rule against remoteness. It limits the period to lives in being, 21 years, and the period of gestation. Phinizy v. Wallace, 136 Ga. 520, 71 S.E. 896.

Hawaii.—Manufacturers Life Ins. Co. v. The von Hamm-Young Co. Ltd., 34 Haw. 288.

Illinois.—The common-law rule is in force. Hale v. Hale, 125 Ill. 399, 17 N.E. 470; Keyes v. Northern Trust Co., 227 Ill. 354, 81 N.E. 384; Armstrong v. Barber, 239 Ill. 389, 88 N.E. 246; French v. Calkins, 252 Ill. 243, 96 N.E. 877; Dime Savings & Trust Co. v. Watson, 254 Ill. 419, 98 N.E. 777; Barrett v. Barrett, 255 Ill. 332, 99 N.E. 625; Kolb v. Landes, 277 Ill. 440, 115 N.E. 539.

Indiana.—Reasoner v. Herman, 191 Ind. 642, 134 N.E. 276. And see Leach, 15 Ind.L.J. 261.

Iowa.—Woodard v. Woodard, 184 Iowa 1178, 169 N.W. 464.

Kansas.—The common-law rule is in force. Keeler v. Lauer, 73 Kan. 388, 85 P. 541; Henderson v. Bell, 103 Kan. 422, 173 P. 1124.

Kentucky.—Ky.St.1936, § 2360, reads as follows: "The absolute

The rule against remoteness of vesting may affect the settlor of a trust in three ways of interest here. First, if he provides that the trust is to begin, and the legal interest of the trustee to

power of alienation shall not be suspended, by any limitation or condition whatever, for a period longer than during the continuance of a life or lives in being at the creation of the estate, and twenty-one years and ten months thereafter." This appears to be a rule against suspension of the power of alienation and to have nothing to do with remoteness, but it seems to have been construed to be a rule against remoteness of vesting. Brown v. Columbia Finance & Trust Co., 123 Ky. 775, 97 S.W. 421, 30 Ky.Law Rep. 110; United States Fidelity & Guaranty Co. v. Douglas' Trustee, 134 Ky. 374, 120 S.W. 328, 20 Ann.Cas. 993; Miller v. Miller, 151 Ky. 563, 152 S.W. 542; Tyler v. Fidelity & Columbia Trust Co., 158 Ky. 280, 164 S.W. 939; Pond Creek Coal Co. v. Runyan, 161 Ky. 64, 170 S.W. 501; Curd's Trustee v. Curd, 163 Ky. 472, 173 S.W. 1148; Ligget v. Fidelity & Columbia Trust Co., 274 Ky. 387, 118 S.W.2d 720. In Tyler v. Fidelity & Columbia Trust Co., supra, the court says (158 Ky. at page 286, 164 S.W. 941): "The test, therefore, for determining the existence of a perpetuity, is not whether the event or contingency named upon which the estate devised may vest in the ultimate takers does happen or may happen, but whether it is possible that it might not happen within that time. If it is possible that the event or contingency upon which the estate will finally vest may not happen within the limit prescribed by the rule against perpetuities, the instrument is void, or at least so much thereof is void as relates to this remote event or contingency. In other words, a possible perpetuity is a perpetuity denounced by the statute." Pond Creek Coal Co. v. Runyan, supra, is, however, repudiated in Kentland Coal &

Coke Co. v. Keen, 168 Ky. 836, 183 S.W. 247, L.R.A.1916D, 924.

Maine.—The common-law rule applies. Slade v. Patten, 68 Me. 380; Towle v. Doe, 97 Me. 427, 54 A. 1072.

Maryland.—The common-law rule is in force. Lee v. O'Donnell, 95 Md. 538, 52 A. 979; Robinson v. Bonaparte, 102 Md. 63, 61 A. 212; Hollander v. Central Metal & Supply Co., 109 Md. 131, 71 A. 442, 23 L.R.A.,N.S., 1135; Starr v. Starr Methodist Protestant Church, 112 Md. 171, 76 A. 595; Gambrill v. Gambrill, 122 Md. 563, 89 A. 1094.

Massachusetts.—The common-law rule governs. Fosdick v. Fosdick, 88 Mass. 41, 6 Allen 41; Otis v. McLellan, 95 Mass. 339, 13 Allen 339; Loring v. Blake, 98 Mass. 253; Lovering v. Worthington, 106 Mass. 86.

Mississippi.—Section 2117 of the Code of 1930 reads as follows: "Estates in fee tail are prohibited; and every estate which, but for this statute, would be an estate in fee tail shall be an estate in fee simple; but any person may make a conveyance or a devise of lands to a succession of donees then living, and after the death of the last of said successors to any person or any heir." This seems to supersede the common law rule as far as real property is concerned. Hanie v. Grissom, 178 Miss. 108, 172 So. 500; Gully v. Neville, 55 So. 289; Gwin v. Hutton, 100 Miss. 320, 56 So. 446; Henry v. Henderson, 101 Miss. 751, 58 So. 354; Redmond v. Redmond, 104 Miss. 512, 61 So. 552. But the common-law rule is in force as to personal property. Thomas v. Thomas, 97 Miss. 697, 53 So. 630.

Michigan has the common law rule as well as its statutory rule. Michigan Trust Co. v. Baker, 226 Mich.

vest, at a future date, this date must not be more remote than twenty-one years after the expiration of named lives in being. Thus, a trust to begin if and when an orchestra is established in

72, 196 N.W. 976; Gardner v. City Nat. Bank & Trust Co., 267 Mich. 270, 255 N.W. 587.

Dean Fraser has expressed the opinion that the common law rule is in force in *Minnesota.* 8 Minn.L.R. 185, 295; 9 id. 314.

Missouri.—The common-law rule applies. Lockridge v. Mace, 109 Mo. 162, 18 S.W. 1145; Bradford v. Blossom, 207 Mo. 177, 105 S.W. 289; Stewart v. Coshow, 238 Mo. 662, 142 S.W. 283; St. Louis Union Tr. Co. v. Bassett, 337 Mo. 604, 85 S.W.2d 569. See Hudson, The Rule against Perpetuities in Missouri, 15 Mo.Law Bul., No. 11, p. 3.

New Hampshire.—The rule is against remoteness. Wood v. Griffin, 46 N.H. 230; Wentworth v. Wentworth, 77 N.H. 400, 92 A. 733.

New Jersey.—The rule is the common-law rule against remoteness. Siedler v. Syms, 56 N.J.Eq. 275, 38 A. 424; In re Corle, 61 N.J.Eq. 409, 48 A. 1027; Van Riper v. Hilton, 78 N.J.Eq. 371, 78 A. 1055; In re Smisson, 79 N.J.Eq. 233, 82 A. 614.

New York.—Recent decisions (In re Wilcox, 194 N.Y. 288, 87 N.E. 497, and Walker v. Marcellus & O. L. Ry. Co., 226 N.Y. 347, 123 N.E. 736) have made it apparent that there exists in New York a rule against remoteness of vesting, as well as against undue suspension of the power of alienation. Thus, this state seems to have two rules against perpetuities. See O. R. Clark, 5 Cornell Law Quarterly, 189.

North Carolina.—The rule is against remoteness. Baker v. Pender, 50 N.C., 351, 5 Jones Law 351; O'Neal v. Borders, 170 N.C. 483, 87 S.E. 340.

Ohio.—A peculiar local statute provides what persons may be grantees and devisees of lands lying within the state: "No estate in fee simple, fee tail, or any lesser estate, in lands or tenements, lying within this state, shall be given or granted by deed or will, to any person or persons but such as are in being, or to the immediate issue or descendants of such as are in being at the time of making such deed or will." Page & A. Ann.Gen.Code, § 8622; Phillips v. Herron, 55 Ohio St. 478, 45 N.E. 720. The rule against remoteness seems also to be in force. Stevenson v. Evans, 10 Ohio St. 307, 315; Dayton v. Phillips, 28 Wkly.Law Bul., Ohio., 327. See White, 1 Cinc.L.R. 36, 136.

The common law rule may be in force in *Oklahoma.* In re Street's Estate, 138 Okl. 115, 280 P. 413; Tipton v. North, 185 Okl. 365, 92 P. 2d 364.

Oregon.—The rule is that of the common law. In re John's Will, 30 Or. 494, 47 P. 341, 50 P. 226, 36 L.R.A. 242.

Pennsylvania.—The common-law rule of remoteness is in force. Briggs v. Davis, *81 Pa. 470; In re Johnston's Estate, 185 Pa. 179, 39 A. 879, 64 Am.St.Rep. 621; Stephens v. Dayton, 220 Pa. 522, 70 A. 127; Barton v. Thaw, 246 Pa. 348, 92 A. 312, Ann.Cas.1916D, 570.

Rhode Island.—The common-law rule applies. Williams v. Herrick, 19 R.I. 197, 32 A. 913; Storrs v. Burgess, 29 R.I. 269, 67 A. 731; In re Tyler, 30 R.I. 590, 76 A. 661.

South Carolina.—The rule is one of remoteness. Breeden v. Moore, 82 S.C. 534, 64 S.E. 604.

Tennessee.—The rule is the common-law rule against remoteness. Davis v. Williams, 85 Tenn. 646, 4

a certain city,[77] or if and when a gravel pit is worked out,[78] or if and when mortgages are paid off out of rents,[79] is a trust the origin or vesting of which is contingent, and the gift to the trustee is void because his interest is not so limited as to be sure to vest within the permitted period.

Secondly, even though the trust be limited to begin at once, or within the permitted period, there may be contingent equitable interests given to the beneficiaries under the trust, and, if so, these must be made to vest within the permitted period. Thus, a trust to provide support for the widow of the settlor and her then living or afterborn children for a period of thirty years, and then to pay the income of the property to the then living lineal descendants of the settlor, would create remote equitable interests in the latter class of persons.[80] Their interests would be contingent, since it could not be told until the end of thirty years who would be such descendants. The period during which this contingency was to last was thirty years, a gross period too long under the

S.W. 8; Armstrong v. Douglass, 89 Tenn. 219, 14 S.W. 604, 10 L.R.A. 85.

Texas.—The rule is one against remoteness. Dulin v. Moore, 96 Tex. 135, 70 S.W. 742; Anderson v. Menefee, Civ.App., 174 S.W. 904; Brooker v. Brooker, 130 Tex. 27, 106 S.W. 2d 247.

Virginia.—The common-law rule is in force. Otterback v. Bohrer, 87 Va. 548, 12 S.E. 1013.

Washington probably has the common law rule. Hoover v. Ford's Prairie Coal Co., 145 Wash. 295, 259 P. 1079.

West Virginia.—The rule is against remoteness. Whelan v. Reilly, 3 W.Va. 597; Starcher Bros .v. Duty, 61 W.Va. 373, 56 S.E. 524, 9 L.R.A.,N.S., 913, 123 Am.St.Rep. 990; Thaw v. Gaffney, 83 S.E. 983, 75 W.Va. 229, 3 A.L.R. 495; Brookover v. Grimm, 118 W.Va. 227, 190 S.E. 697.

In *Wisconsin* there is no rule against remoteness. Miller v. Douglass, 192 Wis. 486, 213 N.W. 320; Rundell, 19 Mich.L.R. 235.

[77] In re Dyer, 1935, Vict.L.R. 273.

[78] In re Wood [1894] 3 Ch. 381. See, also, Taylor v. Crosson, Del. Ch., 98 A. 375; Overby v. Scarborough, 145 Ga. 875, 90 S.E. 67; Ortman v. Dugan, 130 Md. 121, 100 A. 82; Ewalt v. Davenhill, 257 Pa. 385, 101 A. 756; Rhode Island Hospital Trust Co. v. Peck, 40 R.I. 519, 101 A. 430. A provision for the payment of one-half the income of the trust fund to the settlor or his eldest male heir on demand at any time is void, as creating an interest too remote. Amory v. Trustees of Amherst College, 229 Mass. 374, 118 N.E. 933. But discretionary power in the trustee as to the time of payment of the cestui que trust's interest does not cause a violation. Strout v. Strout, 117 Me. 357, 104 A. 577.

[79] In re Bewick, [1911] 1 Ch. 116.

[80] Anderson v. Williams, 262 Ill. 308, 104 N.E. 659, Ann.Cas.1915B, 720; Ortman v. Dugan, 130 Md. 121, 100 A. 82; Clark v. Union County Trust Co., 127 N.J.Eq. 221, 12 A. 2d 365.

§ 72 RULE AGAINST SUSPENSION OF POWER OF ALIENATION 247

rule, and not in any way connected with the period of lives necessarily in being when the trust was created.

Thirdly, it should be noticed that all contingent interests following after trust estates are subject to the rule against remoteness, and may drag the trust down with them, if they violate the rule. For example, if a trust is created to last for seventy-five years, and contingent legal remainders are provided to follow the trust term, it is obvious that these contingent interests violate the rule against remoteness. They need not vest within lives in being and twenty-one years. They are to vest only at the end of a period of years, not in any way connected with lives. Hence, of course, the remainders to take effect and vest at the end of the trust are void for remoteness. It may well be that the falling of these remainders will so destroy the scheme of the testator that it will be necessary, in order to prevent an unjust disposition of the property, to declare the trust for the term of seventy-five years void also. This was done in a Pennsylvania case. The trust was considered valid in itself, but it was destroyed, due to its inseparable connection with an unlawful contingent legal remainder.[81]

On the other hand, although there is a remainder following the trust which is too remote, and therefore void, yet the trust may be separable and may stand alone. In many cases the only effect of the violation of the rule against remoteness by a contingent remainder is that the remainder is void. The trust preceding the remainder is enforced.[82]

RULE AGAINST SUSPENSION OF POWER OF ALIENATION

72. In many states there is a statutory rule that the power of alienation of property shall not be suspended longer than a given period.

In these states trusts are invalid when they result in suspending the power of alienating the trust property for a period longer than that permitted by the statute.

Trusts may result in suspending the power of alienation, either because the instruments creating them expressly require the trustee to retain the trust property, or because they

---

[81] In re Johnston's Estate, 185 Pa. 179, 39 A. 879, 64 Am.St.Rep. 621.

[82] Beers v. Narramore, 61 Conn. 13, 22 A. 1061; Loomer v. Loomer, 76 Conn. 522, 57 A. 167; Wolfe v. Hatheway, 81 Conn. 181, 70 A. 645; Dime Savings & Trust Co. v. Watson, 254 Ill. 419, 98 N.E. 777; Camden Safe Deposit & Trust Co. v. Guerin, 87 N.J.Eq. 72, 99 A. 105.

prohibit the beneficiary from selling his interest, or because a statute forbids alienation of the beneficiary's interest.

The rule against undue restraint upon the alienation of property is called the rule against perpetuities in many states. In substance it provides that every provision in will or deed which suspends the absolute power of alienation of real or personal property beyond a given period shall be void. The period during which suspension may occur is two lives in being in some states, and any number of lives in being in others. In some states a period of years varying from 21 to 30 may be added to lives in being as a period of suspension.

This rule, it will be seen, is aimed at preventing property from being inalienable for too long a period. It aims to keep property in the market. It is different from the rule against remoteness, which is aimed at preventing the fastening of contingent and uncertain interests upon property for too long a period. However, remote contingent interests do clog the alienability of property, either legally or practically.

A statutory rule against undue suspension of the power of alienation has been adopted in fourteen states and the District of Columbia.[83]

---

[83] *Arizona.*—The power of alienation cannot be suspended for more than two lives in being and twenty-one years. Code 1939, § 71-106.

California.—The power of alienation may not be suspended beyond the existence of lives in being and twenty-five years. Civ.Code, §§ 715, 716. See Sacramento Bank v. Montgomery, 146 Cal. 745, 81 P. 138; In re Fay's Estate, 5 Cal.App. 188, 89 P. 1065; In re Heberle's Estate, 155 Cal. 723, 102 P. 935; In re Gregory's Estate, 12 Cal.App. 309, 107 P. 566. See Hohfeld, The Need of Remedial Legislation in the California Law of Trusts and Perpetuities, 1 Cal.Law Rev. 305.

District of Columbia.—The power of alienation shall not be suspended for more than lives in being and twenty-one years. Code 1929, title 25, § 112. But the rule against remoteness is recognized. See page 243, ante.

Idaho.—Suspension beyond lives in being is prohibited. Code 1932, § 54-111.

Indiana.—Suspension of the power of alienation of both real and personal property for longer than lives in being is forbidden. Burns' Ann. St.1933 §§ 51-101, 56-142. See Matlock v. Lock, 38 Ind.App. 281, 73 N. E. 171; Pooler v. Hyne, C.C.A.Ind., 213 F. 154, 129 C.C.A. 506; Hayes v. Martz, 173 Ind. 279, 89 N.E. 303; Reeder v. Antrim, 64 Ind.App. 83, 110 N.E. 568. See 1 Ind.Law J. 220; 2 Ind.Law J. 18; 3 Ind.Law J. 7, 67, 100.

Iowa.—Suspension longer than lives in being and twenty-one years is forbidden. See Code 1939, § 10127. In some cases the rule appears to be considered as one dealing with vesting, while in others emphasis is laid on the power of alienation. Todhunter v. Des Moines, I. & M. R. Co., 58 Iowa 205, 12 N.W. 267; Meek v.

§ 72   RULE AGAINST SUSPENSION OF POWER OF ALIENATION

The effect of this rule against undue suspension of the power of alienation upon the purposes for which trusts can be created is obvious. No trust which contemplates a suspension of the

Briggs, 87 Iowa 610, 54 N.W. 456, 43 Am.St.Rep. 410; In re Hubbell Trust, 135 Iowa 637, 113 N.W. 512, 13 L.R.A.,N.S., 496, 14 Ann.Cas. 640; Phillips v. Harrow, 93 Iowa 92, 61 N.W. 434; In re Ogle's Estate, 146 Iowa 33, 124 N.W. 758.

Kentucky.—Suspension of the power of alienation may not be provided for more than lives in being and twenty-one years. St.1936, § 2360.

Michigan.—The statute limits suspension of the power of alienation to two lives in being. Ann.St., § 26.15. See, also, Trustees, etc., of M. E. Church of Newark v. Clark, 41 Mich. 730, 3 N.W. 207; Fitz Gerald v. City of Big Rapids, 123 Mich. 281, 82 N.W. 56; Casgrain v. Hammond, 134 Mich. 419, 96 N.W. 510, 104 Am.St. Rep. 610; McInerny v. Haase, 163 Mich. 364, 128 N.W. 215. Personal property is not covered by the statute against restraints on alienation. Penny v. Croul, 76 Mich. 471, 43 N.W. 649, 5 L.R.A. 858. The rule against remoteness is recognized in Palms v. Palms, 68 Mich. 355, 36 N.W. 419, and Niles v. Mason, 126 Mich. 482, 85 N.W. 1100.

See Goddard, 22 Mich.L.R. 95.

Minnesota.—The power of alienation must not be suspended longer than during two lives in being. St. 1927, §§ 8044, 8045. See Rong v. Haller, 109 Minn. 191, 123 N.W. 471, 806, 26 L.R.A.,N.S., 825; Buck v. Walker, 115 Minn. 239, 132 N.W. 205, Ann.Cas.1912D, 882. See Fraser, Future Interests in Property in Minnesota, 3 Minn.Law Rev. 320; 4 Id. 318; 8 Id. 185, 295; 9 Id. 314.

Montana.—Suspension of the power of alienation for longer than the period of lives in being is prohibited. Rev.Codes, 1935, § 6705, 6706.

New York.—The rule is against the suspension of the power of alienation for a longer period than two lives in being. Real Property Law, § 42; Personal Property Law, § 11. These statutes have given rise to an enormous amount of litigation. For illustrative cases, see Hawley v. James, 5 Paige 318; Coster v. Lorillard, 14 Wend. 265; Woodgate v. Fleet, 64 N.Y. 566; Schermerhorn v. Cotting, 131 N.Y. 48, 29 N.E. 980; Allen v. Stevens, 161 N.Y. 122, 55 N.E. 568; In re Colegrove's Estate, 221 N.Y. 455, 117 N.E. 813; Carrier v. Carrier, 226 N.Y. 114, 123 N.E. 135. See Dwight on Powers of Sale as Affecting Restraints on Alienation, 7 Col.Law Rev. 589; Powell, 25 Col.L. R. 989; Chaplin, 26 Col.L.R. 671; Whiteside, 13 Cornell L.Q. 31, 167.

North Dakota.—Comp.L.1913, § 5287, prohibits the suspension of the power of alienation for a period longer than lives in being. See Penfield v. Tower, 1 N.D. 216, 46 N.W. 413; Hagen v. Sacrison, 19 N.D. 160, 123 N.W. 518, 26 L.R.A.,N.S., 724.

Oklahoma.—Lives in being is the legal period for suspension of the power of alienation. 60 Okl.St.Ann. § 31.

South Dakota.—The legal period of suspension of the power of alienation is during lives in being. Code 1939, § 51.0231.

Wisconsin.—The rule is against the suspension of the power of alienation for longer than during two lives in being and thirty years. St.1941, §§ 230.14, 230.15. For construction, see Holmes v. Walter, 118 Wis. 409, 95 N.W. 380, 62 L.R.A. 986; In re Adelman's Will, 138 Wis. 120, 119 N.W. 929; Eggleston v. Swartz, 145 Wis. 106, 129 N.W. 48. The statute applies to real property only. Dan-

power of alienation for a time longer than that allowed by the statute will be valid. For example, in New York the statute prohibits the suspension of the power of alienation for longer than two lives. Hence a trust which provided that the trustee should retain the property intact, and should have no power to sell it during the lives of A., B., and C., would suspend the power of alienation of the trust property for three lives, and be void.

What trusts suspend the power of alienation? In what cases does the existence of a trust take the trust property out of the market, and make it impossible for any person or persons to convey to another an absolute and complete title to the trust property?

A trust may suspend the power of alienation because of its own express provisions. It may by its express terms require that the alienation of the trust property shall be suspended during a given period. Thus, the settlor may provide the trustee shall retain title to certain real property, collect the rents therefrom, and deliver them to A., and divide the property between the children of A., at A.'s death. Such a trust prevents the property from being sold for a given period, namely, from the date of the creation of the trust until A.'s death. It suspends the power of alienation during A.'s life. Such a trust would be valid in all states having the rule against undue suspension. But, if the express provision were that the trust should continue under the same terms for fifty years, the trust would be invalid in all the states having the rule against undue suspension of the power of alienation. In none of such states may the power be suspended during a period of years longer than thirty.[84]

As is shown by a decision of a California court, at least two classes of trusts by their own express provisions require a suspension of the power of alienation, namely, those created for the purpose of having rents and profits collected and paid over to a beneficiary, and those created for the purpose of having a sale made at a definite date in the future. Discussing these two classes of trusts, the court says: "Under the first class are included all those whose very purpose and essence it is that

---

forth v. City of Oshkosh, 119 Wis. 262, 97 N.W. 258.

See Rundell, 4 Wis.L.R. 1, 2 id. 449; 19 Mich.L.R. 235.

[84] In re Fay's Estate, 5 Cal.App. 188, 89 P. 1065; Williams v. Williams, 73 Cal. 99, 14 P. 394; Fowler v. Duhme, 143 Ind. 248, 42 N.E. 623; Haug v. Schumacher, 166 N.Y. 506, 60 N.E. 245.

the land shall not be alienated by the trustee during the trust term, and where, consequently, a sale by him would be in direct contravention of the trust. In the case of such express trusts as occasion the suspension of the absolute power of alienation, the term of duration is the vital subject of inquiry. * * * Trusts such as these under consideration in their very nature operate to suspend the power of alienation. That power must be suspended in the one case while the trustee is distributing the rents and profits, and in the other case it is suspended by the express duty imposed upon the trustee to sell only at the expiration of a fixed period."[85]

Not only may a trust suspend the power of alienation by its own provisions, but statutes have in some states caused certain classes of trusts to result in an automatic suspension of the power of alienation. In Michigan, Minnesota, Montana, New York, and Wisconsin there are statutes providing that a beneficiary of a trust to receive the income and profits of property and apply them to the use of another cannot transfer his interest.[86]

The result of these restraining statutes in these five states is that, in all trusts to collect rent and income and apply it to the use of another, there is a suspension of the power of alienation. The beneficiary cannot transfer his interest and, unless he can do so, a perfect title cannot be given. If the trustee, by the terms of the trust, also has no power to sell, then obviously there is a double suspension of the power of alienation. If the trustee has the power to sell the particular property in his hands at the commencement of the trust, other property will be held

---

[85] In re Walkerly's Estate, 108 Cal. 627, 650, 651, 41 P. 772, 49 Am.St.Rep. 97. The statutes of California, North Dakota, Oklahoma, and South Dakota provide that the beneficiary of a trust to collect rents and profits may be restrained from disposing of his interest for a limited period. Cal.Civ. Code § 867; N.D.Comp.L. 1913, § 5377; Okl.L.1941, H.B. 174, § 25, 60 Okl.St.Ann. § 175.25; S.D. Code 1939, § 59.0315. The California statute reads as follows: "The beneficiary of a trust for the receipt of the rents and profits of real property, or for the payment of an annuity out of such rents and profits, may be restrained from disposing of his interest in such trust, during his life or for a term of years, by the instrument creating the trust."

[86] Mich.Ann.St. § 26.29; Minn.St. 1927, § 8098; New York Real Property Law, § 103; New York Personal Property Law, § 15; Wis.St.1941, § 231.19. The New York statute with respect to real property is typical: "The right of a beneficiary of an express trust to receive rents and profits of real property and apply them to the use of any person, cannot be transferred by assignment or otherwise, but the right of the beneficiary of any other trust in real property may be transferred."

by him in its place, and the cestui's interest in the substituted property will be inalienable throughout the life of the trust. Trusts to collect rents and income and apply to the use of another in these five states, therefore, automatically suspend the power of alienation of the property concerned. Their duration must correspond to the statutory period of the rule against suspension of the power of alienation.[87]

In several states it is expressly provided by statute that the power of alienation is suspended by a trust when the trustee cannot absolutely alien his interest, but can only exchange the trust property, or sell it and reinvest the proceeds.[88]

It will be seen that, in these states having the statutory rule against undue suspension of the power of alienation, the question as to the validity of trusts under that rule is a simple one. It depends upon two factors, namely, whether the trust, either by its own express provisions or by virtue of a statute, does actually result in a suspension of the power of alienating a complete and absolute title to the trust property; and, secondly, whether, if there be such suspension, the trust, and therefore the suspension of the power of alienation, continues for a period longer than that allowed by the rule.

The rules laid down in this section apply to private trusts only. The application of these and similar rules to charitable trusts will be considered later.

[87] This period is two lives in being in Michigan, Minnesota, and New York; lives in being in Montana; and lives in being and thirty years in Wisconsin.

For instances in which trusts in these states have resulted in violations of the rule against undue suspension of the power of alienation, see the following cases: Casgrain v. Hammond, 134 Mich. 419, 96 N.W. 510, 104 Am.St.Rep. 610; Niles v. Mason, 126 Mich. 482, 85 N.W. 1100; Rong v. Haller, 109 Minn. 191, 123 N. W. 471, 806 (but see Y. M. C. A. v. Horn, 120 Minn. 404, 139 N.W. 805, as to trust of personalty); Hawley v. James, 5 Paige, N.Y., 318; Coster v. Lorillard, 14 Wend., N.Y., 265; Amory v. Lord, 9 N.Y. 403; Schermerhorn v. Cotting, 131 N.Y. 48, 29 N.E. 980; Schlereth v. Schlereth, 173 N.Y. 444, 66 N.E. 130, 93 Am.St.Rep. 616; Central Trust Co. of New York v. Egleston, 185 N.Y. 23, 77 N.E. 989; Ford v. Ford, 70 Wis. 19, 33 N.W. 188, 5 Am.St.Rep. 117.

[88] Cal.Civ.Code, § 771; Montana Rev.Codes 1935, § 6733; N.D.Comp.L. 1913, § 5314; Oklahoma, 60 Okl.St. Ann. § 33. South Dakota Code 1939, § 51.0412.

RULE AGAINST ACCUMULATIONS

73. At common law the power to provide that the income of property should be accumulated and added to capital was restricted only by the rule against remoteness of vesting. If the ownership of the accumulations was vested, there was no limit on the period for which they could be required; but if the ownership of the accumulations was contingent until a future date, that future date must not be more remote than the end of lives in being and twenty one years. This is still the law with regard to private trusts in most American states.

   In Arizona, Indiana, Michigan, Minnesota, New York, North Dakato, South Dakota, and Wisconsin the period of accumulation is now by statute in some cases restricted to the minority of an infant in being, and the accumulation must be for the benefit of such infant. In Alabama the accumulation may take place during the infancy of the beneficiary, or during a gross period of ten years where no infancy is involved.

   In Pennsylvania and Illinois the English statute known as Thellusson's Act has been followed, and accumulations are subject to greater restrictions than at common law.

For how long a period and for the benefit of what persons may the income of real or personal property be accumulated? May A. devise land to X., as trustee, and provide that X. shall collect the rents, income and profits of the realty for a period of fifty years, place the same in a savings bank at compound interest and at the end of the fifty year period pay over the accumulations to A.'s eldest son, or his descendants, if he be dead? May A. bequeath $10,000 to X., as trustee, with a direction that the money be lent out at interest, the interest accumulated until A.'s youngest son reaches twenty-one and that the trustee then pay over to the son the principal and accumulated interest?

The problems involved here arose in a famous English case.[89] There an accumulation was directed to occur during the continuance of nine lives in being at the time the testator died and at the end of that period the entire capital, original property and accumulations, was to go to the then living eldest lineal descendant of the testator's son, Peter. This was a provision for an accumulation to last for, and to vest at the end of, lives in being at the time the will went into effect. The directions as to accumulations were held valid, the court saying that the period during

---

[89] Thellusson v. Woodford, 4 Ves. 227, 11 Ves. 112.

which accumulations might occur was the same as that during which the vesting of property might be postponed, namely, during lives in being and twenty-one years. "If the law is so as to postponing alienation, another question arises out of this will, which is a pure question of equity: Whether a testator can direct the rents and profits to be accumulated for that period, during which he may direct, that the title shall not vest, and the property shall remain unalienable; and that he can do so is most clear law."[90]

The dangers of the vast accumulation of property which became apparent as a result of the decision in Thellusson v. Woodford led Parliament to enact the so-called Thellusson Act, which restricted accumulations. Under that act there are only four lawful periods of accumulation, namely, during the life of the giver, during twenty-one years after the giver's death, during the minorities of any persons living at the giver's death, or during the minorities of persons who would be entitled to the income of the fund, if no provision for accumulation were made.[91] This act has been later amended by the so-called Accumulations Act, which provides for accumulations for the purpose of purchasing land only during the minorities of the persons who would be entitled to the income, if there were no direction for accumulations.[92] The law regarding accumulations was consolidated and somewhat amended in the Property Act of 1925.[93]

In the American states which are unaffected by local statutes, the common-law rule, as laid down in Thellusson v. Woodford,[94] is now in force. Accumulations for the benefit of private persons, as distinguished from charities, if their ownership is contingent until the end of the accumulation period, are allowed to continue only during the existence of lives in being and twenty-one years. The measuring lives must be in existence when the accumulation begins.

"At common law, the power of controlling the rents and profits was coextensive with the power to dispose of the estate which produced them, the limit of the accumulation of annual income was the same as the limit of the creation of future estates, and the enjoyment of the profits could not be suspended for a longer period than the full power of alienating the estate itself. * * *

---

[90] Lord Eldon, Thellusson v. Woodford, 11 Ves. 112, 146.

[91] St. 39 & 40 George III, c. 98, 1800.

[92] St. 55 & 56 Vict. c. 58, 1892.

[93] 15 & 16 Geo. V, c. 20, §§ 164–166.

[94] 11 Ves. 112.

§ 73 RULE AGAINST ACCUMULATIONS 255

Any directions for accumulation for the benefit of individuals until the happening of a contingency which by possibility may not take place within the period prescribed by the rule against perpetuities are void."[95] The principle is that "trusts for accumulation must be strictly confined within the limits of the rule against perpetuities, and that, if such a trust exceeds those limits, it is void."[96]

Thus, in states which have the common-law rule regarding accumulations, unaffected by local statute, a provision for accumulations for twenty years,[97] or for the life of a person in being at the death of the testator, is valid, even though ownership of the accumulations is left contingent until the end of the accumulation period.[98] On the other hand, in such states a provision that accumulations continue for twenty-five years[99] or for thirty years[1] is void, if the owner of the accumulations cannot be known until the end of the accumulation period, since the gross period involved is beyond the twenty-one years allowed by the rule against perpetuities.

In Arizona, Indiana, Michigan, Minnesota, Montana, New York, North Dakota, South Dakota, and Wisconsin statutes exist which restrict some or all accumulations to the period of the minority of an infant in being at the time the accumulation begins. The accumulation must also be solely for the benefit of the minor. The time at which accumulations may be directed to commence in the future is also restricted.[2] The California

[95] Gray, J., in Odell v. Odell, 10 Allen, Mass., 1, 5, 9.

[96] Hoadley v. Beardsley, 89 Conn. 270, 93 A. 535, 539.

[97] Connecticut Trust & Safe Deposit Co. v. Hollister, 74 Conn. 228, 50 A. 750.

[98] Kasey v. Fidelity Trust Co., 131 Ky. 609, 115 S.W. 739.

See, however, Burdick v. Burdick, D.C.D.C., 33 F.Supp. 921, noted in 54 Harv.L.R. 147, where it was held that it was against the public policy of the District of Columbia to permit a required accumulation of the income of trust property for two lives in being and twenty-one years. The view of the court apparently was that accumulations in private trusts would be allowed for reasonable periods only.

[99] Hoadley v. Beardsley, 89 Conn. 270, 93 A. 535; Kimball v. Crocker, 53 Me. 263.

[1] Andrews v. Lincoln, 95 Me. 541, 50 A. 898, 56 L.R.A. 103.

[2] The New York Revised Statutes furnished the model for these statutes regarding accumulations. The present New York statute regarding accumulations of the profits of realty is typical: "All directions for the accumulation of the rents and profits of real property, except such as are allowed by statute, shall be void. An accumulation of rents and profits of real property, for the benefit of one or more persons, may be directed by

statute was originally similar to that of New York but has been recently amended to permit accumulations for any person for lives in being and twenty-five years.³

These statutes regarding accumulations either expressly provide or have been construed to mean that, where an excessive accumulation is attempted, the entire provision will not be declared void, but only that portion which exceeds the statutory limit. Thus, if a testator attempts to create an accumulation for the benefit of his son A. until he reaches thirty years of age, and the son is an infant at the time the will takes effect, the courts will hold the direction for an accumulation valid as to the infancy of the minor, and will merely strike out that portion of the will which contemplates an accumulation from the age of twenty-one until the age of thirty.⁴

any will or deed sufficient to pass real property, as follows: 1. If such accumulation be directed to commence on the creation of the estate out of which the rents and profits are to arise, it must be made for the benefit of one or more minors then in being, and terminate at or before the expiration of their minority. 2. If such accumulation be directed to commence at any time subsequent to the creation of the estate out of which the rents and profits are to arise, it must commence within the time permitted, by the provisions of this article, for the vesting of future estates, and during the minority of the beneficiaries, and shall terminate at or before the expiration of such minority." New York Real Property Law, § 61. A similar statute as to personal property exists. New York Personal Property Law, § 16.

The statutes of Montana, North Dakota, and South Dakota, modeled after the New York statute, apply alike to real and personal property. Mont.Rev.Codes 1935, § 6711; N.D. Comp.L.1913, § 5292; S.D.Code 1939, § 51.0304. Similar statutes in Arizona, Michigan, Minnesota, and Wisconsin apply only to real property. Ariz. Code 1939, § 71.118; Mich.Ann.St. 1912, 26.37; Minn.St.1927, §§ 8067–8068; Wis.St.1941, § 230.37. The Indiana statute, drawn along similar lines, applies to personal property alone. Burns' Ann.St.1933, § 51-102. For cases construing these statutes, see the following: Shriver v. Montgomery, 181 Ind. 108, 103 N.E. 945; Toms v. Williams, 41 Mich. 552, 2 N. W. 814; Wilson v. Odell, 58 Mich. 533, 25 N.W. 506; Palms v. Palms, 68 Mich. 355, 36 N.W. 419; Loomis v. Laramie, 286 Mich. 707, 282 N.W. 876; In re Pettit's Estate, 135 Minn. 413, 161 N.W. 158; Pray v. Hegeman, 92 N.Y. 508; Hascall v. King, 162 N.Y. 134, 56 N.E. 515, 76 Am.St. Rep. 302; United States Trust Co. v. Soher, 178 N.Y. 442, 70 N.E. 970; Morris v. Morris, 272 N.Y. 110, 5 N.E. 2d 56; Hawthorne v. Smith, 273 N. Y. 291, 7 N.E.2d 139; Scott v. West, 63 Wis. 529, 24 N.W. 161, 25 N.W. 18; In re Stark's Will, 149 Wis. 631, 134 N.W. 389. Under the New York statute a provision that increased capital stock or stock dividends should be added to capital is invalid, so far as accumulation of income is concerned. In re Megrue, 224 N.Y. 284, 120 N.E. 651.

³ Cal.Civ.Code, §§ 723–726, 733, as amended by St.1929, p. 276.

⁴ In re Haines' Estate, 150 Cal. 640, 89 P. 606; French v. Calkins, 252 Ill.

In Alabama, Illinois, and Pennsylvania other statutes regarding accumulations exist, and trusts in those states must comply with such statutes in order to be valid.[5]

DURATION OF TRUSTS

74. **By American common law a private, indestructible trust is void if its duration as provided by the settlor is not limited to the period of the rule against perpetuities, namely, lives in being and twenty one years.**

In some states statutes in effect limit the duration of some trusts.

Although the matter is not entirely free from doubt,[6] the American courts have apparently laid down a common law rule that private, indestructible trusts must be limited in duration. The period of their existence must be measured by the life or lives of some person or persons in existence when the trust started, or by a period of years not more than twenty one, or by a combination of such lives and such period of years. Thus a

---

243, 96 N.E. 877; New York Real Property Law, § 61, subd. 3; New York Personal Property Law, § 16, subd. 3.

[5] *Alabama.*—Code 1940, Tit. 47, § 146; "No trust of estate for the purpose of accumulation only can have any force or effect for a longer term than ten years, unless when for the benefit of a minor in being at the date of conveyance, or if by will, at the death of the testator; in which case the trust may extend to the termination of such minority." See Campbell v. Weakley, 121 Ala. 64, 25 So. 694; Pearce v. Pearce, Ala., 74 So. 952.

Illinois.—See Laws 1907, p. 1; Smith-Hurd Stats. c. 30, § 153. This statute follows the Thellusson Act in England. The legal periods of accumulation are (1) during the life of the settlor; (2) for twenty-one years after the death of the settlor; (3) for the minorities of persons in being at the death of the settlor; (4) for the minorities of the persons who would have been entitled to the profits if no accumulation had been provided for. Kolb v. Landes, 277 Ill. 440, 115 N.E. 539.

Pennsylvania.—See Act Apr. 18, 1853, § 9, 20 P.S. § 3251. The Thellusson Act is followed in the main. Provision is made for an accumulation during the life of the settlor and for a period of twenty-one years after his death, or during the minorities of the persons who would be entitled to the income of the property involved if they were of full age and no provision for an accumulation were made. See In re Neel's Estate, 252 Pa. 394, 97 A. 502; In re McKeown's Estate, 259 Pa. 216, 102 A. 878; In re Neeb's Estate, 263 Pa. 197, 106 A. 317.

[6] See Gray, Rule against Perpetuities, 3rd Ed., § 121i; Kales, Future Interests, §§ 658–661; 19 Harv.L.R. 604n; 20 Harv.L.R. 202; 2 Ill.L.R. 281; Fraser, 9 Minn.L.R. 314, 326; 34 Mich.L.R. 553; 4 U.Pitts.L.R. 157.

trust of this type to last for the life of the testator's son and widow, who were both living when the testator died, or to last twenty years after the testator's death, would be valid; but a trust to continue for fifty years or to last until the testator's line of descendants runs out, would be void.[7]

It should be noted that in a few states statutes expressly limit the duration of some or all trusts;[8] and also that the statutes of other states in effect limit the length of time which trusts to collect and pay over income can last, because they provide that the power of alienation cannot be suspended for more than a certain period and that the interests of beneficiaries under such trusts are not transferrable.[9] These states present peculiar conditions and are not considered in this section. Reference here is entirely to states having no statute directly or indirectly dealing with trust duration.

The common law rule here discussed, to the effect that private, indestructible trusts must be of limited duration, is founded apparently on the conscious or subconscious view of the courts that it is against public policy to permit a grantor of property to fix its status for too long a period in the future, that he ought to be allowed to control his property and his donees for the next generation only, and that frequent shifts in the status of property are in the interest of the state.[10]

It follows that the rule ought not to apply to destructible trusts. If the beneficiaries can at any time demand the capital of the trust and that the trust be ended and they be allowed to manage the property as owners, obviously there is no danger of a static condition. In England,[11] and in some American states,[12] if the cestuis have vested interests and are ascertained, living persons, they can always call for a termination of the trust, and can thenceforth enjoy the property directly. But, as later shown,[13] in many American states this power in living, ascertained beneficiaries, with vested interests, to demand the

---

[7] Van Epps v. Arbuckle, 332 Ill. 551, 164 N.E. 1; Barnum v. Barnum, 26 Md. 119, 90 Am.Dec. 88; Amory v. Trustees of Amherst College, 229 Mass. 374, 118 N.E. 933; Williams v. Herrick, 19 R.I. 197, 32 A. 913.

[8] La.Acts 1938, No. 81, § 4 (ten years from the settlor's death, except that a trust for a minor may last ten years beyond his minority); N.Y. Stock Corporation Law, § 50 (voting trusts limited to ten years).

[9] See § 72, ante.

[10] See Scott, Control of Property by the Dead, 65 Pa.L.R. 632.

[11] See § 169, post.

[12] See § 169, post.

[13] See § 169, post.

BOGERT TRUSTS 2D

trust capital and the end of the trust, is denied, and the beneficiaries are compelled to continue to enjoy the property indirectly through the trust, so long as any purpose of the settlor will be achieved by such continuance. In these latter states the rule about possible duration of private trusts is one of some importance.

It should also be noted that even in England, and the American states which follow her lead as to the destructibility of trusts, in many cases there are no fixed, ascertained beneficiaries, of full competence and of vested interests. There may be unborn, unknown, contingent beneficiaries. The trust may be one where no persons can claim to be its beneficiaries, as in the case of trusts to keep up private cemetery lots or monuments where these are not treated as charitable.[14] In these cases there can be no destruction of the trust by the beneficiaries and therefore the period of its duration may well be of concern to the courts.

The settlor of every private trust in a common law state should carefully fix the duration of his trust, and should limit its continuance to a period of a life or lives in being when the trust begins, or to a period of years not more than twenty one, or to a combination of one or more of these lives and such a period of years. If he does not do so, he runs a strong risk of having his entire trust declared void, since the courts do not hold such a trust valid in part and void in part but strike the whole trust down if it may last for too long a period.[15]

[14] In many cases the reason why the courts are so anxious to decide whether a trust is charitable or non-charitable is that if it is charitable it may endure indefinitely, while if it is not charitable it must be limited to last not longer than the period of the rule against perpetuities and will be void if of indefinite duration. Mason v. Bloomington Library Ass'n, 237 Ill. 442, 86 N.E. 1044, 15 Ann.Cas. 603; Lounsbury v. Trustees of Square Lake Burial Ass'n, 170 Mich. 645, 129 N.W. 36; In re Stephan's Estate, 129 Pa.Super. 396, 195 A. 653;

Bliven v. Borden, 56 R.I. 283, 185 A. 239. As to the theory of "perpetuities" in these cases see Smith, Honorary Trusts and the Rule against Perpetuities, 30 Col.L.R. 60.

[15] Bigelow v. Cady, 171 Ill. 229, 48 N.E. 974, 63 Am.St.Rep. 230; Siedler v. Syms, 56 N.J.Eq. 275, 38 A. 424; but see Story v. First Nat. Bank & Trust Co., 115 Fla. 436, 156 So. 101, and Tillman v. Blackburn, 276 Ky. 550, 124 S.W.2d 755, which apparently merely lop off the excess period and do not declare the whole trust void.

CHAPTER 8

CHARITABLE TRUSTS

Sec.
75. Definition of Charitable Trust.
76. History—Statute of Charitable Uses.
77. Indefiniteness—Purpose and Beneficiaries.
78. Religious Purposes.
79. Gifts for Masses.
80. Cemeteries and Monuments.
81. Educational Purposes.
82. Eleemosynary Purposes.
83. Governmental Trusts.
84. Purposes Not Charitable.
85. The Administration of Charities.
86. The Cy Pres Doctrine.
87. The Rule against Remoteness of Vesting.
88. The Rule against Restraints on Alienation.
89. The Rule against Accumulations.
90. Duration of Charitable Trusts.
91. Other Statutory Restrictions on Charitable Trusts.

DEFINITION OF CHARITABLE TRUST [1]

75. A charitable or public trust is a trust which will accomplish an appreciable amount of social benefit to the public or some reasonably large class thereof.

It is immaterial that the settlor had personal motives in creating the trust, if the trust has charitable effects, but the purpose must not include profit-making by the settlor, trustees, or others.

It is not important whether the charitable trust funds arise from gifts, or are raised by taxation or in part contributed by individuals who will share the benefits of the trust.

A charitable trust is to be distinguished from an absolute gift to a charitable corporation.

If a trust will bring about charitable results but is also intended to bring mere financial benefits to some cestuis, it is in part charitable and in part private, is called a "mixed" trust and, if the amounts to be used for each of the two purposes are not stipulated, the trust must stand or fall as a private trust.

A trust for "benevolent" objects may be declared a valid charitable trust, if the word "benevolent" is used as a synonym of "charitable," but not if "benevolent" is construed as meaning any object which indicates merely good will toward mankind, or mere liberality.

[1] Restatement, Trusts, § 348.

A charitable trust is frequently called a public trust,[2] or merely a charity.[3]

The charitable trust will first be generally defined, and in later sections that definition will be amplified and illustrated.

"A charity, in the legal sense, may be more fully defined as a gift, to be applied consistently with existing laws, for the benefit of an indefinite number of persons, either by bringing their minds or hearts under the influence of education or religion, by relieving their bodies from disease, suffering, or constraint, by assisting them to establish themselves in life, or by erecting and maintaining public buildings or works, or otherwise lessening the burdens of government."[4]

"It [a charitable trust] includes everything that is within the letter and spirit of the Statute of Elizabeth,[5] considering such spirit to be broad enough to include whatever will promote, in a legitimate way, the comfort, happiness, and improvement of an indefinite number of persons."[6] Eminent counsel has stated that it includes "whatever is given for the love of God or for the love of your neighbor in the catholic and universal sense—given from these motives and to these ends—free from the stain or taint of every consideration that is personal, private, or selfish."[7] "Lord Camden defined a charity as 'a gift to a general public use, which extends to the poor as well as to the rich.' * * * This definition is at once concise and comprehensive, and has been adopted by the Supreme Court of the United States. * * * It was also approved by Chancellor Kent. * * *"[8] "The word 'charity,' as used in law, has a broader meaning and includes substantially any scheme or effort to better the condition of society or any considerable part thereof. It has been well said that any gift not inconsistent with existing laws, which is promotive of science or tends to the education, enlightening, benefit, or amelioration of the condition of mankind or the diffusion of useful knowledge, or is for the public convenience, is a

---

[2] Appeal of Eliot, 74 Conn. 586, 51 A. 558; Holman v. Renaud, 141 Mo. App. 399, 125 S.W. 843.

[3] Smith v. Havens Relief Fund Soc., 44 Misc. 594, 90 N.Y.S. 168; In re Centennial & Memorial Ass'n of Valley Forge, 235 Pa. 206, 83 A. 683.

[4] Gray, J., in Jackson v. Phillips, 14 Allen, Mass., 539, 556.

[5] See post, § 76.

[6] Harrington v. Pier, 105 Wis. 485, 520, 82 N.W. 345, 50 L.R.A. 307, 76 Am.St.Rep. 924.

[7] Mr. Binney in Vidal v. Girard's Ex'rs, 2 How. 127, 11 L.Ed. 205.

[8] Grant v. Saunders, 121 Iowa 80, 81, 95 N.W. 411, 100 Am.St.Rep. 310.

charity." [9] Other definitions of the charitable trust in America will be found to be variations of those quoted above.[10]

An analysis of these definitions of the charitable trust and a study of other cases will, it is submitted, show several separate elements in the composition of that trust:

First, the trust must be for the mental, spiritual, or physical improvement of mankind. It must not have a useless or frivolous purpose or merely enrich the beneficiaries financially. It is not sufficient that an indefinite number of persons, to be selected by the trustees from a class, are to receive something under the trust, unless social welfare will thereby be advanced. "A charitable use, where neither law nor public policy forbids, may be applied to almost any thing that tends to promote the well-doing and well-being of social man." [11]

Secondly, a charitable trust is not necessarily confined to almsgiving. It includes relief of the poor, but also connotes the social advancement of rich and poor in education, religion, culture, and civilization. "It [a charitable trust] is not confined to mere alms-giving, or the relief of poverty and distress, but has a wider signification, which embraces the improvement of the happiness of man." [12] "While poverty is the condition generally recognized in the bestowal of public charity upon individuals, it is not the only condition, as abundantly appears from the authorities. Indeed, it is not the fact of poverty alone which makes a person a proper object of charity, and this is shown by the existence of penal laws in England, along with the law of public charities, for the punishment of sturdy beggars. It is the need or want of food, clothing, shelter, or other bodily ministrations, so commonly found among the poor, which prompts the exercise of public charity to that class. But a person who is sick, injured, or afflicted, or in a helpless condition, is none the

[9] Wilson v. First Nat. Bank of Independence, 164 Iowa 402, 145 N.W. 948, 952, Ann.Cas.1916D, 481.

[10] Burke v. Roper, 79 Ala. 138; In re Lennon's Estate, 152 Cal. 327, 92 P. 870, 125 Am.St.Rep. 58, 14 Ann. Cas. 1024; Ford v. Ford's Ex'r, 91 Ky. 572, 16 S.W. 451; Carter v. Whitcomb, 74 N.H. 482, 69 A. 779, 17 L.R.A.,N.S., 733; Johnson v. Bowen, 85 N.J.Eq. 76, 95 A. 370; Miller v. Porter, 53 Pa. 292; Kelly v. Nichols, 18 R.I. 62, 25 A. 840, 19 L.R.A. 413; Maxcy v. City of Oshkosh, 144 Wis. 238, 128 N.W. 899, 31 L.R.A.,N.S., 787.

[11] Ould v. Washington Hospital, 95 U.S. 303, 311, 24 L.Ed. 450. For illustrations of trusts held invalid as charitable trusts, see post, § 84.

[12] New England Sanitarium v. Inhabitants of Stoneham, 205 Mass. 335, 342, 91 N.E. 385.

less a proper object to be included in the purposes of a public charity, although he may not be poor." [13]

Thirdly, the amount of social benefit must be substantial. If the law is to give to a trust the privileges enjoyed by charitable trusts, it must find a considerable advantage to the state in the trust. Hence, the class to be benefited by the charitable trust must not be too small. It must be some considerable portion of the public, as, for example, the poor of a given city, or needy clergymen of a given denomination. Just how small this class may be is difficult to determine. A trust for the benefit of the widows and orphans of the future ministers of a given church has been held to be a valid charitable trust, notwithstanding the fact that the class would doubtless be very small.[14] And so, too, the smallness of the class was held to be no objection to the validity of the charitable trust where the beneficiaries were to be indigent and needy Masons in Boston and vicinity.[15] On the other hand, a trust for the benefit of the testator's lineal descendants, [16] or for the purpose of educating the descendants of two persons named, [17] or to educate one boy or girl, [18] has been held not a valid charitable trust.

Fourthly, the trust must be solely for charitable purposes, if it is to receive the advantages of a charitable trust. If the trust is to aid the poor in Jonesville, and to support my widow and children during their lives, it is for mixed public and private purposes, and must be judged as to validity by the rules relating to private trusts. It could not be of indefinite duration. If part of the trust property is devoted to charity, and another definite

[13] Buchanan v. Kennard, 234 Mo. 117, 136 S.W. 415, 420, 37 L.R.A., N.S., 993, Ann.Cas.1912D, 50. To the same effect, see American Academy of Arts and Sciences v. President, etc., of Harvard College, 78 Mass. 582, 12 Gray 582; Little v. City of Newburyport, 210 Mass. 414, 96 N.E. 1032, Ann.Cas.1912D, 425; Godfrey v. Hutchins, 28 R.I. 517, 68 A. 317.

[14] Sears v. Attorney General, 193 Mass. 551, 79 N.E. 772, 9 Ann.Cas. 1200.

[15] Masonic Education and Charity Trust v. City of Boston, 201 Mass. 320, 87 N.E. 602.

[16] Kent v. Dunham, 142 Mass. 216, 7 N.E. 730, 56 Am.Rep. 667.

[17] Johnson v. De Pauw University, 116 Ky. 671, 76 S.W. 851, 25 Ky. Law Rep. 950. But see Gafney v. Kenison, 64 N.H. 354, 10 A. 706, and Webster v. Morris, 66 Wis. 366, 28 N.W. 353, 57 Am.Rep. 278, where trusts for the benefit of needy relatives were held to be charitable trusts. Such trusts might well be held to lack the unselfish motive necessary to a charitable trust and to be mere private trusts of an indefinite nature. The size of the family might well be important.

[18] Estate of Huebner, 127 Cal.App. 244, 15 P.2d 758.

part to private purposes, the objection is obviated. For example, a trust to apply funds perpetually to the benefit of such charities, institutions of learning and science and to the promotion of such inventions and discoveries as the trustees shall select is a trust for mixed private and public purposes and will be held invalid.[19] And so, too, a perpetual trust for the benefit of "religious, educational or eleemosynary institutions," since it may be used to benefit noncharitable educational institutions, is for purposes which may be partly private and partly public, and is hence void.[20] But that the administration of a charitable trust may incidentally benefit private persons, not beneficiaries of the trust and who needed no aid, is not an objection to a charitable trust. Thus, a trust for the education of poor children within a certain district is valid, even though the administration of it might incidentally lessen the burden of taxation upon the rich as well as the poor in that district.[21] That the settlor provided that his relatives, if they qualified for the charitable benefits, should be given a preference as to those benefits does not make the trust a mixed trust.[22] A trust aimed at profit-making is not charitable, even if incidentally some public good may result, as where there is trust to run a private school for the benefit of the stockholders.[23]

Fifthly, the motive of the settlor of the charitable trust is not important. That he was actuated by vanity, or family pride, or an interest in perpetuating his own name, is not important, if the purposes of his trust are charitable. The law is interested in the effects of the trust, and not in the motives of the settlor. Thus, that a settlor of a trust to establish a drinking fountain for horses provided for the erection of a monument of a certain favorite horse on the fountain, and desired to perpetuate the memory of the horse by his gift, is not important in determining the validity of the gift, since its general result will be to promote kindness to the animals in the community. "Courts, in deter-

---

[19] Sutro's Estate, 155 Cal. 727, 102 P. 920.

[20] In re Shattuck's Will, 193 N.Y. 446, 86 N.E. 455.

[21] Crow ex rel. Jones v. Clay County, 196 Mo. 234, 95 S.W. 369.

[22] Darcy v. Kelley, 153 Mass. 433, 26 N.E. 1110; Gallaher v. Gallaher, 106 W.Va. 588, 146 S.E. 623. Sometimes a trifling and temporary financial benefit to the settlor's relatives has been treated as so unimportant as not to make the trust a mixed trust. Wright's Estate, 284 Pa. 334, 131 A. 188.

[23] Stratton v. Physio-Medical College, 149 Mass. 505, 21 N.E. 874, 5 L.R.A. 33, 14 Am.St.Rep. 442; Institution for Savings v. Roxbury Home for Aged Women, 244 Mass. 583, 139 N.E. 301.

mining whether or not a gift is charitable, will not look to the motives of the donor, but rather to the nature of the gift and the object which will be attained by it." [24]

Nor is the wisdom of the gift made for the benefit of charity an important consideration. If it is for charitable purposes, it should be supported by the courts, even though equity believes that the settlor could have made a wiser disposition of his property.[25]

Lastly, although there has been some tendency to hold that a trust is not charitable if the beneficiaries obtain their advantages under it as a matter of right, [26] it is not believed that this result is sound. If members of a lodge contribute dues in return for an agreement that in their old age they may enter a home for the aged, the home and its endowment should be regarded as charitable in nature because of the social benefit which comes from caring for a large class of aged persons at a time when they will be weak and sickly and will need care.[27] It should be immaterial that the funds arose from voluntary or forced contribution by members of the public who will get benefits under the trust. The sole question should be the effect on society.

If a gift is made to a charitable corporation for any or all of its purposes, with the intent that full title shall vest in the corporation, subject merely to the duty of the corporation to keep within the purposes of its charter, no trust is created.[28] The property will be devoted to charitable purposes, but not through the medium of a trust. The corporation can be compelled to apply the property to its corporate purposes through a quo warranto suit by the attorney general. It is often diffi-

[24] In re Graves' Estate, 242 Ill. 23, 29, 89 N.E. 672, 24 L.R.A.,N.S., 283, 134 Am.St.Rep. 302, 17 Ann.Cas. 137. See, also, In re Coleman's Estate, 167 Cal. 212, 138 P. 992, Ann.Cas.1915C, 682; Haggin v. International Trust Co., Colo., 169 P. 138, L.R.A.1918B, 710; Appeal of Eliot, 74 Conn. 586, 51 A. 558; French v. Calkins, 252 Ill. 243, 96 N.E. 877; Bills v. Pease, 116 Me. 98, 100 A. 146, L.R.A.1917D, 1060; Richardson v. Essex Institute, 208 Mass. 311, 94 N.E. 262, 21 Ann. Cas. 1158.

[25] Chapman v. Newell, 146 Iowa 415, 125 N.W. 324.

[26] Lowe's Estate, 326 Pa. 375, 192 A. 405.

[27] Burke v. Roper, 79 Ala. 138; Coe v. Washington Mills, 149 Mass. 543, 21 N.E. 966; Powers v. Home for Aged Women, 192 A. 770, 110 A.L.R. 1361.

[28] Bradley v. Hill, 141 Kan. 602, 42 P.2d 580; Greek Orthodox Community v. Malicourtis, 267 Mass. 472, 166 N.E. 863; Matter of Hart, 205 N.Y.App.Div. 703, 200 N.Y.S. 63.

cult to determine whether the intent of a donor to a charitable corporation was to have the corporation act as trustee or to have it own the property outright.

"Benevolent" and "Charitable"

It is a mooted question in what cases the use of the word "benevolent" will create a charitable trust. The view that a trust for merely "benevolent" objects is not ordinarily a charitable trust has been voiced by some courts.[29] Gray, J., says in the last-cited case:[30] "The word 'benevolent,' of itself, without anything in the text to qualify or restrict its ordinary meaning, clearly includes not only purposes which are deemed charitable by a court of equity; but also many acts dictated by kindness, good will, or a disposition to do good, the objects of which have no relation to the promotion of education, learning or religion, the relief of the needy, the sick or the afflicted, the support of public works or the relief of public burdens, and cannot be deemed charitable in the technical and legal sense."

But in some recent statutory provisions for charitable trusts the word "benevolent" is treated as the equivalent of charitable.[31]

In a number of cases where the gift has been to "charity and benevolence," it has been held that the use of "benevolence" was merely as an explanatory term, amplifying the meaning of "charity," and that therefore the trust was a valid charitable trust.[32]

"The courts appear to have been in some cases astute to frustrate the charitable intentions of donors who, meaning to devote their property to uses strictly charitable, have, unfortunately, employed language admitting of a wider scope in the use of the gift than is judicially given to the word 'charity.' It would be far more in accordance with enlightened jurisprudence to exercise in such cases the power of construction so as to effectuate, if possible, the intention of the testator. A

---

[29] Chamberlain v. Stearns, 111 Mass. 267.

[30] Chamberlain v. Stearns, 111 Mass. 267, 268.

[31] Conn.Gen.St.1930, § 3556; Mich. Ann.St. § 26.1191; Minn.St.1927, §§ 8090-1 to 8090-4; Neb.Comp.St.1929, § 24-913; N.Y.Personal Property Law, § 12, Real Property Law, § 113; Oh.Gen.Code 1940, § 10092-1; S.C. Code 1932, § 9053; W.Va.Code 1937, § 3501.

[32] Fox v. Gibbs, 86 Me. 87, 29 A. 940; De Camp v. Dobbins, 29 N.J.Eq. 36; People v. Powers, 147 N.Y. 104, 41 N.E. 432, 35 L.R.A. 502; In re Murphy's Estate, 184 Pa. 310, 39 A. 70, 63 Am.St.Rep. 802; In re Dulles' Estate, 218 Pa. 162, 67 A. 49, 12 L. R.A., N.S., 1177.

latitudinarian interpretation of the words 'charity' and 'charitable' has been unhesitatingly given in order to effectuate the intention of testators; why should not, for the same purpose, a restricted one be given to the words 'benevolence' and 'benevolent'? Why may they not be interpreted according to their popular signification, and so be held to mean just what the testator, in the great majority of cases, understands them to mean?" [33]

In cases where the gift was to "charitable *or* benevolent" objects there has been a marked difference of opinion as to whether the gift could be sustained as a charitable trust. Some cases have held that the use of "benevolent" was to be qualified by its connection with "charitable," and that it was practically synonymous with "charitable." [34] "Whatever, therefore, may be the meaning, in the law of Massachusetts, of the word 'benevolence' by itself, there can be no doubt that, when used in connection with 'charity,' as in this will, it is synonymous with it; and the connecting 'or' must be taken in the sense of defining and limiting the nature of the charity intended, and of explaining one word by the other." [35]

But in other cases it has been maintained that the use of the words "benevolent or charitable" indicates an intent to provide for purposes not technically charitable; i. e., for purposes consistent only with a private trust. Hence in these cases it has been held that the trust is for a mixed charitable and private purpose, with no separation of funds to be applied to each, and that, therefore, the whole trust must fail if of perpetual duration.[36]

In a recent English case the trust was for "purposes charitable or philanthropic." The court held the trust invalid as a charitable trust and said: "Then what is the meaning of the word 'philanthropic'? He means by that something distinguished from charitable in the ordinary sense; but I cannot put any definite meaning on the word. All I can say is that a philanthropic purpose must be a purpose which indicates good will to mankind in general. Can anything be looser than that? And

---

[33] De Camp v. Dobbins, 29 N.J.Eq. 36, 50.

[34] Saltonstall v. Sanders, 11 Allen, Mass. 462; Weber v. Bryant, 161 Mass. 400, 37 N.E. 203; Pell v. Mercer, 14 R.I. 412.

[35] Saltonstall v. Sanders, 11 Allen, Mass., 462, 470.

[36] In re Macduff, [1896] 2 Ch. 451; Thomson's Ex'rs v. Norris, 20 N.J.Eq. 489; Hegeman's Ex'r v. Roome, 70 N.J.Eq. 562, 62 A. 392; Smith v. Pond, 90 N.J.Eq. 445, 107 A. 800.

here arises the difficulty of which the Attorney General has availed himself with great skill. He says, 'What philanthropic purpose is not charitable?' My answer is: You are dealing with two words of so vague a meaning that it is extremely difficult to say, but we can suggest purposes which might be philanthropic and not charitable—purposes indicating good will to rich men, to the exclusion of poor men. Such purposes would be philanthropic in the ordinary acceptation of the word—that is to say, in the wide, loose sense of indicating good will towards mankind, or a great portion of them; but I do not think they would be charitable. I am quite aware that a trust may be charitable, though not confined to the poor; but I doubt very much whether a trust would be declared to be charitable which excluded the poor." [37]

It is submitted that the word "benevolent" in a trust instrument should be given a reasonable construction, for the purpose of ascertaining the meaning which the settlor intended to give to it. If the other statements in the instrument and the surrounding circumstances show that he meant by "benevolent" the equivalent of "charitable," then it would seem proper to declare the trust a valid charitable trust. The modern tendency is toward considering the words "benevolent" and "philanthropic" as synonyms of "charitable."

HISTORY—STATUTE OF CHARITABLE USES

76. Prior to 1601 charitable uses were recognized and enforced by the English Court of Chancery. In 1601 the Statute of Charitable Uses was enacted. It enumerated some of the more important charities then in force and provided for their better protection and enforcement.

The Statute of Charitable Uses is considered to be a part of the common law in some states, in others a statute similar to it is enacted, but in most states charitable trusts depend for their enforcement entirely on the general jurisdiction of equity over all trusts. In a few jurisdictions it has required statutes to give validity to charitable trusts.

In 1601 the English Parliament enacted a statute which has come to be known as the Statute of Charitable Uses.[38] This act

---

[37] In re Macduff, [1896] 2 Ch. 451, 464. See, also, Thorp v. Lund, 227 Mass. 474, 116 N.E. 946, Ann.Cas. 1918B, 1204.

[38] St. 43 Eliz. c. 4. It enumerated the following as purposes for which charities had been established at that time: Relief of aged, impotent, and

recited that property had been given for enumerated charitable purposes and that the trustees of the charities were, in many cases, neglecting the performance of their duties, and it then proceeded to provide for the enforcement of these charitable trusts by the appointment of commissioners by the Chancellor.

It seems to have been the view of some courts, manifested in early decisions, that the Statute of Charitable Uses *created* charities and that they had no life separate and apart from that statute and its successors.[39] This question was carefully considered by Mr. Justice Story in the important case of Vidal v. Girard's Ex'rs.[40] That learned judge there showed that charitable uses were known and supported prior to the Statute of Charitable Uses; that the Statute recognized the existence of such uses and merely provided for their enforcement. He referred to the views of English judges which supported his contention and also to the then recent report of the Commissioners of Public Records in England, in which a collection of early chancery cases involving charitable trusts was made. Of these early cases, prior to the Statute of Charitable Uses, he said: "They establish in the most satisfactory and conclusive manner that cases of charities where there were trustees appointed for general and indefinite charities, as well as for specific charities, were familiarly known to, and acted upon, and enforced in the Court of Chancery. In some of these cases the charities were not only of an uncertain and indefinite nature; but, as far as we can gather from the imperfect statement in the printed records, they were also cases where there were either no trustees appointed, or the trustees were not competent to take."[41] To the report of this case is attached a schedule of early cases in chancery, showing the existence of charitable uses prior to the Statute of Elizabeth.[42]

poor people, maintenance of sick and maimed soldiers and mariners, schools of learning, free schools, and scholars in universities, repair of bridges, ports, havens, causeways, churches, seabanks and highways, education and preferment of orphans, relief, stock or maintenance of houses of correction, marriages of poor maids, supportation, aid and help of young tradesmen, handicraftsmen, and persons decayed, relief and redemption of prisoners and captives, aid of any poor inhabitants concerning payments of fifteens, setting out of soldiers, and other taxes. 7 Pickering's English Statutes, p. 43.

[39] Philadelphia Baptist Ass'n v. Hart, 4 Wheat. 1, 4 L.Ed. 499; Gass v. Wilhite, 2 Dana, Ky., 170, 26 Am. Dec. 446; Dashiell v. Attorney General, 5 Har. & J., Md., 392, 9 Am.Dec. 572; Griffin v. Graham, 8 N.C. 96, 1 Hawks 96, 9 Am.Dec. 619.

[40] 2 How. 127, 11 L.Ed. 205.

[41] 2 How. 127, 196, 11 L.Ed. 205.

[42] 2 How. 127, 155, 11 L.Ed. 205.

That charitable uses were not created by the Statute of Charitable Uses, but have an independent existence in chancery, aside from that statute, is now well recognized.[43]

The extent to which the English Statute of Charitable Uses and the English system of charities are recognized in America varies from state to state.[44] In Virginia, West Virginia, and Maryland the courts were early led into error by the decision of the United States Supreme Court in Philadelphia Baptist Ass'n v. Hart,[45] and held that charitable uses depended on the statute, and that, the statute not being in force in those jurisdictions, no charitable trusts could exist.[46] This early mistake has been somewhat rectified by legislation, sanctioning some, though by no means all, charitable trusts.[47]

In New York the English Statute of Charitable Uses was repudiated in 1788.[48] The Revised Statutes of 1830 provided for only four classes of express trusts in land and did not mention charitable trusts.[49] It became a much-disputed question whether charitable trusts had any existence after the adoption of the Revised Statutes. On the one hand, it was claimed that no charita-

---

[43] Carter v. Balfour Adm'r, 19 Ala. 814; In re Hinckley's Estate, 58 Cal. 457; State v. Griffith, 2 Del.Ch. 392; Beall v. Fox's Ex'rs, 4 Ga. 404; Grimes' Ex'rs v. Harmon, 35 Ind. 198, 9 Am.Rep. 690; Miller v. Chittenden, 2 Iowa 315; Tappan v. Deblois, 45 Me. 122; Going v. Emery, 16 Pick., Mass., 107, 26 Am.Dec. 645; Chambers v. City of St. Louis, 29 Mo. 543; Williams v. Williams, 8 N.Y. 525; Griffin v. Graham, 8 N.C. 96, 1 Hawks 96, 9 Am.Dec. 619; Landis v. Wooden, 1 Ohio St. 160, 59 Am.Dec. 615; Zimmerman v. Anders, 6 Watts & S., Pa., 218, 40 Am.Dec. 552; Shields v. Jolly, 1 Rich.Eq., S.C., 99, 42 Am. Dec. 349; Hopkins v. Upshur, 20 Tex. 89, 70 Am.Dec. 375; Burr's Ex'rs v. Smith, 7 Vt. 241, 29 Am. Dec. 154.

[44] It seems to be held to be a part of the common law in seven states. McDonald v. Shaw, 81 Ark. 235, 98 S.W. 952; Haggin v. International Trust Co., 69 Colo. 135, 169 P. 138, L.R.A.1918B, 710; Dickenson v. City of Anna, 310 Ill. 222, 141 N.E. 754, 30 A.L.R. 587; Klumpert v. Vrieland, 142 Iowa 434, 121 N.W. 34; Tappan v. Deblois, 45 Me. 122; Peirce v. Attorney General, 234 Mass. 389, 125 N.E. 609; Buchanan v. Kennard, 234 Mo. 117, 136 S.W. 415, 37 L.R.A., N.S., 993, Ann.Cas.1912D, 50.

[45] 4 Wheat. 1, 4 L.Ed. 499.

[46] Gallego's Ex'rs v. Attorney General, 3 Leigh 450, 24 Am.Dec. 650; American Bible Soc. v. Pendleton, 7 W.Va. 79; State v. Warren, 28 Md. 338.

[47] Va.Code 1936, §§ 37–49, 587–590, 49a; W.Va.Code 1937, § 3491; Md. Code 1939, Art. 93, § 343, art. 23, § 275. See, also, 1 Va.L.Reg., N.S., 161; 4 Id. 21, 147; 34 W.Va.L.Q. 302, 386; Howard, 1 Md.Law Rev. 105.

[48] Laws 1788, c. 46; Beekman v. Bonsor, 23 N.Y. 298, 307, 80 Am.Dec. 269.

[49] See ante, § 70.

ble trust could exist, since the Statute of Charitable Uses was not in force and since the Revised Statutes made no provision for charitable trusts. On the other, it was maintained that the original jurisdiction of chancery over charitable trusts, irrespective of the Statute of Elizabeth, ought to enable the courts to support charitable trusts. This contention went on for many years; the courts at first leaning to the view that charitable trusts could be supported under equity's general jurisdiction, but later taking a definite stand that charitable trusts were not possible in New York, in view of the statute of 1788 and the Revised Statutes of 1830.[50] The only method by means of which a charitable object could be accomplished during this period was by a gift to a charitable corporation absolutely, either by a donation to a corporation already in existence or to one to be formed within the period allowed by the rule against perpetuities; that is, two lives in being.[51] In 1893 the Legislature passed what was known as the Tilden Act, which has restored the English system of charities as it was in force before the Revolution.[52]

In Michigan, Wisconsin, and Minnesota the history of charitable trusts has been somewhat similar to that of New York. Early legislation in these three states repudiated the Statute of Elizabeth and also adopted practically verbatim the New York chapter on uses and trusts, which declared that only four enumerated real property trusts were valid and made no mention of charitable trusts.[53] In Michigan and Minnesota this was held to prohibit charitable trusts both as to real and personal property;[54] in Wisconsin, as a result of this legislation, charitable trusts of realty were held to be impossible,[55] but gifts of personalty in trust for

[50] Williams v. Williams, 8 N.Y. 525; Bascom v. Albertson, 34 N.Y. 584; Holmes v. Mead, 52 N.Y. 332; Holland v. Alcock, 108 N.Y. 312, 16 N.E. 305, 2 Am.St.Rep. 420; Tilden v. Green, 130 N.Y. 29, 28 N.E. 880, 14 L.R.A. 33, 27 Am.St.Rep. 487.

[51] Wetmore v. Parker, 52 N.Y. 450; Cottman v. Grace, 112 N.Y. 299, 19 N.E. 839, 3 L.R.A. 145; Riker v. Leo, 115 N.Y. 93, 21 N.E. 719; Bird v. Merklee, 144 N.Y. 544, 39 N.E. 645, 27 L.R.A. 423.

[52] Allen v. Stevens, 161 N.Y. 122, 55 N.E. 568; Murray v. Miller, 178 N.Y. 316, 70 N.E. 870; Trustees of Sailors' Snug Harbor in City of New York v. Carmody, 211 N.Y. 296, 105 N.E. 543; New York Real Property Law, § 113; New York Personal Property Law, § 12.

[53] Mich.Rev.St.1846, c. 63; Wis. Rev.St.1849, c. 57; Minn.St.1851, c. 44.

[54] Methodist Episcopal Church of Newark v. Clark, 41 Mich. 730, 3 N.W. 207; Hopkins v. Crossley, 132 Mich. 612, 96 N.W. 499; Little v. Willford, 31 Minn. 173, 17 N.W. 282; Shanahan v. Kelly, 88 Minn. 202, 92 N.W. 948.

[55] Danforth v. City of Oshkosh, 119 Wis. 262, 97 N.W. 258.

charitable uses were allowed, because the Statute of Uses and Trusts had no application to personal property.[56] Recent legislation in Michigan and Wisconsin has validated all charitable trusts by statutes modeled after the Tilden Act of New York.[57] A general charitable trust act in Minnesota was declared unconstitutional because of a defect in its title;[58] but a later act restored charitable trusts in full.[59]

In Mississippi a constitutional provision restricts gifts to charity.[60]

In the remainder of the states charitable trusts have from the beginning been enforced, either because of the adoption of the Statute of Elizabeth or the common law of England, or because of the enactment of statutes similar to the Statute of Elizabeth,[61] or merely on the basis of equity's general jurisdiction.[62]

---

[56] Dodge v. Williams, 46 Wis. 70, 1 N.W. 92, 50 N.W. 1103.

[57] Mich.Pub.Acts 1907, No. 122, formerly Mich.How.Ann.St.1912, § 10700, but repealed by Mich.Pub.Acts 1915, No. 280, which re-enacts sections 10700 and 10701, How.Ann.St.1912, and adds the sentence, "Every such trust shall be liberally construed by such court so that the intentions of the creator thereof shall be carried out whenever possible," and validates all gifts under the former statute. See Ann.St. §§ 26.1191, 26.1192; In re Brown's Estate, 198 Mich. 544, 165 N.W. 929; Wis.St.1941, § 231.11(6)(7); Williams v. City of Oconomowoc, 167 Wis. 281, 166 N.W. 322.

See Zollman, 8 Marquette L.R. 168; 10 Id. 177.

[58] Minn.L.1903, c. 132; Watkins v. Bigelow, 93 Minn. 210, 100 N.W. 1104.

[59] Minn.L.1927, c. 180. See E. S. Thurston, Charitable Gifts in Minnesota, 1 Minn.Law Rev. 201.

[60] Miss.Const. §§ 269, 270, provide that gifts of land to any religious corporation or to trustees for charity, and gifts of personal property to religious trustees, are void. Gifts of personal property to non-religious charitable trusts are valid. Old Ladies' Home Ass'n v. Grubbs' Estate, 199 So. 287; Wells, 12 Miss.L.J. 526.

[61] Conn.Gen.St.1930, § 5000; Ga. Code 1933, §§ 108-201 to 108-206; Ky. St.1936, §§ 317–324; N.C.Code 1939, §§ 4033–4035(c).

[62] Carter v. Balfour's Adm'r, 19 Ala. 814; In re Hinckley's Estate, 58 Cal. 457; Doughten v. Vandever, 5 Del.Ch. 51; Erskine v. Whitehead, 84 Ind. 357; Beidler v. Dehner, 178 Iowa 1338, 161 N.W. 32; Miller v. Tatum, 131 Ky. 490, 205 S.W. 557; Succession of Meunier, 52 La.Ann. 79, 26 So. 776, 48 L.R.A. 77; Preachers' Aid Soc. of Maine Conference of Methodist Episcopal Church v. Rich, 45 Me. 552; Bills v. Pease, 116 Me. 98, 100 A. 146, L.R.A.1917D, 1060; Sanderson v. White, 18 Pick., Mass., 328, 29 Am.Dec. 591; Thorp v. Lund, 227 Mass. 474, 116 N.E. 946, Ann.Cas. 1918B, 1204; Mo.Rev.St.1939, § 5439; Catron v. Scarritt Collegiate Institute, 264 Mo. 713, 175 S.W. 571; In re Nilson's Estate, 81 Neb. 809, 116 N.W. 971; In re Hartung's Estate, 40 Nev. 262, 160 P. 782; Gagnon v. Wellman, 78 N.H. 327, 99 A. 786; Board of Education of City of Albuquerque v. School Dist. No. 5

The enumeration of charitable purposes in the Statute of Charitable Uses is not considered exclusive, even in those states where that statute is adopted as a part of the common law. Many other analogous and similar purposes are allowed as valid charitable objects. The statute merely set forth some of the more common charities then in force.[63] "From the foregoing authorities, it clearly appears that the statute cannot be looked to as the sole test of what is a public charity, but that 'many other uses, not named, and not within the strict letter of the statute, but which, coming within its spirit, equity and analogy, are considered charitable.'"[64]

The English law with respect to charitable trusts is affected by recent statutes.[65]

INDEFINITENESS—PURPOSE AND BENEFICIARIES [66]

77. It is often stated by the courts that charitable trusts must have indefinite beneficiaries. While the persons through whom the public is to receive charitable benefits are usually unknown when the trust is created, and are usually to be selected by the trustee later, it is not believed that this characteristic is vital. The important requirement is that an appreciably large amount of social benefit accrue. This may come about through a trust for a large

of Bernalillo County, 21 N.M. 624, 157 P. 668; Hagen v. Sacrison, 19 N. D. 160, 123 N.W. 518, 26 L.R.A.,N.S., 724; Landis v. Wooden, 1 Ohio St. 160, 59 Am.Dec. 615; Pennoyer v. Wadhams, 20 Or. 274, 25 P. 720, 11 L.R.A. 210; In re Close's Estate, 260 Pa. 269, 103 A. 822; Rhode Island Hospital Trust Co. v. Olney, 14 R.I. 449; Shields v. Jolly, 1 Rich.Eq., S.C., 99, 42 Am.Dec. 349; Gibson v. Frye Institute, 137 Tenn. 452, 193 S. W. 1059, L.R.A.1917D, 1062; Hopkins v. Upshur, 20 Tex. 89, 70 Am. Dec. 375; Lightfoot v. Poindexter, Tex.Civ.App., 199 S.W. 1152; United States v. Late Corporation of Church of Jesus Christ of Latter-Day Saints, 8 Utah 310, 31 P. 436; Burr's Ex'rs v. Smith, 7 Vt. 241, 29 Am.Dec. 154; In re Stewart's Estate, 26 Wash. 32, 66 P. 148, 67 P. 723; Susmann v.

Young Men's Christian Ass'n of Seattle, 101 Wash. 487, 172 P. 554.

[63] Clayton v. Hallett, 30 Colo. 231, 70 P. 429, 59 L.R.A. 407, 97 Am.St. Rep. 117; Garrison v. Little, 75 Ill. App. 402; Strother v. Barrow, 246 Mo. 241, 151 S.W. 960; Haynes v. Carr, 70 N.H. 463, 49 A. 638; In re Kimberly's Estate, 249 Pa. 483, 95 A. 86; Harrington v. Pier, 105 Wis. 485, 82 N.W. 345, 50 L.R.A. 307, 76 Am.St.Rep. 924.

[64] Buchanan v. Kennard, 234 Mo. 117, 136 S.W. 415, 420, 37 L.R.A., N.S., 993, Ann.Cas.1912D, 50.

[65] Mortmain and Charitable Uses Act, 51 & 52 Vict. c. 2, 1888; Charitable Uses Act, 54 & 55 Vict. c. 73, 1891, Charitable Trust Acts 1853 to 1925, 15 & 16 Geo. V c. 27.

[66] Restatement, Trusts, §§ 364, 375

group of identifiable persons, but usually it can only come through having the benefits come to a large class and over a long time.

If the trust is vague or indefinite as to its purpose, it may be void and unenforceable, although it appears to be for a charitable object; but a trust for charity in general or one type of charity in general is not objectionable for vagueness or uncertainty.

The courts often state that charitable trusts must have indefinite beneficiaries, and that a charitable trust cannot exist for persons who are known and defined at the time the trust begins.[67] Thus, a trust to aid the poor of Jonesville, a hamlet of 50 people, indefinitely into the future, would undoubtedly be good, although there might at present be only one poor family in the village. The persons to be aided would be those to be selected by the trustees for years to come out of now existing persons and those to be born; while a trust to aid John Brown and his wife and children, who constitute a small group of poor persons, would be invalid as a charity, although it might be a good private trust.

It is believed, however, that the important element is not the definiteness or indefiniteness of the persons to be aided, but rather the amount of social benefit involved. If the group is small, and consists of named living persons, aid of them will bring about a relatively small amount of social benefit and the court will not be justified in calling the trust charitable and giving it all the special privileges which charitable trusts have, such as tax exemption. But if the group is reasonably large, even though its members are identifiable and a list of them could be made, then the aid of them may cause sufficient social advantage to make the trust charitable.[68] Thus, a trust to aid the sufferers from a certain flood, fire, or mine explosion has been treated as charitable.[69]

If a contract is so uncertain, vague, and indefinite that its meaning cannot be ascertained by a court, the court will declare it void for uncertainty, and will not specifically enforce it or give

---

[67] Averill v. Lewis, 106 Conn. 582, 138 A. 815; Russell v. Allen, 107 U. S. 163, 167, 2 S.Ct. 327, 27 L.Ed. 397.

[68] Harrison v. Barker Annuity Fund, C.C.A.Ill., 90 F.2d 286; Dwan, Charities for Definite Persons, 82 U. Pa.L.R. 12.

[69] Pease v. Pattison, 32 Ch.D. 154; In re Northern Ontario Fire Relief Fund, 11 Dom.L.R. 15; Kerner v. Thompson, 365 Ill. 149, 6 N.E.2d 131; Boenhardt v. Loch, 56 Misc. 406, 107 N.Y.S. 786, affirmed 129 N.Y.App.Div. 355, 113 N.Y.S. 747, affirmed 198 N. Y. 631, 92 N.E. 1078.

BOGERT TRUSTS 2D

damages for its breach. Any transaction from which it is claimed legal or equitable rights have arisen may be so ambiguous and equivocal that courts cannot give effect to it. A trust, private or public, is no exception to this rule. If the court cannot tell what the settlor meant to be done by the trustee, it cannot tell whether the trustee has performed his duty, it cannot direct the trustee, and it will decline to sustain the trust.

This rule against too great vagueness and uncertainty of purpose has been variously stated by the courts. The New York Court of Appeals has said that a charitable trust "may be so indefinite and uncertain in its purposes as distinguished from its beneficiaries as to be impracticable, if not impossible for the courts to administer." [70] Thus, a trust to pay the income to "such highly evolved individuals, with much occult knowledge, who are ceaselessly working for the advancement of the Race and the alleviation of the suffering of Humanity, as to him, my said executor and trustee may seem worthy, and be deemed wise", has been held void on account of uncertainty.[71]

The following directions concerning charitable trusts have been held to be sufficiently definite as to purpose and class, and, therefore, to create enforceable trusts: To the vestrymen of a church, to be used as they deem best for the interests of the church;[72] to be devoted perpetually to human beneficence and charity;[73] for the support of the poor of a certain county;[74] for the diffusion of useful knowledge and instruction among the institutes, clubs or meetings of the working classes, or manual laborers, by the sweat of their brows;[75] to be used in the dissemination of the gospel at home and abroad;[76] in trust to be used purely and solely for charitable purposes, for the greatest relief of human suffering, human wants, and for the good of the greatest number;[77] to the cause of Christ, for the benefit and promotion of true evangelical piety and religion;[78] for the propagation of the Christian religion among the heathen.[79]

---

[70] In re Shattuck's Will, 193 N.Y. 446, 451, 86 N.E. 455.

[71] In re Carpenter's Estate, 163 Misc. 474, 297 N.Y.S. 649.

[72] Biscoe v. Thweatt, 74 Ark. 545, 86 S.W. 432, 4 Ann.Cas. 1136.

[73] In re Hinckley's Estate, Myr. Prob., Cal., 189.

[74] Heuser v. Harris, 42 Ill. 425.

[75] Sweeney v. Sampson, 5 Ind. 465.

[76] Attorney General v. Wallace's Devisees, 7 B.Mon., 46 Ky. 611.

[77] Everett v. Carr, 59 Me. 325. "To be spent in charity in Italy and New York City" is not too indefinite. Stewart v. Franchetti, 167 App.Div. 541, 153 N.Y.S. 453.

[78] Going v. Emery, 16 Pick., Mass., 107, 26 Am.Dec. 645.

[79] Phillips Academy v. King, 12 Mass. 546. A gift "for missions and

In a few states statutes require more than the normal amount of definiteness in a charity,[80] and in some decisions a rather illiberal attitude has been shown on the subject of certainty.[81]

It is well settled that gift to charity or a trust for charity,[82] without any further description, or a trust for one type of charity in general, as, for example, a trust for the poor, or a trust to aid in educational work, is not indefinite or vague.[83] The trustee has power to apply the property to specific objects. The general description is sufficient to enable the court to decide whether his administration is proper. If the gift is "to charity", or "to the poor", it is implied that the testator must have contemplated a trustee as a means of administration.[84]

RELIGIOUS PURPOSES [85]

78. **The maintenance and propagation of religion by providing for places of worship, the salaries and maintenance of religious workers, the education of the young in religion, the upkeep of home and foreign missions, and other similar religious objects are valid charitable purposes.**

    The religion to be forwarded need not necessarily be the Christian religion or any branch or sect thereof, but may be any religion which does not teach immoral or criminal doctrines.

The maintenance and encouragement of religious institutions are valid charitable purposes. A charitable trust may be for the benefit of religion in any one of many ways. Thus, the valid charitable trust for religious purposes may provide a site for the erection of a house of worship;[86] or for the erection of

---

like good objects" is valid. Coffin v. Attorney General, 231 Mass. 579, 121 N.E. 397.

[80] Ky.St.1936, § 317 (trust must be for one of the particular charitable purposes named in the act or for some other definite charitable purpose).

[81] Wentura v. Kinnerk, 319 Mo. 1068, 5 S.W.2d 66; Woodcock v. Wachovia Bank & Trust Co., 214 N.C. 224, 199 S.E. 20 (to such corporations or associations as will best promote the cause of preventing cruelty to animals).

[82] Kirwin v. Attorney General, 275 Mass. 34, 175 N.E. 164; Anderson's Estate, 269 Pa. 535, 112 A. 766.

[83] Grant v. Saunders, 121 Iowa 80, 95 N.W. 411, 100 Am.St.Rep. 310; Whicker v. Hume, 7 H.L.C. 124 (to advance learning all over the world).

[84] Jordan's Estate, In re, 329 Pa. 427, 197 A. 150.

[85] Restatement, Trusts, § 370.

[86] Grundy v. Neal, 147 Ky. 729, 145 S.W. 401; Little v. Willford, 31 Minn. 173, 17 N.W. 282; Mott v. Morris, 249 Mo. 137, 155 S.W. 434.

a church building;[87] or to repair a church edifice;[88] or for the construction of a parsonage;[89] for the support of a particular church or denomination;[90] for the support of a course of sermons;[91] for the support of the rector or pastor of a particular church;[92] for the support of home or foreign missions;[93] for the education of young men in the ministry;[94] for the dissemination of religious books;[95] for the use of a Sabbath school or other religious educational institution;[96] or for the benefit of a Young Men's Christian Association.[97]

Must the trust, in order to be valid as a charitable trust, be for the support of any particular religion? Must the religion be some sect or denomination of Christianity? May it be in aid of the Jewish religion, or of Mormonism, or of Mohammedanism?

The original idea of religious charitable trusts in England was undoubtedly that they were for the benefit of the Established Church; but it is now clear that religious trusts for the benefit of dissenting churches are valid,[98] and by statute Jewish and Roman Catholic religious charities have been given the same support accorded to the dissenting Protestant charities.[99]

---

[87] Appeal of Eliot, 74 Conn. 586, 51 A. 558; Attorney General v. Armstrong, 231 Mass. 196, 120 N.E. 678.

[88] Jones v. Habersham, 107 U.S. 174, 2 S.Ct. 336, 27 L.Ed. 401; French v. Calkins, 252 Ill. 243, 96 N.E. 877.

[89] Sandusky v. Sandusky, 261 Mo. 351, 168 S.W. 1150; Van Wagenen v. Baldwin, 7 N.J.Eq. 211.

[90] People v. Braucher, 258 Ill. 604, 101 N.E. 944, 47 L.R.A.,N.S., 1015; Smith v. Gardiner, 36 App.D.C. 485; Attorney General v. Town of Dublin, 38 N.H. 459; Congregational Unitarian Soc. v. Hale, 29 App.Div. 396, 51 N.Y.S. 704; Potter v. Thornton, 7 R.I. 252.

[91] Attorney General v. Rector, etc., of Trinity Church, 9 Allen 422, 91 Mass. 422.

[92] Prettyman v. Baker, 91 Md. 539, 46 A. 1020; Trustees of Cory Universalist Soc. at Sparta v. Beatty, 28 N.J.Eq. 570. Support of superannuated ministers is also naturally charitable. Buckley v. Monck, Mo., 187 S.W. 31.

[93] Hitchcock v. Board of Home Missions of Presbyterian Church, 259 Ill. 288, 102 N.E. 741, Ann.Cas.1915B, 1; Miller v. Tatum, 181 Ky. 490, 205 S. W. 557.

[94] Field v. Drew Theological Seminary, C.C.Del., 41 F. 371.

[95] Simpson v. Welcome, 72 Me. 496, 39 Am.Rep. 349.

[96] Morville v. Fowle, 144 Mass. 109, 10 N.E. 766.

[97] Goodell v. Union Ass'n of Children's Home of Burlington County, 29 N.J.Eq. 32.

[98] Shrewsbury v. Hornby, 5 Hare 406; Attorney General v. Cock, 2 Ves. 273.

[99] St. 8 & 9 Vict. c. 59, § 2; St. 3 & 4 Wm. IV, c. 115; In re Michel's Trusts, 28 Beav. 39; Bradshaw v. Tasker, 2 Myl. & K. 221.

In Thornton v. Howe [1] the nature of the religion which equity would support as a charity was considered. A testatrix created a trust to aid in the propagation of the writings of Joanna Southcote, a person who believed that she was with child by the Holy Ghost and had received divine revelations. The court sustained the trust, notwithstanding that a great part of the writings of Joanna Southcote appeared to the court foolish and profitless. The court said that "the Court of Chancery makes no distinction between one sort of religion and another. * * * Neither does the court, in this respect, make any distinction between one sect and another. It may be that the tenets of a particular sect inculcate doctrines adverse to the very foundations of all religion, and that they are subversive of all morality. In such a case, if it should arise, the court will not assist the execution of the bequest, but will declare it void. * * * But if the tendency were not immoral, and although this court might consider the opinions sought to be propagated foolish or even devoid of foundation, it would not, on that account, declare it void, or take it out of the class of legacies, which are included in the general terms of charitable bequests." [2]

In an early Supreme Court decision [3] Mr. Justice Story, by way of dictum, considered this problem. He seems to have been of the opinion that a charitable trust which repudiated or attacked the Christian religion would not be sustained. Said he: "It is unnecessary for us, however, to consider what would be the legal effect of a devise in Pennsylvania for the establishment of a school or college for the progagation of Judaism, or Deism, or any other form of infidelity. Such a case is not to be presumed to exist in a Christian country, and therefore it must be made out by clear and indisputable proof. Remote inferences, or possible results, or speculative tendencies, are not to be drawn or adopted for such purposes. There must be plain, positive, and express provisions, demonstrating, not only that Christianity is not to be taught, but that it is to be impugned or repudiated." [4]

---

[1] 31 Beav. 14.

[2] 31 Beav. 14, 19–20. In Bowman v. Secular Soc., Limited [1917] App.Cas. 406, the House of Lords manifested a liberal tendency by sustaining a gift to a society the object of which was in part to promote atheism. No trust was involved, but by analogy a trust to oppose religion would seem to be valid. The case was discussed in 31 Harv.Law Rev. 289. Compare Zeisweiss v. James, 63 Pa. 465, 3 Am.Rep. 558, where a gift to aid an infidel society was held void as a charity.

[3] Vidal v. Girard's Ex'rs, 2 How. 127, 11 L.Ed. 205.

[4] 2 How. 127, 198, 199, 11 L.Ed. 205.

Probably in the United States at the present time a trust for the propagation or support of any religion which did not have immoral or criminal tendencies would be supported as a charitable trust. Thus, a trust for the benefit of Shakers has been held valid,[5] as have trusts in aid of the Swedenborgian religion [6] and the Jewish religion, [7] and to promote the doctrines of Christian Science.[8]

In the case involving the propagation of Christian Science the court says: [9] "Mrs. Eddy had the constitutional right to entertain such opinions as she chose, and to make a religion of them, and to teach them to all others; and their rights of belief are as extensive as hers. Her legal right to teach was not ended with her death. She might dispose of her property by a gift in public charity 'for any use that is not illegal.' Whether her opinions are theologically true, 'the court are not competent to decide.' To suffer the civil magistrate to intrude his powers into the field of opinion, and to restrain the profession or propagation of principles on supposition of their ill tendency, is a dangerous fallacy which at once destroys all religious liberty; * * * it is time enough, for the rightful purposes of civil government, for its officers to interfere when principles break out into overt acts against peace and good order."

GIFTS FOR MASSES [10]

79. **In nearly all states trusts for the purpose of having masses said for the soul of the settlor or for the souls of others are valid charitable trusts for religious purposes.**

   In a few jurisdictions gifts for the purpose of having masses said are valid, although not considered charitable trusts.

In England trusts for the purpose of having masses said were formerly held void as for superstitious uses,[11] but a recent decision has held that the effect of modern legislation recognizing

---

[5] Gass v. Wilhite, 2 Dana, Ky., 170, 26 Am.Dec. 446.

[6] In re Kramph's Estate, 228 Pa. 455, 77 A. 814.

[7] Glaser v. Congregation Kehillath Israel, 263 Mass. 435, 161 N.E. 619; In re Steiner's Estate, 172 Misc. 950, 16 N.Y.S.2d 613.

[8] Glover v. Baker, 76 N.H. 393, 83 A. 916.

[9] Glover v. Baker, 76 N.H. 393, 420, 83 A. 916.

A gift for the upkeep of a spiritualistic camp has been held not charitable. In re Stephan's Estate, 129 Pa.Super. 396, 195 A. 653.

[10] Restatement, Trusts, § 371.

[11] In re Fleetwood, 15 Ch.Div. 596; In re Blundell, 30 Beav. 360.

the Catholic religion in England is to make gifts for masses valid.[12] In Ireland they were regarded as valid as honorary trusts, though not legally enforceable.[13] But even in Ireland it was held the trust for masses was void, if it was not limited in duration to lives in being and twenty one years, inasmuch as it was not a charity.[14]

The doctrine of superstitious uses never had any force in America, where freedom of worship is guaranteed to all. The New York Court of Appeals, in discussing a case where a gift for masses was made, said that "in this state, where all religious beliefs, doctrines, and forms of worship are free, so long as the public peace is not disturbed, the trust in question cannot be impeached on the ground that the use to which the fund was attempted to be devoted was a superstitious use. The efficacy of prayers for the dead is one of the doctrines of the Roman Catholic Church, of which the testator was a member; and those professing that belief are entitled in law to the same respect and protection in their religious observances as those of any other denomination. These observances cannot be condemned by any court, as matter of law, as superstitious, and the English statutes against superstitious uses can have no effect here."[15]

In many American states trusts for the purpose of having masses said for the soul of the settlor, or of his family, or of persons generally, are held valid as charitable trusts. They are deemed to be trusts for the purpose of having religious services performed, and the performance of such service is said to be a public benefit, and not merely beneficial to the souls of the deceased persons.[16]

"The nature of the mass, like preaching, prayer, the communion, and other forms of worship, is well understood. It is intended as a repetition of the sacrifice on the cross, Christ offering Himself again through the hands of the priest, and asking pardon for sinners as He did on the cross, and it is the chief

---

[12] Bourne v. Keane, 121 L.T.R. 426.

[13] Reichenbach v. Quin, 21 L.R.Ir. 138; Perry v. Tuomey, 21 L.R.Ir. 480.

[14] Dillon v. Reilly, Ir.R. 10 Eq. 152; Beresford v. Jervis, 11 Ir.L.T.Rep. 128.

[15] Holland v. Alcock, 108 N.Y. 312, 329, 16 N.E. 305, 2 Am.St.Rep. 420.

[16] In re Hamilton's Estate, Cal., 186 P. 587; Burke v. Burke, 259 Ill. 262, 102 N.E. 293; Coleman v. O'Leary's Ex'r, 114 Ky. 388, 70 S.W. 1068; In re Schouler, 134 Mass. 426; Kerrigan v. Tabb, N.J.Ch., 39 A. 701; In re Morris, 227 N.Y. 141, 124 N.E. 724; Appeal of Rhymer, 93 Pa. 142, 39 Am.Rep. 736; In re Kavanaugh's Will, 143 Wis. 90, 126 N.W. 672, 28 L.R.A.,N.S., 470.

and central act of worship in the Roman Catholic Church. It is a public and external form of worship—a ceremonial which constitutes a visible action. It may be said for any special purpose, but from a liturgical point of view every mass is practically the same. The Roman Catholic Church believes that Christians who leave this world without having sufficiently expiated their sins are obliged to suffer a temporary penalty in the other and among the special purposes for which masses may be said is the remission of this penalty. A bequest for such special purpose merely adds a particular remembrance to the mass, and does not, in our opinion, change the character of the religious service and render it a mere private benefit. While the testator may have a belief that it will benefit his soul or the souls of others doing penance for their sins, it is also a benefit to all others who may attend or participate in it. * * * The bequest is not only for an act of religious worship, but it is an aid to the support of the clergy. Although the money is not regarded as a purchase of the mass, yet it is retained by the clergy, and, of course, aids in the maintenance of the priesthood."[17]

In one state it has been suggested that a trust for the purpose of having masses said for the benefit of all souls is valid as a charitable trust, but that a trust for masses for the souls of particular individuals might be a private trust. In a case in which the masses were to be "for the repose of all poor souls" the court said: "It [the mass] is common, and public to all, as a religious ceremony, and is therefore a religious or pious use, and is a public charity, as distinguished from a private charity, which it might be if restricted to masses for the souls of designated persons."[18]

In two states trusts for masses seem to have been held valid as private trusts.[19]

In two other states a gift for the purpose of having masses said is held not to create any trust, but merely to amount to an absolute gift, with a request as to its disposition.[20] In a Kansas

[17] Hoeffer v. Clogan, 171 Ill. 462, 469, 470, 49 N.E. 527, 40 L.R.A. 730, 63 Am.St.Rep. 241.

[18] Ackerman v. Fichter, 179 Ind. 392, 101 N.E. 493, 496, 46 L.R.A.,N.S., 221, Ann.Cas.1915D, 1117.

[19] In re Lannon's Estate, 152 Cal. 327, 92 P. 870, 125 Am.St.Rep. 58, 14 Ann.Cas. 1024 (but see In re Hamilton's Estate, Cal., 186 P. 587); Moran v. Moran, 104 Iowa 216, 73 N.W. 617, 39 L.R.A. 204, 65 Am.St.Rep. 443; Wilmes v. Tiernay, Iowa, 174 N.W. 271, discussed in 5 Iowa Law Bul. 253.

[20] Harrison v. Brophy, 59 Kan. 1, 51 P. 883, 40 L.R.A. 721; Sherman v. Baker, 20 R.I. 446, 40 A. 11, 40 L.R.A. 717.

case the words of gift were: "I give and bequeath to Rev. James Collins, for mass for his grandfather's and grandmother's soul." The court said: "The will does not undertake to create a trust. The language in which it is made is advisory, persuasive, expressive of desire, 'precatory,' as called in the law of wills; but the passing of the gift is not conditioned upon the performance of the act enjoined. Upon the conscience of the donee alone is laid the duty of performing the sacred service named."[21]

Occasionally courts have taken the stand that trusts for masses are invalid, since they are not charities, and since there is no beneficiary to enforce them as private trusts.[22] An Alabama court has thus expressed its view: "The bequest, in the present case, is, according to the religious belief of the testator, for the benefit alone of his soul, and cannot be upheld, as a public charity, without offending every principle of law by which such charities are supported. * * * It is not valid as a private trust, for the want of a living beneficiary. A trust in form, with none to enjoy or enforce the use, is no trust."[23]

Where a trust for masses is regarded as invalid as a trust, it has been held that a contract inter vivos to use money for the purpose of having masses said was valid.[24]

CEMETERIES AND MONUMENTS [25]

80. **A trust for the erection of a monument to the testator or his family is regarded as a valid provision for the payment of his funeral expenses.**

    At common law a trust for the perpetual care and maintenance of a private cemetery or single lot, or for the construction or care of a monument other than one for the testator or his family, is a private trust and void as providing for a perpetuity. Statutes in many American jurisdictions have

---

[21] Harrison v. Brophy, 59 Kan. 1, 2, 51 P. 883, 40 L.R.A. 721.

[22] Festorazzi v. St. Joseph's Catholic Church of Mobile, 104 Ala. 327, 18 So. 394, 25 L.R.A. 360, 53 Am.St.Rep. 48; McHugh v. McCole, 97 Wis. 166, 72 N.W. 631, 40 L.R.A. 724, 65 Am.St. Rep. 106. But this latter case seems overruled by In re Kavanaugh's Will, 143 Wis. 90, 126 N.W. 672, 28 L.R.A., N.S., 470. In Minnesota a trust for masses was declared invalid under the peculiar statutory condition there prevailing. Shanahan v. Kelly, 88 Minn. 202, 92 N.W. 948.

[23] Festorazzi v. St. Joseph's Catholic Church of Mobile, 104 Ala. 327, 330, 18 So. 394, 25 L.R.A. 360, 53 Am.St. Rep. 48.

[24] Gilman v. McArdle, 99 N.Y. 451, 2 N.E. 464, 52 Am.Rep. 41.

[25] Restatement, Trusts, §§ 124, 371, 374.

made these trusts valid, in some cases only when a cemetery association is the trustee, in other states generally, on the theory that such trusts are charitable trusts.

Trusts for the care and maintenance of public cemeteries are generally regarded as valid charitable trusts.

Trusts to erect monuments to public men or national heroes are regarded as charitable.

The erection of a monument to a deceased person, or in honor of his family, is generally regarded as a part of his funeral expenses. The executor or administrator is justified in expending a reasonable portion of the funds coming into his hands for the purpose of the decent interment of the deceased and for the construction of a monument above his grave. Naturally provisions in wills directing executors to perform such acts and bequeathing definite sums of money to the executors for that purpose are valid, and will be enforced by the courts.[26]

"The erection of a suitable headstone at the decedent's own grave may properly be considered as a part of his funeral expenses, in a case where the rights of creditors cannot be defeated thereby." [27]

"We are of opinion that it is legal for a testator to provide in his will for the purchase and erection of a monument to be placed at his grave; that such expense would be a proper and legitimate part of the funeral expenses. In the absence of such a provision in the will, the probate court would be authorized in making provision for the purchase and erection of a suitable monument at the grave of the testator, the amount or cost of which should be regulated by the value of the estate." [28]

At common law a trust to construct an ordinary monument is not charitable, and if it is not a monument to the testator or his family it cannot be treated as part of his funeral expenses. It has been allowed in England as a valid honorary private trust, if limited in duration to lives in being and twenty-one years.[29]

It is generally held that, in the absence of statute, a trust for the perpetual care and maintenance of a private monument or cemetery lot is void as creating a "perpetuity." It is not a trust

---

[26] Bell v. Briggs, 63 N.H. 592, 4 A. 702; Detwiller v. Hartman, 37 N.J. Eq. 347; Emans v. Hickman, 12 Hun, N.Y., 425; In re Frazer, 92 N.Y. 239; Clark v. Halligan, 158 App.Div. 33, 142 N.Y.S. 980; Fite v. Beasley, 12 Lea, Tenn., 328.

[27] Wood v. Vandenburgh, 6 Paige, N.Y., 277, 285.

[28] McIlvain v. Hockaday, 36 Tex. Civ.App. 1, 2, 81 S.W. 54.

[29] Re Jones, 79 T.L.R. 154; Mussett v. Bingle, W.N., 1876, 170.

for a charitable purpose. As a private trust it must be of limited duration, lasting either for a period of years not more than twenty-one, or for lives in being, or for lives and twenty-one years.[30]

"The law is well settled in this country that a perpetual trust cannot be created to take care of a private burial lot, unless the creation of such trust is authorized by statute." [31] "Our law does not permit the creation of trusts in perpetuity, except for charitable or public purposes. It has been repeatedly determined in this court that a trust for the purpose of keeping in repair the burial place of testator is a purely private trust, and is not a trust the object of which is a charity." [32]

In a few states the view has been maintained that a trust for the perpetual care of a private grave, monument, or cemetery lot is a charitable trust. This is apparently on the theory that the public is benefited by the encouragement of reverence for the dead and that such sentiments improve the morals of the members of the community.[33]

In a number of states the care and maintenance of cemeteries is now provided for by statutes allowing gifts to be made to ceme-

---

[30] In re Vaughan, 33 Ch.Div. 187; Johnson v. Holifield, 79 Ala. 423, 58 Am.Rep. 596; In re Gay's Estate, 138 Cal. 552, 71 P. 707, 94 Am.St.Rep. 70; Burke v. Burke, 259 Ill. 262, 102 N.E. 293; Phillips v. Heldt, 33 Ind.App. 388, 71 N.E. 520; Piper v. Moulton, 72 Me. 155; Bates v. Bates, 134 Mass. 110, 45 Am.Rep. 305 (but see statutory change later noted; Lounsbury v. Trustees of Square Lake Burial Ass'n, 170 Mich. 645, 129 N.W. 36; Hilliard v. Parker, 76 N.J.Eq. 447, 74 A. 447; Sherman v. Baker, 20 R.I. 446, 40 A. 11, 40 L.R.A. 717; Drennan v. Agurs, 98 S.C. 391, 82 S.E. 622; Hornberger v. Hornberger, 12 Heisk, Tenn., 635; McIlvain v. Hockaday, 36 Tex.Civ. App. 1, 81 S.W. 54. See Clark, Unenforceable Trusts and the Rule against Perpetuities, 10 Mich.Law Rev. 31, in which the thesis is maintained that trusts of this sort should be held valid if "limited in duration to a period not longer than twenty-one years after lives in being at the creation of the trust."

[31] Mason v. Bloomington Library Ass'n, 237 Ill. 442, 446, 86 N.E. 1044, 15 Ann.Cas. 603, discussed by A. M. Kales in 5 Ill.Law Rev. 379.

[32] Hilliard v. Parker, 76 N.J.Eq. 447, 448, 74 A. 447.

Care includes the placing of flowers on graves at periodic intervals. Gallagher v. Venturini, 124 N.J.Eq. 538, 3 A.2d 157; Rhode Island Hospital Tr. Co. v. Proprietors of Swan Point Cemetery, 62 R.I. 83, 3 A.2d 236.

[33] Ford v. Ford's Ex'r, 91 Ky. 572, 16 S.W. 451; Webster v. Sughrow, 69 N.H. 380, 45 A. 139, 48 L.R.A. 100; Rollins v. Merrill, 70 N.H. 436, 48 A. 1088 (but see Smart v. Town of Durham, 77 N.H. 56, 86 A. 821); Tierney's Estate, 2 Pa.Dist.R. 524; Nauman v. Weidman, 182 Pa. 263, 37 A. 863. In Trustees of Methodist Episcopal Church of Milford v. Williams, 6 Boyce, Del., 62, 96 A. 795, such a gift was upheld without a statement of reasons.

tery associations or corporations, to be held in trust for the perpetual care of the entire cemetery or of any lot or monument.[34]

In still other states a gift to any trustees for the care or maintenance of a public cemetery or any private lot or monument is made a charitable trust by statute.[35]

It is now quite generally held that a trust for the establishment and perpetual maintenance and care of a *public* cemetery is a valid charitable trust.[36] "That the providing and maintenance of a suitable place for the burial of the dead is one of public use and benefit is not open to question. A decent respect for the memory of the dead is a universal characteristic of civilized society." [37]

Trusts for the erection of monuments to soldiers, sailors, and public men are held valid as charitable trusts on the ground that they foster patriotism and encourage the emulation of men of worthy character.[38]

EDUCATIONAL PURPOSES [39]

81. Trusts for the foundation, support, and maintenance of schools, colleges, libraries, art galleries, museums, and other similar institutions, and for the aid of students, teachers, and investigators, are valid charitable trusts. Trusts to procure changes in the laws or constitution of the state or nation are valid charitable trusts.

[34] See, for example, Conn.Gen.St. 1930, §§ 2980–2988; Neb.Comp.St.1929, §§ 13-501 to 13-505; Ohio Gen.Code, §§ 18, 10110. For further references, see Bogert, Trust & Trustees, § 377.

[35] See, for example Ill.Smith-Hurd Ann.Stats. c. 21, § 64; Minn.St.1927, §§ 7629–7631; N. Y. Personal Property Law, § 13a, Real Property Law, § 114a. For further references see Bogert Trusts & Trustees, § 377. The important portion of the New York statute relating to real property reads as follows: "Gifts, grants and devises of real property, in trust for the purpose of applying the proceeds or income thereof to the perpetual care and maintenance, improvement or embellishment of private burial lots and tombs thereon, are permitted and shall be deemed to be for charitable and benevolent uses. * * *"

[36] In re Vaughan, 33 Ch.Div. 187; Hewitt v. Wheeler School and Library, 82 Conn. 188, 72 A. 935; Swasey v. American Bible Soc., 57 Me. 523; Collector of Taxes of Norton v. Oldfield, 219 Mass. 374, 106 N.E. 1014; Stewart v. Coshow, 238 Mo. 662, 142 S.W. 283; Corin v. Glenwood Cemetery, N.J.Ch., 69 A. 1083; Bliss v. Linden Cemetery Ass'n, 81 N.J.Eq. 394, 87 A. 224; Hullman v. Honcomp, 5 Ohio St. 237; Ritter v. Couch, 71 W.Va. 221, 76 S.E. 428, 42 L.R.A.,N.S., 1216; Webster v. Morris, 66 Wis. 366, 28 N.W. 353, 57 Am.Rep. 278.

[37] Chapman v. Newell, 146 Iowa 415, 125 N.W. 324, 327.

[38] Gilmer's Legatees v. Gilmer's Ex'rs, 42 Ala. 9; Beecher v. Yale, Sup., 45 N.Y.S. 622; In re Smith's Estate, 181 Pa. 109, 37 A. 114; Petition of Ogden, 25 R.I. 373, 55 A. 933.

[39] Restatement, Trusts, § 370.

It is elementary law that trusts for the benefit of education are charitable. "Not only are charities for the maintenance and relief of the poor, sick, and impotent charities in the sense of the common law, but also donations for the establishment of colleges, schools, and seminaries of learning, and especially such as are for the education of orphans and poor scholars." [40]

The range of educational benefactions which are valid as charitable trusts is wide. Trusts are valid as educational charitable trusts, if for the purpose of founding or maintaining a school [41] or college; [42] or for the purpose of aiding or supporting public schools,[43] or to procure a site [44] or erect a building for a school; [45] or for the purpose of employing more teachers [46] or paying higher salaries to those already employed; [47] or to aid needy students in obtaining an education,[48] or to found scholarships [49] or award medals for good work in educational institutions;[50] or for the foundation or maintenance of libraries,[51] historical societies,[52]

[40] Story, J., in Vidal v. Girard's Ex'rs, 2 How. 127, 191, 192, 11 L.Ed. 205.

[41] Bolick v. Cox, 145 Ga. 888, 90 S. E. 54; Grand Prairie Seminary v. Morgan, 171 Ill. 444, 49 N.E. 516; Wilson v. First Nat. Bank of Independence, 145 N.W. 948, 164 Iowa 402, Ann.Cas.1916D, 481; Curling's Adm'rs v. Curling's Heirs, 8 Dana, Ky., 38, 33 Am.Dec. 475; Halsey v. Convention of Protestant Episcopal Church, 75 Md. 275, 23 A. 781; Sears v. Chapman, 158 Mass. 400, 33 N.E. 604, 35 Am.St.Rep. 502; Keith v. Scales, 124 N.C. 497, 32 S.E. 809; Price v. Maxwell, 28 Pa. 23; Franklin v. Armfield, 2 Sneed, Tenn., 305; Kelly v. Love's Adm'rs, 20 Grat., Va., 124.

[42] Connecticut College for Women v. Calvert, 87 Conn. 421, 88 A. 633, 48 L.R.A.,N.S., 485; Dexter v. President, etc., of Harvard College, 176 Mass. 192, 57 N.E. 371; Alfred University v. Hancock, 69 N.J.Eq. 470, 46 A. 178; Raley v. Umatilla County, 15 Or. 172, 13 P. 890, 3 Am.St.Rep. 142; In re Stewart's Estate, 26 Wash. 32, 66 P. 148, 67 P. 723.

[43] Trustees of New Castle Common v. Megginson, 1 Boyce, Del., 361, 77 A. 565, Ann.Cas.1914A, 1207; Smart v. Town of Durham, 77 N.H. 56, 86 A. 821; In re John's Will, 30 Or. 494, 47 P. 341, 50 P. 226, 36 L.R.A. 242.

[44] Price v. School Directors, 58 Ill. 452; Baldwin's Ex'rs v. Baldwin, 7 N. J.Eq. 211.

[45] Meeting St. Baptist Soc. v. Hail, 8 R.I. 234.

[46] Webster v. Wiggin, 19 R.I. 73, 31 A. 824, 28 L.R.A. 510.

[47] Price v. Maxwell, 28 Pa. 23.

[48] In re Curtis' Estate, 88 Vt. 445, 92 A. 965. It is not necessary that the trust be to aid poor students only. Hoyt v. Bliss, 93 Conn. 344, 105 A. 699.

[49] In re Miller, 149 App.Div. 113, 133 N.Y.S. 828.

[50] In re Bartlett, 163 Mass. 509, 40 N.E. 899.

[51] Fordyce v. Woman's Christian Nat. Library Ass'n, 79 Ark. 550, 96 S.W. 155, 7 L.R.A.,N.S., 485; Franklin

[52] Missouri Historical Soc. v. Academy of Science, 94 Mo. 459, 8 S.W. 346.

§ 81   EDUCATIONAL PURPOSES   287

schools, laboratories, or museums dedicated to the advancement of science or art;[53] or for the education of certain classes of persons, as, for example, Indians[54] or the poor or orphans;[55] or for education in certain branches of study, as, for example, in preparation for the ministry,[56] or in preparation for admission to the Naval Academy,[57] or in the domestic and useful arts;[58] or for the distribution of books,[59] or the diffusion of knowledge,[60] or for social service work among young men and boys,[61] or for the erection of a monument in a public park dedicated to and illustrative of music.[62]

It is not essential that the instruction to be given in the educational institution should be gratuitous. That the gift aids members of the public in obtaining an education is sufficient, even though they are obliged to bear part of the expense themselves.[63] Nor is the poverty or wealth of the persons to receive the educational benefits of importance.

The question has arisen whether a trust for the purpose of procuring a change in the Constitution or laws of the nation or a state is a valid educational charitable trust. In a Massachusetts

v. Hastings, 253 Ill. 46, 97 N.E. 265, Ann.Cas.1913A, 135; Minns v. Billings, 183 Mass. 126, 66 N.E. 593, 5 L.R.A.,N.S., 686, 97 Am.St.Rep. 420. That a library and lecture room is to have a dance hall attached does not vitiate the charity, even if it be assumed that the furtherance of dancing is not a charitable purpose. Gibson v. Frye Institute, 137 Tenn. 452, 193 S.W. 1059, L.R.A.1917D, 1062.

[53] Richardson v. Essex Institute, 208 Mass. 311, 94 N.E. 262, 21 Ann. Cas. 1158; Lackland v. Walker, 151 Mo. 210, 52 S.W. 414; Farmers' Loan & Trust Co. v. Ferris, 67 App.Div. 1, 73 N.Y.S. 475; Almy v. Jones, 17 R.I. 265, 21 A. 616, 12 L.R.A. 414.

[54] Magill v. Brown, Fed.Cas.No. 8,952.

[55] Moore's Heirs v. Moore's Devisees, 4 Dana, Ky., 354, 29 Am.Dec. 417; Crow ex rel. Jones v. Clay County, 196 Mo. 234, 95 S.W. 369; Green v. Blackwell, N.J.Ch., 35 A. 375; Clement v. Hyde, 50 Vt. 716, 28 Am.Rep.

522; Kinnaird v. Miller's Ex'r, 25 Grat., Va., 107.

[56] Woodroof v. Hundley, 147 Ala. 287, 39 So. 907; Trustees of Washburn College v. O'Hara, 75 Kan. 700, 90 P. 234.

[57] Taylor v. Columbian University, 226 U.S. 126, 33 S.Ct. 73, 57 L.Ed. 152.

[58] Webster v. Morris, 66 Wis. 366, 28 N.W. 353, 57 Am.Rep. 278.

[59] Pickering v. Shotwell, 10 Pa. 23.

[60] Sweeney v. Sampson, 5 Ind. 465. A trust for "the furtherance of the broadest interpretation of metaphysical thought" was sustained in Vineland Trust Co. v. Westendorf, 86 N.J. Eq. 343, 98 A. 314.

[61] Starr v. Selleck, 145 App.Div. 869, 130 N.Y.S. 693.

[62] Rhode Island Hospital Trust Co. v. Benedict, 41 R.I. 143, 103 A. 146.

[63] Burke v. Burke, 259 Ill. 262, 102 N.E. 293.

case [64] the view was taken that a trust for the purpose of obtaining laws granting the suffrage to women was not a valid charitable trust, but the later and apparently better view is that such trusts are lawful as educational trusts.[65] If they encourage progress and change by means of evolution rather than revolution, they ought to be protected as of the highest advantage to the public. So, in a later Illinois case,[66] it has been held that a trust for the purpose of obtaining the passage of laws giving women the right to vote is a valid charitable trust. And in a New Jersey decision [67] a trust for the dissemination of the writings of Henry George was upheld, although these writings advocate a radical change in the method of landholding in the United States and characterize the present system as unjust. Beasley, C. J., makes the following statement: "I cannot perceive for what reason it is incompatible with judicial position to aid, if invested with such power, in the circulation of the works of a learned and ingenious man, putting under examination and discussion any part of the legal system. It would not seem to me that, as a judge, I was called upon to discard the use of means in the development of the law, which, in every other science, are regarded as absolute essentials." In a Washington case [68] a gift to propagate Socialism was sustained as a valid charity.

ELEEMOSYNARY PURPOSES [69]

82. A trust for the promotion of health and the relief of human want or suffering is a valid charitable trust. Such trusts may provide for giving food, shelter, clothing, medical attendance, and other similar necessities to the needy, or for the promotion of health and the curing of disease in the case of all citizens.

A trust to prevent cruelty to animals generally, or to promote the comfort of animals generally, is valid as a charitable trust.

Trusts for eleemosynary purposes, as, for example, for the relief of human want and poverty, are valid charitable trusts. Instances of valid charitable trusts of this sort are found in

---

[64] Jackson v. Phillips, 14 Allen 539.

[65] Collier v. Lindley, 203 Cal. 641, 266 P. 526.

[66] Garrison v. Little, 75 Ill.App. 402.

[67] George v. Braddock, 45 N.J.Eq. 757, 18 A. 881, 6 L.R.A. 511, 14 Am.St. Rep. 754.

[68] Peth v. Spear, 63 Wash. 291, 115 P. 164.

[69] Restatement, Trusts, § 372.

§ 82   ELEEMOSYNARY PURPOSES   289

trusts for the benefit of the poor generally or the poor of a given locality;[70] or for the friendless poor;[71] or for widows or orphans;[72] or for clothing poor children;[73] or for providing shelter and the necessaries of life;[74] or for the benefit of the aged and infirm;[75] or for the aid of freedmen and refugees,[76] fugitive slaves,[77] disabled firemen,[78] or disabled sailors and soldiers.[79]

In this group are also classed trusts to promote health or to relieve or cure sickness. If the object is to prevent or cure disease, or to provide the maximum of comfort and care for those who are injured or diseased, the trust is charitable, even though its benefits may go to the rich or to persons of moderate means. It is advantageous to society that all its members be well and strong and be relieved of suffering and sickness.[80]

The eleemosynary trust may also provide for the establishment of an institution. Provisions for hospitals,[81] or a home for the poor;[82] or a seaman's home,[83] or an orphan asylum;[84]

---

[70] Strong's Appeal, 68 Conn. 527, 37 A. 395; Klumpert v. Vrieland, 142 Iowa 434, 121 N.W. 34; Bills v. Pease, 116 Me. 98, 100 A. 146, L.R.A. 1917D, 1060; State ex rel. Wardens of Poor of Beaufort County v. Gerard, 37 N.C. 210, 2 Ired.Eq. 210; Trim's Estate, 168 Pa. 395, 31 A. 1071. A gift to "a fresh air fund" is a valid charity. White v. City of Newark, 89 N.J.Eq. 5, 103 A. 1042.

[71] Kemmerer v. Kemmerer, 233 Ill. 327, 84 N.E. 256, 122 Am.St.Rep. 169.

[72] De Bruler v. Ferguson, 54 Ind. 549; Rader v. Stubblefield, 43 Wash. 334, 86 P. 560, 10 Ann.Cas. 20.

[73] Eccles v. Rhode Island Hospital Trust Co., 90 Conn. 592, 98 A. 129; Swasey v. American Bible Soc., 57 Me. 523.

[74] In re Robinson's Will, 203 N.Y. 380, 96 N.E. 925, 37 L.R.A.,N.S., 1023.

[75] Fellows v. Miner, 119 Mass. 541.

[76] White Lick Quarterly Meeting of Friends v. White Lick Quarterly Meeting of Friends, 89 Ind. 136.

[77] Jackson v. Phillips, 14 Allen, Mass., 539.

[78] Potts v. Philadelphia Ass'n for Relief of Disabled Firemen, 8 Phila., Pa., 326.

[79] Holmes v. Coates, 159 Mass. 226, 34 N.E. 190.

[80] In re Clarke, 129 L.T. 310; In re Judd's Estate, 242 N.Y.App.Div. 389, 274 N.Y.S. 902, affirmed 270 N.Y. 516, 200 N.E. 297; Sheen v. Sheen, 126 N.J.Eq. 132, 8 A.2d 136.

[81] Ould v. Washington Hospital, 95 U.S. 303, 24 L.Ed. 450; French v. Calkins, 252 Ill. 243, 96 N.E. 877; Dykeman v. Jenkines, 179 Ind. 549, 101 N.E. 1013, Ann.Cas.1915D, 1011; Ware v. City of Fitchburg, 200 Mass. 61, 85 N.E. 951; Hays v. Harris, 73 W.Va. 17, 80 S.E. 827.

[82] Amory v. Attorney General, 179 Mass. 89, 60 N.E. 391.

[83] Trustees of Sailor's Snug Harbor in City of New York v. Carmody, 211 N.Y. 286, 105 N.E. 543.

[84] Green's Adm'rs v. Fidelity Trust Co. of Louisville, 134 Ky. 311, 120 S.W. 283, 20 Ann.Cas. 861.

Bogert Trusts 2d—19

or homes for old men, [85] or old women, [86] or for girls, [87] are held to be valid charitable trusts.

Trusts for carrying on temperance work, [88] for aiding young men to obtain a start in business, [89] and to provide better housing conditions for laboring men [90] have been sustained as charitable trusts of this class.

The charitable nature of an institution is not negatived by the fact that a charge is made to those who are able to pay for its services, [91] so long as income is used for operating expenses and not for the profit of the stockholders or proprietors of the institution.

Trusts to aid in studying and curing diseases of animals useful to man, [92] or to promote prosecution for cruelty to animals, [93] or to provide a fountain where animals may drink, [94] have been held valid charitable trusts. It is probable that the advancement of the spirit of kindness and humanity among men is as important in these trusts as the aid given to animals. They may be said to be educational or moral in their effect, although they bear resemblances in other respects to eleemosynary charitable trusts. In questionable decisions it has been held that a trust to combat vivisection is charitable, but that a trust to provide a game refuge for all animals (including those hostile to man) is not charitable.[95] The social effect of the first trust seems bad, while that of the latter trust seems desirable to the community in that cruelty to any animals is degrading.

A trust to support a single animal, or a small group of animals, is not charitable, because of the small amount of social interest

[85] Cresson v. Cresson, Fed.Cas.No. 3,389.

[86] Norris v. Loomis, 215 Mass. 344, 102 N.E. 419.

[87] Thornton v. Franklin Square House, 200 Mass. 465, 86 N.E. 909, 22 L.R.A.,N.S., 486; In re Daly's Estate, 208 Pa. 58, 57 A. 180.

[88] Haines v. Allen, 78 Ind. 100, 41 Am.Rep. 555; Harrington v. Pier, 105 Wis. 485, 82 N.W. 345, 50 L.R.A. 307, 76 Am.St.Rep. 924.

[89] Franklin's Adm'x v. City of Philadelphia, 2 Pa.Dist.R. 435.

[90] Webster v. Wiggin, 19 R.I. 73, 31 A. 824, 28 L.R.A. 510.

[91] Jensen v. Maine Eye & Ear Infirmary, 107 Me. 408, 78 A. 898, 33 L.R.A.,N.S., 141.

[92] University of London v. Yarrow, 1 De Gex & J. 72.

[93] In re Vallance, Seton on Decrees, 5th Ed., 1141; In re Douglas, 35 Ch.Div. 472.

[94] In re Coleman's Estate, 167 Cal. 212, 138 P. 992, Ann.Cas.1915C, 682.

[95] In re Foveaux, 1895, 2 Ch. 501; In re Grove-Grady, 1929, 1 Ch. 557.

BOGERT TRUSTS 2D

involved.[96] A testator may provide for a dog or cat, however, by making a gift of the animal and money to a friend, on condition that the donee support and care for the animal, with a reverter to the successors of the testator, if the support is ever withdrawn.[97] In England a trust for animals, small in number and clearly identified, is treated as honorary, that is the trustee is allowed to carry out the trust, but if he does not do so, the successors of the testator may claim the property.[98]

GOVERNMENTAL TRUSTS [99]

83. **Trusts for relieving citizens from the burden of supporting the government, for constructing or maintaining necessary public improvements, buildings or institutions, to encourage patriotism, or to promote the general public safety, comfort, and happiness, are valid charitable trusts.**

There is an important class of charitable trusts which do not fall within the subdivisions previously mentioned. They are sometimes called "governmental" trusts. Their nature can best be explained by a reference to typical examples. Thus, trusts for the purpose of assisting in the payment of public debts,[1] or for the benefit of the inhabitants of a given town [2] or state,[3] are valid charitable trusts of this variety. And so, also, a trust to pay the general expenses of a town,[4] or to provide a townhouse [5] or a courthouse,[6] is a trust of this class.

Further illustrations of these charitable trusts may be found in trusts to repair bridges and highways,[7] to provide a fire engine and fire house,[8] to assist a fire company,[9] to aid a life-

---

[96] In re Forrester's Estate, 86 Colo. 221, 279 P. 721; Willett v. Willett, 197 Ky. 663, 247 S.W. 739, 31 A.L.R. 426.

[97] In re Bradley's Estate, 187 Wash. 221, 59 P.2d 1129.

[98] In re Dean, 41 Ch.D. 552.

[99] Restatement, Trusts, § 373.

[1] Girard Trust Co. v. Russell, C.C. A.Pa., 179 F. 446, 102 C.C.A. 592. But see In re Fox's Estate, 63 Barb., N.Y., 157.

[2] Trustees of New Castle Common v. Megginson, 1 Boyce, Del., 361, 77 A. 565, Ann.Cas.1914A, 1207.

[3] Franklin's Adm'x v. City of Philadelphia, 2 Pa.Dist.R. 435.

[4] Collector of Taxes of Norton v. Oldfield, 219 Mass. 374, 106 N.E. 1014.

[5] Coggeshall v. Pelton, 7 Johns.Ch., N.Y., 292, 11 Am.Dec. 471.

[6] Stuart v. City of Easton, C.C.A. Pa., 74 F. 854, 21 C.C.A. 146. But see Kerlin v. Campbell, 15 Pa. 500.

[7] Town of Hamden v. Rice, 24 Conn. 350.

[8] Magill v. Brown, Fed.Cas.No.8,-952.

[9] Bethlehem Borough v. Perseverance Fire Co., 81 Pa. 445.

saving station,[10] to provide a fountain for furnishing drinking water[11] or for ornamental purposes[12] and to construct a children's playhouse and playground in a public park.[13]

Trusts for laying out and improving streets,[14] planting shade trees,[15] beautifying grounds,[16] constructing or improving parks,[17] making agricultural or horticultural improvements[18] or providing municipal improvements,[19] are valid charitable trusts, because of their enhancement of human comfort and happiness and the æsthetic pleasure which they give the residents of the cities or towns concerned.

Trusts for the erection of monuments to soldiers, sailors, and public men encourage and foster patriotism, and are sustained as charitable trusts;[20] so, too, of a trust for the purchase and distribution of flags.[21]

These trusts will be seen to advance the mental, moral, or physical welfare of the citizens generally. They make life safer or more comfortable, or minister to the æsthetic senses of the members of the community. They aid in the support of government and the consequent protection of life and property and

---

[10] Richardson v. Mullery, 200 Mass. 247, 86 N.E. 319.

[11] Roach's Ex'r v. City of Hopkinsville, 13 Ky.Law Rep. 543.

[12] Hosmer v. City of Detroit, 175 Mich. 267, 141 N.W. 657.

[13] In re Smith's Estate, 181 Pa. 109, 37 A. 114.

[14] Beck v. City of Philadelphia, 17 Pa. 104.

[15] Appeal of Cresson, 30 Pa. 437.

[16] Penny v. Croul, 76 Mich. 471, 43 N.W. 649, 5 L.R.A. 858.

[17] In re Bartlett, 163 Mass. 509, 40 N.E. 899; Richardson v. Essex Institute, 208 Mass. 311, 94 N.E. 262, 21 Ann.Cas. 1158; Burr v. City of Boston, 208 Mass. 537, 95 N.E. 208, 34 L.R.A.,N.S., 143; Board of Assessors of City of Quincy v. Cunningham Foundation, 305 Mass. 411, 26 N.E.2d 335; Trusts for establishing an ornamental gate (Haggin v. International Trust Co., 69 Colo. 135, 169 P. 138, L.R.A.1918B, 710), or a tabernacle (Lightfoot v. Poindexter, Tex.Civ.App., 199 S.W. 1152), in a public park, have been held valid charitable trusts.

[18] Rotch v. Emerson, 105 Mass. 431.

[19] Trustees of New Castle Common v. Megginson, 1 Boyce, Del., 361, 77 A. 565, Ann.Cas.1914A, 1207; Franklin's Adm'x v. City of Philadelphia, 2 Pa.Dist.R. 435.

[20] Gilmer's Legatees v. Gilmer's Ex'rs, 42 Ala. 9; Eliot v. Trinity Church, 232 Mass. 517, 122 N.E. 648; Beecher v. Yale, Sup., 45 N.Y.S. 622; In re Smith's Estate, 181 Pa. 109, 37 A. 114; Petition of Ogden, 25 R. I. 373, 55 A. 933. See Keasbey, Gifts for Public Monuments, 29 Yale Law J. 729, discussing particularly Lawrence v. Prosser, 89 N.J.Eq. 248, 104 A. 772.

[21] Sargent v. Town of Cornish, 54 N.H. 18.

the enforcement of law. Thus they enhance the happiness and well-being of mankind.

PURPOSES NOT CHARITABLE

84. **Trusts which are not for the general benefit of the community, as, for example, trusts for the benefit of private persons, or to encourage sport, or for the care of inanimate objects, or for purposes of mere liberality, or for carrying out mere whims, are not charitable trusts.**

In numerous cases the element of public benefit has been lacking and the trusts have been held private. Thus, a trust for the benefit of a private school,[22] or a waterworks corporation,[23] or for the aid and support of the children of the testator and their descendants who may be destitute,[24] or for a social club,[25] or for the maintenance of a private estate,[26] is a private trust. In all these cases it was not the general public, the community at large, which was to be assisted, but named private persons, or a small class, not open to all.

An English court has considered the question whether a trust to aid a game or sport is a charitable trust.[27] The gift was of a fund in trust to provide annually a cup to be given to the most successful yacht of the season. The testator stated that his object was to encourage the sport of yacht racing. It was contended that the gift was charitable, in that it tended to promote the public health and to train men for the navy. The court held that a gift for the encouragement of a mere sport or game was not charitable, although there might result some incidental benefit to the public at large. The leading object was the amusement of private persons. Rigby, L. J., made the following statement:[28] "There are many things which are laudable and useful

---

[22] Greene v. Dennis, 6 Conn. 293, 16 Am.Dec. 58. For a discussion of some eccentric gifts, held invalid as charities, see Scott, Control of Property by the Dead, 65 Pa.Law Rev. 632.

[23] Doughten v. Vandever, 5 Del.Ch. 51.

[24] Kent v. Dunham, 142 Mass. 216, 7 N.E. 730, 56 Am.Rep. 667.

[25] Re Topham, 1938, 1 All Eng. L.R. 181.

[26] Thorp v. Lund, 227 Mass. 474, 116 N.E. 946, Ann.Cas.1918B, 1204.

[27] In re Nottage, [1895] 2 Ch. 649. Accord, In re Clifford, 81 L.J. Ch. 220 (gift to restock river with fish for private anglers' club); In re Thompson, [1934] 1 Ch. 342 (encouragement of fox hunting). If the sport is to be in connection with the army or navy, so as be of advantage to them, it is charitable. In re Grey, 94 L.J. Ch. 430.

[28] [1895] 2 Ch. 649, 656.

to society, which yet cannot be considered charitable, and this, in my opinion is one of them." In this country it would seem that the fostering of games and contests would be charitable, if it promoted public health and enjoyment.

The lack of community aid or improvement is obvious in the following trusts: A gift to keep in perpetual repair the testator's clock;[29] a gift to keep a house open for the reception and entertainment of ministers and others traveling in the service of the truth;[30] a bequest to be used in making Christmas presents to the scholars of a Sunday school.[31] In the case of the first-named trust, no living person would be benefited; in the instances last mentioned certain individuals might receive benefits, but the element of charity was lacking. The bounty of the donor was evidence of liberality rather than charity.

Gifts for the purpose of carrying out mere whims of the testator are, of course, not charitable. Thus a bequest for the erection of a flagstaff in a public park in memory of the testator's father is not charitable;[32] nor is a gift to be applied to the maintenance of a brass band to march to the testator's grave on holidays and other appropriate occasions and play dirges valid as a charity.[33] In one case a gift to aid an infidel society in the discussion of religion and politics was held invalid as a charity, although it might seem to have some educational features.[34]

THE ADMINISTRATION OF CHARITIES

85. **In the administration of charitable trusts the trustee is governed in the main by the same rules as in the case of private trusts.**

    A suit to enforce a charitable trust against the trustee should be brought in the name of the Attorney General of the

[29] Kelly v. Nichols, 17 R.I. 306, 21 A. 906.

[30] Kelly v. Nichols, 18 R.I. 62, 25 A. 840, 19 L.R.A. 413.

[31] Goodell v. Union Ass'n of Children's Home of Burlington County, 29 N.J.Eq. 32.

And see In re Pleasants, 39 L.T.R. 675 (candy for all children of parish); In re Gwyon, 99 L.J. Ch. 104 (knickers for boys, regardless of need).

[32] Morristown Trust Co. v. Town of Morristown, 82 N.J.Eq. 521, 91 A. 736.

[33] Detwiller v. Hartman, 37 N.J. Eq. 347. Upon similar grounds a gift to support and maintain a person, to "show people" where testator's monument was, was held void in Re Palethorp's Estate, 249 Pa. 389, 94 A. 1060.

[34] Zeisweiss v. James, 63 Pa. 465, 3 Am.Rep. 558.

state, and not by individuals who expect to receive benefits from the trust.

The breach or failure of a charitable trust does not ordinarily give the settlor or his successors power to enforce the trust, or to terminate the trust or to claim the trust property.

The law regarding the powers, duties and liabilities of trustees for charity is in the main the same as that regarding trustees of private trusts.[35] Rare exceptions are found, as in the case of the power of a majority of the trustees of a charitable trust to act,[36] and with regard to liability for torts.[37]

The Attorney General of the state is regarded as the appropriate party to start a suit to enforce a charitable trust against the trustee.[38] He represents the people of the state in that regard. If a suit is brought by the trustees in the course of the trust administration, they should make the Attorney General a party.[39]

Occasionally individual citizens are allowed to sue to enforce a charitable trust, either because there is no objection, or on account of a lack of appreciation of the general rule that the Attorney General is the appropriate complainant. Thus, occasionally members of a church have been allowed to sue to enforce a trust for the church,[40] or the parents of children who would attend a school for which a trust has been established have been recognized as plaintiffs in a suit to compel the trustees to operate the school.[41]

A settlor may make a gift to trustees for charitable purposes on condition subsequent, or may convey to them merely a determinable fee, as where he provides that if the charity is neglected the settlor and his heirs shall have a right of re-entry and to resume ownership of the land, or where he conveys to trustees for a church "as long as a Baptist church is maintained on the premises". Obviously in these cases the settlor, or if he is dead his successors, can take action, if the trust is neglected

---

[35] Bristol Baptist Church v. Connecticut Baptist Convention, 98 Conn. 677, 120 A. 497 (sale of trust property); Rand v. McKittrick, 346 Mo. 466, 142 S.W.2d 29 (investments).

[36] See § 95, post.

[37] See § 117, post.

[38] State ex rel. Carmichael v. Bibb, 234 Ala. 46, 173 So. 74; Healy v. Loomis Institute, 102 Conn. 410, 128 A. 774.

[39] Powers v. Homes for Aged, 55 R.I. 187, 179 A. 610.

[40] Brunnenmeyer v. Buhre, 32 Ill. 183; Howe v. School District, 43 Vt. 282.

[41] Dominy v. Stanley, 162 Ga. 211, 133 S.E. 245.

or the church is not maintained. They may assert a right of re-entry for condition broken in the first case,[42] or a possibility of reverter in the second.[43]

But if there is no such condition or determinable estate, a breach of the trust does not give the settlor or his successors a cause of action for the enforcement of the trust, or to have it declared ended, or to recover the trust property,[44] unless, as elsewhere noted, the gift to charity was voluntary and for some reason *cy pres* is not applied and the trust has become impossible of performance.[45]

THE CY PRES DOCTRINE [46]

86. **The attitude of chancery towards charitable trusts is extremely friendly. It exercises great liberality in the establishment and construction of such trusts.**

   The judicial cy pres power is the authority of equity to apply property given to charity to a purpose as nearly like that of the original purpose as possible, when the settlor had a broad charitable intent and the carrying out of the original charitable trust is at the outset, or later becomes, impossible or inexpedient, due to changes in conditions. This power is possessed by a great majority of American courts of equity. It is exercised with varying degrees of liberality.

   The prerogative cy pres power is the authority of the crown of England, through the Court of Chancery, to dispose of property to such charitable uses as it sees fit, when the original charity was unlawful, or when the original charity was too vague to be enforced and there were no trustees to render it certain. This power is rarely used in England. In America it rests in the several Legislatures and is not possessed by the courts of equity.

The attitude of equity is exceedingly favorable to charitable trusts.[47] The court will be keen-sighted to discover an intent to create a charity,[48] and, where a will is capable of two construc-

---

[42] Tappan's Appeal, 52 Conn. 412; McKissick v. Pickle, 16 Pa. 140.

[43] Easterbrooks v. Tillinghast, 5 Gray, Mass., 17; Schwing v. McClure, 120 Ohio St. 335, 166 N.E. 230.

[44] Tyree v. Bingham, 100 Mo. 451, 13 S.W. 952; Gifford v. First National Bank, 285 Mich. 58, 280 N.W. 108; Lassiter v. Jones, 215 N.C. 298, 1 S.E.2d 845.

[45] See p. 301, post.

[46] Restatement, Trusts, §§ 395–401.

[47] In re Goodfellow's Estate, 166 Cal. 409, 137 P. 12; Duggan v. Slocum, 92 F. 806, 34 C.C.A. 676.

[48] Quimby v. Quimby, 175 Ill.App. 367.

tions, one of which sustains a charitable trust and the other of which is unfavorable to such trust, equity will be disposed to accept the former construction.[49] Equity gives them a more liberal construction than it accords to private trusts,[50] and will carry them into effect wherever this can be done consistently with established rules of law.[51]

The general theory of the cy pres doctrine has been well explained in a New Hampshire case.[52] "When the gift cannot be carried out in the precise mode prescribed by the donor, effect has been given to his general purpose by adopting a method which seemed to be as near his intention as existing conditions would permit. Such a construction is not the result of an arbitrary power exercised in disregard of the donor's wishes for the public benefit, but is as truly based upon a judicial finding of his intention as applied to new conditions as is the construction of a will, deed, or other written contract. The making of a gift for charitable purposes, which is unlimited as to the length of time it may continue, presupposes a knowledge on the part of the donor that material changes in the attending circumstances will occur which may render a literal compliance with the terms of the gift impracticable, if not impossible; and it is not unreasonable to infer that under such circumstances the nearest practicable approximation to his expressed wish in the management and development of the trust will promote his intention to make his charitable purpose reasonably effective; for it would be rash to infer that he intended that the trust fund should be used only in such a way that it could not result in a public benefit—in other words, that he wishes his general benevolent purpose to be defeated, if his method of administering the trust should become impracticable."

In some states the doctrine of cy pres has been put in statutory form.[53] Thus, in New York the statutory provision is as follows:[54]

---

[49] In re Robinson's Will, 203 N.Y. 380, 96 N.E. 925, 37 L.R.A.,N.S., 1023.

[50] Ingraham v. Ingraham, 169 Ill. 432, 48 N.E. 561, 49 N.E. 320.

[51] In re Johnston's Estate, 141 Iowa 109, 119 N.W. 275; St. James Orphan Asylum v. Shelby, 60 Neb. 796, 84 N.W. 273, 83 Am.St.Rep. 553.

[52] Walker, J., in Keene v. Eastman, 75 N.H. 191, 193, 72 A. 213.

[53] In re Royer's Estate, 123 Cal. 614, 56 P. 461, 44 L.R.A. 364; Ford v. Thomas, 111 Ga. 493, 36 S.E. 841. And see Cal. Probate Code § 101; Ga.Code 1933, § 108-202; Minn.St. 1927, § 8090-3, Pa., 10 P.S. §§ 13, 15; W.Va.Code 1939, § 3502; Wis. St.1941, § 231.11(d).

[54] New York Real Property Law, § 113. See, also, In re Brundage's Estate, 101 Misc. 528, 167 N.Y.S. 694;

"The Supreme Court shall have control over gifts, grants and devises in all cases provided for by subdivision one of this section, and whenever it shall appear to the court that circumstances have so changed since the execution of an instrument containing a gift, grant or devise to religious, educational, charitable or benevolent uses as to render impracticable or impossible a literal compliance with the terms of such instrument, the court may, upon the application of the trustee or of the person or corporation having the custody of the property, and upon such notice as the court shall direct, make an order directing that such gift, grant or devise shall be administered or expended in such manner as in the judgment of the court will most effectually accomplish the general purpose of the instrument, without regard to and free from any specific restriction, limitation or direction contained therein: Provided, however, that no such order shall be made without the consent of the donor or grantor of the property, if he be living."

The meaning of the cy pres rule can best be explained by illustrations of its application. In the leading case of Jackson v. Phillips,[55] a testator provided for two trusts, the first to create a sentiment which would put an end to slavery, and the second for the aid of fugitive slaves. Shortly after the death of the testator slavery was abolished by the Emancipation Proclamation. The court held that the change in conditions warranted the application of the first trust fund to the education of freedmen in the South and the use of the second fund in aiding needy negroes in the city where the testator had resided. So, too, in Ely v. Attorney General,[56] where the trust was for the founding of a home for deaf children, to be located on the testator's land, but due to the inadequacy of the sum left, the exact intent of the testator could not be carried out, the court allowed the fund to be applied in assistance of a similar home a few miles distant from the testator's former residence.

In Rector, etc., of St. James Church v. Wilson,[57] the trust was for the purpose of building an Episcopal Church at a specified place. When the fund became available, the place would not support a church. It was held that under the cy pres doctrine the fund would not go to the next of kin, but would be applied

Camp v. Presbyterian Soc. of Sackets Harbor, 105 Misc. 139, 173 N.Y.S. 581; Sherman v. Richmond Hose Co., No. 2, 186 App.Div. 417, 175 N.Y.S. 8.

[55] 14 Allen, Mass., 539.

[56] 202 Mass. 545, 89 N.E. 166.

[57] 82 N.J.Eq. 546, 89 A. 519.

to the use of the Episcopal church in that neighborhood according to a scheme to be approved by the court. And so too, in Mason v. Bloomington Library Ass'n,[58] where the trust was for the establishment of an art gallery in connection with a certain library association, but the library association conveyed its property to another institution and ceased to exist before the gift could be carried out, the court applied the cy pres rule and directed that the property given in trust be used for the benefit of the successor association, since the latter had similar purposes. Again, a trust established in the middle of the nineteenth century to assist persons travelling by covered wagon through St. Louis to the far West may be altered in the twentieth century to provide aid to all travellers passing through that city.[59]

Judicial and Prerogative Cy Pres

There are two kinds of cy pres power—the prerogative cy pres and the judicial cy pres. The former is based on the authority of the crown in England. As parens patriæ the crown disposes of gifts made to charitable uses, where the purpose of the gift is unlawful, or where there is no trustee to administer the gift and the charitable purpose is stated in general terms only. This power is exercised comparatively rarely. An illustration of the application of the prerogative cy pres is found in Cary v. Abbot,[60] where property was given to trustees "for the purpose of educating and bringing up poor children in the Roman Catholic faith." At the time of this gift it was unlawful in England as for a superstitious use. The court held that the property involved was not to be given to the next of kin, but was to be applied to such charitable purposes, as the king should direct. Lord Eldon describes[61] another class of cases in which this power is to be applied as those in which "there is a general indefinite purpose, not fixing itself on any object." So, too, a gift to establish readings of the Jewish law as an incident to that religion was applied by the prerogative cy pres to providing a preacher of the Christian religion at a foundling home.[62]

This prerogative cy pres power is not possessed by any courts in America,[63] but may be held to be vested in the several Legis-

[58] 237 Ill. 442, 86 N.E. 1044, 15 Ann. Cas. 603.

[59] City of St. Louis v. McAllister, 281 Mo. 26, 218 S.W. 312.

[60] 7 Ves. 490.

[61] Moggridge v. Thackwell, 7 Ves. 36, 86.

[62] Da Costa v. De Pas, 1 Ambler 228.

[63] Robbins v. Boulder County Com'rs, 50 Colo. 610, 115 P. 526;

latures.[64] "There are some cases, however, which are beyond its jurisdiction, as where, by statute, a gift to certain uses is declared void and the property goes to the king, and in some other cases of failure of the charity. In such cases the king, as parens patriæ under his sign manual, disposes of the fund to such uses, analogous to those intended, as seems to him expedient and wise. * * * In this country, there is no royal person to act as parens patriæ, and to give direction for the application of charities which cannot be administered by the court. * * * But here the Legislature is the parens patriæ, and, unless restrained by constitutional limitations, possesses all the powers in this regard which the sovereign possesses in England."[65]

The judicial cy pres power is that exercised by equity, where the execution of the charitable trust as directed by the settlor is impossible, impracticable, or inexpedient. It is in common use in the United States.[66]

In a few states the doctrine of cy pres is not recognized, although equity treats charitable trusts with great liberality and friendliness,[67] and often reaches results similar to those which

Kemmerer v. Kemmerer, 233 Ill. 327, 84 N.E. 256, 122 Am.St.Rep. 169; Erskine v. Whitehead, 84 Ind. 357; Lepage v. McNamara, 5 Iowa 124; American Academy of Arts and Sciences v. President, etc., of Harvard College, 12 Gray, Mass., 582; In re Nilson's Estate, 81 Neb. 809, 116 N.W. 971; Dickson v. Montgomery, 1 Swan, Tenn., 348; Reagh v. Dickey, 183 Wash. 564, 48 P.2d 941.

[64] Late Corporation of the Church of Jesus Christ of Latter-Day Saints v. United States, 136 U.S. 1, 10 S.Ct. 792, 34 L.Ed. 481.

[65] Mr. Justice Bradley in Late Corporation of the Church of Jesus Christ of Latter-Day Saints v. United States, 136 U.S. 1, 51, 52, 56, 57, 10 S.Ct. 792, 34 L.Ed. 481.

[66] In re Royer's Estate, 123 Cal. 614, 56 P. 461, 44 L.R.A. 364; Lewis v. Gaillard, 61 Fla. 819, 56 So. 281; Heuser v. Harris, 42 Ill. 425; Troutman v. De Boissiere Odd Fellows' Orphans' Home & Industrial School Ass'n, Kan., 64 P. 33, 5 L.R.A.,N.S., 692; Lynch v. South Congregational Parish of Augusta, 109 Me. 32, 82 A. 432; Norris v. Loomis, 215 Mass. 344, 102 N.E. 419; Catron v. Scarritt Collegiate Institute, 264 Mo. 713, 175 S. W. 571; Lackland v. Walker, 151 Mo. 210, 52 S.W. 414; Adams v. Page, 76 N.H. 96, 79 A. 837; Gagnon v. Wellman, 78 N.H. 327, 99 A. 786; Nichols v. Newark Hospital, 71 N.J.Eq. 130, 63 A. 621; Utica Trust & Deposit Co. v. Thomson, 87 Misc. 31, 149 N.Y.S. 392; In re Kramph's Estate, 228 Pa. 455, 77 A. 814; Brice v. Trustees of All Saints Memorial Chapel, 31 R.I. 183, 76 A. 774; Inglish v. Johnson, 42 Tex.Civ.App. 118, 95 S.W. 558.

[67] Universalist Convention of Alabama v. May, 147 Ala. 455, 41 So. 515; McBride v. Murphy, 14 Del.Ch. 242, 124 A. 798; Graff v. Wallace, 59 App.D.C. 64, 32 F.2d 960; Adams v. Bohon, 176 Ky. 66, 195 S.W. 156; McAuley v. Wilson, 16 N.C. 276, 1 Dev.Eq., 276, 18 Am.Dec. 587; Mars v. Gibert, 93 S.C. 455, 77 S.E. 131; Johnson v. Johnson, 92 Tenn. 559, 23

would have come about from applying cy pres.[68]

That the cy pres doctrine exists does not mean that some kind of charitable trust will be enforced every time a testator expresses a charitable intent. The settlor must have had a broad, general intent to aid charity as a whole, or some particular class of charitable objects. His intent must not be narrow and particular. Conditions may be such that to carry out any other than the settlor's exact plan would be obviously unjust and contrary to the settlor's wishes. For example, when a trust was created for the benefit of the First Universalist Society of Lincoln, and later that society abandoned its religious work, and there was no other religious organization in the same vicinity having similar doctrines, equity refused to apply the property to some other charitable use.[69]

A further illustration of the limits of the cy pres doctrine may be seen in a Maine case,[70] where funds were left in trust for the establishment and maintenance of an institution for the education of young women. An effort was made to obtain the authority of the court for the use of these funds to aid a high school in the town concerned. The court held that this would be violating rather than approximating the testator's intent, and that the case was not one for the application of the cy pres rule. Likewise in the case of Bowden v. Brown[71] the court refused to make use of this doctrine where money was left to a town for the erection of a building to be used in aiding the sick and poor. The town refused to accept the legacy or erect the building. The gift was specific, and no other similar charity would satisfy the court.

If cy pres is not applied, either because the doctrine is not used in the state, or because the settlor had a narrow charitable intent, and the trust fails, there is a resulting trust for the

S.W. 114, 22 L.R.A. 179, 36 Am.St. Rep. 104.

[68] Mars v. Gibert, 93 S.C. 455, 77 S.E. 131.

[69] People v. Braucher, 258 Ill. 604, 101 N.E. 944, 47 L.R.A.,N.S., 1015.

[70] Allen v. Trustees of Nasson Institute, 107 Me. 120, 77 A. 638.

[71] 200 Mass. 269, 86 N.E. 351, 128 Am.St.Rep. 419. And so, also, a gift to use a farm for aiding needy unmarried women formerly employed in the straw industry indicated a specific and not a general charitable intent, and, the trust as planned being impracticable, cy pres could not be applied. Gilman v. Burnett, 116 Me. 382, 102 A. 108, L.R.A.1918A, 794. In Eliot v. Trinity Church, 232 Mass. 517, 122 N.E. 648, the court refused to order the substitution of one statue of Phillips Brooks for another under the cy pres doctrine.

settlor or his successors,[72] if the transfer in trust was gratuitous, or if the trustees paid consideration for the transfer to them they are allowed to retain the property on the failure of the trust.[73]

The impracticability of carrying out the settlor's original trust plan need not amount to physical impossibility. It is sufficient to invoke the application of the cy pres doctrine that the difficulty of executing the plan is extreme.[74]

The cy pres power rests entirely with the court of equity and never in the trustees. The latter may not apply the funds, except according to the literal terms of the trust, even though it seems to them obviously desirable.[75]

The cy pres doctrine can have no application, of course, when the settlor expressly provides for the disposition of the trust property in the event of the failure of the charitable use to which he in the first instance directed that it be devoted.[76] But a mere general residuary clause, even if the residuary gift is to charity, does not prevent the use of the cy pres doctrine.[77] The so-called community trusts established in many large cities give power to the managers to vary the original purposes of any gift, when circumstances make a change expedient.[78]

The cy pres doctrine is applied by equity to absolute gifts to charitable corporations or associations, as well as to trusts for charity. Thus, if a gift is made to a home for the blind at a certain city, but at the time the will goes into effect there is no such institution there or in the neighborhood called by the name used, the court will readily apply the funds to aid other institutions intended to relieve and help blind persons.[79]

In order to bring cy pres into action a suit should be begun by the trustees, making the Attorney General of the state a party, as the representative of the people of the state. The

---

[72] King v. Banks, 220 Ala. 274, 124 So. 871.

[73] See p. 296, ante.

[74] Women's Christian Ass'n v. Kansas City, 147 Mo. 103, 48 S.W. 960.

[75] Lakatong Lodge, No. 114, of Quakertown, etc., v. Board of Education of Franklin Tp., 84 N.J.Eq. 112, 92 A. 870.

[76] Larkin v. Wikoff, 75 N.J.Eq. 462,

72 A. 98, 79 A. 365, affirmed 77 N.J. Eq. 589, 78 A. 1134.

[77] Attorney General v. Briggs, 164 Mass. 561, 42 N.E. 118.

[78] See Hayes, Trust Companies, April, 1929, p. 617.

[79] Goree v. Georgia Industrial Home, 187 Ga. 368, 200 S.E. 684; New York City Miss. Soc. v. Board of Pensions of Presbyterian Church, 261 App.Div. 823, 24 N.Y.S.2d 395.

court will, if it finds conditions appropriate for cy pres, refer the matter to a master to take evidence and recommend a substitute scheme for the charity, and the report of the master will be the basis for action by the court.[80]

THE RULE AGAINST REMOTENESS OF VESTING

87. With one exception the rule against remoteness of vesting applies to the vesting of gifts in trust for charity or to charitable corporations and to gifts following charitable trusts. The gift must vest within lives in being and twenty-one years.

The exception exists in the case of a gift to or in trust for one charity, followed by a gift to or in trust for a second charity, to take effect on the happening of a certain event. The event need not be one sure to occur within a time measured by lives in being and twenty-one years, but may be limited to happen at any time.

The statement is frequently found in the decisions that the rule against perpetuities does not apply to charitable trusts. "It is common knowledge that the rule as to perpetuities does not apply to property given to charities."[81] But, for the reason that "the rule against perpetuities" is an ambiguous phrase, these statements have been provocative of much confusion of thought. In some instances the rule against perpetuities means, to the court using it, the rule against remoteness; in other cases it means a rule against suspending the power of alienation. As has been well said by a Maine court:[82] "The statement is often found in the books that the law against perpetuities does not apply to public charities. But the statement is misleading. It is undoubtedly true that the principle of public policy, which declares that estates shall not be *indefinitely inalienable* in the hands of individuals, is held inapplicable to public charities. But it must be remembered that the rule against perpetuities, in its proper legal sense, has relation only to the time of the vesting of an estate, and in no way affects its continuance after it is once vested."

With respect to the application of the rule against too remote vesting to charitable trusts, four main situations may arise: (1)

---

[80] Bruce v. Maxwell, 311 Ill. 479, 143 N.E. 82; Jackson v. Phillips, 14 Allen, Mass., 539.

[81] Lindley, L. J., in In re Tyler, [1891] 3 Ch. 252, 257. See, also, Trustees of New Castle Common v. Megginson, 1 Boyce, Del., 361, 77 A. 565, 570, Ann.Cas.1914A, 1207; Bauer v. Myers, C.C.A.Kan., 244 F. 902, 157 C.C.A. 252.

[82] Whitehouse, J., in Brooks v. City of Belfast, 90 Me. 318, 324, 38 A. 222.

There may be a gift to or in trust for charity, followed by a gift over to a private person; (2) there may be a gift to a private person, followed by a gift to or in trust for charitable uses to take effect upon certain conditions; (3) an instrument may provide for the vesting of property in a trustee for charitable purposes at a future time; (4) provision may be made for a gift to or in trust for one charity which is to end on the happening of certain events, the property then to be given to or held for the benefit of another charity, either by the same trustee, or by a new trustee.[83]

The first problem suggested above is illustrated by the case of In re Bowen.[84] In that case property was given in trust to establish schools in certain parishes; but if the government should at any time establish a general system of education, the charitable trust was to end and the property to go over to certain private persons. The gift over might take effect at any time in the future. The vesting of the property in the private persons was not certain to occur at a time measured by lives in being and twenty-one years. That the gift over followed a charitable trust was no reason why the ordinary rule against remoteness should not be followed. This is the view taken by those American courts which have considered the question.[85]

In the second instance suggested, namely, that of a gift to an individual, followed by a gift over to charity to vest at a future day, the courts are likewise unanimous in holding that the charitable gift must vest at a time which satisfies the rule against remoteness, or it will be void.[86] Thus, in Village of Brattleboro v.

[83] The application of the rule against remoteness to charitable trusts has been learnedly and thoroughly discussed by the late Professor Gray in his Rule against Perpetuities, 3d Ed., §§ 589–628. On the English cases see Sanger, Remoteness and Charitable Gifts, 29 Yale Law J. 46.

[84] [1893] 2 Ch. 491.

[85] Starr v. Minister and Trustees of Starr Methodist Protestant Church, 112 Md. 171, 76 A. 595; Proprietors of Church in Brattle Square v. Grant, 3 Gray, Mass., 142, 63 Am. Dec. 725; Wells v. Heath, 10 Gray, Mass., 17; Society for Promoting Theological Education v. Attorney General, 135 Mass. 285; Rolfe & Rumford Asylum v. Lefebre, 69 N.H. 238, 45 A. 1087. But if the provision is merely that the charitable trust is to end upon the happening of a certain contingency and that the property is then to revert to the settlor's next of kin, this possibility of reverter is not void under the rule against remoteness, even though it may take effect at a time not measured by lives in being and twenty-one years. Hopkins v. Grimshaw, 165 U.S. 342, 17 S. Ct. 401, 41 L.Ed. 739.

[86] Attorney General v. Gill, 2 P. Wms. 369; Merritt v. Bucknam, 77 Me. 253; Merrill v. American Bap-

Mead,[87] the gift was to the testator's son absolutely, with a provision that, if the testator's heirs should fail at any time in the future, the property should be used for the establishment of an industrial school in the village of Brattleboro. It was held that the gift for the school was void as too remote, since the vesting of it was not measured by the period fixed by the rule against remoteness. In this respect it is evident that the rule against remoteness makes no exception of charitable trusts.

In the third division of cases are those in which a gift to a trustee for charity is made, the gift to vest at a future time, but no gift of the intermediate interest in the property is made. This class of cases is illustrated by Girard Trust Co. v. Russell.[88] The settlor in that case provided for the accumulation of the income of a certain fund until it was equal to the debt of the state of Pennsylvania. At that time it was to be paid to the treasurer of the state, to be held by him in trust for the payment of the state debt. The gift in trust to pay off the state debt was a charitable trust of the governmental variety. But its date of vesting was not measured according to the rule against remoteness. The charitable trust might begin at any time in the future. It was held that the trust was void, as conflicting with the rule against remoteness. Such is the general rule.[89] But a gift to a charitable corporation to be formed in the future may escape the rule against remoteness by the application of the cy pres doctrine.[90] And courts are apt to hold that the gift vested in charity at once and that the provision for management by a corporation in the future was merely one as to methods of administration and not as to vesting of the property in charity.[91]

---

tist Missionary Union, 73 N.H. 414, 62 A. 647, 3 L.R.A.,N.S., 1143, 111 Am.St.Rep. 632, 6 Ann.Cas. 646; Leonard v. Burr, 18 N.Y. 96; Smith v. Townsend, 32 Pa. 434; In re Penrose's Estate, 257 Pa. 231, 101 A. 319.

[87] 43 Vt. 556.

[88] C.C.A.Pa., 179 F. 446, 102 C.C.A. 592.

[89] Chamberlayne v. Brockett, 1872, 8 Ch.App. 206; Jocelyn v. Nott, 44 Conn. 55; Washburn v. Acome, 74 Misc. 301, 131 N.Y.S. 963, affirmed 151 App.Div. 948, 136 N.Y.S. 1150; In re Galland's Estate, 103 Wash. 106, 173 P. 740 (semble). *Contra:* French v. Calkins, 252 Ill. 243, 96 N.E. 877; Franklin v. Hastings, 253 Ill. 46, 97 N.E. 265, Ann.Cas.1913A 135.

[90] Gray, Rule against Perpetuities, 3rd Ed., § 608 et seq.

[91] Ould v. Washington Hospital, 95 U.S. 303, 24 L.Ed. 450; Crerar v. Williams, 145 Ill. 625, 34 N.E. 497, 21 L.R.A. 454; Matter of Juillard's Estate, 238 N.Y. 499, 144 N.E. 772; Hunter's Estate, In re, 279 Pa. 349, 123 A. 865.

The only case in which the rule against remoteness makes an exception regarding charitable trusts is in the fourth class mentioned above. Where a provision is made for the transfer of property from one charity to another at a future time, the rule does not apply. The possible remoteness of the event is not important. Thus, in Christ's Hospital v. Grainger [92] property was given in 1624 to the town of Reading, in trust for the poor of the town, with a clause that, if the town neglected to perform the trust, the property should go over to London in trust for Christ's Hospital. The court held that the devise over was not objectionable, saying: "In this case there is a gift in trust for one charity, and, on the happening of a certain contingency, a gift in trust for another charity. There is no more perpetuity created by giving property to two charities, in that form, than by giving it to one. The evil meant to be guarded against by the rule of law against perpetuities is the making of the property inalienable." This view has been generally accepted in England and America.[93]

The reason for this exception to the rule in favor of charities seems to be that where the remote gift over is to a charity the inalienability of the property is not in any way increased. Property held to charitable uses is for all practical purposes inalienable—is withdrawn from commerce. The addition of a provision for a remote gift over, thus making the title uncertain and incapable of absolute alienation, does not render the property inalienable, for it is already so.

Some courts have given as a reason for the exception that the tying up of property through two charitable trusts is no more objectionable than the restriction of the property by means of one charitable trust.[94]

---

[92] 16 Sim. 83.

[93] In re Tyler, [1891] 3 Ch. 252; Jones v. Habersham, 107 U.S. 174, 2 S.Ct. 336, 27 L.Ed. 401; Brigham v. Peter Bent Brigham Hospital, C.C.A. Mass., 134 F. 513, 67 C.C.A. 393; Storrs Agr. School v. Whitney, 54 Conn. 342, 8 A. 141; MacKenzie v. Trustees of Presbytery of Jersey City, 67 N.J.Eq. 652, 61 A. 1027, 3 L.R.A., N.S., 227; Almy v. Jones, 17 R.I. 265, 21 A. 616, 12 L.R.A. 414; Webster v. Wiggin, 19 R.I. 73, 31 A. 824, 28 L.R. A. 510.

[94] Jones v. Habersham, 107 U.S. 174, 185, 2 S.Ct. 336, 27 L.Ed. 401; Storrs Agr. School v. Whitney, 54 Conn. 342, 345, 8 A. 141.

THE RULE AGAINST RESTRAINTS ON ALIENATION

88. It is of the essence of charitable trusts that the principal fund be kept intact and that the duration of the trust be indefinite. In those states which have as their rule against perpetuities the rule that the power of alienating property cannot be restrained for an undue length of time it is universally held that such rule has no application to charitable trusts and that by means of a charitable trust the power of alienating real or personal property may be indefinitely suspended.

As has been previously noted,[95] the rule against perpetuities in many states is not a rule against remoteness, but is a rule that the power of alienating property cannot be suspended longer than a given period. In some states the period is two lives in being; in others, any number of lives in being. In the states which have this form of the rule against perpetuities it is held without exception that the rule has no application to charitable trusts.[96] The charitable trust does naturally result in suspending the power of alienating the property which is subject to the trust. The trustees are expected to retain the principal fund intact and use the income for the carrying out of the charitable purposes of the settlor. The trust results in withdrawing from commerce a certain fund of money or certain other property. But the desirability of encouraging trusts which make for the general benefit of mankind offsets the dislike which the courts and legislators have of suspension of the power of alienating property. The settlor is allowed to suspend the power of alienation of the property involved, so long as he does it for the benefit of the public.

[95] See page 72.

[96] Cal.Const. art. 20, § 9; Chew v. First Presbyterian Church of Wilmington, Del., D.C.,Del., 237 F. 219; In re Coleman's Estate, 167 Cal. 212, 138 P. 992, Ann.Cas.1915C, 682; Phillips v. Heldt, 33 Ind.App. 388, 71 N.E. 520; Dykeman v. Jenkines, 179 Ind. 549, 101 N.E. 1013, Ann.Cas. 1915D, 1011; Wilson v. First Nat. Bank of Independence, 164 Iowa 402, 145 N.W. 948, Ann.Cas.1916D, 481; Penny v. Croul, 76 Mich. 471, 43 N.W. 649, 5 L.R.A. 858; Lounsbury v. Trustees of Square Lake Burial Ass'n, 170 Mich. 645, 129 N.W. 36; In re Brown's Estate, 198 Mich. 544, 165 N.W. 929; Mich.Ann.St. §§ 26.1191, 26.1201; Allen v. Stevens, 161 N.Y. 122, 55 N.E. 568; Decker v. Vreeland, 170 App.Div. 234, 156 N.Y.S. 442; Brown v. Brown, 7 Or. 285; Lightfoot v. Poindexter, Tex.Civ.App., 199 S.W. 1152; Staines v. Burton, 17 Utah 331, 53 P. 1015, 70 Am.St.Rep. 788; Harrington v. Pier, 105 Wis. 485, 82 N.W. 345, 50 L.R.A. 307, 76 Am.St.Rep. 924; Danforth v. City of Oshkosh, 119 Wis. 262, 97 N.W. 258; In re Kavanaugh's Will, 143 Wis. 90, 126 N.W. 672, 28 L.R.A.,N.S., 470; Williams v. City of Oconomowoc, 167 Wis. 281, 166 N.W. 322; Wis.St.1941, § 230.15.

THE RULE AGAINST ACCUMULATIONS

89. The leading American view is that accumulations for charity are subject to the control of equity, and will be allowed when reasonable and not prejudicial to the best interests of society. In England and several states the matter is now controlled by statute.

Attention has previously been directed to the so-called rule against accumulations, which provides that the income of property shall not be accumulated, except for a restricted period and in some states for the benefit of certain persons.[97] An important question is whether this rule applies with equal force to private trusts and charitable trusts. May a settlor direct that the income of property be accumulated for the benefit of a charity with any greater freedom than he may provide for accumulations for his own children? May a testator decree that half the income of the property given to charity shall be accumulated and added perpetually to the principal? Varying answers have been given to these questions by the several courts which have considered them.

In England accumulations for charity were originally affected only by the rule against remoteness and the rule that the cestui of a vested interest could demand a termination of the trust and management of his own property by himself. If the ownership of the accumulations was not vested, provision must be made for the vesting of the accumulations within lives in being and twenty-one years.[98] If the accumulations were vested in a charity, that charity could call for their payment to it and for an ignoring of the accumulation provision.[99] The Law of Property Act of 1925 permits accumulations for charity for not more than twenty-one years.[1]

The question was given careful consideration in St. Paul's Church v. Attorney General.[2] The court said: "In regard to this matter, one of three rules must be true: The accumulation must be valid forever; or it may be controlled by the court within reasonable and desirable bounds; or it must be subject to the same rules as an accumulation for private purposes. There

---

[97] See § 73, ante.

[98] Martin v. Margham, 14 Sim. 230; In re Monk, 1927, 2 Ch. 197.

[99] Wharton v. Masterman, 1895 A.C. 186.

[1] § 164; Berry v. Geen, 1938 A.C. 575; In re Blake, 1937, 1 Ch. 325.

[2] 164 Mass. 188, 203, 204, 41 N.E. 231.

is good reason to suppose that the rule last named should not apply, for, if the object is not subject to the rule against perpetuities, there is no good reason why an accumulation for that object should be. It certainly would be as much the policy of the law to favor an accumulation for charitable objects as to favor charitable objects. It often happens that the charitable purpose cannot be carried out without accumulation of a fund, sometimes for a long period of time. There are also good objections to a compulsory perpetual accumulation even for a charitable purpose. Much would depend on the terms under which the accumulation was to be made. There would be great public danger in allowing an accumulation indefinitely for a charitable purpose that was not to be carried out within some definite time. Such a purpose would be practically no charitable purpose at all. On the other hand, however, there are cases where the income from property might be directed to be accumulated to form a fund, the income of which fund was to be annually applied to charitable purposes, as in the case at bar. Such an accumulation, it is evident, is less objectionable, as the income from the accumulating fund is constantly being applied to the charity year by year in larger amount. There seems to be no more objection to such an accumulation than to the holding of property constantly increasing in value for the benefit of the charity. We are of opinion, however, that the proper course is to hold that the limits of an accumulation for the benefit of charity are subject to the order of a court of equity. By this method of solving the difficulty, on the one hand an unreasonable and unnecessary trust for accumulation can be restrained, and on the other hand a reasonable accumulation can be allowed to carry out the intention of the benefactor and to secure the accomplishment of the trust in the best manner."

This view, that the limit of the accumulation for charity will be prescribed by the court of equity in each individual case, has been followed in Massachusetts and also adopted in Connecticut.[3]

3 Codman v. Brigham, 187 Mass. 309, 72 N.E. 1008, 105 Am.St.Rep. 394; Ripley v. Brown, 218 Mass. 33, 105 N.E. 637; Collector of Taxes of Norton v. Oldfield, 219 Mass. 374, 106 N.E. 1014; Frazier v. Merchants Nat. Bank of Salem, 296 Mass. 298, 5 N.E.2d 550; Brigham v. Peter Bent Brigham Hospital, C.C.A.Mass., 134 F. 513, 67 C.C.A. 393; Woodruff v. Marsh, 63 Conn. 125, 26 Atl. 846, 38 Am.St.Rep. 346; Duggan v. Slocum, C.C.Conn., 92 F. 806, 34 C.C.A. 676. See, also, Girard Trust Co. v. Russell, C.C.A.Pa., 179 F. 446, 452, 102 C.C.A. 592.

See, also, Perkins v. Citizens & Southern Nat. Bank, 190 Ga. 29, 8 S.E.2d 28; Conway v. Third Nat. Bk. & Tr. Co. of Camden, 119 N.J.

Thus, in Woodruff v. Marsh,[4] where the testator had given $400,000 to trustees to establish a children's home, he directed that $10,000 of the income of this $400,000 should be accumulated annually and added to the principal for a period of one hundred years. This was held by the Connecticut court to be a reasonable accumulation for charity.

In New York it has been held that the general statute relative to accumulations, which prohibits accumulations except during a minority for the benefit of a minor, applies to charitable trusts, and that a provision for the accumulation of the income of a fund for the benefit of a charitable corporation, pending the organization of that corporation, is invalid.[5] But by statute limited exceptions are made.[6] An accumulation may be directed to occur until a sufficient sum is raised to accomplish a given charitable object, and the sufficiency of the sum is to be determined by the regents of the University of the State of New York. Likewise an accumulation to make up a deficiency in the capital sum is allowed, and an accumulation may be provided for as to the income of not more than one-fourth of a gift in trust for education (the sum not to exceed $50,000), the accumulation to continue till the sum has been raised to $100,000; and an exception is also made of trusts for employees.

In Pennsylvania and Wisconsin accumulations of income for charitable purposes are governed to some extent by the Legislature.[7]

Eq. 575, 182 A. 916; Penick v. Bank of Wadesboro, 218 N.C. 686, 12 S.E.2d 253; Schreiner v. Cincinnati Altenheim, 61 Ohio App. 344, 22 N.E.2d 587.

[4] 63 Conn. 125, 26 A. 846, 38 Am. St.Rep. 346.

[5] St. John v. Andrews Institute for Girls, 191 N.Y. 254, 83 N.E. 981, 14 Ann.Cas. 708.

[6] Real Property Law, § 61; Personal Property Law, § 16.

[7] Pa. 20 P.S. § 3251 (general exception made for charities); Wis.St. 1941, § 230.37 (accumulations of realty limited to a minority, except that it may occur for twenty one years for a literary or charitable corporation).

The Illinois Thellusson Act seems to apply to accumulations for charity. Summers v. Chicago Title & Trust Co., 335 Ill. 564, 167 N.E. 777; Webb v. Webb, 340 Ill. 407, 172 N.E. 730, 71 A.L.R. 404. An exception is made of cemetery upkeep trusts. Ill. Smith-Hurd Stats. c. 21, §§ 21, 60.

DURATION OF CHARITABLE TRUSTS

90. In all jurisdictions it is lawful to provide for charitable trusts of indefinite or perpetual duration.

That a charitable trust may be perpetual or of indefinite duration, no matter to what extent the trustees are prohibited from alienating the trust property, is not doubted. The social advantages of trusts for charity more than offset the disadvantages of permitting a donor to make provisions for his property far into the future and of allowing him to fix the status of the property indefinitely.[8]

OTHER STATUTORY RESTRICTIONS ON CHARITABLE TRUSTS [9]

91. In some states limitations upon the rights of the settlor of a charitable trust will be found in three classes of statutes, namely:

(a) Acts restricting the amount of property which a charitable corporation may hold or prohibiting it from taking certain property;

(b) Laws declaring void gifts to charity made within a brief period before the death of the donor;

(c) Statutes prohibiting the giving of more than a certain part of the testator's fortune to charity, when such testator leaves near relatives.

Certain statutes, which place restrictions upon a settlor of a charitable trust and often render such trust invalid, deserve brief consideration here. They have to do with the capacity of corporations to receive gifts for charitable uses and with the power of a testator to give property to charity.

In the first place, if the charitable gift is to be made to a corporation, the settlor should ascertain that the corporation has capacity to take the property which he intends to give to it. The general laws of the state or the charter of the corporation may prevent the corporation from taking the property which

---

[8] Dexter v. Gardner, 7 Allen, Mass., 243; Farmers' & Merchants' Bank of Jamesport v. Robinson, 96 Mo.App. 385, 70 S.W. 372; Smart v. Town of Durham, 77 N.H. 56, 86 A. 821; Hilliard v. Parker, 76 N.J.Eq. 447, 74 A. 447; Stanly v. McGowen, 37 N.C., 2 Ired.Eq., 9; In re Smith's Estate, 181 Pa. 109, 37 A. 114; Young v. St. Mark's Lutheran Church, 200 Pa. 332, 49 A. 887; Franklin v. Armfield, 2 Sneed, Tenn., 305.

[9] Restatement, Trusts, § 362.

he desires to give to it. This class of statutes is illustrated by the case of In re McGraw's Estate.[10] A testatrix made a gift to Cornell University, to be held by it for library purposes. That corporation was, by its charter, restricted to holding property not to exceed $3,000,000 in value. The gift in question was declared void, because the University already held property in excess of the value named in the charter. The court held that the next of kin of the testatrix might raise the question of the invalidity of the gift, and that that right did not rest in the state of New York alone. Upon this latter point, namely, that as to the right to contest the validity of a gift to a corporation on the ground of its lack of capacity, there is a difference of opinion; the prevailing view being opposed to that of the New York court, and being that only the state involved is entitled to attack the gift on such ground.[11]

It is also not infrequent that a statute prohibits certain corporations from taking land under a charitable trust or outright, or requires that the corporation be expressly authorized to take property.[12]

A second class of statutes has placed limitations upon the intending charitable settlor by declaring void gifts made to charitable uses a short time before the death of the donor. The theory of such laws is that gifts made to charity on the threshold of death are apt to be made without due consideration, in an unnatural state of mind, and often under undue influence. The Pennsylvania statute is a good illustration. It provides: "No estate, real or personal, shall be bequeathed or devised to any body politic, or to any person in trust for religious or charitable uses, except the same be done by will at least thirty days before the decease of the testator, which period shall be so computed as to exclude the first and include the last day thereof; and all dispositions of property contrary hereto, shall be void and go

---

[10] 111 N.Y. 66, 19 N.E. 233, 2 L.R.A. 387, affirmed Cornell University v. Fiske, 136 U.S. 152, 10 S.Ct. 775, 34 L.Ed. 427.

[11] Brigham v. Peter Bent Brigham Hospital, 134 F. 513, 67 C.C.A. 393; Hewitt v. Wheeler School & Library, 82 Conn. 188, 72 A. 935; Francis v. Preachers' Aid Soc., 149 Iowa 158, 126 N.W. 1027; Farrington v. Putnam, 90 Me. 405, 37 A. 652, 38 L.R.A. 339; Chase v. Dickey, 212 Mass. 555, 99 N.E. 410; In re Kortright's Estate, 237 Pa. 143, 85 A. 111; Heiskell v. Chickasaw Lodge, 87 Tenn. 668, 11 S.W. 825, 4 L.R.A. 699.

[12] Gould v. Board of Home Missions of Presbyterian Church, 102 Neb. 526, 167 N.W. 776; N.Y.Decedent Estate Law, § 12.

to the residuary legatee or devisee, next of kin or heirs, according to law."[13]

Still a third class of restricting statutes is illustrated by the laws of New York: "No person having a husband, wife, child, or descendant, or parent, shall, by his or her last will and testament, devise or bequeath to any benevolent, charitable, literary, scientific, religious or missionary society, association or corporation or purpose, in trust or otherwise, more than one-half part of his or her estate, after the payment of his or her debts, and such devise or bequest shall be valid to the extent of one-half, and no more. The validity of a devise or bequest for more than such one-half may be tested only by a surviving husband, wife, child, descendant or parent. When payment of a devise or bequest to such society, association, corporation or purpose is postponed, in computing the one-half part of such society, association, corporation or purpose, no allowance may be made for such postponement or for any interest or gains which may accrue after the testator's death." [14]

The limitations upon one intending to become the settlor of a charitable trust are obvious. The statutes of the state concerned should be consulted, to learn whether the Legislature has required that the gift be made a certain time before the death of the donor, or whether there is a prohibition placed upon the giving of more than a certain proportion of the testator's fortune. An excessive gift to charity will be void only as to the excess and only the relatives protected by the statute can raise an objection to the size of the gift to charity.[15]

---

[13] Pa. 20 P.S. § 195. See, also, Cal. Probate Code, §§ 41–43; D.C.Code 1929, T. 29, § 42; Ga.Code 1933, § 113-107; Idaho Code 1932, § 14-326; Miss.Code 1930, § 3565; Mont.Rev. Codes 1935, § 7015; Ohio Gen.Code, § 10504-5.

[14] New York Decedent Estate Law, § 17 as amended by L.1929, c. 229, and L.1927, c. 502, and L.1923, c. 301.

For similar provisions, see Cal. Probate Code §§ 41–43 (one-third); Ga.Code 1933, § 113-107, as amended by L.1937, No. 108 (one-third but does not apply to estates over $200,000); Idaho Code 1932, § 14-326 (one-third); Iowa Code 1939, § 11848 (one-fourth); Mont.Rev.Codes 1935, § 7015 (one-third); Miss.Code 1930, § 3565 (one-third).

[15] Karolusson v. Paonessa, 207 Iowa 127, 222 N.W. 431; Unger v. Loewy, 236 N.Y. 73, 140 N.E. 201.

CHAPTER 9

THE POWERS OF THE TRUSTEE—IN GENERAL

Sec.
92. Express and Implied Powers.
93. Discretionary and Imperative Powers.
94. Personal Powers and Powers Attached to the Office of Trustee.
95. Exercise of Powers by Co-Trustees.
96. Delegation of Trust Powers.
97. Notice of Trustee's Powers.

EXPRESS AND IMPLIED POWERS [1]

92. A trustee's powers are said to be "express" if they are granted to him in the trust instrument or by statute in clear, direct language. They are called "implied" if they are not set forth in the trust instrument in so many words, but are deemed by equity to have been intended by the settlor as necessary to the accomplishment of his trust purposes.

In well drawn trust instrument a large number of powers of the trustee are stated.[2] Thus, the trustee is often given a power to sell the original trust property, to invest the proceeds of any property sold, or to collect the income of the trust property and pay it over to the beneficiaries. These powers are called "express powers" because they are expressly or directly granted to the trustee.[3] Their existence is not left to any inference or implication. They are clearly stated. Express powers may also be granted to a trustee by the legislature, as when a statute provides that trustees may sell real property under certain conditions.[4]

But the fact that a certain power is not set forth in the trust instrument or in any applicable statute does not prove that the power in question does not rest in the trustee. Thus, often no power to sell the original trust property is contained in the will or deed which creates the trust, and yet a sale is so convenient and important in bringing about the results which the settlor had

---

[1] Restatement, Trusts, §§ 186–196.

[2] For a detailed statement of powers which may be granted to a trustee see Stephenson, Clauses Recommended for Grant of Maximum Discretionary Powers to a Trustee, published by the Trust Research Department, Graduate School of Banking, American Bankers' Association; reprinted in Bogert's Cases on Trusts, p. 866.

[3] For cases illustrating the grant of express powers, see §§ 121, 124, 127, post, dealing with powers to sell, mortgage and lease.

[4] See § 122, post.

in mind that the court finds that such power is given to the trustee.⁵ Such powers are "implied." The intent of the settlor to have his trustee vested with such powers is inferred or implied because without them the trustee could not do the work which the settlor directed him to do. Thus, if a settlor leaves improved real estate to a trustee, with a direction to collect the income of it and pay it over to his children for their support, and the instrument contains no power to lease the realty, one may easily be implied, since that is the normal way of getting income from improved real estate.⁶

Where express powers are named in the trust instrument, the trustee should follow specifically the directions there given.⁷ If express power to do an act is not given, the trustee will have implied power to do such act, if it is reasonably necessary for the execution of the trust. "Where a trustee conforms with the provisions of the trust in their true spirit and meaning, he has authority 'to adopt measures and to do acts which, though not specified in the instrument, are implied in its general directions, and are reasonable and proper means for making them effectual.' " ⁸

DISCRETIONARY AND IMPERATIVE POWERS ⁹

93. A trustee's powers are "discretionary" if he is given the option of using the power or declining to use it, and are called "imperative" or "mandatory" when the trustee has a duty to exercise the power as soon as possible or when a given event happens.

A court of equity will order a trustee to use an imperative power, if he fails to exercise it; but the court will not compel the trustee to act in any particular way under a discretionary power unless there has been a clear abuse of that discretion by the trustee.

A settlor may leave to the judgment of his trustee the question whether a certain act should be done or not, in order to carry out the trust. The power to do the act in such a case is called a "discretionary" power, because it rests in the discretion of the

---

⁵ Vansant v. Spillman, 193 Ky. 788, 237 S.W. 379; Robinson v. Robinson, 105 Me. 68, 72 A. 883, 32 L.R.A.,N.S., 675, 134 Am.St.Rep. 537; Parker v. Seeley, 56 N.J.Eq. 110, 38 A. 280.

⁶ Hutcheson v. Hodnett, 115 Ga. 990, 42 S.E. 422; City of Richmond v. Davis, 103 Ind. 449, 3 N.E. 130.

⁷ Clark v. Maguire, 16 Mo. 302; Price v. Methodist Episcopal Church, 4 Ohio 515; Haldeman v. Openheimer, 103 Tex. 275, 126 S.W. 566; Atkinson v. Beckett, 34 W.Va. 584, 12 S.E. 717.

⁸ Kipp v. O'Melveny, 2 Cal.App. 142, 144, 83 P. 264, 265.

⁹ Restatement, Trusts, §§ 186, 187.

trustee whether the act is done or not. For example, if a settlor creates a trust for his widow and directs that the income be paid to her and also that such part of the principal be paid to her as in the judgment of the trustee is desirable, the power to pay principal is a discretionary power. It may or it may not be exercised according to the trustee's decision.[10]

But a settlor may intend that the trustee shall in any event perform a certain act in the course of his administration, and so the settlor may direct the trustee to do the act in question. The trustee's power to perform this act is called "imperative" or "mandatory". For example, if the settlor directs the trustee to sell his real property as soon as possible, and invest the proceeds in bonds, the power to sell is an imperative one. There is a duty as well as a power.[11]

If the trustee fails to use his *imperative* powers at the time required by the trust instrument, he is guilty of a breach of trust, and one of the remedies available to the beneficiary is to procure from the court an order that the trustee exercise the power in question.[12] Conceivably the court might give other relief, as, for example, remove the trustee and appoint one who would be willing to do the act in question.

If, however, the trustee fails to take advantage of a *discretionary* power, the attitude of the court is different. The court holds that the discretion has been left to the trustee and not to the court. If the trustee has honestly used his judgment and decided not to do the act, the court will not compel him to do so, even though the court might have decided differently if the discretion has been that of the court. Thus, if there is a discretionary power to pay over the capital of the trust, and the trustee decides that it would not be in the best interest of the beneficiary that this be done, the court will not decree otherwise, if the court believes the trustee has decided the question fairly and after due consideration.[13]

Occasionally, however, the court finds that the trustee has not acted in good faith and with due consideration of the purposes of

---

[10] For examples, see Whitaker v. McDowell, 82 Conn. 195, 72 A. 938, 16 Ann.Cas. 324; Safe Deposit & Trust Co. v. Sutro, 75 Md. 361, 23 A. 732.

[11] For examples, see Williams v. Gardner, 90 Conn. 461, 97 A. 854;

Osborne v. Gordon, 86 Wis. 92, 56 N. W. 334.

[12] See § 149, post.

[13] In re Sam's Estate, 219 Iowa 374, 258 N.W. 682; Wight v. Mason, 134 Me. 52, 180 A. 917.

the trust, but has rather acted arbitrarily, in bad faith, or from other improper motives. In such cases the court may well order the trustee to use the power, or may appoint a new trustee. Thus, if a trustee has discretionary power to pay the widow of the settlor such part of the income of the trust as he thinks necessary for her comfortable support, and the trust produces $5,000 annual income, and the widow is an invalid needing special medical care and hospitalization, but the trustee refuses to provide such care and pays out only $1,000 a year to the widow, the court would almost certainly find an abuse of discretion and direct a larger payment.[14]

PERSONAL POWERS AND POWERS ATTACHED TO THE OFFICE OF TRUSTEE [15]

94. Powers of a trustee are personal when the settlor expresses an intention that only the trustee named may exercise the power. They are attached to the office when the settlor indicates an intent that the power shall be exercisable by any trustee who is in charge of the trust at any time.

If powers are attached to a trusteeship, they pass to successors of the original trustees and may also be exercised by surviving trustees; but if the powers are personal, and appear to have been granted to one or more trustees alone, successors and surviving trustees are not entitled to exercise such powers.

Questions relating to the powers of trustees may also arise because the trustees are not the original trustees, but are successors appointed by the court or otherwise. Do successors have the same powers expressly and impliedly given to their predecessors? They do when these powers were not personal to the trustees, but were attached to the office only. A quotation from a Maryland case states the attitude of the courts of equity clearly: "It is the well-settled law of this state that 'if it appears that the power lodged with the trustees in connection with the trust is a special confidence in a particular trustee or set of trustees, or is to be exercised only upon his or their personal judgment and discretion, such power can only be exercised by the designated donees, and will not pass to a substituted trustee. On the other hand, if it appears that the power is annexed to the office of trustee for the purposes of the trust, and to promote its objects, then

---

[14] Strawn v. Caffee, 235 Ala. 218, 178 So. 430.

[15] Restatement, Trusts, §§ 195, 196.

it will pass with the trust to the successors of the original trustee, and can be exercised by them.'" [16]

It is "purely a matter of intention, to be gathered from a consideration of the whole will and from the nature and objects of the trust created thereby, as to whether a trust is personal in its character or is annexed to the office of trustee." [17] It has been held that, "in the absence of a clearly expressed intent to the contrary, the power of *sale* conferred upon a trustee in a will is regarded as a ministerial duty, annexed to the office, and passing to any person lawfully substituted in the place of the original trustee." [18]

Thus, the power conferred upon a trustee to collect the rents and profits of property and use the income for the care and education of a daughter until she was 30, and pay her such part of the principal as he might think best after the daughter's marriage, is a power annexed to the office of the trustee, and passes to a substituted trustee; [19] while a trust empowering the trustee "and any successor appointed by him" to sell the property confers on such officer a personal trust, not capable of exercise by a successor appointed by the court.[20] Whether any particular power is personal or annexed to the office can only be told from a careful scrutiny of the trust instrument and surrounding cir-

---

[16] Maryland Casualty Co. v. Safe Deposit & Trust Co. of Baltimore, 115 Md. 339, 344, 80 A. 903, 905, Ann. Cas.1913A, 1279.

[17] Dodge v. Dodge, 109 Md. 164, 166, 71 A. 519, 521, 130 Am.St.Rep. 503. Where a settlor gives trustees power to name a trust company as their successor and gives it certain discretionary powers in case of such selection, and the trustees vacate, but do not appoint a successor, if the court appoints the trust company, it will have the discretionary powers named by the settlor. Stein v. Safe Deposit & Trust Co. of Baltimore, 127 Md. 206, 96 A. 349.

[18] Dodge v. Dodge, 109 Md. 164, 71 A. 519, 130 Am.St.Rep. 503. See, also, Shillinglaw v. Peterson, 184 Iowa 276, 167 N.W. 709.

[19] Jacobs v. Wilmington Trust Co., 9 Del.Ch. 400, 80 A. 346. And so a power to inquire into the status of the beneficiary at a stated time and pay him a portion of the corpus, if advisable, has been held to be an imperative power which passed to a successor. Williams v. Gardner, 90 Conn. 461, 97 A. 854. See, also, Jackson v. Matthews, 133 Md. 282, 105 A. 146; Newport Trust Co. v. Chappell, 40 R.I. 383, 101 A. 323. *Contra:* Singleton v. Cuttino, 105 S.C. 44, 89 S.E. 385.

[20] United States Trust Co. v. Poutch, 130 Ky. 241, 113 S.W. 107. See, also, Chandler v. Chandler, 111 Miss. 525, 71 So. 811. Where the power of sale is a mere incident for the convenient administration of the trust, and the settlor does not expressly require the union of all trustees in the exercise of the power, a remaining trustee may sell the property. Striker v. Daly, 223 N.Y. 468, 119 N.E. 882.

cumstances, for the purpose of learning the settlor's intent.[21] Since personal powers are very disadvantageous to trust administration when trustees die or resign, and since the settlor probably desires any powers given to be used at any time throughout the trust, personal powers are rarely decreed to exist, and the courts strongly incline to find that the settlor intended the powers to be attached to the office.[22]

Surviving trustees, after the death, resignation, or removal of one or more trustees, are ordinarily vested with the same powers as were possessed by the original set of trustees.[23] If the change in the trusteeship has occurred through death, as previously pointed out, the survivors take the entire property and trust powers by survivorship, on account of the joint tenancy under which they hold. In certain rare cases the powers of the trustees are purely personal, and the death or removal of one member of the board makes it impossible for the powers to be exer-

[21] In the following cases the power was held personal and not capable of exercise by a successor: Security Co. v. Snow, 70 Conn. 288, 39 A. 153, 66 Am.St.Rep. 107; Whitaker v. McDowell, 82 Conn. 195, 72 A. 938, 16 Ann.Cas. 324; Luquire v. Lee, 121 Ga. 624, 49 S.E. 834; French v. Northern Trust Co., 197 Ill. 30, 64 N.E. 105; Snyder v. Safe-Deposit & Trust Co., 93 Md. 225, 48 A. 719; De Lashmutt v. Teetor, 261 Mo. 412, 169 S.W. 34; Dillingham v. Martin, 61 N.J.Eq. 276, 49 A. 143; Smith v. Floyd, 124 App.Div. 277, 108 N.Y.S. 775; Young v. Young, 97 N.C. 132, 2 S.E. 78. But in many other cases the power has been construed to be attached to the office and, therefore, to be vested in a successor. Doe ex dem. Gosson v. Ladd, 77 Ala. 223; Wilmington Trust Co. v. Jacobs, 9 Del.Ch. 77, 77 A. 78; Vernoy v. Robinson, 133 Ga. 653, 66 S.E. 928; Yates v. Yates, 255 Ill. 66, 99 N.E. 360, Ann. Cas.1913D, 143; Moore v. Isbel, 40 Iowa 383; Cox v. Shelby County Trust Co., 80 S.W. 789, 26 Ky.Law Rep. 50; Chase v. Davis, 65 Me. 102; Jencks v. Safe Deposit & Trust Co. of Baltimore, 120 Md. 626, 87 A. 1031; Parker v. Converse, 5 Gray, Mass., 336; Hicks v. Hicks, 84 N.J.Eq. 515, 94 A. 409; Forman v. Young, 166 App.Div. 815, 152 N.Y.S. 417; Kadis v. Weil, 164 N.C. 84, 80 S.E. 229; Wilson v. Pennock, 27 Pa. 238; In re Blakely, 19 R.I. 324, 33 A. 518.

[22] There is a slight statutory tendency to make powers attached to the office, unless the settlor expressly provided otherwise. Fla.L.1937, c. 18398, § 2(f); Md.Code 1939, art. 16, § 276; Va.L.1936, c. 341; and the Uniform Trusts Act, § 10, adopted in Louisiana (L.1938, no. 81); Nev.L. 1941, c. 136; N.C.L.1939, c. 197; Okl. L.1941, H.B. 174, § 16, 60 Okl.St.Ann. § 175.16.

[23] Parsons v. Boyd, 20 Ala. 112; Haggart v. Ranney, 73 Ark. 344, 84 S.W. 703; La Forge v. Binns, 125 Ill.App. 527; Cooley v. Kelley, 52 Ind.App. 687, 98 N.E. 653; Stewart v. Pettus, 10 Mo. 755; Weeks v. Frankel, 197 N.Y. 304, 90 N.E. 969; Striker v. Daly, 223 N.Y. 468, 119 N. E. 882; Shortz v. Unangst, 3 Watts & S., Pa., 45; Hughes v. Williams, 99 Va. 312, 38 S.E. 138; Bell's Adm'r v. Humphrey, 8 W.Va. 1.

cised, since the trust instrument clearly shows that the powers were to be exercised by the entire board or not at all.[24]

EXERCISE OF POWERS BY COTRUSTEES [25]

95. Where trust powers are vested in two or more trustees of a private trust, and the settlor does not indicate an intent to the contrary, the powers are held jointly by all the trustees and all must unite in their exercise. In the case of charitable trusts a majority of the trustees may exercise a trust power, unless the settlor indicated a contrary intent.

Where some trustees fail to qualify or they disclaim, the trustees who do qualify have all the powers granted in the trust instrument to the entire set of trustees mentioned there, unless the powers were personal to the entire group named.

If the trust is vested in two or more trustees, they are deemed to hold as a unit and by joint tenancy, unless the settlor provides otherwise. There is only one title and that is vested in the entire board of trustees rather than in the several trustees as tenants in common. From this joint tenancy and from the expressed intent of the settlor arises the rule that in exercising their powers, unless the instrument provides otherwise, trustees of a private trust must act as a unit. A majority may not bind the trust estate by any action. "As a general rule, cotrustees cannot act separately; but they must all join in receipts for money payable to them in respect to their office. * * * But there is this distinction, that if an authority delegated to several persons be a private confidence, all must join; but if it was conferred for public purposes, it may be executed by a majority only." [26] The concurrence of all is necessary to any valid action.[27] Thus, the united action of all the trustees is necessary to

[24] Boone v. Clarke, 3 Cranch, C.C. 389, Fed.Cas.No.1,641; Dillard v. Dillard, 97 Va. 434, 34 S.E. 60.

[25] Restatement, Trusts, §§ 194, 383.

[26] Hill v. Josselyn, 13 Smedes & M., Miss., 597, 598.

[27] Learned v. Welton, 40 Cal. 349; Page v. Gillett, 26 Colo.App. 204, 141 P. 866; Hosch Lumber Co. v. Weeks, 123 Ga. 336, 51 S.E. 439; Dingman v. Boyle, 285 Ill. 144, 120 N.E. 487; Cox v. Walker, 26 Me. 504; Latrobe v. Tiernan, 2 Md. Ch. 474; City of Boston v. Robbins, 126 Mass. 384; Shaw v. Canfield, 86 Mich. 1, 48 N.W. 873; White v. Watkins, 23 Mo. 423; Ham v. Ham, 58 N.H. 70; Carr v. Hertz, 54 N.J.Eq. 127, 33 A. 194; Fritz v. City Trust Co., 72 App. Div. 532, 76 N.Y.S. 625, affirmed 173 N.Y. 622, 66 N.E. 1109; Andrews v. Kirk, Sup., 160 N.Y.S. 434; In re McDowell, 97 Misc. 306, 163 N.Y.S. 164; In re McDowell, 102 Misc. 275, 169 N.Y.S. 853; Morley v. Carson, 240 Pa. 546, 87 A. 713; Franklin Inst.

the making of a binding contract for the repair of the trust property,[28] and to the voting of the trust stock,[29] the purchasing of property for the trust,[30] or the leasing of the trust property.[31]

But the trustees of a charitable trust are not bound by this rule requiring unanimous action. A majority of such trustees may act. And so it has been held that a majority of the trustees appointed by the will of Benjamin Franklin to expend money for the benefit of the inhabitants of the city of Boston might decide how the funds should be disposed of; the court saying: "This board is similar to a board of public officers, or a committee appointed by a public body to perform public duties. * * * It is a board appointed to act in a fiduciary capacity in the administration of the affairs of a public charity. A distinction is made between private agents, or agents or trustees of a private trust, and trustees managing business of a public charity like that entrusted to this board. In the performance of duties of this latter kind, a board may act by a majority." [32]

In exceptional cases some courts have allowed one trustee to act for the entire number. This power is usually based on urgent necessity.[33] Thus, it has been held that, where one trustee was residing in England and the other in Georgia, the latter might act with regard to property in Georgia without the concurrence of the trustee in England.[34] In a few states statutes expressly allow a majority of a board of private trustees to act.[35] If a power vested in two or more trustees is delegable, then the trustees may delegate to one or more of their number the power to do the act in question.[36]

for Savings v. People's Sav. Bank, 14 R.I. 632; North Troy Grade Dist. v. Town of Troy, 80 Vt. 16, 66 A. 1033. Where one of two trustees executes a note purporting to bind the trust estate he will be obliged to repay the loan personally. Cornett v. West, 102 Wash. 254, 173 P. 44.

[28] Busse v. Schenck, 12 Daly, N.Y., 12.

[29] Mannhardt v. Illinois Staats-Zeitung Co., 90 Ill.App. 315.

[30] Bagnell v. Ives, C.C.Pa., 184 F. 466.

[31] Winslow v. Baltimore & O. R. Co., 188 U.S. 646, 23 S.Ct. 443, 47 L. Ed. 635; Hoosier Mining Co. v. Union Trust Co., 173 Ky. 505, 191 S.W. 305.

[32] Boston v. Doyle, 184 Mass. 373, 385, 68 N.E. 851, 854.

[33] Appeal of Vandever, 8 Watts & S., Pa., 405, 42 Am.Dec. 305.

[34] Duckworth v. Ocean S. S. Co., 98 Ga. 193, 26 S.E. 736.

[35] Ladd v. Ladd, 75 N.H. 371, 74 A. 1045.

Ill. Smith-Hurd Stats. c. 148, § 33; Ga.Code 1933, § 102-102; N.H. Pub. L.1926, c. 2, § 15; Uniform Trusts Act, § 11, adopted in Louisiana, Nevada, North Carolina and Oklahoma.

[36] Ubhoff v. Brandenburg, 26 App. D.C. 3.

Having appointed more than one trustee, the settlor is, in the case of private trusts, entitled to have the benefit of their several judgments when any act involving discretion is to be performed. Thus, if a mortgage is held by two trustees, payment to one and taking a discharge of the mortgage from that trustee alone, does not constitute payment of the obligation or give an effective release of the mortgage.[37]

Cotrustees may not divide the trust powers and duties among themselves, and thus departmentalize their work. However convenient it may be, it is a breach of trust to assign to one the management of the trust real estate, to another the handling of personal property investments, and to a third the distribution of capital and income to the beneficiaries.[38] The settlor may divide the trust functions among his trustees,[39] but the trustees themselves cannot do so, unless the trust instrument permits them to make such separation.

Cotrustees have a duty to act with reasonable prudence with regard to their fellows. Unreasonably to surrender control,[40] failure to supervise and check the work of the other trustees,[41] or failure to protect the trust after a warning of threatened harm at the hands of one trustee,[42] may make the inactive trustee liable. One who is nominated as a cotrustee and who desires a life of ease and freedom from responsibility should decline the trust and not accept with the notion that he can earn the trust commissions without work and still be free from chance of liability.

The settlor may expressly empower less than the entire number of trustees to act, and his direction will be respected by the courts.[43] And action taken by less than the entire board of trus-

As to what powers are delegable, see § 96, post.

[37] Coxe v. Kriebel, 323 Pa. 157, 185 A. 770, 106 A.L.R. 102.

[38] Caldwell v. Graham, 115 Md. 122, 80 A. 839, 38 L.R.A.,N.S., 1029.

[39] Warner v. Rogers, 255 Ill.App. 78; French v. Northern Trust Co., 197 Ill. 30, 64 N.E. 105.

[40] Barroll v. Forman, 88 Md. 188, 40 A. 883.

[41] Brüen v. Gillet, 115 N.Y. 10, 21 N.E. 676, 4 L.R.A. 529, 12 Am.St.Rep.

764; Richards v. Seal, 2 Del.Ch. 266; Kerr v. Kirkpatrick, 43 N.C. 137, 8 Ire.Eq. 137.

[42] Crane v. Hearn, 26 N.J.Eq. 378; In re Adams' Estate, 221 Pa. 77, 70 A. 436, 128 Am.St.Rep. 727, 15 Ann. Cas. 518. See Bogert, The Liability of an Inactive Trustee, 34 Harv.L.R. 483.

[43] Ratcliffe v. Sangston, 18 Md. 383; Heard v. March, 66 Mass. 580, 12 Cush. 580; Bascom v. Weed, 53 Misc. 496, 105 N.Y.S. 459; Draper v. Montgomery, 108 App.Div. 63, 95 N.Y.S. 904.

tees may be ratified by the trustees who did not join [44] or by the cestui que trust.[45]

Where action is brought by or against the trust estate, all the trustees must be made parties plaintiff or defendant.[46]

DELEGATION OF TRUST POWERS [47]

96. A trustee may delegate to an agent or servant the use of a trust power if reasonably prudent businessmen in the conduct of similar business would employ agents or servants, but otherwise he must exercise the trust power personally.

The trustee is an officer occupying a highly fiduciary relationship. He is selected because of his good judgment, honesty, and experience. The settlor has a right to rely upon the exercise of those qualities in the administration of the trust. He has a right to expect that important acts regarding the trust will not be delegated to agents and servants of the trustee. Accordingly equity has established the rule that the trustee may not delegate to another the doing of an act, unless a reasonably prudent businessman, in carrying on business of the same nature, would have employed subordinates to do the work.[48] It is sometimes said that "ministerial" functions may be delegated, but not "discretionary". These statements are not believed to be accurate, since all acts involve the use of at least slight judgment and discretion. As Story has said: [49] "when a trustee acts by other hands, either from necessity or conformably to the common usage of mankind, he is not to be made answerable for losses." A trustee is bound

---

[44] Hill v. Peoples, 80 Ark. 15, 95 S.W. 990. But see, *contra*, Fritz v. City Trust Co., 72 App.Div. 532, 76 N.Y.S. 625, affirmed 173 N.Y. 622, 66 N.E. 1109.

[45] Appeal of Vanleer, 24 Pa. 224.

[46] Hazard v. Durant, C.C.Mass., 19 F. 471; Caylor v. Cooper, C.C.N.Y., 165 F. 757; Sayre v. Sayre, 17 N.J.Eq. 349; Brinckerhoff v. Wemple, 1 Wend., N.Y., 470; Thatcher v. Candee, 33 How.Prac., N.Y., 145; Jones v. Maffet, 5 Serg. & R., Pa., 523.

[47] Restatement, Trusts, § 171.

[48] North American Trust Co. v. Chappell, 70 Ark. 507, 69 S.W. 546; Chicago Title & Trust Co. v. Zinser, 264 Ill. 31, 105 N.E. 718, Ann.Cas. 1915D, 931; Morville v. Fowle, 144 Mass. 109, 10 N.E. 766; Fowler v. Coates, 201 N.Y. 257, 94 N.E. 997; In re Bohlen's Estate, 75 Pa. 304. In Stevens v. Home Ins. Co., 199 Mo. App. 536, 204 S.W. 44, the power to indorse a draft was held not to be capable of delegation.

That it may be proper to employ a real estate broker, see Newby v. Kingman, 309 Ill.App. 36, 32 N.E.2d 647; In re Romberger's Estate, 39 Pa.D. & C. 604.

[49] 2 Story Eq. Juris, § 1269.

by and liable for the acts of an agent or servant properly employed to do trust business.[50] The act of an agent or servant improperly employed does not bind the beneficiaries, is void, and the trustee is liable for any damage caused by the improper delegation.[51]

But if the acts to be performed are of slight importance and are such as the ordinary businessman would turn over to his employees, then the trustee may appoint an agent or servant for the purpose.[52] For example, where trustees are authorized to sell real estate whenever it is best, they may delegate to an agent the duty of finding a purchaser, but may not delegate to him the power to enter into a contract of sale, since that involves large discretion.[53] Where the power is one of sale, the mechanical duties of posting advertisements, proclaiming the sale at an auction, and receiving bids may be performed by a servant; but the decisions as to the manner of advertisement and sale are discretionary matters, and must pass under the trustee's personal judgment.[54]

[A trustee which is a corporation must necessarily act through agents in the performance of all duties.[55] When it acts by one of its officers or employees, there is no delegation, but rather the doing of an act by the trustee itself.]

[There has been some doubt as to whether a trustee may delegate the power to vote corporate stock by giving another a proxy.[56] It would seem that this should be allowed, if it would be done by a reasonably prudent business man, and if the trustee uses reasonable care in selecting a donee for the proxy and in instructing him.[57] If the amount of stock is very large, and the

[50] Hill v. Peoples, 80 Ark. 15, 95 S.W. 990; Gray v. Lincoln Housing Trust, 229 Mich. 441, 201 N.W. 489; Telford v. Barney, 1 G.Greene, Iowa, 575.

[51] Warner v. Rogers, 255 Ill.App. 78; Earle v. Earle, 93 N.Y. 104.

[52] Gillespie v. Smith, 29 Ill. 473, 81 Am.Dec. 328; Annis v. Annis, 61 Iowa 220, 16 N.W. 97; Turnbull v. Pomeroy, 140 Mass. 117, 3 N.E. 15; O'Fallon v. Tucker, 13 Mo. 262; Keim v. Lindley, N.J.Ch., 30 A. 1063; Sinclair v. Jackson ex dem. Field, 8 Cow., N.Y., 543; Belding v. Archer, 131 N.C. 287, 42 S.E. 800; Olcott v. Gabert, 86 Tex. 121, 23 S.W. 985.

[53] Coleman v. Connolly, 242 Ill. 574, 90 N.E. 278, 134 Am.St.Rep. 347.

[54] Bales v. Perry, 51 Mo. 449.

[55] Chicago Title & Trust Co. v. Zinser, 264 Ill. 31, 105 N.E. 718, Ann. Cas.1915D, 931.

[56] See Spotts, Voting Trustees Stock, 18 Trust Bulletin 7.

[57] There is some legislation allowing the giving of a proxy. See Cal. Civ.Code, § 2270; Conn. Gen.St.1930, § 3405; Pa. 15 P.S. § 107; R. I. Gen. L.1938, c. 486, § 17. By section 8 of the Uniform Trusts Act a trustee may vote stock by proxy but is liable for lack of reasonable care in deciding

trust has a large influence in corporate affairs, the trustee should doubtless vote the stock in person.

Unauthorized discretionary acts performed by an agent to whom a power was improperly delegated may be ratified by the trustees so as to be binding.[58] And it has been held that consent of all parties interested will enable a trustee to delegate the performance of duties involving judgment and discretion.[59]

NOTICE OF TRUSTEE'S POWERS

97. When a third person deals with a trustee, known by the third person to be a trustee, the third person is put on inquiry as to the powers of the trustee and is charged with knowledge of the extent of the trustee's powers.

A person dealing with a trustee, and knowing of the trusteeship, is charged with knowledge of the extent of the trustee's authority. If the third party acts without knowledge of the trustee's powers, he does so at his peril.[60] It is common knowledge that most trustees have limited powers and that their powers are normally disclosed in a trust document, generally a deed or will. It is fair to require the third person to learn whether the trustee has power to sell, mortgage, lease, or perform the other act which the trustee offers to perform.

how to vote the stock and in voting it. This Act has been adopted in Louisiana, Nevada, North Carolina and Oklahoma.

[58] Hill v. Peoples, 80 Ark. 15, 95 S.W. 990.

[59] Seely v. Hills, 49 Wis. 473, 5 N.W. 940.

[60] Findlay v. Florida East Coast Ry. Co., C.C.A.Fla., 68 F.2d 540; Owen v. Reed, 27 Ark. 122; Jones v. Holladay, 2 App.D.C. 279; Trust Company of Chicago v. Jackson Park Bldg. Corp., 303 Ill.App. 531, 25 N.E.2d 616; Zion Church of Evangelical Ass'n of North America in Charles City v. Parker, 114 Iowa, 1, 86 N.W. 60; Horton v. Tabitha Home, 95 Neb. 491, 145 N.W. 1023, 51 L.R.A.,N.S., 161, Ann.Cas.1915D, 1139; Griswold v. Perry, 7 Lans., N.Y., 98.

CHAPTER 10

THE DUTIES OF THE TRUSTEE—IN GENERAL

Sec.
98. Duty to Use Ordinary Skill and Prudence.
99. Duty of Loyalty.
100. Duty to Carry out the Trust.

DUTY TO USE ORDINARY SKILL AND PRUDENCE [1]

98. **In the management of the trust the trustee is bound to display the skill, prudence, and diligence which an ordinary man would use in the conduct of business of a like character and with like aims; but if the trustee in advance of accepting the trust has represented to the settlor that he possessed unusual ability he will be required to display that amount of ability.**

Only ordinary care, skill, and prudence are normally required of trustees. They are not expected to manifest unusual ability or extraordinary care.[2] The rule is "that trustees are bound in the management of all the matters of the trust to act in good faith and employ such vigilance, sagacity, diligence and prudence as in general prudent men of discretion and intelligence in like matters employ in their own affairs. The law does not hold a trustee, acting in accord with such rule, responsible for errors of judgment."[3] The trustee is not liable for every error which occurs in the administration of the trust. He is not required to be infallible.[4] "All that equity requires from trustees is common skill, common prudence, and common caution."[5] If the

---

[1] Restatement, Trusts, § 174.

[2] American Bonding Co. of Baltimore v. Richardson, C.C.A.Ohio, 214 F. 897, 131 C.C.A. 565; Bourquin v. Bourquin, 120 Ga. 115, 47 S.E. 639; Dillivan v. German Sav. Bank, Iowa, 124 N.W. 350; Litchfield v. White, 7 N.Y. 438, 57 Am.Dec. 534; Belding v. Archer, 131 N.C. 287, 42 S.E. 800; Gilbert v. Sutliff, 3 Ohio St. 129; Appeal of Jones, 8 Watts & S., Pa., 143, 42 Am.Dec. 282; Cunningham v. Cunningham, 81 S.C. 506, 62 S.E. 845; Davis v. Harman, 21 Grat., Va., 194; Hutchinson v. Lord, 1 Wis. 286, 60 Am.Dec. 381.

[3] Costello v. Costello, 209 N.Y. 252, 261, 103 N.E. 148. See, also, Ainsa v. Mercantile Trust Co. of San Francisco, 174 Cal. 504, 163 P. 898; Wylie v. Bushnell, 277 Ill. 484, 115 N.E. 618; In re Wanamaker's Trust, 340 Pa. 419, 17 A.2d 380; Shepherd v. Darling, 120 Va. 586, 91 S.E. 737.

[4] Ellig v. Naglee, 9 Cal. 683; Pine v. White, 175 Mass. 585, 56 N.E. 967; Myers' Ex'r v. Zetelle, 21 Grat., Va., 733.

[5] Appeal of Neff, 57 Pa. 91, 96.

trustee has not used the skill of an ordinary man, it is of no avail to him that his motives were good. Good intent will not relieve him from liability for negligent or improvident conduct.[6]

The degree of ability required is not affected by the compensation of the trustee. Even if he is to receive no pay for his work, he will be required to show the same amount of diligence and ability.[7]

While there has been some suggestion that professional trustees like trust companies are required to show more skill and diligence than casual trustees,[8] there is no judicial authority to that effect.[9] It would seem, however, that if any trustee in advance of his appointment declares to the settlor that he (the trustee) possesses and will use extraordinary ability in the trust administration, and the settlor appoints this trustee in reliance on such a representation, the trustee should be required to exhibit the ability which he said he would use.[10]

It does not excuse a trustee from the use of ordinary care in trust work that he was a person of subnormal ability and diligence and in his own private affairs customarily used less than ordinary ability and attention.[11]

A trustee does not conclusively show that he has used reasonable care when he consults an expert, like a lawyer or investment counsel, and then follows the advice given. It may have been unreasonable to take advice from the party in question, and the advice may have been such that a reasonable man, in evaluating the advice, would have known that it was not good advice.[12]

[6] St. Paul Trust Co. v. Strong, 85 Minn. 1, 88 N.W. 256; Moeller v. Poland, 80 Ohio St. 418, 89 N.E. 100. But, in fixing the penalty to be placed upon the trustee, equity may consider the motives of the trustee and view with indulgence honest acts. Ellig v. Naglee, 9 Cal. 683; Diffenderffer v. Winder, 3 Gill & J., Md., 311. So, too, bad health, while not an excuse for inefficient management of a trust, has been considered by the court in fixing the amount of the liability of the trustee. Newman v. Shreve, 229 Pa. 200, 78 A. 79. Freeman v. Cook, 41 N.C. 373, 6 Ired.Eq. 373.

[7] Speight v. Gaunt, 9 A.C. 1; Switzer v. Skiles, 3 Gilman 529, 8 Ill. 529, 44 Am.Dec. 723. But see, *contra*, Clark v. Anderson, 10 Bush, Ky., 99.

[8] See 30 Col.L.R. 1162, 1172; 29 Mich.L.R. 125; In re Clark's Will, 136 Misc. 881, 242 N.Y.S. 210.

[9] In re Clark's Will, 257 N.Y. 132, 177 N.E. 397, 77 A.L.R. 499; Linnard's Estate, 299 Pa. 32, 38.

[10] Ferrell v. Ellis, 129 Iowa 614, 105 N.W. 993; Brown v. Shyne, 242 N.Y. 176, 151 N.E. 197, 44 A.L.R. 1407.

[11] Knox v. Mackinnon, 13 App.Cas. 753, 766.

[12] Miller v. Proctor, 20 Oh.St. 442; Freeman v. Cook, 41 N.C. 373.

The reasonable man whom the trustee must imitate is one who is seeking the same objects in property management as the purposes of the trust. These are normally safety of principal and such income as is consistent with security of the capital of the trust. The trustee is not to follow in the footsteps of a reasonably prudent speculator.

DUTY OF LOYALTY [13]

99. The trustee owes the beneficiary the duty of conducting the trust with the advantage of the cestui que trust solely in mind. The trustee must exclude his own advantage or profit and that of third parties from consideration in making decisions and taking action under the trust.

The trustee owes the cestui que trust the duty of acting solely for the interest of the cestui que trust. In other words the trustee should not, while administering the trust, take any step with a view to his own advantage or his own enrichment. All his proceedings under the trust should be with the aim of advancing the interests of the cestui que trust, and with that aim alone.[14] "It is a general principle that a trustee must act with the most scrupulous good faith. The one great duty arising from this fiduciary relation is to act in all matters relating to the trust wholly for the benefit of the beneficiary. A trustee will not be permitted to manage the affairs of his trust or to deal with the trust property, so as to gain any advantage, either directly or indirectly, for himself."[15]

The illustrations of self-dealing on the part of the trustee are numerous, as, for example, the purchase by the trustee of the trust property at a sale conducted by him as trustee[16] or at a

---

[13] Restatement, Trusts, § 170.

[14] Enslen v. Allen, 160 Ala. 529, 49 So. 430; City of Chicago v. Tribune Co., 248 Ill. 242, 93 N.E. 757; Teegarden v. Lewis, 145 Ind. 98, 40 N.E. 1047, 44 N.E. 9; In re Carmody's Estate, 163 Iowa 463, 145 N.W. 16; Niblack v. Knox, 101 Kan. 440, 167 P. 741; Richardson's Adm'rs v. Spencer, 18 B.Mon., Ky., 450; Arnold v. Brown, 24 Pick., Mass., 89, 35 Am. Dec. 296; Patterson v. Booth, 103 Mo. 402, 15 S.W. 543; Jeffray v. Towar, N.J.Ch., 54 A. 817; Davis v. Wright, 2 Hill., S.C., 560; Newcomb v. Brooks, 16 W.Va. 32; Ludington v. Patton, 111 Wis. 208, 86 N.W. 571.

[15] Linsley v. Strang, 149 Iowa 690, 126 N.W. 941, 942.

[16] Charles v. Dubose, 29 Ala. 367; Haynes v. Montgomery, 96 Ark. 573, 132 S.W. 651; Bellamy v. Bellamy's Adm'r, 6 Fla. 62; Worthy v. Johnson, 8 Ga. 236, 52 Am.Dec. 399; Mettler v. Warner, 249 Ill. 341, 94 N. E. 522; Bank of Old Dominion v. Dubuque & P. R. Co., 8 Iowa 277, 74 Am.Dec. 302; Baker v. Lane, Ky.,

judicial sale under a mortgage or judgment;[17] the sale by the trustee of his own property to the trust;[18] lending money to, or borrowing it from, the trust;[19] investment of the trust funds in an enterprise in which the trustee has an interest;[20] the purchase of mortgages or tax claims against the trust property;[21] the renewal of a lease in his own name, when the original lease was to the trust;[22] employing himself to do work for the trust.[23] In each of these cases the trustee has conflicting interests, one

118 S.W. 963; Clute v. Barron, 2 Mich. 192; St. Paul Trust Co. v. Strong, 85 Minn. 1, 88 N.W. 256; Shelby v. Creighton, 65 Neb. 485, 91 N.W. 369, 101 Am.St.Rep. 630; Carson v. Marshall, 37 N.J.Eq. 213; Jackson v. Walsh, 14 Johns., N.Y., 407; Brothers v. Brothers, 42 N.C. 150, 7 Ired.Eq. 150; McGinn v. Shaeffer, 7 Watts, Pa., 412; Clarke v. Deveaux, 1 S.C. 172; Armstrong's Heirs v. Campbell, 3 Yerg., Tenn., 201, 24 Am.Dec. 556; Hamilton v. Dooly, 15 Utah 280, 49 P. 769; Smith v. Miller, 98 Va. 535, 37 S.E. 10; Reilly v. Oglebay, 25 W.Va. 36; Harrigan v. Gilchrist, 121 Wis. 127, 99 N.W. 909. A transfer to a corporation in which the trustee owns the majority of the stock is equivalent to a sale by the trustee to himself. Otier v. Neiman, 96 Misc. 481, 160 N.Y.S. 610. On sales by and to the trustee see Uniform Trusts Act, § 5, now in force in Louisiana, Nevada, North Carolina, and Oklahoma.

[17] Broder v. Conklin, 121 Cal. 282, 53 P. 699; Kent v. Barger, 264 Ill. 59, 105 N.E. 741; Van Alstyne v. Brown, 77 N.J.Eq. 455, 78 A. 678; contra, Jackson v. Baird, 148 N.C. 29, 61 S.E. 632, 19 L.R.A.,N.S., 591; Calvert v. Woods, 246 Pa. 325, 92 A. 301.

[18] St. Paul Trust Co. v. Strong, 85 Minn. 1, 88 N.W. 256; Matter of Long Island Loan & Trust Co., 92 App.Div. 1, 87 N.Y.S. 65, affirmed 179 N.Y. 520, 71 N.E. 1133.

But see Pike v. Camden Trust Co.,

128 N.J.Eq. 414, 16 A.2d 634 as to bonds acquired by a corporate trustee expressly for allocation to its trusts.

[19] Pike v. Camden Trust Co., 128 N.J.Eq. 414, 16 A.2d 634 (small, temporary advance not objectionable); In re Randolph, 134 N.Y.S. 1117, affirmed 150 App.Div. 902, 135 N.Y.S. 1138; In re Sinkler's Estate, 25 Pa. C.C. 417, 10 Dist. 399; but see In re Binder's Estate, 137 Ohio St. 26, 27 N.E.2d 939, 129 A.L.R. 130 where a loan of a bank's money to its trust with a charge of interest was sanctioned. See Uniform Trusts Act, § 3.

[20] Whitlow v. Patterson, 195 Ark. 173, 112 S.W.2d 35; In re Gutenkunst's Estate, 232 Wis. 81, 286 N.W. 566.

[21] Petrie v. Badenoch, 102 Mich. 45, 60 N.W. 449, 47 Am.St.Rep. 503; Baugh's Ex'r v. Walker, 77 Va. 99.

[22] Walley v. Walley, 1 Vern. 484; Griffin v. Griffin, 1 Sch. & Lef. 352.

[23] Gamble v. Gibson, 59 Mo. 585; Green v. Winter, 1 Johns.Ch.N.Y., 26; Fryberger v. Anderson, 125 Minn. 322, 147 N.W. 107. But modern American authorities quite generally allow a trustee who is a lawyer to collect at least a reasonable sum for legal services rendered to the trust. Babcock v. Hubbard, 56 Conn. 284, 15 A. 791; Shelton v. McHaney, 343 Mo. 119, 119 S.W.2d 951; Norris v. Bishop, 207 Ky. 621, 269 S.W. 751; Willis v. Clymer, 66 N.J.Eq. 284, 57 A. 803.

that of the beneficiaries and the other that of himself. Equity knows that in such cases selfish interest is apt to control, human nature being what it is. Sometimes such transactions would be innocent and harmless, but often they would be prejudicial to the beneficiaries. Since it is often difficult to prove actual wrongdoing or selfish gain in such transactions, equity makes them all voidable at the option of the beneficiary. This rule will tend to keep trustees in the straight and narrow path and to strike down open or concealed chicanery.

The duty of loyalty is also violated if the trustee acts from motives of gain for third persons, as where he sells trust property to a neighbor for the purpose of enabling the latter to make a profit instead of in the interest of the trust.[24]

Other examples of disloyalty are the cases where the trustee uses knowledge obtained in the administration of the trust for his own private benefit;[25] receives a bonus for lending the trust funds;[26] receives a commission for taking out insurance on the trust property;[27] accepts a gift from persons with whom he deals on behalf of the trust estate;[28] uses the trust funds in his own business[29] or lends them to his wife,[30] votes the trust stock for himself as an officer of a corporation in which the trust owns stock and accepts a salary for filling the office.[31]

The disloyalty may be accomplished indirectly and through the use of a dummy, straw man,[32] or subsidiary or affiliated corporation.[33] Equity will look through all subterfuges. Thus, if a trustee has his wife bid in the trust property on a sale of it, or if a corporate trustee buys trust investments from another corporation which has a substantial amount of identity in the

---

[24] North Baltimore Bldg. Ass'n v. Caldwell, 25 Md. 420, 90 Am.Dec. 67; Harrison v. Manson, 95 Va. 593, 29 S.E. 420.

[25] Jarrett v. Johnson, 116 Ill.App. 592.

[26] Sherman v. Lanier, 39 N.J.Eq. 249.

[27] Sherman v. White, 62 Ill.App. 271.

[28] Jacobus v. Munn, 37 N.J.Eq. 48.

[29] In re Jones' Estate, 10 N.Y.St. Rep. 176; Campbell v. Campbell, C.C. Conn., 8 F. 460.

[30] In re Randolph, Sur., 134 N.Y.S. 1117, affirmed 150 App.Div. 902, 135 N.Y.S. 1138.

[31] Mangels v. Tippett, 167 Md. 90, 173 A. 191.

[32] Hartman v. Hartle, 95 N.J.Eq. 123, 122 A. 615; In re Fulton's Will, 253 App.Div. 494, 2 N.Y.S.2d 917.

[33] Cornet v. Cornet, 269 Mo. 298, 190 S.W. 333; Shanley's Estate v. Fidelity Union Trust Co., 108 N.J.Eq. 564, 138 A. 388, 5 N.J.Misc.R. 783.

personnel of its stockholders and officers, there is a voidable transaction on account of disloyalty.

There has been dispute whether it is disloyal for a corporate trustee to sell investments from one of its trusts to another of its trusts. While strictly speaking this involves a possible conflict between the interests of the selling trust, the trustee, and the buying trust,[34] it seems to be sanctioned if it is fairly done.[35] Ordinarily the fairness of a particular disloyal transaction is not examined by the court. The court sets aside the transaction at the request of the beneficiary even though the trustee proves that the deal did not cause the trust any financial loss or even if he shows that the trust gained by it.[36]

If the trustee is guilty of disloyalty, the beneficiary may avoid the transaction and require restoration to the status quo. Thus, if a trustee sells the trust property to himself, the beneficiary may have the transfer set aside and the property returned to the trust on the payment to the trustee of any amount he may have paid into the trust fund in return for the property. Or the beneficiary may elect to confirm the transfer of the property to the trustee but hold him for any profit he made on the deal.[37] In obtaining the return of the original property or the profit the cestui may use the constructive trust as a basis for his suit, as shown in prior sections.[38]

The obligation of the trustee to deal with the beneficiary with the utmost candor and fairness may be said to be an example of the duty of loyalty. It cannot be said that the trustee is under a duty not to make a contract with his beneficiary, as, for example, not to buy the cestui's interest; but, if the trustee does enter into any agreements with the cestui, the trustee must make a full disclosure of all the facts, treat the cestui with the utmost fairness and openness and pay an adequate consideration for all that he receives. If the trustee cannot prove that the transaction was open and honest, equity will declare the trustee a constructive trustee of all property which he has received by virtue of his contract with the beneficiary.[39] Thus, a convey-

---

[34] The transaction is prohibited by section 6 of the Uniform Trusts Act, adopted in Louisiana, Nevada, North Carolina and Oklahoma.

[35] French v. Hall, 198 Mass. 147, 84 N.E. 438, 16 L.R.A.,N.S., 205; Roberts v. Michigan Trust Co., 273 Mich. 91, 262 N.W. 744.

[36] Brothers v. Brothers, 42 N.C. 150; Smith v. Miller, 98 Va. 535, 37 S.E. 10.

[37] Beckley v. Munson, 22 Conn. 299.

[38] See § 62, ante.

[39] Byrne v. Jones, C.C.A.Ark., 159 F. 321, 90 C.C.A. 101; Yonge v. Hoop-

ance by the cestui que trust to the trustee of the property owned by the cestui under the trust in consideration of the support of the cestui by the trustee for life, where the cestui was of sound mind and not influenced by fraud or undue influence, will be upheld.[40] But a purchase by a trustee from a cestui que trust will be set aside and a constructive trust declared where it appears that the cestui was ignorant of his rights and received an inadequate consideration.[41] The duty applies as well to a sale by a trustee to his beneficiary as to a conveyance from cestui que trust to trustee.[42] If the cestui has the transaction with the trustee set aside, of course he must return any consideration paid by the trustee to him.[43]

The conduct of the cestui que trust may be such as to prevent him from insisting upon the enforcement of the rule that the trustee shall not act for his own benefit. The beneficiary may expressly waive the rule.[44] He may consent that the trustee may buy at his own sale, and if this consent is given by a person of full capacity and with a full knowledge of the facts, the purchase by the trustee will not be voidable.[45] So, too, after the transaction has taken place the acts or failure to act on the part

er, 73 Ala. 119; Flowers v. Flowers, 84 Ark. 557, 106 S.W. 949, 120 Am. St.Rep. 84; Bronson v. Thompson, 77 Conn. 214, 58 A. 692; Saunders v. Richard, 35 Fla. 28, 16 So. 679; Fish v. Fish, 235 Ill. 396, 85 N.E. 662; Copeland v. Bruning, 44 Ind.App. 405, 87 N.E. 1000; Avery's Trustee v. Avery, 90 Ky. 613, 14 S.W. 593; Brown v. Cowell, 116 Mass. 461; Schwarz v. Wendell, Walk.Ch., Mich., 267; Tatum v. McLellan, 50 Miss. 1; Davidson v. I. M. Davidson Real Estate & Investment Co., 249 Mo. 474, 155 S.W. 1; Gassert v. Strong, 38 Mont. 18, 98 P. 497; Marr v. Marr, 73 N.J.Eq. 643, 70 A. 375, 133 Am. St.Rep. 742; In re Ledrich, 68 Hun 396, 22 N.Y.S. 978; Appeal of Costen, 13 Pa. 292; Waldrop v. Leaman, 30 S.C. 428, 9 S.E. 466; Cogbill v. Boyd, 77 Va. 450; Ludington v. Patton, 111 Wis. 208, 86 N.W. 571. In a few cases it seems to have been held that a transfer from cestui to trustee is absolutely void. McKnatt v. McKnatt, 10 Del.Ch. 392, 93 A. 367;

Butman v. Whipple, 25 R.I. 578, 57 A. 379.

[40] Barnard v. Stone, 159 Mass. 224, 34 N.E. 272.

[41] Pugh's Heirs v. Bell's Heirs, 1 J. J.Marsh, Ky., 398.

[42] McCants v. Bee, 1 McCord Eq., S.C., 383, 16 Am.Dec. 610.

[43] Saunders v. Richard, 35 Fla. 28, 16 So. 679; Connecticut Mut. Life Ins. Co. v. Stinson, 62 Ill.App. 319.

[44] Miller v. Dodge, 28 Misc. 640, 59 N.Y.S. 1070.

[45] Faucett v. Faucett, 1 Bush., Ky., 511, 89 Am.Dec. 639; De Caters v. Le Ray De Chaumont, 3 Paige, N.Y., 178; Ungrich v. Ungrich, 131 App. Div. 24, 115 N.Y.S. 413; Roberts v. Roberts, 65 N.C. 27; Field v. Arrowsmith, 3 Humph., Tenn., 442, 39 Am. Dec. 185. But see Munro v. Allaire, 2 Caines' Cas., N.Y., 183, 2 Am.Dec. 330.

of the cestui que trust may bar his right to object. By laches or acts of ratification the beneficiary may lose his right to attack a contract made between trustee and beneficiary.[46] By failure to object within a reasonable time, after full knowledge of the facts, the cestui may affirm the purchase by the trustee of the trust property.[47]

Where the parties capable of avoiding a purchase by a trustee on his own sale stand by and permit the trustee to improve the property as his own, they cannot afterwards set aside the sale or have a constructive trust declared.[48]

The court of chancery may, for sufficient reason and under such restrictions as it may impose, permit the trustee to bid at his own sale,[49] or to commit any other act which would otherwise be disloyal and voidable.

DUTY TO CARRY OUT THE TRUST

100. It is the duty of the trustee to carry out the trust according to the terms of the trust instrument.

It is too obvious to require extended explanation that the primary duty of the trustee is to carry out the trust according to the tenor of the trust instrument. Whether the trust is to accumulate income, or to pay it over to beneficiaries, or to partition, or what not, the trustee should learn the settlor's intent and effectuate it.[50] The discussion of the trust duties in detail,

---

[46] Van Gorp v. Van Gorp, 229 Iowa 1257, 296 N.W. 354; Stewart's Adm'r v. Carneal, 51 S.W. 800, 21 Ky.Law Rep. 497; Prince de Bearn v. Winans, 111 Md. 434, 74 A. 626; Bushe v. Wright, 118 App.Div. 368, 103 N.Y.S. 403; Boyd v. Hawkins, 17 N. C. 195, 2 Dev.Eq. 195; Inlow v. Christy, 187 Pa. 186, 40 A. 823.

[47] Hammond v. Hopkins, 143 U.S. 224, 12 S.Ct. 418, 36 L.Ed. 134; James v. James, 55 Ala. 525; Hayward v. Ellis, 13 Pick., Mass., 272; Jones v. Smith, 33 Miss. 215; Scott v. Freeland, 7 Smedes & M., 409, 15 Miss. 409, 45 Am.Dec. 310; Mulford v. Minch, 11 N.J.Eq. 16, 64 Am.Dec. 472; Greagan v. Buchanan, 15 Misc. 580, 37 N.Y.S. 83; Boerum v. Schenck, 41 N.Y. 182; Villines v. Norfleet, 17 N.C. 167, 2 Dev.Eq. 167; Beeson v. Beeson, 9 Pa. 279; Price v. Nesbit, 1 Hill Eq., S.C., 445; Connolly v. Hammond, 51 Tex. 635; Lewis v. Hill, 61 Wash. 304, 112 P. 373.

[48] Davis v. Simpson, 5 Har. & J., Md., 147, 9 Am.Dec. 500.

[49] Hayes v. Hall, 188 Mass. 510, 74 N.E. 935; Gallatian v. Cunningham, 8 Cow., N.Y., 361; Scholle v. Scholle, 101 N.Y. 167, 4 N.E. 334. But see, *contra*, Linsley v. Strang, 149 Iowa 690, 126 N.W. 941.

[50] Morgan v. Clayton, 61 Ill. 35; Dunn v. Morse, 109 Me. 254, 83 A. 795; Sears v. Russell, 8 Gray, Mass.,

which appears later herein, is merely a consideration of the means which are best adapted to the execution of the trust. "The cardinal duties, and therefore liabilities, of trustees, are these: (1) To carry out the trust; (2) to use due care thereabout; and (3) to act in good faith thereabout."[51] That the trustee has not been requested to perform the trust, is no defense. He should proceed of his own initiative.[52]

How this duty to administer the trust is performed in the various situations which may arise will be discussed in the next chapter under the heading of Problems of Administration.

In order to carry out the trust, the trustee should carefully read the trust instrument, and should learn the law applicable to the trust. He cannot plead ignorance of the trust terms or the relevant law.

86; Steward v. Traverse City State Bank, 187 Mich. 387, 153 N.W. 793.

[51] Klugh v. Seminole Securities Co., 103 S.C. 120, 87 S.E. 644, 646.

[52] Cotton v. Rand, Tex.Civ.App., 92 S.W. 266.

CHAPTER 11

TRUST ADMINISTRATION—PROTECTION AND INVESTMENT

Sec.
101. Duty to Defend the Trust.
102. Duty to Take Possession and Collect.
103. Duty to Keep Trust Property Safely.
104. Duty to Make Trust Property Productive.
105. Duty to Use Reasonable Care in Investing.
106. Statute and Court Rules—Effect.
107. Investments Generally Approved.
108. Investments Generally Disapproved.
109. Common Trust Funds.
110. Control by the Settlor, the Court, or the Beneficiary.
111. Duty to Review Trust Investments.
112. Duty to Change Trust Investments.

DUTY TO DEFEND THE TRUST [1]

101. A trustee is under a duty to defend the trust against attack, if there is a reasonable cause to believe that it can be protected from destruction; and the court will not permit him to attack the trust himself and have it terminated or declared void.

A trustee has a duty to defend the trust against actions to terminate it, to have it set aside, or to have it declared illegal.[2] Thus, if the beneficiaries seek to have the trust terminated before the trust purpose is accomplished, or if the relatives of the settlor-testator seek to have the trust set aside on account of the mental incompetency of the testator, or if the settlor sues to have it declared that the trust was obtained by undue influence, and the trustee reasonably believes after taking legal advice that the plaintiff should not succeed, the trustee will be under a duty to defend the action and all expenses reasonably incurred in such defense may be paid out of trust property.[3] The trustee is not under a duty to advance his own money for such defence, but may use trust funds, and if there are no such funds, he should seek to obtain money from the beneficiaries. If a decision in such an action is against the trustee in the lower

---

[1] Restatement, Trusts, § 178.

[2] In re Spencer's Estate, 18 Cal. App.2d 220, 63 P.2d 875; In re Shepherd's Estate, 152 Or. 15, 41 P.2d 444.

[3] In re Lowe's Estate, 326 Pa. 375, 192 A. 405; Koteen v. Bickers, 163 Va. 676, 177 S.E. 904.

court, and he reasonably should know that the decision is erroneous, he has a duty to appeal.[4]

On accepting the trust the trustee impliedly admits the validity of the trust and agrees not to attack it. Hence he will not be heard to allege its invalidity.[5] Thus, where a trust of insurance has been set up for a second wife of the insured and the trustee has accepted the trusteeship, he will not be heard in an action to enforce the trust to defend by alleging that the second marriage was illegal and that the trust, therefore, had the illegal purpose of fostering illicit relations.[6]

DUTY TO TAKE POSSESSION AND COLLECT [7]

102. The trustee should take the trust property into his possession and reduce ordinary choses in action to money as soon as possible. Except in extraordinary cases, where possession will be highly advantageous to him, the cestui que trust is not entitled to demand from the trustee the possession of the trust property. For losses occasioned by lack of reasonable skill and diligence in performing these duties the trustee will be liable.

The first duty of the trustee, after acceptance of the trust and qualification, is to take possession of the trust property. The very definition of a trust indicates that the trustee is an officer who is to have possession and title to property for the benefit of another. So that, whether the property subject to the trust be real or personal, lands or money, bonds, stocks, or negotiable paper, the trustee should take such steps as are necessary to place such property under his control or in his custody.[8] If the trust property consists of ordinary choses in action, such as promissory notes or book accounts, which are not suitable for retention as trust investments, the trustee should proceed with due diligence to their collection.[9] If he is negligent in reducing them to money, and loss results to the trust estate, he will be

---

[4] Republic Nat. Bank & Trust Co. v. Bruce, 130 Tex. 136, 105 S.W.2d 882.

[5] Federal Trust Co. v. Damron, 124 Neb. 655, 247 N.W. 589.

[6] Carter v. Carter, 321 Pa. 391, 184 A. 78.

[7] Restatement, Trusts, §§ 175, 177.

[8] Connolly v. Leonard, 114 Me. 29, 95 A. 269 Nagle v. Conard, 80 N.J. Eq. 252, 87 A. 1119; In re Harbster's Estate, 133 Pa. 351, 19 A. 558.

[9] Waterman v. Alden, 144 Ill. 90, 32 N.E. 972; Cross v. Petree, 10 B.Mon., Ky., 413; Hunt v. Gontrum, 80 Md. 64, 30 A. 620; Speakman v. Tatem, 48 N.J.Eq. 136, 21 A. 466; Vilas v. Bundy, 106 Wis. 168, 81 N.W. 812.

liable for such loss.[10] Thus, if he waits so long after the obligation becomes due that the obligor becomes insolvent, and he could have collected the debt by promptly bringing suit, the trustee will be obliged to make good the loss to the cestui.

However, the trustee need not sue upon a chose in action the instant it becomes due. "There is no peremptory obligation imposed upon a trustee (especially when acting with the knowledge and approbation of much the largest portion of those interested) to sue upon a bond passed to him as trustee, the moment or the month or the year it becomes due. A due regard to the ultimate security of the debt may require him to indulge the debtor, and if, contrary to a reasonable expectation, any portion of the debt be lost, in the exercise of a fair discretion, regulated solely by an anxious effort to increase the ultimate security of the debt, the chancery court will not visit him with the penalty of making good the loss." [11] If the best interests of the trust dictate a compromise of the debt due the trust, the trustee is under a duty to make such a compromise, and equity will uphold his action upon the accounting.[12] Corresponding to the duty of the trustee to reduce the principal of the trust property to possession is the obligation on his part to collect the income and profits of the trust estate and retain control of them.[13]

Ordinarily the trustee is entitled to the possession of the trust property as against all the world, including the cestui que trust.[14] While the cestui is the beneficial owner of the trust property in a certain sense, for a longer or shorter time, still he is expected to obtain the benefit of the property through the trustee, and not directly, except in unusual cases. In applying the general rule an English Court of Chancery has stated the possible exceptions as follows: "There may be cases in which it may be plain, from the nature of the property, that the testator could not mean to exclude the cestui que trust for life from the per-

---

[10] Lowson v. Copeland, 2 Brown Ch.Cas., Eng., 156; Purdy v. Johnson, 174 Cal. 521, 163 P. 893. And a trustee who fails to collect a dividend from an insolvent estate in which he has wrongfully invested trust moneys is liable for the amount of the dividend. Backes v. Crane, 87 N.J.Eq. 229, 100 A. 900.

[11] Waring v. Darnall, 10 Gill & J., Md., 126, 142.

BOGERT TRUSTS 2D—22

[12] Brackett v. Middlesex Banking Co., 89 Conn. 645, 95 A. 12; Pool v. Dial, 10 S.C. 440.

[13] Windsor Trust Co. v. Waterbury, 160 App.Div. 571, 145 N.Y.S. 794.

[14] In re Harbster's Estate, 133 Pa. 351, 19 A. 558; Barkley v. Dosser, 15 Lea, Tenn., 529.

sonal possession of the property, as in the case of a family residence. There may be very special cases in which this court would deliver the possession of the property to the cestui que trust for life, although the testator's intention appeared that it should remain with the trustees, as where the personal occupation of the trust property was beneficial to the cestui que trust, there the court taking means to secure the due protection of the property for the benefit of those in remainder, would, in substance, be performing the trust according to the intention of the testator." [15]

The general rule is illustrated by a case in which a trust was created for the support and education of a son, to last during his life, with remainder to others. In such case the son is not, on reaching his majority, entitled to the possession of the trust property, a farm.[16] But it has been held that the beneficiary was entitled to the possession of such trust property as slaves, where the only benefit to be had from them would necessarily come from personal use.[17] And an equitable life tenant of stocks has been given by chancery the power to collect the dividends upon the stocks, to the exclusion of the trustee, when the only effect of allowing the trustee to collect and pay over the dividends would be to burden the trust estate with the payment of commissions. In this case the trust property remained in the possession of the trustee, but the right to receive its income directly was granted to the cestui.[18]

It is elementary that the settlor may expressly provide that the cestui shall have the custody of the trust property.[19]

In taking possession of the trust property from the settlor,[20] or the settlor's executor in the case of testamentary trusts,[21] or a predecessor trustee,[22] the trustee should be careful that he obtains exactly the property to which the trust is entitled, both in amount and kind. If the person who is to deliver the trust property to the trustee has wasted or stolen it, the trustee should

---

[15] Tidd v. Lister, 5 Madd. 429, 432, 433.

[16] Wickham v. Berry, 55 Pa. 70.

[17] Wade v. Powell, 20 Ga. 645; McKnight v. McKnight, 10 Rich.Eq., S. C., 157.

[18] Williamson v. Wilkins, 14 Ga. 416.

[19] Freeman v. Bristol Sav. Bank, 76 Conn. 212, 56 A. 527.

[20] Speakman v. Tatem, 48 N.J.Eq. 136, 21 A. 466.

[21] In re Kline's Estate, 280 Pa. 41, 124 A. 280, 32 A.L.R. 926.

[22] Ralston v. Easter, 43 App.D.C. 513; Rowe v. Bentley, 70 Va. 756.

recover from him the damages which have ensued.[23] The best precaution for a successor trustee on taking charge is to have a court accounting and a court decree as to what property is due and as to whether the predecessor has been guilty of any breaches of trust.

DUTY TO KEEP TRUST PROPERTY SAFELY [24]

103. **A trustee is under a duty to keep the trust property safely and to protect it against loss or deterioration. This may involve keeping negotiable securities in a safety deposit box, recording deeds and mortgages running to the trustee, earmarking trust securities, depositing cash and negotiable paper in a bank, keeping real property in repair, and similar acts.**

Having obtained possession of the trust property, it is the duty of the trustee to protect it. If there is trespass upon or waste of the trust property, he should bring the appropriate action.[25] If the trust goods are converted, he should sue in trover.[26] If real property of the trust is wrongfully occupied, he should eject the trespasser, lest his own title and the right of the cestui que trust be lost by adverse possession.[27] In keeping the property the trustee should use the same care which he would bestow on his individual property. The degree of diligence required depends upon the nature of the trust res. Thus, a trustee who places negotiable bonds in a safety deposit box will not be responsible for their loss, if they are stolen;[28] whereas, of course, he would be responsible if he left them in an unprotected situation. Greater attention is due from the trustee in the case of negotiable securities than would be expected where ordinary chattels are involved.

"The trustees are the parties in whom the fund is vested, and whose duty it is to maintain and defend it against wrongful attack or injury tending to impair its safety or amount. The title

---

[23] McClure v. Middletown Trust Co., 95 Conn. 148, 110 A. 838.

[24] Restatement, Trusts, § 176.

[25] Stull v. Harvey, 112 Va. 816, 72 S.E. 701. If a cotrustee has taken steps to misappropriate trust funds, the trustee should enjoin his fellow trustee. Crane v. Hearn, 26 N.J.Eq. 378.

[26] Poage v. Bell, 8 Leigh, Va., 604.

[27] Schiffman v. Schmidt, 154 Mo. 204, 55 S.W. 451; Cameron v. Hicks, 141 N.C. 21, 53 S.E. 728, 7 L.R.A.,N.S., 407; Hunter v. Hunter, 63 S.C. 78, 41 S.E. 33, 90 Am.St.Rep. 663.

[28] Carpenter v. Carpenter, 12 R.I. 544, 34 Am.Rep. 716.

to the fund being in them, neither the cestuis que trust nor the beneficiaries can maintain an action in relation to it, as against third parties, except in case the trustees refuse to perform their duty in that respect, and then the trustees should be brought before the court as parties defendant." [29]

The trustee should keep the trust property separate from his private property and also from other trust funds.[30] In order that he may be able to account accurately, and in order that the cestui que trust may be able to trace his property with ease, the trustee should not mingle the trust property with other property. If he does so mingle it, and loss results, the trustee will be personally liable. Thus, if the trust property consists in part of cash or commercial paper, the trustee should deposit it in a separate account, devoted entirely to the funds of that trust and not to mixed private and trust funds or the mixed funds of two or more trusts.[31]

Furthermore, in order to give the maximum of protection to the trust property it should be earmarked or labelled as trust property of the trust in question, where that is possible. Thus, a deed of land to the trust should run to the trustee of a named trust, as should a mortgage in which trust funds are invested, or a stock certificate bought with trust funds.[32] Such identification will be very useful to the beneficiary in case of need to trace the trust property, as where the trustee dies insolvent, or where creditors of the trustee seek to collect from the property, or where the trustee proves to be dishonest and seeks to convey the property away for his own personal benefit.

In recent years there has been an unfortunate tendency to treat failure to earmark the trust property as a mere technical breach of trust, not making the trustee liable unless actual damage were shown to have come from the lack of earmarking.[33] The older rule made the trustee an insurer of the safety of the

---

[29] Western R. Co. v. Nolan, 48 N.Y. 513, 518.

[30] Moore v. McKenzie, 112 Me. 356, 92 A. 296; In re Union Trust Co. of New York, 86 Misc. 392, 149 N.Y.S. 324; Wagner v. Coen, 41 W.Va. 351, 23 S.E. 735. See, also, the discussion under the subject of investments, post, § 105.

[31] Dunn v. Dunn, 137 N.C. 533, 50 S.E. 212; Mason v. Whitthorne, 2 Coldw., Tenn., 242.

[32] In re Buckelew's Estate, 128 N. J.Eq. 81, 13 A.2d 855.

[33] Chapter House Circle of King's Daughters v. Hartford Nat. Bk. & Trust Co., 124 Conn. 151, 199 A. 110; In re Guthrie's Estate, 320 Pa. 530, 182 A. 248, 103 A.L.R. 1186.

property, if he did not earmark it.[34] This was in the nature of a penalty designed to discourage a dangerous practice and one often tinged with fraud.

There are many examples of the duty to protect the trust property. If the trustee has a deed, mortgage, or similar instrument of conveyance running to him, he should record it as soon as possible, in order to avoid loss of the trust property, through a second conveyance by the same grantor.[35] Cash and commercial paper should be deposited in a bank, pending their disbursement.[36] Securities and valuable papers should be placed in a safe or safety deposit box.[37] Buildings should be kept in good repair in order to prevent deterioration.[38] Agricultural land should be fertilized.

In the case of stock certificates there has been a tendency by corporate trustees to have them run to a nominee, an officer or employee of the bank, so as to save time and trouble in the case of the sale of the stock. If the certificates run to the bank as trustee, on transfer proof of the authority of the trustee may have to be made, but if running to an individual without a trust label no proof of that sort will be required. Here is a balance between convenience and strict trust law. In the absence of a statutory[39] or trust instrument authorization, it would seem improper for the trustee to hold any property in the name of a nominee.[40]

At common law it would seem a disloyal act for a corporate trustee, having banking powers, to deposit trust funds with itself, since there would be a conflict of interest.[41] As a bank it

---

[34] In re Yost's Estate, 316 Pa. 463, 175 A. 383.

[35] Partridge v. American Trust Co., 211 Mass. 194, 97 N.E. 925; Miller v. Parkhurst, 45 Hun 590, 9 N.Y.St. Rep. 759.

[36] Wagner v. Coen, 41 W.Va. 351, 23 S.E. 735; Crane v. Moses, 13 S.C. 561.

[37] In re Boyle's Will, 99 Misc. 418, 163 N.Y.S. 1095.

[38] Annett-Mahnken Realty Co. v. Gollin, 110 N.J.Eq. 469, 160 A. 400; In re Farrell's Estate, 152 Misc. 118, 272 N.Y.S. 852.

[39] See Pa. 7 P.S. § 819–1108. By sec. 9 of the Uniform Trusts Act holding stock in the name of a nominee is permitted with some safeguards.

[40] See, however, Potter v. Union & Peoples Nat. Bank of Jackson, C.C.A. Mich., 105 F.2d 437, where holding stock in this way was held to be merely a technical breach of trust, where no damage was caused thereby.

[41] Several important decisions, however, make the transaction legal. Herzog v. Title Guar. & Trust Co., 148 App.Div. 234, 132 N.Y.S. 1114, modified on another point in 210 N.Y. 531, 103 N.E. 885; Hayward v. Plant,

would seek to get as much in deposits as possible, regardless of the condition of the bank, and at as low rates of interest as possible. As a trustee it should seek the safest bank and the highest rate of interest. It is, however, very convenient for a corporate trustee to deposit with itself. Statutes have recently validated the practice on condition that the trustee set aside a fund of investments as security for the trust deposits.[42] Deposits up to $5,000 are of course guaranteed by federal law at present.[43] Some of the statutes require interest to be paid on the account, if the bank pays interest on similar non-trust accounts.

DUTY TO MAKE TRUST PROPERTY PRODUCTIVE [44]

104. Except in rare cases it is the duty of the trustee to make the trust property productive. This is normally done by investing it in securities of the type permitted by law.

The trustee may deposit the trust funds in a bank of good reputation for a reasonable time, while seeking an investment, but should not place the funds on time deposit.

Occasionally the trustee's duty is to allow the beneficiary to enjoy the trust property directly by taking possession of it and using it.[45] In this and similar cases the trustee has no duty to make the trust property produce an income. That burden is on the beneficiary. But in the normal case it is the trustee who is to have possession and the object of the trust is to confer benefits on the beneficiary. This can be done only by the use of the property in such a way as to produce income. Thus the trustee is usually under a duty to put the trust property into such form that it will regularly produce economic benefits like interest, rents, or dividends, which can be paid over to the beneficiary.[46]

The authority of the trustee to invest the trust funds, and his corresponding duty, may be expressly set forth in the trust instrument, or it may be inferred. If the proper administration of the trust requires investment, of course, the duty to invest

---

98 Conn. 374. But see Restatement, Trusts, § 170, comment m.

[42] See, for example, 12 U.S.C.A. sec. 248k and Reg. F. thereunder (national banks); N. Y. Banking Law, § 111; Ore.L.1929, p. 473; and collection of statutes in Bogert on Trusts & Trustees, § 598.

[43] 12 U.S.C.A. § 264(h).

[44] Restatement, Trusts, §§ 181, 379.

[45] See § 43, ante.

[46] Linder v. Officer, 175 Tenn. 402, 135 S.W.2d 445; Moore v. Sanders, Tex.Civ.App., 106 S.W.2d 337; Krauss v. Cornell, Tex.Civ.App., 116 S.W.2d 882.

will be implied.[47] So, too, the power and duty to change investments is one frequently implied. Where the trust administration is to last for some time, the production of a suitable income will frequently require the trustee to shift his investments. A power and duty to do this is liberally implied.[48]

The trustee should invest the funds of the estate within a reasonable time. What is a reasonable time is a question of fact, which will be solved by a consideration of the amount of the fund and the state of the investment market in the community. Two months has been held to be a reasonable time within which the trustee might search for an investment,[49] but more than two years delay in investing the trust funds has been held unreasonable.[50]

A direction to invest the "estate" will be construed to imply the duty to invest the accumulated income, which is to be paid over to the beneficiaries on their majorities.[51] If interest is accumulating, and will be necessarily held for some time in the hands of the trustee, he should invest it.[52]

Naturally some time will be necessary to enable the trustee to find a proper investment. What shall he do with the funds while searching for such investment? It would be unreasonable to require that he keep the money of the trust in his actual possession at his house or place of business, or that he be required to rent a safety deposit box in which to place the funds. An ordinarily prudent business man places funds on deposit in a bank while searching for an investment. It is unquestioned law that a trustee may deposit the funds in a bank for a reasonable time after their receipt. What is a reasonable time is a question of fact, to be determined upon the circumstances of each case. Deposits for three years,[53] two years,[54] fourteen months,[55] and

---

[47] In re Kaiser's Estate, 2 Lanc.Law Rev., Pa., 362; Appeal of Grothe, 135 Pa. 585, 19 A. 1058.

[48] Luxon v. Wilgus, 7 Bush, Ky., 205; Citizens' Nat. Bank v. Jefferson, 88 Ky. 651, 11 S.W. 767; Spencer v. Weber, 163 N.Y. 493, 57 N.E. 753.

[49] Appeal of Witmer, 87 Pa. 120.

[50] Cavender v. Cavender, C.C.Mo., 8 F. 641.

[51] In re Stewart, 30 App.Div. 368, 51 N.Y.S. 1050; affirmed 163 N.Y. 593, 57 N.E. 1125.

[52] Fowler v. Colt, 22 N.J.Eq. 44.

[53] Woodley v. Holley, 111 N.C. 380, 16 S.E. 419.

[54] In re Knight's Estate, Sup., 4 N.Y.S. 412. In re Donohue, 88 Misc. 359, 151 N.Y.S. 1094, a deposit for ten years was held to render the trustee liable.

[55] Cann v. Cann, 33 Wkly.Rep. 40.

ten months [56] have been held to be unreasonably long, and therefore to render the trustee liable when the bank failed during the period of deposit. The Supreme Court of the United States has expressed the view that three months is ordinarily a reasonable time of deposit.[57] In many cases a temporary deposit in a bank of good repute, selected with due care, has been considered a proper act by the trustee, and the failure of such bank has not rendered the trustee liable for the amount of the loss to the trust fund.[58] "So, also, executors, trustees, or guardians will not be liable if, in the ordinary discharge of their duty, they deposit the assets temporarily in a bank, although the bank may fail. * * * A trustee who would continuously keep for any considerable length of time a large sum of money about his person or in his house, rather than deposit it for safe-keeping in a solvent and reputable bank or trust company, where all the precautions may be exercised for its safety, might justly be regarded as derelict in duty." [59] A New York court, in speaking of the duty of the trustee, has said that "the deposit may be continued for so long a period as will enable the trustee, in the use of ordinary diligence, to obtain its secure and proper investment, or the exigencies of the estate may require. But where he fails by his neglect within a reasonable time to secure investments, and allows the money still to remain on deposit, and it is thereby lost, the law charges the trustee with the loss." [60]

If the trustee can obtain interest on a call deposit, there is no objection to his so doing; but he should not place the funds of the estate on a time deposit. Such a deposit is a loan to the bank without security, and is not allowable. The fund should be subject to immediate call by the trustee.[61]

---

[56] Barney v. Saunders, 16 How. 535, 14 L.Ed. 1047.

[57] Barney v. Saunders, 16 How. 535, 14 L.Ed. 1047.

[58] Norwood v. Harness, 98 Ind. 134, 49 Am.Rep. 739; McCollister v. Bishop, 78 Minn. 228, 80 N.W. 1118 (affected by a local statute); Jacobus v. Jacobus, 37 N.J.Eq. 17; Odd Fellows' Beneficial Ass'n of Columbus v. Ferson, 3 Ohio Cir.Ct. 84; In re Law's Estate, 144 Pa. 499, 22 A. 831, 14 L.R.A. 103; Crane v. Moses, 13 S.C. 561.

[59] In re Law's Estate, 144 Pa. 499, 506, 22 A. 831, 14 L.R.A. 103.

[60] In re Knight's Estate, Sup., 4 N.Y.S. 412, 413.

[61] Andrew v. Union Sav. Bk. & Tr. Co., 222 Iowa 881, 270 N.W. 465; Baskin v. Baskin, 4 Lans., N.Y., 90; Frankenfield's Appeal, 127 Pa. 369 note; Baer's Appeal, 127 Pa. 360, 18 A. 1, 4 L.R.A. 609. But see Smith v. Fuller, 86 Ohio St. 57, 99 N.E. 214, L.R.A.1916C, 6 Ann.Cas.1913D, 387.

If a trustee fails to use reasonable care in selecting the bank in which to deposit the trust funds, [62] or in leaving the funds on deposit after he should have known of danger, [63] or if he chooses the bank of deposit from motives of self-interest and not from considerations of the welfare of the beneficiary, [64] the trustee will be liable for any loss ensuing.

DUTY TO USE REASONABLE CARE IN INVESTING [65]

105. In investing the trust funds the trustee is under a duty to act as an ordinarily prudent man would in investing money for similar purposes. In a few states this is the trustee's only guide in investment work.

It has been previously shown[66] that, in the performance of his trust duties, the trustee is under an obligation to exercise the care and skill of an ordinary man in the conduct of his own affairs. This rule applies to the investment of the trust funds, as well as to the other functions of the trustee. "It has long been the rule in this commonwealth that in making investments, as well as in the general management of the trust, a trustee is held only to good faith and sound discretion, and hence that he cannot be held for the consequences of an error in judgment, unless the error is such as to show either that he acted in bad faith or failed to exercise sound discretion."[67] In deciding whether the investments of the settlor shall be continued, and in making new investments, the trustee should be strictly honest and fair toward the cestui que trust, and he should use the diligence and prudence which an ordinary business man would use in investing his own funds for like objects.[68] In determining what is or-

---

[62] Caldwell v. Hicks, D.C.Ga., 15 F.Supp. 46; In re Howison's Estate, 49 Ohio App. 421, 197 N.E. 333.

[63] In re Foster's Estate, 218 Iowa 1202, 256 N.W. 744.

[64] United States ex rel. Willoughby v. Howard, 302 U.S. 445, 58 S.Ct. 309, 82 L.Ed. 352.

[65] Restatement, Trusts, §§ 227, 228.

[66] See, § 98, ante.

[67] Taft v. Smith, 186 Mass. 31, 32, 70 N.E. 1031.

[68] Richardson v. Morey, 18 Pick., Mass., 181; Thayer v. Dewey, 185 Mass. 68, 69 N.E. 1074; Roosevelt v. Roosevelt, 6 Abb.N.C., N.Y., 447; King v. Talbot, 40 N.Y. 76; Nance v. Nance, 1 S.C. 209; Watkins v. Stewart, 78 Va. 111.

For example, it has been held a breach of trust to purchase as a trust investment a mortgage certificate on the representation of its seller that it was a legal trust investment, where the trustee made no investigation of the value and condition of the property. Cobb v. Gramatan Nat. Bk. & Tr. Co., Sup., 21 N.Y.S.2d 49.

dinary skill and diligence, the court will consider extraordinary conditions such as the existence of war.[69]

In making investments the trustee should be guided by the interests of both present cestuis que trust and the remaindermen or future cestuis que trust. The trustee should look to the security of the fund, to the production of a reasonable income, and to the obtaining of an investment which is readily salable.[70] Thus, where a trust fund was for the support and education of infants, the New York court has said that "the first and obvious duty was to place that fifteen thousand dollars in a state of security; second, to see to it that it was productive of interest; and, third, so to keep the fund, that it should always be subject to future recall for the benefit of the cestui que trust."[71]

The propriety of an investment will, of course, be determined as of the time when it was made by the trustee.[72] It is elementary that the trustee should invest the trust funds separately from his own funds and from other trust funds,[73] that he should not invest the trust money in his own name but rather in the name of the trust;[74] that the trustee should not make the investment in such a way as to result in his private gain;[75] and that as far as possible the trust funds should be invested within the jurisdiction where the trust is being administered.[76]

---

[69] Foscue v. Lyon, 55 Ala. 440; Campbell v. Miller, 38 Ga. 304, 95 Am.Dec. 389.

[70] Tarbox v. Tarbox, 111 Me. 374, 89 A. 194; Appeal of Pray, 34 Pa. 100. But if a trustee can deliver securities to a remainderman, and is not under a duty to pay cash, he will not be obliged to consider liquidity of investments as important. In re D'Happart's Estate, 132 Pa.Super. 326, 200 A. 927.

[71] King v. Talbot, 40 N.Y. 76, 88.

[72] Taft v. Smith, 186 Mass. 31, 70 N.E. 1031. If the trust investments depreciate in value, due to causes not involving the negligence of the trustee, he is not liable. In re Blauvelt's Estate, Sur., 20 N.Y.S. 119; In re Menzie's Estate, 54 Misc. 188, 105 N.Y.S. 925; In re Bartol's Estate, 182 Pa. 407, 38 A. 527; In re Gouldey's Estate, 201 Pa. 491, 51 A. 315.

[73] McCullough's Ex'rs v. McCullough, 44 N.J.Eq. 313, 14 A. 642. The trustee should not buy a mortgage on property in which a corporation of which he is president is interested. Strong v. Dutcher, 186 App.Div. 307, 174 N.Y.S. 352.

[74] Morris v. Wallace, 3 Pa. 319, 45 Am.Dec. 642. "One of these rules is that the trustee who invests such funds in his own name becomes personally responsible. * * * Were he permitted to do otherwise, it would place before him the constant temptation to make the trust fund a dumping ground for his own unsatisfactory ventures." Cornet v. Cornet, 269 Mo. 298, 190 S.W. 333, 341.

[75] In re Carr's Estate, 24 Pa.Super. Ct. 369.

[76] McCullough's Ex'rs v. McCullough, 44 N.J.Eq. 313, 14 A. 642.

§ 105   DUTY TO USE REASONABLE CARE IN INVESTING

In making investments a trustee may obtain and pay for advice, if ordinary prudence permits such action, but he must use reasonable skill and wisdom in weighing the advice and in deciding whether to follow it or not. If an ordinarily prudent man would not take or follow the advice in question, a trustee will not be protected by the advice.[77]

The trustee should obtain as high a rate of interest on the trust fund as is consistent with safety. There is no absolute standard. Each case must be solved upon its own facts, and depends upon the investment market in the community and the nature of the trust. It has been held that 4½ per cent. was a proper amount of interest to receive,[78] while in other cases the rates of 2.8 per cent.[79] and from 3 to 4 per cent.[80] have been held unreasonably low.

Investment at too high a rate of interest will show that the trustee has been speculating with the trust fund, and this is universally condemned.[81]

The trust fund should always be kept by the trustee so as to be capable of being easily followed by the cestui que trust. Any assumption of private ownership over the trust property, or mixture of the trust property with his own goods, by the trustee, makes the trust property difficult to trace, and is frowned upon by equity. The deposit of the trust moneys pending investment should, under this general rule, be made in the name of the trustee as trustee, and not on his behalf individually. If the trustee has the account entitled with his own name, without mention of the trust,[82] or places the trust moneys in a pre-exist-

---

[77] Learoyd v. Whiteley, 12 A.C. 727; Matter of Clark's Will, 257 N.Y. 132, 177 N.E. 397, 77 A.L.R. 499; Miller v. Proctor, 20 Ohio St. 442. It has been held proper for an individual trustee, but not for a corporate trustee, to pay out trust funds to secure the advice of a professional investment counsellor. In re Gutman's Estate, 171 Misc. 680, 14 N.Y.S. 2d 473; In re Greata's Will, 172 Misc. 955, 17 N.Y.S.2d 776.

[78] Appeal of Graver, 50 Pa. 189.

[79] In re Shields' Estate, 14 Phila., Pa., 307.

[80] In re Whitecar's Estate, 147 Pa. 368, 23 A. 575.

[81] English v. McIntyre, 29 App.Div. 439, 51 N.Y.S. 697; Davis v. Davis Trust Co., 106 W.Va. 228, 145 S.E. 588. Buying the securities of a new and untried corporation may also constitute speculation.

[82] Chancellor v. Chancellor, 177 Ala. 44, 58 So. 423, 45 L.R.A.,N.S., 1, Ann. Cas.1915C, 47; Gilbert v. Welsch, 75 Ind. 557; Jenkins v. Walter, 8 Gill & J., Md., 218, 29 Am.Dec. 539; Coffin v. Bramlitt, 42 Miss. 194, 97 Am.Dec. 449; Knowlton v. Bradley, 17 N.H. 458, 43 Am.Dec. 609; Baskin v. Baskin, 4 Lans., N.Y., 90; Booth v. Wilkinson, 78 Wis. 652, 47 N.W. 1128, 23 Am.St.Rep. 443.

ing private account,[83] the beneficiary may hold the trustee liable for all losses occurring to the trust fund while it is so deposited. Equity places this penalty upon the trustee for his mingling of private and trust affairs.

While some statutes require trustees to diversify their investments, and not to place an unduly large share of the trust funds in a single security or type of security,[84] there is a tendency to be liberal with trustees who fail to diversify and to hold that concentration of risk is not alone a breach of trust.[85]

In a few states, where there are no court rules or statutes to guide trustees in making investments, the rule of reasonable prudence is the only rule which the trustee has to consider.[86]

The duty to observe loyalty to the beneficiaries in making investments, and hence to exclude all selfish interest of the trustee, has been noticed elsewhere.[87]

STATUTE AND COURT RULES—EFFECT [88]

106. In nearly all states statutes or court rules specify investments lawful for a trustee. In some states the statute provides that a trustee "may" invest in the described securities; in other states it is provided that the trustee "must" make such investments. If the trustee follows the list, he will be protected, provided he used reasonable care in so doing. If the list is permissive, the trustee may invest in securities outside the list, if he sustains the burden of proving the use of reasonable care and skill. If the list

---

[83] Henderson's Adm'r v. Henderson's Heirs, 58 Ala. 582; Webster v. Pierce, 35 Ill. 158; Cartmell v. Allard, 7 Bush, Ky., 482; In re Stafford, 11 Barb., N.Y., 353; McAllister v. Commonwealth, 30 Pa. 536; Mason v. Whitthorne, 2 Cold., Tenn., 242; Vaiden v. Stubblefield's Ex'r, 28 Grat., Va., 153.

[84] In re Dreier's Estate, 204 Wis. 221, 235 N.W. 439. And see at common law Appeal of Davis, 183 Mass. 499, 67 N.E. 604.

[85] In re Gottschalk's Estate, 167 Misc. 397, 4 N.Y.S.2d 13; In re First Nat. Bk. of City of New York, Sup., 25 N.Y.S.2d 221; In re Romberger's Estate, 39 Pa.D. & C. 604; In re Saeger's Estate, 340 Pa. 73, 16 A.2d 19, 131 A.L.R. 1152. See 48 Harv.L.R. 347.

[86] Creed v. McAleer, 275 Mass. 353, 175 N.E. 761, 80 A.L.R. 1117. Missouri has recently approved this rule for investments. St. Louis Union Trust Co. v. Toberman, Mo.App., 140 S.W.2d 68; Rand v. McKittrick, Mo., 142 S.W.2d 29. And see N.H.L.1941, c. 93; Conn.Gen.St.Supp.1939, § 1289e; Mich.Pub.Acts 1939, No. 76.

[87] See § 99, ante; and Vincent v. Werner, 140 Kan. 599, 38 P.2d 687; Calaveras Timber Co. v. Michigan Trust Co., 278 Mich. 445, 270 N.W. 743.

[88] Restatement, Trusts, § 227.

is mandatory, it would seem that an investment outside the list would be a breach of trust, no matter how great the care and judgment used.

In most states the legislature or the court of chancery has set up a list of legal trust investments by statute or court rule. Some of these rules are in permissive form, others are mandatory in wording. Some state that a trustee "may" invest in the classes of securities named, others that he "must" invest in that way. These lists are in many states exceedingly lengthy and detailed. They are changed frequently. No attempt is made here to give the situation in full as to each state. Such information can easily be obtained from other sources.[89] The broad, general effect of these rules will be discussed in this book.

The trustee will normally buy for his trust securities on the legal list in his state and nothing else, and he will then in all probability be protected against any claim of breach of trust; but following the legal list does not absolutely insure protection to the trustee against liability. Whether the list is permissive or mandatory, the trustee must use reasonable care in following it.[90] Perhaps this care will be less than that required of a trustee who is selecting an investment on his own initiative and does not have any legal list to guide him. The trustee may assume that the investments on the legal list are in all probability safe and proper, but he must take at least slight care to see that this is so and he must not ignore plain warnings that securities on the list are not safe. Thus, if it is generally known in the investment world that an obligor on a corporate bond has defaulted, or that a foreign government has been overthrown by a revolution, no trustee would be safe in investing in the bonds of the corporation or the foreign government, even though they were on the legal list.

It is clearly held that if the list is permissive, that is, the legislature has merely stated that a trustee "may invest" in certain types of securities, the trustee is not limited to those on the legal list, but may go outside it. But if he buys a security not on the list, he will be required to show that it was one which

---

[89] Copies of these statutes and court rules are given in McKinney, Trust Investments, and in the various "services" relating to trusts. A digest of them is given in Bogert, Trusts and Trustees, c. 30.

[90] Indiana Trust Co. v. Griffith, 176 Ind. 643, 95 N.E. 573, 44 L.R.A., N.S., 896, Ann.Cas.1914A, 1023; In re Buckelew's Estate, 128 N.J.Eq. 81, 13 A.2d 855; In re Randolph, 134 N.Y.S. 1117, affirmed 150 App.Div. 902, 135 N.Y.S. 1138.

at that time would have been purchased by an ordinarily prudent man for the purposes of the trust.[91] Going outside the list puts a heavier burden on him, as a practical matter, than if he confines himself to the list.

If the list is mandatory, that is, the legislature has provided that a trustee "shall invest" in named securities, it would seem that the trustee is not at liberty to go outside the list and seek purchases which he thinks a reasonably prudent man would buy. While the cases have been somewhat conflicting,[92] it would seem that the purchase of a non-listed security is inevitably a breach of trust, if the beneficiary elects to treat it as such.[93]

A settlor may permit his trustee to invest in any securities, even though they are not on the legal list, and the trustee will be protected in following the settlor's permissions or directions, if he uses ordinary care and prudence in so doing.[94]

Where a trustee purchases an investment which is illegal at the time it is made, but later becomes legal, he is liable only for the depreciation in it which occurred before it became a legal trust investment.[95]

INVESTMENTS GENERALLY APPROVED [96]

107. The investments generally sanctioned for trusts by statutes and court rules in the United States are

(a) Obligations of the United States or of an instrumentality of the United States;

(b) Bonds of the states, where there has been no default within a certain period;

---

[91] Clark v. Beers, 61 Conn. 87, 23 A. 717; In re Cook's Trust Estate, 20 Del.Ch. 123, 171 A. 730; Buckle v. Marshall, 176 Va. 139, 10 S.E.2d 506; but see, contra, In re Trusteeship of First Minn. Trust Co., 202 Minn. 187, 277 N.W. 899; Home Savings & Loan Co. v. Strain, 130 Ohio St. 53, 196 N.E. 770, 99 A.L.R. 903.

[92] Delafield v. Barret, 270 N.Y. 43, 200 N.E. 67, 103 A.L.R. 941; 49 Harv. L.R. 821; 49 Yale L.J. 891.

[93] It has been held that a court has no power to permit a trustee to invest outside the list of required investments. In re Trusteeship of First Minneapolis Trust Co., 202 Minn. 187, 277 N.W. 899; In re Smith, 279 N.Y. 479, 18 N.E.2d 666, dictum; Humphries v. Manhattan Sav. Bank & Trust Co., 174 Tenn. 17, 122 S.W.2d 446.

[94] Marshall v. Frazier, 159 Or. 491, 81 P.2d 132; In re Sparks' Estate, 328 Pa. 384, 196 A. 48.

[95] Geldmacher v. City of New York, 175 Misc. 788, 25 N.Y.S.2d 380; Humphries v. Manhattan Sav. Bank & Trust Co., 174 Tenn. 17, 122 S.W. 2d 446.

[96] Restatement, Trusts, §§ 227–229.

(c) Obligations of cities, counties and other municipal corporations having certain qualifications;

(d) First mortgages on real estate where the loan has a certain margin of security;

(e) The bonds of certain types of private corporations when secured by mortgage.

It is generally recognized that the obligations of the United States, those guaranteed by it, and those of its instrumentalities, are the safest investments for trustees. Hence American statutes and court rules invariably make them legal trust investments.[97] Examples of obligations of federal agencies which are made legal by statute are the bonds of the Home Owners Loan Corporation[98] and of the Federal Home Loan Banks.[99]

The statutes universally permit investment in the obligations of the state in question,[1] and generally of the other states of the Union, provided no default has occurred as to principal or interest for a certain period before the investment.[2]

Municipal bonds are very highly considered, when the municipality is of at least fair size, the value of the property subject to taxation by it is of adequate amount, and the already existing debt is not excessive. Hence statutes generally permit investment by trustees in the bonds of cities, counties, school districts, and other municipal corporations.[3] In most cases, however, the bonds must meet certain qualifications, intended to insure that there is adequate security, as, for example, that the total property liable for taxation has a certain valuation, or that the bonded debt does not exceed a certain proportion of the value of the taxable property.[4]

A type of security very highly regarded and always found on trustees' investment lists is the first mortgage on the fee simple title to real property, where the debt secured does not exceed a certain proportion of the value of the mortgaged land.[5] The margins required differ somewhat from state to state,[6] and depend somewhat on whether the property is improved or unim-

[97] See, for example, Ala. Gen.Acts 1935, No. 33.

[98] See, for example, Ark. L.1933 Sp. Sess., No. 10.

[99] Del. L.1934, c. 37.

[1] Fla. L. 1937, c. 17949.

[2] Ind. L.1937, c. 33, §§ 20–23.

[3] Ky. L.1936, c. 53; La. Acts 1938, No. 81, § 62.

[4] Neb. L.1935, c. 68.

[5] N.J.S.A. 3:16–1.

[6] Ohio Gen.Code, § 710-112 (50%); Ore. L.1935, c. 212(60%).

proved, but the typical requirement is that the debt secured must not exceed fifty, or in some cases sixty, per cent. of the value of the mortgaged land. In England in the days before the investment statute equity allowed a loan of two-thirds of the value of agricultural property but only fifty per cent. of the value of residential or business property.[7] Land is fairly stable in value, but recent history has shown that even it fluctuates in dollar value, and therefore security adequate when the loan is made may become inadequate when the loan becomes due, unless a considerable margin is allowed.

It is common to require also that the loan on real property mortgage shall not be made unless there is an independent valuation of the property which shows adequate margin, unless an appropriate abstract of title or title guaranty policy is obtained, and unless any buildings on the mortgaged property are insured in favor of the mortgagee.[8]

Certain corporation bonds, secured by a mortgage to a trustee for the benefit of the bondholders, are also commonly placed on the legal lists.[9] The bonds of public utility corporations, such as railroads, electric light and power companies, and telephone corporations are frequently made legal for trusts.

Other obligations found on the legal lists from time to time, but not in general approved, are those of the Dominion of Canada and a few other foreign governments,[10] shares of savings and loan associations,[11] notes secured by a pledge of high grade securities,[12] savings bank accounts to a limited extent,[13] and certain types of insurance policies.[14]

A "participating" mortgage is one where the debt is not held by a single person, but is owned by various investors. For example, if a bond issue is floated by a large apartment hotel corporation, the mortgage will be made to a bank or trust company as trustee and the bonds will be sold to the investing public in varying amounts, so that eventually a thousand persons may own the bonds secured by a million dollar mortgage. The mortgage is participated in by all the investors in the bonds.

---

[7] In re Salmon, 42 Ch.D. 351.

[8] See, for example, Wash. Rem. Rev.St. §§ 3255–32551.

[9] Pa. 20 P.S. §§ 814–817; Va. L. 1936, c. 106.

[10] Del. L. 1935, c. 230.

[11] Cal. L.1935, c. 564.

[12] Wis. L.1935, c. 363.

[13] Conn. Gen.St.Supp. 1937, §§ 776d, 777d.

[14] Tenn. Acts 1939, c. 133; and see Mich. L.1941, Act 143.

There has been some doubt as to the propriety of a trustee investing in such a participating interest in a mortgage, although the security is adequate. It has been argued that the investment is not within the sole control of the investing trustee, that there are chances of conflicting interests between the various bondholders in case of default, and that the trustee is mixing the trust fund with other funds in an investment. However, such investments in mortgage participations have been generally sanctioned by the courts[15] and have also been approved by the legislatures in the investment statutes of many states.[16] It would seem that they are no more objectionable than the bonds of public utility companies, secured by mortgages on their plants, where the bond purchaser buys an interest in a mortgage owned by himself and many others, and yet the public utility and similar bond issues are almost universally permitted by statute.

The great practical advantages in mortgage participations and in pools of mortgages are distribution of risk and ease of investment. If a trust has a small interest in many mortgages, instead of a large interest in one mortgage, the failure of one property or changes in the character of one neighborhood will not be so prejudicial to the trust. Small single mortgages are not easy to get. Interests in mortgages of the denomination or $100 or $1,000 are very convenient for the investment of small balances or of the funds of small trusts.

A problem of somewhat similar nature is that of the "mortgage pool" which consists of a collection of mortgages running to a trustee and held by it for various trusts. Thus, the trustee may purchase a million dollars worth of mortgages, given by forty different mortgagors, paying for them with idle trust funds of seventy different trusts of which the corporate trustee is trustee. The trustee will allot interests in this mass of mortgages to the seventy different trusts in accordance with the amount of their investments and these interests will be represented by certificates and will be noted on all appropriate trust accounts. Here again there is an argument that the beneficia-

---

[15] First Nat. Bank v. Basham, 238 Ala. 500, 191 So. 873, 125 A.L.R. 656; In re Lalla's Estate, 362 Ill. 621, 1 N.E.2d 50; Springfield Safe Deposit & Trust Co. v. First Unitarian Society, 293 Mass. 480, 200 N.E. 541; In re Union Trust Co., 219 N.Y. 514, 114 N.E. 1057.

[16] Minn. L.1937, c. 174; Pa. 20 P.S. §§ 801–805.

New York first permitted the purchase of mortgage participations by trustees, and later retracted the remission. Sec. 111, Decedent Estate Law, as amended by L.1936, c. 265, c. 898.

ries of any given trust have a right to object, in that their funds are being mixed with those of other trusts, there is not control of the investment solely for the interest of any one trust, there may be a conflict as to control of the investment when problems like foreclosure or extension of time arise, and the trustee of the investing trusts may be said to be turning over control of the investment of that trust to the trustee of the mortgage pool who represents many persons and trusts.

These mortgage pools have been allowed by statute in a few states.[17] Their depression experiences have not been satisfactory and many complicated problems have arisen regarding their administration.[18] They are similar to the common trust fund mentioned in a later section,[19] except that the mortgage pool contains one type of investment only, whereas the common trust fund may be composed of many different types of investments.

INVESTMENTS GENERALLY DISAPPROVED [20]

108. The following investments are generally disapproved:
(a) Loans without security;
(b) The purchase of common or preferred stocks;
(c) The purchase of real estate or chattels;
(d) The purchase of a business or an interest therein;
(e) Loans secured by encumbrances on property which is located in another state or country;
(f) Loans secured by junior liens;
(g) Loans secured by mortgages on chattels or interests in real property less than the fee.

Unsecured Loans

It is a fundamental rule that investment of trust funds without property security is a violation of the trust. The trustee should not lend the trust moneys to an individual or a corporation and take in return only the bond or note of the borrower. If he cannot obtain security of an approved nature, he should not make the loan. A trustee making a loan without property security will be liable for any losses which occur, due to the fail-

---

[17] Pa. 20 P.S. §§ 801, 804, 805.

[18] Seaboard Trust Co. v. Shea, 118 N.J.Eq. 433, 180 A. 206; Appeal of Commonwealth Trust Co. of Pittsburgh, 324 Pa. 161, 188 A. 200, 107 A.L.R. 1453.

[19] See § 109, post.

[20] Restatement, Trusts, § 227–231.

BOGERT TRUSTS 2D

ure of the debtor to repay,[21] even if he obtained one or more indorsers on the note. "However conflicting in some respects the decisions may appear to be, in one respect they are reasonably uniform. It is a generally accepted rule that it is not prudent to invest trust funds in unsecured notes of an individual or of a partnership. We have found no decision which announces a contrary rule where the trust contemplated an investment of a permanent nature."[22] An English judge has said that this "is a rule that should be rung in the ears of every person who acts in the character of trustee."[23]

The sale of trust property and acceptance in return of the notes of the buyer is not allowed by equity, and the trustee will be liable for a loss resulting from the failure of the maker of the notes.[24] In a few cases the taking of certificates of deposit, which amount to nothing more than loans to a bank without security, has been held a proper procedure for a trustee in the investment of the trust funds.[25] But these holdings are out of line with the majority of the authorities.

The reason for prohibiting investment of trust moneys on personal security is obvious. The borrower may die, or fail in business, or suffer financial reverses. The value of the investment depends partly on the business ability of the borrower and the general financial prosperity of the community. Such an investment is too uncertain for a trustee. He should place the funds so that there will be reasonable assurance of a steady income and

---

[21] Cornet v. Cornet, 269 Mo. 298, 190 S.W. 333; Gray v. Fox, 1 N.J.Eq. 259, 22 Am.Dec. 508; Brewster v. Demarest, 48 N.J.Eq. 559, 23 A. 271; Dufford's Ex'r v. Smith, 46 N.J.Eq. 216, 18 A. 1052; Backes v. Crane, 87 N.J.Eq. 229, 100 A. 900; In re Foster's Will, 15 Hun, N.Y., 387; In re Petrie, 5 Dem.Sur., N.Y., 352; In re Randolph, Sur., 134 N.Y.S. 1117, affirmed 150 App.Div. 902, 135 N.Y.S. 1138; Wilmerding v. McKesson, 103 N.Y. 329, 8 N.E. 665; Deobold v. Oppermann, 111 N.Y. 531, 19 N.E. 94, 2 L.R.A. 644, 7 Am.St.Rep. 760; Collins v. Gooch, 97 N.C. 186, 1 S.E. 653, 2 Am.St.Rep. 284; Roach's Estate, 50 Or. 179, 92 P. 118; Nobles v. Hogg, 36 S.C. 322, 15 S.E. 359; Rowe v. Bentley, 29 Grat., Va., 756. In a few cases it has been held that trustees or persons in similar situations might invest upon personal security in extraodinary cases. Knowlton v. Bradley, 17 N.H. 458, 43 Am. Dec. 609; Scott v. Trustees of Marion Tp., 39 Ohio St. 153; Singleton v. Lowndes, 9 S.C. 465; Barney v. Parsons' Guardian, 54 Vt. 623, 41 Am. Rep. 858.

[22] Michigan Home Missionary Soc. v. Corning, 164 Mich. 395, 402, 129 N.W. 686.

[23] Holmes v. Dring, 2 Cox, Eq.Cas. 1.

[24] Miller v. Holcombe's Ex'r, 9 Grat., Va., 665.

[25] Hunt, Appellant, 141 Mass. 515, 6 N.E. 554; St. Paul Trust Co. v. Kittson, 62 Minn. 408, 65 N.W. 74.

ultimate return of the principal. No matter how prosperous the borrower may be at the time of the loan, the payment of principal and interest depends upon the multitude of uncertainties incident to human affairs. The trustee should obtain a lien upon or interest in some property of reasonable permanence as security for the safety of his investment.

Trade and Business

With but few exceptions, the courts do not sanction the use of trust funds in trade or business.[26] The hazards of buying and selling, manufacturing, and transporting goods are too great to render such operations proper for trustees. The trustee may in breach of trust invest the trust moneys in business in any one of several ways. He may, for example, purchase land and engage in coal mining [27] or buy a farm and pursue agriculture.[28] Neither one of these steps would be a proper one for the trustee to take. They involve too much speculation and risk. The greatest possible assurance that a steady income will be produced and that the principal will be returned is required. Or, although not buying directly the property necessary to engage in trade, the trustee may purchase with the trust funds a share in a partnership which is operating a business. This transaction is likewise a breach of duty on the part of the trustee and renders him liable for losses.[29] Perhaps the most common method adopted by trustees for embarking the trust funds in business is that of the purchase of the stock of corporations engaged in business. A great majority of the American courts condemn such an investment by a trustee as too hazardous and speculative.[30] In recent years, due to the low yield on bonds, there has been an increasing effort to obtain leg-

[26] Adams v. Nelson, 31 Wkly.Law Bul., Ohio., 46; City of Bangor v. Beal, 85 Me. 129, 26 A. 1112; Windmuller v. Spirits Distributing Co., 83 N.J.Eq. 6, 90 A. 249; Nagle v. Von Rosenberg, 55 Tex.Civ.App. 354, 119 S.W. 706.

[27] Butler v. Butler, 164 Ill. 171, 45 N.E. 426.

[28] Wieters v. Hart, 68 N.J.Eq. 796, 64 A. 1135.

[29] Penn v. Fogler, 182 Ill. 76, 55 N. E. 192; Trull v. Trull, 13 Allen, Mass., 407; In re Bannin, 142 App. Div. 436, 127 N.Y.S. 92.

[30] Williams v. Cobb, C.C.A.N.Y., 219 F. 663, 134 C.C.A. 217; White v. Sherman, 168 Ill. 589, 48 N.E. 128, 61 Am.St.Rep. 132; Tucker v. State, 72 Ind. 242; Gilbert v. Welsch, 75 Ind. 557; Cropsey v. Johnston, 137 Mich. 16, 100 N.W. 182; Kimball v. Reding, 31 N.H. 352, 64 Am.Dec. 333; King v. Talbot, 40 N.Y. 76; Adair v. Brimmer, 74 N.Y. 539; In re Hall, 164 N.Y. 196, 58 N.E. 11; English v. McIntyre, 29 App.Div. 439, 51 N.Y.S. 697; Appeal of Worrell, 23 Pa. 44; Appeal of Pray, 34 Pa. 100; Appeal

§ 108   INVESTMENTS GENERALLY DISAPPROVED   357

islative or judicial approval of corporate stock as a trust investment, but the progress of the movement has been slight.[31]

The prevailing view regarding stocks is set forth in the opinion of the New York court in King v. Talbot, where the propriety of investments in railroad, canal company, and bank stocks was under consideration. The court said: [32] "It is not denied that the employment of the fund as capital in trade would be a clear departure from the duty of trustees. If it cannot be so employed under the management of a copartnership, I see no reason for saying that the incorporation of the partners tends, in any degree, to justify it. The moment the fund is invested in bank, or insurance, or railroad stock, it has left the control of the trustees; its safety, and the hazard or risk of loss, is no longer dependent upon their skill, care, or discretion, in its custody or management, and the terms of the investment do not contemplate that it will ever be returned to the trustees. If it be said that, at any time, the trustees may sell the stock (which is but another name for their interest in the property and business of the corporation), and so repossess themselves of the original capital, I reply that is necessarily contingent and uncertain; and so the fund has been voluntarily placed in a condition of uncertainty, dependent upon two contingencies: First, the practicability of making the business profitable; and, second, the judgment, skill, and fidelity of those who have the management of it for that purpose."

The courts of a few states, however, have taken the position that investments in corporate stock are not necessarily improper; that their propriety is to be determined from the nature of the stock and the amount of the investment. In some of these states there is no statutory list and each investment is judged by the rule of ordinary care and prudence. If the stock is one of a reputable company, of strong financial position, and the amount in-

of Ihmsen, 43 Pa. 431. See, however, Costello v. Costello, 209 N.Y. 252, 103 N.E. 148, in which it was held that the statutory and court rules in force in New York, while generally denying the trustee the right to invest in stock, do not invariably make such an investment illegal and that the trustees were in that case authorized to accept corporate stock in exchange for an interest in a partnership.

[31] For efforts to secure court approval of an investment in stocks, see Morris Community Chest v. Wilentz, 124 N.J.Eq. 580, 3 A.2d 808; Reiner v. Fidelity Union Trust Co., 127 N.J.Eq. 377, 13 A.2d 291, 128 A. L.R. 964. Some statutes allow investment in stocks, either with court approval, or in selected stocks named in the statute. Del. L.1935, c. 230, Del.L.1941, c. 224; N.H.L.1941, c. 93; N.J.S.A. 3:16-1; Wash.L.1941, c. 41.

[32] 40 N.Y. 76, 88, 89.

vested therein is not an unduly large proportion of the trust funds, the investment will be approved.[33] Thus, in Dickinson, Appellant,[34] the Massachusetts court held that an investment of more than $3,500 out of a trust fund of $16,200 in the stock of the Union Pacific Railroad Company was improper, on account of the fact that it placed too great a proportion of the funds in the stock of one corporation. The court said:[35] "Our cases, however, show that trustees in this commonwealth are permitted to invest portions of trust funds in dividend-paying stocks and interest-bearing bonds of private business corporations, when the corporations have acquired, by reason of the amount of their property, and the prudent management of their affairs, such a reputation that cautious and intelligent persons commonly invest their own money in such stocks and bonds as permanent investments."

Real Estate and Chattels

Ordinarily a trustee should not invest the trust moneys in real estate.[36] The same rule is applied to quasi trustees, as, for example, guardians.[37] Real property may be productive or unproductive, dependent on many circumstances. Farm land will be productive, if the weather is good, the rainfall proper, and the farmer industrious and skillful. Business and residential property will be productive, if the buildings are kept in good repair,

---

[33] Gray v. Lynch, 8 Gill, Md., 403; McCoy v. Horwitz, 62 Md. 183; Dickinson, Appellant, 152 Mass. 184, 25 N.E. 99, 9 L.R.A. 79; Appeal of Davis, 183 Mass. 499, 67 N.E. 604; Smyth v. Burns' Adm'rs, 25 Miss. 422; Peckham v. Newton, 15 R.I. 321, 4 A. 758; Scoville v. Brock, 81 Vt. 405, 70 A. 1014.

[34] 152 Mass. 184, 25 N.E. 99, 9 L.R.A. 279.

See, also, St. Louis Union Trust Co. v. Toberman, Mo.App., 140 S.W.2d 68. The statutes of two states following the prudent investment rule expressly mention stocks as possible trust investments. Conn. Gen.St. Supp.1939, § 1289e; Mich. Public Acts 1939, No. 76.

[35] 152 Mass. 184, 187, 188, 25 N.E. 99, 9 L.R.A. 279.

[36] Bowman v. Pinkham, 71 Me. 295; West v. Robertson, 67 Miss. 213, 7 So. 224; Williams v. Williams, 35 N.J.Eq. 100; Baker v. Disbrow, 18 Hun, N.Y., 29; Morton's Ex'rs v. Adams, 1 Strob.Eq., S.C., 72; Stone v. Kahle, 22 Tex.Civ.App. 185, 54 S.W. 375. Where the trust funds are partially invested in realty and there is a shortage of income, the court will order a sale of realty and an investment of the proceeds in productive securities. Lesesne v. Cheves, 105 S.C. 432, 90 S.E. 37.

[37] Eckford v. De Kay, 8 Paige, N.Y., 89; Fourth Nat. Bank v. Hopple, 6 Ohio Dec. 482; Scheib v. Thompson, 23 Utah, 564, 65 P. 499; Boisseau v. Boisseau, 79 Va. 73, 52 Am.Rep. 616.

are not destroyed by fire, and the trustee is diligent and skillful in the management of the property. But there are too many contingencies regarding the productivity of real property to make it a safe investment for a trustee. The ordinary trustee is not qualified to operate real estate. In addition real property is often difficult to sell. The trustee may find great trouble in converting the investment into cash when he is required to distribute the trust funds. Nor should a trustee place the trust funds in a leasehold estate in real property.[38] But a loan of the trust funds secured by a mortgage upon real property is not, of course, an investment in lands.[39] The latter investment is approved, providing the margin of security is ample.[40]

In some instances, however, courts have sanctioned a trust investment in real estate, even though such property was without the state in which the trust was to be administered.[41] If the trust instrument expressly authorizes an investment in land, it is obvious that there is sound basis for an approval of the real estate investment.[42] If unusual conditions render desirable an investment in land, the court may grant permission to use the trust funds for such purpose,[43] or the trustee may, in rare cases, so apply the trust funds without express court direction.[44] Thus, where slaves and other property were given to a mother as trustee for her children, for the purpose of supporting the children, and the children had no land upon which the slaves could work, the mother was held entitled to invest in land in order to render the trust property useful and productive.[45] If the settlor places realty in the trust and permits or directs the trustee to retain it, this action will be a protection to the trustee in holding the realty, if he uses reasonable care.

It is obvious that the perishable and temporary character of chattels make them an investment highly unsuited to trusts. Thus, it would be a clear violation of his common law duty, and of

---

[38] In re Anderson, 211 N.Y. 136, 105 N.E. 79.

[39] Milhous v. Dunham, 78 Ala. 48; Zimmerman v. Fraley, 70 Md. 561, 17 A. 560.

[40] See page 351.

[41] Merchants' Loan & Trust Co. v. Northern Trust Co., 250 Ill. 86, 95 N.E. 59, 45 L.R.A.,N.S., 411; Thayer v. Dewey, 185 Mass. 68, 69 N.E. 1074.

[42] Amory v. Green, 13 Allen, Mass., 413; Schaffer v. Wadsworth, 106 Mass. 19.

[43] In re Bellah, 8 Del.Ch. 59, 67 A. 973; Ex parte Jordan, 4 Del.Ch. 615; Ridley v. Dedman, 134 Ky. 146, 119 S.W. 756.

[44] Bethea v. McColl, 5 Ala. 308; Troy Iron & Nail Factory v. Corning, 45 Barb., N.Y., 231.

[45] Bethea v. McColl, 5 Ala. 308.

his duty under all statutes, for a trustee to buy a herd of cattle or an elevator full of grain as a trust investment.

Foreign Investments

As a general rule a trustee should not make an investment outside the jurisdiction in which he is acting. Thus, if he is appointed trustee by a will admitted to probate in New Jersey, and is thus liable to account to the courts of New Jersey for the faithful administration of his trust, he should seek investments within the state of New Jersey. He should not, unless authorized by statute or by the court, invest, for instance, in bonds secured by mortgages on real estate in Kansas. This general principle is recognized in a number of decisions.[46]

In considering the validity of an investment in a bond and mortgage on Ohio real estate, a New York court has well stated the rule:[47] "While, therefore, we are not disposed to say that an investment by a trustee in another state can never be consistent with the prudence and diligence required of him by the law, we still feel bound to say that such an investment, which takes the trust fund beyond our own jurisdiction, subjects it to other laws and the risk and inconvenience of distance and of foreign tribunals, will not be upheld by us as a general rule, and never unless in the presence of a clear and strong necessity, or a very pressing emergency." In that case, however, the court held that a trustee, who was seeking to recover lost trust moneys from the representatives of a defaulting, deceased trustee, was justified in taking a bond secured by a mortgage on foreign real estate as the best satisfaction which he could obtain.

In numerous cases exceptions to this general rule have been made. In some instances the court has allowed foreign investments without any special reason;[48] in other decisions there have been unusual circumstances, as, for example, that the trust instrument gave express authority for the foreign investment,[49] or that the amount invested in foreign real estate was very small in

---

[46] McCullough's Ex'rs v. McCullough, 44 N.J.Eq. 313, 14 A. 642; In re Reed, 45 App.Div. 196, 61 N.Y.S. 50; Collins v. Gooch, 97 N.C. 186, 1 S.E. 653, 2 Am.St.Rep. 284; Pabst v. Goodrich, 133 Wis. 43, 113 N.W. 398, 14 Ann.Cas. 824.

[47] Finch, J., in Ormiston v. Olcott, 84 N.Y. 339, 343.

[48] Merchants' Loan & Trust Co. v. Northern Trust Co., 250 Ill. 86, 95 N.E. 59, 45 L.R.A.,N.S., 411; Stevens v. Meserve, 73 N.H. 293, 61 A. 420, 111 Am.St.Rep. 612.

[49] Amory v. Green, 13 Allen, Mass., 413.

comparison to the size of the whole estate,[50] or that the property taken as security was just across the state boundary and thus within easy reach of the trustee,[51] or that the trustee necessarily took foreign real estate security in order to effect a sale of foreign real estate which the settlor had placed in his hands.[52] The court may permit an investment in foreign real property.[53] In allowing a $200,000 investment in lands located in Illinois, that sum being but a small part of the total trust funds, a Massachusetts court has thus stated the rule: [54] "There is grave objection to the investment of a trust fund in the purchase of real estate in a foreign state, where the property is beyond the jurisdiction of our courts and is subject to laws different from our own. On this account it would not be within the exercise of a sound discretion to make such an investment without some good reason to justify the choice of it. Ordinarily it is very desirable that investments which have a local character, like the ownership of real estate, should be within the jurisdiction of the court that controls the trust. But in this commonwealth there is no arbitrary, universal rule that an investment will not be approved if it consists of fixed property in another state." The investment statutes frequently state whether foreign realty may be the subject of a mortgage taken by a trustee.

Junior Liens

While loans secured by second mortgages on land are sometimes allowed, they are generally disapproved by courts of equity.[55] The trustee should not place the trust funds in a position where they may be endangered by the foreclosure of a prior lien. If he holds a junior mortgage, he may be obliged to pay off the senior encumbrance in order to protect his investment. Such action might involve the investment of too great a proportion of

---

[50] Thayer v. Dewey, 185 Mass. 68, 69 N.E. 1074.

[51] In re Gouldey's Estate, 201 Pa. 491, 51 A. 315.

[52] Denton v. Sanford, 103 N.Y. 607, 9 N.E. 490.

[53] Ridley v. Dedman, 134 Ky. 146, 119 S.W. 756.

[54] Thayer v. Dewey, 185 Mass. 68, 70, 69 N.E. 1074.

[55] New Haven Trust Co. v. Doherty, 75 Conn. 555, 54 A. 209, 96 Am. St.Rep. 239; Shuey v. Latta, 90 Ind. 136; Mattocks v. Moulton, 84 Me. 545, 24 A. 1004; Gilbert v. Kolb, 85 Md. 627, 37 A. 423; Gilmore v. Tuttle, 32 N.J.Eq. 611; In re Petrie, 5 Dem. Sur., N.Y., 352; Savage v. Gould, 60 How.Prac., N.Y. 234; Whitney v. Martine, 88 N.Y. 535; King v. Mackellar, 109 N.Y. 215, 16 N.E. 201; National Surety Co. v. Manhattan Mortg. Co., 185 App.Div. 733, 174 N.Y.S. 9; In re Makin's Estate, 20 Pa.Co.Ct.R. 587.

the trust funds in one piece of property. In rare cases equity will sanction an investment secured by a second mortgage, but only when the security is adequate and unusual circumstances justify the trustee in taking this form of investment.[56]

Mortgages on Chattels or Inferior Realty Interests

Few decisions or statutes [57] approve of an investment of the trust fund in a loan secured by a chattel mortgage or pledge, or secured by a mortgage of a leasehold or life interest in realty.[58] The subject matter of the security is too temporary and evanescent in character.

COMMON TRUST FUNDS [59]

109. At common law it is illegal for a trustee to mingle two or more trust funds in a single investment or a group of investments. But in recent years it has become customary in the case of a few banks to procure permission from settlors to mingle the funds of several trusts in a mass of securities, and also legislation has validated such conduct in some jurisdictions if the trustee complies with certain conditions.

According to the rules laid down by the court of equity it is improper for a trustee who is operating several trusts to mingle in a single investment or in several investments the funds of two or more trusts. Each trust fund must be invested separately from every other fund.[60] Thus, if T. is trustee for A. and also trustee under another trust for B., and has $1,000 of the A. trust funds and $500 of the B. funds on hand for investment, it would be illegal under strict equity doctrines for him to purchase a $1,500 mortgage with these two funds and allot to the A. trust a two-thirds interest and to the B. trust a one-third

---

[56] Taft v. Smith, 186 Mass. 31, 70 N.E. 1031; Sherman v. Lanier, 39 N.J.Eq. 249; In re Blauvelt's Estate, Sur., 20 N.Y.S. 119, semble; In re Bartol's Estate, 182 Pa. 407, 38 A. 527.

[57] Occasionally investment statutes approve of trust investments in mortgages on long term leaseholds, equipment trust obligations where the security is rolling stock of a railroad, or pledges of securities which themselves are legal for trust investment. Ohio Gen.St. § 710-111; Haw.Rev.L. 1935, § 6909, amended by L.1935, p. 205, and L.1937, p. 227.

[58] Sherman v. Lanier, 39 N.J.Eq. 249.

[59] Restatement, Trusts, § 227.

[60] Moore v. McKenzie, 112 Me. 356, 92 A. 296; Jones v. Harsha, 233 Mich. 499, 206 N.W. 979; Heaton v. Bartlett, 87 N.H. 357, 180 A. 244.

interest. He should seek a $1,000 mortgage or bond for the A. trust and a $500 mortgage or bond for the B. trust.

In recent years, however, there has been a tendency to legalize such methods of investment and to permit a trustee of many trusts to set up a common trust fund consisting of many investments which are legal for trusts and invest the funds of its several trusts in shares in this common trust fund. Such a procedure has two important advantages already noticed with regard to participating mortgages and mortgage pools. It spreads the risk and it facilitates quick investment of idle funds, no matter how small they may be. The beneficiaries of each trust have a small fractional interest in the whole mass of securities and the failure of any one security brings them a small loss only. Units of investment in the common fund can be made small so that small balances can be invested without loss of time. If a trustee has to search for a separate investment for $500, more delay may result.[61]

The first method used to validate these common trust funds has been to secure consent of the settlors of trusts. In the case of a few large banks in the East these common trust funds have been set up and the banks have persuaded settlors when they created trusts to insert in the trust instrument a permission that the trustee might invest in shares in the common trust fund.[62]

Secondly, recent legislation has indicated a distinct tendency to permit corporate trustees to set up common trust funds for investments, provided the funds were composed of securities legal for trusts, and the funds were operated under rules protecting the participants.[63] The use of these common trust funds was checked temporarily by a federal court decision [64] that the common trust fund was an "association" for income tax purposes and had to pay a corporation income tax; but Congress remedied this defect by enacting that such funds should not be regarded as associations for federal income tax purposes, if they are operated in accordance with rules laid down by the Federal

[61] See 37 Col.L.R. 1384; 13 Conn. B.J. 14.

[62] For the details of such a composite fund see Bogert, Trusts and Trustees, § 1121.

[63] See statutes of California, Delaware, Hawaii, Kentucky, Massachusetts, New York, Ohio, Oregon, Pennsylvania and Vermont discussed in Bogert on Trusts and Trustees, § 677. A simple enabling act permitting common trust funds is the Uniform Common Trust Fund Act, enacted in Arizona, North Carolina and South Dakota. And see Mass.L.1941, c. 474; Mich.L.1941, S.B. 356.

[64] Brooklyn Trust Co. v. Commissioner of Internal Revenue, C.C.A. N.Y., 80 F.2d 865.

Reserve Board.[65] The Board has recently established rules for the conduct of common trust funds.[66] These rules must be obeyed by any trustee which desires to protect its common trust fund against liability for corporation income taxes which are so much higher than individual income taxes that no common trust fund could survive if treated as an association for income tax purposes.

So far common trust funds have been used in a few cities only. Bookkeeping difficulties in connection with them are serious. But they may afford important sources of investment for small balances and small trusts in the future.

CONTROL BY THE SETTLOR, THE COURT, OR THE BENEFICIARY [67]

110. The trustee's investment duty may be controlled by
   (a) Directions of the settlor expressed in the trust instrument;
   (b) Orders of the court of chancery;
   (c) Conduct of the beneficiary in requesting, consenting to, or acquiescing in, investments.

   In following directions of the settlor the trustee is required to exercise ordinary care and skill.

Settlor's Directions

In considering the duties of a trustee regarding the investment of trust funds, it should be remembered that those duties may be seriously affected or wholly controlled by the directions of the settlor in the trust instrument. The settlor may expressly name the investments which the trustee is under a duty to make, or the settlor may direct the trustee to retain the investments which the settlor had made, or the settlor may give the trustee discretion to invest as he sees fit. "It is fundamental law that a testator or the creator of a trust has unlimited authority to direct how his money may be invested by his trustees, or may leave the manner of such investment completely in the discretion of such trustees." [68]

---

[65] 26 U.S.C.A. Int.Rev.Code, § 169.

[66] Reg.F., Fed.Res. Bd., promulgated in 1937. For text see Bogert, Trusts and Trustees, § 134.

[67] Restatement, Trusts, § 227.

[68] In re Reid, 170 App.Div. 631, 634, 156 N.Y.S. 500. See, also, Merchants' Loan & Trust Co. v. Northern Trust Co., 250 Ill. 86, 91, 95 N.E. 59, 45 L.R.A.,N.S., 411, where the court said: "The creator of a trust may designate how the investments may be made and what security may be taken, or that security may be dis-

If the settlor selects a particular investment as one in which he desires the trust funds to be placed, it is the duty of the trustee to retain the trust funds in such investment, if they are already there, or otherwise to place them in such investment.[69] Thus, a direction of a creator of a trust to invest the shares of the cestuis que trust separately,[70] or to retain certain bonds as the subject-matter of the trust,[71] or to invest in secure stocks or other securities,[72] should be followed by the trustee.

The settlor may, by express direction, give the trustee authority to invest in ways which would ordinarily be unlawful. Thus, a provision for the lending of the trust fund on personal security to a certain business firm,[73] or a clause allowing the purchase of railroad bonds,[74] is valid, and the trustee will be protected in making such investments. But directions by a settlor, allowing a departure from ordinary trust investments, will be strictly construed, and no investment under such authority permitted which is not expressly provided for therein.[75]

It has sometimes been held that equity has no power to direct the trustee to disregard the instructions of the settlor regarding investments, unless all persons interested in the trust consent

pensed with, and the trustees will be bound by the directions." The settlor may reserve the right to direct the investments after the commencement of the trust. Rice v. Halsey, 156 App.Div. 802, 142 N.Y.S. 58.

[69] MacGregor v. MacGregor, 9 Iowa 65; Gray v. Lynch, 8 Gill, Md., 403; Worcester City Missionary Soc. v. Memorial Church, 186 Mass. 531, 72 N.E. 71; Vernon v. Marsh's Ex'rs, 3 N.J.Eq. 502; In re Watson, 81 Misc. 89, 142 N.Y.S. 1058; Seligman v. Seligman, 89 Misc. 194, 151 N.Y.S. 889; Appeal of Ihmsen, 43 Pa. 431. A direction to "preserve" present investments warrants subscribing to additional shares of stock, where such right is given to stockholders, even though the trust instrument also prohibits investments in stock. In re Tower's Estate, 253 Pa. 396, 98 A. 576. If the failure to follow the directions of the settlor results in no loss, the trustee will not be penalized. In re McKinney's Estate, 260 Pa. 123, 103 A. 590. Although the settlor directs investment in railroad bonds, an investment in Liberty Bonds in time of war will be approved. In re London's Estate, 104 Misc. 372, 171 N.Y.S. 981.

[70] In re Watson, 81 Misc. 89, 142 N.Y.S. 1058.

[71] Seligman v. Seligman, 89 Misc. 194, 151 N.Y.S. 889.

[72] Appeal of Ihmsen, 43 Pa. 431.

[73] In re Reid, 170 App.Div. 631, 156 N.Y.S. 500.

[74] In re Bartol's Estate, 182 Pa. 407, 38 A. 527.

[75] In re Franklin Trust Co., 84 Misc. 686, 147 N.Y.S. 885. Thus, a direction to invest in "first-class interest-bearing real estate mortgage securities" does not authorize the purchase of bonds secured by a blanket mortgage protecting the whole issue. The trustee should obtain a mortgage for his benefit alone. In re Mendel's Will, 164 Wis. 136, 159 N.W. 806.

to such change.[76] But, in other cases, where obedience to the settlor's directions would result in loss or disadvantage to the cestuis and all the adult cestuis consent, the court has decreed that the trustee might be relieved from the duty of following the direction of the settlor and might make a more advantageous investment.[77] The court should have power to permit or direct a deviation from the settlor's directions about investments for the purpose of enabling the trustee to accomplish the trust purposes.[78] Thus, where a trust fund amounts to but $2,000, and the trust instrument directs that it be invested in Florida real estate upon which houses are to be built for winter tourists, and it is desirable to make an investment which will yield some income at once for the beneficiaries, a New York court of equity felt justified in directing the trustee to disregard the settlor's direction and make a productive investment.[79]

If the settlor authorizes the trustee to invest the trust funds as may seem best to the trustee or according to his discretion, he has a wide margin for action. He is not required to make his selection from the securities and investments declared by equity or by statute to be legal investments for trust funds. He may choose reasonable investments outside such approved lists.[80] Thus, where the trustee has discretion with respect to the investments, he may lawfully invest in railway and street rail-

[76] Clark v. St. Louis A. & T. H. R. Co., 58 How.Prac., N.Y., 21; Burrill v. Sheil, 2 Barb., N.Y., 457; Snelling v. McCreary, 14 Rich.Eq., S.C., 291. Thus, in International Trust Co. v. Preston, 24 Wyo. 163, 156 P. 1128, it was held that a court had no power to sanction an investment in Mexican bonds when the will directed investment in bonds of the United States or a state or municipality thereof.

[77] Wood v. Wood, 5 Paige, N.Y., 596, 28 Am.Dec. 451; McIntire's Adm'rs v. City of Zanesville, 17 Ohio St. 352; Perronneau v. Perronneau's Ex'rs, 1 Desaus. S.C., 521. In Hackett's Ex'rs v. Hackett's Devisees, 180 Ky. 406, 202 S.W. 864, the court says that the testator's direction must be followed unless no such investment as is directed can be made or the safety of the investment directed has become doubtful by supervening circumstances. As showing the recent tendency of the English courts on this subject, see In re D'Epinoix's Settlement, [1914] 1 Ch. 890.

[78] See § 164, post.

[79] In re Snyder's Will, Sup., 136 N.Y.S. 670.

[80] Cromey v. Bull, 4 Ky.Law Rep. 787; Lawton v. Lawton, 35 App.Div. 389, 54 N.Y.S. 760; In re Vom Saal's Will, 82 Misc. 531, 145 N.Y.S. 307; Willis v. Braucher, 79 Ohio St. 290, 87 N.E. 185, 44 L.R.A., N.S., 873, 16 Ann. Cas. 66. In Lawson v. Cunningham, 275 Mo. 128, 204 S.W. 1100, under such a grant of discretion, an investment in land was sanctioned.

way bonds [81] and in real estate outside the state, [82] if such investments are reasonably prudent.

But the grant of discretion in the making of investments does not protect the trustee in *any* investment which he may make. He must use good faith and reasonable prudence in exercising his discretion.[83] Just because he may go outside the selected list of trust investments approved by the court or the Legislature does not mean that he may invest the trust funds in any wildcat venture. He must select an investment which he honestly believes will be safe and productive, [84] and he must act with reasonable prudence and diligence.[85] The fact that the trustee has authority to exercise his discretion regarding investments does not make it proper for him to invest in a manufacturing plant in another state, when he has little or no knowledge concerning the business,[86] or to invest in stocks,[87] or to speculate in Western lands [88] with the trust funds. In an opinion in which it disapproved of an investment in the stock of an umbrella manufacturing company by a trustee having discretion concerning investments, the New York Court of Appeals has said: [89] "We concede that under the terms of the will the trustees were given a discretion as to the character of the investments they might make, and that they were not limited to the investments required by a court of equity in the absence of any directions from a testator. * * * But such a discretion, in the absence of words in the will giving greater authority, should not be held to authorize investment of the trust fund in new speculative or hazardous ventures. If the trustees had invested in the stock of a railroad, manufacturing, banking, or even business cor-

---

[81] In re Allis' Estate, 123 Wis. 223, 101 N.W. 365.

[82] Merchants' Loan & Trust Co. v. Northern Trust Co., 250 Ill. 86, 95 N.E. 59.

[83] Appeal of Davis, 183 Mass. 499, 67 N.E. 604. Thus, a loan to himself is not warranted by the grant of such discretion. Carrier v. Carrier, 226 N.Y. 114, 123 N.E. 135.

[84] In re Smith, [1896] 1 Ch. 71.

[85] Kimball v. Reding, 31 N.H. 352, 64 Am.Dec. 333; Clark v. Clark, 23 Misc. 272, 50 N.Y.S. 1041; In re Vom Saal's Will, 82 Misc. 531, 145 N.Y.S. 307. The court will review the exercise of the discretion and will disapprove such investments as loans to a corporation in which the trustees are individually interested. In re Keane, 95 Misc. 25, 160 N.Y.S. 200.

[86] In re Hart's Estate, 203 Pa. 480, 53 A. 364.

[87] In re Hirsch's Estate, 116 App. Div. 367, 101 N.Y.S. 893, affirmed 188 N.Y. 584, 81 N.E. 1165.

[88] In re Reed, 45 App.Div. 196, 61 N.Y.S. 50.

[89] In re Hall, 164 N.Y. 196, 199, 200, 58 N.E. 11.

poration, which, by its successful conduct for a long period of time, had achieved a standing in commercial circles and acquired the confidence of investors, their conduct would have been justified, although the investment proved unfortunate. But the distinction between such an investment and the one before us is very marked. Surely there is a mean between a government bond and the stock of an Alaska gold mine, and the fact that a trustee is not limited to the one does not authorize him to invest in the other."

In following any direction of the settlor about investments, the trustee is required to act with ordinary prudence and care.

Court Control

Not only may the duty of the trustee regarding investments be controlled by the settlor, but also by chancery. If the trustee is justifiably in doubt concerning the investments which the trust instrument authorizes him to make, he may apply to the court, and it will give him direction.[90] These decrees should be implicitly obeyed, and the trustee will be protected, no matter what the result of the investment, if it was made in strict accordance with a court order which has been properly obtained.[91] Likewise, disobedience to the court order will render the trustee personally liable for losses. Thus, where a trustee submitted the trust to the jurisdiction of the court and was ordered to invest the funds in government bonds, but instead left the money in a bank in which he was interested, and the bank failed, the trustee was charged with the loss ensuing to the trust estate.[92]

In a few states trustees are required by statute to submit all proposed investments to the court for approval.[93] It seems poor practice for a trustee to attempt to shift responsibility for the selection of investments to the court of equity. The court has no time or facilities for passing on investments and its decree of approval is ordinarily purely formal and does not involve the use of any judgment which will protect the beneficiaries.

---

[90] Drake v. Crane, 127 Mo. 85, 29 S.W. 990, 27 L.R.A. 653; Tillinghast v. Coggeshall, 7 R.I. 383; Whitehead v. Whitehead, 85 Va. 870, 9 S.E. 10.

[91] Wheeler v. Perry, 18 N.H. 307; Wood v. Wood, 5 Paige, N.Y., 596, 28 Am.Dec. 451; In re Old's Estate, 176 Pa. 150, 34 A. 1022.

[92] Whitehead v. Whitehead, 85 Va. 870, 9 S.E. 10.

[93] See Iowa Code 1939, § 12772; In re Nolan's Guardianship, 216 Iowa 903, 249 N.W. 648.

Consent by Cestui

If the trustee makes an improper investment at the request or direction or with the consent of the cestui que trust, the trustee will not be liable for losses ensuing as a result of such improper investment.[94] And so, too, if the beneficiary acquiesces in or ratifies the unlawful investment after it has been made, he will not be heard to complain of losses occurring therefrom.[95] But the consent or ratification must be with full knowledge of the facts and of the legal rights of the beneficiaries, in order that it may relieve the trustee from liability.[96] And the cestui must be of full age and sound mind, and labor under no other disability when he gives his consent or acquiescence, in order that the trustee may be protected.[97] Naturally also a consent or

---

[94] Campbell v. Miller, 38 Ga. 304, 95 Am.Dec. 389; Follansbe v. Kilbreth, 17 Ill. 522, 65 Am.Dec. 691; Phillips v. Burton, 107 Ky. 88, 52 S.W. 1064; Contee v. Dawson, 2 Bland, Md., 264; Appeal of Fidelity & Deposit Co. of Maryland, 172 Mich. 600, 138 N.W. 205; In re Hoffman's Estate, 183 Mich. 67, 148 N.W. 268, 152 N.W. 952; Furniss v. Zimmerman, 90 Misc. 138, 154 N.Y.S. 272; In re Westerfield, 48 App.Div. 542, 63 N.Y.S. 10, appeal dismissed, 163 N.Y. 209, 57 N.E. 403; In re Hall, 164 N.Y. 196, 58 N.E. 11; Hester v. Hester, 16 N.C. 328, 1 Dev.Eq. 328; Dennis v. Dennis, 3 Ohio Dec. 12; In re Clermontel's Estate, 12 Phila., Pa., 139; Arthur v. Master in Equity, Harp.Eq., S.C., 47; Mills v. Swearingen, 67 Tex. 269, 3 S.W. 268; Pownal v. Myers, 16 Vt. 408; Watson v. Conrad, 38 W.Va. 536, 18 S.E. 744. *Contra,* Aydelott v. Breeding, 111 Ky. 847, 64 S.W. 916. Thus, where a portion of the trust assets is a claim against a mining company and the beneficiaries consent to the lending of more money to such company in an attempt to recover the sum already invested, they cannot afterward object to the investment. Mann v. Day, 199 Mich. 88, 165 N.W. 643. And acceptance by a cestui que trust of securities on a distribution bars objection to them as improper investments. In re Kent, 173 App. Div. 563, 159 N.Y.S. 627.

[95] See § 161, post. Failure to object for twenty-seven years was held to bar the cestui que trust from complaint in Backes v. Crane, 87 N.J.Eq. 229, 100 A. 900. See, also, In re Union Trust Co. of New York, 219 N.Y. 514, 114 N.E. 1057; In re Keane, 95 Misc. 25, 160 N.Y.S. 200.

The mere sending of statements by the trustee to the beneficiary showing an investment, and a conversation between trustee and beneficiary about it after a default, do not show ratification. In re Johnston's Estate, 129 N.J.Eq. 104, 18 A.2d 274.

[96] White v. Sherman, 168 Ill. 589, 48 N.E. 128, 61 Am.St.Rep. 132; Appeal of Nichols, 157 Mass. 20, 31 N.E. 683; McKim v. Glover, 161 Mass. 418, 37 N.E. 443; In re Reed, 45 App.Div. 196, 61 N.Y.S. 50; Adair v. Brimmer, 74 N.Y. 539; Appeal of Pray, 34 Pa. 100.

[97] Murray v. Feinour, 2 Md.Ch. 418. A guardian of a minor cestui que trust cannot acquiesce in a wrongful investment and bind the minor. International Trust Co. v. Preston, 24 Wyo. 163, 156 P. 1128.

acquiescence obtained by fraud [98] or undue influence [99] will have no effect upon the cestui's rights. Obviously the beneficiaries who are in existence cannot consent or acquiesce in such a way as to affect the rights of cestuis not yet born.[1]

The law respecting the approval by the beneficiary of improper investments is well set forth in an Illinois decision, in which it was held that the trustee was not protected in investing in railroad stocks by proof that he suggested such investments and the beneficiaries told him to use his own judgment.[2] "In order to bind a cestui que trust by acquiescence in a breach of trust by the trustee, it must appear that the cestui que trust knew all the facts, and was apprised of his legal rights, and was under no disability to assert them. Such proof must be full and satisfactory. The cestui que trust must be shown, in such case to have acted freely, deliberately, and advisedly, with the intention of confirming a transaction which he knew, or might or ought, with reasonable or proper diligence, to have known to be impeachable. His acquiescence amounts to nothing if his right to impeach is concealed from him, or if a free disclosure is not made to him of every circumstance which it is material for him to know. He cannot be held to have recognized the validity of a particular investment, unless the question as to such validity appears to have come before him. The trustee setting up the acquiescence of the cestui que trust must prove such acquiescence. The trustee must also see to it that all the cestuis que trust concur, in order to protect him from a breach of trust. If any of the beneficiaries are not sui juris, they will not be bound by acts charged against them as acts of acquiescence. The trustee cannot escape liability merely by informing the cestuis que trust that he has committed a breach of trust. The trustee is bound to know what his own duty is, and cannot throw upon the cestuis que trust the obligation of telling what such duty is. Mere knowledge and noninterference by the cestui que trust before his interest has come into possession do not always bind him as acquiescing in the breach of trust. As a general rule, acquiescence by a tenant for life, or by a cestui que trust for life, will not bind the person entitled to the remainder."

---

[98] Zimmerman v. Fraley, 70 Md. 561, 17 A. 560; Appeal of Nichols, 157 Mass. 20, 31 N.E. 683.

[99] Wieters v. Hart, 68 N.J.Eq. 796, 64 A. 1135.

[1] Wood v. Wood, 5 Paige, N.Y., 596, 28 Am.Dec. 451. And life tenants cannot affect the rights of remaindermen. International Trust Co. v. Preston, 24 Wyo. 163, 156 P. 1128.

[2] White v. Sherman, 168 Ill. 589, 605, 606, 48 N.E. 128, 61 Am.St.Rep. 132.

It is undesirable trust practice for a trustee to depend on consents and waivers by the beneficiaries to protect him against liability for investments. The settlor has vested the investment powers in the trustee, not in the beneficiaries. The former is, or ought to be, a person of judgment and capacity; the beneficiaries are often not skilled in investment work. The very purpose of the trust is to give the cestuis the benefits of the property, without placing upon them the burdens of management. A trustee who submits every investment to his beneficiaries and secures their written approval is trying to shift his investment burden to the beneficiaries. Their approval does not often represent a considered opinion, but rather a merely formal act.

DUTY TO REVIEW TRUST INVESTMENTS [3]

111. A trustee is under a duty to examine from time to time the trust investments which he holds in order to learn whether they are legal for holding under the trust and are still desirable for retention.

If a trustee makes a lawful and prudent investment for his trust, or receives such an investment from the settlor or a predecessor trustee, he cannot assume that it will continue indefinitely to be a lawful and prudent investment. He cannot place it in his safety deposit box and ignore its status henceforth. He has a duty to examine all his trust investments at reasonable intervals in order to learn the condition of the obligor on bonds and mortgages, the condition of the property in which he holds a security interest, and the status of the corporations whose stock he holds.[4] He should watch out for defaults in payments of principal and interest, financial difficulties experienced by obligors, changes in the condition of real property, and similar matters. He should collect all relevant information through an examination of the property himself, watching corporate statements and reports, and reading financial services which give information regarding the finances of corporations.

The trustee is charged with knowledge of what he could have learned by this review and re-examination, and is liable for damages if he should have known of danger to the trust, could have protected the trust, but did not do so.[5]

[3] Restatement, Trusts, §§ 230–231.

[4] Johns v. Herbert, 2 App.D.C. 485; Matter of Clark's Will, 257 N.Y. 132, 177 N.E. 397, 77 A.L.R. 499.

[5] State Street Trust Co. v. Walker, 259 Mass. 578, 157 N.E. 334; Tannenbaum v. Seacoast Trust Co., 125 N.J. Eq. 360, 5 A.2d 778.

DUTY TO CHANGE TRUST INVESTMENTS [6]

112. When an investment is at the beginning of the trust, or becomes later, an investment not permitted under the terms of the trust and the law of the state in question, the trustee has a duty to sell it and reinvest the proceeds.

On receiving an investment from the settlor, or the settlor's executor, or a predecessor trustee, the trustee has a duty to examine the investment and study the trust instrument and the law of the state. He must at his peril learn whether the investment is a lawful one for him to hold under the terms of the particular trust and under the controlling case and statute law.[7] Thus, if the trust is testamentary and the executor of the settlor delivers to the trustee stock certificates of a manufacturing corporation as part of the trust property, the trustee will have a duty to learn whether stock of such a corporation is a lawful and prudent trust investment for him, in view of what the settlor has said about trust investments in his will and in view of the decisions and statutes of the state.

If the trustee concludes that the investment is not lawful or prudent for him, he has a duty to sell it as soon as possible, without too great sacrifice.[8] What is a reasonable period within which to make the sale depends upon many circumstances, including the market there is for the investment and the price at which it can be sold.

This same duty to convert or sell investments arises when the trustee discovers that an investment originally legal, whether made by him or by a predecessor in title, has now become illegal or imprudent.[9] If in the course of his periodical reviews of the trust investments, for example, he learns that property on which he holds a $10,000 mortgage is rapidly deteriorating due to a change in the neighborhood, so that the margin of security has now vanished, he may come under a duty to sell the mortgage if he can find a purchaser at a reasonable figure, or if there has been a default to foreclose.[10]

---

[6] Restatement, Trusts, §§ 230–231.

[7] Wordin's Appeal from Probate, 71 Conn. 531, 42 A. 659, 71 Am.St.Rep. 219; Mobley v. Phinizy, 42 Ga.App. 33, 155 S.E. 73; Villard v. Villard, 219 N.Y. 482, 114 N.E. 789.

[8] Clark v. Clark, 167 Ga. 1, 144 S.E. 787; Creed v. McAleer, 275 Mass. 353, 175 N.E. 761, 80 A.L.R. 1117; In re Leitsch's Will, 185 Wis. 257, 201 N.W. 284, 37 A.L.R. 547.

[9] Stephens' Ex'rs v. Milnor, 24 N.J. Eq. 358; In re Estate of Dreier, 204 Wis. 221, 235 N.W. 439.

[10] In re Salmon, 42 Ch.D. 351; State Street Trust Co. v. De Kalb, 259 Mass. 578, 157 N.E. 334.

In many trust instruments the settlor expressly *permits* the trustee to retain investments made by the settlor. This, of course, protects the trustee in such retention, if he used reasonable care in so doing. It does not permit the trustee to retain the investment, no matter how bad or dangerous it may become.[11]

If the settlor *directs* a retention of his investments, or directs a sale of them, naturally this instruction will obligate the trustee to hold the investment unless very clear proof arises that the investment is unsound, or to sell as soon as can be done at a reasonable price.[12]

In several states statutes permit the trustee to retain the settlor's investments, but they have been construed to mean that retention is allowed, unless an ordinarily prudent man would know that retention was highly dangerous to the beneficiaries.[13]

The trustee may be relieved from liability for failure to sell an improper investment by a request of the beneficiaries that he retain it.[14]

[11] Fortune v. First Trust Co., 200 Minn. 367, 274 N.W. 524, 112 A.L.R. 346; Fairleigh v. Fidelity Nat. Bank & Trust Co., 335 Mo. 360, 73 S.W.2d 248; In re Dickinson's Estate, 318 Pa. 561, 179 A. 443.

[12] Richardson v. Knight, 69 Me. 285; In re Bartol's Estate, 182 Pa. 407, 38 A. 527.

[13] Fla.L.1937, p. 1283; La.Act No. 81 of 1938, § 65; People by Kerner v. Canton Nat. Bank, 288 Ill.App. 418, 6 N.E.2d 220; In re Riker's Estate, 125 N.J.Eq. 349, 350, 351, 5 A.2d 685; N.Y.L.1938, c. 356; 20 P.S. §§ 865, 866.

[14] In re Bogert's Estate, Sur., 24 N.Y.S.2d 553.

CHAPTER 12

TRUST ADMINISTRATION—LIABILITIES FROM CONTRACTS, TORTS AND PROPERTY OWNERSHIP

Sec.
113. Personal Liability of Trustee on Contracts.
114. Exclusion of Personal Liability.
115. Trustee's right to Indemnity.
116. Contract Creditor's Rights against the Trustee as Such.
117. Personal Liability of Trustee for Torts.
118. Trustee's Right to Indemnity.
119. Tort Creditor's Rights against the Trustee as Such.
120. Liability of the Trustee as Property Owner.

PERSONAL LIABILITY OF TRUSTEES ON CONTRACTS [1]

113. If a trustee makes a contract on behalf of the trust he is personally liable on it, unless the contract provides otherwise. The promisee can recover out of the trustee's private property and not out of the trust property. It is immaterial that the person contracting with the trustee knew of the trust and knew that the trustee was making the contract for the benefit of the trust.

Trustees have express or implied authority to make many contracts.[2] For example, a trustee of an office building may contract for the services of the employees necessary to run the building and for fuel and light to make it usable. If the contract is one which the trustee is empowered to make, he will usually perform his contracts and no difficulty will arise. He will pay the janitor and the coal dealer out of the income of the office building. But frequently the trustee makes contracts in his trust administration and fails to perform them. For example, he may hire a contractor to place a new roof on the office building and not pay the contract price of the work and materials when the price is due. The question then arises as to the liability on such a contract and the remedies of the creditor.[3]

The question is decided by careful consideration of the identity of the person who made the promise. The only legal person recognized by the court of law in which the promise will be en-

---

[1] Restatement, Trusts, §§ 262, 275.

[2] Shelby v. White, 158 Miss. 880, 131 So. 343; Ranzau v. Davis, 85 Or. 26, 158 P. 279.

[3] For valuable articles see Brandeis, 15 Amer.L.R. 449; Stone, 22 Col.L.R. 527; Scott, 28 Harv.L.R. 725.

374

forced is the trustee as an individual, and not in his representative capacity. If Henry Smith is trustee under the will of John Brown, and Smith contracts for work and materials and promises to pay a certain sum therefor, the court of law regards Henry Smith as the person making the promise and liable upon it. It does not recognize Henry Smith, as trustee, as a distinct legal person at all. The trust estate or trust is certainly not a person in the eye of the law, and the beneficiaries of the trust did not make the contract. The trustee is not their agent.[4] They are not liable as principals. Smith is the only legal entity making the promise and liable upon it. Whether his liability is permanent or will finally be shifted to the trust is of no concern to the law court. It leaves that matter to the court of equity.

Thus, it comes about that trustees are personally liable on the contracts they make during trust administration, unless they expressly exclude such liability. For a breach of a contract where personal liability is not excluded the third person who is the promisee can sue the trustee at law and collect out of the trustee's individual property.[5] An action at law cannot be maintained against the trustee as such, or in his representative capacity, and collection cannot be had out of the trust property after judgment obtained.[6]

It is immaterial that the person contracting with the trustee knew the trust existed, knew that the trustee was acting in his fiduciary capacity, and that the contract was one made in the course of the trust administration.[7] If the third person did not expressly agree to relieve the trustee from personal liability, in the contract itself, the trustee is personally liable. That the trust instrument provided that the trustee was not to be liable on contracts he made for the trust, will not excuse the trustee from personal liability, unless the parties contracted with the terms of the trust instrument in mind and in substance incorporated them into their contract.[8]

---

[4] Taylor v. Mayo, 110 U.S. 330, 4 S.Ct. 147, 28 L.Ed. 163; Everett v. Drew, 129 Mass. 150.

[5] Peyser v. American Security & Trust Co., 70 App.D.C. 349, 107 F.2d 625; Slatt v. Thomas, 95 Colo. 382, 36 P.2d 459.

[6] Zehnbar v. Spillman, 25 Fla. 591, 6 So. 214; O'Brien v. Jackson, 167 N.Y. 31, 60 N.E. 238; Smith v. Chambers, 117 W.Va. 204, 185 S.E. 211.

[7] Breid v. Mintrup, 203 Mo.App. 567, 219 S.W. 703; Connally v. Lyons, 82 Tex. 664, 18 S.W. 799, 27 Am. St.Rep. 935.

[8] James Stewart & Co., Inc., v. National Shawmut Bank of Boston, C.C. A.Mass., 75 F.2d 148; Goldwater v.

In a few states as a result of statute law a contract creditor of the trustee may sue the trustee in his representative capacity in an action at law and collect his judgment from trust property.[9] This tendency to recognize the trustee as such as a juridical person is found in the Uniform Trusts Act which permits such an action, if the beneficiaries have been notified and given an opportunity to intervene.[10]

A recent Montana case [11] refuses to hold the trustee personally liable, basing its decision in part on a statute [12] and in part on the argument that the reason for the rule of personal liability was the distinction between law and equity and that this reason has ceased to exist. There is much force to this argument.

If a trustee attempts to make a contract on behalf of the trust, but he lacks power to make it, the contract binds the trustee personally.[13]

EXCLUSION OF PERSONAL LIABILITY [14]

114. A trustee may exclude personal liability by inserting a clause to that effect in a contract, but merely describing himself as trustee in the body of the contract or in his signature does not amount to an expression of a willingness by the other party to forego the personal liability of the trustee.

A trustee may also stipulate for liability of the trust property for the performance of a contract made by the trustee, if the contract is one which is proper for the trustee to make and is beneficial to the beneficiaries.

If the person contracting with the trustee is willing to treat with the trustee on such terms, the trustee may provide express-

---

Oltman, 210 Cal. 408, 292 P.2d 624, 71 A.L.R. 871; Review Printing & Stationery Co. v. McCoy, 291 Ill.App. 524, 10 N.E.2d 506.

[9] Conn.Gen.St.1930, § 5640; Ga. Code 1933, § 108-406; Pa. 20 P.S. § 1171.

[10] Section 12, now adopted in Louisiana, Nevada, North Carolina and Oklahoma.

[11] Tuttle v. Union Bank & Trust Co., Mont., 119 P.2d 884.

[12] Mont.Rev.Code 1935, § 7914. This section was copied from the Field Code in California. See Cal. Civ.Code, § 2267; N.D.Comp.L.1913, § 6305; S.D.Code 1939, § 59.0209. The section reads as follows: "A trustee is a general agent for the trust property. His authority as such is conferred upon him by the declaration of trust and by this chapter, and none other. His acts, within the scope of his authority, bind the trust property to the same extent as the acts of an agent bind his principal."

[13] Downey Co. v. 282 Beacon St. Trust, 292 Mass. 175, 197 N.E. 643.

[14] Restatement, Trusts, §§ 263, 271.

§ 114   EXCLUSION OF PERSONAL LIABILITY   377

ly against any personal obligation upon his part and the trustee cannot be held individually liable for the performance of the contract.[15] "It is equally clear, on the other hand, that although one may covenant as trustee, he may limit and qualify the character in which he is to be held answerable; and where it plainly appears from the face of the instrument that he did not mean to bind himself personally, courts will construe the covenant according to the plainly expressed intention of the parties, and this, too, in cases where the covenantor had no right to bind himself in a fiduciary character. If the plaintiff be without remedy in such cases, he has no one to blame but himself, in accepting a covenant of such a character. He certainly has no right to rely upon the individual liability of the covenantor."[16] Where personal liability is thus excluded, it would seem that the only right of the promisee would be against the trustee in his representative capacity if that liability was contracted for and the contract was within the trustee's powers,[17] or if the contract was not within the trustee's powers a cause of action against the trustee for breach of a warranty of authority.[18] "Where the parties expressly contract that no personal liability shall attach to the trustee, the creditor would necessarily depend upon such liability as might lawfully be created against the estate, and it is possible that his remedy might be limited to a suit in equity."[19]

The trustee, in order to exclude personal liability, should state in the contract that he contracts as trustee and not personally. The mere description of the trustee as such in the body of the contract, and the mere addition of the words "as trustee" following the trustee's signature, do not show an intent to contract against personal liability or an acceptance of such exclusion by the other party.[20]

---

[15] Thayer v. Wendell, 1 Gall. 37, Fed.Cas.No.13,873; Glenn v. Allison, 58 Md. 527; Shoe & Leather Nat. Bank v. Dix, 123 Mass. 148, 25 Am. Rep. 49; Rand v. Farquhar, 226 Mass. 91, 115 N.E. 286; Brackett v. Ostrander, 126 App.Div. 529, 110 N.Y. S. 779; Crate v. Benzinger, 13 App. Div. 617, 43 N.Y.S. 824. In Watling v. Lewis, [1911] 1 Ch. 414, it was held that where the trustees made a contract "as trustees, but not so as to create any personal liability," they were nevertheless liable; the court considering the contract to have two repugnant terms, and saying that the trustees might limit, but could not destroy their personal liability.

[16] Glenn v. Allison, 58 Md. 527, 529.

[17] Hussey v. Arnold, 185 Mass. 202, 70 N.E. 87.

[18] Landow v. Keane, Sup., 10 N.Y.S. 2d 267.

[19] Packard v. Kingman, 109 Mich. 497, 507, 67 N.W. 551, 555.

[20] Hamlen v. Welch, C.C.A.Mass., 116 F.2d 413; Zimmer Construction

Under the terms of the Uniform Negotiable Instruments Law [21] if a trustee signs a negotiable instrument "in a representative capacity" and on behalf of a named or described trust, he is not personally liable on the instrument but is liable in his representative capacity so that collection can be had out of the assets of the trust, assuming that the execution of the instrument was within the powers of the trustee.[22] If the name of the trust does not appear in the instrument, some courts have permitted oral evidence to explain that the name was stated orally to the payee by the maker.[23]

In some cases the trustee has been allowed expressly to obligate the trust estate by his contracts; that is, his promises have resulted in creating rights on behalf of the promisees to proceed in equity directly against the trustee in his representative capacity and collect out of trust property.[24] Thus, in Jessup v. Smith [25] a trustee who was out of funds employed an attorney to perform services beneficial to the estate and expressly stipulated that the estate alone should be liable. It was held that the trust property could be subjected to the payment of the debt; the court saying: [26] "A trustee, who pays his own money for services beneficial to the trust, has a lien for reimbursement. But if he is unable or unwilling to incur liability himself, the law does not leave him helpless. In such circumstances, he 'has the power, if other funds fail, to create a charge, equivalent to his own lien for reimbursement, in favor of another by whom the services are rendered.' * * *" And in Rand v. Farquhar [27] the trust instrument provided that contracts of the trustees should bind the trust estate alone. The trustees executed a contract excluding personal responsibility and providing for liability by the trust estate only.

Co. v. White, 8 Cal.App.2d 672, 47 P.2d 1087; Dolben v. Gleason, 292 Mass. 511, 198 N.E. 762.

[21] Section 20.

[22] Cotton v. Courtright, 215 Ala. 474, 111 So. 7; Tebaldi Supply Co. v. MacMillan, 292 Mass. 384, 198 N.E. 651; First Nat. Bk. of Pennsboro v. Delancey, 109 W.Va. 136, 153 S.E. 908.

[23] American Trust Co. v. Canevin, C.C.A.Pa., 184 F. 657; Magallen v. Gomes, 281 Mass. 383, 183 N.E. 833;
Megowan v. Peterson, 173 N.Y. 1, 65 N.E. 738.

[24] People ex rel. Nelson v. Home Bank & Trust Co., 300 Ill.App. 611, 21 N.E.2d 809; King v. Stowell, 211 Mass. 246, 98 N.E. 91; New v. Nicoll, 73 N.Y. 127, 29 Am.Rep. 111.

[25] 223 N.Y. 203, 119 N.E. 403. See, also, in accord, Noyes v. Blakeman, 6 N.Y. 567, and Randall v. Dusenbury, 39 N.Y.Super.Ct. 174.

[26] 223 N.Y. 203, 207, 119 N.E. 403, 404.

[27] 226 Mass. 91, 115 N.E. 286.

It was held that the object desired could be accomplished under the circumstances. And in some cases where the settlor has directed the carrying on by the trustee of a certain business, and the contract in question has been made by the trustee in connection with such business, the trustee has been held to have power to charge the trust estate by his contract.[28] The contract must be one which is beneficial to the cestuis and within the trustee's powers.[29]

It would seem that if the trustee expressly excludes personal liability, and does not contract for collection from the trust property in so many words, such a provision should nevertheless be implied,[30] since otherwise the remedy of the other party to the contract will be negative or exceedingly difficult.

TRUSTEE'S RIGHT OF INDEMNITY AS TO CONTRACTS[31]

115. A trustee who makes a contract which is within his powers and is prudently made has a right that liability thereunder shall not rest upon him permanently but shall rather be satisfied out of trust property. The trustee may assert this right of indemnity by

(a) Paying the contract creditor out of trust property;

(b) Reimbursing himself out of trust property for advances he has made out of his own funds to meet liability under trust contracts;

(c) Suing in equity to get a decree that initial liability rest on him as trustee, where he is sued individually on a contract which he made as trustee;

(d) Requesting reimbursement for amounts paid from his own property to meet contract obligations, either on his accounting or in a suit to have trust property sold for that purpose.

(e) Retaining possession of trust property under a lien which the law gives him until he is repaid amounts which he has expended from his private funds for contract liability.

The trustee is not ordinarily entitled to indemnity for contract obligations from the beneficiary, even though he cannot get full indemnity from the trust property.

[28] Gisborn v. Charter Oak Life Ins. Co., 142 U.S. 326, 12 S.Ct. 277, 35 L.Ed. 1029; Roberts v. Hale, 124 Iowa 296, 99 N.W. 1075, 1 Ann.Cas. 940; Cannon v. Robinson, 67 N.C. 53; Mathews v. Stephenson, 6 Pa. 496; Woodrop v. Weed, 154 Pa. 307, 26 A. 375, 35 Am.St.Rep. 832; Yerkes v. Richards, 170 Pa. 346, 32 A. 1089.

[29] Terminal Trading Co. v. Babbit, 7 Wash.2d 166, 109 P.2d 564.

[30] Ballentine v. Eaton, 297 Mass. 389, 8 N.E.2d 808; Beggs v. Fite, 130 Tex. 46, 106 S.W.2d 1039.

[31] Restatement, Trusts, §§ 249, 261, 268, 278-279.

It is obvious that final liability for contracts made by the trustee in the proper administration of his trust should be borne by the trust property. The trustee is only a representative. He personally does not gain from the trust administration. The benefits of the contract will go to the beneficiaries of the trust, and any burdens incidental to it should be met from property equitably belonging to the beneficiaries, that is, from the trust property. While as a matter of contract law, and as between the contracting trustee and the third person, the liability of the trustee generally is personal to the trustee, as a matter of equity that burden should ultimately be shifted to the trust property, if the trustee had power to make the contract and made it with reasonable prudence.

In recognition of this principle it is undoubted law that the trustee may meet such contract obligations in the first place out of trust property, that is, by self-help he may shift the burden from himself to the trust property. Or if originally he is forced to meet the contract debt from his own pocket, he may by self help repay himself from trust income later coming into his hands.[32]

Furthermore, if an action is pending against the trustee on a contract he made for the trust, and the trustee wants to avoid having a judgment recovered against him personally, he may sue in equity to have it adjudged that the judgment shall be against him as trustee in the first place, and he will succeed if he can prove that he made the contract lawfully and with ordinary prudence.[33] This is sometimes called the right of "exoneration" from liability.

It is also true that, if the trustee has met the contract obligation out of his own funds, and it is not possible for him to repay himself in the ordinary course of trust administration, he may claim reimbursement on his accounting as a trustee or by petitioning the court of equity to permit him to sell trust property in order to accomplish the reimbursement.[34]

In order to force the reimbursement to which he is entitled,

---

[32] Hamlen v. Welch, C.C.A.Mass., 116 F.2d 413.

[33] Hobbs v. Wayet, 36 Ch.D. 256; In re National Financial Co., L.R. 3 Ch.App. 791.

[34] Sorrels v. McNally, 94 Fla. 1174, 115 So. 540; Warner v. Tullis, 206 Iowa 680, 218 N.W. 575; Barrell v. Joy, 16 Mass. 221.

the trustee may hold possession of the trust property. He is said to have a lien for that purpose.[35]

The trustee is not entitled to indemnity for contract or other liabilities from the beneficiary, except to the extent that the trustee has conveyed trust property to the beneficiary without deducting the amount due the trustee and without an agreement to forego his right to indemnity.[36]

The trustee has no right of indemnity against liability incurred by him in making a contract which was not lawful or proper for him under the terms of the trust instrument.[37]

CONTRACT CREDITOR'S RIGHTS AGAINST THE TRUSTEE AS SUCH [38]

116. Where a trustee makes a contract in the due course of his administration a creditor under it can recover out of the trust property by suing the trustee in his representative capacity in equity, when

(a) The trustee excluded personal liability and expressly contracted that the creditor might recover from trust property; or

(b) Although the trustee did not contract for collection out of trust property, the trustee has a right to indemnity against this claim, and the creditor cannot collect from the trustee personally; or

(c) Performance of the contract has increased the value of the trust property.

It has been shown in a previous section that the trustee has the power to contract for collection by the contract creditor out of the trust property.[39] Such collection should be in a suit against the trustee as trustee, in a court of equity.[40]

---

[35] Woodard v. Wright, 82 Cal. 202, 22 P. 1118; Percy v. Huyck, 252 N.Y. 168, 169 N.E. 127.

[36] The English cases permitting a claim against the beneficiary are not followed in the United States. Hardoon v. Belilios, [1901] A.C. 118, noted in 14 Harv.L.R. 539; Mathews v. Ruggles-Brise, [1911] 1 Ch. 194. In some cases the beneficiary is liable because he agrees to reimburse the trustee. Cunniff v. McDonnell, 196 Mass. 7, 81 N.E. 879; Poland v. Beal, 192 Mass. 559, 78 N.E. 728.

[37] Sheets v. Security First Mtge. Co., 293 Ill.App. 222, 12 N.E.2d 324; Downey Co. v. 282 Beacon St.Trust, 292 Mass. 175, 197 N.E. 643.

[38] Restatement, Trusts, §§ 266–273.

[39] See § 114, ante.

[40] See Vanneman, 9 Univ. of Cinc. L.R. 1.

It is generally conceded that the creditor who has a claim against the trustee because of a proper contract is entitled to the benefit of the trustee's right of indemnity under some circumstances.[41] The courts have not clearly defined the circumstances, nor have they been unanimous in their views. But the large majority of cases in which the creditor has been allowed to step into the trustee's shoes and claim part of the trust property have been cases in which (a) the remedy against the trustee individually was worthless or difficult of enforcement; (b) the trust estate had had the benefit of the creditor's services or property; and (c) the trustee was not in debt to the trust estate, and so would have been entitled to reimbursement himself, had he paid the claim.[42] "A trustee, express or implied, cannot, in the absence of express power conferred upon him, by his contracts or engagements impose a liability upon the trust estate. If he make a contract which is beneficial to the estate, the creditor, or person with whom he contracts, has no equity to charge the estate unless he be insolvent, which must be shown by the exhaustion of legal remedies against him, and the estate is indebted to him. In that event, a court of equity may subrogate the creditor to the right of the trustee to charge the trust estate."[43] The above statement would seem to be erroneous in requiring present indebtedness by the estate to the trustee. It would seem sufficient that the estate would have been indebted to the trustee if he had paid the creditor's claim.

In cases where the trustee has had a right of indemnity and he has been without the jurisdiction, the difficulty of pursuing the remedy against the trustee has induced some courts to allow the creditor to avail himself of the trustee's right of indemnity and collect from the trust estate.[44] In other cases the in-

---

[41] In re Johnson, 15 Ch.Div. 548; In re Richardson, [1911] 2 K.B. 705; Paul v. Wilson, 79 N.J.Eq. 204, 81 A. 835. But if the settlor devoted only part of the trust funds to the business in which the debt was contracted, the trustee's right and hence the creditor's right of indemnity relates to the property devoted to the business only and not to the general trust assets. Cutbush v. Cutbush, 1 Beav. 184; Ex parte Garland, 10 Ves. 110; Ex parte Richardson, 3 Maddock 138; Fridenberg v. Wilson, 20 Fla. 359; Moore v. McFall, 263 Ill. 596, 105 N.E. 723, Ann.Cas.1915C, 364. If the trustee is in arrears in his accounts, he has no right to reimbursement, which he can pass on to the creditor. Wilson v. Fridenberg, 21 Fla. 386.

[42] See, for example, Clopton v. Gholson, 53 Miss. 466; Fowler v. Mutual Life Ins. Co., 28 Hun, N.Y., 195.

[43] Blackshear v. Burke, 74 Ala. 239, 243.

[44] Gates v. McClenahan, 124 Iowa 593, 100 N.W. 479; Norton v. Phelps, 54 Miss. 467; Field v. Wilbur, 49 Vt. 157.

solvency of the trustee has been the moving cause for allowing direct action in equity by the creditor.[45] In other cases the fact that the settlor directed the carrying on of the business in which the contract was made was emphasized as a reason allowing action against the estate, when the trustee was irresponsible.[46] No necessity for such emphasis is seen, since the question should be whether the contract was within the powers of the trustee, and not whether it was in the management of a continued business.

In Norton v. Phelps[47] the Mississippi court states the rule to be that, "where expenditures have been made for the benefit of the trust estate, and it has not paid for them, directly or indirectly, and the estate is either indebted to the trustee, or would have been if the trustee had paid, or would be if he should pay, the demand, and the trustee is insolvent or nonresident, so that the creditor cannot recover his demand from him, or will be compelled to follow him to a foreign jurisdiction, the trust estate may be reached directly by a proceeding in chancery. The principle is that, while persons dealing as creditors with the trustee must look to him personally, and not to the trust estate, yet where the estate has received the benefit of expenditures procured to be made for it by the trustee, and it has not in any way borne the burden of these expenditures properly chargeable to it, and to fasten the charge upon it will do it no wrong, but simply cause it to pay what it is liable for to the trustee, or would be liable for if he had paid it, or should pay it, and because of the insolvency or nonresidence of the trustee, our tribunals cannot afford the creditor a remedy for his demand, he may proceed directly against the trust estate, and assert against it the demand the trustee could maintain if he had paid or should pay the claim, and should himself proceed against the trust estate."

The Massachusetts courts allow the creditor to reach the trust property where the debt was authorized by the trust instrument and the trustee is not in arrears, without proof of impossibility or difficulty of collecting from the trustee, due to his absence or

---

[45] Hewitt v. Phelps, 105 U.S. 393, 26 L.Ed. 1072; Wells-Stone Mercantile Co. v. Aultman, Miller & Co., 9 N.D. 520, 84 N.W. 375; Henshaw v. Freer's Adm'rs, 1 Bailey Eq., S.C., 311.

[46] Willis v. Sharp, 113 N.Y. 586, 21 N.E. 705, 4 L.R.A. 493; Wadsworth, Howland & Co. v. Arnold, 24 R.I. 32, 51 A. 1041.

[47] 54 Miss. 467, 471.

insolvency.[48] They give the claimant the trustee's right of indemnity as an alternative to suit against the trustee individually.

If a contract is made by two or more trustees, each trustee has a right to indemnity, and the creditor can recover from the trust property if one of the trustee's right to indemnity is intact, although the other trustees have defaulted and their right to indemnity has been wiped out. Thus, if trustees A. and B. properly contract with X. for a loan, the debt is not paid, X. is unable to recover from A. or B. personally, and X. sues A. and B. as trustees and seeks to recover from the trust property, and it appears that A. owes the trust estate much more than the amount of X.'s claim because of breaches of trust committed by A. but B. has committed no breaches of trust and owes the trust estate nothing, X. may recover through B., by taking B.'s right of indemnity against liability on this contract.[49]

If the operator of a business dies and leaves it to trustees who continue the business and incur debts in such continuance, and a contest arises between the creditors of the deceased who became such during his life, and the new creditors who contracted with the trustees, the result will depend upon whether the continuance of the business was with the consent of the old creditors. If they consented to it, otherwise than by merely failing to object, then they became in substance beneficiaries of the trust, and must permit the new creditors to be satisfied out of all the trust property before the old creditors and other beneficiaries of the trust receive satisfaction. If, however, the old creditors did not consent, then they are entitled to be paid out of the property which the testator left at his death, in priority to the new creditors.[50]

Even in the case where the contract made by the trustee was without his powers, and normally his personal liability would be the only remedy to the creditor, if the trust property has been increased in value by the performance of the contract, the creditor may recover in equity the amount of such increase in value on quasi-contractual principles. Thus, if a trustee has made a contract to improve trust real estate by the construction of a building thereon, but this contract was not proper or legal under the trust, and the builder has proceeded to perform the

---

[48] Mason v. Pomeroy, 151 Mass. 164, 24 N.E. 202, 7 L.R.A. 771; King v. Stowell, 211 Mass. 246, 98 N.E. 91.

[49] In re Frith, [1902] 1 Ch. 342; Mason v. Pomeroy, 151 Mass. 164, 24 N.E. 202, 7 L.R.A. 771.

[50] Dowse v. Gorton, [1891] A.C. 190; In re Oxley, [1914] 1 Ch. 604; Adelman, 36 Mich.L.R. 185.

contract and to construct a building, the creditor may recover in equity in a suit against the trustee as such the increase in the value of the trust property caused by his work and materials.[51]

PERSONAL LIABILITY OF TRUSTEE FOR TORTS [52]

117. A trustee of a private trust is personally liable for torts committed by himself, or by his servants or agents when they are acting in the course of their work for him. In very few cases is a suit against the trustee as such and recovery from the trust property allowed.

A trustee of a charitable trust is personally liable for torts committed by himself, but not for those committed by agents or servants.

Occasionally while carrying on private trust work the trustee, or his agent or servant, commits a tort and injures a third person. Common examples are the cases where the trustee holds an apartment house in trust, and he personally negligently permits the parts of the building within his control to become in a dangerous condition, or he entrusts the repairs of some stairs to a janitor employed by him and the janitor does his work carelessly, and a tenant is injured due to the defective condition of the premises. Here the common law courts, in which tort liability is enforced, recognize only one legal person, namely, the trustee, as the one who committed the wrong. The trustee as trustee is not recognized as a juristic person, separate and apart from the trustee as an individual, by the court of law. If a trustee named John Doe committed the wrong in question either personally or through another acting for him, the law court holds that John Doe is the tort-feasor. It does not admit the possibility of a tort by John Doe, as trustee. It places the liability on John Doe and leaves to a court of equity the question whether Doe should permanently bear this liability or should be able to shift it to the trust estate.

An action against a trustee who has personally or through an agent or servant committed a tort, such as libel, slander, assault, negligence or conversion, should, therefore, name John Doe as

[51] Brownfield v. McFadden, 21 Cal. App.2d 208, 68 P.2d 993; In re Manning's Estate, 134 Iowa 165, 111 N.W. 409; Henrietta Nat. Bank v. Barrett, Tex.Civ.App., 25 S.W. 456. Some decisions to the contrary effect seem unsound. Johnson v. Leman, 131 Ill. 609, 23 N.E. 435, 7 L.R.A. 656, 19 Am.St.Rep. 63; Downey Co. v. 282 Beacon St. Trust, 292 Mass. 175, 197 N.E. 643.

[52] Restatement, Trusts, §§ 264, 275, 402.

BOGERT TRUSTS 2D—25

the defendant, and omit all reference to his trusteeship, and if judgment is recovered against Doe it may be satisfied out of Doe's own property in full, without regard to the amount of the trust property or the possibility of recovery by Doe from the trust.[53]

In a few states there has been a departure from the orthodox doctrine stated above and courts have allowed recovery at law in an action against the trustee in his representative capacity, and collection from the trust property on execution.[54] By statute, also, there has been a slight tendency to recognize the trustee, as such, as a separate juristic person from the trustee as an individual, and to permit recovery out of the trust property through a law action against the trustee as trustee, if the beneficiaries were notified of the action and given an opportunity to intervene or take other action they deemed appropriate.[55]

If the trustee is acting for charity he is liable only for torts committed by himself personally, and not for those committed by agents or servants in the course of their employment.[56] For example, if the trustee is operating a charitable hospital, and he negligently selects an incompetent doctor or nurse who causes injury to a patient, the trustee is personally liable; but if the trustee used reasonable care in choosing his employees and a nurse negligently caused injury to a patient, the trustee is not liable. This difference from the result outlined above with relation to private trusts is based on the desire of the courts to protect and encourage charities, even at the expense of individuals who may suffer. In minority cases[57] there has been a tendency to criticize this position and to urge that it is better public policy to indemnify all persons wrongfully injured than it is

---

[53] Shepard v. Creamer, 160 Mass. 496, 36 N.E. 475; Smith v. Rizzuto, 133 Neb. 655, 276 N.W. 406; Kirchner v. Muller, 280 N.Y. 23, 19 N.E.2d 665, 127 A.L.R. 681; Belvin's Ex'rs v. French, 84 Va. 81, 3 S.E. 891.

[54] Smith v. Coleman, 100 Fla. 1707, 132 So. 198; Louisville Trust Co. v. Morgan, 180 Ky. 609, 203 S.W. 555, 7 A.L.R. 396; Ewing v. Wm. L. Foley, Inc., 115 Tex. 222, 280 S.W. 499, 44 A.L.R. 627. *Contra:* Wahl v. Schmidt, 307 Ill. 331, 138 N.E. 604; Keating v. Stevenson, 21 App.Div. 604, 47 N.Y.S. 847; Parmenter v. Barstow, 22 R.I. 245, 47 A. 365, 63 L.R.A. 227.

[55] See section 14, Uniform Trusts Act, adopted in Louisiana, Nevada, North Carolina, Oklahoma.

[56] Farrigan v. Pevear, 193 Mass. 147, 78 N.E. 855, 7 L.R.A.,N.S., 481, 118 Am.St.Rep. 484, 8 Ann.Cas. 1109; Herndon v. Massey, 217 N.C. 610, 8 S.E.2d 914.

[57] Geiger v. Simpson Methodist Episcopal Church of Minneapolis, 174 Minn. 389, 219 N.W. 463, 62 A.L.R. 716.

BOGERT TRUSTS 2D

to cause the victims of torts to lose health and property without redress in order that a charity may go on without impairment. The rules laid down for trustees of charitable trusts are also applied to charitable corporations owning property absolutely. Most of the cases are actions against charitable corporations and do not involve trusts.[58]

TRUSTEES RIGHT OF INDEMNITY AS TO TORTS[59]

118. A trustee is entitled to be indemnified against liability for torts in the following cases:
   (a) Where he was not personally at fault;
   (b) Where the tort occurred as a normal incident of the kind of activity in which the trustee was properly engaged;
   (c) Where the commission of the tort increased the value of the trust property.

While the amount of law on the topic is small, it would appear that a trustee who has incurred tort liability is entitled to be indemnified against it by the trust in at least three cases.

In the first place if the tort was one which did not involve any personal blame or fault on the part of the trustee, it would seem fair and reasonable to permit the trustee to shift the burden to the trust.[60] Thus, in a well known English case[61] the trustee of a coal mine had a duty to support the surface of the ground which was owned by another person and which was located above the mine. Although the trustee took reasonable precautions to hold the surface up, he did in fact let it down. This was a violation of an absolute duty imposed on him by the common law, but it was a tort without any personal fault on the part of the trustee. The court held that the trustee was entitled to indemnity against this tort liability.

A similar case arises where the tort liability occurs through the operation of the doctrine of respondeat superior. If the trustee with reasonable care employs, directs and supervises a servant who is doing work for the trust, and the servant commits a tort which causes the trustee to be liable, it would seem

---

[58] See McCaskill, 5 Cornell L.Q. 409; 6 Id. 56; Zollman, 19 Mich.L.R. 395; Taylor, 2 Cinc.L.R. 72; Feezer, 77 Pa.L.R. 191.

[59] Restatement, Trusts, §§ 264, 268, 278-279.

[60] Benett v. Wyndham, 4 De G. F. & J. 259; Smith v. Rizzuto, 133 Neb. 655, 276 N.W. 406; Ewing v. Wm. L. Foley, Inc., 115 Tex. 222, 280 S.W. 499, 44 A.L.R. 627.

[61] In re Raybould, [1900] 1 Ch. 199.

fair that the trustee should be able to shift the burden to the trust.[62] Thus, if a trustee with due care employs a collector to collect rents from tenants on the trust property, and the collector becomes involved in a fight with a tenant while trying to collect the rent, and physically injures the tenant, if the trustee is made personally liable for this tort of his servant it would seem that he should be reimbursed from trust property. It is a tort not involving reprehensible conduct on the part of the trustee. It might be held that the trustee was not personally liable for this tort, since the commission of it was an act outside the collector's work.

So, too, the law should recognize that the commission of occasional torts is an inevitable incident of the conduct of some business. Due to the fallibility of human beings, it is impossible to carry on certain activities without occasionally wronging other persons. Thus, if a trustee is conducting a newspaper, it is probably true that he and his employees will inevitably from time to time commit the torts of libel and negligence. Even the best conducted journals have these experiences. For these liabilities which are the necessary incidents of the trust business, he should not bear permanent responsibility. The risks of the business should fall on the business.[63]

Occasionally a trustee commits a tort which enriches the trust estate. For example, if he converts the personal property of another and mixes it with the trust property, and he is sued in trover and a judgment collected from his personal property, surely the trust estate is enriched to the extent of the value of the converted property which it now owns as a result of the payment of the judgment in the trover action, and surely to the extent of such enrichment the trustee should be allowed to get reimbursement out of trust property. To hold otherwise would be to give a windfall to the trust estate.[64]

Where the trustee has a right of indemnity he may use it in the ways discussed with regard to contracts.[65] He may in the first place pay the tort claim out of trust property, by self-

---

[62] Matter of Lathers' Will, 137 Misc. 226, 243 N.Y.S. 366.

[63] See section 13, Uniform Trusts Act, adopted in Louisiana, Nevada, North Carolina, and Oklahoma, which states the three cases where indemnity is allowed, as set forth in this section.

[64] Willetts v. Schuyler, 3 Ind.App. 118, 29 N.E. 273; Leigh v. Lockwood, 15 N.C. 577; Morgan's Estate, 2 Pa. Dist. 816.

[65] See § 115, ante.

help, reimburse himself for the payment of the claim, secure a decree of exoneration from initial liability, or procure reimbursement through accounting or other proceedings.

In the case of a charitable trust the trustee is liable only for his personal fault, and there is no right of indemnity in favor of a trustee in such case, unless the tort was one usually incident to the trustee's activity for this trust or one which enriched the trust estate. Indemnity for a tort of a servant or agent is not needed since the trustee is not usually held to be liable for such a tort. The charitable trustee's right of indemnity would, therefore, seem to be of very limited application.

TORT CREDITOR'S RIGHTS AGAINST THE TRUSTEE AS SUCH [66]

119. Where a trustee of a private trust is liable for a tort but collection cannot be had from him due to his insolvency or other cause, the injured party may sue the trustee in his representative capacity in equity and collect from trust property, if the trustee would have been entitled to be reimbursed if he had paid the claim out of his own pocket.

It would seem that in the case of a tort claim against a charitable trust, the creditor should be able to take advantage of the trustee's right to indemnity where he has one, and should be able to sue in equity and collect out of the trust property; but the cases generally deny such right, especially where the plaintiff is a beneficiary of the charity at the time he is injured.

Although there is little authority on the subject, it seems clear that a tort creditor of a trustee, who is unable to collect from the trustee out of his private property, can sue in equity, making the trustee as such a defendant, and collect out of the trust property, if the trustee had a right of indemnity against liability in the case in question.[67] To recover in this way the person injured would have to prove inability to collect from the trustee by showing the exhaustion of his remedies at law or at least great difficulty in collecting, as where the trustee is a non-resident, that the tort was one for which the trustee had a right of indemnity, and lastly that the trustee was not indebted to the trust estate in such a way as to destroy his right of indemnity. Thus, if a trustee is lawfully operating an apartment house for

---

[66] Restatement, Trusts, §§ 266–273, 402.

[67] In re Raybould, [1900] 1 Ch. 199; Smith v. Rizzuto, 133 Neb. 655, 276 N.W. 406.

the trust, his servant is negligent and a tenant is injured thereby, the tenant sues the trustee for damages and gets a judgment against him but finds his execution returned unsatisfied, the tenant could sue the trustee in his representative capacity in equity, and if he could prove that the trustee did not owe the trust estate money because of a breach of trust, the plaintiff could get a decree ordering the payment of his claim out of trust property. In this case the trustee had a right of indemnity and it had not been destroyed by his wrongful conduct. The trustee's right of indemnity, and the corresponding right of the creditor, might be extinguished or reduced by a breach of trust on the trustee's part which made him the debtor of the trust estate.

As previously suggested, the trustee of a charitable trust has a very limited right to indemnity, and it would seem that the tort creditor ought to be able to use it; but the strong bent against charitable trust liability has in most cases prevented recovery. If the plaintiff is a beneficiary of the charitable trust, as, for example, a patient in a hospital run by a trustee for charity, the courts mention that fact as a basis for denying recovery.

LIABILITY OF THE TRUSTEE AS PROPERTY OWNER [68]

120. The trustee's liabilities arising from holding title to the trust property are the same as if he owned the property absolutely. Examples of such liability exist in the case of taxes and calls or assessments on the stock of a corporation. He has a right of indemnity against personal liability incurred as title holder.

Certain obligations arise from the mere ownership of property. They do not depend on contract or tort. They are obligations which are inherent in ownership of property of the type in question. For example, the ownership of real property, and sometimes the ownership of personalty, involves liability to a property tax. And the title to stock in a corporation carries with it liability to pay unpaid subscriptions for the stock and assessments in favor of creditors of the corporation.

Unless the tax statute provides otherwise, a trustee holding taxable property is personally liable for taxes due on it,[69] and in

---

[68] Restatement, Trusts, §§ 265, 277.

[69] Ill.Smith-Hurd Stats. c. 120, § 215; Thiebaud v. Tait, 138 Ind. 238, 36 N.E. 525; Dunham v. City of Lowell, 200 Mass. 468, 86 N.E. 951.

the absence of statutory control he is also personally liable for calls and assessments on corporate stock held by the trust.[70] In the case of many statutes creating double liability on the holders of stock in certain corporations, it is provided that if the stock is held by a trustee, and the stock certificate shows the trust, the trustee will not be personally liable but rather the assessment may be collected from the trust property.[71] Double liability in the case of national and many state banks has been abolished under recent statutes.[72]

A trustee who is personally liable as mere title holder has a right to be indemnified out of the trust property. He may meet the liability in the first place from trust property, or may repay himself after he has satisfied the claim from his own funds.[73]

The question whether the trustee's personal liability as title holder is greater than the amount in which he can be indemnified by the trust estate is an unsettled one.[74]

The beneficiary is not liable on obligations arising out of ownership of the trust property vested in the trustee.

---

[70] French v. Busch, C.C.N.Y., 189 F. 480; Union Savings Bank of San Jose v. Willard, 4 Cal.App. 690, 88 P. 1098.

[71] See, for example, Fla.Comp.L. 1927, § 5989; Minn.St.1927, § 7483.

[72] Section 304 of the Banking Act of 1935, 12 U.S.C.A. § 64a; Ky.L. 1938, c. 137; Pa. 7 P.S., §§ 819–614.

[73] Merritt v. Jenkins, 17 Fla. 593; Bourquin v. Bourquin, 120 Ga. 115, 47 S.E. 639.

[74] As tending to show unlimited liability, see City of Bangor v. Peirce, 106 Me. 527, 76 A. 945, 29 L.R.A.,N.S., 770, 138 Am.St.Rep. 363; McLaughlin v. Minnesota Loan & Trust Co., 192 Minn. 203, 255 N.W. 839; but an opposite view was expressed in Smith v. Rizzuto, 133 Neb. 655, 276 N.W. 406.

CHAPTER 13

TRUST ADMINISTRATION—SALES, MORTGAGES AND LEASES

Sec.
121. Trustee's Power to Sell.
122. Court Control of Trustee's Sales.
123. The Conduct of Sales by Trustees.
124. Power of Trustee to Borrow and Give Security.
125. Court Control over Borrowing and Giving Security.
126. Effect of Loans and Giving Security.
127. Express or Implied Power to Lease.
128. Length of Leases Permitted.
129. Trustee's Duties as Lessor.

TRUSTEE'S POWER TO SELL [1]

121. A trustee is very commonly given a power to sell the trust property, and is either permitted or directed to exercise it. He may also be forbidden by the settlor from selling the trust property.

A power of sale will be implied where it is necessary or highly convenient to accomplishing the settlor's purposes.

A trustee should be careful to qualify before contracting to sell the trust property.

A trustee may not ordinarily give options to buy, exercisable in the future, since they deprive him of his power to sell for the best price and under the most advantageous terms.

The power to sell the trust property may be expressly given to the trustee.[2] No technical words are necessary to confer this authority upon him, it being sufficient that the settlor's intent is clear.[3] The power may be made mandatory, or its use may be left to the discretion of the trustee.[4] It is commonly attach-

---

[1] Restatement, Trusts, § 190.

[2] Blair v. Hazzard, 158 Cal. 721, 112 P. 298; Aldersley v. McCloud, 35 Cal.App. 17, 168 P. 1153; Salisbury v. Bigelow, 20 Pick., Mass., 174; Penniman v. Howard, 71 Misc. 598, 128 N.Y.S. 910; Shaw v. Bridgers, 161 N.C. 246, 76 S.E. 827. If an express power is given no application to the court is necessary. Livermore v. Livermore, 231 Mass. 293, 121 N.E. 27.

[3] Holden v. Circleville Light & Power Co., C.C.A.Ohio, 216 F. 490, 132 C.C.A. 550, Ann.Cas.1916D, 443; Reeder v. Reeder, 184 Iowa 1, 168 N.W. 122. Thus a deed to the trustee, "his successors and assigns," implies a power of sale. Crawford v. El Paso Land Imp. Co., Tex.Civ.App., 201 S.W. 233.

[4] Trust Co. of New Jersey v. Glunz, 121 N.J.Eq. 593, 191 A. 795; Peters

§ 121   TRUSTEE'S POWER TO SELL   393

ed to the office of the trustee and not made personal to any particular trustee.[5]

The settlor may prohibit the sale of the trust property,[6] or provide that it shall be sold only if the settlor or a beneficiary consents.[7]

If the law of the particular state requires a trustee to qualify by giving bond, taking an oath, or procuring letters of trust, the trustee desiring to use his power of sale should be careful to complete qualification before making a contract or deed.[8]

It is generally held that a trustee with a power of sale may not give options to buy, since ordinary prudence requires that he reserve power to sell at the price and on the terms which are most advantageous from time to time.[9] If he binds himself to sell at a future date at a price fixed in advance, he may prejudice the trust because of an increase in the value of the property or other change of conditions.

A power of sale in favor of the trustee is implied in equity whenever such power is necessary to carry out the trust.[10] "While it is true that under the original theory of a trust the powers and duties of the trustee were confined substantially to holding and caring for the property, it is equally true that the purposes of the modern trust are of a much broader character, requiring ordinarily much greater powers on the part of the trustee, including a power of sale, which is generally expressly given. The power of sale, where not expressly given, will be

v. Kanawha Banking & Trust Co., 118 W.Va. 484, 191 S.E. 581.

[5] Weeks v. Frankel, 197 N.Y. 304, 90 N.E. 969.

[6] Garrott v. McConnell, 201 Ky. 61, 256 S.W. 14.

[7] Palmer v. Williams, 24 Mich. 328.

[8] Chappus v. Lucke, 246 Mich. 272, 224 N.W. 432.

[9] Moore v. Trainer, 252 Pa. 367, 97 A. 462; 30 Col.L.R. 870.

[10] Preston v. Safe Deposit & Trust Co., 116 Md. 211, 81 A. 523, Ann.Cas. 1913C, 975; Garesche v. Levering Inv. Co., 146 Mo. 436, 48 S.W. 653, 46 L.R.A. 232; Clark v. Fleischmann, 81 Neb. 445, 116 N.W. 290; Crown Co. v. Cohn, 88 Or. 642, 172 P. 804; In re Kaiser's Estate, 2 Lanc.Law Rev. 362; Dorrance v. Greene, 41 R. I. 444, 104 A. 12; Wisdom v. Wilson, 59 Tex.Civ.App. 593, 127 S.W. 1128. A power to sell does not include a power to exchange. Holsapple v. Schrontz, 65 Ind.App. 390, 117 N.E. 547.

Where a trust contains much real estate, part of which is unimproved, and the instrument gives the trustee all powers necessary for management and profitable use of the property, and directs payment of annuities to the settlor's relatives, a power of sale is to be implied. Revoc Co. v. Thomas, 179 Md. 101, 16 A.2d 847, 134 A.L.R. 373.

implied from the fact that the trustee is charged with a duty which cannot be performed without a power of sale." [11]

It is impossible to give details of the instances in which a power of sale has been implied. In many cases where the question of the existence of such a power has arisen, the court has thought it necessary to the proper execution of the trust and has held that it existed, [12] while in others the court has considered a sale unessential and unauthorized.[13]

Whether the trustee of a charitable trust has an implied power of sale depends in part upon whether the particular property is necessary to the carrying on of the trust and whether there is any necessity for a sale of it. Where a settlor has dedicated particular land for lodgeroom, church, and graveyard purposes, the trustees will not be held to have an implied power of sale under ordinary conditions.[14]

The cestui que trust alone can raise the question of the power of the trustee to sell the trust property or the propriety of the sale as conducted.[15] The sale may by the trust instrument be expressly required to be made only when the cestuis que trust

[11] Robinson v. Robinson, 105 Me. 68, 71, 72 A. 883, 32 L.R.A.,N.S., 675, 134 Am.St.Rep. 537.

[12] McDonald v. Shaw, 81 Ark. 235, 98 S.W. 952; Giselman v. Starr, 106 Cal. 651, 40 P. 8; Green v. Bissell, 79 Conn. 547, 65 A. 1056, 8 L.R.A., N.S., 1011, 118 Am.St.Rep. 156, 9 Ann.Cas. 287; Flinn v. Frank, 8 Del. Ch. 186, 68 A. 196; Cherry v. Greene, 115 Ill. 591, 4 N.E. 257; Steinke v. Yetzer, 108 Iowa 512, 79 N.W. 286; Morris v. Winderlin, 92 Kan. 935, 142 P. 944; First Nat. Bank of Carlisle v. Lee, 66 S.W. 413, 23 Ky.Law Rep. 1897; Dodson v. Ashley, 101 Md. 513, 61 A. 299; Smith v. Haynes. 202 Mass. 531, 89 N.E. 158; Mason v. Bank of Commerce, 90 Mo. 452, 3 S. W. 206; Varick v. Smith, 69 N.J.Eq. 505, 61 A. 151; Spencer v. Weber, 163 N.Y. 493, 57 N.E. 753; Foil v. Newsome, 138 N.C. 115, 50 S.E. 597, 3 Ann.Cas. 417; Brown v. Brown, 7 Or. 285; In re Streater's Estate, 250 Pa. 328, 95 A. 459.

[13] Goad v. Montgomery, 119 Cal. 552, 51 P. 681, 63 Am.St.Rep. 145; Bremer v. Hadley, 196 Mass. 217, 81 N.E. 961; Potter v. Ranlett, 116 Mich. 454, 74 N.W. 661; Rolfe & Rumford Asylum v. Lefebre, 69 N. H. 238, 45 A. 1087; Alvord v. Sherwood, 21 Misc. 354, 47 N.Y.S. 749; Robinson v. Ingram, 126 N.C. 327, 35 S.E. 612; Seif v. Krebs, 239 Pa. 423, 86 A. 872; Kennedy v. Pearson, Tex.Civ.App., 109 S.W. 280; Mundy v. Vawter, 3 Grat., Va., 518.

[14] Tate v. Woodyard, 145 Ky. 613, 140 S.W. 1044; and see Bridgeport Public Library and Reading Room v. Burroughs Home, 85 Conn. 309, 82 A. 582.

[15] Herbert v. Hanrick, 16 Ala. 581; Prouty v. Edgar, 6 Iowa 353; Norris v. Hall, 124 Mich. 170, 82 N.W. 832; Schenck v. Ellingwood, 3 Edw.Ch., N.Y., 175; Coxe v. Blanden, 1 Watts., Pa., 533, 26 Am.Dec. 83.

consent, in which case such consent must be procured before a valid sale can be made.[16]

It is generally held that the lack of power on the part of the trustee to sell the trust property may be supplied by showing the consent of the beneficiary in advance that the sale take place;[17] but in some instances such consent has been held insufficient to render the sale valid.[18] After the sale has taken place, the cestui que trust may ratify[19] it, or estop himself to attack its validity.[20] Thus, acceptance of the proceeds of the sale with full knowledge of the facts shows an estoppel to assert that the sale was invalid.[21] Where the trustees are given power to sell land and distribute the proceeds among the beneficiaries of the trust, the beneficiaries may elect to take the land, rather than the proceeds thereof.[22]

COURT CONTROL OF TRUSTEE'S SALE [23]

122. A court of equity has inherent power to order or forbid a sale of trust property, notwithstanding any direction of the settlor. Statutes frequently set forth the court's power to order sales and to control their terms. The power of the court will be exercised with a view to the best interests of the beneficiaries.

The court of equity has power to do whatever is necessary to insure that the trust purpose of the settlor, if lawful, is carried out. This often includes directing a sale of some of the

---

[16] Berrien v. Thomas, 65 Ga. 61; Franklin Sav. Bank v. Taylor, 131 Ill. 376, 23 N.E. 397; Clemens v. Heckscher, 185 Pa. 476, 40 A. 80; Walke v. Moore, 95 Va. 729, 30 S.E. 374; Norvell v. Hedrick, 21 W.Va. 523.

[17] Dykes v. McVay, 67 Ga. 502; Rogers v. Tyley, 144 Ill. 652, 32 N.E. 393; Turner v. Fryberger, 99 Minn. 236, 108 N.W. 1118, 109 N.W. 229; Cooper v. Harvey, 21 S.D. 471, 113 N.W. 717.

[18] Walton v. Follansbee, 165 Ill. 480, 46 N.E. 459; Mauldin v. Mauldin, 101 S.C. 1, 85 S.E. 60.

[19] Long v. Long, 62 Md. 33; Swartz v. Duncan, 38 Neb. 782, 57 N.W. 543; Johnson v. Bennett, 39 Barb., N.Y., 237; In re Post, 13 R.I. 495.

[20] Mitchell v. Berry, 1 Metc., Ky., 602; Matthews v. Thompson, 186 Mass. 14, 71 N.E. 93, 66 L.R.A. 421, 104 Am.St.Rep. 550.

[21] Shepherd v. Todd, 95 Ga. 19, 22 S.E. 32; Lawson v. Cunningham, 275 Mo. 128, 204 S.W. 1100.

[22] Craig v. Leslie, 3 Wheat. 563, 4 L.Ed. 460; Smith v. A. D. Farmer Type Founding Co., 16 App.Div. 438, 45 N.Y.S. 192; Fraser v. Bowerman, 104 Misc. 260, 171 N.Y.S. 835.

[23] Restatement, Trusts, § 190.

trust property.[24] If the trust property is unproductive, for example, but can be sold and the proceeds invested in bonds or mortgages bearing four or five per cent. income, surely the trust purpose of the settlor that the beneficiaries receive support will be achieved better by a sale than by a retention. If the trustee does not voluntarily make a sale, the court may order him to do so. It is immaterial whether the settlor directed a sale or a retention of the property, or whether the instrument gave the trustee a power of sale.[25] Equity has authority to override the settlor and make a decree which will be for the best interests of the beneficiaries.

As a part of this same general control over trusts chancery may forbid a sale, even though directed by the settlor.[26] If, for example, the settlor directed the sale of all his assets and the investment of the proceeds in government bonds, and the court finds that some of the assets are very safe, high-yield bonds, and that governments bear only one or two per cent. interest, and that the cestuis are greatly in need of all possible income, the court may ignore the settlor's command and direct the trustee not to sell.

Settlors of charitable trusts frequently leave their homesteads or residential property to trustees for charity for operation as a home for the aged or an orphan asylum or similar institution and direct retention of the property forever. If, however, the neighborhood has changed, or other events make the original realty unsuited for the charitable object, the court, may order a sale and a location elsewhere.[27]

This inherent power of the court regarding sales is often expressed in statutes.[28] They do not create a power but rather merely give procedure for its use. They are declaratory of well established equitable principles.

---

[24] Bibb v. Bibb, 204 Ala. 541, 86 So. 376 (property depreciated and subject to liens); Dallas Art League v. Weaver, 240 Ala. 432, 199 So. 831; Hewitt v. Beattie, 106 Conn. 602, 138 A. 795 (stone quarry could no longer be operated at a profit).

[25] Suiter v. McWard, 328 Ill. 462, 159 N.E. 799; Young v. Young, 255 Mich. 173, 237 N.W. 535, 77 A.L.R. 963.

[26] Bertron, Storrs & Griscom v. Polk, 101 Md. 686, 61 A. 616; Albright v. Albright, 91 N.C. 220.

[27] Amory v. Attorney General, 179 Mass. 89, 60 N.E. 391; Rolfe & Rumford Asylum v. Lefebre, 69 N.H. 238, 45 A. 1087.

[28] Ga.Civ.Code, §§ 113–1721 to 113–1723; Me.L.1937, c. 79; Mich.Pub. Acts 1939, No. 288, c. VI, § 3, c. IX, § 4; N.Y.L.1937, c. 141; N.D.L.1935, c. 250, § 15.

CONDUCT OF SALES BY TRUSTEES [29]

123. In selling trust property the trustee should carefully follow the instructions of the settlor as expressed in the trust instrument and the orders of any court which have been directed to him. All important acts in connection with the contract to sell and the sale should be performed by co-trustees as a group and should not be delegated.

If the conditions on which he can sell are not laid down for the trustee by the settlor or the court, he is under a duty to use ordinary skill and prudence in selling on terms most advantageous to the beneficiaries.

In giving a bill of sale or a deed the trustee is not obliged to warrant or covenant except against his own acts. All warranties or covenants which he does make will bind him personally, unless he expressly excludes such liability.

Sales ordered by the court must be confirmed by the court, but otherwise, unless a statute or the trust instrument requires confirmation, there need be no application by the trustee to the court for approval of his sale.

In deciding when and how to sell, the trustee should examine the trust instrument, any relevant statute, and any court order made with regard to the sale, and then follow closely any directions which he finds.[30] In these documents he may find instructions as to the time of sale, as to whether the sale shall be at auction or at a private sale, and whether cash must be required or credit may be given.

As previously noted with regard to powers generally,[31] the trustee may not delegate to an employee the performance of important acts of discretion with regard to the sale.[32] Thus, he surely will be required to decide when to sell, at what price the property will be sold, and what terms as to credit shall be given. But he may delegate to a broker the work of advertising the property, seeking offers, posting notices of sale, and other functions which would be delegated by an ordinary business man to subordinates.[33]

The power of sale will normally be vested in co-trustees jointly. They must act together in all transactions relating to the sale,

---

[29] Restatement, Trusts, § 190.

[30] Rooker v. Fidelity Trust Co., 198 Ind. 207, 151 N.E. 610; Patterson v. Lanning, 62 Neb. 634, 87 N.W. 338.

[31] See § 96, ante.

[32] Saunders v. Webber, 39 Cal. 287; Grover v. Hale, 107 Ill. 638.

[33] Tyler v. Herring, 67 Miss. 169, 6 So. 840, 19 Am.St.Rep. 263; Gates v. Dudgeon, 173 N.Y. 426, 66 N.E. 116, 93 Am.St.Rep. 608.

such as, for example, signing a contract of sale or giving a deed.[34] Action in matters of this sort by one trustee alone will be void.

If the trustee finds that there are no express directions regarding the manner of conducting the sale, he will then be bound merely to use the care and ability of an ordinarily prudent man in deciding when and how to sell and on what terms.[35] The nature of the property and the available market for it, as well as the purposes of the trust and the needs of the cestuis will be the most important considerations in leading him to decisions. For example, corporate stock will be sold differently from land, and stock quoted on a stock exchange differently from the stock of a family corporation. In the case of a tract of unimproved land it is a question of judgment whether better results can be achieved by offering it in lots or as a whole.[36]

When the trustee comes to execute the instrument of conveyance which evidences his sale, as, for example, the bill of sale of goods or the deed of realty, he will have to decide whether to insert any warranties of the goods or any covenants as to the title to the land. The law requires him to do nothing more than to agree that the title to the thing conveyed has not been prejudiced by the acts of the trustee, that is, to execute a covenant against his own conduct.[37] But if the buyer demands further assurances, the trustee may insert warranties or covenants of other types. Since these are obligations contractual in nature, the trustee will fasten on himself personal liability for the truth of the warranties or covenants, unless he includes in the bill of sale or deed a statement that the warranty or covenant is not to bind him personally.[38]

The settlor may direct the trustee to apply to the court of equity for confirmation of any sale he makes, and a court order or statute may make such a requirement; but if the trustee finds no duty to seek confirmation expressed in any of these ways, he will not be obliged to ask the court for confirmation of

---

[34] Learned v. Welton, 40 Cal. 349; Page v. Gillett, 26 Colo.App. 204, 141 P. 866.

[35] Reeder v. Lanahan, 111 Md. 372, 74 A. 575; Johnston v. Eason, 38 N.C. 330. Ordinarily a trustee is not justified in selling trust property in return for a contingent interest in the business of the purchaser. Murphy v. Merchants' Nat. Bk. of Mobile, 240 Ala. 688, 200 So. 894.

[36] Goode v. Comfort, 39 Mo. 313; Crown Co. v. Cohn, 88 Or. 642, 172 P. 804.

[37] Barnard v. Duncan, 38 Mo. 170, 90 Am.Dec. 416.

[38] Bloom v. Wolfe, 50 Iowa 286; Glenn v. Allison, 58 Md. 527.

sales which he makes on his own initiative.[39] Naturally in the case of sales ordered by the court confirmation will be needed.[40] Where court confirmation is necessary, it will be refused only where gross unfairness is evident and not for slight disadvantages in the price or terms. If the trust estate has had the benefit of the consideration paid by the purchaser, the sale will be set aside only upon the repayment of such consideration.[41] The cestui que trust may, of course, be estopped to question the validity of a sale, as when he accepts the proceeds of the sale with knowledge of the facts surrounding it.[42]

EXPRESS OR IMPLIED POWER TO BORROW AND GIVE SECURITY [43]

124. A power to borrow and pledge or mortgage trust property as security is frequently expressly given to a trustee, either without qualification or to be used for a particular purpose only.

A power to give a mortgage or pledge is often implied, as, for example, where there is an express power to sell in order to raise a particular sum or where there is an express power to manage and control. A power to sell does not include by implication a power to mortgage, but a power to buy may be found to include a power to give a purchase money mortgage. In each case the question is whether it is reasonable to assume that the settlor wanted to give the power to mortgage, considering the objectives of his trust.

Frequently the trustee is given express authority to mortgage the trust property.[44] This power may be given without qualification, in which case it may be used for any lawful trust purpose, or it may be permitted to be exercised only for a given purpose like improving the trust property,[45] or only on the happening of

---

[39] Goodrich v. Proctor, 1 Gray, Mass., 567; Fleming v. Holt, 12 W. Va. 143.

[40] Rader v. Bussey, 313 Ill. 226, 145 N.E. 192; Offutt v. Jones, 110 Md. 233, 73 A. 629.

[41] Hill v. Shoemaker, 1 McArthur 305, 8 D.C. 305; Goode v. Comfort, 39 Mo. 313; Johnson v. Bennett, 39 Barb., N.Y., 237; Tiffany v. Clark, 1 Thomp. & C., N.Y., 9; Suarez v. De Montigny, 1 App.Div. 494, 37 N.Y.S. 503; Abernathy v. Phillips, 82 Va. 769, 1 S.E. 113.

[42] Childs v. Childs, 150 App.Div. 656, 135 N.Y.S. 972.

[43] Restatement, Trusts, § 191.

[44] Bank of Visalia v. Dillonwood Lumber Co., 148 Cal. 18, 82 P. 374; Guilmartin v. Stevens, 55 Ga. 203; Walter v. Brugger, 78 S.W. 419, 25 Ky.Law Rep. 1597; Boskowitz v. Held, 15 App.Div. 306, 44 N.Y.S. 136, affirmed 153 N.Y. 666, 48 N.E. 1104.

[45] Jones v. Harsha, 225 Mich. 416, 196 N.W. 624.

a certain event like the insufficiency of trust income to pay the living expenses of the beneficiary.[46]

The power to borrow and mortgage or pledge may be given impliedly where it appears that the settlor must have intended such a power to exist in order to make his trust administration more efficient or convenient.[47] A power of this type is, however, not easily implied, since it involves danger of loss of the original trust property.[48]

The express grant of a power to sell is ordinarily held not to include the power to mortgage,[49] nor does the power to change the investments of the trust property permit the trustee to mortgage it.[50]

The trustee will be held to have an implied power to mortgage the trust property whenever the wording of the trust instrument or the necessities of the trust indicate that the settlor meant that such power should exist.[51] A "trustee has 'authority to adopt measures and do acts which, though not specified in the instrument, are implied in its general directions, and are reasonable and proper means for making it effectual.'"[52] Thus, when a trustee is given power to take charge of, manage, and control property for the benefit of a beneficiary, he has implied power to mortgage. In such a case a court has said that, "so long as it was deemed to the interest of the beneficiaries that the trustee should manage and control the property, the power to do so included the power to improve and repair, and if in the exercise of the discretion allowed him under the deed appointing him, he deemed it to

---

[46] Alexander v. Goellert, 153 Kan. 202, 109 P.2d 146.

[47] Fergusson v. Fergusson, 148 Ark. 290, 229 S.W. 738; King v. Stowell, 211 Mass. 246, 98 N.E. 91.

[48] Purdy v. Bank of American Nat. Trust & Savings Ass'n, 2 Cal.2d 298, 40 P.2d 481.

[49] Townsend v. Wilson, 77 Conn. 411, 59 A. 417; Hamilton v. Hamilton, 149 Iowa, 321, 128 N.W. 380; Walter v. Brugger, 78 S.W. 419, 25 Ky.Law Rep. 1597; Stengel v. Royal Realty Corp., 179 Md. 204, 17 A.2d 127; Loring v. Brodie, 134 Mass. 453; Potter v. Hodgman, 178 N.Y. 580, 70 N.E. 1107; Kenworthy v. Levi, 214 Pa. 235, 63 A. 690; Greene v. Greene, 19 R.I. 619, 35 A. 1042, 35 L.R.A. 790; Mansfield v. Wardlow, Tex.Civ.App., 91 S.W. 859. A power to "dispose of" does not include a power to mortgage. Beakey v. Knutson, 90 Or. 574, 174 P. 1149.

[50] Griswold v. Caldwell, 65 App. Div. 371, 73 N.Y.S. 2.

[51] Security Trust Co. v. Merchants' & Clerks' Sav. Bank, 26 Ohio Cir. Ct.R. 381; Harding v. St. Louis Life Ins. Co., 2 Tenn.Ch. 465. In In re Billinger, [1898] 2 Ch. 534, a power to mortgage was implied from a power to carry on a real estate business.

[52] Gilbert v. Penfield, 124 Cal. 234, 238, 56 P. 1107, 1108, quoting 2 Pomeroy's Eq.Jurisp. § 1062.

the advantage of the beneficiaries that they procure the necessary funds by mortgaging the land he had the power and authority to do so." [53] The burden is upon the person taking the mortgage to satisfy himself that the trustee has power to mortgage. "Ordinarily the legal presumption exists that a trustee has no power to sell or mortgage the trust estate. Prospective purchasers and mortgagees must therefore exercise reasonable diligence to ascertain whether the trustee has authority to sell or incumber the real estate." [54]

If no power to mortgage, express or implied, is vested in the trustee, a mortgage by him will, upon objection by the cestui que trust, be held to be void,[55] even though the mortgagee in good faith believed that there was a power to mortgage. In some cases a purchase-money mortgage by the trustee has been held impliedly authorized, where the trustee had power to buy property and inability to pay cash for it was reasonably to be expected.[56]

If the cestuis que trust join with the trustee in the mortgage, or consent to it, or accept its benefits after it is executed, they will be estopped to assert its invalidity.[57]

COURT CONTROL OVER BORROWING AND GIVING SECURITY [58]

125. The court of chancery has inherent power to order or prohibit a mortgage by a trustee, regardless of the terms of the trust instrument. Statutes often declare this power and prescribe the procedure for its use. The court will ordinarily sanction a mortgage of trust property only for the purpose of conserving it or providing for its better management, and not to enable the trustee to enter into new business enterprises or speculation.

[53] Ely v. Pike, 115 Ill.App. 284, 287.

[54] Snyder v. Collier, 85 Neb. 552, 558, 123 N.W. 1023, 1025, 133 Am.St. Rep. 682.

[55] Williamson v. Grider, 97 Ark. 588, 135 S.W. 361; Taylor v. Clark, 56 Ga. 309; Tuttle v. First Nat. Bank of Greenfield, 187 Mass. 533, 73 N.E. 560, 105 Am.St.Rep. 420; Byron Reed Co. v. Klabunde, 76 Neb. 801, 108 N.W. 133.

[56] Mavrich v. Grier, 3 Nev. 52, 93 Am.Dec. 373; Gernert v. Albert, 160 Pa. 95, 28 A. 576. *Contra:* Mathews v. Heyward, 2 S.C. 239.

[57] Boon v. Hall, 76 App.Div. 520, 78 N.Y.S. 557; Magraw v. Pennock, 2 Grant Cas., Pa., 89; Hughes v. Farmers' Savings & Building & Loan Ass'n, Tenn.Ch.App., 46 S.W. 362.

[58] Restatement, Trusts, § 191.

Chancery has authority to permit the trustee to mortgage the trust property when such action is necessary to preserve the property or to enable the trustee to execute the trust as the settlor intended he should.[59]

An example of the cases in which the court authorizes a mortgage may be found in a recent case in which a testator left all his property to his widow in trust for herself and her children. Debts of the testator were a lien upon certain land which he had devised to the trustee, and the creditors were threatening suit. Equity authorized the trustee to mortgage the trust property to raise the money necessary to pay off the debts of the settlor and thus preserve the trust property intact.[60] The beneficiaries are necessary parties to a proceeding to procure the consent of the court to a mortgage of the trust property.[61] The power of the court is usually employed in order to enable the trustee to preserve the trust property, as where it is encumbered by tax liens.[62] It is not usual for a court to permit a trustee to raise money by mortgage in order to improve the trust property, since such action involves new risks and is apt to be somewhat speculative.[63]

In many states the power of the court to sanction mortgages by trustees is stated in statutory form and procedure regarding the application, proof, and confirmation of the mortgage is given.[64] These acts are declaratory of a power already existing, so that the procedural rules are their most important parts.

---

[59] Townsend v. Wilson, 77 Conn. 411, 59 A. 417; Jamison v. McWhorter, 7 Houst., Del., 242, 31 A. 517; Wagnon v. Pease, 104 Ga. 417, 30 S.E. 895; Long v. Simmons Female College, 218 Mass. 135, 105 N.E. 553; Butler v. Badger, 128 Minn. 99, 150 N.W. 233; In re Windsor Trust Co., 142 App.Div. 772, 127 N.Y.S. 586; New York Real Property Law, § 105; Penick v. Bank of Wadesboro, 218 N.C. 686, 12 S.E.2d 253; Shirkey v. Kirby, 110 Va. 455, 66 S.E. 40, 135 Am.St.Rep. 949.

[60] Lyddane v. Lyddane, 144 Ky. 159, 137 S.W. 838.

[61] Sampson v. Mitchell, 125 Mo. 217, 28 S.W. 768.

[62] Burroughs v. Gaither, 66 Md. 171, 7 A. 243; Butler v. Badger, 128 Minn. 99, 150 N.W. 233.

[63] Cruger v. Jones, 18 Barb.N.Y. 467; In re Stevenson's Estate, 186 Pa. 262, 40 A. 473; but see Bond v. Town of Tarboro, 217 N.C. 289, 7 S.E.2d 617, 127 A.L.R. 695; Smith v. Drake, Tex.Civ.App., 94 S.W.2d 236.

[64] Iowa L.1935, c. 114; Mich.Pub. Acts 1939, No. 288, c. IX, § 48; Neb. L.1935, c. 68; N.Y.L.1937, c. 141; N.D.L.1935, c. 250, § 15.

EFFECT OF LOANS AND GIVING SECURITY [65]

126. If a trustee has no power to mortgage under any conditions, or has power to mortgage only on a condition which has not occurred, a mortgage or pledge by him is void; but if the money lent has been used to improve the property which the trustee purported to mortgage, the lender may be given an equitable lien to the extent of the increase in value of the property caused by the use of the money lent.

If a trustee had power to mortgage for a limited purpose only, or for general trust purposes, a mortgage by him is not invalidated by reason of an intent on his part to use the proceeds of the loan for an unlawful purpose and the actual use of them for an illegal object, unless the mortgagee had knowledge of the illegal object when he lent the money and took the mortgage. The mortgagee is not bound to see to the application of the loan made.

The conduct of a trustee with regard to borrowing and mortgaging or pledging may be objectionable on either one of three grounds. The trustee may, in the first place, seek to borrow and hypothecate the trust property when he has no power to do so, that is, when neither the express terms of his trust, nor its implied grants of power, nor a court order or statute, permitted him to enter into the transaction. Here the mortgage given will be null and void.[66] The lender cannot complain of such a holding since he is bound to inquire into the powers of the trustee when he deals with a known trustee.

Secondly, the trustee may have had a power to mortgage, but only on the happening of a condition precedent, as, for example, the direction of the settlor or of a beneficiary. What is the result here if he mortgages but has not obtained the required direction? The mortgage is invalid.[67] The lender is bound to learn whether the power exists. He cannot safely rely on the assertions of the mortgagor-trustee.

However, if the mortgage is invalid and the money lent has been used by the trustee in such a way as to increase the value of the trust property which was covered by the invalid mortgage, it is fair that the lender should have a security interest in that property. Thus, if a trustee represents that he has power to

---

[65] Restatement, Trusts, § 191.

[66] Haimovitz v. Hawk, 80 Fla. 272, 85 So. 668; Kenworthy v. Levi, 214 Pa. 235, 63 A. 690.

[67] First Nat. Bank of Paterson v. National Broadway Bank, 156 N.Y. 459, 51 N.E. 398, 42 L.R.A. 139.

mortgage, and the lender foolishly believes him, although an examination of the trust instrument would clearly have shown the opposite, and the trustee uses the money lent to build a house on the land described in the invalid mortgage, it has been held that the lender ought to have an equitable lien by way of security on the house and lot, to the extent that his money increased its value.[68]

Thirdly, although a trustee may have the power to mortgage, he may use it for an improper purpose. If he has power to mortgage to pay off tax liens, or to repair real estate, but he in reality mortgages in order to use the money for his own purposes or in order to construct a new building on the land, the problem arises as to the effect of such a mortgage, when the money lent has been improperly used by the trustee. If the lender knew of the improper purpose, he is a participant in a breach of trust in lending to the trustee; but if he did not know of the trustee's object the mortgage is valid, even though the trust got no benefit from the mortgage loan or got no benefit to which it was entitled.[69] The lender is not bound to learn the trustee's motives and purposes, or to trace the money after the trustee gets it, or to see to the proper application of the money lent. The lender may assume that the trustee will use the proceeds of the loan for a legitimate purpose.[70]

The effect of notes and mortgages executed by trustees in performance of their trusts is governed by the general rules regarding contract obligations.[71] The trustee will be liable on promises and covenants in the notes and mortgages, unless he expressly excludes such liability.[72]

---

[68] Griley v. Marion Mtge. Co., 132 Fla. 299, 182 So. 297; Griley v. Marion Mtge. Co., 135 Fla. 824, 185 So. 734; Jones v. Swift, 300 Mass. 177, 15 N.E.2d 274.

[69] Seaverns v. Presbyterian Hospital, 173 Ill. 414, 50 N.E. 1079, 64 Am. St.Rep. 125; Parks v. Central Life Assur. Soc., 181 Okl. 638, 75 P.2d 1111; McAuslan v. Union Trust Co., 46 R.I. 176, 125 A. 296.

[70] See § 159, post.

[71] See § 113, ante.

[72] Hamlen v. Welch, C.C.A.Mass., 116 F.2d 413; East River Sav. Bank v. Samuels, 284 N.Y. 470, 31 N.E.2d 906.

EXPRESS OR IMPLIED POWER TO LEASE [73]

127. The power to lease is normally expressly given to a trustee who holds productive real estate, since the trustee cannot be expected to engage in business directly.

The implied authority to lease the trust property exists in the trustee whenever such a step is a reasonably necessary incident of the trust management.

In several states statutes govern leases by trustees and the power of the court to authorize leases. Chancery has jurisdiction to sanction or forbid leases, whenever such action will forward the trust purpose.

Power on the part of the trustee to lease the trust property is frequently found in the trust instrument in plain terms. In such case there can be no doubt about his authority.[74] If the trustee is to hold real estate, he can usually obtain profits from it only by leasing it to others, since he would not normally be permitted or expected to engage in business and obtain profit from the land directly.

A lease is not a "sale or disposal" of the trust property within the prohibition of a trust instrument.[75]

Implied power to lease the trust property exists wherever it is necessary to enable the trustee to perform his trust duties. The power to lease is frequently a necessary incident of the management of trust property.[76] If profits are to be made and distributed, and the trustee holds real estate, the implication that he is to lease the land to others and collect rents is almost inevitable.

It is often a difficult question to determine whether a trustee of a charitable trust has implied power to lease the property which he holds.[77] Thus, where buildings held in trust for charity

---

[73] Restatement, Trusts, § 189.

[74] Denegre v. Walker, 214 Ill. 113, 73 N.E. 409, 105 Am.St.Rep. 98, 2 Ann.Cas. 787; Ohio Oil Co. v. Daughetee, 240 Ill. 361, 88 N.E. 818, 36 L.R.A.,N.S., 1108. On the matters discussed in this section, see Kales, Powers in Trustees to Make Leases, 7 Ill.Law Rev. 427.

[75] In re Hubbell Trust, 135 Iowa 637, 113 N.W. 512, 13 L.R.A.,N.S., 496, 14 Ann.Cas. 640.

[76] Davis v. Harrison, Hawaii, 240 F. 97, 153 C.C.A. 133; Smith v. Jones, 120 Fla. 237, 162 So. 496; Hutcheson v. Hodnett, 115 Ga. 990, 42 S.E. 422; First Nat. Bank in Wichita v. Magnolia Petroleum Co., 144 Kan. 645, 62 P.2d 891; Geer v. Traders' Bank of Canada, 132 Mich. 215, 93 N.W. 437; Betts v. Betts, 4 Abb.N.C., N.Y., 317. For an instance of a case in which the trustee was held to have no implied power to lease, see In re Hoysradt, 20 Misc. 265, 45 N.Y.S. 841.

[77] In the following cases the circumstances of the charity were such that a lease was held to be within the implied powers of the trustee: Appeal

are dilapidated and the trustees have no funds for repairs or maintenance of the charity, a lease of the property to persons who agree to erect new buildings and use the property for the purposes of the trust will be upheld;[78] but, in another case, it has been held that where land was conveyed to trustees to provide a site for a schoolhouse to educate children, a lease of the premises, in consideration of a nominal rent and on the agreement of the lessee that a church should be there erected to be used to educate colored youth, was void, as not impliedly authorized by the deed of trust.[79] As with the private trust, so with the charitable, the authority of the trustee to lease depends upon the necessity of the lease. If the execution of the charity requires a lease to carry out the intent of the founder, implied power to lease will be held to exist.

Courts of equity have inherent power to authorize a trustee to lease and frequently exercise such authority, upon proof of its necessity.[80]

In some states the statutes declare when a trustee may lease trust property,[81] and also set forth the circumstances in which a court may authorize a lease and the procedure for obtaining such authority.[82]

of Trustees of Proprietors, School Fund of Providence, 2 Walk., Pa., 37; Black v. Ligon, 1 Harp.Eq., S.C., 205. But in Hendrix College v. Arkansas Townsite Co., 85 Ark. 446, 108 S.W. 514, a lease was held invalid for lack of power on the part of the trustee.

[78] Trustees of Madison Academy v. Board of Education of Richmond, Ky., 26 S.W. 187.

[79] Thornton v. Harris, 140 N.C. 498, 53 S.E. 341.

[80] Packard v. Illinois Trust & Savings Bank, 261 Ill. 450, 104 N.E. 275; Pedroja v. Pedroja, 152 Kan. 82, 102 P.2d 1012; Hitch v. Davis, 3 Md.Ch. 262. Equity may also validate a lease, which was improper when made. Wilmer v. Philadelphia & Reading Coal & Iron Co., 130 Md. 666, 101 A. 588. The fact, that the interest of all cestuis que trust will be promoted must be shown before equity will authorize a lease. Schroeder v. Woodward, 116 Va. 506, 82 S.E. 192.

[81] In some states the statute permits a trustee to make a lease for not to exceed five years, without court approval. Minn.St.1927, § 8100–8102; N. Y. Real Property Law, §§ 106–107n; Pa. 20 P.S. § 717. Court approval is required for a longer lease.

[82] N.D.L.1935, c. 250, § 15; R.I.Gen. L.1938, c. 486, § 20; Ore.Code 1930, §§ 6-801 to 6-817; Va.Code 1936, §§ 5334–5340.

LENGTH OF LEASES PERMITTED [83]

128. The prevailing view is that a trustee has no power to make a lease extending beyond the end of his trust, and that his lease terminates when the trust ends, no matter what the period fixed in the lease. But courts of equity exercise the power to authorize trustees to make leases which will or may run beyond the term of the trust, where the interests of trust beneficiaries and remaindermen justify such action.

Trustees sometimes find that it is desirable to make a long term lease, as, for example, one for fifty or ninety-nine years. In the case of property in a large city the proposed tenant is sometimes willing, if a long lease can be secured, to improve the land and pay a higher rent than could otherwise be obtained. The tenant will not be willing to construct an office or hotel building on the land leased, unless he can have the use of the land for a long time and thus recover his investment. The life of the ordinary trust is limited to lives in being or a period of years not more than twenty-one, or by lives and twenty-one years. It is often doubtful, therefore, whether the trust will last out a fifty or ninety-nine year lease, or it is certain that it will not. The trustee wants to make a long lease so as to get higher income and improvement of the land, but he doubts his power to lease for such a period.

Some courts have held that a trustee may make a long term lease, running beyond the life of his trust, where this conduct is reasonable in view of all the conditions; [84] but a majority of the cases deny the trustee any such power and require him to procure court sanction for such a lease.[85]

The court has power to grant to the trustee authority to make a lease which will or may last beyond the trust, but it must be shown that the benefits to trust beneficiaries and to remaindermen justify the action and that the remaindermen have no ground for complaint at losing control of their interest for a short period of time.[86] This power of the court is based on its juris-

---

[83] Restatement, Trusts, § 189.

[84] Russell v. Russell, 109 Conn. 187, 145 A. 648, 63 A.L.R. 783; Butler v. Topkis, Del., 63 A. 646; Lindenberger v. Kentucky Title Trust Co., 270 Ky. 579, 110 S.W.2d 301; North v. Augusta Real Estate Ass'n, 130 Me. 254, 155 A. 36; Sweeney v. Hagerstown Trust Co., 144 Md. 612, 125 A. 522.

[85] Hunt v. Lawton, 76 Cal.App. 655, 245 P. 803; Bergengren v. Aldrich, 139 Mass. 259, 29 N.E. 667; Standard Metallic Paint Co. v. Prince Mfg. Co., 133 Pa. 474, 19 A. 411. See 21 Harv. L.R. 211.

[86] Colonial Trust Co. v. Brown, 105 Conn. 261, 135 A. 555; Russell v. Russell, 109 Conn. 187, 145 A. 648, 63 A.

diction to secure for the beneficiaries the advantages which the trust instrument shows the settlor intended for them.

An Iowa court has summed up the law as follows: "(1) The trustees may lease for such reasonable terms as are customary and essential to the proper care of and to procure a reasonable income from the property. (2) Such terms should not, save on showing of reasonable necessity to effectuate the purposes of the trust, extend beyond the period the trust is likely to continue. (3) Should they extend unreasonably beyond such period, the excess only will be void. (4) Only upon a showing of such reasonable necessity, when not given such power by the instrument creating the trust, will the trustees be authorized to bind the estate so as to effectually deprive those ultimately entitled thereto of the property itself." [87]

TRUSTEE'S DUTIES AS LESSOR [88]

129. As lessor the trustee has a duty to make a lease under terms most advantageous to the beneficiaries, to collect the rent and otherwise enforce the lease, and to keep the premises in repair. It is not his duty or privilege to improve the premises before or after lease, unless it is necessary to make the land fit for being leased.

The trustee who leases has a duty to procure terms which are most advantageous to the beneficiaries, as far as possible. While it would seem unreasonable to grant a lessee an option to buy,[89] he may often with prudence give an option to renew the lease.[90]

The trustee is under a duty to enforce the lease, as, for example, to collect rents due under it. If he fails to collect any rent which he could have obtained, by the use of ordinary care and diligence, he will be liable for it.[91]

L.R. 783; Denegre v. Walker, 214 Ill. 113, 73 N.E. 409, 105 Am.St.Rep. 98; In re Hubbell Trust, 135 Iowa 637, 113 N.W. 512, 13 L.R.A.,N.S., 496, 14 Ann.Cas. 640; In re Caswell's Will, 197 Wis. 327, 222 N.W. 235, 61 A.L.R. 1359.

[87] In re Hubbell Trust, 135 Iowa, 637, 664, 665, 113 N.W. 512, 522, 13 L.R.A.,N.S., 496, 14 Ann.Cas. 640.

[88] Restatement, Trusts, § 189.

[89] In re Armory Board, 29 Misc. 174, 60 N.Y.S. 882; Hickok v. Still, 168 Pa. 155, 31 A. 1100, 47 Am.St.Rep. 880.

[90] Raynolds v. Browning, King & Co., 217 App.Div. 443, 217 N.Y.S. 15; but see McCrory v. Beeler, 155 Md. 456, 142 A. 587.

[91] Kinney v. Uglow, 163 Or. 539, 98 P.2d 1006.

§ 129 TRUSTEE'S DUTIES AS LESSOR 409

Insofar as the lease and the law of landlord and tenant place upon the landlord the duty of keeping the leased buildings in repair, the trustee, of course, has a duty to make repairs.

A trustee has implied or general authority to make reasonable, necessary repairs to the trust property. "A trustee cannot ordinarily make improvements, and charge the cost thereof to the beneficiary, unless clearly authorized by the instrument creating the trust. * * * He will, however, be allowed for repairs, when such repairs are necessary to the preservation of the estate." [92] The trustee should consider the value of the trust property, the probable length of the trust, and the effect of the repairs upon the income of the trust property. If, in view of these considerations, a reasonable man in the conduct of his own business would repair the property, the trustee has implied power so to do.[93] "Regard should be had to the probable duration of the trust in determining whether temporary and slight, or more permanent and thorough repairs, should be made." [94] Occasionally the trustee is given express authority to make repairs.[95]

Except as an improvement of real estate may be necessary and reasonably prudent for the purpose of making property tenantable,[96] that is, where the property cannot be rented without the improvement, the trustee has no duty or privilege to improve the premises in anticipation of, or after, a lease.[97]

Thus, in a case where buildings are ancient, unsafe, and untenantable, and the property is in an unproductive condition, the trustee will be considered to have implied power to use a portion of the principal of the trust fund for the purpose of constructing new buildings on the land.[98]

---

[92] Booth v. Bradford, 114 Iowa 562, 570, 87 N.W. 685, 688.

[93] Veazie v. Forsaith, 76 Me. 172; Sohier v. Eldredge, 103 Mass. 345; Rathbun v. Colton, 15 Pick., Mass., 471; Kearney v. Kearney, 17 N.J. Eq. 59; Disbrow v. Disbrow, 46 App. Div. 111, 61 N.Y.S. 614, affirmed 167 N.Y. 606, 60 N.E. 1110; In re Heroy's Estate, 102 Misc. 305, 169 N.Y.S. 807; In re Griffith's Estate, 4 Pa.Dist.R. 495.

[94] Rathbun v. Colton, 15 Pick., Mass., 471, 484.

[95] Stamford Trust Co. v. Mack, 91 Conn. 620, 101 A. 235; In re Rankin's Estate, 5 Pa.Co.Ct.R. 603.

[96] Patterson v. Johnson, 113 Ill. 559; Sohier v. Eldredge, 103 Mass. 345; Stevens v. Stevens, 80 Hun, N. Y., 514, 30 N.Y.S. 625, 62 N.Y.St.Rep. 599.

[97] Booth v. Bradford, 114 Iowa 562, 87 N.W. 685; and see § 103, ante.

[98] Smith v. Keteltas, 62 App.Div. 174, 70 N.Y.S. 1065. But in In re Cole's Estate, 102 Wis. 1, 78 N.W. 402, 72 Am.St.Rep. 854, it was held that, even though the cestuis que trust and remainderman consented,

In other instances the peculiar conditions of the trust have made the expenditure for improvements unreasonable and the trustee has been held to have exceeded his powers in making improvements.[99] Thus, the expenditure of $850,000 in erecting a new building upon land when the value of the entire trust property was only $920,000, has been held to be unreasonable and not within the authority of the trustee.[1] The Massachusetts court stated its position regarding improvements in general in these words: "We have no doubt that a trustee under a Massachusetts trust would be justified in tearing down an old building owned by the trust and erecting a new one in its place, when a prudent business man would do so to secure a fair return by way of income, and at the same time to maintain the corpus of the portion of the principal so invested intact, having regard to the relation which such an investment, when made, would have to the amount of the principal of the trust fund as a whole." [2]

In some states statutes expressly authorize chancery to empower a trustee to sell or mortgage the trust property for the purpose of making repairs or improvements.[3]

---

the trustee had no power to employ a part of the principal in making improvements.

[99] Pope's Ex'r v. Weber, 1 Ky.Law Rep. 329; Green v. Winter, 1 Johns. Ch., N.Y., 26, 7 Am.Dec. 475; Herbert v. Herbert, 57 How.Prac., N.Y., 333; Killebrew v. Murphy, 3 Heisk.,Tenn., 546; Hughes v. Williams, 99 Va. 312, 38 S.E. 138.

[1] Warren v. Pazolt, 203 Mass. 328, 89 N.E. 381.

[2] 203 Mass. 328, 345, 89 N.E. 381, 387.

[3] N.J.S.A. 3:19–1 to 3:19–10; New York Real Property Law, § 105.

CHAPTER 14

TRUST ADMINISTRATION—PAYMENTS—CHANGES IN TRUSTEE PERSONNEL

Sec.
130. Trustee's Duties in Making Payments.
131. Advances of Trust Capital or Income.
132. Resignation by Trustee.
133. Death of Trustee.
134. Vacancies in Trusteeship—Appointment of Successors.

TRUSTEE'S DUTIES IN MAKING PAYMENTS [1]

130. The trustee should make payments to the beneficiaries as directed by the trust instrument. If he fails to do so, he will be liable, even though he used ordinary care in paying out the funds.

The duties of the trustee regarding the payment of the income of the trust property to the beneficiaries are not ordinarily difficult to ascertain. The trust instrument either prescribes that definite sums shall be paid at definite times to the cestui, or it leaves the amounts and times to the discretion of the trustee. If the settlor has determined the amount of property to be delivered to the cestui and the time of such delivery, there will not ordinarily arise any question of difficulty for the trustee. If the amount and time are left to the discretion of the trustee, he may exercise his discretion, and, if he uses good faith, equity will not ordinarily interfere with his acts.[2] Thus, where a testator authorized his trustees to pay over to the cestui que trust a certain sum whenever in their opinion his mental and physical condition was such that he was competent to attend to his affairs, and the trustees did not pay over the sum to the beneficiary during his life, this exercise of discretion was not interfered with by the court.[3] But a direction to the trustees to pay the dividends of certain stock to the beneficiaries "at their discretion" does not authorize the trustees to decline to pay any dividends to the cestuis que trust. It merely gives the trustees discretion as to the time and manner of payment.[4]

---

[1] Restatement, Trusts, §§ 182, 226.

[2] Kimball v. Blanchard, 101 Me. 383, 64 A. 645; Kimball v. Reding, 31 N.H. 352, 64 Am.Dec. 333; In re Wilkin, 183 N.Y. 104, 75 N.E. 1105.

[3] O'Gorman v. Crowley, 81 N.J.Eq. 520, 86 A. 442.

[4] Lembeck v. Lembeck, 73 N.J.Eq. 427, 68 A. 337.

The rules regarding the trustee's duties concerning payments vary so much with the terms of different trust instruments that but little profitable general discussion can be given. However, a few principles are worth noting. Money paid by a trustee to a cestui que trust is presumed to be on account of the profits of the trust estate.[5] If the beneficiary is incompetent, it becomes a question of the construction of the trust instrument whether the trustee should pay income to the guardian of the beneficiary or apply it for the incompetent's benefit.[6] A trustee may make payments by check.[7] If the trust instrument states the times of payment, such directions should be obeyed.[8] Where the trustee has notice that the cestui que trust has assigned his interest, the trustee should make payments to the assignee.[9] A trustee who makes improper payments will, of course, be responsible to the cestuis.[10] If the amounts of the payments to be made are not fixed by the trust instrument and the trustee has no right to fix them, the court of chancery will determine the amounts.[11] If a trustee is directed to divide the settlor's property equally between certain beneficiaries, he is not obliged to give each an equal share of the real property and each an equal amount of the personalty, but must merely give each property equal in value to the shares of the others.[12] A trustee charged with the duty of supporting the cestui que trust may perform that duty without making any money payments to the cestui.[13] If the trustee is charged with the support of a cestui, he must honestly exercise his discretion as to the amount needed for that purpose.[14] Where the trust instrument provides for the investment of money in land and the conveyance of such land to the cestuis que trust, the latter may elect to take the money instead of the land.[15] If the trustee is ordered to pay money to

[5] Woodard v. Wright, 82 Cal. 202, 22 P. 1118.

[6] Rudy's Appeal, Pa., 11 A. 398; Matter of Fisk, 45 Misc. 298, 92 N.Y.S. 394; Everhart v. Everhart, 87 Pa. Super. 184.

[7] In re Jones' Estate, 199 Pa. 143, 48 A. 865.

[8] Brown v. Berry, 71 N.H. 241, 52 A. 870.

[9] Seger v. Farmers' Loan & Trust Co., 73 App.Div. 293, 76 N.Y.S. 721, reversed 176 N.Y. 589, 68 N.E. 1124.

[10] Owings v. Rhodes, 65 Md. 408, 9 A. 903.

[11] In re Riley's Estate, 4 Misc. 338, 24 N.Y.S. 309.

[12] Richardson v. Morey, 18 Pick., Mass., 181.

[13] Conover v. Fisher, N.J.Ch., 36 A. 948.

[14] Collister v. Fassitt, 163 N.Y. 281, 57 N.E. 490, 79 Am.St.Rep. 586.

[15] Ashby v. Smith, 1 Rob., Va., 55.

the beneficiaries, he should not, obviously, offer them stock of a corporation instead.[16] If the beneficiary has disappeared, and an administrator of his estate has been appointed on the theory that he is dead, the trustee may require the administrator to give a bond before he pays money to the administrator.[17]

The duty of the trustee is making payments or deliveries of the trust property is absolute. It is not a duty to use ordinary care to see that the trust benefits come to the proper persons. Thus, if a trustee has a duty to pay net income to the widow of the settlor, he will not be discharged from liability except by a payment to the woman who actually was the settlor's widow at his death. If another woman impersonates the widow and secures the trust income, the trustee will be liable, although he can show that he made a careful investigation and was deceived by forgeries and perjury. A debtor is released by making payment to his creditor, and not by the use of reasonable efforts to make payment. A trustee is an obligor in equity, similar to a debtor at law.[18]

A trust to pay an annuity of a fixed sum of money may, or may not, include a clause permitting or directing the trustee to encroach on trust principal to make up the annuity, if the trust income proves inadequate during any given year.[19] Where there has been an inadequacy of income to pay an annuity, it becomes a question of the settlor's intent whether the trustee should make up a deficiency in the annuity for one year from a surplus of income in a later year.[20]

---

[16] Mitchell v. Carrollton Nat. Bank, 97 S.W. 45, 29 Ky.Law Rep. 1228. The court may permit a trustee who has a duty to pay in money, to pay in securities, if there is a good reason therefor. In re McGuffey's Estate, 123 Pa.Super. 432, 187 A. 298; In re Smith's Estate, 332 Pa. 581, 2 A.2d 779. A duty to turn over the trust property at the end of the trust requires its delivery as it then is, and not a conversion into money. In re Osterling's Estate, 324 Pa. 167, 188 A. 180.

[17] Donovan v. Major, 253 Ill. 179, 97 N.E. 231.

[18] Prince De Bearn v. Winans, 111 Md. 434, 74 A. 626; Ellis v. Kelsey, 241 N.Y. 374, 150 N.E. 148; Moyer v. Norristown-Penn Trust Co., 296 Pa. 26, 145 A. 682.

[19] First Trust Co. of Wichita v. Varney, 142 Kan. 93, 45 P.2d 582; Taylor v. Gardiner, 296 Mass. 411, 6 N.E.2d 357, 109 A.L.R. 714.

[20] Fate v. Fate, 295 Ill.App. 271, 14 N.E.2d 890; In re Lowrie's Estate, 294 Mich. 298, 293 N.W. 656.

ADVANCES OF TRUST CAPITAL OR INCOME [21]

131. Unless the trust instrument authorizes the trustee to do so, he should not expend the trust capital, even though the beneficiaries greatly need it, without receiving court authorization.

Equity has power to hasten the enjoyment of trust capital or income, by ordering a trustee to spend income instead of accumulating it, or to spend trust capital instead of holding it for distribution at a later date; but it has no power to order advances to be made to one who does not have a vested interest in the income or capital advanced. The power to hasten enjoyment is used sparingly for the benefit of infants, and rarely for adults.

A trustee has no duty to advance his own money to a trust beneficiary in anticipation of trust income, but if he does so, he may repay himself out of future trust income belonging to the beneficiary in question.

Where the income of the trust property is insufficient to accomplish the trust purposes, the trustee is sometimes tempted to sell trust capital and use the proceeds to make up the deficiency in income. If the trustee is expressly or impliedly authorized to do this by the trust instrument, of course his action will be legal, if prudently done and if the trust instrument is followed.[22] But unless the trustee is sure of such implied or express power, he should lay the matter before the court of equity and ask for instructions. He should not act on his own initiative. For example, if the object of the trust is the support of the settlor's widow, and the trust income is only $1,000 a year, net, and the widow needs at least $2,000, the trustee should not take the responsibility of selling $1,000 of trust property a year and adding that sum to the widow's income, unless he is advised that the instrument permits it. He should rather ask equity to sanction such action.

The object of the settlor was his widow's comfortable support. He sought to achieve it by providing for the payment of the net income of the trust property to her. The function of the court is to direct such management of the trust as will provide comfortable support for the widow, so long as it can be done without taking the property of someone else and using it for the widow's benefit. Thus, in the case put, if the instrument

---

[21] Restatement, Trusts, §§ 196, 250, 255.

[22] Whitaker v. McDowell, 82 Conn. 195, 72 A. 938, 16 Ann.Cas. 324; Osborne v. Gordon, 86 Wis. 92, 56 N.W. 334.

provided that at the end of ten years, the capital should be paid to the widow, the court might be induced to direct advancement of parts of it year by year during the trust; but if at the end of the widow's life the capital was to be distributed to her children, the court would not direct the use of principal for the widow, since it would be appropriating property of the children for their mother's benefit, if it did so.[23]

This power of the court to order advances of income or principal is not infrequently used for the advantage of infant beneficiaries,[24] but rarely for adults.[25] Thus, if a trust is set up to accumulate the income of the fund until a son reaches twenty-one, and then pay him the accumulations and deliver the fund to him, and it appears that the son is badly in need of money for his education and support before he reaches his majority, the court will be inclined to direct that part or all of the income of the fund be spent for the infant's benefit during his minority, rather than held for him until he comes of age. The court here feels that it is changing methods of administration but not changing ownership of the trust benefits. It is hastening enjoyment, but not giving enjoyment to someone who would not otherwise have obtained it.[26]

If the interest of the temporary beneficiary in the capital is contingent and uncertain, there will be no court order for the use of capital for him. This might be taking another's property and giving it to the income beneficiary. Thus, if a trust is created to pay the income to three daughters during their minorities, with a gift of the capital to them, share and share alike, when the youngest reaches twenty-one, or if any of the three has died before reaching twenty-one, then her share is to go to her issue if any, the court will not order the use of the capital for the three daughters during the trust, since their interests in the capital are subject to the remote possibility of divestment.[27] They might all die before twenty-one, leaving issue, in which case the issue would get the trust capital. It is almost certain that the daughters will receive the trust capital in the future, but it is not absolutely certain.

[23] Mills v. Michigan Trust Co., 124 Mich. 244, 82 N.W. 1046.

[24] Pearce v. Pearce, 199 Ala. 491, 74 So. 952; Matter of Wagner, 81 App.Div. 163, 80 N.Y.S. 785.

[25] First Nat. Bk. of Mobile v. Watters, 220 Ala. 356, 125 So. 222; Post v. Grand Rapids Trust Co., 255 Mich. 436, 238 N.W. 206.

[26] Bennett v. Nashville Trust Co., 127 Tenn. 126, 153 S.W. 840, 46 L.R.A.,N.S., 43, Ann.Cas.1914A, 1045.

[27] Stewart v. Hamilton, 151 Tenn. 396, 270 S.W. 79, 39 A.L.R. 37.

The trustee is under no duty to advance his own funds to the trust beneficiary, in anticipation of the receipt of trust income. Thus, if the beneficiary tells the trustee he is in great need, and asks for an advance until the next payment of trust income is due, the trustee may advance his own money, but need not.[28] If such an advance is made, the trustee is entitled to reimbursement out of later collected trust income which is allocable to the beneficiary, but if the trustee made the advance as the income of a specific mortgage or other investment, he is entitled to reimbursement out of the future income of that investment only.[29]

RESIGNATION BY TRUSTEE [30]

132. The trustee may resign the trust by obtaining a decree of a court of equity accepting his resignation, or by securing the consent of all the beneficiaries, if they are competent to give their consent. The trustee cannot by his own act discharge himself from the obligations of the trust. Equity will accept a resignation for good cause shown and on such terms as seem to it just.

When and by what method may a trustee resign a trusteeship and be freed from its obligations? Chancery has the power to accept a trustee's resignation and discharge him from the trust.[31] It may use its discretion in accepting or rejecting the resignation of a trustee. His resignation will not be accepted as a matter of course, although the unwillingness of the trustee to proceed with the trust is a reason of some force for the acceptance of the resignation. A reluctant trustee is not desirable. The mere filing of the resignation with the court, or notification of the cestuis que trust of his resignation, does not release the trustee.[32]

---

[28] Walker v. Doak, 210 Cal. 30, 290 P. 290; Clark v. Clark, 123 Kan. 646, 256 P. 1012.

[29] In re Klein's Estate, 326 Pa. 393, 190 A. 882.

[30] Restatement, Trusts, §§ 106, 384.

[31] Du Puy v. Standard Mineral Co., 88 Me. 202, 33 A. 976; Bowditch v. Banuelos, 1 Gray, Mass., 220; Craig v. Craig, 3 Barb.Ch., N.Y., 76; Young v. Barker, 141 App.Div. 801, 127 N.Y.S. 211.

For recent statutory statements regarding the resignation of the trustee, see Cal.L.1939, p. 1942, adding § 1125.1 to the Probate Code; La. Acts 1938, No. 81, § 20; Kan.L.1939, c. 180, § 140; Mich.Pub.Acts 1939, No. 288, c. IV, §§ 48, 49; N.Y.L.1940, c. 829.

[32] Tucker v. Grundy, 83 Ky. 540; In re Miller, 15 Abb.Prac., N.Y., 277; Perkins v. McGavock, 3 Hayw., Tenn., 265.

The rule is generally stated to be that the trustee cannot resign without a decree of the court permitting his resignation or the consent of all the cestuis que trust.³³ "But it is a settled rule of law that a trustee, after he has accepted the office, cannot discharge himself from liability by a subsequent resignation merely. He must either be discharged from the trust by virtue of a special provision in the deed, or will, which creates the trust, or by an order or decree of the court of chancery, or with the general consent of all persons interested in the execution of the trust." ³⁴ "The authorities are clear that a trustee cannot divest himself of the obligation to perform the duties of the trust, without an order of the court, or the consent of all the cestuis que trust." ³⁵

The statements sometimes made that the trustee cannot resign without an order of the court *and* the consent of the cestuis que trust are clearly inaccurate. The court may accept the resignation, even though the beneficiaries, or some of them, object to such acceptance.³⁶ Where the cestuis que trust are infants, or otherwise incapable of giving consent to the resignation of the trustee, no resignation based on their consent alone will be valid. In such instances resignation can only occur through a decree of the court.³⁷

The usual method of resignation is by application to the court rather than by securing consents from the beneficiaries. In some states statutory proceedings for resignation are now provided.³⁸

---

³³ Badgett v. Keating, 31 Ark. 400; Jones v. Stockett, 2 Bland, Md., 409; Henderson v. Sherman, 47 Mich. 267, 11 N.W. 153; Green v. Blackwell, 31 N.J.Eq. 37; Shepherd v. M'Evers, 4 Johns.Ch., N.Y., 136, 8 Am.Dec. 561: Thatcher v. Candee, 33 How.Prac., N.Y., 145; Anderson v. Robinson, 57 Or. 172, 110 P. 975; Breedlove v. Stump, 3 Yerg., Tenn., 257.

³⁴ Cruger v. Halliday, 11 Paige, N.Y., 314, 319.

³⁵ Thatcher v. Candee, 33 How. Prac., N.Y., 145, 149.

³⁶ In re Nixon's Estate, 235 Pa. 27, 83 A. 687.

³⁷ Cruger v. Halliday, 11 Paige, N.Y., 314.

Bogert Trusts 2d—27

³⁸ A New York statute upon the subject reads as follows: "An executor, administrator, guardian or testamentary trustee may, at any time, present to the Surrogate's Court a petition, praying that his account may be judicially settled; that a decree may thereupon be made, revoking his letters or permitting him to resign, and discharging him accordingly; and that the same persons may be cited to show cause why such a decree should not be made who must be cited upon a petition for a judicial settlement of his account. The petition must set forth the facts upon which the application is founded; and it must, in all other respects, conform to a petition praying for a judicial settlement of his account. The surrogate may, in his

The trustee must allege some cause for his desire to resign.[39] If it appears that a resignation at that time will be disadvantageous to the beneficiaries, the court will refuse to allow the trustee to resign. An example of such a situation is found in the cases where pending actions brought by the trustee or other unsettled matters render it desirable to retain the trustee in office until the conclusion of the unfinished business.[40] Ordinarily, however, a court will not force an unwilling trustee to continue. The following have been held to be sufficient grounds for resignation: that continuance in office would be inconvenient to the trustee;[41] that the trustee is unwilling to continue and that there has been an increase in the amount of the trust property since the original acceptance;[42] that the trustee is about to leave the United States;[43] that there is friction and disagreement between the trustee and the cestuis que trust.[44]

A trustee may, at any time before the court has taken final action on his resignation, withdraw it and resume his duties as trustee.[45]

In the proceeding to obtain a release from the trust the cestuis que trust are necessary parties.[46] The court may impose a condition upon the acceptance of the trustee's resignation, as, for example, that the trustee waive his commissions.[47] Where the resignation is solely to promote the convenience of the trustee,

---

discretion, entertain or decline to entertain the application." N.Y. Surrogate's Court Act, § 102. See, also, Drane v. Gunter, 19 Ala. 731; Cal.Prob.Code, § 1125.1; Mich.Pub. Acts 1939, No. 288, c. IV, §§ 48, 49; Va.Acts 1938, c. 422.

[39] Craig v. Craig, 3 Barb.Ch., N.Y., 76.

[40] In re Olmstead, 52 App.Div. 515, 66 N.Y.S. 212, affirmed 164 N.Y. 571, 58 N.E. 1090; In re Longstreth's Estate, 12 Phila., Pa., 86.

[41] Bogle v. Bogle, 3 Allen, Mass., 158.

[42] Green v. Blackwell, 31 N.J.Eq. 37.

[43] Tilden v. Fiske, 4 Dem.Sur., N.Y., 357.

[44] In re Bernstein, 3 Redf.Sur.,

N.Y., 20; Parker v. Allen, Sup., 14 N.Y.S. 265. For other cases construing the New York statutes, see In re Cutting, 49 App.Div. 388, 63 N.Y.S. 246; Smith v. Lansing, 24 Misc. 566, 53 N.Y.S. 633; Rothschild v. Goldenberg, 33 Misc. 646, 68 N.Y.S. 955; In re Abbot, 39 Misc. 760, 80 N.Y.S. 1117.

[45] Dillard v. Winn, 60 Ala. 285. But after action upon the resignation by the court, even if no successor has been appointed, the resignation may not be retracted. Lednum v. Dallas Trust & Savings Bank, Tex.Civ.App., 192 S.W. 1127.

[46] Clay's Adm'r v. Edwards' Trustee, 84 Ky. 548, 2 S.W. 147; Riggs v. Moise, 344 Mo. 177, 128 S.W.2d 632.

[47] In re Curtiss, 15 Misc. 545, 37 N.Y.S. 586.

BOGERT TRUSTS 2D

the court will oblige him to pay the costs of the proceeding;[48] but in other instances, where the cause for resignation is not personal with the trustee, the court may direct that the costs be paid out of the trust estate.[49] The court will require an accounting by the resigning trustee before accepting his resignation.[50]

The trust instrument may provide the procedure for resignation, as, for example, that any one of several trustees may resign by filing a written statement of his resignation with the other trustees.[51]

DEATH OF TRUSTEE [52]

133. **The death of the trustee does not of itself affect the life of the trust. Equity will fill the vacancy, and the trust will continue.**

> **In the absence of statute, upon the death of a sole trustee intestate, the title to the trust property vests in the trustee's heirs or personal representative, depending upon the nature of the property, whether real or personal. If the deceased sole trustee left a will, title to the trust property, but not the trust office, passes to the devisees or executor named in the will. Where one of several trustees dies, the surviving trustees become the sole owners of the trust property by virtue of the right of survivorship in joint tenancy.**

> **By statute in several states, on the death of a sole trustee the title to the trust property vests in the court of equity.**

> **There is no right of dower or curtesy in the estate of the trustee.**

> **On the death of the trustee intestate and without heirs, the crown or state takes subject to the rights of cestui que trust.**

The death of the trustee will not of itself terminate the trust. The continuance of the trust is not dependent on the life of any particular trustee. Equity will supply a successor.[53]

---

[48] In re Jones, 4 Sandf.Ch., N.Y., 615.

[49] Green v. Blackwell, 31 N.J.Eq. 37; Richmond v. Arnold, R.I., 68 A. 427.

[50] In re Carson's Will, 227 Iowa 941, 289 N.W. 30; Kan.L.1939, c. 180, § 139.

[51] Cal.Civ.Code, § 2282(3); Douglas Properties v. Stix, 118 Fla. 354, 159 So. 1.

[52] Restatement, Trusts, §§ 103–105, 384.

[53] See ante, § 35. An exception must be made, of course, where the trust was personal. In such cases, on the death of the trustee, equity will not appoint a successor. The trust ends. Rogers v. Rea, 98 Ohio St. 315, 120 N.E. 828. The settlor may, of course, provide in the trust instrument that the trust shall last until the trustee dies and no longer.

After a sole trustee's death, however, it is obvious that the legal title to the trust property which has been vested in him can no longer remain there. It must be transferred to some one upon the trustee's death. It cannot remain in suspense.

By common law the holding is that the ownership of the trust property devolves upon the persons who would take the absolute property of the deceased. "The general principle is not questioned that trusts of real estate upon the trustee's death devolve upon his heir at law, and trusts of personalty devolve upon the executor or administrator for the preservation of the title, until the appointment of a new trustee. * * *"[54] That the heir becomes the owner of real property[55] held in trust, and the personal representative the owner of personal property,[56] upon the death of the sole trustee, is well recognized.

Due to the inconveniences which would arise from tenancy in common, it is generally provided by statute or decision that trustees hold as joint tenants. Where there are several trustees, and one dies, it is preferable that the surviving trustees, who have knowledge of the trust and have been selected by the settlor, should administer the trust, rather than that the administration should be continued by such survivors in common with the heirs or personal representatives of the deceased trustee. Such heirs or personal representatives may have no special fitness for the task of carrying on the trust. It is only when the title can rest nowhere else that it devolves upon them.

---

[54] Baltimore Trust Co. v. George's Creek Coal & Iron Co., 119 Md. 21, 34, 85 A. 949.

[55] Greenleaf v. Queen, 26 U.S. 138, 1 Pet. 138, 7 L.Ed. 85; Lawrence v. Lawrence, 181 Ill. 248, 54 N.E. 918; Bloom v. Ray, Ky., 16 S.W. 714; Laughlin v. Page, 108 Me. 307, 80 A. 753; Hawkins v. Chapman, 36 Md. 83; Ewing v. Shannahan, 113 Mo. 188, 20 S.W. 1065; Kirkman v. Wadsworth, 137 N.C. 453, 49 S.E. 962; Jenks' Lessee v. Backhouse, 1 Bin., Pa., 91; Watkins v. Specht, 7 Cold., Tenn., 585; Williams v. Moliere, 60 Vt. 378, 15 A. 192. But see Birks v. McNeill, 177 Iowa 567, 159 N.W. 210. If the sole trustee devise the real property held in trust, the devisees will be held to hold the title as trustees but not to have the right to administer the trust. Mortimer v. Ireland, 11 Jur. 721; Cresap v. Brown, 82 W.Va. 467, 96 S.E. 66.

[56] Conaway v. Third Nat. Bank of Cincinnati, C.C.A.W.Va., 167 F. 26, 92 C.C.A. 488; Gregg v. Gabbert, 62 Ark. 602, 37 S.W. 232; Tyler v. Mayre, 95 Cal. 160, 27 P. 160, 30 P. 196; Friedley v. Security Trust & Safe Deposit Co., 10 Del.Ch. 74, 84 A. 883; Anderson v. Northrop, 30 Fla. 612, 12 So. 318; Lucas v. Donaldson, 117 Ind. 139, 19 N.E. 758; Safford v. Rantoul, 12 Pick., Mass., 233; Gulick v. Bruere, 42 N.J.Eq. 639, 9 A. 719; Appeal of Baird, 3 Watts & S., Pa., 459; Merriam v. Hemmenway, 26 Vt. 565.

§ 133 DEATH OF TRUSTEE 421

A settlor may by express provision make his cotrustees tenants in common, but this is very rarely done, and joint tenancy is presumed where no express statement is made as to the method of holding.

It is, of course, a characteristic of joint tenancy that, upon the death of one of the joint tenants, the title to the property remains in the surviving joint tenants as a whole, and that no rights descend to the heirs or personal representatives of the deceased joint tenant. Thus, in cases of trusts, if A., B., and C. are trustees, and A. dies, B. and C. will hold the title to the trust property, free from any claims by the heirs or personal representatives of A.[57] "Upon the death of one of several cotrustees, the office of trustee will devolve, with the estate, upon the survivor, and ultimately upon the heir or personal representative of the last survivor. Trusts of real estate, upon the death of the trustee, devolve upon his heir at law. Trusts of personalty vest in his executor or administrator."[58]

Even in states where joint tenancy is generally abolished, it still exists among trustees,[59] and in other states, where all grants to two or more persons are presumed to be to them as tenants in common, there is an exception in the case of trustees, and they are to hold as joint tenants.[60]

In several states statutes modifying the common-law rule regarding the devolution of trust property have been enacted. These statutes vest the title to trust property, upon the death of the sole trustee, in the court having general equity jurisdiction, and require the court to appoint a trustee to carry out the trust to its conclusion.[61]

---

[57] F. G. Oxley Stave Co. v. Butler County, 166 U.S. 648, 17 S.Ct. 709, 41 L.Ed. 1149; Wilson v. Snow, 35 App.D.C. 562; Reichert v. Missouri & I. Coal Co., 231 Ill. 238, 83 N.E. 166, 121 Am.St.Rep. 307; Boyer v. Sims, 61 Kan. 593, 60 P. 309; Rutherford Land & Improvement Co. v. Sanntrock, 60 N.J.Eq. 471, 46 A. 648; In re Ziegler, 168 App.Div. 735, 154 N.Y.S. 652; Maffet v. Oregon & C. R. Co., 46 Or. 443, 80 P. 489; Mattison v. Mattison, 53 Or. 254, 100 P. 4, 133 Am.St.Rep. 829, 18 Ann.Cas. 218. But see, contra, Sander's Heirs v. Morrison's Ex'rs, 7 T.B.Mon., Ky., 54, 18 Am.Dec. 161. The statute in California reads as follows: "On the death, renunciation, or discharge of one of several cotrustees the trust survives to the others." Civ.Code, § 2288.

[58] Schenck v. Schenck, 16 N.J.Eq. 174, 182.

[59] Boyer v. Sims, 61 Kan. 593, 60 P. 309.

[60] New York Real Property Law, § 66.

[61] Ala.Code 1940, Title 47, § 150; Whitehead v. Whitehead, 142 Ala. 163, 37 So. 929; Lecroix v. Malone, 157 Ala. 434, 47 So. 725; Ind.Burns'

Where the title to the trust property passes to the heir or personal representative of a deceased sole trustee, the court will, upon proper application, appoint a new trustee to carry on the trust and relieve the heir or executor.[62]

The modern rule is that if the trustee dies without heirs and escheat takes place, the crown or state holds for the beneficiary of the trust.[63]

It is well settled that the widow of a sole trustee is not entitled to dower in the trust property,[64] and that the widower of a sole trustee has no rights of curtesy.[65] The seizin of the trustee not being beneficial, and his title being the dry legal title only, there is no basis for the award of dower or curtesy. "Where a person holds land in trust for another, the husband or wife of such trustee is not entitled to dower in such premises."[66]

VACANCIES IN TRUSTEESHIP—APPOINTMENT OF SUCCESSORS [67]

134. **The settlor may reserve to himself or vest in others the power of filling vacancies in the trusteeship. If he makes no such provision, or if the method provided by the settlor does not produce a trustee, the court of chancery has power to appoint the new trustee.**

In appointing a trustee, equity will prefer unbiased persons of full legal capacity.

Ann.St. 1933, § 56-617; Kan.Gen.St. 1935, 67-410; Collier v. Blake, 14 Kan. 250; Mich.Ann.St. § 26.118; Minn.St.1927, § 8103; New York Personal Property Law, § 20; New York Real Property Law, § 111; Stewart v. Franchetti, 167 App.Div. 541, 153 N.Y.S. 453; In re Meehan's Estate, 104 Misc. 219, 171 N.Y.S. 766; St. Wis.1941, § 231.24.

[62] Gregg v. Gabbert, 62 Ark. 602, 37 S.W. 232; Cal.Civ.Code § 2289; Ewing v. Shannahan, 113 Mo. 188, 20 S.W. 1065.

[63] St. 47 & 48 Vict. c. 71, § 6; N.Y. Public Lands Law, § 68; New York Cent. & H. R. R. Co. v. Cottle, 102 Misc. 30, 168 N.Y.S. 463.

[64] Barker v. Smiley, 218 Ill. 68, 75 N.E. 787; Gritten v. Dickerson, 202 Ill. 372, 66 N.E. 1090; Sanford v. Sanford, 157 Ill.App. 350; Tevis v. Steele, 4 T.B.Mon., Ky., 339; Miller v. Miller, 148 Mo. 113, 49 S.W. 852; Van Pelt v. Parry, 218 Mo. 680, 118 S.W. 425; Kager v. Brenneman, 47 App.Div. 63, 62 N.Y.S. 339; Hendren v. Hendren, 153 N.C. 505, 69 S.E. 506, 138 Am.St.Rep. 680; Kaphan v. Toney, Tenn.Ch.App., 58 S.W. 909; Wilson v. Wilson, 32 Utah 169, 89 P. 643.

[65] King v. Bushnell, 121 Ill. 656, 13 N.E. 245; Chew v. Commissioners of Southwark, 5 Rawle, Pa., 160.

[66] King v. Bushnell, 121 Ill. 656, 660, 13 N.E. 245.

[67] Restatement, Trusts, § 108.

§ 134 VACANCIES IN TRUSTEESHIP 423

The application for the appointment of a trustee is generally required to be made by a party financially interested in the trust, upon notice to all others so interested.

An administrator with the will annexed does not ordinarily succeed to trust duties conferred upon an executor.

A trustee appointed by the court becomes vested with the title to the trust property by virtue of the decree of the court. No conveyance from the retiring trustee is necessary.

The question next arises as to the method of filling a vacancy in a trusteeship. If the original trustee is removed from office by natural or artificial causes, voluntarily or involuntarily, by whom and in what way will his successor be appointed?

The settlor may devise a method of filling vacancies, and this method must be respected, if reasonable.[68]

Neither a surviving trustee[69] nor a cestui que trust[70] has implied authority to fill a vacancy in the trusteeship. Only when expressly empowered by the trust instrument may they appoint the successor trustee.

The persons whom the settlor may empower to fill vacancies are numerous and restricted only by the settlor's imagination. He may reserve to himself the right to fill vacancies,[71] or may vest such right in the surviving trustees,[72] or in the surviving trustees and the cestuis que trust,[73] or in the beneficiaries alone.[74] The creator of the trust cannot vest this power in a court which has no jurisdiction over the subject of trusts,[75] for this would be allowing an individual to enlarge the jurisdiction

---

[68] Tuckerman v. Currier, 54 Colo. 25, 129 P. 210, Ann.Cas.1914C, 599.

[69] Whitehead v. Whitehead, 142 Ala. 163, 37 So. 929; Mallory v. Mallory, 72 Conn. 494, 45 A. 164; Adams v. Highland Cemetery Co., Mo., 192 S.W. 944; Wilson v. Towle, 36 N.H. 129.

[70] Grundy v. Drye, 104 Ky. 825, 48 S.W. 155, 49 S.W. 469.

[71] Equitable Trust Co. v. Fisher, 106 Ill. 189.

[72] Yates v. Yates, 255 Ill. 66, 99 N.E. 360, Ann.Cas.1913D, 143; Orr v. Yates, 209 Ill. 222, 70 N.E. 731; In re Cleven's Estate, 161 Iowa 289, 142 N.W. 986; Carr v. Corning, 73 N.H. 362, 62 A. 168; Jacobs v. McClintock, 53 Tex. 72; Mitchell v. Stevens, 1 Aikens, Vt., 16; Whelan v. Reilly, 3 W.Va. 597.

[73] Griswold v. Sackett, 21 R.I. 206, 42 A. 868.

[74] March v. Romare, C.C.A.Ala., 116 F. 355, 53 C.C.A. 575; Foster v. Goree, 4 Ala. 440; Leggett v. Grimmett, 36 Ark. 496; McConnell v. Day, 61 Ark. 464, 33 S.W. 731; Fuller v. Davis, 63 Miss. 78; Clark v. Wilson, 53 Miss. 119; Guion v. Pickett, 42 Miss. 77; Frank v. Colonial & United States Mortg. Co., 86 Miss. 103, 38 So. 340, 70 L.R.A. 135, 4 Ann. Cas. 54; Miller v. Knowles, Tex.Civ. App., 44 S.W. 927; Cates v. Mayes, Tex.Sup., 12 S.W. 51.

[75] Harwood v. Tracy, 118 Mo. 631, 24 S.W. 214. Thus in Petition of

of the courts; but the settlor may provide that a court of chancery shall fill vacancies,[76] or that the court shall perform this duty, subject to the approval of the interested parties,[77] or that the trustees shall nominate the successor and the court appoint.[78] But in cases where the power of appointment is given to the trustee or cestui que trust the court will nevertheless supervise the filling of the vacancy.[79]

As a part of its general jurisdiction to protect and enforce trusts, the court of chancery has power to appoint a successor trustee. If the settlor has provided no method of appointment to fill vacancies, the power of the court will be exclusive.[80] On the death of a trustee,[81] or his resignation,[82] or declination [83] of

Straw, 78 N.H. 506, 102 A. 628, it was held that the settlor could not give to the Supreme Court power to fill vacancies, since such power was vested by statute in the probate court.

[76] Cruit v. Owen, 203 U.S. 368, 27 S.Ct. 71, 51 L.Ed. 227; Appeal of Allen, 69 Conn. 702, 38 A. 701; Morrison v. Kelly, 22 Ill. 610, 74 Am. Dec. 169; Shaw v. Paine, 12 Allen, Mass., 293.

[77] Cole v. City of Watertown, 119 Wis. 133, 96 N.W. 538.

[78] Huston v. Dodge, 111 Me. 246, 88 A. 888.

[79] Bailey v. Bailey, 2 Del.Ch. 95; Yates v. Yates, 255 Ill. 66, 99 N.E. 360, Ann.Cas.1913D, 143. Where the persons given the power to appoint successors do not exercise it, a suit may be brought in equity to obtain an appointment, and it is then too late for the settlor's nominees to act. National City Bank of Cleveland v. Schmoltz, OhioApp., 31 N. E.2d 444.

[80] Doe v. Roe, 1 Boyce, Del., 216, 75 A. 704; Thompson v. Hale, 123 Ga. 305, 51 S.E. 383; Mason v. Bloomington Library Ass'n, 237 Ill. 442, 86 N.E. 1044, 15 Ann.Cas. 603; Sawtelle v. Witham, 94 Wis. 412, 69 N.W. 72.

[81] Allison v. Little, 85 Ala. 512, 5 So. 221; In re Gay's Estate, 138 Cal. 552, 71 P. 707, 94 Am.St.Rep. 70;

O'Brien v. Battle, 98 Ga. 766, 25 S.E. 780; People, Use of Brooks, v. Petrie, 191 Ill. 497, 61 N.E. 499, 85 Am.St. Rep. 268; Cruse v. Axtell, 50 Ind. 49; Kennard v. Bernard, 98 Md. 513, 56 A. 793; Hildreth v. Eliot, 8 Pick., Mass., 293; Weiland v. Townsend, 33 N.J.Eq. 393; Farmers' Loan & Trust Co. v. Pendleton, 179 N.Y. 486, 72 N.E. 508; Thornton v. Harris, 140 N.C. 498, 53 S.E. 341; In re Kane Borough Park Lands Trustees' Appointment, 177 Pa. 638, 35 A. 874; Ex parte O'Brien, 11 R.I. 419; Somers v. Craig, 9 Humph., Tenn., 467; Buchanan v. Hart, 31 Tex. 647; Fisher v. Dickenson, 84 Va. 318, 4 S.E. 737; Forsyth v. City of Wheeling, 19 W.Va. 318. But if the trust is personal, so that it ends on the death of the trustee, the court will not appoint a successor. Rogers v. Rea, 98 Ohio St. 315, 120 N.E. 828.

[82] Reese v. Ivey, 162 Ala. 448, 50 So. 223; Vernoy v. Robinson, 133 Ga. 653, 66 S.E. 928; French v. Northern Trust Co., 197 Ill. 30, 64 N.E. 105; Petition of Pierce, 109 Me. 509, 84 A. 1070; Massachusetts General Hospital v. Amory, 12 Pick., Mass., 445; Schehr v. Look, 84 Mich. 263, 47 N.W. 445; In re Pitney, 186 N.Y. 540, 78 N.E. 1110.

[83] Roberts v. Roberts, 259 Ill. 115, 102 N.E. 239; Whallen v. Kellner, 104 S.W. 1018, 31 Ky.Law Rep. 1285;

the trust, or when he is unable to administer the trust,[84] or is removed,[85] or, being a corporation, ceases to exist,[86] equity may appoint a new trustee. In many states statutes prescribe when and how equity may appoint trustees.[87] It is impossible here to enter into a discussion of the jurisdiction of the various state courts over the appointment of new trustees. This subject has been litigated in many cases which are here cited for the convenience of the investigator.[88] The location of general equity jurisdiction is a purely local question.

Whether or not equity will appoint a new trustee is a matter wholly within its discretion.[89] Even though a trustee may have been removed from the trusteeship, the court may deem it unwise to fill his place. Thus, if there is a surviving trustee who is administering the trust successfully, chancery may deem it unnecessary to fill the vacancy;[90] and if the only duty left to the

Greene v. Borland, 4 Metc., Mass., 330; Brush v. Young, 28 N.J.L. 237; Anderson v. Robinson, 57 Or. 172, 110 P. 975; Gamble v. Dabney, 20 Tex. 69.

[84] Spengler v. Kuhn, 212 Ill. 186, 72 N.E. 214; Dean v. Northern Trust Co., 259 Ill. 148, 102 N.E. 244.

[85] In re Burk's Estate, 1 N.Y.St. Rep. 316.

[86] Lanning v. Commissioners of Public Instruction of City of Trenton, 63 N.J.Eq. 1, 51 A. 787; Town of Montpelier v. Town of East Montpelier, 29 Vt. 12, 67 Am.Dec. 748.

[87] Huston v. Dodge, 111 Me. 246, 88 A. 888; Md.Laws 1918, c. 431; Sells v. Delgado, 186 Mass. 25, 70 N. E. 1036; In re Satterthwaite's Estate, 60 N.J.Eq. 347, 47 A. 226; New York Personal Property Law, § 20; New York Real Property Law, § 112; Va.Code 1936, §§ 6298–6298a; Roller v. Catlett, 118 Va. 185, 86 S.E. 909.

[88] Whitehead v. Whitehead, 142 Ala. 163, 37 So. 929; Appeal of Beardsley, 77 Conn. 705, 60 A. 664; Dailey v. City of New Haven, 60 Conn. 314, 22 A. 945, 14 L.R.A. 69; Mitchell v. Pitner, 15 Ga. 319; Woodbery v. Atlas Realty Co., 148 Ga. 712, 98 S.E. 472; Dwyer v. Cahill, 228 Ill. 617, 81 N.E. 1142; Shepard v. Meridian Nat. Bank, 149 Ind. 532, 48 N.E. 346; White v. Hampton, 10 Iowa, 238; Haggin v. Straus, 148 Ky. 140, 146 S.W. 391, 50 L.R.A.,N.S., 642; Coudon v. Updegraf, 117 Md. 71, 83 A. 145; Sells v. Delgado, 186 Mass. 25, 70 N.E. 1036; Bredell v. Kerr, 242 Mo. 317, 147 S.W. 105; Zabriskie's Ex'rs v. Wetmore, 26 N. J.Eq. 18; People v. Norton, 9 N.Y. 176; Sowers v. Cyrenius, 39 Ohio St. 29, 48 Am.Rep. 418; Richards v. Rote, 68 Pa. 248; Mask v. Miller, 7 Baxt., Tenn., 527; In re Cary's Estate, 81 Vt. 112, 69 A. 736; Morse v. Stoddard's Estate, 90 Vt. 479, 98 A. 991; Shelton v. Jones' Adm'x, 26 Grat., Va., 891; McWilliams v. Gough, 116 Wis. 576, 93 N.W. 550.

[89] City Council of Augusta v. Walton, 77 Ga. 517, 1 S.E. 214; Ex parte Knust, Bailey Eq., S.C., 489. The discretion warrants the appointment of a trust company as sole trustee, although the instrument provided for several individual trustees. In re Battin's Estate, 89 N.J.Eq. 144, 104 A. 434.

[90] Mullanny v. Nangle, 212 Ill. 247, 72 N.E. 385; In re Dietz, 132 App.

trustees is to transfer the property to the beneficiaries, equity may deem it superfluous to appoint new trustees and may transfer the property itself.[91]

If equity does fill the vacancy, it will, of course, select a trustee, who will be apt to administer the affairs of the trust with fairness and ability. It will not choose a prejudiced or incompetent person. Thus the court will not appoint, as a trustee of a religious charitable trust, a person hostile to the religion to be promoted;[92] nor will the court name as a successor a person who is biased and apt to favor one or more of the cestuis que trust as against the others.[93] It is the better practice to appoint a resident of the jurisdiction,[94] but circumstances may justify the choice of a nonresident.[95] The court should consider the wishes of the interested parties in its appointment, though not bound to follow them.[96]

Proceeding for Appointment

The application for the appointment of a new trustee may be made by any one interested financially in the execution of the trust. Thus a cestui que trust,[97] or the guardian of an infant cestui que trust,[98] may apply, and, in the case of a religious char-

Div. 641, 117 N.Y.S. 461; In re Zerega, 81 Misc. 113, 142 N.Y.S. 144; In re Physic's Estate, 2 Phila., Pa., 278. And on the removal of two trustees the court may appoint only one in their places. Harvey v. Schwettman, Mo.App., 180 S.W. 413.

[91] In re Kittinger's Estate, 9 Del. Ch. 71, 77 A. 24; Friedley v. Security Trust & Safe Deposit Co., 10 Del.Ch. 74, 84 A. 883; Boyer v. Decker, 5 App.Div. 623, 40 N.Y.S. 469.

[92] Glover v. Baker, 76 N.H. 393, 83 A. 916.

[93] Waller v. Hosford, Iowa, 132 N. W. 426; In re Welch, 20 App.Div. 412, 46 N.Y.S. 689.

[94] Dodge v. Dodge, 109 Md. 164, 71 A. 519, 130 Am.St.Rep. 503.

[95] Appeal of Wilcox, 54 Conn. 320, 8 A. 136. For example, where a trust was to be administered in Germany an Iowa court appointed a resident of Germany as trustee. Beidler v. Dehner, 178 Iowa, 1338, 161 N.W. 32.

[96] Thornburg v. Macauley, 2 Md.Ch. 425; Coster v. Coster, 125 App.Div. 516, 109 N.Y.S. 798. By Civ.Code Cal. § 2287, the cestui que trust, if fourteen years of age, may nominate the trustee and other things being equal, the court is required to give preference to such nominee.

In some cases it has been held an abuse of judicial discretion not to follow the desires of the beneficiaries in appointing a trustee. Central Trust Co. of Illinois v. Harvey, 297 Ill.App. 425, 17 N.E.2d 988; Hodgen's Ex'rs v. Sproul, 221 Iowa 1104, 267 N.W. 692; In re McCaskey's Estate, 293 Pa. 497, 143 A. 209. See 42 Harv.L. R. 446.

[97] Cone v. Cone, 61 S.C. 512, 39 S.E. 748.

[98] Hallinan v. Hearst, 133 Cal. 645, 66 P. 17, 55 L.R.A. 216.

§ 134　　　VACANCIES IN TRUSTEESHIP　　　427

itable trust, a member of the church to be benefited may make application,[99] although the fact that a person is a citizen and taxpayer in the county where the charity is to be carried on does not show sufficient interest to enable one to secure the ear of the court.[1]

The question of notice upon the application for the appointment of a new trustee is one affected by statute to a large extent, and the courts have not been in accord in their views upon the subject.[2] In many instances they have held that the notice necessary to be given was entirely in the discretion of the court,[3] while in other cases notice to all interested parties has been required.[4] Occasionally new trustees seem to have been appointed ex parte.[5] It has been held that the beneficiaries are necessary parties to the application,[6] but not if their interests are of a future or contingent nature.[7] So, too, the heirs of the deceased trustee whose place is to be filled have been called necessary parties,[8] as well as the Attorney General in the case of a charitable trust.[9] But a person claiming the trust property adversely to the trustee is not a necessary party when the question of filling a vacancy in the trusteeship is being considered.[10]

Frequently a sole executor is given the duties of a trustee, and later a vacancy in the executorship occurs. In such a case

[99] Harris v. Brown, 124 Ga. 310, 52 S.E. 610, 2 L.R.A.,N.S., 828.

[1] Harris v. Brown, 124 Ga. 310, 52 S.E. 610, 2 L.R.A.,N.S., 828.

[2] Gray v. Union Trust Co., 213 Ind. 675, 12 N.E.2d 931, 14 N.E.2d 532 (improperly appointed trustees become de facto trustees if they assume charge); State v. Underwood, 54 Wyo. 1, 86 P.2d 707 (if one beneficiary is not notified, only he can avoid the appointment).

[3] Dyer v. Leach, 91 Cal. 191, 27 P. 598, 25 Am.St.Rep. 171; In re Earnshaw, 196 N.Y. 330, 89 N.E. 825; Bransford Realty Co. v. Andrews, 128 Tenn. 725, 164 S.W. 1175.

[4] Simmons v. McKinlock, 98 Ga. 738, 26 S.E. 88; Dexter v. Cotting, 149 Mass. 92, 21 N.E. 230; Greene v. Borland, 4 Metc., Mass., 330; Clarke v. Inhabitants of Andover, 207 Mass. 91, 92 N.E. 1013.

[5] Sullivan v. Latimer, 35 S.C. 422, 14 S.E. 933; Reigart v. Ross, 63 Wis. 449, 23 N.W. 878.

[6] In re Earnshaw, Sup., 112 N.Y.S. 197; Henry v. Doctor, 9 Ohio, 49; Bolling v. Stokes, 7 S.C. 364.

[7] Whallen v. Kellner, 104 S.W. 1018, 31 Ky.Law Rep. 1285; Fitzgibbon v. Barry, 78 Va. 755.

[8] In re Abbott, 55 Me. 580; Plumley v. Plumley, 8 N.J.Eq. 511. But see, contra, Hawley v. Ross, 7 Paige, N.Y., 103.

[9] Lakatong Lodge, No. 114, of Quakertown, etc., v. Board of Education of Franklin Tp., Hunterdon County, 84 N.J.Eq. 112, 92 A. 870.

[10] White River Lumber Co. v. Clark, 75 N.H. 585, 70 A. 247.

an administrator with the will annexed is appointed. The general rule is that under such circumstances the administrator cum testamento annexo does not succeed to the position of trustee, which the former executor held; but that such administrator is vested only with the duties of the executorship, and that a new trustee must be appointed to undertake the separate duties of the trusteeship.[11] However, in some cases the administrator with the will annexed has been held to become vested with the trusteeship as well as with the position of the deceased executor.[12] These latter cases seem to proceed upon the ground of a distinction between cases where the trust duties are attached to the office of the executor and cases where the trust duties are attached to the executor personally and are separated from the executorial functions.

This attempted distinction is[13] illustrated by the statements of a New York court: "The Revised Statutes provide that, in all cases where letters of administration with the will annexed shall be granted, the will of the deceased shall be observed and performed; and that the administrators with such will shall have the rights and powers, and be subject to the same duties, as if they had been named as executors in such will. * * * There can be no doubt, therefore, that in cases where the execution of a trust, or of a power in trust, is confided by a testator to his executors as such, they cannot execute the trust without also taking out letters testamentary, and assuming the office of executors. In such cases the administrator with the will annexed is probably entitled to execute all the trusts of the will, in the same manner as if he had been named therein, by the tesator, as the executor and trustee. The difficulty in the present case, on that subject, is that the testator appears to have intended to give to the three individuals named in his will a distinct character as trustees, entirely independent of their character of executors. * * *" It is difficult to see how an executor can

---

[11] Hayes v. Pratt, 147 U.S. 557, 13 S.Ct. 503, 37 L.Ed. 279; Warfield v. Brand's Adm'r, 13 Bush, Ky., 77; Knight v. Loomis, 30 Me. 204; Stoutenburgh v. Moore, 37 N.J.Eq. 63; Dunning v. Ocean Nat. Bank of City of New York, 61 N.Y. 497, 19 Am.Rep. 293; Kelsey v. McTigue, 171 App.Div. 877, 157 N.Y.S. 730; In re Sheaffer's Estate, 230 Pa. 426, 79 A. 651; Harrison v. Henderson, 7 Heisk., Tenn., 315.

[12] Jones v. Jones, 17 N.C. 387; Mathews v. Meek, 23 Ohio St. 272; Com. v. Barnitz, 9 Watts, Pa., 252; In re Sheet's Estate, 215 Pa. 164, 64 A. 413.

[13] De Peyster v. Clendening, 8 Paige, N.Y., 295, 310, 311; In re Welch, 20 App.Div. 412, 46 N.Y.S. 689; Guion v. Melvin, 69 N.C. 242; Pitzer v. Logan, 85 Va. 374, 7 S.E. 385; Fitzgibbon v. Barry, 78 Va. 755.

be a trustee, also, without having a distinct office and character. His successor in the executorial office ought not to succeed to the trust duties as incidental.

When the new trustee is appointed to fill the vacancy, his title to the trust property is acquired by virtue of the order of the court. No conveyance from the retiring trustee is needed in order to vest the property rights in the succeeding trustee.[14] Where one is appointed trustee in place of another who has declined the trust, the title to the trust property vests in the appointee as of the date of the inception of the trust, by virtue of the doctrine of relation.[15]

[14] Reilly v. Conrad, 9 Del.Ch. 154, 78 A. 1080; Security Trust & Safe Deposit Co. v. Ward, 10 Del.Ch. 408, 93 A. 385; Golder v. Bressler, 105 Ill. 419; Reichert v. Missouri & I. Coal Co., 231 Ill. 238, 83 N.E. 166, 121 Am.St.Rep. 307; Bloodgood v. Massachusetts Ben. Life Ass'n, 19 Misc. 460, 44 N.Y.S. 563; Coster v. Coster, 125 App.Div. 516, 109 N.Y.S. 798; McNish v. Guerard, 4 Strob.Eq., S.C., 66; Wooldridge v. Planter's Bank, 1 Sneed, Tenn., 297. "At common law the appointment of new trustees by parties (not in execution of a special power) did not vest the title in the new trustees without conveyance." Glazier v. Everett, 224 Mass. 184, 187, 112 N.E. 1009 (but common law changed by statute). *Contra:* Koehne v. Beattie, 36 R.I. 316, 90 A. 211.

[15] Parkhill v. Doggett, 135 Iowa 113, 112 N.W. 189.

CHAPTER 15

TRUST ADMINISTRATION—PRINCIPAL AND INCOME ACCOUNTS

Sec.
135. Ordinary Returns.
136. Apportionment of Receipts.
137. Extraordinary Receipts.
138. Unproductive Property.
139. Wasting Property.
140. Cash Dividends.
141. Stock Dividends.
142. Stock Subscription Rights.
143. Source from Which Expenses should be Paid.

ORDINARY RETURNS [1]

135. The ordinary returns from the use of trust property are income of the trust. Examples are interest on bonds and notes and rents on realty leased.

Nearly every trustee acts for two classes of persons, the income beneficiaries, and those entitled to the principal under the trust or after its end. One important part of his administration is maintaining an impartial attitude as between these two classes, and making sure that the benefits and burdens of the trust are allocated and distributed properly between income and principal accounts. The following sections treat some of the more difficult questions which confront the trustee in this field.

The trustee will ordinarily have little doubt about the disposition of the products of the trust property. Receipts arising from the use of the trust property are normally trust income. If the trustee invests the trust fund in corporate or government bonds, or notes secured by mortgages, the interest received will be trust income.[2] It is gain from the use of the trust fund and not a substitute for the trust fund. And similar treatment should be made of rents from trust property which has been leased,[3] or crops grown on a farm owned by the trust,[4] or gains from a business operated by the trustee,[5] or the increase of a herd of

---

[1] Restatement, Trusts, § 233.

[2] In re Wilson's Appeal, 108 Pa. 344, 56 Am.Rep. 214.

[3] Matter of Franklin, 26 Misc. 107, 56 N.Y.S. 858.

[4] Poindexter v. Blackburn, 1 Ired. 286.

[5] Matter of McCollum, 80 App.Div. 362, 80 N.Y.S. 755; Matter of Weaver's Estate, 53 Misc. 244, 104 N.Y.S.

animals held by the trustee.[6] Such receipts constitute gains or profits of the trust property, and not distributions of the trust capital itself.

APPORTIONMENT OF RECEIPTS [7]

136. Where a trust begins or ends, or the right to receive the income shifts from one beneficiary to another during the life of the trust, and the trustee shortly thereafter receives a periodic payment like interest, rent, or a dividend, he is under a duty to apportion the payment in the case of interest only. By statute some other periodic payments are apportionable.

A problem which confronts every trustee is that of the apportionment of periodic income between successive interests. The trustee receives money which is ordinarily trust income, as, for example, rent, interest, or cash dividends on stock held. But during the period since the last periodic payment there has been a change with regard to the trust property which makes it doubtful to whom the latest payment should be delivered. An illustration will best explain the difficulty.

S. owns three pieces of property, namely, a bond of the X. company for $1,000, bearing 4% interest payable semi-annually on January 1st and July 1st; ten shares of stock in the Y. company on which dividends of $30 are customarily declared on January 1st and July 1st; and the lessor's interest under a lease to Z., by the terms of which Z. is obligated to pay $100 a month rent to S. on the first of each month for the preceding month. On January 15, 1941, S. dies leaving a will by which he gives all his property to T., as trustee, to hold for W., the widow of S. for the life of W., and then to deliver the trust property to A., the son of S. Assuming that T. took up his duties as trustee immediately after the death of S., and ignoring the fact that the estate would normally be in the hands of an executor for some time, T. has problems regarding the interest, rent, and dividends which he later receives. The first receipt he will obtain will naturally be the rent due on February 1, 1941, which was payable for the month of January, 1941. During half of

---

475. And see section 7 of the Uniform Principal and Income Act.

[6] Major v. Herndon, 78 Ky. 123. Section 8 of the Uniform Principal and Income Act allots the increase of the herd to income, subject to a duty to maintain the original size of the herd.

[7] Restatement, Trusts, §§ 235, 238.

January S. was the owner of the landlord's interest, and during the second half of that month, W. was the equitable owner of the right to rent. Shall the $100 payment made on February 1 be treated as half the property of S. at his death and half the property of W? The common law answered this question in the negative and decreed that the trustee should treat the entire $100 as income of the trust for W. It explained this result by stating that rent accrues in a lump sum on the rent day, and not day by day, and that therefore there was no rent due until February 1st and at that time the right to the rent was vested in W. This is a declaration that rent is not "apportionable".[8]

Secondly, the trustee will collect on July 1st, 1941, the coupon on the X. company bond amounting to $20, and will have to decide whether he is to divide this between the capital of the trust and the income account of the trust, or treat it all as income. It might be urged that one-twelfth of this $20 interest payment was for the period during which S. owned the bond, namely, from January 1st to January 15th, and that this amount should be treated as a part of the capital of the trust which S. gave to T. as trustee, and that only eleven-twelfths of the $20 should be treated as trust income. This in fact is the view of the common law, which it explains by stating that interest accrues from day to day, and not in a lump sum on the day when it is payable, and hence that interest is apportionable. One-twelfth of the interest had accrued as the property of S. when he died on January 15th.[9] Hence this one-twelfth should be treated by T. as capital of the trust.

Thirdly, T. will receive on July 1st in all probability $30 as the semi-annual regular dividend on the stock which he holds. Shall he treat this as earned in part during the period when S. owned the stock, and so as one-twelfth trust capital and eleven-twelfths trust income, or shall he treat it all as trust income earned on the date when the dividend was paid to T., namely, July 1st, 1941? Here the common law refused apportionment, and held that dividends do not accrue to stockholders until declared by the corporation. They are not paid for any particular period or accruable to the stockholder day by day or month

---

[8] Poole v. Union Trust Co., 191 Mich. 162, 157 N.W. 430, Ann.Cas. 1918E, 622.

[9] Bridgeport Trust Co. v. Marsh, 87 Conn. 384, 87 A. 865; Dexter v. Phillips, 121 Mass. 178, 23 Am.Rep. 261.

by month. Therefore, at common law, T. should treat the entire dividend as trust income as of July 1, 1941.[10]

If T. had been given by S. the right to an annuity, the result would have been the same as with dividends and rents. The annuity payments received by T. would not have been apportionable, but would all have been treated as income of the trust as of the date they became due.[11]

The problem of apportionment may arise not only at the beginning of the trust, but during its life, and at its end. For example, the income may be directed to be paid first to A. for life, and then to B. for his life, and then the trust is to end and C. is to receive the capital. If A. dies during the period between periodic payments, the problem will arise as to whether part of a periodic payment later collected by the trustee shall go to the executor of A. and the rest of it to B., or whether it all goes to B. And if B. dies during the period between payments, the question will be whether the receipts after the death of B. shall go partly to B.'s executor, or entirely to C.[12]

The rules about apportionment are the same whether the trust begins or ends, or a shift in the right to trust income occurs, in the middle of a periodic payment period. At common law the only payment apportioned was interest.

In England and a number of states statutes have been passed providing for the apportionment of receipts other than interest.[13] The Uniform Principal and Income Act requires the apportionment of all receipts except dividends.[14]

---

[10] Bates v. McKinley, 31 Beav. 280; but see Bankers' Trust Co. of New York v. Lobdell, 116 N.J.Eq. 363, 173 A. 918, *contra*. See, also, In re Wuichet's Estate, 138 Ohio St. 97, 33 N.E.2d 15 (time when dividend payable, not when declared, is the important time).

[11] Heizer v. Heizer, 71 Ind. 526, 36 Am.Rep. 202; Nehls v. Sauer, 119 Iowa 440, 93 N.W. 346.

[12] Parker v. Ames, 121 Mass. 220; Kearney v. Cruikshank, 117 N.Y. 95, 22 N.E. 580; Rhode Island Hospital Trust Co. v. Noyes, 26 R.I. 323, 58 A. 999; In re Will of Barron, 163 Wis. 275, 155 N.W. 1087.

[13] 33 & 34 Vict. c. 35; Ky.St.1930, § 2070 (applies to annuities only); Mass.G.L.(Ter.Ed.) c. 197, §§ 26, 27 (apportions all except dividends); N.Y.Real Property Law, § 275, and Surrogate's Court Act, § 204 (apportions all receipts); N.C.Code 1939, § 2346 (apportions all); Pa. 20 P.S. § 634 (all); R.I.Gen.L.1938, c. 566, §§ 37, 38 (like Mass.); Va.Code 1936, §§ 5544–5547 (apportions rents, hire and interest); W.Va.Code 1937, §§ 3688–3691 (like Virginia).

[14] Section 4; now adopted in Alabama, California, Connecticut, Florida, Illinois, Louisiana, Maryland, North Carolina, Oklahoma, Oregon, Utah and Virginia. In the Illinois Act only interest is apportioned.

BOGERT TRUSTS 2D—28

If a periodic payment is due but uncollected by the settlor at the time he creates the trust, and is later collected by his trustee, it is treated as a part of trust capital. Thus, if S. owns corporate stock on which a dividend has been declared as payable to him on a day during his life, but he has not collected the dividend, and he dies leaving the stock to a trustee who later collects the dividend, the trustee should treat the dividend as a part of the capital of the trust and not as income of it.[15]

EXTRAORDINARY RECEIPTS [16]

137. **Sums received by the trustee in settlement of claims are ordinarily awarded to trust capital, unless they represent income of the trust lost or misappropriated. Examples are insurance and eminent domain claims, and causes of action for the withholding or misappropriation of trust property.**

The proceeds of the sale of trust property are to be treated as trust principal, even though they include a profit over cost price or inventory value.

The trustee sometimes receives certain extraordinary benefits which have to be allotted to trust income or capital. For example, he may have insured a building located on trust real estate, and the building may have been destroyed by fire. Since the land and building were trust capital, money received on account of their deterioration in value should also be treated as trust capital.[17] If the life tenant should insure his own interest, he might keep the proceeds of a claim for loss, but insurance taken out by the trustee will be on the entire trust interest in the property.

In North Carolina and Virginia the legislature, in enacting the Uniform Principal and Income Act, with its provision about apportionment, did not expressly repeal the pre-existing statutes in those states on the same subject. Thus, in North Carolina, section 2346 apportions all receipts, while section 4035(4) apportions all but dividends; and in Virginia sections 5544–5547 apportion all receipts except dividends, and section 5133f makes the same provision. The Uniform Principal and Income Act, however, does repeal all laws which are inconsistent with it, and this would seem to mean that in North Carolina dividends are not to be apportioned, as to trusts set up after March 15, 1937.

[15] Matter of Kernochan, 104 N.Y. 618, 11 N.E. 149.

[16] Restatement, Trusts, § 233.

[17] Horton v. Upham, 72 Conn. 29, 43 A. 492; Campbell v. Mansfield, 104 Miss. 533, 61 So. 593, 45 L.R.A., N.S., 446. See section 3 of the Uniform Principal and Income Act for a treatment of ordinary and extraordinary receipts.

§ 137   EXTRAORDINARY RECEIPTS   435

In other cases the origin of the benefit also affords the clue to the appropriate entries. Thus, if land owned by a trustee for life tenant and remainderman is taken by eminent domain for a public park, and an allowance made for the fee taken, this sum should be treated as trust capital, replacing the original trust principal.[18] Separate awards might be made to life tenant and remainderman, if their estates were legal, but would not be made where the res was held in trust.

Sometimes the trustee collects a claim for destruction of, injury to, or misappropriation of, the trust property. Here again the source of the claim should be considered. If the property destroyed, injured, or misappropriated was trust capital, the proceeds of the claim should be treated as a replacement. But if both trust capital and trust income were taken by the wrongdoer, as where a trustee misappropriates both, the money received in settlement of the claim should be divided between trust capital and income in the same proportions as the lost income bore to the lost capital.[19]

Where a trustee sells trust property, the proceeds should be placed in the capital account of the trust, since they are the product of trust principal. This is true, even though those proceeds include a profit over the cost price or original inventory value of the trust property sold. The principal account bears the risk of the trust property decreasing in value, and gets the benefit of its increase in value. Such profits are not treated as trust income.[20]

There has been a tendency in some courts to make a special case of the sale of corporate stock held by the trust, where it is sold at a profit, and where the reason for the increase in value was in whole or in part the failure of the corporation to distribute profits as dividends and the addition of such profits to corporate surplus.[21] Such a dividend policy naturally increases the book value of the stock. Some courts have thought that the sale of such stock at a profit was an indirect way of getting dividends

[18] Gibson v. Cooke, 42 Mass. 75, 1 Metc. 75.

[19] In re Dashiell's Estate, Del.Ch., 181 A. 681; In re Kight's Estate, 167 Misc. 296, 4 N.Y.S.2d 63.

[20] Wood v. Davis, 168 Ga. 504, 148 S.E. 330; Smith v. Hooper, 95 Md. 16, 51 A. 844; Duclos v. Benner, 62 Hun 428, 17 N.Y.S. 168.

[21] In re Sherman Trust, 190 Iowa 1385, 179 N.W. 109; Matter of United States Trust Co., 229 N.Y. 598, 129 N.E. 923, affirmed in memorandum opinion 190 App.Div. 494, 180 N.Y. 12; Nirdlinger's Estate, 290 Pa. 457, 139 A. 200, 56 A.L.R. 1303; Wallace v. Wallace, 90 S.C. 61, 72 S.E. 553.

on the stock, and that the income beneficiary of the trust ought to receive such indirect distributions of corporate income. This view, however, has not received general favor and is not believed to be sound.[22] A practical objection to it is the extraordinary difficulty of learning what part of the sale price of the stock is due to the undistributed earnings of the corporation.

Where there is a duty to sell trust property which has been wasting or unproductive, the proceeds are treated specially, as is shown in subsequent sections.[23] The statements of this section are based on the idea that the sale is made under a mere privilege to sell, or is made under a mandatory power of sale but the property is of an ordinarily productive type.

One type of claim by a trustee is also treated separately in a later section, namely that of a trustee against a defaulting mortgagor, where the trustee buys in the property on foreclosure, holds it, and then sells it.[24] This is in reality a case of a sale of unproductive property under a duty to sell.

The beneficiary who is entitled to the income of the trust property obtains part of the benefit of sale at a profit and reinvestment, for he obtains a greater income from the new trust fund than from the old. The corpus of the estate, no matter what changes of form it undergoes, should be regarded as the same property. That the trust property is originally money, later becomes bonds, and still later real estate, ought not to affect the status of the property as the capital fund. A Pennsylvania court well points out that the capital fund bears losses which occur from investments, and should, therefore, be entitled to the benefit of gains which accrue. "If, then, in case of a loss by reason of an unfortunate investment, it falls on both the legatees for life and in remainder, it seems but equitable that, if there be a profit arising from the sale of a trust security, they should both participate in it in the same manner they would bear a loss, the former receiving more income from the increased corpus and the latter more corpus." [25]

[22] Long v. Rike, C.C.A.Ill., 50 F.2d 124, 81 A.L.R. 521; Guthrie's Trustee v. Akers, 157 Ky. 649, 163 S.W. 1117; Berger v. Burnett, 97 N.J.Eq. 169, 127 A. 160; Matter of Schley's Will, 202 App.Div. 169, 195 N.Y.S. 871, affirmed 234 N.Y. 616, 138 N.E. 469; In re Roebken's Will, 230 Wis. 215, 283 N.W. 815; section 3 of the Uniform Principal and Income Act.

[23] See §§ 138, 139, post.

[24] See § 138, post.

[25] In re Graham's Estate, 198 Pa. 216, 219, 47 A. 1108.

UNPRODUCTIVE PROPERTY [26]

138. If a trustee holds unproductive or underproductive property which he has a duty to sell, and the sale is delayed, the trustee is under a duty to apportion the proceeds of the sale between income and capital accounts in such a way as to bring to trust income the amount it would have received if the property had been sold as soon as the duty to sell arose and the proceeds had been invested in normally productive property. This assumes that the settlor made no express direction about the disposition of such proceeds.

It quite often happens that a trustee holds unproductive property or property which produces less than the average rate of income on trust investments. In this case he may be under a duty to retain the property because of directions in the trust instrument, or he may have a discretionary power to sell the property but no duty to sell, or he may be under a duty to sell either because of a direction of the settlor to that effect or because the investment is not a legal investment for his trust under the law of that state. If the trustee sells such trust property after a delay during which he has been seeking a buyer, a problem arises as to whether part of the proceeds should be transferred to the trust income account, to compensate for the lack of income received during the holding of the unproductive or underproductive property.

If the trustee was directed to retain the investment in question, there will be no sale and no problem. If the trustee had no duty to sell, but merely a discretionary power to sell, the entire proceeds of the sale will go to trust capital, whether there has been a profit over cost price or inventory value or not, as stated in the last section.[27]

But if the trustee sold because of a duty to sell, the law directs a division of the proceeds between trust income and capital. The settlor in such a case is deemed to have intended that the income beneficiary should have a constant flow of normal income, and to have intended that if such income did not come from some of the trust property for a period, this shortage should be made up later. The settlor is said to have a presumed intent that the income beneficiary should get "delayed income" out of the sale proceeds, or in other words that upon the sale the trustee should apportion the proceeds in such a way

---

[26] Restatement, Trusts, § 240.   [27] Love v. Engelke, 368 Ill. 342, 14 N.E.2d 228.

as to give the life tenant the income he would have had if the trustee had been able to carry out his duty to sell at once, and had then invested the net proceeds of his sale in normally productive trust property.[28]

Thus, if the trustee is given vacant suburban land, which the settlor directs him to sell, or he has a duty to sell because it is not a proper trust investment, and after five years the trustee succeeds in selling, he should divide the net proceeds in such a way as to give the life beneficiary the delayed income described above. The trustee is to find what sum, if invested at the time the trustee's duty to sell arose, would have produced at simple interest at the rate earned by average trust investments, the net proceeds of the sale. This sum is subtracted from the proceeds of the sale and the sum thus reached is called trust income, while the remainder of the proceeds is allotted to trust capital.

This computation can be made by the use of a simple formula. Let X equal the principal sum sought to be found. Let P equal the net proceeds of the sale, that is, the gross proceeds less the cost of selling. Let T equal the time in years during which the property was held awaiting a sale. And let R equal the rate of trust income which is assumed to be normal or average, expressed in decimal form.

$$X = \frac{P}{1+TR}$$

Thus, if the unproductive suburban land were held five years and ultimately sold for $100,000 net, and the average trust income rate was 4%, the computation would be as follows:

$$X = \frac{\$100,000}{1+(5 \times .04)} = \frac{\$100,000}{1.20} = \$83,333.33$$

The sum of $83,333.33 should therefore be added to trust principal and the sum of $16,666.67 should be treated as trust income. This assumes that there were no carrying charges on the property during the five year period or that rent of the land paid such charges. If there were carrying charges like taxes or mortgage interest on the land, they should have been paid from trust income, and if they were paid from trust capital, it

---

[28] Edwards v. Edwards, 183 Mass. 581, 67 N.E. 658; Lawrence v. Littlefield, 215 N.Y. 561, 109 N.E. 611; Patterson v. Old Dominion Trust Co., 149 Va. 597, 140 S.E. 810; section 11, Uniform Principal and Income Act.

§ 138   UNPRODUCTIVE PROPERTY   439

should be reimbursed out of the portion of the sale proceeds which would otherwise have been allotted to trust income.[29]

In recent years trustees have often found that mortgages on real estate held by them became unproductive due to a default in the payment of interest, they have been obliged to foreclose and buy in the land, hold it for a time and then sell it at a loss over the amount of principal and income due on the mortgage and the costs of foreclosing and holding the property.

Some courts have treated these mortgage foreclosure operations as merely involving one type of unproductive property and have applied the formula given above to the net proceeds of the foreclosure transaction.[30] Other courts have divided the net proceeds between trust principal and trust income in the same proportion as the investment of trust income and trust capital in the defaulted mortgage.[31] Thus, under this latter rule if the amount of interest defaulted was $1,000 and the defaulted principal was $5,000, one-sixth of the net proceeds would be given to trust income and five-sixths to trust principal.

The complexity of these mortgage salvaging operations has caused some legislatures to enact statutes giving the entire net proceeds to trust capital, on the ground that such a result accomplishes substantial justice between life tenant remainderman, and that it relieves the trustee from much costly and time consuming bookkeeping.[32]

If the property is underproductive, that is, brings in less than average trust income, the life tenant is entitled to the net income of it realized during the delay period, while the trustee is seeking to sell.

Bonds purchased at a discount may be said to be one form of underproductive property. If a trustee buys a bond having a face value of $1,000 at 90 he will pay $900 for it, but the trust principal will receive $1,000 if the bond is held to maturity and paid. Often one reason for the discount at which bonds are sold

---

[29] Matter of Satterwhite's Will, 262 N.Y. 339, 186 N.E. 857. But some recent authorities display a tendency to place upon the capital the burden of carrying charges of unproductive property. Springfield Safe Deposit & Trust Co. v. Wade, 305 Mass. 36, 24 N.E.2d 764; In re Reese's Estate, 173 Misc. 510, 18 N.Y.S.2d 125; Develon's Estate, 26 Pa.D. & C. 19.

[30] Nirdlinger's Estate, 327 Pa. 171, 193 A. 30.

[31] Matter of Chapal, 269 N.Y. 464, 199 N.E. 762, 103 A.L.R. 1268; Matter of Otis, 276 N.Y. 101, 11 N.E.2d 556, 115 A.L.R. 875.

[32] Ill.Smith-Hurd Stats. c. 30, § 171; N.Y.L.1940, c. 452. See Estate of Wacht, N.Y.L.J. Jan. 14, 1942.

is that the interest rate is lower than normal. An argument has been made that trust capital should compensate trust income for the subnormal yield of discount bonds and that this can be done by imposing a duty on the trustee to set up a fund out of trust capital to be added to trust income. However, in the few cases[33] where this matter has been litigated it has been held that there is no such duty, and that the trustee can treat the proceeds of a bond bought at a discount as entirely trust capital, whether the bond is held to maturity and collected or is sold before maturity. The income beneficiary may get a lower rate of interest on the bond bought at a discount than is normal, but he also gets income on the amount of principal left over. If only $900 is required to buy this bond, $100 is left over to be invested in another bond. Furthermore, discounts are based not merely on subnormal interest rates, but also on a smaller degree of security as to principal and income.

The problem of the trustee holding United States Savings Bonds is somewhat similar. Here no interest is paid from year to year, but the bonds appreciate gradually and mature at a figure which in effect compensates for the lack of interest paid during their lives. Thus, if $18.75 is invested in such a bond it produces $25 in ten years, and the sum of $6.25 is equivalent to interest paid at the maturity of the bond. There has been a tendency to provide by statute that the trustee may treat the accruals of value in such bonds as income.[34]

WASTING PROPERTY [35]

139. Where a trustee holds wasting property and is not permitted by the trust instrument to retain it, he should sell it as soon as possible. If there is delay in selling, he should set aside an amortization fund out of the income of this property in order to replace capital which wastes. Upon the sale of wasting property the proceeds should be apportioned between income and capital in such a way as to bring average, normal income to the temporary beneficiary and to preserve the capital of the trust.

[33] In re Gartenlaub's Estate, 198 Cal. 204, 244 P. 348, 48 A.L.R. 677; In re Houston's Will, 19 Del.Ch. 207, 165 A. 132 (and see Del.L.1939, c. 150); section 6, Uniform Principal and Income Act (no duty to accumulate for discounts); Ill.Smith-Hurd Stats. c. 30, § 165.

[34] Del.L.1939, c. 150; Ill.L.1941, p. 411, § 7, Smith-Hurd Stats. c. 30, § 165; Va.L.1940, c. 233.

[35] Restatement, Trusts, § 239.

§ 139   WASTING PROPERTY   441

A trustee sometimes finds himself in possession of wasting assets that is, investments which will gradually wear out and become worthless. Examples are found in the case of leaseholds,[36] annuities,[37] rights to royalties,[38] and tangible personal property of a destructible nature.[39] If a trustee holds a right to collect rent for twenty years, or a right to collect royalties on a book for the life of the book, or a right to obtain an annuity of a certain sum during the life of a named person, his property interest is obviously of a wasting character. It will wear out and become valueless in a short time. At the end of twenty years rent will no longer be payable, when the book ceases to sell there will be no more royalties on it, and when the person whose life measures the annuity dies no further payments will be made under the annuity.

The trustee's problem in the case of these wasting assets is to determine whether all the current income goes to the life tenant, or whether a part of it shall be reserved to take the place of the trust investment when that investment has disappeared. Is there any duty to manage the investment so as to maintain the dollar value of the trust capital, or may the trustee ignore the wasting nature of the property?

The matter may be settled by the terms of the trust instrument which direct the trustee to pay all of the income of the wasting property to the income beneficiary or direct the trustee to hold the wasting asset. But if the trustee has a duty to sell the wasting asset, and there is no express direction to give the life tenant the full income pending sale, then the trustee must protect trust capital by setting up an amortization fund or by apportioning the proceeds of the sale of the wasting asset.

If the wasting asset is held until it disappears, it may be replaced by an amortization fund which has been set up out of the income of the wasting asset. Thus, if a trustee owns a leasehold of twenty years duration, bringing in $1,000 a year, and he holds the lease for twenty years until it becomes worthless, he may replace the trust capital thus wasted by taking out part of the rent every year and laying it aside as trust capital. The

---

[36] Minot v. Thompson, 106 Mass. 583; In re Estate of Wells, 156 Wis. 294, 144 N.W. 174.

[37] Porter v. Baddeley, L.R. 5 Ch. Div. 542.

[38] In re Elsner's Will, 210 App.Div. 575, 206 N.Y.S. 765; and see Industrial Trust Co. v. Parks, 57 R.I. 363, 190 A. 32, 109 A.L.R. 220 (agent's rights to renewal premiums on insurance policies).

[39] Matter of Hopson's Estate, 213 App.Div. 395, 211 N.Y. 128.

deductions should be of such size as to total the value of the leasehold at the beginning of the trustee's holding of the lease.

Thus, if the trustee finds that the twenty year lease when first held by him was worth $18,000, he will be obliged to deduct from each annual rent payment of $1,000 the sum of $900, so that twenty deductions may total $18,000. The income beneficiary will thus receive $100 a year.

Or the trustee may value the wasting asset and pay the income beneficiary only average income on that valuation. Thus, if the leasehold is valued at $18,000, the trustee might pay the income beneficiary 4% a year on that sum, out of the rents received, and treat the remainder of the rent as trust capital.[40]

If the trustee sells the wasting asset one year after receiving it, he can apportion the proceeds between income and capital accounts by finding what sum, if invested at average trust income when the duty to sell arose, would have equalled the net proceeds of the sale.[41] This is the same formula applied to unproductive property.

$$X = \frac{P}{1+TR}, \text{ or } X = \frac{\$18,000}{1+(1\times.04)} = \$17,307.69$$

Thus, $17,307.69 of the proceeds of the sale would be trust capital and $692.31 would be trust income.

If a sale is made after a part of the amortization fund has been set up, the amount taken from income and placed in the amortization fund pending sale should be deducted from the amount otherwise to be allocated to trust capital.

In cases where a trustee holds securities which have been purchased at a premium, he may find it difficult to determine what is his duty regarding the payment of income. If, for example, the trustee has purchased a bond at 105, is it his duty to pay to the person entitled to the income the entire interest received by the payment of coupons, or should the trustee retain a portion of the coupon in order that he may replace the deficiency in the capital fund which will occur when the bond matures? At maturity the bond will produce only $1,000, whereas the original investment of capital in the bond was $1,050. There will thus be a loss of $50 to the principal fund, unless the trustee retains enough of the interest to make up that $50.

---

[40] In re Pennock's Estate, 260 App. Div. 181, 20 N.Y.S.2d 811; Ill.Smith-Hurd Stats. c. 30, § 169.

[41] Industrial Trust Co. v. Parks, 57 R.I. 363, 190 A. 32, 109 A.L.R. 220.

§ 139

The majority of courts which have passed upon the question have held it to be the trustee's duty to create an amortization fund for the purpose of caring for the premium.[42] The theory of these courts is well explained by Cullen, C. J., in Re Stevens,[43] the New York case which fixed the rule where there had previously been some doubt and confusion. This judge said in part: "The justification for the rule is very apparent. The income on a bond having a term of years to run and purchased at a premium is not the sum paid annually on its interest coupons. The interest on a $1,000 ten-year 5 per cent. bond, bought at 120 per cent., is not $50, but a part thereof only, and the remainder is a return of the principal. All large investors in bonds, such as banks, trust companies, and insurance companies, purchase bonds on the basis of the interest the bonds actually return, not the amount they nominally return. Nor is the premium paid on the bond an outlay for the security of the principal. All government bonds have the same security, the faith of the government; yet they vary in price, a variation caused by the difference in the rate of interest and the time they have to run. It is urged that there is often a speculative change in the market value of a bond, and a bond may be worth more at the termination of the trust than at the time of its purchase. This has no bearing on the case. The life tenant should neither be credited with an appreciation nor charged with a loss in the mere market value of the bond. But, apart from any speculative change in the market value, there is from lapse of time an inherent and intrinsic change in the value of the security itself as it approaches maturity. It is this, and this only, with which the life tenant is to be charged. We, therefore, adhere to the rule declared in the Baker case [New York Life Ins. & Trust Co. v. Baker, 165 N.Y. 484, 59 N.E. 257, 53 L.R.A. 544], that in the absence of a clear direction in the will to the contrary, where investments are made by the trustee, the principal must be maintained intact from loss by payment of premium

[42] Curtis v. Osborn, 79 Conn. 555, 65 A. 968; New England Trust Co. v. Eaton, 140 Mass. 532, 4 N.E. 69, 54 Am.Rep. 493; Ballantine v. Young, 74 N.J.Eq. 572, 70 A. 668; In re Stevens, 187 N.Y. 471, 80 N.E. 358, 12 L.R.A.,N.S., 814, 10 Ann.Cas. 511; In re Allis' Estate, 123 Wis. 223, 101 N.W. 365; In re Wells' Estate, 156 Wis. 294, 144 N.W. 174. The amortization fund should be accumulated gradually, and not deducted from a single installment of income. In re Schaefer, 178 App.Div. 117, 165 N.Y.S. 19. See Edgerton, Premiums and Discounts in Trust Accounts, 31 Harv.Law Rev. 447; Vierling, 5 St.L. L.R. 134, 8 Id. 1, 11 Id. 266.

[43] 187 N.Y. 471, 476, 477, 80 N.E. 358, 12 L.R.A.,N.S., 814, 10 Ann.Cas. 511.

on securities having a definite term to run, while if the bonds are received from the estate of the testator, then the rule in the McLouth case [McLouth v. Hunt, 154 N.Y. 179, 48 N.E. 548, 39 L.R.A. 230] prevails, and the whole interest should be treated as income."

The amortization rule does not apply where the settlor purchased the securities at a premium,[44] or where he expressly directed the trustee to buy the securities in question,[45] or when the settlor indicates in any way an intent that the gross income shall be paid to the life beneficiary.[46] In these instances the trustee may treat as income all the interest received upon the securities. In such cases the settlor must be deemed to have intended that the income from the securities should be the actual coupons or interest received.

The minority view is that the trustee is under no duty to accumulate a fund to care for the premium, but that the entire interest upon the security should be paid to the beneficiary, and the loss due to the payment of the premium should fall on the capital fund.[47] The arguments which appeal to the courts taking this minority view are well expressed by the Pennsylvania court in one of its latest discussions of the subject:[48] "If the whole premium is at once charged to income, or if a part of the income is withheld each year, so that the successive deductions

[44] Hemenway v. Hemenway, 134 Mass. 446; Ballantine v. Young, 74 N.J.Eq. 572, 70 A. 668; McLouth v. Hunt, 154 N.Y. 179, 48 N.E. 548, 39 L.R.A. 230; In re Fanoni, 88 Misc. 442, 152 N.Y.S. 218; Robertson v. De Brulatour, 188 N.Y. 301, 80 N.E. 938. Where securities were bought at a premium by the settlor, the trustee is not chargeable for the loss due to the depreciation of the securities as they approach maturity. In re Hunt, 121 App.Div. 96, 105 N.Y.S. 696. *Contra:* In re Wells' Estate, 156 Wis. 294, 144 N.W. 174.

[45] Shaw v. Cordis, 143 Mass. 443, 9 N.E. 794.

[46] In Higgins v. Beck, 116 Me. 127, 100 A. 553, 4 A.L.R. 1245, the bonds had been bought by the settlor and the court held the life beneficiaries entitled to the whole income. See, also, In re Hawk's Estate, 54 Misc. 187, 105 N.Y.S. 856; Lynde v. Lynde, 113 App.Div. 411, 99 N.Y.S. 283; Kemp v. Macready, 165 App.Div. 124, 150 N.Y.S. 618.

[47] American Security & Trust Co. v. Payne, 33 App.D.C. 178; Hite's Devisees v. Hite's Ex'r, 93 Ky. 257, 20 S.W. 778, 19 L.R.A. 173, 40 Am. St.Rep. 189; Liberty Nat. Bank & Trust Co. v. Loomis, 275 Ky. 445, 121 S.W.2d 947, 131 A.L.R. 1419; In re Penn-Gaskell's Estate, 208 Pa. 346, 57 A. 715.

The Uniform Principal and Income Act, § 6, provides that amortization for premiums is not necessary, but the 1941 Illinois Principal and Income Act requires amortization. Ill. Smith-Hurd Stats. c. 30, § 165.

[48] In re Penn-Gaskell's Estate, 208 Pa. 346, 348, 349, 57 A. 715.

will cover the whole time the security has to run, the life tenant, who is the primary and immediate object of the testator's bounty, will be deprived of the income provided. In one case he may be wholly deprived of the means of support for a considerable period, and receive no benefit whatever from the provision made for him; in the other, he will suffer a diminution of what is really income, it may be for the whole period of the trust. * * * The remainder has the advantage of any increase resulting from profits made on investments, and it bears the losses resulting from depreciation in value of ordinary securities. There is no substantial reason why an exception should be made in its favor, where losses result from the payment of premiums made in order to obtain safe and permanent investments. If premiums were paid to secure greater income, they should be charged, of course, to the life tenant, because he could be the only party benefited by the payment. But this is not the case. Securities that command a premium do not bear a proportionately high interest. Premiums do not represent higher interest, but safety and permanency of the investment and facility of transfer and use. These are matters in which the life tenant has less interest than the remainderman, because he has less at stake. And he pays in part for safety and permanency whenever securities are bought at a price above par."

CASH DIVIDENDS [49]

140. Under the Kentucky and Massachusetts rules a trustee who holds stock in a corporation on which he receives cash dividends, either ordinary or extraordinary, should treat them as income of the trust.

Under the Pennsylvania rule an ordinary cash dividend is trust income, but an extraordinary cash dividend is trust capital to the extent necessary to preserve the book value of the trust's interest in the corporation as it was when the trust first obtained the stock.

A dividend payable in cash or stock, at the option of the trustee, is treated as a cash dividend.

A trustee who holds stock in a corporation as a part of his trust capital is obliged to determine what to do with various benefits received by him from the corporation on account of his stock ownership. His problem is whether in fairness and equity part or all of these benefits should be allocated to trust capital, or whether they should all be treated as trust income.

[49] Restatement, Trusts, § 236.

At common law the American courts established three rules for the distribution of these corporate benefits, namely, the Kentucky, the Massachusetts, and the Pennsylvania rules. The Kentucky rule is very simple, namely, that all corporate benefits received by a trustee by virtue of his ownership of stock go to the income account. No inquiry is made as to the source of the benefit or the effect of its distribution or its form. Hence cash and stock dividends, whether usual or extraordinary, go to the trust income account.[50]

The Massachusetts rule is also a simple rule, intended to make the trustee's work easy and sure, and to accomplish approximate justice between income beneficiaries and remaindermen, if not exact justice. The criterion for action is the form of the dividend. If the dividend is in cash, the trustee is entitled to treat it as trust income, without inquiry as to its source or effect. If the dividend is stock of the declaring corporation, the trustee should treat it as trust capital; but if the stock of another corporation than the declaring corporation, then it should be treated as trust income.[51] Cash dividends are usually declared out of current income which has accumulated during the time the trust has been holding the stock. Stock dividends are often declared out of undistributed earnings and surplus which have been piling up for some time and may have accrued before the trust held the stock. A rough and ready, simple rule which will do substantial justice is to be preferred to a more complex rule which strives for ideal justice and causes much trouble and expense. Giving stock dividends to trust capital is of benefit to the life tenant as well as the remainderman, since the life tenant immediately begins to get income on such stock. The settlor can always expressly provide for the method of distribution of stock and cash dividends, if he does not like the simple rule which is fixed by law.

The Pennsylvania courts, on the other hand, have sought to inquire into the source and effect of extraordinary cash and of all stock dividends, in order to determine what is the fairest distribution.[52] They have argued that the income beneficiary is equitably entitled to corporate income earned while he is beneficiary, and that the remainderman is equitably entitled to have

---

[50] Hite's Devisees v. Hite's Ex'r, 93 Ky. 257, 20 S.W. 778, 14 Ky.Law Rep. 385, 19 L.R.A. 173, 40 Am.St.Rep. 189.

[51] Minot v. Paine, 99 Mass. 101, 96 Am.Dec. 705.

Section 5 of the Uniform Principal and Income Act in substance follows the Massachusetts rule.

[52] Earp's Appeal, 28 Pa. 368; Smith's Estate, 140 Pa. 344, 21 A. 438, 23 Am.St.Rep. 237.

§ 146   CASH DIVIDENDS   447

the book or intact value of the stock maintained as large as it was when the trust first obtained the stock. They have tried to distribute the benefits received from the corporation in such a way as to preserve original trust capital value and to give the rest of the benefit to trust income.

Cash dividends are of two types, ordinary and extraordinary. The former are dividends payable in cash which are of the usual size and declared at a customary time. Extraordinary dividends are larger or more frequent than those usually issued by the corporation in question.

In states following the Kentucky [53] and Massachusetts [54] rules all cash dividends should be treated by the trustee as income of his trust, regardless of whether they are ordinary or extraordinary.

In the states following the Pennsylvania rule no inquiry is made as to the source or effect of ordinary cash dividends and they are to be considered trust income;[55] but if the cash dividend is extraordinary its source and effect must be considered by the trustee.[56] Thus, under the Pennsylvania rule if a trustee buys in 1930 ten shares of stock of a par value of $1,000 in the X corporation, and the corporation then has a capital of $100,000 and a surplus of $100,000, the book value of each share of the stock, assuming there are 1,000 shares outstanding, will then be 200. If the trustee holds the stock until 1940 during which time ordinary cash dividends have been paid and the capitalization has remained the same but the surplus has reached $150,000, and in 1940 the corporation issues an extraordinary cash dividend of $100 on each share of stock, it is evident that after this dividend has been paid the corporation will have a capitalization of $100,000 and a surplus of $50,000, and that each share of stock will have a book value of 150. In order to maintain the book value of the trust's original investment in this stock, namely, $2,000, the trustee who receives the $1,000 extraordinary cash dividend will be obliged to treat $500 of it as trust capital. His stock after the dividend will have a book value of 150 a share so that the ten

---

[53] Robinson v. Robinson's Exr., 221 Ky. 245, 298 S.W. 701.

[54] Buchanan v. National Savings & Trust Co., 57 App.D.C. 386, 23 F.2d 994.

[55] Opperman's Estate, 319 Pa. 455, 179 A. 729; In re Boyle's Estate, 235 Wis. 591, 294 N.W. 29, 130 A.L.R. 486.

[56] Foard v. Safe Deposit & Trust Co. of Baltimore, 122 Md. 476, 89 A. 724; Lang v. Lang's Exr., 57 N.J. Eq. 325, 41 A. 705; Stoke's Estate, 240 Pa. 277, 87 A. 971.

shares will be worth $1,500. When bought it had a book value of $2,000. The $500 in book value lost by reason of this extraordinary cash dividend must be replaced by applying $500 of the dividend to trust capital.

It is generally agreed that a dividend payable in stock or cash, as the trustee may elect, is to be treated as a cash dividend.[57]

Where a dividend is declared in order to distribute the assets of the corporation, because it has sold its property and is going out of business, it is generally held that this dividend should be treated by the trustee as trust capital, even though it is in the form of cash.[58] It would seem that in states following the Pennsylvania rule such part of it as is necessary to maintain the dollar value of the trust's investment in the stock should be treated as trust capital, and the balance should go to trust income.[59]

If the directors of a corporation state when they declare a dividend that it is declared out of corporate capital and not out of earnings, the trustee is entitled to treat the dividend as trust capital.[60]

STOCK DIVIDENDS [61]

141. Under the Kentucky rule stock dividends are trust income.

   Under the Massachusetts rule dividends in the stock of the declaring corporation are trust capital, but dividends in the stock of corporations other than the declaring corporation are trust income.

   Under the Pennsylvania rule stock dividends are trust capital to the extent necessary to preserve the dollar value of the trust's original investment in the stock; and beyond that are trust income.

As previously suggested under the Kentucky rule the current income account is entitled to all benefits from corporate stock.

---

[57] Davis v. Jackson, 152 Mass. 58, 25 N.E. 21, 23 Am.St.Rep. 801; Newport Trust Co. v. Van Rensselaer, 32 R.I. 231, 78 A. 1009, 35 L.R.A., N.S., 563; Uniform Principal and Income Act, § 5; but see Ballantine v. Young, 79 N.J.Eq. 70, 81 A. 119; Thompson's Estate, 262 Pa. 278, 105 A. 273.

[58] Powell v. Madison Safe Deposit & Trust Co., 208 Ind. 432, 196 N.E. 324, 101 A.L.R. 1368.

[59] In re Sternbergh's Estate, 337 Pa. 342, 10 A.2d 376; In re Boyle's Estate, 235 Wis. 591, 294 N.W. 29, 130 A.L.R. 486.

[60] Girard Trust Co. v. Mueller, 125 N.J.Eq. 597, 7 A.2d 413.

[61] Restatement, Trusts, § 236.

Hence stock dividends of all corporations, whether the issuing corporation or another, are to be considered trust income.[62]

The Massachusetts rule makes a distinction between stock of the corporation declaring the dividend and stock of another corporation. Thus, if a trustee holds stock of the X corporation and it declares a dividend in its own stock, the dividend is to be treated as capital of the trust;[63] but if the X corporation declares a dividend in stock of the Y corporation, a subsidiary corporation the stock of which is all held by the X corporation, then the trustee should treat the stock of the Y corporation as income of his trust.[64] Doubtless the reason for the difference is that the receipt by the trustee of more stock in the issuing corporation is not regarded as increasing the size of the trust's interest in the corporation, but the receipt of shares in another corporation does produce a real benefit. Thus, if the trust held ten shares out of 1,000 in the X corporation, and the capitalization of the X corporation is increased to 2,000 shares and ten new shares delivered to the trustee, the size of his interest has in a certain sense not been increased. He formerly held ten shares out of 1000, or a one one-hundredth interest; he now holds twenty shares out of 2,000 which is still a one one-hundredth interest in the assets of the corporation. But if the X corporation has a part of its surplus invested in shares of the Y corporation, and the X corpora-

---

[62] Goff v. Evans, 217 Ky. 664, 290 S.W. 490; Lightfoot v. Beard, 230 Ky. 488, 20 S.W.2d 90.

[63] Hyde v. Holmes, 198 Mass. 287, 84 N.E. 318; Lyman v. Pratt, 183 Mass. 58, 66 N.E. 423. This rule is followed by the Supreme Court of the United States, and the courts of Connecticut, District of Columbia, Illinois, Indiana, Maine, Michigan, Missouri, Nebraska, Ohio, Rhode Island, Virginia, and West Virginia.

See Gibbons v. Mahon, 136 U.S. 549, 10 S.Ct. 1057, 34 L.Ed. 525; Second Universalist Church of Stamford v. Colegrove, 74 Conn. 79, 49 A. 902; Smith v. Dana, 77 Conn. 543, 60 A. 117, 69 L.R.A. 76, 107 Am.St. Rep. 51; Jackson v. Maddox, 136 Ga. 31, 70 S.E. 865, Ann.Cas.1912B, 1216 (controlled by statute); De Koven v. Alsop, 205 Ill. 309, 68 N.E. 930, 63 L.R.A. 587; Billings v. Warren, 216 Ill. 281, 74 N.E. 1050, Thatcher v. Thatcher, 117 Me. 331, 104 A. 515; Harris v. Moses, 117 Me. 391, 104 A. 703; Greene v. Smith, 17 R.I. 28, 19 A. 1081; In re Brown, 14 R.I. 371, 51 Am.Rep. 397; Newport Trust Co. v. Van Rensselaer, 32 R.I. 231, 78 A. 1009, 35 L.R.A.,N.S. 563. And see Wilberding v. Miller, 88 Ohio St. 609, 106 N.E. 665, L.R.A.1916A, 718, discussed in Farmers' Loan & Trust Co. v. Whiton, Sup., 173 N.Y.S. 890. The West Virginia court has recently followed Massachusetts. Security Trust Co. v. Rammelsburg, 82 W.Va. 701, 97 S.E. 122. Bonds issued by a corporation to its stockholders are to be added to the corpus. Bishop v. Bishop, 81 Conn. 509, 71 A. 583.

[64] Gray v. Hemenway, 212 Mass. 239, 98 N.E. 789; Creed v. McAleer, 275 Mass. 353, 175 N.E. 761, 80 A.L.R. 1117.

tion distributes these shares of the Y corporation to the shareholders of the X corporation as a dividend, the transaction is not mere bookkeeping. The shareholders of the X corporation are getting a distribution of the property of that corporation, and not merely a piece of paper showing that the trust's interest in the corporation is now represented by two stock certificates instead of one.

In a recent case [65] the Supreme Judicial Court stated the rule as follows: "The rule for determining the respective rights of those entitled to the income and to the principal of trust funds established long ago in this commonwealth, and constantly followed, 'is to regard cash dividends, however large, as income, and stock dividends, however made as capital.'" The leading Massachusetts case is Minot v. Paine,[66] where the reason for the establishment of the rule is thus set forth: "A trustee needs one plain principle to guide him; and the cestuis que trust ought not to be subjected to the expense of going behind the action of the directors, and investigating the concerns of the corporation, especially if it is out of our jurisdiction."

The courts which have followed this Massachusetts rule have admitted that it is not logically perfect. "It was not pretended that this rule, which has been commonly known as the Massachusetts rule, was the ideal rule of reason; nor have the courts of high authority which have given their approval of it ever claimed it to be such, or one which would accomplish justice under all circumstances. What has been claimed for it is that its general application, at least if due regard be had for the substance and intent of the transaction, would prove more beneficent in its consequences, and on the whole lead to results more closely approximating to what was just and equitable, than would the application of any other rule or any attempt to go behind the declaration of the dividend to search out and discover the equities of each case according to some theoretical ideal." [67]

The Pennsylvania rule, as previously stated, calls upon the trustee to investigate the effect of the stock dividend he receives, whether in the stock of the issuing or another corporation. His problem is to learn what the original book value of his interest in the corporation was, and what it now is after the stock dividend has been paid. Thus, if we assume that the trustee bought ten

---

[65] Talbot v. Milliken, 221 Mass. 367, 368, 108 N.E. 1060.

[66] 99 Mass. 101, 108, 96 Am.Dec. 705.

[67] Smith v. Dana, 77 Conn. 543, 548, 549, 60 A. 117, 69 L.R.A. 76, 107 Am.St.Rep. 51.

shares of stock in a corporation having 1,000 shares outstanding, the par value of each being $100, and at the time of the purchase the surplus of the corporation was $100,000, the trustee would find that the original value of his holding in this corporation, from a bookkeeping and not a market point of view, was $200 a share, making a total of $2,000. If after some years the corporation has increased its surplus to $200,000, and decides to issue a stock dividend of 100%, it will award to the trustee ten shares of the new stock. The capital of the corporation will then be $200,000, its surplus $100,000, and the book value of each share $150. This will make the value of the trustee's holding of twenty shares $150 times twenty, or $3,000. The trust's interest has been increased in value from $2,000 to $3,000 by the operation. All that the trustee was required to do was to maintain his book value, $2,000. Therefore, $1,000 in value of the new stock may be sold and the proceeds paid out to the income beneficiary.[68]

This puts the burden on the trustee of learning what the book values of the trust's interest were at two dates. He cannot rely with absolute confidence on the bookkeeping of the corporation. It may have been erroneous. At his peril he must find out original book value and present book value. Either he must employ lawyers and accountants and take a chance that their results are correct, or he must get an agreement between competent beneficiaries, or he must apply to the court of equity for instructions.

[68] Sloan's Estate, 258 Pa. 368, 102 A. 31; In re Harkness' Estate, 283 Pa. 464, 129 A. 458. This rule has been followed in Delaware, California, Hawaii, Iowa, Maryland, New Jersey, South Carolina, Tennessee, Vermont, and Wisconsin. New York follows it as to trusts established before 1926. Matter of Osborne, 209 N.Y. 450, 103 N.E. 723, 823, Ann.Cas.1915A, 298, 50 L.R.A.,N.S., 510; N.Y.L.1926, c. 843 (adopting the Mass. rule as to trusts established after May 17, 1926).

See In re Duffill's Estate, 180 Cal. 748, 183 P. 337; Bryan v. Aikin, 10 Del.Ch. 446, 86 A. 674, 45 L.R.A.,N.S., 477; Kalbach v. Clark, 133 Iowa 215, 110 N.W. 599, 12 L.R.A.,N.S., 801, 12 Ann.Cas. 647; Gilkey v. Paine, 80 Me. 319, 14 A. 205 (semble), overruled in Harris v. Moses, 117 Me. 391, 104 A. 703; Thomas v. Gregg, 78 Md. 545, 28 A. 565, 44 Am.St.Rep. 310; Safe Deposit & Trust Co. v. White, 102 Md. 73, 61 A. 295, 296; Coudon v. Updegraf, 117 Md. 71, 83 A. 145; In re Northern Cent. Dividend Cases, 126 Md. 16, 94 A. 338; Miller v. Safe Deposit & Trust Co. of Baltimore, 127 Md. 610, 96 A. 766; Goodwin v. McGaughey, 108 Minn. 248, 122 N.W. 6; Holbrook v. Holbrook, 74 N.H. 201, 66 A. 124, 12 L.R.A.,N.S., 768; Van Doren v. Olden, 19 N.J.Eq. 176, 97 Am.Dec. 650; Pritchitt v. Nashville Trust Co., 96 Tenn. 472, 36 S.W. 1064, 33 L.R.A. 856; In re Heaton's Estate, 89 Vt. 550, 96 A. 21, L.R.A.1916D, 201; Soehnlein v. Soehnlein, 146 Wis. 330, 131 N.W. 739; Miller v. Payne, 150 Wis. 354, 136 N.W. 811; In re Barron's Will, 163 Wis. 275, 155 N.W. 1087.

The first method is expensive and hazardous, the second not often available, and the third is costly and time-consuming. The Pennsylvania rule is idealistic but impractical. Recent court [69] and legislative [70] trends are against it and in favor of the Massachusetts rule.

An application of the Pennsylvania rule may be found in the leading case of Appeal of Earp.[71] There the testator left to the trustee 540 shares of the stock of the Lehigh Crane Iron Works. At the time of the death of the testator and the beginning of the trust a large surplus fund had been accumulated by the corporation from its earnings, so that the shares had increased from a book value of $50 to a value of $125. The surplus fund continued to increase for a period of six years after the death of the testator, when the corporation canceled the old stock certificates and issued to the trustee in place of the original 540 shares, certificates for 1,350 shares; that is, practically declared a stock dividend of 810 shares of stock. These 1,350 shares were of the value of $80 a share at the time of their issuance. The court reasoned that the 540 shares were worth $67,500 at the time of the settlor's death; that the 1,350 shares at the time of their issuance were worth $108,000; that $67,500 of the new stock was necessary to maintain the book value of the trust's investment in this corporation; and that the difference, or $40,500, represented the profits accumulated during the continuance of the trust. The court, therefore, directed that an amount of the stock equal in value to $40,500 be distributed to the life beneficiary as income, and that the balance be retained by the trustee as capital, to be delivered over to the remainderman.

If the settlor has in so many words stated in the trust instrument that all dividends, cash or stock, no matter when earned or

---

[69] Powell v. Madison Safe Deposit & Trust Co., 208 Ind. 432, 196 N.E. 324, 101 A.L.R. 1368; In re Joy's Estate, 247 Mich. 418, 225 N.W. 878, 72 A.L.R. 973; Hayes v. St. Louis Union Trust Co., 317 Mo. 1028, 298 S.W. 91, 56 A.L.R. 1276.

[70] N.Y.L.1926, c. 843; § 5, Uniform Principal and Income Act, now in force in eleven states.

[71] 28 Pa. 368. For other Pennsylvania cases construing this rule, see Appeal of Wiltbank, 64 Pa. 256, 3 Am.Rep. 585; Appeal of Merchants' Fund Ass'n, 136 Pa. 43, 20 A. 527, 9 L.R.A. 421, 20 Am.St.Rep. 894; In re Thomson's Estate, 153 Pa. 332, 26 A. 652, 653; In re Sloan's Estate, 258 Pa. 368, 102 A. 31; In re Thompson's Estate, 262 Pa. 278, 105 A. 273; In re McKeown's Estate, 263 Pa. 78, 106 A. 189; Mercer v. Buchanan, C.C.Pa., 132 F. 501; Appeal of Philadelphia Trust, Safe-Deposit & Ins. Co., 16 A. 734; In re Eastwick's Estate, 15 Phila. 569; In re Wright's Estate, 5 Pa.Dist.Ct.R. 345.

from what source declared, shall go to the life beneficiary of the trust, there can be no doubt that it will be the duty of the trustee to pay to such life beneficiary all dividends declared.[72] In this case, as in all others, the intent of a testator or grantor, when not in contravention of some rule of law, will control the court.

STOCK SUBSCRIPTION RIGHTS [73]

142. **In most states a trustee who owns corporate stock and receives a stock subscription right should treat the right or its proceeds as trust capital. In a few states following the Pennsylvania rule the effect of the issuance of the stock subscription right on the value of the trust's investment in the corporation is considered and such part of the value of the right as is necessary to preserve the original value of the trust's investment in the corporation is treated as trust capital.**

Corporations sometimes issue to their stockholders rights to subscribe to new stock which is to be issued, the purpose being to raise new capital for the enterprise. It is customary to permit the old stockholders to subscribe to the new stock at par or some other price lower than the market price of the new stock. When a trustee owning stock receives a stock subscription right he must decide whether to credit it to trust income or to trust capital.

The effect of the receipt and use of such a right can be illustrated. Let us suppose that a trustee buys for $2,000 ten shares of stock in the X corporation, each having a par value of $100, the corporation being capitalized at $100,000 and having a $100,-000 surplus. Let us assume that after the trustee has held the stock for some years and received ordinary cash dividends on it, the corporation announces that it is going to increase its capital to $200,000, and that it is distributing to its old stockholders rights to subscribe to the same amount of new stock as they hold of the old stock. The trustee will, therefore, receive a right to subscribe to ten new shares of stock which can be exercised by investing $1,000 more of trust capital, or he can probably sell his stock subscription right for $500, since the book value of the ten shares of new stock will be $1500, assuming that the corpo-

---

[72] In re Robinson's Trust, 218 Pa. 481, 67 A. 775. And see, also, dicta to the same effect in Thomas v. Gregg, 78 Md. 545, 549, 28 A. 565, 44 Am. St.Rep. 310; In re Tod, 85 Misc. 298, 147 N.Y.S. 161.

[73] Restatement, Trusts, § 236.

ration surplus has remained $100,000. There will be 2,000 shares of stock after the new issue is taken up, the capital will be $200,000, and the surplus will be $100,000, so that each share of stock will have a book value of $150.

If the trustee exercises his subscription right and invests $1,000 more of trust capital, he will then have $3,000 invested, and will own twenty shares of stock of a book value of $150 each, making the interest of the trust in the corporation worth $3,000. Thus, the interest of the trust capital in this investment will not have been changed by the issuance and use of the subscription right.

If the trustee sells the subscription right for $500, he will then have $500 in cash and ten shares of stock each of which is worth $150. The stock will be worth $1,500 and there will be $500 in cash, making the total property $2,000, which was exactly the size of the trust's original investment in this corporation.

If the facts are as indicated above, it would seem clear that the entire benefit derived from the stock subscription right or its use should be treated as trust capital. Under the Pennsylvania rule which seeks the preservation of the dollar value of the trust's investment in the corporation, an allocation of the right or its proceeds to trust capital would be necessary in order to preserve the trust capital. Under the Massachusetts rule the form of the benefit, namely, a right to stock, would call for its allocation to trust capital. Only under the Kentucky rule would the right or its proceeds go to trust income.[74]

The great majority of the cases give the right or its proceeds to trust capital, usually stating merely that the right is an "incident" of the ownership of the stock or is "inherent" in it.[75] In Pennsylvania and a few other states,[76] however, the rule of preservation of trust capital is followed, and the right or its proceeds is allotted to trust capital only to the extent necessary to preserve the value of the trust's capital investment in the corporation. Sometimes this rule gives part of the proceeds of the right to trust income, although under the facts of the illustration given

[74] Hite's Devisees v. Hite's Ex'r, 93 Ky. 257, 20 S.W. 778, 14 Ky.Law Rep. 385, 19 L.R.A. 173, 40 Am.St.Rep. 189.

[75] De Koven v. Alsop, 205 Ill. 309, 68 N.E. 930, 63 L.R.A. 587; Chase v. Union Nat. Bank of Lowell, 275 Mass. 503, 176 N.E. 508; Baker v. Thompson, 181 App.Div. 469, 168 N.Y.S. 871, affirmed 224 N.Y. 592, 120 N.E. 858; In re Jenkins' Will, 199 Wis. 131, 225 N.W. 733.

[76] In re Schnur's Estate, Cal., 32 P.2d 970; Holbrook v. Holbrook, 74 N.H. 201, 66 A. 124, 12 L.R.A.,N.S., 768; Hostetter's Estate, 319 Pa. 572, 181 A. 567.

§ 143   SOURCE OF PAYMENT OF EXPENSES   455

above it happened that the entire benefit was necessary to preserve trust capital.

The Uniform Principal and Income Act [77] allots rights to subscribe to the stock of the corporation which issues them to trust capital, but gives to trust income rights to subscribe to the stock of a corporation other than the one which distributes the rights.

SOURCE FROM WHICH EXPENSES SHOULD BE PAID [78]

143. **The trustee should pay the ordinary expenses of administration of the trust out of trust income, but should pay from trust capital any expenses which are extraordinary or solely beneficial to the remainder interests under the trust. While no hard and fast rule can be laid down, in general the cost of keeping the trust property productive and secure is to be borne from trust income.**

In the administration of the trust the trustee must spend large sums of trust money for the expenses of operation, and he must decide whether to take these items out of trust income or to extract them from the capital funds of the trust.

The decisions and statutes lay down the very general and loose rule that the ordinary expenses of administration should be borne by trust income, and other costs should be charged to trust capital.[79] The theory is that the income beneficiaries must bear the burden of keeping the trust property safe and productive and of maintaining the status which existed when the trust began, but that expenditures which increase the value of the trust capital, or enure to the benefit of the remaindermen in particular, or are extraordinary in amount, should be paid from trust capital. Illustrations will show the meaning of these rather vague statements.

The following items have been held to be ordinary or current expenses and so payable from trust income: the interest on a mortgage on the trust property,[80] real or personal property tax-

---

[77] Section 5, adopted in twelve states previously named.

[78] Restatement, Trusts, § 237.

[79] Guthrie v. Wheeler, 51 Conn. 207; Rothschild v. Weinthel, 191 Ind. 85, 132 N.E. 687, 17 A.L.R. 1377; Cogswell v. Weston, 228 Mass. 219, 117 N.E. 37. The Uniform Principal and Income Act, § 12, lays down guides in general harmonious with those established by the courts.

[80] Morton's Case, 74 N.J.Eq. 797, 70 A. 680.

es,[81] the repairs of buildings on trust real estate,[82] rental of a safety deposit box,[83] insurance premiums in the case of fire or liability insurance,[84] the premiums on the trustee's bond,[85] and the compensation of the trustee where it is not expressly allowed as payable out of capital.[86]

The following expenses should normally be borne from trust capital: the principal debt in the case of a mortgage on trust property;[87] special assessments for public improvements or the cost of improvements made by the trustee where the improvement will probably last longer than the income beneficiary's interest;[88] the costs of litigation which has as its object the enforcement or defense of the trust;[89] costs of investment and sale of trust property;[90] and commissions of the trustee when allowed on principal.[91]

The settlor's directions in the trust instrument may control the source of expenditures,[92] and the court may vary the usual rule in special cases by apportioning the expenditure between capital and income or in other ways.[93]

Where real property is unproductive there has been a tendency in recent years to place the carrying charges like mortgage interest and property taxes on the capital of the trust.[94]

---

[81] Hagan v. Varney, 147 Ill. 281, 35 N.E. 219; In re Harris' Will, 170 Minn. 134, 212 N.W. 182.

[82] Alberts v. Steiner, 237 Mich. 143, 211 N.W. 46; Disbrow v. Disbrow, 46 App.Div. 111, 61 N.Y.S. 614, affirmed 167 N.Y. 606, 60 N.E. 1110.

[83] In re Kimber's Will, 172 Misc. 991, 16 N.Y.S.2d 786.

[84] Prudential Ins. Co. of America v. Land Estates, D.C.N.Y., 31 F.Supp. 845; Kingsley v. Spofford, 298 Mass. 469, 11 N.E.2d 487.

[85] Butler v. Builders' Trust Co., 203 Minn. 555, 282 N.W. 462, 124 A. L.R. 1178.

[86] Bridgeport-City Trust Co. v. First Nat. Bank & Trust Co. of Bridgeport, 124 Conn. 472, 200 A. 809, 117 A.L.R. 1148.

[87] Ash v. Ash, 126 N.J.Eq. 531, 10 A.2d 150.

[88] Plympton v. Boston Dispensary, 106 Mass. 544; Peltz v. Learned, 70 App.Div. 312, 75 N.Y.S. 104.

[89] Carter v. Brownell, 95 Conn. 216, 111 A. 182; In re Estate of Cole, 102 Wis. 1, 78 N.W. 402, 72 Am.St.Rep. 854.

[90] In re Fargo's Estate, Sur., 68 Misc. 273; Whittemore v. Beekman, 2 Dem.Surr. 275.

[91] McAfee v. Thomas, 121 Or. 351, 255 P. 333.

[92] Colt v. Duggan, D.C.N.Y., 25 F. Supp. 268; In re Jeffery's Estate, 333 Pa. 15, 3 A.2d 393.

[93] See, for example, the different methods of treating accounting costs. Perrine v. Newell, 49 N.J.Eq. 57, 23 A. 492; Matter of Eddy's Will, 207 App.Div. 162, 201 N.Y.S. 760; Matter of Kelsey's Estate, 89 Misc. 701, 153 N.Y.S. 1095.

[94] Harvard Trust Co. v. Duke, 304 Mass. 414, 24 N.E.2d 144; In re Levy's Estate, 333 Pa. 440, 5 A.2d 98.

Where expenditures occur periodically, as in the case of property taxes, it would seem that their burden should be distributed between successive income beneficiaries. Thus, if a property tax is levied on January 1st for the preceding year, and a trust exists for A. for life, remainder to B. for life, remainder to C.; and A. dies on June 1st, 1941, and taxes are levied on January 1st, 1942, for the year 1941, it would seem that this tax bill should not be met entirely out of the income due to B., but five-twelfths of it should be paid by the estate of A., since he was life tenant for five months of the year 1941, and seven-twelfths of it should be paid by the trustee from income which has been accumulated for B, since B. has been life tenant during seven months of the year 1941. This result has been reached in a recent Massachusetts case and seems highly equitable.[95]

It should be noted that paying trust expenses out of trust capital is in reality apportioning them between life tenant and remaindermen beneficiaries, since the use of capital for such a purpose deprives the income beneficiary of income on that capital for the remainder of the period during which he is entitled to income, and it also reduces the amount of capital which the remaindermen beneficiaries will get at the end of the trust.

[95] Taylor v. Bentinck-Smith, 304 Mass. 430, 24 N.E.2d 146, 126 A.L.R. 857; but see Industrial Trust Co. v. Wilson, 58 R.I. 378, 192 A. 821, 109 A.L.R. 220 (tax not assessed for a particular period).

CHAPTER 16

TRUST ADMINISTRATION—ACCOUNTING AND COMPENSATION

Sec.
144. Duty to Keep Records and Give Information.
145. Duty to Render Court Accountings.
146. Compensation of the Trustee.

DUTY TO KEEP RECORDS AND GIVE INFORMATION [1]

144. The trustee is under a duty to the cestui que trust—
   (a) To keep accurate and complete records of the trust business;
   (b) To furnish the beneficiary with all necessary information regarding the trust;
   (c) To permit the beneficiary to inspect the trust records, papers, and securities.

Ordinarily the management and control of the trust property is solely in the hands of the trustee. The cestui que trust knows nothing of the trust business directly. The nature of the trust investments, the condition of the trust property, the income actually received—these are all matters of which the beneficiary is usually ignorant, except as he obtains information regarding them from the trustee. And yet it is highly proper that the beneficiary should have knowledge of these matters, in order that he may know whether the trust is being properly administered. From this situation arises the duty of the trustee to keep accurate accounts of his transactions, to supply full information to the cestui que trust, and to render a full account of his proceedings in the proper court.

The trustee should keep books which will accurately show his disposition of the trust funds, and he should obtain vouchers for all payments.[2] "He is bound to keep clear and accurate accounts, and if he does not the presumptions are all against him, obscurities and doubts being resolved adversely to him." [3]

---

[1] Restatement, Trusts, §§ 172, 173.

[2] Williamson v. Grider, 97 Ark. 588, 135 S.W. 361; Richardson v. Van Auken, 5 App.D.C. 209; Potter v. Porter, 109 S.W. 344, 33 Ky.Law Rep. 129; Smallwood v. Lawson, 183 Ky. 189, 208 S.W. 808; Ithell v. Malone, Sup., 154 N.Y.S. 275; Raski v. Wise, 56 Or. 72, 107 P. 984; Stockwell v. Stockwell's Estate, 92 Vt. 489, 105 A. 30.

[3] White v. Rankin, 18 App.Div. 293, 295, 46 N.Y.S. 228, affirmed 162 N.Y. 622, 57 N.E. 1128.

It is not necessary that the cestui que trust bring a bill for an accounting in order to obtain information about the trust business. The trustee is under the duty of furnishing all pertinent information upon demand.[4] Thus, in a leading English case it was held that a beneficiary was entitled to an order from the trustee which would enable him to learn whether any of the trust property was incumbered or any interest in it had been assigned. The court said: "The general rule, then, is what I have stated, that the trustee must give information to his cestui que trust as to the investment of the trust estate. Where a portion of the trust estate is invested in consols, it is not sufficient for the trustee merely to say that it is so invested, but his cestui que trust is entitled to an authority from the trustee to enable him to make proper application to the bank, as has been done in this case, in order that he may verify the trustee's own statement. * * *"[5]

Furthermore, if reasonable regard for the interests of the beneficiaries requires it, the trustee is under a duty to volunteer information to the beneficiary, and not merely to furnish it on demand.[6] For example, a trustee of a mortgage for bondholders has been held under a duty to inform the bondholders of a default by the mortgagor, so that the bondholders can unite to force foreclosure, if they desire to do so.[7]

The same rule was well framed in a statement of a Michigan court: "The beneficiaries of a trust have the right to be kept informed at all times concerning the management of the trust, and it is the duty of the trustees to so inform them. It is not generally presumable that the beneficiaries have such information from independent sources."[8] An illustration of the enforcement of this same rule is found in the cases holding that a beneficiary is entitled to examine legal opinions which the trustee obtains for the purpose of guiding him in carrying out the trust.

[4] Wylie v. Bushnell, 277 Ill. 484, 115 N.E. 618; Perrin v. Lepper, 72 Mich. 454, 40 N.W. 859; Woolf v. Barnes, 46 Misc. 169, 93 N.Y.S. 219; Jay v. Squire, 7 Ohio N.P. 345; In re Scott's Estate, 202 Pa. 389, 51 A. 1023. The cestui que trust is entitled to be informed in what securities the trust funds are invested. Baer v. Kahn, 131 Md. 17, 101 A. 596.

[5] In re Tillott, [1892] 1 Ch. 86, 88, 89.

[6] Birmingham Trust & Savings Co. v. Ansley, 234 Ala. 674, 176 So. 465; Moore v. Sanders, Tex.Civ.App., 106 S.W.2d 337.

[7] Lyman v. Stevens, 123 Conn. 591, 197 A. 313; First Trust Co. of Lincoln v. Carlsen, 129 Neb. 118, 261 N. W. 333.

[8] Loud v. Winchester, 52 Mich. 174, 183, 17 N.W. 784.

The trustee is not, however, under the same obligation regarding opinions which he obtains for the purpose of defending himself from charges of misconduct.[9]

The beneficiary is also entitled to an inspection of all books and documents relating to the trust and of trust securities and other property held by the trustee.[10] He may personally examine the books or have an accountant do it for him. He is entitled to know from personal observation whether the trust papers, accounts, and documents are in the condition claimed by the trustee.

Of course, the privilege of obtaining information and of inspecting must be exercised at reasonable hours of the day and at reasonable intervals. The trustee cannot be required to give information and permit inspection outside of business hours or so frequently as to be unnecessary and unreasonable.

DUTY TO RENDER COURT ACCOUNTING [11]

145. A trustee is under a duty to render an accounting in a court of equity when ordered to do so by the court. Any person financially interested in the trust administration may bring a suit to obtain a decree for an accounting.

The trustee may also voluntarily present to the court an account of his administration.

In many states by statute or court rule trustees are required to make accountings in court periodically, and the procedure and effect of such accountings are fixed.

The beneficiaries may object to the account as presented by the trustee, and the court will allow or reject the objections, and disallow, modify, or approve the account.

The approval by the court of a trustee's account prevents the beneficiaries from objecting later to any conduct of the trustee which was fairly stated in the account, but does not prevent the beneficiary from applying for a reopening of the account if there has been fraud or mistake.

Many corporate trustees present voluntary reports of their trust administration to their beneficiaries periodically out of court, and procure their approval by the cestuis. This protects the trustee against later complaint as to his administration, if he fully and fairly stated the facts and was guilty of no misrepresentation or concealment.

---

[9] Wynne v. Humberston, 27 Beav. 421.

[10] Union Trust Co. of San Diego v. Superior Court, in and for San Diego County, 11 Cal.2d 449, 81 P.2d 150, 118 A.L.R. 259; Baydrop v. Second Nat. Bank, 120 Conn. 322, 180 A. 469.

[11] Restatement, Trusts, § 172.

Duty to Account

It is elementary that a trustee is under the obligation of rendering an account of his dealings as trustee in a court having jurisdiction of the trust, under the rules laid down by that court or by the legislature.[12] The details of such accountings will be taken up at a later time. It is sufficient here to state the broad, general duty. This obligation is placed upon the trustee in order that the cestui que trust may learn what property has been received by the trustee and what funds paid out, and may then object to the account, if he desires, and have the propriety of the trustee's actions passed upon. "It is well settled that, when a fiduciary relation is shown to exist, and property or property interests have been intrusted to an agent or trustee, the burden is thrown upon such agent intrusted to render an account and to show that all his trust duties have been fully performed, and the manner in which they have been performed. It is assumed that the agent or trustee has means of knowing and does know what the principal or cestui que trust cannot know, and is bound to reveal the entire truth.[13] * * * It is not necessary in such a case as this that the plaintiff should show that there will be something found due to her on the accounting. That fact can never be known with certainty until the account has been taken. The right to this accounting results from the facts that the fiduciary relation has been created and assumed by the agent or trustee, and that the principal or cestui que trust is not informed and does not know what has been done with reference to the property or property interests confided to the agent or trustee."[14] The duty here is to give information in writing and under oath, in such manner that the beneficiaries and the court can scrutinize it for breaches of trust.

[12] Silver King Consol. Min. Co. of Utah v. Silver King Coalition Mines Co. of Nevada, C.C.A.Utah, 204 F. 166, 122 C.C.A. 402, Ann.Cas.1918B, 571; Bone v. Hayes, 154 Cal. 759, 99 P. 172; Purdy v. Johnson, 174 Cal. 521, 163 P. 893; Barnes v. Century Sav. Bank, 165 Iowa 141, 144 N.W. 367; Dillivan v. German Sav. Bank, Iowa, 124 N.W. 350; Barnes v. Gardiner, 140 App.Div. 395, 125 N.Y.S. 433; Gray v. Heinze, 82 Misc. 618, 144 N.Y. S. 1045; Arnold v. Southern Pine Lumber Co., 58 Tex.Civ.App. 186, 123 S.W. 1162; Geisse v. Beall, 3 Wis. 367. An implied as well as an express trustee may be compelled to account. Tucker v. Weeks, 177 App. Div. 158, 163 N.Y.S. 595. Since the account need not be personally prepared, illness of the trustee is not an excuse for failure to file an account. In re Buchanan's Estate, Sur., 171 N.Y.S. 953.

[13] Citing Marvin v. Brooks, 94 N.Y. 71.

[14] Frethey v. Durant, 24 App.Div. 58, 61, 62, 48 N.Y.S. 839. See, also, State v. Illinois Cent. R. Co., 246 Ill. 188, 92 N.E. 814.

The forum in which the trustee may voluntarily account, or in which he may be compelled to account, is usually the forum having general equitable jurisdiction. It is impossible here to enumerate the courts of the various jurisdictions which possess the power to receive and compel accountings by a trustee.[15] Quite frequently statutes give to the probate courts concurrent or exclusive jurisdiction over accountings by testamentary trustees.[16]

In order to fix the initial liability of trustees as to the amount of trust property received by them, it is required in some states that they file an inventory of the trust property they have obtained, within a short time after taking office. The inventory

[15] For cases discussing the jurisdiction of various courts, see McAdoo v. Sayre, 145 Cal. 344, 78 P. 874; Prindle v. Holcomb, 45 Conn. 111; Jones v. Downs, 82 Conn. 33, 72 A. 589; McHardy v. McHardy's Ex'r, 7 Fla. 301; Cheney v. Langley, 56 Ill.App. 86; Weaver v. Fisher, 110 Ill. 146; Waterman v. Alden, 144 Ill. 90, 32 N.E. 972; Cunningham v. Fraize, 85 Ky. 35, 2 S.W. 551; Boreing v. Faris, 127 Ky. 67, 104 S.W. 1022; Page v. Marston, 94 Me. 342, 47 A. 529; Nelson v. Howard, 5 Md. 327; Hobart v. Andrews, 21 Pick., Mass., 526; Green v. Gaskill, 175 Mass. 265, 56 N.E. 560; Hayes v. Hall, 188 Mass. 510, 74 N.E. 935; McBride v. McIntyre, 91 Mich. 406, 51 N.W. 1113; Sullivan v. Ross' Estate, 113 Mich. 311, 71 N.W. 634, 76 N.W. 309; Montgomery v. Gilbert, Mont., 108 P.2d 616; Evans v. Evans, N.J.Ch., 57 A. 872; Marsh v. Marsh's Ex'rs, 73 N.J.Eq. 99, 67 A. 706; Jones v. Jones, 8 Misc. 660, 30 N.Y.S. 177; In re Widmayer, 28 Misc. 362, 59 N.Y.S. 980; Meeks v. Meeks, 51 Misc. 538, 100 N.Y.S. 667; In re Clyne, 72 Misc. 593, 131 N.Y.S. 1090; Van Sinderen v. Lawrence, 50 Hun 272, 3 N.Y.S. 25; Cass v. Cass, 61 Hun 460, 16 N.Y.S. 229; Rutherfurd v. Myers, 50 App.Div. 298, 63 N.Y.S. 939; In re Fogarty's Estate, 117 App.Div. 583, 102 N.Y.S. 776; Post v. Ingraham, 122 App.Div. 738, 107 N.Y.S. 737; Mildeberger v. Franklin, 130 App.Div. 860, 115 N.Y.S. 903; Runk v. Thomas, 138 App.Div. 789, 123 N.Y.S. 523; Ungrich v. Ungrich, 141 App.Div. 485, 126 N.Y.S. 419; Furniss v. Furniss, 148 App.Div. 211, 133 N.Y.S. 535; Deering v. Pierce, 149 App.Div. 10, 133 N.Y.S. 582; Conant v. Wright, 22 App.Div. 216, 48 N.Y.S. 422, affirmed 162 N.Y. 635, 57 N.E. 1107; Code Civ. Proc.N.Y. § 2723 et seq.; Herron v. Comstock, C.C.A.Ohio, 139 F. 370, 71 C.C.A. 466; In re Roach's Estate, 50 Or. 179, 92 P. 118; Bank of United States v. Biddle, 2 Pars Eq.Cas., Pa., 31; Appeal of Simpson, 9 Pa. 416; Appeal of Jones, 3 Grant, Cas., Pa., 169; In re Apple, 2 Phila., Pa., 171; Appeal of Baskin, 34 Pa. 272; Appeal of Paisley, 70 Pa. 153; In re Walton's Estate, 174 Pa. 195, 34 A. 558; Meurer v. Stokes, 246 Pa. 393, 92 A. 506; Poole v. Brown, 12 S.C. 556; Leach v. Cowan, 125 Tenn. 182, 140 S.W. 1070, Ann.Cas.1913C, 188; Downer v. Downer, 9 Vt. 231; Bailey v. Bailey, 67 Vt. 494, 32 A. 470, 48 Am.St.Rep. 826; In re Cary's Estate, 81 Vt. 112, 69 A. 736; Wilson v. Kennedy, 63 W.Va. 1, 59 S.E. 736.

[16] Hooker v. Goodwin, 91 Conn. 463, 99 A. 1059, Ann.Cas.1918D, 1159; Appeal of Morse, 92 Conn. 286, 102 A. 586; People ex rel. Safford v. Washburn, 105 Misc. 415, 173 N.Y.S. 157, affirmed 188 App.Div. 951, 176 N.Y.S. 833.

§ 145 DUTY TO RENDER COURT ACCOUNTING

is filed with the court having jurisdiction over the enforcement of the trust.[17]

The suit or proceeding for a court accounting may be brought by any person having a contingent or vested, present or future, financial interest in the trust administration. Thus, the following are proper parties plaintiff: any beneficiary,[18] a remainderman who is to take following the trust,[19] a surety on the bond of a trustee,[20] a sole trustee[21] or a cotrustee,[22] the executor of a deceased trustee,[23] or a successor trustee.[24] The settlor as such has no legal interest in the trust and cannot sue for an accounting.[25]

The trustee may be relieved from the duty of rendering an account in a variety of ways. If the remedy at law is adequate, an account may be unnecessary.[26] There may be private settlement between cestuis que trust and trustee, which will excuse the trustee from making a formal report in court.[27] Laches on the part of the beneficiary in demanding an account may relieve the trustee.[28] Thus, in one case the lapse of twenty years was held to bar the right to an account,[29] while in another the passing of eight years was held not to prevent the cestui from demanding an account.[30] Action or failure to act on the part of the cestui may estop him from later claiming an account.[31]

---

[17] See sections 2 and 12, Uniform Trustees Accounting Act; and Minn. L.1933, c. 259.

[18] Brown v. Ricks, 30 Ga. 777; Savage v. Sherman, 87 N.Y. 277.

[19] Franz v. Buder, C.C.A.Mo., 11 F.2d 854.

[20] Pa. 20 P.S. § 2945.

[21] Arnold v. Alden, 173 Ill. 229, 50 N.E. 704.

[22] Bermingham v. Wilcox, 120 Cal. 467, 52 P. 822.

[23] In re Scott's Estate, 202 Pa. 389, 51 A. 1023.

[24] Boreing v. Faris, 127 Ky. 67, 104 S.W. 1022, 31 Ky.Law Rep. 1265.

[25] Boone v. Davis, 64 Miss. 138, 8 So. 202; Marvin v. Smith, 46 N.Y. 571.

[26] Mersereau v. Bennet, 62 Misc. 356, 115 N.Y.S. 20.

[27] Colton v. Stanford, 82 Cal. 351, 23 P. 16, 16 Am.St.Rep. 137; Scudder v. Burrows, 7 N.Y.St.Rep. 605; Appeal of Schoch, 33 Pa. 351; Britton v. Lewis, 8 Rich.Eq., S.C., 271; Maffitt v. Read, 11 Rich.Eq., S.C., 285.

[28] McClane's Adm'x v. Shepherd's Ex'x, 21 N.J.Eq. 76; In re Engel's Estate, 180 Pa. 215, 36 A. 727; In re Rist's Estate, 192 Pa. 24, 43 A. 407.

[29] Snodgrass v. Snodgrass, 176 Ala. 276, 58 So. 201.

[30] Horine v. Mengel, 30 Pa.Super. Ct. 67. See, also, Dyer v. Waters, 46 N.J.Eq. 484, 19 A. 129; Felkner v. Dooly, 27 Utah 350, 75 P. 854.

[31] Wooden v. Kerr, 91 Mich. 188, 51 N.W. 937; Jones v. Jones, 50 Hun 603, 2 N.Y.S. 844. Acceptance by the

Practice on Accounting

The practice upon trustees' accountings is usually governed by statute or court rules to such an extent that any statement of generally applicable principles is difficult.[32] The necessary parties are all those interested in the trust. Thus, all the trustees should be made parties,[33] unless the account is demanded of one trustee alone;[34] and the representatives of a deceased trustee should be joined.[35] Naturally all beneficiaries should be made parties,[36] as well as the representatives of a deceased cestui.[37] Persons in possession of the trust res may properly be joined,[38] but it is not necessary to give notice to transferees from the trustee.[39] Remaindermen are, of course, interested in the property and should be joined when their rights may be affected.[40]

The account is filed with the court and copies of it served on all beneficiaries. After the trustee has presented his account the cestuis que trust are given an opportunity of objecting to any item.[41] The trustee should present vouchers for all payments which he claims he has made,[42] but if satisfactory proof of the payment is made otherwise than by the presentation of a voucher, the claim will be allowed.[43] Where no voucher is

cestui que trust of a part of the property from the trustee does not estop him from requiring an account. Schneider v. Hayward, 231 Mass. 352, 121 N.E. 76.

[32] See, for example, the New York statute having to do with the accountings of testamentary trustees, found in Surrogate's Court Act, §§ 251–274.

[33] McKinley v. Irvine, 13 Ala. 681; People v. Equitable Life Assur. Soc. of United States, 124 App.Div. 714, 109 N.Y.S. 453; German-American Coffee Co. v. Diehl, 86 Misc. 547, 149 N.Y.S. 413.

[34] Fleming v. Gilmer, 35 Ala. 62.

[35] Evans v. Evans, N.J.Ch., 57 A. 872.

[36] Parsons v. Lyman, Fed.Cas.No. 10780; Newman v. Schwerin, C.C.A. Tenn., 61 F. 865, 10 C.C.A. 129; Dill v. McGehee, 34 Ga. 438; Speakman v. Tatem, 45 N.J.Eq. 388, 17 A. 818;

Brewster v. Brewster, 4 Sandf.Ch., N.Y., 22; Adams v. Purser, 126 App. Div. 20 110 N.Y.S. 167.

[37] Cogan v. McCabe, 23 Misc. 739, 52 N.Y.S. 48.

[38] McBride v. McIntyre, 91 Mich. 406, 51 N.W. 1113.

[39] Pondir v. New York, L. E. & W. R. Co., 72 Hun 384, 25 N.Y.S. 560; Felton v. Long, 43 N.C. 224, 8 Ired. Eq. 224.

[40] Leonard v. Barnum, 94 App.Div. 266, 87 N.Y.S. 978, affirmed Same v. Pierce, 182 N.Y. 431, 75 N.E. 313, 1 L.R.A.,N.S., 161. But see Mount v. Mount, 68 App.Div. 144, 74 N.Y.S. 148.

[41] Lycan v. Miller, 56 Mo.App. 79.

[42] Willis v. Clymer, 66 N.J.Eq. 284, 57 A. 803; Smith v. Robinson, 83 N. J.Eq. 384, 90 A. 1063.

[43] Groom v. Thompson, Ky., 16 S. W. 369; Brinkerhoff's Ex'rs v. Banta,

presented and the charge seems questionable, the trustee will not be allowed the amount.[44] While the legal presumption is that a trustee has done his duty and performed the trust,[45] the burden is upon the accounting trustee to show satisfactorily the disposition of all property received by him as trustee, and to prove the necessity and propriety of all expenditures for which he claims credit.[46] He cannot throw upon the cestui que trust the burden of proving the opposite.[47] All presumptions are against the trustee upon the accounting, and obscurities and doubts in the account will be resolved against him.[48]

In many states there are court rules or statutes requiring the trustee to present to the court and the beneficiaries a report of his doings at stated periods.[49] In some states the report must be annual,[50] in others biennial,[51] and in some triennial.[52] These

[26] N.J.Eq. 157; In re United States Mortgage & Trust Co., 114 App.Div. 532, 100 N.Y.S. 12; In re Froelich's Estate, 50 Misc. 103, 100 N.Y.S. 436; In re Davis' Estate, 43 App.Div. 331, 60 N.Y.S. 315.

[44] In re Quinn's Estate, 16 Misc. 651, 40 N.Y.S. 732.

[45] Aldridge v. Aldridge, Ky., 109 S. W. 873, 33 Ky.LawRep. 246.

[46] Chirurg v. Ames, 138 Iowa 697, 116 N.W. 865; Fidelity & Deposit Co. of Maryland v. Husbands, 174 Ky. 200, 192 S.W. 51; Ashley v. Winkley, 209 Mass. 509, 95 N.E. 932; Parker's Adm'r v. Parker, N.J.Ch., 5 A. 586; McCulloch v. Tomkins, 62 N.J. Eq. 262, 49 A. 474; Ithell v. Malone, Sup., 154 N.Y.S. 275; Biddle Purchasing Co. v. Snyder, 109 App.Div. 679, 96 N.Y.S. 356; Choctaw, O. & G. R. Co. v. Sittel, 21 Okl. 695, 97 P. 363; Mintz v. Brock, 193 Pa. 294, 44 A. 417; Heyward v. Glover, 2 Hill, Eq., S.C., 515; Montgomery v. Coldwell, 14 Lea, Tenn., 29; Stockwell v. Stockwell's Estate, 92 Vt. 489, 105 A. 30.

[47] Red Bud Realty Co. v. South, 96 Ark. 281, 131 S.W. 340; Purdy v. Johnson, 174 Cal. 521, 163 P. 893.

[48] Bone v. Hayes, 154 Cal. 759, 99 P. 172; Smith v. Robinson, 83 N.J. Eq. 384, 90 A. 1063; Dufford's Ex'r v. Smith, 46 N.J.Eq. 216, 18 A. 1052; In re Gaston Trust, 35 N.J.Eq. 60; White v. Rankin, 18 App.Div. 293, 46 N.Y.S. 228, affirmed 162 N.Y. 622, 57 N.E. 1128; Landis v. Scott, 32 Pa. 495.

[49] For full details of these accounting statutes or court rules, see Bogert, Trust and Trustees, §§ 965–968.

[50] Connecticut, District of Columbia, Hawaii, Iowa, Louisiana, Michigan, Minnesota, Missouri, New Hampshire, New York, North Carolina, North Dakota, South Carolina, South Dakota, Utah, Vermont, West Virginia and Wisconsin. In Massachusetts an account is required to be filed in court annually and delivered to the beneficiaries, but it is not called up for a court hearing oftener than once in three years unless a party requests it. This rule is followed in the Uniform Trustees Accounting Act, now adopted in Indiana, Kansas and Washington.

[51] Delaware, Kentucky, and Ohio.

[52] Maine, New Jersey, and Pennsylvania.

statutes and rules fix the procedure as to notice, hearings, objections, allowance of the account and the effect of allowance.

The approval of an account by the court to which it is presented prevents the beneficiaries from objecting later to the acts of the trustee which are fully and fairly stated in the account.[53] For example, if a trustee reports in his account that he has invested the trust fund in part in common stock, and this is not a lawful investment for his trust, but the beneficiary makes no objection to the investment when the matter is before the court, and the court approves the account, the investment will be validated and the beneficiary will not be allowed later to claim that the investment was a breach of trust.[54]

But if the trustee conceals facts regarding his conduct, the approval by the court of the account will not grant him immunity from later action.[55] Thus, where a trustee has purchased trust investments from himself, or a corporate trustee has bought them from an affiliated corporation, and the investment is stated in the account but not the seller of it to the trustee, and the court approves the account, there is no validation of the act of disloyalty by the trustee, since that act was not stated in the account.[56]

The decree of a court approving an account, like all court judgments and decrees, will be reopened by the court, on the application of an interested party, where it is shown that there was fraud, concealment, or mistake in the account or in the procuring of the court approval.[57]

In states which do not have compulsory periodic court accountings it is customary with corporate trustees to present to

---

[53] Shearman v. Cameron, 78 N.J.Eq. 532, 80 A. 545; Costello v. Costello, 209 N.Y. 252, 103 N.E. 148. Parties not served with notice of an accounting proceeding are not bound by an adjudication in it. In re Galli's Estate, 340 Pa. 561, 17 A.2d 899. When a trustee for life tenant and remainderman accounts during the life tenancy, a gratuitous statement by the court in a decree approving the account which purports to give the size of the remaindermen's interests, is not binding on them. In re Bayard's Estate, 340 Pa. 488, 17 A.2d 361.

[54] Harvard College v. Amory, 26 Mass. 446, 9 Pick. 446; Beam v. Patterson Safe Deposit & Trust Co., 96 N.J.Eq. 141, 126 A. 25.

[55] Henderson v. Segars, 28 Ala. 352; Wann v. Northwestern Trust Co., 120 Minn. 493, 139 N.W. 1061.

[56] In re Cosgrove's Will, 236 Wis. 554, 295 N.W. 784, 132 A.L.R. 1514; but see In re Colladay's Estate, 33 Pa. D. & C. 597, affirmed 333 Pa. 218, 3 A.2d 787.

[57] Beardsley v. Hall, 291 Mass. 411, 197 N.E. 35, 99 A.L.R. 1129; Richter v. Anderson, 56 Oh.App. 291, 10 N.E. 2d 789.

BOGERT TRUSTS 2D

beneficiaries a statement of the trust work at frequent intervals, say every year or every quarter. These reports are very brief, condensed outlines of the work of the trustee during the period and often do not give all the information which a beneficiary should have. The practice is to request the beneficiaries to give express written approval of the accounts thus rendered, or to state that they will be considered approved if no objection is received within a limited period. Approvals by beneficiaries of full age and sound mind will relieve the trustee from liability for all acts fully described in the report, if there was no misrepresentation or concealment or other unfair practice by the trustee.[58]

On an accounting the trustee is charged with all principal and income received by him during the accounting period, and with all such property which he did not obtain but could have received if he had used ordinary diligence and care, and with all damages caused by his breaches of trust;[59] and the trustee is credited with all sums expended by him from the trust capital and income where the expenditure was lawful under the terms of the trust.[60] The latter includes disbursements for expenses of administration, for investment, and for paying the beneficiaries the amounts due them.

Debits

If the trustee appropriates the trust funds to his own use, he will be charged with the value of the trust property as of the date of the misappropriation.[61] It is obvious that the trustee must be debited on the accounting with the income of the trust property, as well as with the original value of the trust res. Thus, he must account for the rents of lands held in trust, or for their reasonable rental value, where he uses them for his own benefit.[62] Where the negligence of the trustee causes ex-

[58] Fleischmann v. Northwestern Nat. Bank & Trust Co., 194 Minn. 227, 260 N.W. 310.

[59] Farmers' Loan & Trust Co. v. Pendleton, 179 N.Y. 486, 72 N.E. 508; Purdy v. Johnson, 174 Cal. 521, 163 P. 893; In re Roach's Estate, 50 Or. 179, 92 P. 118.

[60] United States v. Swope, C.C.A. N.M., 16 F.2d 215; Patterson v. Northern Trust Co., 286 Ill. 564, 122 N.E. 55.

[61] In re Hart's Estate, 203 Pa. 488, 53 A. 367.

[62] Cunningham v. Cunningham, 81 S.C. 506, 62 S.E. 845. In Van Orden v. Pitts, Tex.Com.App., 206 S.W. 830, one who appropriated property and was made a constructive trustee thereof was charged with interest at the highest rate allowed by law, 10 per cent. And in Campbell v. Napier, 182 Ky. 182, 206 S.W. 271, a trustee who repudiated his trust was

pense, as where a second account has to be rendered, due to the inaccuracy of the first, the trustee will be charged with this expense.[63]

Credits

It is an application of the elementary principles of the law of trusts that a trustee who has paid out money for insurance premiums,[64] or repairs upon the trust property,[65] or taxes,[66] or lawyer's fees,[67] or the costs of an action,[68] or to discharge a claim against the trust estate,[69] or for improvements of the trust property,[70] or for office rent and office expenses,[71] should be credited in his account with such payments. The payments were for the benefit of the cestuis que trust. They should come out of the trust funds, and not out of the private moneys of the trustee. If a trustee neglects to keep proper accounts of his expenditures, the lowest possible estimate will be put upon them in allowing him remuneration.[72]

Other examples of credits allowed are found in the cases where the trustee has advanced his own funds to a beneficiary, pending the accrual of the income from the trust funds;[73] or where the trustee has necessarily used his own funds to buy in

charged with interest from the date of repudiation.

[63] Clark v. Anderson, 13 Bush, Ky., 111.

[64] Fisher v. Fisher, 170 N.C. 378, 87 S.E. 113.

[65] In re Parry's Estate, 244 Pa. 93, 90 A. 443.

[66] Tarbox v. Tarbox, 111 Me. 374, 89 A. 194.

[67] Locke v. Cope, 94 Kan. 137, 146 P. 416; In re Dreier's Estate, 83 N.J. Eq. 618, 92 A. 51; In re Mylin's Estate, 32 Pa.Super.Ct. 504.

[68] Ralston v. Easter, 43 App.D.C. 513.

[69] Curlett v. Emmons, 9 Del.Ch. 62, 85 A. 1079.

[70] Woodard v. Wright, 82 Cal. 202, 22 P. 1118; Condit v. Maxwell, 142 Mo. 266, 44 S.W. 467; Wiley v. Morris, 39 N.J.Eq. 97; Dilworth's Lessee v. Sinderling, 1 Bin., Pa., 488, 2 Am.Dec. 469. But where the trustee has had personal use of the trust property, he may not be allowed for improvements which he has put upon it. Bradford v. Clayton, Ky., 39 S.W. 40. And if the improvements are unnecessary, the trustee will not be reimbursed. Booth v. Bradford, 114 Iowa 562, 87 N.W. 685. Myers v. Myers, 2 McCord, Eq., S.C., 214, 16 Am.Dec. 648.

[71] In re Nesmith, 140 N.Y. 609, 35 N.E. 942.

[72] McDowell v. Caldwell, 2 McCord, Eq., S.C., 43, 16 Am.Dec. 635.

[73] Foscue v. Lyon, 55 Ala. 440; Ellig v. Naglee, 9 Cal. 683; Mallory v. Clark, 9 Abb.Prac., N.Y., 358; In re King's Estate, 9 Pa.Co.Ct.R. 74; In re Crane's Estate, 174 Pa. 613, 34 A. 348.

an outstanding claim against trust property [74] or to remove an encumbrance therefrom, [75] or for the purpose of improving the trust property.[76] In these cases the trust estate has had the benefit of the trustee's money, and it is equitable that the income accruing after the advance should be used for the purpose of making the trustee whole. But it has been held that a trustee has no lien upon the income of a trust for reimbursement on account of a loan to the cestui que trust, [77] or because of payments made to the beneficiary when no income was due to the cestui que trust.[78]

Whether a trustee who has advanced money for the benefit of the cestui shall be entitled to interest upon the sum advanced, as well as to reimbursement for the principal, is within the discretion of the court of chancery.[79] The trust instrument may direct that the trustee be paid interest on advances, in which case there will, of course, be no doubt concerning his rights.[80] Usually the courts have allowed simple interest to trustees who have made advances and have conducted the trust with prudence and honesty.[81] Occasionally courts have taken the attitude that there should be no interest allowed where the advancement was unnecessary because of the existence of trust funds in the hands of the trustee, [82] or have repudiated altogether the right of the trustee to receive interest on advances.[83] A trustee guilty of misconduct may be denied interest on money advanced during

---

[74] Wiswall v. Stewart, 32 Ala. 433, 70 Am.Dec. 549; McClanahan's Heirs v. Henderson's Heirs, 2 A. K. Marsh., Ky., 388, 12 Am.Dec. 412.

[75] Harrison v. Mock, 16 Ala. 616; Garvey v. New York Life Ins. & Trust Co., 54 Hun 637, 7 N.Y.S. 818.

[76] Pratt v. Thornton, 28 Me. 355, 48 Am.Dec. 492. In Wright v. Chilcott, 61 Or. 561, 122 P. 765, one declared a resulting trustee was allowed the amount expended for improvements, which added to the permanent value of the land, and for taxes.

[77] Abbott v. Foote, 146 Mass. 333, 15 N.E. 773, 4 Am.St.Rep. 314.

[78] In re Jones' Estate, 10 N.Y.St. Rep. 176; In re Odell's Estate, Sur., 2 N.Y.S. 752.

[79] Turner v. Turner, 44 Ark. 25.

[80] Booth v. Bradford, 114 Iowa 562, 87 N.W. 685.

[81] Pettingill v. Pettingill, 60 Me. 411; Urann v. Coates, 117 Mass. 41; Cook v. Lowry, 29 Hun, N.Y., 20; Evertson v. Tappen, 5 Johns.Ch., N.Y., 497; Dilworth's Lessee v. Sinderling, 1 Bin., Pa., 488, 2 Am.Dec. 469; Appeal of Carpenter, 2 Grant, Cas., Pa., 381; Jenckes v. Cook, 10 R.I. 215; Yost v. Critcher, 112 Va. 870, 72 S.E. 594; Fisk v. Brunette, 30 Wis. 102.

[82] Cook v. Lowry, 95 N.Y. 103.

[83] Appeal of Dexter, 147 Pa. 410, 23 A. 604.

the conduct of the trust.[84] In rare instances has compound interest been allowed.[85]

An obligation of the cestui que trust running to the trustee, but which arose prior to the existence of the trust, is not ordinarily a proper item of credit in behalf of the trustee in his account.[86] The trustee is entitled to credits which arise in the administration of the trust, but to none other. However, if the trust is for the purpose of paying the debts of the settlor, and the trustee is one of the creditors, he may credit himself with the amount of the debt due him.[87]

Whether the trustee may receive the costs of the accounting as an item of credit is within the discretion of chancery.[88] Usually a trustee who has been guilty of no bad faith or misconduct will be allowed the costs of the accounting.[89] But bad faith or malfeasance by the trustee may cause equity to charge the costs to him personally.[90] In some cases chancery has exercised its discretion by dividing the costs between the parties to the account.[91] Whether the costs of the accounting should be paid out of the income or out of the capital of the estate, assuming that they are to be paid from the trust funds, depends upon the object of the accounting. In the case of an annual accounting, primarily for the benefit of the immediate cestuis que trust, the income should bear the expense.[92] But where both rights of life tenant and remainderman are involved, the costs should be apportioned between capital and income.[93]

---

[84] Adams v. Lambard, 80 Cal. 426, 22 P. 180.

[85] Barrell v. Joy, 16 Mass. 221.

[86] Angell v. Jewett, 58 Ill.App. 596; Knowles v. Goodrich, 60 Ill.App. 506; Willis v. Clymer, 66 N.J.Eq. 284, 57 A. 803.

[87] Smith v. Miller, 98 Va. 535, 37 S.E. 10.

[88] In re Selleck, 111 N.Y. 284, 19 N.E. 66. See, also N.Y.Code Civ.Proc. §§ 2746, 2747.

[89] Lape's Adm'r v. Taylor's Trustee, Ky., 23 S.W. 960; McCloskey v. Bowden, 82 N.J.Eq. 410, 89 A. 528; Appeal of Lowrie, 1 Grant, Cas., Pa., 373; Appeal of Graver, 50 Pa. 189. In Re Starr, N.J.Prerog., 103 A. 392, a trustee whose account was unsuccessfully attacked was allowed a counsel fee.

[90] In re Howell, 215 N.Y. 466, 109 N.E. 572, Ann.Cas.1917A, 527; Harris v. Sheldon, Pa., 16 A. 828; In re Carr's Estate, 24 Pa.Super.Ct. 369; In re Brooke's Estate, 36 Pa.Super.Ct. 332. Thus, a trustee who is removed for fraud is not entitled to charge the costs of the accounting to the trust fund. Cornet v. Cornet, 269 Mo. 298, 190 S.W. 333.

[91] Lyon v. Foscue, 60 Ala. 468; In re Old's Estate, 150 Pa. 529, 24 A. 752.

[92] In re Long Island Loan & Trust Co., 79 Misc. 176, 140 N.Y.S. 752.

[93] In re Cooper, 82 Misc. 324, 144 N.Y.S. 189.

Where an expense actually incurred in the administration of the trust has arisen because of the carelessness of the trustee, or was unnecessary and extravagant, the trustee will not be allowed to credit himself with the amount thus spent. Thus, where the trustee unnecessarily keeps a vehicle for the administration of the trust duties,[94] or pays taxes which are not due,[95] or mingles the trust funds with his own property so that no separate allowance for taxes can be made,[96] he will not be entitled to reimbursement.

Trustee's Lien

For the purpose of protecting the trustee's right to reimbursement for expenditures of the kinds named above the trustee is given a lien on the trust property.[97] "The expenses of a trustee in the execution of the trust, are a lien upon the estate; and he will not be compelled to part with the property, until his disbursements are paid. * * * Trustees have an inherent equitable right to be reimbursed all expenses which they reasonably incur in the execution of the trust, and it is immaterial that there are no provisions for such expenses in the instrument of trust. If a person undertakes an office for another in relation to property, he has a natural right to be reimbursed all the money necessarily expended in the performance of the duty."[98]

Thus, a trustee who has expended his own funds for needful repairs and improvements on the trust property,[99] or for the payment of taxes on the trust estate,[1] or to purchase a title outstanding against the trust,[2] or to make proper payments directly to the cestui,[3] is entitled to hold the trust property as

---

[94] Eysaman v. Nelson, 79 Misc. 304, 140 N.Y.S. 183.

[95] Lorenz v. Weller, 267 Ill. 230, 108 N.E. 306.

[96] Elmer v. Loper, 25 N.J.Eq. 475.

[97] Jones v. Dawson, 19 Ala. 672; King v. Cushman, 41 Ill. 31, 89 Am. Dec. 366; Smith v. Walker, 49 Iowa 289; Feldman v. Preston, 194 Mich. 352, 160 N.W. 655; Fearn v. Mayers, 53 Miss. 458; Matthews v. McPherson, 65 N.C. 189. In Bay Biscayne Co. v. Baile, 73 Fla. 1120, 75 So. 860, the trustee was accorded a lien on the trust property for costs, disbursements, and counsel fees in litigation in defense of the trust.

[98] Rensselaer & S. R. Co. v. Miller, 47 Vt. 146, 152.

[99] Woodard v. Wright, 82 Cal. 202, 22 P. 1118; Turton v. Grant, 86 N.J. Eq. 191, 96 A. 993.

[1] Bourquin v. Bourquin, 120 Ga. 115, 47 S.E. 639.

[2] King v. Cushman, 41 Ill. 31, 89 Am.Dec. 366; Bennett v. Chandler, 199 Ill. 97, 64 N.E. 1052.

[3] Smith v. Greeley, 67 N.H. 377, 30 A. 413.

security for repayment and to cause the property to be sold to satisfy his lien by bringing a bill in equity. But where a trustee is directed by the trust instrument to pay the income of the trust property to the cestui que trust only as it accrues, the trustee has no lien upon the trust property for reimbursement as to advances made to the beneficiary prior to accrual of such income.[4]

COMPENSATION OF THE TRUSTEE [5]

146. Under early English equity rules the trustee served without compensation, but in America the trustee is now generally allowed pay for his work unless he agreed to serve without remuneration.

The amount of compensation is in the discretion of chancery, in the absence of statute or controlling term in the trust instrument or in an agreement between settlor or beneficiaries and trustee. Corporate trustees have fee schedules based on a percentage of the value of the property handled by them.

In many states there are statutes or court rules prescribing the commissions which are to be allowed to trustees.

The amount of property and work involved and the fidelity and efficiency of the trustee will be considered by the court in determining the compensation to be awarded. Usually a percentage upon the amount of property managed by the trustee is awarded, rather than a lump sum.

The trustee may waive his right to compensation or forfeit it by committing a breach of trust.

Joint trustees usually receive but a single commission, which is divided between them in proportion to the amount of work done by each. The compensation due to a trusteeship is divided between successive trustees in proportion to the value of the services rendered by each. A trustee who is also an executor with respect to the same property will receive double compensation, if the offices are distinct, but not if he performs but one function, though under two titles.

Closely akin to the right of the trustee to be credited on the accounting with the amount of the trust funds properly expended on behalf of the trust, and to his corresponding right to be reimbursed for necessary advances, is the right of the trustee to be paid a reasonable sum for his time and trouble. Is a trustee entitled to compensation? Will chancery allow him pay for his services in administering the trust? It was the early rule in

[4] Loring v. Salisbury Mills, 125 Mass. 138.
[5] Restatement, Trusts, § 242.

§ 146   COMPENSATION OF THE TRUSTEE   473

England that a trustee would be allowed no remuneration. In Robinson v. Pett [6] Lord Chancellor Talbot said: "It is an established rule that a trustee, executor, or administrator, shall have no allowance for his care and trouble; the reason of which seems to be, for that on these pretences, if allowed, the trust estate might be loaded, and rendered of little value. Besides, the great difficulty there might be in settling and adjusting the quantum of such allowance, especially as one man's time may be more valuable than that of another; and there can be no hardship in this respect upon any trustee, who may choose whether he will accept the trust, or not." In England now a provision in the instrument for compensation will be respected, and the court may under some circumstances allow a trustee compensation.[7]

Some American courts of chancery were inclined during the early history of the country to refuse compensation to trustees,[8] but the modern rule in this country is to give the trustee a reasonable remuneration for his skill and industry.[9] In all American states the rule of compensation is now established, either by

[6] 3 P.Wms. 249, 251.

[7] Re Thorley, [1891] 2 Ch. 613; Re Freeman, 37 Ch.D. 148; Trustee Act of 1925, § 42.

[8] Brooks v. Egbert, 2 Del.Ch. 83; State v. Platt, 4 Har., Del., 154; Constant v. Matteson, 22 Ill. 546; Huggins v. Rider, 77 Ill. 360; Cook v. Gilmore, 133 Ill. 139, 24 N.E. 524; Miles v. Bacon, 4 J.J.Marsh., Ky., 457; Warbass v. Armstrong, 10 N.J. Eq. 263; Green v. Winter, 1 Johns. Ch., N.Y., 37, 7 Am.Dec. 475; Boyd v. Hawkins, 17 N.C. 195, 2 Dev.Eq. 195; Gilbert v. Sutliff, 3 Ohio St. 129. One argument for denying the trustee compensation was that a right to pay gave him conflicting interests and encouraged disloyalty. He would be tempted to operate the trust so as to magnify his fees instead of administering it solely with the interest of the cestui in mind.

[9] Clark v. Platt, 30 Conn. 282; Muscogee Lumber Co. v. Hyer, 18 Fla. 698, 43 Am.Rep. 332; Arnold v. Allen, 173 Ill. 229, 50 N.E. 704; Jarrett v. Johnson, 116 Ill.App. 592; Compher v. Browning, 219 Ill. 429, 76 N.E. 678, 109 Am.St.Rep. 346; Knight v. Knight, 142 Ill.App. 62; Hendrix's Ex'rs v. Hardin, 5 Ky. Law Rep. 333; Cotton v. Graham, 10 Ky.Law Rep. 402; Patrick v. Patrick, 135 Ky. 307, 122 S.W. 159; Devilbiss v. Bennett, 70 Md. 554, 17 A. 502; Rathbun v. Colton, 15 Pick., Mass., 471; Schwarz v. Wendell, Walk.Ch., Mich., 267; Maginn v. Green, 67 Mo.App. 616; Olson v. Lamb, 56 Neb. 104, 76 N.W. 433, 71 Am.St.Rep. 670; Marston v. Marston, 21 N.H. 491; Boyd v. Hawkins, 17 N.C. 329, 2 Dev.Eq. 329; Raiford v. Raiford, 41 N.C. 490, 6 Ired.Eq. 490; Appeal of Heckert, 24 Pa. 482; In re Rothschild's Assigned Estate, 47 Pa.Super.Ct. 234; Sartor v. Newberry Land & Security Co., 104 S.C. 184, 88 S.E. 467; Leach v. Cowan, 125 Tenn. 182, 140 S.W. 1070, Ann. Cas.1913C, 188; Miller v. Beverleys, 4 Hen. & M., Va., 415. For a discussion of the abolition of the common-law rule and the reasons for such action, see Schriver v. Frommel, 183 Ky. 597, 210 S.W. 165.

rule of equity or by statute. But a passive trustee is entitled to no compensation, since he is a mere dummy.[10] It is not necessary, in order that a trustee should have the right to remuneration for his labors, that there should be any stipulation for remuneration in the trust instrument.[11] Compensation is provided by the rules of equity or by statute rather than through a direction of the settlor.

Compensation Fixed by Trust Instrument

The matter of compensation may be settled by the express provisions of the trust instrument. If the settlor states that the trustee shall receive a certain amount for his services, the trustee will be deemed to have acquiesced in such provision, if he accepts and enters upon the trust.[12] The trust instrument may prohibit any compensation.[13] It may provide for a reasonable compensation, in which case the court is not confined by the statutory allowances.[14] A valid agreement inter vivos may, of course, be made between settlor and trustee with respect to the latter's compensation.[15] Corporate trustees now have schedules of fees. The ordinary charge is a percentage of income and capital. Its size depends on the type of property to be handled, the duration of the trust, and the value of the estate. Larger percentages are charged for the smaller estates.[16]

---

[10] Wetmore v. Brown, 37 Barb., N.Y., 133.

Neither a trustee de son tort, nor any other kind of a constructive trustee, is entitled to compensation. Hale v. Cox, 240 Ala. 622, 200 So. 772.

[11] Burr v. McEwen, Fed.Cas.No.2,-193; Ringgold v. Ringgold, 1 Har. & G., Md., 11, 18 Am.Dec. 250; Bentley v. Shreve, 2 Md.Ch. 215; Wagstaffe v. Lowerre, 23 Barb., N.Y., 209; Sherrill v. Shuford, 41 N.C. 228, 6 Ired.Eq. 228; Fox v. Weckerly, 9 Leg.Int., Pa., 43.

[12] Biscoe v. State, 23 Ark. 592; In re Hanson's Estate, 159 Cal. 401, 114 P. 810; Jarrett v. Johnson, 216 Ill. 212, 74 N.E. 756; Gossom's Adm'r v. Gossom, 142 Ky. 118, 133 S.W. 1162; Schriver v. Frommel, 183 Ky. 597, 210 S.W. 165; Thomas v. Thomas, 97 Miss. 697, 53 So. 630; Opplger v. Sutton, 50 Mo.App. 348; Bigelow v. Tilden, 52 App.Div. 390, 65 N.Y.S. 140; In re Rowe, 42 Misc. 172, 86 N.Y.S. 253; Steinway v. Steinway, 197 N.Y. 522, 90 N.E. 1166; College of Charleston v. Willingham, 13 Rich. Eq., S.C., 195; Southern Ry. Co. v. Glenn's Adm'r, 98 Va. 309, 36 S.E. 395. Where the settlor fixes the compensation, the court may increase it, where it deems such action equitable. In re Battin's Estate, 89 N.J.Eq. 144, 104 A. 434.

[13] Wilson v. Biggama, 73 Wash. 444, 132 P. 43.

[14] See Guide to Trust Fees, Trust Division of the American Bankers Association, 1932.

[15] In re Schell, 53 N.Y. 263.

[16] Louisville Trust Co. v. Warren, 66 S.W. 644, 23 Ky.Law Rep. 2118.

§ 146   COMPENSATION OF THE TRUSTEE   475

The trustee's compensation may likewise be fixed by contract between the trustee and the cestui que trust. An agreement upon that subject between those parties will, if fairly made, be enforced by the courts.[17]

In the absence of stipulation in the trust instrument, or binding contract between the parties, or statutory regulation, the amount of the remuneration is within the discretion of the court of equity.[18] The compensation must be such as is allowed by chancery.[19] The trustee has no right to deduct from the trust funds such allowance as he deems proper.[20] His right to receive compensation must be enforced in equity, and cannot be made the basis of an action of assumpsit.[21]

Controlling Statutes

Frequently statutes control the courts in the award of compensation to trustees.[22] No attempt can be made here to give

---

[17] Bowker v. Pierce, 130 Mass. 262; Ladd v. Pigott, 215 Mo. 361, 114 S.W. 984; Green v. Jones, 78 N.C. 265; Henry v. Hilliard, 157 N.C. 572, 73 S. E. 98. Where for thirteen years the cestuis que trust have received statements showing the deduction of 10 per cent. commissions and have raised no objection, they will not be heard to object. American Colonization Soc. v. Latrobe, 132 Md. 524, 104 A. 120.

[18] Magruder v. Drury, 37 App.D.C. 519; Weiderhold v. Mathis, 204 Ill. App. 3; Jenkins v. Whyte, 62 Md. 427; Taylor v. Denny, 118 Md. 124, 84 A. 369; White v. Ditson, 140 Mass. 351, 4 N.E. 606, 54 Am.Rep. 473; Rothschild v. Dickinson, 169 Mich. 200, 134 N.W. 1035; Appeal of Fidelity & Deposit Co. of Maryland, 172 Mich. 600, 138 N.W. 205; Henderson v. Sherman, 47 Mich. 267, 11 N. W. 153; Marsh v. Marsh, 82 N.J.Eq. 176, 87 A. 91; Appeal of Heckert, 24 Pa. 482.

[19] Robinson v. Tower, 95 Neb. 198, 145 N.W. 348; Lathrop v. Smalley's Ex'rs, 23 N.J.Eq. 192; Beard v. Beard, 140 N.Y. 260, 35 N.E. 488.

[20] In re Mylin's Estate, 32 Pa. Super.Ct. 504. A withdrawal of compensation without order of court constitutes conversion. Robinson v. Tower, 95 Neb. 198, 145 N.W. 348.

[21] Hazard v. Coyle, 26 R.I. 361, 58 A. 987.

[22] In re Prescott's Estate, 179 Cal. 192, 175 P. 895; Lowe v. Morris, 13 Ga. 165; Burney v. Spear, 17 Ga. 223; Warbass v. Armstrong, 10 N. J.Eq. 263; In re New Jersey Title Guarantee & Trust Co., 76 N.J.Eq. 293, 75 A. 232; In re Allen, 96 N.Y. 327; Disbrow v. Disbrow, 46 App. Div. 111, 61 N.Y.S. 614, affirmed 167 N.Y. 606, 60 N.E. 1110; In re Johnson, 170 N.Y. 139, 63 N.E. 63; Conger v. Conger, 185 N.Y. 554, 77 N.E. 1184; Robertson v. De Brulatour, 188 N.Y. 301, 80 N.E. 938; In re Todd, 64 App.Div. 435, 72 N.Y.S. 277; Chisolm v. Hamersley, 114 App.Div. 565, 100 N.Y.S. 38; Whitehead v. Draper, 132 App.Div. 799, 117 N.Y.S. 539; In re Ziegler's Estate, 85 Misc. 673, 148 N.Y.S. 1055; In re Dimond's Estate, Sur., 156 N.Y.S. 268; Moffett v. Eames, Sup., 143 N.Y.S. 357.

the details of the various provisions found in the statute books on this subject.[23]

Basis of Compensation

Where the court is free to fix the compensation of the trustee, not being bound by statute, it will consider a variety of facts. The value of the trust estate,[24] the responsibility involved and the amount of work done,[25] the fidelity with which the trustee has acted,[26] any unusual skill or training which he may possess,[27] the success of his services,[28] are all relevant matters. The court may also consider the pay usually given to agents employed to do similar work.[29] If the trust instrument gives the trustee power to fix his own compensation, the court will nevertheless review the exercise of such discretion.[30] Compensation is ordinarily awarded by way of commissions on the amount received and paid out,[31] but may be made in a gross or lump sum.[32]

If the trustee has merely received the property, he will be entitled to one-half the usual commission.[34] The collection of in-

---

[23] Some statutes merely give discretion to the court to fix fees for trustees. Others prescribe a schedule. See, for example, Kan.L.1939, c. 180, § 147; Ky.L.1938, c. 129; La.Acts 1938, No. 81, §§ 79-80; Md.L.1939, c. 100; Mich.Pub.Acts 1939, No. 288, c. IV, §§ 33-34; N.J.S.A. 3:11-2; N. J.L.1940, c. 172; N. Y. Real Property Law, § 111, Personal Property Law, § 20; N.Y.Surrogate's Court Act, § 285; N.Y.Civil Practice Act, §§ 1548-1548a; N.D.L.1935, c. 250, § 20.

[24] Louisville, N. A. & C. Ry. Co. v. Hubbard, 116 Ind. 193, 18 N.E. 611.

[25] Appeal of Barclay, 2 Walk., Pa., 17; Appeal of Duval, 38 Pa. 112; In re Tidball's Estate, 29 Pa.Super.Ct. 363; In re Harrison's Estate, 217 Pa. 207, 66 A. 354.

[26] Barney v. Saunders, 16 How. 535, 14 L.Ed. 1047.

[27] Follansbee v. Outhet, 182 Ill.App. 213.

[28] Fleming v. Wilson, 6 Bush, Ky., 610; Appeal of Wagner, 3 Walk., Pa., 130. The amount of interest earned is important. In re May's Estate, 197 Mo.App. 555, 196 S.W. 1039.

[29] Barrell v. Joy, 16 Mass. 221.

[30] Ross v. Conwell, 7 Ind.App. 375, 34 N.E. 752.

[31] Girard Trust Co. v. McKinley-Lanning Loan & Trust Co., C.C.Pa., 143 F. 355; Woodruff v. Snedecor, 68 Ala. 437; United States Bank v. Huth, 4 B.Mon., Ky., 423; Ames v. Scudder, 83 Mo. 189; Phœnix v. Livingston, 101 N.Y. 451, 5 N.E. 70; In re Willets, 112 N.Y. 289, 19 N.E. 690; Weisel v. Cobb, 118 N.C. 11, 24 S.E. 782; Hazard v. Coyle, 26 R.I. 361, 58 A. 987.

[32] Appeal of Perkins, 108 Pa. 314, 56 Am.Rep. 208.

[34] Palmer v. Dunham, 53 Hun. 637, 6 N.Y.S. 262; Foote v. Bruggerhof, 66 Hun 406, 21 N.Y.S. 509.

§ 146

terest [35] and other income [36] of trust property should be considered in reckoning the compensation of the trustee. Where the trust is one to sell property and deliver the proceeds to the beneficiaries, the basis for computing the commissions is the sale price which has been received and disbursed.[37] The trustee will be compensated only for the performance of his trust duties,[38] and not for committing wrongful acts [39] or for performing merely ministerial or formal functions.[40] Thus, the formal act of turning over the trust property to a successor does not entitle the trustee to commissions.[41]

Where a trustee is obliged to account annually,[42] or to make payments to the cestui annually,[43] he is entitled to retain his commissions each year; but annual rests are not allowed in the computation of commissions, where such annual payments or accountings are not required.[44] When a commission is to be allowed, equity exercises a large discretion as to the amount. An examination of a number of cases in which the matter was not controlled by statute shows that the percentages allowed varied from one to ten per cent. upon the amount received and disbursed.[45]

[35] Kennedy v. Dickey, 99 Md. 295, 57 A. 621.

[36] Longley v. Hall, 11 Pick., Mass., 120; Appeal of McCauseland, 38 Pa. 466.

[37] Waring v. Darnall, 10 Gill & J., Md., 126; Dorsett v. Houlihan, 95 Ga. 550, 22 S.E. 290; McKee v. Weeden, 1 App.Div. 583, 37 N.Y.S. 465; Ingram v. Kirkpatrick, 43 N.C. 62, 8 Ired.Eq. 62; In re Wistar's Estate, 125 Pa. 526, 17 A. 460; Appeal of Carrier, 79 Pa. 230; Appeal of Shunk, 2 Pa. 304.

[38] Tracy v. Gravois R. Co., 84 Mo. 210; Brown v. Silsby, 10 N.H. 521.

[39] Appeal of Stearly, 38 Pa. 525; Harris v. Sheldon, Pa., 16 A. 828.

[40] Jenkins v. Whyte, 62 Md. 427; Parker v. Hill, 185 Mass. 14, 69 N.E. 336; Appeal of Hemphill, 18 Pa. 303.

[41] Whitehead v. Draper, 132 App. Div. 799, 117 N.Y.S. 539.

[42] In re Meserole, 36 Hun, N.Y., 298; Hancox v. Meeker, 95 N.Y. 528.

[43] In re Roberts' Will, 40 Misc. 512, 82 N.Y.S. 805.

[44] Hosack v. Rogers, 9 Paige, N.Y., 461; Brush v. Smith, 1 Dem.Sur., N. Y., 477.

[45] Marks v. Semple, 111 Ala. 637, 20 So. 791 (lump sum allowed); Wilder v. Hast, 96 S.W. 1106, 29 Ky.Law Rep. 1181 (5 per cent. allowed); Central Trust Co. v. Johnson, 74 S.W. 663, 25 Ky.Law Rep. 55 (5 per cent. on income and 1½ per cent. on principal); Williams v. Mosher, 6 Gill, Md., 454 (5 per cent.); Abell v. Brady, 79 Md. 94, 28 A. 817 (5 per cent.); Jones v. Day, 102 Md. 99, 62 A. 364 (2½ per cent.); Berry v. Stigall, 125 Mo.App. 264, 102 S.W. 585 (5 per cent.); Ladd v. Pigott, 215 Mo. 361, 114 S.W. 984; Wiegand v. Woerner, 155 Mo.App. 227, 134 S. W. 596 (lump sum); Babbitt v. Fidelity Trust Co., 72 N.J.Eq. 745, 66 A. 1076 (4 per cent.); Fisher v. Fisher,

Compensation may, in the discretion of equity, be allowed before the end of the trust.[46] If a trustee dies prior to the termination of his duties, the court may make an allowance for the reasonable value of his services.[47]

If the work of the trustee has been unusually arduous, difficult, or lengthy, chancery may make him an extra allowance;[48] but additional compensation will not be given for the performance of the ordinary duties of the trustee.[49]

A trustee has a lien on the trust property for the amount due him for compensation for his services.[50]

Source of Payment

Whether the compensation of the trustee should be paid out of the capital of the trust fund or out of the income thereof depends upon the nature of the trustee's duties, the character of the trust fund, and the circumstances of the accounting at which the compensation is allowed. Ordinarily the income bears the current expenses of operation, which include the commissions of the trustee;[51] but in exceptional cases the corpus of the fund has

---

170 N.C. 378, 87 S.E. 113 (5 per cent.); Appeal of Marsteller, 4 Watts, Pa., 267 (10 per cent.); Appeal of Lukens, 47 Pa. 356 (1½ per cent.); In re Hemphill's Estate, 9 Phila., Pa., 486 (1¼ per cent.); In re Lafferty's Estate, 5 Pa.Dist.R. 75 (3½ per cent.); In re Bosler's Estate, 161 Pa. 457, 29 A. 57 (5 per cent.); In re Dorrance's Estate, 186 Pa. 64, 40 A. 149 (1 per cent.); In re McCallum's Estate, 211 Pa. 205, 60 A. 903 (5 per cent.); In re McKinney's Estate, 260 Pa. 123, 103 A. 590 (5 per cent.); Cobb v. Fant, 36 S.C. 1, 14 S.E. 959 (2½ per cent. for receiving and 2½ per cent. for paying over); Whitehead v. Whitehead, 85 Va. 870, 9 S.E. 10 (8 per cent.); Thom's Ex'r v. Thom, 95 Va. 413, 28 S.E. 583 (5 per cent. excessive); Darling's Ex'r v. Cumming, 111 Va. 637, 69 S.E. 940 (5 per cent.).

[46] In re Thouron's Estate, 182 Pa. 126, 37 A. 861.

[47] Bentley v. Shreve, 2 Md.Ch. 215; Windener v. Fay, 51 Md. 273.

[48] Grimball v. Cruse, 70 Ala. 534; Clark v. Anderson, 13 Bush, Ky., 111; In re Holden, 58 Hun, 611, 12 N.Y.S. 842, reversed in 126 N.Y. 589, 27 N.E. 1063; In re Gill, 21 Misc. 281, 47 N.Y. S. 706; Appeal of Perkins, 108 Pa. 314, 56 Am.Rep. 208; In re Ashman's Estate, 218 Pa. 509, 67 A. 841.

[49] Fanning v. Main, 77 Conn. 94, 58 A. 472; Parkhill v. Doggett, Iowa, 136 N.W. 665; Doom v. Howard, 64 S.W. 469, 23 Ky.Law Rep. 884; Blake v. Pegram, 101 Mass. 592; In re Froelich, 122 App.Div. 440, 107 N.Y.S. 173; In re Young, 15 App.Div. 285, 44 N.Y. S. 585; In re Brennan's Estate, 215 Pa. 272, 64 A. 537; Southern Ry. Co. v. Glenn's Adm'r, 98 Va. 309, 36 S. E. 395.

[50] Premier Steel Co. v. Yandes, 139 Ind. 307, 38 N.E. 849.

[51] Morgan v. Shields, 4 Ky.Law Rep. 904; Offutt v. Divine's Ex'r, Ky., 53 S.W. 816; Parker v. Ames, 121 Mass. 220; In re Thompson's Estate,

been obliged to bear the expense of compensating the trustee.[52] Under no circumstances is there a duty upon the settlor to pay the trustee's compensation,[53] unless the settlor has expressly contracted to do so. Where the remainder consists of two parts, one real property to be conveyed to the heirs and the other personal property to be delivered to the next of kin, and the commissions are to be charged against this corpus, they should be apportioned between the real and personal property.[54]

The rules regarding the source from which the trustee's compensation should be paid are well stated by a Pennsylvania court:[55] "In the case of a continuous trust, one duty of which is to preserve the fund, as a source of periodic interest, dividends, rents, etc., the authorities do not recognize a right in the trustee, except in extraordinary circumstances, or when the instrument by which the trust is created so indicates, to diminish the fund which is to create the income during the life of the trust. For services rendered by way of collecting and paying over the income, the compensation is a fit charge upon the income and is properly deducted from it. But the labor, care and responsibility pertaining to the conservation of the capital itself are properly a charge on it, and are to be deducted from it when the trust expires, or the particular trustee's relation to it ends. 'The rule which may be safely deduced from the cases' is 'that commissions upon the corpus of a trust estate are never allowable except when the fund is in the course of distribution. The reason is inherent in the nature of a trust. Its purpose is to preserve, and it may be of unlimited duration, while that of administration is to divide, and implies dispatch. Hence, if commissions upon the capital are awarded to the successive trustees who may be called to its management, the fund, instead of being intact, may be absorbed in the payment of its custodians.' * * * So far as we have been able to discover, by a somewhat extended examination of cases, the commission on the corpus is never allowed until the trust has ended, or, at least, the particular trustee has ceased to be such."

Exceptional cases may occur where it is impossible to pay the commissions out of the income of the trust estate, or where such

Sur., 1 N.Y.S. 213; Spangler's Estate, 21 Pa. 335.

[52] Woodruff v. New York, L. E. & W. R. Co., 129 N.Y. 27, 29 N.E. 251; In re Kelsey's Estate, 89 Misc. 701, 153 N.Y.S. 1095; Hubbard v. Fisher, 25 Vt. 539.

[53] Patton v. Cone, 1 Lea, Tenn., 14.

[54] Grimball v. Cruse, 70 Ala. 534.

[55] In re Bosler's Estate, 161 Pa. 457, 462, 463, 29 A. 57.

action is inequitable. "If the commissions can be paid out of the income or interest of the capital, they should be so paid. Cases may occur, however, where this cannot be done, and then the commissions may be paid out of the body of the fund. Suppose a trustee is appointed for one year to the management of a large and troublesome property, occupying much of his time and care, and yet from some unavoidable cause (not arising from fault of his) no income is produced by it during the period of his trust, and up to the time of its termination. At his settlement with the cestui que trust, he would certainly be allowed compensation out of the corpus of the fund, or there would be no remedy for his right." [56]

Waiver or Loss

The trustee's right to receive compensation may be lost, either voluntarily or involuntarily. He may waive his claim to commissions, or he may forfeit his right to be paid for his services.

The possibility of waiver is obvious. The trustee may expressly agree to serve without compensation,[57] or, having earned compensation, he may forego it and decline to receive pay for his work.[58] "The statute allows commissions to executors and trustees; but they may waive them, if they wish, and, if there be any evidence of a waiver, their legal representatives are in no position to dispute it."[59]

An express waiver of commissions in the past is no bar to the recovery of present commissions.[60] That a trustee declines to receive compensation at one time does not prevent him from demanding it at another time. It would seem that the mere failure to ask for commissions would not constitute a waiver

---

[56] Burney v. Spear, 17 Ga. 223, 225.

Because of the low rates of income on trusts at the present time, an effort has been made to procure court permission to charge a part of the trustee's fees to trust capital. But the courts have been loath to permit such action, in the absence of statute or special services rendered by the trustee to the owners of the capital interest, at least until the end of the trust. Bridgeport-City Trust Co. v. First Nat. Bank & Trust Co., 124 Conn. 472, 200 A. 809, 117 A.L.R. 1148.

[57] Ridgely v. Gittings, 2 Har. & G., Md., 58.

[58] Barry v. Barry, 1 Md.Ch. 20; Ten Broeck v. Fidelity Trust & Safety Vault Co., 88 Ky. 242, 10 S.W. 798; Cook v. Stockwell, 206 N.Y. 481, 100 N.E. 131, Ann.Cas.1914B, 491; In re Wiener's Estate, 4 Pa.Dist.R. 422.

[59] Cook v. Stockwell, 206 N.Y. 481, 484, 100 N.E. 131, Ann.Cas.1914B, 491.

[60] Denmead v. Denmead, 62 Md. 321.

of them, in the absence of action on the part of the cestuis que trust sufficient to estop the trustee.[61] But the courts of New York have been inclined to regard the failure to claim commissions as evidence of a waiver of them.[62] "Where, through a long series of years, trustees voluntarily pay the net income from a trust fund to the beneficiary as the full net income thereon, it is a waiver by such trustees of their commissions." [63]

It is well settled that chancery may deprive a trustee of his commissions in cases where he has been guilty of neglect of duty or positive wrongdoing in office.[64] What conduct is sufficient warrant for refusing the trustee compensation rests within the discretion of the court. There may be a reduction of compensation, as well as a total deprivation.[65] The specific causes for the forfeiture of the right to compensation have been numerous, as, for example, general cases of breach of trust,[66] ordinary negligence,[67] gross negligence,[68] repudiation of the trust,[69] misappropriation of the trust funds,[70] failure to keep proper

---

[61] Phillips v. Burton, 107 Ky. 88, 52 S.W. 1064, 21 Ky.Law Rep. 720; Appeal of Wister, 86 Pa. 160.

[62] In re Harper, 27 Misc. 471, 59 N.Y.S. 373; Spencer v. Spencer, 38 App.Div. 403, 56 N.Y.S. 460; In re Haskin, 49 Misc. 177, 98 N.Y.S. 926; Olcott v. Baldwin, 190 N.Y. 99, 82 N.E. 748. The retention of a part only of the commission earned is a waiver of the balance. In re Schaefer, 178 App.Div. 117, 165 N.Y.S. 19, affirmed 222 N.Y. 533, 118 N.E. 1076.

[63] Olcott v. Baldwin, 190 N.Y. 99, 109, 82 N.E. 748.

[64] Jarrett v. Johnson, 116 Ill.App. 592; Clark v. Clark, 87 N.J.Eq. 504, 101 A. 300.

[65] Diffenderffer v. Winder, 3 Gill & J., Md., 311.

[66] Comingor v. Louisville Trust Co., 128 Ky. 697, 108 S.W. 950, 33 Ky.Law Rep. 53, 129 Am.St.Rep. 322; Newton v. Rebenack, 90 Mo.App. 650; Judge of Probate v. Jackson, 58 N.H. 458; Moore v. Zabriskie, 18 N.J.Eq. 51; Dufford's Ex'r v. Smith, 46 N.J.Eq.

216, 18 A. 1052; In re Welling's Estate, 51 App.Div. 355, 64 N.Y.S. 1025; In re Swartswalter's Account, 4 Watts, Pa., 77; Fellows v. Loomis, 204 Pa. 227, 53 A. 999; In re Reich's Estate, 230 Pa. 55, 79 A. 151; Singleton v. Lowndes, 9 S.C. 465.

[67] In re Thompson's Estate, 101 Cal. 349, 35 P. 991, 36 P. 98, 508; Ralston v. Easter, 43 App.D.C. 513; In re Nagle's Estate, 12 Phila., Pa., 25.

[68] Ward v. Shire, 65 S.W. 8, 23 Ky. Law Rep. 1279.

[69] Pollard v. Lathrop, 12 Colo. 171, 20 P. 251; H. B. Cartwright & Bro. v. United States Bank & Trust Co., 23 N.M. 82, 167 P. 436; In re Greenfield's Estate, 24 Pa. 232; Whiteside v. Whiteside, 35 Pa.Super.Ct. 481; Hanna v. Clark, 204 Pa. 145, 53 A. 757; Stone v. Farnham, 22 R.I. 227, 47 A. 211; Fuller v. Abbe, 105 Wis. 235, 81 N.W. 401.

[70] Belknap v. Belknap, 5 Allen, Mass., 468; Harvey v. Schwettman, Mo.App., 180 S.W. 413; McCulloch v. Tomkins, 62 N.J.Eq. 262, 49 A.

records, [71] failure to account, [72] the rendition of a false account, [73] an improper investment, [74] failure to invest the trust funds, [75] refusal to obey the orders of the court, [76] mingling the trust property with private property, [77] removal from office for incompetence, [78] in some instances upon the resignation of the trustee, [79] and cases where the trustee has acted for his private benefit in administering the trust.[80] Mere lack of skill in administering the trust affairs, [81] or slight improprieties of conduct, [82] or errors of judgment, [83] will not ordinarily be regarded as ground for refusal to allow the trustee his commissions.

Co-trustees

Two or more trustees are, in the absence of statute, entitled to one commission only. This commission should be divided between them, in proportion to the amount of work done by each.

474; In re Lafferty's Estate, 5 Pa. Dist.R. 75.

[71] Welsh v. Brown, 50 N.J.Eq. 387, 26 A. 568.

[72] Folk v. Wind, 124 Mo.App. 577, 102 S.W. 1; Gilbert v. Sutliff, 3 Ohio St. 129; Ward v. Funsten, 86 Va. 359, 10 S.E. 415; but see Muckenfuss v. Heath, 1 Hill Eq., S.C., 182, contra.

[73] Elmer v. Loper, 25 N.J.Eq. 475.

[74] Aydelott v. Breeding, 111 Ky. 847, 64 S.W. 916, 23 Ky.Law Rep. 1146; In re Hart's Estate, 203 Pa. 496, 53 A. 370. But see Babbitt v. Fidelity Trust Co., 72 N.J.Eq. 745, 66 A. 1076, and In re Haskin, 111 App. Div. 754, 97 N.Y.S. 827, where it was held that there was no forfeiture if the bad investments resulted in no loss, or the loss was made good by the trustee.

[75] Warbass v. Armstrong, 10 N.J. Eq. 263; McKnight's Ex'rs v. Walsh, 23 N.J.Eq. 136.

[76] French v. Commercial Nat. Bank, 199 Ill. 213, 65 N.E. 252.

[77] Weakley v. Meriwether, 156 Ky. 304, 160 S.W. 1054; In re Hodges' Estate, 66 Vt. 70, 28 A. 663, 44 Am. St.Rep. 820; Beverley v. Miller, 6 Munf., Va., 99. But see In re Patrick's Estate, 162 Pa. 175, 29 A. 639, and Appeal of Biddle, 129 Pa. 26, 18 A. 474, in which mingling of the trust funds with other funds was held not to be sufficient ground for the forfeiture of commissions.

[78] In re Williamsburgh Trust Co., 60 Misc. 296, 113 N.Y.S. 276.

[79] In re Allen, 96 N.Y. 327. But see Linsly v. Bogert, 87 Hun 137, 33 N.Y.S. 975.

But the discharge of the trustee by the court is not necessarily ground for the refusal of commissions. In re Welscher's Estate, 3 Walk., Pa., 241.

[80] Gregg v. Gabbert, 62 Ark. 602, 37 S.W. 232; Loud v. Winchester, 52 Mich. 174, 17 N.W. 784; Royal v. Royal, 30 Or. 448, 47 P. 828, 48 P. 695.

[81] Appeal of Kilgore, Pa., 8 A. 441.

[82] Jacobus v. Munn, 37 N.J.Eq. 48.

[83] In re Johnston's Estate, 129 N.J. Eq. 104, 18 A.2d 274; In re Blodgett's Estate, 261 App.Div. 878, 25 N.Y.2d 39.

BOGERT TRUSTS 2D

The trustees are regarded as a unit which has earned compensation. The trusteeship is awarded one commission, and this is divided between the several trustees. "It is, however, said they are joint trustees. Grant it, and how does it change the attitude of the parties? By becoming joint trustees, each, no doubt, became vested with a legal right to perform one-half of the labor with his entire skill, and, on performing one-half of the duties of the trust, as between him and his cotrustee, he would be entitled to one-half of the compensation. But where he performs but one-third of the duties, he can surely have no claim to more than one-third of the emoluments, unless conceded by the beneficiary as a gratuity; but he can, in justice, have no claim to the earnings of his cotrustee over and above the sum he has himself earned." [84] In some states provision is made for commissions to each of several trustees in cases of large estates.[85]

Where two or more persons successively occupy the trusteeship, they should be compensated on a quantum meruit basis; that is, each should be paid the reasonable value of his services during his term of office. "The practice of allowing a reasonable compensation to the estate of a deceased trustee, who dies before the completion of the trust, is well settled and sanctioned by authority." [86] The succeeding trustee receives compensation only for the work which he actually does.[87] Ordinarily a trustee will not be compensated for the merely formal act of paying over to a successor or receiving from a predecessor the trust funds.[88]

---

[84] Huggins v. Rider, 77 Ill. 360, 364.

[85] "If the gross value of the principal of the estate or fund accounted for amounts to one hundred thousand dollars or more, each executor, administrator, guardian, or testamentary trustee is entitled to the full compensation on principal and income allowed herein to a sole executor, administrator, guardian or testamentary trustee, unless there are more than three, in which case the compensation to which three would be entitled must be apportioned among them according to the services rendered by them, respectively." N.Y. Surrogates Court Act, § 285. For a similar provision applying to trustees appointed otherwise than by will, see N.Y.Civil Practice Act, §§ 1548–1548a. For cases construing these sections, see In re Holbrook's Estate, 39 Misc. 139, 78 N.Y.S. 972; In re Hunt's Estate, 41 Misc. 72, 83 N.Y.S. 652; In re Grossman's Estate, 92 Misc. 656, 156 N.Y.S. 268.

[86] Widener v. Fay, 51 Md. 273, 275. See, also, In re Barker, 186 App.Div. 317, 174 N.Y.S. 230. But awarding compensation to the estate of the deceased trustee is discretionary with the court. In re Bushe, 227 N.Y. 85, 124 N.E. 154, 7 A.L.R. 1590.

[87] In re Leavitt, 8 Cal.App. 756, 97 P. 916; Gibson's Case, 1 Bland, Md., 138, 17 Am.Dec. 257.

[88] Jenkins v. Whyte, 62 Md. 427; In re Fisk, 45 Misc. 298, 92 N.Y.S.

Executors and Trustees

Whether one occupying the office of executor and trustee with respect to the same property shall receive two commissions depends upon the nature of the duties he has performed. If his executorship is separate from his trusteeship, and there are two distinct sets of duties, he should be given double compensation;[89] but if he merely holds two offices and does the same work in both offices, he should be compensated by single commissions only.[90] The rule has been stated by the New York Court of Appeals to be as follows:[91] "Where by the terms of the will the two functions with their corresponding duties coexist and run from the death of the testator to the final discharge, interwoven, inseparable, and blended together so that no point of time is fixed or contemplated in the testamentary intention at which one function should end and the other begin, double commissions or compensation in both capacities cannot be properly allowed. But executors are entitled to commissions as executors and also as trustees where under the will their duties as executors and trustees are separable and their duties as executors having ended they take the estate as trustees and afterward act solely in that capacity." Thus, where executors have had their accounts settled by the court and have been ordered to pay over to themselves as trustees the trust funds, and this act has been performed, there are two separate sets of duties and a right to double commissions, the court saying:[92] "We do not think that this is a case where the two functions of

---

394; In re Ward's Estate, Sur., 112 N.Y.S. 763; Young v. Barker, 141 App.Div. 801, 127 N.Y.S. 211. But see In re Baldwin, 209 N.Y. 601, 103 N.E. 734; In re Affleck, 163 App.Div. 876, 147 N.Y.S. 573.

[89] Arnold v. Alden, 173 Ill. 229, 50 N.E. 704; Dunne v. Cooke, 197 Ill. App. 422; In re Gloyd's Estate, 93 Iowa 303, 61 N.W. 975; In re Gulick, 7 N.J.Law J. 263; In re Jackson, 32 Hun, N.Y., 200; Wildey v. Robinson, 85 Hun 362, 32 N.Y.S. 1018; In re Curtiss, 15 Misc. 545, 37 N.Y.S. 586; In re Garth, 10 App.Div. 100, 41 N.Y.S. 1022; In re Slocum, 60 App. Div. 438, 69 N.Y.S. 1036; Olcott v. Baldwin, 190 N.Y. 99, 82 N.E. 748; In re Harteau, 125 App.Div. 710, 110 N.Y.

S. 59. In Williams v. Bond, 120 Va. 678, 91 S.E. 627, a direction by the testator that the executor-trustee receive $500 as executor was held not to exclude his right to commissions as trustee.

[90] Clark v. Anderson, 10 Bush, Ky., 99; Kennedy v. Dickey, 99 Md. 295, 57 A. 621; McKie v. Clark, 3 Dem. Sur., N.Y., 380; Haglar v. McCombs, 66 N.C. 345; In re Olds' Estate, 150 Pa. 529, 24 A. 752; Thom's Ex'r v. Thom, 95 Va. 413, 28 S.E. 583.

[91] Chase, J., in Olcott v. Baldwin, 190 N.Y. 99, 105, 106, 82 N.E. 748, quoting 18 Cyc. 1160.

[92] In re Willets, 112 N.Y. 289, 296, 19 N.E. 690.

executors and trustees coexist and run from the death of the testator to a final discharge, inseparably blended together. But from the language of the will we think the duties of the respondents, as executors, were to be first discharged, and that they were to assume the duties of trustees, and as such manage the trust funds, to the final termination of the trusts."

It is frequently a difficult matter to determine just when the duties of the executorship have ended and those of the trusteeship begun. "In the absence of any direction in the will, or any evidence in relation thereto, the duties of the trustee named in the will, even though he be the person named therein as executor, would not begin until after the duties of the executor have terminated, * * * and until he commences to exercise his duties as trustee he is not entitled to compensation therefor." [93] The completion of the duties of the executorship may be shown in a variety of ways. "An accounting as executors and a transfer of the trust funds to the trustees pursuant to a decree of a court of competent jurisdiction is the most satisfactory proof of the completion of their duties in one capacity and the commencement of their duties in the other capacity; but such judicial decree is not the only means of proving that the transfer has actually been made." [94]

The same rules would seem applicable to trustees who are also guardians of the cestuis que trust. The combination trustee and guardian should receive but one compensation for performing a single set of duties, although during the performance he may hold two titles.[95] "When the same person is both guardian and trustee, it would be a reproach to the law, and to the courts charged with the protection of such trusts, to allow him to charge full compensation in both capacities for the same service." [96]

---

[93] Bemmerly v. Woodard, 136 Cal. 326, 331, 68 P. 1017.

[94] Olcott v. Baldwin, 190 N.Y. 99, 107, 82 N.E. 748. See, also, Wylie v. Bushnell, 277 Ill. 484, 115 N.E. 618. See N.Y.Surrogates Court Act, § 314, subd. 6, which provides as follows: "The expression, 'testamentary trustee' includes every person, except an executor, an administrator with the will annexed, or a guardian, who is designated by a will, or by any competent authority, to execute a trust created by a will; and it includes such an executor or administrator, where he is acting in the execution of a trust created by the will, which is separable from his functions as executor or administrator." Trustees may enter upon their duties before their final accounting as executors. In re McDowell, 178 App.Div. 243, 164 N.Y. S. 1024.

[95] Foote v. Bruggerhof, 66 Hun 406, 21 N.Y.S. 509.

[96] Blake v. Pegram, 101 Mass. 592, 600.

CHAPTER 17

REMEDIES UNDER TRUSTS

Sec.
147. Advice and Instruction by the Court.
148. Enjoining or Setting Aside Wrongful Acts.
149. Decree for Carrying Out of Trust.
150. Damages against Trustee for Breach of Trust.
151. Personal Liability of Trustee with Lien.
152. Recovery of Trust Res or Its Substitute.
153. Meaning of Bona Fide Purchaser.
154. Tracing Trust Funds—Identification.
155. Necessity of Election between Tracing and Damages.
156. Subrogation and Marshaling.
157. Control of Trust Administration.
158. Recovery from Bondsman or Guaranty Fund.
159. Actions against Third Persons for Participating in a Breach of Trust.
160. Actions against Third Parties for Injuring the Trust Property.

ADVICE AND INSTRUCTION BY THE COURT [1]

147. Either the trustee or a beneficiary may bring a suit in equity to obtain a construction of the trust instrument and the court will settle any real doubts as to its meaning. The trustee may petition the court for advice and instruction on problems where he is justifiably in doubt as to the law.

If the trustee is justifiably in doubt as to whether he possesses certain powers, or concerning the method of exercising powers which it is admitted are vested in him, he may apply to a court of chancery, and that court will instruct him. "He must be honestly in doubt as to the proper construction of the instrument under which he is acting, or as to the disposition of the funds in his hands, or the course of action that he ought to take in any particular case, in order to authorize his application to a court of equity for aid and direction." [2] Hence it was held in the case just cited that equity would not instruct the trustee whether he should pay an attorney's bill for services rendered to the trust estate, there being no showing that there was any dispute as to the validity of the claim. The trustee should exercise his discretion regarding such matters. So, also, where the trustee applies for instructions concerning the method of exercising a power

[1] Restatement, Trusts, § 259.
[2] Warner v. Mettler, 260 Ill. 416, 421, 103 N.E. 259, 261.

of sale, and no difficult questions are involved, the court will put the burden of exercising the discretion upon the trustee. "The questions relate to the administration of a trust, in respect to matters which the testator has expressly confided to the wise discretion of trustees selected by himself. There is no suggestion, from any quarter, that they are likely to abuse that trust, by an arbitrary or capricious exercise of authority. The judgment of this court cannot be substituted for the discretion of the trustees, reasonably and fairly exercised." [3] There must be some question of doubt and some real necessity for advice concerning the powers resting in the trustee.[4] Where there is a question of admitted difficulty,[5] equity will direct the trustee concerning his powers, but not if the question is prematurely presented, and relates to what the trustee's powers in the future will be, rather than to what they are now.[6]

The court will not act as a legal adviser to the trustee to enable him to avoid the expense of hiring counsel,[7] nor will it decide problems which involve merely business judgment.[8]

The beneficiary may also bring a suit in equity for the construction of the trust instrument, in order to learn what his

[3] Proctor v. Heyer, 122 Mass. 525, 529.

[4] Morris v. Boyd, 110 Ark. 468, 162 S.W. 69, Ann.Cas.1916A, 1004; Connolly v. Leonard, 114 Me. 29, 95 A. 269; Bartlett v. Pickering, 113 Me. 96, 92 A. 1008. Thus advice as to the propriety of past action will not be given. Stover v. Webb, 114 Me. 386, 96 A. 721; Hill v. Moors, 224 Mass. 163, 112 N.E. 641. Nor will an opinion be rendered on questions which may never become of practical interest. Bridgeport Trust Co. v. Bartholomew, 90 Conn. 517, 97 A. 758; Passaic Trust & Safe Deposit Co. v. East Ridgelawn Cemetery, N.J. Ch., 101 A. 1026. If the question is not in controversy or is too general, it will not be answered. Bailey v. Smith, 222 Mass. 600, 111 N.E. 684.

[5] Berger v. Butler, 159 Ala. 539, 48 So. 685; Stapyleton v. Neeley, 44 Fla. 212, 32 So. 868; Moore v. Emery, Me., 18 A.2d 781; Hills v. Putnam, 152 Mass. 123, 25 N.E. 40; Thorp v. Lund, 227 Mass. 474, 116 N.E. 946, Ann.Cas.1918B, 1204; Hayden's Ex'rs v. Marmaduke, 19 Mo. 403; Trustees of Princeton University v. Wilson, 78 N.J.Eq. 1, 78 A. 393; Coe v. Beckwith, 31 Barb., N.Y., 339; Meadows v. Marsh, 123 N.C. 189, 31 S.E. 476; Johnson v. Wagner, 219 N.C. 235, 13 S.E.2d 419; Jones v. Creamer, 32 Ohio Cir.Ct.R. 223; Gamel v. Smith, 3 Tex.Civ.App. 22, 21 S. W. 628.

[6] Bullard v. Chandler, 149 Mass. 532, 21 N.E. 951, 5 L.R.A. 104; Wheaton v. Batcheller, 211 Mass. 223, 97 N.E. 924; Tibbetts v. Tomkinson, 217 Mass. 244, 104 N.E. 562; Hewitt v. Green, 77 N.J.Eq. 345, 77 A. 25; Prichard v. Prichard, 83 W.Va. 652, 98 S.E. 877.

[7] City Bank Farmers' Trust Co. v. Smith, 263 N.Y. 292, 189 N.E. 222, 93 A.L.R. 598.

[8] McCarthy v. Tierney, 116 Conn. 588, 165 A. 807.

rights are and what are the duties of the trustee, and the court will entertain the suit if there is any real doubt as to the meaning of the document.

In a few states a distinction is made between court supervised trusts and normal trusts. In the former the court takes control of the trust and directs the trustee by court order in every step of his administration, just as it does with a receiver. The trustee in substance becomes an officer of the court. An application must be made to the court to assume supervision of the trust.[9]

Ordinarily the settlor of a trust in which the fee is granted has no interest in the trust property after the complete creation of the trust.[10] He is as much a stranger to that property as a third person who has had no connection with it. The legal title to the property is in the trustee, and the equitable interest rests in the beneficiary.

It is obvious that the settlor as such has no right to obtain a construction of the trust instrument by a court of equity.[11] What the trust instrument means is of no importance financially to him, for under no construction of it will he be adjudged to have property rights.

ENJOINING OR SETTING ASIDE WRONGFUL ACTS [12]

148. If a trustee threatens to commit a breach of trust, the beneficiary may secure an injunction against the act; and if the breach has already occurred, the transaction may be set aside or avoided if this does not involve taking property from the hands of a bona fide purchaser.

If the trustee is preparing to commit a breach of trust, the beneficiary need not sit idly by and wait until damage has been done. He may sue in a court of equity for an injunction against the wrongful act. The trustee will not be likely to violate the injunction and thus run the danger of liability for contempt of court. Thus, if the trustee is intending to sell the trust property for an unreasonably low price, or on improper conditions, or for

---

[9] McCrory v. Beeler, 155 Md. 456, 142 A. 587; Minn.L.1933, c. 259; N.D.L.1931, c. 122, L.1935, c. 250; N.D.Sup.Ct.Rules, adopted Dec. 1, 1932; S.D.Comp.L.1929, § 1233B, and Sup.Ct.Rules, 46 S.D. ix.

[10] Boone v. Davis, 64 Miss. 138, 8 So. 202; Marvin v. Smith, 46 N.Y. 571.

[11] Carroll v. Smith, 99 Md. 653, 59 A. 131; Levy v. Hart, 54 Barb., N.Y., 248.

[12] Restatement, Trusts, §§ 199, 210, 212.

§ 148 INJUNCTION 489

an improper purpose, the beneficiary may receive the aid of the court in preventing this action.[13]

Instances in which equity has, at the instance of the cestui que trust, enjoined the performance of a specific act on the ground that it would be a breach of the trust, or at least prejudicial to the cestui que trust, are found in the following cases: Where the making of an oil and gas lease would constitute waste as to a remainderman cestui;[14] where the transfer or incumbrance of the trust property or its substitute has been prohibited;[15] and where the act enjoined has been the misappropriation of the trust funds,[16] the submission of a question to arbitration,[17] the voting of stock in a particular way,[18] or the prosecution by persons denying the trust of an action to recover the trust res.[19] If the trust funds are jeopardized, the trustee may be compelled to give a bond.[20] The trustee may also be directed to pay the funds into court pending litigation.[21]

Furthermore, even if the wrongful act of the trustee has been completed before the beneficiary has time to act, it may not be too late to receive the aid of the court in setting aside or avoiding the transaction.[22] Thus, if the trustee releases a mortgage owned by him as trustee, without receiving any consideration for the release, the beneficiary may have the mortgage reinstated where the property formerly subject to the mortgage is still in the hands of the mortgagor or his donees.[23] If a mortgage is attempted to be cancelled by one of two trustees, the release of it will be void, and the beneficiary or a successor trustee

[13] McCreary v. Gewinner, 103 Ga. 528, 29 S.E. 960; Beachey v. Heiple, 130 Md. 683, 101 A. 553; Cohen v. Mainthow, 182 App.Div. 613, 169 N.Y.S. 889.

[14] Ohio Oil Co. v. Daughetee, 240 Ill. 361, 88 N.E. 818, 36 L.R.A.,N.S., 1108.

[15] Preston v. Walsh, C.C.Tex., 10 F. 315; Beachey v. Heiple, 130 Md. 683, 101 A. 553; Chamberlain v. Eddy, 154 Mich. 593, 118 N.W. 499; Raleigh v. Fitzpatrick, 43 N.J.Eq. 501, 11 A. 1; Depau v. Moses, 3 Johns.Ch., N.Y., 349; Cohen v. Mainthow, 182 App.Div. 613, 169 N.Y.S. 889; Hunt v. Freeman, 1 Ohio 490.

[16] Coleman v. McGrew, 71 Neb. 801, 99 N.W. 663; Commonwealth v. Bank of Pennsylvania, 3 Watts & S., Pa., 184.

[17] Crum v. Moore's Adm'r, 14 N.J. Eq. 436, 82 Am.Dec. 262.

[18] McHenry v. Jewett, 90 N.Y. 58, semble.

[19] St. Luke's Hospital v. Barclay, Fed.Cas.No.12,241, 3 Blatchf. 259.

[20] Starr v. Wiley, 89 N.J.Eq. 79, 103 A. 865.

[21] Bullock v. Angleman, 82 N.J.Eq. 23, 87 A. 627.

[22] Towle v. Ambs, 123 Ill. 410, 14 N.E. 689; Price v. Estill, 87 Mo. 378.

[23] Locke v. Andrasko, 178 Wash. 145, 34 P.2d 444.

may have a decree reinstating the mortgage on the records.[24] Naturally, as will be shown later,[25] if the trustee has conveyed trust property away in breach of trust to a bona fide purchaser, the deed cannot be set aside.

DECREE FOR CARRYING OUT OF TRUST [26]

149. In the case of a private trust a beneficiary may sue in equity and obtain a decree that the trustee perform a certain act under the trust or carry out the trust in general. Such an action cannot be maintained by the settlor as such.

In charitable trusts the remedy for breach is a suit by the Attorney General of the state to procure trust enforcement.

In the case of gifts to charitable corporations the donor may reserve visitorial powers to himself and his successors.

Ordinarily the remedy of the cestui que trust for the enforcement of his rights is by suit in equity, but occasionally the beneficiary is allowed to proceed at law, as, for example, where a definite sum is fixed as due from the trustee to the cestui que trust by virtue of a promise from the trustee, or by the terms of the trust, or by an account stated, or an order of court.

The existence of an adequate remedy at law does not bar the cestui que trust from proceeding in equity. The jurisdiction of equity to enforce the rights of cestui que trust is based on its original exclusive recognition of the trust, and not upon proof of the inadequacy of a remedy at law.

The cestui que trust has a right to have the trustee carry out the trust as laid down in the trust instrument and in accordance with the rules of equity. This right is so axiomatic as to need no treatment and has often been described and enforced by the courts on the application of the cestui que trust.[27] One of the most important remedies of a beneficiary is to get a decree from equity directing specific performance of his duties by the trustee.

[24] Coxe v. Kriebel, 323 Pa. 157, 185 A. 770, 106 A.L.R. 102.

[25] See § 153, post.

[26] Restatement, Trusts, § 199.

[27] Robinson v. Mauldin, 11 Ala. 977; Smith v. Wildman, 37 Conn. 384; Cooper v. McClun, 16 Ill. 435; Wyble v. McPheters, 52 Ind. 393; Forsythe v. Lexington Banking & Trust Co., Ky., 121 S.W. 962; Suydam v. Dequindre, Har., Mich., 347; Goble v. Swobe, 64 Neb. 838, 90 N.W. 919; Brock v. Sawyer, 39 N.H. 547; Attorney General ex rel. Bailey v. Moore's Ex'rs, 19 N.J.Eq. 503; In re Scherrer's Estate, 24 Misc. 351, 53 N.Y.S. 714; Fogg v. Middleton, 2 Hill, Eq., S.C., 591; Clark v. Brown, Tex.Civ.App., 108 S.W. 421; Bell's Adm'r v. Humphrey, 8 W.Va. 1; Harrigan v. Gilchrist, 121 Wis. 127, 99 N.W. 909.

Thus, expressing this fundamental idea, a Delaware court has said that "every cestui que trust, whether a volunteer or not, or be the limitation under which he claims with or without a consideration, is entitled to the aid of a court of equity, to avail himself of the benefit of a trust, * * * and that the forbearance of the trustees shall not prejudice him. * * * In these cases the principle seems to be fully established, that the person for whose benefit a trust is created may compel the performance, although he may be no party to the contract." [28]

This right to compel the execution of the trust rests in the cestui que trust alone. Where the interest of the beneficiary is inheritable, obviously, the right to enforce passes to the heirs [29] or personal representative [30] on the cestui's death. The right of enforcement is not affected by the contingent [31] or remote [32] nature of cestui que trust's interest. Where the interest is assignable, the assignee may come into court to demand that the trust be carried out.[33] Where a trust is for a group like a family, any member may enforce the trust.[34] Beneficiaries of resulting [35] and constructive [36] trusts have the same rights as those of an express trust in this respect.

Persons having no financial interest in the trust as, for example, a relative of the cestui, who is only affected by reasons of sentiment,[37] or a claimant of the legal title in hostility to the trust,[38] cannot sue for the enforcement or construction of the trust. Where a private trust is for the aid of an individual pauper, a

---

[28] Rodney v. Shankland, 1 Del.Ch. 35, 45, 46, 12 Am.Dec. 70.

[29] Mendenhall v. Walters, 53 Okl. 598, 157 P. 732.

[30] Schwebel v. Wohlsen, 254 Pa. 281, 98 A. 864; Smith v. Smith, 38 Pa.Super.Ct. 251.

[31] Williams v. Sage, 180 App.Div. 1, 167 N.Y.S. 179; Clarke v. Deveaux, 1 S.C. 172.

[32] Pritchard v. Williams, 175 N. C. 319, 95 S.E. 570; Cooper v. Day, 1 Rich.Eq. 26.

[33] Smith v. Orton, 21 How. 241, 16 L.Ed. 104; Mitchell v. Carrollton Nat. Bank, 97 S.W. 45, 29 Ky.Law Rep. 1228; Clark v. Crego, 47 Barb., N.Y., 599.

[34] Chase v. Chase, 2 Allen, Mass., 101.

[35] Franklin v. Colley, 10 Kan. 260; Sherburne v. Morse, 132 Mass. 469; Leader v. Tierney, 45 Neb. 753, 64 N.W. 226. But the heirs of a person who could have elected to be a resulting trustee, but did not, are not entitled to enforce the trust. Cooper v. Cockrum, 87 Ind. 443.

[36] Fox v. Fox, 77 Neb. 601, 110 N.W. 304; Johnston v. Reilly, 66 N. J.Eq. 451, 57 A. 1049; Trustees of Amherst College v. Ritch, 10 Misc. 503, 31 N.Y.S. 885.

[37] Autrey v. Stubenrauch, 63 Tex. Civ.App. 247, 133 S.W. 531.

[38] Warren v. Warren, 75 N.J.Eq. 415, 72 A. 960.

town cannot maintain a bill to enforce the trust, on the theory that it has a financial interest because the pauper may become a town charge.[39] The interest is incidental.

The cestui may obtain a decree for the performance of a single act by the trustee, as, for example, the sale of the trust realty;[40] or he may secure a decree for performance of all the duties of the trust in general terms.[41]

The settlor has no power to obtain the enforcement of a private trust.[42] Its enforcement will not make him a penny richer. Equity will give aid to such enforcement only on the application of the trustee or a cestui que trust.[43] "It is a general rule that a suit to enforce a trust can only be maintained by the trustee or the cestui que trust. As against a third person, the trustee, he being regarded as the representative of the cestui que trust, is the proper party to bring the action. As against the trustee himself, the suit can only be maintained by the cestui que trust. Where the trust is for a public charity, there being no certain persons who are entitled to it, so as to be able to sue in their own names as cestuis que trust, a suit for the purpose of having the charity duly administered must be brought in the name of the Attorney General. In such a case that officer, as representative of the public, would occupy the relation of cestui que trust to trustees." [44]

The settlor is not entitled to rescind the trust for a breach by the trustee.[45] The creation of a trust does not involve a contract, but rather a conveyance with equitable obligations.

Naturally, if the settlor has an interest in remainder following the trust, he can, after the expiration of the trust, compel a

---

[39] Town of Sharon v. Simons, 30 Vt. 458.

[40] Vrooman v. Virgil, 81 N.J.Eq. 301, 88 A. 372.

[41] Callis v. Ridout, Md., 7 Gill & J. 1.

[42] Padelford v. Real Estate-Land Title & Trust Co., 121 Pa.Super. 193, 183 A. 442.

[43] Rodney v. Shankland, 1 Del.Ch. 35, 12 Am.Dec. 70; Culbertson v. Matson, 11 Mo. 493; Foster v. Friede, 37 Mo. 36; Carter v. Uhlein, N.J. Ch., 36 A. 956. *Contra:* Abbott v. Gregory, 39 Mich. 68, where the agreement of the trustee to carry out the trust is viewed as a contract apparently enforceable by either the cestui or the settlor. The settlor's administrator or executor, of course, stands in his shoes. Kellogg v. White, 103 Misc. 167, 169 N.Y.S. 989; Barrette v. Dooly, 21 Utah 81, 59 P. 718.

[44] Harris, J., in Association for the Relief of Respectable, Aged Indigent Females v. Beekman, 21 Barb., N.Y., 565, 568, 569.

[45] Thornton v. Koch, 317 Pa. 400, 176 A. 3.

§ 149   DECREE FOR CARRYING OUT OF TRUST   493

reconveyance, or the delivery of possession, by the trustee.[46] And obviously, if the trust is for the benefit of the settlor, he may enforce it; but here he occupies a double role, and the enforcement is by him as cestui, and not by him as settlor.[47]

It has likewise been stated that, in jurisdictions where the trustee is empowered to devise the trust res or where it descends to his heirs or representatives at his death, the devisee,[48] heir[49] or representative[50] is bound by the trust, as was the ancestor, and the right of cestui que trust to enforce the trust obligation extends to the devisee, heir, or representative. The same principle applies to a substituted trustee who replaces the original trustee by decree of chancery.[51]

As in the case of a private trust, so with the charitable trust there is a right to have the trustee carry out the trust in the manner provided by the settlor and by the rules of chancery.[52] This right must be enforced by some representative of the public generally, the prospective beneficiaries. The officer usually selected has been the Attorney General,[53] although in some states

[46] Eaton v. Tillinghast, 4 R.I. 276.

[47] Backes v. Crane, 87 N.J.Eq. 229, 100 A. 900; Hamilton v. Muncie, 182 App.Div. 630, 169 N.Y.S. 826.

[48] Ante, § 133; Hill v. True, 104 Wis. 294, 80 N.W. 462.

[49] Ante, § 133; Mendenhall v. Walters, 53 Okl. 598, 157 P. 732; Smalley v. Paine, 62 Tex.Civ.App. 52, 130 S. W. 739.

[50] Ante, § 133; Austin v. Wilcoxson, 149 Cal. 24, 84 P. 417; Smith v. Darby, 39 Md. 268; Anderson v. Thomson, 38 Hun, N.Y., 394; Devoe v. Lutz, 133 App.Div. 356, 117 N.Y.S. 339; Young v. Hughes, 39 Or. 586, 65 P. 987, 66 P. 272; Bible v. Marshall, 103 Tenn. 324, 52 S.W. 1077.

[51] Ante, § 134; In re Appley, Sup., 33 N.Y.S. 724.

[52] Harris v. Cosby, 173 Ala. 81, 55 So. 231; Kauffman v. Foster, 3 Cal. App. 741, 86 P. 1108; Attorney General v. Wallace's Devisees, 7 B.Mon., Ky., 611; Ellenherst v. Pythian, 110 Ky. 923, 63 S.W. 37; Brunnenmeyer v. Buhre, 32 Ill. 183; Lamb v. Cain, 129 Ind. 486, 29 N.E. 13, 14 L.R.A. 518; Peter v. Carter, 70 Md. 139, 16 A. 450; President, etc., of Harvard College v. Society for Promoting Theological Education, 3 Gray, Mass., 280; Sessions v. Doe ex dem Reynolds, 7 Smedes & M., Miss., 130; Chambers v. City of St. Louis, 29 Mo. 543; Adams Female Academy v. Adams, 65 N.H. 225, 18 A. 777, 23 A. 430, 6 L.R.A. 785; Allen v. Stevens, 161 N.Y. 122, 55 N.E. 568; Penfield v. Skinner, 11 Vt. 296; Overseers of Poor of Richmond County v. Tayloe's Adm'r, Gilmer, Va., 336. But, of course, equity will take jurisdiction only to protect a property right. Houston v. Howze, 162 Ala. 500, 50 So. 266. And equity will not interfere merely to control the discretion of the trustee. Society of Cincinnati's Appeal (In re Washington Monument Fund) 154 Pa. 621, 26 A. 647, 20 L.R.A. 323.

[53] People ex rel. Ellert v. Cogswell, 113 Cal. 129, 45 P. 270, 35 L.R.A. 269; Parker v. May, 5 Cush., Mass., 336; Burbank v. Burbank, 152 Mass.

the county prosecuting attorney [54] performs this function. If the trustees are guilty of neglect or maladministration, the Attorney General, or other corresponding officer, may, either on his own initiative or on the relation of any citizen, institute proceedings in chancery for the enforcement of the trust. "Courts of equity have jurisdiction to prevent a misuse or an abuse of charitable trusts. * * * The Attorney General or a state's attorney representing the public is charged with the duty of preventing a breach of a trust for a public charity or to restore a trust fund after it has been diverted." [55] A Massachusetts court has recently voiced the same principle as follows: "If the trustees appointed under the decree neglect or refuse to execute the trust, or abuse their powers, the Attorney General on his own initiative or at the relation of those who are beneficially interested can petition for their removal, and also can have relief in equity for an accounting, or, if the trustees are uncertain or are unable to agree among themselves as to their powers and duties, they can ask for instructions making him a party defendant." [56] Any person may act as a relator in a charitable information, regardless of personal financial interest in the enforcement of the trust.[57]

In the discussion of the rights of the settlor the law was shown to be that, by the weight of authority, the settlor has no capacity to sue to enforce or to obtain a construction of a charitable trust.[58] "Before it was established that a valid trust was created by the will, no question as to its execution could arise. After that was done and it was determined that the trust was charitable, it became the duty of the Attorney General to see that the rights of the public in the trust were protected and that it was properly executed. The heirs had no interest in the question apart from the general public, whose rights were represented by the Attorney General." [59] The court was speaking of the heirs of the set-

---

254, 25 N.E. 427, 9 L.R.A. 748; Attorney General v. Bedard, 218 Mass. 378, 105 N.E. 993; Tyree v. Bingham, 100 Mo. 451, 13 S.W. 952; N.Y.Real Property Law, § 113; N.Y.Personal Property Law, § 12; Buell v. Gardner, Sup., 149 N.Y.S. 803; Association for the Relief of Respectable, Aged Indigent Females v. Beekman, 21 Barb., N.Y. 565; Ewell v. Sneed, 136 Tenn. 602, 191 S.W. 131, 5 A.L.R. 303.

[54] Mich.Ann.St. § 26.1192.

[55] People ex rel. Smith v. Braucher, 258 Ill. 604, 608, 101 N.E. 944, 47 L.R. A.,N.S., 1015.

[56] Crawford v. Nies, 224 Mass. 474, 490, 113 N.E. 408.

[57] Mackenzie v. Trustees of Presbytery of Jersey City, 67 N.J.Eq. 652, 61 A. 1027, 3 L.R.A.,N.S., 227.

[58] Ante, § 85. And see Strong v. Doty, 32 Wis. 381.

[59] Petition of Burnham, 74 N.H. 492, 494, 69 A. 720.

tlor of the charity. A person expecting or hoping to get some personal advantage from a charity is not a proper plaintiff in a bill to enforce the trust.[60]

Visitorial Powers

The visitor of an eleemosynary corporation has no power to enforce the right of the public that the charity be carried on. The power of visitation is the authority retained by the founder for himself and his heirs, or his nominees, to inspect and regulate the internal affairs of a charitable corporation. It is not a power vested in courts of equity in the United States. It is a rule of the law of corporations, rather than of trusts.[61] After considering the common law of England upon the subject of visitation, as laid down in Philips v. Bury [1 Ld.Raym. 5, 2 Term.R. 346], an early case, a Massachusetts court has stated: "By that law the visitor of all eleemosynary corporations is the founder or his heirs, unless he has given the power of visitation to some other person or body, which is generally the case; and to the visitor thus constituted belongs the right and power of inspecting the affairs of the corporation and superintending all officers who have the management of them, according to such regulations and restrictions as are prescribed by the founder in the statutes which he ordains, without any control or revision of any other person or body, except the judicial tribunals by whose authority and jurisdiction they may be restrained and kept within the limits of their granted powers, and made to regard the Constitution and general laws of the land." [62] With respect to the possession of the power of visitation by chancery a New York court has said: "While a court of equity never had visitorial power, yet it always assumed jurisdiction over the charity and its officers when a question arose as to the proper use and disposition of the funds. The power of visitation, therefore, pertained to the supervision and regulation of the work and purpose of the charity, while the court of equity, not as a visitor, but in its inherent power over trusts, assumed jurisdiction to determine whether the funds were being spent in accordance with the trust and purpose of the charity." [63] But in England, when the visitorial power cannot be exercised

---

[60] Association for the Relief of Respectable, Aged Indigent Females v. Beekman, 21 Barb., N.Y., 565.

[61] Allen v. McKean, 1 Sumn. 276, Fed.Cas.No.229; Trustees of Auburn Academy v. Strong, 1 Hopk.Ch., N. Y., 278; Koblitz v. Western Reserve University, 21 Ohio Cir.Ct.R. 144.

[62] In re Murdock, 7 Pick., Mass., 303, 321.

[63] In re Norton, 97 Misc. 289, 299, 161 N.Y.S. 710.

by the founder or his nominee, it results to the crown and will be exercised by the Chancellor as the representative of the crown.[64] And courts have been given quasi-visitorial powers in some cases in America.[65]

It is self-evident that the Legislature, being a law-making rather than a law-enforcing body, has no power to enforce the right of the cestuis que trust of a charitable trust. It cannot enact statutes which modify the terms of the trust, as by a change in trustees or beneficiaries. Such acts have been held to violate the constitutional guaranty against the impairment of the obligation of contracts.[66] "The acceptance by the town [the trustee] of Maria Cary's proposition contained in her letter created a contract, which was executed on her part by the payment of the money, and which continued binding on the town and the trustees as to their conduct in reference to the charity. * * * We are of opinion that the statute which we are considering impairs the obligation of the contract under which this charity is administered."[67] The act referred to by the court changed the trustee.

Beneficiary should Sue in Equity

Since the right of a cestui que trust is equitable in its nature, it may naturally be assumed that courts of chancery, or the equity side of courts having double jurisdiction, will grant a remedy to the beneficiary. Ordinarily relief should be sought by the cestui in equity.[68] Thus the recovery of the trust property from the

---

[64] Lewin on Trusts, 13th Ed., 565, citing St. 36 & 37, Vict. c. 66, § 17.

[65] N. Y. Membership Corporations Law, § 26; N. Y. Religious Corporations Law, § 14.

[66] Tharp v. Fleming, 1 Houst., Del., 580; Town of Greenville, v. Town of Mason, 53 N.H. 515; Brown v. Hummel, 6 Pa. 86, 47 Am.Dec. 431; Plymouth v. Jackson, 15 Pa. 44; Field v. Directors of Girard College, 54 Pa. 233. But acts authorizing a change in the character of the trust property have been allowed as valid. Stanley v. Colt, 5 Wall. 119, 18 L.Ed. 502; Petition of Van Horne, 18 R.I. 389, 28 A. 341. And where the Legislature has appointed a corporation as the trustee (the settlor having appointed none), the Legislature can revoke the charter of the first corporation and create another to take the property in trust. Wambersie v. Orange Humane Soc., 84 Va. 446, 5 S.E. 25.

[67] Cary Library v. Bliss, 151 Mass. 364, 375, 378, 25 N.E. 92, 7 L.R.A. 765.

[68] Clews v. Jamieson, 182 U.S. 461, 21 S.Ct. 845, 45 L.Ed. 1183; Hopkins v. Granger, 52 Ill. 504; Hobart v. Andrews, 21 Pick., Mass., 526; Wright v. Dame, 22 Pick., Mass., 55; Malone v. Malone, 151 Mich. 680, 115 N.W. 716; Ewing v. Parrish, 148 Mo. App. 492, 128 S.W. 538; Husted v. Thomson, 158 N.Y. 328, 53 N.E. 20; McCoy v. McCoy, 30 Okl. 379, 121 P. 176, Ann.Cas.1913C, 146; Washington Nat. Building & Loan Ass'n

trustee [69] or a third person [70] should be demanded in equity. And bills to establish a resulting trust,[71] to protect the trust estate,[72] or for an account and a decree against the sureties on the trustee's bond [73] are properly brought in equity.

In many cases the remedy of a cestui que trust is in equity only. He has no option but to proceed by bill in chancery. The law provides him no means of redress. This is true where the trust is open and the suit is for the statement of an account and the recovery of an unliquidated sum.[74] Equity has exclusive jurisdiction to aid the cestui likewise where the basis of the suit is the negligence of the trustee in managing the trust property,[75] or the wrongful conveyance of the trust property to another,[76] or a breach of trust in neglecting to collect and apply the trust assets according to the trust terms,[77] or damage to the trust property by the trustee which would be waste if committed by a tenant,[78] or where the possession of trust realty [79] or the value of trust property wrongfully sold [80] is sought by the cestui que trust, or where the object is an account of rents and profits of land held in trust,[81] or where the foundation is the conversion by the trustee of the trust property and its proceeds.[82]

v. Heironimus, 62 W.Va. 6, 57 S.E. 256.

[69] McCampbell v. Brown, C.C.Ohio, 48 F. 795; Bullock v. Angleman, 82 N.J.Eq. 23, 87 A. 627; Reade v. Continental Trust Co., 27 Misc. 435, 58 N.Y.S. 321; Clarke v. Deveaux, 1 S.C. 172.

[70] Smith v. American Nat. Bank, C. C.A.Mo., 89 F. 832, 32 C.C.A. 368; Lee v. Simpson, C.C.S.C., 37 F. 12, 2 L.R.A. 659; Lehnard v. Specht, 180 Ill. 208, 54 N.E. 315; Buck v. Lockwood, 193 Mich. 242, 159 N.W. 509; Calhoun v. Burnett, 40 Miss. 599; Luscombe v. Grigsby, 11 S.D. 408, 78 N.W. 357.

[71] Fausler v. Jones, 7 Ind. 277; Johnston v. Sherehouse, 61 Fla. 647, 54 So. 892.

[72] Dorsey's Lessee v. Garey, 30 Md. 489.

[73] Thruston v. Blackiston, 36 Md. 501.

Bogert Trusts 2d—32

[74] Goldschmidt v. Maier, 140 Cal. xvii, 73 P. 984; Robison v. Carey, 8 Ga. 527; Davis v. Coburn, 128 Mass. 377; Upham v. Draper, 157 Mass. 292, 32 N.E. 2; Kendall v. Kendall, 60 N.H. 527; Congdon v. Cahoon, 48 Vt. 49; Goupille v. Chaput, 43 Wash. 702, 86 P. 1058.

[75] Hukill v. Page, 6 Biss. 183, Fed. Cas.No.6,854.

[76] Norton v. Ray, 139 Mass. 230, 29 N.E. 662.

[77] Bishop v. Houghton, 1 E. D. Smith, N.Y., 566.

[78] Kincaird v. Scott, 12 Johns., N. Y., 368.

[79] Matthews v. McPherson, 65 N.C. 189.

[80] Jasper v. Hazen, 1 N.D. 75, 44 N.W. 1018.

[81] Cearnes v. Irving, 31 Vt. 604.

[82] Redwood v. Riddick, 4 Munf., Va., 222.

Occasional Remedy at Law

But in a few cases remedies are open to the cestui que trust in courts of law for the enforcement of rights against the trustee or third parties. Thus, where a third person has trust property under circumstances which entitle the cestui to have him declared a constructive trustee (as, for example, where the property has been obtained by fraud), the cestui may also maintain money had and received against the third party in a court of law.[83] The liability of the surety on the trustee's bond is almost always solely at law.[84] The cestui may proceed at law where the title to realty is involved and the only question is whether trust money has gone into the realty.[85] It has been held that, where the trustee has misapplied the trust fund and it cannot be followed, damages at law for the breach of trust may be recovered.[86] And a similar holding is found in cases where the trustee has broken his trust by a wrongful sale of the trust res,[87] and where the purpose of the trust was accomplished and the trustee had no function to perform.[88]

Perhaps the most common case in which the beneficiary may proceed at law against the trustee is that where the trustee has promised to pay the cestui que trust a definite sum, or the trust has been closed, the accounts settled, a definite sum fixed as that due, and the trustee has no further duty except to pay it to the cestui que trust. In these cases sometimes courts of law have entertained jurisdiction in the action for money had and received or its equivalent and have not obliged the cestui to proceed in equity.[89] "It is well settled that a cestui que trust cannot bring

---

[83] Clifford Banking Co. v. Donovan Commission Co., 195 Mo. 262, 94 S.W. 527; Hanford v. Duchastel, 87 N.J.L. 205, 93 A. 586.

[84] Hite v. Hite's Ex'r, 133 Ky. 554, 118 S.W. 357; Clagett v. Worthington, 3 Gill., Md., 83.

[85] Nanheim v. Smith, 253 Pa. 380, 98 A. 602.

[86] Snyder v. Parmalee, 80 Vt. 496, 68 A. 649.

[87] Holderman v. Hood, 70 Kan. 267, 78 P. 838; Brys v. Pratt, 55 Wash. 122, 104 P. 169. In Davis v. Dickerson, 137 Ark. 14, 207 S.W. 436, the cestui que trust was held to have the alternatives of an action at law for money had and received, or a bill in equity for damages for breach of trust.

[88] Thomas v. Harkness, 13 Bush., Ky., 23.

[89] Vincent v. Rogers, 30 Ala. 471; Sterling v. Tantum, 5 Boyce, Del., 409, 94 A. 176; Guthrie v. Hyatt, 1 Har., Del., 446; Daugherty v. Daugherty, 116 Iowa 245, 90 N.W. 65; O'Neil v. Epting, 82 Kan. 245, 108 P. 107; Crooker v. Rogers, 58 Me. 339; Nelson v. Howard, 5 Md. 327; Rogers v. Daniell, 8 Allen, Mass., 343; Brown v. Cowell, 116 Mass. 461; Johnson v. Johnson, 120 Mass. 465; Arms v.

an action at law against a trustee to recover for money had and received while the trust is still open; but when the trust has been closed and settled, the amount due the cestui que trust established and made certain, and nothing remains to be done but to pay over money, such an action may be maintained." [90] The same doctrine has been framed somewhat differently by a Delaware court, as follows: "Where the only remaining function and duty of a trustee is to pay over to his cestui que trust a sum of money, made certain by the terms of the trust, by an account passed by the trustee, by agreement between them, or by an order of court, the cestui que trust has an action at law against the trustee to recover such amount, and it is attachable in the hands of the trustee by a creditor of the cestui que trust by attachment fi. fa., or in foreign attachment, as the case may be." [91] In Massachusetts and Pennsylvania, before the establishment there of courts of equity, all remedies of cestui que trust had to be worked out through courts of law.[92]

A probate court may of course construe a will purporting to create a trust, for the purpose of determining whether such trust was validly created,[93] and occasionally probate courts have concurrent jurisdiction with courts of equity over trusts created by will; [94] but, aside from statute, probate or surrogate's courts have no jurisdiction to declare or enforce trusts.[95]

Inadequacy of Remedy at Law

It has occasionally been suggested that equity will not take jurisdiction to enforce the rights of a cestui que trust where a complete and adequate remedy at law exists.[96] But it is believed that

[90] Ashley, 4 Pick., Mass., 71; Chase v. Perley, 148 Mass. 289, 19 N.E. 398; Henchey v. Henchey, 167 Mass. 77, 44 N.E. 1075; Collar v. Collar, 75 Mich. 414, 42 N.W. 847, 4 L.R.A. 491; Frank v. Morley's Estate, 106 Mich. 635, 64 N.W. 577; Pitcher v. Rogers' Estate, 199 Mich. 114, 165 N.W. 813; Batchis v. Leask, 149 App.Div. 713, 134 N.Y.S. 350; Van Camp v. Searle, 147 N.Y. 150, 41 N.E. 427; Spencer v. Clarke, 25 R.I. 163, 55 A. 329; Parker v. Parker, 69 Vt. 352, 37 A. 1112.

[90] Johnson v. Johnson, 120 Mass. 465, 466.

[91] Sterling v. Tantum, 5 Boyce, Del., 409, 94 A. 176, 183.

[92] Newhall v. Wheeler, 7 Mass. 189; Martzell v. Stauffer, 3 Pen. & W. 398.

[93] In re Hinckley's Estate, 58 Cal. 457; Carpenter v. Cook, 132 Cal. 621, 64 P. 997, 84 Am.St.Rep. 118.

[94] Green v. Gaskill, 175 Mass. 265, 56 N.E. 560.

[95] In re Dunn's Estate, Myr.Prob., Cal., 122; Haverstick v. Trudel, 51 Cal. 431; Butler v. Lawson, 72 Mo. 227; Hayes v. Hayes, 48 N.H. 219; Koch v. Feick, 81 N.J.Eq. 120, 86 A. 67.

[96] Fidelity Trust Co. v. Alexander, C.C.A.Pa., 243 F. 162, 156 C.C.A. 28;

the prevailing and better view is that the lack of a remedy at law is not a condition precedent to equitable relief, that originally all the remedies of the cestui que trust were in chancery, and that he continues to be entitled to enforce all his rights in that court, even though the courts of law may have conceded to him certain remedies from time to time.[97] In other words historically equity has original and complete jurisdiction over trusts and will enforce the rights of a cestui que trust because they arise out of a trust. No showing of inadequacy of the remedy at law is necessary to give a cestui que trust standing in a court of equity. The statement of Lord Mansfield is applicable, although it was made with reference to another question. He said: "This court will not allow itself to be ousted of any part of its original jurisdiction, because a court of law happens to have fallen in love with the same or a similar jurisdiction, and has attempted (the attempt for the most part is not very successful) to administer such relief as originally was to be had here and here only." [98] To the same purpose is a statement of Leaming, V. C., in a recent New Jersey case: "It is undoubtedly true, as suggested by defendant, that the danger of irreparable injury may be said to constitute the foundation of a great part of equitable jurisdiction, and especially that part of equitable jurisdiction calling for relief by way of injunction, either pendente lite or perpetual; but it is not the sole ground of equitable jurisdiction by any means. Where, as here, a trust is involved, and the suit is for the purpose of preserving for the benefit of the cestui que trust the existence of property rights which have arisen through and by reason of the trust or its breach, it is no answer to a bill seeking the enforcement or preservation of those property rights, with a view of preserving the corpus in which the rights exist, that adequate money dam-

---

Langdon v. Blackburn, 109 Cal. 19, 41 P. 814; Coe v. Turner, 5 Conn. 86; White v. White, 1 Md.Ch. 53; Van Sciver v. Churchill, 215 Pa. 53, 64 A. 322; Downs v. Downs' Ex'r, 75 Vt. 383, 56 A. 9; Franks v. Cravens, 6 W.Va. 185.

[97] Camody v. Webster, 197 Ala. 290, 72 So. 622; Thompson v. Hartline, 105 Ala. 263, 16 So. 711; Humes v. Scott, 130 Ala. 281, 30 So. 788; Hubbard v. United States Mortg. Co., 14 Ill.App. 40; Dorenkamp v. Dorenkamp, 109 Ill.App. 536; First Congregational Soc. in Raynham v. Trustees of Fund, etc., in Raynham, 23 Pick., Mass., 148; Flye v. Hall, 224 Mass. 528, 113 N.E. 366; Farrell v. Farrell, 91 Mo.App. 665; Gutch v. Fosdick, 48 N.J.Eq. 353, 22 A. 590, 27 Am.St.Rep. 473; McCrea v. Purmort, 16 Wend., N.Y., 460, 30 Am.Dec. 103; Farrelly v. Skelly, 130 App.Div. 803, 115 N.Y.S. 522; Goldrick v. Roxana Petroleum Co., Okl., 176 P. 932; Nease v. Capehart, 8 W.Va. 95; Borchert v. Borchert, 132 Wis. 593, 113 N.W. 35.

[98] Eyre v. Everett, 2 Russell 381, 382.

ages might be recovered against the defendant for a breach of his trust. Trusts are enforced, and trust rights are established and preserved, without reference to the possibility of a money judgment in an action for damages affording a measure of compensation for threatened injuries." [99]

MONEY JUDGMENT AGAINST TRUSTEE FOR BREACH OF TRUST [1]

150. If damages have resulted to the beneficiary from a breach of the trust, he may obtain a decree against the trustee, or his representatives if he is dead, providing for the payment of money to the cestui or to a successor trustee.

Co-trustees are jointly and severally liable where they unite in a breach of trust. If they are equally at fault, and one co-trustee is obliged to bear entire liability to the beneficiary, such trustee may have contribution from the other co-trustee.

Where the cestui que trust is not able to trace the trust property or its substitute into the assets of the trustee and claim a lien thereon, he is not a preferred creditor and must share equally with the general creditors of the trustee.

A trustee is liable to the cestui que trust for wrongful acts of an agent or servant properly employed by the trustee when the wrong was committed in the course of the employee's work for the trust, but is not liable for acts outside the scope of the employee's work.

In dealing with a cotrustee a trustee is required to use the care of a reasonably prudent man in dealing with business associates. A co-trustee may become liable if he negligently allows or assists his fellow trustee to obtain or retain exclusive control of the trust property, or negligently fails to supervise the work of his fellow trustee, and the latter embezzles or wastes the trust property.

The cestui que trust may recover interest, simple or compound, when the allowance of interest is necessary to compensate him for the loss of the use of the trust property which has been occasioned by the default of the trustee.

Under many modern statutes the trustee is criminally liable for an appropriation of the trust property.

The personal liability of the trustee to respond in money damages for his acts in the administration of the trust which are wrongful and which cause damage to the cestui que trust is elementary.[2] Thus, the making of unauthorized payments to

[99] Hussong Dyeing Mach. Co. v. Morris, N.J., 89 A. 249, 250.

[1] Restatement, Trusts, §§ 198, 199.

[2] Miller v. Butler, 121 Ga. 758, 49 S.E. 754; Graham v. Graham, 85 Ill. App. 460; West v. Biscoe, 6 Har. & J., Md., 460; Moore v. Robertson, 62 Hun 623, 17 N.Y.S. 554; Burris v. Brooks, 118 N.C. 789, 24 S.E. 521; Robertson v. Sublett, 6 Humph., Tenn., 313; Silliman v. Gano, 90 Tex. 637, 39 S.W. 559, 40 S.W. 391.

other cestuis que trust,[3] the conversion of the trust property,[4] negligence in recording instruments affecting the trust property,[5] or in obtaining security,[6] or in collecting the trust property,[7] or in the retention of property until it is worthless,[8] wrongful sale of the trust res,[9] and negligence or misconduct in the making or retaining of investments,[10] may give rise to a right in favor of cestui que trust to have the trustee pay money damages. Where the trustee is financially responsible this affords a remedy which is usually complete and satisfactory. Such a procedure is sometimes called "surcharging" the trustee.

The burden of proving misconduct by the trustee in these actions is on the cestui que trust. The trustee is aided by the presumption of the regularity of his proceedings.[11]

[3] Kendall v. De Forest, C.C.A.N.Y., 101 F. 167, 41 C.C.A. 259; Prince de Bearn v. Winans, 111 Md. 434, 74 A. 626. In re Tod, 86 Misc. 616, 148 N.Y.S. 618. But the trustee may recover the unauthorized payment from the one to whom it was made. Marks v. Semple, 111 Ala. 637, 20 So. 791.

[4] Milloglav v. Zacharias, 33 Cal.App. 561, 165 P. 977; Appeal of Fisk, 81 Conn. 433, 71 A. 559; White v. Sherman, 168 Ill. 589, 48 N.E. 128, 61 Am.St.Rep. 132; United States Fidelity & Guaranty Co. v. Douglas' Trustee, 134 Ky. 374, 120 S.W. 328, 20 Ann. Cas. 993; Duckett v. National Bank of Baltimore, 88 Md. 8, 41 A. 161, 1062; Brown v. Cowell, 116 Mass. 461; Davis v. Hoffman, 167 Mo. 573, 67 S.W. 234; Madison Trust Co. v. Carnegie Trust Co., 215 N.Y. 475, 109 N.E. 580; Smith v. Frost, 70 N.Y. 65; Brown v. Lambert's Adm'r, 33 Grat., Va., 256.

[5] Appeal of Hatch, Pa., 12 A. 593; Cooper v. Day, 1 Rich.Eq., S.C., 26; Cogbill v. Boyd, 77 Va. 450.

[6] Waterman v. Alden, 144 Ill. 90, 32 N.E. 972.

[7] Kennedy v. Winn, 80 Ala. 165; Cross v. Petree, 10 B.Mon., Ky., 413; Hunt v. Gontrum, 80 Md. 64, 30 A. 620; Bentley v. Shreve, 2 Md.Ch. 215;

Tatem v. Speakman, 50 N.J.Eq. 484, 27 A. 636; In re Willett's Estate, 15 N.Y.St.Rep. 445.

[8] Snyder's Adm'rs v. McComb's Ex'x, C.C.Del., 39 F. 292.

[9] Voorhees' Ex'x v. Melick, 25 N.J. Eq. 523; Weisel v. Cobb, 118 N.C. 11, 24 S.E. 782; Cresap v. Brown, 82 W.Va. 467, 96 S.E. 66.

[10] De Jarnette v. De Jarnette, 41 Ala. 708; Johns v. Herbert, 2 App. D.C. 485; Hitchcock v. Cosper, 164 Ind. 633, 73 N.E. 264; Robertson v. Robertson's Trustee, 130 Ky. 293, 113 S.W. 138, 132 Am.St.Rep. 368; Jordan v. Jordan's Trust Estate, 111 Me. 124, 88 A. 390; Tuttle v. Gilmore, 36 N.J.Eq. 617; Gray v. Fox, 1 N.J. Eq. 259, 22 Am.Dec. 508; Smith v. Smith, 4 Johns.Ch., N.Y., 281; In re Blauvelt's Estate, Sur., 20 N.Y.S. 119; In re Stark's Estate, Sur., 15 N.Y.S. 729; In re Hart's Estate, 203 Pa. 480, 53 A. 364; Metzger v. Lehigh Valley Trust & Safe Deposit Co., 220 Pa. 535, 69 A. 1037; Dunn v. Dunn, 1 S.C. 350; Wynne v. Warren, 2 Heisk., Tenn., 118; Carr's Adm'r v. Morris, 85 Va. 21, 6 S.E. 613; Key v. Hughes' Ex'rs, 32 W.Va. 184, 9 S.E. 77; Simmons v. Oliver, 74 Wis. 633, 43 N.W. 561.

[11] Mead v. Chesbrough Bldg. Co., C.C.A.N.Y., 151 F. 998, 81 C.C.A. 184;

§ 150 DAMAGES AGAINST TRUSTEE FOR BREACH

The remedy of a cestui que trust here treated, namely, that of recovery of money due for breach of the trust, may be asserted against the representatives of the trustee after his death, as well as against the trustee during his life.[12]

The measure of damages for a breach of trust is the amount of financial loss which the beneficiary, or a successor trustee, can prove flowed from the breach. The trust estate is entitled to be placed in the situation which would have existed if the breach of trust had not been committed.[13] Thus, if the breach was a failure to comply with a duty to sell corporate stock which could have been sold at the price of $2,000, if reasonable diligence had been observed, and the stock was held a year and then sold for $1,000, and the stock has been unproductive during the year, the measure of damages will probably be $1,000, plus the estimated income which the $2,000 would have produced if a sale had been made and that amount reinvested in ordinarily productive trust investments.[14] And if the breach was leaving trust funds idle in the bank instead of investing them in any of the legal trust investments of the state, the measure of damages will be the average trust income which could have been obtained by the trustee on the amount involved and for the period of delay.[15]

A trustee who has made two separate unlawful investments, on one of which there has been a profit and on the other of which there has been a loss, is not entitled to offset the profit against the loss. The beneficiary may insist on the profit as earned by his property, and may reject the unprofitable investment, and require the trustee to replace the cash invested and to retain for himself that investment.[16]

Anderson v. Thero, 139 Iowa 632, 118 N.W. 47; Kirby v. State, 51 Md. 383; Offenstein v. Gehner, 223 Mo. 318, 122 S.W. 715.

[12] Hazard v. Durant, C.C.Mass., 19 F. 471; Pryor v. Davis, 109 Ala. 117, 19 So. 440; Hill v. State, 23 Ark. 604; Green v. Brooks, 25 Ark. 318; Benson v. Liggett, 78 Ind. 452; Frank v. Morley's Estate, 106 Mich. 635, 64 N.W. 577; In re Turpin's Estate, 7 Ohio N.P. 569; In re Gaffney's Estate, 146 Pa. 49, 23 A. 163; In re Spatz's Estate, 245 Pa. 334, 91 A. 492.

[13] For numerous illustrations, see Wright, Measure of Trustee's Liability for Improper Investments, 80 Univ. of Pa.L.R. 1105; Restatement, Trusts, §§ 205–213.

[14] Matter of Garvin's Will, 256 N.Y. 518, 177 N.E. 24; In re Dreier's Estate, 204 Wis. 221, 235 N.W. 439.

[15] Wight v. Lee, 101 Conn. 401, 126 A. 218; Whitecar's Estate, 147 Pa. 368, 23 A. 575.

[16] In re Deare, 11 T.L.R. 183; Creed v. McAleer, 275 Mass. 353, 175 N.E. 761, 80 A.L.R. 1117.

Joint and Several Liability

If several trustees unite in a breach of trust, they are jointly and severally liable, and the entire claim of the cestui may be satisfied from the property of one trustee.[17] In the words of a New Jersey court:[18] "A liability to make good a loss resulting from a breach of trust participated in by more than one trustee is both joint and several, so that each guilty trustee is liable for the whole of the loss." But where several persons are constructive trustees each is liable only for the amount of property coming into his hands.[19]

If two trustees are held liable for a breach of trust in which both joined, and the beneficiary pursues one of them and recovers the full amount of the loss from him, the latter may in equity claim a recovery from his co-trustee of one-half of the amount paid, since equity regards it as fair that the liability should be borne equally, where there is no great difference in the blameworthiness of the trustees. If one trustee is deserving of much more condemnation than the other, contribution may be refused to the more guilty defendant.[20]

Cestui Not Preferred

The claim of a cestui que trust based on a money judgment against the trustee is not a preferred debt. He stands on a level with other creditors of the trustee,[21] and has no lien [22] upon the

[17] Heath v. Erie Ry. Co., 8 Blatchf. 347, Fed.Cas.No. 6306; Hazard v. Durant, C.C.Mass., 19 F. 471; Fellrath v. Peoria German School Ass'n, 66 Ill.App. 77; Furman v. Rapelje, 67 Ill.App. 31; Windmuller v. Spirits Distributing Co., 83 N.J.Eq. 6, 90 A. 249; Gilchrist v. Stevenson, 9 Barb., N.Y., 9; Sortore v. Scott, 6 Lans., N. Y., 271; Meldon v. Devlin, 31 App. Div. 146, 53 N.Y.S. 172, affirmed 167 N.Y. 573, 60 N.E. 1116; Deaderick v. Cantrell, 10 Yerg., Tenn., 263, 31 Am. Dec. 576; Thomas v. Scruggs, 10 Yerg., Tenn., 400; Harrigan v. Gilchrist, 121 Wis. 127, 99 N.W. 909.

[18] General Proprietors of Eastern Division of New Jersey v. Force's Ex'rs, 72 N.J.Eq. 56, 68 A. 914, 942.

[19] Hunter v. Hunter, 50 Mo. 445.

[20] Jackson v. Dickinson, [1903] 1 Ch. 947; Sherman v. Parish, 53 N.Y. 483; In re Linsley, [1904] 2 Ch. 785.

[21] Wales v. Sammis & Scott, 120 Iowa 293, 94 N.W. 840; City of Lincoln v. Morrison, 64 Neb. 822, 90 N.W. 905, 57 L.R.A. 885; Mertens v. Schlemme, 68 N.J.Eq. 544, 59 A. 808; Clark v. Timmons, Tenn.Ch.App., 39 S.W. 534; Johnson's Ex'rs v. Johnson's Heirs, 83 W.Va. 593, 98 S.E. 812.

[22] Spokane County v. First Nat. Bank, C.C.A.Wash., 68 F. 979, 16 C. C.A. 81; Burgoyne v. McKillip, C.C.A. Neb., 182 F. 452, 104 C.C.A. 590; Pharis v. Leachman, 20 Ala. 662; Lathrop v. Bampton, 31 Cal. 17, 89 Am.Dec. 141; Lang v. Metzger, 206 Ill. 475, 69 N.E. 493; City of St. Paul v. Seymour, 71 Minn. 303, 74 N.W. 136; In re Mumford, 5 N.Y.St.Rep. 303; MacArthur v. Gordon, 52 Hun

§ 150 DAMAGES AGAINST TRUSTEE FOR BREACH   505

general assets of the trustee. If the trustee is bankrupt, the cestui must take his dividend in the bankruptcy court with the other creditors, unless he can trace the trust res into the property in the hands of the receiver, assignee, or trustee in bankruptcy. If the trust property, or its substitute, can be traced into the property in the hands of the trustee, or his representative, then the cestui is not dependent upon the recovery of a money judgment against the trustee and its collection from the trustee's general assets; but the cestui que trust may elect the remedy of following the trust property,[23] a remedy the limitations of which are hereinafter discussed; or he may elect to take a money judgment with a lien on the property traced, as is later explained.[24] "But to entitle the owner of trust property to a preference over the general creditors of an insolvent trustee it must appear that his property, or its proceeds, went into and became a part of the fund or estate upon which it is sought to impress a trust."[25]

If the trustee, against whom the cestui brings his bill to recover a decree for the payment of money on account of a breach of trust, is also a cestui que trust, and in that capacity has funds due him or property which is equitably his, the plaintiff cestui may have a lien upon this interest of the defendant as cestui que trust for the recovery of the plaintiff's claim.[26]

Where the respective rights of persons claiming to be cestuis que trust of resulting trusts and creditors of the alleged trustee of such trust come into question, a different problem from that just considered is presented. In this latter case the object of the cestui que trust is to recover the res itself, and not a money judgment. The prevailing view is that, in the absence of

615, 5 N.Y.S. 513; Shute v. Hinman, 34 Or. 578, 56 P. 412, 58 P. 882, 47 L.R.A. 265; Appeal of Cross, 97 Pa. 471; Heidelbach v. Campbell, 95 Wash. 661, 164 P. 247.

[23] Weiss v. Haight & Freese Co., C.C.Mass., 152 F. 479; Metropolitan Nat. Bank v. Campbell Commission Co., C.C.Mo., 77 F. 705; Gray v. Perry, 51 Ga. 180; McCutchen v. Roush, 139 Iowa, 351, 115 N.W. 903; Farnsworth v. Muscatine Produce & Pure Ice Co., 177 Iowa 21, 158 N.W. 741; Hartsock v. Russell, 52 Md. 619; State v. Bank of Commerce, 54 Neb. 725, 75 N.W. 28; Lathrop v. Gilbert, 10 N.J.Eq. 344; Warwick v. Warwick, 31 Grat., Va., 70.

[24] See § 151, post.

[25] Morrison v. Lincoln Sav. Bank & Safe Deposit Co., 57 Neb. 225, 227, 77 N.W. 655. A cestui que trust, having the right to take specific assets from the trustee's estate, may waive it and come in as a general creditor. Keller v. Washington, 83 W.Va. 659, 98 S.E. 880.

[26] Raynes v. Raynes, 54 N.H. 201; Miller v. Miller, 148 Mo. 113, 49 S. W. 852.

estoppel, the resulting cestui prevails over the creditors of the resulting trustee.[27] A similar holding has been made in the case of a constructive trust.[28]

Liability from Acts of Employee

As shown previously,[29] a trustee may in some cases entrust to an agent or servant the performance of acts for the trust. If he does properly delegate work, then the acts of the agents or servants are considered those of the trustee in law, and are binding upon him if they are performed in the usual course of the employee's work. If these acts of the employees amount to breaches of trust, the trustee will be liable to the beneficiary for those breaches.[30] Thus, if a trustee properly delegates to an employee some work in making investments or in making leases, and the investments or leases are imprudently made, the trustee may well be liable for the beneficiary for the damage resulting.

But if an agent is employed to perform certain acts for the trust, and he goes outside his designated work and does a wrongful act, the agent but not the trustee will be liable.[31] Thus, if an agent is employed to collect rents from a building belonging to the trust, and the agent collects the rents properly but steals them, the trustee is not liable to the beneficiary for the wrongful act of the agent in committing a crime, since this was not part of the work for which he was employed.

Obviously, if the trustee negligently employs an agent, or negligently supervises him, he may be liable when the agent does a wrongful act like embezzling the trust funds.[32] But here the basis of liability of the trustee is his own omission, and not the act of the employee.

[27] Murphy v. Clayton, 113 Cal. 153, 45 P. 267; Waterman v. Buckingham, 79 Conn. 286, 64 A. 212; McLaurie v. Partlow, 53 Ill. 340; Robinson v. Robinson, 22 Iowa 427; Hudson v. Wright, 204 Mo. 412, 103 S.W. 8. Contra: Buck v. Webb, 7 Colo. 212, 3 P. 211; Roberts v. Broom, 1 Del.Ch. 388.

[28] Arntson v. First Nat. Bank of Sheldon, 39 N.D. 408, 167 N.W. 760, L.R.A.1918F, 1038.

[29] See § 96, ante.

[30] McClure v. Middletown Trust Co., 95 Conn. 148, 110 A. 838.

[31] Speight v. Gaunt, 1883, 9 App. Cas. 1; Darlington's Estate, 245 Pa. 212, 91 A. 486.

[32] Webb's Estate, 165 Pa. 330, 30 A. 827, 44 Am.St.Rep. 666; McCloskey v. Gleason, 56 Vt. 264, 48 Am.Rep. 770.

Liability upon Default by Cotrustee

Frequent instances are found in the books of inactivity by one trustee and a loss to the trust estate resulting immediately from the negligence or fraud of the active cotrustee. Is an inactive trustee liable to the cestui que trust where the trust property has been dissipated by the wrongful act of the active associate in the trusteeship? Great lack of harmony has been shown by the courts in the discussion of a rule to be applied in this case. In the reign of Charles I the Lord Keeper stated the rule to be that the inactive trustee was not liable "unless some purchase, fraud, or evil dealing appear." [33] This doctrine seemed to limit liability to cases of practical joinder by the passive trustee in the breach by the active trustee.

A Pennsylvania judge in 1843 thus formulated the rule: [34] "It is said to be the harshest demand that can be made in equity to compel a trustee to make up a deficiency, where the money has not come into his hands. In such a case equity will not charge him unless he has been guilty of neglect so gross as almost amounts to fraud."

A Tennessee court has made the rule depend upon the discretionary or directory nature of the trust: "A discretionary trust is, when by the terms of the trust no direction is given as to the manner in which the trust funds shall be vested, till the time arrives at which it is to be appropriated in satisfaction of the trust. In such cases, in order to charge a trustee for an abuse by his cotrustee, some act of commission must be shown on his part, by which the trust fund was attained by his cotrustee, or some act of omission amounting, to gross neglect in permitting the fund to be wasted. * * * A directory trust is when by the terms of the trust the fund is directed to be vested in a particular manner, till the period arrives at which it is to be appropriated. In such cases, if the fund be not vested, or vested in a different manner from that pointed out, it is an abuse of trust for which both trustees are responsible, though but one received the money, because both are bound to attend to the directions of the trust, and must be careful to execute it faithfully, according to its terms and the intention of the person by whom it was created." [35]

Sir John Romilly, Master of the Rolls, has said that "giving one trustee the sole and absolute control over the fund was a breach

---

[33] Townley v. Sherborne, J. Bridgman, 35, 37.

[34] Bell, J., in Nyce's Estate, 5 Watts & S. 254, 255, 40 Am.Dec. 498.

[35] Turley, J., in Deaderick v. Cantrell, 10 Yerg. 263, 269, 270, 272, 31 Am.Dec. 576.

of trust." [36] By this principle affirmative action by the passive trustee giving the active trustee sole control seemed to be all that was necessary in order to show liability.

The New York Court of Appeals has taken the position that an inactive trustee is liable only if he "unnecessarily do an act by which the funds are transferred from the joint possession of all to the sole possession of one," and it has said that "an act is unnecessary when done outside of the usual course of business pertaining to the subject." [37]

The Supreme Judicial Court of Massachusetts has formulated the rule as follows: [38] "It is well settled that a trustee is not responsible for the acts or misconduct of a cotrustee in which he has not joined, or to which he does not consent or has not aided or made possible by his own neglect."

This disorder in the statement of the governing principle lends some color to the statement of Woodward, J., in Irwin's Appeal,[39] that "there is, perhaps, no one subject on which English authorities are so contradictory and irreconcilable as upon the question, when is one trustee or executor liable for moneys that have been lost in the hands of a cotrustee or executor?"

The decisions may be placed in four classes, namely: (a) Those in which the inactive trustee has done nothing but passively allow his cotrustee to assume exclusive possession of the trust property; (b) those in which the sole basis of the inactive trustee's alleged liability is an affirmative act on his part giving the active trustee exclusive possession; (c) cases in which there is an intrusting of possession by positive or negative conduct and, in addition, a failure to supervise the administration of the trust after the co-trustee has taken exclusive control; (d) instances in which the intrusting of possession was followed by notice to the inactive trustee of a possible specific danger to the trust fund and thereafter by continued inaction by the passive trustee.

Passively Allowing Cotrustee to Take Exclusive Possession

The earliest case raising the question of an inactive trustee's liability is Townley v. Sherborne.[40] There a trustee who had passively allowed his fellow trustee to receive the rents of the trust realty was held not liable when the funds were lost, the Lord

---

[36] Wiglesworth v. Wiglesworth, 16 Peav. 269, 272.

[37] Purdy v. Lynch, 145 N.Y. 462, 473, 40 N.E. 232.

[38] Ashley v. Winkley, 209 Mass. 509, 528, 95 N.E. 932.

[39] 35 Pa. 294, 295.

[40] J. Bridgman, 35, 37, 38.

Keeper saying that the passive trustee was not liable in the absence of some "purchase, fraud or evil dealing" in allowing the cotrustee exclusive possession, "for they being by law joyntenants or tenants in common, every one by law may receive either all or as much of the profits as he can come by; and it being the case of most men in these days, that their personal estates do not suffice to pay their debts, prefer their children, and perform their wills, they are enforced to trust their friends with some part of their real estate, to make up the same, either by the sale, or perception of profits; and if such of these friends, who carry themselves without fraud, should be chargeable out of their own estate for the faults and deficiencies of their cotrustees, who were not nominated by them, few men would undertake any such trust. And if two executors be, and one of them waste all, or any part of the estate, the devastavit shall by law charge him only, and not his coexecutor; and in that case, 'equitas sequitur legem,' there have been many precedents resolved in this court, that one executor shall not be charged for the act or default of his companion. And it is no breach of trust to permit one of the trustees to receive all or the most part of the profits, it falling out many times that some of the trustees live far from the lands, and are put in trust out of other respects than to be troubled with the receit of profits." This early case which treated exclusive possession by one trustee as natural and the liability of a trustee as confined to his own receipts, in the absence of fraud, has been followed by many English decisions.[41] This rule has also been applied to passively allowing the cotrustee to have exclusive possession of the evidence of trust property, as, for example, title deeds.[42] The court said in the last-cited case [43] that "no laches could be imputed to the trustees for suffering one of their number to hold the deeds. The reason is that the deeds must be held by some one person, unless they are deposited with bankers, or placed in a box secured by a number of different locks, of which each trustee should hold one of the keys, and negligence cannot be imputed to trustees for not taking such precautions as these."

Yet in other cases passively allowing a cotrustee to take exclusive possession has been regarded as a breach of trust, rendering the inactive trustee liable for loss of the funds while in the co-

[41] Spalding v. Shalmer, 1 Vern. 301; Anonymous, 12 Mod. 560; Aplyn v. Brewer, Finch's Prec.Ch. 173; Fellows v. Mitchell, 1 P.Wms. 81; Leigh v. Barry, 3 Atk. 583; In re Fryer, 3 Kay & J. 317.

[42] Cottam v. Eastern Counties Ry. Co., 1 Johns. & H. 243.

[43] Cottam v. Eastern Counties Ry. Co., 1 Johns. & H. 243, 247.

trustee's hands.[44] In Rodbard v. Cooke [45] the court said: "It may be stated as a general rule of law that where there are two trustees, and one of them places a fund so that it is under the sole control of the other, if the money is misapplied by that other, both are equally liable. The object of having two trustees is to double the control over the trust property, and when one trustee thinks fit to give the other the sole power of dealing with the trust property he defeats that object and becomes himself responsible." The words of this quotation suggest active conduct resulting in exclusive control by the cotrustee, but the facts of the case seem to indicate mere passivity.

Rare circumstances may justify the exclusive control by one trustee and thus obviate any dispute as to the inactive trustee's liability. Thus, where the trust property consisted of shares in a company, the deed of creation of which prohibited ownership of shares by two or more jointly, obviously one trustee must hold the shares.[46]

If exclusive possession is obtained without the actual or constructive knowledge of the passive trustee, naturally there is no liability, because there is no acquiescence in the sole control of the active trustee; [47] and the same is true where exclusive control is obtained by fraud, as by altering a check.[48] Here there is lack of real consent.

In a number of American cases the doctrine of Townley v. Sherborne has been approved, passive acquiescence in exclusive possession by a cotrustee has not been regarded as negligence or a breach of trust, and the inactive trustee has been absolved from liability.[49] In support of this attitude Finch, J., said in Orm-

---

[44] Ex parte Shakeshaft, 3 Bro.Ch. 197; Gregory v. Gregory, 2 Y. & C. 313; Lockhart v. Reilly, 25 L.J.Ch. 697; Rodbard v. Cooke, 36 L.T.N.S. 504; Lewis v. Nobbs, 8 Ch.D. 591.

[45] 36 L.T.N.S. 505.

[46] Consterdine v. Consterdine, 31 Beav. 331.

[47] Derbishire v. Home, 3 De G., M. & G. 80.

[48] Barnard v. Bagshaw, 3 De G., J. & S. 355.

[49] Colburn v. Grant, 181 U.S. 601, 21 S.Ct. 737, 45 L.Ed. 1021; Taylor v. Roberts, 3 Ala. 83; Glenn v. Mc-Kim, 3 Gill, Md., 366; Stowe v. Bowen, 99 Mass. 194; Hunter v. Hunter, 50 Mo. 445; Dyer v. Riley, 51 N.J. Eq. 124, 26 A. 327; Bankes v. Wilkes' Ex'rs, 3 Sandf.Ch., N.Y., 99; Kip v. Deniston, 4 Johns., N.Y., 23; Ormiston v. Olcott, 84 N.Y. 339; Purdy v. Lynch, 145 N.Y. 462, 40 N.E. 232; Westerfield v. Rogers, 174 N.Y. 230, 66 N.E. 813; Worth v. McAden, 1 Dev. & B.Eq. 199, 21 N.C. 199; Ochiltree v. Wright, 1 Dev. & B.Eq. 336, 21 N.C. 336; State v. Guilford, 18 Ohio 500, reversing 15 Ohio 593; Stell's Appeal, 10 Pa. 149; Estate of Fesmire, 134 Pa. 67, 19 A. 502, 19 Am. St.Rep. 676; Birely's Estate, 7 Pa.

iston v. Olcott:[50] "There would be neither wisdom nor justice in a rule which would practically end in making a trustee a guarantor of the diligence and good faith of his associates, and hold him responsible for acts which he did not commit and could not prevent."

A smaller number of American courts have considered passively surrendering the trust property to the exclusive possession of a cotrustee to be negligence, and have held the inactive trustee liable.[51] Where the cotrustee was found in exclusive control,[52] or was passively allowed to assume it,[53] and the inactive trustee thereafter did nothing to return the property to joint control, he has been held liable.

If the active trustee has obtained exclusive control of the property without the knowledge or consent of the inactive trustee, obviously there is no basis for a judgment against the latter.[54]

Intrusting Cotrustee with Exclusive Control by Positive Act

The English cases are almost unanimous in regarding as a negligent breach of trust a positive act by the passive trustee (as, for example, the execution of a power of attorney), by means of which the cotrustee is enabled to get exclusive control of trust assets and thereby to waste them.[55] But Mendes v. Guedella [56] seems to run counter to this weight of authority. In that case two trustees placed in the hands of a third the key to a bank box, for the purpose of allowing him to get the coupons from securi-

---

Dist.R. 395; Boyd's Ex'rs v. Boyd's Heirs, 3 Grat., Va., 113; Griffin's Ex'r v. Macaulay's Adm'r, 7 Grat., Va., 476, 578; Keenan v. Scott, 78 W.Va. 729, 90 S.E. 331. See, also, City Bank v. Maulson, 3 Chanc.Ch.R., U.C., 334.

[50] 84 N.Y. 339, 346.

[51] Royall's Adm'r v. McKenzie, 25 Ala. 363; Fox v. Tay, 89 Cal. 339, 24 P. 855, 26 P. 897, 23 Am.St.Rep. 474; Ringgold v. Ringgold, 1 Har. & G., Md., 11, 18 Am.Dec. 250; Maccubbin v. Cromwell's Ex'rs, 7 Gill & J., Md., 157; Laroe v. Douglass, 13 N.J.Eq. 308; Mumford v. Murray, 6 Johns.Ch., N.Y., 1; Bowman v. Rainetaux, Hoff.Ch., N.Y., 150; Spencer v. Spencer, 11 Paige, N.Y., 299; Earle v. Earle, 93 N.Y. 104.

[52] Thomas v. Scruggs, 10 Yerg., Tenn., 400.

[53] Harvey v. Schwettman, Mo.App., 180 S.W. 413.

[54] Lansburgh v. Parker, 41 App.D. C. 549.

[55] Bradwell v. Catchpole, 3 Swanst. 78, note; Chambers v. Minchin, 7 Ves. 186; Hanbury v. Kirkland, 3 Simon, 265; Marriott v. Kinnersley, Tamlyn, 470; Wiglesworth v. Wiglesworth, 16 Beav. 269; Brumridge v. Brumridge, 27 Beav. 5; Cowell v. Gatcombe, 27 Beav. 568; Ingle v. Partridge, 32 Beav. 661; In re Taylor, 81 L.T.N.S. 812.

[56] 2 Johns. & Hen. 259. See, also, Home v. Pringle, 8 Clark & Fin. 264, and Shepherd v. Harris, [1905] 2 Ch. 310.

ties. The bank was instructed to deliver to the active trustee the coupons only, and not the box; but it negligently delivered the box to the active trustee, and he defaulted. The court declined to hold the passive trustees liable, although it would seem that their act enabled the cotrustee to get exclusive control.

The American courts have not been harmonious in their treatment of the inactive trustee, whose sole negligence, if such it be, has been the taking of a positive step for the purpose of intrusting his active cotrustee with exclusive possession of the trust property. In numerous instances the passive trustee, or guardian or other fiduciary treated by the court as a trustee, has been held responsible, upon the loss of the property by the negligence or crime of the active trustee.[57] But the opposite result has been reached in several cases;[58] the courts stating that, in the absence of warning that the active trustee is in financial difficulty or is dishonest, such conduct by the inactive trustee is not negligent. In Purdy v. Lynch[59] the purpose of the trust was the payment of the debts of a bank. One trustee, who was also a receiver of the bank and had a good reputation, was intrusted by the other trustees with exclusive control of the trust property for the purpose of paying off the bank's debts to its depositors. This was approved by the court as reasonable conduct, and liability for the loss of the funds by the active trustee was not fastened upon the inactive trustees.

The act of intrusting the res to a cotrustee may obviously be negligent, if the passive trustee has knowledge, prior to his sur-

---

[57] Wallis v. Thornton's Adm'r, 2 Brock. 422, Fed.Cas.No.17,111; Edmonds v. Crenshaw, 14 Pet. 166, 10 L.Ed. 402; Gray v. Reamer, 11 Bush, Ky., 113; Barroll v. Forman, 88 Md. 188, 40 A. 883; Smith v. Pettigrew, 34 N.J.Eq. 216; Monell v. Monell, 5 Johns.Ch., N.Y., 283, 9 Am.Dec. 298; Bruen v. Gillet, 115 N.Y. 10, 21 N.E. 676, 4 L.R.A. 529, 12 Am.St.Rep. 764; Matter of Litzenberger, 85 Hun 512, 33 N.Y.S. 155; Graham v. Davidson, 2 Dev. & B.Eq., 22 N.C., 155; Hauser v. Lehman, 2 Ired.Eq. 594, 37 N.C. 594; Clark's Appeal, 18 Pa. 175; Donnelly's Estate, 11 Pa.Dist.R. 211; Graham v. Austin, 2 Grat., Va., 273. To the same effect is Mickleburgh v. Parker, 17 Grant.Ch., U.C., 503.

[58] Laurel County Court v. Trustees of Laurel Seminary, 93 Ky. 379, 20 S. W. 258; Adair v. Brimmer, 74 N.Y. 539; Purdy v. Lynch, 145 N.Y. 462, 40 N.E. 232; State v. Guilford, 18 Ohio 500, reversing 15 Ohio 593; Jones' Appeal, 8 Watts & S., Pa., 143, 42 Am.Dec. 282; Appeal of Hatch, Pa., 12 A. 593. In Re McLatchie, 30 Ont. 179, it was held that where affirmative action of the passive trustee would put the cotrustee in sole control only if the cotrustee committed a crime (forgery), there was no negligence by the passive trustee.

[59] 145 N.Y. 462, 40 N.E. 232.

render of possession, that the cotrustee is financially embarrassed.[60]

Failure to Supervise the Conduct of the Active Cotrustee

In many cases the evidence shows, not only exclusive control by the active trustee, obtained through the acquiescence or affirmative aid of the inactive trustee, but also the lapse of a considerable period of time after such intrusting, with no investigation by the inactive trustee of the conduct of the active trustee. This situation raises the question whether failure to supervise the work of a cotrustee, as, for example, failure to examine the investments made by him, is such negligence as makes the inactive trustee liable for damage to the trust estate.

The English cases have been unanimous in asserting a duty to watch an active cotrustee in exclusive control, to examine his accounts, and to inspect his investments. To fail to give such supervision has been held negligence, rendering the passive trustee liable, whether the active trustee acquired exclusive control through the mere passivity of the inactive trustee [61] or through his positive action.[62]

The American cases also very generally place upon the inactive trustee the duty of supervising and inspecting the work of the active trustee. A trustee who has, by failure to act or by direct action, enabled his cotrustee to obtain exclusive possession of the trust subject-matter, must examine the investments and accounts of the active colleague.[63] Thus, in Richards v. Seal [64] an inactive trustee, who for eleven years made no examination of the status

[60] In re Evans' Estate, 2 Ashm., Pa., 470.

[61] Lincoln v. Wright, 4 Beav. 427; Thompson v. Finch, 22 Beav. 316; Wynne v. Tempest, 13 T.L.R. 360. In the last-named case the trustee was held not to be protected by the provision of section 3 of the Judicial Trustees Act of 1896 to the effect that a court might relieve from liability for a breach of trust a trustee who had acted "honestly and reasonably."

[62] Broadhurst v. Balguy, 1 Y. & C. Ch. 16; Wiglesworth v. Wiglesworth, 16 Beav. 269; Trutch v. Lamprell, 20 Beav. 116; Mendes v. Guedella, 2 Johns. & H. 259; Hale v. Adams, 21 W.R. 400; In re Second East Dulwich Soc., 68 L.J.Ch.,N.S., 196. In Horton v. Brocklehurst, 29 Beav. 504, there was the additional fact that the passive trustee had represented to the cestui que trust that the funds had been properly invested by the active cotrustee, although he (the inactive trustee) knew nothing about the investments. Liability was fixed upon the inactive trustee.

[63] In re Adams' Estate, 221 Pa. 77, 84, 70 A. 436, 128 Am.St.Rep. 727, 15 Ann.Cas. 518. But see Kerr v. Kirkpatrick, 8 Ired.Eq. 137, 43 N.C. 137, where it is denied that "one trustee is bound to keep a supervision over the acts of another."

[64] 2 Del.Ch. 266.

of a bond intrusted to a cotrustee, and thus failed to learn that the cotrustee had collected it and held the proceeds uninvested, was held liable for a loss resulting from the inability of the cotrustee to turn over the money.[65] This duty to supervise exists, whether the inactive trustee, at the time he becomes a trustee, finds the cotrustee in control,[66] or has passively allowed the cotrustee to take exclusive possession,[67] or has by his own positive act put the cotrustee into possession.[68]

If the trust settlement directs that the funds be invested in a particular way, as, for example, in mortgages upon real estate, the duty of the inactive trustee to supervise the conduct of the active associate would seem to be accentuated, if anything. For failure to make such inspection, resulting in the continuance of

[65] To the same effect, see Estate of Hilles, 13 Phila. 402. Jones' Appeal, 8 Watts & S., Pa. 143, 42 Am. Dec. 282, held that mere inquiry of a coguardian was sufficient performance of the duty to investigate; Gibson, C. J., saying (page 151): "To require him to have dealt with his colleague as a rogue, by calling for the securities, would require of him the highest and most exact vigilance, a degree of it that would ruin every guardian." This seems a questionable principle as applied to trustees.

[66] Ralston v. Easter, 43 App.D.C. 513.

[67] In the following cases the loss arose from the bad management or improper investments of the active trustee: Ashley v. Winkley, 209 Mass. 509, 95 N.E. 932; Klatt v. Keuthan, 185 Mo.App. 306, 170 S.W. 374; Wilmerding v. McKesson, 103 N.Y. 329, 8 N.E. 665. Whereas, in other instances, the defalcation of the active trustee was the immediate cause of the loss. Bates v. Underhill, 3 Redf.Sur., N.Y., 365; City Bank v. Maulson, 3 Chanc.Ch.R., U. C., 334; Crowe v. Craig, 29 Nov. Scot. 394. In Wilmerding v. McKesson, 103 N.Y. 329, 8 N.E. 665, however, the court refused to hold the passive trustee liable for the conversion of the trust property by the active trustee, saying that there was no duty to guard against such conduct, unless there was reason to suspect the cotrustee, some fact to put the inactive trustee upon inquiry. And in Matter of Halsted, 110 App. Div. 909, 95 N.Y.S. 1131, affirmed without opinion in 184 N.Y. 563, 76 N.E. 1096, a trustee who for five years allowed trust securities to remain in a bank box to which both trustees had keys, without examining the securities, was held not liable when his active cotrustee stole the securities, since the passive trustee had no reason to suspect his cotrustee.

[68] Caldwell v. Graham, 115 Md. 122, 80 A. 839, 38 L.R.A.,N.S., 1029; Thompson v. Hicks, 1 App.Div. 275, 37 N.Y.S. 340; Estate of Fesmire, 134 Pa. 67, 19 A. 502, 19 Am.St.Rep. 676; McMurray v. Montgomery, 2 Swan, Tenn., 374. Contra: In re Cozzens' Estate, Sur., 15 N.Y.S. 771, 39 N.Y.St.Rep. 386. In Caldwell v. Graham the court says, 115 Md. 129, 80 A. 839, 38 L.R.A.,N.S., 1029: "In accepting the appointment the trustees assumed the joint and equal obligation of exercising their discretion and control with respect to the trust in its entirety."

BOGERT TRUSTS 2D

an improper investment, the passive trustee has been charged.[69] The opinion of the Tennessee court is forcefully put by Turley, J., in Deaderick v. Cantrell, as follows: [70] "Two trustees are appointed to execute a trust, the final operation of which is not to be completed for years; they undertake to execute it; they are intended as checks on each other, have an equal control over the fund, are mutually bound to attend to the interest of the trust, and shall one be permitted to go to sleep and trust everything to the management of his cotrustee, and when, in the course of ten or fifteen years, the fund having been wasted, and his cotrustee insolvent, he is called upon to make it good, shall he be heard to say that he had implicit confidence in his companion, and permitted him to retain all the money, and appropriate it as he pleased, and that he ought not therefore to be charged? Surely not; it is neither law nor reason."

Warning of Danger to Trust Fund, Followed by Continued Inactivity

It frequently happens that the active trustee has got exclusive possession of the trust property, by the act of the passive trustee or without his objection, and that the inactive trustee thereafter learns of an act committed or about to be committed by the active trustee, which is or will be dangerous to the interests of the cestui que trust. In such circumstances there can be no doubt of the passive trustee's duty to act to protect the beneficiary, and, if he fails to bestir himself, he will be liable for injury to the trust estate subsequently resulting from the conduct of the active trustee.[71] Robertson, L. P., in Millar's Trustees v. Polson,[72] has graphically described the position of the inactive trustee in this case: "It is, of course, disagreeable to take a cotrustee by the throat; but if a man undertakes to act as a trustee he must face the necessity of doing disagreeable things when they become necessary in order to keep the estate intact. A trustee is not entitled to purchase a quiet life at the expense of the estate, or to act as

---

[69] Beatty's Estate, 214 Pa. 449, 63 A. 975; Deaderick v. Cantrell, 10 Yerg., Tenn., 263, 31 Am.Dec. 576. But in Cocks v. Haviland, 124 N.Y. 426, 26 N.E. 976, a passive trustee was not held liable, notwithstanding a direction to invest in bonds and mortgages, which, to his knowledge, had not been carried out by the cotrustee.

[70] 10 Yerg. 263, 272, 31 Am.Dec. 576.

[71] Boardman v. Mossman, 1 Bro. Ch. 68; Brice v. Stokes, 1 Ves. 319; Booth v. Booth, 1 Beav. 125; Curtis v. Mason, 12 L.J.Ch.,N.S., 452; Millar's Trustees v. Polson, 34 Sc.L.R. 798.

[72] 34 Sc.L.R. 804.

good-natured men sometimes do in their own affairs in letting things slide and losing money rather than create ill feeling."

The American courts have been equally clear that idleness after a warning of danger is a negligent breach of trust. "It is the duty of one trustee to protect the trust estate from any misfeasance by his cotrustee, upon being made aware of the intended act, by obtaining an injunction against him; and, if the wrongful act has been already committed, to take measures, by suit or otherwise, to compel the restitution of the property, and its application in the manner required by the trust." [73] This rule has been applied where the knowledge was of an improper investment,[74] a refusal to return the property to joint control,[75] the insolvency of the active trustee,[76] an interest in the active trustee antagonistic to that of the cestui que trust,[77] or any breach of trust.[78] A recent case of this type is In re Adams' Estate,[79] where a trustee had knowledge that a cotrustee had wrongfully assumed exclusive control of the trust property but, after restoring the property to joint control, the inactive trustee allowed his cotrustee the means of regaining exclusive possession. Such failure to guard the estate was held negligence, rendering the inactive trustee liable.

Statutory Rules

An English statute of 1859 [80] lays down important rules regarding the liabilities of trustees. It provides that every trust instrument shall be deemed to contain a clause to the effect that the several trustees shall be chargeable only for such property "as they shall respectively actually receive notwithstanding any receipt for the sake of conformity,[81] and shall be answerable and

[73] Crane v. Hearn, 26 N.J.Eq. 378, 381; see, also, Elmendorf v. Lansing, 4 Johns.Ch., N.Y., 562.

[74] Bermingham v. Wilcox, 120 Cal. 467, 52 P. 822; Matter of Niles, 113 N.Y. 547, 21 N.E. 687; In re Cozzens' Estate, Sur., 15 N.Y.S. 771, 39 N.Y.St.Rep. 386; Meldon v. Devlin, 31 App.Div. 146, 53 N.Y.S. 172, affirmed without opinion 167 N.Y. 573, 60 N.E. 1116; Pim v. Downing, 11 Serg. & R., Pa., 66.

[75] Ralston v. Easter, 43 App.D.C. 513; *contra*, Stewart's Estate, 21 Pa. Dist.R. 635.

[76] Darnaby v. Watts, Ky., 21 S.W. 333.

[77] Hill v. Hill, 79 N.J.Eq. 521, 82 A. 338.

[78] In re Howard, 110 App.Div. 61, 97 N.Y.S. 23, affirmed without opinion 185 N.Y. 539, 77 N.E. 1189.

[79] 221 Pa. 77, 70 A. 436, 128 Am. St.Rep. 727, 15 Ann.Cas. 518.

[80] St. 22 & 23 Vict. c. 35, § 31.

[81] Some courts in earlier cases made the distinction that trustees acting "for conformity only"—that is, merely formally—were not liable

§ 150   DAMAGES AGAINST TRUSTEE FOR BREACH   517

accountable only for their own acts, receipts, neglects, or defaults, and not for those of each other, nor for any banker, broker, or other person with whom any trust moneys or securities may be deposited. * * *" This act has been copied in Canada, Australia, and New Zealand,[82] and was incorporated into the English Trustee Act of 1893.[83] A statute applicable to Scotch trustees, enacted in 1861, provided that each trustee "shall only be liable for his acts and intromissions, and shall not be liable for the acts and intromissions of cotrustees, and shall not be liable for omissions."[84]

The decisions since 1859 make no mention of the statute. There are a number of cases in which an inactive trustee who had at one time had possession of the trust property has been held liable for neglect which contributed to the loss.[85] This seems logical under the statute. There are also a few cases in which an inactive trustee has been held responsible for property which he never actually received, on the basis of neglect after the receipt of it by his co-trustee.[86] These latter cases are difficult to reconcile with the express provision of the statute that a trustee shall be liable only for what he actually receives.

Another English statute bearing on the liability of trustees is that section of the Judicial Trustees Act[87] which gives the court power to excuse a trustee from liability for a breach of trust, if he has acted "honestly and reasonably." But this statute has been held not to be intended to protect the inactive trustee, who delegates the trust duties and fails to supervise the administra-

---

for the property received by their co-trustees. Gray v. Reamer, 11 Bush., Ky., 113. And the same doctrine has been applied to executors. Terrill v. Mathews, 12 L.J.Ch.,N.S., 31.

[82] Brit.Col.Tr.Act, § 88; New Brunsw.Tr.Act, § 17; Consol.St. Newf., 1892, c. 84, § 14; Nov.Sc.Tr. Act, § 24; Ont.Tr.Act, § 35; Sask. Tr.Act, § 9; New So.Wales Tr.Act, 1898, § 69; Queensl.Tr. & Ex.Act, 1897, § 25; Vict.St.Trusts, 1864, § 78; New Zealand Tr.Act, § 82.

[83] St. 56 & 57 Vict. c. 53, § 24.

[84] St. 24 & 25 Vict. c. 84, § 1.

[85] Hale v. Adams, 21 Week.R. 400; Lewis v. Nobbs, 8 Ch.D. 591; Rodbard v. Cooke, 36 L.T.,N.S., 504; Bacon v. Camphausen, 58 L.T.,N.S., 851; Robinson v. Harkin, 1896, 2 Ch. 415; In re Taylor, 81 L.T.,N.S., 812, semble.

[86] Bahin v. Hughes, 31 Ch.D. 390; Wynne v. Tempest, 13 L.T.R. 360; In re Second East Dulwich Soc., 68 L.J.Ch.,N.S., 196.

[87] St. 59 & 60 Vict., c. 35, § 3. This act has also been copied in the Dominions. Brit.Col.Tr.Act, § 89; New Br.Tr.Act, § 49; Ont.Tr.Act, § 37; New So.Wales Tr.Amend.Act 1902, § 9; Queensl.Tr. & Ex.Act 1897, § 51; New Zeal.Tr.Act, § 89.

tion of the trust. Such conduct is not "reasonable" or "honest."[88] Hence this section would seem to be of little importance in determining the liabilities of inactive trustees.

A few American states have codified the law regarding the liability of an inactive trustee in the following form:[89] "A trustee is responsible for the wrongful acts of a cotrustee to which he consented, or which by his negligence he enabled the other to commit, but for no others." These statutes are not believed to alter the pre-existing rules of equity.

Change of Inactive Trustee's Liability by Stipulation of Parties

A settlor may provide that each of two trustees shall be liable for only a moiety of the trust property,[90] or that four trustees shall take turns in administering the trust for a year each, and that each shall be liable only during the period of his active administration.[91] English courts have not been friendly to clauses in trust instruments excusing trustees from liability except for property actually received by them, and have construed such clauses to mean that the trustee is liable for what he ought to have received, as well as for what he actually did have in his hands.[92] In Brumridge v. Brumridge, Romilly, M. R., said:[93] "This clause is constantly brought forward to sanction the misappropriation of trust property; but until it is provided, by the instrument creating the trust, that the trustee shall be liable for no breach of trust, provided he does not obtain a personal advantage, I shall not consider the clause as giving a trustee the right or liberty of conniving at a breach of trust. Even if an instrument containing such an inconsistent clause were brought before me, I express no opinion on the result; but, until it is, I cannot allow a trustee to say that it is not his business to act properly in the performance of his duty as trustee."

A provision in the trust deed or will that each trustee shall be liable only for his own default does not protect an inactive trustee from liability for allowing a cotrustee to have exclusive possession. Such negligence is a default as much as a positive breach would be.[94]

[88] In re Turner, 1897, 1 Ch. 536. See, also, In re Second East Dulwich Soc., 68 L.J.Ch.,N.S., 196. But see Dover v. Denne, 3 Ont.L.R. 664.

[89] Civ.Code Cal. § 2239; Mont.Rev. Code 1935, § 7899; Comp.Laws N.D. 1913, § 6292; S.D.Code 1939, 59.0116.

[90] Birls v. Betty, 6 Maddock 90.

[91] Atty. Gen. v. Holland, 2 Y. & C. 683.

[92] Mucklow v. Fuller, Jacobs 198; Bone v. Cook, McClelland 168; Brumridge v. Brumridge, 27 Beav. 5.

[93] 27 Beav. 7.

[94] Marriott v. Kinnersley, Tamlyn 470; Dix v. Burford, 19 Beav. 409.

These constructions of the clauses inserted in trust instruments by settlors before 1859 are consistent with the decisions previously referred to as occurring since the English statute of 1859. Both sets of decisions recognize negligence as a default, and both treat a duty to get actual possession as equivalent to actual possession.

As for the American cases, we find that in Walker v. Walker's Ex'rs [95] the settlor's direction that one trustee should have exclusive possession of the trust property was held to excuse the inactive trustee from liability for the loss of such property.[96] But in Graham v. Austin [97] an attempt by the settlor to restrict the liability of a trustee to a moiety of the property was not allowed to have effect. No matter what may be the settlor's power to limit liability by insertions in the trust instrument, it is obvious that oral statements of a testator-settlor to a prospective trustee, not incorporated into the will, can have no effect to restrict the trustee's liability.[98]

The hostility of the courts to settlor's directions that a trustee's liability shall be limited to the property he actually obtains was further shown in Caldwell v. Graham,[99] where such a clause was somewhat remarkably construed to provide merely against liability for depreciation of the property while in the trustee's hands.

A clause restricting the trustee's responsibility to cases of "willful default" was sustained in Crabb v. Young; [1] Ruger, C. J., stating: [2] "The testator had an absolute right to select the agencies by which his bounty should be distributed and to impose the terms and conditions under which it should be done. * * * The court has not the right to increase the measure of their responsibility or impose obligations from the burden of which he has in his will so carefully protected them." But in Litchfield v. White [3] an assignment for the benefit of creditors, containing a provision that the trustee should be liable only for gross negligence and willful default, was held void. A clause excusing the trustees

---

[95] 88 Ky. 615.

[96] The decisions in Duckworth v. Ocean Steamship Co., 98 Ga. 193, 26 S.E. 736, and Markel v. Peck, 168 Mo.App. 358, 151 S.W. 772, allowing the settlor to alter the usual powers of the trustees, would seem to support the principle that the settlor may also change the several liabilities of the trustees.

[97] 2 Grat., Va., 273.

[98] Dover v. Denne, 3 Ont.L.R. 664.

[99] 115 Md. 122, 80 A. 839, 38 L.R.A.,N.S., 1029.

[1] 92 N.Y. 56.

[2] 92 N.Y. 65, 66.

[3] 7 N.Y. 438, 57 Am.Dec. 534.

from all liability for losses occurring without "willful default" was held, in Matter of Howard,[4] not to exempt from liability a trustee who, after knowledge of a breach of trust by his cotrustee, passively allowed the cotrustee to take exclusive control of the property.

The settlor's power over the details of trust administration has frequently been sustained, as, for example, in giving the trustees greater latitude than usual in the selection of investments. It would seem that this power should extend to such limitations of the trustee's liability as are not repugnant to the essential elements of a trust and do not attempt to make crime lawful.

Trustees have no power by agreement among themselves to divide their responsibilities and to limit the liability of any particular trustee to a portion of the trust property.[5] Thus, in Caldwell v. Graham,[6] where trustees divided the trust property among themselves, one taking the realty and the other the personalty, the court declined to excuse one trustee for negligence respecting the property allotted to the other trustee, and said:[7] "It was optional with him to accept or decline the trust; but, having undertaken the duty imposed by the will, it was not competent for him to limit his obligations or divest himself of any part of his fiduciary discretion."

The consent of the cestui que trust to division of responsibility among trustees has been held not to render such division proper.[8] This result is readily understandable where the consenting beneficiary possesses only a temporary interest and the rights of remaindermen cestuis que trust would also be affected.[9] But it would seem patent that any cestui que trust of full age and sound mind might estop himself from asserting liability against any particular trustee, either wholly or in part.

---

[4] 110 App.Div. 61, 97 N.Y.S. 23, affirmed without opinion 185 N.Y. 539, 77 N.E. 1189.

[5] Fellows v. Mitchell, 1 P.Wms. 81; Lewis v. Nobbs, 8 Ch.D. 591; Mickelburgh v. Parker, 17 Grant.Ch., U.C., 503; Bermingham v. Wilcox, 120 Cal. 467, 52 P. 822; In re Stong's Estate, 160 Pa. 13, 28 A. 480; Thomas v. Scruggs, 10 Yerg., Tenn., 400; contra, In re Cozzens' Estate, Sur., 15 N.Y.S. 771, 39 N.Y.St.Rep. 386; Appeal of Jones, 8 Watts & S., Pa., 143, 42 Am.Dec. 282 (case of joint guardians treated as trustees).

[6] 115 Md. 122, 80 A. 839, 38 L.R.A., N.S., 1029.

[7] 115 Md. 127, 80 A. 839, 38 L.R.A., N.S., 1029.

[8] Fellows v. Mitchell, 1 P.Wms. 81.

[9] Mickelburgh v. Parker, 17 Grant Ch., U.C., 503.

A contract made by trustees in the trust instrument to the effect that each shall be liable for the acts of the other is unobjectionable and valid.[10]

The power of equity to make one trustee liable primarily and another secondarily would seem unquestionable;[11] but the action of a federal court [12] in approving the decree of a probate court which divided the trust property between trustees, and in limiting the liability of each trustee to his share of the property, seems to amount to violating the settlor's intent and remaking the trust for him.

The liability of the inactive trustee should, it would seem, be determined in the light of the joint title and powers of trustees, and by the aid of the rule requiring the trustee, whether active or inactive, to use the prudence of an ordinarily careful man in his own affairs, and also the rule prohibiting the delegation of discretionary powers.

The failure of an inactive trustee to act to protect the trust estate after notice of impending danger is assuredly a want of ordinary prudence. The refusal to supervise the administration of the active cotrustee would seem to be a delegation of discretionary powers and also a failure to use reasonable care. Whether the mere exclusive possession of the trust property by the active cotrustee, acquired by the aid of the inactive trustee or with his passive acquiescence, is sufficient to charge the inactive trustee would seem to be a more difficult question. In cases where there was necessity for intrusting the exclusive control to the cotrustee, and there was no apparent danger, it might well be held that such intrusting was not negligence on the part of the inactive trustee. But, on the other hand, where there was no necessity for such intrusting, and the character of the property (as, for example, its negotiability) rendered the intrusting dangerous, the inactive trustee might well be regarded as negligent if he allowed the active trustee sole control.[13]

---

[10] Leigh v. Barry, 3 Atk. 583.

[11] McCartin v. Traphagen, 43 N.J. Eq. 323, 11 A. 156. Upon the question whether a trustee who has been held liable for a breach of trust ever has a right to contribution from his cotrustee, see Fletcher v. Green, 33 Beav. 426; and as to the right of indemnity in the same case, see Lockhart v. Reilly, 25 L.J.Ch. 697; Price v. Price, 42 L.T.R. 654; Bahin v. Hughes, 31 Ch.D. 390; Bacon v. Camphausen, 58 L.T.,N.S., 851; In re Turner, 1897, 1 Ch. 536; Head v. Gould, 1898, 2 Ch. 250; In re Linsley, 1904, 2 Ch. 785.

[12] American Bonding Co. of Baltimore v. Richardson, C.C.A.Ohio, 214 F. 897, 131 C.C.A. 565.

[13] For a discussion of this subject on principle, see Bogert, The Liability of an Inactive Co-Trustee, 34 Harv.Law Rev. 483.

Liability of Trustee for Interest, Simple or Compound

Frequently, where the cestui que trust pursues the remedy of recovering a money judgment or decree against the trustee, interest is included as a part of the amount directed to be paid. The trustee has deprived the cestui of the use of trust property or its proceeds, and the value of that use is estimated by interest. The sole object of allowing the cestui que trust interest is to make him whole, to place him in the position he would have been in if the trustee had performed his duty. When interest will be allowed and at what rate is wholly in the discretion of the court. "As a general rule, in the absence of anything to the contrary, the question of requiring a trustee to pay interest on the trust funds is one which must depend upon the facts and circumstances in each particular case; and where good conscience requires that the trustee be charged with interest, the payment thereof ought to be exacted." [14] This principle has been stated as follows by another court: "Independent of contract or statute, a court of equity in its sound discretion may require one who has converted to his own use the funds of another to pay damages equal to the legal rate of interest, as compensation for the loss of the use of his funds." [15]

Where the property, of the use of which the beneficiary has been deprived, has produced a known income, this furnishes a more satisfactory basis for the award of damages than interest. Thus, where the trustee mingles the trust funds with his own property, and the separate earnings of the trust property are known, recovery of such separate earnings is frequently allowed; [16] but the cestui que trust may elect between such earnings and interest.[17] And so, also, the actual rents received from real property used by the trustee,[18] and the actual interest on money unjustifiably left in a bank,[19] have been allowed as dam-

[14] Stanley's Estate v. Pence, 160 Ind. 636, 644, 66 N.E. 51, 67 N.E. 441.

[15] Cree v. Lewis, 49 Colo. 186, 112 P. 326, 328.

[16] Title Ins. & Trust Co. v. Ingersoll, 158 Cal. 474, 111 P. 360; Rainsford v. Rainsford, McMul.Eq., S.C., 335.

[17] Treacy v. Powers, 112 Minn. 226, 127 N.W. 936; City of Lincoln v. Morrison, 64 Neb. 822, 90 N.W. 905, 57 L.R.A. 885; In re Eisenlohr's Estate, 258 Pa. 431, 102 A. 115.

[18] Percival-Porter Co. v. Oaks, 130 Iowa 212, 106 N.W. 626; Hayes v. Kerr, 40 App.Div. 348, 57 N.Y.S. 1114; Owens v. Williams, 130 N.C. 165, 41 S.E. 93; Hill v. Cooper, 8 Or. 254; Thomson v. Peake, 38 S.C. 440, 17 S.E. 45, 725.

[19] Cornet v. Cornet, 269 Mo. 298, 190 S.W. 333; In re Wiley, 98 App. Div. 93, 91 N.Y.S. 661.

ages, rather than interest or estimated value. The gains actually made from the trust property by the trustee are more apt to be awarded as damages when the trustee has shown good faith than when he has been guilty of fraud.[20]

Occasionally, where the trustee has had the use of trust property, its rental value is used as the measure of damages.[21]

Whether simple or compound interest shall be allowed, where interest is the basis, is a question of discretion and fact in each case. If simple interest will adequately compensate the cestui que trust, it will be added; if compound interest will more accurately make the beneficiary whole, then that standard of computation will be followed. "Although as a general rule it may fairly be stated that, where the trustee is guilty of gross neglect or fraud, or mingles the money with his own, he should be charged with interest at the legal rate, with annual rests, and, if he is guilty of mere neglect, with simple interest only, this rule is subject to exceptions, and the real question is what the equities of the particular case demand." [22]

If the trustee has converted the trust property to his own use, simple interest on the value of the property at the time of conversion is ordinarily allowed.[23] Simple interest has also been frequently charged when the trustee has failed to invest the funds, although directed to do so by the trust instrument,[24] or when he has allowed the funds to lie idle in the absence of any

---

[20] Van Buskirk v. Van Buskirk, 148 Ill. 9, 35 N.E. 383; Phillips v. Burton, 107 Ky. 88, 52 S.W. 1064; Beale v. Kline, 183 Pa. 149, 38 A. 897; Watson v. Dodson, Tex.Civ.App., 143 S.W. 329.

[21] Johnson v. Richey, 5 Miss. 233, 4 How. 233; Weltner v. Thurmond, 17 Wyo. 268, 98 P. 590, 99 P. 1128, 129 Am.St.Rep. 1113.

[22] Backes v. Crane, 87 N.J.Eq. 229, 100 A. 900, 904, 905.

[23] Primeau v. Granfield, C.C.N.Y., 184 F. 480; Hall v. Glover, 47 Ala. 467; Clapp v. Vatcher, 9 Cal.App. 462, 99 P. 549; Cree v. Lewis, 49 Colo. 186, 112 P. 326; Stanley's Estate v. Pence, 160 Ind. 636, 66 N.E. 51, 67 N.E. 441; Campbell v. Napier, 182 Ky. 182, 206 S.W. 271; McKim v. Hibbard, 142 Mass. 422, 8 N.E. 152; Darling v. Potts, 118 Mo. 506, 24 S.W. 461; Van Rensselaer v. Morris, 1 Paige, N.Y., 12; Mabie v. Bailey, 95 N.Y. 206; Hazard v. Durant, 14 R.I. 25; Cresap v. Brown, 82 W.Va. 467, 96 S.E. 66.

[24] Nicholson v. McGuire, 4 Cranch, C.C. 194, Fed.Cas.No.10249; Boreing v. Faris, 127 Ky. 67, 104 S.W. 1022; Ringgold v. Ringgold, 1 Har. & G., Md., 11, 18 Am.Dec. 250; Smith v. Darby, 39 Md. 268; Backes v. Crane, 87 N.J.Eq. 229, 100 A. 900; In re Muller, 31 App.Div. 80, 52 N.Y.S. 565; Breneman v. Frank, 28 Pa. 475; Landis v. Scott, 32 Pa. 495; Appeal of McCausland, 38 Pa. 466; Appeal of Stearly, 38 Pa. 525; Baker v. Lafitte, 4 Rich.Eq., S.C., 392.

express direction for investment,[25] or when he has been negligent in collecting the funds and reinvesting them.[26]

Simple interest has also been awarded on funds improperly invested, from the date of the investment,[27] on money held by the trustee after he should have paid it over to the beneficiary,[28] and on trust moneys used by the trustee in his own business.[29]

Occasionally the trustee has a good reason for holding the trust property in an unproductive condition, and he will not be liable to pay to the cestui interest or the value of the use measured in any other way. Thus, where the money is held under a mistake of law,[30] or where the money is held during a period when there is no duty to pay over or invest,[31] or where the trustee has in good faith paid the money to the wrong party under a mistake of law,[32] or where the trustee is holding the money to await the determination of conflicting claims to it,[33]

[25] McComb v. Frink, 149 U.S. 629, 13 S.Ct. 993, 37 L.Ed. 876; Jennings' Ex'rs v. Davis, 5 Dana, Ky., 127; Comegys v. State, 10 Gill & J., Md., 175; Weisel v. Cobb, 118 N.C. 11, 24 S.E. 782; Landis v. Scott, 32 Pa. 495; Appeal of Lukens, 47 Pa. 356; Pettus v. Sutton, 10 Rich.Eq., S.C., 356; Smith v. Thomas, 8 Baxt., Tenn., 417.

[26] Hamilton v. Reese, 18 Ga. 8.

[27] Hitchcock v. Cosper, 164 Ind. 633, 73 N.E. 264; Cogbill v. Boyd, 79 Va. 1.

[28] Lasker-Morris Bank & Trust Co. v. Gans, 132 Ark. 402, 200 S.W. 1029; Knapp v. Marshall, 56 Ill. 362; Haines v. Hay, 169 Ill. 93, 48 N.E. 218; Mathewson v. Davis, 191 Ill. 391, 61 N.E. 68; Glenn's Ex'rs v. Cockey, 16 Md. 446; Rowland v. Maddock, 183 Mass. 360, 67 N.E. 347; McBride v. McIntyre, 100 Mich. 302, 58 N.W. 994; Judd v. Dike, 30 Minn. 380, 15 N.W. 672; Macklanburg v. Griffith, 115 Minn. 131, 131 N.W. 1063; Isler v. Brock, 134 N.C. 428, 46 S.E. 951; Knight v. Reese, 2 Dall. 182, 1 L.Ed. 340; Lomax v. Pendleton, 3 Call, Va., 538.

[29] Lehmann v. Rothbarth, 111 Ill. 185; Dorsey's Ex'rs v. Dorsey's Adm'r, 4 Har. & McH., Md., 231; Union Trust Co. v. Preston Nat. Bank, 144 Mich. 106, 107 N.W. 1109; St. Paul Trust Co. v. Strong, 85 Minn. 1, 88 N.W. 256; Kerr v. Laird, 27 Miss. 544; Knowlton v. Bradley, 17 N.H. 458, 43 Am.Dec. 609; First Congregational Soc. v. Pelham, 58 N.H. 566; Lathrop v. Smalley's Ex'rs, 23 N.J.Eq. 192; Mumford v. Murray, 6 Johns.Ch., N.Y., 1; In re Muller, 31 App.Div. 80, 52 N.Y.S. 565; In re Jones, 143 App.Div. 692, 128 N.Y.S. 215; In re Bosler's Estate, 161 Pa. 457, 29 A. 57; Reid v. Reid, 237 Pa. 176, 85 A. 85; In re Hodges' Estate, 66 Vt. 70, 28 A. 663, 44 Am.St. Rep. 820; Miller v. Beverleys, 4 Hen. & M., Va., 415.

[30] Southern Ry. Co. v. Glenn's Adm'r, 102 Va. 529, 46 S.E. 776.

[31] Mathewson v. Davis, 191 Ill. 391, 61 N.E. 68; January v. Poyntz, 2 B. Mon., Ky., 404; Martin v. Martin, 43 Or. 119, 72 P. 639.

[32] Calkins v. Bump, 120 Mich. 335, 79 N.W. 491.

[33] Calkins v. Bump, 120 Mich. 335, 79 N.W. 491.

or there is no unreasonable delay in applying the trust money and no use of it by the trustee for his own purposes,[34] or where the money is held as probably necessary to pay debts,[35] there will be no liability to pay interest. And if, due to the neglect of the cestui que trust, there is no opportunity to pay over or invest accrued income, the trustee will not be liable for interest on it.[36]

Compound interest will be allowed where it is necessary to compensate the beneficiary. It is not awarded as punishment, but as compensation. "The rule which makes an executor or other trustee chargeable with compound interest upon trust funds used by him in his own business is not adopted for the purpose of punishing him for any intentional wrongdoing in the use of such fund, but rather to carry into effect the principle, enforced by courts of equity, that the trustee shall not be permitted to make any profit from the unauthorized use of such funds."[37] As Chancellor Walworth said: "Stating the account with periodical rests, and compounding interest, is only a convenient mode, adopted by the court, to charge the trustee with the amount of profits supposed to have been made by him in the use of the money; where the actual amount of profits, which he has made, beyond simple interest, cannot be ascertained."[38] Compound interest is generally allowed in case of fraud,[39] willful misconduct,[40] or other gross delinquency.[41]

Perhaps the most common instance of the collection of compound interest from the defaulting trustee is found where he has used the trust fund in his own business and the actual profits earned by the trust fund are not claimed or are impossible of computation,[42] or where there is a strong presumption that

---

[34] Minuse v. Cox, 5 Johns.Ch., N.Y., 441, 9 Am.Dec. 313; In re Selleck, 111 N.Y. 284, 19 N.E. 66.

[35] Fulton v. Davidson, 3 Heisk., Tenn., 614.

[36] Cassels v. Vernon, 5 Mason 332, Fed.Cas.No. 2,503.

[37] Miller v. Lux, 100 Cal. 609, 616, 35 P. 345, 639.

[38] Utica Ins. Co. v. Lynch, 11 Paige, N.Y., 520, 524.

[39] St. Paul Trust Co. v. Strong, 85 Minn. 1, 88 N.W. 256.

[40] Adams v. Lambard, 80 Cal. 426, 22 P. 180. But it may be awarded in the absence of any misconduct. Page's Ex'r v. Holman, 82 Ky. 573.

[41] Mathewson v. Davis, 191 Ill. 391, 61 N.E. 68.

[42] In re Thompson's Estate, 101 Cal. 349, 35 P. 991, 36 P. 98, 508; Faulkner v. Hendy, 103 Cal. 15, 36 P. 1021; Bemmerly v. Woodward, 124 Cal. 568, 57 P. 561; State v. Howarth, 48 Conn. 207; Clement v. Brainard, 46 Conn. 174; Lehman v. Rothbarth, 159 Ill. 270, 42 N.E. 777; Page's Ex'r v. Holman, 82 Ky. 573; Clemens v.

the trustee has used the funds in his own business, because he renders no account and in no way shows the disposition of the trust money.[43] Compound interest has also been granted on money unlawfully invested,[44] and upon money not invested after a decree of a court directing its investment.[45]

The expenses incurred by the trustee in carrying on the trust business or protecting the trust property should clearly be paid by the beneficiary as a condition of relief against the trustee.[46] But claims by the trustee against the cestui que trust arising out of other transactions unconnected with the trust cannot be required to be paid as a condition precedent to the enforcement of the trust.[47]

Neither a demand[48] nor a previous action at law[49] are ordinarily conditions precedent to the maintenance of a suit in equity to enforce the trust.

Criminal Liability of Trustee

Until the enactment of recent statutes a breach of trust by a trustee, even though fraudulent, was not a crime. The trustee had the legal title, and his original possession was lawful. In discussing a fraudulent appropriation of trust funds, a New York court recently said:[50] "The acts of the defendant were not larceny at common law, and not cognizable in a criminal prosecution. The underlying concept of larceny at common law was an initial *trespass* and *trover*. Where there was no trespass, there was no larceny, though trespass and trover in themselves were not necessarily larceny. * * * The defendant's conduct amounted to what was known formerly as 'a criminal

---

[43] Voorhees' Adm'rs v. Stoothoff, 11 N.J.L. 145.

[44] White v. Sherman, 168 Ill. 589, 48 N.E. 128, 61 Am.St.Rep. 132.

Caldwell, 7 B.Mon., Ky., 171; Montjoy v. Lashbrook, 2 B.Mon., Ky., 261; Ringgold v. Ringgold, 1 Har. & G., Md., 11, 18 Am.Dec. 250; Diffenderffer v. Winder, 3 Gill & J., Md., 311; Pullis v. Somerville, 218 Mo. 624, 117 S.W. 736; Bobb v. Bobb, 89 Mo. 411, 4 S.W. 511; Cornet v. Cornet, 269 Mo. 298, 190 S.W. 333; McKnight's Ex'rs v. Walsh, 23 N.J.Eq. 136; Cook v. Lowry, 95 N.Y. 103; In re Reed, 45 App.Div. 196, 61 N.Y.S. 50.

[45] Latimer v. Hanson, 1 Bland, Md., 51.

[46] Pujol v. McKinlay, 42 Cal. 559; Wagenseller v. Prettyman, 7 Ill.App. 192.

[47] Waller v. Jones, 107 Ala. 331, 18 So. 277; Fitzgerald v. Hollan, 44 Kan. 499, 24 P. 957.

[48] Garard v. Garard, 135 Ind. 15, 34 N.E. 442, 809.

[49] Neresheimer v. Smyth, 167 N.Y. 202, 60 N.E. 449.

[50] People v. Shears, 158 App.Div. 577, 580, 143 N.Y.S. 861.

breach of trust,' and until quite recent times was cognizable only in a court of equity and punishable only as contempt of court, where restitution was not made in obedience to a judgment so decreeing. * * * Nor did the defendant's act come within the scope of the early statutes creating the crime of embezzlement, which statutes were enacted to meet some of the deficiencies of the common-law rules as to larceny."

But modern statutes frequently make the appropriation of the trust property by the trustee larceny or embezzlement, so that the cestui que trust has the additional remedy of prosecuting the trustee for a crime, and in some cases collecting a fine from him under the criminal law.[51]

---

[51] The New York statute, Penal Law, § 1302, may be taken as a sample. It reads as follows: "A person acting as executor, administrator, committee, guardian, receiver, collector or trustee of any description, appointed by a deed, a will, or other instrument, or by an order or judgment of a court or officer, who secretes, withholds, or otherwise appropriates to his own use, or that of any person other than the true owner, or person entitled thereto, any money, goods, thing in action, security, evidence of debt or of property, or other valuable thing, or any proceeds thereof, in his possession or custody by virtue of his office, employment, or appointment, is guilty of grand or petit larceny in such degree as is herein prescribed, with reference to the amount of such property; and upon conviction, in addition to the punishment in this article prescribed for such larceny, may be adjudged to pay a fine, not exceeding the value of the property so misappropriated or stolen, with interest thereon from the time of the misappropriation, withholding, concealment, and twenty per centum thereon, in addition, and to be imprisoned for not more than five years in addition to the term of his sentence for larceny, according to this article, unless the fine is sooner paid." The fine, if collected, is payable to the injured party to the extent of his loss, plus interest and expenses of collection.

See, also, Ariz.Code 1939, § 43-5510, construed in Wooddell v. Arizona, C.C.A.Ariz., 187 F. 739, 109 C.C.A. 487; Ga.Code 1933, § 26-2805; Pa. 18 P.S. § 2591, construed in Commonwealth v. Levi, 44 Pa.Super.Ct. 253.

PERSONAL LIABILITY OF TRUSTEE WITH LIEN [52]

151. Where the trustee has wrongfully disposed of trust property, and has in his hands the proceeds of such trust property, the beneficiary may hold the trustee liable for the loss, and also have a lien on the proceeds of the trust property as a means of collecting his decree.

In some cases the beneficiary is aided in the collection of his judgment against the trustee for breach of trust. He is given a lien, or right to the use of specific property for the purpose of collecting his claim.

Where the trustee has wrongfully disposed of trust property, and has in his hands the product or substitute for that particular trust property, equity considers it fair to give the beneficiary a lien on the product or substitute as a means of helping him to collect his decree for the payment of money.[53] Thus, if the trustee in breach of trust buys land with the trust money, and has the deed run to himself as trustee or to himself without trust label, the land is the product or proceeds of trust property which has been mismanaged by the trustee. The beneficiary is undoubtedly entitled to a decree against the trustee for the amount of the trust fund invested in the land, and can make the trustee keep the land as his, the trustee's, personal investment. But, in addition, since the land is the product of trust funds, the court of equity considers it just to give the plaintiff beneficiary a lien on the land, for the purpose of enabling him to collect the decree against the trustee for the payment of the amount of trust money wrongfully invested. If the trustee invested $1,000 of trust money in the land, there will be a decree against him requiring him to pay into the trust fund $1,000 of his own money; and there will be a lien on the land which will enable the beneficiary to have the land sold and its proceeds applied on the decree. If the sale of the land realizes $500 net, then the decree for $1,000, will be reduced to $500, and $500 only will be collectible out of the other property of the trustee.

---

[52] Restatement, Trusts, § 202.

[53] Primeau v. Granfield, C.C.N.Y., 184 F. 480; Citizens' Bank of Paso Robles v. Rucker, 138 Cal. 606, 72 P. 46; Hinsey v. Supreme Lodge K. of P., 138 Ill.App. 248; Newis v. Topfer, 121 Iowa 433, 96 N.W. 905; Bohle v. Hasselbroch, 64 N.J.Eq. 334, 51 A. 508, 61 L.R.A. 323.

Where the product of a wrongful disposition of trust property is of less value than the trust property was, and there is some chance of collecting out of the general assets of the trustee, this method is preferable to tracing. On the other hand if the product is greater in value than the original trust property, tracing will be a preferable remedy. Thus, if $1,000 of trust funds has been wrongfully invested in land by the trustee, and the land has shrunk in value to $800, a money judgment plus lien on the land will be advisable. But if the land has increased in value to $1,200, tracing into the land will give the beneficiary a more advantageous remedy.

In Will of Mendel a trustee was directed to invest the funds in "first-class interest-bearing real estate mortgage securities." It being held that the securities actually purchased were improper investments under this direction, the cestuis were allowed to hold the trustee personally liable and to enforce an equitable lien upon the securities. The court said:[54] "Counsel for appellant contend that the judgment, affording respondents the benefit of the securities, so far as money can be realized therefrom, to restore the trust funds, is inconsistent with the judgment against the guilty trustee for the money improperly diverted; that appellant cannot have the securities in question and have a judgment for a recovery of the money invested therein, as well. The difficulty with that is that the judgment does not proceed upon the theory that the title to the securities is in the trustees, or that they are to have them; but rather upon the ground that the securities have been rejected, subject to an equitable lien thereon in favor of the trust fund. We do not perceive any difficulty in that. This is not a case of following the trust fund into the property in which it has been improperly invested, and claiming such property, and, at the same time, claiming to recover the fund upon personal liability therefor. * * * The [successor] trustees do not claim the securities. They claim that, in equity, they are entitled to hold them as property of the wrongdoer, charged with a lien to make good, so far as practicable, the damage caused by the wrong. There can be no doubt but what the cestui que trust, in such circumstances as exist here, may retain the property and thereby ratify

[54] 164 Wis. 136, 143–144, 159 N.W. 806.

the wrong, or reject it and claim damages for the wrongful investment therein, or claim such damages and charge such property, as belonging to the wrongdoer, with a lien for the damages suffered."

RECOVERY OF THE TRUST RES OR ITS SUBSTITUTE [55]

152. The cestui que trust, or a substitute trustee representing him, may follow the trust res or its substitute into the hands of all persons except purchasers without notice of the trust, and procure a decree for the return of the trust property or its product to the trust fund.

An important remedy available to the beneficiary or a trustee representing him, is the recovery of the trust property or its product from one who holds it after the trustee has committed a breach of trust.[56] That this remedy exists, subject to qualifications to be explained, whether the property or its product is in the wrongdoing trustee's hands [57] or is held by a third person,[58] is unquestioned. The beneficiary naturally must elect to take one or the other, the original trust property or the substitute, where both are capable of identification.[59] "The law is now well settled that as between the cestui que trust and trustee, and all parties claiming under the trustee otherwise than by purchase for a valuable consideration without notice, all property be-

---

[55] Restatement, Trusts, § 202.

[56] Oliver v. Piatt, 3 How. 333, 11 L.Ed. 622; General Petroleum Corporation of California v. Dougherty, C.C.A.Cal., 117 F.2d 529; Cooper v. Landis, 75 N.C. 526; In re Freas' Estate, 231 Pa. 256, 79 A. 513.

[57] Taber v. Bailey, 22 Cal.App. 617, 135 P. 975; Breit v. Yeaton, 101 Ill. 242; Clifford v. Farmer, 79 Ind. 529; Brothers v. Porter, 6 B.Mon., Ky., 106; Freeman v. Maxwell, 262 Mo. 13, 170 S.W. 1150; Lucia Mining Co. v. Evans, 146 App.Div. 416, 131 N.Y. S. 280; Frank v. Firestone, 132 App. Div. 932, 116 N.Y.S. 700; Berry v. Evendon, 14 N.D. 1, 103 N.W. 748; O'Neill v. O'Neill, 227 Pa. 334, 76 A.

26; Wilkinson v. Wilkinson, 1 Head, Tenn., 305; Kaphan v. Toney, Tenn. Ch.App., 58 S.W. 909; Mitchell v. Blanchard, 72 Vt. 85, 47 A. 98; Overseers of Poor of Norfolk v. Bank of Virginia, 2 Grat., Va., 544, 44 Am. Dec. 399; Crumrine v. Crumrine, 50 W.Va. 226, 40 S.E. 341, 88 Am.St.Rep. 859; Hubbard v. Burrell, 41 Wis. 365.

[58] Cobb v. Knight, 74 Me. 253; Chaves v. Myer, 13 N.M. 368, 85 P. 233, 6 L.R.A.,N.S., 793; Barnard v. Hawks, 111 N.C. 333, 16 S.E. 329.

[59] Bonner v. Holland, 68 Ga. 718; Cadieux v. Sears, 258 Ill. 221, 101 N. E. 542.

BOGERT TRUSTS 2D

longing to a trust, however much it may be changed or altered in its nature or character, and all the fruit of such property, whether in its original or altered state, continues to be subject to or affected by the trust." [60] This doctrine has recently been expressed by the Supreme Court of California in the following words: "It is well settled that the beneficiary of a trust may follow and recover the trust fund, if any property in the hands of the trustee or of those taking with notice can be identified, either as the original property of the cestui que trust or as the product of it." [61]

The cestui's right is not that of a lienholder or a preferred creditor. It is based on a property right in the res or its substitute. "The right of the beneficiary to pursue a fund and impose upon it the character of a trust is based on the principle that it is the property of the beneficiary, not upon any right of lien against the wrongdoer's general estate; and this, whether the property sought to be recovered is in the form in which the beneficiary parted with its possession or in a substituted form." [62]

This remedy may be illustrated. If A. is trustee for B., and the original trust res is certain land, A. violates the trust by selling the land to X., who knows of the breach, and A. then deposits the proceeds of the sale in a bank; B. may follow the original property into the hands of X. and recover it, or he may follow the proceeds of the original property into the bank account and take the claim against the bank as his property. By following and recovering the trust property or its substitute it is meant that the beneficiary, or a trustee acting for him, may obtain a decree that the property in question is subject to the trust and is to be treated henceforth as a part of the trust property. This will involve delivery of it to a trustee for the complainant beneficiary.

This right to recover the property is, however, qualified. Its exercise depends upon two considerations, namely: (a) The status of the holder of the property sought to be recovered;

[60] Hill v. Fleming, 128 Ky. 201, 107 S.W. 764, 766, 16 Ann.Cas. 840.

[61] People v. California Safe Deposit & Trust Co., 175 Cal. 756, 167 P. 388, 389, L.R.A.1918A, 1151.

[62] Heidelbach v. Campbell, 95 Wash. 661, 665, 164 P. 247. See, also, Chase & Baker Co. v. Olmsted, 93 Wash. 306, 160 P. 952.

and (b) the ability of the cestui que trust to identify the property in question as the original trust res or its substitute. These conditions of the exercise of the remedy will be separately considered.

If the beneficiary is not sure whether there is trust property or its product which he can trace, he may bring a bill of discovery;[63] if he is ignorant of the status of the trust, he is entitled to a decree compelling the trustee to give him information or to account.[64]

Where the suit is to recover the trust res or its substitute from a third person, and such third person has performed services or made expenditures for which the cestui should equitably pay, reimbursement will be a prerequisite to relief.[65] For example, an action to recover the trust res from a taker who has paid no consideration will succeed only upon the payment to the holder of the property of advances which he has made to cancel incumbrances on the property.[66] Frequently in bills to charge the defendants as constructive trustees because of wrongdoing this principle has been applied.[67] Thus, an attorney charged as a constructive trustee because he acquired an adverse interest while acting for the plaintiff is entitled to be reimbursed for money spent to acquire titles adverse to those of the cestui que trust.[68]

On principle it would seem that a purchaser of the trust property with notice of the trust ought not to be allowed to charge

---

[63] Ferguson v. Rogers, 129 Ark. 197, 195 S.W. 22; Indian Land & Trust Co. v. Owen, Okl., 162 P. 818.

[64] Alexander v. Fidelity Trust Co., C.C.A.Pa., 249 F. 1, 161 C.C.A. 61; Peters v. Rhodes, 157 Ala. 25, 47 So. 183; Green v. Brooks, 81 Cal. 328, 22 P. 849; People v. Bordeaux, 242 Ill. 327, 89 N.E. 971; Dodge v. Black, 53 S.W. 1039, 21 Ky.Law Rep. 992; Taft v. Stow, 174 Mass. 171, 54 N.E. 506. See §§ 144–145, ante.

[65] Wormley v. Wormley, 8 Wheat. 421, 5 L.Ed. 651; Bates v. Kelly, 80 Ala. 142; Hawley v. Tesch, 88 Wis. 213, 59 N.W. 670.

[66] Feingold v. Roeschlein, 276 Ill. 79, 114 N.E. 506.

[67] McKibben v. Diltz's Ex'r, 138 Ky. 684, 128 S.W. 1082, 137 Am.St.Rep. 408; Coburn v. Page, 105 Me. 458, 74 A. 1026, 131 Am.St.Rep. 575; Iddings v. Bruen, 4 Sandf.Ch., N.Y., 223; McKennan v. Pry, 6 Watts, Pa., 137; Haight v. Pearson, 11 Utah 51, 39 P. 479; Soderberg v. McRae, 70 Wash. 235, 126 P. 538.

[68] Home Inv. Co. v. Strange, Tex., 195 S.W. 849.

the cestui que trust with the payment of the cost of improvements as a condition to the recovery of the property;[69] but the opposite view has sometimes found judicial approval.[70]

MEANING OF BONA FIDE PURCHASER [71]

153. A bona fide purchaser is one who acquires a legal property interest without notice that there is an outstanding trust or other equitable interest in the thing in question, and who gives value for the property interest he acquires by paying money, delivering other property, or changing his status. The prevalent view is that merely making a promise is not giving value, but that taking property as security for, or in payment of, an old debt does make one a purchaser for value.

The purchaser must have paid his value and acquired his legal title with an innocent mind. The purchaser of an equitable interest does not get the benefit of the rule.

Notice may be actual or constructive, and it may exist because the purchaser had knowledge of facts putting him on inquiry which, if investigated, would have disclosed the trust.

The rule is similar to, but separate from, the holder in due course rule in the law of negotiable instruments and the application of the recording acts.

"Giving value" is not the same thing as furnishing consideration in the law of contracts.

Status of Holder of Property

The cestui que trust can always recover the res or its substitute from the trustee, assuming satisfactory identification; but recovery from a third person depends upon the so-called "bona fide purchaser rule." Mr. Justice Story stated the rule in Oliver v. Piatt as follows:[72] "It is a clearly established principle in that jurisprudence that, whenever the trustee has been guilty of a breach of the trust and has transferred the property,

---

[69] Hawley v. Tesch, 88 Wis. 213, 59 N.W. 670.

[70] Rines v. Bachelder, 62 Me. 95.

[71] Restatement, Trusts, §§ 284–294.

[72] Oliver v. Piatt, 3 How. 333, 401, 11 L.Ed. 622. For a criticism of the rule, see Jenks, The Legal Estate, 24 Law Quart.Rev. 147.

See, also, Ames, 1 Harv.Law Rev. 3, 16; Kenneson, Purchaser for Value Without Notice, 23 Yale Law J. 193; Searey, Purchaser for Value Without Notice, 23 Yale Law J. 447.

by sale or otherwise, to any third person, the cestui que trust has a full right to follow such property into the hands of such third person, unless he stands in the predicament of a bona fide purchaser, for a valuable consideration, without notice."

This rule has been frequently applied, and the holder, where he was a purchaser in good faith, has been protected in his ownership and possession of the property.[73]

On the other hand are many cases holding that, if the third person from whom the cestui que trust seeks to recover the trust property either has not paid value therefor, or has been affected with notice of the trust, the cestui or his representative may take the property.[74]

---

[73] Cole v. Thompson, C.C.W.Va., 169 F. 729; Sorrells v. Sorrells, 4 Ark. 296; Ricks v. Reed, 19 Cal. 551; In re Lyon's Estate, 163 Cal. 803, 127 P. 75; Learned v. Tritch, 6 Colo. 432; Saunders v. Richard, 35 Fla. 28, 16 So. 679; Lewis v. Equitable Mortg. Co., 94 Ga. 572, 21 S.E. 224; McCaskill v. Lathrop, 63 Ga. 96; Carrie v. Carnes, 145 Ga. 184, 88 S.E. 949; Prevo v. Walters, 5 Ill. 35, 4 Scam. 35; Lennartz v. Popp's Estate, 118 Ill.App. 31; Beckett v. Bledsoe, 4 Ind. 256; Dillon v. Farley, 114 Iowa 629, 87 N.W. 677; Bailey v. Dyer, 65 S.W. 595, 23 Ky.Law Rep. 1585; Bromley v. Gardner, 79 Me. 246, 9 A. 621; Newell v. Hadley, 206 Mass. 335, 92 N.E. 507, 29 L.R.A.,N.S., 908; Curtis v. Brewer, 140 Mich. 139, 103 N.W. 579; Clark v. Rainey, 72 Miss. 151, 16 So. 499; Shirley v. Shattuck, 28 Miss. 13; Groye v. Robards' Heirs, 36 Mo. 523; McWaid v. Blair State Bank, 58 Neb. 618, 79 N.W. 620; Doremus v. Doremus, 66 Hun 111, 21 N.Y.S. 13; Petrie v. Myers, 54 How.Prac., N.Y., 513; Lincoln Soc. of Friends v. Joel, Sup., 163 N.Y.S. 860; McClelland v. Myers, 7 Watts, Pa., 160; Price v. Krasnoff, 60 S.C. 172, 38 S.E. 413; Schneider v. Sellers, 98 Tex. 380, 84 S.W. 417; Magnolia Park Co. v. Tinsley, 96 Tex. 364, 73 S.W. 5; Martin v. Granger, Tex.Civ.App., 204 S.W. 666; Waterman v. Cochran, 12 Vt. 699; Love v. Braxton, 5 Call, Va., 537; Chancellor v. Ashby, 2 Pat. & H., Va., 26.

[74] Pennington v. Smith, C.C.N.Y., 69 F. 188; Harrington v. Atlantic & Pac. Tel. Co., C.C.N.Y., 143 F. 329; Hallett v. Collins, 10 How. 174, 13 L.Ed. 376; Jones' Adm'r v. Shaddock, 41 Ala. 262; Randolph v. East Birmingham Land Co., 104 Ala. 355, 16 So. 126, 53 Am.St.Rep. 64; Clemmons v. Cox, 114 Ala. 350, 21 So. 426; Pindall v. Trevor, 30 Ark. 249; Crouse-Prouty v. Rogers, 33 Cal.App. 246, 164 P. 901; Bean v. Bean, 39 Cal.App. 785, 180 P. 23; Gale v. Harby, 20 Fla. 171; Harris v. Brown, 124 Ga. 310, 52 S.E. 610, 2 L.R.A.,N.S., 828; Masters v. Mayes, 246 Ill. 506, 92 N.E. 945; Boyer v. Libey, 88 Ind. 235; Sleeper v. Iselin, 62 Iowa, 583, 17 N.W. 922; Gray v. Ulrich, 8 Kan. 112; Farmers' & Traders' Bank of Shelbyville v. Fidelity & Deposit Co. of Maryland, 108 Ky. 384, 56 S.W. 671; Safe-Deposit & Trust Co. v. Cahn, 102 Md. 530, 62 A. 819; Elliott v. Landis Mach. Co., 236 Mo. 546, 139 S.W. 356; Logan v. Aabel, 90 Neb. 754, 134 N.W. 523; Mazzolla v. Wilkie, 72 N.J.Eq. 722, 66 A. 584; Shepherd v. M'Evers, 4 Johns.Ch., N.Y., 136, 8 Am.Dec. 561; Havana Cent.

Purchaser Must have Title

In order that one may be a bona fide purchaser he must have become the owner of the property, and he must have paid the purchase price. If he has merely contracted to buy the trust res at the time he receives notice of the trust, he is bound by the trust, even though he has paid part or all of the consideration.[75] And if he has received the title to the trust property, but has not yet paid the consideration at the time he receives notice, he cannot hold the property against the cestui que trust.[76] In the words of Chancellor Kent: [77] "A plea of a purchase for a valuable consideration, with notice, must be *with the money actually paid;* or else, according to Lord Hardwicke, you are not hurt. The averment must be, not only that the purchaser had not notice, at or before the time of the execution of the deeds, but that the purchase money was paid before notice. There must not only be a denial of notice before the purchase, but a denial of notice before payment of the money." And, as

---

R. R. Co. v. Knickerbocker Trust Co., 135 App.Div. 313, 119 N.Y.S. 1035; Reynolds v. Ætna Life Ins. Co., 28 App.Div. 591, 51 N.Y.S. 446, affirmed 160 N.Y. 635, 55 N.E. 305; English v. McIntyre, 29 App.Div. 439, 51 N.Y.S. 697; Moloney v. Tilton, 22 Misc. 682, 51 N.Y.S. 19; Winters v. Winters, 34 Nev. 323, 123 P. 17; United States Fidelity & Guaranty Co. v. Citizens' State Bank of Langdon, 36 N.D. 16, 161 N.W. 562, L.R.A.1918E, 326; Fidelity & Deposit Co. of Maryland v. Rankin, 33 Okl. 7, 124 P. 71; Lane v. Wentworth, 69 Or. 242, 138 P. 468; Hall v. Vanness, 49 Pa. 457; Coble v. Nonemaker, 78 Pa. 501; Jackson v. Thomson, 222 Pa. 232, 70 A. 1095; Sullivan v. Lattimer, 35 S.C. 422, 14 S.E. 933; Folk v. Hughes, 100 S.C. 220, 84 S.E. 713; Rabb v. Flenniken, 29 S.C. 279, 7 S.E. 597; Luscombe v. Grigsby, 11 S.D. 408, 78 N.W. 357; Bass v. Whelass, 2 Tenn.Ch. 531; Merchants' Nat. Bank of Ft. Worth v. Phillip & Wiggs Machinery Co., 15 Tex.Civ.App. 159, 39 S.W. 217; Chadwick v. Arnold, 34 Utah 48, 95 P. 527; Haslam v. Haslam, 19 Utah 1, 56 P. 243; Schenck v. Wicks, 23 Utah 576, 65 P. 732; Towle v. Mack, 2 Vt. 19.

[75] Louisville & N. R. R. Co. v. Boykin, 76 Ala. 560; Dugan v. Vattier, 3 Blackf., Ind., 246, 25 Am.Dec. 105; Corn v. Sims, 3 Metc., Ky., 391; Grimstone v. Carter, 3 Paige, N.Y., 421, 24 Am.Dec. 230; Hoover v. Donally, 3 Hen. & M., Va., 316. *Contra:* Wheaton v. Dyer, 15 Conn. 307, 311.

[76] Burgett v. Paxton, 99 Ill. 288; Kitteridge v. Chapman, 36 Iowa 348; Paul v. Fulton, 25 Mo. 156; Patten v. Moore, 32 N.H. 382; Dean v. Anderson, 34 N.J.Eq. 496; Frost v. Beekman, 1 Johns.Ch., N.Y., 288; Murray v. Finster, 2 Johns.Ch., N.Y., 155; Jewett v. Palmer, 7 Johns.Ch., N.Y., 65, 11 Am.Dec. 401; Everts v. Agnes, 4 Wis. 343, 65 Am.Dec. 314.

[77] Jewett v. Palmer, 7 Johns.Ch., N. Y., 65, 68, 11 Am.Dec. 401.

said by a Kentucky court: [78] "It is the well-settled doctrine that a purchaser of land takes subject to the claim of the holder of a prior equity, although such second purchaser may have made his contract, and fully paid the purchase money before he had notice of it, provided he has such notice before his own equity is clothed with the legal title."

The purchaser must have acquired a legal interest in order to get the benefit of the rule. If he has merely obtained an equity or equitable interest, then he is not a bona fide purchaser under the rule.[79] Equity applies to him the general doctrine that where there are two equities in the same property, and there is no other way of deciding their priority, then time of origin of the equities controls, and the one which is prior in time of origin is superior.[80] Thus, if A. owns the fee in a tract of land, and is induced by B. to contract to sell the land to B., on the basis of fraudulent representations by B. to A., B. acquires an equitable interest in the land because of the doctrine of specific performance. If B. sells his rights under the contract to C., who knows nothing of B.'s fraud and pays B. the full value of B.'s interest, C. is not a bona fide purchaser so as to prevent A. from avoiding the contract on account of B.'s fraud. C. acquired in good faith and for value an equitable interest merely. A. already had the legal title and an equity to avoid the contract between him and B. Even if A. had no legal title, his older equity would prevail over C.'s junior equity.[1]

So, too, if the facts of the above illustration are used, and it is assumed that after B. had sold his equity to C., B. later pur-

---

[78] Corn v. Sims, 3 Metc., Ky., 391, 400, 401.

[79] Louisville & Nashville R. R. Co., v. Boykin, 76 Ala. 560; Dugan v. Vattier, 3 Blackf. 245, 25 Am.Dec. 105; Grimstone v. Carter, 3 Paige 421, 24 Am.Dec. 230. In a few cases where the purchaser has obtained an equitable interest plus a power on his own part or through an independent third person to acquire the legal title, the purchaser is protected by the rule. Examples are the cases where a deed has been deposited in escrow (Winlock v. Munday, 156 Ky. 806, 162 S.W. 76), or stock has been sold but registration not changed on the corporation's books (Otis v. Gardner, 105 Ill. 436), or the deed to the purchaser was ineffective only for lack of acknowledgment, or the purchaser bought from a sheriff selling at public sale and has not yet obtained his deed (Duff v. Randall, 116 Cal. 226, 48 P. 66, 58 Am.St.Rep. 158).

[80] Southern Bank of Fulton v. Nichols, 235 Mo. 401, 138 S.W. 881; Mayer v. Kane, 69 N.J.Eq. 733, 61 A. 374.

[1] Duncan Townsite Co. v. Lane, 245 U.S. 308, 38 S.Ct. 99, 62 L.Ed. 309.

ported to sell the same equity to D., who paid value and did not know of the prior sale to C., C. would be superior to D. They both hold equities in good faith. There is no other basis for deciding between them except priority in time.[2]

So, too, if A. furnishes the money to pay for land and directs his agent, B., to buy the land in the name of A., but B. uses own money and buys the land in the name of B., A. has a right to have B. charged as constructive trustee, and this right is an equitable interest. If B. sells his legal title to C. who buys it in good faith and for value, C. will be superior to A., as a bona fide purchaser of the legal title; but if B. merely contracts to sell his legal interest to C., who in good faith and for value makes the contract, and then the interest of A. appears, A. will be superior to C., since both have mere equities, and A.'s is earlier in time.[3]

It will be noticed that the rule applies to cut off equities of any type, and not merely to cut off the interests of beneficiaries under trusts. For example, it governs such equities as those of contract vendees in specifically enforceable contracts, the equities of defrauded vendors who have conveyed away the legal title, and many others.

If a purchaser from a trustee in breach of trust has paid only part of the price before he receives notice of the trust and its breach, equity will protect him only in part. Whatever result is fairest in the circumstances will be directed by the court. Either the purchaser will be allowed to keep the legal title on paying into the trust the balance of the price, or the purchaser will be directed to reconvey to the trust his legal title on being reimbursed for the part of the price paid, or the purchaser will be given an interest in the property proportionate to the amount of the part payment made.[4] It will be important to learn whether the price contracted to be paid was reasonable, whether the property can be partitioned, what portion of the price has been paid, whether the purchaser has made improvements, and other surrounding circumstances.

---

[2] See § 43, ante.

[3] Johnson v. Hayward, 74 Neb. 157, 103 N.W. 1058, 5 L.R.A.,N.S., 112, 12 Ann.Cas. 800.

[4] Henry v. Phillips, 163 Cal. 135, 124 P. 837, Ann.Cas.1914A, 39; Paul v. Fulton, 25 Mo. 156; Haughwout v. Murphy, 22 N.J.Eq. 531; Durst v. Daugherty, 81 Tex. 650, 17 S.W. 388.

The bona fide purchaser may hold the trust res against the cestui que trust even though the former purchased from a volunteer,[5] or from a purchaser with notice of the trust;[6] and a purchaser with notice from a bona fide purchaser without notice is superior to the beneficiary.[7] An Illinois court quotes with approval Story's statement that "a purchaser with notice may protect himself by purchasing the title of another bona fide purchaser for a valuable consideration without notice; for, otherwise, such bona fide purchaser would not enjoy the full benefit of his own unexceptionable title."[8] If the title of the bona fide purchaser is good, it must be good for sale purposes, as well as a foundation for use and occupation. But the wrongdoing trustee, himself, may not get good title from a bona fide purchaser.[9] If he could, the door would be open for grave frauds on his part. If the trustee wrongfully transfers the trust res, and later purchases it from one who holds it innocently as a purchaser for value, the res will be affected with the trust in the hands of the trustee, just as it was originally.

Reason for Rule

The reason for the bona fide purchaser rule has been shown by Langdell to lie in the nature of equitable jurisdiction. "The reason why all equitable rights to property are lost the moment

[5] Richardson v. Haney, 76 Iowa 101, 40 N.W. 115. But see Martin v. Fix, 44 Kan. 540, 24 P. 954, *contra*.

[6] Bartlett v. Varner's Ex'r, 56 Ala. 580; Hampson v. Fall, 64 Ind. 382; Hoffman Steam Coal Co. v. Cumberland Coal & Iron Co., 16 Md. 456, 77 Am.Dec. 311; Wamburzee v. Kennedy, 4 Desaus., S.C., 474; Bracken v. Miller, 4 Watts & S., Pa., 102.

[7] Brodie v. Skelton, 11 Ark. 120; Lathrop v. White, 81 Ga. 29, 6 S.E. 834; St. Joseph Mfg. Co. v. Daggett, 84 Ill. 556; Bracken v. Miller, 4 Watts & S., Pa., 102. But such purchaser is charged with a trust, if the trust is recognized and administered. Appeal of Booth, 35 Conn. 165. "Undoubtedly if a person, though with notice, purchases from one without notice, he is entitled to stand in his shoes, and take shelter under his bona fides. If it were not so the bona fide purchaser without notice might be unable to dispose of the property, and thus its value in his hands be materially deteriorated. But if the second purchaser in such case be the original trustee, who reacquires the estate, he will be fixed with the trust. * * *" Church v. Ruland, 64 Pa. 432, 444.

[8] St. Joseph Mfg. Co. v. Daggett, 84 Ill. 556, 564.

[9] Oliver v. Piatt, 3 How. 333, 11 L. Ed. 622; Church v. Church, 25 Pa. 278; Church v. Ruland, 64 Pa. 432.

the legal ownership is transferred for value to a person who has no notice that it is subject to any equitable rights will be found in the fundamental nature of equitable jurisdiction, as explained in previous paragraphs. It is only by a figure of speech that a person who has not the legal title to property can be said to be the equitable owner of it. What is called equitable ownership, or equitable title, or an equitable estate, is in truth only a personal claim against the real owner; for equity has no jurisdiction in rem, and cannot, therefore, confer a true ownership, except by its power over the person with whom the ownership resides, i. e., by compelling him to convey. Thus, if A. has been clothed with the ownership of property for the sole purpose of holding it for the benefit of B., or if, being the owner, he has made a valid agreement with B. to convey it to him, or if A., though the owner of the property, acquired his title from B. by fraud; in each of these cases, equity will compel A. to convey to B.; and it is only because of this personal right of B. against A. (and because equity often creates a semblance of true ownership by treating what ought to be done as having been done), that B. can be said to be the owner of the property in equity. If, therefore, A. transfer the property to C., B.'s remedy in respect to the property will be gone, unless C. be privy to B.'s equity; i. e., unless he have notice of it express or implied. If he paid nothing for the property (e. g., if he received it as a gift, or in payment of a debt, or upon credit), the law will imply notice against him, and thus establish privity; but if he paid for the property its full value, and had no knowledge or notice of B.'s equity when he made the payment, it will be impossible to subject the property to B.'s claim without holding that the latter is a right in rem." [10]

The courts have sometimes suggested that the reason for the rule lay in the maxim, "Where the equities are equal, the law shall prevail," or in the fact that the conduct of the cestui in placing the property in the hands of the trustee has made possible the wrongdoing of the trustee; [11] or in the rule that "an innocent person shall not in general have his title impeached." [12]

Burden of Proof

Upon the subject of the burden of proof in the application of the bona fide purchaser rule the authorities are not harmonious.

[10] Summary of Equity Pleading, 90.

[11] Behrmann v. Seybel, 178 App. Div. 862, 869, 166 N.Y.S. 254.

[12] Groye v. Robards' Heirs, 36 Mo. 523, 525. See, also, Scott v. Gallagher, 14 Serg. & R., Pa., 333, 16 Am. Dec. 508.

Some cases require the cestui que trust to allege and prove that the holder of the property was not a purchaser for value without notice;[13] but other decisions put the onus on the property holder to prove good faith and payment of value.[14]

What is Notice?

To affect a purchaser with notice it is not essential that it be shown that he knew who the cestuis que trust were or the precise terms of the trust. It is sufficient that he knew there was a trust and either actually or constructively knew that the transfer was in breach of that trust.[15] Notice to an agent acting within the scope of his authority is notice to the principal.[16] Thus, knowledge of a bank cashier may prevent a bank from being a purchaser in good faith;[17] but a corporation is not charged with the knowledge of an officer of it who acted solely for his own benefit in the transaction,[18] nor is notice to a mere advisor sufficient.[19] Where a trustee buys an interest in a partnership with trust funds, the other partners are not charged with notice of the trust.[20] Notice to a trustee affects the cestuis que trust.[21]

[13] Bartlett v. Varner's Ex'r, 56 Ala. 580; Wyrick v. Weck, 68 Cal. 8, 8 P. 522; Warnock v. Harlow, 96 Cal. 298, 31 P. 166, 31 Am.St.Rep. 209; Harris v. Stone, 15 Iowa 273; Oaks v. West, Tex.Civ.App., 64 S.W. 1033.

[14] Wright-Blodgett Co. v. United States, 236 U.S. 397, 35 S.Ct. 339, 59 L.Ed. 637; Buford v. McCormick, 57 Ala. 428; Kaiser v. Waggoner, 59 Iowa 40, 12 N.W. 754; Hume v. Franzen, 73 Iowa 25, 34 N.W. 490; Kringle v. Rhomberg, 120 Iowa 472, 94 N.W. 1115; Ripley v. Seligman, 88 Mich. 177, 50 N.W. 143; Newton v. Newton, 46 Minn. 33, 48 N.W. 450; Stevens v. Brennan, 79 N.Y. 254; Levy v. Cooke, 143 Pa. 607, 22 A. 857.

[15] Mayfield v. Turner, 180 Ill. 332, 54 N.E. 418; Zuver v. Lyons, 40 Iowa 510; Jeffray v. Towar, 63 N.J.Eq. 530, 53 A. 182. But see Conner v. Tuck, 11 Ala. 794.

[16] Chapman v. Hughes, 134 Cal. 641, 58 P. 298, 60 P. 974, 66 P. 982; Watson v. Sutro, 86 Cal. 500, 24 P. 172, 25 P. 64; Webber v. Clark, 136 Ill. 256, 26 N.E. 360, 32 N.E. 748; Stewart v. Greenfield, 16 Lea, Tenn., 13.

[17] Duncan v. Jaudon, 15 Wall. 165, 21 L.Ed. 142; Gaston v. American Exch. Nat. Bank, 29 N.J.Eq. 98.

[18] Weber v. Richardson, 76 Or. 286, 147 P. 522, 1199.

[19] McNamara v. McNamara, 62 Ga. 200.

[20] Gilruth v. Decell, 72 Miss. 232, 16 So. 250; Hollembaek v. More, 44 N.Y.Super.Ct. 107.

[21] In Newell v. Hadley, 206 Mass. 335, 92 N.E. 507, 29 L.R.A.,N.S., 908, B. was trustee of the N. trust and of the P. trust. Having stolen money from the P. trust, he stole funds from the N. trust and replaced his withdrawals from the P. trust. The beneficiaries under the P. trust were held liable to the N. trust for the N. funds so used by B. to make good his

If the trust property is represented by a document, as, for example, a bond, certificate of stock, or note, and it appears on the face of such document that the holder owns as trustee, a purchaser will be held to have notice of the trust.[22] But in some cases the bare word "trustee" in the paper has not been deemed sufficient to charge a purchaser with notice, [23] as, for example, where a search to learn the extent of the trustee's power of sale would have been fruitless, because it would have led the purchaser to records from which no information could have been obtained, or to the trustee who might have deceived the purchaser.[24]

Frequently the purchaser receives constructive notice as to the existence of a trust and the trustee's powers, [25] or is put on inquiry as to such matters, [26] by the record of a deed or other instrument in his chain of title; but a deed which is not a link in that chain, but is between third parties, will not act as constructive notice.[27] A voidable deed in the chain of title, as, for

thefts. B. represented the beneficiaries of the P. trust, and his knowledge of the transaction bound them. For a criticism of this case, see West, Money Stolen by a Trustee from One Trust and Used for Another, 25 Harv. Law Rev. 602.

[22] Duncan v. Jaudon, 15 Wall. 165, 21 L.Ed. 142; Eldridge v. Turner, 11 Ala. 1049; Watson v. Sutro, 86 Cal. 500, 24 P. 172, 25 P. 64; Turner v. Hoyle, 95 Mo. 337, 8 S.W. 157; Gaston v. American Exch. Nat. Bank, 29 N.J.Eq. 98; Harrison v. Fleischman, 70 N.J.Eq. 301, 61 A. 1025; Swan v. Produce Bank, 24 Hun, N.Y., 277; Stoddard v. Smith, 11 Ohio St. 581; Clemens v. Heckscher, 185 Pa. 476, 40 A. 80; Simons v. Southwestern R. Bank, 5 Rich.Eq., S.C., 270.

[23] Ashton v. President, etc., of Atlantic Bank, 3 Allen, Mass., 217; Rua v. Watson, 13 S.D. 453, 83 N. W. 572; Lincoln Sav. Bank v. Gray, 12 Lea, Tenn., 459.

[24] Grafflin v. Robb, 84 Md. 451, 35 A. 971.

[25] Gaines v. Summers, 50 Ark. 322, 7 S.W. 301; Bazemore v. Davis, 55 Ga. 504; Dean v. Long, 122 Ill. 447, 14 N.E. 34; Hagan v. Varney, 147 Ill. 281, 35 N.E. 219; Martin v. Fix, 44 Kan. 540, 24 P. 954; Knowles v. Williams, 58 Kan. 221, 48 P. 856; Hagthorp v. Hook's Adm'rs, 1 Gill & J., Md., 270; Turner v. Edmonston, 210 Mo. 411, 109 S.W. 33, 124 Am.St. Rep. 739; Johnson v. Prairie, 91 N. C. 159; Barrett v. Bamber, 81 Pa. 247; Simmons v. Dinsmore, 56 Tex. 404; Stone v. Kahle, 22 Tex.Civ.App. 185, 54 S.W. 375; Mansfield v. Wardlow, Tex.Civ.App., 91 S.W. 859; Graff v. Castleman, 5 Rand., Va., 195, 16 Am.Dec. 741; Heth v. Richmond, F. & P. R. Co., 4 Grat., Va., 482, 50 Am. Dec. 88; Justis v. English, 30 Grat., Va., 565; Morgan v. Fisher's Adm'r, 82 Va. 417. But see Riley v. Cummings, 37 App.Div. 512, 56 N.Y.S. 60.

[26] Hassey v. Wilke, 55 Cal. 525; Webber v. Clark, 136 Ill. 256, 26 N. E. 360, 32 N.E. 748; Mercantile Nat. Bank of Cleveland v. Parsons, 54 Minn. 56, 55 N.W. 825, 40 Am.St. Rep. 299.

[27] Moore v. Hunter, 6 Ill. 317, 1 Gilman 317; Murray v. Ballou, 1

example, from an executor to himself, does give the purchaser notice of a constructive trust.[28] A lis pendens may prevent the purchaser of the trust res from being a purchaser in good faith.[29]

Open, notorious, and exclusive possession [30] of real property by a cestui que trust has been held to give a purchaser notice of the rights of the cestui, [31] or at least to put him on inquiry.[32] "What shall be deemed constructive notice in cases of this kind has been much discussed in courts, and we consider it as perfectly well settled that open exclusive possession is sufficient notice to all the world of any claim which one who is so in possession has upon the land. It is not to be supposed that any man, who wishes to purchase land honestly, will buy it without knowing what are the claims of a person who is in the open possession of it." [33] In the words of the Supreme Court of North Dakota: "An open, notorious, and adverse possession of real property is notice to the world of every right or interest owned or held by the person in possession, whether such right be legal or equitable." [34] But where a widow claims that heirs hold land in trust for her, joint occupancy by the widow and the heirs is not notice of the widow's claim to a purchaser from the heirs;[35] nor is there constructive notice of a claim by a mother-in-law, when the occupation is joint between her and her son-in-law, [36] or of an alleged equity in favor of a housekeeper, where she lives with her employer.[37] Exclusive and open possession

Johns.Ch., N.Y., 566; Claiborne v. Holland, 88 Va. 1046, 14 S.E. 915.

[28] Cox v. Barber, 68 Ga. 836.

[29] Murray v. Ballou, 1 Johns.Ch., N.Y., 566.

[30] Beaubien v. Hindman, 38 Kan. 471, 16 P. 796.

[31] McVey v. McQuality, 97 Ill. 93; McDaniel v. Peabody, 54 Iowa 305, 6 N.W. 538; Rogers v. Scarff, 3 Gill, Md., 127; Jones v. Johnson Harvester Co., 8 Neb. 446, 1 N.W. 443; Oberlender v. Butcher, 67 Neb. 410, 93 N.W. 764; Pritchard v. Brown, 4 N.H. 397, 17 Am.Dec. 431; Ferrin v. Errol, 59 N.H. 234; Flaherty v. Cramer, 62 N.J.Eq. 758, 48 A. 565; Grimstone v. Carter, 3 Paige, N.Y., 421, 24 Am.Dec. 230; Ross v. Hendrix, 110 N.C. 403, 15 S.E. 4; Krause v. Krause, 30 N.D.

54, 151 N.W. 991; Petrain v. Kiernan, 23 Or. 455, 32 P. 158. *Contra:* Scott v. Gallagher, 14 Serg. & R., Pa., 333, 16 Am.Dec. 508.

[32] Witter v. Dudley, 42 Ala. 616; Morrison v. Kelly, 22 Ill. 609, 74 Am.Dec. 169; Bowman v. Anderson, 82 Iowa 210, 47 N.W. 1087, 31 Am. St.Rep. 473.

[33] Pritchard v. Brown, 4 N.H. 397, 404, 17 Am.Dec. 431.

[34] Krause v. Krause, 30 N.D. 54, 151 N.W. 991, 996.

[35] Carroll v. Draughon, 173 Ala. 327, 56 So. 207.

[36] Ellis v. Young, 31 S.C. 322, 9 S.E. 955.

[37] Harris v. McIntyre, 118 Ill. 275, 8 N.E. 182.

of part of a single tract by a cestui is constructive notice of his claim to the whole,[38] and possession by one of several cestuis que trust of part of the land binds a purchaser with notice of the claims of all cestuis to all the land.[39]

Gross inadequacy of consideration paid by the alleged bona fide purchaser may amount to a fact putting the buyer on inquiry, since in such a case an ordinarily prudent man would be led to suspect that the title of his seller was defective or subject to an equity or burden.[40] A purchaser at a sheriff's or other judicial sale is held to be a purchaser in good faith, in the absence of actual notice. The character of the sale to him charges him with no constructive notice of equities.[41]

Facts Putting on Inquiry

If the purchaser learns of facts which, while not conclusively showing the existence of a trust with respect to the property in question, tend to excite suspicion or arouse doubt regarding the title, he will be charged with notice of such further facts as he could have ascertained by the use of reasonable diligence.[42] Thus, that the purchaser knew that a note which he bought was given for property sold by a trustee,[43] or that his grantor paid an inadequate consideration to the trustee for the property,[44] or that another had made some kind of claim to the property,[45] or that suits affecting the property were pending,[46] or that his

---

[38] Davis v. Hendrix, 192 Ala. 215, 68 So. 863.

[39] Ramirez v. Smith, 94 Tex. 184, 59 S.W. 258.

[40] Carpenter v. Robinson, Fed.Cas. No.2431; Gaines v. Summers, 50 Ark. 322, 7 S.W. 301; Storrs v. Wallace, 61 Mich. 437, 28 N.W. 662; Condit v. Bigalow, 64 N.J.Eq. 504, 54 A. 160; Hanrick v. Gurley, 93 Tex. 458, 54 S. W. 347, 55 S.W. 119, 56 S.W. 330.

[41] Fahn v. Bleckley, 55 Ga. 81; Elting v. First Nat. Bank of Biggsville, 173 Ill. 368, 50 N.E. 1095; Hampson v. Fall, 64 Ind. 382; Catherwood v. Watson, 65 Ind. 576; Gifford v. Bennett, 75 Ind. 528; Rooker v. Rooker, 75 Ind. 571; Jackson ex dem. Lansing v. Chamberlain, 8 Wend., N.Y., 620; Lessee of Paine v. Mooreland, 15 Ohio 435, 45 Am.Dec. 585.

[42] Bradley v. Merrill, 88 Me. 319, 34 A. 160; Condit v. Maxwell, 142 Mo. 266, 44 S.W. 467; Prall v. Hamil, 28 N.J.Eq. 66; Jeffray v. Towar, 63 N.J.Eq. 530, 53 A. 182; Federal Heating Co. v. City of Buffalo, 182 App.Div. 128, 170 N.Y.S. 515; Blaisdell v. Stevens, 16 Vt. 179.

[43] Bunting v. Ricks, 22 N.C. 130, 32 Am.Dec. 699.

[44] Hume v. Franzen, 73 Iowa 25, 34 N.W. 490.

[45] Austin v. Dean, 40 Mich. 386; Cain v. Cox, 23 W.Va. 594.

[46] Swoope v. Trotter, 4 Port., Ala., 27.

assignor had been described as "trustee" in a paper affecting the property, [47] or that securities were trust securities and being pledged by a trustee to secure a private debt, [48] or that the records showed an indirect transfer of the property from the trustee to himself, [49] will put the purchaser upon inquiry. Information should be sought from other sources than the trustee, for he is not impartial.[50] If he was a trustee and wrongfully transferred the trust property, or committed another breach of trust, he will not be apt to admit it. "It is well established that one who has reason to believe that another is offering property for sale, which he holds either as trustee or agent for a third person, cannot become a bona fide purchaser of the property for value by reliance on the statements of the suspected trustee or agent, either as to his authority or as to his beneficial ownership of the thing sold. In such a case, inquiry must be made of some one other than the agent or trustee—of some one who will have a motive to tell the truth, in the interest of the cestui que trust or principal." [51]

Who is a Purchaser?

A purchaser is one paying money or money's worth for the property. Therefore a donee inter vivos, [52] a legatee or devisee of the trustee, [53] or one taking by operation of law from the trustee, [54] is not entitled to protection, even though he may have taken the property innocently. "A person to whose hands a

[47] Pendleton v. Fay, 2 Paige, N.Y., 202.

[48] Loring v. Brodie, 134 Mass. 453.

[49] Beckett v. Tyler, 3 MacArthur, D.C., 319.

[50] Jonathan Mills Mfg. Co. v. Whitehurst, C.C.A.Ohio, 72 F. 496, 19 C.C.A. 130; Golson v. Fielder, 2 Tex. Civ.App. 400, 21 S.W. 173. Contra: Mercantile Nat. Bank of Cleveland v. Parsons, 54 Minn. 56, 55 N.W. 825, 40 Am.St.Rep. 299.

[51] Jonathan Mills Mfg. Co. v. Whitehurst, C.C.A.Ohio, 72 F. 496, 502, 19 C.C.A. 130.

[52] Joslyn v. Downing, Hopkins & Co., C.C.A.Wash., 150 F. 317, 80 C.C.A. 205; Lehnard v. Specht, 180 Ill. 208, 54 N.E. 315; Jacobs v. Jacobs, 130 Iowa 10, 104 N.W. 489, 114 Am. St.Rep. 402; Otis v. Otis, 167 Mass. 245, 45 N.E. 737; Davis v. Downer, 210 Mass. 573, 97 N.E. 90; Attorney General v. Bedard, 218 Mass. 378, 105 N.E. 993; Edwards v. Welton, 25 Mo. 379; Johnson v. Johnson, 51 Ohio St. 446, 38 N.E. 61; Weber v. Richardson, 76 Or. 286, 147 P. 522; Appeal of Sadler, 87 Pa. 154; Metzger v. Lehigh Valley Trust & Safe Deposit Co., 220 Pa. 535, 69 A. 1037.

[53] Evans v. Moore, 247 Ill. 60, 93 N.E. 118, 139 Am.St.Rep. 302; Talbott v. Barber, 11 Ind.App. 1, 38 N. E. 487, 54 Am.St.Rep. 491; McCants v. Bee, 1 McCord, Eq., S.C., 383, 16 Am.Dec. 610; Kluender v. Fenske, 53 Wis. 118, 10 N.W. 370.

[54] Derry v. Derry, 74 Ind. 560.

trust fund comes by conveyance from the original trustee is chargeable as a trustee in his turn, if he takes it without consideration, whether he has notice of the trust or not. This has been settled for three hundred years, since the time of uses."[55]

The giving of a note for the price does not constitute the maker of the note a purchaser, unless the note has been negotiated by the payee and thus the maker absolutely bound upon it.[56] Merely promising to pay money, render services, or do another act does not make the promisor a payer of value under the rule.

"Giving value" is not the same thing as furnishing consideration in the law of contract. A mere promise is consideration but is not giving value. Giving value is a narrower concept than furnishing consideration.

There has been a sharp division of authority as to whether one who takes property as security for, or in payment of, an antecedent debt is a purchaser for value. The modern tendency is to treat him as such, since he has changed his position in an important way, been lulled into security for a time, and will have to take action to get restored to his former status.[57] But many common law cases deny him the position of a purchaser for value, claiming that he has not given up anything substantial but rather has improved his position.[58] The uniform statutes define value as anything sufficient to support a contract, and make cancelling a debt or taking as security for it "giving value".[59]

---

[55] Holmes, J., in Otis v. Otis, 167 Mass. 245, 246, 45 N.E. 737.

[56] Davis v. Ward, 109 Cal. 186, 41 P. 1010, 50 Am.St.Rep. 29; Partridge v. Chapman, 81 Ill. 137; Jones v. Glathart, 100 Ill.App. 630; Kitteridge v. Chapman, 36 Iowa 348; Rush v. Mitchell, 71 Iowa 333, 32 N.W. 367; Freeman v. Deming, 3 Sandf.Ch., N.Y., 327. In Citizens' Bank of Parker v. Shaw, 14 S.D. 197, 84 N.W. 779, it was held the note constituted value, even though not negotiated.

[57] Schluter v. Harvey, 65 Cal. 158, 3 P. 659; Phelps v. American Mortgage Co., 40 Cal.App.2d 361, 104 P.2d 880; First Nat. Bank of Ottawa v. Kay Bee Co., 366 Ill. 202, 7 N.E.2d 860; Adams v. Vanderbeck, 148 Ind. 92, 45 N.E. 645, 62 Am.St.Rep. 497; Merchants' Ins. Co. of Providence v. Abbott, 131 Mass. 397; Payne v. Allen, 178 Okl. 328, 62 P.2d 1227; Akin v. Security Savings & Trust Co., 157 Or. 172, 68 P.2d 1047; W. Horace Williams Co. Inc., v. Vandaveer, Brown & Stoy, Tex.Civ.App., 84 S.W.2d 333.

[58] Levant State Bank v. Shults, 142 Kan. 318, 47 P.2d 80; Aetna Life Ins. Co. of Hartford, Conn. v. Morlan, 221 Iowa 110, 264 N.W. 58; Howells v. Hettrick, 160 N.Y. 308, 54 N.E. 677; Home Owners' Loan Corporation v. Tognoli, 127 N.J.Eq. 390, 13 A.2d 571.

[59] See, for example, Uniform Negotiable Instruments Law, § 25; Uniform Stock Transfer Act, § 22.

An assignee for the benefit of creditors or trustee in bankruptcy stands in the shoes of the debtor, and takes subject to all equities which affected the property in the debtor's hands. He is not a purchaser.[60]

A judgment creditor is not,[61] in the absence of a statute,[62] a purchaser. Property seized by him will be held subject to equities attaching to it in the hands of his debtor. "Attaching creditors, even though without notice of the equitable claims of third parties, who, in the transactions in which the debts sought to be collected were incurred, gave no credit to, and had no knowledge of, the apparent or record title of the debtor to the property attached, do not, as to the equitable owners of such property, stand in the position of bona fide purchasers for value, unless by force of some statute law to that effect." [63]

A corporation which issues its stock in return for the transfer to it of property is a purchaser,[64] as is also one receiving property in consideration of marriage; [65] but "love and affection," being merely "good" consideration, does not constitute value under the rule.[66]

A change of status is sometimes held to be giving value, as where one makes a promise of marriage in return for a conveyance of property on the engagement. The mere act of becoming betrothed is treated as giving value.[67]

---

[60] Chace v. Chapin, 130 Mass. 128; Martin v. Bowen, 51 N.J.Eq. 452, 26 A. 823; Stainback v. Junk Bros. Lumber & Mfg. Co., 98 Tenn. 306, 39 S.W. 530. *Contra,* Wickham v. Martin, 13 Grat., Va., 427; Marshall v. McDermitt, 79 W.Va. 245, 90 S.E. 830, L.R.A.1917C, 883 (under the recording act).

[61] Flanders v. Thompson, Fed.Cas. No. 4853; Houghton v. Davenport, 74 Me. 590; Harney v. First Nat. Bank, 52 N.J.Eq. 697, 29 A. 221.

[62] Marshall v. Lister, 195 Ala. 591, 71 So. 411; Guin v. Guin, 196 Ala. 221, 72 So. 74.

[63] Waterman v. Buckingham, 79 Conn. 286, 291, 64 A. 212.

[64] Whittle v. Vanderbilt Min. & Mill. Co., C.C.Cal., 83 F. 48.

[65] Johnson v. Petersen, 101 Neb. 504, 163 N.W. 869, 1 A.L.R. 1235.

[66] Waddail v. Vassar, 196 Ala. 184, 72 So. 14.

[67] Smith v. Allen, 5 Allen, Mass., 454, 81 Am.Dec. 758; De Hierapolis v. Reilly, 44 App.Div. 22, 60 N.Y.S. 417. *Contra:* Lionberger v. Baker, 88 Mo. 447.

TRACING TRUST FUNDS—IDENTIFICATION [68]

154. In order that the beneficiary or a trustee representing him may recover the trust property or its proceeds he must identify the property claimed as the original trust property or the product of it. If the disposition of the original trust property or its product is unknown, or it has been dissipated so that no substitute for it remains, or used to pay the debts of the trustee, the beneficiary will not be able to trace and recover any property.

In some states the so-called "swollen assets" doctrine is followed, and if trust property or its product is used to pay the debts of its holder, the beneficiary may recover the value of the property or product out of the general assets of the holder.

If the beneficiary traces trust funds into a bank account containing the private funds of the trustee, withdrawals therefrom for the trustee's personal purposes or for unknown objects are presumed to be from the trustee's portion of the account as long as any private credit remains.

If the beneficiary traces trust funds into a bank account containing the funds of another trust and nothing else, withdrawals from the mixed account for purposes which are not known or which are purely for the trustee's private benefit, should be deducted from the credit due to each trust, in proportion to their several amounts of credit at that time; but in some cases the rule of "first in, first out" is applied and such wrongful withdrawals are attributed to the funds first deposited in the account.

If the beneficiary traces trust funds into an account containing private funds of the trustee, and later the trustee purchases an investment from the mixed account without designating the object of the investment or from what funds made, and later all the remainder of the fund is withdrawn for the trustee's private purposes, the beneficiary may elect to treat the investment as made from the trust portion of the account.

If a trustee mixes trust funds and his private funds in a bank account, and later misappropriates part of the trust funds in the account, a later deposit by the trustee of his own money in the account is not presumed to be a replacement of the stolen trust funds, unless the account is labelled a trust account.

The beneficiary is not aided by a presumption that trust funds traced into an account or mass of property remained there.

[68] Restatement, Trusts, § 202.

Identification

The remedy of recovery of the trust property, or its substitute, is necessarily dependent on proof that the property in question is the trust res or its product. The property which the cestui seeks to have equity decree to belong to him must be shown to be the original subject-matter of the trust, or its successor. If the claim is made that the realty or personalty in dispute was once in the hands of the trustee as trust property, the question of identification will not ordinarily be extremely difficult; but if the cestui que trust seeks to show that certain land or chattels or a bank account are the avails of trust property, that trust property has, perhaps through several transactions, been traced into this land or these chattels or this bank account, the problem is apt to be more difficult. The courts have not always agreed on what is sufficient identification.

Burden of Proof and Presumptions

If the cestui que trust alleges that certain property is trust property, or that the proceeds of trust property have gone into it, the burden is on the cestui to prove that fact.[69] In this proof he may be aided by certain presumptions, which will now be stated.

If the beneficiary proves that the trust property or its substitute was in the hands of the trustee at a given date, prior to the death or insolvency of the trustee, is there any presumption that it remained among the assets of the trustee at his death or insolvency? A few courts have held that proof of receipt of the property and the existence of similar property in the estate at insolvency or death raises a presumption that the trust property was among the trustee's assets, or in other words that the burden is on the trustee or his representative to show that the property has been transferred or dissipated.[70] A somewhat similar presumption regarding the retention of property is found in a case where a trustee was ordered to invest trust funds in certain securities, he made such investment, and at his death securities of the kind ordered to be bought were found among his possessions; it was held that the securities on hand at his death were pre-

[69] Schuyler v. Littlefield, 232 U.S. 707, 34 S.Ct. 466, 58 L.Ed. 806; Waddell v. Waddell, 36 Utah 435, 104 P. 743; Chase & Baker Co. v. Olmsted, 93 Wash. 306, 160 P. 952.

[70] Farnsworth v. Muscatine Produce & Pure Ice Co., 177 Iowa 20, 158 N.W. 741; State v. Bank of Commerce of Grand Island, 61 Neb. 181, 85 N.W. 43, 52 L.R.A. 858; Widman v. Kellogg, 22 N.D. 396, 133 N.W. 1020, 39 L.R.A.,N.S., 563.

sumed to be trust securities.[71] But the majority of courts considering this question have determined that the cestui que trust is aided by no presumption of the retention of the trust property; that he must show not only its receipt by the trustee, but also that it remained among the assets of the trustee at the death or insolvency of the trustee, or other event fixing the rights of the parties.[72] Thus, a cestui que trust who merely proves that a bank collected trust moneys, and does not show their disposition, has not made out a case for following trust funds.[73] He must show that such trust funds remained in the hands of the bank or its representative at the time he brought suit.

The beneficiary is occasionally aided in following trust property by a rule which is sometimes called a presumption, but which is really referable to the doctrine of the loss of property by confusion of goods. If the trustee mingles trust funds with his own, and the entire mingled fund is on hand, the burden will be on the trustee to make a separation and to show the amount of his individual property in the mass,[74] and if the trustee cannot separate trust and private funds, the whole will be treated as trust property.[75] An example is found in the case where trust money is traced into a stock of goods bought partly with trust money and partly with the trustee's money, but the beneficiary cannot prove the exact amount contributed to the purchase price by trust money. If the trustee cannot make this proof, the entire stock will be treated as trust property.

Rule in Clayton's Case

Several important presumptions regarding withdrawals by a trustee have been established. In Clayton's Case[76] it was held

[71] Kauffman v. Foster, 3 Cal.App. 741, 86 P. 1108.

[72] Mathewson v. Wakelee, 83 Conn. 75, 75 A. 93; Shields v. Thomas, 71 Miss. 260, 14 So. 84, 42 Am.St.Rep. 458; Rockwood v. School District of Brookline, 70 N.H. 388, 47 A. 704; Collins v. Lewis, 60 N.J.Eq. 488, 46 A. 1098; Ellicott v. Kuhl, 60 N.J.Eq. 333, 46 A. 945; In re Hicks, 170 N.Y. 195, 63 N.E. 276; Gardner v. Whitford, 24 R.I. 253, 52 A. 1082.

[73] Windstanley v. Second Nat. Bank of Louisville, 13 Ind.App. 544, 41 N.E. 956.

[74] Evans v. Evans, 200 Ala. 329, 76 So. 95, semble; Atkinson v. Ward, 47 Ark. 533, 2 S.W. 77; Moore v. First Nat. Bank of Kansas City, 154 Mo. App. 516, 135 S.W. 1005; Yellowstone County v. First Trust & Savings Bank, 46 Mont. 439, 128 P. 596; Watson v. Thompson, 12 R.I. 466.

[75] Byrom v. Gunn, 102 Ga. 565, 31 S.E. 560; Ward v. Armstrong, 84 Ill. 151; Hunt v. Smith, 58 N.J.Eq. 25, 43 A. 428; Waddell v. Waddell, 36 Utah 435, 104 P. 743.

[76] Clayton's Case, 1 Meriv. 572, 608.

that a banking firm, receiving deposits from Clayton and making payments to him, presumably applied the first money paid in to the first drafts on the account. "Presumably it is the sum first paid in that is first drawn out." If but one cestui que trust is interested in a fund, and no moneys of the trustee are mixed with the trust moneys, this rule will not be of great importance, for ordinarily it will be immaterial to the cestui whether the trustee is regarded as having paid out first the money first deposited or the money later added to the fund. But if one trustee has mixed two or more trust funds, made a number of deposits in the joint fund to the credit of each trust fund and a number of withdrawals from the common fund, it may be of prime importance to know to which trust fund the withdrawals are to be charged. Conceivably it might be held that the balance should be divided among the several trusts in proportion to the total deposits made to the credit of each fund. Under this theory the withdrawals would be presumed to be from the several trust funds pro rata; that is, if the total credits to the A. trust were $1,000, and the total credits to the B. trust were $2,000, on March 1, 1941, one-third of the money then withdrawn for an unknown object or for a purpose personal to the trustee would be presumed to have been drawn from the A. fund and two-thirds from the B. fund, regardless of the dates of the various deposits.[77] This theory has the merit of reaching some degree of justice. It distributes the loss between the two trusts proportionately. It does not rest on any presumed or supposed intent of the trustee, since it would be immaterial to him from which trust he stole. It has been followed in some decisions and is the preferable view.[78] But in other decisions the rule of thumb known as the rule in Clayton's Case has been applied, a rule admittedly not based on fair play or intent, and it has been held that the trust funds first deposited will be presumed to be those first drawn out by the trustee.[79] Thus, if the trustee deposits $500 of the money of the

[77] Plano Mfg. Co. v. Auld, 14 S.D. 512, 86 N.W. 21, 86 Am.St.Rep. 769.

[78] Andrew v. State Bank of New Hampton, 205 Iowa 1064, 217 N.W. 250; County Commissioners of Frederick County v. Page, 163 Md. 619, 164 A. 182; Yesner v. Commissioner of Banks, 252 Mass. 358, 148 N.E. 224. This is the rule applied in section 15 of the Uniform Trusts Act.

[79] In re Hallett's Estate, 13 Ch.Div. 696; Spokane County v. First Nat. Bank, C.C.A.Wash., 68 F. 979, 16 C. C.A. 81; Empire State Surety Co. v. Carroll County, C.C.A.Iowa, 194 F. 593, 114 C.C.A. 435; In re Bolognesi & Co., C.C.A.,N.Y., 254 F. 770, 166 C.C.A. 216; In re Walter J. Schmidt & Co., D.C.N.Y., 298 F. 314; Hewitt v. Hayes, 205 Mass. 356, 91 N.E. 332, 137 Am.St.Rep. 448; Cole v. Cole, 54 App.Div. 37, 66 N.Y.S. 314.

A. trust on January 1st and $500 of the money of the B. trust in the same account on June 1st, and no other moneys have entered into the fund, and on July 1st the trustee withdraws $500 and dissipates it, it will be presumed that it was the money of the A. trust which he withdrew, and the B. trust will be entitled to the entire balance of $500.

Mixed Personal and Trust Funds

If, however, the fund in question contains, not merely trust funds, but also the funds of the trustee, the presumption with respect to withdrawals will be different. In such case the presumption that the trustee will perform his duty and will not be guilty of a breach of trust enters into the situation. If funds are withdrawn from this mixed account for the use of the trustee, or for an unknown object, it may be assumed that he withdrew his own money for his own use before he touched the trust money. As long as any of the money of the trustee remains in the mixed fund, the withdrawals for his private benefit will be treated as being made from his private funds, and only after the private funds are exhausted will the trust funds be deemed to be invaded.[80] The leading case in establishing this rule is In re Hallett's Estate,[81] where Jessel, M. R., referred to the principle "that, where a man does an act which may be rightfully performed, he cannot say that that act was intentionally and in fact

[80] Bank of British North America v. Freights, etc., of The Hutton, C.C.A.N.Y., 137 F. 534, 70 C.C.A. 118; In re Berry, C.C.A.N.Y., 147 F. 208, 77 C.C.A. 434; Board of Com'rs of Crawford County, Ohio, v. Strawn, C.C.A. Ohio, 157 F. 49, 84 C.C.A. 553, 15 L. R.A.,N.S., 1100; In re City Bank of Dowagiac, D.C.Mich., 186 F. 413; Empire State Surety Co. v. Carroll County, C.C.A. Iowa, 194 F. 593, 114 C.C.A. 435; Clark Sparks & Sons Mule & Horse Co. v. Americus Nat. Bank, D.C.Ga., 230 F. 738; Covey v. Cannon, 104 Ark. 550, 149 S.W. 514; People v. California Safe Deposit & Trust Co., 175 Cal. 756, 167 P. 388, L.R.A.1918A, 1151; Keeney v. Bank of Italy, 33 Cal.App. 515, 165 P. 735; Hewitt v. Hayes, 205 Mass. 356, 91 N.E. 332, 137 Am.St.Rep. 448; Board of Fire & Water Com'rs of City of Marquette v. Wilkinson, 119 Mich. 655, 78 N.W. 893, 44 L.R.A. 493; Harrison v. Smith, 83 Mo. 210, 53 Am.Rep. 571; State v. Bank of Commerce of Grand Island, 61 Neb. 181, 85 N.W. 43, 52 L.R.A. 858; Standish v. Babcock, 52 N.J.Eq. 628, 29 A. 327; Heidelbach v. National Park Bank, 87 Hun 117, 33 N.Y.S. 794; Blair v. Hill, 50 App.Div. 33, 63 N.Y. S. 670, affirmed 165 N.Y. 672, 59 N.E. 1119; Widman v. Kellogg, 22 N.D. 396, 113 N.W. 1020, 39 L.R.A.,N.S., 563; Continental Nat. Bank v. Weems, 69 Tex. 489, 6 S.W. 802, 5 Am.St.Rep. 85; Waddell v. Waddell, 36 Utah 435, 104 P. 743; Emigh v. Earling, 134 Wis. 565, 115 N.W. 128, 27 L.R.A.,N.S., 243; State v. Foster, 5 Wyo. 199, 38 P. 926, 29 L.R.A. 226, 63 Am.St.Rep. 47.

[81] In re Hallett's Estate, 13 Ch. Div. 696, 727, 728.

done wrongly," and then said: "When we come to apply that principle to the case of a trustee who has blended trust moneys with his own, it seems to me perfectly plain that he cannot be heard to say that he took away the trust money when he had a right to take away his own money. The simplest case put is the mingling of trust moneys in a bag with money of the trustee's own. Suppose he has a hundred sovereigns in a bag and he adds to them another hundred sovereigns of his own, so that they are commingled in such a way that they cannot be distinguished, and the next day he draws out of his own purposes £100, is it tolerable for anybody to allege that what he drew out was the first £100, the trust money, and that he misappropriated it, and left his own £100 in the bag? It is obvious he must have taken away that which he had a right to take away, his own £100. What difference does it make if, instead of being in a bag, he deposits it with his banker, and then pays in other money of his own, and draws out some money for his own purposes? Could he say that he had actually drawn out anything but his own money? His money was there, and he had a right to draw it out, and why should the natural act of simply drawing out the money be attributed to anything except to his ownership of money which was at his bankers."

But this doctrine of In re Hallett's Estate has not been followed to its logical conclusion in all cases. If a trustee has trust and private funds in a single account, and then withdraws a sum less than the amount of the private funds and invests it in securities in his own name, it would seem logical that the securities would be presumed to belong to the trustee personally since he would be presumed to use his own funds to make individual investments. But generally where such withdrawal and investment has been made, and later the trustee has withdrawn and dissipated the balance of the fund, the cestui has been allowed to take the investments made with the first withdrawals.[82] Thus, in In re

[82] Brennan v. Tillinghast, C.C.A. Mich., 201 F. 609, 120 C.C.A. 37; Mitchell v. Dunn, 211 Cal. 129, 294 P. 386; Glidden v. Gutelius, 96 Fla. 834, 119 So. 140; Erie County v. Lamberton, 297 Pa. 406, 147 A. 86; City of Lincoln v. Morrison, 64 Neb. 822, 90 N.W. 905, 57 L.R.A. 885. But *contra:* Covey v. Cannon, 104 Ark. 550, 149 S.W. 514; Farmers' Bank of White Plains v. Bailey, 221 Ky. 55, 297 S.W. 938; Standish v. Babcock, 52 N.J.Eq. 628, 29 A. 327; and State v. Foster, 5 Wyo. 199, 38 P. 926, 29 L.R.A. 226, 63 Am.St.Rep. 47 (where it was held that where a bank loaned money while its balance on hand exceeded the trust fund, it would be presumed that the notes resulting from such loans represented private funds of the bank and not trust funds, even though the balance later became reduced below the amount of the trust fund). And see,

Oatway[83] the trustee paid for shares in the Oceana Company by a check on an account containing trust funds and sufficient private funds to meet the check. Later the trustee withdrew and dissipated the balance of the account. The beneficiary was allowed to take the Oceana stock; Joyce, J., saying: "It is, in my opinion, equally clear that when any of the money drawn out has been invested, and the investment remains in the name or under the control of the trustee, the rest of the balance having been afterwards dissipated by him, he cannot maintain that the investment which remains represents his own money alone, and that what has been spent and can no longer be traced and recovered was the money belonging to the trust. In other words, where the private money of the trustee and that which he held in a fiduciary capacity have been mixed in the same banking account, from which various payments have from time to time been made, then, in order to determine to whom any remaining balance or any investment that may have been paid for out of the account ought to be deemed to belong, the trustee must be debited with all the sums that have been withdrawn and applied to his own use, so as to be no longer recoverable, and the trust money in like manner debited with any sums taken out and duly invested in the names of the proper trustees." Thus, if this presumption is advantageous to the cestui que trust, it operates; if it is disadvantageous, it is not applied. If the trustee withdraws the money and wastes it, he is deemed to withdraw his own money; but if he withdraws funds and purports to make an investment on his own account, he is presumed to be making an investment for the cestui que trust.

Presumption Regarding Deposits

It might be supposed that if the trustee reduces the mixed account below the amount of the trust funds by withdrawals for his own use, and later makes deposits of private moneys in the account, the trustee would be presumed to be restoring the trust funds; that is, that the presumption of the performance of duty would again apply. But whether because the trustee has, in such a situation, already shown an express intent not to perform his duty, or for other reason, the courts have held that subsequent

also, Burnham v. Barth, 89 Wis. 362, 62 N.W. 96, where it was held that a bank using part of a mixed fund to pay debts and expenses and part to buy securities, and having securities on hand at its insolvency in an amount less than the trust fund, was not presumed to have invested the trust funds in the securities.

[83] [1903] 2 Ch. 356, 360.

deposits to the credit of an account which stands in the name of the trustee individually, but which contains trust funds as well as private funds, do not inure to the benefit of the cestui que trust. The subsequent deposits are added to the private portion of the account. Hence, if trustee A. has a bank account entitled merely "A.," and into such account $500 of trust moneys have entered, and at some time in the history of the account the balance is reduced below $500,[84] or the account is wholly exhausted,[85] by withdrawals of funds for the use of A., deposits by A. after such reduction below $500, or after such exhaustion, when no express intent to make the deposit as a restoration is shown, will not operate as a restoration of the trust funds, and will inure to the benefit of A. But if the account is entitled "A., Trustee," it has been held that subsequent deposits, under the circumstances just narrated, will be credited to the trust funds.[86] And it has been held that where a trustee has a mixed account, and has on hand trust funds not deposited, and later deposits in the mixed account an amount equal to the trust funds which he was holding, it will be presumed that the funds so deposited were trust funds or trust fund replacements.[87] And, of course, there may be a restoration of misapplied trust funds by express action, as where a defaulting trustee uses his own money to buy land in his own name but with the express intent of making a restoration.[88] The principal doctrine regarding subsequent deposits is thus stated by the Supreme Court:[89] "Where one has deposited

[84] James Roscoe (Bolton), Ltd., v. Winder, [1915] 1 Ch. 62; Mercantile Trust Co. v. St. Louis & S. F. R. Co., C.C.Mo., 99 F. 485; Board of Com'rs of Crawford County, Ohio, v. Strawn, C.C.A.Ohio, 157 F. 49, 84 C.C.A. 553, 15 L.R.A.,N.S., 1100; In re M. E. Dunn & Co., D.C.Ark., 193 F. 212; Covey v. Cannon, 104 Ark. 550, 149 S.W. 514; Hewitt v. Hayes, 205 Mass. 356, 91 N.E. 332, 137 Am. St.Rep. 448. But see *contra*, In re T. A. McIntyre & Co., C.C.A.N.Y., 181 F. 960, 104 C.C.A. 424; State Sav. Bank v. Thompson, 88 Kan. 461, 128 P. 1120. Supreme Lodge of Portuguese Fraternity of United States v. Liberty Trust Co., 215 Mass. 27, 102 N.E. 96 (where the withdrawal was a mistake and the subsequent deposit was expressly made as a replacement, is a different case).

[85] Schuyler v. Littlefield, 232 U.S. 707, 34 S.Ct. 466, 58 L.Ed. 806, affirming decrees in In re Brown, C.C. A.N.Y., 193 F. 24, 113 C.C.A. 348, and In re A. O. Brown & Co., C.C.A.N.Y., 193 F. 30, 113 C.C.A. 354.

[86] United Nat. Bank of Troy v. Weatherby, 70 App.Div. 279, 75 N.Y. S. 3.

[87] Jeffray v. Towar, 63 N.J.Eq. 530, 53 A. 182; Baker v. New York Nat. Exch. Bank, 100 N.Y. 31, 2 N.E. 452, 53 Am.Rep. 150.

[88] Houghton v. Davenport, 74 Me. 590.

[89] Schuyler v. Littlefield, 232 U.S. 707, 710, 34 S.Ct. 466, 58 L.Ed. 806.

trust funds in his individual bank account, and the mingled fund is at any time wholly depleted, the trust fund is thereby dissipated, and cannot be treated as reappearing in sums subsequently deposited to the credit of the same account."

As a result of the presumptions regarding withdrawals and deposits which have just been discussed, it follows that the cestui que trust can never recover from a mixed account a sum greater than the lowest balance since the admixture of the funds. Thus, if trustee A. have an account standing in his own name in a bank, containing $1,000 of his own funds, and he deposits $1,000 of trust funds in the account on January 1st, makes deposits of his own moneys and withdrawals for his own benefit until July 1st, when he is declared a bankrupt, and when the balance in the account is $1,500, the cestui's right to follow his money into the claim against the bank will depend upon the state of the account between January and July 1st; and if it appear that on March 1st the account had been reduced to $500, the beneficiary will be confined to the recovery of that amount.[90] The sums added to the fund since March 1st do not benefit the cestui, for they are not deemed to be restorations of the trust money; and after the balance went below $1,000 it is obvious that the trustee must have been withdrawing and dissipating trust funds.

Degree of Identification Required—(a) Specific Property Rule

Neither the number nor the character of the changes which have affected the trust property will prevent the cestui que trust from following it, if he can make sufficient identification.[91] If the trust property is money and it has been mixed with other money, the beneficiary need not identify particular coins and bills in order to establish a right to trace his property; it is suf-

[90] Schuyler v. Littlefield, 232 U.S. 707, 34 S.Ct. 466, 58 L.Ed. 806; Mercantile Trust Co. v. St. Louis & S. F. Ry. Co., C.C.Mo., 99 F. 485; Board of Com'rs of Crawford County, Ohio, v. Patterson, C.C.Ohio, 149 F. 229; Board of Com'rs of Crawford County, Ohio, v. Strawn, C.C.A.Ohio, 157 F. 49, 84 C.C.A. 553, 15 L.R.A., N.S., 1100; Southern Cotton Oil Co. v. Elliotte, C.C.A.Tenn., 218 F. 567, 134 C.C.A. 295; Covey v. Cannon, 104 Ark. 550, 149 S.W. 514; Hill v. Miles, 83 Ark. 486, 104 S.W. 198; Powell v. Missouri & Arkansas Land & Mining Co., 99 Ark. 553, 139 S.W. 299; Porter v. Anglo & London Paris Nat. Bank of San Francisco, 36 Cal.App. 191, 171 P. 845; Hewitt v. Hayes, 205 Mass. 356, 91 N.E. 332, 137 Am. St.Rep. 448; Gray v. Board of Sup'rs of Tompkins County, 26 Hun, N.Y., 265, affirmed 93 N.Y. 603; Cole v. Cole, 54 App.Div. 37, 66 N.Y.S. 314; Chase & Baker Co. v. Olmsted, 93 Wash. 306, 160 P. 952. *Contra:* Myers v. Board of Education, 51 Kan. 87, 32 P. 658, 37 Am.St.Rep. 263.

[91] Bostwick-Gooddell Co. v. Wolff, 19 Ga.App. 61, 90 S.E. 975.

ficient if he show that his money has gone into a certain fund and remained there.[92] And so, too, where cash or commercial paper is deposited in a bank the rules as to tracing are liberal. The mass of cash in the bank, plus credits in other banks, is considered a single fund, and if it remains above the amount of the trust cash and commercial paper deposited, there is a basis for tracing.[93]

The majority of the courts which have considered the degree of identification required have held that the cestui que trust must be able to trace the trust res to some particular piece of property, and that proof that the trust res or its substitute is located at some unknown place among the assets of the trustee is not satisfactory. The trust fund must be traced into a particular bond, or tract of land, or bank account, for example. As said by Lewis, J., in Thompson's Appeal:[94] "Whenever a trust fund has been wrongfully converted into another species of property, if its identity can be traced, it will be held, in its new form, liable to the rights of the cestui que trust. No change in its state and form can divest it of such trust. So long as it can be identified either as the *original property* of the cestui que trust, or as the *product of it,* equity will follow it; and the right of reclamation attaches to it until detached by the superior equity of a bona fide purchaser, for a valuable consideration, without notice. The substitute for the original thing follows the nature of the thing itself so long as it can be ascertained to be such. But the right of pursuing it fails when the means of ascertainment fail." This same rule is expressed thus in a Massachusetts case:[95] "The court will go as far as it can in thus tracing and following trust money; but when, as a matter of fact, it cannot be traced, the equitable right of the cestui que trust to follow it fails. Under such circumstances, if the trustee has become bankrupt, the court cannot say that the trust money is to be found somewhere in the general estate of the trustee that still remains; he may have lost it with property of his own, and in such case the cestui que

---

[92] Western German Bank v. Norvell, C.C.A.Fla., 134 F. 724, 69 C.C.A. 330; School Trustees v. Kirwin, 25 Ill. 62 (orig. ed. p. 73); Shopert v. Indiana Nat. Bank, 41 Ind.App. 474, 83 N.E. 515; Farmers' & Mechanics' Nat. Bank v. King, 57 Pa. 202, 98 Am.Dec. 215; Wulbern v. Timmons, 55 S.C. 456, 33 S.E. 568. See Scott, The Right to Follow Money Wrongfully Mingled with Other Money; 27 Harv.L.R. 125.

[93] Erie Trust Company's Case, 326 Pa. 198, 191 A. 613.

[94] 22 Pa. 16, 17.

[95] Little v. Chadwick, 151 Mass. 109, 110, 111, 23 N.E. 1005, 7 L.R.A. 570.

trust can only come in and share with the general creditors." This rule requiring the cestui to trace his trust property to specific property, rather than to rely on a mere general lien or interest in the whole estate of the trustee, has been applied in many cases.[96]

[96] Illinois Trust & Savings Bank of Chicago, Ill. v. First Nat. Bank, C.C. N.Y., 15 F. 858; American Can Co. v. Williams, C.C.A.N.Y., 178 F. 420, 101 C.C.A. 634; Bettendorf Metal Wheel Co. v. P. P. Mast & Co., C.C.A. Ohio, 187 F. 590, 109 C.C.A. 420; In re Brown, C.C.A.N.Y., 193 F. 24, 113 C.C.A. 348, affirmed sub nom. First Nat. Bank of Princeton, Ill., v. Littlefield, 226 U.S. 110, 33 S.Ct. 78, 57 L.Ed. 145; In re Larkin & Metcalf, D.C.S.D., 202 F. 572; In re See, C.C.A.N.Y., 209 F. 172, 126 C.C.A. 120; State Bank of Winfield v. Alva Security Bank, C.C.A.Okl., 232 F. 847, 147 C.C.A. 41; Parker v. Jones' Adm'r, 67 Ala. 234; Goldthwaite v. Ellison, 99 Ala. 497, 12 So. 812; Hutchinson v. National Bank of Commerce, 145 Ala. 196, 41 So. 143; Lummus Cotton Gin Co. v. Walker, 195 Ala. 552, 70 So. 754; Korrick v. Robinson, Ariz., 180 P. 446; Hill v. Miles, 83 Ark. 486, 104 S.W. 198; Red Bud Realty Co. v. South, 96 Ark. 281, 131 S.W. 340; School Trustees v. Kirwin, 25 Ill. 73; Wetherell v. O'Brien, 140 Ill. 146; Seiter's Estate v. Mowe, 182 Ill. 351, 55 N.E. 526; Hauk v. Van Ingen, 196 Ill. 20, 63 N.E. 705; Richelieu Hotel Co. v. Miller, 50 Ill.App. 390; Kneisley v. Weir, 81 Ill.App. 251; Moninger v. Security Title & Trust Co., 90 Ill. App. 246; Arnold Inv. Co. v. Citizens' State Bank of Chautauqua, 98 Kan. 412, 158 P. 68, L.R.A.1916F, 822; McCormick v. McCormick's Adm'r, Ky., 121 S.W. 450; Goodell v. Buck, 67 Me. 514; Portland & H. Steamboat Co. v. Locke, 73 Me. 370; Cushman v. Goodwin, 95 Me. 353, 50 A. 50; Gault v. Hospital for Consumptives of Maryland, 121 Md. 591, 89 A. 105; Lowe v. Jones, 192 Mass. 94, 78 N.E. 402, 6 L.R.A.,N.S., 487, 116 Am.St.Rep. 225, 7 Ann.Cas. 551; Hewitt v. Hayes, 205 Mass. 356, 91 N.E. 332, 137 Am.St.Rep. 448; Board of Fire & Water Com'rs of City of Marquette v. Wilkinson, 119 Mich. 655, 78 N.W. 893, 44 L.R.A. 493; Watson v. Wagner, 202 Mich. 397, 168 N.W. 428; Neely v. Rood, 54 Mich. 134, 19 N.W. 920, 52 Am.Rep. 802; Twohy Mercantile Co. v. Melbye, 83 Minn. 394, 86 N.W. 411; Morrison v. Kinstra, 55 Miss. 71; Phillips v. Overfield, 100 Mo. 466, 13 S.W. 705; Pearson v. Haydel, 90 Mo.App. 253; City of Lincoln v. Morrison, 64 Neb. 822, 90 N.W. 905, 57 L.R.A. 885; Ellicott v. Kuhl, 60 N.J.Eq. 333, 46 A. 945; Heinisch v. Pennington, 73 N.J.Eq. 456, 68 A. 233; Pierson v. Phillips, 85 N.J. Eq. 60, 95 A. 622; Van Alen v. American Nat. Bank, 52 N.Y. 1; Ferris v. Van Vechten, 73 N.Y. 113; Welch v. Polley, 177 N.Y. 117, 69 N.E. 279; Brown v. Spohr, 180 N. Y. 201, 73 N.E. 14; Jaffe v. Weld, 155 App.Div. 110, 139 N.Y.S. 1101; People v. Bank of Dansville, 39 Hun, N.Y., 187; Virginia-Carolina Chemical Co. v. McNair, 139 N.C. 326, 51 S.E. 949; Widman v. Kellogg, 22 N. D. 396, 133 N.W. 1020, 39 L.R.A., N.S., 563; Muhlenberg v. Northwest Loan & Trust Co., 26 Or. 132, 38 P. 932, 29 L.R.A. 667; Ferchen v. Arndt, 26 Or. 121, 37 P. 161, 29 L. R.A. 664, 46 Am.St.Rep. 603; Dunham v. Siglin, 39 Or. 291, 64 P. 661; Appeal of Thompson, 22 Pa. 16; Appeal of Cross, 97 Pa. 471; McLaughlin v. Fulton, 104 Pa. 161; Commonwealth v. Tradesmen's Trust Co., 250 Pa. 372, 95 A. 574; Appeal of Hopkins, Pa., 9 A. 867; Groff v. City Savings Fund & Trust Co.,

558 REMEDIES UNDER TRUSTS Ch. 17

In the following illustrative cases the courts have held that, under the specific property rule, the cestui que trust identified the property sufficiently to enable him to follow it: Where the cestui sent money to the bankrupt to enable the latter to buy cotton for the former, and the bankrupt bought some cotton, used some of the funds for his own purposes, employed some of his own funds to buy cotton for the beneficiary, and placed all the cotton in a warehouse belonging to the cestui que trust;[97] where an agent to operate a store used the proceeds of sales to buy land, taking title in his own name, the land clearly might be followed as the substitute for the trust res;[98] where trust money was used to purchase a drug store which was conducted by the trustee in his own name for four years it was held that, notwithstanding the shifting stock, the trust funds were sufficiently identified as being in the store;[99] where trust moneys were used to pay off a mortgage, it has been held that the cestui que trust could not trace the funds into the land, but would be entitled to have a lien on the land in his favor;[1] where a trustee used trust funds to pay insurance premiums on a policy of life insurance on his own life, payable to his wife, it has been held that the cestui could trace the trust funds into the proceeds of the policy upon the death of the trustee.[2]

If trust money paid only part of the premiums on insurance payable to a relative of the trustee, the trust should obtain only

46 Pa.Super.Ct. 423; Slater v. Oriental Mills, 18 R.I. 352, 27 A. 443; Buist v. Williams, 88 S.C. 252, 70 S.E. 817; Continental Nat. Bank v. Weems, 69 Tex. 489, 6 S.W. 802, 5 Am.St.Rep. 85; Texas Moline Plow Co. v. Kingman Texas Implement Co., 32 Tex.Civ.App. 343, 80 S.W. 1042; Hoopes v. Mathis, 40 Tex.Civ. App. 121, 89 S.W. 36; Waddell v. Waddell, 36 Utah 435, 104 P. 743; Kent v. Kent, 50 Utah 48, 165 P. 272; Overseers of Poor of Norfolk v. Bank of Virginia, 2 Grat., Va., 544, 44 Am.Dec. 399; Watts v. Newberry, 107 Va. 233, 57 S.E. 657; Chase & Baker Co. v. Olmsted, 93 Wash. 306, 160 P. 952; Gianella v. Momsen, 90 Wis. 476, 63 N.W. 1018; Burnham v. Barth, 89 Wis. 362, 62 N.W. 96; Emigh v. Earling, 134 Wis. 565, 115 N.W. 128, 27 L.R.A.,N.S., 243; State v. Foster, 5 Wyo. 199, 38 P. 926, 29 L.R.A. 226, 63 Am.St.Rep. 47. See Williston, The Right to Follow Trust Property When Confused with Other Property, 2 Harv.Law Rev. 28.

[97] Southern Cotton Oil Co. v. Elliotte, C.C.A.Tenn., 218 F. 567, 134 C.C.A. 295.

[98] Atkinson v. Ward, 47 Ark. 533, 2 S.W. 77.

[99] Byrne v. McGrath, 130 Cal. 316, 62 P. 559, 80 Am.St.Rep. 127. But see Byrne v. Byrne, 113 Cal. 294, 45 P. 536.

[1] Standish v. Babcock, 52 N.J.Eq. 628, 29 A. 327.

[2] Holmes v. Gilman, 138 N.Y. 369, 34 N.E. 205, 20 L.R.A. 566, 34 Am. St.Rep. 463.

that proportion of the insurance purchased by its share of the premiums; but if all the premiums were paid by trust funds, then all the insurance should go to the trust, even though the amount of it is much larger than the amount of the trust money used to pay the premiums.[3] True, the trust gets a windfall in this way, but it is because it involuntarily invested in a profitable way. The insurance recovery is exclusively the product of trust funds. The beneficiary of the policy did not pay for the insurance and has no legal right to it.

On the other hand, the identification has been held to be defective where there was merely a showing of the receipt of the trust funds, their misappropriation, and the death of the trustee leaving an estate;[4] where the proof showed $1,400 of the trust money invested in the trustee's mercantile business, that the trustee for five years did an annual business of $10,000, and that at the end of the five years he died leaving a stock worth less than $1,000;[5] where the trustee had $10,000 in trust funds, used it indiscriminately in his business, and the money was not shown to have gone into any particular remaining property;[6] and where a draft was deposited for collection, was collected, and the proceeds used to pay the debts of the collecting bank.[7]

The payment of interest on the trust fund by the trustee till his death is strong evidence that he had the fund among his assets at his death.[8] If the beneficiary can follow the trust funds, even though the property into which he is able to trace them is now worthless, he will be obliged to accept such worthless property, if he wishes to seek a remedy in rem, and he cannot have a lien on the general assets of the trustee.[9]

Where the trust res is money, and the trustee invests it and his own funds in property, the cestui que trust may claim a charge thereon for his money, or he may demand a proportion-

---

[3] Vorlander v. Keyes, C.C.A.Minn., 1 F.2d 67; Shaler v. Trowbridge, 28 N.J.Eq. 595; Truelsch v. Miller, 186 Wis. 239, 202 N.W. 352, 38 A.L.R. 914; but see *contra*, and to the effect that the trust merely recovers the premiums paid: Summers v. Summers, 218 Ala. 420, 118 So. 912; Hubbard v. Stapp, 32 Ill.App. 541; Thum v. Wolstenholme, 21 Utah 446, 61 P. 537.

[4] Holden v. Piper, 5 Colo.App. 71, 37 P. 34.

[5] Robinson v. Woodward, 48 S.W. 1082, 20 Ky.Law Rep. 1142.

[6] Little v. Chadwick, 151 Mass. 109, 23 N.E. 1005, 7 L.R.A. 570.

[7] Nonotuck Silk Co. v. Flanders, 87 Wis. 237, 58 N.W. 383.

[8] In re Holmes, 37 App.Div. 15, 55 N.Y.S. 708, affirmed 159 N.Y. 532, 53 N.E. 1126.

[9] Cotting v. Berry, 50 Colo. 217, 114 P. 641.

ate interest in the property, on the basis of a constructive trust.[10] This right to a lien or the property itself has been previously stated.[11]

Degree of Identification Required—(b) "Swollen Assets" Theory

But some courts have held that the cestui que trust may trace and recover his property, if he can show that the assets in the hands of the trustee at his death or bankruptcy have been "swollen" or increased by the use of the trust property, even though no particular piece of property can be pointed to as the product of the trust res. Their theory seems to have been that, if the estate of the trustee was larger because of the use of the trust property, then the cestui que trust ought to have a specific lien on the estate, a preference over general creditors of the trustee. Thus, in the Kansas case of Peak v. Ellicott[12] a bank received money to pay a note, used the money for its own purposes, there was no proof that the trust fund was in the assets of the bank at its insolvency, and yet the cestui was allowed a preference and recovery of the full amount deposited, apparently on the theory that the use of his money to pay checks on the bank had freed other money of the bank which was to be found in the insolvent bank's assets. And in a later case in the same state[13] a treasurer of a school board wrongfully deposited school moneys in the bank of which he was manager, the funds of the bank later became reduced below the amount of the school fund, and the cestui was allowed the entire fund on hand at the time of the bank's failure, although obviously there could be no tracing into specific property; the court saying: "As the estate was augmented by the conversion of the trust funds, no reason is seen, under the equitable principle which has been mentioned, why they should not become a charge upon the entire estate." And in a Missouri case[14] tracing was allowed and recovery from the general property of the trustee granted where the trustee had deposited trust funds in a private bank account, checked out all but a trifling sum, and then became insolvent. In a recent Montana case[15] county funds were wrongfully deposited in a bank,

[10] Primeau v. Granfield, C.C.N.Y., 184 F. 480.

[11] See ante, § 152.

[12] 30 Kan. 156, 1 P. 499, 46 Am. Rep. 90. See, also, Ellicott v. Barnes, 31 Kan. 170, 1 P. 767.

[13] Myers v. Board of Education, 51 Kan. 87, 32 P. 658, 37 Am.St.Rep. 263.

[14] Evangelical Synod of North America v. Schoeneich, 143 Mo. 652, 45 S.W. 647.

[15] Yellowstone County v. First Trust & Savings Bank, 46 Mont. 439, 128 P. 596.

§ 154   TRACING TRUST FUNDS—IDENTIFICATION   561

which resulted in making the bank a trustee of them, and recovery by the county of the entire balance due on the county account was allowed out of the assets of the insolvent bank, regardless of the state of the bank's cash account between the date of deposit and the date of failure; the court saying that it was sufficient to justify recovery that the trust fund "enhanced the apparent value of the bank's total assets." A case similar to that last mentioned is State v. Bruce,[16] in which state funds were wrongfully deposited in a bank, became thereby a trust fund in the bank's hands, were paid out to cancel checks and expenses of the bank, and yet the cestui was allowed a lien on all the property of the bank at the time of its insolvency, and not merely on the cash on hand in the bank.

This theory that mere proof of benefit to the estate of the trustee is sufficient to allow tracing has been accepted by other courts.[17] The Supreme Court of Idaho has explained the reasoning on which it founds this rule in the following words:[18] "It is conceded that it [the trust money] went into the general funds of the bank, and was paid out from day to day, together with general deposits, on the checks of depositors and in the purchase of securities and other assets. No pretense is made by the bank or its receiver that this money was embezzled, stolen, or dissipated. It was used in the due course of business as transacted by the bank. It is also conceded that no part of this fund can

[16] 17 Idaho 1, 102 P. 831, L.R.A. 1916C, 1, 134 Am.St.Rep. 245.

[17] Town of Lafayette v. Williams, 232 Ala. 502, 168 So. 668; Word v. Sparks, 191 Ark. 893, 82 S.W.2d 5; Hopkins v. Burr, 24 Colo. 502, 52 P. 670, 65 Am.St.Rep. 238; Bryan v. Coconut Grove Bank & Trust Co., 101 Fla. 947, 132 So. 481; In re Knapp, 101 Iowa 488, 70 N.W. 626; Bradley v. Chesebrough, 111 Iowa 126, 82 N.W. 472; Hubbard v. Alamo Irrigation & Mfg. Co., 53 Kan. 637, 36 P. 1053, 37 P. 625; Kansas State Bank v. First State Bank, 62 Kan. 788, 64 P. 634; Carley v. Graves, 85 Mich. 483, 48 N.W. 710, 24 Am.St. Rep. 99; Blythe v. Kujawa, 175 Minn. 88, 220 N.W. 168, 60 A.L.R. 330; Stoller v. Coates, 88 Mo. 514; Hawaiian Pineapple Co. v. Browne, 69 Mont. 140, 220 P. 1114; McColl v. Fraser, 40 Hun, N.Y., 111; State v. Farmers' State Bank, 121 Neb. 532, 237 N.W. 857, 82 A.L.R. 7; State v. Farmers' State Bank, 62 N.D. 426, 244 N.W. 45; First State Bank v. O'Bannon, 130 Okl. 206, 266 P. 472; Lane v. First State Bank, 131 Or. 350, 270 P. 476; Deering Harvester Co. v. Keifer, 20 Ohio Cir.Ct.R. 311; Plano Mfg. Co. v. Auld, 14 S.D. 512, 86 N.W. 21, 86 Am.St.Rep. 769; Ex parte Bank of Aynor, 144 S.C. 147, 142 S.E. 239; State ex rel. Robertson v. Thomas W. Wrenne & Co., 170 Tenn. 131, 92 S.W.2d 416; First Nat. Bank v. Commercial Bank & Trust Co., 163 Va. 162, 175 S.E. 775; McLeod v. Evans, 66 Wis. 401, 28 N.W. 173, 214, 57 Am.Rep. 287.

[18] State v. Bruce, 17 Idaho 1, 102 P. 831, 833, L.R.A.1916C, 1, 134 Am. St.Rep. 245.

BOGERT TRUSTS 2D—36

be traced into any particular securities, paper, or assets. The bulk of it was doubtless paid out on depositors' checks during the closing days the bank did business, and while it was struggling to maintain its credit and to continue business. We fail to see what difference it can make in point of fact, reason, or law whether the money was used in buying bonds, mortgages, and other paper to add to the general assets of the bank, or in discharging the debts of the bank. In either event, it adds to or appreciates the body and value of the bank's assets. If the money is used to-day to pay the bank's debts, and it suspends business to-morrow, the indebtedness of the bank will be just as much less than it would otherwise have been as the amount paid out represents."

The fallacy of the "swollen assets" theory lies in its failure to recognize that a trust requires specific property as its subject-matter, and that the very essence of the cestui's right to follow is his ability to point to the trust res or its exact substitute. As a creditor a cestui que trust is entitled to no preference over any other creditor. It is only as a property owner that he is entitled to take particular chattels or realty. The matter is illuminated by the statements of Stiness, J., in Slater v. Oriental Mills:[19] "While one who has been wronged may follow and take his own property, or its visible product, it is quite a different thing to say that he may take the property of somebody else. The general property of an insolvent debtor belongs to his creditors, as much as particular trust property belongs to a cestui que trust. Creditors have no right to share in that which is shown not to belong to the debtor, and conversely a claimant has no right to take from creditors that which he cannot show to be equitably his own. But right here comes the argument that it is equitably his own because the debtor has taken the claimant's money and mingled it with his estate, whereby it is swelled just so much. But, as applicable to all cases, the argument is not sound. Where the property or its substantial equivalent remains, we concede its force; but, where it is dissipated and gone, the appropriation of some other property in its stead simply takes from creditors that which clearly belongs to them. In the former case, as in Pennell v. Deffell, 4 De G.,M.&G. 372, and In re Hallett's estate, Knatchbull v. Hallett, L.R. 13 Ch.Div. 696, the illustration may be used of a debtor mingling trust funds with his own in a chest or bag. Though the particular money cannot be identified the amount is swelled just so much, and the amount added belongs

[19] 18 R.I. 352, 353, 27 A. 443.

to the cestui que trust. But in the latter case there is no swelling of the estate, for the money is spent and gone; or, as respondent's counsel pertinently suggests, 'Knight Bruce's chest, Jessel's bag, is empty.' Shall we therefore order a like amount to be taken out of some other chest or bag, or out of the debtor's general estate?"

A further fallacy in the swollen assets doctrine lies in its assumption that the use of the trust funds to pay the trustee's personal debts has swollen the estate which he leaves. As a matter of fact it has paid one debt and created another of exactly the same size, so that the estate is neither swollen nor diminished. Thus, if T. is trustee of the A. trust, and has in his hands $1,000 of trust money, and owes personally to X. $500 and to Y. $1,000, and the only property which T. owns personally is a bond worth $500, it is apparent that T. is insolvent. He owes $1,500 and owns $500. The trust property does not count in the private affairs of T., either as an asset or a liability, as long as T. is carrying out his trust. Now if T. used the $1,000 of trust money to pay his creditor, Y., and dies, it cannot be said that the use of the trust money has "swollen" the estate left by T. The estate owes $1,500 and owns $500. Now instead of owing Y. $1,000, his estate owes the trust $1,000, on account of the misappropriated funds.

It may be noticed that many of the cases in which the "increased assets" rule has been applied were cases where public funds were in danger of being lost and the temptation to prefer the public claim to private creditors perhaps caused the courts to strain the law and the logic of the situation.

NECESSITY OF ELECTION BETWEEN TRACING AND DAMAGES [20]

155. Where the trustee or a third person has rendered himself personally liable to the cestui que trust by committing or joining in a breach of trust, and the trust res involved, or its substitute, can be traced into the hands of one not a bona fide taker for value, the cestui que trust must elect between recovery of damages and tracing as to each transaction.

It frequently happens that the trustee has committed a breach of trust and rendered himself personally liable, and that the trust property affected by this breach of trust, or its substitute,

[20] Restatement, Trusts, § 202.

can be traced into the hands of the trustee or a third person. And also a third person may make himself personally liable by a joinder in a breach of trust or by other tort, and the trust res or its substitute may likewise be available. The question arising in these situations is whether the cestui que trust is confined to a money decree against the trustee or third person, or whether he must pursue his trust property, or whether he may have the benefit of both remedies, or whether he must make an election.

It is universally held that the cestui must elect between taking a money judgment against the wrongdoer and tracing the trust property.[21] This right to elect exists, whether the property involved is in the hands of the trustee [22] or of a third person, [23] so long as the third person is affected by notice of the trust or has not paid value for the property. The trustee cannot compel the beneficiary to resort to either remedy. "Now, it is well settled that, when a trustee uses the property of the trust for his own benefit, the true owner is not compelled to follow the property, even though he might be able, by proving notice, to follow it successfully. He has his option, in such a case, to sue the trustee or follow the property. It would be monstrous to permit the trustee, in such cases, to say: 'Yes; I have used the trust property; I have got the benefit of that use; but you can prove that the party now in possession had notice of your claim. He trusted, it is true, to my statements; but he ought to have known me better. Your remedy is on him.' The rule is well established that the cestui que trust may sue the trustee, even though it appear that he has a right also to sue the person dealing with the trustee." [24]

---

[21] Oliver v. Piatt, 3 How. 333, 11 L.Ed. 622; Lathrop v. Bampton, 31 Cal. 17, 89 Am.Dec. 141; Woodrum v. Washington Nat. Bank, 60 Kan. 44, 55 P. 333.

[22] Small v. Hockinsmith, 158 Ala. 234, 48 So. 541; Phinizy v. Few, 19 Ga. 66; Baughman v. Lowe, 41 Ind. App. 1, 83 N.E. 255; MacGregor v. MacGregor, 9 Iowa 65; Peabody v. Tarbell, 2 Cush., Mass., 226; Isom v. First Nat. Bank, 52 Miss. 902; Prewitt v. Prewitt, 188 Mo. 675, 87 S.W. 1000; Prondzinski v. Garbutt, 10 N.D. 300, 86 N.W. 969; In re Carr's Estate,

[24] Pa.Super.Ct. 369; Shanks v. Edmondson, 28 Grat., Va., 804.

[23] Roberts v. Mansfield, 38 Ga. 452; Parker v. Straat, 39 Mo.App. 616; Treadwell v. McKeon, 7 Baxt., Tenn., 201; D. Sullivan & Co. v. Ramsey, Tex.Civ.App., 155 S.W. 580.

[24] Roberts v. Mansfield, 38 Ga. 452, 458, 459. But in Crutchfield v. Haynes, 14 Ala. 49, it was held that, where the trustee was amply able to respond in damages, the title of a purchaser from the trustee should not be disturbed, even though the prop-

§ 155   ELECTION BETWEEN TRACING AND DAMAGES   565

Examples of the exercise of this right of election are found in cases where the trustee has made an unlawful investment, and the cestui que trust has had the option of taking the investment or of holding the trustee for the trust money thus invested, with interest.[25] And likewise where the trustee wrongfully withdraws money from the trust funds, the cestui may sue for conversion or have the money or its product impounded in the hands of a third party.[26] An administrator who used trust money to buy realty in his own name may be compelled to restore the money or the real property may be subjected to the trust.[27]

But where a trustee makes several wrongful investments, the beneficiary may elect to hold him for damages in one case and trace the trust funds into the unlawful investment in another case.[28] It is only as to each separate transaction that the trustee must make his choice between damages and recovery of trust property or its product.

The remedies in rem and in personam are naturally mutually exclusive.[29] It would be unjust to compel a trustee to restore funds unlawfully invested and at the same time to take from him the securities in which he had placed the money. This would be double recovery; it would do more than restore the cestui que trust to his former position. Hence it has been held that bringing action [30] or recovering judgment [31] against the trustee on a claim of personal liability bars later attempts to take the res or its substitute as the property of the beneficiary. The Supreme Court of Oregon in a recent decision has stated the principle as follows: [32] "When a trustee has violated the trust by purchasing property with trust funds and taking the title in his own name, the cestui que trust has the right to elect either to proceed to fasten the trust upon the purchased property, or to proceed against the trustee personally. When with knowledge of

erty could have been followed into his hands.

[25] Clark v. Anderson, 13 Bush., Ky., 111; Baker v. Disbrow, 18 Hun, N.Y., 29.

[26] Robinson v. Tower, 95 Neb. 198. 145 N.W. 348.

[27] Merket v. Smith, 33 Kan. 66, 5 P. 394.

[28] Title Insurance & Trust Co. v. Ingersoll, 158 Cal. 474, 111 P. 360; Abell v. Howe, 43 Vt. 403.

[29] Barker v. Barker, 14 Wis. 131.

[30] Stoller v. Coates, 88 Mo. 514; Bettencourt v. Bettencourt, 70 Or. 384, 142 P. 326.

[31] Carter v. Gibson, 61 Neb. 207, 85 N.W. 45, 52 L.R.A. 468.

[32] Bettencourt v. Bettencourt, 70 Or. 384, 142 P. 326, 330.

the facts he thus makes an election, it is binding upon him, and it cannot be revoked. When a cestui que trust, with knowledge of the facts, elects to proceed against the trustee personally, he waives all right to have the trust impressed upon property purchased with trust funds, but conveyed to the trustee * * *."

Reference has already been made to the right of the beneficiary to claim a lien on the product of the trustee's wrongful disposition of trust property in connection with a claim for damages; and also to the need to choose between tracing the original trust property and the product of it, where both are available.

SUBROGATION AND MARSHALING [33]

156. Where the trust property is used to pay the debts of the trustee or a person not connected with the trust, the trust is entitled to be subrogated to the rights of the creditor paid.

Where trust property is used to discharge an encumbrance on property not belonging to the trust, the trust is entitled to have the encumbrance restored for its benefit.

Where the beneficiary can trace trust funds into an asset owned by the trustee or another, and this asset is also subject to a lien in favor of another creditor, but the latter has other property security for his claim, the trust beneficiary may employ the marshaling of assets doctrine and compel the creditor having two sources of collection to resort first to that one which is open to him exclusively.

Sometimes a trustee unlawfully uses trust funds to pay his own debts, or the debts of another person who is not a trust beneficiary. Here, according to the better view, there can be no tracing of trust property into any asset in the hands of the trustee or of the other party whose debt has been discharged. The discharge of a debt leaves no affirmative product. It has a negative result from the point of view of the debtor, namely, that it relieves him of a burden but does not increase his property. But the court of equity has felt that the beneficiaries of the trust whose money has been used to pay the debt of another should be permitted to stand in the place formerly occupied by the creditor who has been paid. The trust should have the cause of action and remedies which the creditor formerly had. It should be subrogated to the position of that creditor.

This result is based on the benefit which the trust has involuntarily conferred on the creditor who has been paid. An

[33] Restatement, Trusts, § 202.

example of the application of the rule can be found in the cases where T. is trustee of two trusts, the A. trust and the B. trust, and T. steals money from the A. trust funds and uses it to pay the debts of the B. trust.[34] Here it is fair that the beneficiaries of the A. trust, or a trustee who is a successor of T. and acts for the beneficiaries, should have the rights formerly held by the creditors of T., as trustee of the B. trust. If these creditors were secured and have released their security, it should be restored for the benefit of the A. trust. If the creditors were unsecured, the A. trust should be able to sue T. for the amount of the debt paid, and if it cannot recover from T., personally it should be able to proceed in equity against T., as trustee of the B. trust, and take his right to indemnity and collect out of the B. trust funds, provided T. could have collected from such funds if he had paid the debt from his own pocket. This result is reached in some cases, although there has been a tendency to ignore the fact that the A. trust must take through T., and that its rights will be of no value if T. was in default to the B. trust to an amount greater than the claim of the A. trust.

Secondly, trust funds are sometimes used illegally by a trustee to discharge an encumbrance on his own property, or on the property of one not a party to the trust. For example, the trustee may steal trust money and pay off a mortgage on his home. Here there can be no tracing in a strict sense, since the result is the cancellation of a debt and the discharge of a mortgage; but equity can and does restore the debt and mortgage in favor of the trust which has been injured, and permits it to enforce the mortgage on the trustee's home.[35]

Lastly, the doctrine of marshaling of assets is sometimes useful to a beneficiary whose trust property has been improperly used by the trustee.[36] This doctrine is one which runs all the way through the administration of the estates of debtors, whether trust claimants are involved or not. It is merely the rule

[34] Newell v. Hadley, 206 Mass. 335, 92 N.E. 507, 20 L.R.A.,N.S., 908; Whiting v. Hudson Trust Co., 234 N.Y. 394, 138 N.E. 33, 25 L.R.A. 1470; Fidelity & Casualty Co. v. Maryland Casualty Co., 222 Wis. 174, 268 N.W. 226; Weston, 25 Harv.L.R. 602; Baker, 59 Pa.L.R. 225; Jacob, 25 Ill. L.R. 19.

[35] Shinn v. Macpherson, 58 Cal. 596; Title Guarantee & Trust Co. v. Haven, 196 N.Y. 487, 89 N.E. 1082, 25 L.R.A.,N.S., 1308, 17 Ann.Cas 1131; Erie County v. Lamberton, 297 Pa. 406, 147 A. 86.

[36] M'Mahon v. Featherstonhaugh, 1895, 1 Ir.R. 83; Metzger v. Emmel, 289 Ill. 52, 124 N.E. 360; Broadway Nat. Bank v. Hayward, 285 Mass. 459, 189 N.E. 199; Farmers' Loan & Trust Co. v. Kip, 192 N.Y. 266, 85 N.E. 59.

that where there are two creditors, one of whom has a security interest in the A. property, and the other of whom has a security interest in the A. property and also in the B. property, the second creditor can be compelled to exhaust the B. property before he resorts to the A. property. It is immaterial, ordinarily, to the second creditor whether he uses A. property or B. property, but it makes a great difference to the first creditor. This makes it fair that the court force the second creditor to resort first to the security which is exclusively his.

For example, if T. is trustee for A. and steals trust money which he invests in land in the name of T., without trust label; and then T. mortgages the land to X. as security for a loan which X. makes to T., and X. is a bona fide purchaser; and X. also takes as security for this loan a pledge of jewelry owned by T.; and T. becomes insolvent and his creditors seek to enforce their claims, the beneficiaries of the A. trust can compel X. to resort first to the pledge of jewelry as a means of satisfying his claim, since that security is exclusively his, and to resort to the land mortgaged only secondarily in case he is not satisfied from the pledged jewelry. As to the mortgaged land X. would be superior to X., because of the application of the bona fide purchaser rule.

CONTROL OF TRUST ADMINISTRATION [37]

157. On the application of a cestui que trust equity will control the administration of the trust for his benefit by appointing or removing a trustee, or appointing a receiver.

Unless the power of removal is expressly reserved to the settlor, beneficiary, or other person, in the trust instrument, a court of equity alone may remove the trustee.

Equity will in its discretion remove a trustee, upon notice to the trustee and all other parties interested in the trust, if the trustee is shown to have been guilty of such misconduct in office that the financial interests of the cestui que trust have been greatly damaged or are seriously endangered.

The remedies of cestui que trust stated in the preceding paragraphs have had to do with the recovery of the trust property or its substitute, or of money, from the trustee or a third person, following a breach of the trust. But the beneficiary also has other remedies connected with the enforcement of the trust.

---

[37] Restatement, Trusts, §§ 107, 199.

Under this heading comes the right of the cestui que trust to apply for the appointment of a trustee, [38] as in the case where none has been lawfully appointed, or where the trustee has disappeared.[39] Equity will also remove the trustee on cause shown,[40] and if the trust fund is in danger will appoint a receiver, either pending the determination of the action, or for an indefinite period.[41] "It is said that the appointing of a receiver rests in discretion. This proposition does not teach much. A receiver is proper, if the fund is in danger; and this principle reconciles the cases found in the books. There is no case, in which the court appoints a receiver, merely because the measure can do no harm; and still less, when the trustee is such under the appointment of a testator."[42] The doctrine regarding receivers has been thus stated by a Georgia court:[43] "Besides it is an established rule of the Court of Chancery that, when a trust fund is in danger of being wasted or misapplied, it will interfere on the application of those interested in the fund, and by the appointment of a receiver, or in some other mode, secure the fund from loss."

The general rule is that the sole power of removing a trustee rests in the court of equity. That court is admitted to have plenary power to revoke the trustee's authority, upon cause shown.[44] Neither the settlor [45] nor the cestui que trust [46] has the implied power to remove a trustee, but the settlor may reserve to himself [47] or vest in the cestui que trust, [48] or in the cestui que

---

[38] Howard v. Gilbert, 39 Ala. 726; Wilson v. Russ, 17 Fla. 691. See discussion of the appointment of a trustee, ante, § 134.

[39] Beachey v. Heiple, 130 Md. 683, 101 A. 553.

[40] Lasley's Ex'r v. Lasley, 1 Duv., Ky., 117. See, also, ante, § 134.

[41] Hagenbeck v. Hagenbeck Zoological Arena Co., C.C.Ill., 59 F. 14; Hogg v. Hoag, C.C.N.Y., 80 F. 595; Vose v. Reed, 1 Woods, 647, Fed.Cas. No. 17,011; Calhoun v. King, 5 Ala. 523; Jones v. Dougherty, 10 Ga. 273; Gale v. Sulloway, 62 N.H. 57; Bowling v. Scales, 2 Tenn.Ch. 63; McCandless v. Warner, 26 W.Va. 754.

[42] Orphan Asylum Society v. McCartee, Hopk.Ch., N.Y., 429, 435.

[43] Jones v. Dougherty, 10 Ga. 273, 287, 288.

[44] Williamson v. Suydam, 6 Wall. 723, 18 L.Ed. 967; Parker v. Kelley, C.C.N.Y., 166 F. 968; Mazelin v. Rouyer, 8 Ind.App. 27, 35 N.E. 303; Waller v. Hosford, 152 Iowa 176, 130 N.W. 1093; City of St. Louis v. Wenneker, 145 Mo. 230, 47 S.W. 105, 68 Am.St.Rep. 561; Gaston v. Hayden, 98 Mo.App. 683, 73 S.W. 938; Quackenboss v. Southwick, 41 N.Y. 117; In re McGillivray, 138 N.Y. 308, 33 N.E. 1077; Appeal of Piper, 20 Pa. 67; Bailey v. Rice, 1 Tenn.Ch.App. 645; Lamp v. Homestead Bldg. Ass'n, 62 W.Va. 56, 57 S.E. 249.

[45] Pierce v. Weaver, 65 Tex. 44.

[46] Bouldin v. Alexander, 15 Wall. 131, 21 L.Ed. 69.

[47] Bowditch v. Banuelos, 1 Gray, Mass., 220.

[48] May v. May, 167 U.S. 310, 17 S. Ct. 824, 42 L.Ed. 179.

trust and a cotrustee,[49] or in a person totally unconnected with the trust, the authority to remove a trustee from office. All reasonable provisions which the settlor makes regarding removal in the trust instrument will, of course, be respected.

No attempt can be made here to show in what courts in the several states the general equity jurisdiction which gives the right of removal is vested.[50] In many states there are now statutes which state the procedure to be followed in removal cases and the grounds upon which removal will be ordered.[51]

What are sufficient grounds for the removal of the trustee rests in the discretion of the court of equity, in the absence of statute.[52] The trustee will not be relieved of his office, except upon a showing of clear necessity in order to preserve the interests of the beneficiaries.[53] It has been said that fraud, negligence, or willful breach of trust alone justify the removal,[54] while another court has required proof that the trustee has been acting wrongfully or in a manner which constitutes mischievous or negligent conduct in relation to the trust,[55] and still another court has stated that danger to the trust fund alone would justify removal.[56] Where the trustee has been guilty only of a misunderstanding[57] or of an honest mistake[58] he will not ordi-

[49] May v. May, 167 U.S. 310, 17 S. Ct. 824, 42 L.Ed. 179.

[50] For some decisions on the subject, see Attorney General v. Barbour, 121 Mass. 568; Widmayer v. Widmayer, 76 Hun 251, 27 N.Y.S. 773; Jones v. Jones, 8 Misc. 660, 30 N.Y. S. 177; Stafford v. American Missionary Ass'n, 22 Ohio Cir.Ct.R. 399; Baird's Case, 1 Watts & S., Pa., 288; Ex parte Hussey, 2 Whart., Pa., 330; Jenkins v. Wilkins, 10 Heisk., Tenn., 52; Lewis' Adm'r v. Glenn, 84 Va. 947, 6 S.E. 866.

[51] Parker v. Kelley, C.C.N.Y., 166 F. 968 (construing Massachusetts statute).; Nutt v. State, 96 Miss. 473, 51 So. 401; Holman v. Renaud, 141 Mo. App. 399, 125 S.W. 843; N. Y. Surrogate's Court Act, § 99; Real Property Law, § 112; Ohio Gen.Code, § 10506-53; In re Strickler's Estate, 28 Pa.Super.Ct. 455; In re Price's Estate, 209 Pa. 210, 58 A. 280.

[52] Scott v. Rand, 118 Mass. 215; Ward v. Dortch, 69 N.C. 277; Lamp v. Homestead Bldg. Ass'n, 62 W.Va. 56, 57 S.E. 249.

[53] Preston v. Wilcox, 38 Mich. 578; Waller v. Hosford, 152 Iowa, 176, 130 N.W. 1093; Wiegand v. Woerner, 155 Mo.App. 227, 134 S.W. 596; Appeal of Williams, 73 Pa. 249.

[54] Thompson v. Thompson, 2 B. Mon., Ky., 161.

[55] Mannhardt v. Illinois Staats-Zeitung Co., 90 Ill.App. 315.

[56] Satterfield v. John, 53 Ala. 127.

[57] Matthews v. Murchison, C.C.N.C., 17 F. 760.

[58] In re Durfee, 4 R.I. 401.

For recent cases showing the reluctance of the court to remove a trustee, especially when he has been appointed by the settlor, see Chicago Title & Trust Co. v. Rogers Park

narily be removed. In determining the question of removal the court should consider the wishes of the beneficiary.[59] In many of the statutes grounds of removal are set forth at length,[60] but these are illustrative merely and not an exclusive list of reasons for removal.

Grounds for Removal

The following have been held to be good reasons for the removal of a trustee; insolvency;[61] mingling the trust funds with private property;[62] inability to produce the trust funds upon an accounting;[63] misconduct in office;[64] use of the trust property for his own benefit;[65] placing himself in a position where his private interests conflict with his interests as trustee;[66] non-

---

Apartments Bldg. Corp., 375 Ill. 599, 32 N.E.2d 137; In re Crawford, 340 Pa. 187, 16 A.2d 521.

[59] In re Morgan, 63 Barb., N.Y., 621, affirmed 66 N.Y. 618.

[60] Thus, by the New York statute having to do with testamentary trustees removal may be had where the trustee has become incompetent or disqualified to act; or has wasted or improperly applied or invested the funds, or otherwise improvidently managed or injured the property committed to his charge, or by reason of other misconduct in the execution of his office, or dishonesty, drunkenness, improvidence, or want of understanding, is unfit for the due execution of his office; or where he has refused to obey an order of the court; or where his appointment was procured by fraud. N. Y. Surrogate's Court Act, § 99.

[61] In re Wiggins, 29 Hun, N.Y., 271; Cohn v. Ward, 32 W.Va. 34, 9 S.E. 41.

[62] Sparhawk v. Sparhawk, 114 Mass. 356; Gaston v. Hayden, 98 Mo.App. 683, 73 S.W. 938; Lowe v. Montgomery, 117 Mo.App. 273, 92 S.W. 916; Deen v. Cozzens, 30 N.Y.Super.Ct. 178; In re Strickler's Estate, 28 Pa.Super. 455.

[63] In re Mallon's Estate, 38 Misc. 27, 76 N.Y.S. 879.

[64] Ehlen v. Ehlen, 63 Md. 267; Scott v. Rand, 118 Mass. 215; Billings v. Billings, 110 Mass. 225; Lister v. Weeks, 60 N.J.Eq. 215, 46 A. 558; In re McGillivray, 138 N.Y. 308, 33 N.E. 1077; Haight v. Brisbin, 100 N.Y. 219, 3 N.E. 74; Appeal of Johnson, 9 Pa. 416; Gilbert v. Johnson, 49 Pa.Super. 191; Cooper v. Day, 1 Rich.Eq., S.C., 26. A practical repudiation of the trust was held sufficient ground for removal in Keating v. Keating, 182 Iowa 1056, 165 N.W. 74.

[65] Wheatcraft v. Wheatcraft, 55 Ind.App. 283, 102 N.E. 42; State v. Ausmus, Tenn.Ch.App., 35 S.W. 1021.

[66] Clemens v. Caldwell, 7 B.Mon., Ky., 171; Barbour v. Weld, 201 Mass. 513, 87 N.E. 909; In re Keller, 142 App.Div. 454, 127 N.Y.S. 16, affirmed 201 N.Y. 590, 95 N.E. 1131; Elias v. Schweyer, 13 App.Div. 336, 43 N.Y.S. 55; In re Etgen, 146 App.Div. 932, 132 N.Y.S. 308; Pyle v. Pyle, 137 App.Div. 568, 122 N.Y.S. 256; Warren v. Burnham, 125 App.Div. 169, 109 N.Y.S. 202; In re Hirsch's Estate, 188 N.Y. 584, 81 N.E. 1165; Dickerson v. Smith, 17 S.C. 289; Fisk v. Patton, 7 Utah 399, 27 P. 1.

residence or removal from the jurisdiction; [67] inattention to the trust business; [68] refusal to obey the orders of the court; [69] disagreement and friction with the fellow trustees, [70] or with the cestuis que trust; [71] refusal to give information regarding the trust business; [72] failure to furnish the bond required; [73] intemperance; [74] lunacy [75] or other incompetency; [76] lack of discre-

[67] Ketchum v. Mobile & O. R. Co., Fed.Cas.No.7737; Letcher's Trustee v. German Nat. Bank, 134 Ky. 24, 119 S.W. 236, 20 Ann.Cas. 815; Dorsey v. Thompson, 37 Md. 25; Barkley Cemetery Ass'n v. McCune, 119 Mo. App. 349, 95 S.W. 295; Lane v. Lewis, 4 Dem.Sur., N.Y., 468; Ex parte Tunno, Bailey Eq., S.C., 395; Carr v. Bredenberg, 50 S.C. 471, 27 S.E. 925; Maxwell v. Finnie, 6 Cold., Tenn., 434. But see, contra, La Forge v. Binns, 125 Ill.App. 527; Bonner v. Lessley, 61 Miss. 392.

[68] In re Boyle, 166 App.Div. 504, 151 N.Y.S. 1022.

[69] Appeal of Morse, 92 Conn. 286, 102 A. 586; In re Pott's Petition, 1 Ashm., Pa., 340; Tunstall v. Wormley, 54 Tex. 476.

[70] Quackenboss v. Southwick, 41 N.Y. 117; In re Morgan, 63 Barb., N. Y., 621, affirmed 66 N.Y. 618; McKenna v. O'Connell, 84 Misc. 582, 147 N.Y.S. 922; In re Myers' Estate, 205 Pa. 413, 54 A. 1093. Contra: Cornett v. West, 102 Wash. 254, 173 P. 44.

[71] May v. May, 167 U.S. 310, 17 S.Ct. 824, 42 L.Ed. 179; Polk v. Linthicum, 100 Md. 615, 60 A. 455, 69 L.R.A. 920; Wilson v. Wilson, 145 Mass. 490, 14 N.E. 521, 1 Am.St.Rep. 477; Gartside v. Gartside, 113 Mo. 348, 20 S.W. 669; Austin v. Austin, 18 Neb. 306, 22 N.W. 116; In re Chapman, Sup., 2 N.Y.S. 248; Disbrow v. Disbrow, 46 App.Div. 111, 61 N.Y.S. 614, affirmed 167 N.Y. 606, 60 N.E. 1110; In re Martin's Estate, 4 Pa.Dist.R. 219; In re Marsden's Estate, 166 Pa. 213, 31 A. 46; In re Price's Estate, 209 Pa. 210, 58 A. 280; In re Nathan's Estate, 191 Pa. 404, 43 A. 313. But if the disagreement between trustee and cestui que trust is not dangerous to the best interest of the trust, but a mere personal difference, the trustee will not be removed on that account. McPherson v. Cox, 96 U.S. 404, 24 L.Ed. 746; Nickels v. Philips, 18 Fla. 732; Parsons v. Jones, 26 Ga. 644; Lorenz v. Weller, 267 Ill. 230, 108 N.E. 306; Anderson v. Kemper, 116 Ky. 339, 76 S.W. 122; Clark v. Anderson, 73 Ky. 99, 10 Bush. 99; Polk v. Linthicum, 100 Md. 615, 60 A. 455, 69 L.R.A. 920; Starr v. Wiley, 89 N.J.Eq. 79, 103 A. 865; Trask v. Sturges, 170 N.Y. 482, 63 N.E. 534; In re Price's Estate, 209 Pa. 210, 58 A. 280; In re Neafie's Estate, 199 Pa. 307, 49 A. 129; Gibbes v. Smith, 2 Rich.Eq., S.C., 131. But where the trustee has discretion as to the amount to be given the cestui que trust and hostility will thus result disadvantageously to the cestui, friction will authorize removal even though the trustee has been capable and honest. Maydwell v. Maydwell, 135 Tenn. 1, 185 S.W. 712, Ann.Cas. 1918B, 1043.

[72] Gartside v. Gartside, 113 Mo. 348, 20 S.W. 669.

[73] Suit v. Creswell, 45 Md. 529.

[74] Bayles v. Staats, 5 N.J.Eq. 513; In re Cady's Estate, 103 N.Y. 678, 9 N.E. 442, affirming In re Cady, 36 Hun, N.Y., 122; In re Bell's Estate, 44 Pa.Super. 60.

[75] In re Wadsworth, 2 Barb.Ch., N.Y., 381.

[76] Savage v. Gould, 60 How.Prac., N.Y., 234; In re Smith's Estate, Sur., 7 N.Y.S. 327.

tion;[77] failure to carry out the trust.[78] The court may also remove a trustee on the ground that it is expedient to intrust the management of the estate to a smaller number of trustees.[79]

But it has been held that the trustee will not be removed on the ground of insolvency, if the trust fund is guarded by a proper bond;[80] nor will he be removed on the ground of negligence alone,[81] nor because of a failure to carry out the provisions of the trust due to a misconception of his duties,[82] nor because of misconduct in office,[83] when the safety of the trust fund is not endangered; nor merely because of enemy alienage and internment.[84] And in many other cases slight misconduct, inefficiency, or impropriety has been held insufficient ground for the removal of the trustee, where the trust fund was not placed in serious jeopardy.[85]

[77] Attorney General v. Garrison, 101 Mass. 223; but see Preston v. Wilcox, 38 Mich. 578.

[78] Cavender v. Cavender, 114 U.S. 464, 5 S.Ct. 955, 29 L.Ed. 212; Frisbie v. Fogg, 78 Ind. 269; Robinson v. Cogswell, 192 Mass. 79, 78 N.E. 389; In re Mechanics' Bank, 2 Barb., N.Y., 446; In re McKeon, 37 Misc. 658, 76 N.Y.S. 312; In re Hoysradt, 20 Misc. 265, 45 N.Y.S. 841; Anderson v. Robinson, 63 Or. 228, 126 P. 988. Acquiescence in a breach by a cotrustee may also be a ground. Harvey v. Schwettman, Mo.App., 180 S.W. 413. Threatened insolvency of the trust estate may authorize the transfer of the charity to a municipal corporation. Woods v. Bell, Tex.Civ.App., 195 S.W. 902.

[79] Barker v. Barker, 73 N.H. 353, 62 A. 166, 1 L.R.A.,N.S., 802, 6 Ann. Cas. 596.

[80] Moorman v. Crockett, 90 Va. 185, 17 S.E. 875.

[81] Waterman v. Alden, 144 Ill. 90, 32 N.E. 972.

[82] In re Rothaug's Estate, 51 Misc. 548, 101 N.Y.S. 973; In re Ward's Estate, Sur., 175 N.Y.S. 655.

[83] Haines v. Elliot, 77 Conn. 247, 58 A. 718; Wylie v. Bushnell, 277 Ill. 484, 115 N.E. 618; Lathrop v. Smalley's Ex'rs, 23 N.J.Eq. 192; Corlies v. Corlies' Ex'rs, 23 N.J.Eq. 197; In re Engel, 83 Misc. 675, 146 N.Y.S. 793; Brackett v. Seavey, Sup., 131 N.Y.S. 664; In re Thieriot, 117 App. Div. 686, 102 N.Y.S. 952; In re O'Hara, 62 Hun 531, 17 N.Y.S. 91.

[84] In re Amsinck's Estate, 103 Misc. 124, 169 N.Y.S. 336.

[85] Chambers v. Mauldin, 4 Ala. 477; Williamson v. Grider, 97 Ark. 588, 135 S.W. 361; McNair v. Montague, 260 Ill. 465, 103 N.E. 450; Olive v. Olive, 117 Iowa 383, 90 N.W. 827; Berry v. Williamson, 11 B.Mon., Ky., 245; Dailey v. Wight, 94 Md. 269, 51 A. 38; Preston v. Wilcox, 38 Mich. 578; Wiegand v. Woerner, 155 Mo. App. 227, 134 S.W. 596; Jacobus v. Munn, 37 N.J.Eq. 48; Wiggins v. Burr, 54 Misc. 149, 105 N.Y.S. 649; In re Wallace's Estate, 206 Pa. 105, 55 A. 848; Curran v. Green, 18 R.I. 329, 27 A. 596; Carr v. Bredenberg, 50 S.C. 471, 27 S.E. 925; Clausen v. Jones, 18 Tex.Civ.App. 376, 45 S.W. 183; Wisconsin Universalist Convention v. Union Unitarian and Universalist Soc. of Prairie du Sac, 152 Wis. 147, 139 N.W. 753.

Where trust duties are attached to the office of executor, and the executor is removed or resigns, he will be treated as having been relieved of his duties as trustee also;[86] but if the offices of executor and trustee are expressly made separate by the will, but the same person occupies both offices, the revocation of the appointment as executor will not affect the trusteeship.[87]

Proceeding for Removal

The application for the removal of the trustee may be made by any one having a financial interest in the execution of the trust. It may be made by one or all of the cestuis que trust,[88] whether their interests are vested or contingent.[89] The Attorney General should apply for the removal of an improper trustee of a charitable trust.[90] The settlor as such has not the interest requisite to enable him to apply for the removal of the trustee.[91]

In a proceeding for the removal of the trustee, the cestuis que trust should all be made parties or their interests represented;[92] and all other persons interested in the trust should be joined in the action.[93] If one of several trustees is to be removed, the co-trustees should be made parties to the proceeding.[94] The trustee surely should be given notice of the proceeding to remove him, in order that he may have the opportunity to defend himself.[95]

---

[86] Randall v. Gray, 80 N.J.Eq. 13, 83 A. 482; Cushman v. Cushman, 191 N.Y. 505, 84 N.E. 1112, affirming 116 App.Div. 763, 102 N.Y.S. 258.

[87] Tuckerman v. Currier, 54 Colo. 25, 129 P. 210, Ann.Cas.1914C, 599.

[88] Barbour v. Weld, 201 Mass. 513, 87 N.E. 909; Goncelier v. Foret, 4 Minn. 13, Gil. 1; Cooper v. Day, 1 Rich.Eq., S.C., 26.

[89] Wilson v. Wilson, 145 Mass. 490, 14 N.E. 521, 1 Am.St.Rep. 477; In re Bartells' Will, 109 App.Div. 586, 96 N.Y.S. 579; Bailey v. Rice, 1 Tenn.Ch.App. 645.

[90] State v. Fleming, 3 Del.Ch. 153.

[91] Thompson v. Childress, 4 Baxt., Tenn., 327.

[92] Farmers' Loan & Trust Co. v. Lake St. El. R. Co., 177 U.S. 51, 20 S.Ct. 564, 44 L.Ed. 667; Jones v. Bryant, 204 Ill.App. 609; Butler v. Butler, 164 Ill. 171, 45 N.E. 426; Elias v. Schweyer, 13 App.Div. 336, 43 N.Y.S. 55.

[93] Goodwin v. Goodwin, 69 Mo. 617. But see In re Gilbert's Estate, 3 N.Y.St.Rep. 208, holding that the matter of parties is within the discretion of the court.

[94] Hamilton v. Faber, 33 Misc. 64, 68 N.Y.S. 144.

[95] Ex parte Kilgore, 120 Ind. 94, 22 N.E. 104; Hitch v. Stonebraker, 125 Mo. 128, 28 S.W. 443; Holcomb v. Kelly, Sup., 114 N.Y.S. 1048; In re Sterling, 68 Misc. 3, 124 N.Y.S. 894; Foss v. Sowles, 62 Vt. 221, 19 A. 984. But see Letcher's Trustee v. German Nat. Bank, 134 Ky. 24, 119 S.W. 236, 20 Ann.Cas. 815, and State,

§ 158   RECOVERY FROM BONDSMAN OR GUARANTY FUND   575

A trustee who unsuccessfully resists an application for his removal may be held liable for the costs of the proceeding;[96] but, if he shows that there is no cause for his removal and that he has been performing his duties satisfactorily, the court may charge the costs of the proceeding to the trust estate.[97]

RECOVERY FROM BONDSMAN OR GUARANTY FUND

158. **Where a trustee has given a bond with sureties, and he has committed a breach of trust, the beneficiary or his representative may recover from the bondsmen.**

Where a corporate trustee is required by statute to make a deposit of a security fund with a state official as a guaranty of the faithful administration of its trusts, a beneficiary suffering from a breach of trust may secure satisfaction out of the guaranty fund.

On a showing of necessity equity will require a bond where none has existed, or order an increase in the size of the trustee's bond.

Actions against Sureties

As has been previously shown,[98] the trustee often gives a bond for the faithful performance of his duties and is joined in this bond by sureties. The question when such a bond will afford a cestui a remedy against a surety upon it depends partly upon the language and intent of the bond. Ordinarily the misapplication of trust funds by the trustee,[99] the failure of the trustee to turn over the trust property to his successor[1] or to render an account required by statute,[2] or the mixture of trust and private funds by the trustee with consequent loss[3] is a default which will render the surety liable. Whether the surety becomes liable

to Use of Napton, v. Hunt, 46 Mo. App. 616, where no actual notice was given to the trustee. Where the trustee is a defaulter and a fugitive from justice, and his whereabouts unknown, he may be removed without citation served upon him. Commonwealth v. Allen, 254 Pa. 474, 98 A. 1056.

[96] Lape's Adm'r v. Taylor's Trustee, Ky., 23 S.W. 960.

[97] Appeal of Bloomer, 83 Pa. 45.

[98] See ante, § 38.

[99] State v. Thresher, 77 Conn. 70, 58 A. 460; McKim v. Blake, 139 Mass. 593, 2 N.E. 157; McIntire v. Linehan, 178 Mass. 263, 59 N.E. 767.

[1] State v. Howarth, 48 Conn. 207; State v. Hunter, 73 Conn. 435, 47 A. 665; Haddock v. Perham, 70 Ga. 572; Bogard v. Planters' Bank & Trust Co., Ky., 112 S.W. 872; Bassett v. Granger, 136 Mass. 174; McKim v. Doane, 137 Mass. 195.

[2] Prindle v. Holcomb, 45 Conn. 111.

[3] Knowlton v. Bradley, 17 N.H. 458, 43 Am.Dec. 609.

for defaults occurring before the execution of the bond is a question the answer to which depends upon the wording and intention of the bond. In some cases the wording has been broad enough to cover transactions occurring prior to the bond,[4] while in others the wording has been prospective, and led to a decision that future acts of the trustee only were to be covered.[5]

In whose name the action against the surety should be brought depends upon the terms of the bond or statutory control. Such bonds frequently run to the judge of the probate court,[6] the county judge,[7] or to the state.[8] The public officer or body, however, is merely the nominal plaintiff, and the cestuis que trust are the real parties in interest,[9] as is illustrated where the statute of limitations is involved.[10] When the bond runs to the clerk or master of an equity court, the cestui cannot sue without leave of court.[11]

The nature of the surety's liability and the conditions precedent to fixing responsibility upon him are questions of the law of suretyship, not of trusts. Ordinarily the surety's liability is secondary to that of the trustee, and co-sureties are equally liable among themselves.[12] In pursuance of this rule the cestui has been required to prosecute an action against the trustee to have the amount of the default decreed before seeking recovery from the surety;[13] but in cases where the trustee is a non-resident,[14] or a bankrupt, fugitive from justice, and of unknown residence,[15] this requirement of prior action against the trustee has been dispensed with. The courts are not in harmony upon

---

[4] Ladd v. Smith, Ala., 10 So. 836; Comegys v. State, 10 Gill. & J., Md., 175; Commonwealth v. Fidelity & Deposit Co. of Maryland, 224 Pa. 95, 73 A. 327, 132 Am.St.Rep. 755.

[5] State v. Hunter, 73 Conn. 435, 47 A. 665; Lamar v. Walton, 99 Ga. 356, 27 S.E. 715; State v. Banks, 76 Md. 136, 24 A. 415; Thomson v. American Surety Co. of New York, 170 N.Y. 109, 62 N.E. 1073.

[6] Bassett v. Granger, 136 Mass. 174.

[7] Meyer v. Barth, 97 Wis. 352, 72 N.W. 748, 65 Am.St.Rep. 124.

[8] Commonwealth v. Allen, 254 Pa. 474, 98 A. 1056; State v. Graham, 115 Md. 520, 81 A. 31.

[9] Close v. Farmers' Loan & Trust Co., 195 N.Y. 92, 87 N.E. 1005.

[10] Pearson v. McMillan, 37 Miss. 588.

[11] Floyd v. Gilliam, 59 N.C. 183.

[12] Clagett v. Worthington, 3 Gill., Md., 83. But in Harmon v. Weston, 215 Mass. 242, 102 N.E. 470, the surety and the principal were held jointly liable.

[13] Crane v. Moses, 13 S.C. 561.

[14] Yates v. Thomas, 35 Misc. 552, 71 N.Y.S. 1113.

[15] Commonwealth v. Allen, 254 Pa. 474, 98 A. 1056.

the effect to be given to a decree against the trustee adjudging him in default and fixing the amount of the defalcation. Some have held such decree prima facie evidence of the fact and amount of the surety's liability; [16] others have treated it as conclusive upon the surety.[17] Yet other courts have held that the surety was not at all bound by a proceeding against the trustee to which he was not a party, [18] or that he was bound only when he had agreed by his bond to be bound by such adjudication.[19] In discussing the question a Pennsylvania court recently said: [20] "As to official bonds, bonds of indemnity, and bonds to insure the faithful performance of duty and to secure a proper accounting by persons in fiduciary relations, the rule of our cases seems to be that a judgment against the principal is conclusive against his sureties as to his misconduct and failure properly to account. In this class of cases, the surety submits himself to the acts of his principal and to the judgment as a legal consequence, following the scope of the suretyship." And Winslow, J., speaking in a Wisconsin case, has said: [21] "Whatever may be the rule in other jurisdictions, this court has definitely adopted the rule that sureties upon a probate bond are, in the absence of fraud or collusion, concluded by the decree of the proper court, rendered upon an accounting by their principal, as to the amount of the principal's liability; and this is the rule, even though the sureties be not parties to the accounting."

If the court believes that a bond ought to be required, although one was not originally given by the trustee, or that the size of the bond should be increased, it will, on application of the beneficiary make an order accordingly.[22] The cestui will be obliged to make a showing of a change in circumstances, as, for example, that the conduct of the trustee has given ground for

[16] Haddock v. Perham, 70 Ga. 572; Cully v. People, to Use of Dunlap, 73 Ill.App. 501.

[17] State v. Banks, Md., 24 A. 540; Appeal of Glover, 167 Mass. 280, 45 N.E. 744; Commonwealth v. Fidelity & Deposit Co. of Maryland, 224 Pa. 95, 73 A. 327, 132 Am.St.Rep. 755; Meyer v. Barth, 97 Wis. 352, 72 N. W. 748, 65 Am.St.Rep. 124.

[18] Thomson v. American Surety Co. of New York, 170 N.Y. 109, 62 N.E. 1073.

[19] People ex rel. Collins v. Donohue, 70 Hun 317, 24 N.Y.S. 437.

[20] Commonwealth v. Fidelity & Deposit Co. of Maryland, 224 Pa. 95, 102, 73 A. 327, 132 Am.St.Rep. 755.

[21] Meyer v. Barth, 97 Wis. 352, 355, 72 N.W. 748, 65 Am.St.Rep. 124.

[22] McClernan v. McClernan, 73 Md. 283, 20 A. 908; Starr v. Wiley, 89 N.J.L. 79, 103 A. 865; Fidelity & Deposit Co. v. Wolfe, 100 Oh.St. 332, 126 N.E. 414.

apprehension as to the safety of the trust property, or that the size of the estate has increased.

Statutes quite commonly provide that a corporate trustee must, as a condition precedent to accepting trusts, deposit with a state official securities having a named value as a guaranty fund for the faithful performance of its trusts. It is obvious that if such a fund is deposited, and there is a breach of trust by the corporate trustee, the state official as pledgee of the fund may be required by the trust beneficiaries to use the fund for the purpose of satisfying the claim for damages.[23]

ACTIONS AGAINST THIRD PERSONS FOR PARTICIPATING IN A BREACH OF TRUST [24]

159. The cestui que trust has a right that third persons (that is, strangers to the trust) shall not participate in a breach of the trust by the trustee, and an action for damages for such participation may be brought by the beneficiary or by the trustee.

A purchaser of known trust property is put on inquiry as to the power of the trustee to sell, and if the trustee has no power to sell, the purchaser will participate in a breach of trust by attempting to buy from the trustee. But if the trustee has power to sell, there is no duty on the part of the buyer to inquire into the propriety of the purpose of the trustee, or to see to the application of the purchase money to trust purposes.

Where corporate stock held by a trustee is presented to the issuing corporation or a transfer agent for a change in the registration of the stock, there is no duty on the part of the corporation or its agent to inquire into the propriety of the transfer, and the transfer may be safely made if there is no actual knowledge of an intended breach and no knowledge of highly suspicious circumstances.

A person who takes known trust property in satisfaction of a personal debt of the trustee is guilty of taking part in a breach of trust.

A bank is not guilty of taking part in a breach of trust merely because it permits the trustee to deposit known trust funds in his personal bank account.

If the trustee draws a check on an account, known by the bank to be a trust account, and the payee is the trustee

---

[23] Carcaba v. McNair, C.C.A.Fla., 68 F.2d 795, certiorari denied 292 U. S. 646, 54 S.Ct. 780, 78 L.Ed. 1497; In re Schmitt's Estate, 288 Ill.App. 250, 6 N.E.2d 444; Huntington Nat. Bank v. Fulton, 49 Ohio App. 268, 197 N.E. 204.

[24] Restatement, Trusts, §§ 321–326.

BOGERT TRUSTS 2D

or a third person not the bank, the bank may assume that the check is properly drawn and may pay it without being a participator in a breach of trust, if it does not know of an intended breach or have knowledge of highly suspicious circumstances.

Every property owner, be his interest legal or equitable, has a fundamental right to have third persons refrain from injuring or appropriating the subject of his property right. It is therefore a truism that cestui que trust, being the owner of an equitable property right, has the support of the courts in his claim that strangers shall not cause damage to the trust res or prevent the application of it to the purposes of the trust.[25] An elevated railroad company which erects structures injurious to the trust property must respond in damages to the trust.[26] If a stranger converts to his own use slaves which are the subject-matter of the trust, an action of trover may be maintained.[27] If persons unconnected with the trust wrongfully retain possession of the trust estate, replevin or ejectment or a similar possessory action will lie.[28] In whose name these actions must be brought is not here the question.[29] The actions inure to the benefit of cestui que trust. They represent rights which belong to him, or, viewed otherwise, duties owed to him by the public at large.

That the third person violates his duty to the beneficiary, or infringes upon the cestui's rights, in cooperation with the trustee is naturally of no importance as far as the liability of such third person is concerned. Such liability exists, nevertheless. "There can be no dispute that as a general principle all persons who knowingly participate or aid in committing a breach of trust are responsible for the money and may be compelled to replace the fund which they have been instrumental in diverting."[30] Thus, a cestui que trust of a trust for creditors may maintain a bill in equity against a third person who has induced the trustees to transfer the trust assets to him;[31] and individual creditors of the trustee, who knowingly accept trust funds from the trustee

[25] Ripperger v. Shroder-Rockefeller Co., D.C.N.Y., 37 F.Supp. 375.

[26] Roberts v. N. Y. El. R. R. Co., 155 N.Y. 31, 49 N.E. 262.

[27] Jones v. Cole, 2 Bailey, S.C., 330.

[28] Warren v. Howard, 99 N.C. 190, 5 S.E. 424.

[29] For a fuller discussion of this matter, see § 162, post.

[30] Duckett v. National Mechanics' Bank, 86 Md. 400, 403, 38 A. 983, 39 L.R.A. 84, 63 Am.St.Rep. 513.

[31] Kentucky Wagon Mfg. Co. v. Jones & Hopkins Mfg. Co., C.C.A. Miss., 248 F. 272, 160 C.C.A. 350.

as payment of their debts, are liable therefor to the cestui que trust.[32]

The wrongdoing trustee, or his successor, may maintain the action against the third person who has taken part in a breach of trust. The wrongdoing trustee is allowed to repent and to try to remedy the wrong.[33]

Rights against Banks

This right of the beneficiary to have third persons refrain from interfering with the trust property and from aiding in a breach of trust has been frequently discussed in cases involving the rights and duties of banks holding trust funds on deposit. To what extent, if at all, may the bank apply the trust funds to its own use by taking them to satisfy a debt of the trustee to it? To what extent is the bank obliged to scrutinize the withdrawals by the trustee from the trust fund to ascertain that the trustee is not diverting the trust funds to improper uses?

It has been almost universally held that a bank, which has notice that funds deposited with it are trust funds has no lien upon such deposit for the personal debts of the trustee to it, has no right to apply such trust funds to the satisfaction of the individual debt of the trustee, with or without his consent, and will be liable to the cestui que trust if it makes such application. This doctrine applies to all fiduciary accounts, even though not strictly trust accounts. It has been used in cases of funds deposited by agents, guardians, executors, and commission merchants. The bank may not take the trust money to pay the trustee's debt to it, whether the account be entitled a trust account,[34] or whether it

---

[32] Stratton v. Stratton's Adm'r, 149 Ky. 473, 149 S.W. 900.

[33] Wetmore v. Porter, 92 N.Y. 76; Stall v. Cincinnati, 16 Ohio St. 169; Abbott's Ex'r v. Reeves, 49 Pa. 494, 88 Am.Dec. 510.

[34] Cuthbert v. Robarts, Lubbock & Co., [1909], 2 Ch. 226; Ex parte Kingston, L.R. 6 Ch.App. 632; United States Fidelity & Guaranty Co. v. Union Bank & Trust Co., C.C.A.Tenn., 228 F. 448, 143 C.C.A. 30; Central Nat. Bank v. Connecticut Mut. L. Ins. Co., 104 U.S. 54, 26 L.Ed. 693; Bank of Guntersville v. Crayter, 199 Ala. 599, 75 So. 7, L.R.A.1917F, 460;

Sayre v. Weil, 94 Ala. 466, 10 So. 546, 15 L.R.A. 544; Keeney v. Bank of Italy, 33 Cal.App. 515, 165 P. 735; Lowndes v. City Nat. Bank of South Norwalk, 82 Conn. 8, 72 A. 150, 22 L.R.A.,N.S., 408; American Trust & Banking Co. v. Boone, 102 Ga. 202, 29 S.E. 182, 40 L.R.A. 250, 66 Am.St. Rep. 167; Miami County Bank v. State ex rel. Peru Trust Co., 61 Ind. App. 360, 112 N.E. 40; Washbon v. Linscott State Bank, 87 Kan. 698, 125 P. 17; Farmers' & Traders' Bank of Shelbyville v. Fidelity & Deposit Co. of Maryland, 108 Ky. 384, 56 S. W. 671; Allen v. Puritan Trust Co., 211 Mass. 409, 97 N.E. 916, L.R.A.

§ 159 PARTICIPATION IN BREACH 581

be a personal account in which the bank knows trust funds have been deposited.[35] Where a check on a trust account in the A. bank is deposited by the trustee in his individual account in the B. bank when such latter account is overdrawn, the bank is liable to the cestui for the full amount of the check so deposited and used to pay the overdraft.[36] In a recent New York case [37] it

1915C, 518; State Bank of St. Johns v. McCabe, 135 Mich. 479, 98 N.W. 20; Jeffray v. Towar, 63 N.J.Eq. 530, 53 A. 182; McStay Supply Co. v. Stoddard, 35 Nev. 284, 132 P. 545; Fidelity & Deposit Co. of Maryland v. Rankin, 33 Okl. 7, 124 P. 71; United States Fidelity & Guaranty Co. v. Adoue & Lobit, 104 Tex. 379, 137 S.W. 648, 138 S.W. 383, 37 L.R.A., N.S., 409, Ann.Cas.1914B, 667; Boyle v. Northwestern Nat. Bank, 125 Wis. 498, 103 N.W. 1123, 104 N.W. 917, 1 L.R.A.,N.S., 1110, 110 Am.St.Rep. 827. In First Nat. Bank of Sharon v. Valley State Bank, 60 Kan. 621, 57 P. 510, it was held that the depositary was not liable when the account from which the bank received payment was an individual account and the trustee had withdrawn from it more than the amount of the trust fund and the bank had had a right to suppose that such withdrawals were paid to the cestui. See Thulin, "Misappropriation of Funds by Fiduciaries; the Bank's Liability," 6 Cal.Law Rev. 171; Scott, "Participation in a Breach of Trust," 34 Harv.Law Rev. 454.

[35] Santa Marina Co. v. Canadian Bank of Commerce, D.C.Cal., 242 F. 142; Miami County Bank v. State ex rel. Peru Trust Co., 61 Ind.App. 360, 112 N.E. 40; Nehawke Bank v. Ingersoll, 2 Neb.Unoff. 617, 89 N.W. 618; Globe Sav. Bank v. Nat. Bank of Commerce, 64 Neb. 413, 89 N.W. 1030; Interstate Nat. Bank v. Claxton, 97 Tex. 569, 80 S.W. 604, 65 L.R. A. 820, 104 Am.St.Rep. 885; Pratt v. Commercial Trust Co., 105 Misc. 324, 174 N.Y.S. 88, affirmed, Sup., 175 N.Y.S. 918; Hale v. Windsor Sav. Bank, 90 Vt. 487, 98 A. 993. But it has been held that the bank is not liable if it merely credited the trust deposit to a personal account of the trustee which was then overdrawn and thus paid the overdraft, without any intent to make a profit (Coleman v. Bucks & Oxon Union Bank [1897] 2 Ch. 243); nor is there liability if the bank did not know that the funds deposited in the personal account were trust funds (First Denton Nat. Bank v. Kenney, 116 Md. 24, 81 A. 227, Ann.Cas.1913B, 1337); or if the trustee's individual account, since the trust deposit has been mingled with his own moneys, has been reduced below the amount of the trust money and there is no proof that the trust money is still in the account (Mayer v. Citizens' Bank of Sturgeon, 86 Mo. App. 422.)

[36] Allen v. Puritan Trust Co., 211 Mass. 409, 97 N.E. 916, L.R.A.1915C, 518.

[37] Bischoff v. Yorkville Bank, 218 N.Y. 106, 112 N.E. 759, L.R.A.1916F, 1059. See, also, Corn Exch. Bank v. Manhattan Sav. Inst'n, 105 Misc. 615, 173 N.Y.S. 799; Atwood-Stone Co. v. Lake County Bank, 38 S.D. 377, 161 N.W. 539, and United States Fidelity & Guaranty Co. v. Adoue & Lobit, 104 Tex. 379, 137 S.W. 648, 138 S.W. 383, 37 L.R.A.,N.S., 409, Ann.Cas.1914B, 667. But in Interstate Nat. Bank v. Claxton, 97 Tex. 569, 80 S.W. 604, 65 L.R.A. 820, 104 Am.St.Rep. 885, while holding the bank liable for the benefit it received from the payment of its debt out of the trust fund, the court did not extend the liability to money thereafter withdrawn by the

was held that, where a trustee drew a check on his trust account in the A. bank, deposited it to his private credit in the B. bank, and then paid the funds to the B. bank to satisfy his own debt to such bank, the B. bank was liable to the cestui que trust for the amounts it received. In another case a check payable to "A, guardian," was deposited by the guardian to his individual account and part of the credit used to pay A.'s debt to the depositary. This rendered the depositary liable to the cestui for the amount received by it.[38]

This rule affects all creditors of the trustee who knowingly take trust property in satisfaction of his debt to them. The transaction inevitably is a breach of trust and the creditor should know this.

Basis of Liability

The basis of liability in this class of cases has been clearly stated by the courts. "The principle governing the defendant's liability is, that a banker who knows that a fund on deposit with him is a trust fund cannot appropriate that fund for his private benefit, or where charged with notice of the conversion join in assisting others to appropriate it for their private benefit, without being liable to refund the money if the appropriation is a breach of the trust."[39] Or, as the New York Court of Appeals has put it: "Inasmuch as the defendant knew that the credits to Poggenburg created by the proceeds of the checks were of a fiduciary character and were equitably owned by the executor, it had not the right to participate in a diversion of them from the estate or the proper purposes under the will. Its participation in a diversion of them would result from either (a) acquiring an advantage or benefit directly through or from the diversion, or (b) joining in a diversion, in which it was not interested with actual notice or knowledge that the diversion was intended or was being executed, and thereby becoming privy to it."[40]

trustee and used to pay debts of other creditors.

[38] United States Fidelity & Guaranty Co. v. Adoue & Lobit, 104 Tex. 379, 137 S.W. 648, 138 S.W. 383, 37 L.R.A., N.S., 409, Ann.Cas.1914B, 667; Brovan v. Kyle, 166 Wis. 347, 165 N.W. 382.

[39] Allen v. Puritan Trust Co., 211 Mass. 409, 422, 97 N.E. 916, L.R.A. 1915C, 518.

[40] Bischoff v. Yorkville Bank, 218 N.Y. 106, 112, 112 N.E. 759, L.R.A. 1916F, 1059.

When Bank Not Liable

When a trustee checks on a trust account, or on his individual account known by the bank to contain trust funds, the bank is entitled to presume that the withdrawal is made for the proper purposes of the trust. The mere fact that the check is payable to the trustee in his private capacity or is not payable to a beneficiary of the trust places no duty on the bank to inquire into the disposition of the trust money. It is usually only when the bank has actual notice of an intended misappropriation of the trust fund that it is warranted in refusing to honor the trustee's check, and is liable if it does honor it, according to the great weight of authority. Thus, the mere deposit of trust funds in an individual account is not of itself wrongful and creates no liability on the part of the bank for later withdrawals.[41] "An administrator or other person having charge of trust funds may deposit them in a bank to the credit of his personal account and check them out in the usual course of business, and the bank, though it has knowledge of the character of the funds so deposited, is not thereby made liable to the beneficial, or actual, owners of such funds, in the absence of any knowledge on its part that the funds are being misappropriated or misapplied by such trust officer."[42] But when a bank is expressly directed to credit a check to a trust account and the bank credits it to an individual account,[43] or when a certificate of deposit belonging to a trust estate is applied by the trustee to pay his debt to the bank and to pay other debts by check, and this use of the certificate is regarded as a single fraudulent transaction,[44] the bank will be liable.[45] In some extraordinary cases where the bank has knowledge of extremely suspicious circumstances, it may be liable as for participating in a breach

---

[41] Miami County Bank v. State ex rel. Peru Trust Co., 61 Ind.App. 360, 112 N.E. 40; Batchelder v. Central Nat. Bank, 188 Mass. 25, 73 N.E. 1024; United States Fidelity & Guaranty Co. v. Adoue & Lobit, Tex.Civ. App., 128 S.W. 636. But, if the bank knows that the deposit of trust funds in the individual account is wrongful, it will be liable for subsequent misappropriations. British America El. Co. v. Bank of British N. A., [1919] A. C. 658.

[42] Miami County Bank v. State ex rel. Peru Trust Co., 61 Ind.App. 360, 112 N.E. 40, 43.

[43] Blanton v. First Nat. Bank of Forrest City, 136 Ark. 441, 206 S.W. 745; Duckett v. National Mechanics' Bank, 86 Md. 400, 38 A. 983, 39 L.R. A. 84, 63 Am.St.Rep. 513.

[44] United States Fidelity & Guaranty Co. v. Adoue & Lobit, 104 Tex. 379, 137 S.W. 648, 138 S.W. 383, 37 L.R.A., N.S., 409, Ann.Cas.1914B, 667.

[45] Farmers' Loan & Trust Co. v. Fidelity Trust Co., C.C.A.Wash., 86 F. 541, 30 C.C.A. 247.

where it honors the trustee's checks on a known trust account. These are the cases referred to in the Uniform Fiduciaries Act as cases where the bank has knowledge of such facts that its action amounts to bad faith. An example might be the case where the bank honored a series of checks by a trustee on a known trust account in favor of a stock broker, with strong suspicions that the trustee was gambling.[46]

Ordinarily the honoring by the bank of a check on a trust account to the order of the trustee does not render a bank liable, if it turns out that the trustee has misappropriated the money so paid.[47] The bank is not required to demand proof that he intends to use the proceeds of the check for trust purposes. The presumption is to the contrary. It would be an intolerable burden on a bank to require it to investigate the intent and powers of every trustee doing business with it. The obligation of watching for dishonesty is rather on the cestuis que trust. But it has been held that where a trustee checked on trust funds to take up notes of a corporation in which he was interested, the bank was liable for the amount of the checks when it had previous notice of breaches of the trust by use of trust funds to pay debts of the trustee to the bank, and when the bank officials had been negligent in supervising the affairs of the bank.[48]

Nor, in the absence of special circumstances implicating the bank in the breach, is a bank liable where it honors checks of the trustee upon the trust account and these checks run to the individual creditors of the trustee. Without other facts showing

---

[46] Farmers' Loan & Trust Co. v. Fidelity Trust Co., C.C.A.Wash., 86 F. 541; Lowndes v. City Nat. Bank, 82 Conn. 8, 72 A. 150, 22 L.R.A.,N.S., 408; Pearce v. Dill, 149 Ind. 136, 48 N.E. 788.

[47] Lowndes v. City Nat. Bank, 82 Conn. 8, 72 A. 150, 22 L.R.A.,N.S., 408; First Nat. Bank of Sharon v. Valley State Bank, 60 Kan. 621, 57 P. 510; Allen v. Fourth Nat. Bank, 224 Mass. 239, 112 N.E. 650; Kendall v. Fidelity Trust Co., 230 Mass. 238, 119 N.E. 861; Town of Eastchester v. Mt. Vernon Trust Co., 173 App.Div. 482, 159 N.Y.S. 289; Fidelity & Deposit Co. of Maryland v. Queens County Trust Co., 174 App.Div. 160, 159 N.Y.S. 954; Taylor v. Astor Nat. Bank, 105 Misc. 386, 174 N.Y.S. 279.

[48] Lowndes v. City Nat. Bank of South Norwalk, 82 Conn. 8, 72 A. 150, 22 L.R.A.,N.S., 408. And so, too, where a bank is charged with notice that an account is a trust account, and, by reason of a section of the Bankruptcy Act and the countersignature of some checks, is also charged with notice that withdrawals from the fund could not lawfully be made without the signature of the clerk of the court, it is liable for moneys paid out on checks payable to the trustee individually and not countersigned. Fidelity & Deposit Co. of Maryland v. Queens County Trust Co., 226 N.Y. 225, 123 N.E. 370.

an intended breach, the bank is entitled to assume that the payees are creditors of the trust estate, or that the payments are for the benefit of the cestuis que trust.[49] The bank is not obliged to require the payees to prove that the checks satisfy valid claims against the trust, or were issued in the trust business. But where a bank allows a trustee to check on the trust account to pay bucket shop debts, with full knowledge of the nature of the account and the use to which the checks were being put, it will be liable to the beneficiary.[50]

Where a trustee draws a check on his personal account, known by the bank to contain trust funds, and the check is to pay debts of the trustee to third persons, the bank will not be liable in the absence of knowledge of an intended breach.[51]

Liability on the part of the B. bank has been denied when the trustee drew a check on the trust account in the A. bank, deposited it to his individual account in the B. bank, the A. bank paid the check, and thereafter the trustee checked out the funds for his own benefit.[52]

In cases where a trustee has had in his possession a check payable to "A., trustee," and has deposited it to his individual account and checked it out for his individual benefit, the courts have disagreed upon the question of the liability of the bank, a few courts taking the view that such action was a participation

---

[49] Gray v. Johnston, L.R. 3 H.L. 1; Pa. Title & Trust Co. v. Meyer, 201 Pa. 299, 50 A. 998; Merchants' & Planters' Nat. Bank of Union v. Clifton Mfg. Co., 56 S.C. 320, 33 S.E. 750; First State Bank of Bonham v. Hill, Tex.Civ.App., 141 S.W. 300; Anderson v. Walker, 93 Tex. 119, 53 S.W. 821; Boyle v. Northwestern Nat. Bank, 125 Wis. 498, 103 N.W. 1123, 104 N.W. 917, 1 L.R.A.,N.S., 1110, 110 Am.St.Rep. 844. But see Farmers' Loan & Trust Co. v. Fidelity Trust Co., C.C.A.Wash., 86 F. 541, 30 C.C.A. 247.

[50] Pearce v. Dill, 149 Ind. 136, 48 N.E. 788.

[51] Coleman v. Bucks & Oxon Union Bank [1897] 2 Ch. 243; Interstate Nat. Bank v. Claxton, 97 Tex. 569, 80 S.W. 604, 65 L.R.A. 820, 104 Am. St.Rep. 885. Where the indorsement of the instrument enabling the trustee to place it to his private account was a forgery, the bank was liable for the funds thereafter withdrawn for the trustee's benefit. Hope Vacuum Cleaner Co. v. Commercial Nat. Bank of Independence, 101 Kan. 726, 168 P. 870.

[52] Havana Cent. R. Co. v. Central Trust Co. of New York, C.C.A.N.Y., 204 F. 546, 123 C.C.A. 72, L.R.A.1915B, 715; Allen v. Puritan Trust Co., 211 Mass. 409, 97 N.E. 916, L.R.A.1915C, 518; Kendall v. Fidelity Trust Co., 230 Mass. 238, 119 N.E. 861; Havana Central R. Co. v. Knickerbocker Trust Co., 198 N.Y. 422, 92 N.E. 12, L.R.A. 1915B, 720; Bischoff v. Yorkville Bank, 218 N.Y. 106, 112 N.E. 759, L. R.A.1916F, 1059.

in the breach by the bank,[53] while most courts hold that the facts did not necessarily imply a breach of trust and that the bank was not liable in the absence of evidence of actual knowledge of intended fraud.[54]

If a trustee holds a check to his order as trustee, indorses it to B., and B. deposits it and checks out the fund, the bank of deposit is not liable if the trustee misappropriated the moneys represented by the check.[55]

While in a few cases the courts have held that after a bank has knowledge that the trustee is violating his trust, the bank comes under a duty to investigate the propriety of his future actions with the bank account, and is charged with knowledge of what it could have learned by such investigation,[56] this view is not generally accepted and is repudiated by the Uniform Fiduciaries Act.[57]

The rules regarding what amounts to a participation in a breach of trust have been codified in the Uniform Fiduciaries Act which is now in force in several jurisdictions.[58] In a general way it restricts the third person's liability to cases where he accepts trust property in satisfaction of the trustee's debt to him, and where he actually knows of an intended breach of trust or acts with knowledge of such facts about the trustee and his conduct that the third person's action amounts to a display of bad faith. The latter test is honesty and not the use of ordinary care, it will be observed.

[53] Bank of Hickory v. McPherson, 102 Miss. 852, 59 So. 934; United States Fidelity & Guaranty Co. v. People's Bank, 127 Tenn. 720, 157 S. W. 414.

[54] Safe Deposit & Trust Co. v. Diamond Nat. Bank, 194 Pa. 334, 44 A. 1064; United States Fidelity & Guaranty Co. v. Home Bank for Savings, 77 W.Va. 665, 88 S.E. 109.

[55] Hood v. Kensington Nat. Bank, 230 Pa. 508, 79 A. 714.

[56] Bischoff v. Yorkville Bank, 218 N.Y. 106, 112 N.E. 759, L.R.A.1916F, 1059.

[57] Sections 5 and 6.

[58] Approved in 1922 and now adopted in Colorado, District of Columbia, Idaho, Illinois, Indiana, Louisiana, Maryland, Nevada, New Jersey, New Mexico, New York, North Carolina, Pennsylvania, Rhode Island, Utah, Wisconsin, Wyoming.

See Scott, Participation in a Breach of Trust, 34 Harv.L.R. 454.

For construction of this Act, see Colby v. Riggs, 67 App.D.C. 259, 92 F.2d 183, 114 A.L.R. 1065; New Amsterdam Casualty Co. v. National Newark & Essex Banking Co., 119 N.J.Eq. 540, 182 A. 824.

Notice to the Bank

If the bank does not know that funds are trust funds, it is not liable for their disposition by the trustee.[59] Notice of the existence of the trust acquired by an officer of the bank while acting in his official capacity will bind the bank,[60] but otherwise if the officer acquired the information outside his official duties.[61]

Where corporations deal with trustees, knowledge of their employees acquired in the course of their business binds the corporation.[62] But an exception is made where the employee was knowingly assisting for his own benefit in the breach of trust of which he knew, and so would naturally not notify his employer of it.[63] The basis of the imputation of the knowledge of the agent to the principal is the likelihood that he will pass the information on. This does not apply where it would be to the personal disadvantage of the agent to tell his principal the facts of the case.

The theory of the bank's liability in these cases is well stated in Duckett v. National Mechanics' Bank,[64] as follows: "It is true, undoubtedly, that a bank is bound to honor the checks of its customer so long as he has funds on deposit to his credit, unless such funds are intercepted by a garnishment or other like process, or are held under the bank's right of set-off. It is equally true that whenever money is placed in bank on deposit and the bank's offi-

---

[59] Martin v. Kansas Nat. Bank, 66 Kan. 655, 72 P. 218; First State Bank of Bonham v. Hill, Tex.Civ. App., 141 S.W. 300.

[60] Lowndes v. City Nat. Bank of South Norwalk, 82 Conn. 8, 72 A. 150, 22 L.R.A.,N.S., 408; Tesene v. Iowa State Bank, 186 Iowa 1385, 173 N.W. 918; Atwood-Stone Co. v. Lake County Bank, 38 S.D. 377, 161 N.W. 539.

[61] Bank of Hartford v. McDonald, 107 Ark. 232, 154 S.W. 512; First Denton Nat. Bank v. Kenney, 116 Md. 24, 81 A. 227, Ann.Cas.1913B, 1337.

[62] Chapman v. Hughes, 134 Cal. 641, 58 P. 298, 60 P. 974, 66 P. 982; Hedrick v. Beeler, 110 Mo. 91, 19 S.W. 492; Cowan v. Withrow, 111 N.C. 306, 16 S.E. 397.

[63] Neagle v. McMullen, 334 Ill. 168, 165 N.E. 605; Leach v. State Sav. Bank, 202 Iowa 265, 209 N.W. 422; Henry v. Allen, 151 N.Y. 1, 45 N.E. 355, 36 L.R.A. 658; Knobeloch v. Germania Sav. Bank, 50 S.C. 259, 27 S.E. 962.

[64] 86 Md. 400, 405, 406, 38 A. 983, 39 L.R.A. 84, 63 Am.St.Rep. 513. For further discussions of the principles underlying these bank cases, see Gray v. Johnston, L.R. 3 H.L. 1; United States Fidelity & Guaranty Trust Co. v. Union Bank & Trust Co., C.C.A.Tenn., 228 F. 448, 143 C.C.A. 30; Lowndes v. City Nat. Bank of South Norwalk, 82 Conn. 8, 72 A. 150, 22 L.R.A.,N.S., 408; Allen v. Puritan Trust Co., 211 Mass. 409, 97 N.E. 916, L.R.A.1915C, 518; Bischoff v. Yorkville Bank, 218 N.Y. 106, 112 N. E. 759, L.R.A.1916F, 1059; United States Fidelity & Guaranty Co. v. Home Bank for Savings, 77 W.Va. 665, 88 S.E. 109.

cers are unaware that the fund does not belong to the person depositing it, the bank upon paying the fund out on the depositor's check will be free from liability even though it should afterwards turn out that the fund in reality belonged to some one else than the individual who deposited it. It is immaterial, so far as respects the duty of the bank to the depositor, in what capacity the depositor holds or possesses the fund which he places on deposit. The obligation of the bank is simply to keep the fund safely and to return it to the proper person or to pay it to his order. If it be deposited by one as trustee, the depositor as trustee has the right to withdraw it, and the bank, in the absence of knowledge or notice to the contrary, would be bound to assume that the trustee would appropriate the money, when drawn, to a proper use. Any other rule would throw upon a bank the duty of inquiring as to the appropriation made of every fund deposited by a trustee or other like fiduciary; and the imposition of such a duty would practically put an end to the banking business, because no bank could possibly conduct business if, without fault on its part, it were held accountable for the misconduct or malversation of its depositors who occupy some fiduciary relation to the fund placed by them with the bank. In the absence of notice or knowledge a bank cannot question the right of its customer to withdraw funds, nor refuse (except in the instances already noted) to honor his demands by check; and therefore, even though the deposit be to the customer's credit in trust, the bank is under no obligation to look after the appropriation of the trust funds when withdrawn, or to protect the trust by setting up a jus tertii against a demand. But if the bank has notice or knowledge that a breach of trust is being committed by an improper withdrawal of funds or if it participates in the profits or fruits of the fraud, then it will undoubtedly be liable."

Negligence by Bank

Occasionally gross negligence by the bank or palpable aid in the breach will make liability certain. Thus, where the trustee has an individual and trust account in the same bank, and the bank charges individual checks against the trust account, it is openly aiding a breach.[65] And where the cashier of the bank and the

[65] United States Fidelity & Guaranty Co. v. United States Nat. Bank, 80 Or. 361, 157 P. 155, L.R.A.1916E, 610. And so in Tesene v. Iowa State Bank, 186 Iowa 1385, 173 N.W. 918, a bank which had knowledge of the lack of authority by a mother to receive money for her children, but which paid moneys, standing in her name as guardian for the children, to her personally, was held to have aided in a breach.

trustee are one and the same person, and the directors, after breaches of trust with notice of which they were charged, failed to exercise any supervision over the affairs of the bank, they may be held liable to the beneficiaries of the trust on the ground of negligence.[66]

Seeing to Application of Purchase Money

The doctrine of early English equity [67] that a purchaser of trust property from a trustee was bound to see to the application of the purchase money, that is, was bound to pay direct to the cestuis que trust or make sure that they received the money, has been abolished by statute in England,[68] and has either never been accepted or has been abandoned in America.[69] An occasional trace of the old rule may be found in early cases,[70] and some courts have declared that it should be applied unless the trust is a general and unlimited trust.[71] It has been held that if the purchaser or other debtor pays money to the trustee, knowing that the latter is on the verge of insolvency and will surely misappropriate the money, the purchaser will remain liable to the cestui after payment to the trustee.[72] If the purchaser knows that the sale constitutes a breach of trust, naturally he is not an innocent purchaser, and the trust property will be subject to the

[66] Lowndes v. City Nat. Bank of South Norwalk, 82 Conn. 8, 72 A. 150, 22 L.R.A.,N.S., 408.

[67] Lewin on Trusts, 13th Ed., 1081.

[68] 56 & 57 Vict., c. 53, § 20.

[69] Dawson v. Ramser, 58 Ala. 573; Jacks v. State, 44 Ark. 61; Colesbury v. Dart, 61 Ga. 620; Davis v. Freeman, 148 Ga. 117, 95 S.E. 980; Ely v. Pike, 115 Ill.App. 284; Bevis v. Heflin, 63 Ind. 129; Pike v. Baldwin, 68 Iowa 263, 26 N.W. 441; Henriott v. Cood, 153 Ky. 418, 155 S.W. 761; Burroughs v. Gaither, 66 Md. 171, 7 A. 243; Cady v. Lincoln, 100 Miss. 765, 57 So. 213; Gate City Building & Loan Ass'n v. National Bank of Commerce, 126 Mo. 82, 28 S.W. 633, 27 L.R.A. 401, 47 Am.St.Rep. 633; Conover v. Stothoff, 38 N.J.Eq. 55; Doscher v. Wyckoff, 132 App.Div. 139, 116 N.Y.S. 389; N.Y.Real Property Law, § 108; Kadis v. Weil, 164 N.C. 84, 80 S.E. 229; Stall v. City of Cincinnati, 16 Ohio St. 169; In re Streater's Estate, 250 Pa. 328, 95 A. 459; Petition of Van Horne, 18 R.I. 389, 28 A. 341; Campbell v. Virginia-Carolina Chemical Co., 68 S.C. 440, 47 S. E. 716; Spencer v. Lyman, 27 S.D. 471, 131 N.W. 802; Weakley v. Barrow, 137 Tenn. 224, 192 S.W. 927; Whatley v. Oglesby, Tex.Civ.App., 44 S.W. 44; Redford v. Clarke, 100 Va. 115, 40 S.E. 630; Woodwine v. Woodrum, 19 W.Va. 67.

By section 2 of the Uniform Fiduciaries Act there is no duty to see to the application of purchase money.

[70] Indiana I. & I. R. Co. v. Swannell, 54 Ill.App. 260.

[71] Duffy v. Calvert, 6 Gill, Md., 487; St. Mary's Church of Burlington v. Stockton, 8 N.J.Eq. 520.

[72] Darnaby v. Watts, 28 S.W. 338, 16 Ky.Law Rep. 321.

trust in his hands.[73] And every person dealing with a known trustee is put on inquiry as to the extent of the trustee's powers, and charged with knowledge of what he could have learned by a reasonable inquiry.[74]

Where a trustee holds stock in a corporation and he or a transferee from him presents to the corporation or its transfer agent the stock certificate with an indorsement, and requests a change in the registration of the stock to the name of the transferee, there is no duty on the part of the corporation or its transfer agent to inquire into the propriety and validity of the transfer.[75] It may be assumed that the trustee has power to transfer and that he is doing it for a lawful purpose. There will be no participation in a breach of trust, unless the corporation or agent either knows of a breach or knows such facts that its assistance in the transfer is an act of bad faith.[76]

ACTIONS AGAINST THIRD PARTIES FOR INJURING THE TRUST PROPERTY [77]

160. If a third person injures or misappropriates the trust property, a cause of action arises in favor of the trustee which is ordinarily enforceable by him alone; but where he will not or cannot enforce it, the beneficiary is allowed to sue in the place of the trustee.

The title to, and possession of, the trust property normally rest in the trustee. He is the owner in the courts of law. It is therefore natural that a cause of action in favor of the trustee is held to arise when a third person interferes with the possession of the trust property, or misappropriates or damages it. Ordinarily the trustee, and he alone, is permitted to sue the wrongdoer. Thus, an action to recover the trust property or for injury to it,[78] to restrain the wrongful taxation of the trust res,[79] to recover on a

---

[73] Grider v. Driver, 46 Ark. 109; Leake v. Watson, 58 Conn. 332, 20 A. 343, 8 L.R.A. 666, 18 Am.St.Rep. 270; Kenworthy v. Levi, 214 Pa. 235, 63 A. 690; Cardwell v. Cheatham, 2 Head, Tenn., 14.

[74] See § 97, ante.

[75] Section 3 of the Uniform Fiduciaries Act, and many statutes in other states collected in Bogert on Trusts and Trustees, p. 2618.

[76] Marbury v. Ehlen, 72 Md. 206, 19 A. 648, 20 Am.St.Rep. 467; In re Bohlen's Estate, 75 Pa. 304.

[77] Restatement, Trusts, §§ 280, 393.

[78] Robinson v. Adams, 81 App.Div. 20, 80 N.Y.S. 1098, affirmed 179 N.Y. 558, 71 N.E. 1139.

[79] Western R. Co. v. Nolan, 48 N.Y. 513.

bond payable to the trustee,[80] to recover for use and occupation of the trust property,[81] in ejectment,[82] to recover on a covenant,[83] or to recover hire for the trust property,[84] should be brought by the trustee, in the absence of special circumstances.

The cestui que trust may not ordinarily sue a third person for injury to or recovery of the trust property, in the absence of one or more of the special facts hereinafter mentioned.[85] Thus, the cestui has been denied relief against a third person in actions of trover,[86] ejectment,[87] for the recovery of damages to the trust property,[88] and to recover the trust fund.[89]

When Cestui may Sue

If the purposes of the trust are accomplished, and the trust is therefore a dry trust, the cestui que trust may maintain ejectment.[90] And likewise the beneficiary may bring ejectment, if he is entitled to the possession of the trust property, even though the trust is active.[91] And if the cestui que trust is in possession he may recover at law for an injury to that possession,[92] or enjoin a disturbance of the possession by a third party.[93]

[80] Forrest v. O'Donnell, 42 Mich. 556, 4 N.W. 259.

[81] Grady v. Ibach, 94 Ala. 152, 10 So. 287.

[82] Simmons v. Richardson, 107 Ala. 697, 18 So. 245.

[83] Lovell v. Nelson, 6 J.J.Marsh., Ky., 247.

[84] Denton's Guardians v. Denton's Ex'rs, 17 Md. 403.

[85] Weetjen v. Vibbard, 5 Hun, N.Y., 265; Thompson v. Remsen, 27 Misc. 279, 58 N.Y.S. 424; Woolf v. Barnes, 46 Misc. 169, 93 N.Y.S. 219; Dameron v. Gold, 17 N.C. 17.

[86] Myers v. Hale, 17 Mo.App. 204; Poage v. Bell, 8 Leigh, Va., 604.

[87] Obert v. Bordine, 20 N.J.L. 394; Bruce v. Faucett, 49 N.C. 391.

[88] Lindheim v. Manhattan Ry. Co., 68 Hun 122, 22 N.Y.S. 685; Pennsylvania R. Co. v. Duncan, 111 Pa. 352, 5 A. 742.

[89] Morrow v. Morrow, 113 Mo.App. 444, 87 S.W. 590.

[90] Doggett v. Hart, 5 Fla. 215, 58 Am.Dec. 464; Cable v. Cable, 146 Pa. 451, 23 A. 223; Hopkins v. Stephens, 2 Rand., Va., 422; Hopkins v. Ward, 6 Munf., Va., 38.

[91] Glover v. Stamps, 73 Ga. 209, 54 Am.Rep. 870; School Directors v. Dunkleberger, 6 Pa. 29; Presbyterian Congregation v. Johnston, 1 Watts & S., Pa., 9; Cape v. Plymouth Congregational Church, 117 Wis. 150, 93 N. W. 449. In McCoy v. Anderson, 137 Ark. 45, 207 S.W. 213, the cestui que trust had been in possession for many years, the trustee was dead, and the beneficiary was allowed to bring ejectment.

[92] Yates v. Big Sandy R. Co., Ky., 89 S.W. 108; Stearns v. Palmer, 10 Metc., Mass., 32.

[93] Reed v. Harris, 30 N.Y.Super.Ct. 151.

If the trustee refuses to bring the action, after demand,[94] or fails to act,[95] or the trusteeship is vacant,[96] or the trustee has been absent for many years,[97] or the trustee has an adverse interest,[98] the cestui may bring the action against the third person. To wait until a new trustee could be appointed, or until the present trustee saw fit to act, or his disabilities were removed, would endanger the cause of action. The necessities of the case entitle the cestui que trust to proceed directly, in place of the trustee, to enforce the cause of action which the trustee has.

The principle is illustrated by a New York case, in which a bondholder cestui que trust was allowed to maintain a bill to foreclose a mortgage, because of the absence of the trustee in a foreign country. There was the additional allegation that the trustee was insane. The court, through Finch, J., said:[99] "It is conceded that the beneficiary may sue where the trustee refuses, but that is because there is no other remedy, and the right of the bondholder, otherwise, will go unredressed. The doctrine does not rest rigidly upon a technical ground, but upon a substantial necessity. * * * What occurred in the present case was tantamount to and an equivalent of a refusal by the trustee. He had gone beyond the jurisdiction; the whole apprehended mischief would be consummated before he could be reached; and if reached there was sufficient reason to believe that he was incompetent. But the Special Term say that in such event a new trustee should have been appointed. That simply reproduces the difficulty in another form, for a court would hardly remove a trustee without notice to him and giving him an opportunity to be heard. And why should a new appointment be made when any one of the bondholders can equally do the duty of pursuing the foreclosure? The court, in such an action, takes hold of the trust, dictates and

---

[94] Bowdoin College v. Merritt, C.C. Ind., 54 F. 55; Reinach v. Atlantic & G. W. R. Co., C.C.Ohio, 58 F. 33; Blackburn v. Fitzgerald, 130 Ala. 584, 30 So. 568 (semble); Eagan v. Mahoney, 24 Colo.App. 285, 174 P. 1119; Canada v. Daniel, 175 Mo.App. 55, 157 S.W. 1032; De Kay v. Hackensack Water Co., 38 N.J.Eq. 158; O'Beirne v. Allegheny & K. R. Co., 151 N.Y. 372, 45 N.E. 873; Anderson v. Daley, 38 App.Div. 505, 56 N.Y.S. 511, appeal dismissed 159 N.Y. 146, 53 N.E. 753; Phœbe v. Black, 76 N. C. 379.

[95] Wheeler v. Brown, 26 Ill. 369.

[96] Zimmerman v. Makepeace, 152 Ind. 199, 52 N.E. 992; Judd v. Dike, 30 Minn. 380, 15 N.W. 672.

[97] Hemmerich v. Union Dime Sav. Inst., 144 App.Div. 413, 129 N.Y.S. 267.

[98] Webb v. Vermont Cent. R. Co., C.C.Vt., 9 F. 793; Hale v. Nashua & L. R. R., 60 N.H. 333.

[99] Ettlinger v. Persian Rug & Carpet Co., 142 N.Y. 189, 192, 193, 36 N.E. 1055, 40 Am.St.Rep. 587.

controls its performance, distributes the assets as it deems just, and it is not vitally important which of the two possible plaintiffs set the court in motion. The bondholders are the real parties in interest; it is their right which is to be redressed, and their loss which is to be prevented; and any emergency which makes a demand upon the trustee futile or impossible and leaves the right of the bondholder without other reasonable means of redress should justify his appearance as plaintiff in a court of equity for the purpose of foreclosure."

The trustee and cestui que trust may unite in an action to recover the trust fund, although the addition of the cestui as a party plaintiff is ordinarily unnecessary.[1]

[1] Jennings' Ex'rs v. Davis, 5 Dana, Ky., 127; Marble v. Whaley, 33 Miss. 157.

CHAPTER 18

THE BARRING OF REMEDIES

Sec.
161. Act or Omission of the Beneficiary.
162. Statute of Limitations.

ACT OR OMISSION OF THE BENEFICIARY [1]

161. An act of the beneficiary may bar his remedy, as where he expressly releases his claim, or elects to take an alternative remedy, or consents to a wrongful act in advance, or approves it after its commission, or in any other way conducts himself so as to render it unfair to grant him relief.

Regardless of statutes of limitation, if the beneficiary, without reasonable excuse, fails to assert his right and seek his remedy for a long period, and because of this inaction the position of the beneficiary's opponent is prejudiced, the beneficiary may be held guilty of laches, and his remedy regarded as barred.

Having in the sections next preceding, considered the remedies available to the beneficiary and trustee upon the breach of the trust or in aid of its enforcement, the methods by which such remedies may be lost, barred or destroyed will now be discussed.

Remedy Barred by Acts of Beneficiary

A large number of confusing and ill-defined terms have come into use in connection with the barring or destruction of rights. Courts and text-writers have joined in using in different senses and with different implications such words as "release," "waiver," "election," "acquiescence," "adoption," "ratification," "confirmation," "estoppel," and "laches." The hopeless confusion in the use of the word "waiver" has been strikingly shown by an eminent author.[2] It is believed that clarity will ensue from the abandonment of these terms as far as possible and the description of the acts which result as a bar, without trying to give them technical names.

At the outset it is obvious that the remedy of the beneficiary may be barred either by his act or his failure to act. The destruction of his remedy by his positive conduct will be treated first. The most direct way of barring his remedy is to execute

[1] Restatement, Trusts, §§ 208-212, 216, 219, 295, 315, 327, 409.

[2] Ewart, Waiver Distributed.

§ 161   ACT OR OMISSION OF THE BENEFICIARY   595

a release to the trustee or third person against whom he has the right of action. As any one having a cause of action may discharge it, so it is elementary that the cestui que trust may contract to cancel his cause of action; that is, may release.[3] Thus, where the cestui has filed a bill for an account, a compromise has been offered, and after an examination of the accounts with the aid of attorneys the offer of compromise is accepted and a release executed by the beneficiary to the trustee, the cestui's remedy is clearly destroyed.[4] Since the release of one joint tortfeasor under the common law releases both, a beneficiary should be wary in his settlements with wrongdoing co-trustees, and in the case of third persons joining with the trustee in a breach of trust.[5]

Releases by the beneficiary are of course subject to attack on the ground of the lack of capacity of the beneficiary, as, for example, in the case of infancy;[6] and they must be given with a full knowledge of the facts, and without concealment or fraud, if they are to be binding.[7]

Election

The beneficiary may also do an act, which, while not intended by him as a bar to his remedies under the trust, will be so treated in equity because to do otherwise would be unconscionable. In such a case the beneficiary has placed himself and his opponent in such positions that he cannot fairly ask equity to grant him the remedy in question. Thus, the beneficiary may have an election between two remedies, and if he takes one he cannot thereafter demand the other. His own conduct in taking the first remedy has barred the second.[8] For example, if a trustee makes a voidable sale of the trust property, the cestui has the option of accepting the proceeds of such sale and treating it as valid or of seeking to recover the res sold and avoiding the sale; and

---

[3] Cocks v. Barlow, 5 Redf.Sur., N.Y., 406; Dearing v. Selvey, 50 W. Va. 4, 40 S.E. 478.

[4] Forbes v. Forbes, 5 Gill., Md., 29.

[5] First & Merchants' Nat. Bank v. Bank of Waverly, 170 Va. 496, 197 S.E. 462, 116 A.L.R. 1156.

[6] Parker v. Hayes' Adm'r, 39 N.J. Eq. 469; Clark v. Law, 22 How.Prac., N.Y., 426.

[7] Jones v. Lloyd, 117 Ill. 597, 7 N.E. 119; Huddleston v. Henderson, 181 Ill.App. 176; Barton v. Fuson, 81 Iowa 575, 47 N.W. 774; Appeal of Berryhill's Adm'x, 35 Pa. 245.

[8] Wiswall v. Stewart, 32 Ala. 433, 70 Am.Dec. 549; Hyatt v. Vanneck, 82 Md. 465, 33 A. 972; Washburn v. Rainier, 149 App.Div. 800, 134 N.Y.S. 301.

where he has clearly shown his intention to adopt the former course, he has lost the second remedy.[9]

The cestui que trust may also bar his remedy by consenting to the alleged wrongful act in advance, or by requesting that the act of which he now complains be done.[10] Thus, beneficiaries who consent in advance to the continuance of a business by a trustee,[11] or to the making of a wrongful investment,[12] may not thereafter question the legality of the conduct of the trustee. This doctrine was stated by Lord Eldon as follows:[13] "It is established by all the cases that if the cestui que trust joins with the trustees in that which is a breach of the trust, knowing the circumstances, such a cestui que trust can never complain of such a breach of trust. I go further, and agree that either concurrence in the act, or acquiescence without original concurrence, will release the trustees. * * *" And a Missouri court has stated the rule to be that "a concurring and acquiescing cestui que trust is denied redress against a defaulting trustee, on account of any injury sustained by the latter's misconduct at the former's request or with his approval."[14]

Approval of Wrongful Act

After the breach of trust or other wrong to the cestui que trust has been committed, he may approve or excuse the act in such a way as to bar his remedy. Examples of the approval of wrongful acts are frequent.[15] Thus, a cestui who joins in a petition to a court to confirm a voidable act by a trustee will not be heard

---

[9] Marx v. Clisby, 130 Ala. 502, 30 So. 517. But such election is not shown by inaction without knowledge of the right to set aside the transaction. Branch v. Bulkley, 109 Va. 784, 65 S.E. 652.

[10] Chirurg v. Ames, 138 Iowa 697, 116 N.W. 865; Preble v. Greenleaf; 180 Mass. 79, 61 N.E. 808; Richards v. Keyes, 195 Mass. 184, 80 N.E. 812; Newton v. Rebenack, 90 Mo.App. 650; Town of Verona v. Peckham, 66 Barb., N.Y., 103; Sherman v. Parish, 53 N.Y. 483; Woodbridge v. Bockes, 59 App.Div. 503, 69 N.Y.S. 417, affirmed 170 N.Y. 596, 63 N.E. 362; Ungrich v. Ungrich, 131 App.Div. 24, 115 N.Y.S. 413; Ungrich v. Ungrich, 141 App.Div. 485, 126 N.Y.S. 419.

[11] Quimby v. Uhl, 130 Mich. 198, 89 N.W. 722.

[12] In re Fidelity & Deposit Co. of Maryland, 172 Mich. 600, 138 N.W. 205.

[13] Walker v. Symonds, 3 Swanst. 1, 64.

[14] Newton v. Rebenack, 90 Mo.App. 650, 663, 670.

[15] Pope v. Farnsworth, 146 Mass. 339, 16 N.E. 262; Bennett v. Pierce, 188 Mass. 186, 74 N.E. 360; In re Armitage's Estate, 195 Pa. 582, 46 A. 117.

See Adams v. Whitmarsh, R.I., 17 A.2d 433 (acquiescence in conduct of

later to question the act;[16] and, where the trustee has been guilty of neglect of duty in delaying to bring suit, approval of the suit when it is brought will prevent the cestui que trust from holding the trustee liable.[17] "There is no illegality in a cestui que trust authorizing an act which otherwise would be a breach of trust towards himself, or in his releasing or agreeing to hold harmless his trustee for such an act after it is done."[18]

But when the cestui que trust performs the act of approval he must have full knowledge of the wrong which has been committed.[19] "To establish a ratification by a cestui que trust, the fact must not only be clearly proved, but it must be shown that the ratification was made with a full knowledge of all the material particulars and circumstances, and also in a case like the present that the cestui que trust was fully apprised of the effect of the acts ratified, and of his or her legal rights in the matter. Confirmation and ratification imply, to legal minds, knowledge of a defect in the act to be confirmed and of the right to reject or ratify it. The cestui que trust must therefore not only have been acquainted with the facts, but apprised of the law, how these facts would be dealt with by a court of equity."[20]

The approval, ratification, or confirmation of the wrongful act may not only be expressly given, but also impliedly, as where the cestui que trust accepts the benefits of the wrongful act.[21] Thus, a beneficiary, who joins the trustee in a wrongful conveyance of the trust property to a third person and thereafter takes the benefits of such transfer, will clearly be barred from suing the trustee.[22]

The cestui's act may have caused the trustee to neglect his duty, as where a beneficiary assured a trustee that he would pay the taxes and water rents, and as a result the trustee failed to

---

trust through incorporation for long time).

[16] Richards v. Keyes, 195 Mass. 184, 80 N.E. 812.

[17] Ellig v. Naglee, 9 Cal. 683.

[18] Pope v. Farnsworth, 146 Mass. 339, 344, 16 N.E. 262.

[19] Luers v. Brunjes, 5 Redf.Sur., N.Y., 32; Smith v. Howlett, 29 App. Div. 182, 51 N.Y.S. 1018; Smith v. Miller, 98 Va. 535, 37 S.E. 10.

[20] Adair v. Brimmer, 74 N.Y. 539, 553, 554.

[21] Willis v. Holcomb, 83 Ohio St. 254, 94 N.E. 486; Farish v. Wayman, 91 Va. 430, 21 S.E. 810; Trethewey v. Horton, 71 Wash. 402, 128 P. 632. But there must be knowledge of the unlawful nature of the act when the benefits are accepted. St. Paul Trust Co. v. Strong, 85 Minn. 1, 88 N.W. 256.

[22] Hamilton v. Hamilton, 231 Ill. 128, 83 N.E. 125.

look after them. The cestui's act here barred his remedy against the trustee for neglect of duty in failing to pay the taxes and water rents.[23]

Remedy Barred by Omissions of the Cestui Que Trust

The failure of the beneficiary to act, his delay in asserting his rights, may also bar his remedy. This is the doctrine of "laches," the following statement of which has been approved by the United States Supreme Court:[24] "But there is a defense peculiar to courts of equity, founded on lapse of time and the staleness of the claim, where no statute of limitations governs the case. In such cases, courts of equity act upon their own inherent doctrine of discouraging, for the peace of society, antiquated demands, refuse to interfere where there has been gross laches in prosecuting the claim, or long acquiescence in the assertion of adverse rights." A Colorado court has stated that: "The term 'laches,' in its broad legal sense, as interpreted by courts of equity, signifies such unreasonable delay in the assertion of and attempted securing of equitable rights as should constitute in equity and good conscience a bar to recovery."[25]

The defense of laches is independent of the statute of limitations. The fact that a statutory period for the barring of causes of action has been set, and that this period has not elapsed, does not prove that the cestui que trust has not been guilty of laches. Delay for a period shorter than the statutory limit may be sufficient to destroy the cestui's remedy.[26] "Independently of any statute of limitations, courts of equity uniformly decline to assist a person who has slept upon his rights and shows no excuse for his laches in asserting them."[27] But if the statutory period has expired there is a strong presumption of laches.[28]

Laches may bar the remedy in the case of express as well as implied trusts,[29] but the courts are reluctant to apply the doctrine to the rights of a cestui que trust.[30] Laches is a defense which must be pleaded.[31]

[23] Vreeland v. Van Horn, 17 N.J. Eq. 137.

[24] Badger v. Badger, 2 Wall. 87, 94, 17 L.Ed. 836.

[25] Graff v. Portland Town & Mineral Co., 12 Colo.App. 106, 112, 54 P. 854.

[26] Nettles v. Nettles, 67 Ala. 599; Appeal of Evans, 81 Pa. 278.

[27] Speidel v. Henrici, 120 U.S. 377, 387, 7 S.Ct. 610, 30 L.Ed. 718.

[28] Taylor v. Coggins, 244 Pa. 228, 90 A. 633.

[29] Preston v. Horwitz, 85 Md. 164, 36 A. 710.

[30] Fellrath v. Peoria German School Ass'n, 66 Ill.App. 77; Jenkins v. Hammerschlag, 38 App.Div. 209, 56 N.Y.S. 534.

[31] Davis v. Downer, 210 Mass. 573, 97 N.E. 90.

Laches Founded on Estoppel

Various reasons have been given by the courts for the laches principle, but at bottom they are found to be estoppel. Ewart, in his work on Estoppel,[32] has approved Jacob's definition that estoppel is "an impediment or bar, by which a man is precluded from alleging, or denying, a fact, in consequence of his own previous act, allegation, or denial to the contrary." And in a large number of cases it has been held that there must be something besides mere lapse of time in order to establish laches. The one who is sought to be held as trustee, or the third party sued, must have changed his position in reliance on the delay, or his position must have changed from external causes.[33] The definition of a learned judge has met with frequent approval: "Laches, in legal significance, is not delay, but delay that works a disadvantage to another. So long as parties are in the same condition, it matters little whether one presses a right promptly or slowly, within limits allowed by law; but when, knowing his rights, he takes no step to enforce them until the condition of the other party has, in good faith, become so changed that he cannot be restored to his former state, if the right be then enforced, delay becomes inequitable, and operates as estoppel against the assertion of the right."[34]

Other courts have laid stress on the inability of the courts to do complete or certain justice where long delay has occurred, and have said that the basis of the doctrine of laches is the powerlessness of the courts to ascertain the truth after great lapse of

---

[32] Ewart, Estoppel, p. 4.

[33] Etting v. Marx, C.C.Va., 4 F. 673; Haney v. Legg, 129 Ala. 619, 30 So. 34, 87 Am.St.Rep. 81; Lasker-Morris Bank & Trust Co. v. Gans, 132 Ark. 402, 200 S.W. 1029; Chamberlain v. Chamberlain, 7 Cal.App. 634, 95 P. 659; Woodruff v. Williams, 35 Colo. 28, 85 P. 90, 5 L.R.A.,N.S., 986; Evans v. Moore, 247 Ill. 60, 93 N.E. 118, 139 Am.St.Rep. 302; Jones v. Henderson, 149 Ind. 458, 49 N.E. 443; Harvey v. Hand, 48 Ind.App. 392, 95 N.E. 1020; In re Mahin's Estate, 161 Iowa 459, 143 N.W. 420; Cantwell v. Crawley, 188 Mo. 44, 86 S.W. 251; Hudson v. Cahoon, 193 Mo. 547, 91 S.W. 72; O'Day v. Annex Realty Co., Mo., 191 S.W. 41; Van Alstyne v. Brown, 77 N.J.Eq. 455, 78 A. 678; Evans' Appeal, 81 Pa. 278; Bruner v. Finley, 187 Pa. 389, 41 A. 334; Stephens v. Dubois, 31 R.I. 138, 76 A. 656, 140 Am.St.Rep. 741; Ruckman v. Cox, 63 W.Va. 74, 59 S.E. 760; Roush v. Griffith, 65 W.Va. 752, 65 S.E. 168; Ash v. Wells, 76 W.Va. 711, 86 S.E. 750. "Of course, delay without neglect, or which does not operate to the prejudice of the rights of the opposite party, is not sufficient to constitute laches." Norfleet v. Hampson, 137 Ark. 600, 209 S.W. 651, 653.

[34] Stiness, J., in Chase v. Chase, 20 R.I. 202, 203, 37 A. 804. See, also, Ruckman v. Cox, 63 W.Va. 74, 59 S.E. 760, 762.

time.[35] Thus, a New Jersey court[36] has held that delay will be "fatal when it is operative to render the court unable to feel confident of its ability to ascertain the truth as well as it could have done when the subject for investigation was recent and before the memories of those who had knowledge of the material facts had become faded and weakened by time." And a Pennsylvania court, in referring to an attempt to establish equities on facts which occurred fifty-two years before, has said:[37] "Of the men who were then in active life, and capable of being witnesses, not one in twenty thousand is now living. Written documents whose production might have settled this dispute instantly, have been, in all human probability, destroyed, or lost, or thrown away as useless. The matter belongs to a past age of which we can have no knowledge, except what we derive from history, through whose medium we can dimly discern the outlines of great public events, but all that pertains to men's private affairs is wholly invisible, or only visible in such a sort as to confound the sense and mislead the judgment." The statement that the court will not act when it feels the delay has been such that the truth cannot be learned is essentially based on the idea of estoppel. The delay has caused the loss of evidence and thus placed the party against whom the trust is sought to be enforced in a disadvantageous position. The trust asserter ought to be estopped to set up the trust.

Still other courts have placed emphasis on the thought that the doctrine of laches is founded on the public policy of encouraging repose.[38] This is perhaps but another way of expressing the "inability to do justice" idea.

Some courts have given a presumption of abandonment or release as a reason for the application of the doctrine of laches.[39]

---

[35] Badger v. Badger, 2 Wall. 87, 17 L.Ed. 836; Huntington Nat. Bank v. Huntington Distilling Co., C.C.W. Va., 152 F. 240, 248; Monroe v. Gregory, 147 Ga. 340, 94 S.E. 219; Taylor v. Blair, 14 Mo. 437; Hendrickson v. Hendrickson, 42 N.J.Eq. 657, 9 A. 742; Kellogg v. Kellogg, 169 App.Div. 395, 155 N.Y.S. 310; Harrison v. Gibson, 23 Grat., Va., 212; Woods v. Stevenson, 43 W.Va. 149, 27 S.E. 309.

[36] Cox v. Brown, 87 N.J.Eq. 462, 464, 101 A. 260.

[37] Strimpfler v. Roberts, 18 Pa. 283, 299, 57 Am.Dec. 606.

[38] Jewell v. Trilby Mines Co., C.C.A. Colo., 229 F. 98, 143 C.C.A. 374; Veitch v. Woodward Iron Co., 200 Ala. 358, 76 So. 124; Kleinclaus v. Dutard, 147 Cal. 245, 81 P. 516; Sprinkle v. Holton, 146 N.C. 258, 59 S. E. 680.

[39] Sanchez v. Dow, 23 Fla. 445, 2 So. 842; Newberry v. Winlock's Ex'x, 168 Ky. 822, 182 S.W. 949; In re Kelly's

According to them, after the lapse of a long period, equity presumes that the trust has been satisfied and terminated. But this is an arbitrary and artificial reason, and the notion of estoppel is behind it.

Length of Time

The mere fact that a long period of time has elapsed between the date of the accrual of a right and the date of the commencement of an action to enforce the right will not alone show laches.[40] "It has long since been settled by this court that mere lapse of time, short of the period fixed by the Statute of Limitations, will not bar a claim to equitable relief, when the right is clear, and there are no countervailing circumstances."[41] But the passage of a long interval has led many courts to find laches without the placing of any emphasis on any facts of estoppel, and in some cases with little, if any proof of change of position by others than the claimant.[42] Delay for a short period, as, for example, two years,[43] has been held to be laches under certain circumstances. No rule can be set. Each case must depend on its own peculiar facts—on the reasons for and the effects of the delay.

Estate, 37 Pa.Super. 320; Lafferty v. Turley, 3 Sneed, Tenn., 157.

[40] Pryor v. McIntire, 7 App.D.C. 417; Percival-Porter Co. v. Oaks, 130 Iowa 212, 106 N.W. 626; Reihl v. Likowski, 33 Kan. 515, 6 P. 886; Cantwell v. Crawley, 188 Mo. 44, 86 S.W. 251.

[41] Cantwell v. Crawley, 188 Mo. 44, 57, 86 S.W. 251.

[42] Kansas City Southern Ry Co. v. Stevenson, C.C.Ark., 135 F. 553 (9 years); Froneberger v. First Nat. Bank, C.C.A.N.C., 203 F. 429, 121 C.C.A. 539 (40 years); Benedict v. City of New York, C.C.A.N.Y., 247 F. 758, 159 C.C.A. 616 (17 years); Ewald v. Kierulff, 175 Cal. 363, 165 P. 942 (43 years); Martin v. Martin, Del.Ch., 74 A. 864 (26 years); Mayfield v. Forsyth, 164 Ill. 32, 45 N.E. 403 (31 years); Moore v. Taylor, 251 Ill. 468, 96 N.E. 229 (30 years); Rittenhouse v. Smith, 255 Ill. 493, 99 N.E. 657 (30 years); Cecil's Committee v. Cecil, 149 Ky. 605, 149 S.W. 965 (25 years); Sizemore v. Davidson, 183 Ky. 166, 208 S.W. 810 (30 years); Thorne v. Foley, 137 Mich. 649, 100 N.W. 905 (45 years); Sprague v. Trustees of Protestant Episcopal Church of Diocese of Michigan, 186 Mich. 554, 152 N.W. 996 (30 years); Quairoli v. Italian Beneficial Society of Vineland, 64 N.J.Eq. 205, 53 A. 622 (20 years); Phillips v. Vermeule, 88 N.J.Eq. 500, 102 A. 695 (50 years); Jackson v. Farmer, 151 N.C. 279, 65 S.E. 1008 (29 years); Person v. Fort, 64 S.C. 502, 42 S.E. 594; Stianson v. Stianson, 40 S.D. 322, 167 N.W. 237, 6 A.L.R. 280 (24 years); Spaulding v. Collins, 51 Wash. 488, 99 P. 306 (20 years).

For a recent case see Chandler v. Lally, 308 Mass. 41, 31 N.E.2d 1 (25 years delay after trustee's refusal to account).

[43] Curtis v. Lakin, C.C.A.Utah, 94 F. 251, 36 C.C.A. 222. In Cowan v. Union Trust Co. of San Francisco, 38 Cal.App. 203, 175 P. 799, the period was three years and four months.

When laches are pleaded and the delay is shown, the burden then falls on the cestui que trust to explain the delay.[44] This he may do by showing that he had no knowledge of the existence of any cause of action until very shortly before the commencement of his suit.[45] If he did not know that he had been wronged, naturally he is charged with no negligence in failing to seek a remedy. "It has been said that the laches which will deprive a party of claiming equitable relief is the 'intentional failure to resist the assertion of an adverse right' and that consequently there cannot be acquiescence, 'without knowledge on the part of the person of the infringement of his legal rights.'"[46]

Excuses for Delay

But mere proof of ignorance is not enough to excuse delay. The ignorance must have been reasonable—must have existed despite the exercise of due care to learn the facts and to protect the cestui's rights.[47] A cestui que trust cannot sit idly by and close his eyes to what is going on around him. "One who would repel the imputation of laches on the score of ignorance of his rights must be without fault in remaining so long in ignorance of those rights. Indolent ignorance and indifference will no more avail than will voluntary ignorance of one's rights."[48] As a Penn-

---

[44] Robb v. Day, C.C.A.Mich., 90 F. 337, 33 C.C.A. 84; Alexander v. Fidelity Trust Co., D.C.Pa., 215 F. 791; Ewald v. Kierulff, 175 Cal. 363, 165 P. 942; Martin v. Martin, Del.Ch., 74 A. 864; Blaul v. Dalton, 264 Ill. 193, 106 N.E. 196; Sackman v. Campbell, 15 Wash. 57, 45 P. 895; Richardson v. McConaughey, 55 W.Va. 546, 47 S.E. 287.

[45] Stanwood v. Wishard, C.C.Iowa, 134 F. 959; Bay State Gas Co. of Delaware v. Rogers, C.C.Mass., 147 F. 557; Huntington Nat. Bank v. Huntington Distilling Co., C.C.W.Va., 152 F. 240; Russel v. Huntington Nat. Bank, C.C.A., 162 F. 868, 89 C. C.A. 558; Haney v. Legg, 129 Ala. 619, 30 So. 34, 87 Am.St.Rep. 81; Mullen v. Walton, 142 Ala. 166, 39 So. 97; Cliff v. Cliff, 23 Colo.App. 183, 128 P. 860; Anderson v. Northrop, 30 Fla. 612, 12 So. 318; Manning v. Manning, 135 Ga. 597, 69 S.E. 1126;

Southern Bank of Fulton v. Nichols, 235 Mo. 401, 138 S.W. 881; Delmoe v. Long, 35 Mont. 139, 88 P. 778; In re Roney's Estate, 227 Pa. 127, 75 A. 1061; Weltner v. Thurmond, 17 Wyo. 268, 98 P. 590, 129 Am.St.Rep. 1113. The record of a will in a foreign state is not such notice as to create laches. Mullen v. Walton, 142 Ala. 166, 39 So. 97.

[46] Mullen v. Walton, 142 Ala. 166, 172, 39 So. 97.

[47] Swift v. Smith, C.C.A.Colo., 79 F. 709, 25 C.C.A. 154; McMonagle v. McGlinn, C.C.Cal., 85 F. 88; Jewell v. Trilby Mines Co., C.C.A.Colo., 229 F. 98, 143 C.C.A. 374; Weber v. Chicago & W. I. R. Co., 246 Ill. 464, 92 N.E. 931; Taylor v. Coggins, 244 Pa. 228, 90 A. 633; Redford v. Clarke, 100 Va. 115, 40 S.E. 630.

[48] Redford v. Clarke, 100 Va. 115, 122, 123, 40 S.E. 630.

sylvania court has said:[49] "Laches is not excused by simply saying: 'I did not know.' If by diligence a fact can be ascertained, the want of knowledge so caused is no excuse for a stale claim. The test is, not what the plaintiff knows, 'but what he might have known, by the use of the means of information within his reach, with the vigilance the law requires of him.'"

If the cestui que trust has, throughout the period of alleged laches, continuously asserted his rights as a beneficiary,[50] as, for example, by maintaining exclusive possession of the trust res,[51] he will, of course, be guilty of no laches. And joint possession by the beneficiary and trustee rebuts the idea of laches,[52] since it shows a recognition of the interest of the beneficiary. Payment of taxes by the beneficiary shows an assertion of his right and militates against laches.[53] That the land which is the subject of contention has been unoccupied during the period of laches is no excuse for inaction on the part of the cestui.[54]

Strong evidence in contradiction of the allegation of laches is found in the continuous acknowledgment and fulfillment of the trust by the trustee during the period of alleged laches. If the trustee admits the trust and performs it, either there is no breach or other wrong, or it is so concealed from the beneficiary that he may reasonably remain ignorant of it.[55] Other facts excus-

[49] Taylor v. Coggins, 244 Pa. 228, 231, 90 A. 633.

[50] Grayson v. Bowlin, 70 Ark. 145, 66 S.W. 658; Howe v. Howe, 199 Mass. 598, 85 N.E. 945, 127 Am.St. Rep. 516.

[51] Dufour v. Weissberger, 172 Cal. 223, 155 P. 984; Boyd v. Boyd, 163 Ill. 611, 45 N.E. 118; Dorman v. Dorman, 187 Ill. 154, 58 N.E. 235, 79 Am. St.Rep. 210; Flaherty v. Cramer, 62 N.J.Eq. 758, 48 A. 565; Houston, E. & W. T. R. Co. v. Charwaine, 30 Tex.Civ. App. 633, 71 S.W. 401.

[52] Wright v. Wright, 242 Ill. 71, 89 N.E. 789, 26 L.R.A.,N.S., 161; Doyle v. Doyle, 268 Ill. 96, 108 N.E. 796; Cox v. Brown, 87 N.J.Eq. 462, 101 A. 260.

[53] Johnson v. Bayley, 15 Vt. 595.

[54] Lloyd v. Kirkwood, 112 Ill. 329.

[55] Sternfels v. Watson, C.C.Or., 139 F. 505; Small v. Hockinsmith, 158 Ala. 234, 48 So. 541; Woodruff v. Jabine, Ark., 15 S.W. 830; Kleinclaus v. Dutard, 147 Cal. 245, 81 P. 516; Cooney v. Glynn, 157 Cal. 583, 108 P. 506; Fleming v. Shay, 19 Cal.App. 276, 125 P. 761; Marshall v. Marshall, 11 Colo.App. 505, 53 P. 617; Madison v. Madison, 206 Ill. 534, 69 N.E. 625; Snyder v. Snyder, 280 Ill. 467, 117 N.E. 465; Jones v. Henderson, 149 Ind. 458, 49 N.E. 443; Johnson v. Foust, 158 Iowa 195, 139 N.W. 451; Reihl v. Likowski, 33 Kan. 515, 6 P. 886; Chadwick v. Chadwick, 59 Mich. 87, 26 N.W. 288; Lamberton v. Youmans, 84 Minn. 109, 86 N. W. 894; Murry v. King, 153 Mo.App. 710, 135 S.W. 107; Gutch v. Fosdick, 48 N.J.Eq. 353, 22 A. 590, 27 Am.St.Rep. 473; Carter v. Uhlein, N.J.Ch., 36 A. 956; Jones v. Haines, 79 N.J.Eq. 110, 80 A. 943; Laughlin v. Laughlin, 219 Pa. 629, 69 A.

ing delay and rebutting the imputation of laches are family relationship between the alleged cestui and trustee, making a settlement of differences out of court more natural;[56] a proven desire on the part of the beneficiary to avoid litigation;[57] and infancy of the beneficiary during the period of inaction.[58] The poverty of the beneficiary during the delay will not excuse him, for the courts consider it possible for him to seek relief, even though he can advance no money to counsel.[59] That the beneficiary sought other and fruitless remedies does not excuse him from delay in seeking the correct remedy or rebut the inference of laches.[60]

If material witnesses have died during the delay of the beneficiary,[61] and especially if the person who the cestui claims was a trustee has died[62] or become insane,[63] the courts will be apt to regard the inaction as amounting to laches. So, too, the loss of documentary evidence during the period when the beneficiary

288; Cetenich v. Fuvich, 41 R.I. 107, 102 A. 817; Miller v. Saxton, 75 S. C. 237, 55 S.E. 310; Goode v. Lowery, 70 Tex. 150, 8 S.W. 73; Nuckols v. Stanger, Tex.Civ.App., 153 S.W. 931; Hammond v. Ridley's Ex'rs, 116 Va. 393, 82 S.E. 102; Gentry v. Poteet, 59 W.Va. 408, 53 S.E. 787; Campbell v. O'Neill, 69 W.Va. 459, 72 S.E. 732.

[56] Delkin v. McDuffie, 134 Ga. 517, 68 S.E. 93; Madison v. Madison, 206 Ill. 534, 69 N.E. 625; Wright v. Wright, 242 Ill. 71, 89 N.E. 789, 26 L.R.A.,N.S., 161; Snyder v. Snyder, 280 Ill. 467, 117 N.E. 465; Cetenich v. Fuvich, 41 R.I. 107, 102 A. 817.

[57] Pearson v. Treadwell, 179 Mass. 462, 61 N.E. 44.

[58] Patrick v. Stark, 62 W.Va. 602, 59 S.E. 606.

[59] Naddo v. Bardon, C.C.A.Minn., 51 F. 493, 2 C.C.A. 335.

[60] Carpenter v. M. J. & M. & M., Consolidated, C.C.A.Cal., 212 F. 868, 129 C.C.A. 388; Hotchkin v. McNaught-Collins Improvement Co., 102 Wash. 161, 172 P. 864.

[61] C. H. Venner Co. v. Central Trust Co. of New York, C.C.A.N.Y., 204 F. 779, 123 C.C.A. 591; Elliott v. Clark, 5 Cal.App. 8, 89 P. 455; Smick's Adm'r v. Beswick's Adm'r, 113 Ky. 439, 68 S.W. 439; Streitz v. Hartman, 35 Neb. 406, 53 N.W. 215; Heinisch v. Pennington, 73 N.J. Eq. 456, 68 A. 233; Backes v. Crane, 87 N.J.Eq. 229, 100 A. 900; Coxe v. Carson, 169 N.C. 132, 85 S.E. 224; Newman v. Newman, 60 W.Va. 371, 55 S.E. 377, 7 L.R.A.,N.S., 370.

[62] Hume v. Beale, 17 Wall. 336, 21 L.Ed. 602; Hughes v. Letcher, 168 Ala. 314, 52 So. 914; Veitch v. Woodward Iron Co., 200 Ala. 358, 76 So. 124; Reese v. Bruce, 136 Ark. 378, 206 S.W. 658; Van Hook v. Frey, 13 App.D.C. 543; Benson v. Dempster, 183 Ill. 297, 55 N.E. 651; Smith's Guardian v. Holtheide, 74 S.W. 718, 25 Ky.Law Rep. 125; Gaither v. Gaither, 3 Md.Ch. 158; Love v. Rogers, 118 Md. 525, 85 A. 771; Reid v. Savage, 59 Or. 301, 117 P. 306; Groome v. Belt, 171 Pa. 74, 32 A. 1132; Pilcher v. Lotzgesell, 57 Wash. 471, 107 P. 340; Smith v. Turley, 32 W.Va. 14, 9 S.E. 46; Russell v. Fish, 149 Wis. 122, 135 N.W. 531.

[63] Whitney v. Fox, 166 U.S. 637, 17 S.Ct. 713, 41 L.Ed. 1145.

was idle will operate against him;[64] and if the property in question has greatly increased in value,[65] or the rights of third parties have in the meantime attached,[66] or if the beneficiary has recognized the legal title holder as the beneficial owner,[67] there will be a strong tendency to treat the delay of the beneficiary as laches which bar his remedy. In all these cases there is a basis for estoppel which, it is believed, is at the foundation of all laches.

THE STATUTE OF LIMITATIONS [68]

162. Where there are no statutes of limitations expressly applying to equitable causes of action, equity follows the law and by analogy applies the legal statutes of limitation to equitable rights.

The remedies of the beneficiary of an express trust against the trustee may be barred by a statute of limitation, but the statute does not run against the beneficiary until he has notice of a breach of the trust, a repudiation of it by the trustee, or its termination.

Causes of action in favor of the trustee or beneficiary and against third persons are subject to the normal operation of the statute of limitations.

By the weight of authority a resulting trustee is deemed to hold in subordination to his beneficiary and not adversely, unless he has repudiated the trust. The statute of limitations, therefore, does not affect the beneficiary's remedy until notice of the trustee's repudiation reaches the beneficiary.

One who may be held as a constructive trustee holds wrongfully and adversely, and the statute of limitations operates to bar the remedy of the possible constructive cestui que trust from the date of his knowledge of the facts upon which the constructive trust might be based.

Having observed that by rule of chancery in certain cases lapse of time and inaction will bar the remedy of the beneficiary, it remains to inquire how statutory bars to the maintenance of

[64] Amory v. Trustees of Amherst College, 229 Mass. 374, 118 N.E. 933.

[65] Alaska Northern R. Co. v. Alaska Cent. Ry. Co., 5 Alaska 377; Russell v. Miller, 26 Mich. 1; Delmoe v. Long, 35 Mont. 139, 88 P. 778; Graham v. Donaldson, 5 Watts, Pa., 451.

[66] Lady Ensley Coal, Iron & R. Co. v. Gordon, 155 Ala. 528, 46 So. 983; Butt v. McAlpine, 167 Ala. 521, 52 So. 420.

[67] Higginbotham v. Boggs, C.C.A. Va., 234 F. 253, 148 C.C.A. 155; Havenor v. Pipher, 109 Wis. 108, 85 N.W. 203.

[68] Restatement, Trusts, § 327.

actions have affected trusts. Legislatures have established periods after the expiration of which actions may not be maintained. Do these statutes expressly or impliedly affect the remedies of the beneficiary or trustee?

Express Trusts

The expression, "the statute of limitations has no application to express trusts," is frequently found in opinions.[69] From this one might at first thought be led to believe that no statute of limitations would ever bar the remedy of a cestui que trust or trustee of an express trust; that after a breach of the trust by a trustee the beneficiary might sue at any time and would never be met by a statutory bar. But the users of this expression have not intended to convey any such comprehensive meaning. They have merely meant that, so long as the express trust continued to be recognized and enforced by the trustee, there was no running of the statute of limitations. For example, that a trust had been in existence for forty years, during all of which time the trustee had possessed the trust property, collected the income, and turned it over to the beneficiary, would be no reason for barring the rights of the beneficiary to the trust property. If one had had the adverse possession of property for forty years, he would, of course, be entitled to hold it as against all the world; but the trustee in the case put did not have adverse possession of the trust property, but had possession in subordination to the rights of the beneficiary. Hence the statement that the statute of limitations has no application to express trusts merely means that so long as the trust is continuing and enforced there is no cause of action in favor of the beneficiary and against the trustee, and the possession of the trustee is not adverse.

When the trustee denies the trust, repudiates his obligations under it, claims the trust property as his own, then of course a cause of action arises in favor of the beneficiary, and then the statute of limitations starts to run. It is well settled that in express trusts, and as between beneficiary and trustee, the statute of limitations runs from the date when the beneficiary has actual or constructive notice of a repudiation of the trust by the

---

[69] McDonald v. Sims, 3 Ga. 383; Whetsler v. Sprague, 224 Ill. 461, 79 N.E. 667; Decouche v. Savetier, 3 Johns.Ch., N.Y., 190, 8 Am.Dec. 478 (semble); Neilly v. Neilly, 23 Hun, N.Y., 651; In re Passmore's Estate, 194 Pa. 632, 45 A. 417; Horine v. Mengel, 30 Pa.Super. 67; Pinson v. Ivey, 1 Yerg., Tenn., 296; Charter Oak Life Ins. Co. v. Gisborne, 5 Utah 319, 15 P. 253; Redwood v. Riddick, 4 Munf., Va., 222.

trustee.[70] "As between the trustee and beneficiary, in the case of an express or direct trust, the statute of limitations has no application, unless the trustee has repudiated the trust and claims the trust estate adversely, and such repudiation and adverse claim have been brought to the knowledge of the cestui que trust, after the latter is sui juris, and the connection is so wholly at an end as to indicate that the cestui que trust is no longer controlled by the influence proceeding from the trustee, which existed during the continuance of the trust." [71] "It is well settled that, as between trustee and cestui que trust, the statute of limitations does not operate, in cases of express or direct trusts, so long as such trusts continue. But when the trustee denies the trust and assumes ownership of the trust property, or denies his liability or obligation under the trust relation, in such a manner that the cestui que trust has actual, or even constructive, notice of the repudiation of the trust, then the statute of limitations attaches, and begins to run from that time, for such denial or adverse claim is an abandonment of the fiduciary character in which the trustee has stood to the prop-

---

[70] Cholmondeley v. Clinton, 2 Meriv. 171, 360; Oliver v. Piatt, 3 How. 333, 11 L.Ed. 622; Seymour v. Freer, 75 U.S. 202, 8 Wall. 202, 19 L.Ed. 306; De Bardelaben v. Stoudenmire, 82 Ala. 574, 2 So. 488; Alaska Northern R. Co. v. Alaska Cent. R. Co., 5 Alaska 304; Williams v. Young, 71 Ark. 164, 71 S.W. 669; Lamb v. Lamb, 171 Cal. 577, 153 P. 913; Warren v. Adams, 19 Colo. 515, 36 P. 604; Keaton v. Greenwood, 8 Ga. 97; Olympia Min. & Mill. Co. v. Kerns, 24 Idaho 481, 135 P. 255; Albretch v. Wolf, 58 Ill. 186; Parks v. Satterthwaite, 132 Ind. 411, 32 N.E. 82; Cooley v. Gilliam, 80 Kan. 278, 102 P. 1091; Bates v. Bates, 182 Ky. 566, 206 S.W. 800; Owens v. Crow, 62 Md. 491; Second Religious Soc. of Boxford v. Harriman, 125 Mass. 321; Pitcher v. Roger's Estate, 199 Mich. 114, 165 N.W. 813; Johnston v. Johnston, 107 Minn. 109, 119 N.W. 652; Moulden v. Train, 199 Mo. App. 509, 204 S.W. 65; Holmes v. Doll, 101 Neb. 156, 162 N.W. 487; Smith v. Combs, 49 N.J.Eq. 420, 24 A. 9; Woolley v. Stewart, 169 App.Div. 678, 155 N.Y.S. 169; Rouse v. Rouse, 176 N.C. 171, 96 S.E. 986; Paschall v. Hinderer, 28 Ohio St. 568; Manaudas v. Mann, 22 Or. 525, 30 P. 422; Davidson v. Davidson, 262 Pa. 520, 106 A. 64; McDonald v. May's Ex'rs, 1 Rich. Eq., S.C., 91; Armstrong's Heirs v. Campbell, 3 Yerg., Tenn., 201, 24 Am. Dec. 556; Hunter v. Hubbard, 26 Tex. 537; Thomas v. Glendinning, 13 Utah 47, 44 P. 652; Drake v. Wild, 65 Vt. 611, 27 A. 427; Garvey v. Garvey, 52 Wash. 516, 101 P. 45; Key v. Hughes' Ex'rs, 32 W.Va. 184, 9 S. E. 77; In re McClear's Estate, 147 Wis. 60, 132 N.W. 539; Weltner v. Thurmond, 17 Wyo. 268, 98 P. 590, 99 P. 1128, 129 Am.St.Rep. 1113. But an action by the heir of the settlor to set aside the trust instrument is judged by the date of the trust instrument. Mackenzie v. Los Angeles Trust & Savings Bank, 39 Cal.App. 247, 178 P. 557.

[71] Drake v. Wild, 65 Vt. 611, 614, 27 A. 427.

erty." [72] Thus, where one transfers stock to a friend to vote and collect the dividends, and the transferee admits the trust when called upon for the dividends, but fails to deliver the dividends, the statute of limitations has not run against the rights of the cestui que trust because he has not demanded an accounting for eight years. The holding of the stock was not adverse, but was as trustee at all times.[73]

Trustee's Normal Possession Not Adverse

During the continuance and recognition of the trust the possession of the trustee is the possession of the cestui que trust. There is no adverse or hostile holding.[74] "But in express or direct trusts, created by the contract of the parties, the statute of limitations does not operate. In such cases the trustee takes possession and holds for another. His possession is the possession of that other, and there can be no adverse holding, until the trustee denude himself of his trust, by assuming to hold for himself, and notifies the cestui que trust of his treachery." [75] "In the nature of things, however, the statute must act upon express technical trusts less frequently than upon any other class, since it is only through the *breach* of such a trust that it is set in motion. The statute never runs except against a *cause of action,* and a cause of action implies, not only the existence of a right, but such a denial of it, either actual or constructive, as puts the party entitled under a necessity to *act* if he would preserve it. An open, subsisting, and acknowledged *trust* is not within the operation of the statute, for, as said by Lord Redesdale, in the old case of Hovenden v. Annesley, 2 Sch. & Lef. 607: 'If a trustee is in possession, and does not execute his trust, the possession of the trustee is the possession of the cestui que trust; and if the only circumstance is that he does not perform his trust, his possession operates nothing as a bar, because his possession is according to his title.' " [76] In numerous cases where the disavowal of the trust was brought to the notice of the cestui que trust, he has been held barred by the statute.[77]

[72] Thomas v. Glendinning, 13 Utah 47, 56, 44 P. 652.

[73] Hovey v. Bradbury, 112 Cal. 620, 44 P. 1077.

[74] Anderson v. Dunn, 19 Ark. 650; Huntley v. Huntley, 43 N.C. 250; Howard's Adm'rs v. Aiken, 3 McCord, S.C., 467; Marr's Heirs v. Gilliam, 1 Cold., Tenn., 488

[75] Haynie v. Hall's Ex'r, 5 Humph. Tenn., 290, 292, 42 Am.Dec. 427.

[76] Cooper v. Cooper, 61 Miss. 676, 696.

[77] Goodno v. Hotchkiss, D.C., Conn., 237 F. 686; McGuire v. Inhabitants of Linneus, 74 Me. 344; Stanton v. Helm, 87 Miss. 287, 39 So. 457; Mantle v. Speculator Min. Co., 27 Mont.

But where a trustee mixed trust funds with his own and lent the mixed funds, but this wrong was not brought to the attention of the beneficiary, it has been held that the lack of notice prevented the running of the statute.[78]

Whether a given act is consistent with the continuance of the trust, or indicates an intent to repudiate the trust and claim adversely, is a question of fact for the determination of the court in each individual case. A conveyance by the trustee in violation of the trust is clearly a repudiation of it.[79] The mere payment of taxes by the trustee out of his own funds does not necessarily show a claim to the property as private property.[80] Where the cestui que trust remains in possession of the trust property, acts of the trustee are not ordinarily construed as a repudiation of the trust, since he has so far recognized the trust as to allow the beneficial owner possession.[81]

Termination of Trust

Not only repudiation of the trust, but also the termination of the trust, may start the statute of limitations running against the claims of the cestui que trust. Thus, if the trustee effects a settlement and is discharged as trustee, his possession of the trust property, if he retains any, will be adverse to the cestui que trust, and the statute of limitations will run against the right of the cestui to reclaim the property, or to allege fraud or impropriety in the account.[82] In the words of Finch, J.: "In the case of a direct trust the statute will begin to run when it ends, and the trustee has no longer a right to hold the fund or property as such, but is bound to pay it over or transfer it dis-

---

473, 71 P. 665; Congregational Society and Church in Newington v. Town of Newington, 53 N.H. 595; Boydstun v. Jacobs, 38 Nev. 175, 147 P. 447; Williams v. First Presbyterian Soc. in Cincinnati, 1 Ohio St. 478; Baillie v. Columbia Gold Min. Co., 86 Or. 1, 166 P. 965, 167 P. 1167; Hayes v. Walker, 70 S.C. 41, 48 S.E. 989; Moffatt v. Buchanan, 11 Humph., Tenn., 369, 54 Am.Dec. 41; Robertson v. Wood, 15 Tex. 1, 65 Am.Dec. 140; Felkner v. Dooly, 27 Utah 350, 75 P. 854; Felkner v. Dooly, 28 Utah 236, 78 P. 365.

[78] Watson v. Dodson, Tex.Civ.App. 143 S.W. 329.

[79] Adams v. Holden, 111 Iowa 54, 82 N.W. 468.

[80] Warren v. Adams, 19 Colo. 515, 36 P. 604.

[81] American Mining Co. v. Trask, 28 Idaho 642, 156 P. 1136; Clark v. Clark, 21 Neb. 402, 32 N.W. 157.

[82] Clarke v. Boorman, 18 Wall. 493, 21 L.Ed. 904; Wellborn v. Rogers, 24 Ga. 558; Spallholz v. Sheldon, 216 N.Y. 205, 110 N.E. 431, Ann.Cas.1917C, 1017; Starke v. Starke, 3 Rich., S.C., 438; Sollee v. Croft, 7 Rich.Eq., S.C., 34; Coleman v. Davis, 2 Strob.Eq., S.C., 334; Van Winkle v. Blackford, 33 W.Va. 573, 11 S.E. 26.

charged of the trust."[83] When the relation of trustee and beneficiary changes to that of debtor and creditor, obviously the statute of limitations applicable to contract claims will control.[84] Where the death of the beneficiary causes the end of the trust, the holding by the trustee will be adverse after such death, and the statute will operate against the persons equitably entitled to the property on the death.[85] But it has been held that the mere ending of the trust, with no account rendered, or settlement had or demanded, does not cause the statute to run, simply because the cestui leaves the trust property with the trustee.[86]

The statute of limitations does not begin to run against a remainderman beneficiary until the expiration of the precedent estate.[87] Until his right to the benefits or use of the property accrues, the possession of the trustee or another will not be adverse to the remainderman beneficiary, but will be adverse only to the owners of the preceding interest.

What Statutes Control Equity

The original statute of limitations,[88] which, as amended from time to time, forms the basis for modern American legislation, was directed to bar legal causes of action only. It did not expressly mention equitable rights. But courts of equity, in adjudicating with respect to legal rights, are bound by the legal statutes of limitations, and in dealing with equitable rights they have followed the law, and applied the legal statutes of limitations to equitable causes of action.[89] "But it is said that courts of equity are not within the statutes of limitations. This is true in one respect: They are not within the words of the statutes, because the words apply to particular legal remedies; but they are within the spirit and meaning of the statutes, and have been always so considered. * * * I think, therefore, courts of equity are bound to yield obedience to the statute of limitations upon all legal titles and legal demands, and cannot act contrary

---

[83] Gilmore v. Ham, 142 N.Y. 1, 10, 36 N.E. 826, 40 Am.St.Rep. 554.

[84] Treadwell v. Treadwell, 176 Mass. 554, 57 N.E. 1016, 51 L.R.A. 190.

[85] Snodgrass v. Snodgrass, 185 Ala. 155, 64 So. 594.

[86] Jones v. Home Sav. Bank, 118 Mich. 155, 76 N.W. 322, 74 Am.St. Rep. 377.

[87] Pritchard v. Williams, 175 N.C. 319, 95 S.E. 570; Stewart v. Conrad's Adm'r, 100 Va. 128, 40 S.E. 624.

[88] 21 James I, c. 16, 1623, as printed in 4 Chitty's Stats., 4th Ed., 85.

[89] Holloway v. Eagle, 135 Ark. 206, 205 S.W. 113; Appeal of Kutz, 40 Pa. 90; Redford v. Clarke, 100 Va. 115, 40 S.E. 630.

to the spirit of its provisions. I think the statute must be taken virtually to include courts of equity; for when the Legislature by statute limited the proceedings at law in certain cases, and provided no express limitations for proceedings in equity, it must be taken to have contemplated that equity followed the law, and therefore it must be taken to have virtually enacted in the same cases a limitation for courts of equity also." [90] "In respect of the statute of limitations, equity follows the law, and a demand that would be barred if asserted in a legal forum will be equally barred in equity." [91] In America frequently statutes have been enacted creating limitations peculiar to trusts, or to all equitable causes of action.[92]

Actions against Third Persons

An adverse claim to the trust property by a third person for the statutory period will bar both trustee and cestui que trust. Causes of action against third persons for the recovery of the trust res or for damages on account of its injury are subject to the ordinary statutes of limitation, and delay or negligence by the trustee in enforcing the causes of action will operate to bar the beneficiary's rights.[93] "The rule in this court, that the Stat-

---

[90] Hovenden v. Annesley, 2 Sch. & Lef. 607, 630, 631.

[91] Redford v. Clarke, 100 Va. 115, 121, 40 S.E. 630. See, also, Kent, Ch., in Kane v. Bloodgood, 7 Johns.Ch. 90, 113, 11 Am.Dec. 417.

[92] In Mississippi there is a ten-year statute applicable to trusts. Stanton v. Helm, 87 Miss. 287, 39 So. 457; Code 1930, § 2316. In New York rights of action under trusts are barred by a blanket section covering all cases not otherwise provided for and creating a ten-year limitation. Civil Practice Act § 53. The Pennsylvania statute reads: "No right of entry shall accrue, or actions be maintained for a specific performance of any contract for the sale of any real estate, or for damages for non-compliance with any such contract, or to enforce any equity of redemption, after re-entry made for any condition broken, or to enforce any implied or resulting trust as to realty, but within five years after such contract was made or such equity or trust accrued, with the right of entry; unless such contract shall give a longer time for its performance, or there has been in part, a substantial performance, or such contract, equity of redemption, or trust, shall have been acknowledged by writing to subsist, by the party to be charged therewith, within the same period; Provided, that as to any one affected with a trust, by reason of his fraud, the said limitation shall begin to run only from the discovery thereof, or when, by reasonable diligence, the party defrauded might have discovered the same. * * *" 12 P.S. § 83. See Carson v. Painter, 69 Pa.Super. 490.

[93] Cruse v. Kidd, 195 Ala. 22, 70 So. 166, 2 A.L.R. 36; Fleck v. Ellis, 144 Ga. 732, 87 S.E. 1055; Hart v. Citizens' Nat. Bank, 105 Kan. 434, 185 P. 1, 7 A.L.R. 933; Stoll v. Smith, 129 Md. 164, 98 A. 530. See §§ 159, 160, ante.

ute of Limitations does not bar a trust estate, holds only as between cestui que trust and trustee, not between cestui que trust and trustee on the one side and strangers on the other, for that would be to make the statute of no force at all, because there is hardly an estate of consequence without such trust, and so the act would never take place; therefore, where a cestui que trust and his trustee are both out of possession for the time limited, the party in possession has a good bar against them both." [94]

It is immaterial that the beneficiary has been an infant or otherwise under disability during part or all of the time when the statute has been running against the trustee.[95]

Where a third person joins with a trustee in committing a breach of trust, in collusion with the trustee, the beneficiary has a cause or action against the third person in his own right, and the trustee also has a cause of action against the third person. The former will be affected by disabilities of the cestui, like infancy; the latter will not.[96]

If the third person innocently joined with the trustee in committing a breach of trust, that is, his action was based on mistake, the cases have held that the only cause of action arising is in favor of the trustee, and is barred by the trustee's inaction, even though the cestui may have been incompetent.[97]

Resulting Trusts

Resulting trusts are based on an inferred or presumed intent that they shall exist. The most common example of them is found in the case of the payment of the consideration for a conveyance by one and the taking of the title in the name of another, with the consent of the payor of the consideration. The question has frequently arisen whether the statute of limitations begins to run against the rights of the beneficiary of a resulting trust from the date when the trustee obtained title, on the theory of an adverse holding from that date, or only from the date of a repudiation by the resulting trustee of the trust, on the theory

---

[94] Lord Hardwicke in Lewellin v. Mackworth, as quoted in 2 Eq. Cases Abr. 579.

[95] Crittenden v. Dorn, C.C.A.Cal., 274 F. 520, certiorari denied 257 U.S. 648, 42 S.Ct. 57, 66 L.Ed. 415; Molton v. Henderson, 62 Ala. 426; Wilmerding v. Russ, 33 Conn. 67.

[96] Elliott v. Landis Machine Co., 236 Mo. 546, 139 S.W. 356; In re Marshall's Estate, 138 Pa. 285, 22 A. 24.

[97] Chase v. Cartright, 53 Ark. 358, 14 S.W. 90, 22 Am.St.Rep. 207; Smilie v. Biffle, 2 Pa. 52, 44 Am.Dec. 156; Evans, the Colluding and the Mistaken Trustee, 17 Ky.L.J. 382.

§ 162 THE STATUTE OF LIMITATIONS 613

of a friendly holding until the appearance of the contrary. Many courts have taken a position that a resulting trustee is like an express trustee, that his normal position is that of a holder in subordination to the rights of the beneficiary, and that, from the date of the event which makes possible the trust until the contrary appears, he should be regarded as holding for the beneficiary and not adversely to him.[98] This would seem sound. "In such cases [those of resulting trusts] the title to the property is generally taken in the name of the trustee, with his knowledge and approval, and upon his recognition of the relation thereby created. It is hardly conceivable that a trustee should fail to recognize the trust at the time of the conveyance, unless he intends to deceive the beneficiary and acquire an absolute title by fraud. In that event, there would be a practical disavowal of the trust at the outset, and the statute would begin to run as in the case of a constructive trust. But so long as the trustee recognizes the trust, the beneficiary may rely upon the recognition, and ordinarily will not be in fault for omitting to bring an action to enforce his rights. The case then resembles an express trust of a continuing nature, and is subject to the statute of limitations in like manner. If the trustee is in possession by permission of the cestui que trust, the possession will be that of the latter." [99]

Other courts have seemed to take the position that the attitude of a resulting trustee is equivocal; that it may sometimes be in subordination to the rights of the cestui que trust, and sometimes adverse to such rights. Thus, according to these decisions, whether the statute of limitations started to run at the time of the conveyance to the resulting trustee can only be told by examining the attitude of the resulting trustee from the date of such conveyance. If he has throughout recognized the alleged cestui que trust as a beneficiary, then the statute will not have commenced to run; but if his position has been hostile to the cestui que trust, the statute will run from the date of the conveyance. In this class of cases fall a number of decisions to the effect that where the resulting trustee has recognized the trust,

---

[98] Lasker-Morris Bank & Trust Co. v. Gans, 132 Ark. 402, 200 S.W. 1029; Faylor v. Faylor, 136 Cal. 92, 68 P. 482; In re Mahin's Estate, 161 Iowa 459, 143 N.W. 420; Hanson v. Hanson, 78 Neb. 584, 111 N.W. 368; Crowley v. Crowley, 72 N.H. 241, 56 A. 190; White v. Sheldon, 4 Nev. 280; Levy v. Ryland, 32 Nev. 460, 109 P. 905.

[99] Crowley v. Crowley, 72 N.H. 241, 245–246, 56 A. 190. See, also, Lufkin v. Jakeman, 188 Mass. 528, 530, 531, 74 N.E. 933.

the statute does not run until repudiation;[1] and allowing the cestui que trust to have possession rebuts the notion of repudiation and shows a recognition of the trust by the trustee.[2] On the other hand, in other cases founded on this theory, where there was no recognition of the trust, the statute was held to have run from the date of acquisition of title by the resulting trustee.[3] "It is true that the statute of limitations runs against a resulting trust on the ground that the holding of the title in such case is adverse to the right of the true owner. * * * In the present case the existence of the trust has at all times been acknowledged. The trustee has at all times admitted the right of the cestui que trust. As the reason has failed, so the rule has failed. There has been no adverse holding."[4]

Constructive Trusts

The application of the statutes of limitation to constructive trusts ought not to be difficult. These trusts are involuntary, and are imposed upon the trustee because of wrong doing. They are founded upon the notion of wrongful or adverse possession. It would seem clear, therefore, that from the instant when the constructive trustee obtains the property the statute should run. From the date when the wrongful act is committed there is a cause of action, a right to have a constructive trust declared. From that date, therefore, the statute of limitations should operate. In accordance with this theory a great majority of the American courts have held that the statute runs against a constructive trust from the time when the existence of the facts on which the trust is based became known to the beneficiary.[5]

---

[1] Appeal of Corr, 62 Conn. 403, 26 A. 478; Miller v. Saxton, 75 S.C. 237, 55 S.E. 310; Cole v. Noble, 63 Tex. 432.

[2] McNamara v. Garrity, 106 Ill. 384; Doyle v. Doyle, 268 Ill. 96, 108 N.E. 796 (semble); Norton v. McDevit, 122 N.C. 755, 30 S.E. 24; Snider v. Johnson, 25 Or. 328, 35 P. 846 (semble); Clark v. Trindle, 52 Pa. 492; Williard v. Williard, 56 Pa. 119; Henderson v. Maclay, Pa., 6 A. 52; Miller v. Baker, 160 Pa. 172, 28 A. 648.

[3] Currier v. Studley, 159 Mass. 17, 33 N.E. 709; Best v. Campbell, 62 Pa. 476; McNinch v. Trego, 73 Pa. 52.

[4] Appeal of Corr, 62 Conn. 403, 408, 26 A. 478.

[5] Lide v. Park, 135 Ala. 131, 33 So. 175, 93 Am.St.Rep. 17; Holloway v. Eagle, 135 Ark. 206, 205 S.W. 113; Benoist v. Benoist, 178 Cal. 234, 172 P. 1109; Cliff v. Cliff, 23 Colo.App. 183, 128 P. 860; Harrison v. Adcock, 8 Ga. 68; Terry v. Davenport, 185 Ind. 561, 112 N.E. 998; Burch v. Nicholson, 157 Iowa 502, 137 N.W. 1066; Washbon v. Linscott State Bank, 87 Kan. 698, 125 P. 17; Blakley v. Hanberry, 137 Ky. 283, 125 S.W. 703; Brawner v. Staup, 21 Md. 328; Cooper v. Cooper, 61 Miss. 676; Hudson v. Cahoon, 193 Mo. 547, 91 S.W.

Thus, where a trustee has wrongfully conveyed trust property to a third person, and the latter is sought to be held as a constructive trustee, the date of the conveyance will govern; [6] where a trustee purchased the trust res at his own sale, the right to have a constructive trust declared arose at once, and was barred in ten years from the date of the purchase; [7] and where one standing in a fiduciary relation, as that of principal and agent, bought his principal's property, the statute ran against the right to have a constructive trust declared from the date of the purchase.[8] Constructive notice, or notice of facts which should have led to the discovery of the fraud, is sufficient to start the statute running.[9] If the person obtaining the property by fraud conceals his fraud, [10] or for any other reason, not involving negligence of the claimant, the one claiming as beneficiary of a constructive trust is ignorant of the fraud, the statute of limitations does not operate.[11]

The correct rule regarding constructive trusts and the statute of limitations is well stated in an early Wisconsin case, [12] as follows: "It follows that the cause of action set forth was barred in the lifetime of William Howell unless, as counsel supposed, it was necessary that there should have been a denial of the trust before the statute would begin to run. But that doctrine is applicable only to express or *acknowledged* trusts, where the trustee has afterwards repudiated the rights of the cestui que trust, and set up a claim to the trust property in his own right, and not to those implied or equitable trusts which spring from the originally wrongful and fraudulent acts of the party to be

---

72; Markley v. Camden Safe Deposit & Trust Co., 74 N.J.Eq. 279, 69 A. 1100; Lammer v. Stoddard, 103 N.Y. 672, 9 N.E. 328; Dunn v. Dunn, 137 N.C. 533, 50 S.E. 212; In re Marshall's Estate, 138 Pa. 285, 22 A. 24; In re Post, 13 R.I. 495; Beard v. Stanton, 15 S.C. 164; Haynie v. Hall's Ex'r, 5 Humph., Tenn., 290, 42 Am.Dec. 427; Kennedy v. Baker, 59 Tex. 150; Sheppard v. Turpin, 3 Grat., Va., 373; Beecher v. Foster, 51 W.Va. 605, 42 S.E. 647; Buttles v. De Baun, 116 Wis. 323, 93 N.W. 5.

[6] Smith v. Dallas Compress Co., 195 Ala. 534, 70 So. 662.

[7] Hubbell v. Medbury, 53 N.Y. 98.

[8] McKean & Elk Land & Imp. Co. v. Clay, 149 Pa. 277, 24 A. 211; Ackerson v. Elliott, 97 Wash. 31, 165 P. 899.

[9] Rider v. Maul, 70 Pa. 15; Frost v. Bush, 195 Pa. 544, 46 A. 80; Cooper v. Lee, 75 Tex. 114, 12 S.W. 483.

[10] Jacobs v. Snyder, 76 Iowa 522, 41 N.W. 207, 14 Am.St.Rep. 235; West v. Sloan, 56 N.C. 102.

[11] Prewitt v. Prewitt, 188 Mo. 675, 87 S.W. 1000; Freeland v. Williamson, 220 Mo. 217, 119 S.W. 560; Johnson v. Petersen, 100 Neb. 255, 159 N.W. 414; Wamburzee v. Kennedy, 4 Desaus, S.C., 474.

[12] Howell v. Howell, 15 Wis. 55, 58.

charged, and which were never recognized or admitted by him. It was of such express or acknowledged trusts that the court was speaking in the case referred to, and it would be as absurd to apply that doctrine to these implied trusts as it would be to apply the ten years' limitation to those where a denial of the trust has never taken place. It would be to abrogate the statute of limitations altogether in actions of this nature, or to say that it was not intended to apply to them; for as the party to be charged has no occasion to deny the trust until called upon to execute it, which is usually done by action, and as this might be delayed until after the expiration of the ten years, so it might be postponed for an indefinite period in the future. This was clearly not the intention. The trust in such cases originates in a fraud, which is in itself as complete and absolute a denial of the rights of the injured party as it is possible to have, and every day which passes without reparation of the injury is a continuation or repetition of it."

Minority View

In a few cases the courts seem to have overlooked the fact that constructive trusts are founded on adverse holding from the beginning. In these cases the courts hold that constructive trusts are on the same footing with regard to the statute of limitations as express trusts, [13] and consequently that the statute does not run until the constructive trustee has repudiated the trust.[14] This peculiar doctrine has been applied to a few cases of constructive trusts arising out of confidential relationships, [15] and to others where an attempt was made to follow trust property.[16] Of course, if there has been a disavowal by the constructive trustee, that is, an express statement that he declines to hold for the beneficiary, such evidence, while not necessary to cause the statute to run, will certainly not impede its operation.[17] The view that the statute operates alike on all trusts is thus expressed by an Illinois court: [18] "When the possession of

---

[13] Case v. Goodman, 250 Mo. 112, 156 S.W. 698; Canada v. Daniel, 175 Mo.App. 55, 157 S.W. 1032.

[14] Dennison v. Barney, 49 Colo. 442, 113 P. 519; Schlosser v. Schlosser, 62 Colo. 270, 162 P. 153.

[15] Newis v. Topfer, 121 Iowa 433, 96 N.W. 739; Home Inv. Co. v. Strange, Tex., 195 S.W. 849.

[16] Harvey v. Bank of Marrowbone, 178 Ky. 793, 200 S.W. 28; Goodman v. Smith, 94 Neb. 227, 142 N.W. 521.

[17] Young v. Walker, 224 Mass. 491, 113 N.E. 363.

[18] Reynolds v. Sumner, 126 Ill. 58, 71, 18 N.E. 334, 1 L.R.A. 327, 9 Am.St. Rep. 523.

the trust property is taken by the trustee, under the trust, it is the possession of the cestui que trust, whether the trust be express or implied, and cannot be adverse until the trust is openly disavowed or denied, and this fact is brought home to the knowledge of the cestui que trust." An illustration of the application of this rule is found in an Iowa case, [19] where a woman in feeble health conveyed realty to her stepfather upon an oral understanding that he would care for her children. The court raised a constructive trust upon the ground of the confidential relation, and held that, since the constructive trustee had never repudiated the trust, the statute of limitations had not operated to bar the rights of the cestuis que trust.

Constructive Trustee may Consent to Trust

Yet other courts have taken the position that the possession of the constructive trustee should be treated as adverse or not, dependent on whether the constructive trustee recognized the rights of the beneficiary. If the trustee, after committing the fraud which gave rise to the right to have the constructive trust declared, admitted the rights of the defrauded person and denied any intention of holding for his own benefit, these courts have held that the statute of limitations did not run, unless and until there was a change of attitude by the constructive trustee.[20] Thus, where a husband used his wife's money to buy land without her consent, and took the title in his name, but thereafter at all times recognized the wife's ownership of the land and made no claim to it for himself, an Alabama court has held that the possession of the husband was not adverse, though obtained fraudulently, and the statute had not begun to run against the wife's rights.[21]

In this class of cases fall those in which an agent takes title to property in his own name, but the principal remains in pos-

[19] Newis v. Topfer, 121 Iowa 433, 96 N.W. 739.

[20] Moore v. Worley, 24 Ind. 81; Milner v. Hyland, 77 Ind. 458; Johnson v. Foust, 158 Iowa 195, 139 N.W. 451; Hunnicut v. Oren, 84 Kan. 460, 114 P. 1059; Donahue v. Quackenbush, 62 Minn. 132, 64 N.W. 141; Donovan v. Driscoll, 93 Pa. 509; Preston v. Preston, 202 Pa. 515, 52 A. 192; Pearce v. Dyess, 45 Tex.Civ. App. 406, 101 S.W. 549. *Contra:* Parks v. Satterthwaite, 132 Ind. 411, 32 N.E. 82. In Nougues v. Newlands, 118 Cal. 102, 50 P. 386, it was held that the recognition of the constructive trust must be by writing, if the res is real property, in order that the recognition be effective to prevent the running of the statute.

[21] Haney v. Legg, 129 Ala. 619, 30 So. 34, 87 Am.St.Rep. 81. For a similar case, see Fawcett v. Fawcett, 85 Wis. 332, 55 N.W. 405, 39 Am.St.Rep. 844.

session. Here, though the agent be guilty of fraud which might be made the basis of a constructive trust, yet possession by the principal amounts to a recognition of the trust and prevents the statutory bar from being imposed.[22] "The rule, however, is different with respect to constructive or resulting trusts; the general rule in such cases being that the statute commences to run from the time the act occurs which creates the trust, or, in other words, when the cestui que trust could bring an action to enforce the trust, and that no repudiation of the trust by the trustee is necessary to start the running of the statute. But to that general rule there is a well defined and recognized exception, viz., when the cestui que trust is in possession, and the trustee has done nothing inconsistent with a recognition of the trust, or has not asserted an adverse claim." [23] The holdings of many courts amount substantially to a rule that the statute of limitations commences to run against a constructive trust from the date of knowledge by the beneficiary of the act which gives rise to the trust, unless there is a recognition of the trust by the constructive trustee.[24] The presumption is in favor of adverse holding. Holding in subordination to the cestui que trust is abnormal and exceptional.

It would seem that the possession of the constructive trustee should be regarded as adverse, unless he recognizes the trust in such a way as to change his status to that of an express trustee. So long as the person obtaining the property wrongfully has not made himself an express trustee, or been made a constructive trustee by act of equity, he holds the property adversely and for his own benefit, and the statute should operate in his favor.

[22] Ackley v. Croucher, 203 Ill. 530, 68 N.E. 86; Franks v. Morris, 9 W. Va. 664; Cook v. Elmore, 25 Wyo. 393, 171 P. 261.

[23] Cook v. Elmore, 25 Wyo. 393, 171 P. 261, 263.

[24] Martin v. Branch Bank of Decatur, 31 Ala. 115; Brackin v. Newman, 121 Ala. 311, 26 So. 3; Broder v. Conklin, 121 Cal. 282, 53 P. 699; Barker v. Hurley, 132 Cal. 21, 63 P. 1071, 64 P. 480; Earle v. Bryant, 12 Cal.App. 553, 107 P. 1018; Earhart v. Churchill Co., 169 Cal. 728, 147 P. 942; Wilmerding v. Russ, 33 Conn. 67; Gebhard v. Sattler, 40 Iowa 152; Otto v. Schlapkahl, 57 Iowa 226, 10 N.W. 651; Manion's Adm'r v. Titsworth, 18 B.Mon., Ky., 582; Commonwealth v. Clark, 119 Ky. 85, 83 S.W. 100, 9 L.R.A.,N.S., 750; Harlow v. Dehon, 111 Mass. 195; Prewett v. Buckingham, 28 Miss. 92; Mills v. Hendershot, 70 N.J.Eq. 258, 62 A. 542; Seitz v. Seitz, 59 App.Div. 150, 69 N.Y.S. 170; Stianson v. Stianson, 40 S.D. 322, 167 N.W. 237, 6 A.L.R. 280.

CHAPTER 19

ALTERATION OR TERMINATION OF THE TRUST

Sec.
163. Alteration of Trust by Trust Parties.
164. Alteration of Private Trusts by the Court.
165. Revocation of the Trust.
166. Natural Termination.
167. Purpose Accomplished or Becomes Impossible of Accomplishment.
168. Merger of Interests.
169. Termination at Request of Beneficiary.

ALTERATION OF TRUST BY TRUST PARTIES [1]

163. Except as the power to alter or modify the trust is expressly reserved to the settlor, or granted to others by the settlor, neither the trust parties nor others, nor any combination of trust parties, have power to change the terms of the trust.

Sometimes after a trust has been created the settlor or others desire to change the terms of the trust. There may be a wish to deprive some persons of their interests as beneficiaries, to add new cestuis, to alter the shares of the beneficiaries, to change methods of administration, to modify the investment provisions of the instrument, or to alter the methods of replacing trustees who die or resign. The settlor may expressly provide for changes in the trust, either in general or of specific types, and he may reserve to himself the power to make them, or he may grant such power to the trustee, or to one or more beneficiaries, or to an outsider.[2]

But if there is no clause in the trust instrument giving to someone the power of amendment of the trust, neither the trust parties, nor any combination of them, nor any other persons have power to alter the trust.[3] Application must be made to the court

---

[1] Restatement, Trusts, §§ 167, 331, 332.

[2] Riddle v. Cutter, 49 Iowa 547; Sieling v. Sieling, 151 Md. 536, 135 A. 376; Lippincott v. Williams, 63 N.J. Eq. 30, 51 A. 467; Yard v. Pittsburgh & L. E. R. Co., 13 Pa. 205, 18 A. 874.

[3] Master v. Second Parish of Portland, D.C.Me., 36 F.Supp. 918; Childs v. Gross, 41 Cal.App.2d 680, 107 P.2d 424; Farwell v. Illinois Merchants Trust Co., 264 Ill.App. 49; Bayless v. Wheller-Kelly-Hagny Trust Co., 153 Kan. 81, 109 P.2d 108; Krause v. Jeannette Inv. Co., 333 Mo. 509, 62 S.W.2d 890.

of equity, which will act in some circumstances, as stated in the following section.

The creation of a trust amounts to a conveyance of property interests to the beneficiaries. The grantor of them is not able to change his conveyance after it has operated, unless he so provided in the instrument of conveyance. The grantees of these interests, that is, the beneficiaries, ought not to be able to enlarge their gifts or the interests which they have bought. And surely strangers to the trust should have no such power as a matter of law or implication.

An example of a futile attempt by the trustee and a beneficiary to change a trust is found in a recent Wisconsin case. The will provided that the trustee should hold $50,000 in trust for a son of the settlor and spend $5,000 in buying a farm for the son. By agreement between the trustee and the son the trustee did not set up any trust or buy any farm, but paid the son 6% on $55,000. The court held that this was an ineffective arrangement, even when sanctioned by the county court, and that the trustee should carry out the trusts as set forth in the will.[4]

These rules apply to charitable trusts as well as private trusts. Thus, where land was given in trust for school purposes, the settlor could not later add to the trust the restriction that the school should admit white children only.[5] The settlor of a passive trust cannot change it to an active one.[6]

ALTERATION OF PRIVATE TRUSTS BY THE COURT [7]

164. **The court of equity possesses power to alter the administrative provisions of a private trust instrument where, due to circumstances not known to the settlor or anticipated by him, a change is necessary or highly convenient to insure the accomplishment of the settlor's purposes; but the court has no power to change the financial interests of the beneficiaries or to add new beneficiaries.**

The power of equity to alter charitable trusts has been discussed under the heading of cy pres.[8] The court possesses a somewhat similar power with relation to private trusts. Not infrequently the trustee is met with a situation which was either

---

[4] In re Stanley's Will, 223 Wis. 345, 269 N.W. 550.

[5] Price v. School Directors, 58 Ill. 452.

[6] Fish v. Prior, 16 R.I. 566, 18 A. 162.

[7] Restatement, Trusts, § 167.

[8] See § 86, ante.

§ 164   ALTERATION OF PRIVATE TRUSTS BY THE COURT   621

in existence at the time the trust was created but was unknown to the settlor, or arose after the creation of the trust and was not anticipated by the settlor. This situation may be one which renders the carrying out of the trust, in exact accordance with the terms of the trust as laid down in the trust instrument, either impossible or very difficult. Unless the trustee is authorized to deviate from the administrative provisions of the trust instrument, he will be unable to accomplish the settlor's objects. Here the court asserts its inherent jurisdiction to take such action as is necessary to secure the accomplishment of all lawful trust purposes, and assumes a power to direct the trustee to ignore some of the directions of the settlor as to methods of administration.[9] Thus, the settlor may have directed a sale of real estate, or the investment of the trust property in business, or may have prohibited leases by the trustee in excess of one year, or have prohibited a mortgage by the trustee of the trust real estate, and a change in circumstances may have arisen which seriously handicaps the trustee in his administration if these provisions of the instrument are followed. In such cases equity is ready to act and to direct a deviation from the settlor's directions to whatever extent necessary to secure the results the settlor desired.

However, the court has no power to make over the settlor's conveyances or to enlarge or diminish his gifts. It cannot change the subject matter of the trust, or alter the shares of the cestuis, or add new beneficiaries to the list.[10] To do so would be to remake the deed or will of the settlor and to assume the power of distributing his property without his consent.

Some real, unforeseen necessity must exist to move the court to alter the administrative provisions. It will not do so merely to facilitate the work of the trustee or to make his labors easier or to gratify a whim of the cestui.[11]

---

[9] Hale v. Hale, 146 Ill. 227, 33 N.E. 858, 20 L.R.A. 247; Price v. Long, 87 N.J.Eq. 578, 101 A. 195; Cutter v. American Trust Co., 213 N. C. 686, 197 S.E. 542; Penick v. Bank of Wadesboro, 218 N.C. 686, 12 S.E. 2d 253.

[10] Stewart v. Hamilton, 151 Tenn. 396, 270 S.W. 79, 39 A.L.R. 37; In re Stanley's Will, 223 Wis. 345, 269 N.W. 550.

[11] Johns v. Johns, 172 Ill. 472, 50 N.E. 337; Anglo California Nat. Bank of San Francisco v. Stafford, 25 Cal. App.2d 225, 77 P.2d 263; First M. E. Church of Ottumwa v. Hull, 225 Iowa 306, 280 N.W. 531. See Scott, Deviations from the Terms of Trust, 44 Harv.L.R. 1025.

REVOCATION OF THE TRUST [12]

165. Unless the settlor reserves to himself or grants to another the power of revocation of the trust, by an express term in the trust instrument, or if the trust was created without writing by express oral statement, the trust is irrevocable.

If a power of revocation was omitted by mistake, the trust instrument may be reformed so as to include it; but the omission of such a power in a voluntarily created trust is not evidence of a mistake.

If a power of revocation is reserved or granted, it must be exercised in accordance with the method prescribed in the instrument.

May the settlor destroy or revoke the trust after its complete creation? If the settlement is founded on consideration, obviously it is without the powers of the settlor to revoke the trust, unless he has bargained for such a right. And so, also, if the settlement of the trust was voluntary, there may be no revocation unless that right was reserved. Of course, frequently the right to revoke is expressly provided, and in such case there can be no dispute about the power of the settlor to destroy the trust.[13] The power to destroy the trust may likewise be given by the settlor, by a term in the trust instrument, to another than the grantor.[14]

But where such right of revocation is not retained by the settlor, and he effects a complete trust, he has lost all control over the property. There is no implied power of revocation.[15]

---

[12] Restatement, Trusts, §§ 330, 332.

[13] Kansas City Theological Seminary v. Kendrick, Mo.App., 203 S.W. 628; Van Cott v. Prentice, 104 N.Y. 45, 10 N.E. 257; Wood v. Paul, 250 Pa. 508, 95 A. 720. Where a settlor creates a trust for herself for life and after death for her children, with a provision that, if the settlor at any time convey the land by deed, the trustee should thereafter hold for such grantee, a power to revoke the trust is reserved, and the settlor is in the position of a fee-simple owner. Culpeper Nat. Bank v. Wrenn, 115 Va. 55, 78 S.E. 620. If the right to revoke is made dependent on the consent of the trustee, of course the settlor alone cannot destroy the trust. Downs v. Security Trust Co., 175 Ky. 789, 194 S.W. 1041.

When the settlor exercises a power to revoke, the trustee is allowed to keep possession of the trust property until he has accounted and been discharged. Neary v. City Bank Farmers Trust Co., 260 App.Div. 791, 24 N.Y.S.2d 264.

[14] Farlow v. Farlow, 83 Md. 118, 34 A. 837; Falk v. Turner, 101 Mass. 494; Richardson v. Stephenson, 193 Wis. 89, 213 N.W. 673, 52 A.L.R. 681.

[15] Gray v. Union Trust Co. of San Francisco, 171 Cal. 637, 154 P. 306; Lovett v. Farnham, 169 Mass. 1, 47 N.E. 246; Thorp v. Lund, 227 Mass.

The case of Viney v. Abbott[16] is a good illustration of this rule. There one William Viney had transferred personal property to a trustee, to be held for the support of Viney during his life, and after his death for the benefit of certain relatives. No power of revocation was expressed in the instrument. Only a week after the creation of this trust Viney married, and desired to destroy the trust and retake the property. The court said: "It is immaterial whether there was any other consideration than appears upon the face of the indenture; for, even if the settlement was purely voluntary, the case falls within the doctrine, now well established in equity, that a voluntary settlement, completely executed, without any circumstances tending to show mental incapacity, mistake, fraud, or undue influence, is binding and will be enforced against the settlor and his representatives, and cannot be revoked, except so far as a power of revocation has been reserved in the deed of settlement, and that the fact that by the terms of the deed the income of the property is to be applied by the trustee to the benefit of the settlor during his lifetime does not impair the validity or effect of the further trusts declared in the instrument."[17]

If the settlor directed that a power of revocation be inserted in his trust instrument, but it was omitted by mistake or fraud, he may have the instrument reformed so as to include the power.[18]

474, 116 N.E. 946, Ann.Cas.1918B, 1204 (semble); Stein v. Nat. Bank of Commerce, Mo.App., 181 S.W. 1072; New Jersey Title Guarantee & Trust Co. v. Parker, 84 N.J.Eq. 351, 93 A. 196; Hammerstein v. Equitable Trust Co. of New York, 156 App.Div. 644, 141 N.Y.S. 1065; Dorman v. Balestier, Sup., 175 N.Y.S. 677; Fishblate v. Fishblate, 238 Pa. 450, 86 A. 469; In re Greenfield's Estate, 14 Pa. 489; Reidy v. Small, 154 Pa. 505, 26 A. 602, 20 L.R.A. 362; Barber v. Thompson, 49 Vt. 213; Sargent v. Baldwin, 60 Vt. 17, 13 A. 854; Howard v. Howard, 60 Vt. 362, 14 A. 702.

In California in 1931 voluntary trusts were made revocable, unless the instrument expressly stipulated that they should be irrevocable. Civ. Code, § 2280. A North Carolina statute permits the revocation of a voluntary trust so far as the interests of unborn persons are concerned. N. C.Code 1939, § 996.

In Richards v. Wilson, 185 Ind. 335, 112 N.E. 780, it is held that, upon a subscription to a charitable trust fund without mention of revocation, there is an implied condition against revocation. Obviously a completed trust with no power of revocation reserved cannot be revoked by a will of the settlor. McElveen v. Adams, 108 S.C. 437, 94 S.E. 733.

[16] 109 Mass. 300.

[17] Gray, J., in Viney v. Abbott, 109 Mass. 300, 302, 303. For similar views see Appeal of Fellows, 93 Pa. 470; Kraft v. Neuffer, 202 Pa. 558, 52 A. 100.

[18] Garnsey v. Mundy, 24 N.J.Eq. 243; Bristor v. Tasker, 135 Pa. 110, 19 A. 851, 20 Am.St.Rep. 853.

The courts of Rhode Island have taken the position that in a voluntary trust the insertion of a power of revocation is so natural and reasonable that failure to reserve such power will be regarded as prima facie evidence of mistake,[19] but this doctrine has not received general acceptance.[20] In New York by statute, upon the written consent of all persons beneficially interested in a trust, the creator thereof may revoke it.[21] This statute has given rise to a great deal of litigation as to the meaning of "persons beneficially interested in the trust". It has been held in some cases that if the trust is for the settlor for his life, and then for his heirs or next of kin or his appointees by his will, during the life of the settlor he is the only person beneficially interested.[22] His prospective successors by intestacy or appointment are not beneficially interested under the trust. The entire beneficial interest in the property of the trust is in the settlor, and if the heirs, next of kin, or appointees ever take, it will be by a virtue of the operation of the laws of intestacy or a new act by the settlor. But other cases seem to treat the prospective successors of the settlor as presently beneficially interested.[23]

[19] Aylsworth v. Whitcomb, 12 R.I. 298.

And see Sharp v. Leach, 31 Beav. 491; In re Rick's Appeal, 105 Pa. 528.

[20] Du Pont v. Du Pont, 19 Del.Ch. 131, 164 A. 238; Patterson v. Johnson, 113 Ill. 559; Riddle v. Cutter, 49 Iowa 547; Rogers v. Rogers, 97 Md. 573, 55 A. 450; Sands v. Old Colony Trust Co., 195 Mass. 575, 81 N.E. 300, 12 Ann.Cas. 837.

[21] New York Personal Property Law, § 23. The wording of the statute is as follows: "Upon the written consent of all the persons beneficially interested in a trust in personal property or any part thereof heretofore or hereafter created, the creator of such trust may revoke the same as to the whole or such part thereof, and thereupon the estate of the trustee shall cease in the whole or such part thereof." In 1932 a similar section was added as to real property trusts. Real Property Law, § 118. For cases construing this statute, see Cazzain v. Title Guarantee & Trust Co., 175 App.Div. 369, 161 N.Y.S. 884, affirmed 220 N.Y. 683, 116 N.E. 1040; Sperry v. Farmers' Loan & Trust Co., 154 App.Div. 447, 139 N.Y.S. 192; Crackanthorpe v. Sickles, 156 App.Div. 753, 141 N.Y. S. 370; Whittemore v. Equitable Trust Co., 162 App.Div. 607, 147 N.Y. S. 1058; Goodwin v. Broadway Trust Co., 87 Misc. 130, 149 N.Y.S. 1033; Court v. Bankers' Trust Co., Sup., 160 N.Y.S. 477; Cruger v. Union Trust Co. of New York, 173 App.Div. 797, 160 N.Y.S. 480; Cram v. Walker, 173 App.Div. 804, 160 N.Y.S. 486; In re Berry, 178 App.Div. 144, 164 N.Y.S. 990; Williams v. Sage, 180 App.Div. 1, 167 N.Y.S. 179.

[22] Whittemore v. Equitable Trust Co., 162 App.Div. 607, 147 N.Y.S. 1058; Berlenbach v. Chemical Bank & Trust Co., 235 App.Div. 170, 256 N. Y.S. 563, affirmed 260 N.Y. 539, 184 N.E. 83.

[23] Whittemore v. Equitable Trust Co., 250 N.Y. 298, 165 N.E. 454; En-

§ 165

Neither the absence[24] nor the presence[25] of a power of revocation has any effect upon the validity of a trust. Either the absence or presence of such power is consistent with a completed trust. However, under the tax laws revocable trusts are exceedingly vulnerable. A clause permitting revocation by the settlor alone, or with another, makes the income of the trust taxable to the settlor, and makes the capital of the trust a part of the settlor's estate for estate tax purposes on his death.[26] On elementary principles, a voluntary agreement to convey upon trust may be abandoned without obligation.[27]

If a power of revocation is reserved or granted in the trust instrument, the holder of it must exercise it in the manner required by the instrument. Thus, if the instrument states that the trust can be revoked by the settlor by a written statement of that intent, addressed to the trustee, that method must be followed, and an oral effort to revoke will be without effect.[28]

The trustee is ordinarily a mere instrument for the execution of the trust, and has no control over its duration. In the absence of an express grant of that power to him in the trust instrument, therefore, the trustee has no power to end the trust or to call

gel v. Guaranty Trust Co. of New York, 280 N.Y. 43, 19 N.E.2d 673.

[24] Lawrence v. Lawrence, 181 Ill. 248, 54 N.E. 918; Riddle v. Cutter, 49 Iowa 547; Middleton v. Shelby County Trust Co., 51 S.W. 156, 21 Ky. Law Rep. 183; Carroll v. Smith, 99 Md. 653, 59 A. 131; Rogers v. Rogers, 97 Md. 573, 55 A. 450; Brown v. Mercantile Trust & Deposit Co., 87 Md. 377, 40 A. 256.

[25] Stone v. Hackett, 78 Mass. 227, 12 Gray 227; Seaman v. Harmon, 192 Mass. 5, 78 N.E. 301; Mize v. Bates County Nat. Bank, 60 Mo.App. 358; Schreyer v. Schreyer, 101 App. Div. 456, 91 N.Y.S. 1065; Locke v. Farmers' Loan & Trust Co., 140 N.Y. 135, 35 N.E. 578; Brown v. Spohr, 180 N.Y. 201, 73 N.E. 14; Witherington v. Herring, 140 N.C. 495, 53 S.E. 303, 6 Ann.Cas. 188; Springs v. Hopkins, 171 N.C. 486, 88 S.E. 774; First Wisconsin Trust Co. v. Wisconsin Dept. of Taxation, 237 Wis. 135, 294

N.W. 868. "The reservation of a reversion is not inconsistent with the creation of a trust to continue until the death of the reversioner." Doctor v. Hughes, 225 N.Y. 305, 311, 122 N.E. 221. A power of revocation in a deed of trust does not render the instrument testamentary. Wilcox v. Hubbell, 197 Mich. 21, 163 N.W. 497.

[26] Helvering v. City Bank Farmers Trust Co., 296 U.S. 85, 56 S.Ct. 70, 80 L.Ed. 62; 26 U.S.C.A. Int.Rev. Code, §§ 166, 811.

[27] McCartney v. Ridgway, 160 Ill. 129, 43 N.E. 826, 32 L.R.A. 555.

[28] Security Trust Co. v. Spruance, 20 Del.Ch. 195, 174 A. 285; Chase Nat. Bank v. Tomagno, 172 Misc. 63, 14 N.Y.S.2d 759; In re Lau's Estate, 27 Pa. D. & C. 157. If a power of revocation is exercisable by two persons jointly, it is not usable by the survivor. In re Solomons' Trust Estate, 332 Pa. 462, 2 A.2d 825.

BOGERT TRUSTS 2D—40

on chancery to end it.[29] A reconveyance by trustee to settlor has been held to have no effect on the life of the trust,[30] and, where there is reason for the continuance of the trust, a transfer of the legal title from trustee to cestui que trust has likewise been regarded as not determining the relationship.[31] By merely delivering to a court his resignation, the trustee cannot extinguish the trust.[32] The failure of a trustee to sell for the benefit of creditors within the time limited by the trust instrument will not cause the trust to cease to exist.[33] The change of the trust res does not destroy the trust,[34] but where a trustee has power to alienate trust property the trust is naturally ended as to the property alienated.[35] The settlor may confer on the trustee the power to end the trust;[36] and the failure of the trustee to act may result in the title to trust property being lost by adverse possession and the trust thus extinguished.[37]

In many cases the trustee is expressly given authority to convey the principal to the cestuis. In such cases there can be no doubt about the validity of the transfer.[38] Where it is the duty of the trustee to convey to the cestui the trust res, after a long time it will be presumed that such duty has been performed and that a conveyance has been executed;[39] but where a conveyance would be a breach of duty, possession by the beneficiary will be pre-

[29] Cox v. Cox, 95 Va. 173, 27 S.E. 834; Heiskell v. Powell, 23 W.Va. 717; Harrigan v. Gilchrist, 121 Wis. 127, 99 N.W. 909. But if the trustee improperly end the trust, transfer the property to the cestuis que trust, and take releases from them, no one has a standing in court to complain of the destruction of the trust. Partridge v. Clary, 228 Mass. 290, 117 N.E. 332.

[30] Ewing v. Warner, 47 Minn. 446, 50 N.W. 603.

[31] Hartley v. Unknown Heirs of Wyatt, 281 Ill. 321, 117 N.E. 995; Douglas v. Cruger, 80 N.Y. 15 (on statutory grounds).

[32] Tucker v. Grundy, 83 Ky. 540.

[33] Smith v. Kinney's Ex'rs, 33 Tex. 283.

[34] United States v. Thurston Co., C.C.A.Neb., 143 F. 287, 74 C.C.A. 425;

Moore v. O'Hare, 224 Mass. 283, 112 N.E. 863.

[35] Thatcher v. Wardens, etc., of St. Andrew's Church of Ann Arbor, 37 Mich. 264.

[36] In re Spring's Estate, 216 Pa. 529, 66 A. 110.

[37] Nelson v. Ratliff, 72 Miss. 656, 18 So. 487.

[38] Halper v. Wolff, 82 Conn. 552, 74 A. 890; Jarboe v. Griffith, 150 Ky. 549, 150 S.W. 839; Lord v. Comstock, 240 Ill. 492, 88 N.E. 1012; Mt. Morris Co-op. Building & Loan Ass'n v. Smith, Sup., 120 N.Y.S. 676; Paine v. Sackett, 27 R.I. 300, 61 A. 753.

[39] Reilly v. Conrad, 9 Del.Ch. 154, 78 A. 1080; Marr's Heirs v. Gilliam, 1 Cold., Tenn., 488.

sumed not to be under a conveyance from the trustee.[40] These cases are, of course, following the general rule that a trustee is presumed to have performed his duty.[41] Where a trustee is required to execute a conveyance to a cestui que trust, he should not be required to warrant the title except as against his own acts.[42]

Ordinarily a third party to the trust can have no power to destroy the trust. However, if he be the owner of a mortgage or other lien on the trust property, which lien existed prior to the creation of the trust, he may, by the foreclosure of the lien, wipe the trust res out of existence and thus terminate the trust.[43] As was said in a Kentucky case,[44] where the rights of creditors of the testator and those of cestuis que trust under a will came into conflict: "The rights of the creditors to subject the property to the satisfaction of the debts is superior to the rights of the devisees under the will. They do not have to wait on the expiration of the trust by time. If the property is sold to satisfy the debts, this removes the authority of the trustees over it, and hence the further execution of the trust becomes impossible, and the rights devised to the beneficiaries of the trust must fail. A judicial sale of the trust property under an incumbrance, which was made prior to the creation of the trust, necessarily renders the trust impossible of accomplishment."

NATURAL TERMINATION [47]

166. The length of time for which the trust is to last is usually fixed expressly in the trust instrument and the trust ends when this period expires.

If the instrument does not expressly fix the duration of the trust, it will be deemed to have been intended that the trust last until the settlor's purposes have been accomplished.

Neither the death of the settlor, trustee, or a beneficiary causes the trust to terminate, in the absence of express or implied provision to that effect.

[40] Brewster v. Striker, 2 N.Y. 19.

[41] See § 154, ante.

[42] Hoare v. Harris, 11 Ill. 24; Dwinel v. Veazie, 36 Me. 509.

[43] De Bevoise v. Sandford, 1 Hoff.
Ch., N.Y., 192; Marquam v. Ross, 47 Or. 374, 78 P. 698, 83 P. 852, 86 P. 1.

[44] Miller's Ex'rs v. Miller's Heirs and Creditors, 172 Ky. 519, 528, 529, 189 S.W. 417.

[47] Restatement, Trusts, § 334.

Expiration of Trust Term

The termination of the trust does not ordinarily involve difficulty. Normally the term is fixed by the trust instrument or the oral settlement. Where the settlor states the period for which the trust is to continue, and this period is a lawful one, there can be little room for contention concerning the extinction of the trust by natural means. The trust will last till the date set and then naturally cease.[48] Thus, a period of years,[49] or a life,[50] may be fixed as the trust term; or the settlor may provide that the trust shall continue for a period of years, unless a life expires prior to that time.[51] A life may be fixed as the trust term, with a proviso that the trustee may in his discretion earlier end the trust.[52] The settlor may prescribe that the trust shall last during a minority,[53] or until a cestui que trust reaches a given age,[54] or until the marriage of a given person.[55]

The happening of any one of a large number of events may be fixed as the date of the termination of the trust; as, for example, the alienation of the interest of the cestui que trust,[56] a breach of trust by the trustee,[57] the failure of the cestui to perform a condition,[58] the discharge of the beneficiary from all his debts,[59] or the good moral conduct of the cestui que trust for seven years.[60]

Instead of fixing the end of the trust himself, the settlor may give that right to another. The trust period will not then be certain, but will be capable of being rendered certain by the exer-

---

[48] Yedor v. Chicago City Bank & Trust Co., 376 Ill. 121, 33 N.E.2d 220.

[49] Watkins v. Greer, 52 Ark. 65, 11 S.W. 1019; In re Hanson's Estate, 159 Cal. 401, 114 P. 810; Montgomery v. Trueheart, Tex.Civ.App., 146 S.W. 284.

[50] Laughlin v. Page, 108 Me. 307, 80 A. 753; In re 110th St., 81 App. Div. 27, 81 N.Y.S. 32; Embury v. Sheldon, 68 N.Y. 227; Dunn v. Dunn, 137 N.C. 533, 50 S.E. 212; In re Wilson's Estate, 49 Pa. 241; Bearden v. White, Tenn.Ch.App., 42 S.W. 476.

[51] McCosker v. Brady, 1 Barb.Ch., N.Y., 329.

[52] Cutter v. Hardy, 48 Cal. 568.

[53] Kuykendall v. Zenn, 78 Md. 537, 28 A. 412; Fogarty v. Stange, 72 Misc. 225, 129 N.Y.S. 610; Mason v. Paschal, 98 Tenn. 41, 38 S.W. 92.

[54] Anderson v. Messinger, C.C.A. Ohio, 146 F. 929, 77 C.C.A. 179, 7 L. R.A.,N.S., 1094.

[55] Thornquist v. Oglethorpe Lodge Number One, 140 Ga. 297, 78 S.E. 1086; In re Rose's Will, 156 Wis. 570, 146 N.W. 916.

[56] Cherbonnier v. Bussey, 92 Md. 413, 48 A. 923.

[57] Rolfe & Rumford Asylum v. Lefebre, 69 N.H. 238, 45 A. 1087.

[58] Short v. Wilson, 13 Johns., N.Y., 33.

[59] In re Ames, 22 R.I. 54, 46 A. 47.

[60] Ordway v. Gardner, 107 Wis. 74, 82 N.W. 696.

cise of the power of termination given to the trustee,[61] the trustee and the cestui que trust jointly,[62] the cestui que trust,[63] a majority of the beneficiaries,[64] or such other party as the settlor may select. Where the settlor nominates another to end the trust in its entirety, it is a question of fact whether he also impliedly granted the power to end the trust in part.[65]

Although a settlor may not have expressly stated the trust term, or measured it by lives, years, or similar standards, he may impliedly have fixed the duration of the trust by his statement of its purpose. It is rudimentary law that a trust will last no longer than necessary for the accomplishment of its purpose. If the settlor has not otherwise fixed the end of the trust, he will be deemed to have intended that it should last till the trust purpose was attained.[66] Thus, a trust to collect the net income and pay it over to a beneficiary may naturally be measured by the life of the beneficiary, since the object of supporting the beneficiary would not be accomplished until his death;[67] and a trust for a married woman, to protect her property from her husband, may reasonably be construed to last during the marriage only.[68]

In some jurisdictions statutes provide that certain trusts suspend the power of alienation, and other statutes limit the lawful period of such suspension.[69] In these states the trust period must be carefully fixed, in order to avoid the rules against unlawful suspension of the power of alienation.

The rules regarding the express or implied limits of the trust term are well stated by an Illinois court, as follows:[70] "Where a testator by his will creates a trust and fixes the duration thereof, his direction will, if not in violation of the rule against perpetui-

---

[61] Schreyer v. Schreyer, 101 App. Div. 456, 91 N.Y.S. 1065, affirmed 82 N.Y. 555, 75 N.E. 1134; In re Wilkin, 90 App.Div. 324, 86 N.Y.S. 360.

[62] Lippincott v. Williams, 63 N.J. Eq. 130, 51 A. 467.

[63] In re Stone, 138 Mass. 476.

[64] Culver v. Culver, 58 Ohio St. 172, 50 N.E. 505.

[65] In re Columbia Trust Co., 97 Misc. 566, 163 N.Y.S. 536.

[66] Edwards v. Edwards, 142 Ala. 267, 39 So. 82; Smith v. Dunwoody, 19 Ga. 237; Cornwell v. Wulff, 148 Mo. 542, 50 S.W. 439, 45 L.R.A. 53; Augustus v. Graves, 9 Barb., N.Y., 595; Burke v. O'Brien, 115 App.Div. 574, 100 N.Y.S. 1048; Mackrell v. Walker, 172 Pa. 154, 33 A. 337.

[67] In re Leavitt, 8 Cal.App. 756, 97 P. 916.

[68] Smith v. Metcalf, 1 Head, Tenn., 64.

[69] Jessup v. Witherbee Real Estate & Imp. Co., 63 Misc. 649, 117 N.Y.S. 276. See discussion, ante, § 72.

[70] Kohtz v. Eldred, 208 Ill. 60, 72, 69 N.E. 900.

ties, be given effect and the trust will continue for the time indicated; but where a testator does not specifically indicate the time for which the trust is to continue, his intention must, if possible, be determined from the entire will. Where the evident purpose of a trust is the accomplishment of a particular object, the trust will terminate so soon as that object has been accomplished, and the fact that a fee is given to the trustee does not show the testator's intention that the trust estate shall continue after the active duties connected with the trust have been accomplished."

Death of Party

The death of settlor, trustee, or cestui que trust will not cause the trust to terminate unless the life of one or the other has in some way been made the measure of the life of the trust. In other words, the death of one or all of these parties will not prematurely end the trust, will not cut it off in advance of the time fixed by the settlor.

A trust is not like an agency, where the death of the principal revokes the relationship. The death of the settlor will, unless the settlor's life has been made a measuring life, have no effect on the continuance of the trust.[71]

So, too, under the application of the doctrine that equity never allows a trust to fail for want of a trustee, the death of the trustee will not extinguish the trust relationship.[72] A substitute trustee will be supplied. But if the powers of the deceased trustee were personal, that is, if an intention had been expressed by the settlor that the deceased trustee alone should exercise the powers, then his death will end the trust.[73] The life of the trustee may, of course, be made the measure of the trust's duration, expressly or by implication.[74] Where the deceased trustee had the sole power to appoint his successor and appointed none, the trust will

---

[71] Lyle v. Burke, 40 Mich. 499.

[72] Williams v. McConico, 36 Ala. 22; Spence v. Widney, Cal., 46 P. 463; Shillinglaw v. Peterson, 184 Iowa 276, 167 N.W. 709.

[73] Hadley v. Hadley, 147 Ind. 423, 46 N.E. 823; Hinckley v. Hinckley, 79 Me. 320, 9 A. 897. But merely giving discretion to the trustee to deliver part of the principal to the cestui que trust does not show that the trust was personal. Russell v. Hartley, 83 Conn. 654, 78 A. 320.

[74] Fidelity Trust Co. v. Alexander, C.C.A.Pa., 243 F. 162, 156 C.C.A. 28; Brock v. Conkwright, 179 Ky. 555, 200 S.W. 962; Farrelly v. Ladd, 10 Allen, Mass., 127; Barbour v. Weld, 201 Mass. 513, 87 N.E. 909; Baker v. McAden, 118 N.C. 740, 24 S.E. 531; Appeal of Shoemaker, 91 Pa. 134.

end at the death of the trustee.[75] Where a husband is trustee for his wife, the object of the trust being to protect the property from interference by the husband during the marriage, the death of the husband trustee naturally results in the accomplishment of the trust purpose and indirectly causes the end of the trust.[76]

The death of the cestui que trust has ordinarily no effect on the life of the trust.[77] His interest, if inheritable, passes to his representatives, or goes to the succeeding cestui que trust, if provision is made for two or more successive beneficiaries. But frequently the settlor expressly or impliedly provides that the trust shall endure only during the life of the cestui que trust.[78] In the so-called "savings bank" trusts, where A. deposits his money in a bank and directs that the account be entitled "A., in trust for B.," the death of B. may prevent the trust having any existence.[79] Unless A. makes the trust irrevocable by notice to B., or delivery of the book, or in some similar way, the deposit will not result in the creation of a trust, unless B. survives A. Here the death of a tentative cestui que trust prevents him from becoming a permanent beneficiary.

End Presumed

In a few cases, where there has been great lapse of time since the establishment of the trust, or gross laches in its enforcement, equity has presumed the end of the trust.[80] Thus, where the trust was for the children of the settlor during their dependency on their father, it will be presumed to have been extinguished after thirty years;[81] and where the trust is to sell property and distribute the proceeds, equity will presume that it has been closed, when fourteen months have elapsed since the sale and part of the proceeds are shown to have been paid out.[82]

---

[75] Brock v. Conkwright, 179 Ky. 555, 200 S.W. 962.

[76] Coughlin v. Seago, 53 Ga. 250.

[77] Slevin v. Brown, 32 Mo. 176; Mendenhall v. Walters, 53 Okl. 598, 157 P. 732.

[78] Snodgrass v. Snodgrass, 185 Ala. 155, 64 So. 594; Bradstreet v. Kinsella, 76 Mo. 63; Norton v. Norton, 2 Sandf., N.Y., 296; Deering v. Pierce, 149 App.Div. 10, 133 N.Y.S. 582; Ivory v. Burns, 56 Pa. 300; Appeal of Stokes, 80 Pa. 337. By Ind.Acts 1915, p. 98, unexplained absence of the cestui que trust for five years is regarded as equivalent to his death, and authorizes a termination of the trust. See Ind.Burns' Ann.St. 1933, § 6-1422.

[79] In re United States Trust Co. of New York, 117 App.Div. 178, 102 N.Y.S. 271, affirmed 189 N.Y. 500, 81 N.E. 1177.

[80] Jones v. Haines, 79 N.J.Eq. 110, 80 A. 943.

[81] Bozarth v. Watts, Tenn.Ch.App., 61 S.W. 108.

[82] Holderman v. Hood, 70 Kan. 267, 78 P. 838.

In fixing the term for his trust the settlor should take note of a recent Supreme Court decision regarding "short term" trusts. In Helvering v. Clifford,[83] it was held that where a settlor declared himself trustee for five years for his wife, with reversion in himself, the income of the trust was taxable to the settlor, since he remained for practical purposes the owner of the property after creating the trust.

PURPOSE ACCOMPLISHED OR BECOMES IMPOSSIBLE OF ACCOMPLISHMENT [84]

167. If the trust purpose of a private trust becomes accomplished before the date for the natural termination of the trust, equity will consider the trust terminated, either because of the application of the Statute of Uses to a passive real property trust, or because equity will not compel the futile and useless act of holding the property in trust for a longer period.

If it becomes impossible to accomplish the purposes of the settlor at a time before the natural date for trust termination, the court will terminate the trust or consider it terminated in the case of a private trust.

Accomplishment of Purpose

Not only may the trust terminate because of the expiration of the period stated by the settlor to be the trust period, but also because the continuance of the trust would be useless. If the result sought to be reached by the establishment of the trust has been achieved, equity will either regard the trust as ended or will end it. Many courts have held that, on the accomplishment of the purpose of a private trust, the legal title of the trustee ceases and the person entitled to the property after the end of the trust becomes automatically the holder of the legal title.[85]

[83] 309 U.S. 331, 60 S.Ct. 554, 84 L. Ed. 788.

[84] Restatement, Trusts, § 334.

[85] Comby v. McMichael, 19 Ala. 747; Cherry v. Richardson, 120 Ala. 242, 24 So. 570; Snell v. Payne, 78 S.W. 885, 25 Ky.Law Rep. 1836; In re Hagerstown Trust Co., 119 Md. 224, 86 A. 982; Taylor v. Richards, 153 Mich. 667, 117 N.W. 208; Bellinger v. Shafer, 2 Sandf.Ch., N.Y., 293; Peck v. Brown, 25 N.Y.Super. Ct. 119; Quin v. Skinner, 49 Barb., N.Y., 128; Sharman v. Jackson, 98 App.Div. 187, 90 N.Y.S. 469; Kahn v. Tierney, 135 App.Div. 897, 120 N.Y.S. 663, affirmed 201 N.Y. 516, 94 N.E. 1095; Steacy v. Rice, 27 Pa. 75, 67 Am.Dec. 447; Appeal of Bush, 33 Pa. 85; Appeal of Koenig, 57 Pa. 352; Appeal of Williams, 83 Pa. 377; In re Lee's Estate, 207 Pa. 218, 56 A. 425; Wilson v. Heilman, 219 Pa. 237, 68 A. 674; Packer's Estate, 246 Pa. 97, 92 A. 65; Warland v. Colwell, 10 R.I.

Other courts have reached the same result on a different theory by holding that the accomplishment of the trust purpose caused the original trust to end, and left the trustee the holder of the legal title under a passive trust for the person next entitled.[86] This latter view would seem more logical and less apt to produce confusion in titles than a change of title without action or record.

The effect of the accomplishment of the objects of a charitable trust has been discussed elsewhere.[87]

"The duration of a trust depends upon the purposes of the trust. When the purposes have been accomplished the trust ceases."[88] In Koenig's Appeal[89] a trust for a married woman had been created and divorce had later occurred. In discussing the termination of the trust the court said: "But if the sole purpose of the trust was to protect the wife's estate against her husband, it is manifest that purpose was fully accomplished when the coverture ceased. The divorce of the parties terminated all possibility of the husband's interference with the property bequeathed and devised to the wife, as completely as his death would have done. Then why should the trust be continued after its exigencies have been met? It matters not what may be the nominal duration of an estate given by will to a trustee. It continues in equity no longer than the thing sought to be secured by the trust demands. Even a devise to trustees and their heirs will be cut down to an estate for life, or even for years, if such lesser estate be sufficient for the purpose of the trust."

Examples of trusts terminating naturally or prematurely through the accomplishment of their purposes are found in trusts for married women where the marriage ends, either by the death of the husband,[90] or the death of the wife,[91] or by divorce.[92] Once such a trust is extinguished, it does not revive

---

369; Temple v. Ferguson, 110 Tenn. 84, 72 S.W. 455, 100 Am.St.Rep. 791; Millsaps v. Johnson, Tex.Civ.App., 196 S.W. 202.

[86] Ringrose v. Gleadall, 17 Cal.App. 664, 121 P. 407; Kohtz v. Eldred, 208 Ill. 60, 69 N.E. 900; Cary v. Slead, 220 Ill. 508, 77 N.E. 234; Browning v. Fiklin's Adm'r, 12 S.W. 714, 26 Ky.Law Rep. 470; Adams v. Adams, 56 S.W. 151, 21 Ky.Law Rep. 1756; Harlow v. Cowdrey, 109 Mass. 183; Dodson v. Ball, 60 Pa. 492, 100 Am.Dec. 586; Carman v. Bumpus, 244 Pa. 136, 90 A. 544.

[87] See § 86, ante.

[88] Winters v. March, 139 Tenn. 496, 501, 202 S.W. 73.

[89] 57 Pa. 352, 355.

[90] O'Brien v. Ash, 169 Mo. 283, 69 S.W. 8.

[91] Liptrot v. Holmes, 1 Ga. 381.

[92] In re Cornils' Estate, 167 Iowa 196, 149 N.W. 65, L.R.A.1915E, 762;

on the remarriage of the cestui que trust.[93] Similarly a trust to pay debts is ended by the cancellation of the debts through other means.[94] But where a trust was created for one who happened to be an inebriate at the time of the commencement of the trust, but the object of the trust did not appear to have been to guard against improvidence arising from such habits, a change in the condition of the cestui que trust to that of sobriety did not cause the trust to terminate.[95]

The principle that achievement of purpose causes the end of a trust is, in some states, incorporated in statutory form.[96]

The accomplishment of the trust purpose makes the trust passive. If the subject-matter is a freehold estate, the Statute of Uses will terminate the trust in this event.[97]

Impossibility of Performance

The effect on private, express trusts of imperfection in the declaration, or illegality or impossibility, has been previously discussed.[98] If the imperfection, illegality, or impossibility existed at the time it was sought to create the trust, the express trust never comes into being. Title passes by virtue of the settlement, but the trustee holds as a resulting trustee and not under the intended express trust. If, however, the illegality or impossibility did not exist at the commencement of the trust, but arose during its execution, a different question is presented. In this latter case the express trust has admittedly had existence. The impossibility or illegality which changes it into a resulting trust will therefore cause the termination of the express trust. Such situation, therefore, presents another example of the methods by which a trust may be extinguished. For example, if a trust is created by deed to aid creditors named in an assignment for the benefit of creditors previously made by the settlor's husband, and the husband's assignment is set aside after the trust created by the wife has commenced, obviously there is an im-

McNeer v. Patrick, 93 Neb. 746, 142 N.W. 283. But, if the trust is expressly settled to last for the life of the husband, divorce will not terminate it. Pelton v. Macy, 124 App. Div. 367, 108 N.Y.S. 713.

[93] Hamersley v. Smith, 4 Whart., Pa., 126.

[94] Selden v. Vermilya, 3 N.Y. 525.

[95] Anderson v. Kemper, 116 Ky. 339, 76 S.W. 122.

[96] "When the purpose for which an express trust is created ceases, the estate of the trustee shall also cease." New York Real Property Law, § 109.

[97] Hooper v. Felgner, 80 Md. 262, 30 A. 911; Morgan v. Moore, 3 Gray, Mass., 319.

[98] See ante, § 53.

possibility. The execution of a trust auxiliary to the husband's assignment has been prevented because the husband's assignment has been wiped out of existence. Therefore the original express trust ceases and the trustee holds as a resulting trustee for the settlor. The court says: "It will not be disputed, we presume, that where a trust is created by deed, and the object of such trust fails, the property conveyed by the deed reverts to the grantor or his heirs by way of resulting trust." [99]

It has been previously shown that impossibility of performance has a different effect in charitable trusts from that given to it in the case of private trusts.[1] Ordinarily if a charitable trust becomes impossible of execution as directed by the settlor, equity will apply the cy pres doctrine and carry out the settlor's intention as nearly as possible. But in a few cases impossibility of performance has had the effect of terminating a charitable trust. Thus, it has been held that where the trust funds become exhausted, the charity should be declared extinguished.[2] And where the application of the cy pres doctrine is impossible, because no other charity than the one prescribed would approximately carry out the settlor's ideas, the trust will be held to have failed and fund revert to the donor.[3] A few courts have held that where a settlor voluntarily creates a charitable trust and there is a subsequent abandonment of the charity by the trustees, there will be a reverter.[4] And in a few states, due to the failure of the court to recognize the cy pres rule, or for other reason, impossibility of performance has had the effect of the destruction of the trust.[5]

On the other hand, in the great majority of the cases considering the question, impossibility of carrying out the charitable trust as originally planned has been no bar to its continuance.

[99] Witt v. Carroll, 37 S.C. 388, 393, 16 S.E. 130.

[1] Ante, § 85.

[2] Bronson v. Strouse, 57 Conn. 147, 17 A. 699; Acklin v. Paschal, 48 Tex. 147.

[3] People ex rel. Smith v. Braucher, 258 Ill. 604, 101 N.E. 944, 47 L.R.A., N.S., 1015.

[4] Grundy v. Neal, 147 Ky. 729, 145 S.W. 401 (but see, contra, Lutes v. Louisville & N. R. Co., 158 Ky. 259, 164 S.W. 792, where the reason for the abandonment of the premises was the necessity to convey them to a railroad to avoid condemnation proceedings and where other property was substituted); Cone v. Wold, 85 Minn. 302, 88 N.W. 977; Appeal of Gumbert, 110 Pa. 496, 1 A. 437, semble.

[5] Taylor v. Rogers, 130 Ky. 112, 112 S.W. 1105; Golding v. Gaither, 113 Md. 187, 77 A. 333; Pringle v. Dorsey, 3 S.C. 502.

Thus, the dissolution of the corporation made trustee under the trust instrument does not affect the life of the trust, for a new trustee may be supplied.[6] In the absence of a clause providing for a reverter and a termination of the trust in case of impossibility of performance according to the original directions, equity will apply the property cy pres for charitable objects as nearly like those stated by the settlor as possible.[7] "Where lands have been donated and become vested in a trustee, as herein for charitable uses, neither the donor nor his or her heirs can ever reclaim it, and all right and interest therein or thereto is gone forever."[8] For abuse of the charitable trust the remedy is not a termination of the trust, but removal of the trustee or action in equity to compel performance. From nonuse or abuse by the trustee no termination of the trust results.[9] An unreasonable delay by the trustee of the charitable trust has no effect on the life of the trust.[10]

MERGER OF INTERESTS [11]

168. **Where during the life of the trust the interests of the trustee and beneficiaries become vested in the same person or persons, equity will sometimes decree the trust ended on account of a merger of the equitable and legal interests.**

Where in the course of trust administration the interests of all beneficiaries and remaindermen become vested in one person or in the same group of persons, equity frequently

---

[6] Green v. Blackwell, N.J.Ch., 35 A. 375; In re Orthodox Congregational Church in Union Village, 6 Abb. N.C., N.Y. 398; In re Centennial & Memorial Ass'n of Valley Forge, 235 Pa. 206, 83 A. 683.

[7] Barnard v. Adams, C.C.Iowa, 58 F. 313; Bridgeport Public Library & Reading Room v. Burroughs Home, 85 Conn. 309, 82 A. 582; Huger v. Protestant Episcopal Church, 137 Ga. 205, 73 S.E. 385; Goode v. McPherson, 51 Mo. 126; Women's Christian Ass'n v. City of Kansas City, 147 Mo. 103, 48 S.W. 960; Keene v. Eastman, 75 N.H. 191, 72 A. 213; Maxcy v. City of Oshkosh, 144 Wis. 238, 128 N.W. 899, 1136, 31 L.R.A.,N.S., 787.

[8] Women's Christian Ass'n v. City of Kansas City, 147 Mo. 103, 126, 127, 48 S.W. 960.

[9] Bolick v. Cox, 145 Ga. 888, 90 S.E. 54; People ex rel. Ellert v. Cogswell, 113 Cal. 129, 45 P. 270, 35 L.R.A. 269; American Colonization Soc. v. Soulsby, 129 Md. 605, 99 A. 944, L.R.A. 1917C, 937; Sanderson v. White, 18 Pick., Mass., 328, 29 Am.Dec. 591; Stewart v. Franchetti, 167 App.Div. 541, 153 N.Y.S. 453; Barr v. Weld, 24 Pa. 84; In re Sellers M. E. Church's Petition, 139 Pa. 61, 21 A. 145, 11 L.R.A. 282; In re Toner's Estate, 260 Pa. 49, 103 A. 541; Clark v. Oliver, 91 Va. 421, 22 S.E. 175.

[10] Tainter v. Clark, 5 Allen, Mass., 66.

[11] Restatement, Trusts, §§ 337, 341.

decrees the termination of the trust on the grounds of merger and frustration of trust purpose.

Equity, however, will not apply the doctrine of merger where the application would defeat intent or bring about hardship.

The effect of identity of personnel of trustees and beneficiaries at the beginning of the trust has been discussed previously. It sometimes happens that this identity springs up in the course of the life of the trust, although it did not exist at the beginning. Thus, A. may be made trustee for B., and later B. may sell his interest to A.; or A. may be appointed trustee for A. and B., and later B. may die and the interest of B. may pass to A. by virtue of a gift in the will of B.; or A. and B. may be created trustees for A. and B. for their lives, remainder to C., and C. may transfer his interest to A. and B. Here undoubtedly the legal and equitable interests in the same property become vested in the same person or group, and a suitable situation for the merger of the two interests might seem to have arisen. If that merger occurred, of course the trust would end. However, equity does not regard the doctrine of merger as one which should be automatically applied. It looks at the effect of its application to see whether injustice and hardship would be achieved, or whether the intent of the settlor would be frustrated or accomplished.[12] In cases where the result will be beneficial or harmless, the court sometimes applies the doctrine of merger in these cases and decrees that the trust is ended. But in other instances it appoints a new trustee or new trustees and directs the continuance of the trust.[13]

Another instance of a union of interests occurring during the history of the trust is that of the joinder of the beneficiaries' rights. All equitable interests under the trust may be acquired by one person or group, or such equitable interests and also legal interests following the trust may come into the ownership of the same person or group. Here again there is a situation where equity can give as a reason for the termination of the trust that all beneficial interests in the property have become united in one person or set of persons and that merger of these interests has occurred and therefore the trust is ended. It would seem that the primary problem should be whether the union of the interests makes the trust passive or prevents the accomplishment

---

[12] Wenzel v. Powder, 100 Md. 36, 59 A. 194, 108 Am.St.Rep. 380; Tifft v. Ireland, 273 Mass. 56, 172 N.E. 865.

[13] Cunningham v. Bright, 228 Mass. 385, 117 N.E. 909; Healey v. Alston, 25 Miss. 190; Hickman v. Wood's Ex'r, 30 Mo. 199.

of the settlor's purposes. If the joinder of the beneficial interests defeats the object of the trust, it should be decreed to be terminated whether merger is given as the reason or it is stated that equity will not require the doing of useless acts.

In some cases merger has been used in this latter situation.[14] Thus, if a trust is created to pay the income to A. during her life in order to give her comfortable support, and at her death to deliver the property to B., and A. purchases the interest of B. so that A. now becomes the owner of life and remainder interests in the trust property, it can be argued that merger should cause the trust's extinction. The objects of having the property managed for A. during his life and conserved for B. have now become impossible of accomplishment, and it will do no harm to allow the merger of the two interests in the hands of A. to cause a termination of the trust.[15]

TERMINATION AT REQUEST OF BENEFICIARY [16]

169. If the trust is passive or its purpose has been accomplished, the court will terminate the trust or consider it ended, at the request of the beneficiaries.

If the trust is active and its purpose not accomplished, the majority American view is that the court will not end the trust, even if requested to do so by all the beneficiaries and even if they are of full competency and all interests under the trust are vested. If there are any possible unborn or unascertained beneficiaries, or if any of them are minors or incompetent, the court will not terminate the trust.

In some cases, however, even though no power of revocation was reserved there has been a tendency to terminate the trust when the sole beneficiary was also the sole settlor and requested such action, and also in the case where the settlor and all the beneficiaries joined in a like request, even though the trust purpose was not yet achieved.

Occasionally the court terminates a trust in part and releases part of the trust property, although it will not ordinarily do this, where the trust purpose is not yet fulfilled.

Ordinarily a spendthrift trust will not be terminated at the request of the beneficiaries, since this would always frus-

---

[14] Davis v. Goodman, 17 Del.Ch. 231, 152 A. 115; Ormsby v. Dumesnil, 91 Ky. 601, 16 S.W. 459, 13 Ky. Law Rep. 209; Brooks v. Davis, 82 N.J.Eq. 118, 88 A. 178; Brown v. Fidelity Union Trust Co., 128 N.J.Eq. 197, 15 A.2d 788.

[15] Simmons v. Northwestern Trust Co., 136 Minn. 357, 162 N.W. 450, L.R.A.1917F, 736.

[16] Restatement, Trusts, §§ 335–347.

trate the object of the settlor to protect the beneficiaries against their own imprudent conduct or misfortune.

One beneficiary, or all beneficiaries, may, if competent, surrender their interests to the trustee, and end the trust in whole or in part. If real property is involved, some states require the surrender to be manifested by a writing, signed by the surrenderer.

Whether the cestui que trust may call upon equity to terminate the trust is a question not without difficulty. The cases may be divided into several classes. There are first those in which the trust is passive and all cestuis que trust have vested interests, are sui juris, and unite in a demand for the termination of the trust and the vesting of the legal title in them. These cases present no difficulty. The courts are unanimous in granting the demand of the cestuis que trust and determining the trust.[17] As was said by a Massachusetts court in deciding a case of this class: [18] "In the case before us the trustees hold the fund in question upon a simple trust; the plaintiff is the absolute equitable owner of the fund and its income; he may alienate them and they can be reached by his creditors. If the testator had the intention of guarding against his possible improvidence or misfortune, he failed to carry his intention into effect, and thus the reason for the existence of a trust fails." As previously shown, [19] whether the property is realty or personalty, the court has been inclined to treat the title in such cases as in the beneficiaries, on the theory that the Statute of Uses had operated or that the court would not continue the operation of a useless trust.

The second class of cases comprises those in which the objects of the trust have been accomplished and there is no benefit to be obtained by continuing the trust. As previously shown, [20] in these cases the courts have allowed a destruction of the trust

[17] Ringrose v. Gleadall, 17 Cal.App. 664, 121 P. 407; Fox v. Fox, 250 Ill. 384, 95 N.E. 498; Reuling's Ex'x v. Reuling, 137 Ky. 637, 126 S.W. 151; Fidelity & Columbia Trust Co. v. Williams, 268 Ky. 671, 105 S.W.2d 814. Tilton v. Davidson, 98 Me. 55, 56 A. 215; Root v. Blake, 14 Pick., Mass., 271; Rector v. Dalby, 98 Mo.App. 189, 71 S.W. 1078; Hill v. Hill, 90 Neb. 43, 132 N.W. 738, 38 L.R.A.,N.S., 198; Supreme Lodge, Knights of Pythias v. Rutzler, 87 N.J.Eq. 342, 100 A. 189; McKenzie v. Sumner, 114 N.C. 425, 19 S.E. 375; Fisher v. Wister, Pa., 25 A. 1015; Taylor v. Taylor, 9 R.I. 119; Kennedy v. Badgett, 19 S.C. 591.

[18] Sears v. Choate, 146 Mass. 395, 398, 399, 15 N.E. 786, 4 Am.St.Rep. 320.

[19] See § 68, ante.

[20] See § 167, ante.

at the request of the cestuis que trust, although the normal period of its existence had not expired.[21] The settlor's intent is not violated by such termination of the trust, for his intent has been effectuated. It is reasonable and equitable under such circumstances to allow the sole parties in interest to decide for themselves whether they prefer to enjoy their property as legal owners or indirectly through the use of a trust. In Georgia, where trusts are limited by statute to those for the benefit of spendthrifts and persons non sui juris, if a spendthrift becomes thrifty and the trust is no longer needed for his protection, the trust purpose fails, and the cestui que trust may call for its end.[22] Where the object of a trust is the protection of the corpus of the fund during the life of the first beneficiary, and the remainderman beneficiary acquires the interest of the life beneficiary, there is an accomplishment of purpose, and the sole party in interest may call for a conveyance. In a case involving this situation a Pennsylvania court has recently said:[23] "In the case now before us, all present and future interests in the trust property having been acquired by the remainderman, the 'thing sought to be secured,' i. e., the protection of the corpus pending the duration of the life estates, has become unessential. Under such circumstances, it is the right of a cestui que trust to have the legal estate of the trustee declared terminated. * * *"

In numerous other cases where the cestui que trust and the remainderman were either identical in person at the commencement of the trust, or became so by purchase during the trust life, and the purpose of the trust had been accomplished, extinguishment of the trust has been allowed.[24] Upon this same

---

[21] Coltman v. Moore, D.C., 1 MacArthur 197; Bowditch v. Andrew, 8 Allen, Mass., 339; Sands v. Old Colony Trust Co., 195 Mass. 575, 81 N.E. 300, 12 Ann.Cas. 837; Donaldson v. Allen, 182 Mo. 626, 81 S.W. 1151; Coram v. Davis, 39 Mont. 495, 104 P. 518; Beideman v. Sparks, 64 N. J.Eq. 374, 55 A. 1132; In re Wood's Estate, 261 Pa. 480, 104 A. 673; Megargee v. Naglee, 64 Pa. 216; Ives v. Harris, 7 R.I. 413; Angell v. Angell, 28 R.I. 592, 68 A. 583; Armistead's Ex'rs v. Hartt, 97 Va. 316, 33 S.E. 616.

[22] De Vaughn v. Hays, 140 Ga. 208, 78 S.E. 844.

[23] In re Stafford's Estate, 258 Pa. 595, 598, 599, 102 A. 222.

[24] Whall v. Converse, 146 Mass. 345, 15 N.E. 660; Simmons v. Northwestern Trust Co., 136 Minn. 357, 162 N. W. 450, L.R.A.1917F, 736; Camden Safe Deposit & Trust Co. v. Guerin, 89 N.J.Eq. 556, 105 A. 189; Gloyd v. Roff, 2 Ohio Cir.Ct.R. 253; Taylor v. Huber's Ex'rs, 13 Ohio St. 288; Appeal of Yerkes, 2 Chest. Co. Rep. 410; In re Harrar's Estate, 244 Pa. 542, 91 A. 503; Thom's Ex'r v. Thom, 95 Va. 413, 28 S.E. 583.

principle a partial extinction of the trust has been allowed where the trust purpose as to a portion of the cestuis que trust has been accomplished and their interests could be severed.[25] Thus, where a portion of the trust property was being held for the purpose of ascertaining whether a son of the settlor would have any afterborn children to share in the fund, and the son died childless, it was held that the trust object was, as to this property, achieved and the property might be distributed to the cestuis entitled thereto, freed from the trust.[26] But the court is not apt to terminate the trust in part on the request of part of the beneficiaries, where there is some result to be achieved which was in the mind of the settlor as a trust purpose.[27]

English and Minority View

A third set of decisions have proceeded yet further in recognizing the rights of the cestui que trust. They have allowed a person, or a group of persons, possessing the sole equitable interests in the trust property, to call for a termination of the trust, even though the trust was still active, its natural term not completed, and the purposes of the settlor not carried out.[28] These courts have declined to respect the intent of the settlor. They have said that the sole person interested in the property might determine for himself whether he should enjoy his gift through the medium of a trust or as legal owner, even though his donor stated that he should enjoy it through a trust. This theory is exemplified by a recent Maine case [29] in which the trust was created for the aid of certain relatives in time of need. Obviously its purposes would not be rendered impossible of accomplishment until the beneficiaries had died, for they might at

---

[25] Williams v. Thacher, 186 Mass. 293, 71 N.E. 567; Welch v. Trustees of Episcopal Theological School, 189 Mass. 108, 75 N.E. 139; Harlow v. Weld, R.I., 104 A. 832.

[26] Wayman v. Follansbee, 253 Ill. 602, 98 N.E. 21.

[27] Hills v. Travellers' Bank & Trust Co., 125 Conn. 640, 7 A.2d 652; McDonnell v. McDonnell, 72 App.D.C. 317, 114 F.2d 478, Fox v. Greene, 289 Mich. 179, 286 N.W. 203; Wachovia Bank & Trust Co. v. Laws, 217 N.C. 171, 7 S.E.2d 470; In re Stack's Will, 217 Wis. 94, 258 N.W. 324, 97 A.L.R. 316.

[28] Saunders v. Vautier, 4 Beav. 115; Wharton v. Masterman, [1895] A. C. 186; Taber v. Bailey, 22 Cal.App. 617, 135 P. 975; Eakle v. Ingram, 142 Cal. 15, 75 P. 566, 100 Am.St.Rep. 99; Smith v. Harrington, 4 Allen, Mass., 566; Spooner v. Dunlap, 87 N.H. 384, 180 A. 256; Newlin v. Girard Trust Co., 116 N.J.Eq. 498, 174 A. 479; Huber v. Donoghue, 49 N.J.Eq. 125, 23 A. 495; Turnage v. Greene, 55 N.C. 63, 62 Am.Dec. 208.

[29] Dodge v. Dodge, 112 Me. 291, 92 A. 49.

any time fall into need; but the court terminated the trust upon the written request of all the beneficiaries and allowed them to divide the property among themselves. In a New Jersey case it was held that, where a trust to last for ten years was created for the benefit of a widow and children, the beneficiaries to receive the principal at the end of the trust, the cestuis might demand the conveyance of the property to them prior to the expiration of the trust.[30]

If the cestui que trust is non sui juris, as for, example, an infant, he will not be entitled to end the trust, regardless of its state, for his act in releasing the trustee would be voidable at least.[31]

If the cestuis que trust demanding a termination possess vested interests, but there is a possibility that other cestuis may come into being, the existing cestuis que trust will not be entitled to call for a conveyance;[32] and so, to, where the beneficiaries demanding an extinction of the trust and a conveyance to themselves are contingent cestuis only, the court will not grant their request.[33]

If the settlor has created a trust for himself alone, and desires to get the court's consent to its termination, even though the purposes he originally had in mind have not been achieved, and even though he did not reserve a power of revocation, some courts have been inclined to grant the request. After all the settlor-cestui is merely changing his mind about how he wants to enjoy his own property. He is not seeking to retract a gift.[34]

And even if a trust was created for others than the settlor, and so amounted to the gift of equitable interests, if the settlor and all beneficiaries unite in a request for a court termination, and

[30] Huber v. Donoghue, 49 N.J.Eq. 125, 23 A. 495.

[31] Wirth v. Wirth, 183 Mass. 527, 67 N.E. 657.

[32] Allen v. Allen's Trustee, 141 Ky. 689, 133 S.W. 543; Battle v. Petway, 27 N.C. 576, 44 Am.Dec. 59; In re Eshelman's Estate, 191 Pa. 68, 43 A. 201; In re Lewis' Estate, 231 Pa. 60, 79 A. 921; Greene v. Aborn, 10 R.I. 10; Dial v. Dial, 21 Tex. 529.

[33] Sanders v. First Nat. Bank, 189 Ga. 450, 6 S.E.2d 294; Olsen v. Youngerman, 136 Iowa 404, 113 N.W. 938; In re McKenney's Will, 169 Md. 640, 182 A. 425; Bennett v. Fidelity Union Trust Co., 122 N.J.Eq. 455, 194 A. 449; Deal v. Wachovia Bank & Trust Co., 218 N.C. 483, 11 S.E.2d 464; In re Thistle's Estate, 263 Pa. 60, 106 A. 94.

[34] Vlahos v. Andrews, 362 Ill. 593, 1 N.E.2d 59; Sutliff v. Aydelott, 373 Ill. 633, 27 N.E.2d 529; Raffel v. Safe Deposit & Trust Co., 100 Md. 141, 59 A. 702; Cole v. Nickel, 43 Nev. 12, 177 P. 409, 185 P. 565; Bottimore v. First & Merchants' Nat. Bank of Richmond, 170 Va. 221, 196 S.E. 593; but see, *contra*, Kauffman v. Hiestand, 131 Pa. Super. 219, 200 A. 251.

all are competent and have vested interests, a strong argument can be made for termination. Donees with the consent of their donor are seeking to enjoy their gifts in a different way from that originally prescribed by the donor. The donees could in most cases give their interests back to the donor, and then he could give legal interests instead of equitable. The termination of the trust prevents the need for this circumlocution. Some courts have accepted these arguments.[35]

Majority View

Even though all the persons equitably interested in the property join, and all have vested interests and are sui juris, yet if the trust is active and its purposes therefore not accomplished, they will not be allowed to call for a termination of the trust, according to the weight of authority in America.[36] The larger number of the courts which have considered the question respect the intention of the testator, give him the power to restrict and define the way in which the beneficiaries shall take the benefits of the trust property, and refuse to allow the beneficiaries to elect how they shall enjoy the property. As has been well said by the Supreme Court of Pennsylvania in a recent case:[37] "It may,

[35] Fowler v. Lanpher, 193 Wash. 308, 75 P.2d 132.

[36] Ballantine v. Ballantine, C.C.A. N.J., 160 F. 927, 88 C.C.A. 109; DeLadson v. Crawford, 93 Conn. 402, 106 A. 326; Lunt v. Van Gorden, 229 Iowa 263, 294 N.W. 351; Webster v. Bush, 39 S.W. 411, 42 S.W. 1124, 19 Ky.Law Rep. 565; Nunn v. Peak, 130 Ky. 405, 113 S.W. 493; Miller's Ex'rs v. Miller's Heirs and Creditors, 172 Ky. 519, 189 S.W.417; Downs v. Security Trust Co., 175 Ky. 789, 194 S.W. 1041; Kimball v. Blanchard, 101 Me. 383, 64 A. 645; Russell v. Grinnell, 105 Mass. 425; Claflin v. Claflin, 149 Mass. 19, 20 N.E. 454, 3 L.R.A. 370, 14 Am.St.Rep. 393; Watson v. Watson, 223 Mass. 425, 111 N. E. 904; Easton v. Demuth, 179 Mo. App. 722, 162 S.W. 294; Robbins v. Smith, 72 Ohio St. 1, 73 N.E. 1051; Hill v. Hill, 49 Okl. 424, 152 P. 1122; Twining v. Girard Life Ins. Annuity & Trust Co., 14 Phila., Pa., 74; Wickham v. Berry, 55 Pa. 70; Van Leer v. Van Leer, 221 Pa. 195, 70 A. 716; In re Shirk's Estate, 242 Pa. 95, 88 A. 873; In re Stewart's Estate, 253 Pa. 277, 98 A. 569, Ann.Cas.1918B, 1216; Barkley v. Dosser, 15 Lea, Tenn., 529; Glasscock v. Tate, 107 Tenn. 486, 64 S.W. 715; Lanius v. Fletcher, 100 Tex. 550, 101 S.W. 1076; McNeill v. St. Aubin, Tex.Civ. App., 209 S.W. 781; Carney v. Kain, 40 W.Va. 758, 23 S.E. 650; Bussell v. Wright, 133 Wis. 445, 113 N.W. 644. In Stier v. Nashville Trust Co., C.C.A., 158 F. 601, 85 C.C.A. 423, it is said that equity may in its discretion refuse to end a trust, where it is active and has an unaccomplished purpose.

The payment of fees to the trustee is not a trust purpose, and therefore the mere opposition of the trustee to termination on the ground that he will lose money is not material. In re Musser's Estate, 341 Pa. 1, 17 A.2d 411.

[37] In re Henderson's Estate, 258 Pa. 510, 515, 102 A. 217. For a dis-

therefore, be regarded as settled that a testamentary direction to a trustee to hold, invest and manage the corpus of a fund for a definite period, and pay the income therefrom at stated times to a beneficiary creates an active trust which the statute does not execute and which will continue to be operative and cannot be terminated until the purpose for which the trust was created has been accomplished. The rule has its foundation in the well-established principle that, within the limits of the law, every man may do as he pleases with his own property. He may, therefore, dispose of it in fee, or create estates therein in different persons, or grant or devise it on such conditions or under such restrictions as he may desire." It follows, a fortiori, that a portion of the beneficiaries cannot cause the termination of a trust, the purpose of which is unaccomplished.[38]

In a leading Massachusetts case the court declined to order a conveyance under similar circumstances and said: "This court has ordered trust property to be conveyed by the trustee to the beneficiary when there was a dry trust, or when the purposes of the trust had been accomplished, or when no good reason was shown why the trust should continue, and all the persons interested in it were sui juris and desired that it be terminated; but we have found no expression of any opinion in our reports that provisions requiring a trustee to hold and manage the trust property until the beneficiary reached an age beyond that of twenty-one years are necessarily void if the interest of the beneficiary is vested and absolute."[39]

The trustee and cestuis que trust have been allowed to terminate active, unaccomplished trusts in jurisdictions where the policy of the court permits the cestuis que trust to achieve the same result.[40] On the other hand, those courts which refuse to the cestuis the right to extinguish the trust, so long as its purpose remains unaccomplished, have declined to decree an end of the trust upon the application of both trustee and cestuis que

---

cussion of the policy of this rule, see Scott, Control of Property by the Dead, 65 Pa.Law Rev. 632, 647.

[38] Gray v. Union Trust Co. of San Francisco, 171 Cal. 637, 154 P. 306; Lobdell v. State Bank of Neuvoo, 180 Ill. 56, 54 N.E. 157; Petition of Thurston, 154 Mass. 596, 29 N.E. 53, 26 Am.St.Rep. 278; Smith v. Smith, 70 Mo.App. 448; Harris v. Harris, 205 Pa. 460, 55 A. 30; Carney v. Byron, 19 R.I. 283, 36 A. 5; Guye v. Guye, 63 Wash. 340, 115 P. 731, 37 L.R.A., N.S., 186.

[39] Claflin v. Claflin, 149 Mass. 19, 22, 20 N.E. 454, 3 L.R.A. 370, 14 Am. St.Rep. 393.

[40] Armour v. Murray, 74 N.J.L. 351, 68 A. 164; Short v. Wilson, 13 Johns., N.Y., 33 (decided prior to the Revised Statutes).

§ 169   TERMINATION AT REQUEST OF BENEFICIARY   645

trust.[41] Thus, in Young v. Snow, the trust was to keep the property in repair and to pay the income over for twenty years; all the cestuis que trust and the trustee united in asking equity to end the trust before the expiration of the twenty years; but the court, following the leading case of Claflin v. Claflin,[42] declined.[43] Where contingent interests exist, the joinder of the trustee with the cestuis que trust will not induce the court to terminate the trust.[44]

The termination of a spendthrift trust at the request of the beneficiaries will always defeat the aim of the settlor to protect them against creditors and the folly of the beneficiaries. The case for court termination is, therefore, often deemed very weak;[45] but, some courts seem to make no distinction between spendthrift and nonspendthrift trusts.[46]

In some states statutes forbid the beneficiaries of trusts to collect and pay over the income and profits from alienating their interests. These statutes have been construed to prevent the abrogation of such trusts by act of the cestuis que trust.[47] A New York court in considering the question has said:[48] "Whatever view may be taken of the general jurisdiction of courts of equity, in the absence of any statutory or legislative policy, to abrogate continuing trusts, created for the purpose of providing a sure support for the widow or children of a testator, or other beneficiary, the indestructibility of such trusts here, by judicial decree, results, we think, from the inalienable character impressed upon them by statute. The beneficiaries of trusts for the receipt of

---

[41] Backburn v. Blackburn, 167 Ky. 113, 180 S.W. 48; In re Unruh's Estate, 248 Pa. 185, 93 A. 1000; In re Simonin's Estate, 260 Pa. 395, 103 A. 927.

[42] 167 Mass. 287, 45 N.E. 686.

[43] 149 Mass. 19, 20 N.E. 454, 3 L. R.A. 370, 14 Am.St.Rep. 393.

[44] Anderson v. Williams, 262 Ill. 308, 104 N.E. 659, Ann.Cas.1915B, 720; Bailey's Trustee v. Bailey, 97 S.W. 810, 30 Ky.Law Rep. 127; Newton v. Rebenack, 90 Mo.App. 650; Isham v. Delaware L. & W. R. Co., 11 N.J.Eq. 227; Mauldin v. Mauldin, 101 S.C. 1, 85 S.E. 60.

[45] Mason v. Rhode Island Hospital Trust Co., 78 Conn. 81, 61 A. 57; Rose v. Southern Michigan Nat. Bank, 255 Mich. 275, 238 N.W. 284; Rehr v. Fidelity-Philadelphia Trust Co., 310 Pa. 301, 165 A. 380, 91 A.L.R. 99; In re Smaltz' Estate, 329 Pa. 21, 195 A. 880.

[46] Botzum v. Havanna Nat. Bank, 367 Ill. 539, 12 N.E.2d 203; Dunnett v. First Nat. Bank & Trust Co. of Tulsa, 184 Okl. 82, 85 P.2d 281.

[47] Dale v. Guaranty Trust Co., 168 App.Div. 601, 153 N.Y.S. 1041, 1 Cornell Law Quarterly, 209; Patton v. Patrick, 123 Wis. 218, 101 N.W. 408.

[48] Lent v. Howard, 89 N.Y. 169, 181.

the rents and profits of land are prohibited from assigning or disposing of their interest, * * * and this provision is held to apply, by force of other sections of the statute, to the interest of beneficiaries in similar trusts of personalty. * * * This legislative policy cannot, we think, be defeated by the action of the court permitting such alienation, or abrogating the trust."

The beneficiary of a non-spendthrift trust may surrender his interest to the trustee and thus extinguish the trust in whole or in part, since the trustee will then become the absolute owner.[49] It would seem that if real property is the subject of the trust where the cestui seeks to surrender, a careful examination of the Statute of Frauds should be made to learn whether the surrender must be in writing and signed by the surrenderer. Oral surrenders have been held valid in the case of many trusts of realty,[50] but in some cases a writing has been required.[51]

[49] First Nat. Bank of Lincoln v. Cash, 220 Ala. 319, 125 So. 28; Keaton v. McGwier, 24 Ga. 217; Owings v. Owings, 3 Ind. 142; Dearing v. Selvey, 50 W.Va. 4, 40 S.E. 478.

[50] See Scott, Parol Extinguishment of Trusts in Land, 42 Harv.L.R. 849.

[51] Coleman v. Coleman, 48 Ariz. 337, 61 P.2d 441, 106 A.L.R. 1309; Matthews v. Thompson, 186 Mass. 14, 71 N.E. 93, 66 L.R.A. 421, 104 Am.St.Rep. 550.

TABLE OF CASES

Figures refer to pages

A

Aaron Frank Clothing Co. v. Deegan, 181.
Abbott, In re, 418, 427.
Abbott v. Foote, 469.
Abbott v. Gregory, 492.
Abbott's Ex'r v. Reeves, 580.
Abell v. Brady, 477.
Abell v. Howe, 565.
Abernathy v. Phillips, 399.
Abert v. Lape, 98.
Ackerman v. Fichter, 281.
Ackerson v. Elliott, 615.
Ackley v. Croucher, 618.
Acklin v. Paschal, 635.
Adair v. Brimmer, 356, 369, 512, 597.
Adams v. Adams, 34, 96, 100, 126, 127, 633.
Adams v. Bohon, 300.
Adams v. Canutt, 89.
Adams v. Highland Cemetery Co., 113, 423.
Adams v. Holden, 609.
Adams v. Lambard, 470, 525.
Adams v. Nelson, 356.
Adams v. Page, 300.
Adams v. Perry, 135.
Adams v. Purser, 464.
Adams v. Vanderbeck, 545.
Adams v. Whitmarsh, 596.
Adams' Estate, In re, 322, 513, 516.
Adams Female Academy v. Adams, 493.
Adamson v. Paonessa, 148.
Adelman's Will, In re, 249.
Ætna Life Ins. Co. of Hartford, Conn. v. Morlan, 545.
Affleck, In re, 484.
Ahrens v. Simon, 186.
Aicardi v. Craig, 124.
Ainsa v. Mercantile Trust Co. of San Francisco, 326.
Ainsworth v. Harding, 205.
Akin v. Akin, 177.
Akin v. Jones, 24.
Akin v. Security Savings & Trust Co., 545.

BOGERT TRUSTS 2D

Alaska Northern R. Co. v. Alaska Cent. Ry. Co., 605, 607.
Alberts v. Steiner, 456.
Albretch v. Wolf, 607.
Albright v. Albright, 396.
Aldersley v. McCloud, 392.
Aldridge v. Aldridge, 465.
Alexander v. Fidelity Trust Co., 532.
Alexander v. Goellert, 400.
Alexander v. Spaulding, 84.
Alexander v. Tams, 182.
Alexander v. Warrance, 145.
Alexander County Nat. Bank v. Conner, 24.
Alford v. Bennett, 231, 233.
Alfred University v. Hancock, 286.
Alger v. North End Savings Bank, 68, 69.
Allen, Appeal of, 424.
Allen, In re, 475, 482.
Allen v. Allen, 112.
Allen v. Allen's Trustee, 642.
Allen v. Almy, 243.
Allen v. Arkenburgh, 213.
Allen v. Baskerville, 57.
Allen v. Craft, 232.
Allen v. Fourth Nat. Bank, 584.
Allen v. Hawley, 146.
Allen v. Hendrick, 117.
Allen v. Jones, 195.
Allen v. McKean, 495.
Allen v. Puritan Trust Co., 580, 581, 582, 585, 587.
Allen v. Stevens, 249, 271, 307, 493.
Allen v. Trustees of Nasson Institute, 301.
Aller v. Crouter, 87.
Allis' Estate, In re, 367, 443.
Allison v. Little, 424.
Almy v. Jones, 287, 306.
Alston v. McGonigal, 83.
Alvord v. Sherwood, 394.
Ambrosius v. Ambrosius, 97.
American Academy of Arts and Sciences v. President, etc., of Harvard College, 127, 263, 300.
American Barrel Co. v. Commissioner of Banks, 23.

CASES CITED
Figures refer to pages

American Bible Soc. v. Pendleton, 270.
American Bonding Co. of Baltimore v. Richardson, 326, 521.
American Can Co. v. Williams, 24, 557.
American Colonization Soc. v. Gartrell, 135.
American Colonization Soc. v. Latrobe, 475.
American Colonization Soc. v. Soulsby, 636.
American Mining Co. v. Trask, 609.
American Nat. Bank v. Owensboro Savings Bank & Trust Co.'s Receiver, 24.
American Security & Trust Co. v. Payne, 444.
American Trust Co. v. Canevin, 378.
American Trust & Banking Co. v. Boone, 580.
Ames, In re, 628.
Ames v. Scudder, 476.
Amherst College, Trustees of, v. Ritch, 227.
Amidon v. Snouffer, 82.
Amory v. Attorney General, 289, 396.
Amory v. Green, 359, 360.
Amory v. Lord, 118, 252.
Amory v. Trustees of Amherst College, 238, 246, 258, 605.
Amsinck's Estate, 573.
Anderson, In re, 359.
Anderson v. Anderson, 179.
Anderson v. Biddle, 150.
Anderson v. Crist, 56.
Anderson v. Daley, 592.
Anderson v. Dunn, 608.
Anderson v. Earle, 126.
Anderson v. Fry, 56.
Anderson v. Gile, 181.
Anderson v. Hultberg, 189.
Anderson v. Kemper, 572, 634.
Anderson v. Menefee, 246.
Anderson v. Messinger, 628.
Anderson v. Northrop, 420, 602.
Anderson v. Robinson, 417, 425, 573.
Anderson v. Thero, 503.
Anderson v. Thomson, 493.
Anderson v. Walker, 585.
Anderson v. Williams, 246, 645.
Anderson's Estate, 276.
Andrew v. Andrew, 215.
Andrew v. State Bank of Blairsburg, 84.
Andrew v. State Bank of New Hampton, 550.
Andrew v. Union Sav. Bk. & Tr. Co., 344.

Andrews v. Aikens, 203.
Andrews v. Andrews, 198.
Andrews v. Hunneman, 40.
Andrews v. Kirk, 320.
Andrews v. Lincoln, 255.
Andrews v. Rice, 238.
Angell v. Angell, 640.
Angell v. Jewett, 470.
Anglo California Nat. Bank of San Francisco v. Stafford, 621.
Angus v. Noble, 56, 237.
Anheuser-Busch Brewing Ass'n v. Morris, 24.
Annett-Mahnken Realty Co. v. Gollin, 341.
Annis v. Annis, 324.
Anonymous, 10, 509.
A. O. Brown & Co., In re, 554.
Apgar v. Connell, 218.
Aplyn v. Brewer, 509.
Apple, In re, 462.
Appley, In re, 493.
Archer-Shee v. Garland, 140.
Armistead's Ex'rs v. Hartt, 640.
Armitage's Estate, In re, 596.
Armory Board, In re, 408.
Armour Fertilizer Works v. Lacy, 136.
Armour v. Murray, 644.
Arms v. Ashley, 498.
Armstrong v. Barber, 243.
Armstrong v. Douglass, 246.
Armstrong's Heirs v. Campbell, 329, 607.
Arnold v. Alden, 463, 484.
Arnold v. Allen, 473.
Arnold v. Brown, 328.
Arnold v. Cord, 213.
Arnold v. Searing, 46, 206.
Arnold v. Southern Pine Lumber Co., 461.
Arnold Inv. Co. v. Citizens' State Bank of Chautauqua, 557.
Arnot v. Bingham, 24.
Arntson v. First Nat. Bank of Sheldon, 85, 124, 224, 506.
Arrowsmith v. Van Harlingen's Ex'rs, 16.
Arthur v. Master in Equity, 369.
Asam v. Asam, 176.
Ash v. Ash, 145, 456.
Ash v. Wells, 599.
Ashby v. Smith, 412.
Ashhurst, Appeal of, 136, 162.
Ashhurst v. Given, 134.
Ashley v. Winkley, 465, 508, 514.
Ashley's Admrs. v. Denton, 33.
Ashman's Estate, In re, 478.

CASES CITED
Figures refer to pages

Ashton v. President, etc., of Atlantic Bank, 541.
Ashurst v. Given, 133.
Aspinall v. Jones, 197.
Association for the Relief of Respectable, Aged Indigent Females v. Beekman, 492, 494, 495.
Astreen v. Flanagan, 179.
Atkins v. Atkins, 230.
Atkinson, Petition of, 69, 74, 77.
Atkinson v. Beckett, 315.
Atkinson v. Ward, 549, 558.
Attorney General v. Armstrong, 277.
Attorney General v. Barbour, 570.
Attorney General v. Bedard, 494, 544.
Attorney General v. Briggs, 302.
Attorney General v. Cock, 277.
Attorney General v. Garrison, 573.
Attorney General v. Gill, 304.
Attorney General v. Goodell, 121.
Attorney General v. Holland, 518.
Attorney General v. Rector, etc., of Trinity Church, 277.
Attorney General v. Town of Dublin, 277.
Attorney General v. Wallace's Devisees, 275, 493.
Attorney General ex rel. Bailey v. Moore's Ex'rs, 490.
Attwill v. Dole, 126, 131.
Atwater v. Russell, 132.
Atwood v. Shenandoah Val. R. Co., 122.
Atwood-Stone Co. v. Lake County Bank, 581, 587.
Augustus v. Graves, 629.
Aultman, Miller & Co. v. Loring, 204.
Anstice v. Brown, 134.
Austin v. Austin, 572.
Austin v. Central Sav. Bank of Baltimore, 67.
Austin v. Dean, 543.
Austin v. Shaw, 136.
Austin v. Wilcoxson, 493.
Autrey v. Stubenrauch, 491.
Averill v. Lewis, 274.
Avery v. Stewart, 196.
Avery's Trustee v. Avery, 332.
Avey v. Burnley, 49.
Aydelott v. Breeding, 369, 482.
Aylsworth v. Whitcomb, 624.
Ayres v. Farmers' & Merchants' Bank, 23.

B

Babbitt v. Fidelity Trust Co., 477, 482.

Babcock v. African Methodist Episcopal Zion Society, 122.
Babcock v. Hubbard, 329.
Babcock v. Monypeny, 159.
Backburn v. Blackburn, 645.
Backes v. Crane, 337, 355, 369, 493, 523, 604.
Bacon v. Barber, 138.
Bacon v. Bonham, 109.
Bacon v. Camphausen, 517, 521.
Bacon v. Ransom, 64.
Bacon v. Taylor, 15.
Badger v. Badger, 598, 600.
Badgett v. Keating, 140, 417.
Badgley v. Votrain, 102.
Baer v. Kahn, 459.
Baer's Appeal, 344.
Bagnell v. Ives, 321.
Bahin v. Hughes, 517, 521.
Baiar v. O'Connell, 29.
Bailey v. Bailey, 129, 199, 424, 462.
Bailey v. Buffalo Loan, Trust & Safe Deposit Co., 190.
Bailey v. Dyer, 534.
Bailey v. Rice, 569, 574.
Bailey v. Smith, 487.
Bailey v. Wood, 85, 98.
Bailey v. Worster, 137.
Bailey's Trustee v. Bailey, 645.
Baillie v. Columbia Gold Min. Co., 609.
Bain v. Brown, 42.
Bainbridge v. Stoner, 47, 190, 195.
Baird, Appeal of, 420.
Baird v. Howison, 239.
Baird's Case, 570.
Baker v. Baker, 62, 82, 88, 173.
Baker v. Brown, 36.
Baker v. Disbrow, 358, 565.
Baker v. Heiskell, 145.
Baker v. Lafitte, 523.
Baker v. Lane, 328.
Baker v. McAden, 630.
Baker v. New York Nat. Exch. Bank, 28, 554.
Baker v. Pender, 245.
Baker v. Terrell, 177, 188.
Baker v. Thompson, 454.
Baker v. Vining, 185.
Balbach v. Frelinghuysen, 22.
Baldwin, In re, 484.
Baldwin v. Campfield, 177.
Baldwin v. Humphrey, 87.
Baldwin v. Porter, 125.
Baldwin's Ex'rs v. Baldwin, 286.
Bales v. Perry, 324.
Ball v. Ball, 145.
Ballantine v. Ballantine, 643.

CASES CITED
Figures refer to pages

Ballantine v. Young, 443, 444, 448.
Ballentine v. Eaton, 379.
Baltimore Trust Co. v. George's Creek Coal & Iron Co., 420.
Bangor Trust Co., In re, 198.
Bank v. Rice, 57.
Bank of America v. Waydell, 22.
Bank of America Nat. Trust & Savings Ass'n v. Hazelbud, 74.
Bank of Aynor, Ex parte, 561.
Bank of Berkeley Springs v. Green, 140.
Bank of Blackwell v. Dean, 28.
Bank of British North America v. Freights, etc., of The Hutton, 551.
Bank of Columbia v. Ross, 16.
Bank of Commerce v. Russell, 24.
Bank of Guntersville v. Crayter, 580.
Bank of Hartford v. McDonald, 587.
Bank of Hickory v. McPherson, 586.
Bank of Old Dominion v. Dubuque & P. R. Co., 328.
Bank of Oregon, In re, 24.
Bank of Sherman v. Weiss, 26.
Bank of United States v. Biddle, 462.
Bank of Visalia v. Dillonwood Lumber Co., 56, 399.
Bankers' Trust Co. of New York v. Lobdell, 433.
Bankes v. Wilkes' Ex'rs, 510.
Bannin, In re, 356.
Barber v. Thompson, 623.
Barbey's Estate, In re 73, 74.
Barbour v. Weld, 571, 574, 630.
Barclay, Appeal of, 476.
Barclay v. Goodloe's Ex'r, 125.
Bare v. Cole, 156.
Barefield v. Rosell, 69.
Barker, In re, 483.
Barker v. Barker, 565, 573.
Barker v. Hurley, 618.
Barker v. Smiley, 422.
Barker's Trusts, In re, 115.
Barkley v. Dosser, 337, 643.
Barkley v. Lane's Ex'r, 57, 132.
Barkley Cemetery Ass'n v. McCune, 572.
Barnard v. Adams, 636.
Barnard v. Bagshaw, 510.
Barnard v. Duncan, 398.
Barnard v. Hawks, 530.
Barnard v. Stone, 332.
Barnes v. Century Sav. Bank, 461.
Barnes v. Dow, 36.
Barnes v. Gardiner, 461.
Barnes v. Spencer, 124, 180.
Barnet v. Dougherty, 213.

Barney v. Parsons' Guardian, 355.
Barney v. Saunders, 344, 476.
Barnum v. Barnum, 190, 258.
Barr v. Schroeder, 96, 138.
Barr v. Weld, 636.
Barrell v. Joy, 380, 470, 476.
Barrett v. Bamber, 204, 541.
Barrett v. Barrett, 243.
Barrett v. Thielen, 224.
Barrette v. Dooly, 492.
Barroilhet v. Anspacher, 182.
Barroll v. Forman, 322, 512.
Barron, In re Will of, 433.
Barron v. Stuart, 225.
Barron's Will, In re, 451.
Barrows v. Bohan, 178, 183.
Barry v. Abbot, 153.
Barry v. Barry, 480.
Bartells' Will, In re, 574.
Bartlett, In re, 286, 292.
Bartlett v. Bartlett, 174.
Bartlett v. Pickering, 487.
Bartlett v. Remington, 75.
Bartlett v. Sears, 243.
Bartlett v. Varner's Ex'r, 538, 540.
Bartol's Estate, In re, 346, 362, 365, 373.
Barton v. Fuson, 595.
Barton v. Magruder, 187.
Barton v. Thaw, 245.
Bascom v. Albertson, 271.
Bascom v. Weed, 322.
Baskin, Appeal of, 462.
Baskin v. Baskin, 344, 347.
Bass v. Scott, 233.
Bass v. Whelass, 535.
Bassett v. Granger, 575, 576.
Batchelder v. Central Nat. Bank, 583.
Batchis v. Leask, 499.
Bates v. Bates, 284, 607.
Bates v. Hurd, 87.
Bates v. Kelly, 181, 532.
Bates v. McKinley, 433.
Bates v. Spooner, 243.
Bates v. Underhill, 514.
Bath Savings Inst. v. Hathorn, 68, 70, 74.
Battin's Estate, In re, 425, 474.
Battle v. Petway, 642.
Batty v. Greene, 197.
Bauer v. Myers, 303.
Baughman v. Lowe, 564.
Baugh's Ex'r v. Walker, 329.
Baumann v. Ballantine, 155.
Baumgartner v. Guessfeld, 187.
Bayard's Estate, In re, 466.
Bay Biscayne Co. v. Baile, 83, 471.
Baydrop v. Second Nat. Bank, 460.

CASES CITED
Figures refer to pages

Bayer v. Cockerill, 146.
Bayles v. Baxter, 172, 178.
Bayles v. Crossman, 174.
Bayles v. Staats, 572.
Bayless v. Wheller-Kelly-Hagny Trust Co., 619.
Baylies v. Payson, 224.
Baylor v. Fulkerson's Ex'rs, 211.
Bay State Gas Co. of Delaware v. Rogers, 602.
Bazemore v. Davis, 541.
Beachey v. Heiple, 489, 569.
Beakes Dairy Co. v. Berns, 74.
Beakey v. Knutson, 400.
Beal v. City of Somerville, 23.
Beale v. Kline, 523.
Beall v. Fox's Ex'rs, 270.
Beam v. Patterson Safe Deposit & Trust Co., 466.
Beaman's Estate, In re, 70, 72.
Bean v. Bean, 534.
Bear v. Millikin Trust Co., 91.
Beard v. Beard, 55, 475.
Beard v. Stanton, 615.
Bearden v. White, 628.
Beardsley, Appeal of, 425.
Beardsley v. Hall, 466.
Bearinger's Estate, In re, 67.
Beatty v. Guggenheim Exploration Co., 195.
Beatty's Estate, 515.
Beaubien v. Hindman, 542.
Beaver v. Beaver, 66.
Beck v. City of Philadelphia, 292.
Becker v. Neurath, 196, 215.
Beckett v. Bledsoe, 534.
Beckett v. Tyler, 544.
Beckley v. Munson, 331.
Bedford v. Bedford's Adm'r, 112.
Beecher v. Cosmopolitan Trust Co., 30.
Beecher v. Foster, 615.
Beecher v. Wilson, 182.
Beecher v. Yale, 285, 292.
Beegle v. Wentz, 213.
Beekman v. Bonsor, 240, 270.
Beers v. Bridgeport Bridge Co., 46.
Beers v. Narramore, 247.
Beeson v. Beeson, 333.
Beggs v. Fite, 379.
Behrmann v. Seybel, 539.
Beideman v. Sparks, 640.
Beidler v. Dehner, 116, 272, 426.
Belding v. Archer, 324, 326.
Belknap v. Belknap, 148, 481.
Belknap v. Northwestern Mut. Life Ins. Co., 110.
Belknap v. Tillotson, 226.

Bell v. Briggs, 283.
Bell v. Watkins, 159, 169.
Bell County v. Alexander, 113.
Bell's Adm'r v. Humphrey, 319, 490.
Bell's Estate, In re, 572.
Bellah, In re, 359.
Bellamy v. Bellamy's Adm'r, 328.
Bellinger v. Shafer, 632.
Bellows v. Page, 232.
Belvin's Ex'rs v. French, 386.
Bemmerly v. Woodard, 485, 525.
Benbrook v. Yancy, 224, 226.
Benedict v. City of New York, 601.
Benett v. Wyndham, 387.
Bennett v. Bennett, 126.
Bennett v. Chandler, 471.
Bennett v. Fidelity Union Trust Co., 642.
Bennett v. Garlock, 140.
Bennett v. Harper, 224, 226.
Bennett v. McKrell, 81.
Bennett v. Nashville Trust Co., 415.
Bennett v. Pierce, 596.
Benoist v. Benoist, 614.
Benson v. Dempster, 604.
Benson v. Liggett, 503.
Bentley v. Shreve, 474, 478, 502.
Beresford v. Jervis, 280.
Bergengren v. Aldrich, 407.
Berger v. Burnett, 436.
Berger v. Butler, 487.
Bergmann v. Lord, 152, 162.
Berlenbach v. Chemical Bank & Trust Co., 624.
Bermingham v. Wilcox, 463, 516, 520.
Bernstein, In re, 418.
Berrien v. Thomas, 395.
Berry, In re, 551, 624.
Berry v. Dunham, 161.
Berry v. Evendon, 530.
Berry v. Geen, 308.
Berry v. Stigall, 477.
Berry v. Williamson, 129, 146, 573.
Berry v. Wooddy, 231.
Berryhill's Adm'x, Appeal of, 595.
Bertron, Storrs & Griscom v. Polk, 396.
Best v. Campbell, 614.
Bethea v. McColl, 359.
Bethlehem Borough v. Perseverance Fire Co., 291.
Bethune v. Beresford, 16.
Bettencourt v. Bettencourt, 565.
Bettendorf Metal Wheel Co. v. P. P. Mast & Co., 557.
Bettinger v. Bridenbecker, 235.
Betts v. Betts, 405.
Beuley v. Curtis, 146.

CASES CITED
Figures refer to pages

Beurhaus v. Cole, 108.
Beverley v. Miller, 482.
Bevis v. Heflin, 589.
Bewick, In re, 246.
Bibb v. Bibb, 396.
Bible v. Marshall, 493.
Biddle, Appeal of, 482.
Biddle Purchasing Co. v. Snyder, 465.
Bigelow v. Cady, 259.
Bigelow v. Tilden, 474.
Biggars, In re, 70, 73, 74, 76, 77.
Billinger, In re, 400.
Billings v. Billings, 571.
Billings v. Shaw, 206.
Billings v. Warren, 449.
Bills v. Pease, 265, 272, 289.
Binder's Estate, In re, 329.
Bingham v. National Bank of Montana, 180.
Binns v. La Forge, 153.
Bird v. Bird, 239.
Bird v. Merklee, 271.
Bird's Will, In re, 40.
Birdsall v. Coon, 37.
Birdsall v. Hewlett, 34.
Birely's Estate, 510.
Birge v. Nucomb, 56.
Birks v. McNeill, 420.
Birls v. Betty, 518.
Birmingham Trust & Savings Co. v. Ansley, 459.
Bisceglia v. Bisceglia, 173.
Bischoff v. Yorkville Bank, 581, 582, 585, 586, 587.
Biscoe v. State, 474.
Biscoe v. Thweatt, 275.
Bishop v. Bishop, 449.
Bishop v. Houghton, 497.
Bishop v. Seaman's Bank, 75, 76.
Bither v. Packard, 197.
Black v. Ligon, 406.
Blackburn v. Fitzgerald, 592.
Blackshear v. Burke, 382.
Blaha v. Borgman, 85.
Blair v. Commissioner of Internal Revenue, 142, 147.
Blair v. Hazzard, 392.
Blair v. Hill, 26, 551.
Blaisdell v. Stevens, 543.
Blake, In re, 308.
Blake v. Dexter, 56, 190.
Blake v. O'Neal, 140, 232, 233.
Blake v. Pegram, 478, 485.
Blakely, In re, 319.
Blakely v. Tisdale, 135.
Blakeshere v. Trustees, 58.
Blakeslee v. Starring, 197.
Blakley v. Hanberry, 614.

Blanchard v. Chapman, 61.
Blanchard v. Taylor's Heirs, 155.
Bland v. Talley, 202.
Blanton v. First Nat. Bank of Forrest City, 583.
Blasdel v. Locke, 178.
Blaul v. Dalton, 602.
Blauvelt's Estate, In re, 346, 362, 502.
Bliss v. Bliss, 63.
Bliss v. Linden Cemetery Ass'n, 285.
Bliven v. Bordon, 259.
Blodgett's Estate, In re, 482.
Bloodgood v. Massachusetts Ben. Life Ass'n, 429.
Bloom v. Ray, 420.
Bloom v. Wolfe, 398.
Bloomer, Appeal of, 575.
Blundell, In re, 279.
Blythe v. Kujawa, 561.
Boardman v. Mossman, 515.
Board of Assessors of City of Quincy v. Cunningham Foundation, 292.
Board of Charities & Corrections of City of Philadelphia v. Lockard, 162.
Board of Com'rs of Crawford County, Ohio, v. Patterson, 555.
Board of Com'rs of Crawford County, Ohio, v. Strawn, C.C.A.Ohio, 551, 554, 555.
Board of Domestic Missions of Reformed Church in America v. Mechanics' Sav. Bank, 70.
Board of Domestic Missions of Reformed Church in America v. Mechanics' Sav. Bank, 74.
Board of Education of City of Albuquerque v. School Dist. No. 5 of Bernalillo County, 272.
Board of Fire & Water Com'rs of City of Marquette v. Wilkinson, 551, 557.
Board of Trustees of M. E. Church South v. Odom, 98.
Board of Trustees of Schools for Industrial Education in City of Hoboken v. City of Hoboken, 113.
Bobb v. Bobb, 526.
Bodwell v. Nutter, 182.
Boenhardt v. Loch, 274.
Boerum v. Schenck, 333.
Bogard v. Planters' Bank & Trust Co., 575.
Bogert v. Perry, 150.
Bogert's Estate, In re, 373.
Bogle v. Bogle, 418.
Bohle v. Hasselbroch, 528.

CASES CITED
Figures refer to pages

Bohlen's Estate, In re, 323, 500.
Bohm v. Bohm, 196.
Boisseau v. Boisseau, 358
Bolick v. Cox, 286, 636.
Bolles v. State Trust Co., 118, 119.
Bolling v. Stokes, 427.
Bolognesi & Co., In re, 550.
Bond v. Lockwood, 205.
Bond v. Town of Tarboro, 402.
Bone v. Cook, 518.
Bone v. Hayes, 206, 461, 465.
Bonner v. Holland, 530.
Bonner v. Lessley, 572.
Boon v. Hall, 401.
Boone v. Clarke, 320.
Boone v. Davis, 143, 463, 488.
Booth, Appeal of, 538.
Booth v. Booth, 515.
Booth v. Bradford, 468, 469.
Booth v. Mason, 213.
Booth v. Oakland Bank of Savings, 68.
Booth v. Wilkinson, 347.
Boqua v. Marshall, 37.
Borchert v. Borchert, 500.
Boreing v. Faris, 120, 462, 463, 523.
Bork v. Martin, 84, 188.
Boskowitz v. Continental Ins. Co., 131.
Boskowitz v. Held, 399.
Bosler's Estate, In re, 478, 479, 524.
Boston v. Doyle, 321.
Boston Safe Deposit Co. v. Collier, 161.
Boston Safe Deposit & Trust Co. v. Luke, 146.
Bostwick-Gooddell Co. v. Wolff, 555.
Botsford v. Burr, 186.
Bottimore v. First & Merchants' Nat. Bank of Richmond, 642.
Botzum v. Havanna Nat. Bank, 645.
Boughman v. Boughman, 59.
Bouldin v. Alexander, 569.
Bourne v. Keane, 280.
Bourquin v. Bourquin, 326, 391, 471.
Bowden v. Brown, 126, 301.
Bowditch v. Andrew, 640.
Bowditch v. Banuelos, 416, 569.
Bowdoin College v. Merritt, 592.
Bowen, In re, 304.
Bowen v. Hughes, 182.
Bowker v. Pierce, 475.
Bowler v. Curler, 211.
Bowlin v. Citizens' Bank & Trust Co., 136, 160.
Bowling v. Scales, 569.
Bowman v. Anderson, 542.
Bowman v. First Nat. Bank, 24.

Bowman v. Long, 232.
Bowman v. Pinkham, 358.
Bowman v. Rainetaux, 511.
In Bowman v. Secular, Soc., Limited, 278.
Boyd v. Boyd, 603.
Boyd v. Hawkins, 333, 473.
Boyd v. Mutual Fire Ass'n of Eau Claire, 47.
Boyd v. Small, 146.
Boyd v. Winte, 174.
Boyd's Ex'rs v. Boyd's Heirs, 511.
Boydstun v. Jacobs, 609.
Boyer v. Decker, 426.
Boyer v. Libey, 534.
Boyer v. Sims, 421.
Boyes, In re, 223.
Boyle, In re, 572.
Boyle v. Northwestern Nat. Bank, 28, 581, 585.
Boyle's Estate, In re, 447, 448.
Boyle's Will, In re, 341.
Boynton v. Gale, 99.
Bozarth v. Watts, 631.
Brabrook v. Boston Five Cents Sav. Bank, 69, 75, 78.
Bracken v. Miller, 538.
Brackenbury v. Hodgkin, 87.
Brackett v. Middlesex Banking Co., 337.
Brackett v. Ostrander, 377.
Brackett v. Seavey, 573.
Brackin v. Newman, 618.
Bradford v. Blossom, 245.
Bradford v. Clayton, 468.
Bradford v. Eastman, 83.
Bradley v. Chesebrough, 561.
Bradley v. Hill, 265.
Bradley v. Merrill, 543.
Bradley Co. v. Bradley, 218.
Bradley's Estate, In re, 291.
Bradshaw v. Tasker, 277.
Bradstreet v. Everson, 26.
Bradstreet v. Kinsella, 631.
Bradwell v. Catchpole, 511.
Bragg v. Geddes, 174.
Brahmey v. Rollins, 159.
Brain v. Bailey, 146.
Brainard v. Commissioner of Internal Revenue, 109.
Branch v. Bulkley, 596.
Branch v. Griffin, 147.
Brandan v. McCurley, 105.
Brandau v. Greer, 211.
Brandon v. Carter, 126, 127.
Brandon v. Robinson, 159.
Brannin v. Brannin, 196.
Brannock v. Magoon, 93, 102.

CASES CITED

Figures refer to pages

Bransford Realty Co. v. Andrews, 427.
Braswell v. Downs, 126.
Braun v. First German Evangelical Lutheran Church, 88, 215.
Brawner v. Staup, 614.
Brearley School v. Ward, 156, 162.
Bredell v. Collier, 143.
Bredell v. Kerr, 425.
Breeden v. Moore, 232, 245.
Breedlove v. Stump, 138, 417.
Breid v. Mintrup, 375.
Breit v. Yeaton, 530.
Breitenbucher v. Oppenheim, 178, 182.
Bremer v. Hadley, 394.
Breneman v. Frank, 523.
Brennaman v. Schell, 172.
Brennan, Matter of, 69.
Brennan v. Tillinghast, 552.
Brennan v. Vogler, 137.
Brennan's Estate, In re, 478.
Brewer v. Slater, 51.
Brewster v. Brewster, 464.
Brewster v. Demarest, 355.
Brewster v. Striker, 627.
Brice v. Stokes, 515.
Brice v. Trustees of All Saints Memorial Chapel, 300.
Bridgeport-City Trust Co. v. First Nat. Bank & Trust Co. of Bridgeport, 456, 480.
Bridgeport Public Library and Reading Room v. Burroughs Home, 394, 636.
Bridgeport Trust Co. v. Bartholomew, 487.
Bridgeport Trust Co. v. Marsh, 432.
Briggs v. Central Nat. Bank of New York, 26.
Briggs v. Davis, 245.
Brigham v. Peter Bent Brigham Hospital, 306, 309, 312.
Brinckerhoff v. Wemple, 323.
Brindley v. Brindley, 215.
Brinkerhoff's Ex'rs v. Banta, 464.
Bristol v. Bristol, 191.
Bristol Baptist Church v. Connecticut Baptist Convention, 295.
Bristor v. Tasker, 623.
Bristow v. McCall, 150, 152.
British America El. Co. v. Bank of British N. A., 583.
Brittin v. Handy, 213.
Britton v. Lewis, 463.
Broadhurst v. Balguy, 513.
Broadrup v. Woodman, 190.
Broadway Nat. Bank v. Adams, 161, 163.

Broadway Nat. Bank v. Hayward, 567.
Brock v. Conkwright, 630, 631.
Brock v. Sawyer, 490.
Broder v. Conklin, 189, 204, 329, 618.
Brodie v. Skelton, 538.
Bromley v. Gardner, 534.
Bronson v. Strouse, 635.
Bronson v. Thompson, 151, 332.
Brook v. Chappell, 226.
Brooke, Appeal of, 128.
Brooke's Estate, In re, 470.
Brooker v. Brooker, 246.
Brooklyn Trust Co. v. Commissioner of Internal Revenue, 363.
Brookover v. Grimm, 246.
Brooks v. Brooks, 180.
Brooks v. City of Belfast, 303.
Brooks v. Davis, 161, 638.
Brooks v. Egbert, 473.
Brooks v. Fowler, 189.
Brooks v. Shelton, 182.
Brothers v. Brothers, 329, 331.
Brothers v. Porter, 530.
Broughton v. West, 107.
Broussard v. Mason, 48.
Brovan v. Kyle, 582.
Brown, In re, 449, 554, 557.
Brown v. Alexander, 176.
Brown v. Barngrover, 124.
Brown v. Berry, 412.
Brown v. Brown, 211, 239, 307, 394.
Brown v. Burdett, 135.
Brown v. Columbia Finance & Trust Co., 244.
Brown v. Cowell, 210, 332, 498, 502.
Brown v. Doane, 217.
Brown v. Fidelity Union Trust Co., 638.
Brown v. Fletcher, 147.
Brown v. Ford, 148.
Brown v. Hall, 232.
Brown v. Harris, 230.
Brown v. Hummel, 496.
Brown v. Kausche, 224.
Brown v. Kelsey, 122.
Brown v. Knapp, 34.
Brown v. Lambert's Adm'r, 199, 502.
Brown v. Mercantile Trust & Deposit Co., 625.
Brown v. Reeder, 232.
Brown v. Richter, 123.
Brown v. Ricks, 463.
Brown v. Shyne, 327.
Brown v. Silsby, 477.
Brown v. Spohr, 102, 557, 625.
Brown's Estate, In re, 272, 307.
Brown's Lessee v. Brown, 58.

CASES CITED
Figures refer to pages

Browne v. Browne, 226.
Browne's Estate, In re, 61.
Brownfield v. McFadden, 385.
Browning v. Fiklin's Adm'r, 633.
Bruce v. Faucett, 591.
Bruce v. Maxwell, 303.
Bruen v. Gillet, 322, 512.
Bruere v. Cook, 122.
Brumridge v. Brumridge, 511, 518.
Brundage v. Cheneworth, 237.
Brundage's Estate, In re, 297.
Bruner v. Finley, 599.
Brunnenmeyer v. Buhre, 295, 493.
Brunson v. Henry, 138.
Brush v. Smith, 477.
Brush v. Young, 425.
Bryan v. Aikin, 451.
Bryan v. Bigelow, 88, 222.
Bryan v. Coconut Grove Bank & Trust Co., 561.
Bryan v. Duncan, 210.
Bryan v. Hawthorne, 130.
Bryan v. Milby, 62.
Bryant v. Allen, 187.
Bryant v. Bryant, 200.
Brys v. Pratt, 498.
Buchanan v. Hart, 424.
Buchanan v. Kennard, 263, 270, 273.
Buchanan v. National Savings & Trust Co., 447.
Buchanan's Estate, In re, 461.
Buck v. Lockwood, 497.
Buck v. Pike, 176.
Buck v. Swazey, 147, 187.
Buck v. Voreis, 196.
Buck v. Walker, 249.
Buck v. Webb, 506.
Buckelew's Estate, In re, 340, 349.
Buckingham v. Clark, 226.
Buckle v. Marshall, 350.
Buckley v. Monck, 122, 277.
Bucknam v. Bucknam, 165.
Bucknell v. Johnson, 189.
Budd v. Walker, 29.
Buder v. Franz, 49.
Buell v. Gardner, 494.
Buffinton v. Maxam, 31, 36.
Buffum v. Town, 61.
Buford v. McCormick, 540.
Buist v. Williams, 558.
Bull v. Bull, 63.
Bull v. Odell, 118.
Bullard v. Attorney General, 130.
Bullard v. Chandler, 487.
Bullock, In re, 169.
Bullock v. Angleman, 489, 497.
Bulwinkle, In re, 71, 72, 75.
Bundy v. Bundy, 119, 120.

Bunn v. Winthrop, 94, 96.
Bunt, In re, 72.
Bunt, Matter of, 68.
Bunting v. Ricks, 543.
Burbach v. Burbach, 118.
Burbank v. Burbank, 493.
Burch v. Nicholson, 197, 614.
Burden v. Sheridan, 206.
Burdick v. Burdick, 255.
Burgess v. Wheate, 144.
Burgett v. Paxton, 535.
Burgoyne v. McKillip, 504.
Burke v. Burke, 107, 122, 280, 284, 287.
Burke v. Morris, 151, 153.
Burke v. O'Brien, 629.
Burke v. Roper, 262, 265.
Burke Grain Co. v. St.Paul-Mercury Indemnity Co., 199.
Burke's Estate, In re, 128.
Burks v. Burks, 53.
Burk's Estate, In re, 425.
Burleigh v. White, 181.
Burnes v. Burnes, 64.
Burnett v. Hawpe's Ex'r, 147.
Burney v. Spear, 475, 480.
Burnham, Petition of, 494.
Burnham v. Barth, 553, 558.
Burns v. Ross, 176.
Burr v. City of Boston, 292.
Burr v. McEwen, 474.
Burr's Ex'rs v. Smith, 270, 273.
Burrill v. Sheil, 366.
Burris v. Brooks, 501.
Burroughs v. Gaither, 402, 589.
Burt v. Wilson, 215.
Bush, Appeal of, 632.
Bush v. Bush, 145.
Bushe, In re, 483.
Bushe v. Wright, 333.
Busse v. Schenck, 321.
Bussell v. Wright, 643.
Butler v. Badger, 402.
Butler v. Builders Trust Co., 130, 456.
Butler v. Butler, 356, 574.
Butler v. Carpenter, 173.
Butler v. Godley, 116.
Butler v. Hyland, 211.
Butler v. Lawson, 499.
Butler v. Rutledge, 176.
Butler v. Taggart's Trustee, 129.
Butler v. Topkis, 407.
Butman v. Whipple, 332.
Butt v. McAlpine, 605.
Butterfield v. Butterfield, 182.
Buttles v. De Baun, 615.
Byington v. Moore, 205.
Bynum v. Bostick, 135.

CASES CITED
Figures refer to pages

Byrne v. Byrne, 558.
Byrne v. Jones, 331.
Byrne v. McGrath, 558.
Byrnes v. Commissioner of Internal Revenue, 165.
Byrnes v. Missouri Nat. Bank, 48.
Byrom v. Gunn, 549.
Byron Reed Co. v. Klabunde, 401.

C

Cable v. Cable, 591.
Cable v. St. Louis Marine Ry. & Dock Co., 38.
Cadieux v. Sears, 530.
Cady, In re, 572.
Cady v. Lincoln, 161, 589.
Cady's Estate, In re, 572.
Cagney v. O'Brien, 221.
Cahlan v. Bank of Lassen County, 99, 103.
Cain v. Cox, 543.
Calaveras Timber Co. v. Michigan Trust Co., 348.
Caldwell v. Graham, 322, 514, 519, 520.
Caldwell v. Hicks, 345.
Caldwell v. Williams, 94.
Calhoun v. Burnett, 497.
Calhoun v. King, 569.
Calkins v. Bump, 524.
Callis v. Ridout, 492.
Calvert v. Woods, 329.
Camden Safe Deposit & Trust Co. v. Guerin, 247, 640.
Camden Safe Deposit & Trust Co. v. Schellenger, 147, 161.
Cameron v. Hicks, 339.
Cameron v. Lewis, 196.
Camody v. Webster, 500.
Camp v. Presbyterian Soc. of Sackets Harbor, 298.
Camp v. Thompson, 237.
Campbell v. Campbell, 189, 330.
Campbell v. Mansfield, 434.
Campbell v. Miller, 346, 369.
Campbell v. Napier, 467, 523.
Campbell v. Noble, 175.
Campbell v. O'Neill, 604.
Campbell v. Virginia-Carolina Chemical Co., 589.
Campbell v. Weakley, 257.
Campbell-Kawannanakoa v. Campbell, 239.
Canada v. Daniel, 592, 616.
Canfield v. Security-First Nat. Bk. of Los Angeles, 163.
Cann v. Cann, 343.
Cannon v. Nicholas, 110.

Cannon v. Robinson, 379.
Canton Exchange Bank v. Zazoo County, 148.
Cantwell v. Crawley, 599, 601.
Cape v. Plymouth Congregational Church, 591.
Caple v. McCollum, 172.
Capuano v. Boghosian, 197.
Carcaba v. McNair, 578.
Cardwell v. Cheatham, 590.
Carley v. Graves, 561.
Carman v. Bumpus, 633.
Carmody's Estate, In re, 328.
Carnegie-Illinois Steel Corp. v. Berger, 32.
Carney v. Byron, 644.
Carney v. Kain, 643.
Carozza v. Boxley, 37.
Carpenter, Appeal of, 469.
Carpenter v. Arnett, 239.
Carpenter v. Carpenter, 204, 339.
Carpenter v. Cook, 238, 499.
Carpenter v. Kingham, 210.
Carpenter v. M. J. & M. & M., Consolidated, 604.
Carpenter v. Robinson, 543.
Carpenter's Estate, In re, 200, 275.
Carpenteria School Dist. v. Heath, 122.
Carr v. Bredenberg, 572, 573.
Carr v. Carr, 56, 72.
Carr v. Corning, 423.
Carr v. Hertz, 320.
Carr's Adm'r v. Morris, 502.
Carr's Estate, In re, 346, 470, 564.
Carrie v. Carnes, 534.
Carrier, Appeal of, 477.
Carrier v. Carrier, 249, 367.
Carrier v. Heather, 204.
Carroll v. Adams, 63.
Carroll v. Draughon, 542.
Carroll v. Smith, 488, 625.
Carruth v. Carruth, 120, 124.
Carson v. Carson, 134.
Carson v. Fuhs, 145, 146.
Carson v. Marshall, 329.
Carson v. Painter, 611.
Carson's Will, In re, 419.
Carstairs v. Bates, 23.
Carter v. Balfour Adm'r, 270, 272.
Carter v. Brownell, 456.
Carter v. Carter, 336.
Carter v. Gibson, 565.
Carter v. Strickland, 64.
Carter v. Uhlein, 492, 603.
Carter v. United Ins. Co., 38.
Carter v. Whitcomb, 262.
Cartmell v. Allard, 348.

CASES CITED
Figures refer to pages

Caruthers v. Williams, 181.
Cary v. Abbot, 299.
Cary v. Slead, 633.
Cary Library v. Bliss, 496.
Cary's Estate, In re, 425, 462.
Case v. Carroll, 204.
Case v. Goodman, 616.
Case v. Hasse, 122.
Casey v. Casey, 224.
Casgrain v. Hammond, 249, 252.
Cashion v. Bank of Arizona, 81.
Cass v. Cass, 462.
Cassagne v. Marvin, 240.
Cassels v. Finn, 226.
Cassels v. Vernon, 525.
Caswell's Will, In re, 408.
Cates v. Mayes, 423.
Catherwood v. Watson, 543.
Catlin, Matter of, 131.
Catron v. Scarritt Collegiate Institute, 272, 300.
Cauhape v. Barnes, 128.
Cavender v. Cavender, 343, 573.
Cavin v. Gleason, 29.
Cawthon v. Stearns Culver Lumber Co., 243.
Caylor v. Cooper, 323.
Cazzain v. Title Guarantee & Trust Co., 624.
Cearnes v. Irving, 497.
Cecil's Committee v. Cecil, 601.
Cecil's Trustee v. Robertson & Bro., 159.
Centennial & Memorial Ass'n of Valley Forge, In re, 261, 636.
Central Nat. Bank v. Connecticut Mut. Life Ins. Co., 28, 580.
Central Nat. Bank, Savings & Trust Co. v. Gilchrist, 40.
Central Trust Co. v. East Tennessee Land Co., 45.
Central Trust Co. v. Gaffney, 93.
Central Trust Co. v. Johnson, 477.
Central Trust Co. of Illinois v. Harvey, 426.
Central Trust Co. of New York v. Egleston, 252.
Central Trust Co. of New York v. Falck, 105.
Cetenich v. Fuvich, 604.
Chace v. Chapin, 546.
Chace v. Gardner, 84.
Chadwick v. Arnold, 202, 535.
Chadwick v. Chadwick, 603.
Chadwick v. Felt, 186.
Chadwick v. Perkins, 88.
Chalk v. Daggett, 180.
Chamberlain v. Chamberlain, 599.

Bogert Trusts 2d—42

Chamberlain v. Eddy, 489.
Chamberlain v. Stearns, 266.
Chamberlain v. Thompson, 57.
Chamberlayne v. Brockett, 305.
Chambers v. City of St. Louis, 270, 493.
Chambers v. Mauldin, 573.
Chambers v. Minchin, 511.
Champlin v. Champlin, 180.
Chancellor v. Ashby, 534.
Chancellor v. Chancellor, 347.
Chandler v. Chandler, 318.
Chandler v. Georgia Chemical Works, 215.
Chandler v. Lally, 601.
Chandler v. Riley, 213.
Chandler v. Roe, 197.
Chanslor v. Chanslor's Trustees, 205.
Chantland v. Midland Nat. Bank, 189.
Chapal, Matter of, 439.
Chapin v. School Dist. No. 2 in Winchester, 113.
Chaplin v. Givens, 125.
Chapman, In re, 572.
Chapman v. Abrahams, 181.
Chapman v. Hughes, 540, 587.
Chapman v. Newell, 113, 265, 285.
Chapman v. Whitsett, 224.
Chapman's Ex'r v. Chapman, 226.
Chappus v. Lucke, 131, 393.
Chapter House Circle of King's Daughters v. Hartford Nat. Bk. & Trust Co., 340.
Charles v. Dubose, 328.
Charter Oak Life Ins. Co. v. Gisborne, 606.
Chase v. Cartright, 612.
Chase v. Chase, 491, 599.
Chase v. Davis, 319.
Chase v. Dickey, 312.
Chase v. Perley, 499.
Chase v. Union Nat. Bank of Lowell, 454.
Chase Nat. Bank v. Tomagno, 625.
Chase Nat. Bank of City of New York v. Citizens Gas Co. of Indianapolis, 125.
Chase & Baker Co. v. Olmsted, 531, 548, 555, 558.
Chaves v. Myer, 530.
Cheney v. Langley, 462.
Cherbonnier v. Bussey, 628.
Cherry v. Cape Fear Power Co., 147.
Cherry v. Greene, 394.
Cherry v. Richardson, 632.
Chew v. Commissioners of Southwark, 422.

CASES CITED
Figures refer to pages

Chew v. First Presbyterian Church of Wilmington, 307.
Chew v. Sheldon, 36.
Cheyney v. Geary, 140.
Chicago Title & Trust Co. v. Rogers Park Apartments Bldg. Corp., 570.
Chicago Title & Trust Co. v. Suter, 51.
Chicago Title & Trust Co. v. Zinser, 323, 324.
Chilcott v. Hart, 243.
Childs v. Childs, 399.
Childs v. Gross, 619.
Childs v. Waite, 120.
Chilvers v. Race, 97.
Chippewa Indians of Minnesota v. United States, 136.
Chirurg v. Ames, 465, 596.
Chisolm v. Hamersley, 475.
Choctaw, O. & G. R. Co. v. Sittel, 465.
Cholmondeley v. Clinton, 607.
Christian v. Yancey, 126, 127.
Christian Moerlein Brewing Co., v. Rusch, 83.
Christopher v. Mungen, 123.
Christ's Hospital v. Budgin, 175.
Christ's Hospital v. Grainger, 306.
Church v. Church, 538.
Church v. Ruland, 224, 538.
Church of St. Stanislaus v. Algemeine Verein, 189.
C. H. Venner Co. v. Central Trust Co. of New York, 604.
Ciffo v. Ciffo, 179.
Citizens' Bank of Parker v. Shaw, 545.
Citizens' Bank of Paso Robles v. Rucker, 528.
Citizens' Loan & Trust Co. v. Herron, 56.
Citizens' Nat. Bank v. Jefferson, 343.
Citizens' Nat. Bank v. Watkins, 140.
Citizens' Nat. Bank of Danville, Ky., v. Haynes, 24.
City Bank v. Maulson, 511, 514.
City Bank Farmers' Trust Co. v. Kennard, 165.
City Bank Farmers' Trust Co. v. Smith, 487.
City Bank of Dowagiac, In re, 551.
City Council of Augusta v. Walton, 425.
City of Bangor v. Beal, 356.
City of Bangor v. Peirce, 391.
City of Boston v. Dolan, 119.
City of Boston v. Robbins, 320.

City of Boston v. Santosuosso, 197.
City of Boston v. Turner, 99.
City of Chicago v. Tribune Co., 328.
City of Fulton v. Home Trust Co., 30.
City of Lincoln v. Morrison, 504, 522, 552, 557.
City of Marquette v. Wilkinson, 4, 99.
City of Minneapolis v. Canterbury, 206.
City of Richmond v. Davis, 315.
City of St. Louis v. McAllister, 299.
City of St. Louis v. Wenneker, 569.
City of St. Paul v. Seymour, 504.
City of Sturgis v. Meade County Bank, 20.
Claflin v. Claflin, 643, 644, 645.
Claflin Co. v. King, 124.
Clagett v. Worthington, 498, 576.
Claiborne v. Holland, 542.
Clapp v. Vatcher, 523.
Clark, Appeal of, 233.
Clark v. Anderson, 327, 468, 478, 484, 565, 572.
Clark v. Baker, 136.
Clark v. Beers, 350.
Clark v. Brown, 490.
Clark v. Clark, 68, 75, 367, 372, 416, 481, 609.
Clark v. Crego, 491.
Clark v. Creswell, 179.
Clark v. Fleischmann, 393.
Clark v. Frazier, 108, 187.
Clark v. Halligan, 283.
Clark v. Law, 595.
Clark v. McCue, 190.
Clark v. Maguire, 315.
Clark v. Oliver, 636.
Clark v. Platt, 473.
Clark v. Rainey, 534.
Clark v. St. Louis A. & T. H. R. Co., 366.
Clark v. Stanfield, 243.
Clark v. Timmons, 504.
Clark v. Trindle, 614.
Clark v. Union County Trust Co., 246.
Clark v. Wilson, 423.
Clark Sparks & Sons Mule & Horse Co. v. Americus Nat. Bank, 551.
Clark's Appeal, 512.
Clark's Will, In re, 327, 347, 371.
Clarke, In re, 136, 289.
Clarke v. Boorman, 609.
Clarke v. Deveaux, 329, 491, 497.
Clarke v. Inhabitants of Andover, 427.
Clarke v. Saxon, 115, 128.

BOGERT TRUSTS 2D

CASES CITED
Figures refer to pages

Clarke v. Sisters of Society of the Holy Child Jesus, 56.
Clarke v. Windham, 151.
Clarkson v. De Peyster, 205.
Clary v. Spain, 115, 180.
Clausen v. Jones, 573.
Clay v. Clay's Guardian, 189.
Clay v. Wood, 64.
Clay's Adm'r v. Edwards' Trustee, 418.
Clayton v. Hallett, 112, 273.
Clayton's Case, 549.
Cleland v. Waters, 135.
Clemens v. Caldwell, 525, 571.
Clemens v. Heckscher, 395, 541.
Clement v. Brainard, 525.
Clement v. Hyde, 287.
Clemmons v. Cox, 534.
Clermontel's Estate, In re, 369.
Clester v. Clester, 195, 197.
Cleveland v. Hallett, 123.
Cleveland v. Hampden Savings Bank, 67, 70.
Cleveland Trust Co. v. White, 91.
Cleven's Estate, In re, 423.
Clews v. Jamieson, 496.
Cliff v. Cliff, 602, 614.
Clifford, In re, 293.
Clifford v. Farmer, 530.
Clifford Banking Co. v. Donovan Commission Co., 498.
Clopton v. Gholson, 382.
Close v. Farmers' Loan & Trust Co., 576.
Close's Estate, In re, 273.
Cloud v. Calhoun, 126, 138.
Clowser v. Noland, 183.
Clute v. Barron, 329.
Clyne, In re, 462.
Coate, Appeal of, 63.
Coates v. Lunt, 126.
Cobb v. Fant, 478.
Cobb v. Gramatan Nat. Bk. & Tr. Co., 345.
Cobb v. Knight, 530.
Coble v. Nonemaker, 535.
Cobleigh v. Matheny, 45.
Coburn v. Page, 532.
Cochran v. O'Hern, 145.
Cochrane v. Schell, 240.
Cocks v. Barlow, 118, 595.
Cocks v. Haviland, 515.
Codman v. Brigham, 309.
Codman v. Krell, 239.
Coe v. Beckwith, 487.
Coe v. Coe, 179.
Coe v. Turner, 500.
Coe v. Washington Mills, 265.

Coffey v. Sullivan, 174.
Coffin v. Attorney General, 276.
Coffin v. Bramlitt, 347.
Coffin v. McIntosh, 173.
Cogan v. McCabe, 464.
Cogbill v. Boyd, 332, 502, 524.
Coggeshall v. Coggeshall, 43.
Coggeshall v. Pelton, 291.
Cogswell v. Weston, 455.
Cohen v. Mainthow, 489.
Cohn v. McClintock, 41.
Cohn v. Ward, 571.
Colburn v. Grant, 510.
Colburn v. Hodgdon, 39.
Colby v. Riggs, 586.
Estate of Cole, In re, 456.
Cole v. City of Watertown, 424.
Cole v. Cole, 550, 555.
Cole v. Fickett, 198.
Cole v. Nickel, 642.
Cole v. Noble, 614.
Cole v. Thompson, 534.
Cole's Estate, In re, 409.
Colegrove's Estate, In re, 249.
Coleman, In re, 148, 167.
Coleman v. Bucks & Oxon Union Bank, 581, 585.
Coleman v. Coleman, 239, 646.
Coleman v. Connolly, 324.
Coleman v. Davis, 609.
Coleman v. Dickenson, 16.
Coleman v. McGrew, 489.
Coleman v. O'Leary's Ex'r, 280.
Coleman's Estate, In re, 113, 265, 290, 307.
Colesbury v. Dart, 589.
Colladay's Estate, In re, 466.
Collar v. Collar, 499.
Collector of Taxes of Norton v. Oldfield, 285, 291, 309.
College of Charleston v. Willingham, 474.
Collier v. Blake, 422.
Collier v. Lindley, 288.
Collins v. Collins, 174.
Collins v. Gooch, 355, 360.
Collins v. Lewis, 549.
Collister v. Fassitt, 63, 412.
Colmary v. Fanning, 55.
Colonial Trust Co. v. Brown, 407.
Colquitt v. Howard, 46.
Colt v. Colt, 40.
Colt v. Duggan, 456.
Coltman v. Moore, 640.
Colton v. Colton, 63.
Colton v. Stanford, 463.
Colton Imp. Co. v. Richter, 46, 206.
Columbia Trust Co., In re, 629.

CASES CITED
Figures refer to pages

Colvin v. Martin, 136.
Comby v. McMichael, 632.
Comegys v. State, 524, 576.
Comingor v. Louisville Trust Co., 481.
Commercial Bank, In re, 25.
Commercial Merchants' Nat. Bank & Trust Co. v. Kloth, 207.
Commercial Nat. Bank v. Armstrong, 22, 26.
Commercial & Farmers' Bank of Raleigh v. Vass, 87.
Commercial & Farmers' Nat. Bank of Baltimore v. Davis, 24.
Commissioner of Internal Revenue v. Allen, 106.
Commissioner of Internal Revenue v. McIlvaine, 109.
Commissioner of Internal Revenue v. Smiley, 34.
Commissioners of Sinking Fund v. Walker, 105.
Commonwealth v. Allen, 575, 576.
Commonwealth v. Bank of Pennsylvania, 489.
Commonwealth v. Barnitz, 428.
Commonwealth v. Clark, 618.
Commonwealth v. Fidelity & Deposit Co. of Maryland, 576, 577.
Commonwealth v. Levi, 527.
Commonwealth v. Louisville Public Library, 230, 232.
Commonwealth v. Naile, 144.
Commonwealth v. Tradesmen's Trust Co., 557.
Commonwealth Trust Co. of Pittsburgh, Appeal of, 354.
Compher v. Browning, 473.
Conant v. Wright, 462.
Conaway v. Third Nat. Bank of Cincinnati, 420.
Condit v. Bigalow, 543.
Condit v. Maxwell, 468, 543.
Condit v. Reynold, 57.
Cone v. Cone, 426.
Cone v. Wold, 635.
Congdon v. Cahoon, 497.
Conger v. Conger, 475.
Congregational Society and Church in Newington v. Town of Newington, 609.
Congregational Unitarian Soc. v. Hale, 277.
Connally v. Lyons, 375.
Connecticut College for Women v. Calvert, 286.
Connecticut Mut. Life Ins. Co. v. Stinson, 332.
Connecticut River Savings Bank v. Albee's Estate, 68, 69, 72, 73, 74, 79.
Connecticut Trust & Safe Deposit Co. v. Hollister, 255.
Conner v. Tuck, 540.
Connolly v. Hammond, 333.
Connolly v. Leonard, 336, 487.
Conover v. Fisher, 412.
Conover v. Stothoff, 589.
Conrad, Ex parte, 128.
Constant v. Matteson, 473.
Consterdine v. Consterdine, 510.
Contee v. Dawson, 369.
Continental Nat. Bank v. Weems, 25, 551, 558.
Continental Oil & Cotton Co. v. E. Van Winkle Gin & Machine Works, 37.
Converse v. Noyes, 147.
Conway v. Third Nat. Bk. & Tr. Co. of Camden, 309.
Cook v. Barr, 88.
Cook v. Blazis, 178.
Cook v. Doggett, 217.
Cook v. Elmore, 618.
Cook v. Gilmore, 473.
Cook v. Lowry, 469, 526.
Cook v. Stockwell, 480.
Cook's Trust Estate, In re, 350.
Cooke v. Platt, 240.
Cooley v. Gilliam, 607.
Cooley v. Kelley, 319.
Cooley v. Miller, 208.
Cooney v. Glynn, 603.
Coons v. Tome, 47.
Cooper, In re, 470.
Cooper v. Cockrum, 491.
Cooper v. Cooper, 608, 614.
Cooper v. Day, 491, 502, 571, 574.
Cooper v. Harvey, 395.
Cooper v. Landis, 530.
Cooper v. Lee, 615.
Cooper v. McClun, 490.
Copeland v. Bruning, 150, 332.
Copeland v. Mercantile Ins. Co., 42.
Copeland v. Summers, 125.
Coram v. Davis, 640.
Corbett v. Hospelhorn, 30.
Corby v. Corby, 62.
Cordon v. Gregg, 143.
Corin v. Glenwood Cemetery, 285.
Corle, In re, 245.
Corlies v. Corlies' Ex'rs, 573.
Corn v. Sims, 535, 536.
Corn Exch. Bank v. Manhattan Sav. Inst'n, 581.
Cornelison v. Roberts, 98.

CASES CITED
Figures refer to pages

Cornell University v. Fiske, 312.
Cornet v. Cornet, 330, 346, 355, 470, 522, 526.
Cornett v. West, 321, 572.
Cornils' Estate, In re 633.
Cornwell v. Orton, 140.
Cornwell v. Wulff, 629.
Corr, Appeal of, 614.
Corse v. Leggett, 88.
Cosgrove's Will, In re, 466.
Costello v. Costello, 326, 357, 466.
Costen, Appeal of, 332.
Coster v. Coster, 426, 429.
Coster v. Lorillard, 249, 252.
Cottam v. Eastern Counties Ry. Co., 509.
Cotting v. Berry, 559.
Cottman v. Grace, 271.
Cotton v. Courtright, 378.
Cotton v. Graham, 473.
Cotton v. Rand, 334.
Coudon v. Updegraff, 40, 125, 130, 425, 451.
Coughlin v. Farmers & Mechanics Sav. Bank, 91.
Coughlin v. Seago, 631.
Coulson v. Alpaugh, 62.
County Commissioners of Frederick County v. Page, 550.
Court v. Bankers' Trust Co., 624.
Covey v. Cannon, 551, 552, 554, 555.
Cowan v. Henika, 132.
Cowan v. Storms, 156.
Cowan v. Union Trust Co. of San Francisco, 601.
Cowan v. Withrow, 587.
Cowee v. Cornell, 212.
Cowell v. Gatcombe, 511.
Cowles v. Cowles, 176.
Cowles v. Mathews, 61.
Cox v. Arnsmann, 124.
Cox v. Barber, 542.
Cox v. Brown, 600, 603.
Cox v. Cox, 626.
Cox v. Shelby County Trust Co., 319.
Cox v. Walker, 320.
Cox v. Wills, 62.
Cox's Lessee v. Grant, 16.
Coxe v. Blanden, 394.
Coxe v. Carson, 604.
Coxe v. Kriebel, 322, 490.
Coyne v. Plume, 151.
Cozzens, In re, 100.
Cozzens' Estate, In re, 514, 516, 520.
Crabb v. Young, 519.
Crackanthorpe v. Sickles, 624.
Craig v. Craig, 416, 418.
Craig v. Hone, 118.

Craig v. Leslie, 395.
Cram v. Walker, 624.
Cramer v. Hoose, 183.
Crandall v. Hoysradt, 36.
Crane v. Hearn, 322, 339, 516.
Crane v. Moses, 341, 344, 576.
Crane's Estate, In re, 468.
Crane's Will, In re, 65.
Crate v. Benzinger, 377.
Crawford, In re, 571.
Crawford v. Creswell, 129.
Crawford v. El Paso Land Imp. Co., 392.
Crawford v. Manson, 181, 187.
Crawford v. Mound Grove Cemetery Ass'n, 108.
Crawford v. Nies, 494.
Crawford's Estate, In re, 122.
Cree v. Lewis, 522, 523.
Creed v. McAleer, 348, 372, 449, 503.
Creed v. President, etc., of Lancaster Bank, 176.
Crerar v. Williams, 305.
Cresap v. Brown, 420, 502, 523.
Cresson, Appeal of, 113, 292.
Cresson v. Cresson, 290.
Crickard's Ex'r v. Crickard's Legatees, 121.
Crinkley v. Rogers, 224.
Crissman v. Crissman, 59.
Crittenden v. Dorn, 612.
Crocheron v. Savage, 209.
Crockett v. Crockett, 215.
Cromey v. Bull, 366.
Cromwell v. Norton, 215.
Cronheim v. Postal Telegraph-Cable Co., 24.
Crooke v. County of Kings, 140.
Crooker v. Rogers, 498.
Crop v. Norton, 184.
Cropsey v. Johnston, 356.
Crosby v. Davis, 146.
Cross, Appeal of, 182, 505, 557.
Cross v. Petree, 336, 502.
Cross v. United States Trust Co. of New York, 239.
Crouse-Prouty v. Rogers, 534.
Crow ex rel. Jones v. Clay County, 264, 287.
Crowe v. Craig, 514.
Crowley v. Crowley, 57, 180, 613.
Crown Co. v. Cohn, 393, 398.
Croyle v. Guelich, 37.
Cruger v. Halliday, 417.
Cruger v. Jones, 402.
Cruger v. Union Trust Co. of New York, 624.
Cruit v. Owen, 424.

CASES CITED
Figures refer to pages

Crum v. Moore's Adm'r, 489.
Crumrine v. Crumrine, 530.
Cruse v. Axtell, 120, 424.
Cruse v. Kidd, 611.
Crutchfield v. Haynes, 564.
Culbertson v. Matson, 492.
Cully v. People, to Use of Dunlap, 577.
Culp v. Price, 173.
Culpeper Nat. Bank v. Wrenn, 622.
Culross v. Gibbons, 238.
Culver v. Avery, 196.
Culver v. Culver, 629.
Culver v. Lompoc Valley Sav. Bank, 72, 122.
Cumberland Coal & Iron Co. v. Parish, 46.
Cunniff v. McDonnell, 137, 381.
Cunningham v. Bright, 164, 234, 637.
Cunningham v. Cunningham, 326, 467.
Cunningham v. Davenport, 69, 74, 75, 77.
Cunningham v. Fraize, 462.
Cunningham v. Pettigrew, 197.
Cunningham v. Wood, 150.
Cunningham's Estate, In re, 154.
Curd's Trustee v. Curd, 244.
Curdy v. Berton, 221, 224.
Curlett v. Emmons, 468.
Curling's Adm'rs v. Curling's Heirs, 286.
Curran v. Green, 573.
Currie v. Look, 189, 197.
Currier v. Studley, 614.
Curtis v. Brewer, 534.
Curtis v. Lakin, 601.
Curtis v. Mason, 515.
Curtis v. Osborn, 443.
Curtis' Estate, In re, 286.
Curtiss, In re, 418, 484.
Cushing v. Blake, 145, 146.
Cushman v. Cushman, 574.
Cushman v. Goodwin, 557.
Cushney v. Henry, 127.
Cutbush v. Cutbush, 382.
Cuthbert v. Robarts, Lubbock & Co., 580.
Cutler v. Tuttle, 185.
Cutler v. Winberry, 231, 241.
Cutter v. American Trust Co., 621.
Cutter v. Hardy, 628.
Cutting, In re, 418.

D

Da Costa v. De Pas, 299.
Dailey v. City of New Haven, 122, 124, 425.
Dailey v. Kinsler, 215.
Dailey v. Wight, 573.
Dale v. Guaranty Trust Co., 645.
Daley v. Daley, 127.
Dallas Art League v. Weaver, 396.
Dalrymple v. Security Loan & Trust Co., 124.
Daly v. Bernstein, 125.
Daly v. Butchers' & Drovers' Bank, 25.
Daly's Estate, In re, 290.
Dalzell v. Dalzell, 189.
Dameron v. Gold, 591.
Dammert v. Osborn, 239.
Dana v. Bank of United States, 105.
Danford, In re, 208.
Danforth v. City of Oshkosh, 116, 249, 271, 307.
Daniel v. Wade, 114.
Danner v. Trescot, 146.
D'Arcy v. Blake, 145.
Darcy v. Kelley, 122, 264.
Darling v. Potts, 523.
Darling v. Witherbee, 232.
Darling's Ex'r v. Cumming, 478.
Darlington's Estate, 506.
Darnaby v. Watts, 516, 589.
Dashiell v. Attorney General, 269.
Dashiell's Estate, In re, 435.
Daugherty v. Daugherty, 498.
Davenport v. Stephens, 124.
Davidson v. Davidson, 607.
Davidson v. I. M. Davidson Real Estate & Investment Co., 332.
Davies v. Harrison, 165.
Davies v. Otty, 215.
Davies' Estate, In re, 130.
Davis, Appeal of, 348, 358, 367.
Davis, Matter of, 70, 76, 77.
Davis v. Coburn, 497.
Davis v. Davis Trust Co., 347.
Davis v. Dickerson, 498.
Davis v. Downer, 173, 544, 598.
Davis v. Freeman, 589.
Davis v. Goodman, 638.
Davis v. Harman, 326.
Davis v. Harrison, Hawaii, 148, 405.
Davis v. Hendrix, 543.
Davis v. Heppert, 140.
Davis v. Hoffman, 502.
Davis v. Jackson, 448.
Davis v. Las Ovas Co., 206.
Davis v. Rossi, 91.
Davis v. Settle, 197.
Davis v. Simpson, 333.
Davis v. Stambaugh, 215.
Davis v. Ward, 545.
Davis v. Williams, 245.

CASES CITED
Figures refer to pages

Davis v. Wright, 328.
Davis' Estate, In re, 132, 465.
Davison v. Wyman, 132.
Dawson v. Copeland, 208.
Dawson v. Ramser, 589.
Day v. Devitt, 213.
Day v. Roth, 83.
Day v. Wright, 208.
Dayton v. Phillips, 245.
Dayton v. Stewart, 125.
Deacon v. Cobson, 61.
Deaderick v. Cantrell, 504, 507, 515.
Deal v. Wachovia Bank & Trust Co., 642.
Dean, In re, 135, 291.
Dean v. Anderson, 535.
Dean v. Long, 541.
Dean v. Northern Trust Co., 425.
Deare, In re, 503.
Dearing v. Selvey, 595, 646.
Deaven's Estate, In re, 129.
De Bardelaben v. Stoudenmire, 607.
De Bevoise v. Sandford, 627.
De Bruler v. Ferguson, 289.
De Camp v. Dobbins, 113, 266, 267.
De Caters v. Le Ray De Chaumont, 332.
Decker v. Directors of Poor, 152.
Decker v. Gardner, 49.
Decker v. Union Dime Sav. Inst., 70, 73.
Decker v. Vreeland, 307.
Decouche v. Savetier, 606.
Dee v. Dee, 36.
Deen v. Cozzens, 571.
Deering v. Pierce, 462, 631.
Deering Harvester Co. v. Keifer, 561.
Deese v. Deese, 180.
Defrees v. Brydon, 123.
Dehaven v. Sterrit, 181.
De Hierapolis v. Reilly, 546.
De Jarnette v. De Jarnette, 502.
De Kay v. Hackensack Water Co., 592.
De Koven v. Alsop, 449, 454.
DeLadson v. Crawford, 643.
Delafield v. Barret, 350.
De Lashmutt v. Teetor, 319.
De Laurencel v. De Boom, 224, 226.
Delkin v. McDuffie, 604.
Delmoe v. Long, 602, 605.
Delvol v. Citizen's Bank, 85.
De Mallagh v. De Mallagh, 196.
Denegre v. Walker, 405, 408.
Denis' Estate, In re, 238.
Denmead v. Denmead, 480.
Dennis v. Dennis, 369.
Dennison v. Barney, 616.

Dennison v. Goehring, 92, 95.
Denniston v. Pierce, 118.
Denton v. McKenzie, 88, 213.
Denton v. Sanford, 361.
Denton's Guardians v. Denton's Ex'rs, 591.
Deobold v. Oppermann, 355.
Depau v. Moses, 489.
De Peyster v. Clendening, 428.
D'Epinoix's Settlement, In re, 366.
Derbishire v. Home, 510.
De Roboam v. Schmidtlin, 176.
Derry v. Derry, 187, 544.
De Rousse v. Williams, 152, 153, 164.
De Rycke's Will, In re, 232.
De Silver's Estate, In re, 122.
Des Moines Ins. Co. v. McIntire, 115.
Detwiler v. Detwiler, 180.
Detwiller v. Hartman, 283, 294.
Deutsche Presbyterische Kirche v. Trustees of Presbytery of Elizabeth, 174.
Deval v. Farris, 213.
De Vaughn v. Hays, 640.
Develon's Estate, 439.
Devilbiss v. Bennett, 473.
Devin v. McCoy, 161.
Devlin v. Hinman, 69, 73, 77.
Devoe v. Lutz, 493.
De Vol v. Citizens' Bank, 29.
Devol v. Dye, 138.
Dewey v. Commercial State Bank, 31.
Dewey v. Long, 150.
Dewey's Estate, In re, 61.
Dexter, Appeal of, 469.
Dexter v. Cotting, 129, 427.
Dexter v. Evans, 63.
Dexter v. Gardner, 311.
Dexter v. Phillips, 432.
Dexter v. President, etc., of Harvard College, 286.
D'Happart's Estate, In re, 346.
Dial v. Dial, 642.
Dibrell v. Carlisle, 146.
Dickel v. Smith, 197.
Dicken v. McKinlay, 201.
Dickenson v. City of Anna, 270.
Dickerson v. Smith, 571.
Dickinson v. Davis, 179.
Dickinson, Appellant, 358.
Dickinson's Estate, In re, 373.
Dickison v. Ogden's Ex'r, 152.
Dickson v. Montgomery, 300.
Dickson v. Stewart, 213.
Dietrich v. O'Brien, 48.
Dietz, In re, 425.
Diffenderffer v. Winder, 327, 481, 526.

CASES CITED
Figures refer to pages

Dill v. McGehee, 464.
Dillard v. Dillard, 320.
Dillard v. Winn, 418.
Dillingham v. Martin, 319.
Dillivan v. German Sav. Bank, Iowa, 326, 461.
Dillon v. Connecticut Mut. Life Ins. Co., 28.
Dillon v. Farley, 534.
Dillon v. Reilly, 280.
Dillwyn v. Llewellyn, 94.
Dilworth's Lessee v. Sinderling, 468, 469.
Dime Savings & Trust Co. v. Watson, 243, 247.
Dimmick v. Rosenfield, 124.
Dimond's Estate, In re, 475.
Dingman v. Beall, 41.
Dingman v. Boyle, 320.
Disbrow v. Disbrow, 409, 456, 475, 572.
Disston v. Board of Trustees of Internal Improvement Fund, 235.
Dix v. Burford, 518.
Dixon v. Helena Soc. of Free Methodist Church of North America, 36.
Doane's Ex'r v. Doane, 146.
Dockray v. Mason, 152.
Doctor v. Hughes, 625.
Dodge v. Black, 532.
Dodge v. Dodge, 126, 318, 426, 641.
Dodge v. Williams, 272.
Dodson v. Ashley, 394.
Dodson v. Ball, 633.
Doe v. Knight, 96.
Doe v. Roe, 424.
Doggett v. Hart, 591.
Doheny v. Lacy, 212.
Dohms v. Mann, 211.
Dolben v. Gleason, 378.
Doll v. Doll, 181.
Doll v. Gifford, 179.
Dolph v. Cross, 29.
Dominy v. Stanley, 295.
Donahue v. Quackenbush, 617.
Donaldson v. Allen, 640.
Donaldson v. Eaton & Estes, 208.
Donlin v. Bradley, 174.
Donnelly's Estate, 512.
Donohue, In re, 343.
Donovan v. Driscoll, 617.
Donovan v. Griffith, 145.
Donovan v. Major, 413.
Doom v. Brown, 213.
Doom v. Howard, 478.
Doran v. Kennedy, 143.
Doremus v. Doremus, 534.

Dorenkamp v. Dorenkamp, 500.
Dorman v. Balestier, 623.
Dorman v. Dorman, 603.
Dorr v. Wainwright, 120.
Dorrance v. Greene, 393.
Dorrance's Estate, In re, 478.
Dorsett v. Houlihan, 477.
Dorsey v. Thompson, 572.
Dorsey's Ex'rs v. Dorsey's Adm'r, 16, 524.
Dorsey's Lessee v. Garey, 497.
Doscher v. Wyckoff, 117, 589.
Dougherty v. Dougherty, 68.
Doughten v. Vandever, 272, 293.
Douglas, In re, 290.
Douglas v. Cruger, 626.
Douglas Properties v. Stix, 419.
Douthitt v. Stinson, 114.
Dover v. Denne, 518, 519.
Dowd v. Tucker, 226.
Dowland v. Staley, 2.
Downard v. Hadley, 205.
Downer v. Downer, 462.
Downey Co. v. 282 Beacon St. Trust, 376, 381, 385.
Downing v. Marshall, 241.
Downs v. Downs' Ex'r, 500.
Downs v. Security Trust Co., 622, 643.
Dowse v. Gorton, 384.
Doyle v. Doyle, 180, 603, 614.
Drake v. Crane, 368.
Drake v. Price, 41.
Drake v. Wild, 607.
Drane v. Gunter, 418.
Draper v. Montgomery, 322.
Drees v. Gosling, 189.
Dreier's Estate, In re, 348, 372, 468, 503.
Drennan v. Agurs, 284.
Drennen v. Heard, 146.
Dresser v. Dresser, 128.
Drinkhouse v. German Savings & Loan Soc., 57, 72.
Drudge v. Citizens' Bank of Akron, 2.
Druker v. Druker, 185.
Drummond, In re 136.
Drury v. Inhabitants of Natick, 128.
Dryden v. Hanway, 181.
Dry Dock Co. v. Stillman, 241.
D. Sullivan & Co. v. Ramsey, 564.
Dubs v. Dubs, 145.
Duckett v. National Bank of Baltimore, 502, 579, 583, 587.
Duckworth v. Ocean Steamship Co., 321, 519.
Duclos v. Benner, 435.
Dudley v. Bachelder, 183.

Duff v. Randall, 536.
Duffill's Estate, In re, 451.
Dufford's Ex'r v. Smith, 355, 465, 481.
Duffy, In re, 71, 75.
Duffy v. Calvert, 589.
Dufour v. Weissberger, 603.
Dugan v. Vattier, 535, 536.
Duggan v. Slocum, 296, 309.
Duke of Beaufort v. Berty, 44.
Dulin v. Moore, 246.
Dulles' Estate, In re, 266.
Duly v. Duly, 107.
Dumesnil v. Reeves, 110.
Duncan v. Jaudon, 540, 541.
Duncan Townsite Co. v. Lane, 536.
Duncanson v. Lill, 143.
Dunephant v. Dickson, 161.
Dunham v. Armitage, 90.
Dunham v. City of Lowell, 390.
Dunham v. Siglin, 557.
Dunkerson v. Goldberg, 140.
Dunn v. Dunn, 340, 502, 615, 628.
Dunn v. Morse, 333.
Dunn v. Zwilling, 215.
Dunn's Estate, In re, 499.
Dunne v. Cooke, 484.
Dunnett v. First Nat. Bank & Trust Co. of Tulsa, 645.
Dunning v. Ocean Nat. Bank of City of New York, 428.
Dunscomb v. Dunscomb, 128.
Dunshee v. Goldbacher, 58.
Du Pont v. Du Pont, 624.
Dupont v. Jonet, 83.
Du Puy v. Standard Mineral Co., 416.
Durand, In re, 56.
Durand v. Gray, 153.
Durant v. Muller, 140.
Durant v. Ritchie, 105.
Durant Lumber Co. v. Sinclair & Simms Lumber Co., 37.
Durel, In re, 39.
Durfee, In re, 570.
Durfee v. Pavitt, 189.
Durst v. Daugherty, 537.
Duval, Appeal of, 476.
Duwe's Estate, In re, 138.
Dwinel v. Veazie, 627.
Dwyer v. Cahill, 425.
Dyer, Appeal of, 88, 132.
Dyer, In re, 246.
Dyer v. Dyer, 176.
Dyer v. Leach, 427.
Dyer v. Riley, 510.
Dyer v. Waters, 463.
Dyett v. Central Trust Co., 230.

Dykeman v. Jenkines, 113, 122, 289, 307.
Dykes v. McVay, 395.

E

Eadie v. Hamilton, 84, 213.
Eagan v. Mahoney, 592.
Eagle Mining & Imp. Co. v. Hamilton, 80.
Eakle v. Ingram, 641.
Earhart v. Churchill Co., 618.
Earle v. Bryant, 618.
Earle v. Earle, 324, 511.
Earll v. Picken, 51.
Early v. Arnold, 133.
Earnshaw, In re, 427.
Earp, Appeal of, 446, 452.
Easterbrooks v. Tillinghast, 296.
Easterly v. Keney, 156.
Eastland v. Jordan, 155.
Easton v. Demuth, 134, 643.
Easton's Estate, In re, 166.
East River Sav. Bank v. Samuels, 404.
Eastwick's Estate, In re, 452.
Eaton v. Barnes, 53.
Eaton v. Tillinghast, 493.
Eaton v. Watts, 61.
Eaton's Estate, In re, 191.
Eberhardt v. Perolin, 62.
Eccles v. Rhode Island Hospital Trust Co., 120, 289.
Eckerson v. McCulloh, 213.
Eckert v. Eckert, 179.
Eckford v. De Kay, 358.
Eddy's Will, Matter of, 456.
Edgerly v. Edgerly, 179.
Edmonds v. Crenshaw, 512.
Edson v. Bartow, 225, 226.
Edwards v. Barstow, 148.
Edwards v. Culberson, 197.
Edwards v. Edwards, 438, 629.
Edwards v. Welton, 544.
Egbert v. De Solms, 152.
Ege v. Medlar, 145.
Egerton v. Jones, 179.
Eggleston v. Swartz, 249.
Ehlen v. Ehlen, 571.
Ehlen v. Mayor of Baltimore, 149.
Eisenberg v. Goldsmith, 181.
Eisenlohr's Estate, In re, 522.
Eisert v. Bowen, 204.
Eldredge v. Mill Ditch Co., 124.
Eldridge v. See Yup Co., 131.
Eldridge v. Turner, 541.
Elias v. Schweyer, 571, 574.
Eliot, Appeal of, 121, 261, 265, 277.

CASES CITED
Figures refer to pages

Eliot v. Trinity Church, 292, 301.
Elizalde v. Elizalde, 125.
Ellenborough, In re, 109.
Ellenherst v. Pythian, 493.
Ellerson v. Westcott, 200.
Ellett v. Tyler, 199.
Ellicott v. Barnes, 560.
Ellicott v. Kuhl, 549, 557.
Ellig v. Naglee, 326, 327, 468, 597.
Elliott v. Armstrong, 147.
Elliott v. Clark, 604.
Elliott v. Landis Mach. Co., 534, 612.
Ellis v. Cary, 217.
Ellis v. Fisher, 123.
Ellis v. Kelsey, 413.
Ellis v. Nimmo, Lloyd & Goold, 94.
Ellis v. Young, 542.
Ellison v. Ellison, 92.
Ellison v. Ganiard, 87.
Ellsworth College of Iowa Falls v. Emmet County, 140.
Elmendorf v. Lansing, 516.
Elmer v. Loper, 471, 482.
Elrod v. Cochran, 179.
Elsner's Will, In re, 441.
Elting v. First Nat. Bank of Biggsville, 543.
Ely v. Attorney General, 298.
Ely v. Pike, 401, 589.
Emans v. Hickman, 283.
Embury v. Sheldon, 628.
Emerson v. Ayres, 213.
Emery v. Farmers' State Bank, 124.
Emigh v. Earling, 551, 558.
Empire State Surety Co. v. Carroll County, 550, 551.
Enders' Ex'r v. Tasco, 64.
Engel, In re, 573.
Engel v. Guaranty Trust Co. of New York, 624.
Engel's Estate, In re, 463.
English v. McIntyre, 239, 347, 356, 535.
Enslen v. Allen, 328.
Eppig, In re, 58.
Equitable Trust Co. v. Fisher, 423.
Erben v. Lorillard, 217.
Erdmân v. Kenney, 218.
Erickson v. Erickson, 163, 165.
Erickson v. Willard, 63.
Erie County v. Lamberton, 552, 567.
Erie Trust Company's Case, 556.
Erskine v. Whitehead, 272, 300.
Eshbach's Estate, In re, 96.
Eshelman's Estate, In re, 642.
Estabrook v. Earle, 156.
Estill v. Estill, 197.
Etgen, In re, 571.

Etting v. Marx, 599.
Ettlinger v. Persian Rug & Carpet Co., 592.
Euans v. Curtis, 179.
Euler v. Schroeder, 176.
Evangelical Synod of North America v. Schoeneich, 560.
Evans, Appeal of, 598.
Evans v. Evans, 462, 464, 549.
Evans v. King, 57.
Evans v. Moore, 222, 544, 599.
Evans' Appeal, 599.
Evans' Estate, In re, 513.
Everett v. Carr, 275.
Everett v. Drew, 43, 375.
Everett v. Everett, 189.
Everhart v. Everhart, 412.
Everitt v. Haskins, 161.
Everts v. Agnes, 535.
Everts v. Everts, 232, 233.
Evertson v. Tappen, 469.
Evinger v. MacDougall, 67.
Ewald v. Kierulff, 601.
Ewald v. Kierulff, 602.
Ewalt v. Davenhill, 246.
Ewell v. Sneed, 122, 494.
Ewing v. Ewing, 196.
Ewing v. Parrish, 496.
Ewing v. Shannahan, 57, 420, 422.
Ewing v. Warner, 626.
Ewing v. Wm. L. Foley, Inc., 386, 387.
Exter v. Sawyer, 46, 206.
Eyre v. Everett, 500.
Eyrick v. Hetrick, 115.
Eysaman v. Nelson, 208, 471.

F

Fahn v. Bleckley, 543.
Fairchild v. Edson, 58, 227.
Fairchild v. Fairchild, 188.
Fairchild v. Rasdall, 196.
Fairfax v. Savings Bank of Baltimore, 155.
Fairhurst v. Lewis, 177.
Fairleigh v. Fidelity Nat. Bank & Trust Co., 373.
Fair's Estate, In re, 191.
Falk v. Hoffman, 197.
Falk v. Turner, 622.
Falls City Woolen Mills v. Louisville Nat. Banking Co., 25.
Fanning v. Main, 478.
Fanoni, In re, 444.
Fargo's Estate, In re, 456.
Farish v. Wayman, 597.
Farleigh v. Cadman, 69, 71, 73, 76.
Farley v. Fullerton, 133.

CASES CITED
Figures refer to pages

Farlow v. Farlow, 622.
Farmers Bank of Clinch Valley v. Kinser, 61.
Farmers' Bank of White Plains v. Bailey, 552.
Farmers' Loan & Trust Co. v. Ferris, 287.
Farmers' Loan & Trust Co. v. Fidelity Trust Co., 583, 584, 585.
Farmers' Loan & Trust Co. v. Kip, 567.
Farmers' Loan & Trust Co. v. Lake St. El. R. Co., 574.
Farmers' Loan & Trust Co. v. Pendleton, 424, 467.
Farmers' Loan & Trust Co. v. Whiton, 449.
Farmers' & Mechanics' Nat. Bank v. King, 28, 556.
Farmers' & Mechanics' Sav. Bank v. Brewer, 239.
Farmers' & Merchants' Bank of Jamesport v. Robinson, 311.
Farmers' & Merchants' Ins. Co. v. Jensen, 231.
Farmers' & Traders' Bank of Shelbyville v. Fidelity & Deposit Co. of Maryland, 534, 580.
Farnsworth v. Muscatine Produce & Pure Ice Co., 505, 548.
Farrell v. Farrell, 500.
Farrell v. Mentzer, 215.
Farrell v. Wallace, 195.
Farrell's Estate, In re, 341.
Farrelly v. Ladd, 630.
Farrelly v. Skelly, 500.
Farrigan v. Pevear, 386.
Farrington v. Barr, 174.
Farrington v. Putnam, 312.
Farwell v. Illinois Merchants Trust Co., 619.
Fate v. Fate, 413.
Faucett v. Faucett, 332.
Faulkner v. Hendy, 525.
Faunce v. McCorkle, 86.
Fausler v. Jones, 497.
Fawcett v. Fawcett, 617.
Faylor v. Faylor, 613.
Fay's Estate, In re, 248, 250.
Feagan v. Metcalfe, 124.
Fearn v. Mayers, 471.
Fearson v. Dunlop, 160.
Federal Heating Co. v. City of Buffalo, 543.
Federal Trust Co. v. Damron, 336.
Feeney v. Howard, 84.
Feesner v. Cooper, 215.
Feingold v. Roeschlein, 185, 532.

Feldman v. Preston, 152, 156, 471.
Felkner v. Dooly, 463, 609.
Fellows, Appeal of, 623.
Fellows v. Loomis, 481.
Fellows v. Miner, 289.
Fellows v. Mitchell, 509, 520.
Fellows v. Ripley, 232.
Fellrath v. Peoria German School Ass'n, 504, 598.
Felton v. Long, 464.
Fenton v. Hall, 41.
Ferchen v. Arndt, 557.
Fergusson v. Fergusson, 400.
Ferguson v. Robinson, 171, 195, 215.
Ferguson v. Rogers, 532.
Fernald v. First Church of Christ, Scientist, in Boston, 130.
Ferrell v. Ellis, 327.
Ferrin v. Errol, 542.
Ferris v. Van Vechten, 557.
Fesmire, Estate of, 510, 514.
Festorazzi v. St. Joseph's Catholic Church of Mobile, 282.
F. G. Oxley Stave Co. v. Butler County, 127, 421.
Fidelity Trust Co. v. Alexander, 499, 630.
Fidelity Trust Co. v. Butler, 210.
Fidelity Trust & Safety Vault Co. v. Walker, 155.
Fidelity & Casualty Co. v. Maryland Casualty Co., 567.
Fidelity & Columbia Trust Co. v. Williams, 639.
Fidelity & Deposit Co. v. Wolfe, 577.
Fidelity & Deposit Co. of Maryland, Appeal of, 369, 475, 596.
Fidelity & Deposit Co. of Maryland v. Husbands, 465.
Fidelity & Deposit Co. of Maryland v. Queens County Trust Co., 584.
Fidelity & Deposit Co. of Maryland v. Rankin, 535, 581.
Field v. Arrowsmith, 332.
Field v. Biddle, 16.
Field v. Directors of Girard College, 496.
Field v. Drew Theological Seminary, 277.
Field v. Middlesex Banking Co., 210.
Field v. Wilbur, 382.
Fields v. Hoskins, 202.
Fifth Nat. Bank v. Armstrong, 26.
Filkins v. Severn, 131.
Findlay v. Florida East Coast Ry. Co., 325.
Fine v. Receiver of Dickenson County Bank, 23.

CASES CITED
Figures refer to pages

Fiocchi v. Smith, 74.
Fireman's Ins. Co. v. Oregon R. Co., 38.
First Congregational Soc. v. Pelham, 524.
First Congregational Soc. in Raynham v. Trustees of Fund, etc., in Raynham, 500.
First Denton Nat. Bank v. Kenney, 581, 587.
First M. E. Church of Ottumwa v. Hull, 621.
First Nat. Bank v. Armstrong, 25, 26.
First Nat. Bank v. Basham, 353.
First Nat. Bank v. Burns, 150, 161.
First Nat. Bank v. Commercial Bank & Trust Co., 561.
First Nat. Bank v. Hinkle, 83.
First Nat. Bank v. Nashville Trust Co., 162.
First Nat. Bank v. Union Trust Co., 25.
First Nat. Bank of Atlanta v. Southern Cotton Oil Co., 50.
First Nat. Bank of Carlisle v. Lee, 394.
First Nat. Bank of Catonsville v. Carter, 124.
First Nat. Bank of City of New York, In re, 348.
First Nat. Bank of Elkhart v. Armstrong, 23.
First Nat. Bank of Joplin v. Woelz, 237.
First Nat. Bank of Lincoln v. Cash, 646.
First Nat. Bank of Mobile v. Watters, 415.
First Nat. Bank of Ottawa v. Kay Bee Co., 545.
First Nat. Bank of Paterson v. National Broadway Bank, 403.
First Nat. Bank of Pawnee City v. Sprague, 25.
First Nat. Bk. of Pennsboro v. Delancey, 378.
First Nat. Bank of Princeton, Ill., v. Littlefield, 557.
First Nat. Bank of Raton v. Dennis, 25.
First Nat. Bank of Sharon v. Valley State Bank, 581, 584.
First Nat. Bank of Spartanburg, S. C. v. Dougan, 152, 156.
First Nat. Bank in Wichita v. Magnolia Petroleum Co., 405.
First Presbyterian Soc. of Town of Chili v. Bowen, 132.
First State Bank v. O'Bannon, 561.
First State Bank of Bonham v. Hill, 585, 587.
First Trust Co. of Lincoln v. Carlsen, 459.
First Trust Co. of Wichita v. Varney, 413.
First Wisconsin Trust Co. v. Wisconsin Dept. of Taxation, 42, 625.
First & Merchants' Nat. Bank v. Bank of Waverly, 595.
Fischbeck v. Gross, 218.
Fish v. Fish, 332.
Fish v. Prior, 620.
Fishblate v. Fishblate, 623.
Fisher v. Dickenson, 424.
Fisher v. Fisher, 57, 468, 477.
Fisher v. Fobes, 189.
Fisher v. Wister, 639.
Fisk, Appeal of, 218, 239, 502.
Fisk, In re, 483.
Fisk, Matter of, 412.
Fisk v. Brunette, 469.
Fisk v. Patton, 176, 571.
Fitchie v. Brown, 120.
Fite v. Beasley, 283.
Fitz Gerald v. City of Big Rapids, 249.
Fitzgerald v. Hollan, 526.
Fitzgibbon v. Barry, 427, 428.
Flaherty v. Cramer, 542, 603.
Flaherty v. O'Connor, 43.
Flanary v. Kane, 176.
Flanders v. Thompson, 546.
Flanner v. Butler, 179.
Fleck v. Ellis, 56, 611.
Fleenor v. Hensley, 81, 99, 138.
Fleetwood, In re, 221, 226, 279.
Fleischmann v. Northwestern Nat. Bank & Trust Co., 467.
Fleming v. Gilmer, 464.
Fleming v. Holt, 399.
Fleming v. Shay, 603.
Fleming v. Wilson, 124, 476.
Fletcher v. Fletcher, 105.
Fletcher v. Green, 521.
Flinn v. Frank, 394.
Flowers v. Flowers, 332.
Floyd v. Duffy, 196.
Floyd v. Gilliam, 576.
Floyd v. Smith, 62.
Flye v. Hall, 500.
Foard v. Safe Deposit & Trust Co. of Baltimore, 447.
Fogarty v. Hunter, 232.
Fogarty v. Stange, 628.
Fogarty's Estate, In re, 462.
Fogg v. Middleton, 38, 105, 490.

CASES CITED
Figures refer to pages

Fogler's Lessee v. Evig, 16.
Foil v. Newsome, 394.
Foley v. Hastings, 167.
Folk v. Hughes, 134, 535.
Folk v. Wind, 482.
Follansbe v. Kilbreth, 369.
Follansbee v. Outhet, 476.
Foord, In re, 191.
Fooshee v. Kasenberg, 174.
Foote v. Bruggerhof, 476, 485.
Foote v. Bryant, 189.
Forbes v. Forbes, 595.
Force v. Force, 120.
Ford v. Caldwell, 159.
Ford v. Ford, 252.
Ford v. Ford's Ex'r, 262, 284.
Ford v. Fowler, 61.
Ford v. Thomas, 297.
Fordyce v. Woman's Christian Nat. Library Ass'n, 286.
Forest v. Rogers, 85.
Forman v. Young, 319.
Forrest v. O'Donnell, 591.
Forrester's Estate, In re, 291.
Forster v. Hale, 83.
Forster v. Winfield, 133.
Forsyth v. City of Wheeling, 424.
Forsythe v. Lexington Banking & Trust Co., 490.
Fort v. First Baptist Church of Paris, 204.
Fortner v. Phillips, 140.
Fortune v. First Trust Co., 373.
Foscue v. Lyon, 346, 468.
Fosdick v. Fosdick, 244.
Foss v. Sowles, 574.
Foster v. Coe, 136.
Foster v. Elsley, 107.
Foster v. Foster, 161, 167.
Foster v. Friede, 147, 492.
Foster v. Goree, 423.
Foster v. Treadway, 179.
Foster v. Willson, 63.
Foster's Estate, In re, 345.
Foster's Will, In re, 355.
Foster's Estate, Matter of, 165.
Fourth Nat. Bank v. Hopple, 358.
Foveaux, In re, 290.
Fowler, Appeal of, 140.
Fowler v. Bowery Sav. Bank, 74.
Fowler v. Coates, 57, 323.
Fowler v. Colt, 343.
Fowler v. Duhme, 250.
Fowler v. Gowing, 99.
Fowler v. Lanpher, 643.
Fowler v. Mutual Life Ins. Co., 382.
Fowler & Lee v. Webster, 162.
Fox v. Fox, 89, 491, 639.

Fox v. Gibbs, 266.
Fox v. Greene, 151, 641.
Fox v. Peoples, 213.
Fox v. Tay, 511.
Fox v. Weckerly, 474.
Fox's Estate, In re, 117, 291.
Francis v. Preachers' Aid Soc., 312.
Frank v. Bingham, 25.
Frank v. Colonial & United States Mortg. Co., 423.
Frank v. Firestone, 530.
Frank v. Morley's Estate, 499, 503.
Frankenfield's Appeal, 344.
Franklin, Matter of, 430.
Franklin v. Armfield, 286, 311.
Franklin v. Colley, 189, 491.
Franklin v. Hastings, 286, 305.
Franklin Inst. for Savings v. People's Sav. Bank, 320.
Franklin Sav. Bank v. Taylor, 395.
Franklin's Adm'x v. City of Philadelphia, 290, 291, 292.
Franklin Trust Co., In re, 365.
Franks v. Cravens, 500.
Franks v. Morris, 618.
Franz v. Buder, 463.
Fraser v. Bowerman, 395.
Frasier v. Findley, 187.
Frazer, In re, 283.
Frazier v. Merchants Nat. Bank of Salem, 309.
Frazier v. St. Luke's Church, 135.
Freas' Estate, In re, 530.
Freeland v. Williamson, 615.
Freeman v. Bristol Sav. Bank, 338.
Freeman v. Brown, 125.
Freeman v. Cook, 327.
Freeman v. Deming, 545.
Freeman v. Maxwell, 147, 530.
Freeman v. Perry, 150.
Freeman's Estate, In re, 121.
French v. Busch, 391.
French v. Calkins, 108, 243, 256, 265, 277, 289, 305.
French v. Commercial Nat. Bank, 482.
French v. Hall, 331.
French v. Northern Trust Co., 319, 322, 424.
Frethey v. Durant, 461.
Frey v. Allen, 145.
Frick Co. v. Taylor, 197.
Fridenberg v. Wilson, 382.
Friedley v. Security Trust & Safe Deposit Co., 420, 426.
Friedrich v. Huth, 189.
Frierson v. General Assembly of Presbyterian Church of U. S., 63.
Frisbie v. Fogg, 573.

CASES CITED
Figures refer to pages

Frith, In re, 384.
Fritz v. City Trust Co., 320, 323.
Froelich, In re, 478.
Froelich's Estate, In re, 465.
Froemke v. Marks, 176.
Froneberger v. First Nat. Bank, 601.
Frost v. Beekman, 535.
Frost v. Bush, 615.
Frost v. Frost, 2.
Frost v. Perfield, 204.
Fryberger v. Anderson, 329.
Fryer, In re, 509.
Fulbright v. Yoder, 57.
Fuller v. Abbe, 481.
Fuller v. Davis, 423.
Fulton v. Davidson, 525.
Fulton's Will, In re, 330.
Funk v. Grulke, 167.
Furber v. Barnes, 28.
Furman v. Fisher, 138.
Furman v. Rapelje, 504.
Furniss v. Furniss, 462.
Furniss v. Zimmerman, 369.
Furniture Workers' Union Local 1007 v. United Brotherhood of Carpenters and Joiners of America, 136.

G

Gadsden's Ex'rs v. Lord's Ex'rs, 16.
Gaffney's Estate, In re, 70, 74, 503.
Gafney v. Kenison, 263.
Gagnon v. Wellman, 272, 300.
Gaines v. Summers, 541, 543.
Gaither v. Gaither, 226, 604.
Gale v. Harby, 534.
Gale v. Sulloway, 58, 88, 569.
Gallagher v. Venturini, 284.
Gallaher v. Gallaher, 264.
Galland's Estate, In re, 305.
Gallatian v. Cunningham, 333.
Gallego's Ex'rs v. Attorney General, 270.
Galli's Estate, In re, 466.
Gamble v. Dabney, 425.
Gamble v. Gibson, 329.
Gambrill v. Gambrill, 244.
Gamel v. Smith, 487.
Garard v. Garard, 526.
Gardner, In re, 62.
Gardner v. City Nat. Bank & Trust Co., 245.
Gardner v. Rowe, 106.
Gardner v. Whitford, 549.
Garesche v. Levering Inv. Co., 393.
Garfield v. Hatmaker, 150.
Garland, Ex parte, 382.
Garner v. Dowling, 126.
Garnsey v. Gothard, 87.
Garnsey v. Mundy, 623.
Garrigus v. Burnett, 76.
Garrison v. Little, 122, 273, 288.
Garrott v. McConnell, 393.
Garten v. Trobridge, 189.
Gartenlaub's Estate, In re, 440.
Garth, In re, 484.
Gartside v. Gartside, 130, 572.
Garvey v. Clifford, 72, 75.
Garvey v. Garvey, 607.
Garvey v. New York Life Ins. & Trust Co., 469.
Garvin's Will, Matter of, 503.
Garwols v. Bankers' Trust Co., 200.
Gaskill v. Gaskill, 129.
Gass v. Wilhite, 269, 279.
Gassert v. Strong, 332.
Gaston v. American Exch. Nat. Bank, 540, 541.
Gaston v. Hayden, 569, 571.
Gaston v. King, 204.
Gaston Trust, In re, 465.
Gate City Building & Loan Ass'n v. National Bank of Commerce, 589.
Gates v. Dudgeon, 397.
Gates v. McClenahan, 382.
Gates v. Paul, 88.
Gault v. Hospital for Consumptives of Maryland, 557.
Gaylord v. City of Lafayette, 81, 86, 93, 230.
Gay's Estate, In re, 284, 424.
Gebhard v. Sattler, 618.
Geer v. Traders' Bank of Canada, 405.
Geiger v. Simpson Methodist Episcopal Church of Minneapolis, 386.
Geisse v. Beall, 461.
Geldmacher v. City of New York, 350.
Gemmel v. Fletcher, 226.
General Convention of New Church in United States v. Smith, 215.
General Petroleum Corporation of California v. Dougherty, 530.
General Proprietors of Eastern Division of New Jersey v. Force's Ex'rs, 504.
Gentry v. Poteet, 604.
Geoghegan v. Smith, 97.
George v. Braddock, 288.
George v. George, 62.
Gerety v. O'Sheehan, 185.
German v. Heath, 186.
German Land Ass'n v. Scholler, 132, 136.
German-American Coffee Co. v. Diehl, 464.

CASES CITED
Figures refer to pages

German Fire Ins. Co. v. Kimble, 24.
Gernert v. Albert, 401.
Gerrish v. New Bedford Inst. for Sav., 69, 72.
Gianella v. Momsen, 558.
Gibbes v. Smith, 572.
Gibbons v. Mahon, 449.
Gibney v. Allen, 130.
Gibson v. Cooke, 435.
Gibson v. Foote, 183.
Gibson v. Frye Institute, 273, 287.
Gibson's Case, 483.
Gibley v. Lovenberg, 121.
Gifford v. Bennett, 543.
Gifford v. First National Bank, 296.
Gilbert v. Chapin, 61.
Gilbert v. Johnson, 571.
Gilbert v. Kolb, 361.
Gilbert v. Penfield, 400.
Gilbert v. Sutliff, 326, 473, 482.
Gilbert v. Welsch, 347, 356.
Gilbert's Estate, In re, 574.
Gilchrist v. Stevenson, 504.
Giles v. Palmer, 124.
Giles v. Perkins, 22.
Gilkey v. Paine, 451.
Gill, In re, 478.
Gill's Heirs v. Logan's Heirs, 143.
Gillespie v. Smith, 324.
Gillespie v. Winston's Trustee, 159.
Gillett v. Bowen, 46.
Gilman v. American Producers' Controlling Co., 37.
Gilman v. Burnett, 301.
Gilman v. McArdle, 282.
Gilmer's Legatees v. Gilmer's Ex'rs, 135, 285, 292.
Gilmore v. Ham, 610.
Gilmore v. Tuttle, 361.
Gilpatrick v. Glidden, 196, 226.
Gilpin v. Columbia Nat. Bank, 26.
Gilruth v. Decell, 540.
Girard Life Ins. & Trust Co. v. Chambers, 155.
Girard Trust Co. v. McKinley-Lanning Loan & Trust Co., 476.
Girard Trust Co. v. Mueller, 448.
Girard Trust Co. v. Russell, 291, 305, 309.
Gisborn v. Charter Oak Life Ins. Co., 108, 379.
Giselman v. Starr, 394.
Glaser v. Congregation Kehillath Israel, 279.
Glasgow v. Missouri Car & Foundry Co., 233.
Glasscock v. Tate, 643.
Glazier v. Everett, 429.

Glenn v. Allison, 377, 398.
Glenn v. McKim, 510.
Glenn's Ex'rs v. Cockey, 524.
Glidden v. Gutelius, 552.
Glieberman v. Fine, 84.
Globe Sav. Bank v. Nat. Bank of Commerce, 581.
Glover, Appeal of, 577.
Glover v. Baker, 57, 113, 279, 426.
Glover v. Stamps, 591.
Gloyd v. Roff, 640.
Gloyd's Estate, In re, 484.
Glynn v. Maxfield, 143.
Goad v. Montgomery, 394.
G. Ober & Sons Co. v. Cochran, 25.
Goble v. Swobe, 490.
Godfrey v. Hutchins, 263.
Goelz v. Goelz, 179.
Goff v. Evans, 449.
Goff v. Goff, 84, 202.
Goffe v. Goffe, 122.
Gogherty v. Bennett, 177.
Going v. Emery, 270, 275.
Golder v. Bressler, 429.
Golding v. Gaither, 635.
Goldman v. Cohen, 213.
Goldman v. Moses, 110.
Goldrick v. Roxana Petroleum Co., 500.
Goldschmidt v. Maier, 497.
Goldsmith v. Goldsmith, 83, 218, 219.
Goldthwaite v. Ellison, 557.
Goldwater v. Oltman, 375.
Golson v. Dunlap, 210.
Golson v. Fielder, 544.
Goncelier v. Foret, 574.
Gonyer v. Williams, 24.
Goodbar v. Daniel, 150.
Goode v. Comfort, 398, 399.
Goode v. Lowery, 604.
Goode v. McPherson, 636.
Goodell v. Buck, 557.
Goodell v. Union Ass'n of Children's Home of Burlington County, 277, 294.
Goodfellow's Estate, In re, 296.
Goodman v. Smith, 616.
Goodman v. White, 46.
Goodno v. Hotchkiss, 608.
Goodrich v. City Nat. Bank & Trust Co., 91.
Goodrich v. Proctor, 399.
Goodrick v. Harrison, 211.
Goodrum v. Goodrum, 121.
Goodwin v. Broadway Trust Co., 624.
Goodwin v. Goodwin, 574.
Goodwin v. McGaughey, 451.
Goodwin v. Wilbur, 46.

CASES CITED
Figures refer to pages

Gordon v. Kaplan, 196.
Gordon v. Rasines, 24.
Gore v. Bingaman, 132.
Goree v. Georgia Industrial Home, 302.
Gorham, In re, 181.
Gorham v. Daniels, 231.
Gorrell v. Alspaugh, 53.
Goss v. Singleton, 127.
Gossom's Adm'r v. Gossom, 474.
Gosson v. Ladd, 319.
Gottschalk's Estate, In re, 348.
Gottstein v. Wist, 53.
Gould v. Board of Home Missions of Presbyterian Church, 122, 312.
Gould v. Lynde, 174.
Gouldey's Estate, In re, 346, 361.
Goupille v. Chaput, 497.
Govin v. De Miranda, 96.
Gowell v. Twitchell, 177.
Grady v. Ibach, 591.
Graff v. Castleman, 541.
Graff v. Portland Town & Mineral Co., 598.
Graff v. Wallace, 300.
Grafflin v. Robb, 541.
Grafing v. Heilmann, 69, 72, 73, 74.
Graham v. Austin, 512, 519.
Graham v. Davidson, 512.
Graham v. Donaldson, 605.
Graham v. Graham, 501.
Graham's Estate, In re, 436.
Grandjean's Estate, In re, 145.
Grand Prairie Seminary v. Morgan, 122, 286.
Grant v. Bradstreet, 226.
Grant v. Saunders, 261, 276.
Grant Trust & Savings Co. v. Tucker, 120.
Graver, Appeal of, 347, 470.
Graves v. Dolphin, 159.
Graves v. Graves, 107.
Graves' Estate, In re, 265.
Gray v. Beard, 174.
Gray v. Board of Sup'rs of Tompkins County, 555.
Gray v. Chase, 150.
Gray v. Corbit, 160.
Gray v. Emmons, 208.
Gray v. Fox, 355.
Gray v. Gray, 179.
Gray v. Heinze, 461.
Gray v. Hemenway, 449.
Gray v. Johnston, 585, 587.
Gray v. Lincoln Housing Trust, 324.
Gray v. Lynch, 358, 365.
Gray v. Perry, 505.
Gray v. Reamer, 512, 517.

Gray v. Ulrich, 534.
Gray v. Union Trust Co., 427.
Gray v. Union Trust Co. of San Francisco, 622, 644.
Grayson v. Bowlin, 603.
Greagan v. Buchanan, 333.
Greata's Will, In re, 347.
Great Berlin Steamboat Co., In re, 239.
Greek Orthodox Community v. Malicourtis, 265.
Green v. Beatty, 16.
Green v. Bissell, 394.
Green v. Blackwell, 287, 417, 418, 419, 636.
Green v. Brooks, 503, 532.
Green v. Gaskill, 462, 499.
Green v. Jones, 475.
Green v. Winter, 329, 410, 473.
Green's Adm'rs v. Fidelity Trust Co. of Louisville, 289.
Greene v. Aborn, 642.
Greene v. Borland, 425, 427.
Greene v. Dennis, 293.
Greene v. Greene, 117, 400.
Greene v. Smith, 449.
Greenfield's Estate, In re, 88, 481, 623.
Greenleaf v. Queen, 420.
Greenville Academies, Ex parte, 113.
Gregg v. Gabbert, 420, 422, 482.
Gregory v. Bowlsby, 218.
Gregory v. Gregory, 510.
Gregory's Estate, In re, 248.
Greifer's Estate, In re, 201.
Grey, In re, 293.
Gribbel v. Gribbel, 59.
Grider v. Driver, 590.
Gridley v. Gridley, 34.
Grieves v. Keane, 156.
Griffin v. Chase, 24.
Griffin v. Graham, 269, 270.
Griffin v. Griffin, 329.
Griffin v. Schlenk, 213.
Griffith's Estate, In re, 409.
Griffin's Ex'r v. Macaulay's Adm'r, 511.
Griggs v. Griggs, 205.
Griley v. Marion Mtge. Co., 404.
Grimball v. Cruse, 478, 479.
Grimes' Ex'rs v. Harmon, 270.
Grimstone v. Carter, 535, 536, 542.
Grist v. Forehand, 45.
Griswold v. Caldwell, 400.
Griswold v. Perry, 325.
Griswold v. Sackett, 423.
Gritten v. Dickerson, 422.
Grodsky v. Sipe, 49.

CASES CITED

Groel v. United Electric Co. of New Jersey, 46.
Groening v. McCambridge, 166.
Groff v. City Savings Fund & Trust Co., 557.
Groff v. Rohrer, 174.
Groom v. Thompson, 464.
Groome v. Belt, 604.
Gross v. Moore, 192.
Grossman's Estate, In re, 483.
Grote v. Grote, 218.
Grothe, Appeal of, 162, 343.
Groton v. Ruggles, 120, 130.
Grove-Grady, In re, 290.
Grover v. Hale, 397.
Groye v. Robards' Heirs, 534, 539.
Gruby v. Smith, 208.
Grundy v. Drye, 423.
Grundy v. Neal, 276, 635.
Grymes v. Hone, 101.
Guernsey v. Lazear, 162.
Guest v. Guest, 182.
Gueutal v. Gueutal, 237.
Guidise v. Island Refining Corp., 31.
Guild v. Allen, 122, 123, 230.
Guilmartin v. Stevens, 399.
Guin v. Guin, 182, 546.
Guion v. Melvin, 428.
Guion v. Pickett, 423.
Gulick, In re, 484.
Gulick v. Bruere, 420.
Gully v. Neville, 244.
Gumbert, Appeal of, 635.
Gutch v. Fosdick, 500, 603.
Gutenkunst's Estate, In re, 329.
Guthrie v. Hyatt, 498.
Guthrie v. Wheeler, 455.
Guthrie's Estate, In re, 340.
Guthrie's Trustee v. Akers, 436.
Gutknecht v. Sorge, 28.
Gutman's Estate, In re, 347.
Guye v. Guye, 644.
Gwin v. Hutton, 244.
Gwynn v. Gwynn, 138.
Gwyon, In re, 294.

H

Haack v. Weicken, 189.
Haaven v. Hoaas, 189.
Hackett's Ex'rs v. Hackett's Devisees, 366.
Hackett's Trustee v. Hackett, 159.
Hackley v. Littell, 136.
Haddock v. Perham, 575, 577.
Hadley v. Hadley, 630.
Hagan v. Varney, 456, 541.
Hagen v. Sacrison, 249, 273.

Bogert Trusts 2d—43

Hagenbeck v. Hagenbeck Zoological Arena Co., 569.
Hagerstown Trust Co., In re, 232, 632.
Haggart v. Ranney, 319.
Haggin v. International Trust Co., 265, 270, 292.
Haggin v. Straus, 425.
Haglar v. McCombs, 484.
Hagthorp v. Hook's Adm'rs, 541.
Haguewood v. Britain, 180.
Haight v. Brisbin, 571.
Haight v. Pearson, 532.
Haight v. Royce, 63.
Haimovitz v. Hawk, 403.
Haines v. Allen, 290.
Haines v. Elliot, 573.
Haines v. Hay, 524.
Haines' Estate, In re, 256.
Haldeman v. Openheimer, 315.
Hale v. Adams, 513, 517.
Hale v. Bowler, 161.
Hale v. Cox, 474.
Hale v. Hale, 243, 621.
Hale v. Nashua & L. R. R., 592.
Hale v. Windsor Sav. Bank, 581.
Haley v. Palmer, 152.
Hall, In re, 356, 367, 369.
Hall v. Crabb, 145.
Hall v. Doran, 197.
Hall v. Edwards, 189.
Hall v. Farmers' & Merchants' Bank, 88.
Hall v. Glover, 523.
Hall v. Miller, 195.
Hall v. Vanness, 535.
Hall v. Williams, 161.
Hall v. Young, 187.
Hallam v. Tillinghast, 24.
Hallett v. Collins, 534.
Hallett's Estate, In re, 550, 551, 552, 562.
Halliday v. Croom, 237.
Halligan's Estate, Matter of, 69, 71, 74.
Hallinan v. Hearst, 426.
Hallowell Sav. Inst. v. Titcomb, 93, 140.
Hallyburton v. Slagle, 232.
Halper v. Wolff, 626.
Halsey v. Convention of Protestant Episcopal Church, 286.
Halsted, Matter of, 514.
Ham v. Ham, 320.
Ham v. Twombly, 226.
Hamersley v. Smith, 634.
Hames v. Stroud, 208.
Hamilton v. Dooly, 329.

CASES CITED
Figures refer to pages

Hamilton v. Drogo, 167.
Hamilton v. Faber, 574.
Hamilton v. Hall's Estate, 93.
Hamilton v. Hamilton, 400, 597.
Hamilton v. Muncie, 493.
Hamilton v. Reese, 524.
Hamilton's Estate, In re, 280, 281.
Hamlen v. Welch, 377, 380, 404.
Hamlin, In re, 49.
Hamlin v. Mansfield, 232.
Hammekin v. Clayton, 134.
Hammer, In re, 74.
Hammerstein v. Equitable Trust Co. of New York, 241, 623.
Hammond v. Hopkins, 333.
Hammond v. Messenger, 38.
Hammond v. Ridley's Ex'rs, 604.
Hampson v. Fall, 538, 543.
Hanbury v. Kirkland, 511.
Hancock v. Ship, 147.
Hancock v. Twyman, 155.
Hancox v. Meeker, 477.
Handley v. Palmer, 121.
Handley v. Wrightson, 62.
Handy v. McKim, 140.
Haney v. Legg, 599, 602, 617.
Hanford v. Duchastel, 498.
Hanie v. Grissom, 244.
Hankwitz v. Barrett, 37.
Hanna v. Clark, 481.
Hannig v. Mueller, 233.
Hannon v. Mechanics Bldg. & Loan Ass'n of Spartanburg, 48.
Hanold v. Bacon, 197.
Hanrick v. Gurley, 543.
Hanrion v. Hanrion, 189.
Hanson v. Hanson, 613.
Hanson v. Svarverud, 196, 218.
Hanson v. Worthington, 128.
Hanson's Estate, In re, 474, 628.
Harbster's Estate, In re, 336, 337.
Hardenburgh v. Blair, 161.
Hardesty v. Smith, 23.
Harding v. St. Louis Life Ins. Co., 400.
Harding v. St. Louis Union Trust Co., 93.
Hardoon v. Belilios, 381.
Hardwick v. Cotterill, 40.
Hardy v. Hardy, 61.
Harkness' Estate, In re, 451.
Harlan v. Eilke, 180.
Harley v. Platts, 232.
Harlow v. Cowdrey, 633.
Harlow v. Dehon, 618.
Harlow v. Weld, 641.
Harmon v. Best, 48.
Harmon v. Weston, 576.

Harney v. First Nat. Bank, 546.
Harper, In re, 481.
Harper v. Perry, 204.
Harrar's Estate, In re, 640.
Harras v. Harras, 213.
Harrigan v. Gilchrist, 329, 490, 504, 626.
Harrington v. Atlantic & Pac. Tel. Co., 534.
Harrington v. Pier, 261, 273, 290, 307.
Harris v. Brown, 427, 534.
Harris v. Cassells, 179.
Harris v. Cosby, 493.
Harris v. Ferguy, 58.
Harris v. Fly, 34.
Harris v. Harris, 644.
Harris v. McIntyre, 180, 542.
Harris v. Moses, 449, 451.
Harris v. Rucker, 121.
Harris v. Sheldon, 470, 477.
Harris v. Stone, 198, 540.
Harris Banking Co. v. Miller, 83, 92.
Harris' Will, In re, 456.
Harrison v. Adcock, 614.
Harrison v. Andrews, 124.
Harrison v. Barker Annuity Fund, 274.
Harrison v. Brophy, 281, 282.
Harrison v. Fleischman, 541.
Harrison v. Gibson, 600.
Harrison v. Harrison, 181.
Harrison v. Henderson, 428.
Harrison v. McMennomy, 59.
Harrison v. Manson, 330.
Harrison v. Mock, 469.
Harrison v. Smith, 29, 551.
Harrison v. Totten, 73, 74, 76.
Harrison's Estate, In re, 476.
Harrisons v. Harrison's Adm'x, 62.
Hart, Matter of, 265.
Hart v. Cannon, 210.
Hart v. Citizens' Nat. Bank, 611.
Hart v. Seymour, 135.
Hart's Estate, In re, 140, 367, 467, 482, 502.
Harteau, In re, 484.
Hartley v. Hartley, 179.
Hartley v. Phillips, 43.
Hartley v. Unknown Heirs of Wyatt, 161, 626.
Hartman v. Hartle, 330.
Hartman v. Loverud, 83.
Harton v. Amason, 185.
Hartsock v. Russell, 505.
Hartung's Estate, In re, 272.
Harvard College v. Amory, 466.
Harvard Trust Co. v. Duke, 456.
Harvey v. Bank of Marrowbone, 616.

BOGERT TRUSTS 2D

CASES CITED
Figures refer to pages

Harvey v. Gardner, 58.
Harvey v. Hand, 599.
Harvey v. Schwettman, 426, 481, 511, 573.
Harwood v. Tracy, 423.
Hascall v. King, 256.
Haskell v. First Nat. Bank, 84.
Haskin, In re, 481, 482.
Haslam v. Haslam, 535.
Hassey v. Wilke, 541.
Hatch, Appeal of, 502, 512.
Hatcher v. Hatcher, 218.
Hatcheson v. Tilden, 16.
Hatheway v. Sackett, 113.
Haug v. Schumacher, 250.
Haughwout v. Murphy, 537.
Hauk v. Van Ingen, 557.
Haulman v. Haulman, 107.
Hauser v. Lehman, 512.
Haux v. Dry Dock Sav. Inst., 75, 77.
Havana Cent. R. Co. v. Central Trust Co. of New York, 585.
Havana Cent. R. R. Co. v. Knickerbocker Trust Co., 534, 585.
Havenor v. Pipher, 605.
Havens, In re, 64.
Haverstick v. Trudel, 499.
Hawaiian Pineapple Co. v. Browne, 561.
Hawkins v. Chapman, 420.
Hawkins v. Sneed, 150.
Hawk's Estate, In re, 444.
Hawley, In re, 56.
Hawley v. James, 241, 249, 252.
Hawley v. Ross, 427.
Hawley v. Tesch, 532, 533.
Hawley v. Wells, 47.
Hawthorne v. Smith, 256.
Hayden v. Denslow, 85.
Hayden v. Hayden, 114.
Hayden's Ex'rs v. Marmaduke, 487.
Hayes v. Hall, 333, 462.
Hayes v. Hayes, 499.
Hayes v. Horton, 179.
Hayes v. Kerr, 522.
Hayes v. Kershow, 94.
Hayes v. Martz, 248.
Hayes v. Pratt, 428.
Hayes v. St. Louis Union Trust Co., 452.
Hayes v. Walker, 609.
Haynes v. Carr, 108, 273.
Haynes v. Montgomery, 328.
Haynie v. Hall's Ex'r, 608, 615.
Hays v. Gloster, 197.
Hays v. Harris, 289.
Hays v. Hollis, 182.
Hayward v. Andrews, 38.

Hayward v. Cain, 177.
Hayward v. Ellis, 333.
Hayward v. Plant, 341.
Hayward's Estate, In re, 94.
Haywood v. Ensley, 213.
Haywood v. Wachovia Loan & Trust Co., 58.
Hazard v. Coyle, 475, 476.
Hazard v. Durant, 323, 503, 504, 523.
Hazlett v. Commercial Nat. Bank, 22.
Hazlewood v. Webster, 62.
H. B. Cartwright & Bro. v. United States Bank & Trust Co., 86, 138, 481.
Head v. Gould, 521.
Healey v. Alston, 637.
Healy v. Loomis Institute, 295.
Heard v. March, 322.
Hearst v. Pujol, 125.
Heath v. Bishop, 151, 159.
Heath v. Erie Ry. Co., 504.
Heaton v. Bartlett, 362.
Heaton v. Dickson, 152, 153.
Heaton's Estate, In re, 451.
Heberle's Estate, In re, 248.
Heckert, Appeal of, 473, 475.
Hedges v. Paquett, 47.
Hedrick v. Beeler, 587.
Heermans v. Burt, 240.
Heermans v. Schmaltz, 132.
Heffern Co-Op. Consol. Gold Min. & Mill Co. v. Gauthier, 47.
Hegeman's Ex'r v. Roome, 267.
Hegstad v. Wysiecki, 189.
Heidelbach v. Campbell, 505, 531.
Heidelbach v. National Park Bank, 551.
Heil v. Heil, 53.
Heinisch v. Pennington, 226, 227, 557, 604.
Heiskell v. Chickasaw Lodge, 312.
Heiskell v. Powell, 626.
Heitman v. Cutting, 125.
Heizer v. Heizer, 433.
Helfenstine's Lessee v. Garrard, 231.
Hellman v. McWilliams, 102.
Hellman v. Messmer, 189.
Helms v. Goodwill, 209.
Helvering v. City Bank Farmers Trust Co., 625.
Helvering v. Clifford, 632.
Hemenway v. Hemenway, 444.
Hemmerich v. Union Dime Sav. Inst., 75, 592.
Hemphill, Appeal of, 477.
Hemphill's Estate, In re, 478.
Hempstead v. Dickson, 155.
Henchey v. Henchey, 499.

CASES CITED
Figures refer to pages

Henderson v. Adams, 232.
Henderson v. Bell, 243.
Henderson v. Hughes, 101.
Henderson v. McDonald, 125.
Henderson v. Maclay, 614.
Henderson v. Murray, 211.
Henderson v. O'Conor, 24.
Henderson v. Segars, 237, 466.
Henderson v. Sherman, 147, 417, 475.
Henderson v. Sunseri, 156.
Henderson's Adm'r v. Henderson's Heirs, 348.
Henderson's Estate, In re, 91, 643.
Hendren v. Hendren, 422.
Hendrickson v. Hendrickson, 600.
Hendrix College v. Arkansas Townsite Co., 406.
Hendrix's Ex'rs v. Hardin, 473.
Henrietta Nat. Bank v. Barrett, 385.
Henriott v. Cood, 589.
Henry v. Allen, 587.
Henry v. Doctor, 427.
Henry v. Henderson, 244.
Henry v. Hilliard, 475.
Henry v. Phillips, 537.
Henry v. Raiman, 205.
Henshaw v. Freer's Adm'rs, 383.
Henson v. Wright, 147.
Henyan v. Trevino, 205.
Heppenstall v. Baudouine, 156.
Herbert v. Hanrick, 394.
Herbert v. Herbert, 410.
Herbert v. Simson, 101.
Herndon v. Massey, 386.
Heroy's Estate, In re, 409.
Herrick v. Low, 122.
Herrick v. Newell, 217.
Herron v. Comstock, 462.
Hershey v. Northern Trust Co., 28.
Herzog v. Title Guar. & Trust Co., 341.
Hessen v. McKinley, 69, 73, 74.
Hester v. Hester, 369.
Heth v. Richmond, F. & P. R. Co., 541.
Heuser v. Harris, 275, 300.
Hewitt, Matter of, 69, 74.
Hewitt v. Beattie, 396.
Hewitt v. Green, 487.
Hewitt v. Hayes, 550, 551, 554, 555, 557.
Hewitt v. Phelps, 383.
Hewitt v. Rankin, 146.
Hewitt v. Wheeler School and Library, 285, 312.
Heyward v. Glover, 465.
Heyward-Williams Co. v. McCall, 133.
Heywood's Estate, In re, 56.

Hexter v. Clifford, 164.
Hickey v. Kahl, 75.
Hickman v. Wood's Ex'r, 637.
Hickok v. Still, 408.
Hicks, In re, 549.
Hicks v. Hicks, 319.
Hickson v. Culbert, 183, 189.
Higbee v. Brockenbrough, 161.
Higginbotham v. Boggs, 176, 605.
Higgins v. Beck, 444.
Higginson v. Turner, 113.
Highberger v. Stiffler, 209.
Highland Park Mfg. Co. v. Steele, 136.
Hildreth v. Eliot, 424.
Hill v. Cooper, 522.
Hill v. Fleming, 531.
Hill v. Fulmer, 156.
Hill v. Hill, 61, 121, 231, 516, 639, **643**.
Hill v. Hill's Ex'rs, 16.
Hill v. Josselyn, 320.
Hill v. Miles, 555, 557.
Hill v. Moors, 487.
Hill v. Peoples, 323, 324, 325.
Hill v. Shoemaker, 399.
Hill v. State, 503.
Hill v. True, 493.
Hilles, Estate of, 514.
Hilliard v. Parker, 284, 311.
Hills v. Putnam, 487.
Hills v. Travellers' Bank & Trust Co. 641.
Hillyer v. Hynes, 218.
Hinckley v. Hinckley, 630.
Hinckley's Estate, In re, 270, 272, 275, 499.
Hindman v. O'Connor, 211.
Hinsey v. Supreme Lodge K., 528.
Hinshaw v. Russell, 182, 184.
Hirsch's Estate, In re, 367, 571.
Hiss v. Hiss, 88, 89, 90, 146.
Hitch v. Davis, 406.
Hitch v. Stonebraker, 574.
Hitchcock v. Board of Home Missions of Presbyterian Church, 121, 277.
Hitchcock v. Cosper, 29, 502, 524.
Hitchins, Matter of, 116.
Hite v. Hite's Ex'r, 498.
Hite's Devisees v. Hite's Ex'r, 444, 446, 454.
Hitz v. National Metropolitan Bank, 125.
Hoadley v. Beardsley, 255.
Hoare v. Harris, 627.
Hobart v. Andrews, 462, 496.
Hobbs v. Smith, 159.
Hobbs v. Wayet, 380.
Hobson v. Hale, 239.

CASES CITED
Figures refer to pages

Hodge v. Churchward, 35, 36.
Hodgen's Ex'rs v. Sproul, 426.
Hodges' Estate, In re, 482, 524.
Hoeffer v. Clogan, 281.
Hoff v. Hoff, 239.
Hoffman v. Beltzhoover, 162.
Hoffman v. First Nat. Bank of Jersey City, 23.
Hoffman v. Mackall, 50.
Hoffman v. Union Dime Saving Inst'n, 59, 102.
Hoffman Steam Coal Co. v. Cumberland Coal & Iron Co., 538.
Hoffman's Estate, In re, 369.
Hoffman's Will, In re, 237.
Hofsas v. Cummings, 238.
Hogan v. Jaques, 152, 174.
Hoge v. Hoge, 222.
Hogg v. Hoag, 569.
Hogg's Ex'rs v. Ashe, 16.
Hojnacki v. Hojnacki, 174.
Holbrook v. Harrington, 120.
Holbrook v. Holbrook, 451, 454.
Holbrook's Estate, In re, 483.
Holcomb v. Coryell, 128, 129.
Holcomb v. Kelly, 574.
Holden, In re, 478.
Holden v. Circleville Light & Power Co., 392.
Holden v. Piper, 559.
Holder v. Melvin, 123.
Holder v. Western German Bank, 26.
Holderman v. Hood, 498, 631.
Holland v. Alcock, 271, 280.
Hollander v. Central Metal & Supply Co., 244.
Hollembaek v. More, 540.
Hollis v. Hollis, 225.
Holloway v. Eagle, 610, 614.
Holman v. Renaud, 261, 570.
Holmes, In re, 559.
Holmes v. Coates, 289.
Holmes v. Dalley, 63.
Holmes v. Doll, 607.
Holmes v. Dring, 355.
Holmes v. Gilman, 558.
Holmes v. Holmes, 204.
Holmes v. Mead, 271.
Holmes v. Walter, 229, 232, 249.
Holsapple v. Schrontz, 53, 86, 393.
Home v. Pringle, 511.
Home Inv. Co. v. Strange, 532, 616.
Home Owners' Loan Corporation v. Tognoli, 545.
Home Savings & Loan Co. v. Strain, 350.
Honaker v. Duff, 159.
Honnett v. Williams, 140, 146, 160.

Hooberry v. Harding, 153, 162.
Hood v. Kensington Nat. Bank, 586.
Hooker v. Axford, 224, 226, 227.
Hooker v. Goodwin, 462.
Hooper v. Felgner, 634.
Hoopes v. Mathis, 558.
Hoosier Mining Co. v. Union Trust Co., 321.
Hoover v. Donally, 535.
Hoover v. Ford's Prairie Coal Co., 246.
Hope v. Valley City Salt Co., 47.
Hope Vacuum Cleaner Co. v. Commercial Nat. Bank of Independence, 585.
Hopkins, Appeal of, 557.
Hopkins v. Burr, 561.
Hopkins v. Crossley, 271.
Hopkins v. Glunt, 64.
Hopkins v. Granger, 496.
Hopkins v. Grimshaw, 243, 304.
Hopkins v. Hopkins, 14.
Hopkins v. Stephens, 591.
Hopkins v. Upshur, 270, 273.
Hopkins v. Ward, 591.
Hopkinson v. Dumas, 145.
Hopkinson v. Swaim, 157, 161.
Hoppe v. Manhattan Co., 67.
Hopson's Estate, Matter of, 441.
Horine v. Mengel, 463, 606.
Hornbeck v. Barker, 184.
Hornberger v. Hornberger, 284.
Hornsby v. City Nat. Bank, 238.
Horsley v. Hrenchir, 217.
Horton v. Brocklehurst, 513.
Horton v. Moore, 154.
Horton v. Tabitha Home, 325.
Horton v. Upham, 434.
Hosack v. Rogers, 477.
Hosch Lumber Co. v. Weeks, 320.
Hosmer v. City of Detroit, 292.
Hospes v. Northwestern Mfg. & Car Co., 47.
Hossack v. Ottawa Development Ass'n, 113.
Hostetter's Estate, 454.
Hotchkin v. McNaught-Collins Improvement Co., 604.
Houghton v. Davenport, 546, 554.
Houghton v. Tiffany, 161.
Houston v. Farley, 202.
Houston v. Howze, 493.
Houston's Will, In re, 440.
Houston, E. & W. T. R. Co. v. Charwaine, 603.
Hovenden v. Annesley, 608, 611.
Hovey v. Bradbury, 608.
Howard, In re, 516.

Howard, Matter of, 520.
Howard v. American Peace Society, 122.
Howard v. Gilbert, 569.
Howard v. Howard, 623.
Howard's Adm'rs v. Aiken, 608.
Howe v. Howe, 176, 181, 603.
Howe v. School District, 295.
Howell, In re, 470.
Howell v. Howell, 615.
Howells v. Hettrick, 545.
Howison's Estate, In re, 345.
Hoye v. Hipkins, 162.
Hoysradt, In re, 405, 573.
Hoyt v. Bliss, 286.
Hoyt v. Hoyt, 36.
Hubbard v. Alamo Irrigation & Mfg. Co., 561.
Hubbard v. Burrell, 530.
Hubbard v. Fisher, 479.
Hubbard v. Goodwin, 134.
Hubbard v. Hayes, 159.
Hubbard v. Housley, 240.
Hubbard v. McMahon, 179.
Hubbard v. Stapp, 559.
Hubbard v. United States Mortg. Co., 500.
Hubbell v. Medbury, 615.
Hubbell Trust, In re, 249, 405, 408.
Huber v. Donoghue, 641, 642.
Huddleston v. Henderson, 595.
Hudson v. Cahoon, 599, 614.
Hudson v. Wright, 506.
Huebner, Estate of, 263.
Huff v. Byers, 80.
Huff v. Fuller, 58.
Huffine v. Lincoln, 215.
Huffine v. McCampbell, 86.
Huger v. Protestant Episcopal Church, 233, 636.
Huggins v. Rider, 473, 483.
Hughes v. Farmers' Savings & Building & Loan Co., 401.
Hughes v. Fitzgerald, 56.
Hughes v. Jackson, 132.
Hughes v. Letcher, 604.
Hughes v. Pritchard, 58.
Hughes v. Williams, 319, 410.
Hukill v. Page, 497.
Hullman v. Honcomp, 285.
Hume v. Beale, 604.
Hume v. Franzen, 540, 543.
Humes v. Scott, 500.
Hummel v. Marshall, 180.
Humphrey v. Gerard, 155.
Humphries v. Manhattan Sav. Bank & Trust Co., 350.
Hun v. Cary, 46.
Hunnell v. Zinn, 173.
Hunnicut v. Oren, 617.
Hunnicutt v. Alabama Great Southern R. Co., 150, 152.
Hunt, Appellant, 355.
Hunt, In re, 444.
Hunt v. Freeman, 489.
Hunt v. Gontrum, 336, 502.
Hunt v. Hunt, 60, 81, 140.
Hunt v. Lawton, 407.
Hunt v. Satterwhite, 145.
Hunt v. Smith, 549.
Hunt v. Townsend, 25.
Hunt's Estate, In re, 483.
Hunter v. Feild, 173, 202.
Hunter v. Hubbard, 607.
Hunter v. Hunter, 212, 339, 504, 510.
Hunter v. Lawrence's Adm'r, 45.
Hunter's Estate, In re, 305.
Huntington v. Jones, 151, 153, 154.
Huntington v. Spear, 232.
Huntington Nat. Bank v. Fulton, 578.
Huntington Nat. Bank v. Huntington Distilling Co., 600, 602.
Huntley v. Huntley, 608.
Huse v. Den, 96, 97.
Hussey, Ex parte, 570.
Hussey v. Arnold, 124, 377.
Hussong Dyeing Mach. Co. v. Morris, 501.
Husted v. Thomson, 496.
Huston v. Dodge, 424, 425.
Hutcheson v. Hodnett, 315, 405.
Hutchins v. Dresser, 44.
Hutchins v. Heywood, 155, 177.
Hutchins v. Van Vechten, 81, 88.
Hutchinson v. Lord, 326.
Hutchinson v. Maxwell, 140, 159.
Hutchinson v. National Bank of Commerce, 557.
Huxley v. Rice, 197.
Hyams v. Old Dominion Co., 47.
Hyatt v. Vanneck, 595.
Hyde v. Holmes, 449.
Hyde v. Kitchen, 72.

I

Iddings v. Bruen, 532.
Ide's Ex'rs v. Clark, 63.
Ihmsen, Appeal of, 356, 365.
Ilgenfritz v. Ilgenfritz, 179.
Illinois Steel Co. v. Konkel, 88.
Illinois Trust & Savings Bank v. First Nat. Bank, 25, 557.
Indian Land & Trust Co. v. Owen, 532.

CASES CITED
Figures refer to pages

Indiana I. & I. R. Co. v. Swannell, 589.
Indiana Trust Co. v. Griffin, 349.
Indig v. National City Bank of Brooklyn, 25.
Industrial Trust Co. v. Parks, 441, 442.
Industrial Trust Co. v. Wilson, 457.
Ingersoll, Appeal of, 238.
Ingle v. Partridge, 511.
Inglis v. Sailor's Snug Harbor, 57.
Inglish v. Johnson, 300.
Ingraham v. Ingraham, 297.
Ingram v. Kirkpatrick, 477.
Ingram v. Fraley, 57.
Inlow v. Christy, 333.
Innis v. Carpenter, 237.
Institution for Savings v. Roxbury Home for Aged Women, 264.
Interborough Consol. Corp., In re, 31.
International Shoe Co. v. U. S. Fidelity & Guaranty Co., 49.
International Trust Co. v. Preston, 366, 369, 370.
Interstate Nat. Bank v. Claxton, 581, 585.
Irvine v. Marshall, 177.
Irwin v. Monongahela River Consol. Coal & Coke Co., 204.
Irwin's Appeal, 508.
Isaac v. Emory, 132.
Isham v. Delaware L. & W. R. Co., 645.
Isler v. Brock, 524.
Isom v. First Nat. Bank, 564.
Ithell v. Malone, 458, 465.
Ives v. Beecher, 155.
Ives v. Harris, 147, 640.
Ivory v. Burns, 87, 631.

J

J. A. B. Holding Co. v. Nathan, 89.
Jacks v. State, 589.
Jackson, In re, 484.
Jackson v. Baird, 329.
Jackson v. Becktold Printing & Book Mfg. Co., 145.
Jackson v. Cleveland, 174.
Jackson v. Dickinson, 504.
Jackson v. Farmer, 601.
Jackson v. Jackson, 179.
Jackson v. Ludeling, 46.
Jackson v. Maddox, 449.
Jackson v. Matthews, 318.
Jackson v. Phillips, 261, 288, 289, 298, 303.
Jackson v. Pleasonton, 206.
Jackson v. Sternbergh, 16.
Jackson v. Thomson, 535.
Jackson v. Walsh, 329.
Jackson v. West, 148.
Jackson ex dem. Benson v. Matsdorf, 179.
Jackson ex dem. Lansing v. Chamberlain, 543.
Jackson ex dem. Livingston v. Bateman, 150.
Jackson ex dem. Ten Eyck v. Walker, 150.
Jackson Square Loan & Sav. Ass'n v. Bartlett, 161.
Jacobs v. Jacobs, 544.
Jacobs v. McClintock, 423.
Jacobs v. Snyder, 615.
Jacobs v. Wilmington Trust Co., 318.
Jacobus v. Jacobus, 344.
Jacobus v. Munn, 330, 482, 573.
Jacoby v. Jacoby, 232.
Jaffe v. Weld, 557.
James, Matter of, 94.
James v. City of Newton, 38.
James v. James, 333.
James Roscoe (Bolton), Ltd., v. Winder, 554.
James Stewart & Co., Inc., v. National Shawmut Bank of Boston, 375.
Jamison v. McWhorter, 402.
Jamison v. Mississippi Valley Trust, 164.
Jamison v. Zausch, 125, 145.
Janes v. Falk, 95, 96, 99.
January v. Poyntz, 524.
Jarboe v. Griffith, 626.
Jarboe v. Hey, 161.
Jarrett v. Johnson, 330, 473, 474, 481.
Jarvis v. Babcock, 132.
Jasper v. Hazen, 497.
Jay v. Squire, 459.
Jefferys v. Jefferys, 94.
Jeffery's Estate, In re, 456.
Jeffray v. Towar, 328, 540, 543, 554, 581.
Jelinek v. Stepan, 146.
Jenckes v. Cook, 213, 469.
Jencks v. Safe Deposit & Trust Co. of Baltimore, 319.
Jenkins v. Baker, 73, 76.
Jenkins v. Hammerschlag, 598.
Jenkins v. Walter, 347.
Jenkins v. Wilkins, 570.
Jenkins v. Whyte, 475, 477, 483.
Jenkins' Will, In re, 454.
Jenkinson v. New York Finance Co., 147.

CASES CITED

Jenks v. Title Guaranty & Trust Co., 154.
Jenks' Lessee v. Backhouse, 420.
Jennings v. Coleman, 152.
Jennings v. Hennessy, 70.
Jennings v. Sellick, 175.
Jennings' Ex'rs v. Davis, 524, 593.
Jensen v. Maine Eye & Ear Infirmary, 290.
Jeremiah v. Pitcher, 188, 218.
Jersey Island Packing Co., In re, 154.
Jervis v. Wolferstan, 138.
Jessup v. Smith, 378.
Jessup v. Witherbee Real Estate & Imp. Co., 629.
Jevon v. Bush, 115.
Jewell v. Barnes' Adm'r, 107.
Jewell v. Trilby Mines Co., 600, 602.
Jewett v. Palmer, 535.
Jewett v. Shattuck, 73.
J. I. Case Threshing Mach. Co. v. Walton Trust Co., 124.
Jimmerson v. Ferguson, 224.
Jobe v. Dillard, 162.
Jocelyn v. Nott, 305.
John G. Myers Co. v. Reynolds, 156.
Johns v. Herbert, 371, 502.
Johns v. Johns, 621.
John's Will, In re, 245, 286.
Johnson, Appeal of, 571.
Johnson, In re, 382, 475.
Johnson v. Amberson, 99.
Johnson v. Bayley, 603.
Johnson v. Bennett, 395, 399.
Johnson v. Bowen, 262.
Johnson v. Candage, 87.
Johnson v. Cook, 125.
Johnson v. De Pauw University, 263.
Johnson v. Foust, 603, 617.
Johnson v. Hayward, 537.
Johnson v. Holifield, 284.
Johnson v. Johnson, 187, 189, 300, 498, 499, 544.
Johnson v. Leman, 385.
Johnson v. Muller, 117.
Johnson v. New York Life Ins. Co., 111.
Johnson v. Outlaw, 204.
Johnson v. Petersen, 546, 615.
Johnson v. Prairie, 541.
Johnson v. Richey, 523.
Johnson v. Sage, 237.
Johnson v. Wagner, 487.
Johnson v. Williams, 56.
Johnson's Ex'rs v. Johnson's Heirs, 504.
Johnston v. Eason, 398.
Johnston v. Jickling, 85.

Johnston v. Johnston, 607.
Johnston v. Little, 206.
Johnston v. Redd, 152.
Johnston v. Reilly, 491.
Johnston v. Sherehouse, 497.
Johnston v. Smith, 152.
Johnston v. Spicer, 144.
Johnston's Estate, In re, 245, 247, 297, 369, 482.
Jonas, Ex parte, 140.
Jonathan Mills Mfg. Co. v. Whitehurst, 544.
Jones, Appeal of, 326, 462, 520.
Jones, In re, 129, 283, 419, 524.
Jones v. Broadbent, 41.
Jones v. Bryant, 574.
Jones v. Cole, 579.
Jones v. Coon, 168.
Jones v. Creamer, 487.
Jones v. Davis, 87.
Jones v. Dawson, 471.
Jones v. Day, 477.
Jones v. Dougherty, 569.
Jones v. Downs, 462.
Jones v. Glathart, 545.
Jones v. Habersham, 277, 306.
Jones v. Haines, 603, 631.
Jones v. Harsha, 362, 399.
Jones v. Henderson, 599, 603.
Jones v. Holladay, 325.
Jones v. Home Sav. Bank, 610.
Jones v. Johnson Harvester Co., 542.
Jones v. Jones, 147, 232, 239, 428, 462, 463, 570.
Jones v. Jones' Ex'r, 145.
Jones v. Kilbreth, 23.
Jones v. Lloyd, 595.
Jones v. McKee, 224, 226.
Jones v. Maffet, 323.
Jones v. Old Colony Trust Co., 91.
Jones v. Reest, 159.
Jones v. Roberts, 115.
Jones v. Smith, 333.
Jones v. Swift, 404.
Jones v. Stockett, 417.
Jones v. Van Doren, 82.
Jones v. Watford, 121.
Jones v. Weakley, 102.
Jones' Adm'r v. Shaddock, 534.
Jones' Appeal, 512, 514.
Jones' Estate, In re, 330, 412, 469.
Jordan, Ex parte, 359.
Jordan v. Jordan, 181, 193.
Jordan v. Jordan's Trust Estate, 502.
Jordan's Estate, In re, 276.
Jordan & Davis v. Annex Corporation, 45.

CASES CITED
Figures refer to pages

Joslyn v. Downing, Hopkins & Co., 544.
Jourdan v. Andrews, 88.
Joy v. Midland State Bank, 123.
Joy's Estate, In re, 452.
Judd v. Dike, 524, 592.
Judd's Estate, In re, 289.
Judge of Probate v. Jackson, 481.
Judson v. Walker, 45.
Juillard's Estate, Matter of, 305.
Juniper v. Batchelor, 222.
Justis v. English, 541.

K

Kadis v. Weil, 319, 589.
Kager v. Brenneman, 422.
Kahn v. Tierney, 632.
Kain v. Gibboney, 136.
Kaiser v. Waggoner, 540.
Kaiser's Estate, In re, 343, 393.
Kalbach v. Clark, 451.
Kane v. Bloodgood, 611.
Kane Borough Park Lands Trustees' Appointment, In re, 424.
Kansas City Southern Ry. Co. v. Stevenson, 601.
Kansas City Theological Seminary v. Kendrick, 622.
Kansas Pacific Ry. Co. v. Cutter, 41.
Kansas State Bank v. First State Bank, 24, 25, 561.
Kaphan v. Toney, 422, 530.
Karolusson v. Paonessa, 313.
Kasey v. Fidelity Trust Co., 255.
Kaufman v. Federal National Bank, 131.
Kauffman v. Foster, 493, 549.
Kauffman v. Hiestand, 642.
Kavanaugh's Estate, In re, 122, 280, 282, 307.
Kay v. Scates, 230, 233.
Kayser v. Maugham, 53.
Keane, In re, 367, 369.
Kearney v. Cruikshank, 433.
Kearney v. Kearney, 409.
Keating v. Keating, 161, 571.
Keating v. Stevenson, 386.
Keaton v. Greenwood, 607.
Keaton v. McGwier, 646.
Keeler v. Lauer, 243.
Keeler's Estate, In re, 166, 168.
Keenan v. Scott, 209, 511.
Keene v. Eastman, 297, 636.
Keene's Estate, In re, 130.
Keeney v. Bank of Italy, 2, 551, 580.
Keim v. Lindley, 324.
Keith v. Scales, 286.

Keller, In re, 571.
Keller v. Keller, 177.
Keller v. Washington, 29, 505.
Kelley v. Snow, 69.
Kelley's Estate, In re, 129.
Kellogg, In re, 127, 128.
Kellogg v. Kellogg, 600.
Kellogg v. White, 492.
Kellogg v. Wood, 150.
Kellum v. Smith, 213.
Kelly v. Anderson, 122.
Kelly v. Kelly, 165, 166.
Kelly v. Love's Adm'rs, 286.
Kelly v. Nichols, 135, 238, 262, 294.
Kelly's Estate, In re, 600.
Kelsey v. McTigue, 428.
Kelsey v. Western, 34.
Kelsey's Estate, Matter of, 456, 479.
Kemmerer v. Kemmerer, 289, 300.
Kemp v. Macready, 444.
Kemp v. Porter, 138.
Kendall v. Chase, 31.
Kendall v. De Forest, 502.
Kendall v. Fidelity Trust Co., 584, 585.
Kendall v. Kendall, 497.
Kendrick v. Ray, 88.
Kennard v. Bernard, 424.
Kennedy v. Badgett, 639.
Kennedy v. Baker, 615.
Kennedy v. Dickey, 477, 484.
Kennedy v. Fury, 16.
Kennedy v. Kennedy, 179.
Kennedy v. Pearson, 394.
Kennedy v. Winn, 125, 502.
Kennerson v. Nash, 181.
Kent, In re, 369.
Kent v. Barger, 329.
Kent v. Dunham, 263, 293.
Kent v. Kent, 558.
Kentland Coal & Coke Co. v. Keen, 244.
Kentucky Wagon Mfg. Co. v. Jones & Hopkins Mfg. Co., 579.
Kenworthy v. Levi, 400, 403, 590.
Keplinger v. Keplinger, 1, 60.
Kerlin v. Campbell, 291.
Kern v. Beatty, 179, 195.
Kerner v. Thompson, 274.
Kernochan, Matter of, 434.
Kerns v. Carr, 162.
Kerr v. Kirkpatrick, 322, 513.
Kerr v. Laird, 524.
Kerr v. White, 129, 130, 239.
Kerrigan v. Tabb, 280.
Kessner v. Phillips, 161.
Ketchum v. Mobile & O. R. Co., 572.
Key v. Hughes' Ex'rs, 502, 607.

CASES CITED
Figures refer to pages

Keyes v. Northern Trust Co., 243.
Keyser v. Mitchell, 168.
Kiah v. Grenier, 240.
Kidd v. Borum, 121.
Kidd v. Cruse, 231.
Kidder's Ex'rs v. Kidder, 63.
Kiffner v. Kiffner, 161.
Kight's Estate, In re, 435.
Kilgore, Appeal of, 482.
Kilgore, Ex parte, 574.
Killebrew v. Murphy, 410.
Kimball v. Blanchard, 411, 643.
Kimball v. Crocker, 255.
Kimball v. De Graw, 88.
Kimball v. Reding, 356, 367, 411.
Kimball v. Tripp, 212.
Kimberly's Estate, In re, 273.
Kimber's Will, In re, 456.
Kimmell v. Tipton, 106.
Kimmick v. Linn, 189.
Kincaird v. Scott, 497.
King v. Banks, 302.
King v. Bushnell, 85, 422.
King v. Cushman, 471.
King v. Denison, 35, 36.
King v. Irving, 156.
King v. Mackellar, 361.
King v. Merritt, 120.
King v. Remington, 205.
King v. Stowell, 378, 384, 400.
King v. Talbot, 345, 346, 356, **357**.
King v. Townshend, 136.
King's Estate, In re, 468.
King's Will, In re, 70, 74, 76.
Kingman v. Winchell, 146.
Kingsbury v. Burnside, 87.
Kingsley v. Spofford, 456.
Kingston, Ex parte, 580.
Kinnaird v. Miller's Ex'r, 287.
Kinney v. St. Louis Union Trust Co., 106.
Kinney v. Uglow, 408.
Kip v. Deniston, 510.
Kipp v. O'Melveny, **315**.
Kirby v. State, 503.
Kirchner v. Muller, 386.
Kirkman v. Wadsworth, 420.
Kirstein Leather Co. v. Deitrick, 23.
Kirwin v. Attorney General, 276.
Kitteridge v. Chapman, 535, 545.
Kittinger's Estate, In re, 426.
Klatt v. Keuthan, 514.
Kleinclaus v. Dutard, 600, 603.
Klein's Estate, In re, 416.
Kline's Estate, In re, 338.
Kluender v. Fenske, 544.
Klugh v. Seminole Securities Co., 334.

Klumpert v. Vrieland, 270, 289.
Knapp, In re, 561.
Knapp v. Marshall, 524.
Knatchbull v. Hallett, 562.
Knefler v. Shreve, 152.
Kneisley v. Weir, 557.
Knettle v. Knettle, 156.
Knight v. Knight, 61, 473.
Knight v. Leary, 189.
Knight v. Loomis, 428.
Knight v. Reese, 16, 524.
Knight's Estate, In re, 343, 344.
Knobeloch v. Germania Sav. Bank, 587.
Knowles v. Goodrich, 470.
Knowles v. Williams, 541.
Knowles' Estate, In re, **49**.
Knowlton v. Atkins, 140.
Knowlton v. Bradley, 347, **355**, **524**, 575.
Knox v. Knox, 63.
Knox v. Mackinnon, **327.**
Knust, Ex parte, 425.
Koblitz v. Western Reserve University, 495.
Koch v. Feick, 499.
Koefoed v. Thompson, 211.
Koehler v. Koehler, 107, 189.
Koehne v. Beattie, 429.
Koenig, Appeal of, 632, 633.
Koeninger v. Toledo Trust Co., 91.
Kohtz v. Eldred, 629, 633.
Kolb v. Landes, 243, 257.
Korrick v. Robinson, 557.
Kortright's Estate, In re, 312.
Koteen v. Bickers, 335.
Kountze v. Smith, 143.
Kountze Bros., In re, **29.**
Koyer v. Willmon, 205.
Kraft v. Neuffer, 623.
Kramph's Estate, In re, 279, **300.**
Krause v. Jeannette Inv. Co., **619.**
Krause v. Krause, 542.
Krauss v. Cornell, 342.
Krauth v. Thiele, 182.
Krickerberg v. Hoff, 94.
Kringle v. Rhomberg, 540.
Kroll v. Coach, 196.
Kronheim v. Johnson, 106.
Kronson v. Lipschitz, 230.
Krouskop v. Krouskop, 215.
Kuhn v. Kuhn, 200.
Kuncl v. Kuncl, 180.
Kutz, Appeal of, 610.
Kuykendall v. Zenn, 628.
Kyle v. Barnett, 205.

CASES CITED
Figures refer to pages

L

Lacey, Ex parte, 204.
Lach v. Weber, 86.
Lackland v. Davenport, 130.
Lackland v. Walker, 287, 300.
La Cotts v. La Cotts, 213.
Ladd v. Judson, 153, 156.
Ladd v. Ladd, 129, 321.
Ladd v. Pigott, 475, 477.
Ladd v. Smith, 576.
Lady Ensley Coal, Iron & R. Co. v. Gordon, 605.
Lafferty v. Turley, 601.
Lafferty's Estate, In re, 478, 482.
Lafkowitz v. Jackson, 177.
La Forge v. Binns, 319, 572.
Lagarde v. Anniston Lime & Stone Co., 205.
Lakatong Lodge, No. 114, of Quakertown, etc., v. Board of Education of Franklin Tp., Hunterdon County, 302, 427.
Lalla's Estate, In re, 353.
Lamar v. Walton, 576.
Lamb v. Cain, 493.
Lamb v. First Huntington Nat. Bk., 117, 143.
Lamb v. Ladd, 28.
Lamb v. Lamb, 607.
Lamb v. Rooney, 199.
Lamb v. Schiefner, 198.
Lambert v. Morgan, 148.
Lamberton v. Pereles, 147.
Lamberton v. Youmans, 603.
Lammer v. Stoddard, 615.
Lamp v. Homestead Bldg. Ass'n, 569, 570.
Lancaster Trust Co. v. Long, 213.
Lander v. Persky, 176.
Landis v. Scott, 465, 523, 524.
Landis v. Wooden, 270, 273.
Landon v. Hutton, 94.
Landow v. Keane, 377.
Lane v. Black, 209.
Lane v. First State Bank, 561.
Lane v. Lewis, 572.
Lane v. Wentworth, 535.
Lang v. Everling, 36.
Lang v. Lang's Ex'r, 447.
Lang v. Metzger, 504.
Lang v. Shell Petroleum Corporation, 199.
Langdon v. Blackburn, 500.
Lanius v. Fletcher, 239, 643.
Lanning v. Commissioners of Public Instruction of City of Trenton, 425.

Lannon's Estate, In re, 281.
Lansburgh v. Parker, 511.
Lantry v. Lantry, 218.
Lape's Adm'r v. Taylor's Trustee, 470, 575.
Larisey v. Larisey, 176, 178.
Larkin v. Wikoff, 302.
Larkin & Metcalf, In re, 557.
Larmon v. Knight, 196.
Laroe v. Douglass, 511.
Lasker-Morris Bank & Trust Co. v. Gans, 178.
Lasker-Morris Bank & Trust Co. v. Gans, 524, 599, 613.
Lasley v. Delano, 85.
Lasley's Ex'r v. Lasley, 569.
Lassiter v. Jones, 296.
Late Corporation of the Church of Jesus Christ of Latter-Day Saints v. United States, 300.
Lathers' Will, Matter of, 388.
Lathrop v. Bampton, 504, 564.
Lathrop v. Gilbert, 505.
Lathrop v. Smalley's Ex'rs, 475, 524, 573.
Lathrop v. White, 538.
Latimer v. Hanson, 526.
Latrobe v. Tiernan, 320.
Latshaw v. Western Townsite Co., 113.
Lattan v. Van Ness, 71, 73, 74.
Laughlin v. Laughlin, 603.
Laughlin v. Page, 140, 420, 628.
Laurel County Court v. Trustees of Laurel Seminary, 512.
Lau's Estate, In re, 625.
Lavender v. Lee, 124.
Law v. Law, 180.
Law's Estate, In re, 344.
Lawrence v. Lawrence, 97, 136, 420, 625.
Lawrence v. Littlefield, 438.
Lawrence v. Prosser, 292.
Lawson v. Cunningham, 366, 395.
Lawson v. Lawson, 215.
Lawton v. Lawton, 366.
Leach v. Cowan, 462, 473.
Leach v. Leach, 210.
Leach v. State Sav. Bank, 587.
Leader v. Tierney, 491.
Leake v. Benson, 152.
Leake v. Garrett, 196.
Leake v. Watson, 590.
Learned v. Tritch, 534.
Learned v. Welton, 320, 398.
Learoyd v. Whiteley, 347.
Leary v. Corvin, 186.
Leavitt, In re, 483, 629.

CASES CITED
Figures refer to pages

Le Blanc, Matter of, 32.
Lecroix v. Malone, 421.
Lednum v. Dallas Trust & Savings Bank, 418.
Ledrich, In re, 332.
Lee v. Enos, 124.
Lee v. Fox, 44.
Lee v. Kennedy, 73.
Lee v. Oates, 136, 232.
Lee v. O'Donnell, 244.
Lee v. Randolph, 120.
Lee v. R. H. Elliott & Co., 182.
Lee v. Simpson, 497.
Lee's Estate, In re, 632.
Lee's Lessee v. Tiernan, 16.
Leggett v. Dubois, 134, 177.
Leggett v. Grimmett, 423.
Leggett v. Perkins, 240.
Legniti v. Mechanics' & Metals Nat. Bank of New York, 30.
Lehmann v. Rothbarth, 524, 525.
Lehnard v. Specht, 497, 544.
Lehrling v. Lehrling, 173.
Leigh v. Barry, 509, 521.
Leigh v. Harrison, 161.
Leigh v. Laughlin, 140.
Leigh v. Lockwood, 388.
Leitsch's Will, In re, 372.
Lejee's Estate, In re, 58.
Leman v. Whitley, 174.
Lembeck v. Lembeck, 411.
Lemmond v. Peoples, 235.
Lennartz v. Popp's Estate, 534.
Lennon's Estate, In re, 262.
Lent v. Howard, 645.
Leonard, In re, 41.
Leonard v. Barnum, 464.
Leonard v. Burr, 305.
Leonard v. Haworth, 120.
Leonard v. Pierce, 464.
Lepage v. McNamara, 300.
Leroy v. Norton, 176.
Lescaleet v. Rickner, 182.
Lesesne v. Cheves, 358.
Leslie v. Leslie, 88, 90.
Lester v. Stephens, 136.
Letcher's Trustee v. German Nat. Bank, 572, 574.
Levant State Bank v. Shults, 545.
Levara v. McNeny, 204.
Levin v. Ritz, 115.
Levy v. Cooke, 540.
Levy v. Hart, 488.
Levy v. Levy, 112.
Levy v. Ryland, 613.
Levy's Estate, In re, 456.
Lewellin v. Mackworth, 612.
Lewis v. Broun, 209.

Lewis v. Curnutt, 99, 138.
Lewis v. Equitable Mortg. Co., 534.
Lewis v. Gaillard, 300.
Lewis v. Helm, 208.
Lewis v. Hill, 333.
Lewis v. Nobbs, 510, 517, 520.
Lewis v. Williams, 213.
Lewis' Adm'r v. Glenn, 570.
Lewis' Estate, In re, 642.
Lexington Brewing Co. v. Hamon, 148.
Libby v. Frost, 137, 138.
Liberty Nat. Bank & Trust Co. v. Loomis, 444.
Lich v. Lich, 144.
Lide v. Park, 614.
Liesemer v. Burg, 129.
Ligget v. Fidelity & Columbia Trust Co., 244.
Lightfoot v. Beard, 449.
Lightfoot v. Davis, 199.
Lightfoot v. Poindexter, 122, 273, 292, 307.
Lillard v. Lillard, 193.
Lincoln v. Alexander, 45.
Lincoln v. Wright, 513.
Lincoln Sav. Bank v. Gray, 541.
Lincoln Soc. of Friends v. Joel, 534.
Lindenberger v. Kentucky Title Trust Co., 407.
Linder v. Officer, 342.
Lindheim v. Manhattan Ry. Co., 591.
Lindsay v. Harrison, 160.
Lindsay v. Lindsay's Adm'rs, 16.
Lindsey v. Rose, 162.
Lines v. Darden, 61, 62.
Linn v. Downing, 169.
Linnard's Estate, 327.
Linsley, In re, 504, 521.
Linsley v. Strang, 328, 333.
Linsly v. Bogert, 482.
Linton v. Brown's Adm'rs, 96.
Linton's Estate, In re, 144.
Lionberger v. Baker, 546.
Lipp v. Lipp, 218.
Lippincott v. Williams, 619, 629.
Lippitt v. Thames Loan & Trust Co., 25.
Liptrot v. Holmes, 633.
Lister v. Weeks, 571.
Litchfield v. White, 326, 519.
Littig v. Vestry of Mt. Calvary Protestant Episcopal Church, 68, 72, 74.
Little v. Chadwick, 556, 559.
Little v. City of Newburyport, 263.
Little v. Willford, 271, 276.
Litzenberger, Matter of, 512.

CASES CITED
Figures refer to pages

Livermore v. Aldrich, 177.
Livermore v. Livermore, 392.
Lloyd v. Brooks, 103.
Lloyd v. Kirkwood, 603.
Lloyd v. Woods, 177.
Lobdell v. State Bank of Neuvoo, 644.
Locke v. Andrasko, 489.
Locke v. Farmers' Loan & Trust Co., 625.
Locke v. Cope, 468.
Lockhart v. Reilly, 510, 521.
Lockridge v. Mace, 245.
Lockward v. Evans, 197.
Loder v. Hatfield, 34, 35, 36.
Loften v. Witboard, 180.
Logan v. Aabel, 534.
Logan v. Glass, 34, 36.
Lomax v. Pendleton, 524.
London's Estate, In re, 365.
Long v. Blackall, 243.
Long v. King, 182.
Long v. Long, 179, 395.
Long v. Rike, 436.
Long v. Simmons Female College, 402.
Long's Estate, In re, 133.
Long Island Loan & Trust Co., In re, 470.
Long Island Loan & Trust Co., Matter of, 329.
Longley v. Hall, 477.
Longmire v. Pilkington, 44.
Longstreth's Estate, In re, 418.
Loomer v. Loomer, 243, 247.
Loomis v. Laramie, 256.
Lord v. Comstock, 626.
Lord v. Lord, 34.
Lorenz v. Weller, 471, 572.
Loring v. Blake, 244.
Loring v. Brodie, 400, 544.
Loring v. Hildreth, 96, 98.
Loring v. Palmer, 132.
Loring v. Salisbury Mills, 472.
Loud v. Winchester, 459, 482.
Loughney v. Page, 150.
Louisville, N. A. & C. Ry. Co. v. Hubbard, 476.
Louisville Trust Co. v. Morgan, 386.
Louisville Trust Co. v. Warren, 474.
Louisville & N. R. Co. v. Boykin, 535, 536.
Louisville & N. R. Co. v. Powers, 125.
Lounsbury v. Purdy, 183.
Lounsbury v. Trustees of Square Lake Burial Ass'n, 259, 284, 307.
Love v. Braxton, 534.
Love v. Engelke, 437.
Love v. Rogers, 604.
Lovell v. Briggs, 210.

Lovell v. Felkins, 204.
Lovell v. Nelson, 591.
Lovering v. Worthington, 244.
Lovett v. Farnham, 622.
Lovett v. Taylor, 53, 174, 175, 215.
Low v. Marco, 150.
Lowe v. Jones, 557.
Lowe v. Montgomery, 571.
Lowe v. Morris, 475.
Lowe's Estate, In re, 265, 335.
Lowell v. Lowell, 186.
Lowndes v. City Nat. Bank of South Norwalk, 580, 584, 587, 589.
Lowrie, Appeal of, 470.
Lowrie's Estate, In re, 413.
Lowry's Lessee v. Steele, 145.
Lowson v. Copeland, 337.
Lozier v. Hill, 201.
Lucas v. Dixon, 86.
Lucas v. Donaldson, 420.
Lucas v. Lockhart, 62.
Lucia Mining Co. v. Evans, 530.
Ludington v. Patton, 210, 328, 332.
Ludlam v. Holman, 132.
Ludlow v. Rector, etc., of St. Johns Church, 133.
Luers v. Brunjes, 597.
Lufkin v. Jakeman, 180, 613.
Lugar v. Lugar, 146.
Lukens, Appeal of, 478, 524.
Lummus v. Davidson, 150, 152.
Lummus Cotton Gin Co. v. Walker, 557.
Lundie v. Walker, 132.
Lunt v. Van Gorden, 643.
Luntz v. Greve, 145.
Luquire v. Lee, 319.
Lurie v. Sabath, 59.
Luscombe v. Grigsby, 204, 497, 535.
Luscombe's Will, In re, 58.
Lutes v. Louisville & N. R. Co., 635.
Luxon v. Wilgus, 343.
Lycan v. Miller, 464.
Lyddane v. Lyddane, 402.
Lyle v. Burke, 43, 125, 630.
Lyman v. Pratt, 449.
Lyman v. Stevens, 459.
Lynch v. Herrig, 182, 183, 189.
Lynch v. South Congregational Parish of Augusta, 300.
Lynch's Will, In re, 65.
Lynde v. Lynde, 444.
Lynn v. Lynn, 230.
Lyon v. Foscue, 470.
Lyon v. Safe Deposit & Trust Co., 123.
Lyon's Estate, In re, 534.

Lyons v. Bass, 202.
Lytle's Ex'r v. Pope's Adm'r, 138.

M

Mabie v. Bailey, 68, 70, 73, 76, 78, 79, 523.
McAdoo v. Sayre, 462.
McAfee v. Green, 136.
McAfee v. Thomas, 456.
McAllister v. Commonwealth, 348.
McArthur v. Gordon, 86, 504.
McAuley v. Wilson, 300.
McAuslan v. Union Trust Co., 404.
McBreen v. McBreen, 145.
McBride v. Elmer's Ex'rs, 122.
McBride v. McIntyre, 125, 462, 464, 524.
McBride v. Murphy, 300.
McCallum's Estate, In re, 478.
McCampbell v. Brown, 497.
McCandless v. Warner, 569.
McCants v. Bee, 332, 544.
McCarthy v. Provident Institution for Savings, 108.
McCarthy v. Tierney, 487.
McCartin v. Traphagen, 521.
McCartney v. Bostwick, 150, 189.
McCartney v. Ridgway, 625.
McCarty v. McCarty's Ex'rs, 16.
McCaskey's Estate, In re, 426.
McCaskill v. Lathrop, 534.
McCauseland, Appeal of, 477, 523.
McClanahan's Heirs v. Henderson's Heirs, 469.
McClane's Adm'x v. Shepherd's Ex'x, 463.
McClean v. McClean, 61.
McClear's Estate, In re, 607.
McClellan v. McClellan, 81, 86, 87, 88, 115.
McClelland v. Myers, 534.
McClenahan v. Stevenson, 174.
McClernan v. McClernan, 130, 577
McCloskey v. Bowden, 470.
McCloskey v. Gleason, 506.
McCloskey v. McCloskey, 215.
McClung v. Colwell, 177.
McClure v. Middletown Trust Co., 339, 506.
McColl v. Fraser, 561.
McColl v. Weatherly, 45.
McCollister v. Bishop, 344.
McCollister v. Willey, 172.
McCollum, Matter of, 430.
McComb v. Frink, 524.
McConnell v. Day, 423.
McConville v. Ingham, 211.

McCormick v. Cooke, 180.
McCormick v. McCormick's Adm'r, 557.
McCormick v. Malin, 208.
McCormick Harvesting Mach. Co. v. Yankton Sav. Bank, 24.
McCosker v. Brady, 140, 628.
McCoy v. Anderson, 591.
McCoy v. Horwitz, 358.
McCoy v. Houck, 161.
McCoy v. McCoy, 53, 496.
McCrea v. Purmort, 500.
McCrea v. Yule, 147.
McCreary v. Gewinner, 88, 489.
McCreary v. McCreary, 189.
McCreary v. Robinson, 162.
McCrory v. Beeler, 408, 488.
Maccubbin v. Cromwell's Ex'rs, 127, 511.
McCulloch v. Tomkins, 465, 481.
McCulloch v. Valentine, 145.
McCullough's Ex'rs v. McCullough, 346, 360.
McCurdy v. McCallum, 61.
McCutchen v. Roush, 505.
McDaniel v. Peabody, 542.
McDermith v. Voorhees, 192.
McDermott v. Eborn, 237.
McDonald v. Carr, 180.
McDonald v. May's Ex'rs, 607.
McDonald v. Shaw, 270, 394.
McDonald v. Sims, 606.
McDonnell v. McDonnell, 641.
McDonogh v. Murdoch, 113.
McDowell, In re, 320, 485.
McDowell v. Caldwell, 468.
McDowell v. McDowell, 226.
McDowell v. Rees, 232.
Macduff, In re, 267, 268.
McDuffie v. McIntyre, 45.
McDuffie v. Montgomery, 63.
McElveen v. Adams, 83.
McEvoy v. Boston Five Cent Sav. Bank, 90.
McElroy v. McElroy, 190.
McElveen v. Adams, 623.
McFall v. Kirkpatrick, 123, 127, 140, 233, 234.
Macfarlane v. Dorsey, 152.
McFarland v. McFarland, 189.
McGee v. McGee, 179.
McGee v. Wells, 187.
McGill v. Chappelle, 173.
McGillivray, In re, 569, 571.
McGinn v. Shaeffer, 329.
McGinness v. Barton, 84.
McGinnis v. McGinnis, 179.
McGowan v. McGowan, 184, 186.

CASES CITED
Figures refer to pages

McGraw's Estate, In re, 312.
MacGregor v. MacGregor, 365, 564.
McGregor-Noe Hardware Co. v. Horn, 152, 153.
McGuffey's Estate, In re, 413.
McGuire v. Inhabitants of Linneus, 608.
McHardy v. McHardy's Ex'r, 234, 462.
McHenry v. Jewett, 489.
McHugh v. McCole, 282.
McIlvain v. Hockaday, 283, 284.
McInerny v. Haase, 249.
McIntire v. Hughes, 94.
McIntire v. Linehan, 575.
McIntire's Adm'rs v. City of Zanesville, 366.
McIntosh v. City of Charleston, 113.
McIntyre v. McIntyre, 202.
Mack v. Champion, 146.
McKay v. Atwood, 44.
McKeage v. Coleman, 35.
McKean & Elk Land & Imp. Co. v. Clay, 615.
McKee v. Weeden, 477.
McKenna v. O'Connell, 572.
McKennan v. Pry, 532.
McKenney's Will, In re, 642.
Mackenzie v. Los Angeles Trust & Savings Bank, 607.
McKenzie v. Sumner, 639.
MacKenzie v. Trustees of Presbytery of Jersey City, 306, 494.
McKeon, In re, 573.
McKeown's Estate, In re, 257, 452.
Mackersy v. Ramsays, 24, 26.
McKibben v. Diltz's Ex'r, 532.
McKie v. Clark, 484.
McKim v. Blake, 575.
McKim v. Doane, 575.
McKim v. Glover, 369.
McKim v. Hibbard, 523.
McKimmon v. Rodgers, 153.
McKinley v. Irvine, 464.
McKinney's Estate, In re, 365, 478.
McKissick v. Pickle, 296.
Macklanburg v. Griffith, 524.
McKnatt v. McKnatt, 332.
McKnight v. McKnight, 338.
McKnight's Ex'rs v. Walsh, 482, 526.
Mackrell v. Walker, 629.
McLatchie, In re, 512.
McLaughlin v. Fulton, 557.
McLaughlin v. Minnesota Loan & Trust Co., 391.
McLaurie v. Partlow, 87, 506.
McLean v. Nelson, 122.
McLellan v. McLean, 224, 226.

McLeod v. Cooper, 156.
McLeod v. Evans, 561.
McLouth v. Hunt, 444.
M'Mahon v. Featherstonhaugh, 567.
McMonagle v. McGlinn, 602.
McMullen v. Lank, 150.
McMurray v. Montgomery, 514.
McNair v. Montague, 573.
McNamara v. Garrity, 614.
McNamara v. McNamara, 540.
McNeer v. Patrick, 634.
McNeil v. Gates, 196.
McNeill v. St. Aubin, 643.
McNinch v. Trego, 614.
McNish v. Guerard, 429.
McParland v. Larkin, 211.
McPherrin v. Fair, 205.
McPherson v. Cox, 572.
McRarey v. Huff, 197.
McStay Supply Co. v. Stoddard, 581.
McTigue v. McTigue, 145.
McVey v. McQuality, 542.
McWaid v. Blair State Bank, 534.
McWilliams v. Gough, 425.
Macy v. Williams, 68, 71, 72, 73, 74, 75, 77.
Madison v. Madison, 603, 604.
Madison Trust Co. v. Carnegie Trust Co., 502.
Madison Trust Co. v. Skogstrom, 101.
Madler v. Kersten, 131.
Mad River Nat. Bank of Springfield v. Melhorn, 25.
Madsen v. Madsen, 179.
Maffet v. Oregon & C. R. Co., 421.
Maffitt v. Read, 463.
Magallen v. Gomes, 378.
Magill v. Brown, 287, 291.
Maginn v. Green, 473.
Magner v. Crooks, 163.
Magnolia Park Co. v. Tinsley, 534.
Magraw v. Pennock, 401.
Magruder v. Drury, 475.
Mahan v. Mahan, 94.
Mahin's Estate, In re, 599, 613.
Mahorner v. Harrison, 176.
Major v. Herndon, 431.
Makeever v. Yeoman, 189.
Makin's Estate, In re, 361.
Malady v. McEnary, 189.
Malim v. Keighley, 61.
Malin v. Malin, 87.
Mallon's Estate, In re, 61, 571.
Mallory v. Clark, 468.
Mallory v. Mallory, 423.
Mallott v. Wilson, 127.
Malone v. Kelley, 210.
Malone v. Malone, 496.

688 CASES CITED
Figures refer to pages

Maltbie v. Olds, 195.
Maltz v. Westchester County Brewing Co., 205.
Manaudas v. Mann, 607.
Mangan v. Shea, 147.
Mangels v. Tippett, 330.
Mangold v. Adrian Irr. Co., 45.
Manheim v. Woods, 208.
Manion's Adm'r v. Titsworth, 618.
Manley v. Fiske, 61.
Manley v. Hunt, 124.
Mann v. Day, 369.
Mann v. McDonald, 211.
Mannhardt v. Illinois Staats-Zeitung Co., 321, 570.
Manning v. Manning, 189, 602.
Manning's Estate, In re, 385.
Mannix v. Purcell, 81.
Mansfield v. Wardlow, 400, 541.
Manson v. Felton, 44.
Mantle v. Speculator Min. Co., 608.
Manufacturers Life Ins. Co. v. The von Hamm-Young Co., Ltd., 243.
Manufacturers' Nat. Bank v. Continental Bank, 22, 26.
Marble v. Whaley, 593.
Marbury v. Ehlen, 590.
March v. Romare, 423.
Marie M. E. Church v. Trinity M. E. Church, 86.
Markel v. Peck, 519.
Markey v. Markey, 71.
Markley v. Camden Safe Deposit & Trust Co., 615.
Marks v. Loewenberg, 7.
Marks v. Semple, 477, 502.
Marquam v. Ross, 627.
Marr v. Marr, 332.
Marr's Heirs v. Gilliam, 608, 626.
Marriott v. Kinnersley, 511, 518.
Mars v. Gibert, 300, 301.
Marsden's Estate, In re, 572.
Marsh v. Keogh, 73, 74, 76, 77.
Marsh v. Marsh, 475.
Marsh v. Marsh's Ex'rs, 462.
Marshall v. Fisk, 231.
Marshall v. Frazier, 350.
Marshall v. Lister, 546.
Marshall v. McDermitt, 546.
Marshall v. Marshall, 603.
Marshall's Adm'r v. Marshall, 99.
Marshall's Estate, In re, 612, 615.
Marshall's Trustee v. Rash, 153.
Marsteller, Appeal of, 478.
Marston v. Marston, 473.
Martin v. Baird, 88.
Martin v. Bowen, 546.

Martin v. Branch Bank of Decatur, 618.
Martin v. Davis, 146.
Martin v. Fix, 538, 541.
Martin v. Funk, 72, 74, 103.
Martin v. Granger, 534.
Martin v. Kansas Nat. Bank, 587.
Martin v. Margham, 308.
Martin v. Martin, 68, 71, 74, 189, 202, 524, 601, 602.
Martin v. Moore, 56.
Martin v. Thomas, 181.
Martin's Estate, In re, 572.
Martin & Garrett v. Mask, 37.
Martling v. Martling, 233.
Martzell v. Stauffer, 499.
Marvel v. Marvel, 84.
Marvel v. Wilmington Trust Co., 233.
Marvin v. Brooks, 42, 43, 461.
Marvin v. Smith, 463, 488.
Marx v. Clisby, 596.
Marx v. McGlynn, 134, 140.
Maryland Casualty Co. v. Safe Deposit & Trust Co. of Baltimore, 318.
Maryland Grange Agency v. Lee, 161.
Mask v. Miller, 425.
Mason v. Bank of Commerce, 394.
Mason v. Bloomington Library Ass'n, 259, 284, 299, 424.
Mason v. Mason's Ex'rs, 118.
Mason v. Paschal, 628.
Mason v. Pomeroy, 384.
Mason v. Rhode Island Hospital Trust Co., 645.
Mason v. Whitthorne, 340, 348.
Mason's Estate, In re, 202.
Masonic Education and Charity Trust v. City of Boston, 263.
Massachusetts General Hospital v. Amory, 424.
Massey v. Huntington, 93.
Master v. Second Parish of Portland, 619.
Masters v. Mayes, 176, 534.
Mastin v. Marlow, 109.
Mathew v. Brise, 44.
Mathews v. Heyward, 401.
Mathews v. Meek, 428.
Mathews v. Ruggles-Brise, 381.
Mathews v. Stephenson, 379.
Mathewson v. Davis, 524, 525.
Mathewson v. Wakelee, 549.
Mathias v. Fowler, 140.
Matlock v. Lock, 248.
Matthews v. Brooklyn Sav. Bank, 69, 71, 73, 74.
Matthews v. McPherson, 471, 497.

CASES CITED

Matthews v. Murchison, 570.
Matthews v. Thompson, 395, 646.
Matthews v. Ward, 144.
Mattison v. Mattison, 162, 421.
Mattocks v. Moulton, 361.
Mauldin v. Armistead, 107.
Mauldin v. Mauldin, 395, 645.
Mavrich v. Grier, 401.
Maxcy v. City of Oshkosh, 113, 262, 636.
Maxwell v. Finnie, 572.
Maxwell v. Vaught, 155.
May v. Baker, 156.
May v. May, 195, 569, 570, 572.
May's Estate, In re, 476.
Maydwell v. Maydwell, 572.
Mayer v. Citizens' Bank of Sturgeon, 581.
Mayer v. Kane, 180, 536.
Mayer v. Wilkins, 150.
Mayfield v. Forsyth, 601.
Mayfield v. Turner, 540.
Maynard's Case, 204.
Mayor of Colchester v. Lowten, 105.
Mays v. Jackson, 178.
Mazelin v. Rouyer, 569.
Mazzolla v. Wilkie, 534.
Mead v. Chesbrough Bldg. Co., 502.
Mead v. Robertson, 225.
Meade v. Fullerton's Adm'x, 211.
Meador v. Manlove, 224.
Meadows v. Marsh, 487.
Mechanics' Bank, In re, 573.
M. E. Dunn & Co., In re, 554.
Medwedeff v. Fisher, 165.
Mee v. Gordon, 56.
Meehan's Estate, In re, 422.
Meek v. Briggs, 248.
Meek v. Meek, 218.
Meek v. Perry, 211.
Meeks v. Meeks, 462.
Meeting St. Baptist Soc. v. Hail, 286.
Megargee v. Naglee, 640.
Megowan v. Peterson, 378.
Megrue, In re, 256.
Meier v. Bell, 189.
Meier v. Blair, 156.
Meier v. Hess, 148.
Meislahn v. Meislahn, 69, 72, 74, 76, 78.
Meldahl v. Wallace, 163.
Meldon v. Devlin, 504, 516.
Melick v. Pidcock, 232.
Mellon v. Driscoll, 165.
Mendel's Will, In re, 365.
Mendenhall v. Walters, 491, 493, 631.
Mendes v. Guedella, 511, 513.
Menken Co. v. Brinkley, 162.

BOGERT TRUSTS 2D—44

Menzie's Estate, In re, 346.
Mercantile Nat. Bank of Cleveland v. Parsons, 541, 544.
Mercantile Trust Co. v. St. Louis & S. F. R. Co., 554, 555.
Mercer v. Buchanan, 239, 452.
Mercer v. Coomler, 181.
Mercer v. Safe-Deposit & Trust Co., 140.
Merchants' Fund Ass'n, Appeal of, 452.
Merchants' Ins. Co. of Providence v. Abbott, 545.
Merchants' Loan & Trust Co. v. Northern Trust Co., 359, 360, 364, 367.
Merchants' Nat. Bank v. Crist, 36, 161.
Merchants' Nat. Bank of Ft. Worth v. Phillip & Wiggs Machinery Co., 535.
Merchants' & Planters' Nat. Bank of Union v. Clifton Mfg. Co., 585.
Meredith v. Citizens' Nat. Bank, 181.
Mereness v. Delemos, 176.
Merigan v. McGonigle, 68, 70, 74, 77, 78.
Merino v. Munoz, 29.
Merket v. Smith, 565.
Merriam v. Hemmenway, 420.
Merrick v. Waters, 204.
Merrill v. American Baptist Missionary Union, 304.
Merritt v. Bucknam, 304.
Merritt v. Corlies, 239.
Merritt v. Jenkins, 391.
Merryman v. Euler, 209.
Mersereau v. Bennet, 56, 463.
Mershon v. Duer, 176.
Mertens v. Schlemme, 504.
Merton v. O'Brien, 35.
Meserole, In re, 477.
Methodist Episcopal Church of Newark v. Clark, 271.
Metropolis Trust & Savings Bank v. Monnier, 210.
Metropolitan Life Ins. Co. v. Hall, 83, 98.
Metropolitan Nat. Bank v. Campbell Commission Co., 505.
Metropolitan Nat. Bank of New York v. Loyd, 23.
Metropolitan Trust & Savings Bank v. Perry, 181.
Mettler v. Warner, 328.
Metzger v. Emmel, 567.
Metzger v. Lehigh Valley Trust & Safe Deposit Co., 502, 544.

CASES CITED
Figures refer to pages

Metzger v. Metzger, 218.
Meunier, Succession of, 272.
Meurer v. Stokes, 462.
Meyer v. Barth, 576, 577.
Miami County Bank v. State ex rel. Peru Trust Co., 580, 581, 583.
Michel's Trusts, In re, 277.
Michigan Home Missionary Soc. v. Corning, 355.
Michigan Trust Co. v. Baker, 244.
Mickleburgh v. Parker, 512, 520.
Middleton v. Shelby County Trust Co., 625.
Mildeberger v. Franklin, 462.
Miles v. Bacon, 473.
Miles v. Ervin, 204.
Miles v. Miles, 87, 230.
Milholland v. Whalen, 69, 70, 73.
Milhous v. Dunham, 359.
Millar's Trustees v. Polson, 515.
Miller, In re, 286, 416.
Miller v. Baker, 614.
Miller v. Beverleys, 473, 524.
Miller v. Blose's Ex'r, 179.
Miller v. Butler, 501.
Miller v. Chittenden, 270.
Miller v. Davis, 177.
Miller v. Dodge, 332.
Miller v. Douglass, 246.
Miller v. Hill, 59, 224.
Miller v. Holcombe's Ex'r, 355.
Miller v. Knowles, 423.
Miller v. London, 191.
Miller v. Lux, 525.
Miller v. Miller, 195, 202, 244, 422, 505.
Miller v. Parkhurst, 341.
Miller v. Payne, 451.
Miller v. Porter, 262.
Miller v. Proctor, 327, 347.
Miller v. Rosenberger, 136.
Miller v. Safe Deposit & Trust Co. of Baltimore, 451.
Miller v. Saxton, 604, 614.
Miller v. Seaman's Bank for Savings, 77.
Miller v. Silverman, 101.
Miller v. Tatum, 272, 277.
Miller's Ex'rs v. Miller's Heirs and Creditors, 627, 643.
Miller's Heirs v. Antle, 213.
Millerstown Borough v. Receivers of Millerstown Deposit Bank, 32.
Milloglav v. Zacharias, 218, 502.
Mills v. Hendershot, 618.
Mills v. Michigan Trust Co., 415.
Mills v. Mills, 208.
Mills v. Newberry, 57.

Mills v. Swearingen, 369.
Millsaps v. Johnson, 633.
Milner v. Hyland, 617.
Milton v. Pace, 233.
Minasian v. Aetna Life Ins. Co., 201.
Minnich's Estate, In re, 162.
Minns v. Billings, 287.
Minor v. Rogers, 70.
Minot v. Paine, 446, 450.
Minot v. Thompson, 441.
Minot v. Tilton, 126.
Minturn v. Seymour, 94.
Mintz v. Brock, 465.
Minuse v. Cox, 525.
Missouri Historical Soc. v. Academy of Science, 286.
Mitchell v. Berry, 395.
Mitchell v. Bilderback, 107.
Mitchell v. Blanchard, 530.
Mitchell v. Carrollton Nat. Bank, 413, 491.
Mitchell v. Colby, 208.
Mitchell v. Colglazier, 189.
Mitchell v. Dunn, 552.
Mitchell v. Pitner, 425.
Mitchell v. Stevens, 423.
Mitchell's Estate, In re, 63.
Mize v. Bates County Nat. Bank, 103, 625.
M. J. Hoey & Co., In re, 108.
Mobley v. Phinizy, 372.
Moeller v. Poland, 327.
Moffatt v. Buchanan, 609.
Moffett v. Eames, 475.
Moggridge v. Thackwell, 299.
Moke v. Norrie, 118.
Molk's Estate, In re, 63.
Moll v. Gardner, 150.
Moloney v. Tilton, 96, 535.
Molton v. Henderson, 612.
Monell v. Monell, 512.
Moninger v. Security Title & Trust Co., 557.
Monk, In re, 308.
Monroe v. Gregory, 600.
Monroe's Trustee v. Monroe, 147.
Montague v. Hayes, 87.
Montfort v. Montfort, 120.
Montgomery v. Coldwell, 465.
Montgomery v. Gilbert, 462.
Montgomery v. Trueheart, 123, 628.
Montjoy v. Lashbrook, 526.
Mooney's Estate, In re, 193.
Moore v. Crump, 197.
Moore v. Emery, 487.
Moore v. First Nat. Bank of Kansas City, 549.
Moore v. Hazelton, 44.

BOGERT TRUSTS 2D

CASES CITED
Figures refer to pages

Moore v. Hegeman, 240.
Moore v. Hunter, 541.
Moore v. Isbel, 319.
Moore v. McClain, 202.
Moore v. McFall, 382.
Moore v. McKenzie, 340, 362.
Moore v. O'Hare, 626.
Moore v. Reaves, 146.
Moore v. Robertson, 501.
Moore v. Sanders, 342, 459.
Moore v. Sinnott, 160.
Moore v. Taylor, 601.
Moore v. Trainer, 393.
Moore v. Worley, 617.
Moore v. Zabriskie, 481.
Moore's Appeal, In re, 40.
Moore's Heirs v. Moore's Devisees, 287.
Moorman v. Crockett, 573.
Moran v. Joyce, 121.
Moran v. Moran, 222, 281.
Morey v. Herrick, 183, 187.
Morford v. Stephens, 177.
Morgan, In re, 571, 572.
Morgan v. Clayton, 333.
Morgan v. Fisher's Adm'r, 541.
Morgan v. Moore, 634.
Morgan v. Morgan, 147.
Morgan v. Shields, 478.
Morgan's Estate, 388.
Morice v. Bishop of Durham, 132.
Morley v. Carson, 320.
Morris, In re, 280.
Morris v. Boyd, 487.
Morris v. Joseph, 199.
Morris v. Linton, 230.
Morris v. Morris, 256.
Morris v. Reigel, 196.
Morris v. Wallace, 346.
Morris v. Winderlin, 394.
Morris Community Chest v. Wilentz, 357.
Morrison v. Kelly, 424, 542.
Morrison v. Kinstra, 557.
Morrison v. Lincoln Sav. Bank & Safe Deposit Co., 505.
Morrison v. Roehl, 49.
Morrison v. Smith, 208.
Morriss v. Virginia State Ins. Co., 51.
Morristown Trust Co. v. Town of Morristown, 294.
Morrow v. Morrow, 591.
Morse, Appeal of, 462, 572.
Morse v. Morse, 56.
Morse v. Stoddard's Estate, 425.
Morsman v. Commissioner of Internal Revenue, 134.
Mortimer v. Ireland, 420.

Mortimer v. Jackson, 147.
Morton's Case, 455.
Morton's Ex'rs v. Adams, 358.
Morville v. Fowle, 277, 323.
Motherwell v. Taylor, 182.
Mott v. Morris, 276.
Moulden v. Train, 56, 83, 87, 607.
Moultrie v. Wright, 187.
Mount v. Mount, 464.
Mt. Morris Co-op. Building & Loan Ass'n v. Smith, 626.
Moyer v. Norristown-Penn Trust Co., 413.
Muckenfuss v. Heath, 482.
Mucklow v. Fuller, 518.
Mueller, Matter of, 69, 75.
Muhlenberg v. Northwest Loan & Trust Co., 557.
Muir's Ex'rs v. Howard, 159.
Mulford v. Minch, 333.
Mullanny v. Nangle, 425.
Mullen v. Walton, 602.
Muller, In re, 523, 524.
Muller v. Benner, 44.
Mullin v. Mullin, 198.
Mumford, In re, 504.
Mumford v. Murray, 511, 524.
Mundy v. Vawter, 394.
Munro v. Allaire, 332.
Munroe v. Whitaker, 128.
Murdock, In re, 495.
Murphey v. Cook, 241.
Murphy v. Carlin, 63.
Murphy v. Clayton, 506.
Murphy v. Merchants' Nat. Bk. of Mobile, 398.
Murphy's Estate, In re, 266.
Murray v. Ballou, 541, 542.
Murray v. Brooklyn Sav. Bank, 91.
Murray v. Feinour, 369.
Murray v. Finster, 535.
Murray v. Miller, 240, 271.
Murray v. Ray, 56.
Murry v. King, 147, 603.
Muscogee Lumber Co. v. Hyer, 473.
Musselman v. Myers, 182.
Musser's Estate, In re, 643.
Mussett v. Bingle, 283.
Mutual Life Ins. Co. v. Woods, 126.
Myer v. Thomson, 156.
Myers v. Board of Education, 555, 560.
Myers v. Hale, 591.
Myers v. Jackson, 215.
Myers v. Luzerne County, 208.
Myers v. Myers, 85, 87, 468.
Myers' Estate, In re, 572.

CASES CITED

Myers' Ex'r v. Zetelle, 326.
Mylin's Estate, In re, 468, 475.

N

Naddo v. Bardon, 604.
Nagle v. Conard, 336.
Nagle v. Von Rosenberg, 356.
Nagle's Estate, In re, 481.
Naglee's Estate, In re, 120.
Nance v. Nance, 345.
Nanheim v. Smith, 498.
Nash v. Bremner, 222.
Nashville Trust Co. v. Weaver, 124.
Nathan's Estate, In re, 572.
National Butchers' & Drovers' Bank v. Hubbell, 22, 24.
National Butchers' & Drovers' Bank v. Wilkinson, 25.
National City Bank of Cleveland v. Schmoltz, 424.
National Exch. Bank v. Beal, 26.
National Financial Co., In re, 380.
National Life Ins. Co. of Montpelier, Vt., v. Hood's Adm'r, 201.
National Mahaiwe Bank v. Barry, 199.
National Surety Co. v. Manhattan Mortg. Co., 361.
Nauman v. Weidman, 284.
Neafie's Estate, In re, 572.
Neagle v. McMullen, 587.
Neale, Appeal of, 134.
Neary v. City Bank Farmers Trust Co., 622.
Nease v. Capehart, 500.
Neathery v. Neathery, 185, 186.
Neblett v. Valentino, 45.
Nebraska Power Co. v. Koenig, 199.
Neeb's Estate, In re, 257.
Neel's Estate, In re, 257.
Neel's Ex'r v. Noland's Heirs, 189.
Neely v. Rood, 557.
Neff, Appeal of, 326.
Nehawke Bank v. Ingersoll, 581.
Nehls v. Sauer, 433.
Neikirk v. Boulder Nat. Bank, 50.
Neill v. Keese, 187.
Neilly v. Neilly, 606.
Neilson v. Blight, 16, 99.
Neilson v. Lagow, 135.
Nellis v. Rickard, 116.
Nelson v. Davis, 146.
Nelson v. Gossage, 210.
Nelson v. Howard, 462, 498.
Nelson v. Nelson, 179.
Nelson v. Ratliff, 626.
Neresheimer v. Smyth, 526.

Nesbit v. Lockman, 209.
Nesbitt v. Onaway-Alpena Til. Co., 197.
Nesbitt v. Stevens, 87, 88, 89.
Nesmith, In re, 468.
Nester v. Gross, 205.
Nettles v. Nettles, 598.
Nevitt v. Woodburn, 48.
New v. Nicoll, 378.
New Amsterdam Casualty Co. v. National Newark & Essex Banking Co., 586.
Newberry v. Winlock's Ex'x, 600.
Newby v. Kingman, 323.
Newcomb v. Brooks, 204, 328.
Newcomb v. Masters, 231.
Newell v. Hadley, 534, 540, 567.
New England Sanitarium v. Inhabitants of Stoneham, 262.
New England Trust Co. v. Eaton, 443.
Newhall v. Wheeler, 147, 499.
New Haven Trust Co. v. Doherty, 361.
Newis v. Topfer, 211, 218, 528, 616, 617.
New Jersey Title Guarantee & Trust Co., In re, 475.
New Jersey Title Guarantee & Trust Co. v. Parker, 623.
Newlin v. Girard Trust Co., 641.
Newman v. Newman, 604.
Newman v. Schwerin, 464.
Newman v. Shreve, 327.
Newport Trust Co. v. Chappell, 159, 318.
Newport Trust Co. v. Van Rensselaer, 448, 449.
New South Building & Loan Ass'n v. Gann, 97.
Newton v. Hunt, 140.
Newton v. Jay, 148.
Newton v. Newton, 540.
Newton v. Nutt, 45.
Newton v. Rebenack, 481, 596, 645.
Newton v. Taylor, 199.
New York Cent. & H. R. R. Co. v. Cottle, 422.
New York City Miss. Soc. v. Board of Pensions of Presbyterian Church 302.
New York Dry Dock Co. v. Stillman, 240.
New York Life Ins. Co. v. Conrad, 111.
New York Life Ins. Co. of New York, N. Y., v. Clemens, 195.
New York Life Ins. & Trust Co. v. Baker, 443.

CASES CITED
Figures refer to pages

Neyens v. Hossack, 37.
Neyland v. Bendy, 59.
Niblack v. Knox, 328.
Nichols, Appeal of, 369, 370.
Nichols v. Eaton, 160.
Nichols v. Newark Hospital, 300.
Nichols v. Nichols, 117.
Nicholson v. McGuire, 523.
Nickels v. Clay, 173.
Nickels v. Philips, 572.
Niemaseck v. Bernett Holding Co., 174.
Niles, Matter of, 516.
Niles v. Mason, 249, 252.
Nilson's Estate, In re, 272, 300.
Nirdlinger's Estate, 435, 439.
Nixon v. Nixon, 123.
Nixon State Bank v. First State Bank of Bridgeport, 24.
Nixon's Estate, In re, 417.
Noble v. Learned, 83.
Nobles v. Hogg, 355.
Noe v. Kern, 62, 64.
Noe v. Roll, 189.
Nolan v. Garrison, 87.
Nolan v. Nolan, 238.
Nolan's Guardianship, In re, 368.
Nonotuck Silk Co. v. Flanders, 25, 559.
Norfleet v. Hampson, 599.
Norman's Ex'x v. Cunningham, 145.
Norris v. Bishop, 329.
Norris v. Frazer, 226.
Norris v. Hall, 394.
Norris v. Johnston, 162.
Norris v. Kendall, 197.
Norris v. Loomis, 290, 300.
North v. Augusta Real Estate Ass'n, 407.
North American Trust Co. v. Chappell, 323.
North Baltimore Bldg. Ass'n v. Caldwell, 330.
North Carolina Corporation Commission v. Merchants' & Farmers' Bank, 24.
Northcraft v. Martin, 213.
Northern Cent. Dividend Cases, In re, 451.
Northern Ontario Fire Relief Fund, In re, 274.
Northern Sugar Corp. v. Thompson, 31.
North Troy Grade Dist. v. Town of Troy, 321.
Norton, In re, 495.
Norton v. McDevit, 614.
Norton v. Norton, 631.

Norton v. Phelps, 382, 383.
Norton v. Ray, 497.
Norvell v. Hedrick, 395.
Norwood v. Harness, 344.
Nottage, In re, 293.
Nougues v. Newlands, 617.
Noyes v. Blakeman, 378.
Noyes v. Noyes, 152.
Nuckols v. Stanger, 604.
Nunn v. Peak, 643.
Nunn v. Titche-Goettinger Co., 162.
Nutt v. Morse, 69, 71, 72.
Nutt v. State, 570.
Nyce's Estate, 507.

O

Oaks v. West, 540.
Oatway, In re, 552.
O'Beirne v. Allegheny & K. R. Co., 592.
Oberlender v. Butcher, 542.
Obert v. Bordine, 591.
Oberthier v. Stroud, 177.
O'Brien, Ex parte, 424.
O'Brien v. Ash, 633.
O'Brien v. Bank of Douglas, 99, 122, 138.
O'Brien v. Battle, 424.
O'Brien v. Gill, 189.
O'Brien v. Jackson, 375.
O'Brien v. Williamsburgh Sav. Bank, 74.
Ochiltree v. Wright, 510.
O'Day v. Annex Realty Co., 213, 599.
Odd Fellows' Beneficial Ass'n of Columbus v. Ferson, 344.
Odell v. Odell, 255.
O'Dell v. Rogers, 204.
Odell's Estate, In re, 469.
O'Donnell v. McCool, 186.
O'Donnell v. White, 186.
O'Fallon v. Tucker, 324.
Offenstein v. Gehner, 503.
Offutt v. Divine's Ex'r, 478.
Offutt v. Jones, 120, 399.
Ogden, Appeal of, 134, 136.
Ogden, Petition of, 285, 292.
Ogden v. Ogden, 145.
Ogilby v. Hickok, 120.
Ogle's Estate, In re, 249.
Oglesby v. Durr, 156.
O'Gorman v. Crowley, 411.
O'Hara, In re, 573.
O'Hara's Will, In re, 225, 226.
O'Hare v. Johnston, 161.
Ohio Oil Co. v. Daughetee, 405, 489.
Oklahoma Nat. Bank v. Cobb, 85.

CASES CITED
Figures refer to pages

Olcott v. Baldwin, 481, 484, 485.
Olcott v. Bynum, 186.
Olcott v. Gabert, 53, 324.
Olcott v. Tope, 185.
Old Colony Trust Co. v. Cleveland, 91.
Old Company's Lehigh, Inc., v. Meeker, 27.
Old Dominion Copper Mining & Smelting Co. v. Bigelow, 46, 206.
Old Ladies' Home Ass'n v. Grubbs' Estate, 272.
Old Nat Bank v. German-American Bank, 26.
Old's Estate, In re, 368, 470, 484.
Olive v. Olive, 573.
Oliver v. Piatt, 530, 533, 538, 564, 607.
Olliffe v. Wells, 221.
Olmstead, In re, 418.
Olsen v. Youngerman, 642.
Olson v. Lamb, 204, 473.
Olson v. Washington, 198.
Olympia Min. & Mill. Co. v. Kerns, 607.
O'Neal v. Borders, 245.
110th St., In re, 628.
O'Neil v. Epting, 498.
O'Neil v. Greenwood, 56.
O'Neill v. O'Neill, 180, 530.
Opperman's Estate, 447.
Opplger v. Sutton, 474.
Ordway v. Gardner, 628.
Orear v. Farmers' State Bank & Trust Co., 181, 215.
Ormiston v. Olcott, 360, 510.
Ormsby v. Dumesnil, 638.
O'Rourke v. Beard, 132.
Orphan Asylum Society v. McCartee, 569.
Orr v. Perky Inv. Co., 196.
Orr v. Yates, 423.
Orth v. Orth, 224.
Orthodox Congregational Church in Union Village, In re, 636.
Ortman v. Dugan, 246.
Osborne, Matter of, 451.
Osborne v. Gordon, 316, 414.
Osgood v. Eaton, 147.
Osterling's Estate, In re, 413.
Ostheimer v. Single, 182, 202.
Otier v. Neiman, 329.
Otis, Matter of, 439.
Otis v. Beckwith, 103.
Otis v. Gardner, 536.
Otis v. McLellan, 244.
Otis v. Otis, 544, 545.
Otjen v. Frohbach, 59.
Otterback v. Bohrer, 246.
Otto v. Schlapkahl, 618.

Ould v. Washington Hospital, 262, 289, 305.
Oulvey v. Converse, 39.
Overby v. Scarborough, 246.
Overseers of Poor of Norfolk v. Bank of Virginia, 530, 558.
Overseers of Poor of Richmond County v. Tayloe's Adm'r, 493.
Owen v. Reed, 325.
Owens v. Cowan's Heirs, 127.
Owens v. Crow, 607.
Owens v. Williams, 522.
Owings v. Owings, 646.
Owings v. Rhodes, 412.
Owings' Case, 226.
Ownes v. Ownes, 105.
Oxley, In re, 384.

P

Pabst v. Goodrich, 360.
Pacific Nat. Bank v. Windram, 164.
Packard v. Illinois Trust & Savings Bank, 406.
Packard v. Kingman, 377.
Packard v. Old Colony R. Co., 57.
Packard v. Putnam, 88.
Packer v. Johnson, 147.
Packer's Estate, 632.
Padelford v. Real Estate-Land Title & Trust Co., 492.
Padfield v. Padfield, 92.
Page v. Gillett, 320, 398.
Page v. Marston, 462.
Page v. Page, 179, 181.
Page v. Stubbs, 204.
Page's Ex'r v. Holman, 525.
Pain v. Farson, 181.
Paine, Lessee of, v. Mooreland, 543.
Paine v. Sackett, 626.
Paisley, Appeal of, 462.
Palethorp's Estate, In re, 294.
Palmer v. City of Chicago, 123.
Palmer v. Dunham, 476.
Palmer v. Schribb, 64.
Palmer v. Stevens, 146.
Palmer v. Williams, 393.
Palms v. Palms, 249, 256.
Palms' Adm'rs v. Howard, 208.
Parker v. Allen, 418.
Parker v. Ames, 433, 478.
Parker v. Converse, 319.
Parker v. Cowell, 114.
Parker v. Hayes' Adm'r, 595.
Parker v. Hill, 477.
Parker v. Hood ex rel. Central Bank & Trust Co., 30.
Parker v. Jones' Adm'r, 557.

CASES CITED
Figures refer to pages

Parker v. Kelley, 569, 570.
Parker v. May, 493.
Parker v. Parker, 499.
Parker v. Sears, 129.
Parker v. Seeley, 315.
Parker v. Straat, 564.
Parker's Adm'r v. Parker, 465.
Parkes v. Burkhart, 202.
Parkhill v. Doggett, 146, 429, 478.
Parkhurst v. Hosford, 197.
Parkman v. Suffolk Savings Bank for Seamen, 67, 78.
Parks v. Central Life Assur. Soc., 404.
Parks v. Parks, 189.
Parks v. Satterthwaite, 607, 617.
Parmenter v. Barstow, 386.
Parnall v. Parnall, 64.
Parrish v. Parrish, 197, 218.
Parry's Estate, In re, 468.
Parsons v. Boyd, 319.
Parsons v. Jones, 572.
Parsons v. Lyman, 464.
Partridge v. American Trust Co., 341.
Partridge v. Cavender, 161.
Partridge v. Chapman, 545.
Partridge v. Clary, 626.
Paschall v. Hinderer, 607.
Passaic Trust & Safe Deposit Co. v. East Ridgelawn Cemetery, 487.
Passmore's Estate, In re, 606.
Patrick v. Patrick, 473.
Patrick v. Stark, 604.
Patrick's Estate, In re, 482.
Patten v. Chamberlain, 87.
Patten v. Herring, 162.
Patten v. Moore, 535.
Patterson v. Booth, 328.
Patterson v. Humphries, 63.
Patterson v. Johnson, 125, 409, 624.
Patterson v. Lanning, 397.
Patterson v. Northern Trust Co., 467.
Patterson v. Old Dominion Trust Co., 438.
Patterson v. Woodward, 48.
Patton v. Beecher, 215, 216.
Patton v. Cone, 479.
Patton v. Patrick, 645.
Paul v. Fulton, 535, 537.
Paul v. Wilson, 382.
Paul Trust Co. v. Strong, 524.
Paulsen's Guardianship, In re, 45.
Paulson v. Paulson, 179.
Payne v. Allen, 545.
Payne v. Avery, 208.
Payne v. Payne, 145.
Peabody, In re, 179.
Peabody v. Burri, 204.

Peabody v. Tarbell, 564.
Peak v. Ellicott, 560.
Pearce v. Dill, 584, 585.
Pearce v. Dyess, 183, 617.
Pearce v. Pearce, 257, 415.
Pearse v. National Lead Co., 40.
Pearson v. Haydel, 557.
Pearson v. McMillan, 576.
Pearson v. Pearson, 84.
Pearson v. Treadwell, 604.
Pease v. Pattison, 274.
Peck v. Brown, 632.
Peck v. Scofield, 68, 69, 71.
Peckham v. Newton, 358.
Pedrick v. Guarantee Trust Co., 190.
Pedroja v. Pedroja, 406.
Peer v. Peer, 89, 178, 179.
Pegge v. Skynner, 115.
Peirce v. Attorney General, 270.
Pell v. Mercer, 267.
Pelton v. Macy, 634.
Peltz v. Learned, 456.
Pendleton v. Fay, 544.
Pendleton v. Whiting, 16.
Penfield v. Skinner, 493.
Penfield v. Tower, 239, 249.
Penick v. Bank of Wadesboro, 310, 402, 621.
Peninsular Sav. Bank v. Union Trust Co., 156.
Penn v. Fogler, 199, 356.
Penn-Gaskell's Estate, In re, 444.
Pennell v. Deffell, 562.
Penniman v. Howard, 392.
Pennington v. Smith, 534.
Pennock's Estate, In re, 63, 442.
Pennoyer v. Wadhams, 229, 273.
Pennsylvania R. Co. v. Duncan, 591.
Pennsylvania Steel Co. v. New York City Ry. Co., 48.
Pennsylvania Title & Trust Co. v. Meyer, 585.
Penny v. Croul, 121, 249, 292, 307.
Penrose's Estate, In re, 305.
People v. Bank of Dansville, 24, 557.
People v. Bordeaux, 532.
People v. Braucher, 277, 301.
People v. Byron, 45.
People v. California Safe Deposit & Trust Co., 531, 551.
People v. City Bank of Rochester, 24.
People v. Dennett, 47.
People v. Equitable Life Assur. Soc. of United States, 464.
People v. Meadows, 20.
People v. Norton, 425.
People v. Powers, 61, 266.
People v. Schaefer, 83, 222, 224.

CASES CITED
Figures refer to pages

People v. Shears, 526.
People v. Stockbrokers' Bldg. Co., 240.
People by Kerner v. Canton Nat. Bank, 373.
People ex rel. Barrett v. Union Bank & Trust Co., 27.
People ex rel. Collins v. Donohue, 577.
People ex rel. Ellert v. Cogswell, 493, 636.
People ex rel. Nelson v. Home Bank & Trust Co., 378.
People ex rel. Safford v. Washburn, 462.
People ex rel. Smith v. Braucher, 494, 635.
People's Bank of Madison, Ind., v. Deweese, 152.
People's Savings Bank v. Webb, 67, 69, 70, 77.
People's Trust Co. v. Harman, 147.
People, Use of Brooks, v. Petrie, 424.
Pepper v. Stone, 45.
Percival-Porter Co. v. Oaks, 522, 601.
Percy v. Huyck, 381.
Perin v. Carey, 113.
Perkins, Appeal of, 476, 478.
Perkins v. Citizens & Southern Nat. Bank, 309.
Perkins v. McGavock, 416.
Perkinson v. Clarke, 189.
Perrin v. Lepper, 459.
Perrine v. Newell, 148, 456.
Perronneau v. Perronneau's Ex'rs, 366.
Perry v. McHenry, 185.
Perry v. Strawbridge, 200.
Perry v. Tuomey, 280.
Person v. Fort, 601.
Peter v. Carter, 493.
Peters v. Kanawha Banking & Trust Co., 392.
Peters v. Rhodes, 532.
Peterson v. Farnum, 150.
Peth v. Spear, 288.
Petrain v. Kiernan, 542.
Petrie, In re, 355, 361.
Petrie v. Badenoch, 329.
Petrie v. Myers, 534.
Pettingill v. Pettingill, 469.
Pettit's Estate, In re 256.
Pettus v. Sutton, 524.
Petty v. Moores Brook Sanitarium, 238.
Petzold v. Petzold, 189.
Peyser v. American Security & Trust Co., 375.
Pharis v. Leachman, 504.

Phelps v. American Mortgage Co., 545.
Philadelphia Baptist Ass'n v. Hart, 269, 270.
Philadelphia Nat. Bank v. Dowd, 25.
Philadelphia Trust, Safe-Deposit & Ins. Co., Appeal of, 452.
Philadelphia, W. & B. R. Co. v. Cowell, 47.
Philbin v. Thurn, 131.
Philbrook v. Delano, 174.
Philips v. Bury, 495.
Philips v. Crammond, 134.
Phillips v. Burton, 369, 481, 523.
Phillips v. Edsall, 38.
Phillips v. Frye, 94.
Phillips v. Grayson, 160.
Phillips v. Harrow, 113, 249.
Phillips v. Heldt, 284, 307.
Phillips v. Herron, 245.
Phillips v. Hines, 199.
Phillips v. Overfield, 557.
Phillips v. Phillips, 60, 61, 181.
Phillips v. Vermeule, 601.
Phillips Academy v. King, 275.
Phinizy v. Few, 564.
Phinizy v. Wallace, 243.
Phipps v. Willis, 208.
Phœbe v. Black, 592.
Phœnix v. Livingston, 476.
Physic's Estate, In re, 426.
Pickering v. Coates, 134.
Pickering v. Shotwell, 287.
Pickler v. Pickler, 182.
Pierce, Matter of, 69, 70.
Pierce, Petition of, 424.
Pierce v. McKeehan, 36.
Pierce v. Pierce, 64, 187.
Pierce v. Weaver, 569.
Pierowich v. Metropolitan Life Ins. Co., 111.
Pierson v. Phillips, 557.
Piester v. Ideal Creamery Co., 33.
Pietsch v. Milbrath, 46.
Pike v. Baldwin, 589.
Pike v. Camden Trust Co., 329.
Pilcher v. Lotzgesell, 604.
Pim v. Downing, 516.
Pindall v. Trevor, 534.
Pine v. White, 326.
Pinney v. Fellows, 187.
Pinnock v. Clough, 182.
Pinson v. Ivey, 112, 606.
Pioneer Mining Co. v. Tyberg, 199.
Piper, Appeal of, 569.
Piper v. Moulton, 113, 284.
Pitcher v. Rogers' Estate, 499, 607.
Pitney, In re, 424.

CASES CITED
Figures refer to pages

Pittock v. Pittock, 176.
Pitts v. McWhorter, 150.
Pittsburgh Nat. Bank of Commerce v. McMurray, 30.
Pitzer v. Logan, 428.
Plano Mfg. Co. v. Auld, 25, 550, 561.
Pleasants, In re, 294.
Plitt v. Yakel, 161.
Plum Trees Lime Co. v. Keeler, 53.
Plumas County Bank v. Bank of Rideout, Smith & Co., 24.
Plumb v. Cooper, 176.
Plumley v. Plumley, 427.
Plunkett v. Le Huray, 156.
Plymouth v. Jackson, 496.
Plympton v. Boston Dispensary, 456.
Poage v. Bell, 339, 591.
Podhajsky's Estate, In re, 69.
Poindexter v. Blackburn, 430.
Poirot v. Gundlach, 101.
Poland v. Beal, 381.
Polk v. Boggs, 85.
Polk v. Linthicum, 572.
Pollard v. Lathrop, 481.
Pollard v. McKenney, 218.
Polley v. Hicks, 102.
Pollock v. Pollock, 185.
Pomroy v. Lewis, 126.
Pond Creek Coal Co. v. Runyan, 244.
Pondir v. New York, L. E. & W. R. Co., 464.
Pool v. Dial, 337.
Pool v. Potter, 129, 131.
Poole v. Brown, 462.
Poole v. Oliver, 179.
Poole v. Union Trust Co., 432.
Pooler v. Hyne, 248.
Poor v. Bradbury, 64.
Pope v. Farnsworth, 596, 597.
Pope's Ex'r v. Weber, 410.
Porter v. Anglo & London Paris Nat. Bank of San Francisco, 555.
Porter v. Baddeley, 441.
Porter v. Bank of Rutland, 122.
Porter v. Doby, 146, 230.
Porter v. Douglass, 189.
Portland & H. Steamboat Co. v. Locke, 557.
Post, In re, 395, 615.
Post v. Grand Rapids Trust Co., 415.
Post v. Ingraham, 462.
Post v. Moore, 63.
Potter v. Hodgman, 400.
Potter v. Porter, 458.
Potter v. Ranlett, 394.
Potter v. Thornton, 277.
Potter v. Union & Peoples Nat. Bank of Jackson, 341.

Potts v. Philadelphia Ass'n for Relief of Disabled Firemen, 289.
Pott's Petition, In re, 572.
Poulet v. Johnson, 172.
Povey v. Colonial Beacon Oil Co., 29.
Powell v. Madison Safe Deposit & Trust Co., 448, 452.
Powell v. Missouri & Arkansas Land & Mining Co., 555.
Powell v. Powell, 204.
Powell v. Yearance, 224, 227.
Powell's Will, In re, 121.
Power v. First Nat. Bank, 26.
Powers v. Home for Aged Women, 265.
Powers v. Homes for Aged, 295.
Powers v. Provident Institution for Savings, 67.
Pownal v. Myers, 369.
Pozzuto's Estate, In re, 67.
Prall v. Hamil, 543.
Pratt v. Clark, 196.
Pratt v. Commercial Trust Co., 581.
Pratt v. Griffin, 55.
Pratt v. Thornton, 469.
Pratt v. Trustees of Sheppard & Enoch Pratt Hospital, 57, 65.
Pray, Appeal of, 346, 356, 369.
Pray v. Hegeman, 256.
Preachers' Aid Soc. of Maine Conference of Methodist Episcopal Church v. Rich, 272.
Preble v. Greenleaf, 596.
Premier Steel Co. v. Yandes, 478.
Presbyterian Congregation v. Johnston, 591.
Prescott's Estate, In re, 475.
President, etc., of Harvard College v. Society for Promoting Theological Education, 493.
Presley v. Rodgers, 152.
Preston v. Horwitz, 598.
Preston v. Preston, 617.
Preston v. Safe Deposit & Trust Co., 393.
Preston v. Walsh, 112, 489.
Preston v. Wilcox, 570, 573.
Prettyman v. Baker, 277.
Prevo v. Walters, 534.
Prevost v. Gratz, 59.
Prewett v. Buckingham, 618.
Prewitt v. Prewitt, 564, 615.
Price v. Estill, 489.
Price v. Hicks, 187.
Price v. Kane, 58, 179.
Price v. Krasnoff, 534.
Price v. Long, 621.
Price v. Maxwell, 286.

CASES CITED
Figures refer to pages

Price v. Methodist Episcopal Church, 315.
Price v. Nesbit, 333.
Price v. Price, 521.
Price v. Reeves, 213.
Price v. School Directors, 286, 620.
Price v. Taylor, 155.
Price's Estate, In re, 570, 572.
Prichard v. Prichard, 487.
Pride v. Andrew, 239.
Primeau v. Granfield, 523, 528, 560.
Prince v. Barrow, 120.
Prince de Bearn v. Winans, 232, 333, 413, 502.
Prindle v. Holcomb, 462, 575.
Pringle v. Dorsey, 635.
Printup v. Patton, 180.
Pritchard v. Brown, 542.
Pritchard v. Williams, 491, 610.
Pritchitt v. Nashville Trust Co., 451.
Proctor v. Heyer, 487.
Prondzinski v. Garbutt, 564.
Proprietors of Church in Brattle Square v. Grant, 304.
Proseus v. Porter, 70, 71.
Prouty v. Edgar, 394.
Prudential Ins. Co. of America v. Land Estates, 456.
Pryor v. Davis, 503.
Pryor v. McIntire, 601.
Pryor v. Morgan, 102.
Puckett v. Benjamin, 186.
Pugh's Heirs v. Bell's Heirs, 332.
Pujol v. McKinlay, 526.
Pullis v. Pullis Bros. Iron Co., 125.
Pullis v. Somerville, 526.
Pumphry v. Brown, 187.
Pungs v. Hilgendorf, 126.
Purcell's Estate, In re, 62.
Purdy v. Bank of American Nat. Trust & Savings Ass'n, 400.
Purdy v. Johnson, 337, 461, 465, 467.
Purdy v. Lynch, 508, 510, 512.
Purinton v. Dyson, 197.
Pusey v. Gardner, 58.
Putnam v. Lincoln Safe Deposit Co., 56.
Putnam v. Story, 148.
Pyle v. Pyle, 571.

Q

Quackenboss v. Southwick, 569, 572.
Quairoli v. Italian Beneficial Society of Vineland, 601.
Quimby v. Quimby, 296.
Quimby v. Uhl, 596.
Quin v. Skinner, 632.
Quinn's Estate, In re, 465.

R

Rabalsky v. Kook, 109.
Rabb v. Flenniken, 535.
Racek v. First Nat. Bank of North Bend, 237.
Rader v. Bussey, 399.
Rader v. Stubblefield, 289.
Raffel v. Safe Deposit & Trust Co., 642.
Ragsdale v. Ragsdale, 226.
Raiford v. Raiford, 473.
Rainsford v. Rainsford, 522.
Raleigh v. Fitzpatrick, 489.
Raley v. Umatilla County, 286.
Ralston v. Easter, 338, 468, 481, 514, 516.
Ralston's Estate, In re, 190.
Rambo v. Armstrong, 37.
Rambo v. Pile, 67, 73, 75, 77, 78.
Ramirez v. Smith, 543.
Ramsden v. O'Keefe, 199.
Rand v. Farquhar, 377, 378.
Rand v. McKittrick, 295, 348.
Randall v. Constans, 88, 241.
Randall v. Dusenbury, 378.
Randall v. Gray, 574.
Randolph, In re, 329, 330, 349, 355.
Randolph v. East Birmingham Land Co., 534.
Randolph v. Read, 229.
Rankin v. Barcroft, 115.
Rankin v. Harper, 179.
Rankin's Estate, In re, 409.
Rankine v. Metzger, 119.
Ransdel v. Moore, 88, 224.
Rantz v. Dale, 56.
Ranzau v. Davis, 230, 374.
Raski v. Wise, 458.
Ratcliffe v. Sangston, 322.
Rathbun v. Colton, 409, 473.
Ratigan v. Ratigan, 85.
Ratliff v. Elwell, 176.
Ratliff's Ex'rs v. Commonwealth, 159.
Rausch's Will, Matter of, 91.
Rawlings v. Adams, 145.
Ray v. Fowler, 132.
Ray v. Simmons, 68, 69, 71, 72, 77.
Raybould, In re, 387, 389.
Raynes v. Raynes, 505.
Reynolds v. Browning, King & Co., 408.
Reynolds v. Hanna, 151.
Rea v. Steamboat Eclipse, 146.
Read v. Robinson, 128.
Read v. Williams, 131.

CASES CITED
Figures refer to pages

Reade v. Continental Trust Co., 497.
Reagh v. Dickey, 300.
Reardon v. Reardon, 140.
Reasoner v. Herman, 243.
Rector v. Dalby, 230, 639.
Rector, etc., of St. James Church v. Wilson, 298.
Red Bud Realty Co. v. South, 465, 557.
Redfield v. Redfield, 34.
Redford v. Clarke, 589, 602, 610, 611.
Redmond v. Redmond, 244.
Redwood v. Riddick, 497, 606.
Reed, In re, 360, 367, 369, 526.
Reed v. Harris, 591.
Reed v. Munn, 155.
Reeder v. Antrim, 248.
Reeder v. Cartwright, 16.
Reeder v. Lanahan, 398.
Reeder v. Reeder, 56, 128, 131, 392.
Reese v. Bruce, 604.
Reese v. Ivey, 424.
Reese's Estate, In re, 439.
Reeve v. Strawn, 181.
Reeves v. Howard, 212.
Regan v. West, 129.
Rehr v. Fidelity-Philadelphia Trust Co., 645.
Reichenbach v. Quin, 280.
Reichert v. Missouri & I. Coal Co., 421, 429.
Reich's Estate, In re, 481.
Reid, In re, 364, 365.
Reid v. Reid, 86, 524.
Reid v. Savage, 604.
Reidy v. Small, 623.
Reiff v. Horst, 105.
Reigart v. Ross, 427.
Reihl v. Likowski, 601, 603.
Reilly v. Conrad, 429, 626.
Reilly v. Oglebay, 329.
Reinach v. Atlantic & G. W. R. Co., 592.
Reiner v. Fidelity Union Trust Co., 357.
Reios v. Mardis, 37.
Reitz v. Reitz, 189.
Reizenberger v. Shelton, 177.
Reminger v. Joblonski, 181.
Rensselaer & S. R. Co. v. Miller, 471.
Rentoul v. Sweeney, 80.
Republic Nat. Bank & Trust Co. v. Bruce, 336.
Resor v. Resor, 180.
Reuling's Ex'x v. Reuling, 639.
Revel v. Albert, 202.
Review Printing & Stationery Co. v. McCoy, 376.

Revoc Co. v. Thomas, 393.
Reynolds, In re, 154.
Reynolds v. Ætna Life Ins. Co., 535.
Reynolds v. Kenney, 177.
Reynolds v. Reynolds, 220, 221.
Reynolds v. Sumner, 616.
Reynolds v. Thompson, 56.
Reynolds v. Title Guaranty Trust Co., 46.
Rhode Island Hospital Trust Co. v. Benedict, 287.
Rhode Island Hospital Trust Co. v. Noyes, 433.
Rhode Island Hospital Trust Co. v. Olney, 273.
Rhode Island Hospital Trust Co. v. Peck, 246.
Rhode Island Hospital Trust Co. v. Proprietors of Swan Point Cemetery, 284.
Rhode Island Hospital Trust Co. v. Town Council of Warwick, 126.
Rhymer, Appeal of, 280.
Rice v. Dougherty, 53.
Rice v. Halsey, 365.
Rice Stix Dry Goods Co. v. W. S. Albrecht & Co., 224.
Richards v. Church Home for Orphan & Destitute Children, 122.
Richards v. Crocker, 89.
Richards v. Keyes, 596, 597.
Richards v. Merrimack & C. R. R. R., 156.
Richards v. Pitts, 210.
Richards v. Rote, 425.
Richards v. Seal, 322, 513.
Richards v. Wilson, 83, 113, 623.
Richardson, Ex parte, 382.
Richardson, In re, 382.
Richardson v. Adams, 226.
Richardson v. Essex Institute, 127, 265, 287, 292.
Richardson v. Haney, 538.
Richardson v. Inglesby, 55.
Richardson v. Knight, 373.
Richardson v. McConaughey, 602.
Richardson v. Morey, 345, 412.
Richardson v. Mounce, 150.
Richardson v. Mullery, 126, 292.
Richardson v. New Orleans Coffee Co., 22.
Richardson v. Stephenson, 622.
Richardson v. Stodder, 145.
Richardson v. Van Auken, 458.
Richardson's Adm'rs v. Spencer, 328.
Richelieu Hotel Co. v. Miller, 557.
Richmond v. Arnold, 419.
Richter v. Anderson, 466.

CASES CITED
Figures refer to pages

Ricks v. Reed, 534.
Rick's Appeal, In re, 624.
Riddle v. Cutter, 619, 624, 625.
Ridenour v. Wherritt, 125.
Rider v. Maul, 615.
Ridgely v. Carey, 16.
Ridgely v. Gittings, 480.
Ridley v. Dedman, 359, 361.
Riechauer v. Born, 64.
Rienzi v. Goodin, 165.
Riggs v. Moise, 418.
Riggs v. Palmer, 200.
Riker v. Leo, 271.
Riker's Estate, In re, 373.
Riley v. Cummings, 541.
Riley's Estate, In re, 412.
Rines v. Bachelder, 533.
Ringe v. Kellner, 64.
Ringgold v. Ringgold, 474, 511, 523, 526.
Ringrose v. Gleadall, 232, 633, 639.
Riordan v. Schlicher, 147.
Ripley v. Brown, 309.
Ripley v. Seligman, 540.
Ripperger v. Shroder-Rockefeller Co., 579.
Rist's Estate, In re, 463.
Rittenhouse v. Smith, 601.
Ritter v. Couch, 285.
Rives v. Lawrence, 213.
Rixford v. Zeigler, 114.
Roach's Estate, In re, 355, 462, 467.
Roach's Ex'r v. City of Hopkinsville, 292.
Robb v. Day, 602.
Robb v. Washington & Jefferson College, 103, 238, 240.
Robbins v. Boulder County Com'rs, 299.
Robbins v. Robbins, 85, 188.
Robbins v. Smith, 643.
Robert, Ex parte, 129.
Roberts, Appeal of, 87.
Roberts v. Broom, 506.
Roberts v. Hale, 379.
Roberts v. Mansfield, 564.
Roberts v. Michigan Trust Co., 331.
Roberts v. Moseley, 125.
Roberts v. N. Y. El. R. R. Co., 579.
Roberts v. Roberts, 332, 424.
Roberts v. Stevens, 161.
Roberts' Will, In re, 477.
Robertson v. De Brulatour, 118, 119, 444, 475.
Robertson v. Howerton, 85.
Robertson v. Johnston, 159.
Robertson v. McCarty, 73.

Robertson v. Robertson's Trustee, 502.
Robertson v. Sublett, 501.
Robertson v. Summeril, 215.
Robertson v. Wood, 609.
Robinson, In re, 126, 128.
Robinson v. Adams, 590.
Robinson v. Appleby, 68, 71, 73, 76.
Robinson v. Bonaparte, 244.
Robinson v. Cogswell, 58, 573.
Robinson v. Crutcher, 122.
Robinson v. Cruzen, 213.
Robinson v. Harkin, 517.
Robinson v. Ingram, 394.
Robinson v. Mauldin, 490.
Robinson v. Pett, 473.
Robinson v. Robinson, 315, 394, 506.
Robinson v. Robinson's Exr., 447.
Robinson v. Springfield Co., 150.
Robinson v. Tower, 475, 565.
Robinson v. Woodward, 559.
Robinson's Trust, In re, 453.
Robinson's Will, In re, 289, 297.
Robison v. Carey, 497.
Robison v. Codman, 145.
Roche v. George's Ex'r, 103.
Roche v. Roche, 215.
Rochefoucauld v. Bonstead, 215.
Rochester Trust Co. v. White, 172.
Rockafellow v. Peay, 146.
Rockwood v. School District of Brookline, 549.
Rodbard v. Cooke, 510, 517.
Roddy v. Roddy, 57.
Rodney v. Shankland, 491, 492.
Roe v. Doe, 113.
Roebken's Will, In re, 436.
Rogan v. Walker, 181.
Rogers v. Colt, 147.
Rogers v. Daniell, 498.
Rogers v. Donnellan, 187.
Rogers v. Genung, 206.
Rogers v. Murray, 182.
Rogers v. Rea, 419, 424.
Rogers v. Rogers, 59, 118, 624, 625.
Rogers v. Scarff, 542.
Rogers v. Tyley, 395.
Roger's Estate, In re, 62.
Rolfe v. Atkinson, 39.
Rolfe & Rumford Asylum v. Lefebre, 304, 394, 396, 628.
Rolikatis v. Lovett, 204.
Roller v. Catlett, 425.
Roller v. Paul, 48.
Rollins v. Marsh, 45.
Rollins v. Merrill, 284.
Romberger's Estate, In re, 323, 348.
Roney's Estate, In re, 602.

CASES CITED
Figures refer to pages

Rong v. Haller, 238, 249, 252.
Rooker v. Fidelity Trust Co., 397.
Rooker v. Rooker, 543.
Roosevelt v. Carow, 97.
Roosevelt v. Roosevelt, 345.
Root v. Blake, 639.
Rosa v. Hummel, 172.
Rose v. Rose, 115.
Rose v. Southern Michigan Nat. Bank, 645.
Rose's Will, In re, 628.
Rosenberg's Will, In re, 165.
Ross v. Ashton, 156.
Ross v. Conwell, 476.
Ross v. Hegeman, 173.
Ross v. Hendrix, 542.
Rosso v. Freeman, 48.
Rotch v. Emerson, 292.
Rothaug's Estate, In re, 573.
Rothenberger v. Garrett, 121.
Rothschild v. Dickinson, 475.
Rothschild v. Goldenberg, 418.
Rothschild v. Weinthel, 455.
Rothschild's Assigned Estate, In re, 473.
Rouse v. Rouse, 607.
Roush v. Griffith, 599.
Rousseau v. Call, 93.
Rowe, In re, 474.
Rowe v. Bentley, 338, 355.
Rowe v. Rand, 43.
Rowe v. Rowe, 126.
Rowland v. Maddock, 524.
Royal v. Royal, 482.
Royall's Adm'r v. McKenzie, 511.
Royer's Estate, In re, 297, 300.
Rozell v. Vansyckle, 83.
Rua v. Watson, 541.
Ruckman v. Cox, 599.
Ruddick v. Albertson, 135, 136.
Rudolph, Matter of, 70.
Rudy's Appeal, 412.
Rugely v. Robinson, 159.
Ruhe v. Ruhe, 198.
Runk v. Thomas, 462.
Runnels v. Jackson, 183.
Rush v. McPherson, 213.
Rush v. Mitchell, 545.
Rush v. South Brooklyn Sav. Inst., 73, 75.
Rusling v. Rusling's Ex'rs, 29.
Russel v. Huntington Nat. Bank, 602.
Russell v. Allen, 274.
Russell v. Fish, 59, 604.
Russell v. Grinnell, 643.
Russell v. Hartley, 630.
Russell v. Hilton, 240.
Russell v. Jackson, 225.

Russell v. Meyers, 169.
Russell v. Miller, 605.
Russell v. Milton, 156.
Russell v. Russell, 407.
Russell v. United States Trust Co. of New York, 63.
Russell's Patent, In re, 107.
Rutherford Land & Improvement Co. v. Sanntrock, 421.
Rutherfurd v. Carpenter, 226.
Rutherfurd v. Myers, 462.
Rutledge's Adm'r v. Smith's Ex'rs, 226.
Ryan v. Ashton, 208.
Ryan v. Dox, 213, 214.
Ryan v. Lofton, 85.
Ryan v. Williams, 215.
Ryder v. Lyon, 56.
Ryder v. Ryder, 215.
Ryland v. Banks, 146.

S

Saar v. Weeks, 198.
Sackman v. Campbell, 602.
Sacramento Bank v. Montgomery, 248.
Sadler, Appeal of, 544.
Saeger's Estate, In re, 348.
Safe-Deposit & Trust Co. v. Cahn, 534.
Safe Deposit & Trust Co. v. Diamond Nat. Bank, 586.
Safe Deposit & Trust Co. v. Sutro, 316.
Safe Deposit & Trust Co. v. White, 451.
Safe Deposit & Trust Co. of Baltimore v. Independent Brewing Ass'n, 161.
Safford v. Rantoul, 420.
St. James Orphan Asylum v. Shelby, 297.
St. John v. Andrews Institute for Girls, 310.
St. Joseph Mfg. Co. v. Daggett, 538.
St. Leger, Appeal of, 208.
St. Louis Union Tr. Co. v. Bassett, 245.
St. Louis Union Trust Co. v. Toberman, 348, 358.
St. Louis & S. F. R. Co. v. Johnston, 22.
St. Luke's Hospital v. Barclay, 489.
St. Mary's Church of Burlington v. Stockton, 589.
St. Mary's Hospital v. Perry, 125.
St. Nicholas Bank of New York v. State Nat. Bank, 26.

702 CASES CITED
Figures refer to pages

St. Paul's Church v. Attorney General, 308.
St. Paul Trust Co. v. Kittson, 355.
St. Paul Trust Co. v. Strong, 327, 329, 525, 597.
Sale v. Thornberry, 64.
Salem Capital Flour Mills Co. v. Stayton Water-Ditch & Canal Co., 133.
Salisbury v. Bigelow, 392.
Salisbury v. Clarke, 174.
Salisbury v. Slade, 240.
Salmon, In re, 352, 372.
Salter v. Salter, 125.
Saltonstall v. Sanders, 267.
Sampson v. Mitchell, 402.
Sam's Estate, In re, 316.
Sanchez v. Dow, 600.
Sanders v. First Nat. Bank, 242, 642.
Sander's Heirs v. Morrison's Ex'rs, 421.
Sanderson v. White, 272, 636.
Sandlin v. Robbins, 238.
Sands v. Old Colony Trust Co., 624, 640.
Sandusky v. Sandusky, 277.
Sanford v. Sanford, 422.
San Francisco Nat. Bank v. American Nat. Bank of Los Angeles, 26.
Sangston v. Gordon, 136.
Sangston v. Hack, 125.
Sansom v. Ayer & Lord Tie Co., 56.
Santa Marina Co. v. Canadian Bank of Commerce, 581.
Sapp v. Houston Nat. Exch. Bank, 137.
Sargent v. Baldwin, 623.
Sargent v. Town of Cornish, 113, 292.
Sartor v. Newberry Land & Security Co., 473.
Satterfield v. John, 570.
Satterthwaite's Estate, In re, 129, 425.
Satterwhite's Will, Matter of, 439.
Saunders v. Edwards, 230.
Saunders v. Richard, 332, 534.
Saunders v. Vautier, 641.
Saunders v. Webber, 397.
Savage v. Burnham, 240.
Savage v. Gould, 361, 572.
Savage v. Sherman, 463.
Sawtelle v. Witham, 424.
Sawyer v. Issenhuth, 205.
Sayles v. Tibbitts, 147.
Saylor v. Plaine, 221.
Sayre v. Sayre, 323.
Sayre v. Townsend, 184, 186.

Sayre v. Weil, 69, 580.
Sayre's Will, In re, 135.
Scallan v. Brooks, 71, 74.
Schaefer, In re, 443, 481.
Schafer v. Olson, 24.
Schaffer v. Wadsworth, 359.
Schehr v. Look, 424.
Scheib v. Thompson, 358.
Schell, In re, 474.
Schenck v. Barnes, 140, 164.
Schenck v. Ellingwood, 394.
Schenck v. Schenck, 421.
Schenck v. Wicks, 535.
Schenectady Dutch Church v. Veeder, 233.
Schermerhorn v. Cotting, 249, 252.
Scherrer's Estate, In re, 490.
Schiffman v. Schmidt, 339.
Schierloh v. Schierloh, 185, 187.
Schlereth v. Schlereth, 252.
Schley's Will, Matter of, 436.
Schloss v. Powell, 32.
Schlosser v. Schlosser, 616.
Schluter v. Bowery Savings Bank, 115.
Schluter v. Harvey, 545.
Schmitt's Estate, In re, 578.
Schneider v. Hayward, 464.
Schneider v. Kloepple, 114.
Schneider v. Schneider, 212.
Schneider v. Sellers, 534.
Schnur's Estate, In re, 454.
Schoch, Appeal of, 463.
Scholle v. Scholle, 333.
School Directors v. Dunkleberger, 591.
School Trustees v. Kirwin, 556, 557.
Schouler, Ex parte, 120, 135, 280.
Schrager v. Cool, 196.
Schreiner v. Cincinnati Altenheim, 310.
Schreyer v. Schreyer, 98, 103, 625, 629.
Schriver v. Frommel, 473, 474.
Schroeder v. Woodward, 406.
Schuler v. Post, 163.
Schultz's Appeal, 223.
Schumacher v. Draeger, 123.
Schur, Appeal of, 211.
Schuyler v. Littlefield, 548, 554, 555.
Schwager v. Schwager, 165.
Schwartz, In re, 241.
Schwarz v. Wendell, 332, 473.
Schwebel v. Wohlsen, 491.
Schwing v. McClure, 296.
Scott v. Calladine, 179.
Scott v. Freeland, 333.
Scott v. Gallagher, 539, 542.
Scott v. Gittings, 144.

CASES CITED
Figures refer to pages

Scott v. Harbeck, 73.
Scott v. Ocean Bank in City of New York, 22.
Scott v. Rand, 570, 571.
Scott v. Scott, 49.
Scott v. Trustees of Marion Tp., 355.
Scott v. West, 256.
Scott's Estate, In re, 459, 463.
Scoville v. Brock, 358.
Screws v. Williams, 31.
Scribner v. Meade, 202.
Scrivens v. North Easton Sav. Bank, 71, 72.
Scudder v. Burrows, 463.
Seaboard Trust Co. v. Shea, 354.
Seabrook v. Grimes, 55.
Seacoast R. Co. v. Wood, 205.
Seaman v. Harmon, 145, 625.
Sears, In re, 129.
Sears v. Attorney General, 263.
Sears y. Chapman, 286.
Sears v. Choate, 639.
Sears v. Cunningham, 61.
Sears v. Russell, 333.
Seaverns v. Presbyterian Hospital, 404.
Second East Dulwich Soc., In re, 513, 517, 518.
Second Nat. Bank of Columbia v. Cummings, 22.
Second Religious Soc. of Boxford v. Harriman, 607.
Second Universalist Church of Stamford v. Colegrove, 449.
Security Bank of New York v. Callahan, 146.
Security Co. v. Snow, 319.
Security National Bank v. Sternberger, 232.
Security Trust Co. v. Merchants' & Clerks' Sav. Bank, 400.
Security Trust Co. v. Rammelsburg, 449.
Security Trust Co. v. Spruance, 625.
Security Trust & Safe Deposit Co. v. Farrady, 99.
Security Trust & Safe Deposit Co. v. Martin, 146.
Security Trust & Safe Deposit Co. v. Ward, 429.
See, In re, 557.
Seefried v. Clarke, 63.
Seely v. Hills, 325.
Sefton v. San Diego Trust & Sav. Bank, 151, 153.
Seger v. Farmers' Loan & Trust Co., 412.
Seif v. Krebs, 394.

Seilert v. McAnally, 45.
Seiter's Estate v. Mowe, 557.
Seitz v. Seitz, 618.
Selby v. Case, 94.
Selden v. Vermilya, 241, 634.
Seligman v. Seligman, 365.
Selleck, In re, 470, 525.
Sellers M. E. Church's Petition, In re, 636.
Sells v. Delgado, 126, 425.
Selwyn & Co. v. Waller, 206.
Sentill v. Robeson, 145.
Sessions v. Doe ex dem. Reynolds, 493.
Seven Corners Bank, In re, 25.
Sewell v. Sewell, 239.
Seymour v. Freer, 607.
Seymour v. McAvoy, 160.
Seymour v. Sanford, 62.
Shackleford v. Elliott, 143.
Shakeshaft, Ex parte, 510.
Shaler v. Trowbridge, 559.
Shanahan v. Kelly, 271, 282.
Shanks v. Edmondson, 564.
Shanley's Estate v. Fidelity Union Trust Co., 330.
Sharman v. Jackson, 632.
Sharp v. Leach, 624.
Shattuck's Will, In re, 264, 275.
Shaw v. Bernal, 180.
Shaw v. Bridgers, 392.
Shaw v. Canfield, 320.
Shaw v. Cordis, 444.
Shaw v. Paine, 424.
Shaw v. Shaw, 181.
Shaw v. Ward, 135.
Shawnee Commercial & Savings Bank v. Miller, 46, 206.
Sheaffer's Estate, In re, 428.
Shearman v. Cameron, 466.
Sheedy v. Roach, 237.
Sheehan v. Sullivan, 59.
Sheen v. Sheen, 289.
Sheets v. Security First Mtge. Co., 381.
Sheet's Estate, In re, 428.
Shelby v. Creighton, 329.
Shelby v. White, 374.
Sheldon v. Chappel, 135.
Shellenberger v. Ransom, 200.
Shelton v. Harrison, 182, 231.
Shelton v. Jones' Adm'x, 425.
Shelton v. King, 160.
Shelton v. McHaney, 329.
Shepard v. Abbott, 43.
Shepard v. Creamer, 386.
Shepard v. Meridian Nat. Bank, 425.
Shepherd v. Darling, 326.

CASES CITED
Figures refer to pages

Shepherd v. Harris, 511.
Shepherd v. M'Evers, 417, 534.
Shepherd v. Todd, 395.
Shepherd v. White, 179.
Shepherd's Estate, 335.
Sheppard v. Turpin, 615.
Sherburne v. Morse, 491.
Sherman v. Baker, 281, 284.
Sherman v. Lanier, 330, 362.
Sherman v. Richmond Hose Co., 298.
Sherman v. Havens, 161.
Sherman v. Parish, 504, 596.
Sherman v. Skuse, 161, 165.
Sherman v. White, 330.
Sherman Trust, In re, 435.
Sherrill v. Shuford, 474.
Shields v. Jolly, 121, 270, 273.
Shields v. McAuley, 224.
Shields v. Thomas, 549.
Shields' Estate, In re, 347.
Shillinglaw v. Peterson, 318, 630.
Shinn v. Macpherson, 567.
Shippey v. Bearman, 85.
Shirkey v. Kirby, 402.
Shirk's Estate, In re, 643.
Shirley v. Shattuck, 534.
Shoemaker, Appeal of, 630.
Shoemaker v. Board of Com'rs of Grant County, 112.
Shoemaker v. Hinze, 20.
Shoemaker v. Smith, 187.
Shoe & Leather Nat. Bank v. Dix, 377.
Shope v. Unknown Claimants, 136.
Shopert v. Indiana Nat. Bank, 556.
Short v. Wilson, 628, 644.
Shortz v. Unangst, 319.
Shotwell v. Mott, 122.
Shotwell v. Stickle, 179.
Shrader v. Shrader, 177.
Shrewsbury v. Hornby, 277.
Shriver v. Montgomery, 256.
Shryock v. Waggoner, 115.
Shuey v. Latta, 361.
Shunk, Appeal of, 477.
Shute v. Hinman, 505.
Siedler v. Syms, 245, 259.
Sieling v. Sieling, 619.
Siemon v. Schurck, 188.
Signs v. Bush's Estate, 189.
Silliman v. Gano, 501.
Silver King Consol. Min. Co. of Utah v. Silver King Coalition Mines Co. of Nevada, 461.
Silvers v. Canary, 124.
Simmons v. Dinsmore, 541.
Simmons v. McKinlock, 427.

Simmons v. Northwestern Trust Co., 638, 640.
Simmons v. Oliver, 502.
Simmons v. Richardson, 591.
Simonds v. Simonds, 232.
Simonin's Estate, In re, 645.
Simons v. Southwestern R. Bank, 541.
Simpson, Appeal of, 462.
Simpson v. Corder, 60.
Simpson v. Simpson, 106.
Simpson v. Waldby, 26.
Simpson v. Welcome, 277.
Sims v. Sims, 232.
Sinclair v. Gunzenhauser, 147.
Sinclair v. Jackson ex dem. Field, 324.
Singleton v. Cuttino, 318.
Singleton v. Lowndes, 355, 481.
Sinkler's Estate, In re, 329.
Sinnott v. Moore, 160, 238.
Sisemore v. Pelton, 182.
Sizemore v. Davidson, 601.
Skahen v. Irving, 183.
Skeen v. Marriott, 105, 230.
Skehill v. Abbott, 184, 186.
Skett v. Whitmore, 83.
Slade v. Patten, 244.
Slater v. Oriental Mills, 558, 562.
Slater v. Rudderforth, 232.
Slatt v. Thomas, 375.
Slee v. Bloom, 47.
Sleeper v. Iselin, 534.
Slevin v. Brown, 232, 631.
Sloan v. Birdsall, 136.
Sloan's Estate, In re, 451, 452.
Sloane v. Cadogan, 102.
Slocum, In re, 484.
Small v. Hockinsmith, 564, 603.
Smalley v. Paine, 493.
Smallwood v. Lawson, 458.
Smaltz' Estate, In re, 645.
Smart v. Town of Durham, 284, 286, 311.
Smick's Adm'r v. Beswick's Adm'r, 604.
Smilie v. Biffle, 612.
Smisson, In re, 245.
Smith, In re, 350, 367.
Smith v. A. D. Farmer Type Founding Co., 395.
Smith v. Allen, 546.
Smith v. American Nat. Bank, 497.
Smith v. Barnes, 177.
Smith v. Chambers, 375.
Smith v. Chenault, 146.
Smith v. Coleman, 386.
Smith v. Collins, 152.
Smith v. Combs, 607.

CASES CITED
Figures refer to pages

Smith v. Dallas Compress Co., 615.
Smith v. Dana, 449, 450.
Smith v. Darby, 493, 523.
Smith v. Drake, 402.
Smith v. Dunwoody, 629.
Smith v. Floyd, 319.
Smith v. Frost, 502.
Smith v. Fuller, 344.
Smith v. Gardiner, 277.
Smith v. Greeley, 471.
Smith v. Hainline, 83.
Smith v. Harrington, 641.
Smith v. Havens Relief Fund Soc., 261.
Smith v. Haynes, 394.
Smith v. Hooper, 435.
Smith v. Howell, 86, 87.
Smith v. Howlett, 597.
Smith v. Jones, 405.
Smith v. Keteltas, 409.
Smith v. Kinney's Ex'rs, 626.
Smith v. Lansing, 418.
Smith v. McWhorter, 232.
Smith v. Metcalf, 629.
Smith v. Miller, 329, 331, 470, 597.
Smith v. Orton, 491.
Smith v. Pettigrew, 512.
Smith v. Pond, 267.
Smith v. Rizzuto, 386, 387, 389, 391.
Smith v. Robinson, 464, 465.
Smith v. Security Loan & Trust Co., 232.
Smith v. Simmons, 44, 90.
Smith v. Smith, 136, 187, 197, 232, 491, 502, 644.
Smith v. Speer, 69, 72.
Smith v. Strahan, 178.
Smith v. Stratton, 198.
Smith v. Thomas, 524.
Smith v. Towers, 161.
Smith v. Townsend, 305.
Smith v. Turley, 182, 604.
Smith v. Walker, 471.
Smith v. Walser, 198.
Smith v. Wildman, 490.
Smith v. Witter, 147.
Smith v. Wright, 197.
Smith's Estate, In re, 75, 76, 77, 88, 96, 99, 285, 292, 311, 413, 446, 572.
Smith's Ex'r v. Cockrell, 150.
Smith's Guardian v. Holtheide, 604.
Smitheal v. Gray, 150.
Smullin v. Wharton, 224, 226, 237.
Smyth v. Burns' Adm'rs, 358.
Snead v. Bell, 37.
Sneer v. Stutz, 129.
Snell v. Payne, 632.
Snelling v. McCreary, 366.

Bogert Trusts 2d—45

Snider v. Johnson, 614.
Snodgrass v. Snodgrass, 463, 610, 631.
Snyder v. Collier, 401.
Snyder v. O'Conner, 165.
Snyder v. Parmalee, 498.
Snyder v. Safe-Deposit & Trust Co., 319.
Snyder v. Snyder, 86, 603, 604.
Snyder v. Toler, 64.
Snyder's Adm'r v. McComb's Ex'x, 502.
Snyder's Will, In re, 120, 366.
Socher, Appeal of, 224.
Society for Promoting Theological Education v. Attorney General, 304.
Soderberg v. McRae, 532.
Soehnlein v. Soehnlein, 451.
Sohier v. Eldredge, 409.
Sollee v. Croft, 609.
Solomons' Trust Estate, In re, 625.
Somers v. Craig, 424.
Sorrels v. McNally, 380.
Sorrells v. Sorrells, 534.
Sortore v. Scott, 504.
Soulard's Estate, In re, 56.
South End Mining Co. v. Tinney, 197.
Southern Bank of Fulton v. Nichols, 180, 536, 602.
Southern Cotton Oil Co. v. Elliotte, 555, 558.
Southern Nat. Life Ins. Co. v. Ford's Adm'r, 152, 153.
Southern Pac. R. R. Co. v. Doyle, 140.
Southern Ry. Co. v. Glenn's Adm'r, 474, 478, 524.
Souverbye v. Arden, 96.
Souza v. First Nat. Bank of Hanford, 83.
Sowers v. Cyrenius, 425.
Spalding v. Shalmer, 509.
Spallholz v. Sheldon, 609.
Spangler's Estate, 479.
Sparhawk v. Allen, 204.
Sparhawk v. Cloon, 168.
Sparhawk v. Sparhawk, 571.
Sparks' Estate, In re, 350.
Sparrow v. Sparrow, 159.
Spatz's Estate, In re, 503.
Spaulding v. Collins, 601.
Speakman v. Tatem, 336, 338, 464.
Speed v. St. Louis M. B. T. R. Co., 232.
Speer v. Colbert, 108.
Speidel v. Henrici, 598.
Speight v. Gaunt, 327, 506.
Spence v. Widney, 630.

CASES CITED
Figures refer to pages

Spencer, In re, 176.
Spencer v. Clarke, 499.
Spencer v. Lyman, 589.
Spencer v. Richmond, 152.
Spencer v. Spencer, 481, 511.
Spencer v. Weber, 343, 394.
Spencer's Estate, In re, 335.
Spengler v. Kuhn, 425.
Sperry v. Farmers' Loan & Trust Co., 624.
Spies v. Price, 84.
Spokane County v. First Nat. Bank, 504, 550.
Spooner v. Dunlap, 641.
Spooner v. Lovejoy, 58.
Spradling v. Spradling, 176, 179.
Sprague v. Moore, 147.
Sprague v. Trustees of Protestant Episcopal Church of Diocese of Michigan, 601.
Sprague v. Woods, 98.
Spreckel's Estate, In re, 123.
Spring v. Hight, 179.
Spring v. Hollander, 49.
Springer v. Arundel, 134.
Springer v. Berry, 115.
Springfield Safe Deposit & Trust Co. v. First Unitarian Society, 353.
Springfield Safe Deposit & Trust Co. v. Wade, 439.
Springs v. Hopkins, 232, 625.
Spring's Estate, In re, 626.
Sprinkle v. Hayworth, 222.
Sprinkle v. Holton, 600.
Squire v. Princeton Lighting Co., 49.
Stack's Will, In re, 641.
Stafford, In re, 348.
Stafford v. American Missionary Ass'n, 570.
Stafford v. Stafford, 214.
Stafford's Estate, In re, 640.
Stahl v. Stahl, 218.
Stainback v. Junk Bros. Lumber & Mfg. Co., 546.
Staines v. Burton, 307.
Stall v. City of Cincinnati, 580, 589.
Stamford Trust Co. v. Mack, 409.
Standard Metallic Paint Co. v. Prince Mfg. Co., 407.
Standish v. Babcock, 551, 552, 558.
Stanley v. Colt, 496.
Stanley v. Thornton, 159.
Stanley's Estate v. Pence, 522, 523.
Stanley's Will, In re, 620, 621.
Stanly v. McGowen, 311.
Stanton v. Helm, 608, 611.
Stanwood v. Wishard, 602.
Stapleton v. Brannan, 238.

Stapyleton v. Neeley, 487.
Starbuck v. Farmers' Loan & Trust Co., 108.
Starcher Bros. v. Duty, 246.
Starke v. Starke, 609.
Stark's Estate, In re, 502.
Stark's Will, In re, 256.
Starr, In re, 470.
Starr v. Minister and Trustees of Starr Methodist Protestant Church, 304.
Starr v. Selleck, 287.
Starr v. Starr Methodist Protestant Church, 244.
Starr v. Wiley, 489, 572, 577.
Starr v. Wright, 105.
State v. Ausmus, 571.
State v. Bank of Commerce, 505.
State v. Bank of Commerce of Grand Island, 26, 548, 551.
State v. Banks 576, 577.
State v. Bruce, 561.
State v. City of Toledo, 113.
State v. Farmers' State Bank, 561.
State v. Fleming, 574.
State v. Foster, 551, 552, 558.
State v. Graham, 576.
State v. Griffith, 270.
State v. Guilford, 510, 512.
State v. Higby Co., 113.
State v. Howarth, 525, 575.
State v. Hunter, 575, 576.
State v. Illinois Cent. R. Co., 461.
State v. Johnson, 208.
State v. Platt, 473.
State v. President, etc., of Bank of Maryland, 105.
State v. Thresher, 575.
State v. Underwood, 427.
State v. Warren, 270.
State Bank v. Macy, 155.
State Bank of St. Johns v. McCabe, 581.
State Bank of Winfield v. Alva Security Bank, 557.
State ex rel. Carmichael v. Bibb, 295.
State ex rel. Hindman v. Reed, 16.
State ex rel. Jones v. Jones, 210.
State ex rel. Robertson v. Thomas W. Wrenne & Co., 561.
State ex rel. Village of Warrensville Heights v. Fulton, 30.
State ex rel. Wardens of Poor of Beaufort County v. Gerard, 289.
State Nat. Bank of Little Rock v. First Nat. Bank of Atchison, Kan., 24.
State Sav. Bank v. Thompson, 554.

BOGERT TRUSTS 2D

CASES CITED
Figures refer to pages

State Street Trust Co. v. De Kalb, 372.
State Street Trust Co. v. Walker, 371.
State to Use of Napton v. Hunt, 574.
Staub v. Williams, 162.
Steacy v. Rice, 632.
Stead, In re, 227.
Stearly, Appeal of, 477, 523.
Stearns v. Newport Hospital, 113.
Stearns v. Palmer, 591.
Stebbins v. Lathrop, 126.
Steele v. Lowry, 96.
Steere v. Steere, 86.
Stein v. Kemp, 29.
Stein v. Nat. Bank of Commerce, 623.
Stein v. Safe Deposit & Trust Co. of Baltimore, 318.
Steiner's Estate, In re, 279.
Steinke v. Yetzer, 394.
Steinmetz v. Kern, 218.
Steinmetz's Estate, In re, 145.
Steinway v. Steinway, 474.
Stellmacher v. Bruder, 203.
Stell's Appeal, 510.
Stengel v. Royal Realty Corp., 400.
Stephan's Estate, In re, 259, 279.
Stephens v. Dayton, 245.
Stephens v. Dubois, 599.
Stephens v. St. Louis Union Trust Co., 181.
Stephens' Ex'rs v. Milnor, 372.
Sterling, In re, 574.
Sterling v. Tantum, 498, 499.
Sternberg & Co. v. Lehigh Val. R. Co., 37.
Sternbergh's Estate, In re, 448.
Sternfels v. Watson, 603.
Stevens, In re, 443.
Stevens y. Bagwell, 105.
Stevens v. Brennan, 540.
Stevens v. Burgess, 130.
Stevens v. Fitzpatrick, 53.
Stevens v. Hince, 155.
Stevens v. Home Ins. Co., 323.
Stevens v. Meserve, 360.
Stevens v. Stevens, 409.
Stevens' Estate, In re, 121.
Stevenson v. Evans, 245.
Stevenson's Estate, In re, 402.
Steward v. Hackler, 173.
Steward v. Traverse City State Bank, 334.
Stewart, In re, 115, 343.
Stewart v. Conrad's Adm'r, 610.
Stewart v. Coshow, 245, 285.
Stewart v. Franchetti, 275, 422, 636.
Stewart v. Greenfield, 540.
Stewart v. Hamilton, 415, 621.

Stewart v. Pettus, 319.
Stewart's Adm'r v. Carneal, 333.
Stewart's Estate, In re, 165, 233, 273, 286, 516, 643.
Stianson v. Stianson, 601, 618.
Stier v. Nashville Trust Co., 643.
Still v. Ruby, 115.
Stirk's Estate, 225.
Stockert v. Dry Dock Sav. Inst., 71, 76, 77.
Stocks v. Inzer, 127.
Stock's Ex'x v. Stock's Ex'r, 16.
Stockton v. Ford, 204.
Stockwell v. Stockwell's Estate, 458, 465.
Stoddard v. Smith, 541.
Stokes, Appeal of, 631.
Stokes v. McKibbin, 145.
Stoke's Estate, 447.
Stoll v. Smith, 611.
Stoller v. Coates, 561, 565.
Stone, In re, 629.
Stone v. Bishop, 75.
Stone v. Farnham, 481.
Stone v. Griffin, 127.
Stone v. Hackett, 92, 625.
Stone v. Kahle, 358, 541.
Stone v. King, 92, 98, 138.
Stonebraker v. First National Bank, 29.
Stong's Estate, In re, 520.
Storm v. McGrover, 186.
Storrs v. Burgess, 245.
Storrs v. Wallace, 543.
Storr's Agr. School v. Whitney, 127, 306.
Story v. First Nat. Bank & Trust Co., 259.
Story v. Palmer, 118.
Stoutenburgh v. Moore, 428.
Stover v. Webb, 487.
Stowe v. Bowen, 510.
Strasner v. Carroll, 213.
Stratton v. Edwards, 88.
Stratton v. Physio-Medical College, 264.
Stratton v. Stratton's Adm'r, 580.
Straw, Petition of, 423.
Strawn v. Caffee, 317.
Strayhorn v. Green, 128.
Streater's Estate, In re, 394, 589.
Street's Estate, In re, 245.
Streitz v. Hartman, 604.
Strickler's Estate, In re, 570, 571.
Striker v. Daly, 318, 319.
Strimpfler v. Roberts, 178, 232, 600.
Stringer v. Montgomery, 85.
Stringer v. Young, 162.

CASES CITED
Figures refer to pages

Strobel's Estate, In re, 129.
Strong v. Doty, 494.
Strong v. Dutcher, 346.
Strong's Appeal, 289.
Strother v. Barrow, 273.
Strout v. Strout, 246.
Stuart v. City of Easton, 291.
Stubinger v. Frey, 208.
Stull v. Harvey, 339.
Stump v. Warfield, 148.
Sturdivant Bank, In re, 32.
Sturgis v. Citizens' Nat. Bank of Pocomoke, 117.
Sturtevant v. Jaques, 83.
Sturtevant v. Sturtevant, 215.
Suarez v. De Montigny, 399.
Suit v. Creswell, 572.
Suiter v. McWard, 396.
Sullivan v. Babcock, 239.
Sullivan v. Latimer, 427, 535.
Sullivan v. McLenans, 187.
Sullivan v. Ross' Estate, 462.
Summers v. Chicago Title & Trust Co., 310.
Summers v. Higley, 137.
Summers v. Moore, 176.
Summers v. Summers, 559.
Sunderland v. Sunderland, 179.
Supreme Lodge, Knights of Pythias v. Rutzler, 639.
Supreme Lodge of Portuguese Fraternity of United States v. Liberty Trust Co., 554.
Susmann v. Young Men's Christian Ass'n of Seattle, 273.
Sutliff v. Aydelott, 146, 642.
Sutro's Estate, 264.
Suydam v. Dequindre, 138, 490.
Swabenland, 239.
Swan v. Produce Bank, 541.
Swartswalter's Account, In re, 481.
Swartwood's Estate, In re, 81.
Swartz v. Duncan, 395.
Swasey v. American Bible Soc., 285, 289.
Swearingham v. Stull's Ex'rs, 16.
Sweeney v. Hagerstown Trust Co., 407.
Sweeney v. Sampson, 275, 287.
Swetland v. Swetland, 91.
Swift v. Craighead, 210.
Swift v. Smith, 602.
Switzer v. Skiles, 327.
Swoope v. Trotter, 543.
Sydnor v. Palmer, 133.

T

Taber v. Bailey, 530, 641.

Taber v. Zehner, 83.
Taft v. Smith, 345, 346, 362.
Taft v. Stow, 532.
Tainter v. Broderick Land & Investment Co., 174.
Tainter v. Clark, 636.
Talbott v. Barber, 544.
Talbot v. Milliken, 450.
Talbot v. Talbot, 98.
Talcott v. American Board Com'rs for Foreign Missions, 93.
Talley v. Ferguson, 169.
T. A. McIntyre & Co., In re, 554.
Tannenbaum v. Seacoast Trust Co., 371.
Tantum v. Miller, 239.
Tappan v. Deblois, 270.
Tappan's Appeal, 296.
Tarbox v. Grant, 96, 102, 108.
Tarbox v. Tarbox, 199, 346, 468.
Tarrant v. Swain, 146.
Tate v. Woodyard, 394.
Tatem v. Speakman, 502.
Tatum v. McLellan, 332.
Taylor, In re, 511, 517.
Taylor v. Astor Nat. Bank, 584.
Taylor v. Bentinck-Smith, 457.
Taylor v. Blair, 600.
Taylor v. Brown, 124.
Taylor v. Calvert, 210.
Taylor v. Clark, 401.
Taylor v. Coggins, 598, 602, 603.
Taylor v. Columbian University, 287.
Taylor v. Crosson, 246.
Taylor v. Davis, 43.
Taylor v. Denny, 475.
Taylor v. Fox's Ex'rs, 224.
Taylor v. Gardiner, 413.
Taylor v. Harwell, 151, 153.
Taylor v. Huber's Ex'rs, 640.
Taylor v. Kelley, 202.
Taylor v. Mayo, 375.
Taylor v. Mullins, 196.
Taylor v. Richards, 632.
Taylor v. Roberts, 510.
Taylor v. Rogers, 635.
Taylor v. Taylor, 639.
Taylor v. Thompson, 174.
Taylor v. Turner, 33.
Taylor v. Watkins, 121.
Teal v. Pleasant Grove Local Union, No. 204, 2, 56.
Tebaldi Supply Co. v. MacMillan, 378.
Tecumseh Nat. Bank v. Russell, 199.
Teegarden v. Lewis, 328.
Teel v. Hilton, 41.
Telford v. Barney, 324.
Teller v. Hill, 232.

CASES CITED
Figures refer to pages

Temple v. Ferguson, 233, 633.
Templeton v. Bockler, 2.
Ten Broeck v. Fidelity Trust & Safety Vault Co., 480.
Tennant v. Tennant, 222.
Tenney v. Simpson, 88.
Terminal Trading Co. v. Babbit, 379.
Terrill v. Mathews, 517.
Terry v. Davenport, 614.
Terry v. Smith, 120.
Tesene v. Iowa State Bank, 587, 588.
Tetlow v. Rust, 197.
Tevis v. Doe, 150.
Tevis v. Steele, 422.
Texas Moline Plow Co. v. Kingman Texas Implement Co., 558.
Thackara v. Mintzer, 162.
Tharp v. Fleming, 496.
Thatcher v. Candee, 323, 417.
Thatcher v. Thatcher, 449.
Thatcher v. Trenton Trust Co., 91.
Thatcher v. Wardens, etc., of St. Andrew's Church of Ann Arbor, 100, 626.
Thaw v. Gaffney, 246.
Thayer v. Dewey, 345, 359, 361.
Thayer v. Pressey, 108.
Thayer v. Wendell, 377.
Thellusson v. Woodford, 253, 254.
Thiebaud v. Dufour, 129.
Thiebaud v. Tait, 390.
Thiede v. Startzman, 209.
Thieriot, In re, 573.
Thistle's Estate, In re, 642.
Thistlethwaite, In re, 107.
Thomas v. Glendinning, 607, 608.
Thomas v. Goodbread, 213.
Thomas v. Gregg, 451, 453.
Thomas v. Harkness, 498.
Thomas v. National Bank of Commerce of Seattle, 119.
Thomas v. Newburgh Sav. Bank, 72, 76, 78.
Thomas v. Reynolds, 61.
Thomas v. Scruggs, 504, 511, 520.
Thomas v. Thomas, 244, 474.
Thomas v. Walker, 150.
Thomassen v. Van Wyngaarden, 38.
Thompson, Appeal of, 557.
Thompson, In re, 135, 293.
Thompson v. Adams, 58.
Thompson v. Childress, 574.
Thompson v. Conant, 232.
Thompson v. Finch, 513.
Thompson v. Gloucester City Sav. Inst., 24.
Thompson v. Hale, 424.
Thompson v. Hart, 240.

Thompson v. Hartline, 500.
Thompson v. Hicks, 514.
Thompson v. Remsen, 591.
Thompson v. Thompson, 2, 199, 570.
Thompson's Appeal, 556.
Thompson's Estate, In re, 75, 448, 452, 478, 481, 525.
Thom's Ex'r v. Thom, 478, 484, 640.
Thomson v. American Surety Co. of New York, 576, 577.
Thomson v. Peake, 522.
Thomson v. Thomson, 183.
Thomson's Estate, In re, 452.
Thomson's Ex'rs v. Norris, 267.
Thorley, Re, 473.
Thornburg v. Macauley, 426.
Thorne v. Foley, 601.
Thornquist v. Oglethorpe Lodge Number One, 628.
Thornton v. Franklin Square House, 290.
Thornton v. Harris, 406, 424.
Thornton v. Howe, 278.
Thornton v. Koch, 492.
Thorp v. Lund, 138, 268, 272, 293, 487, 622.
Thouron's Estate, In re, 478.
Thruston v. Blackiston, 497.
Thum v. Wolstenholme, 559.
Thurston, Petition of, 644.
Tibbetts v. Tomkinson, 487.
Tidball's Estate, In re, 476.
Tidd v. Lister, 338.
Tierney v. Fitzpatrick, 68.
Tierney v. Wood, 106.
Tierney's Estate, 284.
Tiffany v. Clark, 118, 399.
Tifft v. Ireland, 637.
Tift v. Mayo, 147.
Tilden v. Fiske, 418.
Tilden v. Green, 271.
Tillinghast v. Bradford, 159, 160.
Tillinghast v. Coggeshall, 145, 368.
Tillman v. Blackburn, 259.
Tillott, In re, 459.
Tillson v. Moulton, 148.
Tilton v. Davidson, 161, 639.
Tinkham v. Heyworth, 24.
Tinkler v. Swaynie, 215.
Tippett v. Brooks, 209.
Tipton v. North, 245.
Titcomb v. Morrill, 174, 215.
Title Guarantee & Trust Co. v. Haven, 43, 567.
Title Insurance & Trust Co. v. Ingersoll, 522, 565.
Tobin v. Tobin, 188.
Tod, In re, 453, 502.

CASES CITED
Figures refer to pages

Todd, In re, 475.
Todd's Ex'rs v. Todd, 167.
Todhunter v. Des Moines, I. & M. R. Co., 248.
Tolles v. Wood, 161.
Toms v. Owen, 62.
Toms v. Williams, 256.
Toner's Estate, In re, 636.
Toney v. Toney, 179.
Topham, Re, 293.
Torrey v. Toledo Portland Cement Co., 46.
Totten, Matter of, 73, 74.
Touli v. Santa Cruz County Title Co., 50.
Tower's Estate, In re, 365.
Towle v. Ambs, 489.
Towle v. Doe, 244.
Towle v. Mack, 535.
Towle v. Nesmith, 127.
Towles v. Burton, 224.
Towles v. Towles, 179.
Town of Eastchester v. Mt. Vernon Trust Co., 584.
Town of Greenville v. Town of Mason, 496.
Town of Hamden v. Rice, 291.
Town of Lafayette v. Williams, 29, 561.
Town of Montpelier v. Town of East Montpelier, 425.
Town of Sharon v. Simons, 137, 492.
Town of Verona v. Peckham, 596.
Townley v. Sherborne, 507, 508, 510.
Townsend v. Allen, 239.
Townsend v. Wilson, 400, 402.
Townsend's Estate, In re, 121.
Townshend v. Frommer, 241.
Trabue v. Reynolds, 129.
Tracy v. Gravois R. Co., 477.
Trask v. Green, 232.
Trask v. Sturges, 572.
Travers v. Reid, 91.
Treacy v. Powers, 522.
Treadwell v. McKeon, 564.
Treadwell v. Treadwell, 610.
Tremmel v. Kleiboldt, 145.
Trenton Banking Co. v. McKelway, 205.
Trethewey v. Horton, 597.
Trim's Estate, 289.
Trotter v. Blocker, 134.
Trotter v. Lisman, 153, 154.
Troutman v. De Boissiere Odd Fellows' Orphans' Home & Industrial School Ass'n, 300.
Troy Iron & Nail Factory v. Corning, 359.

Troy & North Carolina Gold Min. Co. v. Snow Lumber Co., 232.
True Real Estate Co. v. True, 148.
Truelsch v. Miller, 559.
Trull v. Trull, 356.
Trunkey v. Van Sant, 191.
Trust Co. of Chicago v. Jackson Park Bldg. Corp., 325.
Trust Co. of New Jersey v. Glunz, 392.
Trustees, etc., of M. E. Church of Newark v. Clark, 249.
Trustees of Amherst College v. Ritch, 225, 491.
Trustees of Auburn Academy v. Strong, 495.
Trustees of Cory Universalist Soc. at Sparta v. Beatty, 277.
Trustees of McIntire Poor School v. Zanesville Canal & Mfg. Co., 57.
Trustees of Madison Academy v. Board of Education of Richmond, 406.
Trustees of Methodist Episcopal Church v. Trustees of Jackson Square Church, 191.
Trustees of Methodist Episcopal Church of Milford v. Williams, 284.
Trustees of New Castle Common v. Megginson, 286, 291, 292, 303.
Trustees of Princeton University v. Wilson, 487.
Trustees of Proprietors, School Fund of Providence, Appeal of, 405.
Trustees of Sailors' Snug Harbor in City of New York v. Carmody, 271, 289.
Trustees of Washburn College v. O'Hara, 287.
Trusteeship of First Minneapolis Trust Co., In re, 350.
Trutch v. Lamprell, 513.
Tryon v. Huntoon, 177.
Tucker v. Grundy, 416, 626.
Tucker v. State, 356.
Tucker v. Weeks, 461.
Tuckerman v. Currier, 423, 574.
Tunno, Ex parte, 572.
Tunstall v. Wormley, 572.
Turley v. Massengill, 232.
Turnage v. Greene, 641.
Turnbull v. Pomeroy, 324.
Turner, In re, 518, 521.
Turner v. Barber, 133, 134.
Turner v. Edmonston, 541.
Turner v. Fryberger, 395.
Turner v. Home Ins. Co., 177.

CASES CITED
Figures refer to pages

Turner v. Hoyle, 541.
Turner v. Sawyer, 205.
Turner v. Turner, 204, 469.
Turpin's Estate, In re, 503.
Turton v. Grant, 471.
Tuttle v. First Nat. Bank of Greenfield, 401.
Tuttle v. Gilmore, 502.
Tuttle v. Union Bank & Trust Co., 376.
Twining v. Girard Life Ins. Annuity & Trust Co., 643.
Twohy Mercantile Co. v. Melbye, 557.
Tyler, In re, 245, 303, 306.
Tyler v. Fidelity & Columbia Trust Co., 244.
Tyler v. Granger, 88.
Tyler v. Herring, 397.
Tyler v. Mayre, 117, 420.
Tyler v. Stitt, 225, 226.
Tyler v. Triesback, 57.
Tyree v. Bingham, 296, 494.
Tyrrel's Case, 14.

U

Ubhoff v. Brandenburg, 321.
Ullman v. Cameron, 161.
Ulmer v. Fulton, 105.
Unger v. Loewy, 313.
Ungrich, In re, 156.
Ungrich v. Ungrich, 332, 462, 596.
Union Nat. Bank v. Citizens' Bank, 24.
Union Savings Bank of San Jose v. Willard, 391.
Union Stockyards Nat. Bank v. Gillespie, 28.
Union Trust Co., In re, 353.
Union Trust Co. of New York, In re, 340, 369.
Union Trust Co. v. Preston Nat. Bank, 524.
Union Trust Co. of San Diego v. Superior Court, in and for San Diego County, 460.
United Nat. Bank of Troy v. Weatherby, 554.
U. S. v. Devereux, 140.
U. S. v. Getzelman, 112.
U. S. v. Jackson, 112.
U. S. v. Klein, 144.
U. S. v. Late Corporation of Church of Jesus Christ of Latter-Day Saints, 273.
U. S. v. Oregon & C. R. Co., 132.
U. S. v. Swope, 467.
U. S. v. Thurston Co., 626.

U. S. Bank v. Huth, 476.
U. S. ex rel. Willoughby v. Howard, 345.
U. S. Fidelity & Guaranty Co. v. Adoue & Lobit, 581, 582, 583.
U. S. Fidelity & Guaranty Co. v. Citizens' State Bank of Langdon, 535.
U. S. Fidelity & Guaranty Co. v. Douglas' Trustee, 244, 502.
U. S. Fidelity & Guaranty Co. v. Home Bank for Savings, 586, 587.
U. S. Fidelity & Guaranty Co. v. People's Bank, 586.
U. S. Fidelity & Guaranty Co. v. Union Bank & Trust Co., 580, 587.
U. S. Fidelity & Guaranty Co. v. U. S. Nat. Bank, 588.
U. S. Mortgage & Trust Co., In re, 465.
U. S. Trust Co., Matter of, 70, 435.
U. S. Trust Co. v. Poutch, 318.
U. S. Trust Co. v. Soher, 256.
U. S. Trust Co. of New York, In re, 631.
U. S. Trust Co. of New York, Matter of, 75.
Universalist Convention of Alabama v. May, 300.
University of London v. Yarrow, 290.
Unruh's Estate, In re, 645.
Upham v. Draper, 497.
Urann v. Coates, 81, 86, 87, 97, 469.
Ussery v. Ussery, 215.
Utica Ins. Co. v. Lynch, 525.
Utica Trust & Deposit Co. v. Thomson, 300.
Utter's Will, In re, 133.

V

Vaiden v. Stubblefield's Ex'r, 348.
Vail v. Vail, 191.
Valentine v. Richardt, 197.
Vallance, In re, 290.
Vallette v. Tedens, 205, 206.
Van Alen v. American Nat. Bank, 28, 557.
Van Alstyne v. Brown, 329, 599.
Vanasse v. Reid, 209.
Van Buskirk v. Van Buskirk, 523.
Van Camp v. Searle, 499.
Van Cott v. Prentice, 88, 92, 622.
Vanderheyden v. Crandall, 233.
Vanderpool v. Vanderpool, 197.
Van Deuzen v. Trustees of Presbyterian Congregation, 233.

CASES CITED
Figures refer to pages

Vandever, Appeal of, 321.
Van Doren v. Everitt, 45.
Van Doren v. Olden, 451.
Van Duyne v. Van Duyne, 61.
Van Epps v. Arbuckle, 190, 258.
Van Gorp v. Van Gorp, 333.
Van Hook v. Frey, 604.
Van Horne, Petition of, 496, 589.
Van Horne v. Fonda, 213.
Vanleer, Appeal of, 323.
Van Leer v. Van Leer, 643.
Van Orden v. Pitts, 467.
Van Pelt v. Parry, 422.
Van Rensselaer v. Morris, 523.
Van Riper v. Hilton, 245.
Vansant v. Spillman, 315.
Van Schoonhoven, In re, 128.
Van Sciver v. Churchill, 500.
Van Sinderen v. Lawrence, 462.
Van't Hof v. Jemison, 207.
Van Vacter v. McWillie, 232.
Van Wagenen v. Baldwin, 277.
Van Winkle v. Blackford, 609.
Varner, Appeal of, 57.
Varick v. Smith, 394.
Vaughan, In re, 284, 285.
Vaughan v. Wise, 162.
Veazie v. Forsaith, 409.
Veitch v. Woodward Iron Co., 600, 604.
Verdin v. Slocum, 233.
Vernon v. Marsh's Ex'rs, 365.
Vernoy v. Robinson, 319, 424.
Verzier v. Convard, 174, 215.
Vidal v. Girard's Ex'rs, 261, 269, 278, 286.
Viele v. Curtis, 87.
Vilas v. Bundy, 336.
Vilas Nat. Bank of Plattsburgh v. Newton, 237.
Village of Brattleboro v. Mead, 304.
Villard v. Villard, 372.
Villines v. Norfleet, 333.
Vincent v. Rogers, 498.
Vincent v. Werner, 348.
Vineland Trust Co. v. Westendorf, 287.
Viney v. Abbott, 238, 623.
Virginia-Carolina Chemical Co. v. McNair, 557.
Viser v. Bertrand, 43.
Vlahos v. Andrews, 642.
Vom Saal's Will, In re, 366, 367.
Von Trotha v. Bamberger, 215, 217.
Voorhees v. Presbyterian Church of Village of Amsterdam, 233.
Voorhees' Adm'rs v. Stoothoff, 526.
Voorhees' Ex'x v. Melick, 502.

Vorlander v. Keyes, 559.
Vorse v. Vorse, 212.
Vose v. Reed, 569.
Vreeland v. Van Horn, 598.
Vrooman v. Virgil, 492.

W

Wachovia Bank & Trust Co. v. Laws, 641.
Waddail v. Vassar, 546.
Waddell v. Waddell, 548, 549, 551, 558.
Wade v. Powell, 338.
Wadsworth, In re, 572.
Wadsworth, Howland & Co. v. Arnold, 383.
Wagenseller v. Prettyman, 526.
Wagner, Appeal of, 476.
Wagner, Matter of, 415.
Wagner v. Coen, 340, 341.
Wagner v. Wagner, 157, 161.
Wagnon v. Pease, 402.
Wagstaffe v. Lowerre, 474.
Wahl v. Schmidt, 386.
Wait v. Society for Political Study of New York City, 74.
Waldron v. Merrill, 189.
Waldrop v. Leaman, 332.
Waldstein v. Barnett, 211.
Wales v. Sammis & Scott, 504.
Walke v. Moore, 395.
Walker v. Brooks, 38.
Walker v. Crews, 97.
Walker v. Doak, 416.
Walker v. James, 119.
Walker v. Marcellus & O. L. Ry. Co., 245.
Walker v. Quigg, 63.
Walker v. Scott, 123.
Walker v. Symonds, 596.
Walker v. Walker's Ex'rs, 519.
Walkerly's Estate, In re, 251.
Wall v. Pfanschmidt, 200.
Wallace v. Berdell, 89.
Wallace v. Bowen, 179.
Wallace v. Foxwell, 161.
Wallace v. Lincoln Sav. Bank, 46.
Wallace v. Long, 201.
Wallace v. Smith, 159.
Wallace v. Wallace, 435.
Wallace & Sons v. Castle, 21, 28.
Wallace's Estate, In re, 573.
Wallach, Matter of, 107.
Waller v. Hosford, 426, 569, 570.
Waller v. Jones, 526.
Walley v. Walley, 329.
Wallis v. Thornton's Adm'r, 512.
Walsh v. Walsh, 115.

CASES CITED
Figures refer to pages

Walso v. Latterner, 68.
Walter v. Brugger, 399, 400.
Walter v. Klock, 213.
Walter J. Schmidt & Co., In re, 550.
Walton v. Follansbee, 395.
Walton's Estate, In re, 462.
Wambersie v. Orange Humane Soc., 496.
Wamburzee v. Kennedy, 538, 615.
Wanamaker's Trust, In re, 326.
Wann v. Northwestern Trust Co., 466.
Warbass v. Armstrong, 473, 475, 482.
Warburton Ave. Baptist Church v. Clark, 74.
Ward v. Armstrong, 549.
Ward v. Brown, 204.
Ward v. Buchanan, 2.
Ward v. Conklin, 211.
Ward v. Dortch, 570.
Ward v. Funsten, 482.
Ward v. Marie, 237.
Ward v. Shire, 481.
Ward's Estate, In re, 484, 573.
Wardens etc., of St. Paul's Church v. Attorney General, 190.
Ware v. City of Fitchburg, 289.
Ware v. Richardson, 123.
Warfield v. Brand's Adm'r, 428.
Waring v. Darnall, 337, 477.
Warland v. Colwell, 632.
Warner v. Bates, 63.
Warner v. Mettler, 486.
Warner v. Morse, 182.
Warner v. Rice, 156.
Warner v. Rogers, 322, 324.
Warner v. Tullis, 380.
Warnock v. Harlow, 540.
Warren v. Adams, 607, 609.
Warren v. Burnham, 571.
Warren v. Holbrook, 43.
Warren v. Howard, 579.
Warren v. Pazolt, 410.
Warren v. Steer, 177.
Warren v. Tynan, 187.
Warren v. Warren, 491.
Warren-Scharf Asphalt Paving Co. v. Dunn, 24.
Warsco v. Oshkosh Savings & Trust Co., 90.
Warwick v. Warwick, 505.
Washbon v. Linscott State Bank, 580, 614.
Washburn v. Acome, 305.
Washburn v. Rainier, 595.
Washington Monument Fund, In re, 493.
Washington Nat. Building & Loan Ass'n v. Heironimus, 496.

Washington's Estate, In re, 83.
Waterman v. Alden, 336, 462, 502, 573.
Waterman v. Buckingham, 506, 546.
Waterman v. Cochran, 534.
Waters v. Hall, 189.
Watkins v. Bigelow, 272.
Watkins v. Greer, 628.
Watkins v. Reynolds, 233.
Watkins v. Specht, 420.
Watkins v. Stewart, 345.
Watling v. Lewis, 377.
Watson, In re, 365.
Watson v. Conrad, 369.
Watson v. Dodson, 523, 609.
Watson v. Erb, 202, 206.
Watson v. Kennard, 155.
Watson v. Payne, 230.
Watson v. Sutro, 540, 541.
Watson v. Thompson, 549.
Watson v. Wagner, 557.
Watson v. Watson, 643.
Watt v. Watt, 189.
Watts v. McCloud, 59.
Watts v. Newberry, 558.
Wayman v. Follansbee, 641.
Way's Trusts, In re, 96, 100.
Weakley v. Barrow, 589.
Weakley v. Meriwether, 482.
Weaver v. Emigrant, etc., Savings Bank, 70, 74, 76.
Weaver v. Fisher, 462.
Weaver v. Spurr, 237.
Weaver's Estate, Matter of, 430.
Webb, Estate of, 93.
Webb v. Hayden, 229.
Webb v. Vermont Cent. R. Co., 592.
Webb v. Webb, 310.
Webb's Estate, 506.
Webber v. Clark, 540, 541.
Weber v. Bryant, 267.
Weber v. Chicago & W. I. R. Co., 602.
Weber v. Richardson, 540, 544.
Weber v. Weber, 69, 73, 77, 79.
Webster v. Bush, 643.
Webster v. Morris, 263, 285, 287.
Webster v. Pierce, 348.
Webster v. Sughrow, 284.
Webster v. Wiggin, 286, 290, 306.
Weed, In re, 120.
Weekly v. Ellis, 181.
Weeks v. Cornwell, 240.
Weeks v. Frankel, 117, 118, 319, 393.
Weer v. Gand, 43, 53.
Weetjen v. Vibbard, 591.
Weiderhold v. Mathis, 475.
Weiland v. Townsend, 424.
Weisel v. Cobb, 476, 502, 524.

CASES CITED
Figures refer to pages

Weiss v. Haight & Freese Co., 505.
Weiss v. Heitkamp, 183, 215.
Welch, In re, 426, 428.
Welch v. Allen, 57.
Welch v. City of Boston, 123.
Welch v. Henshaw, 97.
Welch v. Polley, 557.
Welch v. Trustees of Episcopal Theological School, 641.
Wellborn v. Rogers, 609.
Weller v. Noffsinger, 161.
Welles v. Cowles, 44.
Welling's Estate, In re, 481.
Wellington v. Heermans, 102.
Wells v. German Ins. Co. of Freeport, 126.
Wells v. Heath, 304.
Wells v. McCall, 134.
Wells v. Wells, 211.
Wells, Estate of In re, 441, 443, 444.
Wells-Stone Mercantile Co. v. Aultman, Miller & Co., 383.
Welscher's Estate, In re, 482.
Welsh v. Brown, 482.
Welsh's Estate, 49.
Weltner v. Thurmond, 523, 602, 607.
Wemyss v. White, 161.
Wentura v. Kinnerk, 276.
Wentworth v. Wentworth, 245.
Wenzel v. Powder, 164, 637.
West, In re, 35.
West v. Bailey, 130.
West v. Biscoe, 501.
West v. Fitz, 57.
West v. Raymond, 209.
West v. Robertson, 358.
West v. Sloan, 615.
West's Estate, In re, 232.
Westcott v. Edmunds, 233.
Westerfield, In re, 369.
Westerfield v. Kimmer, 182.
Westerfield v. Rogers, 510.
Western German Bank v. Norvell, 24, 556.
Western R. Co. v. Nolan, 340, 590.
Westphal v. Heckman, 215.
Westport Paper-Board Co. v. Staples, 243.
Wetherell v. O'Brien, 29, 557.
Wetmore v. Brown, 474.
Wetmore v. Parker, 271.
Wetmore v. Porter, 580.
Whall v. Converse, 640.
Whallen v. Kellner, 424, 427.
Wharton v. Masterman, 308, 641.
Whatley v. Oglesby, 589.
Wheatcraft v. Wheatcraft, 571.
Wheaton v. Batcheller, 487.

Wheaton v. Dyer, 535.
Wheeler v. Brown, 592.
Wheeler v. Kidder, 179.
Wheeler v. Kirtland, 186.
Wheeler v. Perry, 120, 368.
Wheeler v. Reynolds, 215.
Wheeler v. Willard, 204.
Whelan v. Reilly, 121, 246, 423.
Whetsler v. Sprague, 606.
Whicker v. Hume, 276.
Whitaker v. McDowell, 316, 319, 414.
Whitaker v. Whitaker, 94.
Whitcomb's Estate, In re, 64.
White v. Carpenter, 184.
White v. City of Newark, 289.
White v. Commercial & Farmers' Bank, 25.
White v. Ditson, 475.
White v. Fitzgerald, 81, 86.
White v. Hampton, 425.
White v. Kavanaugh, 150.
White v. Rankin, 458, 465.
White v. Rice, 113.
White v. Sheldon, 183, 613.
White v. Sherman, 356, 369, 370, 502, 526.
White v. Watkins, 320.
White v. White, 126, 500.
White Lick Quarterly Meeting of Friends v. White Lick Quarterly Meeting of Friends, 289.
White River Lumber Co. v. Clark, 427.
White's Ex'r v. White, 156, 162.
Whitecar's Estate, In re, 347, 503.
Whitehead, In re, 128.
Whitehead v. Draper, 475, 477.
Whitehead v. Whitehead, 368, 421, 423, 425, 478.
Whitehouse v. Bolster, 225.
Whitesel v. Whitesel, 62.
Whiteside v. Whiteside, 481.
Whiting v. Gould, 87, 182.
Whiting v. Hudson Trust Co., 567.
Whitlow v. Patterson, 329.
Whitney v. Fox, 604.
Whitney v. Hay, 196.
Whitney v. Martine, 361.
Whittemore v. Beekman, 456.
Whittemore v. Equitable Trust Co., 624.
Whittingham v. Schofield's Trustee, 63.
Whittle v. Vanderbilt Min. & Mill. Co. 546.
W. Horace Williams Co. Inc., v. Vandaveer, Brown & Stoy, 545.
Wickham v. Berry, 338, 643.

CASES CITED
Figures refer to pages

Wickham v. Martin, 546.
Widener v. Fay, 483.
Widman v. Kellogg, 548, 551, 557.
Widmayer, In re, 462.
Widmayer v. Widmayer, 570.
Wiegand v. Woerner, 477, 570, 573.
Wiener's Estate, In re, 480.
Wieters v. Hart, 356, 370.
Wiggins, In re, 571.
Wiggins v. Burr, 573.
Wiggs v. Winn, 88.
Wight v. Lee, 503.
Wight v. Mason, 316.
Wiglesworth v. Wiglesworth, 508, 511, 513.
Wilberding v. Miller, 449.
Wilce v. Van Anden, 108, 191.
Wilcox, Appeal of, 426.
Wilcox, In re, 245.
Wilcox v. Gilchrist, 131.
Wilcox v. Hubbell, 625.
Wilcox v. Wilcox, 195, 218.
Wilde v. Smith, 62.
Wilder v. Hast, 477.
Wilder v. Haughey, 146.
Wilder v. Howard, 74, 91.
Wilder v. Ireland, 233.
Wildey v. Robinson, 484.
Wiley, In re, 522.
Wiley v. Dunn, 173.
Wiley v. Morris, 468.
Wilkin, In re, 411, 629.
Wilkinson v. May, 230.
Wilkinson v. Wilkinson, 530.
Willard v. Willard, 69, 70.
Willats v. Bosworth, 86.
Willets, In re, 476, 484.
Willets v. Willets, 61.
Willett v. Willett, 291.
Willett's Estate, In re, 502.
Willetts v. Schuyler, 388.
Williams, Appeal of, 136, 570, 632.
Williams, In re, 60, 163.
Williams v. Bond, 484.
Williams v. Brooklyn Sav. Bank, 74, 76, 78.
Williams v. City of Oconomowoc, 272, 307.
Williams v. Cobb, 356.
Williams v. Committee of Baptist Church, 64, 65.
Williams v. Cushing, 130, 131.
Williams v. Davison's Estate, 211.
Williams v. First Presbyterian Soc. in Cincinnati, 57, 609.
Williams v. Fullerton, 124.
Williams v. Gardner, 316, 318.
Williams v. Haskin's Estate, 99.

Williams v. Herrick, 245, 258.
Williams v. McConico, 630.
Williams v. Moliere, 420.
Williams v. Moodhard, 87.
Williams v. Mosher, 477.
Williams v. Nichol, 34.
Williams v. Palmer, 210.
Williams v. Powell, 210.
Williams v. Sage, 491, 624.
Williams v. Smith, 163.
Williams v. Thacher, 641.
Williams v. Thorn, 161, 162, 163.
Williams v. Vreeland, 224, 226.
Williams v. Wager, 184.
Williams v. Williams, 87, 250, 270, 271, 358.
Williams v. Worthington, 62, 64.
Williams v. Young, 607.
Williams' Estate, In re, 144.
Williamsburgh Trust Co., In re, 482.
Williamson v. Grider, 401, 458, 573.
Williamson v. Suydam, 569.
Williamson v. Wilkins, 338.
Williamson v. Yager, 103.
Williard v. Williard, 614.
Williford v. Williford, 204.
Willis v. Alvey, 122.
Willis v. Braucher, 366.
Willis v. Clymer, 329, 464, 470.
Willis v. Curtze, 156.
Willis v. Holcomb, 597.
Willis v. Rice, 211.
Willis v. Sharp, 383.
Willis v. Smyth, 72, 73, 74, 76.
Willis v. Willis, 183.
Wills v. Maddox, 243.
Wills v. Nehalem Coal Co., 45.
Wills v. Wood, 209.
Wilmer v. Philadelphia & Reading Coal & Iron Co., 406.
Wilmerding v. McKesson, 355, 514.
Wilmerding v. Russ, 40, 612, 618.
Wilmes v. Tiernay, 281.
Wilmington Trust Co. v. Jacobs. 319.
Wilmington Trust Co. v. Wilmington Trust Co., 243.
Wilmoth v. Wilmoth, 64.
Wilson v. Biggama, 474.
Wilson v. Castro, 198.
Wilson v. Featherston, 102.
Wilson v. First Nat. Bank of Independence, 262, 286, 307.
Wilson v. Fridenberg, 382.
Wilson v. Heilman, 632.
Wilson v. Hughes Bros. Mfg. Co., 101.
Wilson v. Kennedy, 462.
Wilson v. Odell, 256.

CASES CITED

Figures refer to pages

Wilson v. Pennock, 319.
Wilson v. Russ, 569.
Wilson v. Snow, 125, 421.
Wilson v. Towle, 423.
Wilson v. Warner, 80, 179.
Wilson v. Wilson, 16, 422, 572, 574.
Wilson's Appeal, In re, 430.
Wilson's Estate, In re, 628.
Wiltbank, Appeal of, 452.
Winans v. Winans' Estate, 189.
Windener v. Fay, 478.
Winder v. Scholey, 222, 224, 226, 227.
Windmuller v. Spirits Distributing Co., 356, 504.
Windsor Trust Co., In re, 402.
Windsor Trust Co. v. Waterbury, 337.
Windstanley v. Second Nat. Bank of Louisville, 549.
Winlock v. Munday, 536.
Winn v. Dillon, 205.
Winona & St. P. R. Co. v. St. Paul & S. C. R. Co., 197.
Winslow v. Baltimore & O. R. Co., 321.
Winslow v. Rutherford, 162.
Winslow v. Stark, 126.
Winters v. March, 633.
Winters v. Winters, 55, 535.
Winthrop Co. v. Clinton, 162.
Wirth v. Wirth, 642.
Wisconsin Universalist Convention v. Union Unitarian and Universalist Soc. of Prairie du Sac, 573.
Wisdom v. Wilson, 393.
Wistar's Estate, In re, 477.
Wister, Appeal of, 481.
Wiswall v. Stewart, 469, 595.
Witherington v. Herring, 625.
Withers v. Jenkins, 98.
Witmer, Appeal of, 343.
Witt v. Carroll, 635.
Witte v. Storm, 204.
Witter v. Dudley, 542.
Wittner v. Burr Ave. Development Corporation, 189.
Witzel v. Chapin, 72, 74.
Wolf v. Pearce, 89.
Wolfe v. Croft, 34, 36.
Wolfe v. Hatheway, 243, 247.
Wolford v. Herrington, 213.
Women's Christian Ass'n v. City of Kansas City, 302, 636.
Wood, In re, 246.
Wood v. Cox, 36.
Wood v. Davis, 435.
Wood v. Griffin, 245.
Wood v. Kice, 140.
Wood v. McClelland, 162.

Wood v. Paul, 622.
Wood v. Rabe, 196.
Wood v. Vandenburgh, 283.
Wood v. Wood, 239, 366, 368, 370.
Wood's Estate, In re, 640.
Woodard v. Cohron, 213.
Woodard v. Woodard, 243.
Woodard v. Wright, 412, 468, 471.
Woodbery v. Atlas Realty Co., 425.
Woodbridge v. Bockes, 596.
Woodbury v. Hayden, 35, 36, 191.
Woodcock v. Wachovia Bank & Trust Co., 276.
Wooddell v. Arizona, 527.
Wooden v. Kerr, 463.
Woodgate v. Fleet, 249.
Woodley v. Holley, 343.
Woodroof v. Hundley, 287.
Woodrop v. Weed, 379.
Woodruff v. Jabine, 603.
Woodruff v. Marsh, 192, 309, 310.
Woodruff v. New York, L. E. & W. R. Co., 479.
Woodruff v. Snedecor, 476.
Woodruff v. Williams, 599.
Woodruff v. Woodruff, 120.
Woodrum v. Washington Nat. Bank, 564.
Woodward v. Camp, 98.
Woodward v. James, 117.
Woodward v. Stubbs, 230.
Woodward v. Woodward, 145, 179.
Woodwine v. Woodrum, 589.
Wooldridge v. Planter's Bank, 429.
Woolf v. Barnes, 459, 591.
Woolley v. City of Natchez, 32.
Woolley v. Stewart, 607.
Woods v. Bell, 573.
Woods v. Stevenson, 600.
Worcester City Missionary Soc. v. Memorial Church, 365.
Word v. Sparks, 561.
Worden v. Worden, 202.
Wordin's Appeal from Probate, 372.
Wormley v. Wormley, 532.
Worrell, Appeal of, 356.
Worth v. McAden, 510.
Worthy v. Johnson, 328.
Wright v. Chilcott, 178, 469.
Wright v. Dame, 496.
Wright v. Keasbey, 123.
Wright v. Leupp, 161.
Wright v. Miller, 140.
Wright v. Pond, 132.
Wright v. Security-First Nat. Bank of Los Angeles, 143.
Wright v. Wright, 603, 604.
Wright v. Yates, 189.

CASES CITED
Figures refer to pages

Wright v. Young, 58, 215.
Wright-Blodgett Co. v. United States, 540.
Wright's Estate, In re, 264, 452.
Wrightsman v. Rogers, 183.
Wuichet's Estate, In re, 433.
Wulbern v. Timmons, 556.
Wulff v. Roseville Trust Co. of Newark, N. J., 124.
Wyble v. McPheters, 490.
Wylie v. Bushnell, 326, 459, 485, 573.
Wylie v. White, 152, 159.
Wynn v. Sharer, 189.
Wynne v. Humberston, 460.
Wynne v. Tempest, 513, 517.
Wynne v. Warren, 502.
Wyrick v. Weck, 540.
Wyse v. Dandridge, 239.

Y

Yale College, In re, 112, 124.
Yard v. Pittsburgh & L. E. R. Co., 134, 619.
Yates v. Big Sandy R. Co., 591.
Yates v. Thomas, 576.
Yates v. Yates, 319, 423, 424.
Yeamans v. James, 208, 209.
Yedor v. Chicago City Bank & Trust Co., 628.
Yeiser v. United States Board & Paper Co., 45.
Yellowstone County v. First Trust & Savings Bank, 549, 560.
Yerkes, Appeal of, 640.
Yerkes v. Crum, 209.
Yerkes v. Richards, 379.
Yesner v. Commissioner of Banks, 550.
Yetman v. Hedgeman, 183.

Yokem v. Hicks, 116.
Yonge v. Hooper, 331.
Yost v. Critcher, 469.
Yost's Estate, In re, 341.
Young, In re, 478.
Young v. Barker, 416, 484.
Young v. Cardwell, 103, 125.
Young v. Easley, 168.
Young v. Holland, 58.
Young v. Hughes, 493.
Young v. Mercantile Trust Co., 33.
Young v. Murphy, 208.
Young v. St. Mark's Lutheran Church, 311.
Young v. Snow, 146, 645.
Young v. Walker, 616.
Young v. Young, 93, 319, 396.
Y. M. C. A. v. Horn, 252.
Younger v. Moore, 238.

Z

Zabriskie's Ex'rs v. Wetmore, 425.
Zaremba v. Woods, 197.
Zehnbar v. Spillman, 375.
Zerega, In re, 426.
Zeigler v. Hughes, 209.
Zeisweiss v. James, 278, 294.
Ziegler, In re, 421.
Ziegler's Estate, In re, 475.
Zimmer v. Sennott, 36.
Zimmer Construction Co. v. White, 377.
Zimmerman v. Anders, 270.
Zimmerman v. Fraley, 359, 370.
Zimmerman v. Makepeace, 592.
Zion Church of Evangelical Ass'n of North America in Charles City v. Parker, 325.
Zuver v. Lyons, 540.

INDEX

Figures refer to pages

ACCEPTANCE
By beneficiary, 137.
By trustee, 124.

ACCOUNTING
Advances by trustee, 469.
Costs of, 470.
Credits on, 468.
Debits on, 467.
Duties of trustee as to, 458.
Duty of trustee to render, in court, 460
Lien of trustee on, 471.
Practice on, 464.

ACCUMULATIONS
Charitable trusts, 308.
Private trusts, 253.

ACQUIESCENCE
Barring remedy, 596.

ACTIVE TRUSTS
Distinguished from passive, 228.
Statutory restrictions on purpose, 240.
Validity of purpose, 233.

ADMINISTRATOR
Trustee distinguished, 41.

ADVANCES
By trustee, effect on accounting, 469.
Duties of trustee as to, 414.

ADVICE
Court's power to give, 486.

AGENCY
Trust distinguished, 41.

AGENTS
Money paid to, debt or trust, 27.

ALIENATION
Beneficiary's interest, 146.

ALTERATION OF TRUST
By act of parties, 619.
By the court, 620.

BOGERT TRUSTS 2D   719

INDEX
Figures refer to pages

AMENDMENT OF TRUST
By act of parties, 619.
By the court, 620.

APPOINTMENT
Successor trustees, 422.

APPORTIONMENT
Receipts, between principal and income, 431.

ASSIGNMENT
Beneficiary's interest, 148.
Of chose, trust distinguished, 36.

BAILMENT
Distinguished from trust, 32.

BANK DEPOSITS
Debt or trust, 30.

BANKERS' COLLECTION CODE
Effect of, 27.

BANKS
Collection items, debt or trust, 22.
Liabilities for participation in breach of trust, 578.
Savings bank trusts, 65.

BARRING OF REMEDIES
Laches, 598.
Statute of Limitations, 605.
When it occurs, 594.

BENEFICIARY
Acceptance by, 137.
Claim of, not preferred, 504.
Control of investments, 364.
Creditors of, rights against his interest, 149.
In charitable trusts, 273.
Incidents of interest of, 143.
Nature of interest of, 139.
Need for, 131.
Remedies of, 486.
Remedy barred by own acts, 594.
Requesting end of trust, 638.
Rights of, 4.
Right to information from trustee, 458.
Who may be, 134.

BENEVOLENCE
As related to charity, 260.

BLENDED TRUST
Creation of, 168.

BONA FIDE PURCHASER
Notice, 540.
Rule regarding, 533.
Value, meaning of, 545.
Who is a purchaser, 544.

BOND
Recovery on, 575.
Trustee giving, 129.

BORROWING
Court control of, 401.
Effect of, 403.
Power of trustee as to, 399.

BREACH OF CONTRACT
Basis for constructive trust, 201.

CAPITAL
Duty of trustee to advance, 414.

CAPITAL AND INCOME
See Principal and Income.

CEMETERIES
Trusts for, 282.

CERTAINTY
In express trust creation, 57.

CESTUI QUE TRUST
See Beneficiary.

CHARGE
Equitable, distinguished from trust, 34.

CHARITABLE TRUSTS
Accumulations under, 308.
Administration of charities, 294.
Cemeteries and monuments, 282.
Cy pres doctrine, 296.
Definition of, 260.
Distinguished from private, 228.
Duration, 311.
Educational purposes, 285.
Eleemosynary purposes, 288.
Governmental purposes, 291.
History of, 268.
History of in America, 270.
How enforced, 294.
Indefiniteness of purpose and beneficiaries, 273.
Masses, 279.
Purposes not charitable, 293.
Religious purposes, 276.
Remedy to procure execution of, 493.
Restraints on alienation, 307.
Rule against remoteness, 303.
Statutory restrictions on creation, 311.
Visitorial powers, 495.

CHARITY
See Charitable Trusts.

CHOSE IN ACTION
Assignment of, trust distinguished, 36.

CLASSIFICATION
Trusts, 52.

Bogert Trusts 2d—46

CLAYTON'S CASE
Rule in, 549.

CODES
Of trust law, 16.

COLLECTION
Trust property, duties of trustee, 336.

COLLECTION ITEMS
Bankers' Collection Code, 27.
Trust or debt, 22.

COMMERCIAL PAPER
Collection items, debt or trust, 22.

COMMISSIONS
See Compensation.

COMMON TRUST FUNDS
As trust investments, 362.

COMPENSATION
Co-trustees, 482.
Court may reduce or forfeit, 481.
Executors and trustees, 484.
Trustee's, 472.
Waiver or loss, 480.

CONFIDENTIAL RELATION
Direct dealing, constructive trust, 207.
Disloyalty, constructive trust, 203.
Oral trust, 218.

CONFLICT OF LAWS
Trust purpose, 239.

CONSENT
Barring remedy, 596.

CONSIDERATION
Creation express trusts, 92.

CONSTRUCTIVE TRUSTS
Breach of contract to convey, 201.
Classification of, 170.
Conveyance of land on oral trust, 214.
Creation of, 194.
Definition of, 194.
Direct dealing with beneficiary, 207.
Disloyalty by fiduciary, 203.
Duress, 198.
Fraudulent misrepresentation, 196.
Gift by will or intestacy on oral trust, 219.
Larceny or conversion, 199.
Mistake, 198.
Property obtained by homicide, 200.
Purchase at judicial sale, 212.
Statute of Frauds, 195.
Statute of Limitations, 614.
Undue influence, 198.

CONTRACTS
Creditor's right against trust estate, 381.
Distinguished from trust, 18.
Liabilities of trustee on, 374.
Trustee's exclusion of personal liability, 376.
Trustee's right to indemnity, 379.

CONTROL
Trust property, by co-trustees, 511.

CONVERSION
Proceeds of, constructive trust, 199.

CO-TRUSTEES
Compensation of, 482.
Control of trust property, 511.
Division of responsibility among, 520.
Division of work, 322.
Liabilities affected by agreement, 518.
Liabilities of, statutory rules, 516.
Liability for acts of fellow trustee, 507.
Nature of liabilities of, 504.
Powers of, 320.
Supervision of each other, 513.
Warning of danger from one trustee, 515.

COUPON ACCOUNT
Debt or trust, 31.

COURT
Control of borrowing and giving security, 401.
Control of investments, 364.
Control of trustee's sale, 395.
Control over compensation, 481.
Permitting alteration of private trust, 620.
Termination of trust at request of beneficiary, 638.

CREATION
Express trusts, 52.
    Acceptance by beneficiary, 137.
    Acceptance by trustee, 124.
    Beneficiary, who may be, 134.
    Blended trusts, 168.
    Certainty of intent, 57.
    Consideration, 92.
    Delivery trust instrument, 95.
    Discretionary trusts, 166.
    Estate of trustee, 122.
    Evidence, 59.
    Expression trust intent, 55.
    Incident's of beneficiary's interest, 143.
    Interest of beneficiary and creditors, 149.
    Methods of, 54.
    Nature of beneficiary's interest, 139.
    Need for beneficiary, 131.
    Notice of the trust, 99.
    Original appointment of trustee, 119.
    Precatory expressions, 59.
    Qualification by trustee, 128.
    Qualifications of settlor, 104.

CREATION—Continued
Express trusts—Continued
    Savings bank trusts, 65.
    Spendthrift trusts, 156.
    Statute of Frauds, 79.
    Subject matter, 107.
    Support trusts, 168.
    Transfer of possession, 102.
    Transfer of title to trustee, 101.
    Trust elements, 104.
    Trust not to fail for want of trustee, 121.
    Who may be trustee, 111.
    Wills Acts, 89.
    Words required, 56.

CREATION CONSTRUCTIVE TRUSTS
How accomplished, 194.

CREATION RESULTING TRUSTS
How accomplished, 170.

CREDITOR'S SUIT
Against trust beneficiary, 151.

CREDITORS
Of beneficiary, 149.
    Blended trust, 168.
    Discretionary trust, 166.
    Spendthrift trusts, 156.
    Support trust, 168.

CURTESY
Beneficiary's interest, 145.

CY PRES
Doctrine of, 296.

DEATH
Of trustee, effect, 419.

DEBT
Debtor making himself trustee, 31.
Distinguished from trust, 18.
    Specific property criterion, 21.

DEED OF TRUST
In nature of mortgage, trust distinguished, 50.

DEFENDING TRUST
Duty of trustee, 335.

DEFINITIONS
Fundamental terms, 1.

DELEGATION
Powers, 323.

DELIVERY
Trust instrument, need for, 95.

DEVIATION
From trust terms, court consent to, 620.

INDEX
Figures refer to pages

DILIGENCE
Required of trustee, 326.

DIRECT DEALING
Fiduciary and beneficiary, constructive trust, 207.

DISCLAIMER
By beneficiary, 137.
By trustee, 124.

DISCOUNTS
Duty of trustee, when bonds bought at, 439.

DISCRETIONARY POWERS
Of trustee, 315.

DISCRETIONARY TRUSTS
Creation of, 166.

DISLOYALTY
Fiduciary, constructive trust, 203.

DISTINCTIONS
Active and passive trusts, 228.
Agency, 41.
Assignment of chose, 36.
Bailment, 32.
Debt, 18.
    Specific property criterion, 21.
Debt or trust,
    Bank deposits, 30.
    Debtor making self trustee, 31.
    Money for investment, 29.
    Money to pay deliveror's debt, 28.
    Security deposits, 29.
    Transmission of funds, 30.
Deeds of trust in the nature of mortgages, 50.
Equitable charge, 34.
Executorship, 39.
Guardianship, 44.
Life tenant and remainderman, 49.
Private and charitable trusts, 228.
Promoters and officers of corporations, 45.
Receivership, 48.

DIVIDEND ACCOUNT
Debt or trust, 31.

DIVIDENDS
Cash, principal and income accounts, 445.
Stock, principal and income accounts, 448.

DOWER
Beneficiary's interest, 145.

DRY TRUSTS
See Passive Trusts.

DURATION
Charitable trusts, 311.
Of trust, see Termination of Trust.
Private trusts, what permissible, 257.

INDEX
Figures refer to pages

DURESS
Constructive trusts based on, 198.

DUTIES OF TRUSTEE
Accounting, 458.
Advances, 414.
As lessor, 408.
Care in investments, 345.
Carry out trust, 333.
Change trust investments, 372.
Contracts, 374.
Defending trust, 335.
Division among co-trustees, 520.
Earmarking, 340.
Expenses, source from which paid, 455
Information to beneficiary, 458.
In general, 326.
Investments,
    Common trust funds, 362.
    Control by settlor, court or beneficiary, 364
    Statutes and court rules, 348.
Investments generally allowed, 350.
Investments generally disapproved, 354.
Keep records, 458.
Keeping property safely, 339.
Loyalty, 328.
Make trust property productive, 342.
Payments, 411.
Possession and custody, 336.
Principal and income accounts, 430.
Protection and investment, 335.
Relating to co-trustee, 507.
Review of investments, 371.
Supervision of co-trustee, 513.

EARMARKING
Duties of trustee, 340.

EDUCATION
Charitable trusts, 285.

ELECTION
Barring remedy of beneficiary, 595.
Tracing and damages, 563.

ELEEMOSYNARY PURPOSES
Charitable trusts, 288.

ELEMENTS
Of the trust, 104.

EMPLOYEE
Of trustee, liability for acts of, 506.

EQUITABLE CHARGE
Distinguished from trust, 34.

ESCHEAT
Interest of beneficiary, 144.

ESTATE
Of trustee, 122.

INDEX

Figures refer to pages

EVIDENCE
Express trust creation, burden proof, 59.

EXCULPATORY CLAUSE
Regarding co-trustees, 519.

EXECUTORSHIP
Trust distinguished, 39.

EXPENSES
Source from which paid, principal and income accounts, 455.

EXPRESS TRUST
Creation of, 52.
Distinguished from implied, 52.
Failure of, resulting trust, 190.

EXTINCTION OF TRUST
See Termination of Trust.

FAILURE OF EXPRESS TRUST
Resulting trust on, 190.

FEES
See Compensation.

FIDUCIARY
Direct dealing with beneficiary, constructive trust, 207.
Disloyalty, constructive trust, 203.
Duty of loyalty, 328.

FIDUCIARY RELATION
Definition, 2.

FOLLOWING TRUST PROPERTY
Remedy of beneficiary, 530.

FOREIGN EXCHANGE
Debt or trust, 30.

FRAUD
See, also, Statute of Frauds.
Constructive trusts based on, 196.

FUNCTIONS
Of trust, common ones described, 235.

GOVERNMENTAL PURPOSES
Charitable trusts, 291.

GUARANTY FUND
Recovery from, for breach of trust, 575.

GUARDIAN
Trustee distinguished, 44.

HISTORY
Trusts, in early America, 15.

HOMICIDE
Property obtained by, constructive trust, 200.

IDENTIFICATION
Trust funds, 547.

ILLEGAL PURPOSES
Of trusts, effect, 233.

IMPERATIVE POWERS
Of trustee, 315.

IMPLIED TRUSTS
Classification of, 170.
Distinguished from express, 52.

IMPOSSIBILITY
Of trust purpose being accomplished, 634.

IMPROVEMENTS,
Duty of trustee as to, 408.

INCOME
Duty of trustee to advance, 414.
Duty trustee to make trust property produce, 342

INDEFINITENESS
In charitable trusts, 273.

INDEMNITY
Contract liability, 379.
Tort liability, 387.

INFORMATION
Duties of trustee as to requests for, 458.

INJUNCTION
Against breach of trust, 488.

INQUIRY
Facts putting on, 543.

INSTRUCTION
Court's power to give, 486.

INSURANCE
Tracing trust funds into, 558.

INSURANCE TRUSTS
Creation of, 110.

INTENT
Trust, need for expression of, 55.

INTEREST
Liabilities of trustee for, 522.

INTESTACY
Gift by, on oral trust, constructive trust, 219.

INVESTMENTS
Care in making, 345.
Common trust funds, 362.
Control by beneficiary, 364.
Control by court, 364.
Control by settlor, 364.
Duty of trustee to change, 372.
Duty to review, 371.
Generally allowed, 350.

INDEX

Figures refer to pages

INVESTMENTS—Continued
Generally disapproved, 354.
Statutes and court rules, 348.

JUDICIAL SALE
Purchase at, constructive trust, 212.

LACHES
Barring remedy, 598.

LARCENY
Proceeds of, constructive trust, 199.

LEASE
Duties of trustee as lessor, 408.
Length permitted, 407.
Power of trustee to make, 405.

LETTERS OF TRUSTEESHIP
Trustee obtaining, 130.

LIABILITIES OF TRUSTEE
Act of employee, 506.
As property owner, 390.
As such,
    For torts, 389.
    In contract cases, 381.
Contracts, 374.
Co-trustees, joint and several, 504.
Criminal, 526.
For act of co-trustee, 507.
Indemnity on contract liability, 379.
Interest, simple or compound, 522.
Money judgment for breach of trust, 501.
Personal, with lien, 528.
Recovery of trust property or substitute, 530.
Torts, 385.

LIEN
Against trust property, with personal liability of trustee, 528.
Of trustee, on accounting, 471.

LIFE TENANT
Not a trustee, 49.

LIMITATIONS
See Statute of Limitations.

LIVING TRUSTS
When testamentary, 90.

LOUISIANA
Trust law in, 17.

LOYALTY
Duty of, 328.

MARSHALING
As a trust remedy, 566.

MASSES
Charitable trusts, 279.

MERGER
In creation express trusts, 116.
Termination of trust by, 636.

METHODS
Trust creation, 54.

MISTAKE
Constructive trusts based on, 198.

MIXED TRUSTS
Meaning and effect of, 260.

MODIFICATION OF TRUST
By act of parties, 619.
By the court, 620.

MONUMENTS
Trusts for, 282.

MORTGAGE
Court control of, 401.
Deed of trust in nature of, trust distinguished, 50.
Effect of trustee's, 403.
Power of trustee to give, 399.

MORTMAIN ACTS
Restrictions of, 311.

NOTICE
Facts putting on inquiry, 543.
Meaning of, under bona fide purchaser rule, 540.
Of trust, need for, in trust creation, 99.
Powers of trustee, 325.

OATH
Trustee giving, 130.

OFFICERS
Of corporations, trustees distinguished, 45.

ORAL TRUST
Actual fraud by trustee, 217.
Confidential relations, 218.
Gift by will or intestacy on, constructive trust, 219.
Of land, constructive trust from breach, 214.

ORIGIN
Uses and trusts, 6.

OWNER
Liabilities of trustee as, 390.

PAROL EVIDENCE
Statute of Frauds, 88.

PART PERFORMANCE
Statute of Frauds, 84.

PARTIAL ASSIGNMENTS
Trusts distinguished, 38.

PARTICIPATION
In breach of trust, liability, 578.

PASSIVE TRUSTS
Distinguished from active, 228.
Present status, 230.
Statute of Uses and, 230.

PAYMENT OF CONSIDERATION
Purchase money resulting trust, 175.

PAYMENTS
Duties of trustee as to, 411.

PAYROLL ACCOUNT
Debt or trust, 31.

PERFORMANCE
Part, Statute of Frauds, 84.

PERPETUITIES
Duration of private trusts, 257.
Remoteness, charitable trusts, 303.
Remoteness of vesting, private trusts, 242.
Supension power of alienation, private trusts, 247.

PERSONAL POWERS
Of trustee, 317.

PERSONAL PROPERTY
Creation trusts of, formality, 83.

POSSESSION
Transfer to trustee, need for, 102.
Trust property,
    By co-trustees, 511.
    Duties of trustee, 336.

POWER OF ALIENATION
Undue suspension of, private trusts, 247.

POWER OF REVOCATION
Of trust, 622.

POWER OF SALE
When trustee has, 392.

POWERS OF TRUSTEE
Attached to office, 317.
Borrow and give security, 399.
    Court control, 401.
    Effect of, 403.
Delegation of, 323.
Discretionary, 315.
Effect of co-trusteeship, 320.
Express, 314.
Imperative, 315.
Implied powers, 314.
In general, 314.
Lease, 405.
    Length of term permitted, 407.
Notice of, to third persons, 325.
Personal, 317.

POWERS OF TRUSTEE—Continued
Sale,
    Conduct of, 397.
    Court control of, 395.
To sell, 392.

PRECATORY EXPRESSIONS
Effect of, 59.

PREFERRED CLAIM
Beneficiary has none, 504.

PREMIUM
Duty of trustee when bond bought at, 442.

PRESUMPTION
In tracing trust funds, 548.
Termination of trust, 631.

PRINCIPAL AND INCOME
Apportionment of receipts, 431.
Cash dividends, 445.
Compensation of trustee, source of, 478.
Duties as to accounts, 430.
Expenses, source from which paid, 455.
Extraordinary receipts, 434.
Ordinary returns, 430.
Stock dividends, 448.
Stock subscription rights, 453.
Unproductive property, 437.
Wasting property, 440.

PRIVATE TRUSTS
Distinguished from charitable, 228
Purposes of, 228.

PRODUCTIVITY
Duty trustee to procure, 342.

PROMOTERS
Trustees distinguished, 45.

PROPERTY
See Subject-Matter.

PROPERTY OWNER
Liabilities of trustee as, 390.

PROTECTION
Trust property, duty of trustee, 335.

PUBLIC TRUSTS
See Charitable Trusts.

PURCHASE MONEY RESULTING TRUST
Creation of, 175.

PURCHASER
Who is, under bona fide purchaser rule, 544.

PURCHASER FOR VALUE
See Bona Fide Purchaser.

INDEX
Figures refer to pages

PURPOSES
Active trusts, statutory restrictions, 240.
Indefiniteness, in charitable trusts, 273.
Of active trusts, what valid, 233.
Of trusts,
    Accomplished or impossible, 632.
    Classified, 228.
    Common functions described, 235.
Private trusts,
    Accumulations, 253.
    Duration of trust, 257.
    Rule against remoteness of vesting, 242.
    Undue suspension of power of alienation, 247.

QUALIFICATION
By trustee, 128.

RECEIVER
Appointment of, for trust, 568.

RECEIVERSHIP
Trust distinguished, 48.

RECORDING
Trust instrument, 98.

RECORDS
Duty of trustee to keep, 458.

RELEASE
By beneficiary, 594.

RELIGION
Charitable trusts, 276.

REMAINDERMAN
Not a trust beneficiary, 49.

REMEDIES
Advice and instruction by court, 486.
Against third person for injuring trust property, 590.
Against third persons participating in breach, 578.
Barred by acquiescence, 596.
Barred by consent, 596.
Barred by election, 595.
Barred by laches, 598.
Barred by release, 595.
Barred by Statute of Limitations, 605.
Barring of, 594.
Bona fide purchaser rule, 533.
Control of trust administration, 568.
Decree for execution of trust, 490.
Election between tracing and damages, 563.
Enjoining breach of trust, 488.
Equity ordinarily enforces trust, 496.
Inadequacy of remedy at law, not necessary, 499.
Law occasionally enforces trust, 498.
Marshaling, 566.
Money judgment against trustee, 501.
Personal liability of trustee, with lien, 528.
Receivership, 568.

INDEX
Figures refer to pages

REMEDIES—Continued
Recovery from bondsmen, 575.
Recovery from state guaranty fund, 575.
Recovery of trust property or substitute, 530.
Removal of trustee, 568.
Setting aside wrongful acts, 488.
Subrogation, 566.
Tracing trust funds, identification, 547.
Visitorial powers, 495.

REMOTENESS
Charitable trusts, 303.
Private trusts, 242.

REMOVAL OF TRUSTEE
Grounds for, 571.
Proceedings for, 574.
When court will make, 568.

RENT
Duty to collect, 408.

REPAIRS
Duty to make, 408.

REPORT
Trustee's, see Accounting.

RES
See Subject-Matter.

RESIGNATION
By trustee, 416.

RESTATEMENT OF TRUSTS
Purpose of, 17.

RESTRAINTS ON ALIENATION
Charitable trusts, 307.

RESTRICTIONS
On trust purpose, statutory, 240.

RESULTING TRUSTS
Creation of, 170.
Failure of express trust, 190.
Introduction to, 170.
Purchase money, 175.
Statute of Frauds, 172.
Statute of Limitations, 612.
Voluntary conveyances, 173.
Where trust res proves excessive, 192.

REVIEW
Duty to make, 371.

REVOCATION
Of trust, 622.

RIGHTS OF TRUSTEE
Compensation, 472.

INDEX
Figures refer to pages

SAFE-KEEPING
Duties of trustee, 339.

SALE
Court control of trustee's, 395.
Power of trustee as to, 392.
Trustee's, conduct of, 397.

SAVINGS BANK TRUSTS
Effect of, 65.

SETTLOR
Charitable trusts, statutory restrictions on, 311.
Control of investments, 364.
Control of liabilities of co-trustees, 519.
Power of, over compensation of trustee, 474.
Qualifications of, 104.
Revocation of trust by, 622.

SKILL
Required of trustee, 326.

SPENDTHRIFT TRUSTS
Creation of, 156.

STATUTE OF CHARITABLE USES
History of, 268.

STATUTE OF FRAUDS
Constructive trusts, 195.
Creation express trusts, 79.
Oral trust, constructive trust from breach, 214.
Resulting trusts, 172.
Satisfaction of, 86.

STATUTE OF LIMITATIONS
Actions against third persons, 611.
Application to trusts, 605.
Constructive trusts, 614.
Resulting trusts, 612.

STATUTE OF USES
Effect of, 13.
Passive trusts and, 230.
Purpose of, 11.
Trusts and Uses before, 9.

STATUTES
To what extent codify trust law, 16.

STOCK
Subscription rights, principal and income accounts, 453.

SUBJECT-MATTER
Of trust, 107.
Where excessive, resulting trust, 192.

SUBROGATION
As a remedy, 566.

SUBSCRIPTION RIGHTS
Principal and income accounts, 453.

SUCCESSOR TRUSTEES
How appointed, 422.

SUPERVISION
Among co-trustees, 513.

SUPPORT
Agreement for, debt or trust, 31.

SUPPORT TRUSTS
Creation, 168.

SURCHARGE
Of trustee, for breach of trust, 501.

SURETIES
Action against trustee's, 575.

SURRENDER
By beneficiaries, ending trust, 639.

SUSPENSION
Power of alienation, private trusts, 247.

SWOLLEN ASSETS
Theory of, in tracing, 560

TERMINATION OF TRUST
Death of trust party, 630.
End presumed, 631.
Merger of interests, 636.
Natural, 627.
Purpose accomplished or impossible, 632.
Request of beneficiary, 638.
Surrender by beneficiary, 639.

TESTAMENTARY TRUSTS
Distinguished from living, 90.
Formality requirements, 89.

THIRD PERSON
Injuring trust property, action for, 590.
Liability for participating in breach of trust, 578.

TITLE
Transfer to trustee, need for, 101.

TORTS
Creditor's right against trust estate, 389.
Liabilities of trustee for, 385.
Trustee's right to indemnity, 387.

TRACING
Burden of proof and presumptions, 548.
Election between, and damages, 563.
Identification, specific property rule, 555.
Insurance monies, 558.
Trust funds, identification, 547.
Trust property, bona fide purchaser rule, 533.
Trust property or substitute, 530.
Swollen assets theory, 560.

TRANSFER
Title, to trustee, need for, 101.

TRUST INSTRUMENT
Delivery of, 95.
Recording, 98.

TRUST PARTIES
Definition, 3.

TRUST PROPERTY
See, also, Subject-Matter.
Definition, 3.

TRUST PURPOSE
See Purposes.

TRUSTEE
Acceptance by, 124.
Delegation of powers, 323.
Duties of, 4.
    In general, 326.
Estate of, 122.
Notice to, in trust creation, 100.
Original appointment of, 119.
Power, when a co-trustee, 320.
Powers of, in general, 314.
Qualification by, 128.
Removal of, 568.
Trust not to fail for want of, 121.
Who may be, 111.

TRUSTS
Before Statute of Uses, 9.
Definition of, 1.
History, in early America, 15.
Origin of, 6.

UNDUE INFLUENCE
Constructive trusts based on, 198.

UNIFORM FIDUCIARIES ACT
Participation in breach of trust, 578.

UNIFORM LAWS
Relating to trusts, 16.

UNPRODUCTIVE PROPERTY
Principal and income accounts, 437.

USES
    See, also, Statute of Uses.
Before Statute of Uses, 9.
Origin, 6.
Reasons for, 8.
What not executed by Statute of Uses, 13.

VACANCIES
Appointment of successors, 422.

VALUE
Meaning of, under bona fide purchaser rule, 545.
    Bogert Trusts 2d—47

VISITORIAL POWERS
Gift to charitable corporation, 495.

VOLUNTARY CONVEYANCE
Resulting trust on, 173.

WAIVER
Compensation by trustee, 480.

WASTING PROPERTY
Principal and income accounts, 440.

WILL
Gift by, on oral trust, constructive trust, 219.

WILLS ACTS
Creation express trusts, 89.

END OF VOLUME